The Big Book
of Color in Design

edited by
David E .Carter

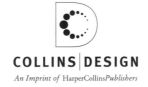

COLLINS | DESIGN
An Imprint of HarperCollinsPublishers

HarperCollins books may be purchased for educational, business, or sales promotional use.
For information, please write: Special Markets Department, HarperCollins Publishers,
10 East 53rd Street, New York, NY 10022.

First published in 2003 by:
Harper Design International
An Imprint of HarperCollins*Publishers*

First Published in Paperback in 2004 by:
Collins Design
An Imprint of HarperCollins*Publishers*
10 East 53rd Street
New York, NY 10022
Tel: (212) 207-7000
Fax: (212) 207-7654
collinsdesign@harpercollins.com
www.harpercollins.com

Distributed throughout the world by:
HarperCollins*Publishers*
10 East 53rd Street
New York, NY 10022
Fax: (212) 207-7654

Library of Congress Control Number: 2005926117

ISBN-10: 0-06-074800-1
ISBN-13: 978-0-06-074800-5

All images in this book have been reproduced with the knowledge and prior consent
of the individuals concerned. No responsibility is accepted by producer, publisher, or printer
for any infringement of copyright or otherwise arising from the contents of this publication.
Every effort has been made to ensure that credits accurately comply with information supplied.

Printed in China by Everbest Printing Company through Four Colour Imports,
Louisville, Kentucky.

Third Printing, 2006

To paraphrase an old TV commercial, this is TWO, TWO, TWO books in one.

First of all, this is a great design resource book. There are hundreds upon hundreds of design ideas within these pages. For those who do what I call "solitary brainstorming," this is another excellent source of design ideas.

But this book is much more. The focus of the book is how color is used to create moods and images. The index shows more than thirty different descriptors: classy, corporate, cool, etc. And within each of those sections, you will find interesting and, often, innovative use of colors in design.

And when you see a particular color or combination of colors that you like, you will find that each image shown in this book has the CMYK formula on how to create that exact color.

All in all, I think this book is one that creative people will find very useful.

For every book that I produce, that is my basic goal.

Table of Contents

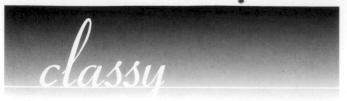

classy • Black is always classy (ask any woman about the "little black dress") • Black and gold are even classier • Grey is classy (it's a variation of black) • So is silver (it's related to gold) • Deep blue is also very classy (maybe because it's a variation of black)

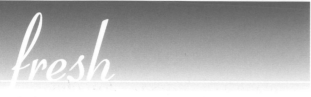

fresh • Green is the color of gardens and grass and springtime • Yellow is the morning light • Yellow is fresh flowers in springtime • Sky blue is the promise of a new day • Pink is a newborn baby, fresh as can be • Black and white is fresh morning e-mail

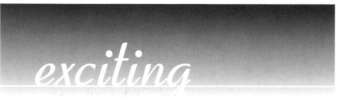

exciting • Red is fireworks • Red is a new Corvette • Yellow is icing on a birthday cake • Green is a ticket to the World Series • Black is the small box that holds a diamond ring • Blue is exciting, especially if you're a Duke fan • Tea leaf green, at the Boston Tea Party •

• Yellow is balloons • Yellow is picking daisies on a spring day • Orange is several different colors in a box of crayons, especially fun if you have the 64 box • Carolina blue is fun, especially at the Dean Dome •

rich • Brown is hardwood floors and chestnuts • Rich is a black sports car • With red accents in the interior • A white Rolls Royce is very rich • Gold is rich, especially when it wraps around a Liz Taylor diamond • Pearl-colored pearls are very rich •

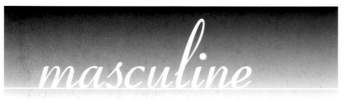

masculine • Black tuxedo is masculine •Camel cashmere is also masculine (not to mention rich) • Navy blue (just like sailors wear) is very masculine • Black bathroom fixtures are masculine • Dark green is masculine (and if it's the color of money, it's also rich) •

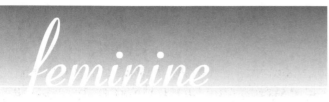

feminine • Baby girls wear pink • So do grown-up girls • Yellow ribbons in her hair. • Cream-colored sweaters are feminine too • Lacy black stockings • Earth tone sweaters, ditto • Tan (as in sun tan) is very feminine •

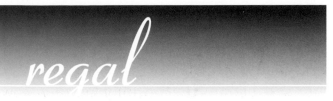

corporate

• Blue, as in IBM blue • Navy blue with pinstripes • Gray flannel suits are corporate, as in the movie "The Man in the Gray Flannel Suit" • Multiple neon colors at Times Square in New York City •

regal

• Centuries ago, in many societies, only royalty could wear purple • Purple is still a color associated with royalty • Gold, of course is royal, as in golden crowns • Mother of pearl, a cream-colored elegance • Multiple gemstone colors, as in the crown jewels •

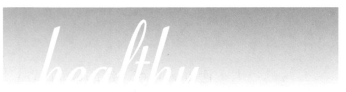

hot

• Orange is hot (at 2,700°F, molten steel is orange) • The sunset is orange, or maybe yellow, or a variation of red • Red is spicy sauce • Red is the 4th of July• Red is hot summer days • Orange is a hot time at a Tennessee football game •

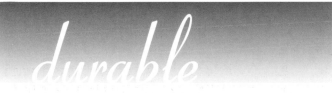

healthy

• Pink cheeks, rosy pink cheeks • Red lips • Green vegetables • Orange-colored vitamin pills • Healthy is a black Volvo, because it's a very safe car • Red wine makes you live longer they say (white wine isn't as healthy—nor as pretty) •

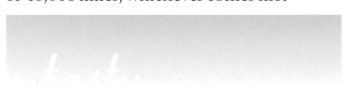

durable

• Gray is steel, which seems to last forever • Brownish gray is the color of tree trunks, trees which have been around longer than we have • Black is steel-belted radial tires, which last forever or 40,000 miles, whichever comes first •

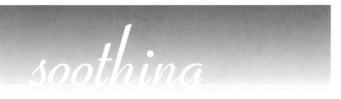

tasty

• Yellow is the taste of honey • Red is a fresh apple, just off the tree • Green is veggies, like beans on the vine • Green (in many shades) is a watermelon • Pink is the inside of the watermelon • Black and white Oreo • Honey and chestnut colors, beautiful and tasty •

soothing

• Brown is morning coffee, easing the start of a new day • Green aloe lotion is soothing, especially after a (fresh) pink sunburn • Light green is the color of an income tax refund check, which is much more soothing than owing the IRS money •

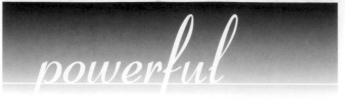

powerful

• Black is powerful; imagine a black business suit • Green is money, which translates into power • Blue is powerful, as in New York Yankees pinstripe blue • Gold is powerful, like the gold at Ft. Knox • Yellow is powerful, as in Caterpillar dozers •

sexy

• Black, as in the little black dress • Purple, as in lacy lingerie • Red, as in wet, red lips • Yellow can be very sexy, even a plain yellow shirt • White, pure simple white, can also be very sexy • Actually, any color can be sexy, given the right place and time... •

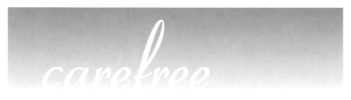

carefree

• Black & white saddle oxfords • With pink shoelaces • Yellow ties • Gray sweatshirts • Pink bubble gum • Blue skies • Yellow sunshine • Green oceans • Brown tree trunks, while walking casually in the woods • Green grass, as in center field • White popcorn •

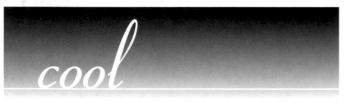

cool

• Ice blue is cool • Light green is cool; just like the Kool cigarette package (although smoking is definitely not "cool") • White snow is cool, or to be more precise, cold • Snow White is cool, if you like fairy tales • Sky blue is cool on a Chicago windy day •

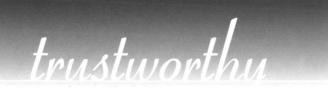

trustworthy

• Khaki is the Boy Scout uniform; a Scout is trustworthy • Green is trustworthy; our currency says "In God We Trust" • Blue is a policeman's uniform • Brown is a plain brown envelope, which is how confidential materials are mailed •

relaxing

• Black is the midnight sky • Pink is the morning sky, just before sunrise • Relaxing is a powder blue, knitted afghan • Fresh white, wool sweat socks are relaxing • Green is the placid emerald ocean • Blue is the sky on a cloudless day •

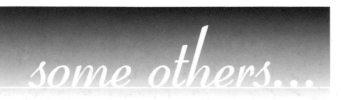

some others...

• Plaid skirts • Argyle socks • Blue Monday • Brown nose • Green grocers • Jet Blue • Black Friday • Pink flamingos • Curious yellow • Statutory grape • Envy green • Blue-nosed censors • Yellow bellies • White Christmas • Green party • Purple monsters •

comunicazione creativa

design firm
Tangram Strategic Design
Novara (Italy)
client
Borsani Comunicazione

C - 0	C - 0
M - 100	M - 0
Y - 100	Y - 0
K - 0	K - 100

C - 14	C - 9	C - 73	C - 0
M - 43	M - 69	M - 57	M - 0
Y - 81	Y - 92	Y - 47	Y - 0
K - 10	K - 12	K - 25	K - 100

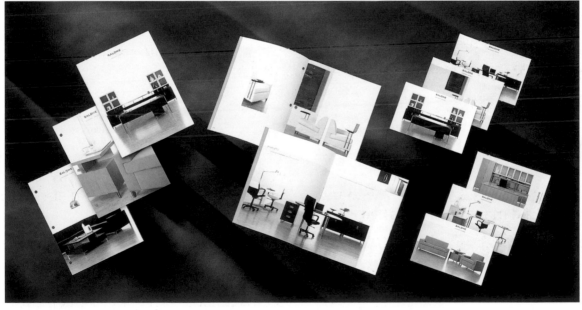

design firm
5D Studio
Malibu, California
client
Tuohy

C - 0	C - 0
M - 0	M - 11
Y - 0	Y - 44
K - 100	K - 30

design firm
The Wecker Group
Monterey, California

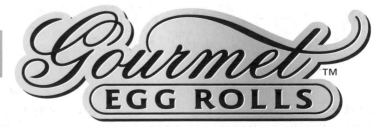

7

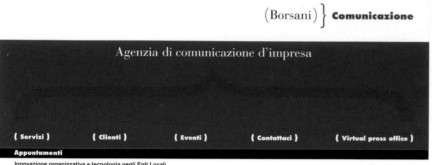

(Borsani) } **Comunicazione**

Agenzia di comunicazione d'impresa

(Servizi)   (Clienti)   (Eventi)   (Contattaci)   (Virtual press office)

Appuntamenti

**Innovazione organizzativa e tecnologia negli Enti Locali
09/10/2002.**
Convegno organizzato dal mensile Pubblica.
Milano, Hotel Executive.
Per informazioni: Edipi Conference - Moira Bellocchio - tel. 0267100340, fax 0267100448, e-mail: mbellocchio@edipi.it, http://www.edipi.com/conference

L'Economia Digitale nel Settore dei Servizi Finanziari 16/10/2002.
La manifestazione è organizzata da Assintel e dalla Federazione per l'Economia Digitale in collaborazione con la Camera di Commercio di Milano.
Milano, Palazzo Castiglioni, Corso Venezia 49.

design firm
Tangram Strategic Design
Novara (Italy)
client
Borsani Comunicazione

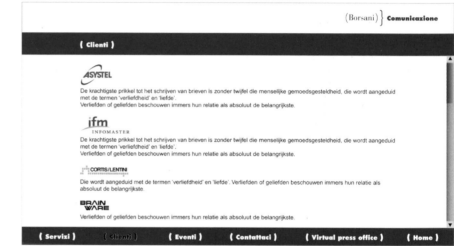

(Borsani) } **Comunicazione**

(Clienti)

ASYSTEL

De krachtigste prikkel tot het schrijven van brieven is zonder twijfel die menselijke gemoedsgesteldheid, die wordt aangeduid met de termen 'verliefdheid' en 'liefde'.
Verliefden of geliefden beschouwen immers hun relatie als absoluut de belangrijkste.

ifm
INFOMASTER

De krachtigste prikkel tot het schrijven van brieven is zonder twijfel die menselijke gemoedsgesteldheid, die wordt aangeduid met de termen 'verliefdheid' en 'liefde'.
Verliefden of geliefden beschouwen immers hun relatie als absoluut de belangrijkste.

CORTIS/LENTINI

Die wordt aangeduid met de termen 'verliefdheid' en 'liefde'. Verliefden of geliefden beschouwen immers hun relatie als absoluut de belangrijkste.

BRAIN WARE

Verliefden of geliefden beschouwen immers hun relatie als absoluut de belangrijkste.

(Servizi)   (Clienti)   (Eventi)   (Contattaci)   (Virtual press office)   (Home)

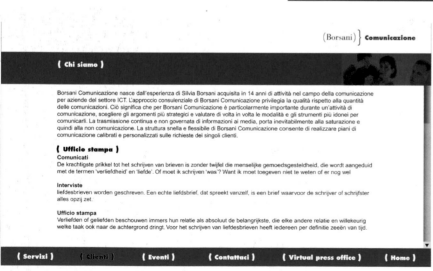

(Borsani) } **Comunicazione**

(Chi siamo)

Borsani Comunicazione nasce dall'esperienza di Silvia Borsani acquisita in 14 anni di attività nel campo della comunicazione per aziende del settore ICT. L'approccio consulenziale di Borsani Comunicazione privilegia la qualità rispetto alla quantità delle comunicazioni. Ciò significa che per Borsani Comunicazione è particolarmente importante durante un'attività di comunicazione, scegliere gli argomenti più strategici e valutare di volta in volta le modalità e gli strumenti più idonei per comunicarli. La trasmissione continua e non governata di informazioni ai media, porta inevitabilmente alla saturazione e quindi alla non comunicazione. La struttura snella e flessibile di Borsani Comunicazione consente di realizzare piani di comunicazione calibrati e personalizzati sulle richieste dei singoli clienti.

(Ufficio stampa)
Comunicati
De krachtigste prikkel tot het schrijven van brieven is zonder twijfel die menselijke gemoedsgesteldheid, die wordt aangeduid met de termen 'verliefdheid' en 'liefde'. Of moet ik schrijven 'was'? Want ik moet toegeven niet te weten of er nog wel

Interviste
liefdesbrieven worden geschreven. Een echte liefdsbrief, dat spreekt vanzelf, is een brief waarvoor de schrijver of schrijfster alles opzij zet.

Ufficio stampa
Verliefden of geliefden beschouwen immers hun relatie als absoluut de belangrijkste, die elke andere relatie en willekeurig welke taak ook naar de achtergrond dringt. Voor het schrijven van liefdesbrieven heeft iedereen per definitie zeeën van tijd.

(Servizi)   (Clienti)   (Eventi)   (Contattaci)   (Virtual press office)   (Home)

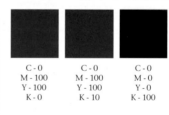

C - 0
M - 100
Y - 100
K - 0

C - 0
M - 100
Y - 100
K - 10

C - 0
M - 0
Y - 0
K - 100

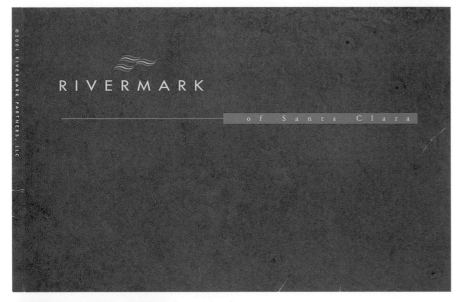

RIVERMARK

of Santa Clara

design firm
Gauger + Santz
San Francisco, California
client
Rivermark

C - 28
M - 89
Y - 83
K - 4

C - 14
M - 55
Y - 68
K - 1

C - 76
M - 42
Y - 0
K - 0

C - 92
M - 84
Y - 65
K - 51

C - 57
M - 27
Y - 6
K - 0

C - 47
M - 42
Y - 70
K - 8

design firm
Rule29
Elgin, Illinois
client
Rule29

Creative Matter | *volume 1*

RULE29

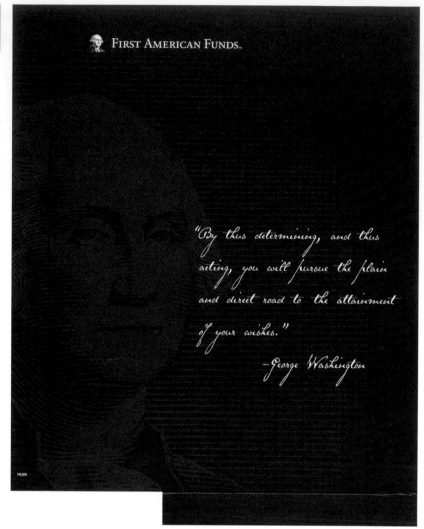

C - 35	C - 38
M - 98	M - 99
Y - 56	Y - 72
K - 13	K - 20

design firm
U.S. Bancorp Asset Management
Minneapolis, Minnesota

FIRST AMERICAN FUNDS.

"By thus determining, and thus acting, you will pursue the plain and direct road to the attainment of your wishes."

—George Washington

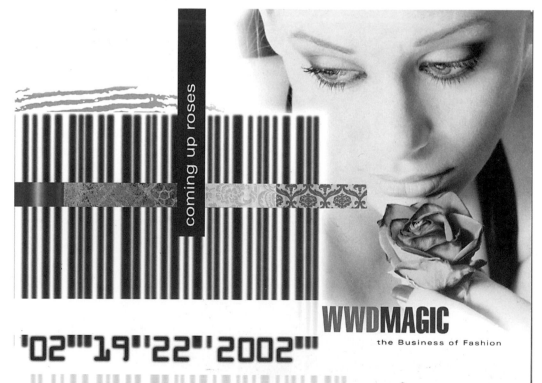

coming up roses

WWDMAGIC
the Business of Fashion

'02'''19''22''2002'''

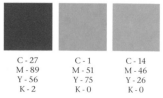

design firm
Marketing Design Group
San Diego, California
client
Magic International

C - 27	C - 1	C - 14
M - 89	M - 51	M - 46
Y - 56	Y - 75	Y - 26
K - 2	K - 0	K - 0

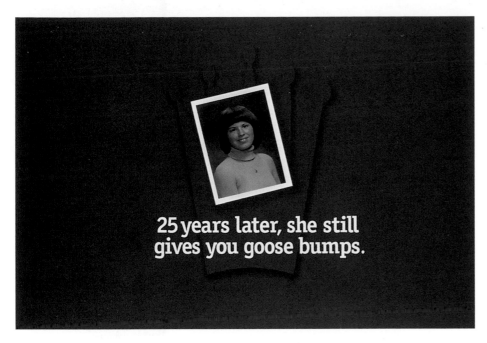

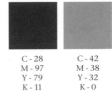

C - 28   C - 42
M - 97   M - 38
Y - 79   Y - 32
K - 11   K - 0

design firm
SevenTwenty Group
Indianapolis, Indiana
client
    Indiana Basketball Hall of Fame

25 years later, she still gives you goose bumps.

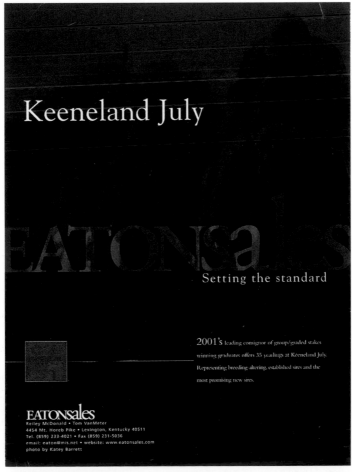

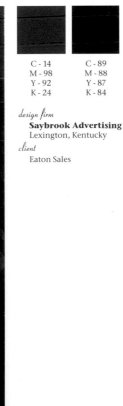

C - 14   C - 89
M - 98   M - 88
Y - 92   Y - 87
K - 24   K - 84

design firm
Saybrook Advertising
Lexington, Kentucky
client
    Eaton Sales

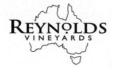

REYNOLDS
VINEYARDS

As Distinctive As The Land It Comes From.

design firm
Trinchero Family Vineyards
St. Helena, California
client
Trinchero Family Estates

C - 64	C - 40
M - 88	M - 60
Y - 91	Y - 60
K - 25	K - 0

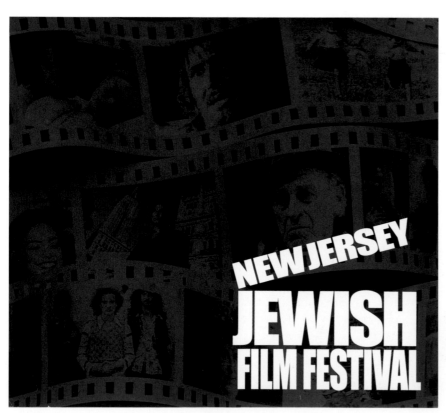

NEW JERSEY JEWISH FILM FESTIVAL

design firm
Creative, Ink.
Short Hills, New Jersey
client
JCC MetroWest

C - 87	C - 70
M - 88	M - 66
Y - 84	Y - 61
K - 80	K - 36

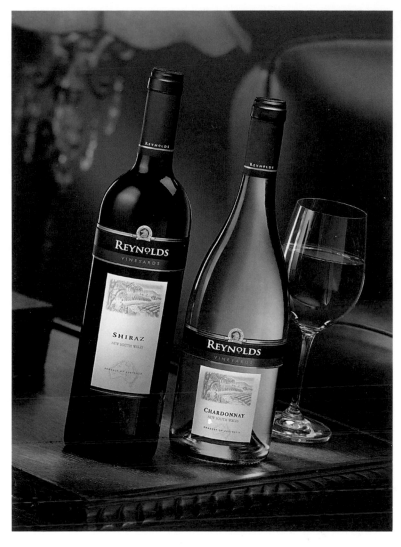

C - 86	C - 19	C - 51
M - 68	M - 33	M - 53
Y - 20	Y - 58	Y - 91
K - 18	K - 0	K - 15

design firm
Trinchero Family Vineyards
St. Helena, California
client
Trinchero Family Estates

STRAITS

| C - 39 |
| M - 46 |
| Y - 72 |
| K - 0 |

design firm
Design Objectives Pte Ltd
Singapore (Singapore)
client
Straits Advisors Pte Ltd

ADVISORS

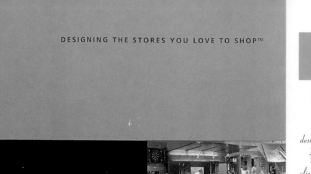

DESIGNING THE STORES YOU LOVE TO SHOP™

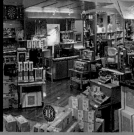

C - 40   C - 0
M - 24   M - 61
Y - 99   Y - 97
K - 0   K - 0

design firm
JGA, Inc.
Southfield, Michigan
client
JGA, Inc.

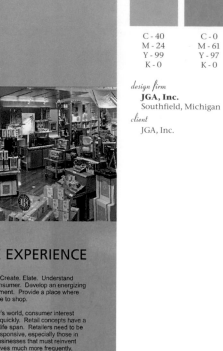

RETAIL FOCUS

NEWS & VIEWS FROM **JGA, INC.**

www·jga·com

RESTORE THE EXPERIENCE

Relate. Create. Elate. Understand your consumer. Develop an energizing environment. Provide a place where they love to shop.

In today's world, consumer interest passes quickly. Retail concepts have a shorter life span. Retailers need to be more responsive, especially those in trend businesses that must reinvent themselves much more frequently. Restore the shopping experience to form a dynamic bond between buyer and seller and as the consumer pie is reallocated, innovative retailers grab a bigger bite of sales.

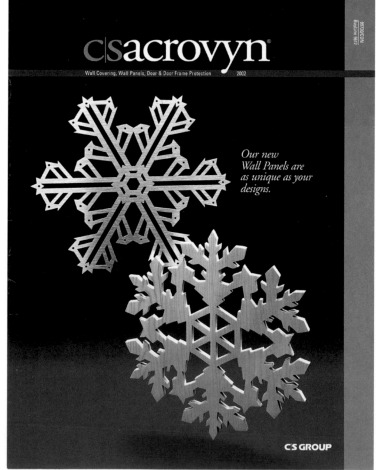

design firm
Brian J. Ganton & Associates
Cedar Grove, New Jersey
client
Construction Specialties, Inc.

C - 21   C - 88   C - 5
M - 65   M - 86   M - 49
Y - 80   Y - 88   Y - 80
K - 1   K - 77   K - 0

14

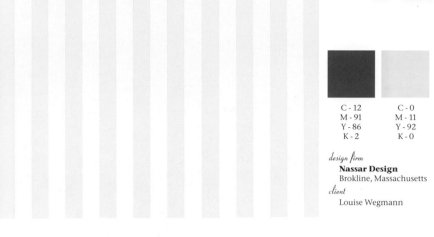

C - 12   C - 0
M - 91   M - 11
Y - 86   Y - 92
K - 2   K - 0

design firm
Nassar Design
Brokline, Massachusetts
client
Louise Wegmann

Collège Louise Wegmann

مدرسة لويز فكمان

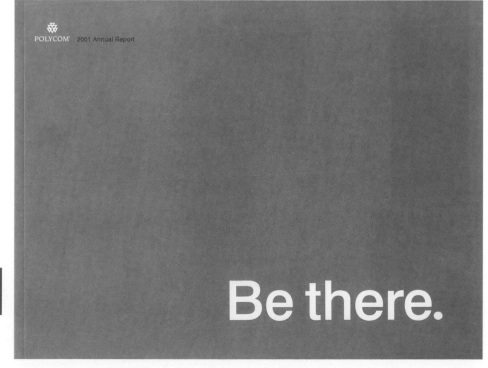

design firm
viadesign
San Diego, California
client
Polycom

C - 6   C - 69
M - 66 M - 76
Y - 99 Y - 42
K - 0   K - 1

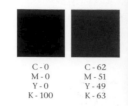

C - 0   C - 62
M - 0   M - 51
Y - 0   Y - 49
K - 100 K - 63

design firm
Paradowski Graphic Design
St. Louis, Missouri
client
Paradowski Graphic Design

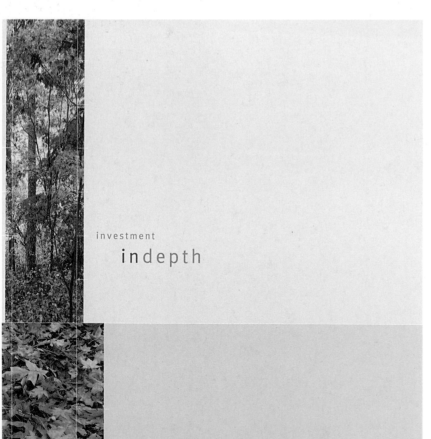

investment
in depth

design firm
Phinney/Bischoff Design House
Seattle, Washington
client
Sirach Capital Management

C - 17   C - 0   C - 0
M - 15   M - 61   M - 83
Y - 49   Y - 79   Y - 62
K - 0   K - 0   K - 0

SIRACH

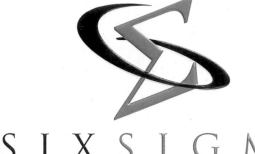

SIX SIGMA
CANADA INC

C - 44	C - 0
M - 47	M - 0
Y - 74	Y - 0
K - 7	K - 100

design firm
Hardball Sports
Jacksonville, Florida
client
Six Sigma Canada

design firm
Barbour Design Inc.
New York, New York
client
The ESPY Awards

C - 87	C - 85	C - 58	C - 54
M - 50	M - 77	M - 93	M - 44
Y - 73	Y - 45	Y - 93	Y - 42
K - 7	K - 6	K - 9	K - 0

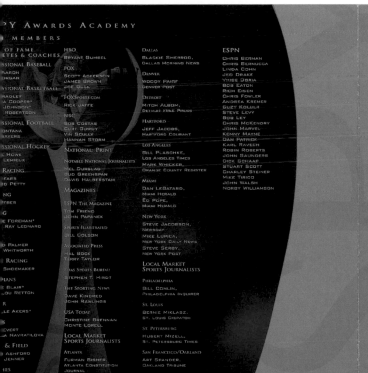

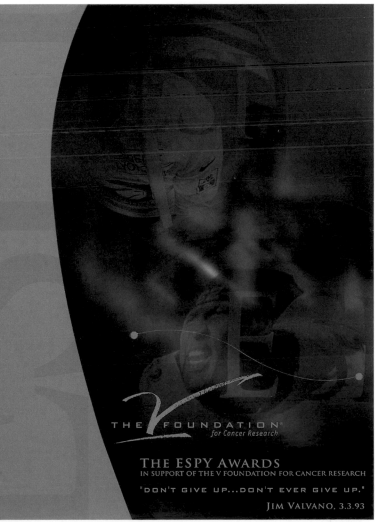

THE ESPY AWARDS
IN SUPPORT OF THE V FOUNDATION FOR CANCER RESEARCH

"DON'T GIVE UP...DON'T EVER GIVE UP."

JIM VALVANO, 3.3.93

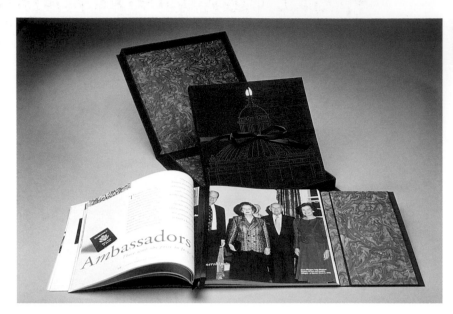

C - 11   C - 71
M - 100   M - 73
Y - 71   Y - 49
K - 16   K - 44

design firm
Dever Designs
Laurel, Maryland
client
James Madison Council

C - 70   C - 0
M - 100   M - 0
Y - 0   Y - 0
K - 15   K - 100

design firm
Praxis Diseñadores, S.C.
México City (Mexico)
client
Valle Redondo

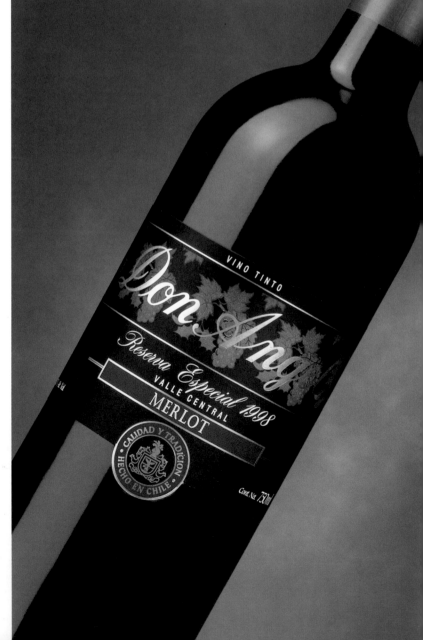

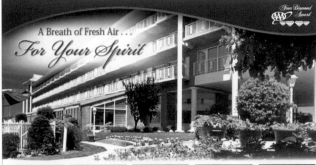

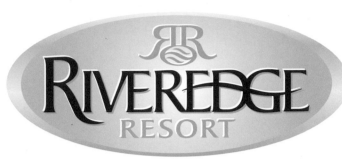

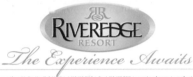

C - 0	C - 0
M - 100	M - 23
Y - 65	Y - 100
K - 47	K - 27

design firm
McElveney & Palozzi Design Group
Rochester, New York
client
Riveredge Resort

C - 85	C - 75
M - 14	M - 60
Y - 29	Y - 49
K - 7	K - 51

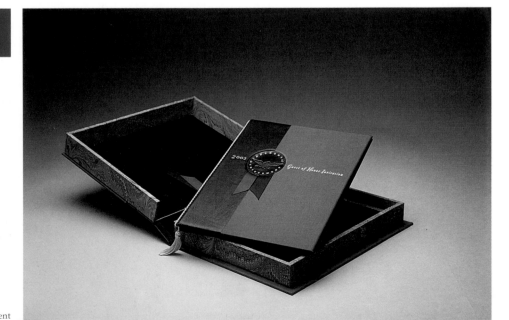

design firm
Dever Designs
Laurel, Maryland
client
Academy of Achievement

Creative Matter | volume 2

ANNUAL REPORTS

design firm
Rule29
Elgin, Illinois
client
Rule29

C - 92　　C - 57　　C - 0
M - 84　　M - 27　　M - 67
Y - 65　　Y - 6　　 Y - 80
K - 51　　K - 0　　 K - 0

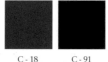

C - 18　　C - 91
M - 99　　M - 86
Y - 99　　Y - 90
K - 24　　K - 74

design firm
Mike Salisbury L.L.C.
Venice, California
client
Polygram Record Group

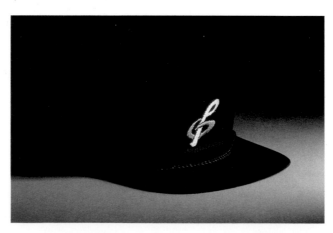

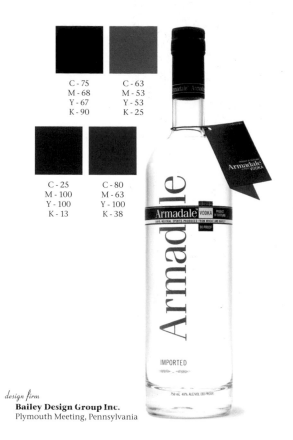

C - 75
M - 68
Y - 67
K - 90

C - 63
M - 53
Y - 53
K - 25

C - 25
M - 100
Y - 100
K - 13

C - 80
M - 63
Y - 100
K - 38

design firm
Bailey Design Group Inc.
Plymouth Meeting, Pennsylvania

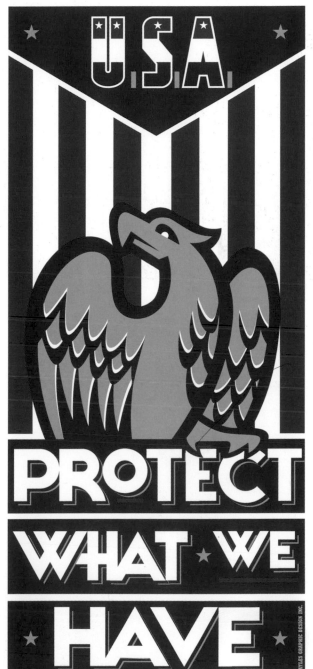

design firm
Sayles Graphic Design
Des Moines, Iowa
client
"Art Fights Back"

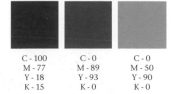

C - 100
M - 77
Y - 18
K - 15

C - 0
M - 89
Y - 93
K - 0

C - 0
M - 50
Y - 90
K - 0

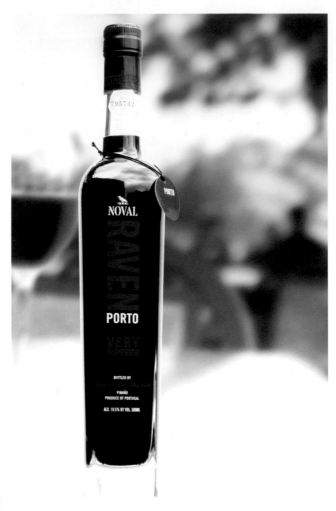

C - 6   C - 0
M - 90   M - 0
Y - 100 Y - 0
K - 1   K - 100

design firm
Bailey Design Group Inc.
Plymouth Meeting, Pennsylvania

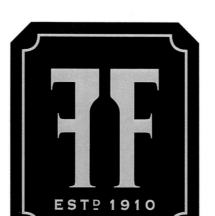

C - 13   C - 0
M - 25   M - 0
Y - 56   Y - 0
K - 0   K - 100

design firm
Lewis Moberly
London (England)
client
Fina Flichman S.A.

FINCA FLICHMAN
WINERY

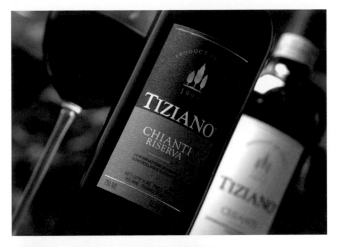

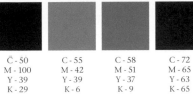

C - 50
M - 100
Y - 39
K - 29

C - 55
M - 42
Y - 39
K - 6

C - 58
M - 51
Y - 37
K - 9

C - 72
M - 65
Y - 63
K - 65

design firm
Klündt Hosmer Design
Spokane, Washington
client
Linesoft

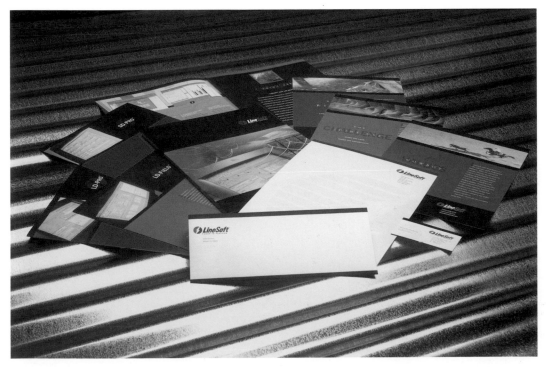

C - 47
M - 32
Y - 67
K - 47

C - 74
M - 49
Y - 12
K - 29

C - 13
M - 26
Y - 80
K - 6

C - 22
M - 82
Y - 90
K - 35

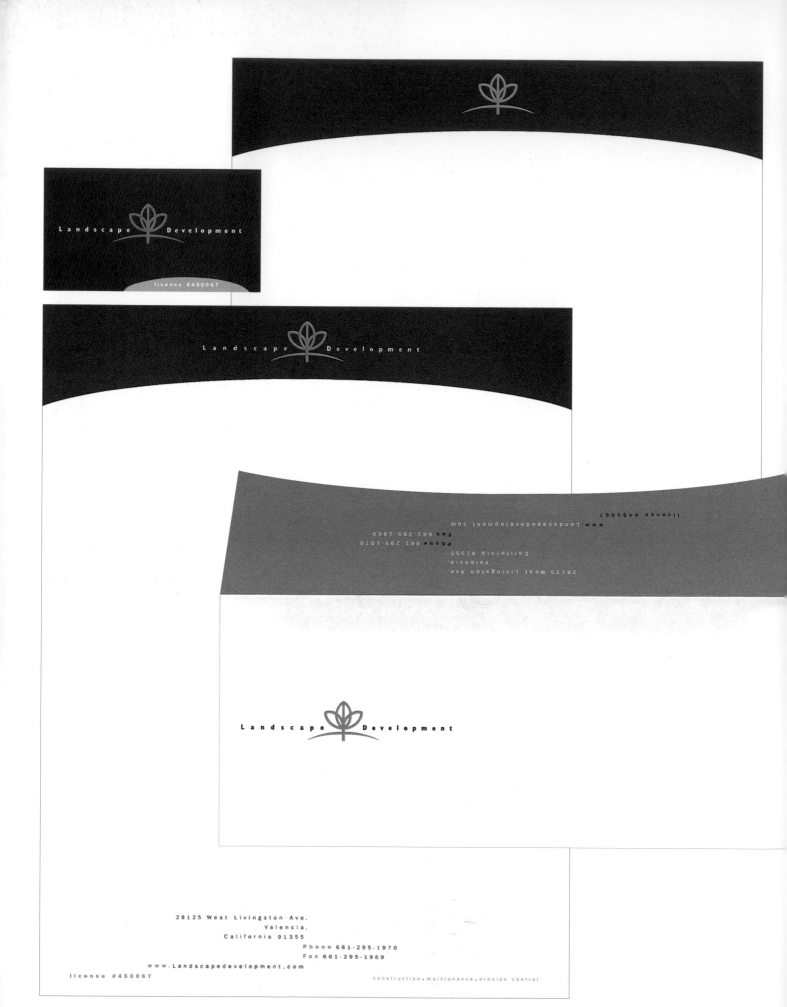

Landscape Development

license #450067

Landscape Development

28125 West Livingston Ave.
Valencia,
California 91355
Phone 661·295·1970
Fax 661·295·1969
www.landscapedevelopment.com
license #450067

Landscape Development

28125 West Livingston Ave.
Valencia,
California 91355
Phone 661·295·1970
Fax 661·295·1969
www.Landscapedevelopment.com
license #450067

construction·maintenance·erosion control

24

(opposite) design firm
Erbe Design
South Pasadena, California
client
Landscape Development

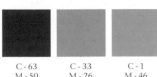

C - 63	C - 33	C - 1
M - 50	M - 26	M - 46
Y - 55	Y - 82	Y - 89
K - 73	K - 16	K - 0

C - 0	C - 0	C - 60
M - 10	M - 8	M - 39
Y - 40	Y - 30	Y - 67
K - 30	K - 23	K - 55

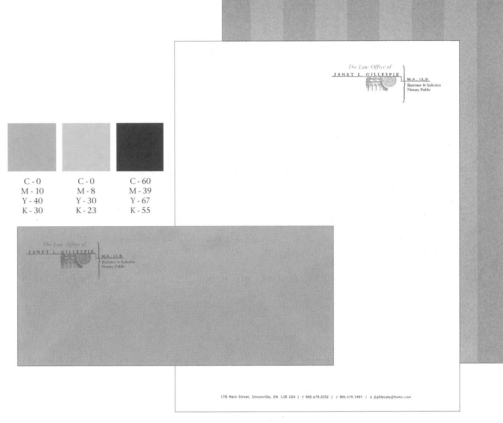

design firm
The Riordon Design Group Inc
Oakville, Ontario
(Canada)
client
Janet Gillespie Law Office

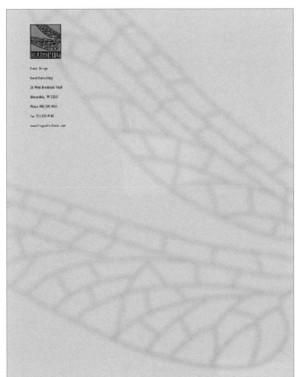

design firm
Gibson Creative
Washington, D.C.
client
Dragonfly

C - 27	C - 20
M - 19	M - 70
Y - 40	Y - 100
K - 15	K - 400

C - 0
M - 30
Y - 50
K - 10

C - 0
M - 0
Y - 0
K - 100

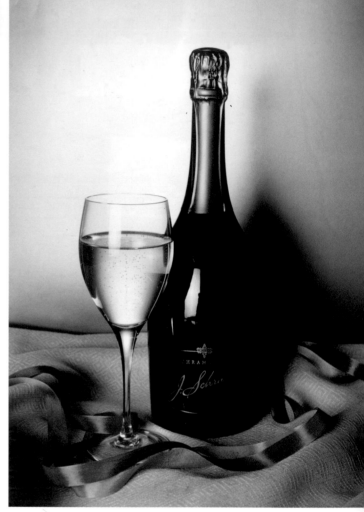

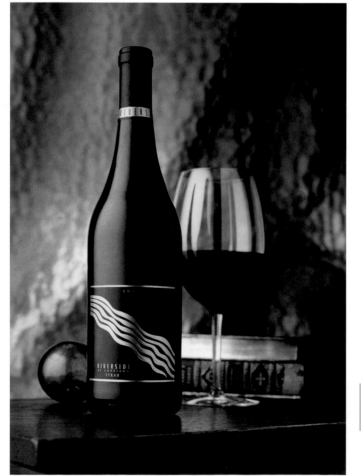

C - 0
M - 25
Y - 30
K - 10

C - 0
M - 0
Y - 0
K - 100

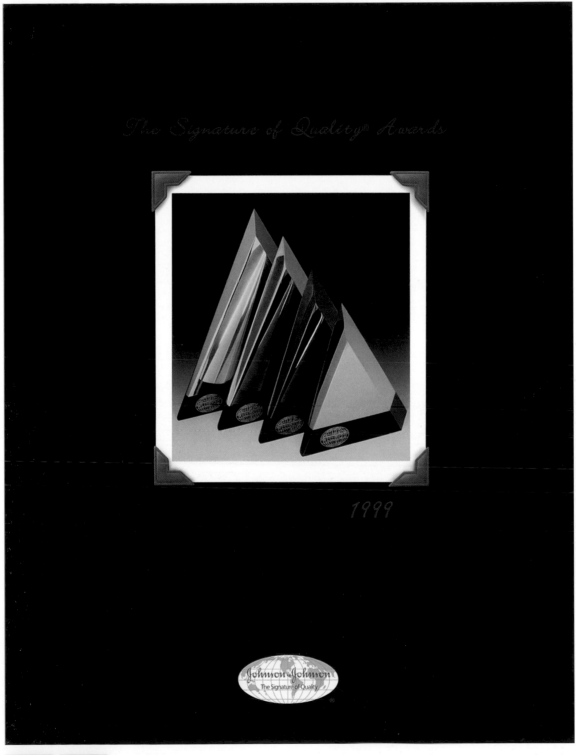

design firm
Checkman Design
New York, New York
client
Johnson & Johnson

C - 0
M - 100
Y - 100
K - 0

C - 0
M - 0
Y - 0
K - 100

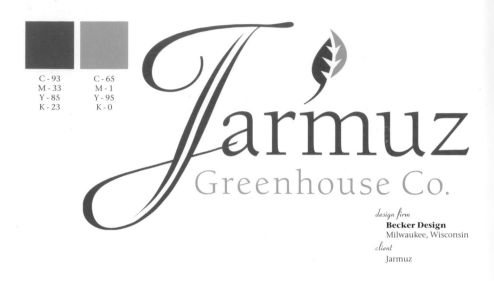

C - 93
M - 33
Y - 85
K - 23

C - 65
M - 1
Y - 95
K - 0

Jarmuz
Greenhouse Co.

design firm
Becker Design
Milwaukee, Wisconsin
client
Jarmuz

C - 30
M - 9
Y - 56
K - 0

C - 24
M - 10
Y - 3
K - 0

C - 19
M - 31
Y - 5
K - 0

C - 29
M - 27
Y - 55
K - 1

C - 20
M - 37
Y - 34
K - 0

design firm
Louis & Partners Design
Bath, Ohio
client
Souper Salad

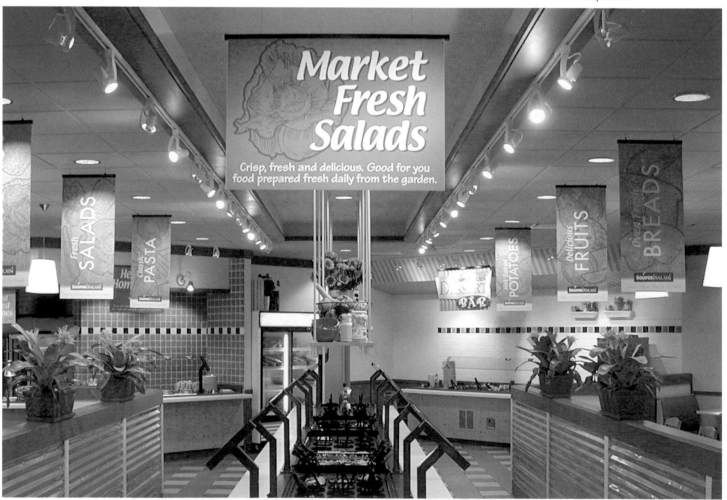

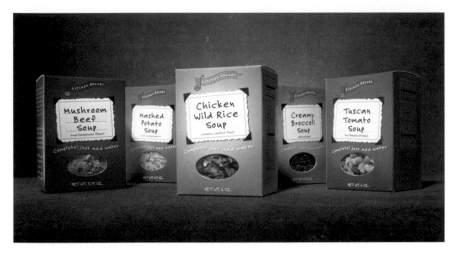

C - 33	C - 62	C - 0	C - 31	C - 1
M - 86	M - 18	M - 27	M - 31	M - 82
Y - 23	Y - 35	Y - 93	Y - 90	Y - 72
K - 17	K - 11	K - 0	K - 20	K - 0

design firm
Compass Design
Minneapolis, Minnesota

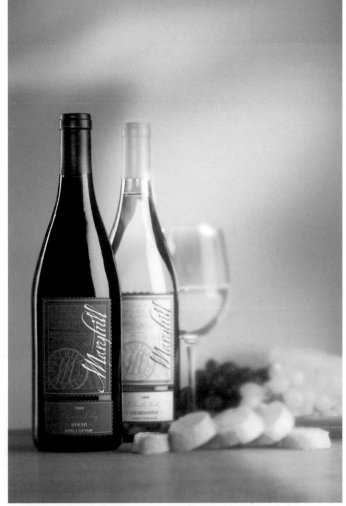

C - 37	C - 7
M - 65	M - 14
Y - 54	Y - 80
K - 51	K - 1

design firm
Klündt Hosmer Design
Spokane, Washington
client
Maryhill Winery

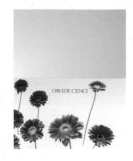

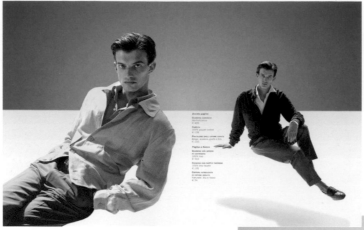

design firm
Tangram Strategic Design
Novara (Italy)
client
Davide Cenci

C - 5
M - 81
Y - 90
K - 1

C - 0
M - 21
Y - 84
K - 1

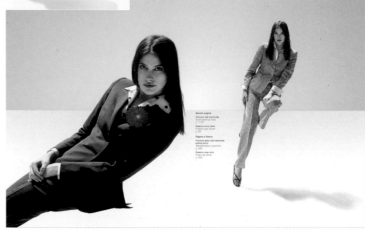

design firm
**Hornall Anderson
Design Works**
Seattle, Washington

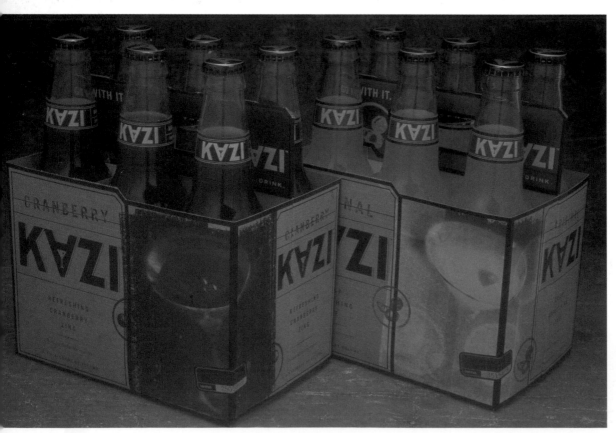

C - 25
M - 47
Y - 63
K - 15

C - 4
M - 87
Y - 69
K - 30

C - 25
M - 27
Y - 75
K - 63

design firm
**Hornall Anderson
Design Works**
Seattle, Washington

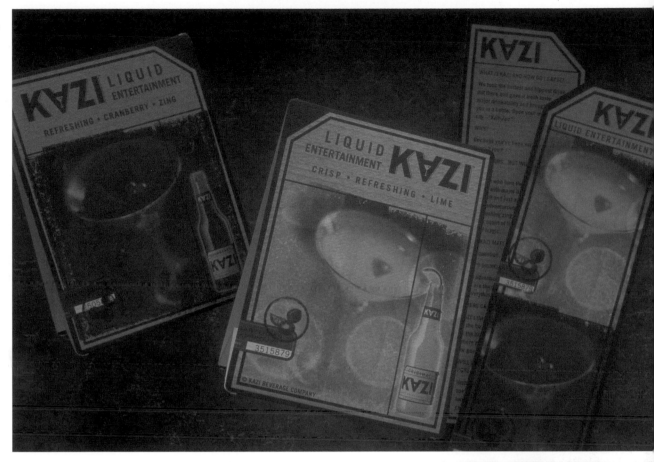

C - 25	C - 4	C - 25
M - 4/	M - 87	M - 27
Y - 63	Y - 69	Y - 75
K - 15	K - 30	K - 63

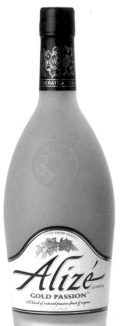
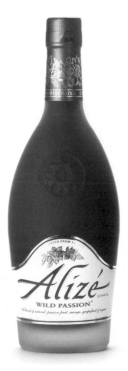
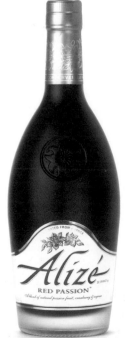

C - 100	C - 0	C - 0	C - 30
M - 94	M - 30	M - 84	M - 95
Y - 34	Y - 87	Y - 70	Y - 63
K - 27	K - 0	K - 0	K - 22

design firm
Pearlfisher
London (England)

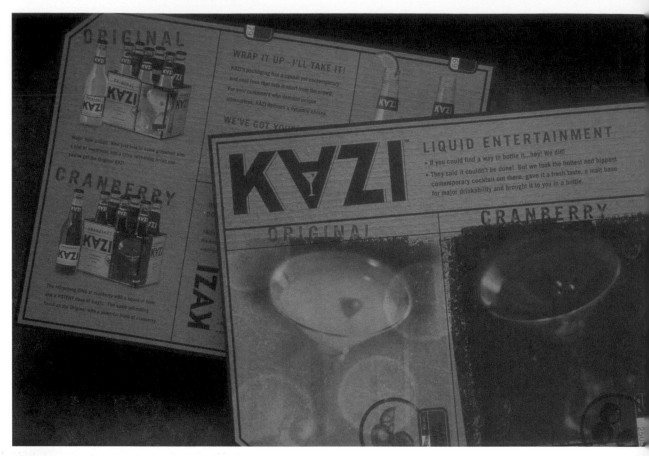

design firm
Hornall Anderson Design Works
Seattle, Washington

C - 25	C - 4	C - 25
M - 47	M - 87	M - 27
Y - 63	Y - 69	Y - 75
K - 15	K - 30	K - 63

design firm
Pearlfisher
London (England)

C - 18	C - 63
M - 79	M - 7
Y - 7	Y - 99
K - 0	K - 0

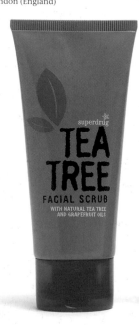 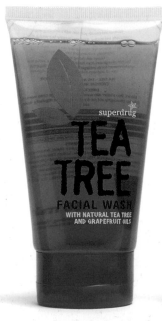 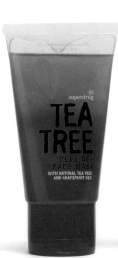 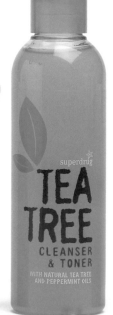 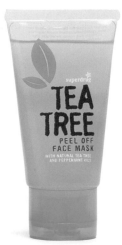

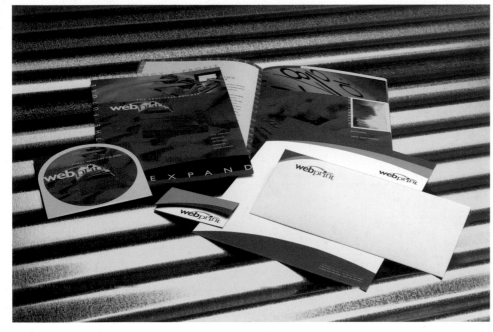

C - 17	C - 62	C - 12	C - 58
M - 12	M - 82	M - 91	M - 18
Y - 97	Y - 20	Y - 86	Y - 94
K - 3	K - 22	K - 2	K - 11

design firm
Klündt Hosmer Design
Spokane, Washington
client
Webprint

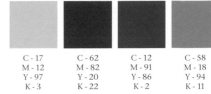

design firm
Hornall Anderson Design Works
Seattle, Washington

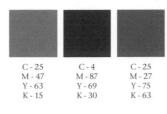

C - 25	C - 4	C - 25
M - 47	M - 87	M - 27
Y - 63	Y - 69	Y - 75
K - 15	K - 30	K - 63

C - 81
M - 58
Y - 0
K - 0

C - 21
M - 3
Y - 1
K - 0

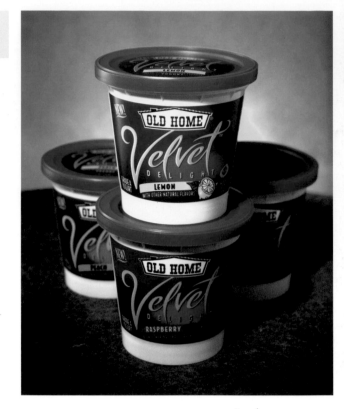

design firm
Compass Design
Minneapolis, Minnesota

C - 13
M - 88
Y - 63
K - 5

C - 73
M - 52
Y - 0
K - 0

C - 0
M - 0
Y - 98
K - 0

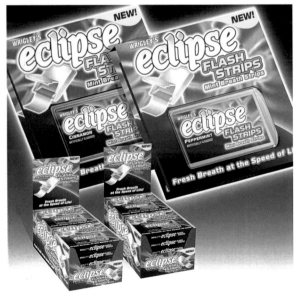

design firm
Cassata & Associates
Schaumbug, Illinois
client
Wm Wrigley Jr. Company

design firm
Dever Designs
Laurel, Maryland
client
American Academy
of Physician Assistants

C - 10
M - 100
Y - 10
K - 15

C - 75
M - 0
Y - 80
K - 0

C - 90
M - 100
Y - 0
K - 0

31st ANNUAL

AAPA'S

New Orleans

PHYSICIAN
ASSISTANT
CONFERENCE

May 22-27, 2003

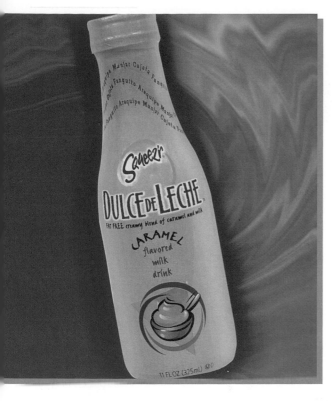

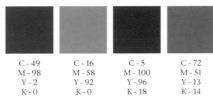

C - 49	C - 16	C - 5	C - 72
M - 98	M - 58	M - 100	M - 51
Y - 2	Y - 92	Y - 96	Y - 13
K - 0	K - 0	K - 18	K - 14

design firm
s²design Group
New York, New York
client
Brooklyn Bottling

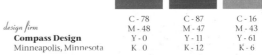

Jamie Stedman-Novo   Tel 646 486 7470

design firm
Compass Design
Minneapolis, Minnesota

C - 78	C - 87	C - 16
M - 48	M - 47	M - 43
Y - 0	Y - 11	Y - 61
K 0	K - 12	K - 6

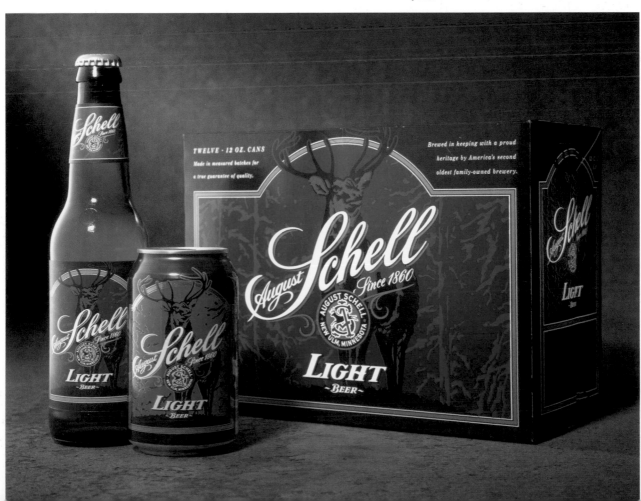

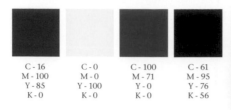

C - 16
M - 100
Y - 85
K - 0

C - 0
M - 0
Y - 100
K - 0

C - 100
M - 71
Y - 0
K - 0

C - 61
M - 95
Y - 76
K - 56

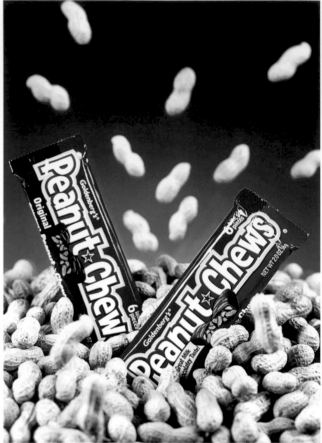

design firm
Bailey Design Group Inc.
Plymouth Meeting, Pennsylvania

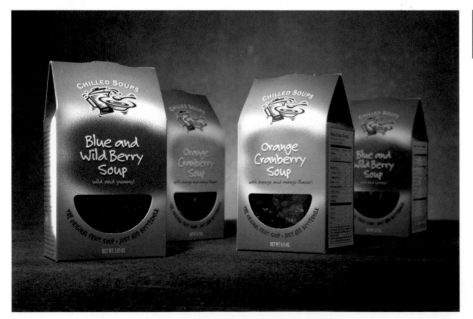

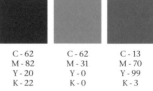

C - 62
M - 82
Y - 20
K - 22

C - 62
M - 31
Y - 0
K - 0

C - 13
M - 70
Y - 99
K - 3

design firm
Compass Design
Minneapolis, Minnesota

36

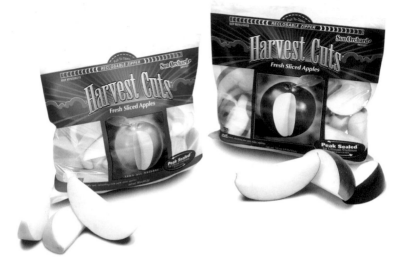

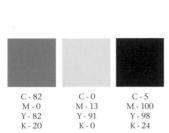

C - 82	C - 0	C - 5
M - 0	M - 13	M - 100
Y - 82	Y - 91	Y - 98
K - 20	K - 0	K - 24

design firm
McElveney & Palozzi Design Group
Rochester, New York

client
Sun Orchard Brand

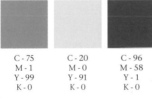

C - 75	C - 20	C - 96
M - 1	M - 0	M - 58
Y - 99	Y - 91	Y - 1
K - 0	K - 0	K - 0

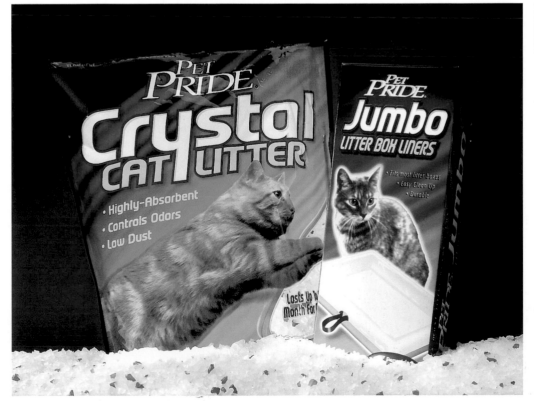

design firm
Interbrand Hulefeld
Cincinnati, Ohio

client
Kroger Company

37

SAN FRANCISCO MUSEUM OF MODERN ART

C - 0
M - 100
Y - 100
K - 0

C - 80
M - 0
Y - 100
K - 0

C - 100
M - 50
Y - 0
K - 0

C - 0
M - 50
Y - 100
K - 0

C - 0
M - 10
Y - 100
K - 0

C - 39
M - 80
Y - 0
K - 0

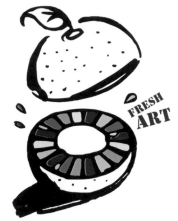

SAN FRANCISCO MUSEUM OF MODERN ART

design firm
Michael Osborne Design
San Francisco, California
client
San Francisco Museum of Modern Art

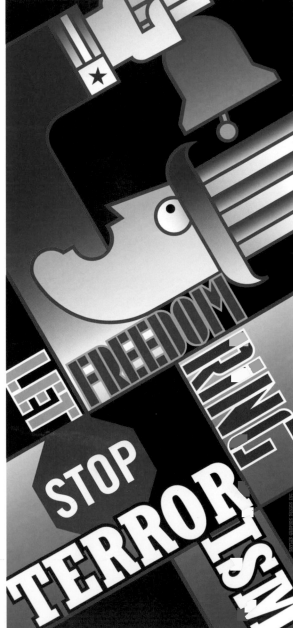

design firm
Sayles Graphic Design
Des Moines, Iowa
client
"Art Fights Back"

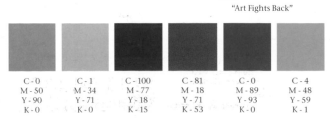

C - 0
M - 50
Y - 90
K - 0

C - 1
M - 34
Y - 71
K - 0

C - 100
M - 77
Y - 18
K - 15

C - 81
M - 18
Y - 71
K - 53

C - 0
M - 89
Y - 93
K - 0

C - 4
M - 48
Y - 59
K - 1

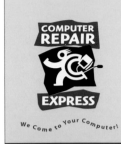

COMPUTER REPAIR EXPRESS

We Come to Your Computer!

P. O. Box 495
Monterey, CA 93942

831.373.3000

Fax 831.620.1845

www.ComputerRepairExpress.com

C - 1
M - 96
Y - 89
K - 0

C - 69
M - 91
Y - 2
K - 0

C - 2
M - 13
Y - 92
K - 0

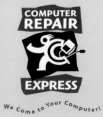

P. O. Box 495
Monterey, CA 93942

831.373.3000

Fax 831.620.1845

MICHAEL ANTONCICH

www.ComputerRepairExpress.com

COMPUTER REPAIR EXPRESS

We Come to Your Computer!

design firm
The Wecker Group
Monterey, California
client
Computer Repair Express

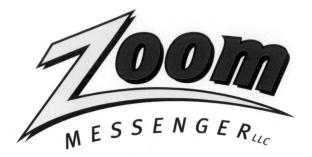

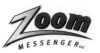

Get it there.

P.O. Box 1834 Milwaukee, Wisconsin 53201 Phone 414 289 9999 Fax 414 289 8388

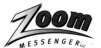

Get it there.

Zoom Messenger, LLC
P.O. Box 1834
Milwaukee, WI 53201

C - 2   C - 3
M - 91   M - 1
Y - 76   Y - 91
K - 0   K - 0

design firm
Becker Design
Milwaukee, Wisconsin
client
Zoom Messenger

This year Cook Communications Ministries, will host three worship together/children's worship & discipleship conferences in Canada. Each conference is two conferences (WORSHIP TOGETHER & CHILDREN'S WORSHIP AND DISCIPLESHIP) simultaneously at the same venue. There will be several general sessions that the delegates from both conferences will attend together for times of refreshing and inspiration. The registration fee for one conference will allow delegates to chose workshops from either conference.

For Example: You are attending the Vancouver conference. You are a CE Director, and your plan is to focus most of your time at the Children's Worship & Discipleship conference. As you look through the workshop listings, you would also like to hear Mike Pilavachi & Matt Redman's workshop on "The Heart of Worship" as found at the Worship Together conference. Or perhaps you're a worship pastor attending the Waterloo conference and you want to hear Bob Hartman's workshop on "The Art of Storytelling" as found at the Children's Worship & Discipleship conference. We have good news! You will be able to attend these sessions at no extra cost. It truly is two conferences in one! This year, Alpha Canada will be joining us and running workshops for those interested in learning more about Alpha.

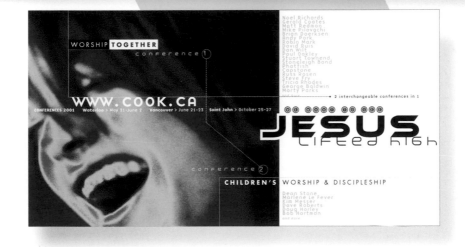

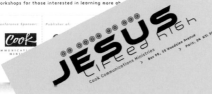

WORSHIP *TOGETHER*

Great Ideas For Worship ›
· Worship for Small Groups · Personal Worship · Creative Expression in Worship · Senior Pastor as Head Worship Leader · The Pastors Point of View · Out of the Abundance · Ways to Get Inspired for Song Writing · Worship Leader or Lead Worshiper? Looking at the Holy Spirit as the Ultimate Worship Leader and What This Means for Us · Finding God in the Desert · Worship & Evangelism · Worship & the Fatherhood of God · Commanded Blessing, Worship, Healing & Reconciliation · Songwriting a "Practical" Focus · Songwriting Panel · Creative Worship Concepts · Actor's Improvisation · Script Writing · Basics in Acting · Hands-on Directing

PR & Sound › · Be equipped, informed & resourced ›
· Basic Sound Systems · Successful Soundchecks · Overcoming Acoustic Problems · Recording Techniques · Mixing Skills

Developing the Heart of a Worship Leader ›
· Worship & Grace · Justice & Mercy · Loving the Father Who Loves Us · In His Presence · The Father Heart of God · Intimacy with the Father · Developing the Heart of a Worship Leader

‹ **Revival Generation** › · Aimed specifically, but not exclusively, at people involved in youth worship · How to be a Worship Leader Without Being a Donkey · Writing Songs for a New Generation · The Heart of Worship · Worship & Evangelism · Worship & Contemporary Culture · The Modern Worship Band · Walking on the Wild Side · Leading Worship as a Band · Rearranging songs in Modern Music Styles · Computer-Based Recording

‹ **Releasing the Prophetic in Worship** ›
· Worship & Intercession · Prophecy · the Biblical Pattern · Spiritual Songs · How to Prophecy in Song · The Heart of the Musical Prophet · Spirituality & Creativity in Worship

‹ **Leading in Worship** › · Foundational skills for the worship leader · The Senior Pastor as Head Worship Leader · How to Excel as a Worship Leader · Breaking Out of the 'Verse-Chorus' Rut · Rhythn of the Saints · Worship Group Skills · Worship Group Leadership · Come & Learn New Songs · Transitioning From Traditional to Contemporary Worship · The Arts in Worship · Drama in Worship · Rehearsing the Band · Surviving the Worship Wars

‹ **Musical Skills** ›
· Keyboards Masterclass · Vocals Masterclass · Acoustic Guitar Master Class

Sharpen your skills by joining us for 8 General Sessions and go home even further equipped having chosen from over 40 Seminars, Panels, and Workshops.

WORKSHOPS

CHILDREN'S WORSHIP & DISCIPLESHIP

Communications
· Drama for Kids · Surviving an All-Age Service · Writing for Children · Incorporating Stories, Songs & Prayers in an All-Age Service · Puppets in the Classroom · Puppet Manipulation · Illusions You Can Make & Use · Children & Creativity · The Theology of Storytelling · The Art of Storytelling

Children and Worship
· Worship for 21st Century Kids · Writing Songs for Children · Discipling Through Dance · Children Serving Others · What Is God Doing with Kids · Preschool Worship · Working with a Children's Worship Band · The Purpose of Flags · Flag Ideas You Can Use

Foundations
· Generation K's Children · Brain Growth · Church in a Postmodern World

Discipleship
· Shepherding Children · Linking Church & Home · The Spiritual Journey of a Child · Prayer with Children · Prayer Ideas

Special Interest/Misc.
· Big Ideas for Small Churches · Children & the Holy Spirit *and more*

WORSHIP **TOGETHER**
conference ①

WWW.COOK.CA

CONFERENCES 2001 Waterloo › May 31-June 2 Vancouver › June 21-23 Saint John › October 25-27

conference ②

CHILDREN'S WORSHIP & DISCIPLESHIP

Noel Richards
Gerald Coates
Matt Redman
Mike Pilavachi
Brian Doerksen
Andy Park
Robin Mark
David Ruis
Dan Wilt
Paul Oakley
Stuart Townend
Stoneleigh Band
Phatfish
Capstone
Ross Rosen
Steve Fry
Tricia Rhodes
George Baldwin
Marty Parks

› 2 interchangeable conferences in 1

JESUS
Lifted high

Dean Stone
Marlene Le Fever
Kim Mesier
Dave Roberts
Doug Horley
Bob Hartman
and more

design firm
The Riordon Design Group Inc.
Oakville, Ontario
(Canada)

C - 0	C - 0	C - 90	C - 0	C - 0
M - 100	M - 60	M - 100	M - 100	M - 15
Y - 20	Y - 80	Y - 0	Y - 100	Y - 100
K - 0	K - 0	K - 0	K - 0	K - 10

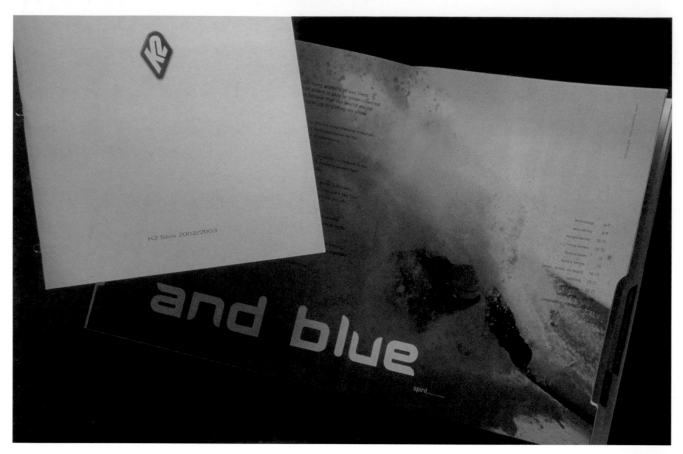

design firm
Hornall Anderson Design Works
Seattle, Washington

C - 12   C - 45
M - 72   M - 49
Y - 59   Y - 45
K - 37   K - 35

IVARA

WORK SMART

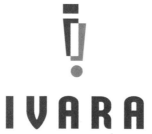

design firm
The Riordon Group Inc.
Oakville, Ontario
(Canada)

C - 55   C - 14
M - 19   M - 0
Y - 0   Y - 50
K - 46   K - 30

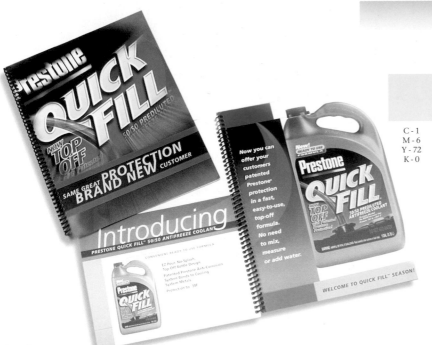

C - 1	C - 0	C - 86	C - 33
M - 6	M - 83	M - 58	M - 44
Y - 72	Y - 99	Y - 0	Y - 74
K - 0	K - 0	K - 0	K - 8

design firm
Tom Fowler, Inc.
Norwalk, Connecticut
client
Honeywell Consumer Products

design firm
DGWB
Santa Ana, California
client
South Coast Plaza

C - 53	C - 63
M - 84	M - 52
Y - 0	Y - 51
K - 0	K - 100

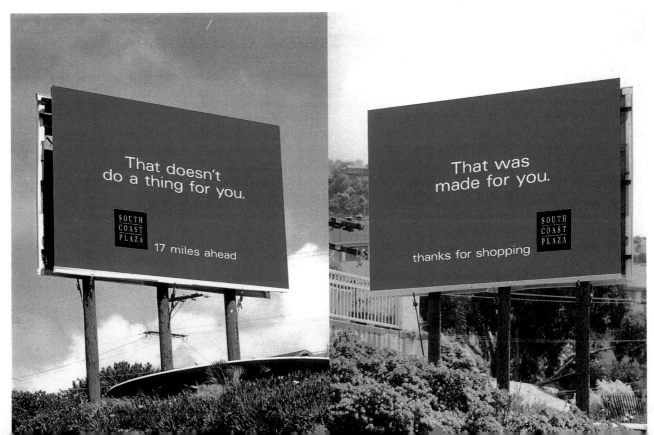

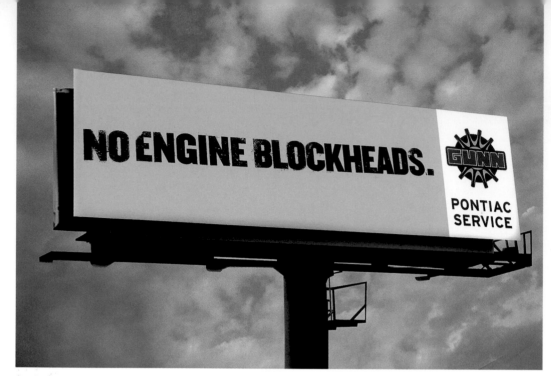

NO ENGINE BLOCKHEADS.

GUNN
PONTIAC
SERVICE

C - 0
M - 27
Y - 96
K - 0

C - 0
M - 99
Y - 82
K - 12

C - 0
M - 0
Y - 0
K - 100

design firm
Toolbox Studios, Inc.
San Antonio, Texas
client
Gunn Automotive

C - 53
M - 85
Y - 16
K - 0

C - 0
M - 25
Y - 94
K - 0

C - 48
M - 7
Y - 89
K - 0

C - 0
M - 66
Y - 99
K - 0

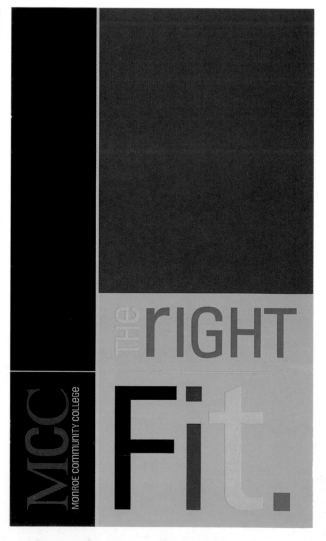

THE riGHT
Fit.

MCC
MONROE COMMUNITY COLLEGE

design firm
Buck & Pulleyn
Pittsford, New York
client
MCC

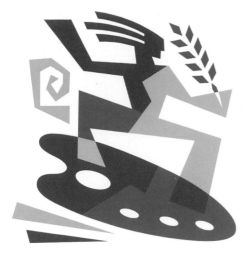

C - 69	C - 0	C - 0
M - 65	M - 79	M - 31
Y - 0	Y - 94	Y - 94
K - 31	K - 0	K - 0

design firm
Greteman Group
Wichita, Kansas

design firm
Funk/Levis & Associates
Eugene, Oregon
client
Sony

C - 18	C - 79
M - 12	M - 83
Y - 89	Y - 1
K - 3	K - 0

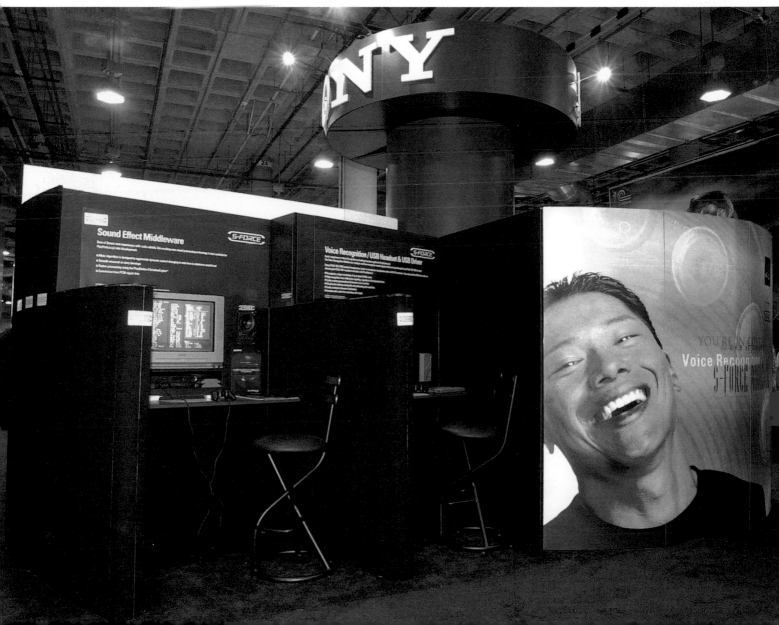

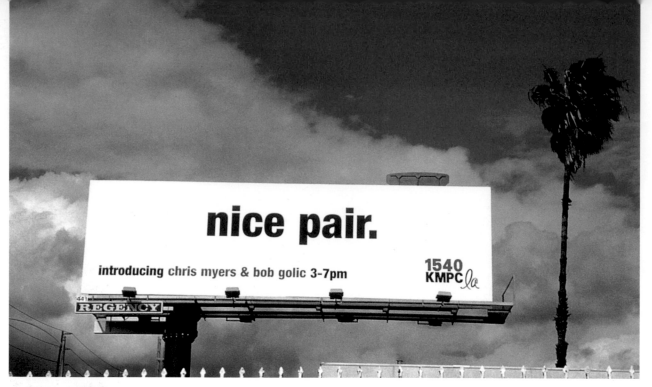

nice pair.

introducing chris myers & bob golic 3-7pm

1540 KMPC la

C - 25
M - 76
Y - 50
K - 4

C - 0
M - 0
Y - 0
K - 100

design firm
Campbell-Ewald Advertising
Warren, Michigan
client
KMPC Sporting News

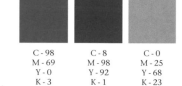

C - 98
M - 69
Y - 0
K - 3

C - 8
M - 98
Y - 92
K - 1

C - 0
M - 25
Y - 68
K - 23

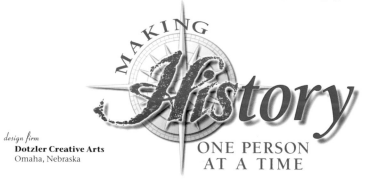

design firm
Dotzler Creative Arts
Omaha, Nebraska

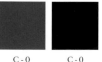

C - 0
M - 99
Y - 95
K - 11

C - 0
M - 0
Y - 0
K - 100

redgraf!x
design&illustrationstudio

design firm
Redgrafix Design & Illustration Studio
New Berlin, Wisconsin
client
Redgrafix Design & Illustration Studio

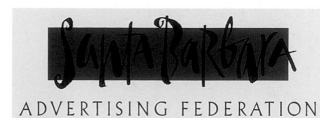

ADVERTISING FEDERATION

C - 26
M - 99
Y - 73
K - 20

design firm
Mark Oliver, Inc.
Solvang, California
client
Santa Barbara Ad Federation

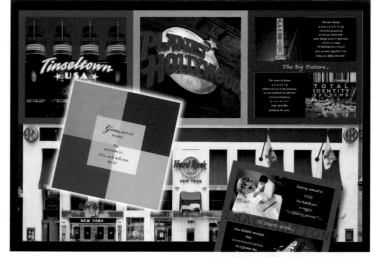

C - 25　　C - 0　　C - 90　　C - 0
M - 0　　M - 100　M - 65　　M - 35
Y - 95　　Y - 100　Y - 0　　Y - 100
K - 27　　K - 22　　K - 15　　K - 0

design firm
McElveney & Palozzi Design Group
Rochester, New York
client
Empire Forster

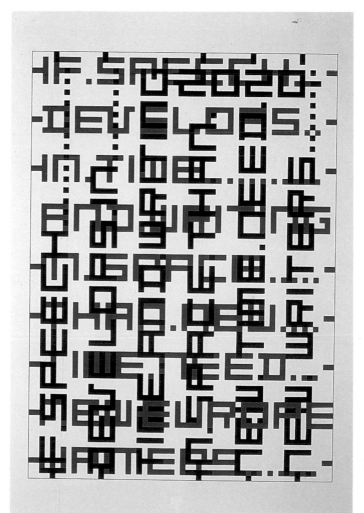

design firm
Kontrapunkt
Ljubljana (Slovenia)
client
Ministry for European Integration, Croatia

C - 12　　C - 62
M - 91　　M - 51
Y - 86　　Y - 49
K - 2　　K - 63

47

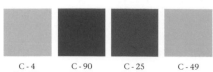

C - 4
M - 30
Y - 78
K - 0

C - 90
M - 71
Y - 0
K - 6

C - 25
M - 85
Y - 0
K - 0

C - 49
M - 5
Y - 99
K - 0

design firm
ProWolfe Partners
St. Louis, Missouri
client
Tripos

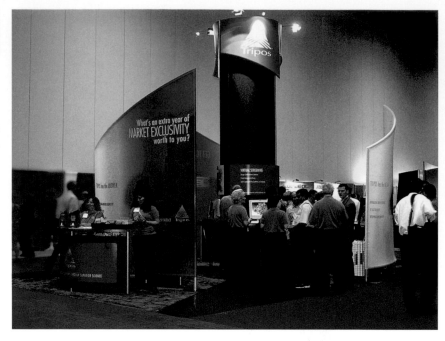

C - 45
M - 25
Y - 57
K - 0

C - 5
M - 15
Y - 68
K - 0

design firm
McClain Finlon Advertising
Denver, Colorado
client
Mutual UFO Network Museum

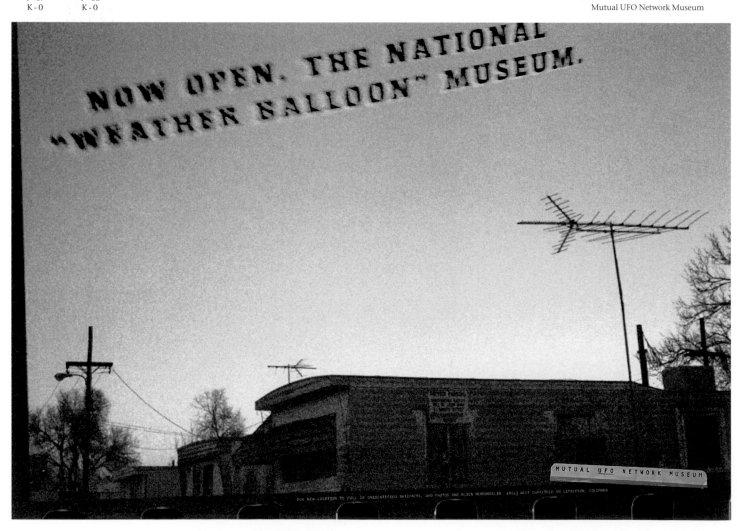

48

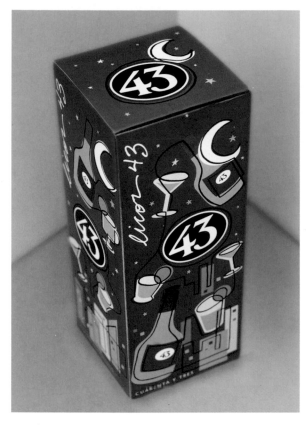

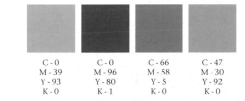

C - 4	C - 82	C - 6	C - 74
M - 41	M - 92	M - 100	M - 29
Y - 96	Y - 6	Y - 99	Y - 100
K - 0	K - 1	K - 1	K - 15

design firm
Bailey Design Group Inc.
Plymouth Meeting, Pennsylvania

C - 0	C - 0	C - 66	C - 47
M - 39	M - 96	M - 58	M - 30
Y - 93	Y - 80	Y - 5	Y - 92
K - 0	K - 1	K - 0	K - 0

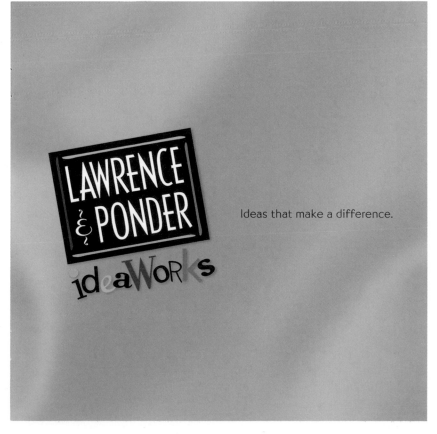

Ideas that make a difference.

design firm
Lawrence & Ponder Ideaworks
Newport Beach, California
client
Lawrence & Ponder Ideaworks

design firm
Belyea
Seattle, Washington
client
ColorGraphics

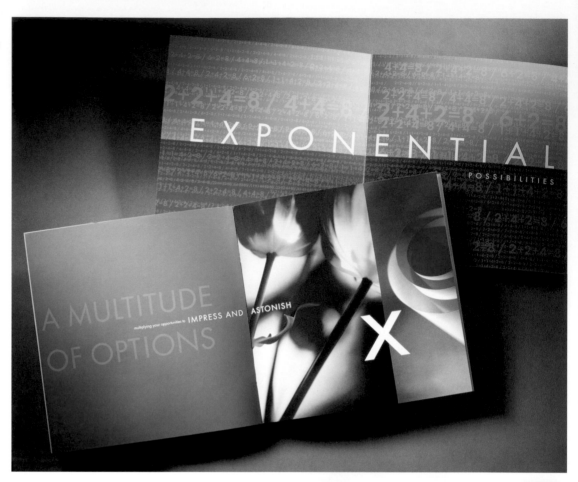

C - 27	C - 44	C - 71	C - 0	C - 100
M - 81	M - 17	M - 20	M - 13	M - 80
Y - 55	Y - 65	Y - 13	Y - 64	Y - 0
K - 4	K - 2	K - 0	K - 0	K - 12

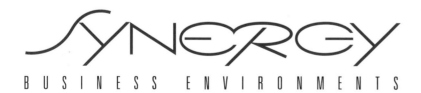

C - 0	C - 75	C - 3
M - 100	M - 75	M - 20
Y - 100	Y - 0	Y - 54
K - 0	K - 0	K - 0

design firm
Tom Ventress Design
Nashville, Tennessee
client
Synergy Business Environments

COVANCE ™

design firm
Addison
San Francisco, California
client
Covance

C - 91   C - 1
M - 9   M - 93
Y - 11   Y - 65
K - 0   K - 0

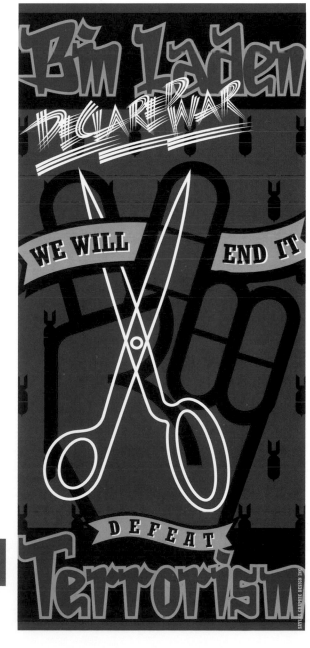

design firm
Sayles Graphic Design
Des Moines, Iowa
client
"Art Fights Back"

C - 0   C - 0   C - 61
M - 89   M - 50   M - 31
Y - 93   Y - 90   Y - 83
K - 0   K - 0   K - 54

51

C - 0
M - 90
Y - 73
K - 0

C - 0   C - 15
M - 68   M - 69
Y - 78   Y - 52
K - 0   K - 55

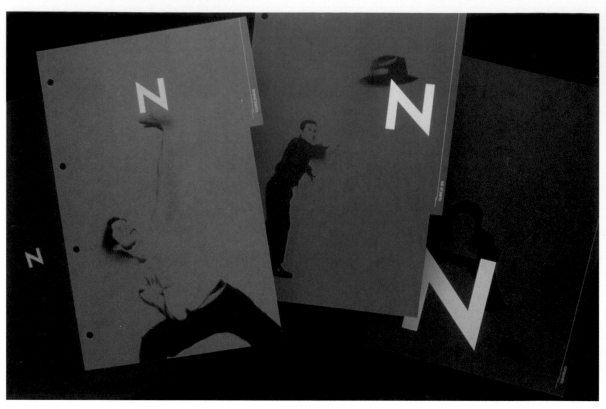

design firm
**Hornall Anderson
Design Works**
Seattle, Washington

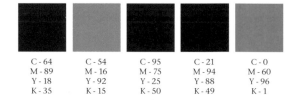

C - 64   C - 54   C - 95   C - 21   C - 0
M - 89   M - 16   M - 75   M - 94   M - 60
Y - 18   Y - 92   Y - 25   Y - 88   Y - 96
K - 35   K - 15   K - 50   K - 49   K - 1

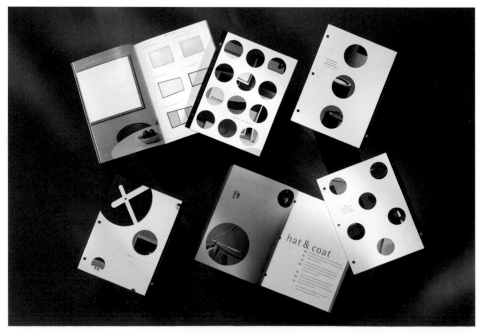

design firm
5D Studio
Malibu, California
client
Peter Pepper Products

52

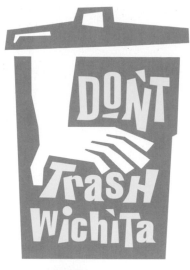

C - 0	C - 0
M - 57	M - 0
Y - 87	Y - 100
K - 0	K - 0

design firm
Greteman Group
Wichita, Kansas

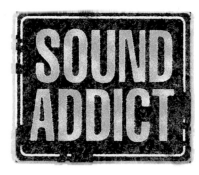

C - 27	C - 80	C - 3	C - 0
M - 0	M - 67	M - 0	M - 49
Y - 63	Y - 67	Y - 49	Y - 80
K - 0	K - 50	K - 0	K - 0

design firm
Louis & Partners Design
Bath, Ohio
client
Sound Addict

design firm
Klündt Hosmer Design
Spokane, Washington
client
Webprint

C - 35	C - 55	C - 0
M - 100	M - 0	M - 0
Y - 0	Y - 100	Y - 0
K - 0	K - 0	K - 100

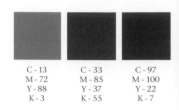

C - 13
M - 72
Y - 88
K - 3

C - 33
M - 85
Y - 37
K - 55

C - 97
M - 100
Y - 22
K - 7

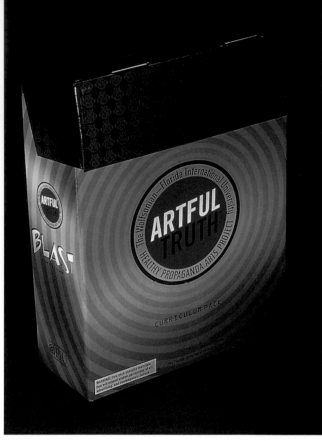

design firm
Mobium Creative Group
Chicago, Illinois

client
Neovation

design firm
Pinkhaus
Miami, Florida

client
Wolfsonian Institute

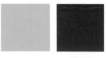

C - 40
M - 2
Y - 93
K - 1

C - 0
M - 0
Y - 0
K - 100

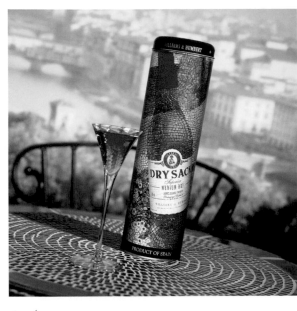

C - 78	C - 0	C - 13	C - 95	C - 1
M - 30	M - 75	M - 100	M - 81	M - 11
Y - 100	Y - 99	Y - 100	Y - 49	Y - 98
K - 19	K - 0	K - 7	K - 21	K - 0

design firm
Bailey Design Group Inc.
Plymouth Meeting, Pennsylvania

C 54	C - 10
M - 72	M - 10
Y - 0	Y - 10
K - 0	K - 1

design firm
Dentz & Cristina
New York, New York
client
Paco Rabanne

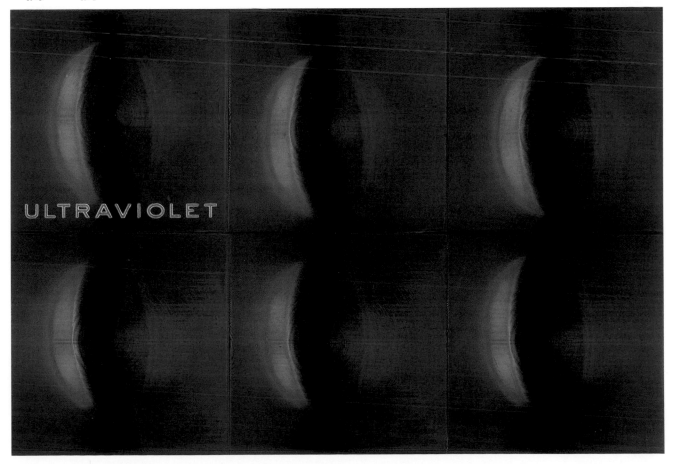

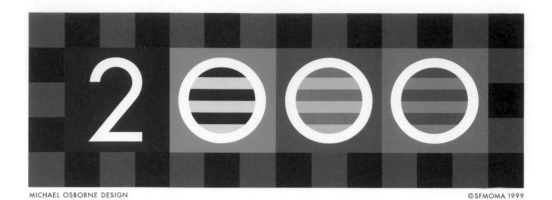

MICHAEL OSBORNE DESIGN   ©SFMOMA 1999

SAN FRANCISCO MUSEUM OF MODERN ART

design firm
Michael Osborne Design
San Francisco, California
client
San Francisco Museum of Modern Art

C - 0	C - 100	C - 70	C - 0	C - 39
M - 100	M - 10	M - 70	M - 65	M - 5
Y - 100	Y - 0	Y - 0	Y - 87	Y - 100
K - 0	K - 0	K - 0	K - 0	K - 0

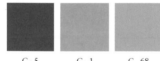

C - 5	C - 1	C - 68
M - 91	M - 47	M - 13
Y - 93	Y - 69	Y - 6
K - 0	K - 0	K - 1

design firm
Becker Design
Milwaukee, Wisconsin
client
GraphicSource

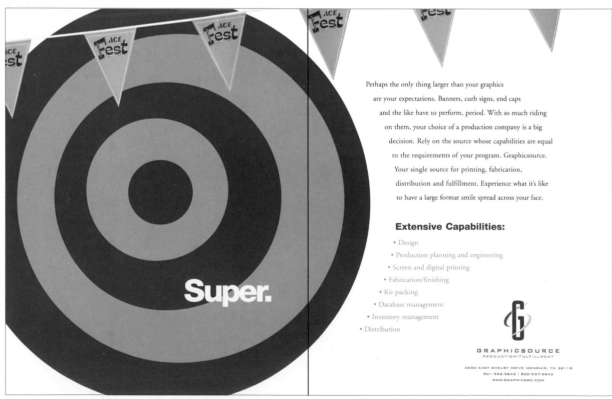

Perhaps the only thing larger than your graphics
are your expectations. Banners, curb signs, end caps
and the like have to perform, period. With so much riding
on them, your choice of a production company is a big
decision. Rely on the source whose capabilities are equal
to the requirements of your program. Graphicsource.
Your single source for printing, fabrication,
distribution and fulfillment. Experience what it's like
to have a large format smile spread across your face.

Extensive Capabilities:

• Design
• Production planning and engineering
• Screen and digital printing
• Fabrication/finishing
• Kit packing
• Database management
• Inventory management
• Distribution

GRAPHICSOURCE
PRODUCTION/FULFILLMENT

4500 EAST SHELBY DRIVE MEMPHIS, TN 38118
901-366-5842 / 800-237-5842
WWW.GRAPHICSRC.COM

C - 40
M - 5
Y - 100
K - 0

C - 45
M - 70
Y - 0
K - 0

C - 80
M - 5
Y - 20
K - 0

C - 0
M - 40
Y - 100
K - 0

C - 5
M - 100
Y - 100
K - 0

C - 80
M - 10
Y - 0
K - 0

C - 3
M - 80
Y - 0
K - 0

C - 0
M - 5
Y - 100
K - 0

C - 100
M - 45
Y - 0
K - 0

design firm
Michael Osborne Design
San Francisco, California

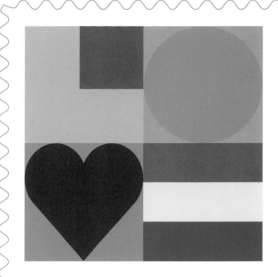

LOVE 37 USA

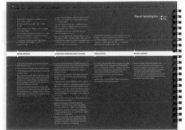

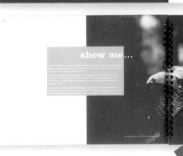

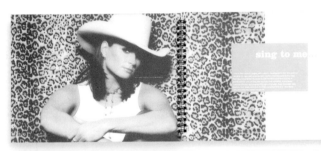

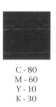

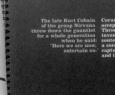

C - 80
M - 60
Y - 10
K - 30

C - 0
M - 90
Y - 95
K - 10

C - 80
M - 5
Y - 100
K - 0

C - 0
M - 25
Y - 80
K - 5

C - 55
M - 60
Y - 0
K - 0

design firm
The Riordon Design Group Inc.
Oakville, Ontario
(Canada)
client
Corus Entertainment

The late Kurt Cobain
of the group Nirvana
threw down the gauntlet
for a whole generation
when he said:
'Here we are now,
entertain us.'

Corus Entertainment has
accepted that challenge.
Through its versatile and
inventive programming and
content, Corus has established
a connection to its audiences,
capturing their hearts, minds
and imaginations.

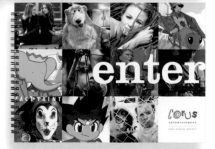

C - 0
M - 40
Y - 90
K - 0

C - 100
M - 50
Y - 0
K - 0

C - 30
M - 70
Y - 0
K - 10

C - 30
M - 0
Y - 100
K - 0

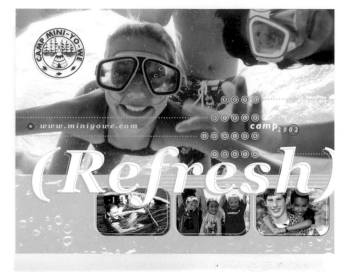

(Refresh)

design firm
The Riordon Design Group Inc.
Oakville, Ontario
(Canada)

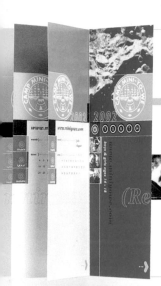

(React)

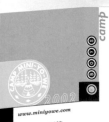

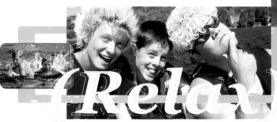

(Relax)

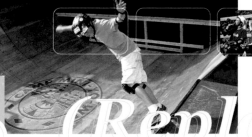

(Replay)

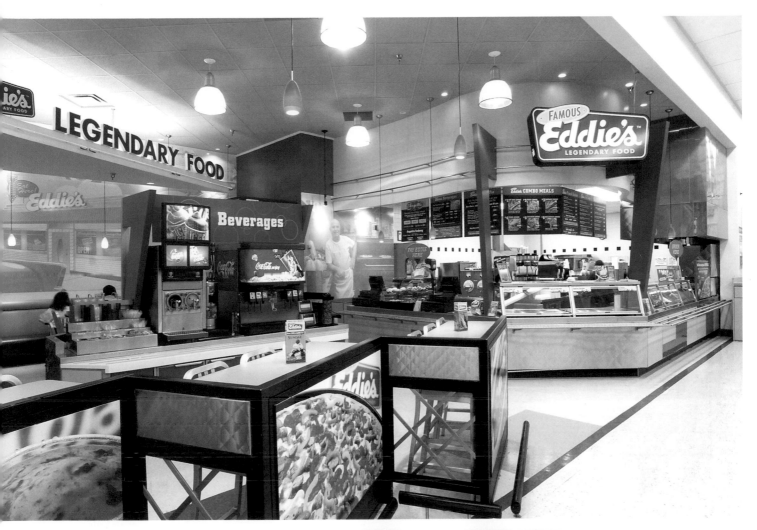

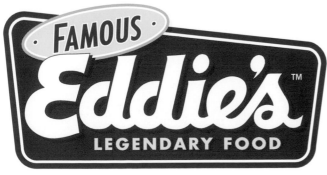

C - 0	C - 0	C - 100	C - 47
M - 100	M - 9	M - 56	M - 95
Y - 91	Y - 94	Y - 0	Y - 93
K - 0	K - 0	K - 34	K - 22

design firm
Louis & Partners Design
Bath, Ohio
client
Famous Eddie's

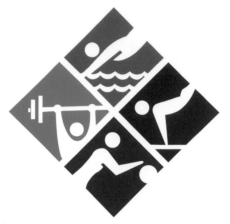

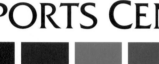

MONTEREY
SPORTS CENTER

C - 50	C - 0	C - 100	C - 100
M - 100	M - 100	M - 0	M - 50
Y - 0	Y - 50	Y - 100	Y - 0
K - 0	K - 0	K - 0	K - 0

design firm
The Wecker Group
Monterey, California
client
Monterey Sports Center

C - 1	C - 15	C - 66
M - 96	M - 12	M - 80
Y - 89	Y - 9	Y - 0
K - 0	K - 0	K - 0

C - 50	C - 0	C - 60
M - 0	M - 30	M - 4
Y - 0	Y - 100	Y - 80
K - 0	K - 0	K - 0

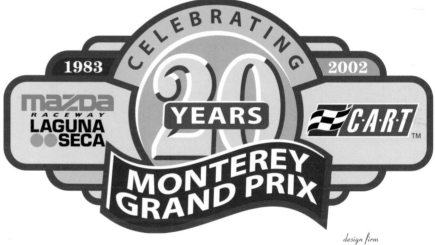

design firm
The Wecker Group
Monterey, California

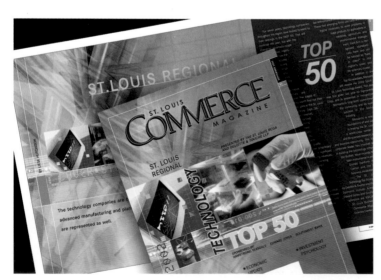

design firm
Stan Gellman Graphic Design
St. Louis, Missouri

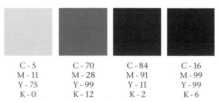

C - 5	C - 70	C - 84	C - 16
M - 11	M - 28	M - 91	M - 99
Y - 75	Y - 99	Y - 11	Y - 99
K - 0	K - 12	K - 2	K - 6

fun

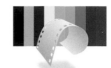

JIM PINCKNEY

137 Littlefield Road
Monterey, CA
93940
Tel 831-375-1964
Fax 831-375-1676
Email jim@jimpinckney.com
jimpinckney.com

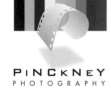

PINCkNEY
PHOTOGRAPHY

design firm
The Wecker Group
Monterey, California
client
Pinckney Photography

C - 100
M - 100
Y - 100
K - 0

C - 33
M - 24
Y - 15
K - 0

C - 0
M - 100
Y - 100
K - 0

C - 0
M - 0
Y - 100
K - 0

C - 50
M - 0
Y - 100
K - 0

C - 75
M - 0
Y - 0
K - 0

C - 100
M - 20
Y - 0
K - 0

C - 35
M - 90
Y - 0
K - 0

C - 65
M - 80
Y - 0
K - 0

PINCkNEY
PHOTOGRAPHY

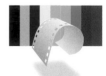

PINCkNEY
PHOTOGRAPHY

JIM PINCKNEY

137 Littlefield Road
Monterey, CA
93940

JIM PINCKNEY

137 Littlefield Road
Monterey, CA
93940
Tel 831-375-1964
Fax 831-375-1676
Email jim@jimpinckney.com
jimpinckney.com

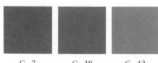

C - 7
M - 19
Y - 0
K - 50

C - 18
M - 61
Y - 81
K - 0

C - 43
M - 0
Y - 30
K - 27

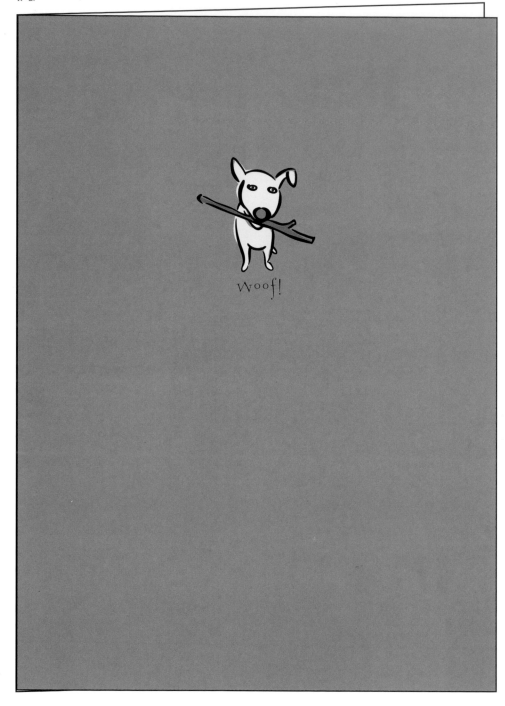

design firm
After Hours Creative
Phoenix, Arizona

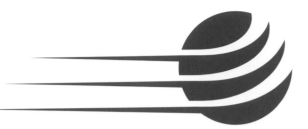

World Wide Packets®

ACCESS BRILLIANCE

design firm
Klündt Hosmer Design
Spokane, Washington
client
WorldWide Packets

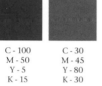

C - 100	C - 30
M - 50	M - 45
Y - 5	Y - 80
K - 15	K - 30

EXPRESS Theatre
northwest

design firm
Klündt Hosmer Design
Spokane, Washington
client
Express Theatre

C - 100	C - 15	C - 4
M - 5	M - 75	M - 22
Y - 20	Y - 100	Y - 30
K - 45	K - 0	K - 0

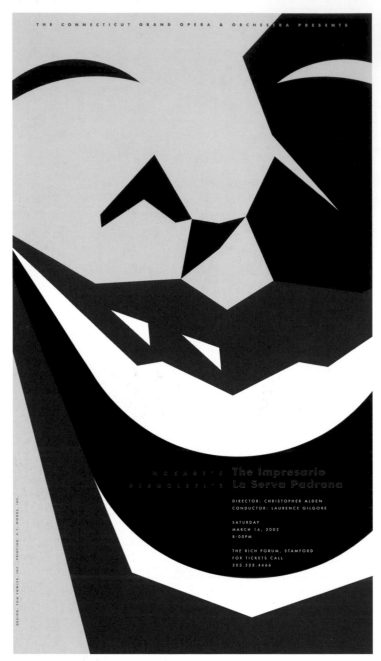

MOZART'S **The Impresario**
PERGOLESI'S **La Serva Padrona**

DIRECTOR: CHRISTOPHER ALDEN
CONDUCTOR: LAURENCE GILGORE

SATURDAY
MARCH 16, 2002
8:00PM

THE RICH FORUM, STAMFORD
FOR TICKETS CALL
203.325.4466

DESIGN: TOM FOWLER, INC. PRINTING: M.T. WOODS, INC.

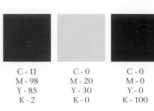

C - 11	C - 0	C - 0
M - 98	M - 20	M - 0
Y - 85	Y - 30	Y - 0
K - 2	K - 0	K - 100

design firm
Tom Fowler, Inc.
Norwalk, Connecticut

client
Connecticut Grand Opera & Orchestra

design firm
Wallace Church, Inc.
New York, New York

client
Kodak

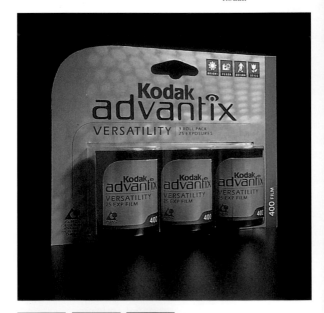

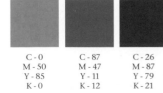

C - 0	C - 87	C - 26
M - 50	M - 47	M - 87
Y - 85	Y - 11	Y - 79
K - 0	K - 12	K - 21

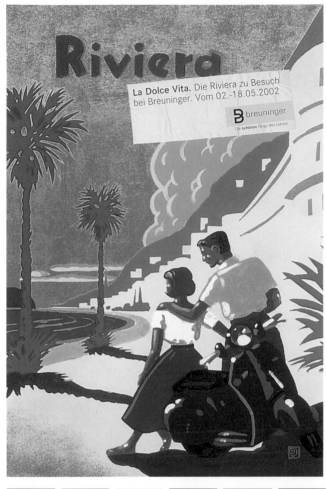

C - 9	C - 7	C - 2	C - 75	C - 61	C - 97
M - 87	M - 45	M - 7	M - 34	M - 16	M - 52
Y - 99	Y - 99	Y - 56	Y - 99	Y - 28	Y - 2
K - 0	K - 0	K - 0	K - 0	K - 0	K - 0

design firm
Heye
Unerhaching/Muclich (Germany)
client
Breuninger

design firm
Greteman Group
Wichita, Kansas

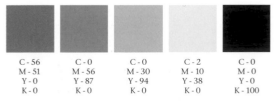

C - 56	C - 0	C - 0	C - 2	C - 0
M - 51	M - 56	M - 30	M - 10	M - 0
Y - 0	Y - 87	Y - 94	Y - 38	Y - 0
K - 0	K - 0	K - 0	K - 0	K - 100

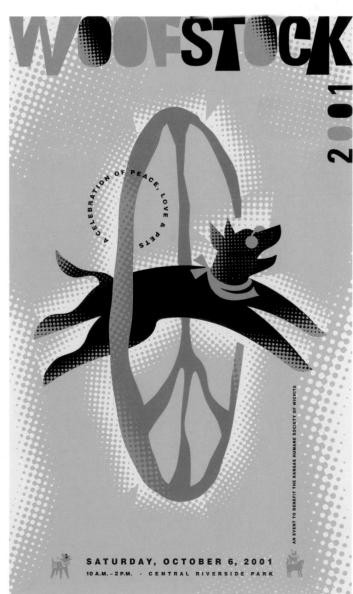

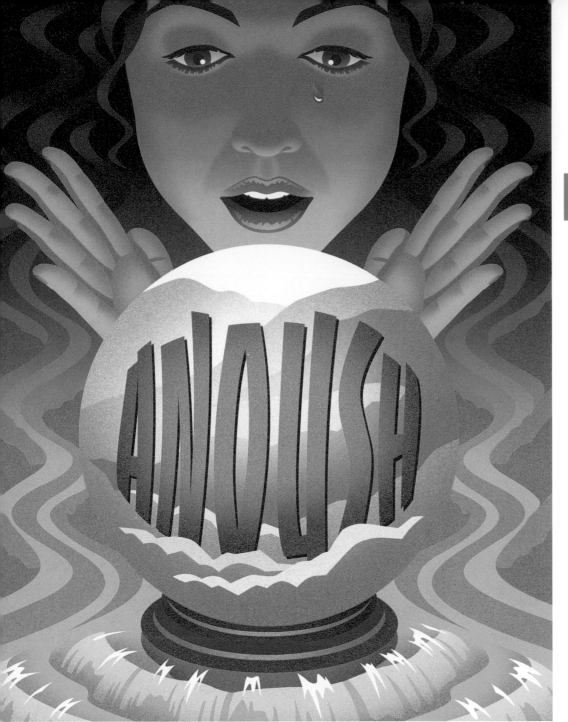

C - 60
M - 4
Y - 22
K - 0

C - 89
M - 18
Y - 76
K - 0

C - 36
M - 54
Y - 69
K - 0

C - 1
M - 0
Y - 43
K - 0

C - 25
M - 54
Y - 69
K - 0

design firm
Fusion/Design Communications
Madison Heights, Michigan
client
Michigan Opera Theatre

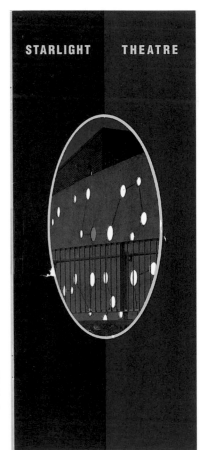

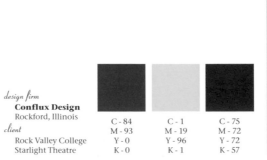

design firm
Conflux Design
Rockford, Illinois
client
Rock Valley College
Starlight Theatre

C - 84
M - 93
Y - 0
K - 0

C - 1
M - 19
Y - 96
K - 1

C - 75
M - 72
Y - 72
K - 57

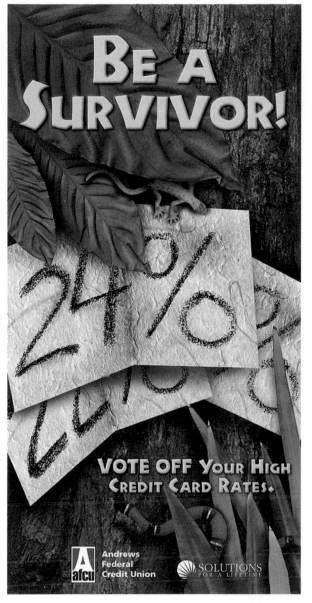

C - 73 | C - 18 | C - 42 | C - 6
M - 37 | M - 19 | M - 62 | M - 85
Y - 91 | Y - 56 | Y - 86 | Y - 85
K - 0 | K - 0 | K - 15 | K - 6

design firm
Rottman Creative Group, LLC
La Plata, Maryland
client
Andrews Federal Credit Union

C - 5 | C - 85 | C - 91 | C - 6 | C - 30 | C - 0
M - 4 | M - 11 | M - 79 | M - 6 | M - 8 | M - 96
Y - 30 | Y - 32 | Y - 1 | Y - 97 | Y - 96 | Y - 88
K - 0 | K - 0 | K - 13 | K - 0 | K - 0 | K - 6

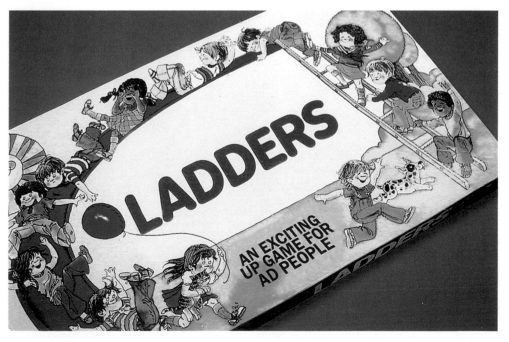

design firm
AMP
Costa Mesa, California
client
Adjobs.com

C - 0
M - 9
Y - 86
K - 0

C - 24
M - 96
Y - 79
K - 9

C - 73
M - 16
Y - 21
K - 0

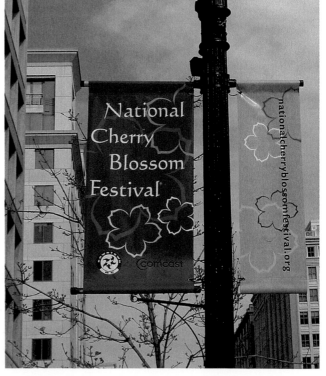

design firm
Marshall Fenn Communications
Toronto (Canada)
client
Casino Rama

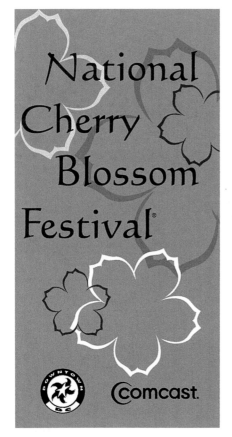

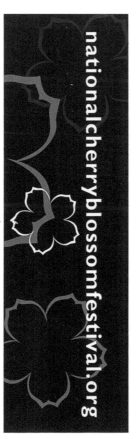

C - 95
M - 99
Y - 20
K - 13

C - 17
M - 98
Y - 11
K - 0

C - 12
M - 51
Y - 21
K - 0

design firm
Pensaré Design Group, Ltd.
Washington, D.C.
client
National Cherry Blossom Festival

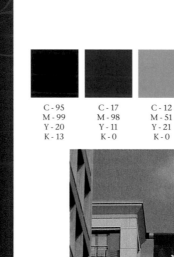

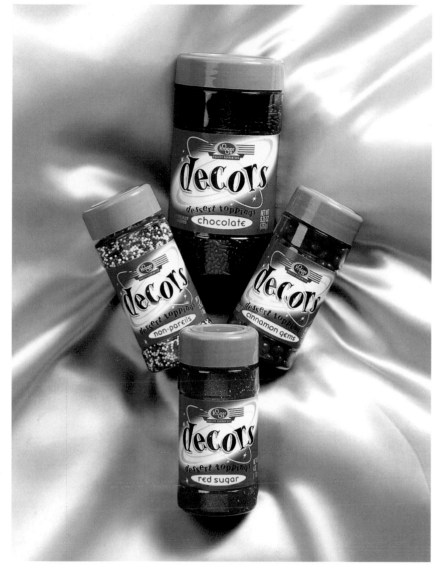

C - 0
M - 0
Y - 0
K - 0

C - 0
M - 0
Y - 0
K - 0

C - 0
M - 0
Y - 0
K - 100

design firm
Interbrand Hulefeld
Cincinnati, Ohio

client
Kroger Company

C - 18
M - 99
Y - 0
K - 0

C - 99
M - 80
Y - 4
K - 2

C - 91
M - 2
Y - 9
K - 0

C - 75
M - 8
Y - 81
K - 0

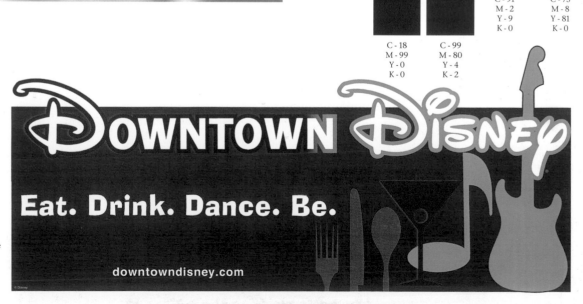

design firm
**Disneyland Creative
Print Services**
Anaheim, California

client
Brand Management

C - 38
M - 99
Y - 95
K - 0

C - 97
M - 71
Y - 2
K - 3

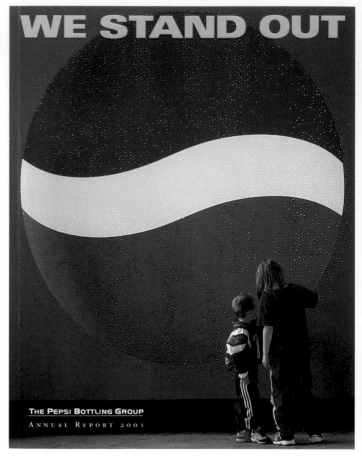

WE STAND OUT

THE PEPSI BOTTLING GROUP
ANNUAL REPORT 2001

design firm
Champ Cohen Design
Del Mar, California
client
Abbott Animal Health

design firm
Davidoff Associates Inc.
New York, New York
client
The Pepsi Bottling Group, Inc.

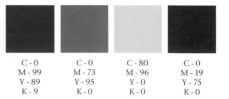

Abbott Crown Club

Top Dog Rewards

C - 0
M - 99
Y - 89
K - 9

C - 0
M - 73
Y - 95
K - 0

C - 80
M - 96
Y - 0
K - 0

C - 0
M - 19
Y - 75
K - 0

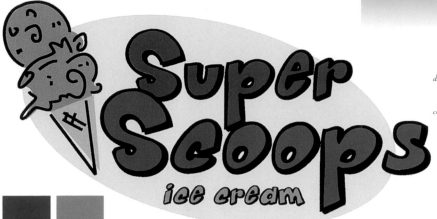

design firm
Bridge Creative Inc.
Kennebunk, Maine
client
Stu Small

C - 0
M - 98
Y - 97
K - 1

C - 35
M - 56
Y - 8
K - 0

C - 88
M - 84
Y - 0
K - 9

C - 76
M - 53
Y - 73
K - 22

C - 0
M - 22
Y - 95
K - 0

C - 92
M - 68
Y - 10
K - 6

C - 8
M - 35
Y - 63
K - 0

C - 0
M - 11
Y - 98
K - 0

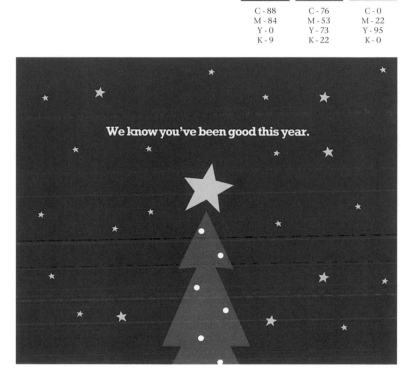

We know you've been good this year.

design firm
[i]e design, Los Angeles
Manhattan Beach, California
client
[i]e design, Los Angeles

design firm
Sterrett Dymond Stewart Advertising
Charlotte, North Carolina
client
Sterrett Dymond Stewart Advertising

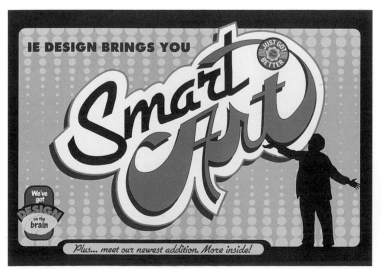

IE DESIGN BRINGS YOU

Plus... meet our newest addition. More inside!

C - 65
M - 51
Y - 10
K - 0

C - 33
M - 4
Y - 56
K - 0

C - 6
M - 67
Y - 80
K - 1

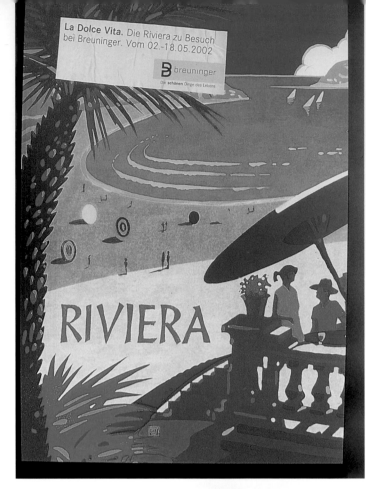

design firm
Heye
Unterhaching/Munich (Germany)
client
Breuninger

C - 9 M - 87 Y - 99 K - 0	C - 7 M - 45 Y - 99 K - 0	C - 2 M - 7 Y - 56 K - 0	C - 75 M - 34 Y - 99 K - 0	C - 61 M - 16 Y - 28 K - 0	C - 97 M - 52 Y - 2 K - 0

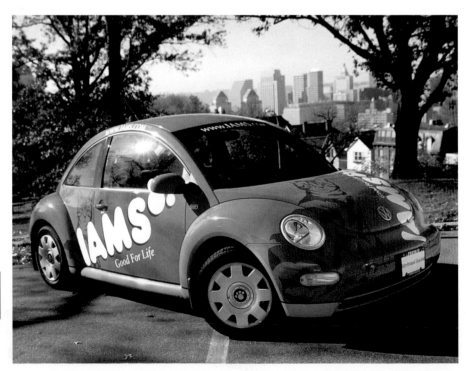

C - 0 M - 57 Y - 100 K - 0	C - 62 M - 95 Y - 100 K - 27

design firm
Interbrand Hulefeld
Cincinnati, Ohio
client
Procter & Gamble

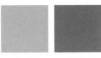

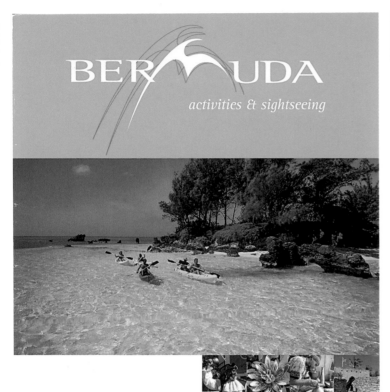

BER UDA

activities & sightseeing

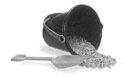

INFORMATION & PRICE GUIDE

BERMUDA DEPARTMENT OF TOURISM

C - 46	C - 71
M - 0	M - 55
Y - 93	Y - 0
K - 0	K - 0

design firm
Advantage Ltd.
Hamilton (Bermuda)
client
Bermuda Tourism

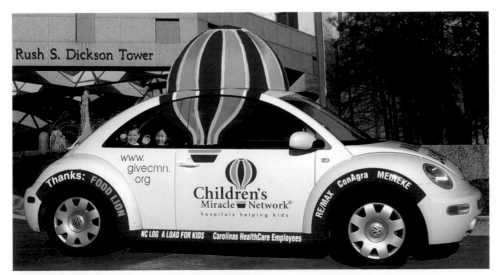

design firm
**Performance Graphics
of Lake Norman**
Cornelius, North Carolina
client
LimeAide
Refreshing Delivery

C - 0	C - 11
M - 24	M - 98
Y - 86	Y - 85
K - 0	K - 2

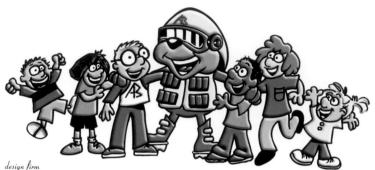
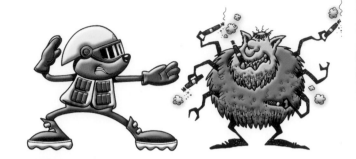

design firm
Dotzler Creative Arts
Omaha, Nebraska

C - 1	C - 61	C - 0	C - 100	C - 3
M - 0	M - 0	M - 60	M - 50	M - 87
Y - 87	Y - 88	Y - 86	Y - 0	Y - 90
K - 0	K - 0	K - 0	K - 16	K - 5

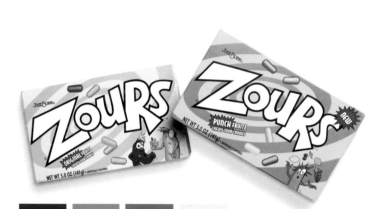

design firm
Bailey Design Group Inc.
Plymouth Meeting, Pennsylvania

C - 0	C - 44	C - 84	C - 0
M - 100	M - 0	M - 16	M - 0
Y - 89	Y - 100	Y - 26	Y - 85
K - 0	K - 22	K - 8	K - 0

design firm
Bailey Design Group Inc.
Plymouth Meeting, Pennsylvania

C - 4	C - 0	C - 100	C - 53	C - 100
M - 80	M - 35	M - 100	M - 100	M - 100
Y - 84	Y - 95	Y - 4	Y - 5	Y - 4
K - 1	K - 1	K - 6	K - 2	K - 6

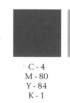
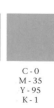

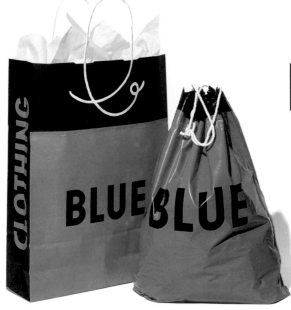

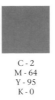

design firm
Sagmeister Inc.
New York, New York

C - 82   C - 2
M - 82   M - 64
Y - 85   Y - 95
K - 58   K - 0

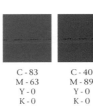 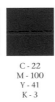   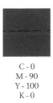

C - 83   C - 40   C - 4   C - 22   C - 68   C - 0
M - 63   M - 89   M - 6   M - 100   M - 0   M - 90
Y - 0   Y - 0   Y - 99   Y - 41   Y - 100   Y - 100
K - 0   K - 0   K - 0   K - 3   K - 0   K - 0

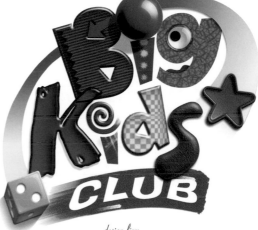

design firm
McElveney & Palozzi Design Group
Rochester, New York
client
McElveney & Palozzi Design Group

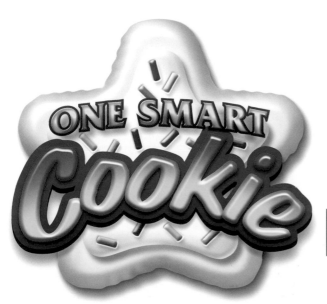

C - 0   C - 3   C - 85   C - 4
M - 80   M - 14   M - 71   M - 0
Y - 100   Y - 99   Y - 0   Y - 50
K - 0   K - 0   K - 0   K - 0

design firm
McElveney & Palozzi Design Group
Rochester, New York
client
McElveney & Palozzi Design Group

C - 13	C - 4	C - 65	C - 71	C - 58
M - 100	M - 0	M - 83	M - 0	M - 0
Y - 12	Y - 88	Y - 0	Y - 100	Y - 1
K - 0	K - 0	K - 0	K - 0	K - 0

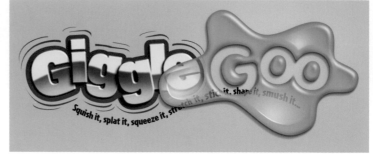

design firm
McElveney & Palozzi Design Group
Rochester, New York
client
McElveney & Palozzi Design Group

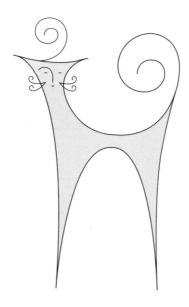

C - 0
M - 14
Y - 0
K - 0

a very stylish girl®

design firm
After Hours Creative
Phoenix, Arizona

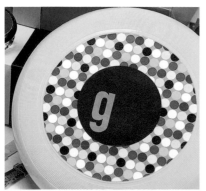

design firm
Michael Osborne Design
San Francisco, California
client
Gymboree

C - 2	C - 2	C - 75	C - 40	C - 69	C - 6
M - 41	M - 10	M - 33	M - 91	M - 70	M - 6
Y - 92	Y - 93	Y - 9	Y - 20	Y - 29	Y - 56
K - 0	K - 0	K - 7	K - 12	K - 59	K - 1

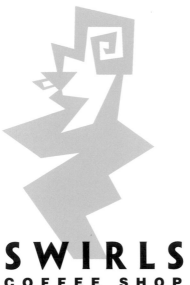

SWIRLS
COFFEE SHOP

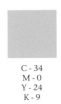

C - 34 C - 0
M - 0   M - 0
Y - 24 Y - 0
K - 9   K - 100

design firm
Greteman Group
Wichita, Kansas

C - 0   C - 39   C - 100 C - 70
M - 10   M - 5   M - 10   M - 70
Y - 100 Y - 100 Y - 0   Y - 0
K - 0   K - 0   K - 0   K - 0

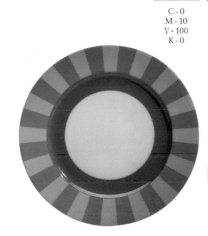
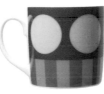

design firm
Michael Osborne Design
San Francisco, California
client
San Francisco Museum of Modern Art

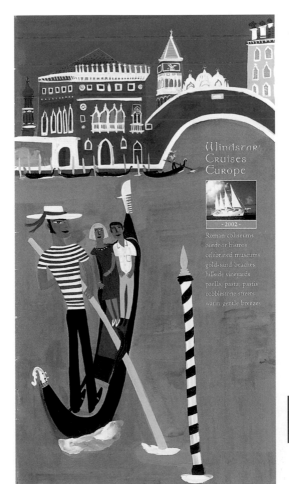

Windstar Cruises Europe

- 2002 -

Roman coliseums
outdoor bistros
celebrated museums
gold-sand beaches
hillside vineyards
paella, pasta, pastis
cobblestone streets
warm gentle breezes

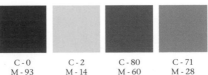

C - 0   C - 2   C - 80   C - 71
M - 93   M - 14   M - 60   M - 28
Y - 82   Y - 92   Y - 0   Y - 29
K - 3   K - 0   K - 0   K - 5

design firm
Besser Design Group
Santa Monica, California
client
Windstar Cruises

77

C - 0
M - 79
Y - 94
K - 0

C - 0
M - 31
Y - 94
K - 0

C - 56
M - 56
Y - 0
K - 0

design firm
Greteman Group
Wichita, Kansas

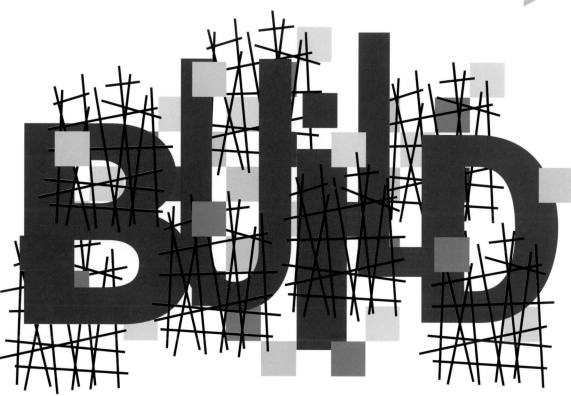

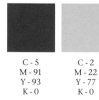

C - 5
M - 91
Y - 93
K - 0

C - 2
M - 22
Y - 77
K - 0

C - 86
M - 22
Y - 2
K - 0

C - 94
M - 69
Y - 5
K - 0

design firm
Bruce Yelaska Design
San Fransico, California
client
Saarman Construction

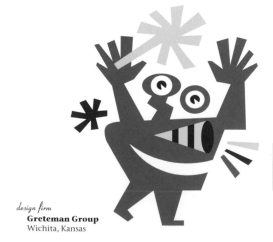

design firm
Greteman Group
Wichita, Kansas

C - 0
M - 80
Y - 100
K - 0

C - 78
M - 94
Y - 0
K - 0

C - 0
M - 15
Y - 100
K - 0

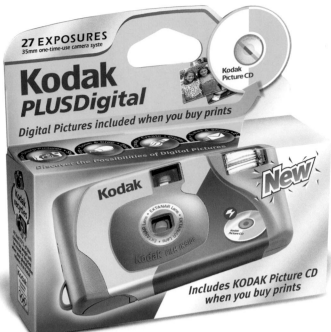

design firm
McElveney & Palozzi Design Group
Rochester, New York
client
Eastman Kodak Company

C - 0	C - 0	C - 85	C - 0
M - 100	M - 18	M - 47	M - 0
Y - 100	Y - 100	Y - 0	Y - 0
K - 0	K - 0	K - 0	K - 31

design firm
Becker Design
Milwaukee, Wisconsin
client
Beta Systems

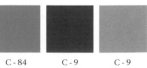

C - 84	C - 9	C - 9
M - 1	M - 93	M - 45
Y - 100	Y - 63	Y - 80
K - 0	K - 1	K - 1

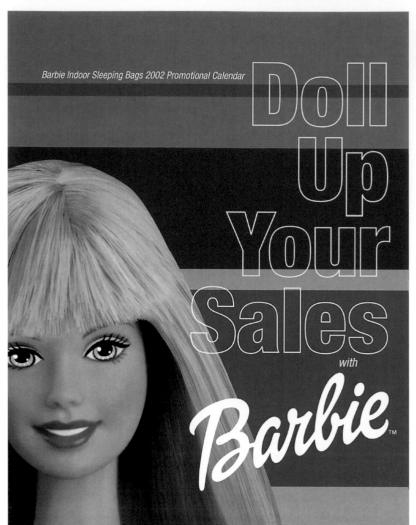

Barbie Indoor Sleeping Bags 2002 Promotional Calendar

Doll Up Your Sales *with* *Barbie*™

C - 0	C - 0	C - 1	C - 20
M - 72	M - 56	M - 90	M - 99
Y - 97	Y - 18	Y - 29	Y - 31
K - 0	K - 0	K - 0	K - 0

design firm
Launch Creative Marketing
Hillside, Illinois
client
Hedstrom Corporation

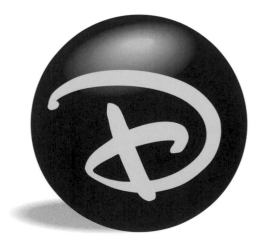

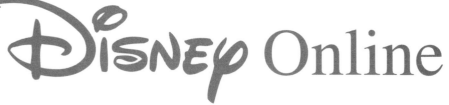

design firm
Disney Online
Los Angeles, California
client
The Walt Disney Company

C - 1	C - 2	C - 43
M - 96	M - 13	M - 30
Y - 89	Y - 92	Y - 41
K - 0	K - 0	K - 14

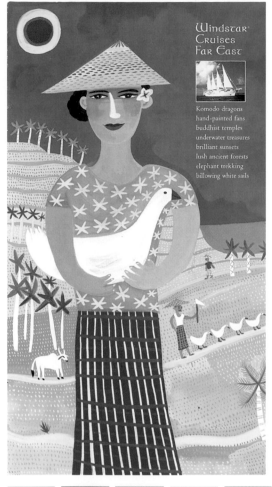

Windstar Cruises Far East

Komodo dragons
hand-painted fans
buddhist temples
underwater treasures
brilliant sunsets
lush ancient forests
elephant trekking
billowing white sails

C - 5	C - 13	C - 0	C - 9	C - 61
M - 49	M - 99	M - 78	M - 0	M - 11
Y - 14	Y - 50	Y - 84	Y - 93	Y - 85
K - 0	K - 0	K - 0	K - 0	K - 0

design firm
Besser Design Group
Santa Monica, California
client
Windstar Cruises

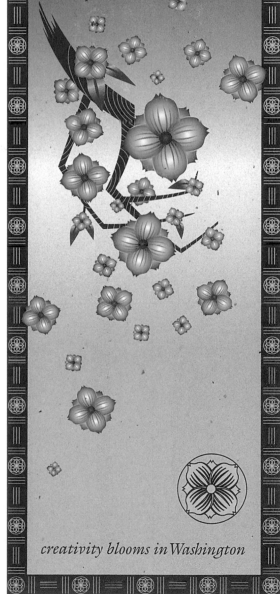

creativity blooms in Washington

design firm
Greenfield/Belser Ltd.
Washington, D.C.
client
Greenfield/Belser Ltd.

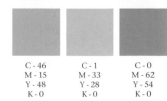

C - 46	C - 1	C - 0
M - 15	M - 33	M - 62
Y - 48	Y - 28	Y - 54
K - 0	K - 0	K - 0

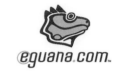

C - 48   C - 7   C - 0
M - 14   M - 1   M - 0
Y - 97   Y - 87   Y - 0
K - 5   K - 0   K - 100

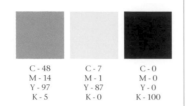

5207 Grant Avenue   Cleveland, Ohio 44125

5207 Grant Avenue   Cleveland, Ohio 44125
t 216 641-7148   f 216 641-7147   e info@eguana.com

design firm
Design Room
Cleveland, Ohio
client
eguana.com

C - 0   C - 2   C - 82   C - 50
M - 100   M - 5   M - 24   M - 100
Y - 100   Y - 93   Y - 96   Y - 0
K - 0   K - 0   K - 18   K - 40

design firm
Sunspots Creative, Inc.
Hoboken, New Jersey
client
Power Play Billiards

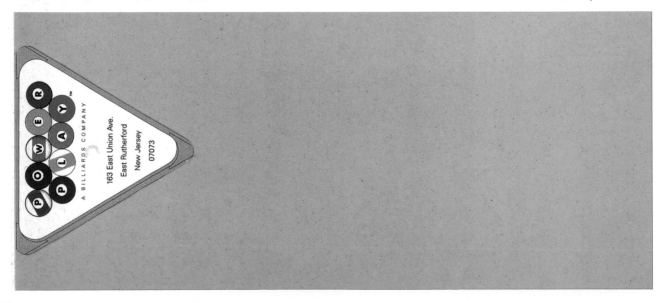

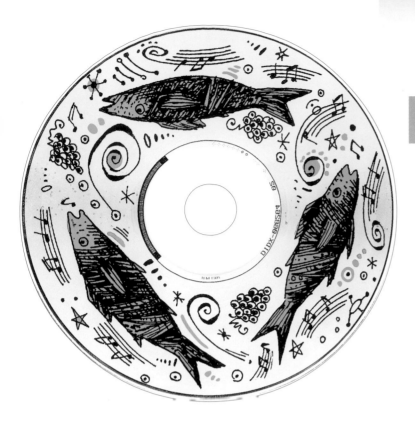

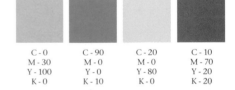

design firm
Oakley Design Studios
Portland, Oregon
client
Sokol Blosser Winery

C - 56   C - 0
M - 0   M - 0
Y - 27   Y - 0
K - 0   K - 100

C - 0   C - 90   C - 20   C - 10
M - 30   M - 0   M - 0   M - 70
Y - 100   Y - 0   Y - 80   Y - 20
K - 0   K - 10   K - 0   K - 20

design firm
Hughes Design
Norwalk, Connecticut
client
Mott's U.S.A.

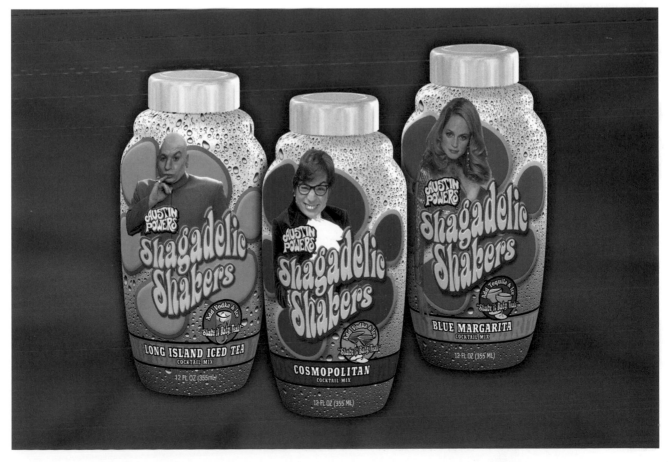

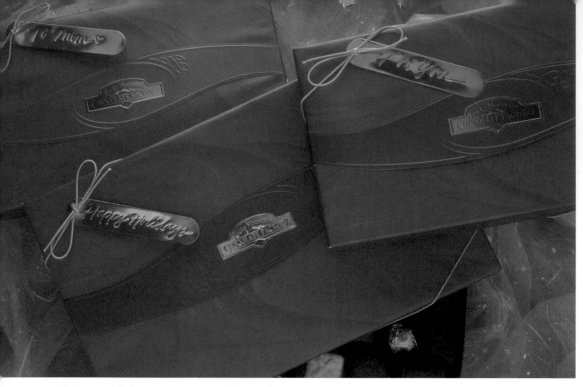

design firm
Hornall Anderson Design Works
Seattle, Washington

C - 18	C - 13	C - 47	C - 51
M - 72	M - 85	M - 62	M - 50
Y - 75	Y - 64	Y - 33	Y - 62
K - 16	K - 12	K - 7	K - 61

C - 52	C - 59	C - 5
M - 70	M - 17	M - 1
Y - 65	Y - 0	Y - 35
K - 57	K - 0	K - 0

design firm
Pearlfisher
London (England)

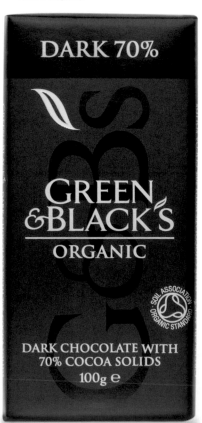 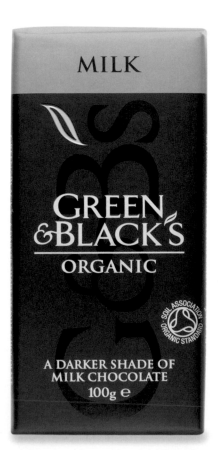 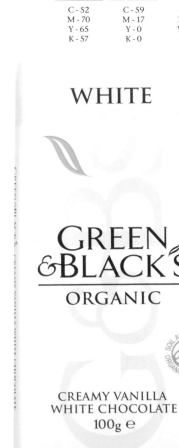

84

Scheid

VINEYARDS

design firm
The Wecker Group
Monterey, California

client
Scheid Vineyards

C - 75
M - 90
Y - 0
K - 0

C - 32
M - 43
Y - 76
K - 19

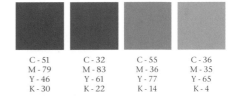

C - 51
M - 79
Y - 46
K - 30

C - 32
M - 83
Y - 61
K - 22

C - 55
M - 36
Y - 77
K - 14

C - 36
M - 35
Y - 65
K - 4

design firm
Michael Osborne Design
San Francisco, California

client
Canyon Road

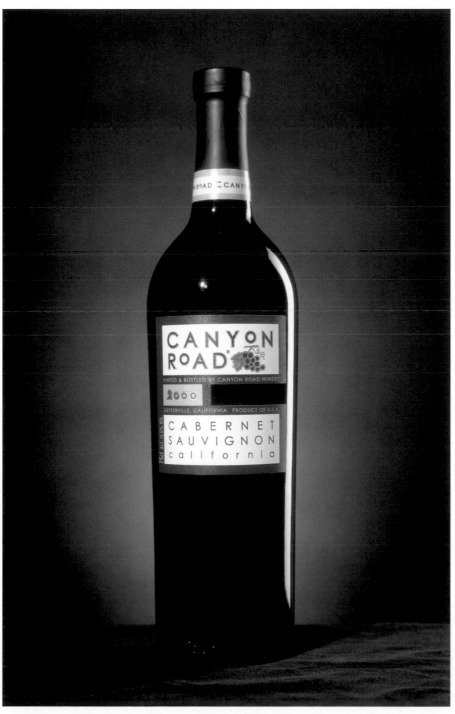

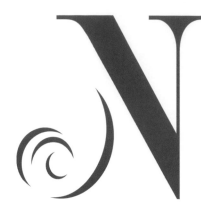

NORWEGIAN WOODS

design firm
Becker Design
Milwaukee, Wisconsin
client
Beta Systems

C - 32	C - 0
M - 83	M 0
Y - 76	Y - 0
K - 23	K - 100

C - 0	C - 40	C - 22
M - 60	M - 60	M - 46
Y - 79	Y - 57	Y - 59
K - 0	K - 80	K - 2

design firm
Hornall Anderson Design Works
Seattle, Washington

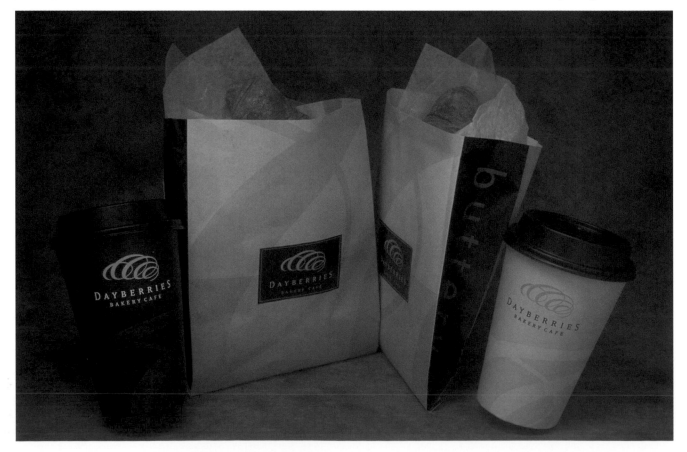

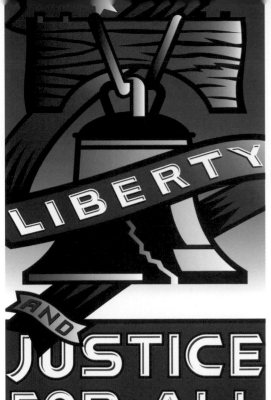

C - 100	C - 24	C - 19	C - 0
M - 77	M - 84	M - 97	M - 72
Y - 18	Y - 99	Y - 96	Y - 90
K - 15	K - 19	K - 8	K - 0

design firm
Sayles Graphic Design
Des Moines, Iowa

client
"Art Fights Back"

C - 23	C - 36	C - 7	C - 6
M - 51	M - 47	M - 80	M - 71
Y - 67	Y - 58	Y - 70	Y - 72
K - 71	K - 57	K - 52	K - 6

design firm
**Hornall Anderson
Design Works**
Seattle, Washington

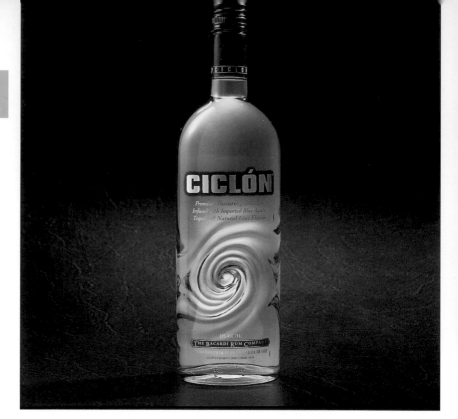

design firm
Bacardi USA
New York, New York
client
Ciclón

C - 69
M - 63
Y - 36
K - 13

C - 0
M - 34
Y - 99
K - 0

C - 1
M - 6
Y - 72
K - 0

C - 12
M - 91
Y - 86
K - 2

C - 34
M - 70
Y - 54
K - 52

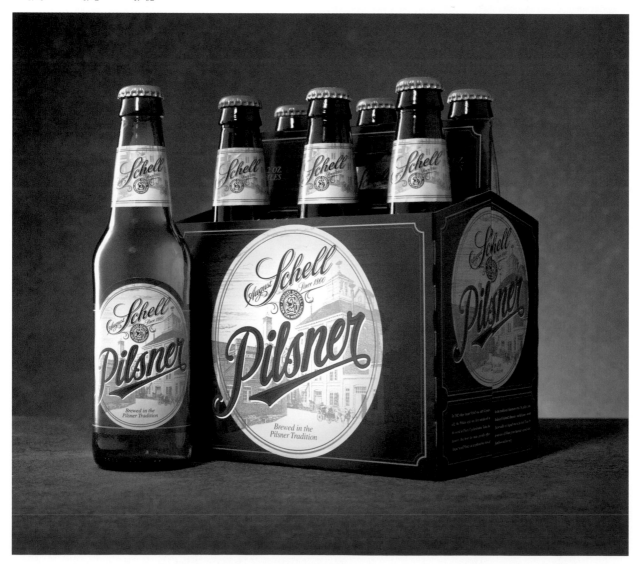

design firm
Compass Design
Minneapolis,
Minnesota

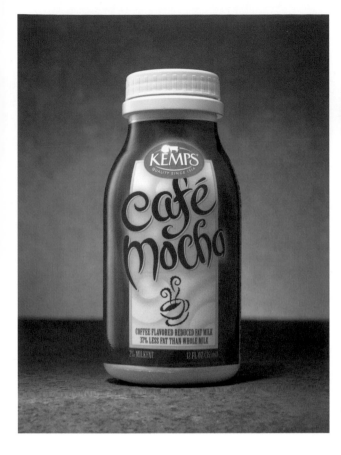

C - 26　　C - 0
M - 87　　M - 51
Y - 79　　Y - 95
K - 21　　K - 0

design firm
Compass Design
Minneapolis, Minnesota

C - 0　　C - 26　　C - 54
M - 24　　M - 87　　M - 43
Y - 86　　Y - 79　　Y - 42
K - 0　　K - 21　　K - 31

design firm
Compass Design
Minneapolis, Minnesota

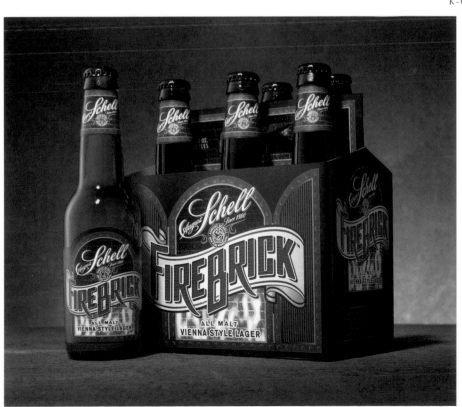

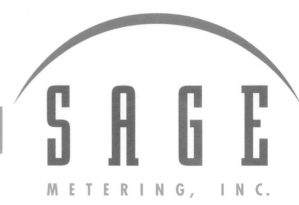

design firm
The Wecker Group
Monterey, California
client
Sage Metering, Inc.

C - 32
M - 38
Y - 81
K - 18

C - 58
M - 30
Y - 96
K - 14

C - 24
M - 28
Y - 56
K - 10

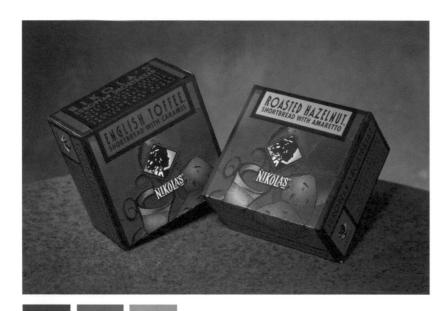

C - 12
M - 91
Y - 86
K - 2

C - 13
M - 72
Y - 88
K - 3

C - 0
M - 50
Y - 85
K - 0

design firm
Compass Design
Minneapolis, Minnesota

C - 25
M - 57
Y - 83
K - 25

C - 7
M - 96
Y - 97
K - 1

C - 1
M - 6
Y - 72
K - 0

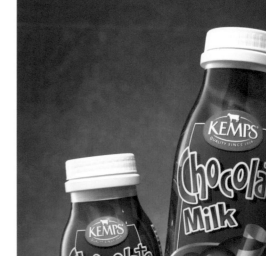

design firm
Compass Design
Minneapolis, Minnesota

design firm
Shields Design
Fresno, California
client
maltwhiskey.com

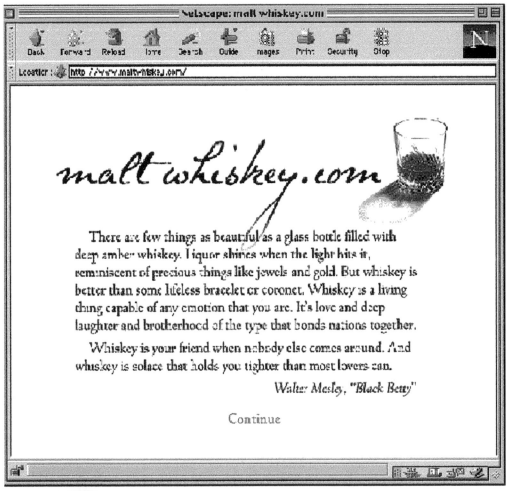

Netscape: malt whiskey.com

Back Forward Reload Home Search Guide Images Print Security Stop

Location: http://www.maltwhiskey.com/

malt whiskey.com

There are few things as beautiful as a glass bottle filled with deep amber whiskey. Liquor shines when the light hits it, reminiscent of precious things like jewels and gold. But whiskey is better than some lifeless bracelet or coronet. Whiskey is a living thing capable of any emotion that you are. It's love and deep laughter and brotherhood of the type that bonds nations together.

Whiskey is your friend when nobody else comes around. And whiskey is solace that holds you tighter than most lovers can.

Walter Mosley, "Black Betty"

Continue

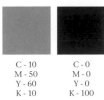

C - 10   C - 0
M - 50   M - 0
Y - 60   Y - 0
K - 10   K - 100

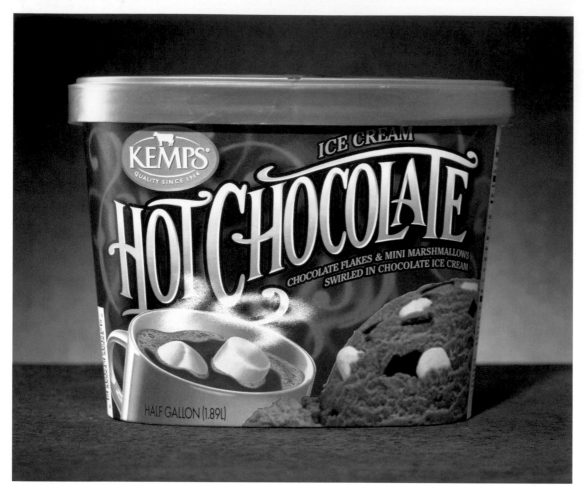

design firm
Compass Design
Minneapolis, Minnesota

C - 1	C - 4	C - 27	C - 41
M - 6	M - 58	M - 82	M - 67
Y - 67	Y - 65	Y - 75	Y - 62
K - 0	K - 1	K - 37	K - 69

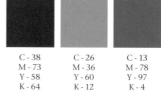

C - 38	C - 26	C - 13
M - 73	M - 36	M - 78
Y - 58	Y - 60	Y - 97
K - 64	K - 12	K - 4

design firm
Tom Fowler, Inc.
Norwalk, Connecticut
client
Playtex Products, Inc.

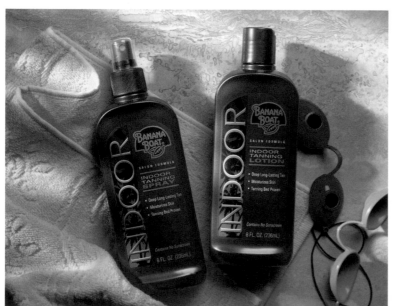

design firm
Ortega Design Studio
St. Helena, California
client
Simi Winery

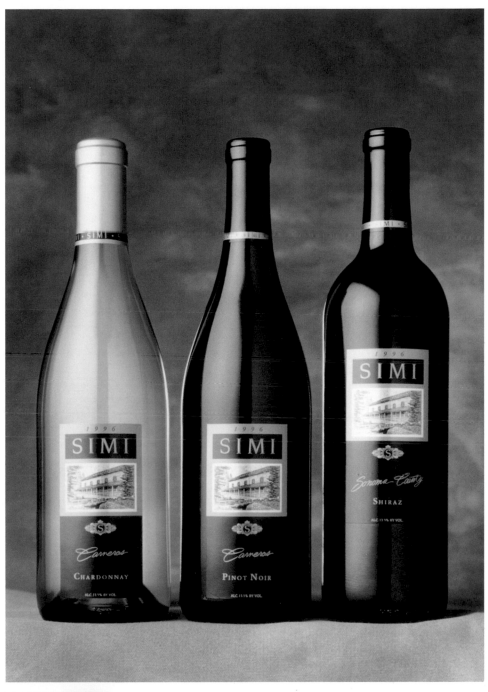

C - 15	C - 0
M - 30	M - 0
Y - 70	Y - 0
K - 0	K - 100

C - 75	C - 0	C - 70	C - 100
M - 60	M - 0	M - 70	M - 10
Y - 70	Y - 0	Y - 0	Y - 0
K - 14	K - 100	K - 0	K - 0

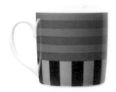
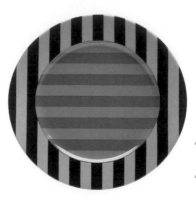

design firm
Michael Osborne Design
San Francisco, California
client
San Francisco Museum of Modern Art

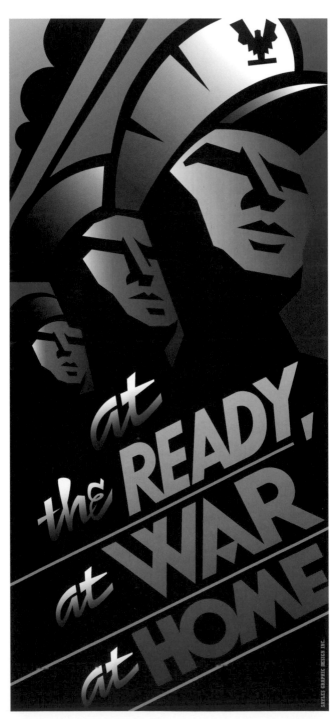

design firm
Sayles Graphic Design
Des Moines, Iowa
client
"Art Fights Back"

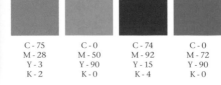

C - 75	C - 0	C - 74	C - 0
M - 28	M - 50	M - 92	M - 72
Y - 3	Y - 90	Y - 15	Y - 90
K - 2	K - 0	K - 4	K - 0

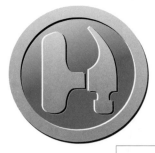

C - 60	C - 18
M - 45	M - 12
Y - 18	Y - 10
K - 5	K - 1

design firm
The Wecker Group
Monterey, California
client
Hammer Golf

HAMMER GOLF
PERFORMANCE & FITNESS

HAMMER GOLF
PERFORMANCE & FITNESS

Andrea Hammer MS, PT, CSCS
Physical Therapist
Certified Strength &
Conditioning Specialist

891 E. Hamilton Ave.
Campbell, CA 95008
Tel (408) 558-9518
Fax (408) 558-9528
www.hammergolf.net
andrea@hammergolf.net

Combining Biomechanical Analysis with Manual Therapy, Strength Training and Conditioning

Combining Biomechanical
Analysis with Manual
Therapy, Strength Training
and Conditioning

891 E. HAMILTON AVE.
CAMPBELL, CA 95008
TEL (408) 558-9518
FAX (408) 558-9528
www.hammergolf.net

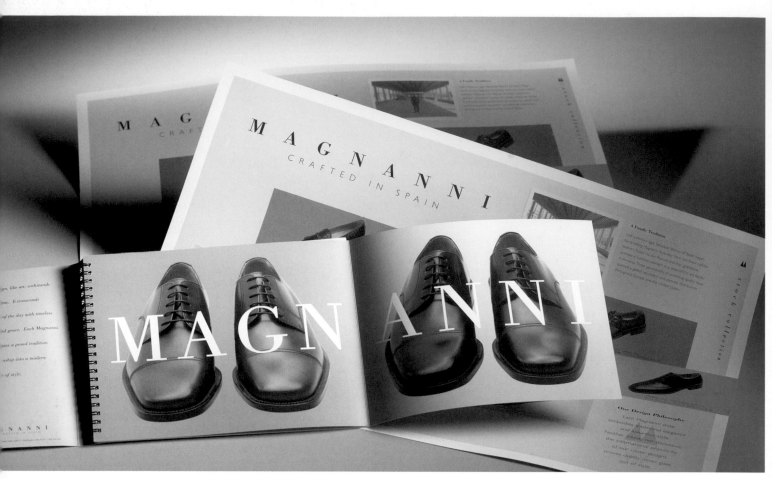

design firm
Louis & Partners Design
Bath, Ohio

client
Magnanni

C - 10	C - 12	C - 39	C - 15
M - 10	M - 21	M - 20	M - 14
Y - 13	Y - 20	Y - 16	Y - 29
K - 0	K - 5	K - 0	K - 0

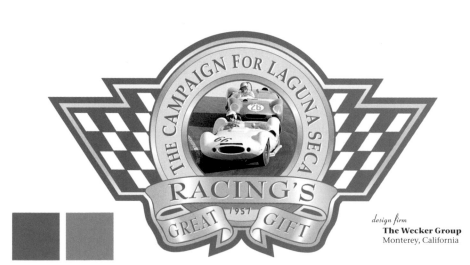

C - 38	C - 42
M - 58	M - 30
Y - 73	Y - 28
K - 6	K - 12

design firm
The Wecker Group
Monterey, California

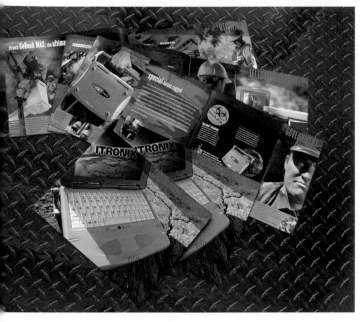

design firm
Klündt Hosmer Design
Spokane, Washington
client
GoBookMax

C - 53	C - 29	C - 68	C - 0
M - 40	M - 87	M - 28	M - 58
Y - 43	Y - 94	Y - 34	Y - 80
K - 11	K - 29	K - 8	K - 0

C - 28	C - 66
M - 60	M - 86
Y - 74	Y - 83
K - 0	K - 51

design firm
After Hours Creative
Phoenix, Arizona

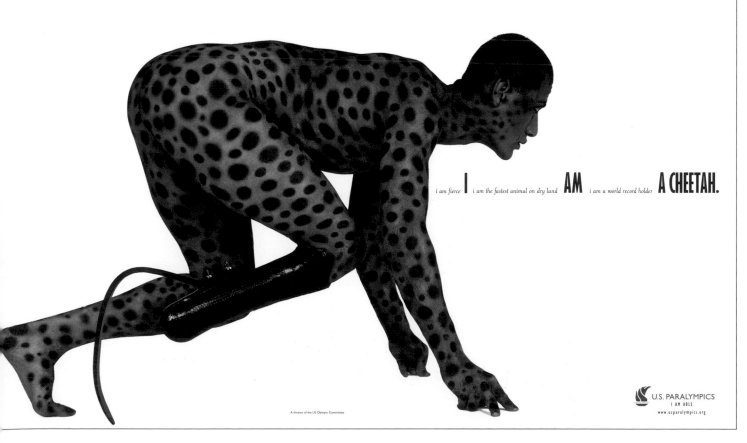

Marlon Shirley
lost leg at the age of 5
paralympic sprinter 2000
world-record holder

i am fierce **I** i am the fastest animal on dry land **AM** i am a world record holder **A CHEETAH.**

A division of the US Olympic Committee

U.S. PARALYMPICS
I AM ABLE
www.usparalympics.org

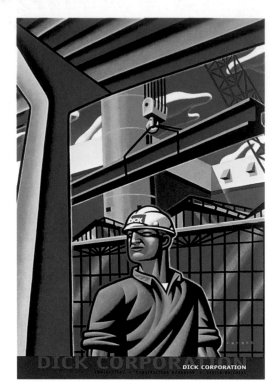

design firm
Bradley Brown Design Group
Carnegie, Pennsylvania
client
Dick Corporation

C - 76	C - 44	C - 65	C - 2	C - 1	C - 57	C - 0
M - 62	M - 27	M - 38	M - 79	M - 27	M - 77	M - 0
Y - 12	Y - 11	Y - 89	Y - 87	Y - 81	Y - 64	Y - 0
K - 9	K - 0	K - 1	K - 0	K - 0	K - 34	K - 100

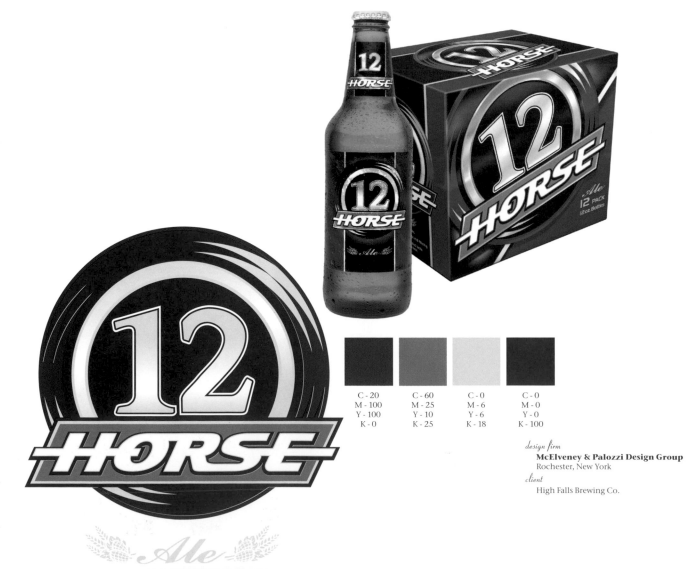

C - 20	C - 60	C - 0	C - 0
M - 100	M - 25	M - 6	M - 0
Y - 100	Y - 10	Y - 6	Y - 0
K - 0	K - 25	K - 18	K - 100

design firm
McElveney & Palozzi Design Group
Rochester, New York
client
High Falls Brewing Co.

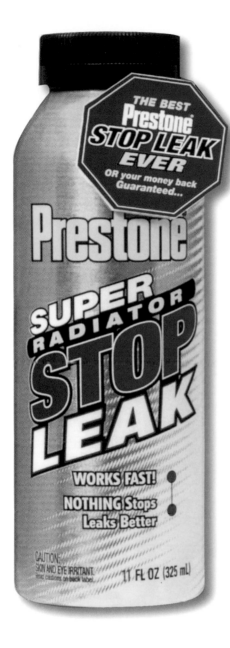

C - 37   C - 16   C - 0
M - 20   M - 87   M - 24
Y - 22   Y - 96   Y - 86
K - 11   K - 24   K - 0

design firm
Tom Fowler, Inc.
Norwalk, Connecticut
client
Honeywell Consumer Products

design firm
Greteman Group
Wichita, Kansas

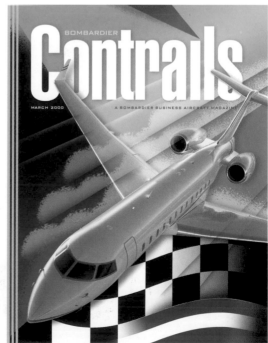

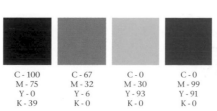

C - 100   C - 67   C - 0   C - 0
M - 75   M - 32   M - 30   M - 99
Y - 0   Y - 6   Y - 93   Y - 91
K - 39   K - 0   K - 0   K - 0

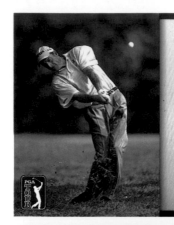
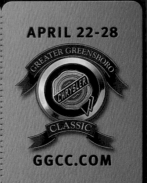

AS CLOSE TO BALLET

AS YOU CAN GET AND STILL

RETAIN YOUR DIGNITY.

APRIL 22-28

GREATER GREENSBORO CHRYSLER CLASSIC

GGCC.COM

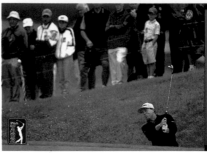
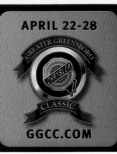

STALK FAMOUS PEOPLE

WITHOUT RISKING

A RESTRAINING ORDER.

APRIL 22-28

GREATER GREENSBORO CHRYSLER CLASSIC

GGCC.COM

design firm
Bouvier Kelly
Greensboro, North Carolina

client
Greater Greensboro Chrysler Classic

C - 6 M - 11 Y - 64 K - 0	C - 84 M - 86 Y - 44 K - 16	C - 21 M - 45 Y - 65 K - 0

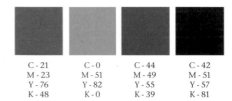

C - 21 M - 23 Y - 76 K - 48	C - 0 M - 51 Y - 82 K - 0	C - 44 M - 49 Y - 55 K - 39	C - 42 M - 51 Y - 57 K - 81

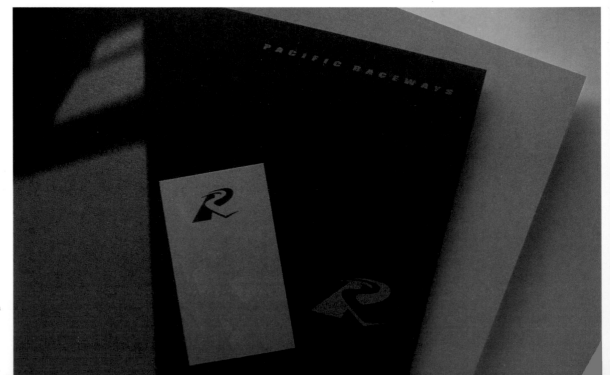

design firm
**Hornall Anderson
Design Works**
Seattle, Washington

100

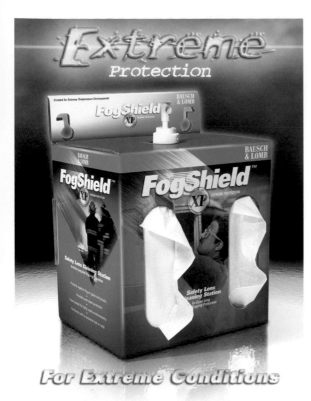

design firm
McElveney & Palozzi Design Group
Rochester, New York
client
Bausch & Lomb

C - 100	C - 100	C - 0	C - 0
M - 9	M - 96	M - 68	M - 0
Y - 0	Y - 0	Y - 99	Y - 95
K - 16	K - 50	K - 0	K - 0

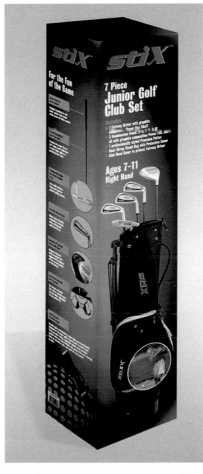

design firm
Goldforest
Miami, Florida
client
Continuum Sales & Marketing

C - 2	C - 74	C - 87
M - 55	M - 41	M - 25
Y - 99	Y - 50	Y - 48
K - 0	K - 68	K - 33

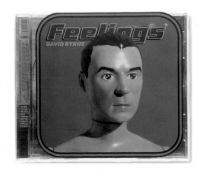

design firm
Sagmeister Inc.
New York, New York

C - 91	C - 24
M - 59	M - 60
Y - 12	Y - 51
K - 7	K - 2

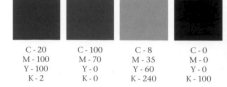

C - 20   C - 100   C - 8   C - 0
M - 100   M - 70   M - 35   M - 0
Y - 100   Y - 0   Y - 60   Y - 0
K - 2   K - 0   K - 240   K - 100

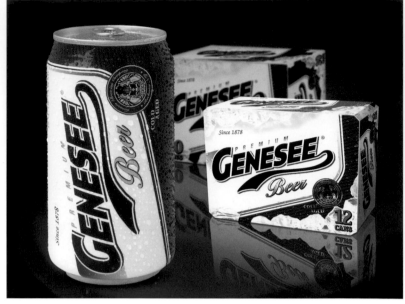

design firm
McElveney & Palozzi Design Group
Rochester, New York
client
High Falls Brewing Co.

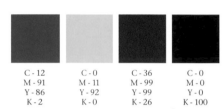

C - 12   C - 0   C - 36   C - 0
M - 91   M - 11   M - 99   M - 0
Y - 86   Y - 92   Y - 99   Y - 0
K - 2   K - 0   K - 26   K - 100

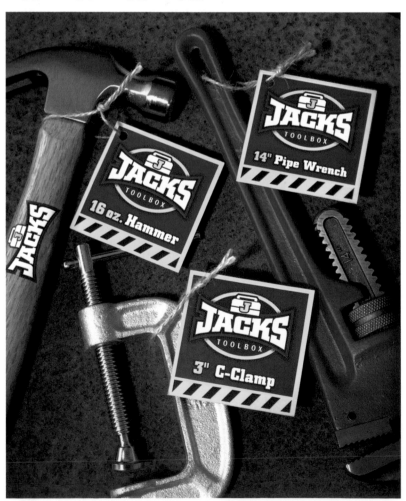

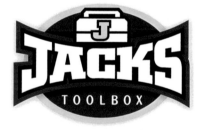

IF YOU DON'T KNOW JACKS
YOU DON'T KNOW TOOLS!

design firm
Compass Design
Minneapolis, Minnesota
client
Jack Toolbox Company

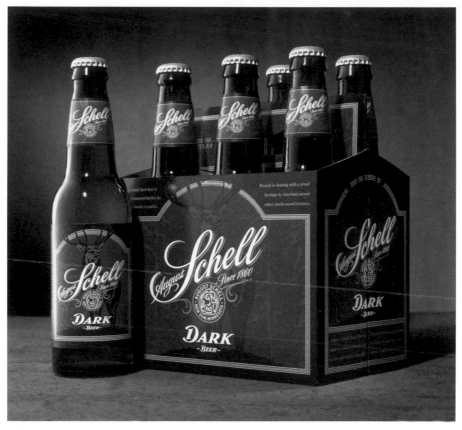

C - 44	C - 62	C - 15
M - 61	M - 51	M - 44
Y - 60	Y - 49	Y - 81
K - 61	K - 63	K - 9

design firm
Compass Design
Minneapolis, Minnesota
client
August Schell Brewing Co.

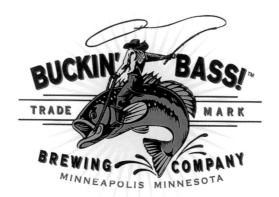

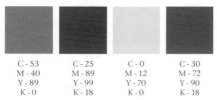

C - 53	C - 25	C - 0	C - 30
M - 40	M - 89	M - 12	M - 72
Y - 89	Y - 99	Y - 70	Y - 90
K - 0	K - 18	K - 0	K - 18

design firm
Compass Design
Minneapolis, Minnesota
client
Buckin' Bass Brewing Co.

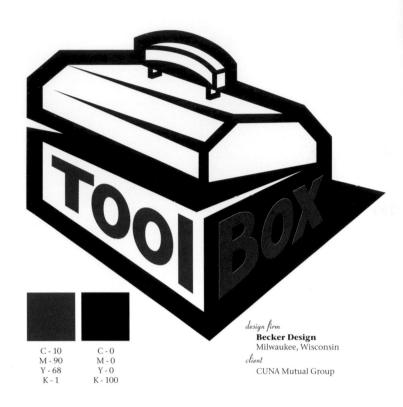

design firm
Becker Design
Milwaukee, Wisconsin
client
CUNA Mutual Group

C - 10	C - 0
M - 90	M - 0
Y - 68	Y - 0
K - 1	K - 100

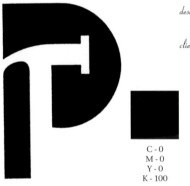

design firm
Pat Taylor Inc.
Washington, D.C.
client
Palis Gen. Contracting

C - 0
M - 0
Y - 0
K - 100

design firm
The Wecker Group
Monterey, California
client
Myrick Photographic

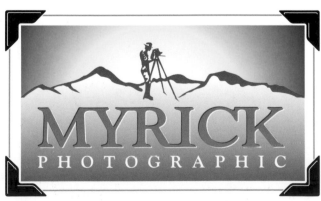

C - 0	C - 0	C - 10
M - 100	M - 0	M - 20
Y - 80	Y - 100	Y - 0
K - 0	K - 0	K - 60

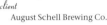

blue fin
CAFE & BILLIARDS

C - 0	C - 81
M - 0	M - 6
Y - 0	Y - 5
K - 100	K - 0

design firm
The Wecker Group
Monterey, California
client
Blue Fin Cafe & Billiards

design firm
Compass Design
Minneapolis, Minnesota
client
August Schell Brewing Co.

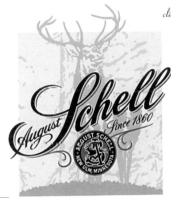

C - 50	C - 34	C - 23
M - 98	M - 64	M - 26
Y - 87	Y - 91	Y - 56
K - 25	K - 0	K - 0

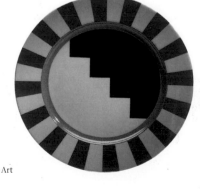

design firm
Michael Osborne Design
San Francisco, California
client
San Francisco Museum of Modern Art

C - 0	C - 0	C - 70	C - 0
M - 100	M - 65	M - 70	M - 0
Y - 100	Y - 87	Y - 0	Y - 0
K - 0	K - 0	K - 0	K - 100

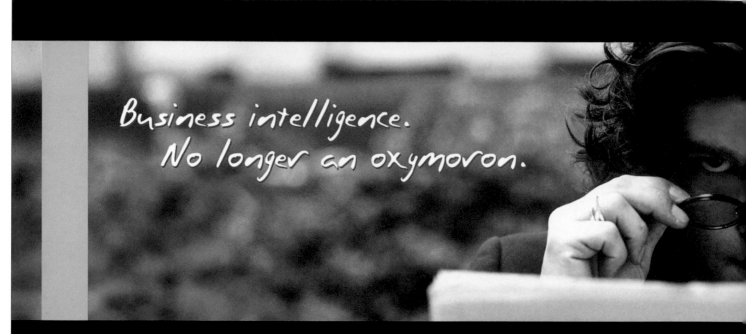

Business intelligence.
No longer an oxymoron.

New rules. New solutions.

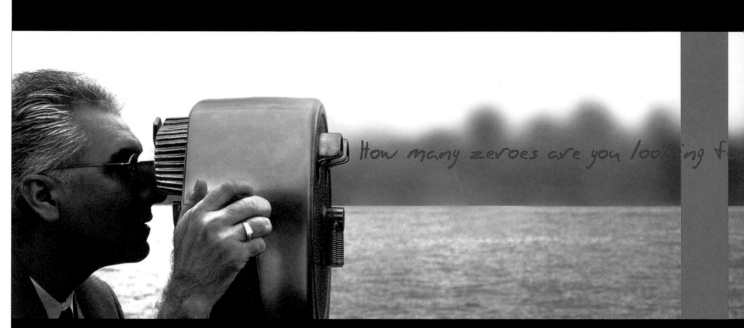

How many zeroes are you looking f

New rules.   New solutions.

C - 35	C - 4	C - 83	C - 10	C - 0
M - 6	M - 59	M - 14	M - 38	M - 0
Y - 93	Y - 88	Y - 3	Y - 88	Y - 0
K - 1	K - 1	K - 1	K - 15	K - 100

design firm
Amber Design Associates
Hackettstown, New Jersey
client
Microsoft

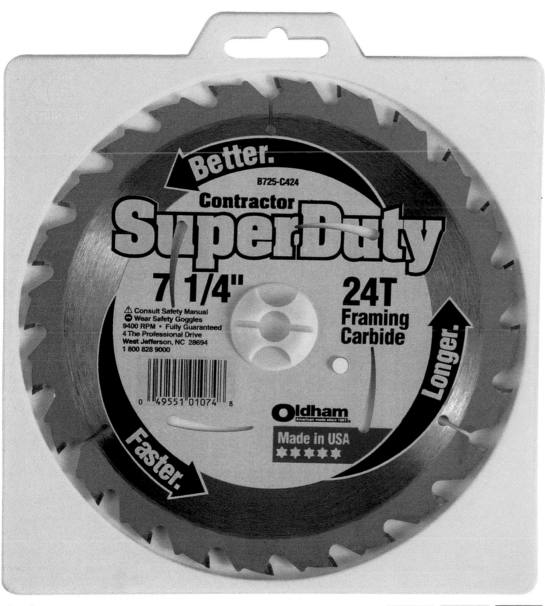

design firm
Ball Advertising & Design
Statesville, North Carolina
client
Oldham

C - 0	C - 20	C - 0
M - 10	M - 0	M - 0
Y - 90	Y - 0	Y - 0
K - 0	K - 20	K - 100

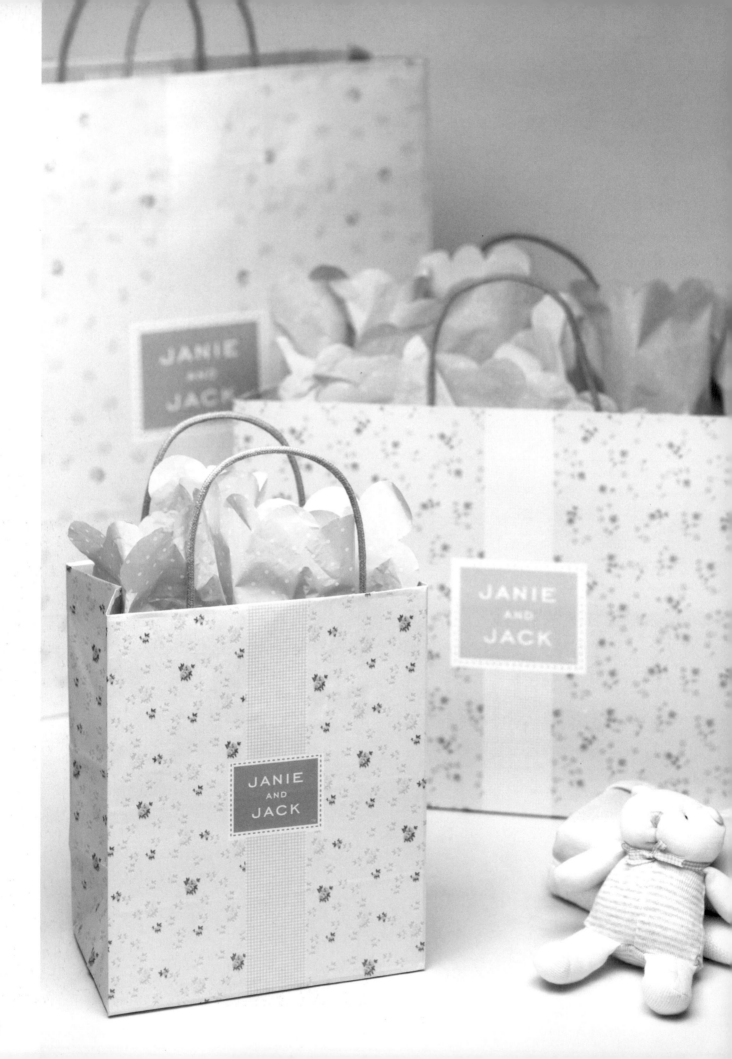

PLASTIC SURGERY

ROBERT L. COOPER M.D.

C - 45
M - 42
Y - 3
K - 0

C - 0
M - 34
Y - 50
K - 0

C - 0
M - 8
Y - 32
K - 0

design firm
Klündt Hosmer Design
Spokane, Washington

client
Robert L. Cooper, M.D.

C - 13
M - 72
Y - 27
K - 3

C - 22
M - 59
Y - 31
K - 5

C - 65
M - 51
Y - 84
K - 19

design firm
After Hours Creative
Phoenix, Arizona

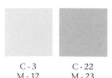

C - 3
M - 12
Y - 40
K - 0

C - 22
M - 23
Y - 4
K - 0

C - 0
M - 22
Y - 11
K - 0

C - 16
M - 4
Y - 26
K - 0

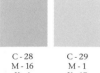

C - 28
M - 16
Y - 4
K - 1

C - 29
M - 1
Y - 17
K - 0

(opposite) design firm
Michael Osborne Design
San Francisco, California

client
Janie and Jack

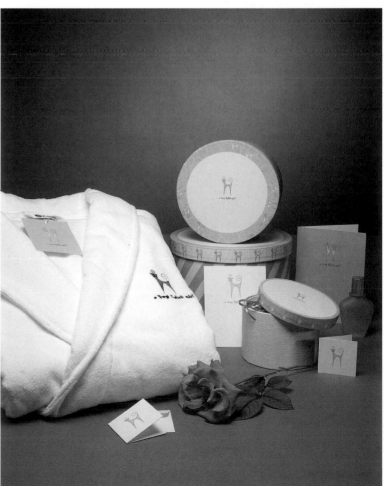

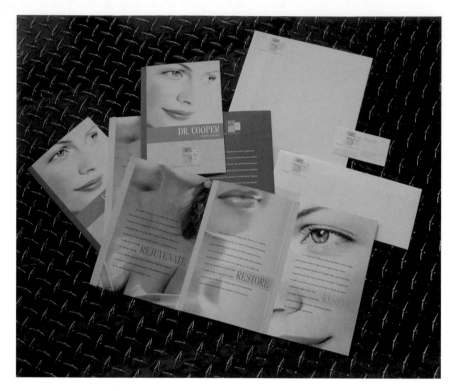

design firm
Klündt Hosmer Design
Spokane, Washington
client
Robert L. Cooper, M.D.

C - 57	C - 25	C - 50	C - 25
M - 53	M - 53	M - 17	M - 35
Y - 20	Y - 32	Y - 40	Y - 40
K - 30	K - 10	K - 5	K - 4

design firm
The Wecker Group
Monterey, California
client
Chateau Valeria

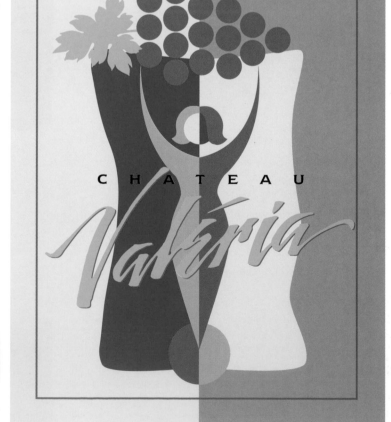

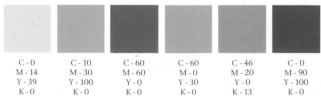

C - 0	C - 10	C - 60	C - 60	C - 46	C - 0
M - 14	M - 30	M - 60	M - 0	M - 20	M - 90
Y - 39	Y - 100	Y - 0	Y - 30	Y - 0	Y - 100
K - 0	K - 0	K - 0	K - 0	K - 13	K - 0

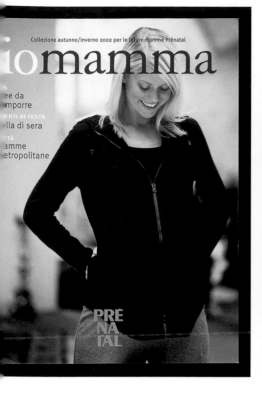

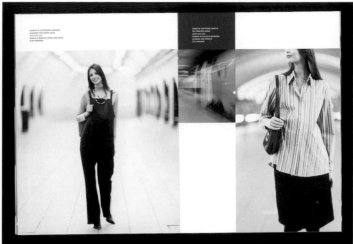

C - 21
M - 99
Y - 100
K - 5

C - 7
M - 47
Y - 85
K - 3

C - 96
M - 73
Y - 33
K - 33

C - 41
M - 29
Y - 87
K - 1

design firm
Tangram Strategic Design
Novara (Italy)
client
Prénatal

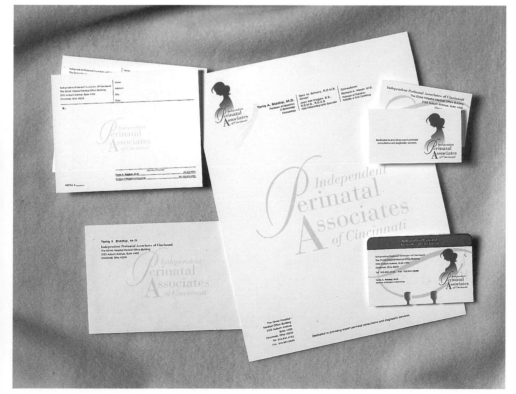

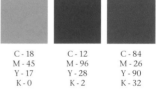

C - 18
M - 45
Y - 17
K - 0

C - 12
M - 96
Y - 28
K - 2

C - 84
M - 26
Y - 90
K - 32

design firm
Interbrand Hulefeld
Cincinnati, Ohio
client
Independent Perinatal Associates of Cincinnati

111

C - 1   C - 14
M - 42   M - 0
Y - 52   Y - 12
K - 0   K - 0

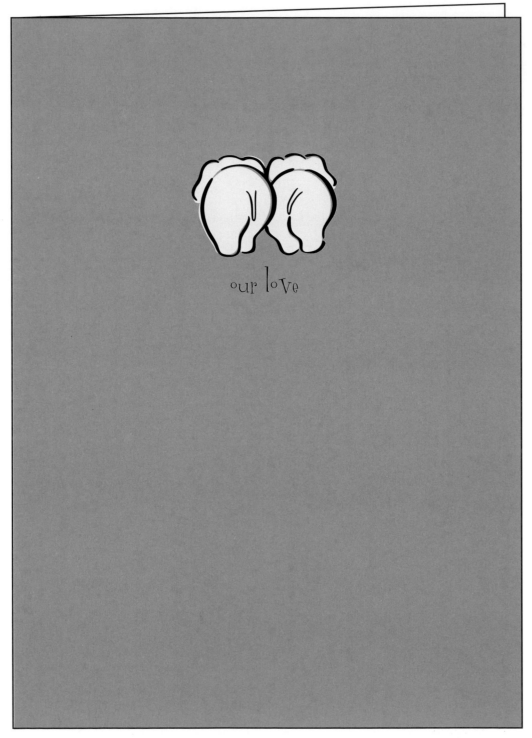

our love

design firm
After Hours Creative
Phoenix, Arizona

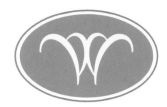

WEĪSHÄÄR

SUE WEISHAAR . DDS

C - 50
M - 35
Y - 0
K - 0

C - 10
M - 60
Y - 80
K - 0

design firm
Klündt Hosmer Design
Spokane, Washington
client
Sue Weishaar, D.D.S.

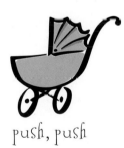

push, push

design firm
After Hours Creative
Phoenix, Arizona

C - 35
M - 35
Y - 0
K - 0

C - 0
M - 0
Y - 30
K - 0

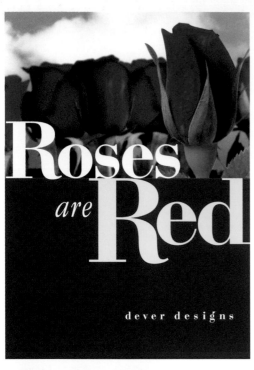

Roses are Red

dever designs

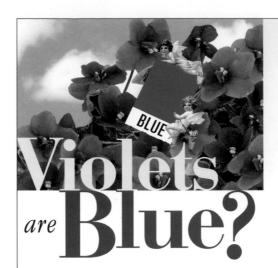

Violets are Blue?

BLUE

Clichéd poetry and color correc-
tions aside, Dever Designs would
love to work with you. We're in the
business of creating fresh communication graphics, the kind your
competitors will lust after. So as

you plan your next project call on

us so we can lovingly create for you.

Conference Kits

Magazines

Corporate Identity

Annual Reports

Books

Consultation

dever designs
The point where art and communication meet
301-776-2812

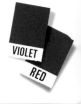

VIOLET
RED

C - 76	C - 96	C - 2	C - 2
M - 83	M - 60	M - 96	M - 5
Y - 3	Y - 2	Y - 85	Y - 93
K - 1	K - 1	K - 0	K - 0

design firm
Dever Designs
Laurel, Maryland
client
Dever Designs

C - 0	C - 100
M - 30	M - 100
Y - 10	Y - 0
K - 0	K - 10

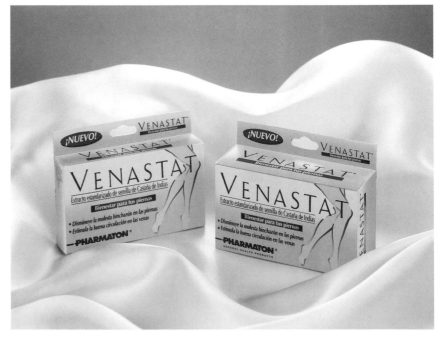

design firm
Praxis Diseñadores, S.C.
México City (Mexico)
client
Laboratorios Promeco

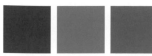

C - 100	C - 100	C - 100	C - 94
M - 60	M - 0	M - 0	M - 94
Y - 0	Y - 30	Y - 70	Y - 0
K - 6	K - 6	K - 15	K - 0

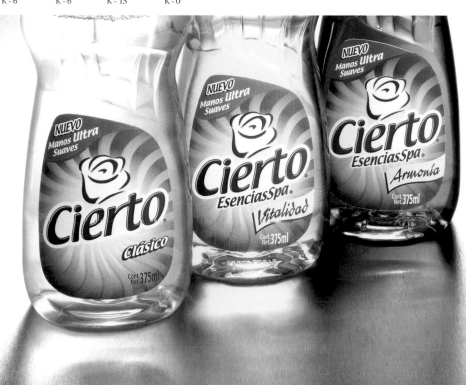

design firm
Praxis Diseñadores, S.C.
México City (Mexico)
client
Procter & Gamble Argentina

C - 0	C - 90
M - 10	M - 90
Y - 100	Y - 0
K - 0	K - 0

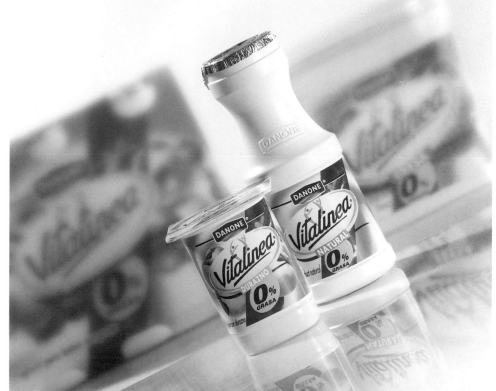

design firm
Praxis Diseñadores, S.C.
México City (Mexico)
client
Danone de México

C - 18
M - 44
Y - 26
K - 5

C - 17
M - 95
Y - 84
K - 6

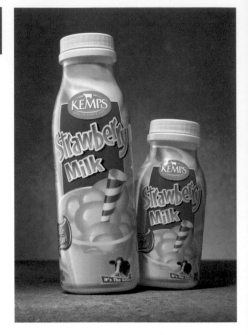

design firm
Compass Design
Minneapolis, Minnesota

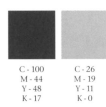

C - 100
M - 44
Y - 48
K - 17

C - 26
M - 19
Y - 11
K - 0

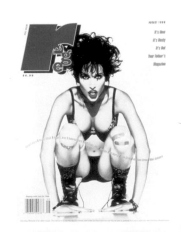

design firm
Allen Bell Solutions Inc.
Agoura Hills, California
client
Essential Skin Inc.

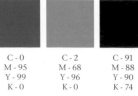

design firm
Mike Salisbury L.L.C.
Venice, California
client
LFP

C - 0
M - 95
Y - 99
K - 0

C - 2
M - 68
Y - 96
K - 0

C - 91
M - 88
Y - 90
K - 74

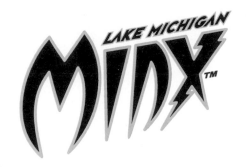

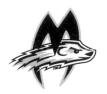

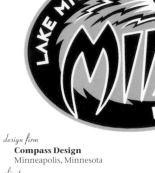

 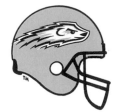

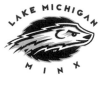

design firm
Compass Design
Minneapolis, Minnesota
client
Womens Professional Football League

1 2 3 4 5
6 7 8 9 0

C - 0	C - 0
M - 34	M - 0
Y - 92	Y - 0
K - 0	K - 100

C 1	C 1	C - 44	C - 1	C - 45
M - 0	M - 56	M - 11	M - 64	M - 20
Y - 46	Y - 26	Y - 2	Y - 32	Y - 4
K - 51	K - 1	K - 30	K - 46	K - 60

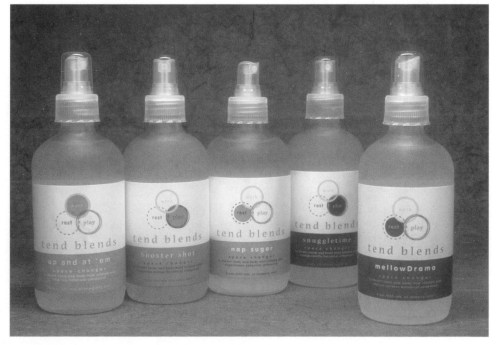

design firm
Hornall Anderson Design Works
Seattle, Washington

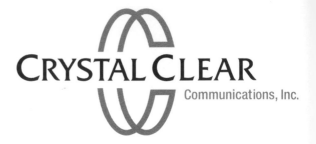

CRYSTAL CLEAR
Communications, Inc.

YOU KNOW
your stuff.
WE HELP YOU
USE IT.

CRYSTAL CLEAR

The Accelerators

CRYSTAL CLEAR

design firm
Becker Design
Milwaukee, Wisconsin
client
Crystal Clear

...iness
...lence.
...ETHING
...E WAY?

In today's business climate of rapid change, it is not unusual for top executives to feel that their organizations are not reaching their potential. This is especially the case when everything seems to have been done by the book: A strategic plan has been developed. Goals have been established. The company's mission has been communicated. Yet performance lags expectations and change is not occurring fast enough.

The temptation is often to fault the company's strategy and change direction again. Unfortunately, this typically results in even less clarity and obscures the real problem: behaviors and attitudes that block the transformation of a good company into a great one.

Crystal Clear helps leaders perform better and organizations attain greater success.

Transformation:
Action, not more information.

How do businesses reach the next level? Seldom by amassing more data. In fact, most companies are awash in information, from research reports to marketing studies to strategic plans. Rather, what they need is a means of utilizing the data they already have to implement meaningful change. Since 1986, Crystal Clear has fulfilled this role with numerous Fortune 1000 companies.

As consultants to key executives, Crystal Clear helps clients identify the factors that are inhibiting performance. Is the company's strategic direction thoroughly understood? Has there been "buy-in" at every level? Are there points of resistance? Have executives misidentified strengths as weaknesses and vice versa? Are the words and deeds of management consistent?

The process of asking tough questions discerns critical issues and provides an accurate assessment of a company's "business reality." Connecting this with the company's strategy, Crystal Clear works in partnership with executives to act as a catalyst for change.

Access your wisdom.

Unlike most consultants, Crystal Clear makes a bold assumption: you already have the answers you need to take your company to the next level. You may, however, be mired down and deterred from acting on what you know. Crystal Clear helps executives regain focus to improve company performance. Through our interaction, you'll heighten your awareness and be able to clarify your vision and goals.

Whether it's during your strategic planning process or implementing a plan that's already created, Crystal Clear brings an action orientation to the wisdom that is already in place. Consistent follow-through on the part of Crystal Clear, developed in long-term relationships with clients, helps companies stay on track and on strategy.

ASSUMPTIO...

You kno...

what

needs t...

get don...

People don't change.
But the way they do business can.

When to consult wit...
Crystal Clear.

It's not a matter of business structure...

We've worked with:

> PUBLIC CORPORATIONS > PRIVATELY HELD CORPORATIONS
> FAMILY OWNED COMPANIES

It's not a matter of the business field.
We've worked with firms in:

> RETAIL
> SERVICE
> MANUFACTURING
> MARKETING
> SALES
> DISTRIBUTION

It's not a matter of the current state.
We've worked with firms that are:

> GROWING
> SHRINKING
> PROFITABLE
> NOT PROFITABLE
> HIGHLY SUCCESSFUL
> DYSFUNCTIONAL

Clarifying

DIRECTION

and improving

implementation

since

1986.

IT'S A MATTER OF THE **COMMITMENT** TO CHANGE.
AND WE ARE THE CATALYSTS.

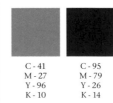

C - 41	C - 95
M - 27	M - 79
Y - 96	Y - 26
K - 10	K - 14

HR
VALUEGROUP

C - 91	C - 44
M - 94	M - 25
Y - 71	Y - 96
K - 22	K - 9

design firm
Becker Design
Milwaukee, Wisconsin
client
HR Value Group

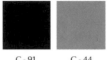

design firm
**Stan Gellman
Graphic Design**
St. Louis, Missouri
client
FMC Technologies

Technologies

Build *Your* **Future**

C - 99	C - 76	C - 12	C - 73
M - 75	M - 35	M - 100	M - 63
Y - 23	Y - 7	Y - 87	Y - 20
K - 7	K - 0	K - 2	K - 2

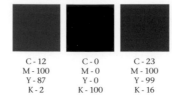

C - 12　　C - 0　　C - 23
M - 100　M - 0　　M - 100
Y - 87　　Y - 0　　Y - 99
K - 2　　K - 100　K - 16

design firm
Stan Gellman Graphic Design
St. Louis, Missouri
client
LaBarge Inc.

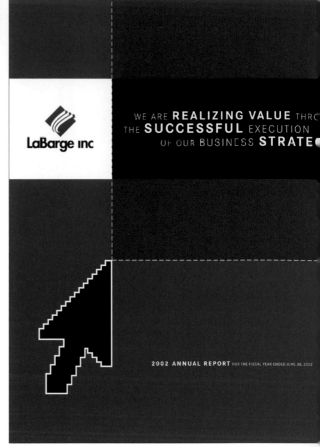

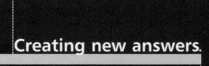

Creating new answers.

2001 | ANNUAL REPORT

ASHLAND
THE WHO IN HOW THINGS WORK™

design firm
Inc Design
New York, New York
client
Ashland

C - 31　　C - 50　　C - 40
M - 99　　M - 10　　M - 3
Y - 86　　Y - 72　　Y - 2
K - 0　　K - 0　　K - 0

120

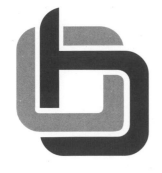

BETHEL
CONSTRUCTION

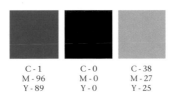

C - 1	C - 0	C - 38
M - 96	M - 0	M - 27
Y - 89	Y - 0	Y - 25
K - 0	K - 100	K - 90

design firm
The Wecker Group
Monterey, California
client
Bethel Construction

design firm
Sagmeister Inc.
New York, New York

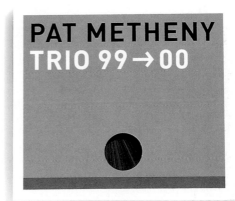

PAT METHENY
TRIO 99→00

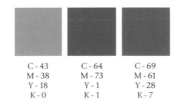

C - 43	C - 64	C - 69
M - 38	M - 73	M - 61
Y - 18	Y - 1	Y - 28
K - 0	K - 1	K - 7

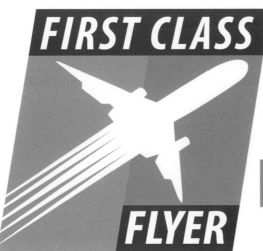

FIRST CLASS

FLYER

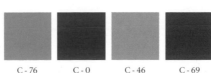

C - 76	C - 0	C - 46	C - 69
M - 23	M - 100	M - 38	M - 94
Y - 0	Y - 91	Y - 36	Y - 0
K - 9	K - 0	K - 4	K - 0

design firm
The Wecker Group
Monterey, California

GREEN JESPERSEN

Certified Public Accountants

A PROFESSIONAL CORPORATION

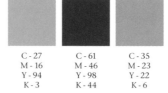

C - 27	C - 61	C - 35
M - 16	M - 46	M - 23
Y - 94	Y - 98	Y - 22
K - 3	K - 44	K - 6

design firm
The Wecker Group
Monterey, California
client
Green Jespersen

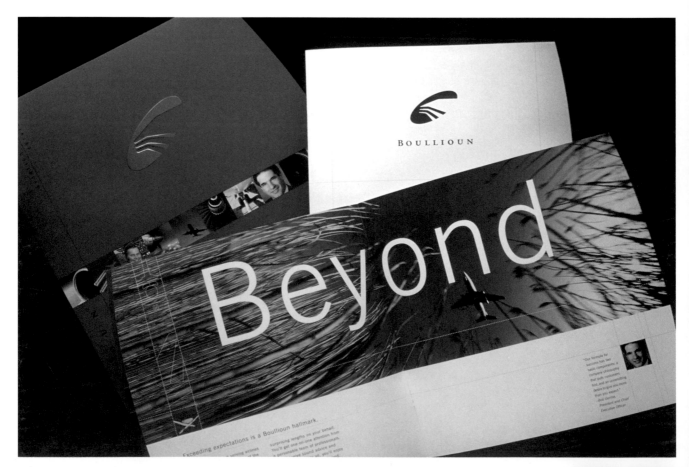

design firm
Hornall Anderson Design Works
Seattle, Washington

C - 70	C - 25
M - 56	M - 59
Y - 11	Y - 58
K - 7	K - 44

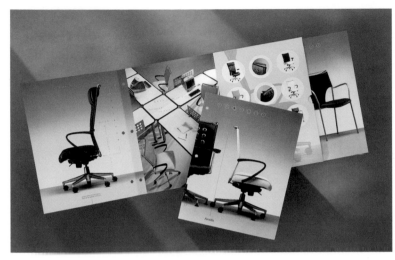

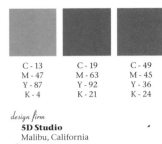

C - 13   C - 19   C - 49
M - 47   M - 63   M - 45
Y - 87   Y - 92   Y - 36
K - 4   K - 21   K - 24

design firm
5D Studio
Malibu, California

client
Arcadia

design firm
Hornall Anderson Design Works
Seattle, Washington

C - 22   C - 0   C - 31
M - 51   M - 5   M - 29
Y - 52   Y - 5   Y - 44
K - 40   K - 0   K - 29

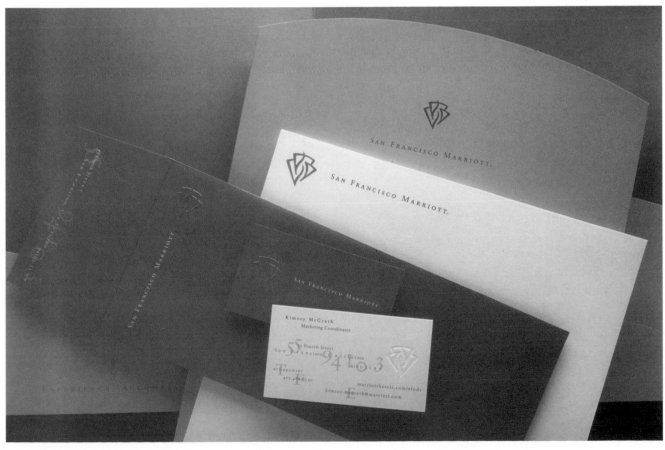

C - 89   C - 55
M - 57   M - 24
Y - 84   Y - 40
K - 26   K - 2

design firm
Greenfield/Belser Ltd.
Washington, D.C.
client
Weil Gotshal + Manges

expand your reach

SHAPE AN INDUSTRY

cure the system

foster competition

CONNECT WITH OPPORTUNITY

energize wall street

protect the franchise

cover ground

manage crisis

reach out

Annual Report : 2001
WEIL, GOTSHAL & MANGES LLP

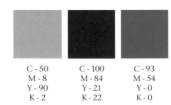

C - 50   C - 100   C - 93
M - 8   M - 84   M - 54
Y - 90   Y - 21   Y - 0
K - 2   K - 22   K - 0

design firm
Bailey Design Group Inc.
Plymouth Meeting, Pennsylvania

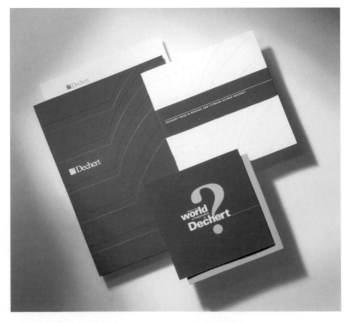

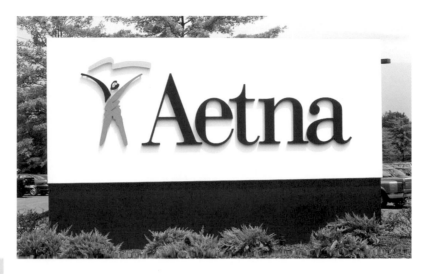

design firm
Bailey Design Group Inc.
Plymouth Meeting, Pennsylvania

C - 75
M - 28
Y - 0
K - 0

C - 0
M - 23
Y - 68
K - 0

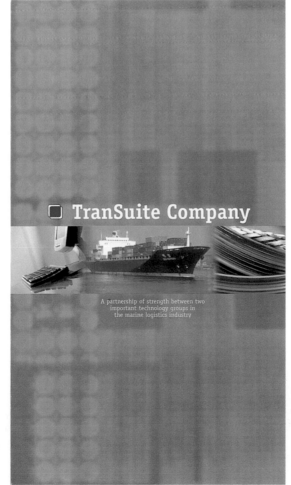

TranSuite Company

A partnership of strength between two
important technology groups in
the marine logistics industry

design firm
Jiva Creative
Alameda, California
client
Embarcadero Systems Corp.

C - 59
M - 51
Y - 46
K - 9

C - 71
M - 72
Y - 25
K - 7

C - 11
M - 71
Y - 82
K - 0

C - 35
M - 37
Y - 77
K - 0

C - 100
M - 43
Y - 0
K - 0

C - 100
M - 94
Y - 0
K - 27

C - 47
M - 11
Y - 0
K - 0

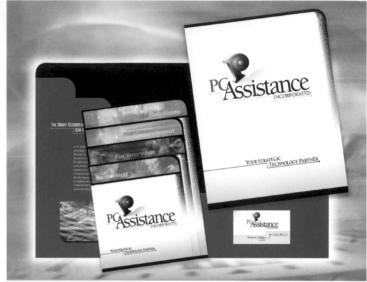

design firm
McElveney & Palozzi Design Group
Rochester, New York
client
PC Assistance, Inc.

AVERY DENNISON

design firm
Addison
San Francisco, California
client
Avery Dennison

C - 0
M - 91
Y - 87
K - 0

C - 0
M - 0
Y - 0
K - 100

C - 88
M - 48
Y - 0
K - 2

C - 0
M - 0
Y - 0
K - 100

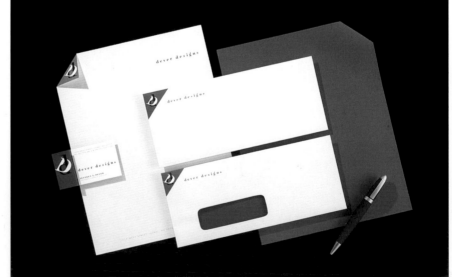

design firm
Dever Designs
Laurel, Maryland
client
Dever Designs

FedEx ®

Federal Express

C - 90	C - 0
M - 100	M - 65
Y - 0	Y - 100
K - 0	K - 0

design firm
Addison
San Francisco, California
client
FedEx

C - 78	C - 10	C - 58
M - 38	M - 79	M - 46
Y - 18	Y - 98	Y - 40
K - 38	K - 0	K - 60

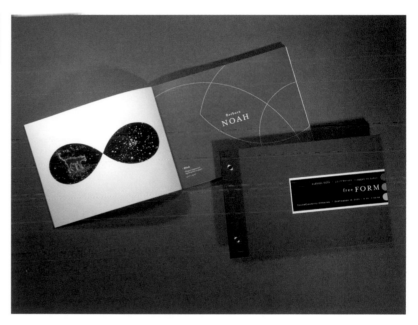

design firm
Belyea
Seattle, Washington
client
ColorGraphics

design firm
Addison
San Francisco, California
client
Alliant Energy

C - 95	C - 2
M - 71	M - 26
Y - 10	Y - 76
K - 1	K - 0

ALLIANT ENERGY™

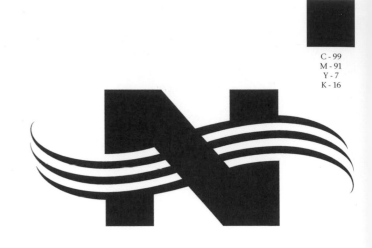

C - 99
M - 91
Y - 7
K - 16

NEWTON LEARNING

design firm
Funk/Levis & Associates
Eugene, Oregon
client
Newton Learning Corp.

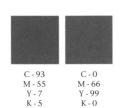

C - 93
M - 55
Y - 7
K - 5

C - 0
M - 66
Y - 99
K - 0

DataComm Plus

design firm
Lynn Cyr Design
Franklin, Massachusetts
client
Data Comm Plus

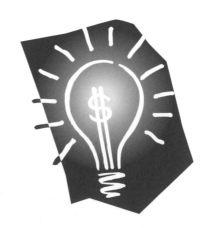

DISTINCTIVE
SOFTWARE

Better Ideas in Accounting!

C - 0
M - 15
Y - 94
K - 0

C - 94
M - 73
Y - 7
K - 1

design firm
The Wecker Group
Monterey, California

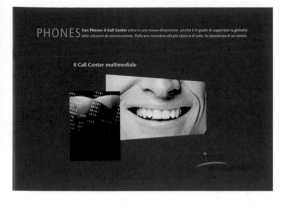

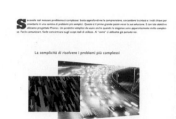

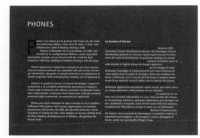

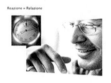

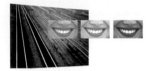

design firm
Tangram Strategic Design
Novara, Italy
client
IFM Infomaster

C - 8	C - 88
M - 100	M - 89
Y - 86	Y - 32
K - 11	K - 18

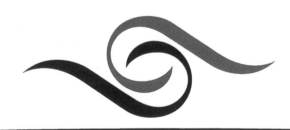

1.2.1
RELATIONSHIP
BANKING
嘉 惠 银 行 服 务

design firm
Design Objectives Pte Ltd
Singapore (Singapore)
client
United Overseas Bank

C - 40	C - 99
M - 69	M - 98
Y - 99	Y - 22
K - 0	K - 22

design firm
ZGraphics, Ltd.
East Dundee, Illinois
client
ASAP Software Express

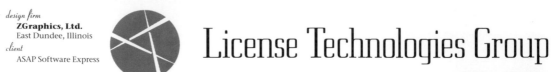

License Technologies Group

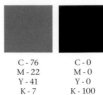

C - 76   C - 0
M - 22   M - 0
Y - 41   Y - 0
K - 7   K - 100

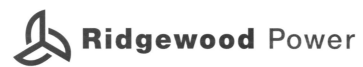

Ridgewood Power

design firm
Straightline Int'l.
New York, New York
client
Ridgewood Power

C - 0   C - 100
M - 0   M - 0
Y - 0   Y - 70
K - 65   K - 45

design firm
Corey McPherson Nash
Watertown, Massachusetts
client
Tribecca

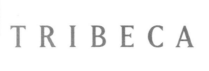

T R I B E C A      **S O F T W A R E**

C - 45   C - 95
M - 29   M - 82
Y - 32   Y - 26
K - 11   K - 14

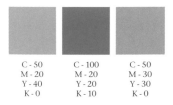

C - 50
M - 20
Y - 40
K - 0

C - 100
M - 20
Y - 20
K - 10

C - 50
M - 30
Y - 30
K - 0

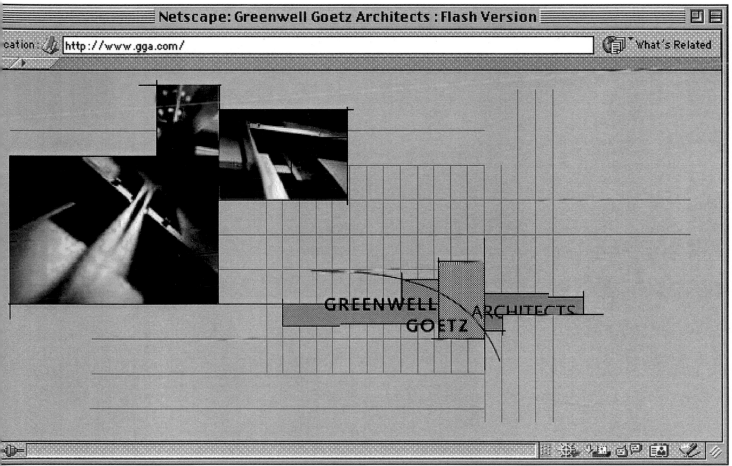

design firm
Grafik
Alexandria, Virginia
client
Thomas Arledge

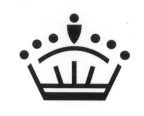

LONDON *by* DESIGN

design firm
Becker Design
Milwaukee, Wisconsin
client
London by Design

C - 91   C - 61
M - 91   M - 47
Y - 33   Y - 67
K - 25   K - 45

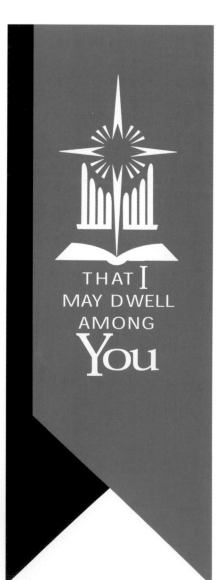

THAT **I** MAY DWELL AMONG **You**

C - 100   C - 70
M - 0   M - 100
Y - 35   Y - 0
K - 20   K - 40

design firm
Dever Designs
Laurel, Maryland
client
Sligo Seventh-Day Adventist Church

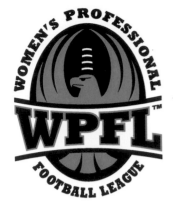

C - 0
M - 61
Y - 95
K - 0

C - 0
M - 0
Y - 0
K - 100

design firm
Compass Design
Minneapolis, Minnesota
client
Women's Professional Football League

design firm
Sayles Graphic Design
Des Moines, Iowa
client
"Art Fights Back"

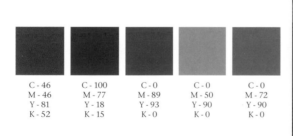

C - 46
M - 46
Y - 81
K - 52

C - 100
M - 77
Y - 18
K - 15

C - 0
M - 89
Y - 93
K - 0

C - 0
M - 50
Y - 90
K - 0

C - 0
M - 72
Y - 90
K - 0

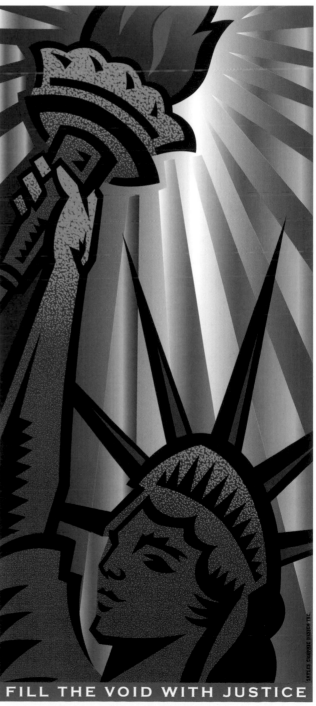

FILL THE VOID WITH JUSTICE

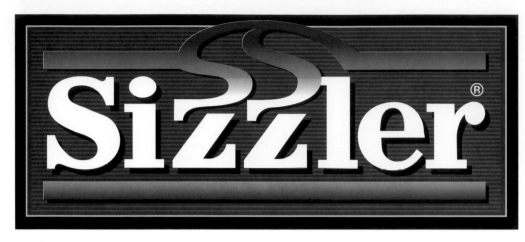
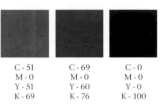

C - 0 M - 100 Y - 91 K - 0	C - 0 M - 27 Y - 100 K - 9

C - 51 M - 0 Y - 51 K - 69	C - 69 M - 0 Y - 60 K - 76	C - 0 M - 0 Y - 0 K - 100

design firm
Louis & Partners Design
Bath, Ohio

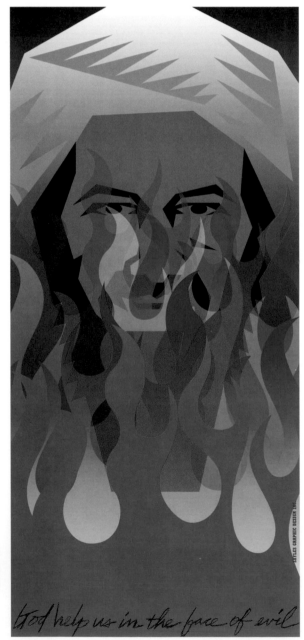

C - 47 M - 35 Y - 33 K - 14	C - 22 M - 70 Y - 89 K - 13	C - 0 M - 89 Y - 93 K - 0	C - 0 M - 72 Y - 90 K - 0	C - 1 M - 34 Y - 71 K - 0

design firm
Sayles Graphic Design
Des Moines, Iowa
client
"Art Fights Back"

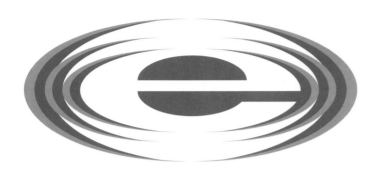

ENERPHAZE

design firm
Klündt Hosmer Design
Spokane, Washington

C - 20   C - 0
M - 70   M - 50
Y - 100   Y - 70
K - 0   K - 0

design firm
Sayles Graphic Design
Des Moines, Iowa
client
"Art Fights Back"

C - 0   C - 0   C - 99   C - 0
M - 89   M - 50   M - 62   M - 0
Y - 93   Y - 90   Y - 2   Y - 0
K - 0   K - 0   K - 1   K - 100

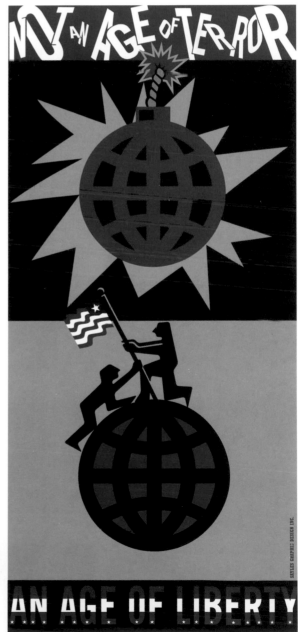

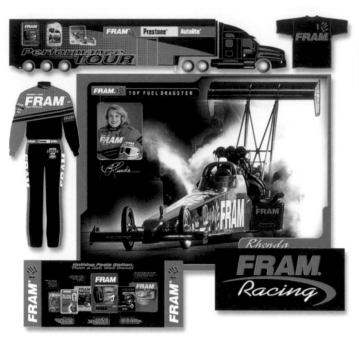

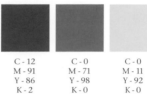

C - 12	C - 0	C - 0
M - 91	M - 71	M - 11
Y - 86	Y - 98	Y - 92
K - 2	K - 0	K - 0

design firm
Tom Fowler, Inc.
Norwalk, Connecticut
client
Honeywell Consumer Products

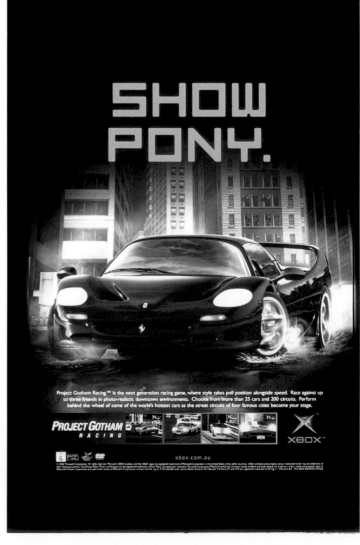

design firm
McCann-Erickson
Sydney (Australia)
client
Microsoft

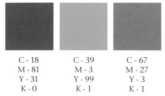

C - 18	C - 39	C - 67
M - 81	M - 3	M - 27
Y - 31	Y - 99	Y - 3
K - 0	K - 1	K - 1

C - 0
M - 100
Y - 100
K - 0

C - 14
M - 100
Y - 100
K - 0

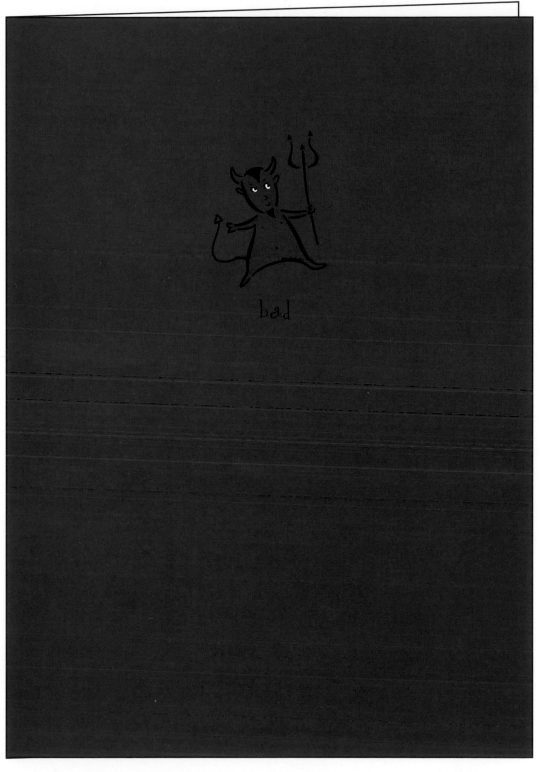

bad

design firm
After Hours Creative
Phoenix, Arizona

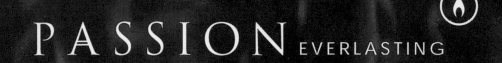

PASSION EVERLASTING

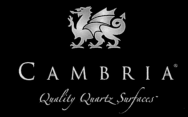

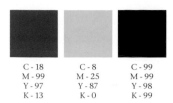

(opposite) design firm
Design Guys
Minneapolis, Minnesota
client
Cambria

C - 18
M - 99
Y - 97
K - 13

C - 8
M - 25
Y - 87
K - 0

C - 99
M - 99
Y - 98
K - 99

C - 13
M - 92
Y - 71
K - 2

C - 1
M - 29
Y - 94
K - 0

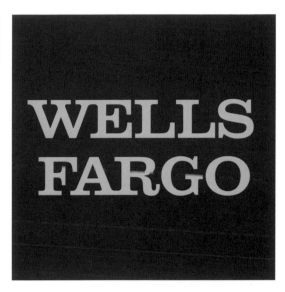

design firm
Addison
San Francisco, California
client
Wells Fargo

C - 9
M - 93
Y - 76
K - 8

C - 5
M - 18
Y - 89
K - 0

C - 0
M - 0
Y - 0
K - 100

design firm
Michael Osborne Design
San Francisco, California
client
Gymboree

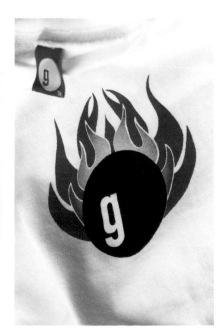

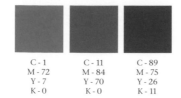

C - 1
M - 72
Y - 7
K - 0

C - 11
M - 84
Y - 70
K - 0

C - 89
M - 75
Y - 26
K - 11

design firm
Sagmeister Inc.
New York, New York

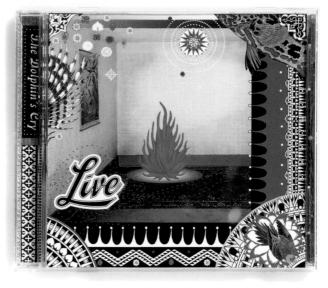

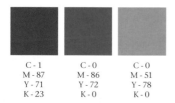

C - 1
M - 87
Y - 71
K - 23

C - 0
M - 86
Y - 72
K - 0

C - 0
M - 51
Y - 78
K - 0

design firm
Hornall Anderson Design Works
Seattle, Washington

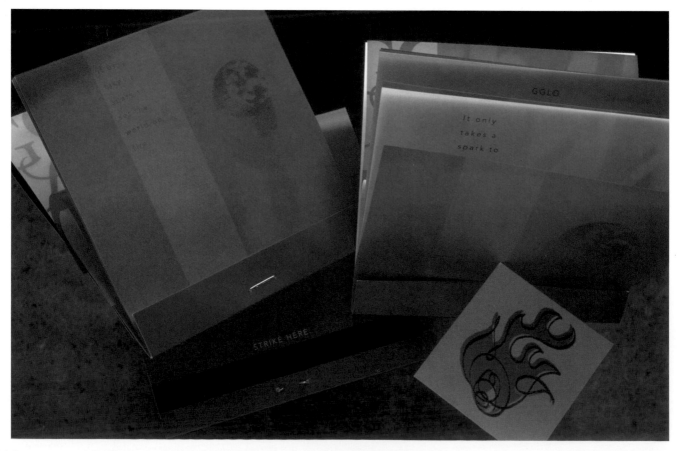

140

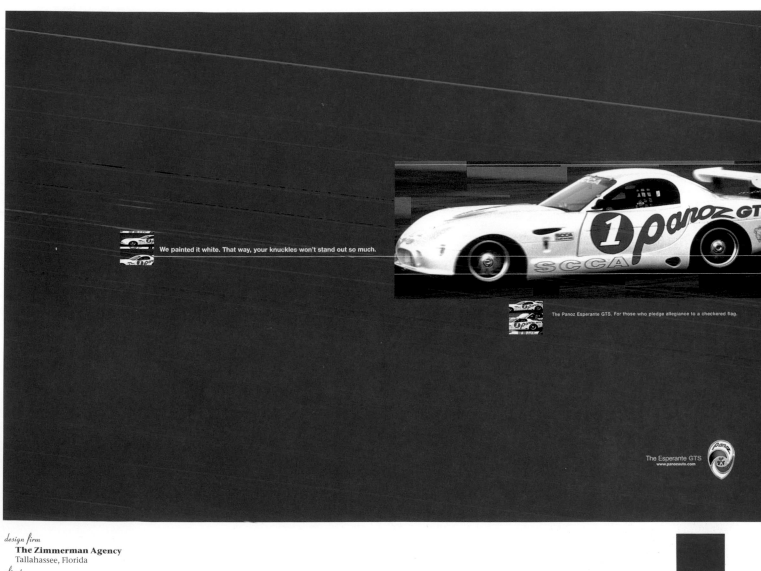

We painted it white. That way, your knuckles won't stand out so much.

The Panoz Esperante GTS. For those who pledge allegiance to a checkered flag.

The Esperante GTS
www.panozauto.com

design firm
The Zimmerman Agency
Tallahassee, Florida
client
Panoz

C - 0
M - 99
Y - 91
K - 5

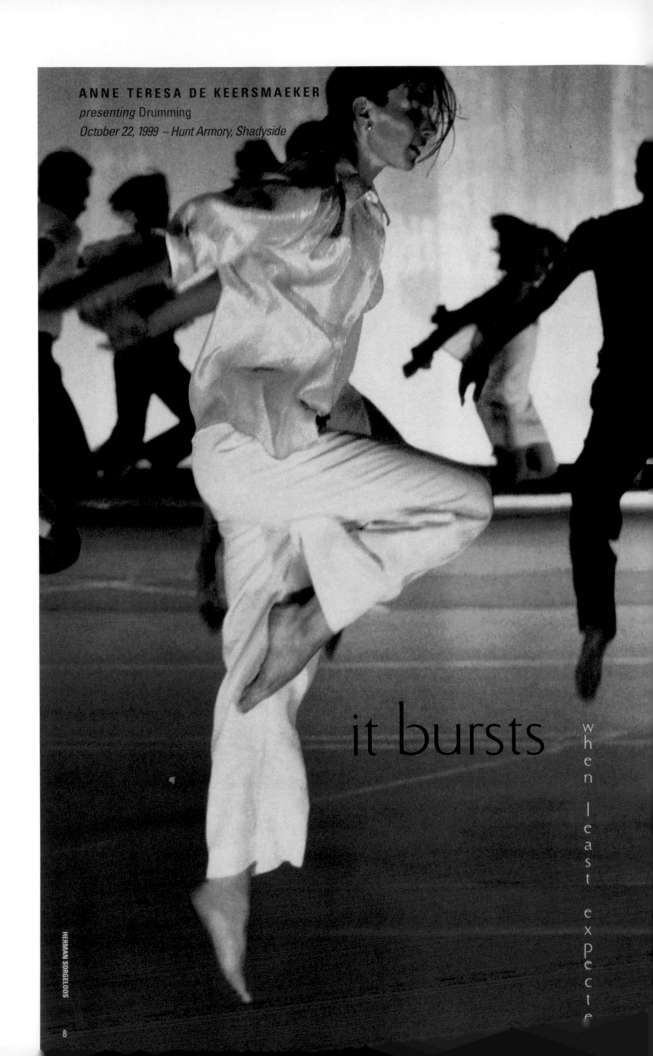

ANNE TERESA DE KEERSMAEKER
presenting Drumming
October 22, 1999 — Hunt Armory, Shadyside

it bursts when least expected

HERMAN SORGELOOS

8

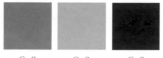

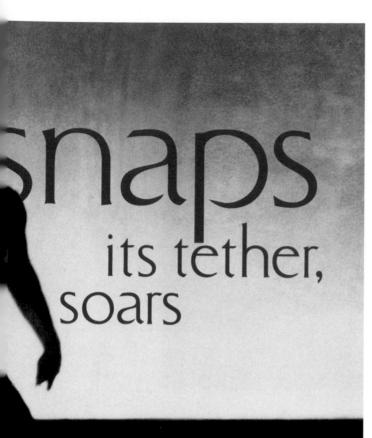

snaps
its tether,
soaps

"An explosion of energies . . . " — Le Soir

Drumming, a percussion piece by noted minimalist composer Steve Reich, made its first appearance in De Keersmaeker's *Just Before*. Now, presented in full, it provides the title and material for the choreographer's latest creation. The music is based on rhythms— simple at first, then gradually gaining complexity as they multiply and overlap. So, too, the choreography. A single motion phrase, exhaustively explored through myriad combinations, variations, and transformations, is slowed down, speeded up, and reversed.

Rhythmic, unremitting, yet endlessly varied, as De Keersmaeker says, *"Drumming* is like a machine that is switched on and then goes its own way, like an unstoppable natural phenomenon."

9

C - 0	C - 0	C - 0
M - 70	M - 40	M - 0
Y - 80	Y - 90	Y - 0
K - 0	K - 0	K - 100

design firm
Agnew Moyer Smith Inc.
Pittsburgh, Pennsylvania
client
Pittsburgh Dance Council

design firm
Full Steam Marketing & Design
Salinas, California
client
Stoked Media

C - 1	C - 33	C - 0
M - 50	M - 31	M - 0
Y - 89	Y - 27	Y - 0
K - 0	K - 6	K - 100

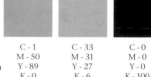

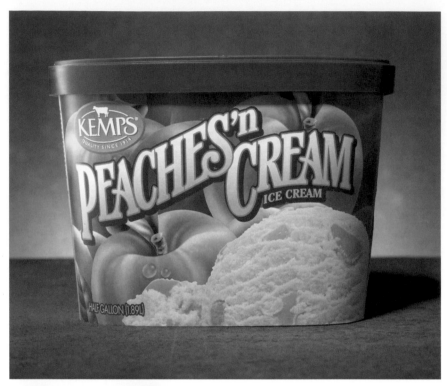

C - 44
M - 29
Y - 91
K - 32

C - 0
M - 24
Y - 86
K - 0

C - 5
M - 78
Y - 91
K - 1

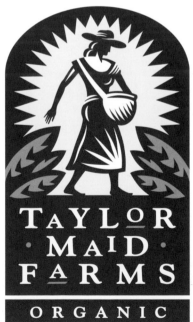

C - 34
M - 0
Y - 72
K - 83

C - 0
M - 76
Y - 76
K - 60

C - 0
M - 5
Y - 43
K - 0

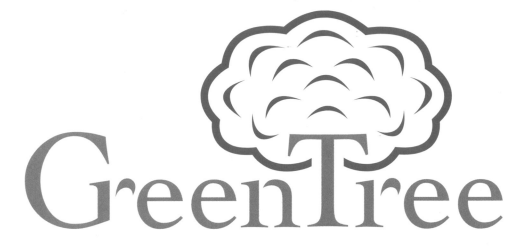

LENDING GROUP

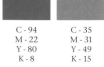

C - 94   C - 35
M - 22   M - 31
Y - 80   Y - 49
K - 8   K - 15

design firm
Becker Design
Milwaukee, Wisconsin
client
HR Value Group

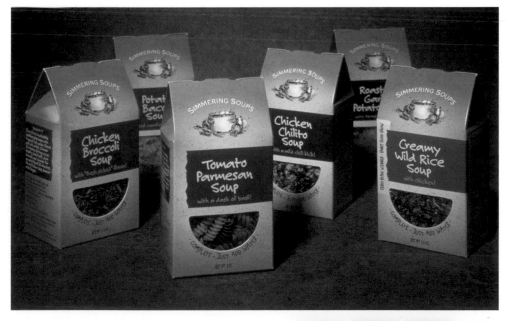

design firm
Compass Design
Minneapolis, Minnesota

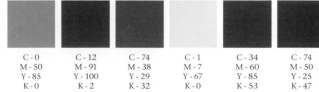

C - 0   C - 12   C - 74   C - 1   C - 34   C - 74
M - 50   M - 91   M - 38   M - 7   M - 60   M - 50
Y - 85   Y - 100   Y - 29   Y - 67   Y - 85   Y - 25
K - 0   K - 2   K - 32   K - 0   K - 53   K - 47

joint replacement
center

C - 76   C - 35
M - 64   M - 14
Y - 64   Y - 22
K - 12   K - 0

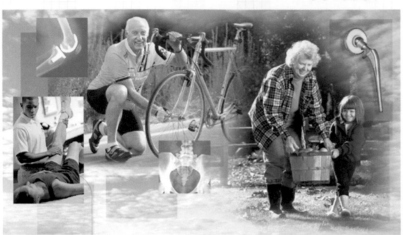

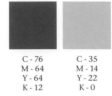 **Alegent** Health
Orthopaedic Services

design firm
Dotzler Creative Arts
Omaha, Nebraska

C - 95   C - 88
M - 85   M - 15
Y - 0   Y - 99
K - 2   K - 0

design firm
Levine & Associates
Washington, D.C.
client
The Kellog Foundation

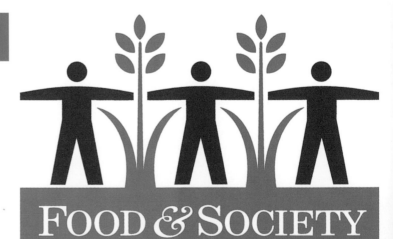

FOOD & SOCIETY

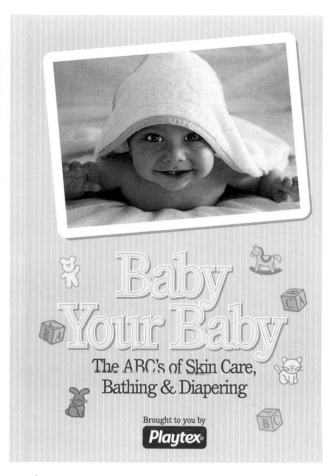

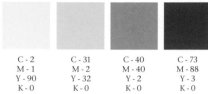

C - 2	C - 31	C - 40	C - 73
M - 1	M - 2	M - 40	M - 88
Y - 90	Y - 32	Y - 2	Y - 3
K - 0	K - 0	K - 0	K - 0

design firm
Tom Fowler, Inc.
  Norwalk, Connecticut
client
  Playtex Products, Inc.

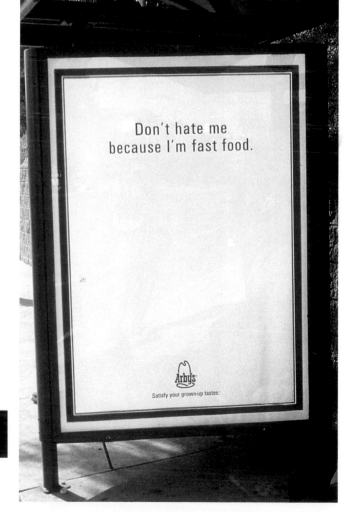

design firm
Bald & Beautiful
  Venice, California
client
  Arby's

C - 33	C - 0
M - 86	M - 0
Y - 23	Y - 0
K - 17	K - 100

C - 35
M - 12
Y - 2
K - 0

C - 44
M - 9
Y - 89
K - 3

C - 43
M - 96
Y - 3
K - 1

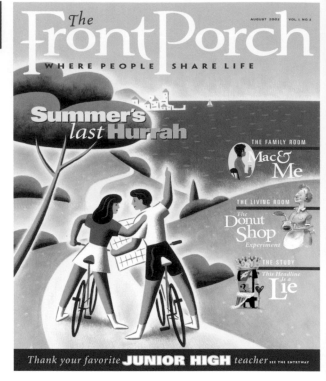

design firm
Dever Designs
Laurel, Maryland
client
The Front Porch Magazine

design firm
Compass Design
Minneapolis, Minnesota
client
Kemps Marigold

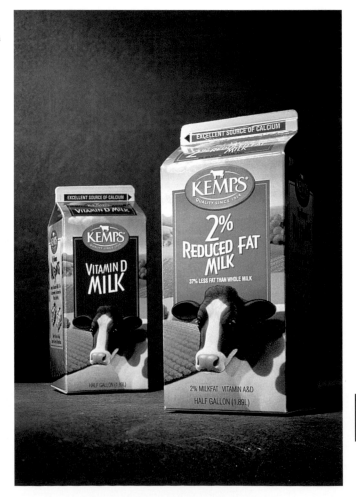

C - 9	C - 78	C - 44	C - 36	C - 5
M - 99	M - 13	M - 26	M - 80	M - 49
Y - 96	Y - 0	Y - 76	Y - 82	Y - 88
K - 11	K - 0	K - 0	K - 7	K - 0

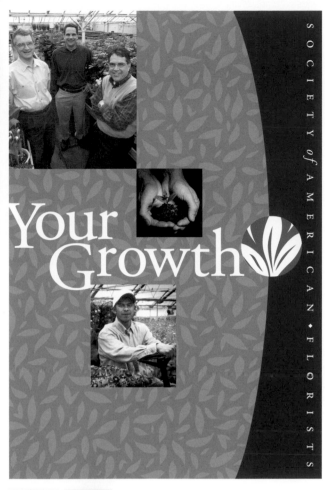

SOCIETY of AMERICAN • FLORISTS

design firm
Dever Designs
Laurel, Maryland
client
Society of American Florists

C - 35	C - 100
M - 0	M - 35
Y - 100	Y - 0
K - 40	K - 60

design firm
Tom Ventress Design
Nashville, Tennessee
client
Walker Foods

C - 0	C - 0	C - 0	C - 100
M - 100	M - 0	M - 5	M - 0
Y - 100	Y - 0	Y - 50	Y - 100
K - 0	K - 100	K - 0	K - 0

149

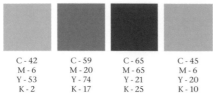

C - 42
M - 6
Y - 53
K - 2

C - 59
M - 20
Y - 74
K - 17

C - 65
M - 65
Y - 21
K - 25

C - 45
M - 6
Y - 20
K - 10

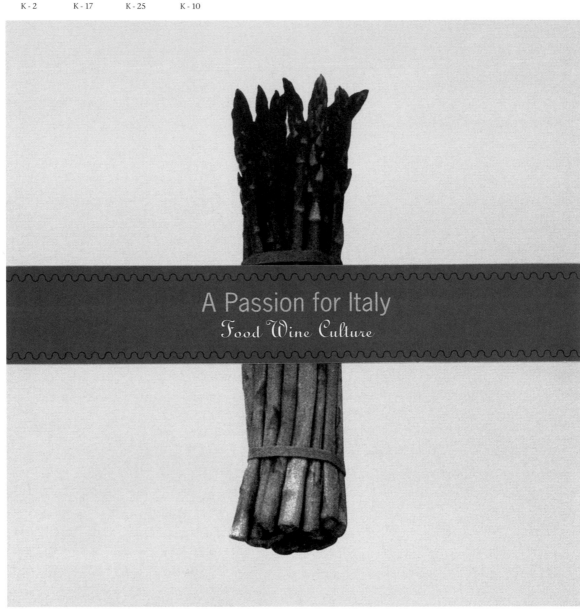

A Passion for Italy

Food Wine Culture

design firm
John Kneapler Design
New York, New York
client
The James Beard Foundation

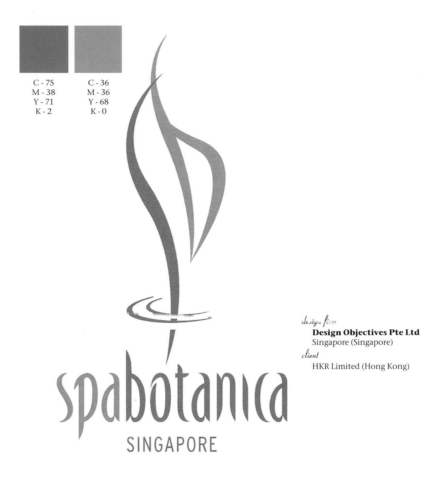

C - 75	C - 36
M - 38	M - 36
Y - 71	Y - 68
K - 2	K - 0

design firm
Design Objectives Pte Ltd
Singapore (Singapore)
client
HKR Limited (Hong Kong)

spabotanica
SINGAPORE

design firm
Tangram Strategic Design
Novara (Italy)
client
Prénatal

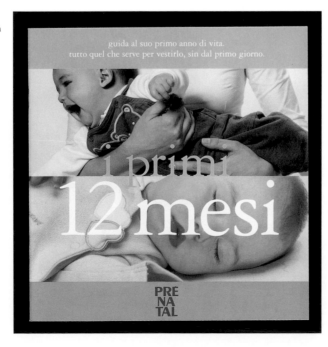

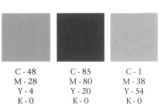

C - 48	C - 85	C - 1
M - 28	M - 80	M - 38
Y - 4	Y - 20	Y - 54
K - 0	K - 0	K - 0

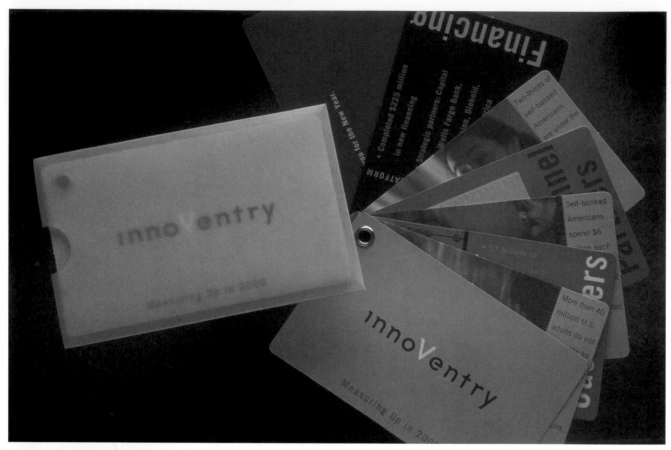

C - 2	C - 6	C - 44
M - 62	M - 87	M - 38
Y - 71	Y - 67	Y - 42
K - 3	K - 20	K - 48

design firm
Hornall Anderson Design Works
Seattle, Washington

Medical Rehabilitation Consultants

Contain Costs. Add Value. Improve Care.

C - 80	C - 0
M - 60	M - 0
Y - 0	Y - 0
K - 0	K - 100

design firm
Klündt Hosmer Design
Spokane, Washington

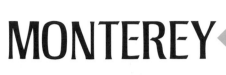 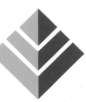 **MONTEREY PACIFIC**

APPLIED
AGRICULTURAL
TECHNOLOGIES

design firm
The Wecker Group
Monterey, California

C - 0	C - 100	C - 50
M - 0	M - 50	M - 0
Y - 0	Y - 100	Y - 100
K - 100	K - 0	K - 0

design firm
Sayles Graphic Design
Des Moines, Iowa
client
"Art Fights Back"

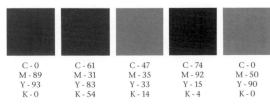

C - 0	C - 61	C - 47	C - 74	C - 0
M - 89	M - 31	M - 35	M - 92	M - 50
Y - 93	Y - 83	Y - 33	Y - 15	Y - 90
K - 0	K - 54	K - 14	K - 4	K - 0

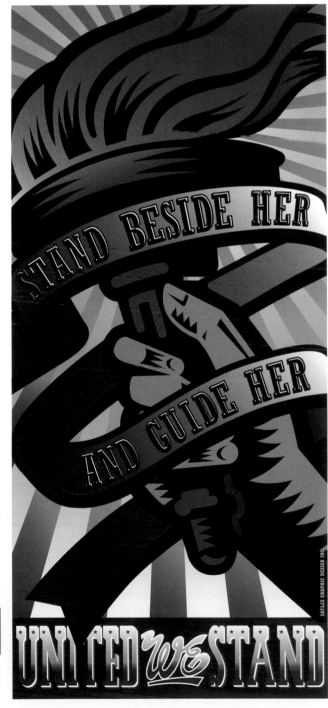

153

design firm
Lemley Design Company
Seattle, Washington
client
REI

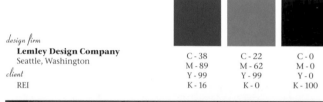

C - 38	C - 22	C - 0
M - 89	M - 62	M - 0
Y - 99	Y - 99	Y - 0
K - 16	K - 0	K - 100

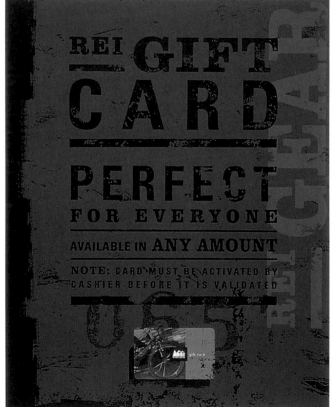

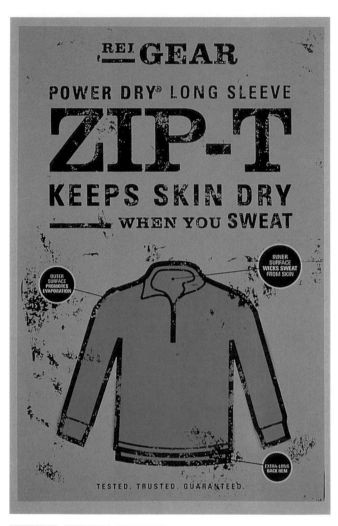

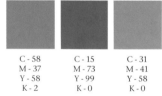

C - 58	C - 15	C - 31
M - 37	M - 73	M - 41
Y - 58	Y - 99	Y - 58
K - 2	K - 0	K - 0

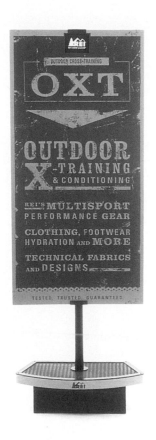

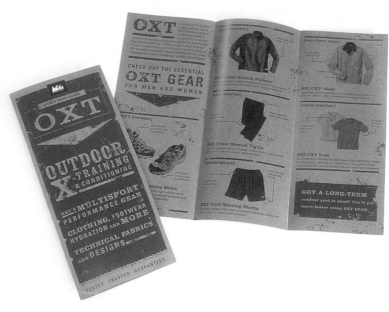

design firm
Lemley Design Company
Seattle, Washington

client
REI

C - 25
M - 57
Y - 83
K - 25

C - 16
M - 43
Y - 61
K - 6

design firm
Klündt Hosmer Design
Spokane, Washington

client
Telect

C - 45
M - 37
Y - 82
K - 38

C - 15
M - 43
Y - 88
K - 5

C - 91
M - 78
Y - 22
K - 24

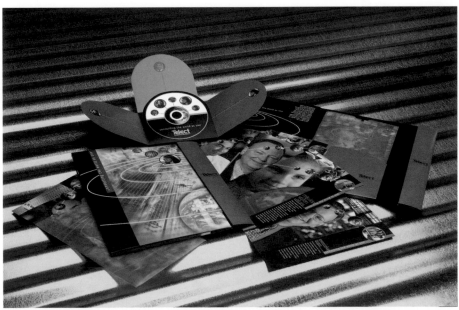

C - 12
M - 26
Y - 44
K - 0

C - 23
M - 68
Y - 56
K - 0

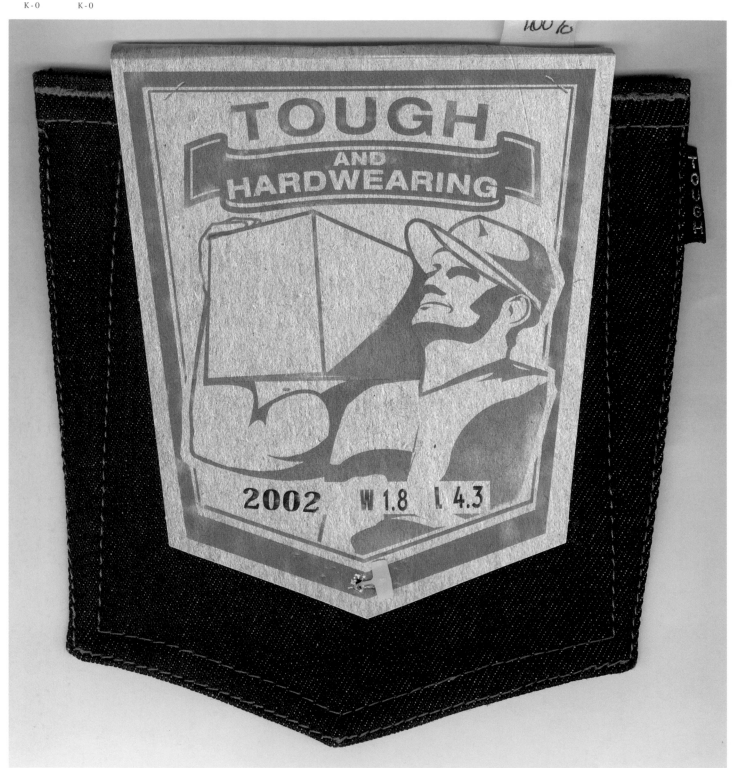

design firm
Burrows
Shenfield (United Kingdom)
client
Ford Motor Company

durable

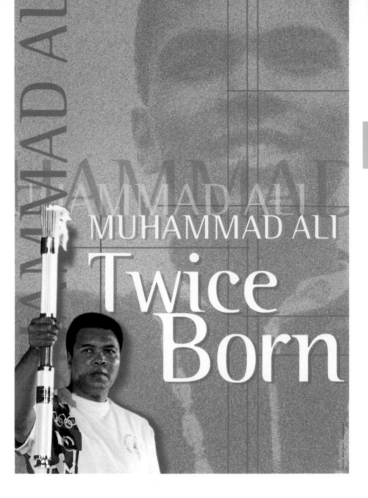

design firm
Designation
New York, New York

C - 25   C - 41
M - 25   M - 45
Y - 25   Y - 48
K - 2   K - 24

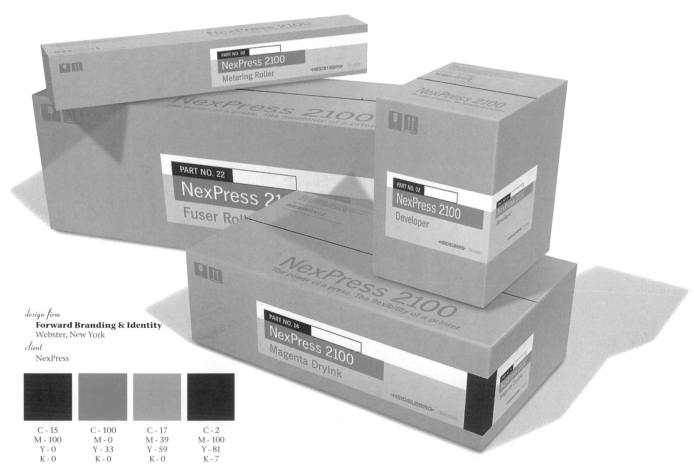

design firm
Forward Branding & Identity
Webster, New York
client
NexPress

C - 15   C - 100   C - 17   C - 2
M - 100   M - 0   M - 39   M - 100
Y - 0   Y - 33   Y - 59   Y - 81
K - 0   K - 0   K - 0   K - 7

C - 0
M - 26
Y - 95
K - 0

C - 0
M - 99
Y - 84
K - 13

C - 0
M - 0
Y - 0
K - 100

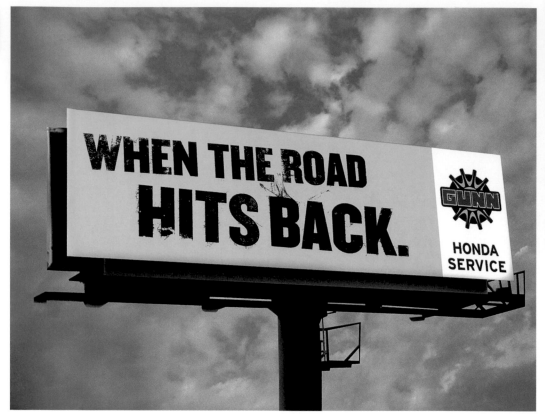

design firm
Toolbox Studios, Inc.
San Antonio, Texas
client
Gunn Automotive

design firm
Baer Design Group
Evanston, Illinois
client
Appropriate Temporaries, Inc.

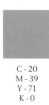

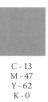

C - 88
M - 71
Y - 45
K - 9

C - 20
M - 39
Y - 71
K - 0

C - 39
M - 82
Y - 80
K - 0

C - 13
M - 47
Y - 62
K - 0

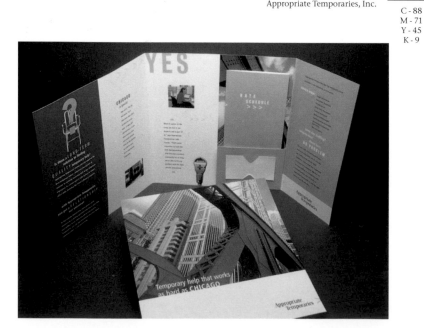

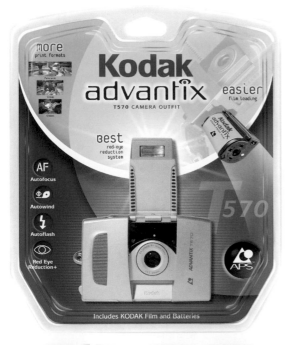

design firm
McElveney & Palozzi Design Group
Rochester, New York
client
Eastman Kodak Company

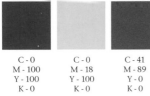

C - 0	C - 0	C - 41	C - 76
M - 100	M - 18	M - 89	M - 95
Y - 100	Y - 100	Y - 0	Y - 0
K - 0	K - 0	K - 0	K - 0

design firm
Dever Designs
Laurel, Maryland
client
Liberty Magazine

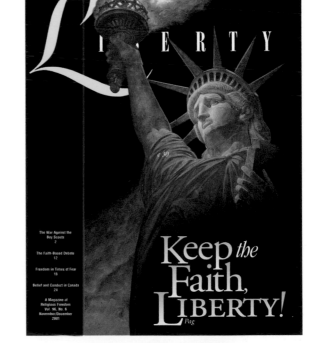

design firm
Supon Design Group
Washington, D.C.
client
Ulman Paper Bag Company

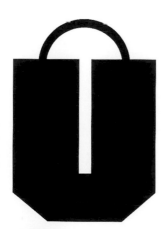

| C - 0 |
| M - 0 |
| Y - 0 |
| K - 100 |

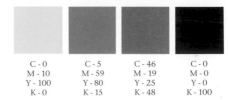

C - 0	C - 5	C - 46	C - 0
M - 10	M - 59	M - 19	M - 0
Y - 100	Y - 80	Y - 25	Y - 0
K - 0	K - 15	K - 48	K - 100

C - 75	C - 0	C - 0	C - 72	C - 83	C - 100	C - 2
M - 28	M - 89	M - 72	M - 8	M - 23	M - 77	M - 20
Y - 3	Y - 93	Y - 90	Y - 64	Y - 83	Y - 18	Y - 25
K - 2	K - 0	K - 0	K - 2	K - 18	K - 15	K - 0

design firm
Sayles Graphic Design
Des Moines, Iowa
client
"Art Fights Back"

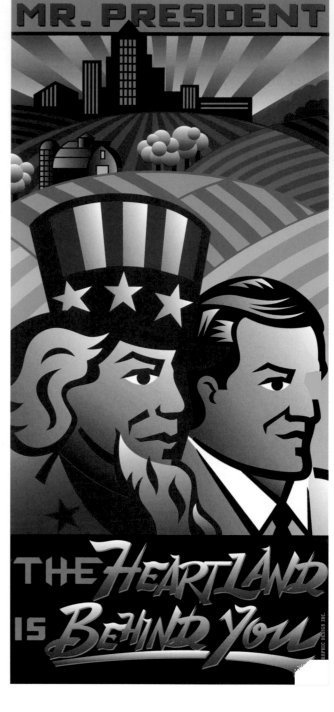

Meta • **logic**

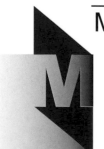

design firm
Ron Bartels Design
Lincoln, Nebraska
client
Meta•Logic Software Developer

C - 0	C - 0	C - 0
M - 100	M - 0	M - 0
Y - 100	Y - 0	Y - 0
K - 0	K - 42	K - 100

C - 8	C - 32	C - 0
M - 93	M - 25	M - 0
Y - 85	Y - 32	Y - 0
K - 1	K - 2	K - 100

design firm
Studio Archetype
San Francisco, California
client
Studio Archetype

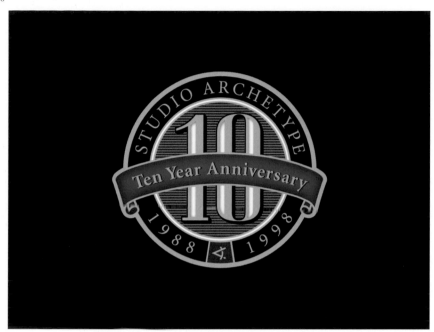

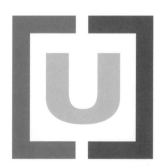

UNIVERSITYSQUARE

design firm
Bailey Design Group
Plymouth Meeting, Pennsylvania

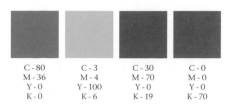

C - 80	C - 3	C - 30	C - 0
M - 36	M - 4	M - 70	M - 0
Y - 0	Y - 100	Y - 0	Y - 0
K - 0	K - 6	K - 19	K - 70

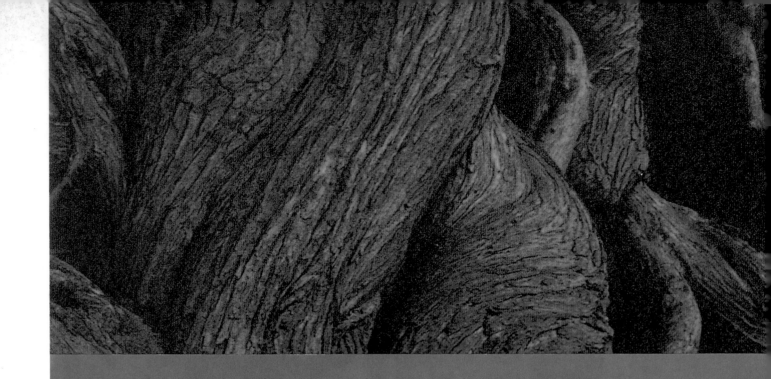

Keiler & Company is proud to present this book of trees. We have been privileged
to explore and communicate many topics and points of view for corporate and business
clients since 1973. **AMONG TREES** is an inspiring example of creative collaboration at its
best, and a reminder that the art of communication is as much alive as the science.
We hope you enjoy this unique photographic journey.

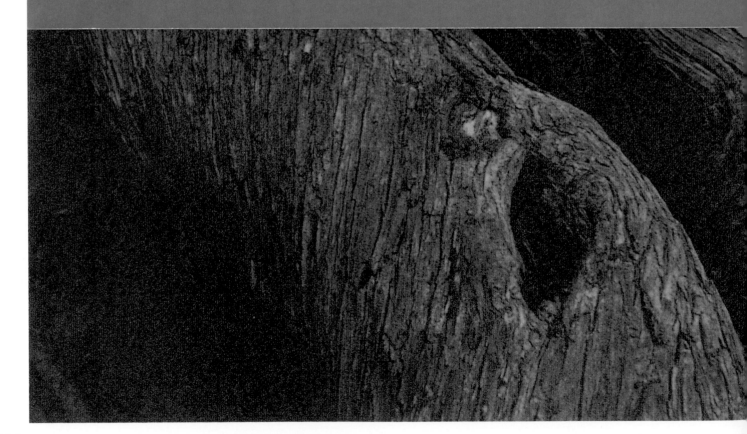

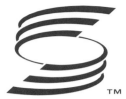

Spokane Chamber
SPOKANE REGIONAL CHAMBER OF COMMERCE

C - 79
M - 72
Y - 100
K - 0

C - 0
M - 87
Y - 83
K - 30

design firm
Klündt Hosmer Design
Spokane, Washington

C - 23
M - 15
Y - 15
K - 1

C - 0
M - 0
Y - 0
K - 100

design firm
Tiffany + Company
New York, New York
client
Tiffany + Company

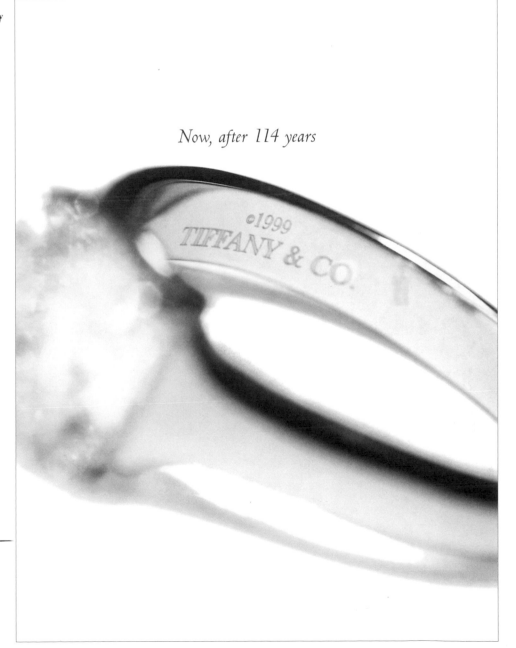

Now, after 114 years

©1999
TIFFANY & CO.

(opposite) design firm
Keiler & Company
Farmington, Connecticut
client
Sean Kernan Photo/
Keiler & Allied Printing

C - 40
M - 50
Y - 60
K - 10

C - 54
M - 46
Y - 43
K - 35

C - 0
M - 0
Y - 0
K - 100

design firm
Louis & Partners Design
Bath, Ohio
client
San Francisco Oven

C - 0
M - 91
Y - 100
K - 40

C - 0
M - 24
Y - 76
K - 0

C - 6
M - 9
Y - 24
K - 0

C - 60
M - 50
Y - 15
K - 0

C - 10
M - 15
Y - 40
K - 0

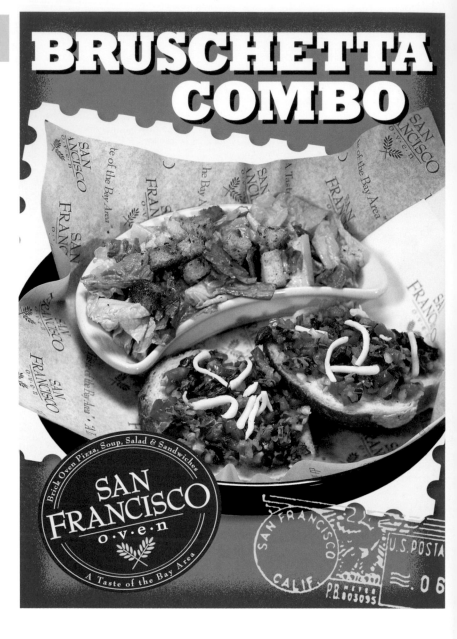

C - 0
M - 100
Y - 91
K - 0

C - 57
M - 0
Y - 100
K - 0

C - 16
M - 31
Y - 56
K - 0

C - 0
M - 0
Y - 0
K - 100

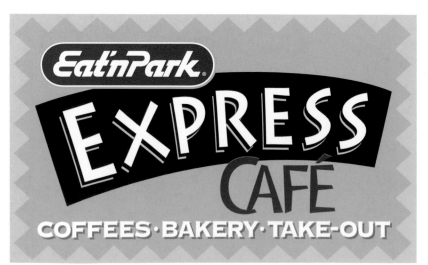

design firm
Louis & Partners Design
Bath, Ohio
client
Eat N' Park

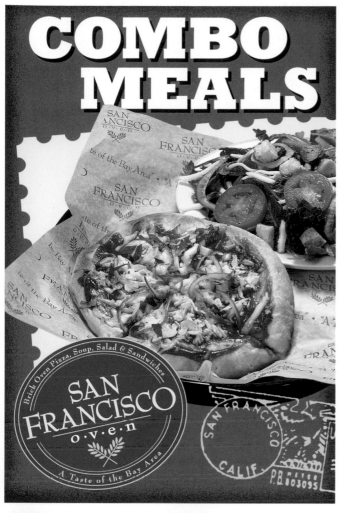

COMBO MEALS

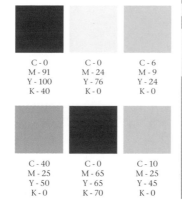

C - 0 M - 91 Y - 100 K - 40	C - 0 M - 24 Y - 76 K - 0	C - 6 M - 9 Y - 24 K - 0	C - 0 M - 50 Y - 50 K - 50	C - 10 M - 25 Y - 45 K - 0

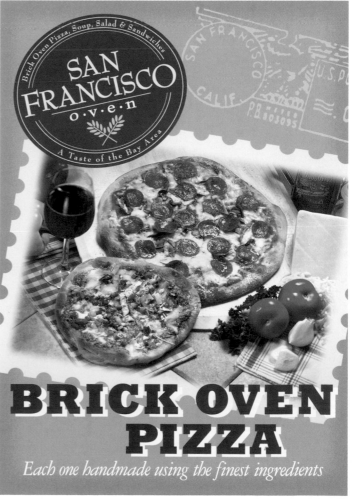

design firm
Louis & Partners Design
Bath, Ohio
client
San Francisco Oven

design firm
Louis & Partners Design
Bath, Ohio
client
San Francisco Oven

C - 0 M - 91 Y - 100 K - 40	C - 0 M - 24 Y - 76 K - 0	C - 6 M - 9 Y - 24 K - 0
C - 40 M - 25 Y - 50 K - 0	C - 0 M - 65 Y - 65 K - 70	C - 10 M - 25 Y - 45 K - 0

BRICK OVEN PIZZA

Each one handmade using the finest ingredients

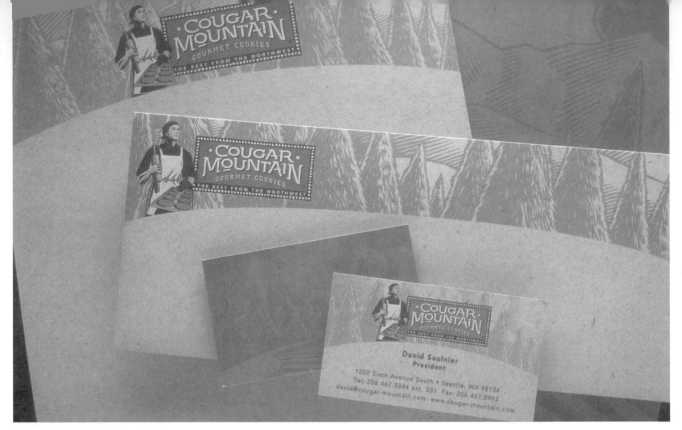

C - 0	C - 36	C - 0
M - 58	M - 13	M - 26
Y - 31	Y - 3	Y - 35
K - 46	K - 55	K - 45

design firm
Hornall Anderson Design Works
Seattle, Washington

design firm
Pearlfisher
London (England)

C - 16	C - 69	C - 20	C - 30
M - 89	M - 80	M - 100	M - 44
Y - 84	Y - 35	Y - 30	Y - 100
K - 5	K - 20	K - 1	K - 7

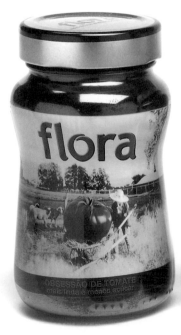 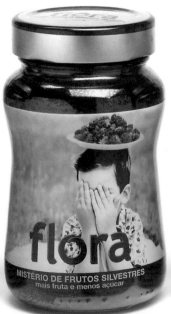 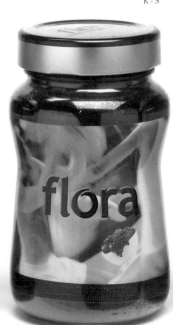 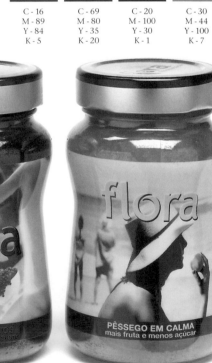

design firm
Klündt Hosmer Design
Spokane, Washington
client
Maryhill Winery

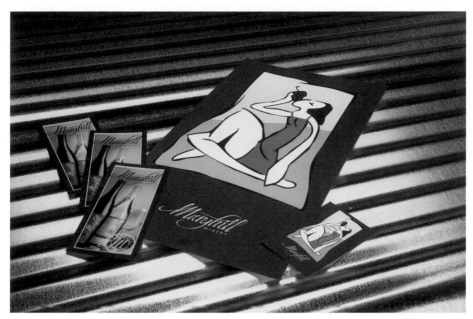

C - 17	C - 18	C - 0	C - 0
M - 80	M - 20	M - 71	M - 17
Y - 54	Y - 58	Y - 81	Y - 50
K - 52	K - 13	K - 10	K - 4

C - 27	C - 38	C - 12	C - 2
M - 88	M - 0	M - 86	M - 36
Y - 10	Y - 75	Y - 80	Y - 86
K - 0	K - 0	K - 2	K - 0

design firm
Pearlfisher
London (England)

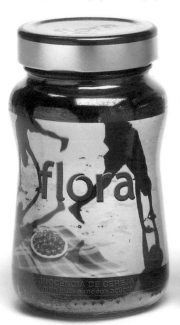

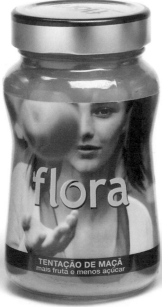

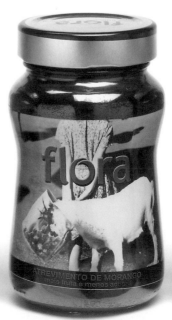

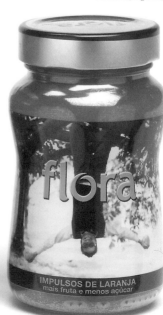

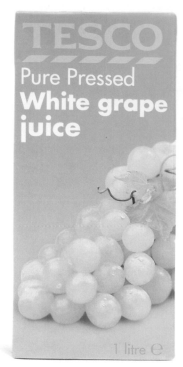

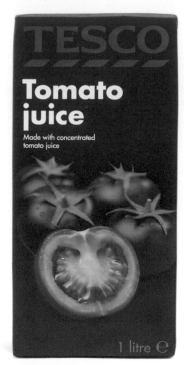

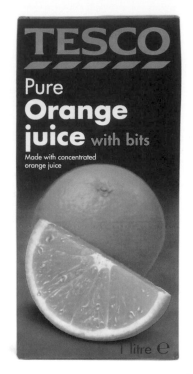

design firm
Pearlfisher
London (England)

C - 46	C - 33	C - 28	C - 11	C - 100	C - 74	C - 19
M - 5	M - 5	M - 91	M - 86	M - 85	M - 27	M - 39
Y - 83	Y - 50	Y - 61	Y - 57	Y - 3	Y - 12	Y - 78
K - 0	K - 0	K - 16	K - 1	K - 0	K - 0	K - 1

C - 25	C - 18	C - 65	C - 69
M - 99	M - 63	M - 113	M - 66
Y - 100	Y - 99	Y - 61	Y - 15
K - 19	K - 7	K - 6	K - 21

design firm
Tom Fowler, Inc.
Norwalk, Connecticut
client
Tom Fowler

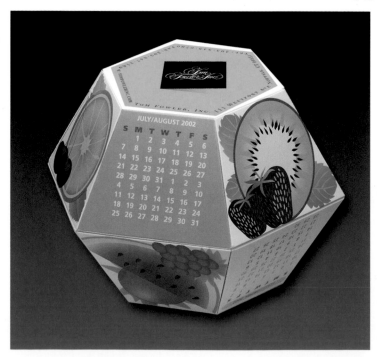

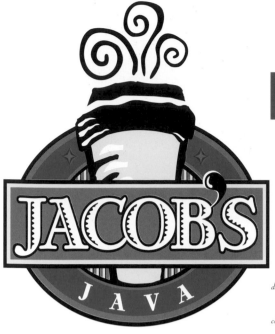

C - 100	C - 0	C - 0	C - 0
M - 43	M - 60	M - 11	M - 0
Y - 0	Y - 100	Y - 47	Y - 0
K - 18	K - 18	K - 0	K - 100

design firm
Klündt Hosmer Design
Spokane, Washington
client
Jacob's Java

design firm
Hornall Anderson Design Works
Seattle, Washington

C - 2	C - 73	C - 58	C - 5
M - 91	M - 62	M - 29	M - 31
Y - 65	Y - 43	Y - 59	Y - 52
K - 1	K - 20	K - 15	K - 1

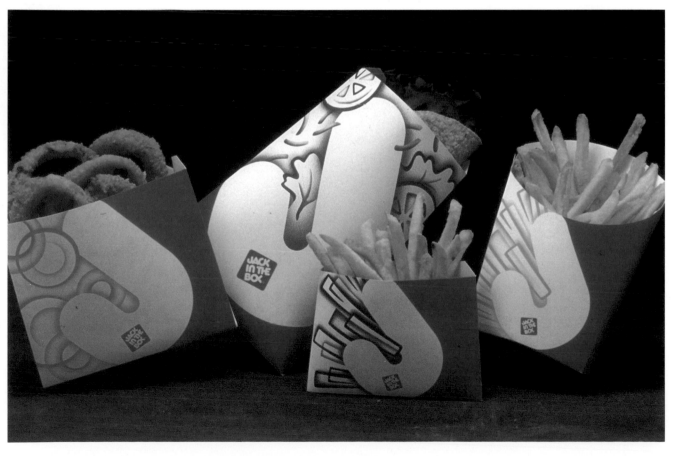

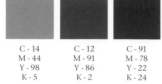

C - 14
M - 44
Y - 98
K - 5

C - 12
M - 91
Y - 86
K - 2

C - 91
M - 78
Y - 22
K - 24

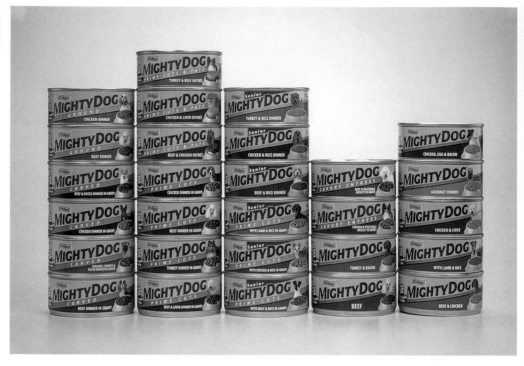

design firm
Thompson Design Group
San Francisco, California
client
Nestlé Purina Pet Care Division

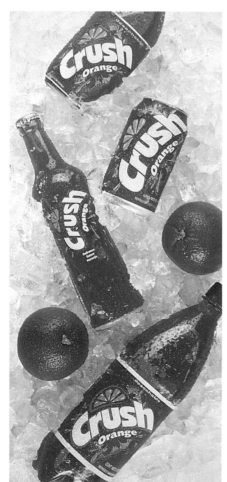

C - 67
M - 78
Y - 27
K - 8

C - 14
M - 34
Y - 82
K - 0

C - 39
M - 88
Y - 67
K - 5

C - 20
M - 66
Y - 75
K - 0

C - 10
M - 28
Y - 75
K - 0

C - 66
M - 52
Y - 69
K - 15

design firm
LIFT Creative
Atlanta, Georgia
client
Cadbury Beverages

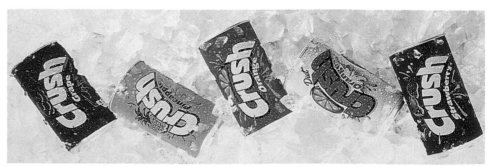

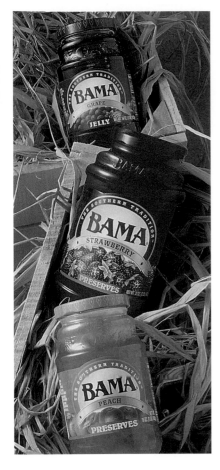

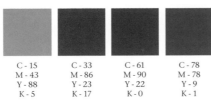

C - 15	C - 33	C - 61	C - 78
M - 43	M - 86	M - 90	M - 78
Y - 88	Y - 23	Y - 22	Y - 9
K - 5	K - 17	K - 0	K - 1

design firm
LIFT Creative
Atlanta, Georgia

client
Welch

design firm
Be.Design
San Rafael, California

client
Williams-Sonoma, Inc.

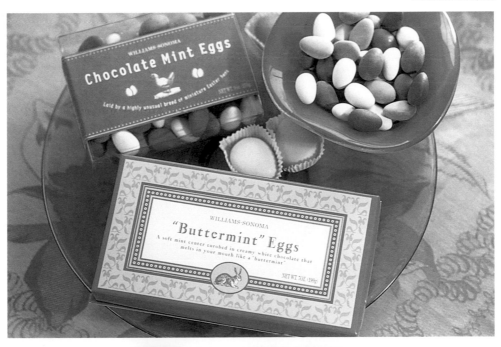

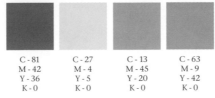

C - 81	C - 27	C - 13	C - 63
M - 42	M - 4	M - 45	M - 9
Y - 36	Y - 5	Y - 20	Y - 42
K - 0	K - 0	K - 0	K - 0

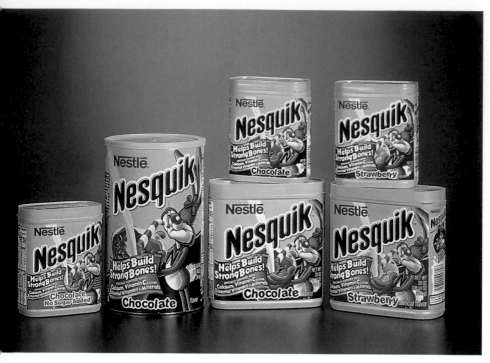

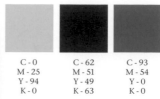

C - 0	C - 62	C - 93
M - 25	M - 51	M - 54
Y - 94	Y - 49	Y - 0
K - 0	K - 63	K - 0

design firm
Thompson Design Group
San Francisco, California
client
Nestle USA, Inc – Beverage

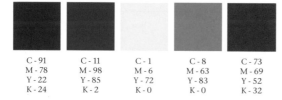

C - 91	C - 11	C - 1	C - 8	C - 73
M - 78	M - 98	M - 6	M - 63	M - 69
Y - 22	Y - 85	Y - 72	Y - 83	Y - 52
K - 24	K - 2	K - 0	K - 0	K - 32

design firm
Cornerstone
New York, New York
client
Goodmark Foods

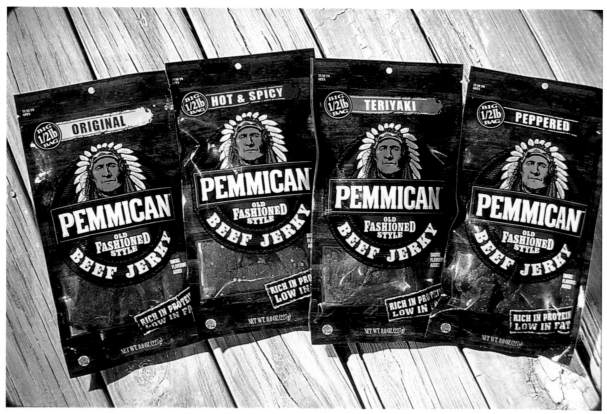

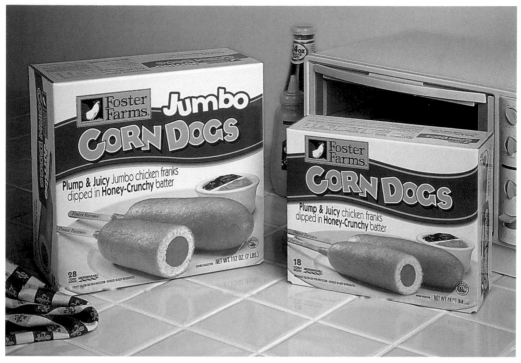

design firm
Thompson Design Group
San Francisco, California
client
Foster Farms

C - 11	C - 0
M - 98	M - 51
Y - 85	Y - 95
K - 2	K - 0

design firm
Thompson Design Group
San Francisco, California
client
Nestlé USA, Inc.—Beverage Division

C - 0	C - 11	C - 65
M - 25	M - 98	M - 74
Y - 94	Y - 85	Y - 35
K - 0	K - 2	K - 70

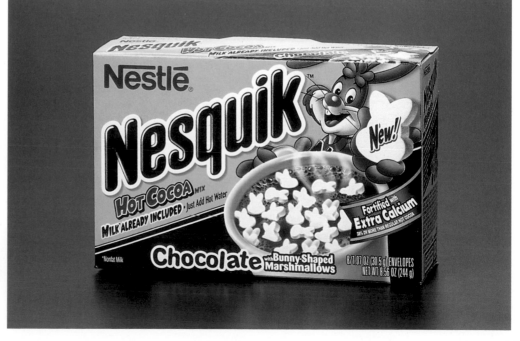

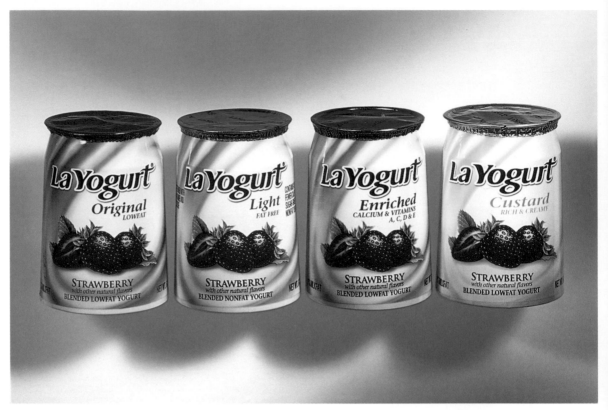

design firm
Cornerstone
New York, New York
client
Johanna Foods

C - 4	C - 56	C - 29	C - 12	C - 0
M - 55	M - 24	M - 99	M - 68	M - 13
Y - 7	Y - 0	Y - 77	Y - 0	Y - 65
K - 0	K - 0	K - 0	K - 0	K - 0

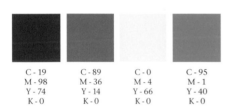

C - 19	C - 89	C - 0	C - 95
M - 98	M - 36	M - 4	M - 1
Y - 74	Y - 14	Y - 66	Y - 40
K - 0	K - 0	K - 0	K - 0

design firm
Gammon Ragonesi Associates
New York, New York
client
Beer Nuts

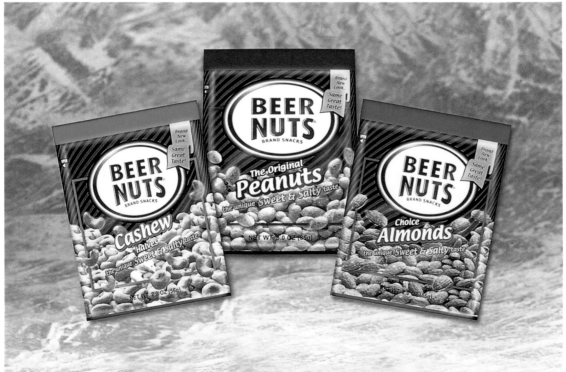

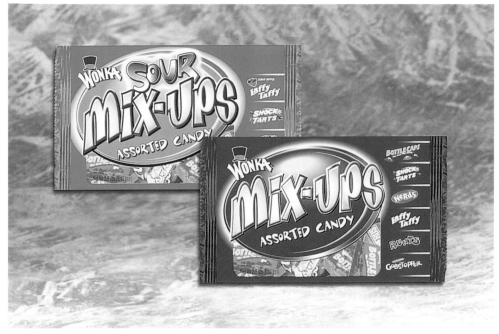

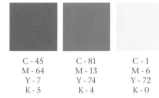

C - 45	C - 81	C - 1
M - 64	M - 13	M - 6
Y - 7	Y - 74	Y - 72
K - 5	K - 4	K - 0

design firm
Gammon Ragonesi Associates
New York, New York

client
Nestlé USA

C - 58	C - 80	C - 21	C - 99
M - 99	M - 47	M - 34	M - 60
Y - 27	Y - 99	Y - 97	Y - 6
K - 0	K - 0	K - 0	K - 2

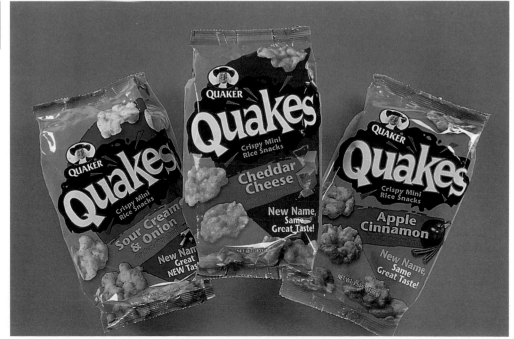

design firm
Haugaard Creative Group
Chicago, Illinois

client
Quaker Oats

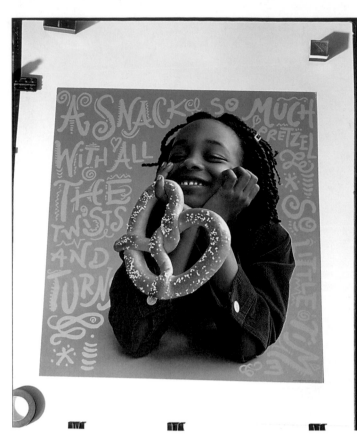

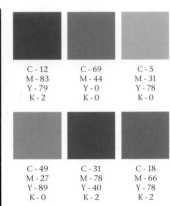

C - 12	C - 69	C - 5
M - 83	M - 44	M - 31
Y - 79	Y - 0	Y - 78
K - 2	K - 0	K - 0

C - 49	C - 31	C - 18
M - 27	M - 78	M - 66
Y - 89	Y - 40	Y - 78
K - 0	K - 2	K - 2

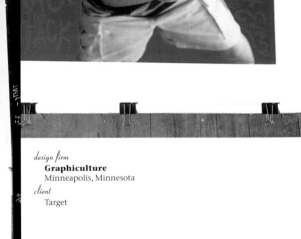

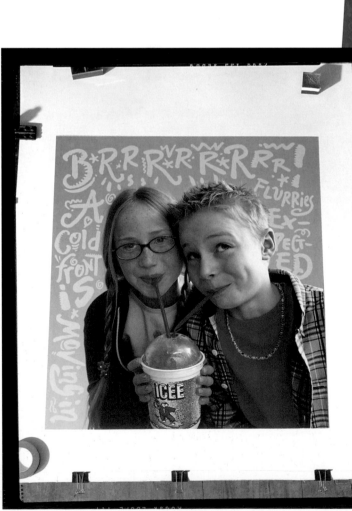

design firm
Graphiculture
Minneapolis, Minnesota
client
Target

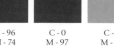

Wholesome Goodness Naturally!

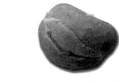
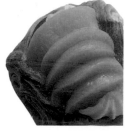
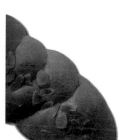
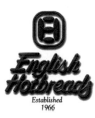

C - 96	C - 0	C - 0
M - 74	M - 97	M - 47
Y - 3	Y - 97	Y - 100
K - 0	K - 0	K - 0

English Hotbreads
Established 1966

design firm
Fixgo Advertising (M) Sdn Bhd
Subang Jaya (Malaysia)
client
English Hotbreads (Sel) Sdn Bhd

design firm
Zunda Design Group
South Norwalk, Connecticut
client
Sbarro Corporation

C - 96	C - 0	C - 0
M - 4	M - 100	M - 13
Y - 99	Y - 100	Y - 69
K - 0	K - 11	K - 0

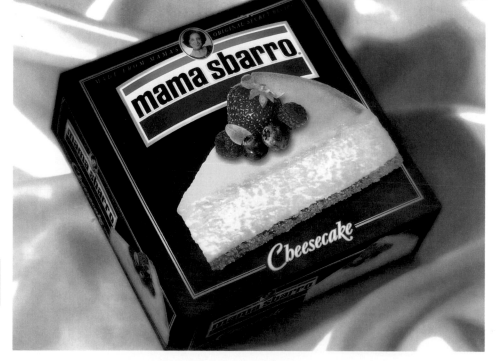

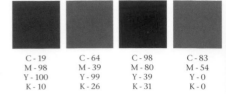

C - 19
M - 98
Y - 100
K - 10

C - 64
M - 39
Y - 99
K - 26

C - 98
M - 80
Y - 39
K - 31

C - 83
M - 54
Y - 0
K - 0

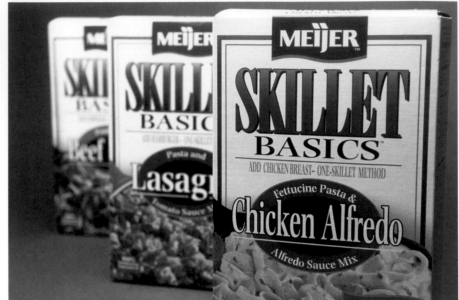

design firm
Baer Design Group
Evanston, Illinois
client
Meijer

design firm
Praxis Diseñadores, S.C.
México City (Mexico)
client
Valle Redondo

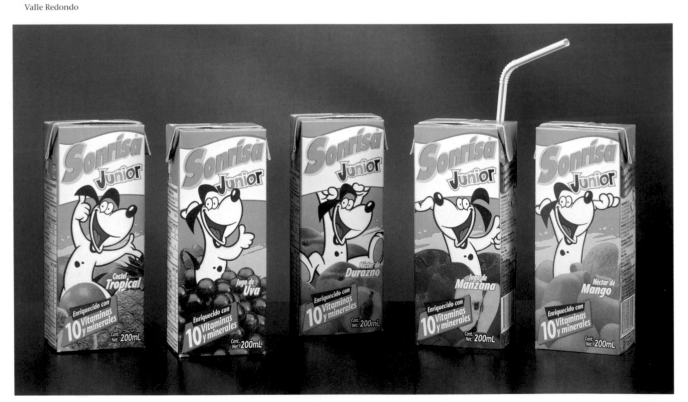

C - 80
M - 0
Y - 90
K - 0

C - 0
M - 10
Y - 100
K - 0

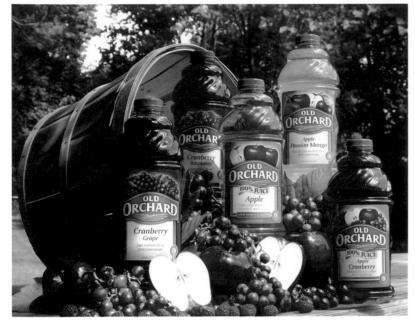

C - 72　　C - 11
M - 0　　 M - 100
Y - 100　　Y - 97
K - 0　　 K - 3

design firm
Bailey Design Group Inc
Plymouth Meeting, Pennsylvania

design firm
McElvency & Palozzi Design Group
Rochester, New York
client
Ahold USA—Tops Division

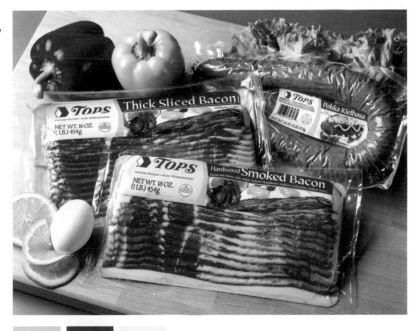

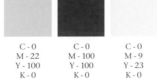

C - 0　　　C - 0　　　C - 0
M - 22　　 M - 100　　M - 9
Y - 100　　Y - 100　　Y - 23
K - 0　　　K - 0　　　K - 0

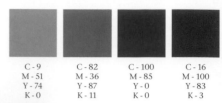

C - 9
M - 51
Y - 74
K - 0

C - 82
M - 36
Y - 87
K - 11

C - 100
M - 85
Y - 0
K - 0

C - 16
M - 100
Y - 83
K - 3

design firm
Tangram Strategic Design
Novara, Italy
client
MDO

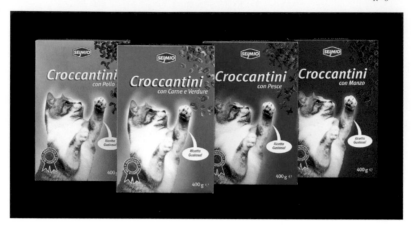

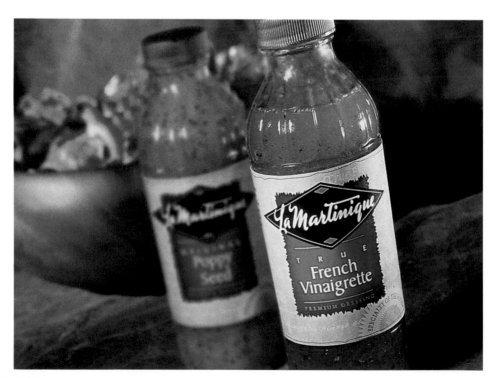

design firm
Interbrand
New York, New York
client
Reily Foods

C - 83
M - 14
Y - 43
K - 4

C - 12
M - 91
Y - 86
K - 2

C - 13
M - 72
Y - 88
K - 3

C - 26
M - 99
Y - 73
K - 20

C - 0
M - 25
Y - 67
K - 0

C - 91
M - 78
Y - 22
K - 24

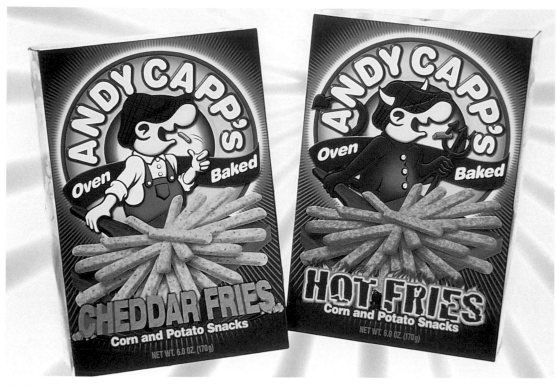

design firm
Cornerstone
New York, New York

client
Goodmark Foods

C - 62
M - 51
Y - 49
K - 63

C - 11
M - 98
Y - 85
K - 2

C - 20
M - 12
Y - 71
K - 3

design firm
Gauger + Santz
San Francisco, California

client
Atkins Nutritionals

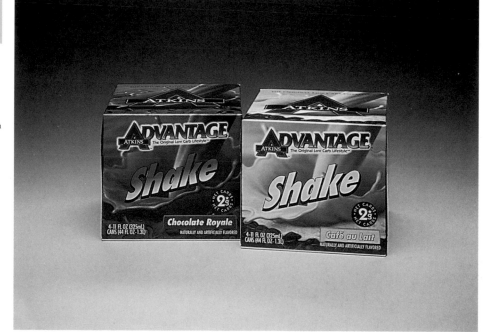

design firm
Design Forum
Dayton, Ohio
client
Dunkin' Donuts

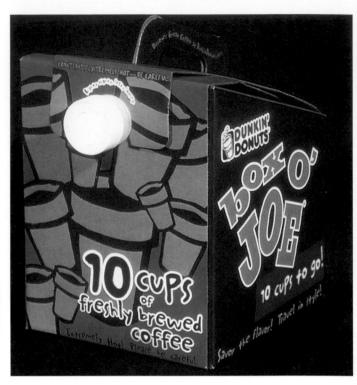

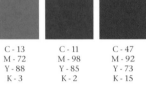

C - 13	C - 11	C - 47
M - 72	M - 98	M - 92
Y - 88	Y - 85	Y - 73
K - 3	K - 2	K - 15

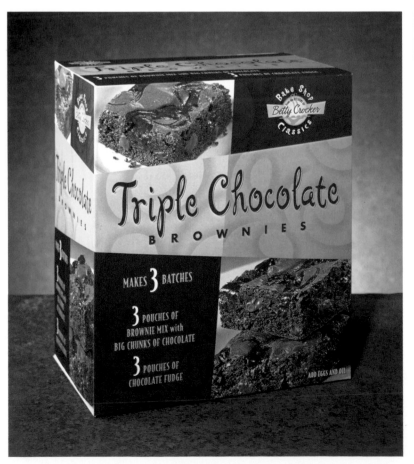

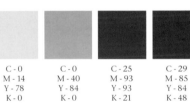

C - 0	C - 0	C - 25	C - 29
M - 14	M - 40	M - 93	M - 85
Y - 78	Y - 84	Y - 93	Y - 84
K - 0	K - 0	K - 21	K - 48

design firm
Compass Design
Minneapolis, Minnesota

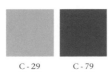

C - 29
M - 29
Y - 39
K - 0

C - 79
M - 60
Y - 51
K - 23

C - 45
M - 99
Y - 76
K - 5

C - 0
M - 21
Y - 75
K - 0

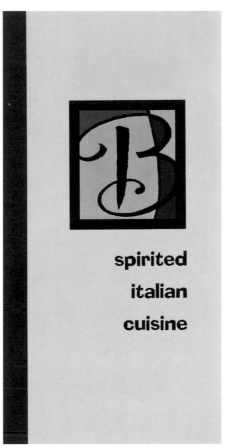

spirited

italian

cuisine

design firm
The Lemonides Design Group, Inc.
Glen Mills, Pennsylvania
client
Bellissimo

design firm
Wallace Church, Inc.
New York, New York
client
Ciao Bella Gelato Co., Inc.

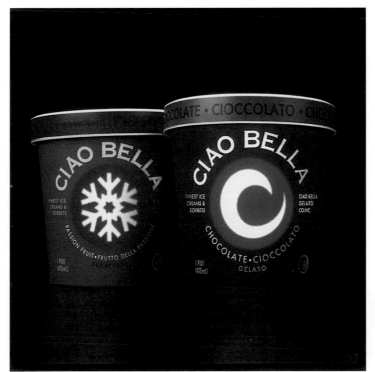

C - 15
M - 82
Y - 100
K - 0

C - 73
M - 80
Y - 29
K - 20

C - 41
M - 95
Y - 66
K - 6

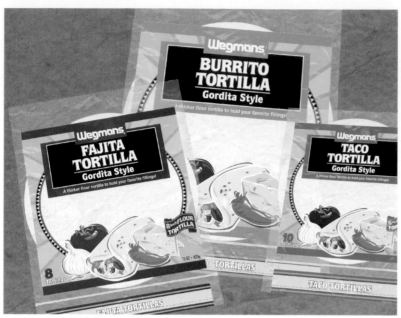

(opposite) design firm
Finished Art, Inc.
Atlanta, Georgia
client
The Coca-Cola Company

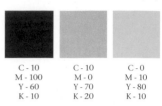

C - 10	C - 10	C - 0
M - 100	M - 0	M - 10
Y - 60	Y - 70	Y - 80
K - 10	K - 20	K - 10

design firm
McElveney & Palozzi Design Group
Rochester, New York
client
Wegmans Food Markets

C - 10	C - 0	C - 65	C - 0
M - 0	M - 100	M - 0	M - 65
Y - 100	Y - 0	Y - 100	Y - 83
K - 0	K - 24	K - 0	K - 0

C - 33	C - 0
M - 86	M - 25
Y - 23	Y - 67
K - 17	K - 0

design firm
Gammon Ragonesi Associates
New York, New York
client
Nestlé Ice Cream Company

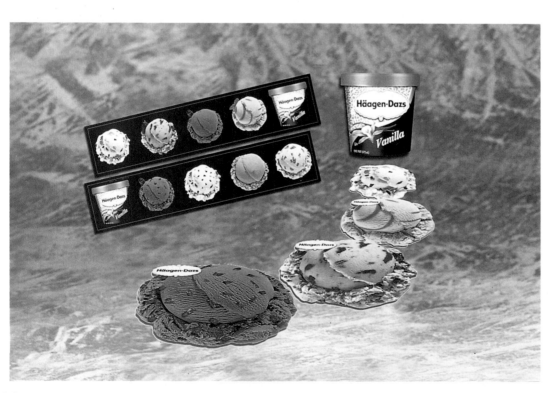

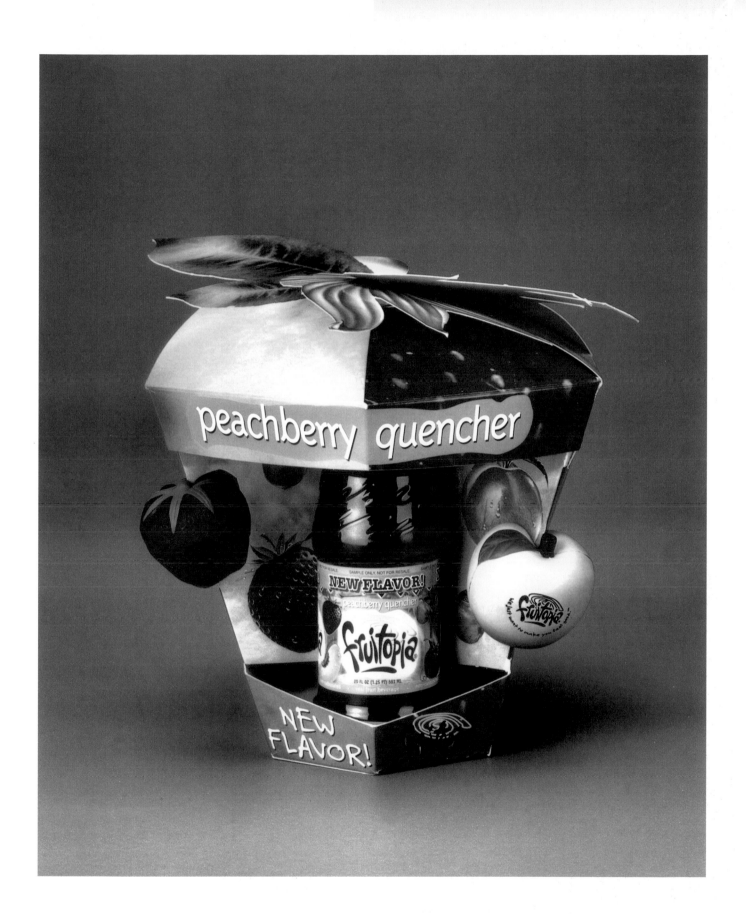

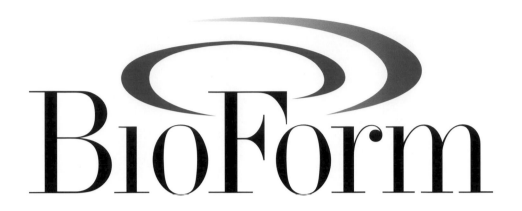

BioForm

Coaptite™ *soft tissue bulking material*

THE NEW FORMULA FOR THE TREATMENT OF STRESS INCONTINENCE.

BioForm

C - 100	C - 14	C - 32	C - 58
M - 60	M - 3	M - 11	M - 12
Y - 0	Y - 3	Y - 95	Y - 13
K - 6	K - 0	K - 3	K - 3

design firm
Becker Design
Milwaukee, Wisconsin

client
BioForm

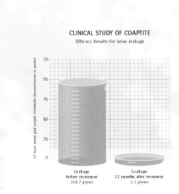

THE FORMULA FOR LONG–TERM SATISFACTION

CLINICAL STUDY OF COAPTITE
Efficacy Results for urine leakage

Physicians can choose Coaptite with confidence. During its development, it has undergone extensive assessments for toxicology and safety, including long-term animal testing. A Phase II clinical study with patients in the U.S. and the U.K. was completed in 1997, with extremely positive results. BioForm has received certification for and a declaration of conformity to ISO 9001, EN 46001 and MDD 93/42/EEC. Ultimately, it is performance with patients that counts. Coaptite has proven its effectiveness, as demonstrated with pad weight measurements. The natural biocompatibility of Coaptite, combined with ease of use and long-term effectiveness, prove to be the formula for satisfaction with both patients and their physicians.

Coaptite information from two prospective Phase II, non-comparative clinical trials conducted in 1996 through 1997

Leakage
before treatment
104.7 grams

Leakage
12 months after treatment
1.3 grams

design firm
Sayles Graphic Design
Des Moines, Iowa

client
"Art Fights Back"

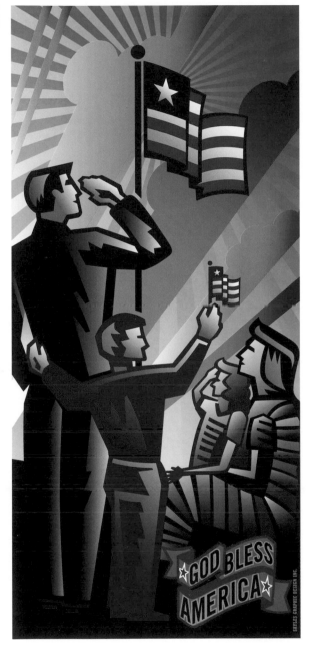

C - 72	C - 94	C - 0	C - 1	C - 13
M - 5	M - 81	M - 89	M - 34	M - 84
Y - 4	Y - 25	Y - 93	Y - 71	Y - 74
K - 1	K - 42	K - 0	K - 0	K - 3

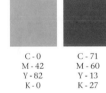

C - 0	C - 71
M - 42	M - 60
Y - 82	Y - 13
K - 0	K - 27

design firm
Hornall Anderson Design Works
Seattle, Washington

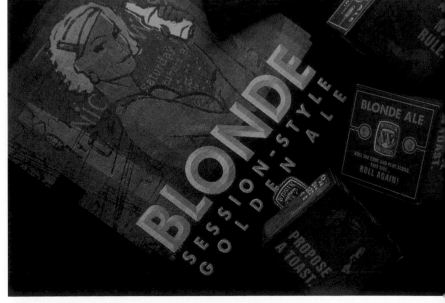

ecri i

EARLY CHILDHOOD RESEARCH INSTITUTE ON INCLUSION

design firm
Vanderbilt University Publication & Design
Nashville, Tennessee

client
Early Childhood Research Institute on Inclusion

C - 50	C - 0
M - 65	M - 0
Y 0	Y - 0
K - 0	K - 100

C - 0	C - 98
M - 9	M - 81
Y - 86	Y - 1
K - 0	K - 0

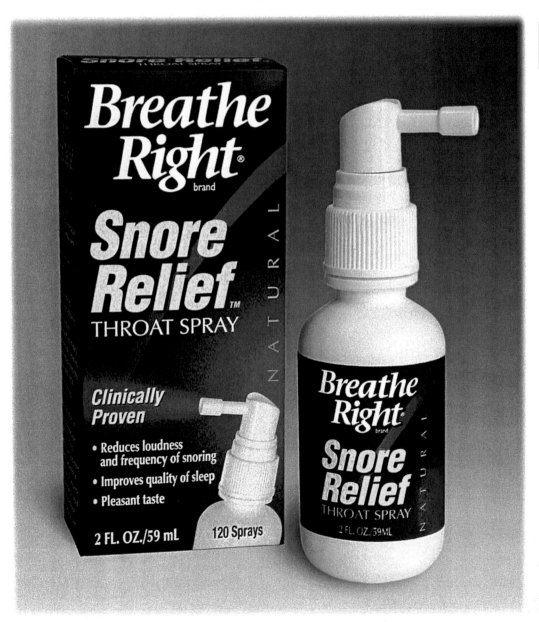

design firm
MackeySzar
Minneapolis, Minnesota

client
CNS

188

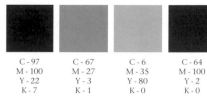

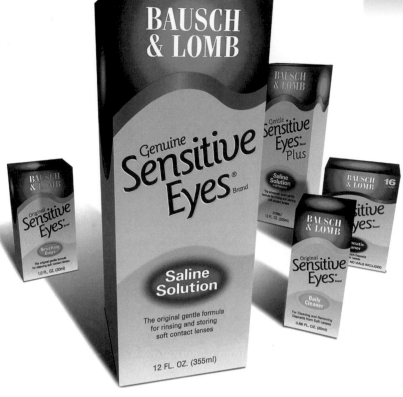

C - 97	C - 67	C - 6	C - 64
M - 100	M - 27	M - 35	M - 100
Y - 22	Y - 3	Y - 80	Y - 2
K - 7	K - 1	K - 0	K - 0

design firm
Forward Branding & Identity
Webster, New York
client
Bausch & Lomb

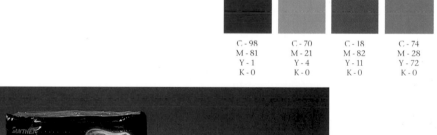

C - 98	C - 70	C - 18	C - 74
M - 81	M - 21	M - 82	M - 28
Y - 1	Y - 4	Y - 11	Y - 72
K - 0	K - 0	K - 0	K - 0

design firm
Cornerstone
New York, New York
client
Santher

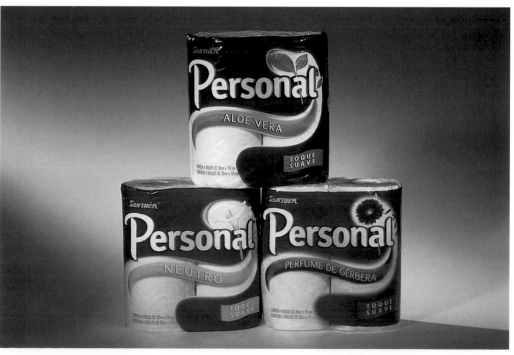

189

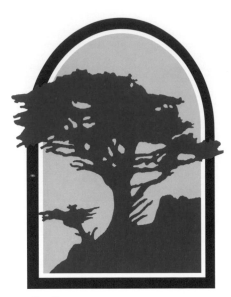

MONTEREY PENINSULA CHAMBER OF COMMERCE

C - 14
M - 19
Y - 80
K - 0

C - 50
M - 100
Y - 90
K - 0

C - 100
M - 60
Y - 100
K - 0

design firm
The Wecker Group
Monterey, California

design firm
Klündt Hosmer Design
Spokane, Washington
client
Whitworth

C - 0
M - 49
Y - 60
K - 0

C - 13
M - 72
Y - 88
K - 3

C - 0
M - 6
Y - 35
K - 2

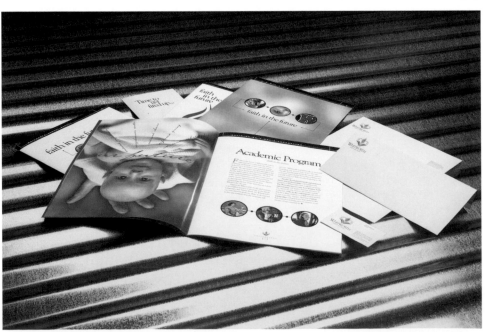

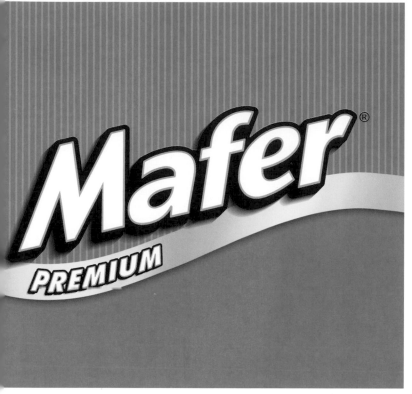

C - 0
M - 70
Y - 100
K - 0

C - 0
M - 27
Y - 80
K - 6

C - 0
M - 0
Y - 0
K - 100

design firm
Praxis Diseñadores, S.C.
México City (Mexico)
client
Alegro Internacional

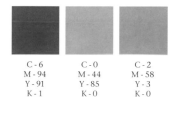

C - 6
M - 94
Y - 91
K - 1

C - 0
M - 44
Y - 85
K - 0

C - 2
M - 58
Y - 3
K - 0

design firm
Compass Design
Minneapolis, Minnesota

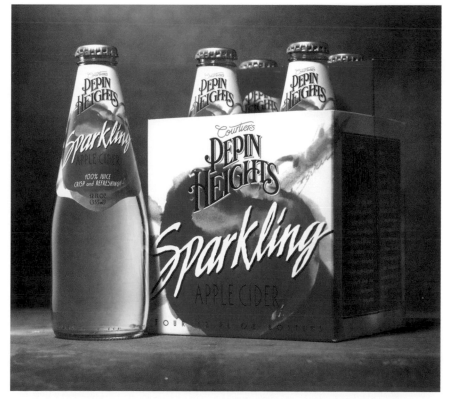

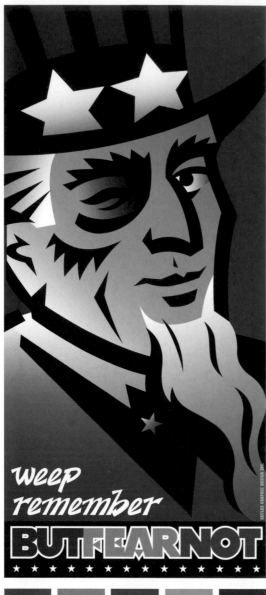

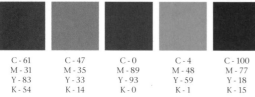

C - 61	C - 47	C - 0	C - 4	C - 100
M - 31	M - 35	M - 89	M - 48	M - 77
Y - 83	Y - 33	Y - 93	Y - 59	Y - 18
K - 54	K - 14	K - 0	K - 1	K - 15

design firm
Sayles Graphic Design
Des Moines, Iowa

client
"Art Fights Back"

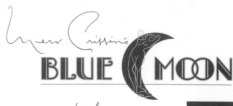

design firm
Mike Salisbury L.L.C.
Venice, California

client
Merv Griffin

C - 97
M - 66
Y - 1
K - 0

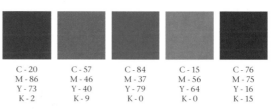

C - 20	C - 57	C - 84	C - 15	C - 76
M - 86	M - 46	M - 37	M - 56	M - 75
Y - 73	Y - 40	Y - 79	Y - 64	Y - 16
K - 2	K - 9	K - 0	K - 0	K - 15

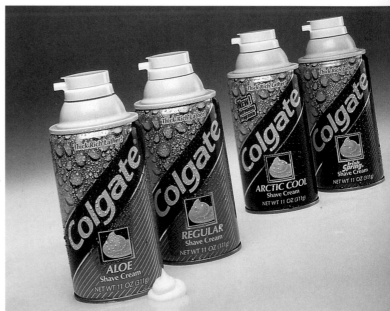

design firm
Bronz/Esposito Inc.
New York, New York

client
Colgate-Palmolive Company

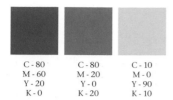

C - 80
M - 60
Y - 20
K - 0

C - 80
M - 20
Y - 0
K - 20

C - 10
M - 0
Y - 90
K - 10

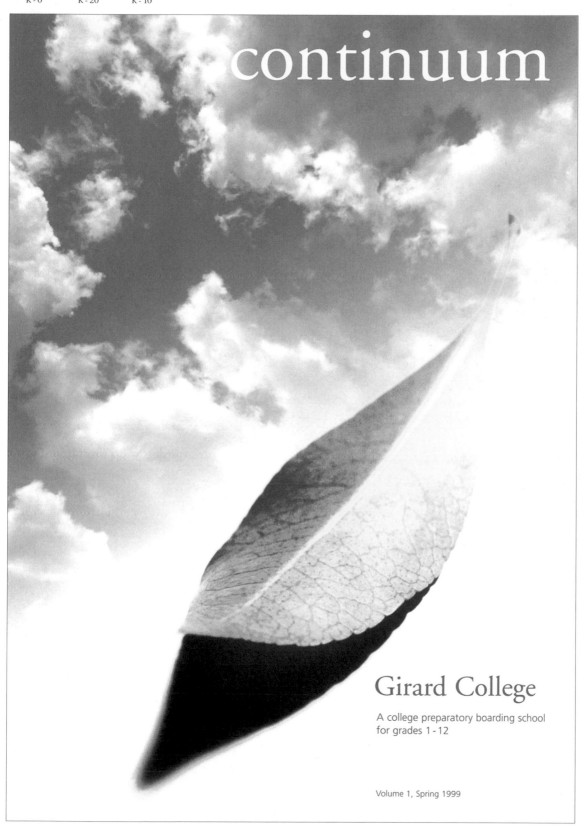

continuum

Girard College

A college preparatory boarding school
for grades 1 - 12

Volume 1, Spring 1999

design firm
kor group
Boston, Massachusetts
client
Girard College

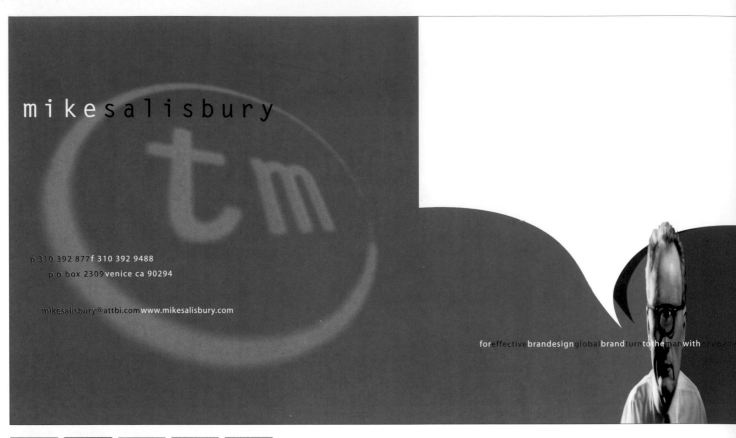

m i k e s a l i s b u r y

p 310 392 877f 310 392 9488
p o box 2309venice ca 90294

mikesalisbury@attbi.comwww.mikesalisbury.com

for effective brandesign global brand turn to the man with one hell a

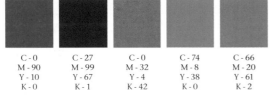

C - 0 M - 90 Y - 10 K - 0	C - 27 M - 99 Y - 67 K - 1	C - 0 M - 32 Y - 4 K - 42	C - 74 M - 8 Y - 38 K - 0	C - 66 M - 20 Y - 61 K - 2

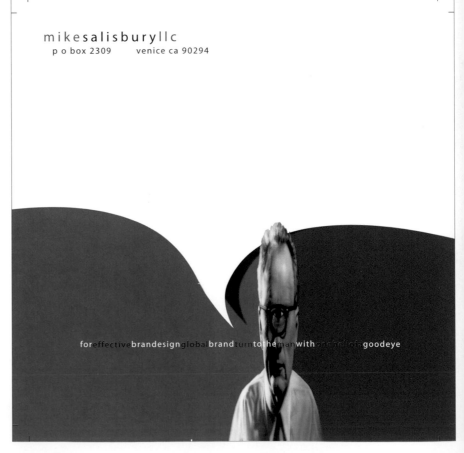

m i k e s a l i s b u r y l l c
p o box 2309   venice ca 90294

for effective brandesign global brand turn to the man with one hell of a goodeye

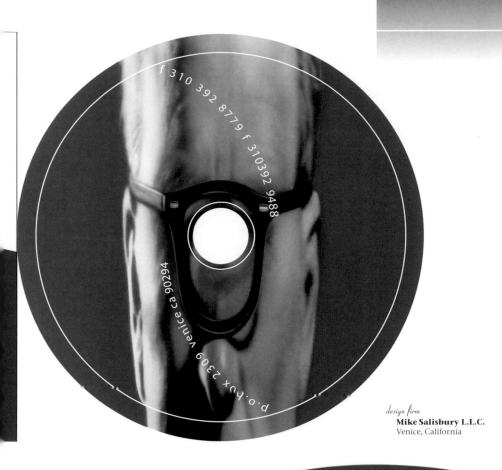

f 310 392 8779 f 310392 9488

p.o.box 2309 venice ca 90294

design firm
Mike Salisbury L.L.C.
Venice, California

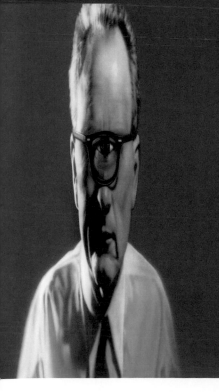

foreffectivebrandesignglobalbrandsturntothemanwithonehelofagoodey

C - 1　　C - 0
M - 96　M - 0
Y - 91　Y - 0
K - 0　　K - 100

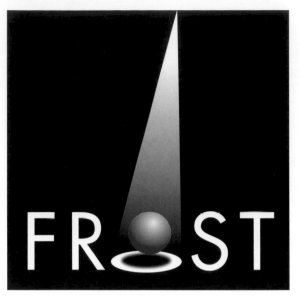

SPECIALTY RISK

design firm
Tom Ventress Design
Nashville, Tennessee
client
Frost Specialty Risk

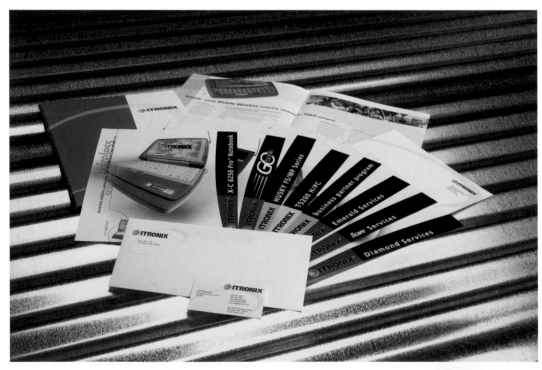

design firm
Klündt Hosmer Design
Spokane, Washington
client
Itronix

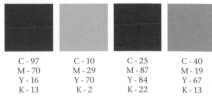

C - 97　　C - 10　　C - 25　　C - 40
M - 70　　M - 29　　M - 87　　M - 19
Y - 16　　Y - 70　　Y - 84　　Y - 67
K - 13　　K - 2　　　K - 22　　K - 13

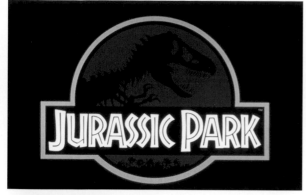

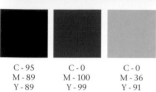

C - 95
M - 89
Y - 89
K - 86

C - 0
M - 100
Y - 99
K - 29

C - 0
M - 36
Y - 91
K - 0

design firm
Mike Salisbury L.L.C.
Venice, California
client
Universal Pictures Amblin

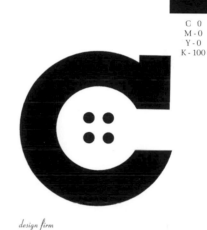

C 0
M - 0
Y - 0
K - 100

design firm
Supon Design Group
Washington, D.C.
client
Charles Button Company

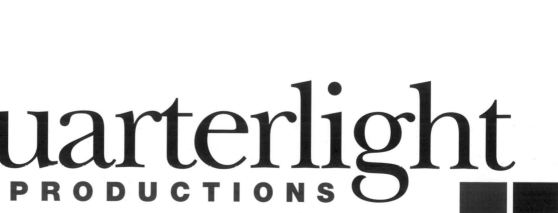

design firm
Tom Ventress Design
Nashville, Tennessee
client
Quarterlight Productions

C - 0
M - 100
Y - 100
K - 0

C - 0
M - 0
Y - 0
K - 100

C - 27
M - 0
Y - 63
K - 0

C - 0
M - 0
Y - 0
K - 100

C - 3
M - 0
Y - 49
K - 0

C - 0
M - 49
Y - 80
K - 0

design firm
Louis & Partners Design
Bath, Ohio
client
Sound Addict

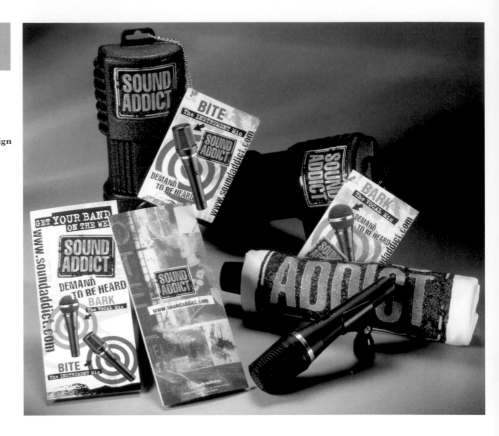

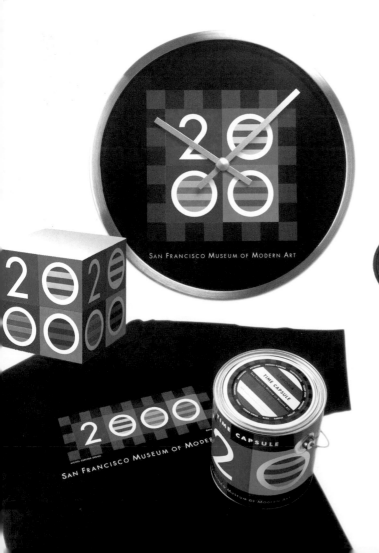

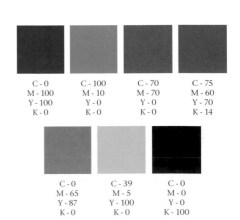

design firm
Michael Osborne Design
San Francisco, California
client
San Francisco Museum of Modern Art

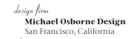

C - 0
M - 100
Y - 100
K - 0

C - 100
M - 10
Y - 0
K - 0

C - 70
M - 70
Y - 0
K - 0

C - 75
M - 60
Y - 70
K - 14

C - 0
M - 65
Y - 87
K - 0

C - 39
M - 5
Y - 100
K - 0

C - 0
M - 0
Y - 0
K - 100

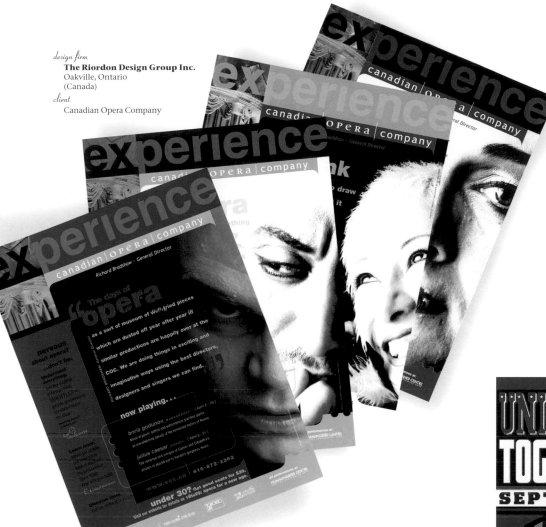

design firm
The Riordon Design Group Inc.
Oakville, Ontario
(Canada)
client
Canadian Opera Company

C - 0	C - 65	C - 50
M - 100	M - 45	M - 10
Y - 100	Y - 0	Y - 0
K - 20	K - 15	K - 0

C - 0	C - 30
M - 0	M - 0
Y - 0	Y - 0
K - 100	K - 75

C - 10	C - 0
M - 10	M - 30
Y - 100	Y - 100
K - 30	K - 10

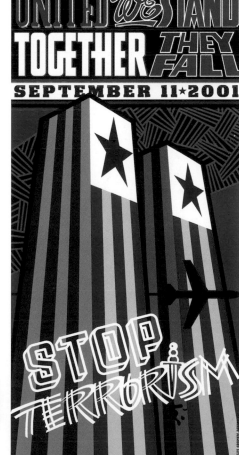

design firm
Sayles Graphic Design
Des Moines, Iowa
client
"Art Fights Back"

C - 1	C - 99	C - 99	C - 61
M - 93	M - 62	M - 75	M - 50
Y - 93	Y - 2	Y - 21	Y - 49
K - 0	K - 1	K - 27	K - 59

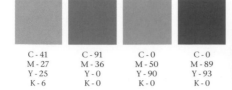

C - 41
M - 27
Y - 25
K - 6

C - 91
M - 36
Y - 0
K - 0

C - 0
M - 50
Y - 90
K - 0

C - 0
M - 89
Y - 93
K - 0

C - 61
M - 31
Y - 83
K - 54

C - 94
M - 81
Y - 25
K - 42

C - 0
M - 50
Y - 90
K - 0

C - 0
M - 89
Y - 93
K - 0

C - 0
M - 72
Y - 90
K - 0

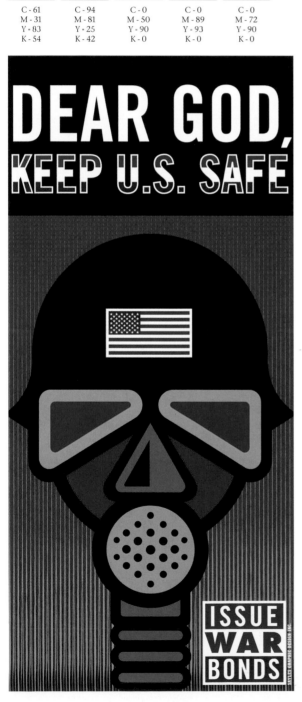

design firm
Sayles Graphic Design
Des Moines, Iowa
client
"Art Fights Back"

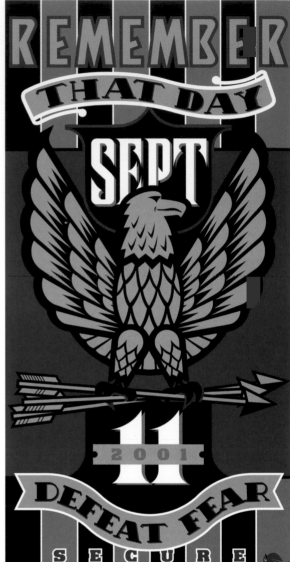
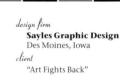

design firm
Sayles Graphic Design
Des Moines, Iowa
client
"Art Fights Back"

200

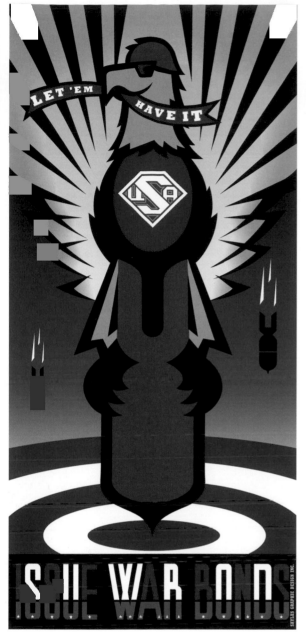

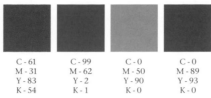

C - 61	C - 99	C - 0	C - 0
M - 31	M - 62	M - 50	M - 89
Y - 83	Y - 2	Y - 90	Y - 93
K - 54	K - 1	K - 0	K - 0

design firm
Sayles Graphic Design
Des Moines, Iowa
client
"Art Fights Back"

C - 100	C - 56	C - 0
M - 72	M - 11	M - 6
Y - 0	Y - 0	Y - 6
K - 38	K - 18	K - 27

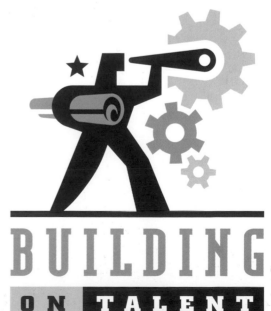

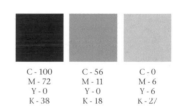

design firm
Greteman Group
Wichita, Kansas

201

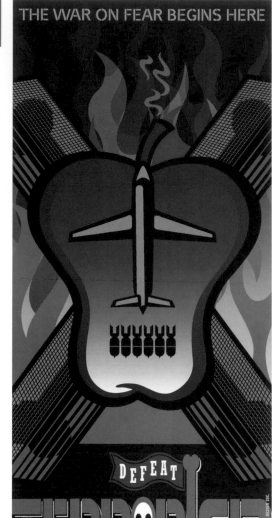

THE WAR ON FEAR BEGINS HERE

DeFEAT TERRORISM

C - 94   C - 28   C - 0   C - 85   C - 0
M - 81   M - 91   M - 72   M - 27   M - 81
Y - 25   Y - 58   Y - 90   Y - 14   Y - 81
K - 42   K - 34   K - 0   K - 14   K - 0

design firm
Sayles Graphic Design
Des Moines, Iowa

client
"Art Fights Back"

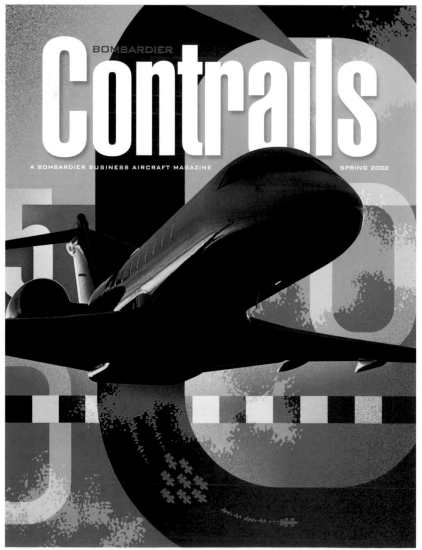

BOMBARDIER
Contrails
A BOMBARDIER BUSINESS AIRCRAFT MAGAZINE   SPRING 2002

design firm
Greteman Group
Wichita, Kansas

C - 64   C - 0   C - 18
M - 69   M - 74   M - 31
Y - 4   Y - 95   Y - 56
K - 8   K - 0   K - 0

202

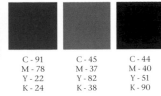

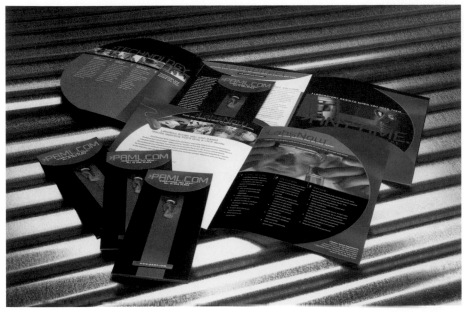

C - 91
M - 78
Y - 22
K - 24

C - 45
M - 37
Y - 82
K - 38

C - 44
M - 40
Y - 51
K - 90

design firm
Klündt Hosmer Design
Spokane, Washington
client
PAML

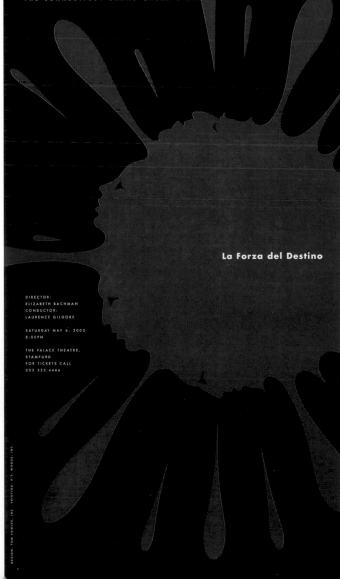

THE CONNECTICUT GRAND OPERA & ORCHESTRA PRESENTS VERDI'S

La Forza del Destino

DIRECTOR:
ELIZABETH BACHMAN
CONDUCTOR:
LAURENCE GILGORE

SATURDAY MAY 4, 2002
8:00PM

THE PALACE THEATRE,
STAMFORD
FOR TICKETS CALL
203.325.4466

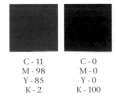

C - 11
M - 98
Y - 85
K - 2

C - 0
M - 0
Y - 0
K - 100

design firm
Tom Fowler, Inc.
Norwalk, Connecticut
client
Connecticut Grand Opera & Orchestra

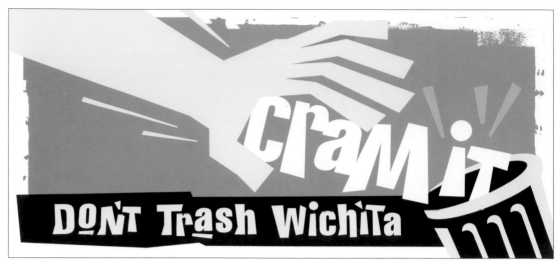

design firm
Greteman Group
Wichita, Kansas

C - 0	C - 0	C - 0
M - 0	M - 0	M - 56
Y - 100	Y - 0	Y - 87
K - 0	K - 100	K - 0

design firm
Hornall Anderson Design Works
Seattle, Washington

C - 0	C - 55
M - 65	M - 22
Y - 78	Y - 60
K - 0	K - 50

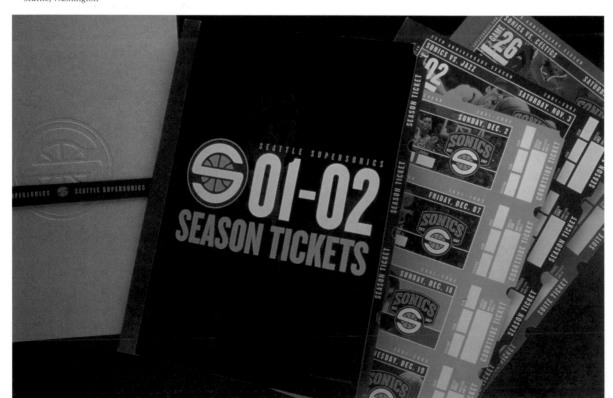

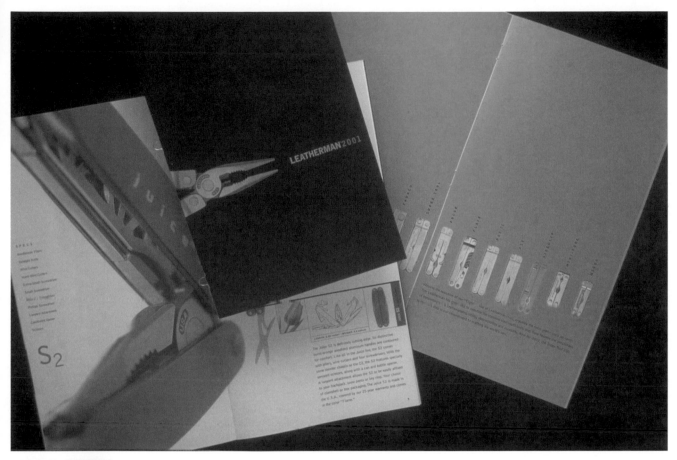

design firm
Hornall Anderson Design Works
Seattle, Washington

C - 0	C - 0
M - 60	M - 0
Y - 85	Y - 0
K - 0	K - 100

design firm
Greteman Group
Wichita, Kansas

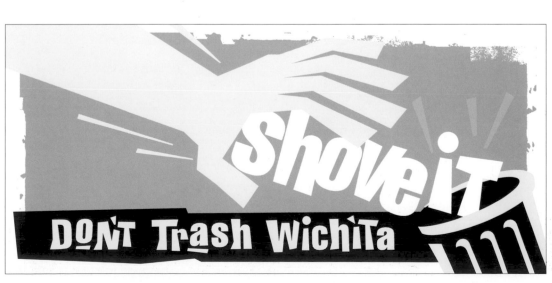

C - 0	C - 0	C - 43
M - 0	M - 0	M - 0
Y - 100	Y - 0	Y - 79
K - 0	K - 100	K - 15

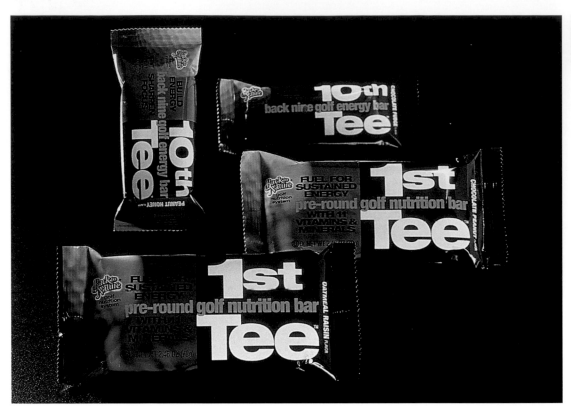

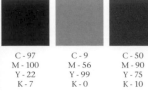

C - 97	C - 9	C - 50
M - 100	M - 56	M - 90
Y - 22	Y - 99	Y - 75
K - 7	K - 0	K - 10

design firm
Mark Oliver, Inc.
Solvang, California
client
Organic Milling, Co.

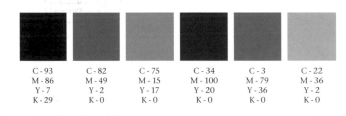

C - 93	C - 82	C - 75	C - 34	C - 3	C - 22
M - 86	M - 49	M - 15	M - 100	M - 79	M - 36
Y - 7	Y - 2	Y - 17	Y - 20	Y - 36	Y - 2
K - 29	K - 0	K - 0	K - 0	K - 0	K - 0

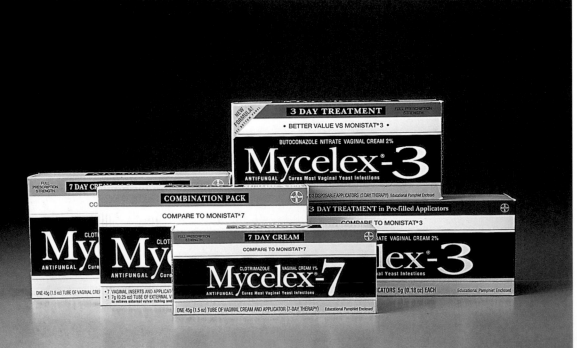

design firm
Szylinski Associates Inc.
New York, New York
client
Bayer Corporation

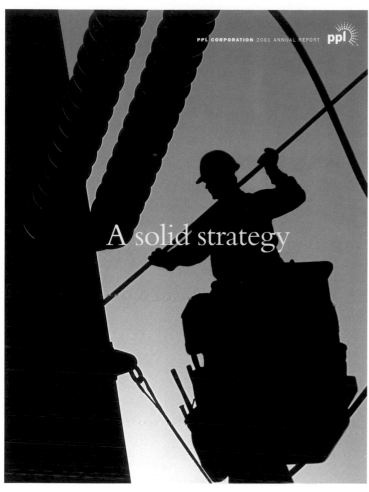

PPL CORPORATION 2001 ANNUAL REPORT

ppl

A solid strategy

C - 79
M - 33
Y - 0
K - 0

C - 93
M - 83
Y - 75
K - 85

design firm
Boller Coates & Neu
Chicago, Illinois
client
PPL Corporation

design firm
Colgate–Palmolive
In-House Design Studio
New York, New York
client
Colgate–Palmolive Company

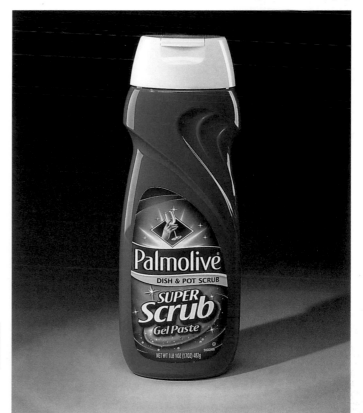

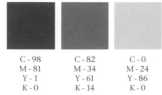

C - 98
M - 81
Y - 1
K - 0

C - 82
M - 34
Y - 61
K - 14

C - 0
M - 24
Y - 86
K - 0

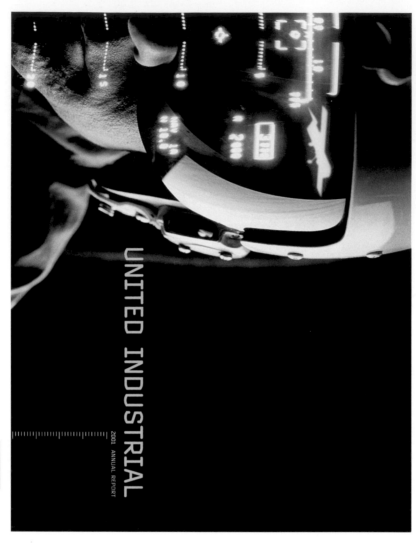

UNITED INDUSTRIAL

2001 ANNUAL REPORT

C - 73	C - 91
M - 45	M - 86
Y - 78	Y - 78
K - 18	K - 85

design firm
Taylor & Ives Incorporated
New York, New York
client
United Industrial Corporation

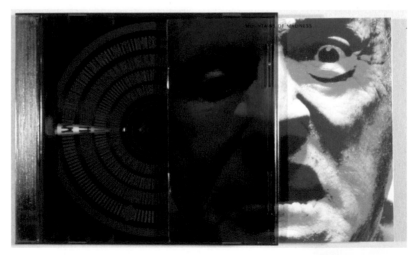

design firm
Sagmeister Inc.
New York, New York

C - 2	C - 67
M - 100	M - 1
Y - 95	Y - 67
K - 4	K - 0

208

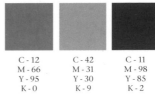

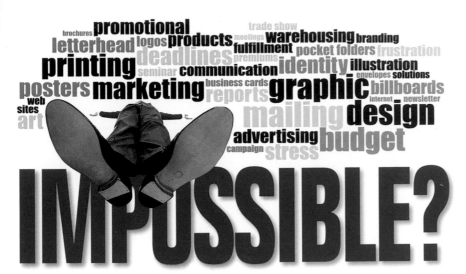

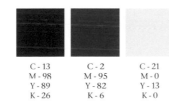

IMPOSSIBLE?

C - 12	C - 42	C - 11
M - 66	M - 31	M - 98
Y - 95	Y - 30	Y - 85
K - 0	K - 9	K - 2

design firm
Resco Print Graphics
Hudson, Wisconsin
client
Resco Print Graphics

design firm
The Sloan Group
New York, New York
client
B.M.I.

C - 13	C - 2	C - 21
M - 98	M - 95	M - 0
Y - 89	Y - 82	Y - 13
K - 26	K - 6	K - 0

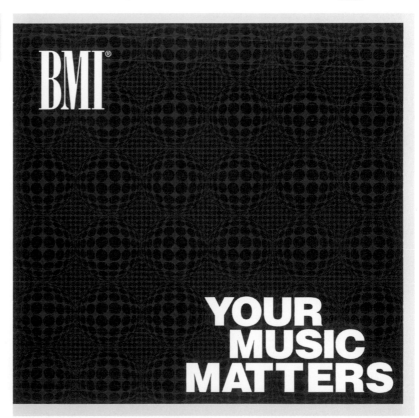

C - 16
M - 10
Y - 1
K - 0

C - 30
M - 28
Y - 1
K - 0

C - 74
M - 50
Y - 20
K - 4

C - 2
M - 47
Y - 84
K - 0

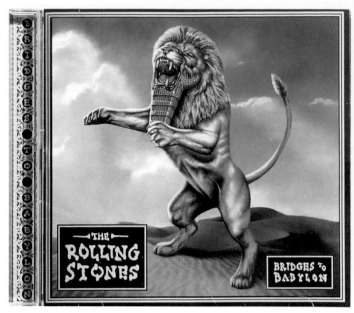

design firm
Sagmeister Inc.
New York, New York

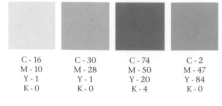

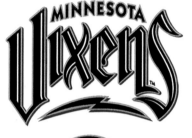

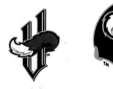 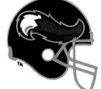

C - 1
M - 99
Y - 88
K - 2

C - 46
M - 36
Y - 30
K - 0

C - 0
M - 0
Y - 0
K - 100

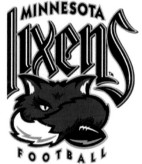

design firm
Compass Design
Minneapolis, Minnesota
client
Women's Professional Football League

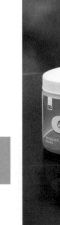

design firm
Praxis Diseñadores, S.C.
México City (Mexico)
client
SmithKline Beecham

C - 100
M - 60
Y - 0
K - 0

C - 80
M - 10
Y - 0
K - 0

210

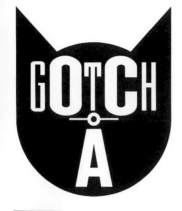

C - 0
M - 0
Y - 0
K - 100

design firm
Mike Salisbury L.L.C.
Venice, California
client
Gotcha

C - 2
M - 91
Y - 86
K - 0

C - 39
M - 0
Y - 0
K - 100

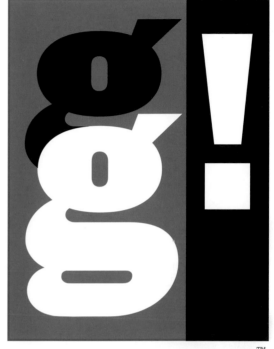

design firm
Addison
San Francisco, California
client
The Good Guys

good guys ™

C - 65
M - 69
Y - 64
K - 69

C - 18
M - 98
Y - 66
K - 18

C - 7
M - 99
Y - 79
K - 16

C - 6
M - 43
Y - 62
K - 4

design firm
Dever Designs
Laurel, Maryland
client
Liberty Magazine

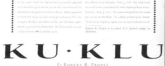

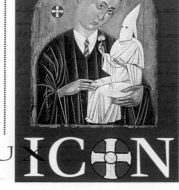

C-0
M-96
Y-73
K-0

C-9
M-59
Y-77
K-0

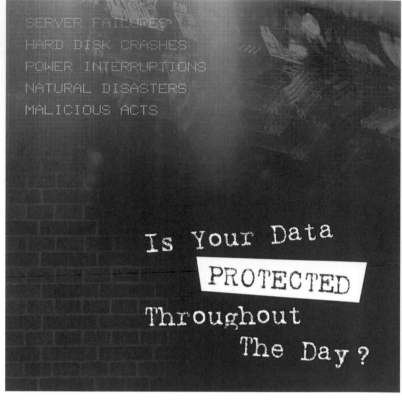

SERVER FAILURES
HARD DISK CRASHES
POWER INTERRUPTIONS
NATURAL DISASTERS
MALICIOUS ACTS

Is Your Data
PROTECTED
Throughout
The Day?

design firm
Ad Formula Design Studio
Singapore (Singapore)
client
C.A.

C-84
M-55
Y-0
K-0

C-11
M-98
Y-85
K-2

C-0
M-24
Y-86
K-0

C-81
M-13
Y-74
K-4

design firm
**Szylinski Associates Inc./
Protocol**
New York, New York
client
Bayer—Pursell, LLC

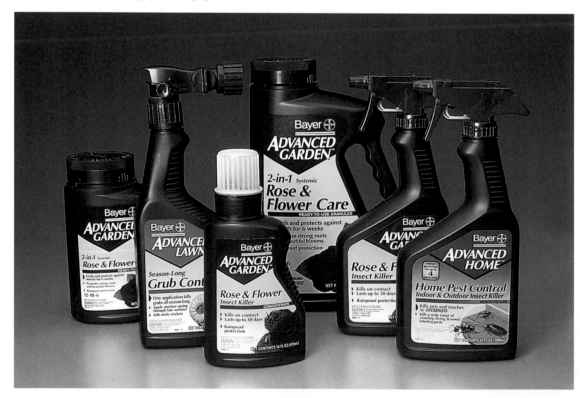

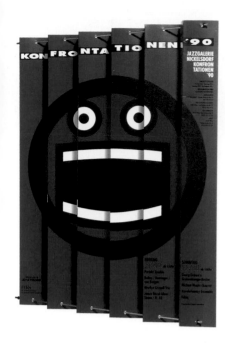

C - 0
M - 100
Y - 86
K - 0

C - 96
M - 66
Y - 5
K - 0

C - 92
M - 89
Y - 90
K - 82

design firm
Sagmeister Inc.
New York, New York

design firm
Designation
New York, New York

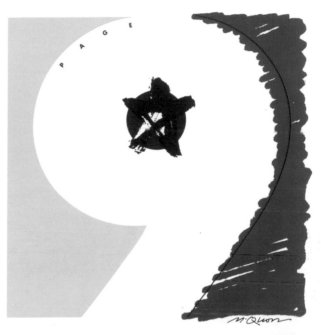

C - 1
M - 90
Y - 88
K - 0

C - 1
M - 21
Y - 91
K - 0

C - 91
M - 60
Y - 21
K - 47

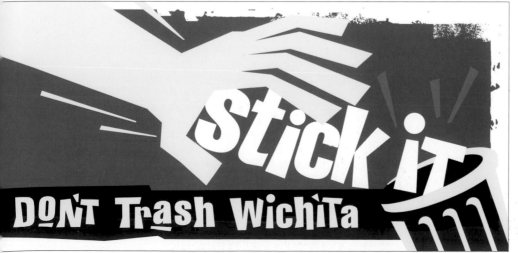

design firm
Greteman Group
Wichita, Kansas

C - 0
M - 0
Y - 100
K - 0

C - 91
M - 51
Y - 0
K - 0

C - 0
M - 0
Y - 0
K - 100

213

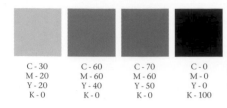

C - 30	C - 60	C - 70	C - 0
M - 20	M - 60	M - 60	M - 0
Y - 20	Y - 40	Y - 50	Y - 0
K - 0	K - 0	K - 0	K - 100

design firm
Tom Fowler, Inc.
Norwalk, Connecticut
client
Connecticut Grand Opera & Orchestra

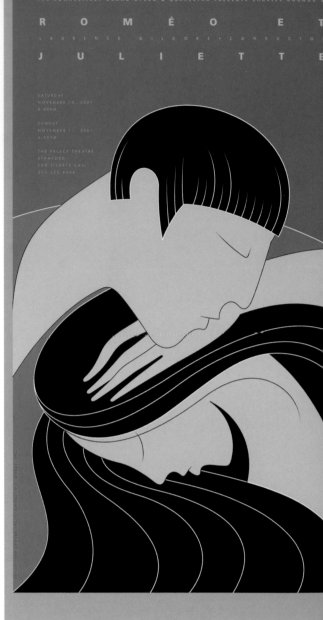

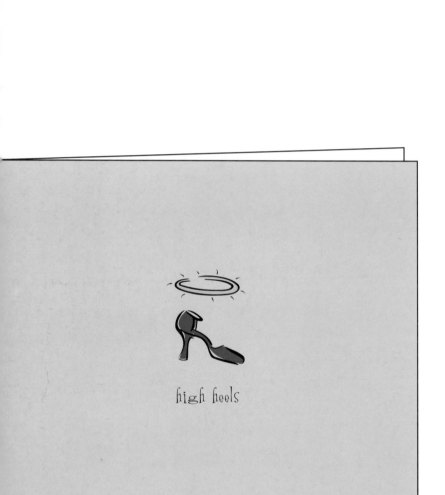

high heels

design firm
After Hours Creative
Phoenix, Arizona

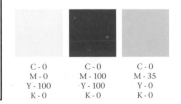

C - 0	C - 0	C - 0
M - 0	M - 100	M - 35
Y - 100	Y - 100	Y - 0
K - 0	K - 0	K - 0

THE

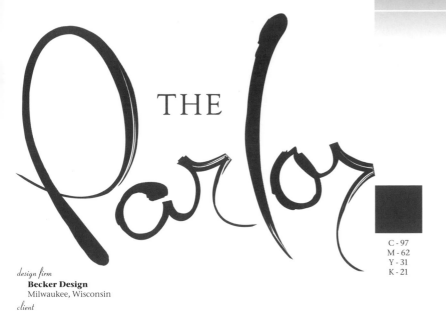

Parlor

C - 97
M - 62
Y - 31
K - 21

design firm
Becker Design
Milwaukee, Wisconsin

client
Parlor

design firm
After Hours Creative
Phoenix, Arizona

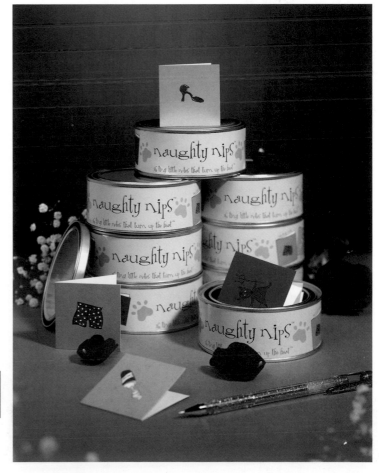

C - 16	C - 7	C - 24
M - 98	M - 58	M - 70
Y - 66	Y - 0	Y - 4
K - 9	K - 0	K - 0

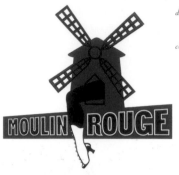

design firm
Mike Salisbury L.L.C.
Venice (California)
client
20th Century Fox

C - 5
M - 99
Y - 73
K - 9

C - 83
M - 88
Y - 86
K - 73

C - 18
M - 48
Y - 96
K - 1

C - 0
M - 79
Y - 94
K - 0

C - 0
M - 31
Y - 94
K - 0

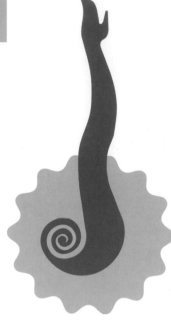

design firm
Greteman Group
Wichita, Kansas

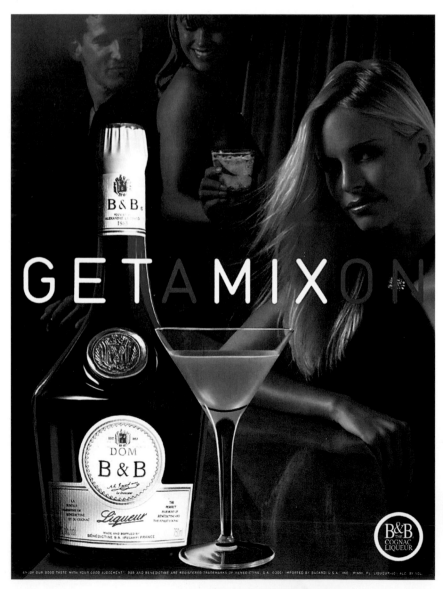

design firm
Pinkhaus
Miami, Florida
client
Bacardi USA, Inc.

C - 0
M - 94
Y - 79
K - 0

C - 12
M - 75
Y - 89
K - 0

C - 0
M - 0
Y - 0
K - 100

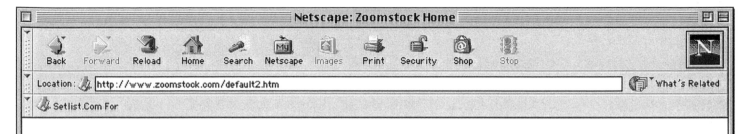

Netscape: Zoomstock Home

Back | Forward | Reload | Home | Search | Netscape | Images | Print | Security | Shop | Stop

Location: http://www.zoomstock.com/default2.htm — What's Related

Setlist.Com For

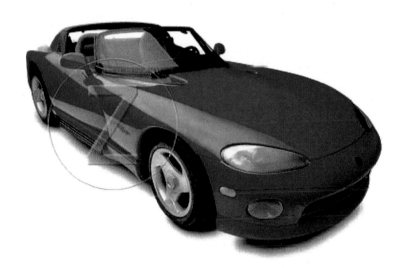

ZOOMSTOCK

Welcome to **Zoomstock.com**.

The one stop shop for images of cool cars. Classics, hot rods, dream cars. We've got them all in stock.

So take our collection of hundreds of top-notch automotive images for a test drive.

Contact us with your inquiries and orders.

Check out Cars 101 to learn more about everything automotive.

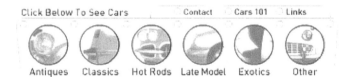

Click Below To See Cars   Contact   Cars 101   Links

Antiques | Classics | Hot Rods | Late Model | Exotics | Other

C - 0
M - 100
Y - 100
K - 0

C - 0
M - 0
Y - 0
K - 100

design firm
Liska + Associates, Inc.
Chicago, Illinois
client
Zoomstock Stock Photography

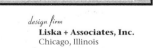

C - 0	C - 10	C - 0
M - 40	M - 10	M - 0
Y - 60	Y - 10	Y - 0
K - 40	K - 200	K - 100

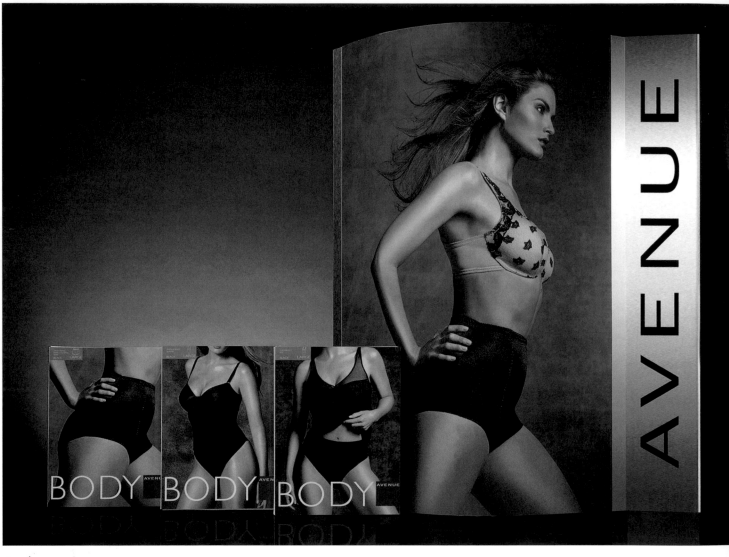

design firm
United Retail Group
Rochelle Park, New Jersey

client
Urgi

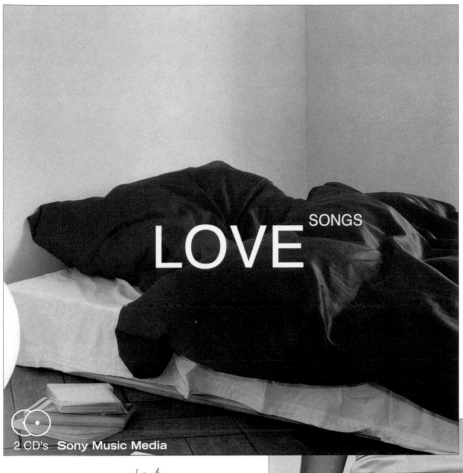

LOVE SONGS

2 CD's Sony Music Media

C - 0	C - 0	C - 50
M - 100	M - 20	M - 8
Y - 100	Y - 50	Y - 15
K - 0	K - 10	K - 0

design firm
Heye + Partner GmbH
Unterhaching (Germany)
client
McDonald's Promotion GmbH

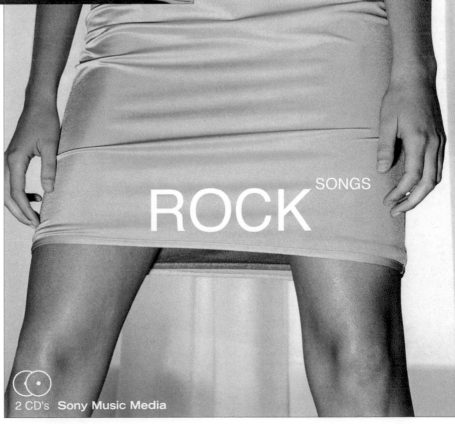

ROCK SONGS

2 CD's Sony Music Media

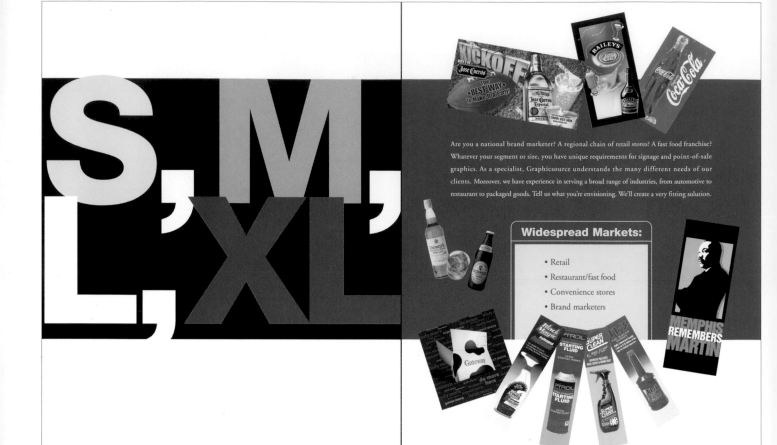

Are you a national brand marketer? A regional chain of retail stores? A fast food franchise? Whatever your segment or size, you have unique requirements for signage and point-of-sale graphics. As a specialist, Graphicsource understands the many different needs of our clients. Moreover, we have experience in serving a broad range of industries, from automotive to restaurant to packaged goods. Tell us what you're envisioning. We'll create a very fitting solution.

Widespread Markets:

- Retail
- Restaurant/fast food
- Convenience stores
- Brand marketers

design firm
Becker Design
Milwaukee, Wisconsin
client
Graphic Source

C - 2	C - 37	C - 78	C - 0
M - 8	M - 22	M - 68	M - 0
Y - 91	Y - 24	Y - 7	Y - 0
K - 0	K - 5	K - 2	K - 100

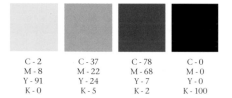

C - 0	C - 60
M - 14	M - 0
Y - 34	Y - 0
K - 60	K - 30

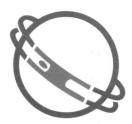

Traveleze.com
Changing the way the world travels

design firm
The Wecker Group
Monterey, California
client
Traveleze.com

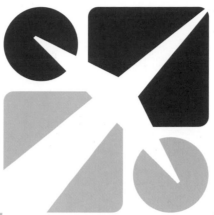

design firm
Greteman Group
Wichita, Kansas

C - 100 | C - 0
M - 72 | M - 34
Y - 0 | Y - 91
K - 38 | K - 0

C - 67 | C - 12 | C - 0
M - 39 | M - 71 | M - 54
Y - 23 | Y - 74 | Y - 82
K - 15 | K - 25 | K - 0

design firm
Hornall Anderson Design Works
Seattle, Washington

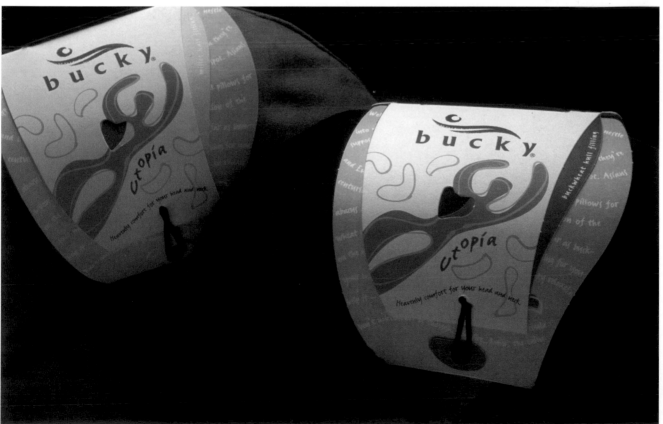

C - 10
M - 100
Y - 100
K - 18

C - 0
M - 0
Y - 0
K - 100

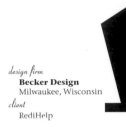

design firm
Becker Design
Milwaukee, Wisconsin
client
RediHelp

RediHelp

design firm
Hornall Anderson Design Works
Seattle, Washington

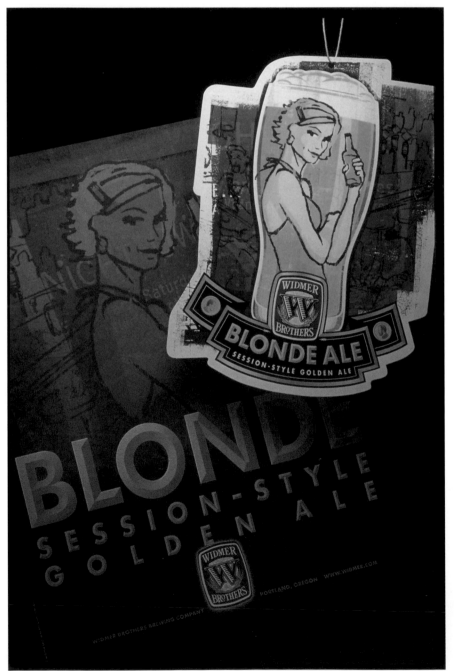

C - 0
M - 42
Y - 82
K - 0

C - 71
M - 60
Y - 13
K - 27

222

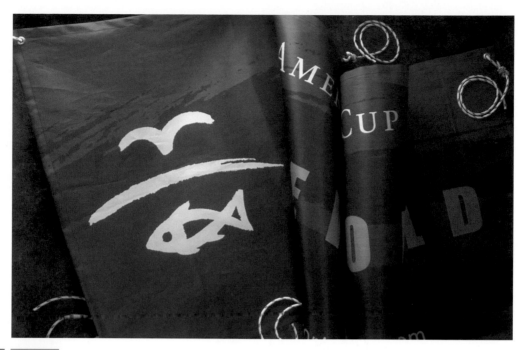

design firm
Hornall Anderson Design Works
Seattle, Washington

C - 57	C - 62	C - 0
M - 44	M - 43	M - 59
Y - 27	Y - 15	Y - 95
K - 43	K - 22	K - 2

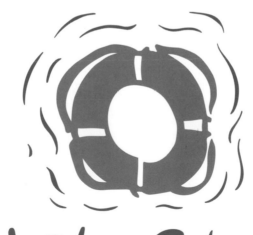

LakeCity
Community Church

design firm
Klündt Hosmer Design
Spokane, Washington
client
LakeCity Community Church

C - 93	C - 2
M - 58	M - 69
Y - 15	Y - 91
K - 4	K - 0

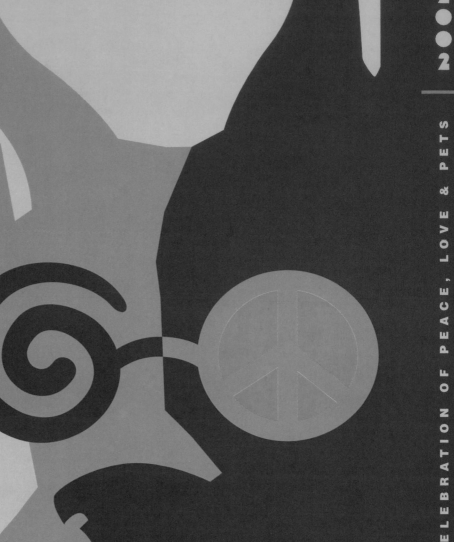

WOOFSTOCK

2002

A CELEBRATION OF PEACE, LOVE & PETS

SATURDAY · OCTOBER 5

10 A.M. – 2 P.M. · CENTRAL RIVERSIDE PARK

AN EVENT TO BENEFIT
THE KANSAS HUMANE
SOCIETY OF WICHITA

PRESENTED BY WARREN
THEATRES AND THE KANSAS
HUMANE SOCIETY OF WICHITA

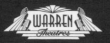

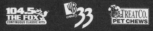

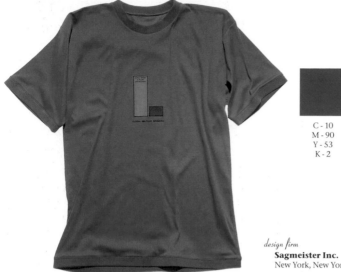

C - 10
M - 90
Y - 53
K - 2

C - 3
M - 64
Y - 81
K - 1

C - 88
M - 65
Y - 0
K - 0

C - 91
M - 25
Y - 76
K - 10

design firm
Sagmeister Inc.
New York, New York

design firm
Tom Fowler, Inc.
Norwalk, Connecticut
client
Unilever Home & Personal Care USA

C - 71
M - 30
Y - 0
K - 1

C - 38
M - 82
Y - 2
K - 1

C - 25
M - 93
Y - 74
K - 16

C - 4
M - 83
Y - 99
K - 1

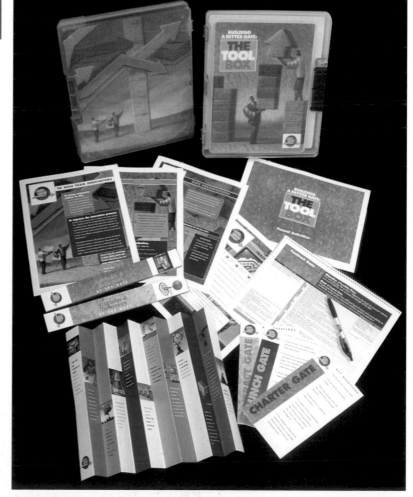

(opposite) design firm
Greteman Group
Wichita, Kansas

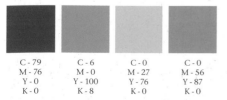

C - 79
M - 76
Y - 0
K - 0

C - 6
M - 0
Y - 100
K - 8

C - 0
M - 27
Y - 76
K - 0

C - 0
M - 56
Y - 87
K - 0

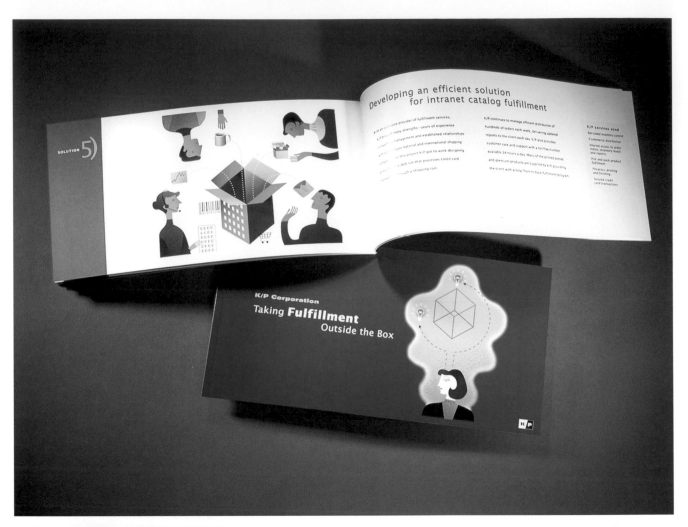

Within the brochure image:

SOLUTION 5)

Developing an efficient solution for intranet catalog fulfillment

K/P Corporation

Taking Fulfillment Outside the Box

C - 0	C - 97	C - 44	C - 0
M - 12	M - 36	M - 31	M - 49
Y - 100	Y - 9	Y - 96	Y - 90
K - 0	K - 5	K - 9	K - 0

design firm
Belyea
Seattle, Washington
client
K/P Corporation

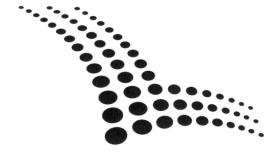

LEAP™

design firm
Addison
San Francisco, California
client
Leap

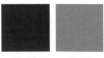

C - 98	C - 45
M - 94	M - 33
Y - 27	Y - 31
K - 14	K - 16

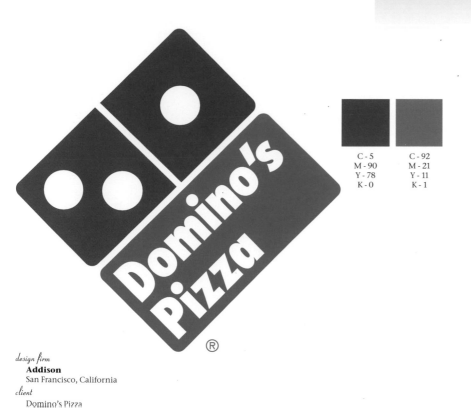

C - 5
M - 90
Y - 78
K - 0

C - 92
M - 21
Y - 11
K - 1

design firm
Addison
San Francisco, California
client
Domino's Pizza

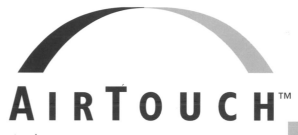

design firm
Addison
San Francisco, California
client
AirTouch

C - 1
M - 33
Y - 91
K - 0

C - 94
M - 62
Y - 6
K - 0

C - 0
M - 91
Y - 76
K - 0

C - 0
M - 0
Y - 0
K - 1090

design firm
Addison
San Francisco, California
client
ConocoPhillips

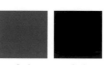

ConocoPhillips

momentum ®

Ⓑ Built by Belyea

C - 0	C - 0
M - 0	M - 0
Y - 50	Y - 0
K - 0	K - 100

STRATEGY + MESSAGING

passion ®

Ⓑ Built by Belyea

G N

belyea.

206.682.4895   belyea.com

design firm
Belyea
Seattle, Washington
client
Belyea

wow ®

Ⓑ Built by Belyea

STRATEGY + MESSAGING ╋ DESIGN

belyea.

206.682.4895   belyea.com

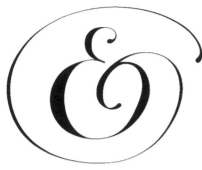

design firm
Pat Taylor Inc.
Washington, D.C.
client
Northern Va. Comm. College

C - 0
M - 0
Y - 0
K - 100

C - 100	C - 10
M - 0	M - 20
Y - 79	Y - 70
K - 60	K - 0

design firm
The Wecker Group
Monterey, California
client
Del Monte Aviation

DEL MONTE
AVIATION

design firm
LarsonLogosEtc
Rockford, Illinois
client
Washington Park Christian Church

C - 0
M - 0
Y - 0
K - 25

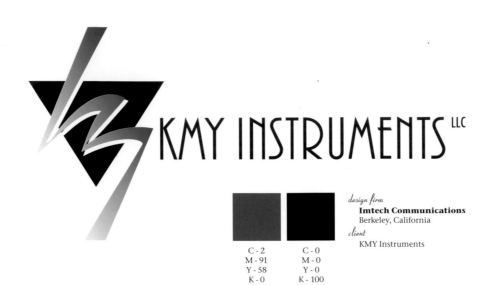

KMY INSTRUMENTS LLC

design firm
Imtech Communications
Berkeley, California

client
KMY Instruments

C - 2
M - 91
Y - 58
K - 0

C - 0
M - 0
Y - 0
K - 100

design firm
über, inc
New York, New York

client
Utopia Marketing

C - 20
M - 40
Y - 50
K - 5

C - 30
M - 90
Y - 100
K - 5

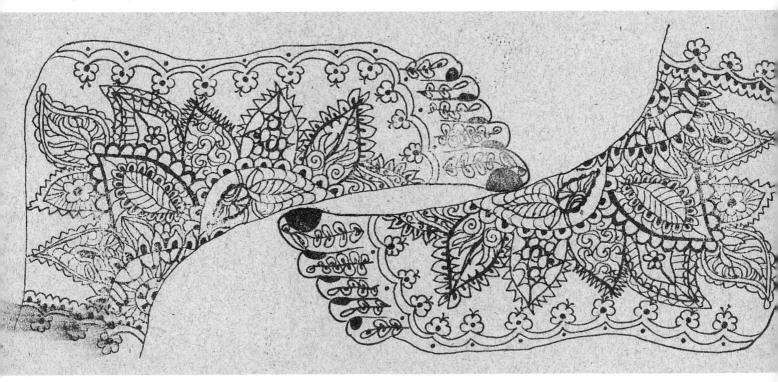

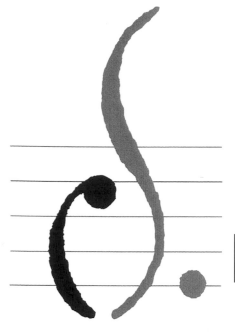

C - 89
M - 89
Y - 31
K - 25

C - 38
M - 35
Y - 100
K - 25

design firm
merish design
New York, New York

client
Riverside Symphony

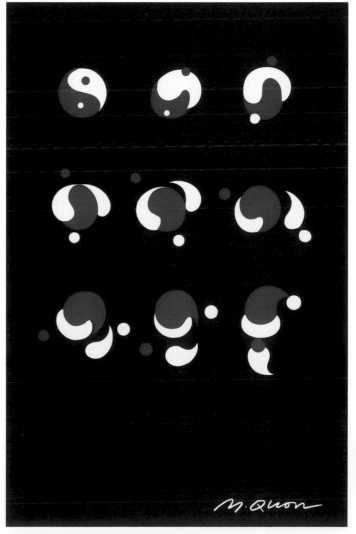

design firm
Designation
New York, New York

C - 2
M - 92
Y - 97
K - 1

C - 63
M - 52
Y - 50
K - 90

C - 44
M - 4
Y - 70
K - 1

C - 100
M - 50
Y - 10
K - 10

C - 0
M - 100
Y - 100
K - 0

C - 0
M - 50
Y - 100
K - 0

C - 5
M - 25
Y - 100
K - 0

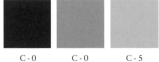

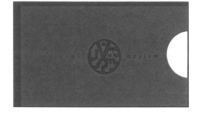

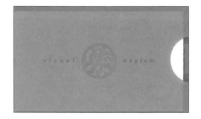

visual asylum 205 WEST DATE SAN DIEGO CA 92101 Y 619.233.9633 F 619.233.9637

33.9637

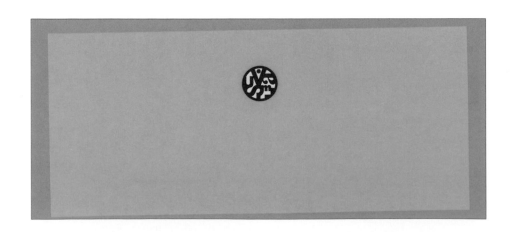

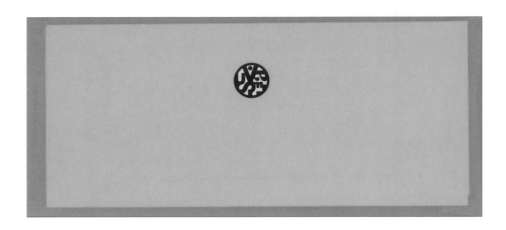

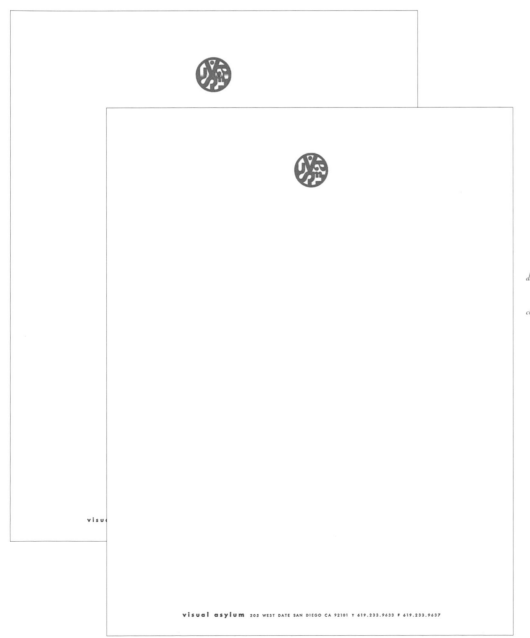

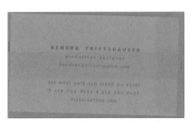

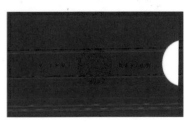

design firm
Visual Asylum
San Diego, California
client
Visual Asylum

visual asylum 205 WEST DATE SAN DIEGO CA 92101 T 619.233.9633 F 619.233.9637

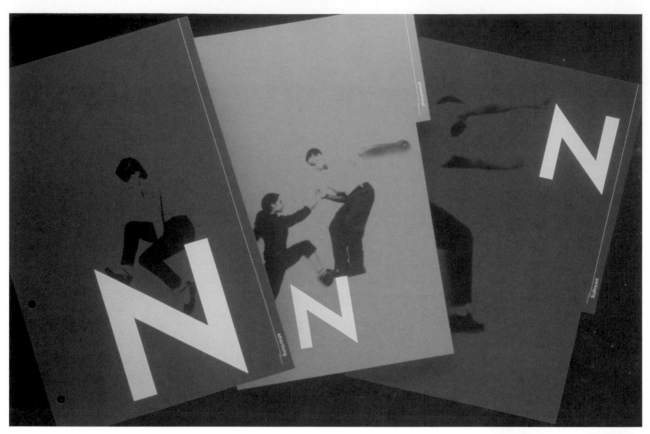

design firm
Hornall Anderson Design Works
Seattle, Washington

C - 32	C - 42	C - 70
M - 53	M - 7	M - 37
Y - 17	Y - 21	Y - 3
K - 50	K - 15	K - 44

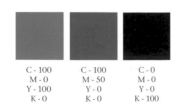

MORGAN
WINERY

C - 100	C - 100	C - 0
M - 0	M - 50	M - 0
Y - 100	Y - 0	Y - 0
K - 0	K - 0	K - 100

design firm
The Wecker Group
Monterey, California
client
Morgan Winery

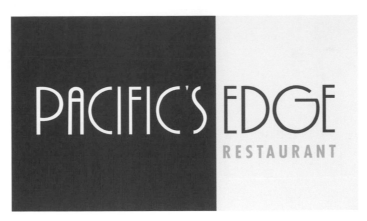

design firm
The Wecker Group
Monterey, California
client
Pacific's Edge

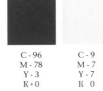

C - 96	C - 9
M - 78	M - 7
Y - 3	Y - 7
K - 0	K - 0

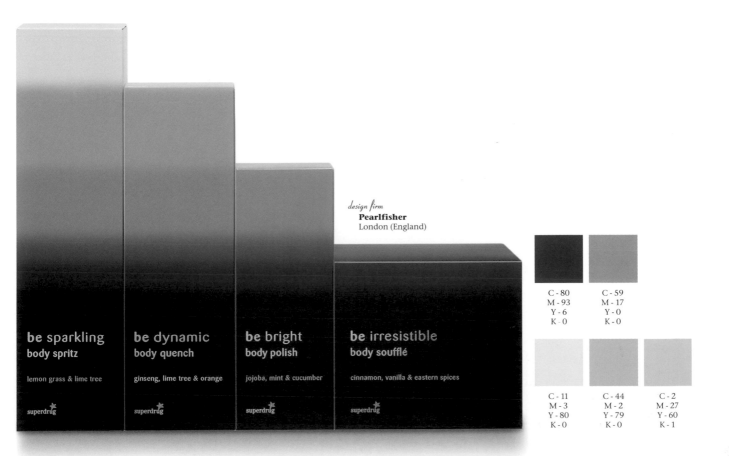

design firm
Pearlfisher
London (England)

be sparkling
body spritz

lemon grass & lime tree

superdrug

be dynamic
body quench

ginseng, lime tree & orange

superdrug

be bright
body polish

jojoba, mint & cucumber

superdrug

be irresistible
body soufflé

cinnamon, vanilla & eastern spices

superdrug

C - 80	C - 59
M - 93	M - 17
Y - 6	Y - 0
K - 0	K - 0

C - 11	C - 44	C - 2
M - 3	M - 2	M - 27
Y - 80	Y - 79	Y - 60
K - 0	K - 0	K - 1

235

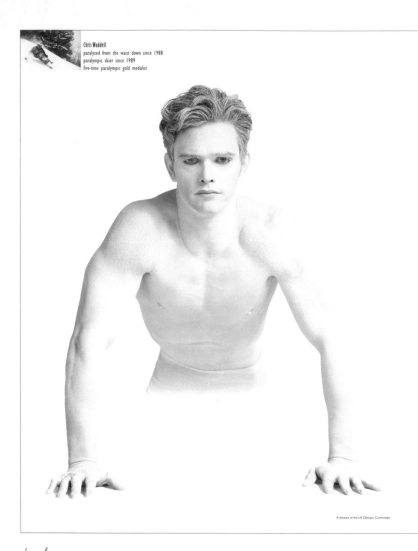

Chris Waddell
paralyzed from the waist down since 1988
paralympic skier since 1989
five-time paralympic gold medalist

I

i am powerful

i am the fastest thing on a mountain

AM

i am speed and precision rolled into one

i am a 5-time gold medalist

AN AVALANCHE.

U.S. PARALYM
I AM ABLE
www.paralympics2002.

A division of the US Olympic Committee

design firm
After Hours Creative
Phoenix, Arizona

C - 47	C - 14
M - 22	M - 2
Y - 6	Y - 1
K - 0	K - 0

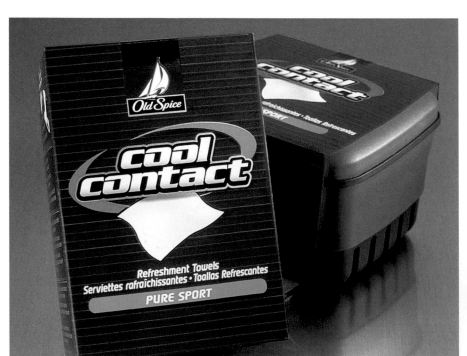

design firm
Interbrand
New York, New York
client
Proctor & Gamble

C - 12	C - 97	C - 56
M - 94	M - 89	M - 12
Y - 73	Y - 1	Y - 1
K - 0	K - 22	K - 0

236

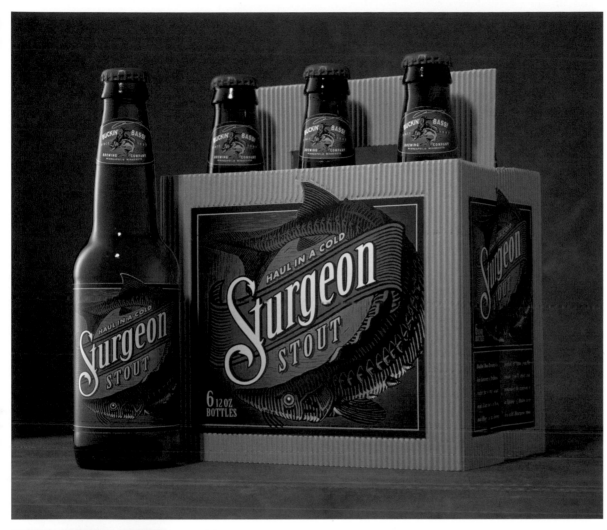

design firm
Compass Design
Minneapolis, Minnesota

C - 42	C - 69	C - 34
M - 31	M - 55	M - 70
Y - 30	Y - 9	Y - 54
K - 9	K - 9	K - 52

design firm
Becker Design
Milwaukee, Wisconsin
client
Suburban

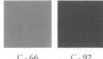

C - 66	C - 92
M - 17	M - 33
Y - 23	Y - 40
K - 3	K - 21

Suburban
COUNSELING SERVICES

C - 88	C - 100	C - 5	C - 1
M - 50	M - 100	M - 28	M - 2
Y - 3	Y - 28	Y - 100	Y - 23
K - 1	K - 16	K - 0	K - 0

design firm
McElveney & Palozzi Design Group
Rochester, New York
client
High Falls Brewing Co.

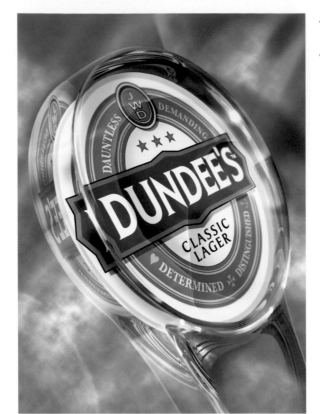

design firm
American Airlines Publishing
Ft. Worth, Texas
client
American Way Magazine

C - 7	C - 31
M - 23	M - 23
Y - 99	Y - 25
K - 0	K - 0

ALTERNATIVE AUTOS

CARMAKERS' LATEST VENTURES INTO HIGH-TECH ENGINES MAKE AUTOS THE LEADING EDGE OF ALTERNATIVE ENERGY SOURCES. BY BARRY LYNN

At the controls of a General Motors electric-powered EV1, cruising nose to nose with a pickup truck, I stared at the point in the road where two lanes become one. Rather than carefully sliding behind my neighbor, I tapped the accelerator. By the time I glanced at the dashboard a few seconds later, the speedometer read 85 and the truck was a distant reflection.

It was at that moment, hurtling toward the morning sun on Washington's Southwest Freeway, that I first really began to wonder why automakers seemingly don't want to build or sell powerful electric cars.

Nor was my borrowed EV1 simply a fine highway machine. Cruising the winding upper stretches of Rock Creek Park, I floated forward in near silence, through sunlight dappled by leafless branches. Not a bad way, all in all, to run errands or get to work, tucked in a smooth, snug roadster that on any stretch of empty asphalt will, with the slightest of prodding, shoot forward like one of those wheeled rockets that set land-speed records at the Bonneville Salt Flats.

64 | AMERICAN WAY | 03.15.02

238

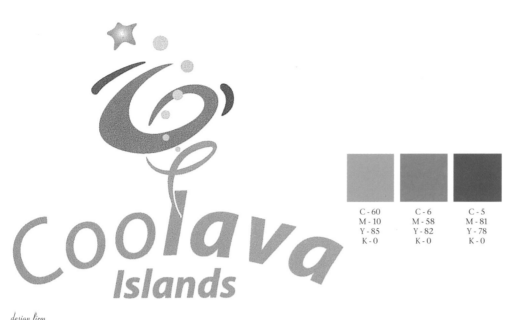

C - 60	C - 6	C - 5
M - 10	M - 58	M - 81
Y - 85	Y - 82	Y - 78
K - 0	K - 0	K - 0

design firm
Julia Tam Design
Palos Verdes, California
client
Coolava Islands

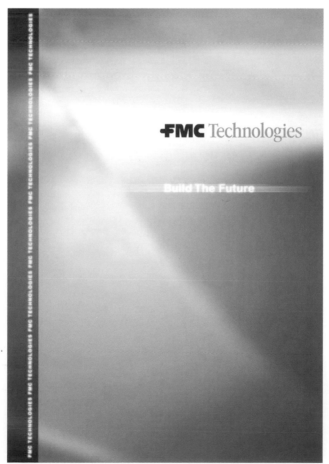

design firm
Stan Gellman Graphic Design
St. Louis, Missouri
client
FMC Technologies

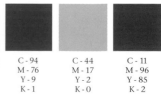

C - 94	C - 44	C - 11
M - 76	M - 17	M - 96
Y - 9	Y - 2	Y - 85
K - 1	K - 0	K - 2

RiverMill

PLAZA

design firm
Klündt Hosmer Design
Spokane, Washington

C - 95   C - 0
M - 75   M - 0
Y - 13   Y - 0
K - 3   K - 100

design firm
Compass Design
Minneapolis, Minnesota

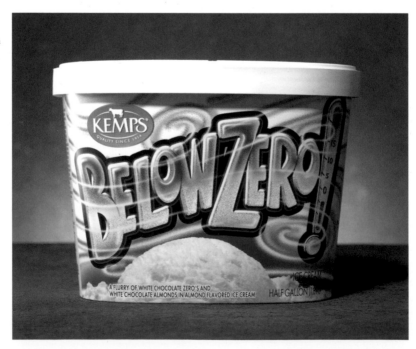

C - 99   C - 23
M - 86   M - 16
Y - 24   Y - 16
K - 29   K - 1

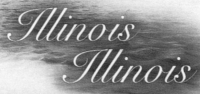

BY THY RIVERS GENTLY FLOWING,

*Illinois
Illinois*

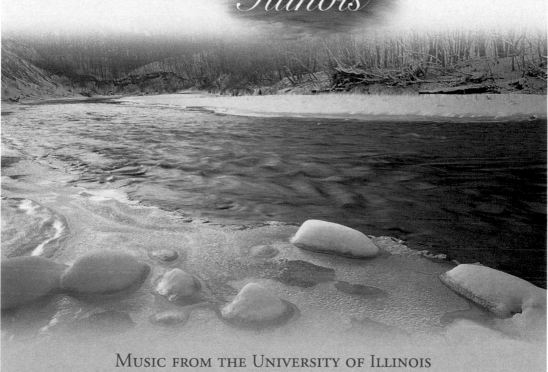

MUSIC FROM THE UNIVERSITY OF ILLINOIS
PRESENTED BY THE UNIVERSITY OF ILLINOIS FOUNDATION

C - 5   C - 80   C - 100
M - 0   M - 40   M - 70
Y - 0   Y - 0   Y - 0
K - 0   K - 30   K - 30

design firm
Stan Gellman Graphic Design Inc.
St. Louis, Missouri
client
University of Illinois Foundation

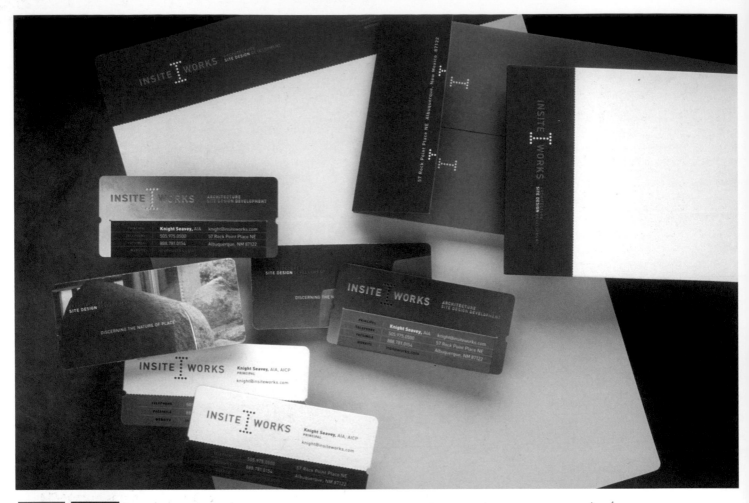

C - 1   C - 81
M - 87   M - 55
Y - 81   Y - 40
K - 1   K - 53

design firm
Hornall Anderson Design Works
Seattle, Washington

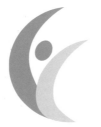

Community
Foundation
for Monterey County

design firm
The Wecker Group
Monterey, California
client
Community Foundation
for Monterey County

C - 36   C - 77
M - 1   M - 9
Y - 12   Y - 4
K - 0   K - 0

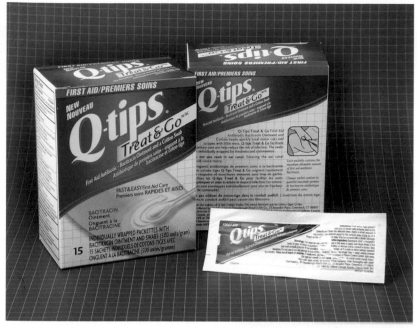

C - 100   C - 1   C - 8
M - 77   M - 87   M - 20
Y - 0   Y - 99   Y - 89
K - 0   K - 0   K - 1

design firm
Tom Fowler, Inc.
Norwalk, Connecticut
client
Unilever Home & Personal Care USA

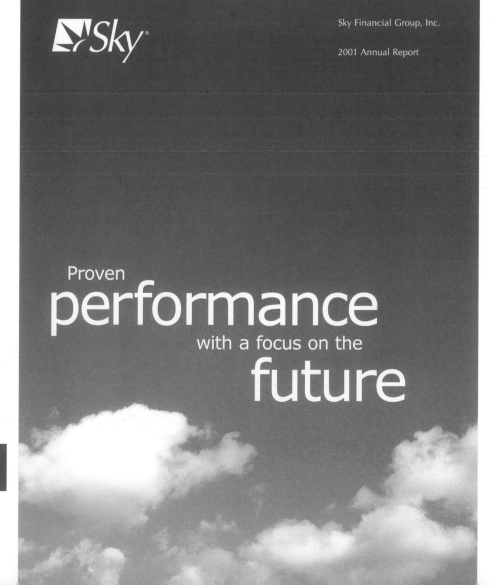

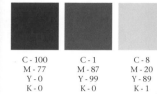 Sky Financial Group, Inc.

2001 Annual Report

Proven
performance
with a focus on the
future

design firm
Lesniewicz Associates
Toldeo, Ohio
client
Sky Bank

C - 98
M - 49
Y - 3
K - 0

BOMBARDIER

Contrails

FALL 2000   A BOMBARDIER BUSINESS AIRCRAFT MAGAZINE

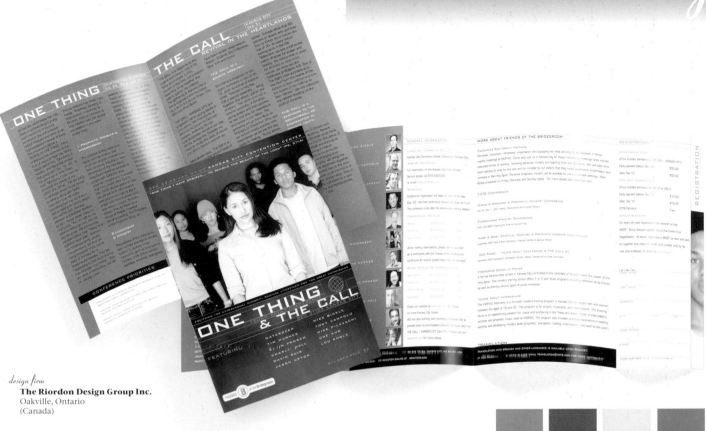

design firm
The Riordon Design Group Inc.
Oakville, Ontario
(Canada)

C - 0	C - 35	C - 0	C - 65
M - 50	M - 50	M - 10	M - 30
Y - 100	Y - 80	Y - 60	Y - 0
K - 5	K - 40	K - 0	K - 0

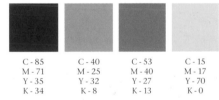

C - 85	C - 40	C - 53	C - 15
M - 71	M - 25	M - 40	M - 17
Y - 35	Y - 32	Y - 27	Y - 70
K - 34	K - 8	K - 13	K - 0

design firm
5D Studio
Malibu, California
client
Brown Jordan

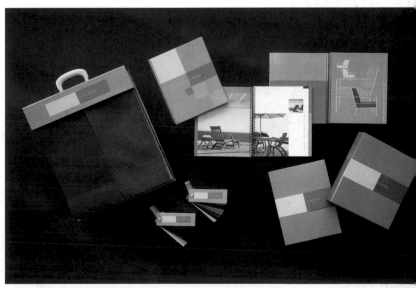

(opposite) **design firm**
Greteman Group
Wichita, Kansas

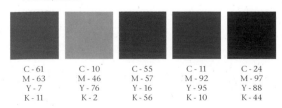

C - 61	C - 10	C - 55	C - 11	C - 24
M - 63	M - 46	M - 57	M - 92	M - 97
Y - 7	Y - 76	Y - 16	Y - 95	Y - 88
K - 11	K - 2	K - 56	K - 10	K - 44

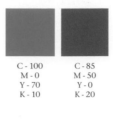

C - 100
M - 0
Y - 70
K - 10

C - 85
M - 50
Y - 0
K - 20

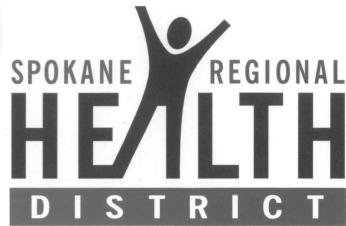

design firm
Klündt Hosmer Design
Spokane, Washington
client
Spokane Regional Health District

CORNETS

SNARE
DRUMS

FRENCH
HORNS

TUBAS

VIBRAPHONES   CELLOS

TIMPANI

BASSOONS   PICCOLOS

VIOLINS

TROMBONES

FLUTES

TRUMPETS   SAXOPHONES

OBOES

PIANOS

CLARINETS

2001
ANNUAL REPORT

STEINWAY MUSICAL INSTRUMENTS, INC.

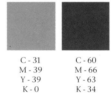

C - 31
M - 39
Y - 39
K - 0

C - 60
M - 66
Y - 63
K - 34

design firm
The Wyant Simboli Group, Inc.
Norwalk, Connecticut
client
Steinway Musical Instruments, Inc.

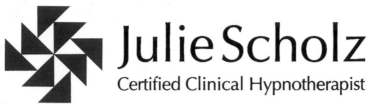

Julie Scholz
Certified Clinical Hypnotherapist

C - 100	C - 0
M - 87	M - 0
Y - 0	Y - 0
K - 13	K - 100

design firm
Jiva Creative
Alameda, California
client
Julie Scholz, CCHT

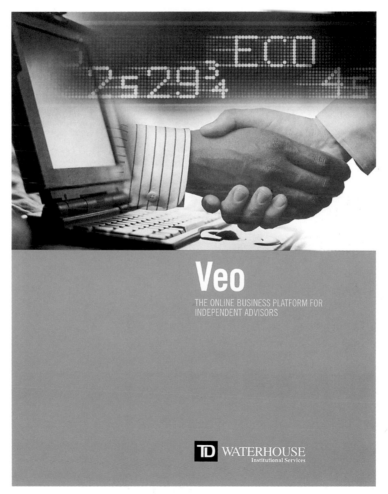

Veo
THE ONLINE BUSINESS PLATFORM FOR
INDEPENDENT ADVISORS

TD WATERHOUSE
Institutional Services

design firm
Berni Marketing & Design
Greenwich, Connecticut
client
TD Waterhouse

C - 34	C - 65
M - 24	M - 3
Y - 23	Y - 82
K - 0	K - 0

design firm
Designation
New York, New York

C - 1
M - 14
Y - 91
K - 0

C - 24
M - 92
Y - 100
K - 18

C - 86
M - 28
Y - 32
K - 30

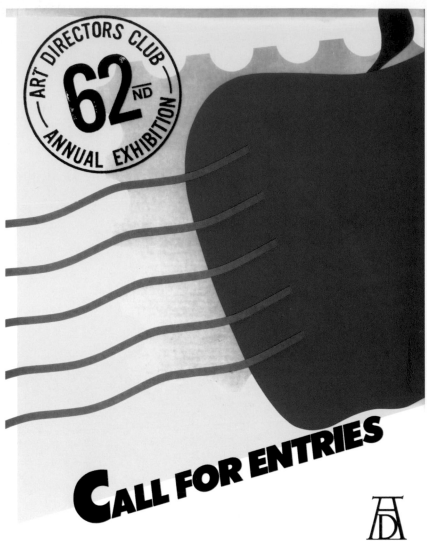

THE SIXTY-SECOND ANNUAL EXHIBITION OF THE ART DIRECTORS CLUB

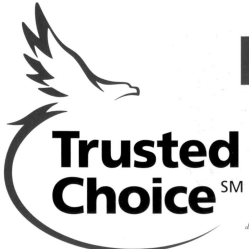

C - 95
M - 71
Y - 10
K - 1

C - 0
M - 0
Y - 0
K - 100

design firm
Addison
San Francisco, California
client
Trusted Choice

248

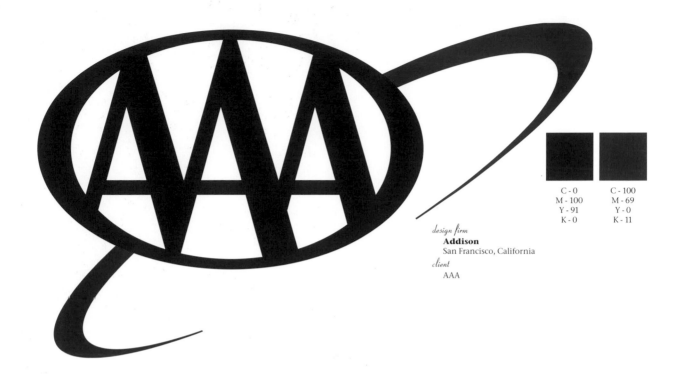

C - 0	C - 100
M - 100	M - 69
Y - 91	Y - 0
K - 0	K - 11

design firm
Addison
San Francisco, California
client
AAA

C - 94	C - 5
M - 69	M - 13
Y - 5	Y - 94
K - 0	K - 0

design firm
Addison
San Francisco, California
client
Guidance Financial Group

C - 8
M - 15
Y - 40
K - 0

C - 0
M - 0
Y - 0
K - 100

C - 54
M - 35
Y - 76
K - 4

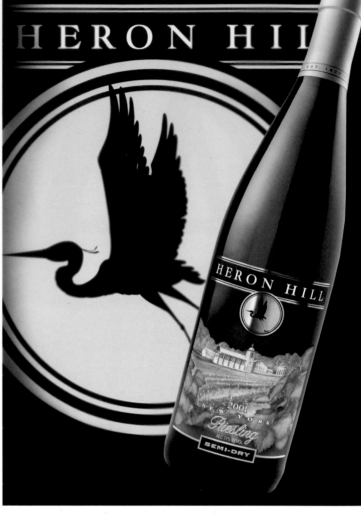

design firm
McElveney & Palozzi Design Group
Rochester, New York
client
Heron Hill Winery

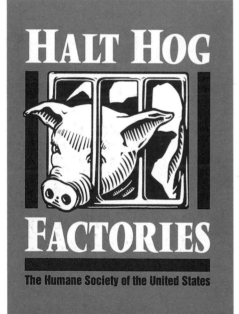

design firm
The Humane Society of the United States
Washington, D.C.
client
The Humane Society of the United States

C - 91
M - 78
Y - 22
K - 24

C - 13
M - 72
Y - 88
K - 3

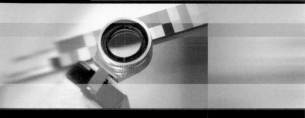

PERFECTION

It's not too much to ask.

design firm
Belyea
Seattle, Washington
client
ColorGraphics

Seattle's Printing Experts

ColorGraphics

1421 SOUTH DEAN STREET | 206.682.7171 | colorgraphics.net

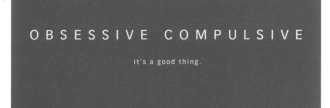

OBSESSIVE COMPULSIVE

It's a good thing.

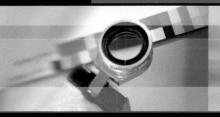

Seattle's Printing Experts

ColorGraphics

1421 SOUTH DEAN STREET | 206.682.7171 | colorgraphics.net

PEACE OF MIND

By far the most popular service we provide.

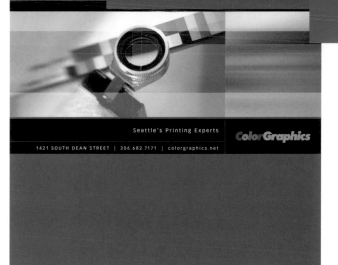

Seattle's Printing Experts

ColorGraphics

1421 SOUTH DEAN STREET | 206.682.7171 | colorgraphics.net

PICKY PICKY PICKY

Thanks for the compliment.

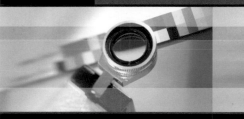

Seattle's Printing Experts

ColorGraphics

1421 SOUTH DEAN STREET | 206.682.7171 | colorgraphics.net

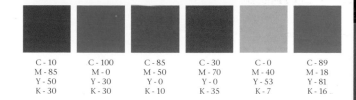

C - 10	C - 100	C - 85	C - 30	C - 0	C - 89
M - 85	M - 0	M - 50	M - 70	M - 40	M - 18
Y - 50	Y - 30	Y - 0	Y - 0	Y - 53	Y - 81
K - 30	K - 30	K - 10	K - 35	K - 7	K - 16

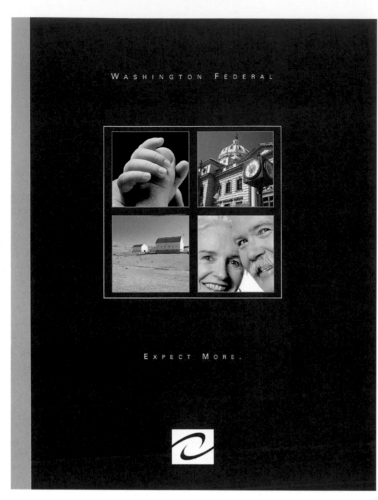

WASHINGTON FEDERAL

EXPECT MORE.

design firm
Desbrow
Pittsburgh, Pennsylvania
client
Washington Federal

C - 95	C - 46	C - 27	C - 7
M - 86	M - 15	M - 84	M - 40
Y - 6	Y - 80	Y - 55	Y - 98
K - 33	K - 0	K - 3	K - 0

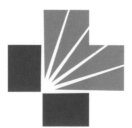

LaserCosmedics

REVEAL A WHOLE NEW YOU

C - 15	C - 90
M - 70	M - 65
Y - 90	Y - 0
K - 0	K - 10

design firm
Klündt Hosmer Design
Spokane, Washington
client
LaserCosmedics

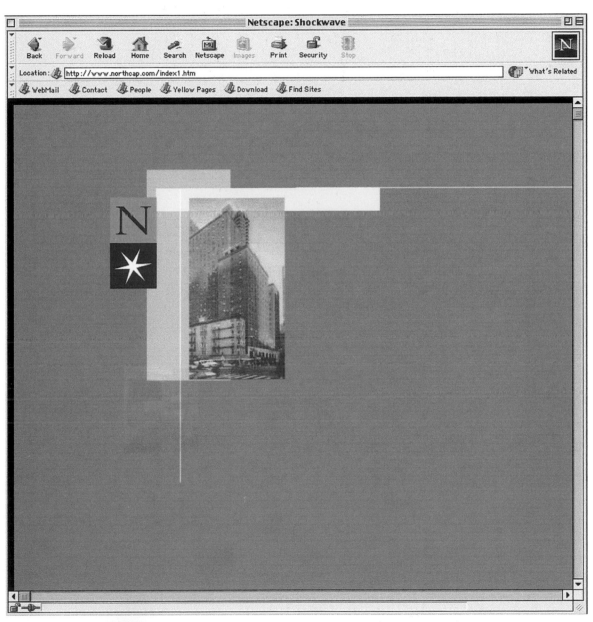

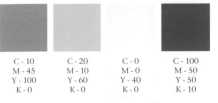

C - 10	C - 20	C - 0	C - 100
M - 45	M - 10	M - 0	M - 50
Y - 100	Y - 60	Y - 40	Y - 50
K - 0	K - 0	K - 0	K - 10

design firm
Suka & Friends Design, Inc.
New York, New York
client
Northstar Capital Investment Corp.

C - 50
M - 100
Y - 20
K - 30

C - 40
M - 95
Y - 65
K - 20

C - 100
M - 0
Y - 50
K - 55

C - 10
M - 40
Y - 100
K - 10

CISCO SYSTEMS

The Brand

Logo Standards

Tag Line/Program Logos

Merchandising/Ingredient Brands

Building the
Cisco brand
from the **inside out**

design firm
Cisco Systems
San Jose, California
client
Cisco Systems

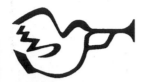

design firm
LarsonLogosEtc
Rockford, Illinois
client
Gloria Dei Lutheran Church

C - 100
M - 100
Y - 0
K - 0

C - 72
M - 100
Y - 0
K - 0

NATROL®

design firm
Gauger & Silva
San Francisco, California
client
Natrol

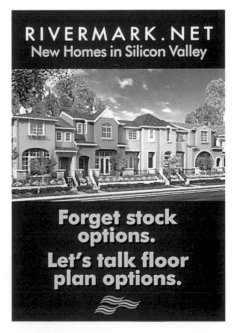

design firm
Gauger + Santz
San Francisco, California
client
Rivermark

C - 71	C - 0	C - 80
M - 99	M - 25	M - 19
Y - 21	Y - 67	Y - 6
K - 7	K - 0	K - 3

JANIE AND JACK ™

JANIE AND JACK ™

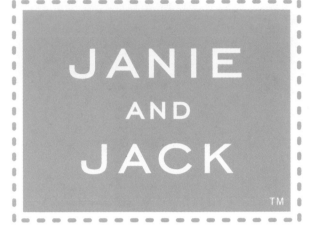

JANIE AND JACK ™

JANIE AND JACK ™

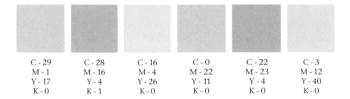

C - 29	C - 28	C - 16	C - 0	C - 22	C - 3
M - 1	M - 16	M - 4	M - 22	M - 23	M - 12
Y - 17	Y - 4	Y - 26	Y - 11	Y - 4	Y - 40
K - 0	K - 1	K - 0	K - 0	K - 0	K - 0

design firm
Michael Osborne Design
San Francisco, California
client
Janie and Jack

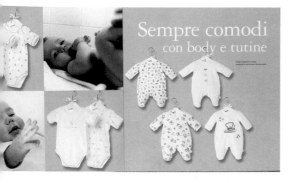

Sempre comodi
con body e tutine

C - 0
M - 18
Y - 13
K - 0

C - 27
M - 18
Y - 4
K - 0

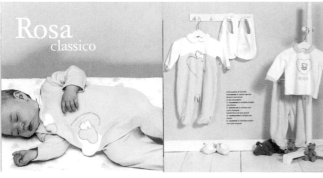

Rosa
classico

design firm
Tangram Strategic Design
Novara, Italy
client
Prénatal

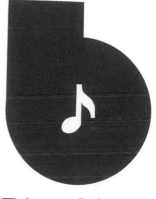

C - 86
M - 67
Y - 1
K - 2

design firm
Mike Salisbury L.L.C.
Venice, California
client
Blue Note Records

Blue Note

C - 75
M - 0
Y - 100
K - 40

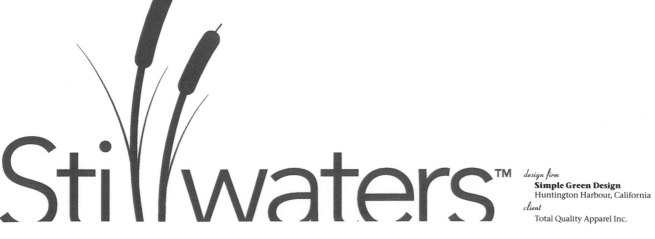

Stillwaters™

design firm
Simple Green Design
Huntington Harbour, California
client
Total Quality Apparel Inc.

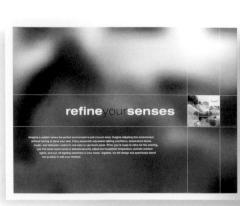
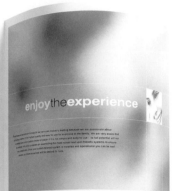

refineyour**senses**

enjoythe**experience**

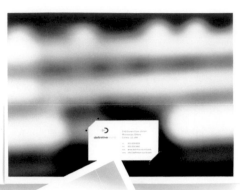

defineyour**environment**

definitive**sound**

C - 0
M - 95
Y - 90
K - 25

C - 80
M - 20
Y - 0
K - 10

C - 55
M - 10
Y - 80
K - 30

design firm
The Riordon Design Group Inc.
Oakville, Ontario
(Canada)
client
Definitive Sound

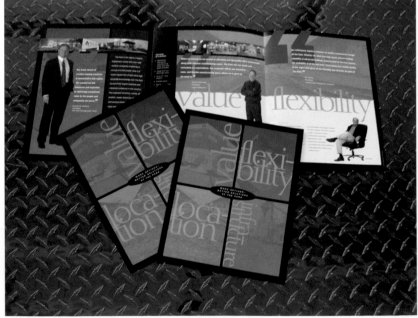

design firm
Klündt Hosmer Design
Spokane, Washington
client
Spokane Industrial

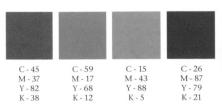

C - 45
M - 37
Y - 82
K - 38

C - 59
M - 17
Y - 68
K - 12

C - 15
M - 43
Y - 88
K - 5

C - 26
M - 87
Y - 79
K - 21

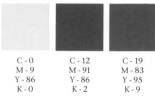

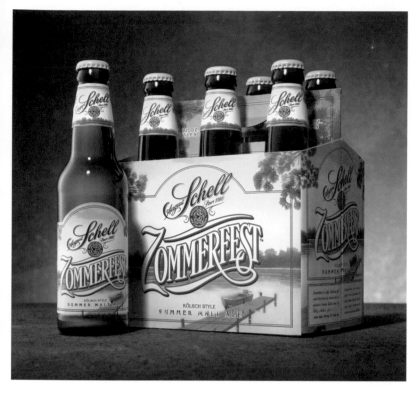

C - 0
M - 9
Y - 86
K - 0

C - 12
M - 91
Y - 86
K - 2

C - 19
M - 83
Y - 95
K - 9

design firm
Compass Design
Minneapolis, Minnesota

design firm
Stan Gellman Graphic Design
St. Louis, Missouri
client
Federal Reserve Bank of St. Louis

C - 100
M - 80
Y - 26
K - 22

C - 76
M - 13
Y - 20
K - 0

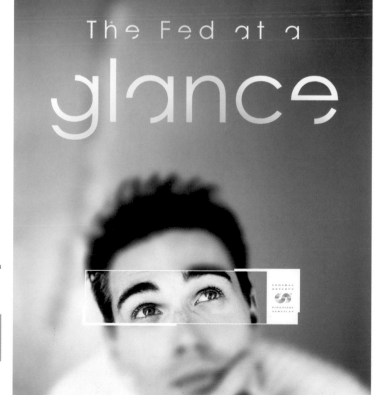

An eye for our world

All the sand on our beaches is made up of individual grains.

From tiny droplets come all our oceans' waters.

At bpTT, we're committed to addressing the problem of global pollution, by acting locally to promote safer personal and industrial use of the environment.

After all, it's our world too.

Investing beyond petroleum...

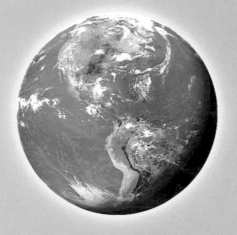

bp

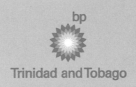

Trinidad and Tobago

bpTT – Education • Culture • Environment • Community

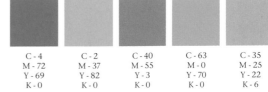

relaxing

(opposite) design firm
All Media Projects Limited (AMPLE)
Port of Spain (Trinidad & Tobago)
client
bp Trinidad and Tobago LLC (bpTT)

C - 4	C - 33	C - 65	C - 70
M - 0	M - 2	M - 11	M - 27
Y - 64	Y - 74	Y - 65	Y - 24
K - 0	K - 0	K - 0	K - 0

C - 4	C - 2	C - 40	C - 63	C - 35
M - 72	M - 37	M - 55	M - 0	M - 25
Y - 69	Y - 82	Y - 3	Y - 70	Y - 22
K - 0	K - 0	K - 0	K - 0	K - 6

THE JEWISH
HOME & HOSPITAL
LIFECARE SYSTEM

MANHATTAN ▪ BRONX ▪ SARAH NEUMAN CENTER/WESTCHESTER ▪ LIFECARE SERVICES

design firm
Bailey Design Group
Plymouth Meeting, Pennsylvania
client
The Jewish Home & Hospital Lifecare System

C - 11	C - 18	C - 43	C - 0
M - 31	M - 99	M - 86	M - 0
Y - 100	Y - 95	Y - 10	Y - 0
K - 0	K - 1	K - 3	K - 100

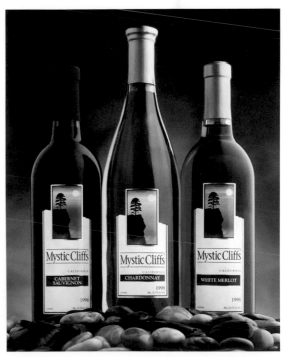

design firm
McElveney & Palozzi Design Group
Rochester, New York
client
Canandaigua Wine Co.

261

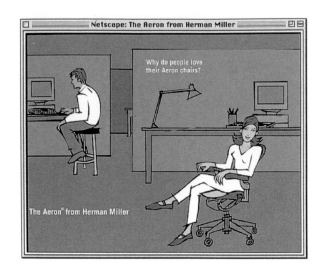

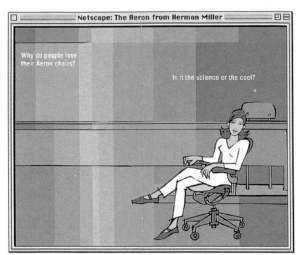

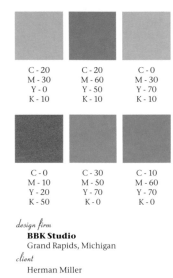

C - 20
M - 30
Y - 0
K - 10

C - 20
M - 60
Y - 50
K - 10

C - 0
M - 30
Y - 70
K - 10

C - 0
M - 10
Y - 20
K - 50

C - 30
M - 50
Y - 70
K - 0

C - 10
M - 60
Y - 70
K - 0

design firm
BBK Studio
Grand Rapids, Michigan

client
Herman Miller

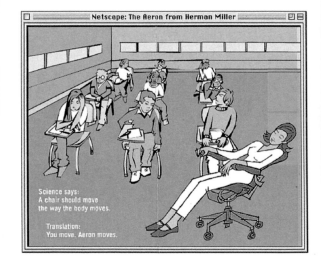

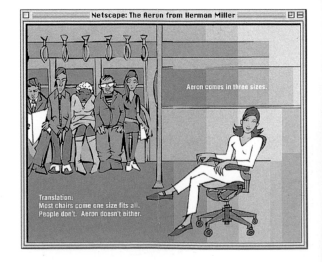

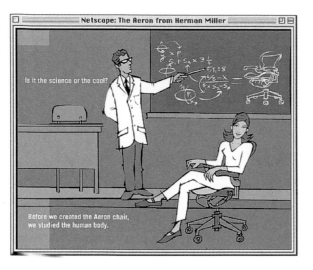

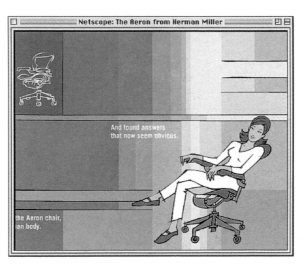

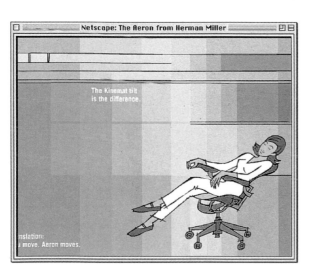

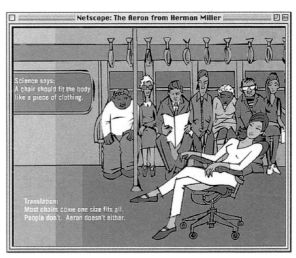

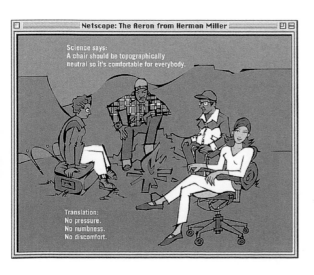

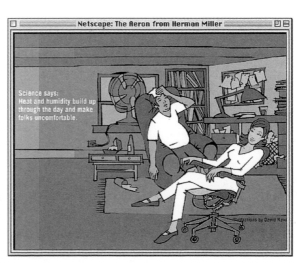

263

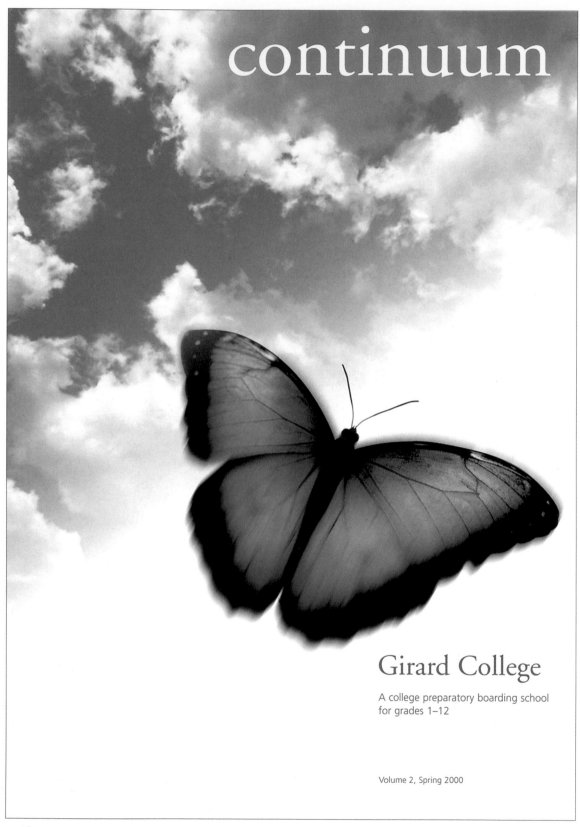

continuum

Girard College

A college preparatory boarding school
for grades 1–12

Volume 2, Spring 2000

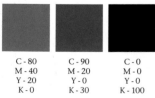

C - 80   C - 90   C - 0
M - 40   M - 20   M - 0
Y - 20   Y - 0   Y - 0
K - 0   K - 30   K - 100

design firm
kor group
Boston, Massachusetts
client
Girard College

264

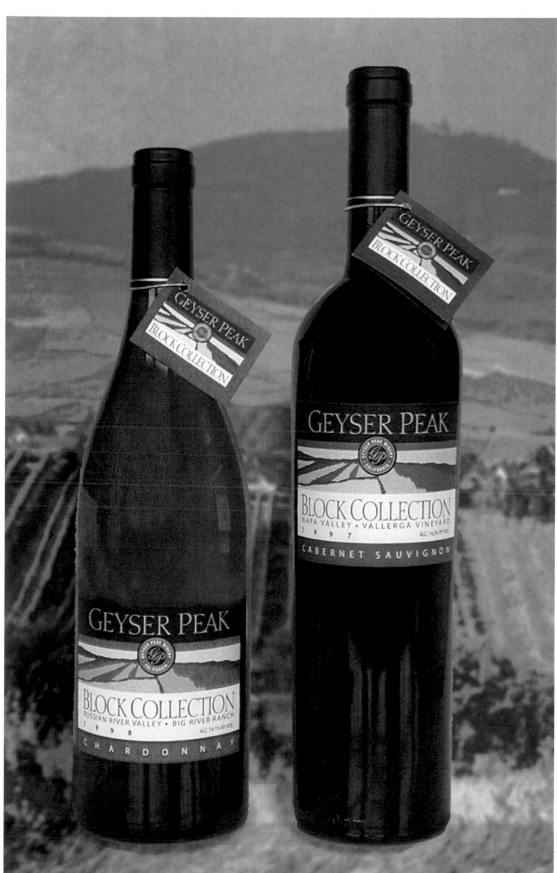

design firm
Di Donato Associates
Chicago, Illinois
client
Jim Beam Brands Company

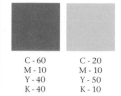

C - 60	C - 20
M - 10	M - 10
Y - 40	Y - 50
K - 40	K - 10

C - 60	C - 30
M - 60	M - 60
Y - 30	Y - 10
K - 20	K - 20

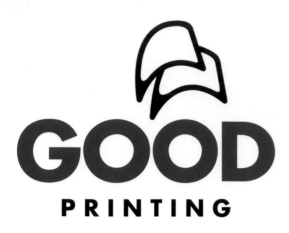

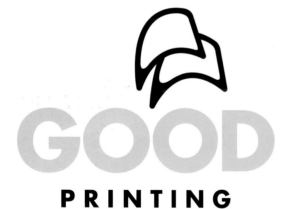

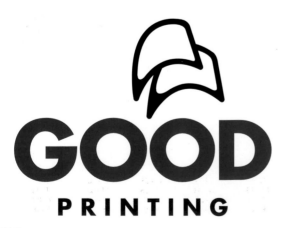

design firm
Becker Design
Milwaukee, Wisconsin
client
Good Printing

7933 North 73rd Street
Milwaukee, Wisconsin 53223

7933 North 73rd Street Milwaukee, Wisconsin 53223 Phone 414 355-4444 Fax 414 355-7746 www.itsgoodprinting.com

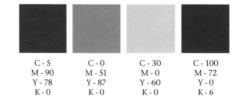

C - 5	C - 0	C - 30	C - 100
M - 90	M - 51	M - 0	M - 72
Y - 78	Y - 87	Y - 60	Y - 0
K - 0	K - 0	K - 0	K - 6

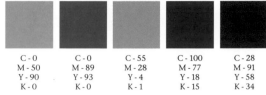

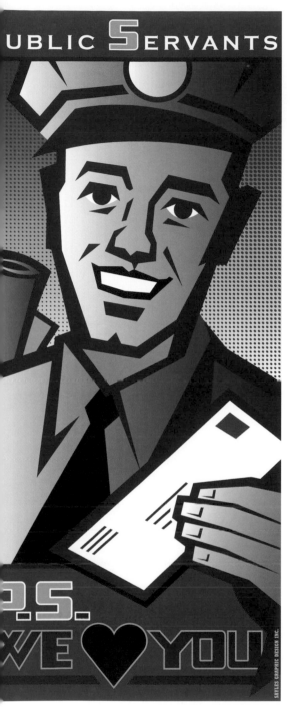

UBLIC SERVANTS

P.S.
WE ♥ YOU

SAYLES GRAPHIC DESIGN INC.

C - 0	C - 0	C - 55	C - 100	C - 28
M - 50	M - 89	M - 28	M - 77	M - 91
Y - 90	Y - 93	Y - 4	Y - 18	Y - 58
K - 0	K - 0	K - 1	K - 15	K - 34

design firm
Sayles Graphic Design
Des Moines, Iowa

client
"Art Fights Back"

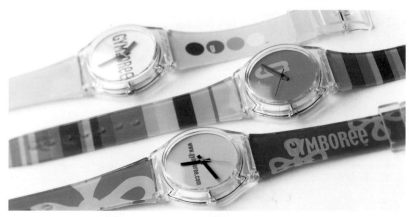

design firm
Michael Osborne Design
San Francisco, California

client
Gymboree

C - 75	C - 5	C - 73	C - 25	C - 10	C - 34
M - 24	M - 43	M - 84	M - 18	M - 82	M - 14
Y - 4	Y - 93	Y - 58	Y - 97	Y - 85	Y - 88
K - 0	K - 0	K - 11	K - 0	K - 3	K - 0

cheerful

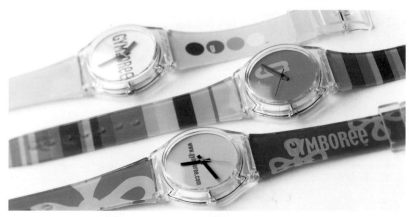

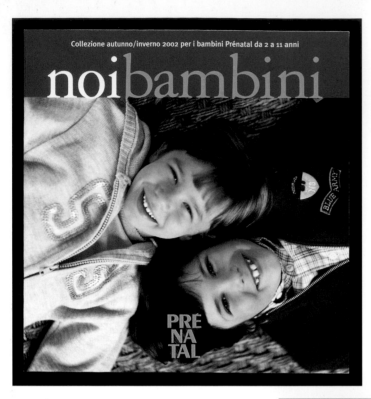

Collezione autunno/inverno 2002 per i bambini Prénatal da 2 a 11 anni

noibambini

PRÉ
NA
TAL

C - 0	C - 0
M - 91	M - 50
Y - 57	Y - 35
K - 13	K - 0

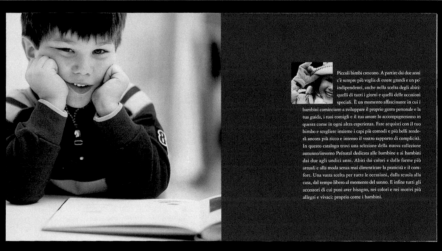

Piccoli bimbi crescono. A partire dai due anni c'è sempre più voglia di essere grandi e un po' indipendenti, anche nella scelta degli abiti: quelli di tutti i giorni e quelli delle occasioni speciali. È un momento affascinante in cui i bambini cominciano a sviluppare il proprio gusto personale e la tua guida, i tuoi consigli e il tuo amore lo accompagneranno in questa come in ogni altra esperienza. Fare acquisti con il tuo bimbo e scegliere insieme i capi più comodi e più belli renderà ancora più ricco e intenso il vostro rapporto di complicità. In questo catalogo trovi una selezione della nuova collezione autunno/inverno Prénatal dedicata alle bambine e ai bambini dai due agli undici anni. Abiti dai colori e dalle forme più attuali e alla moda senza mai dimenticare la praticità e il comfort. Una vasta scelta per tutte le occasioni, dalla scuola alla casa, dal tempo libero al momento del sonno. E infine tutti gli accessori di cui puoi aver bisogno, nei colori e nei motivi più allegri e vivaci: proprio come i bambini.

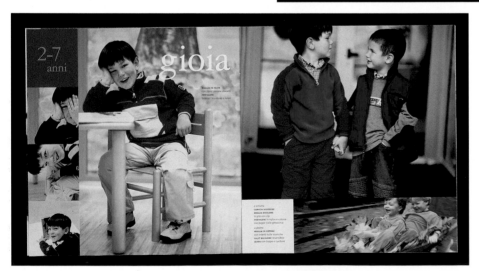

design firm
Tangram Strategic Design
Novara (Italy)
client
Prénatal

Disco\/ery school

design firm
Klündt Hosmer Design
Spokane, Washington
client
Discovery School

C - 80   C - 0
M - 40   M - 60
Y - 0   Y - 100
K - 0   K - 0

design firm
After Hours Creative
Phoenix, Arizona

C - 0   C - 0   C - 30
M - 100   M - 12   M - 0
Y - 100   Y - 90   Y - 90
K - 0   K - 0   K - 15

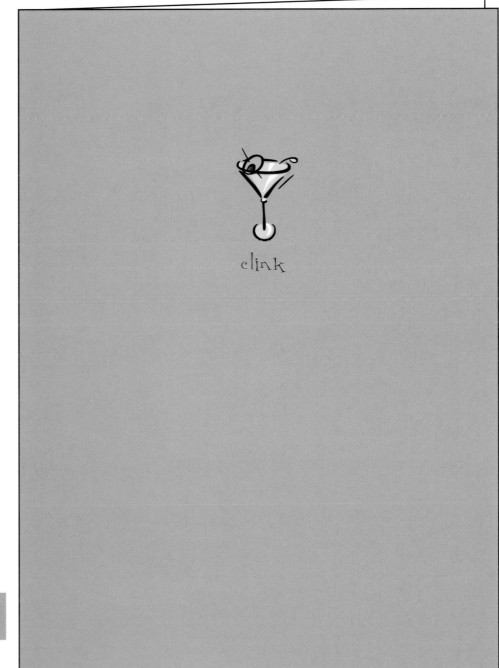

clink

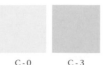

C - 0
M - 14
Y - 0
K - 0

C - 3
M - 27
Y - 3
K - 0

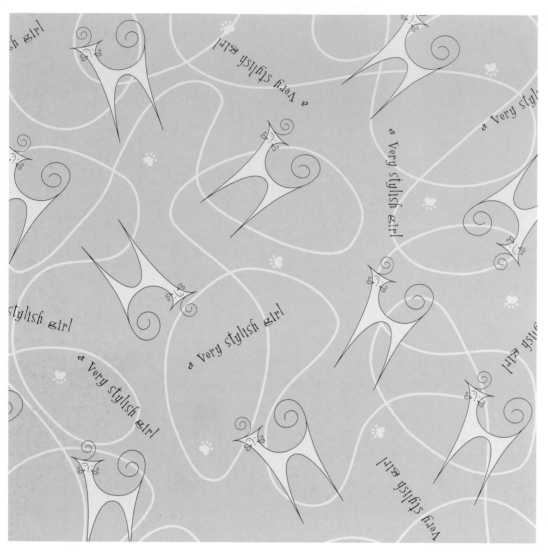

design firm
After Hours Creative
Phoenix, Arizona

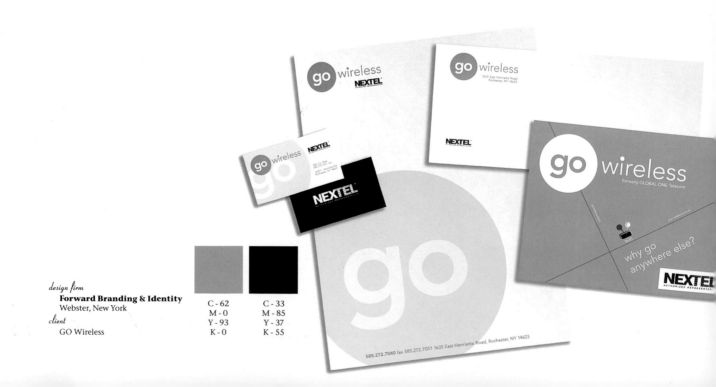

design firm
Forward Branding & Identity
Webster, New York
client
GO Wireless

C - 62
M - 0
Y - 93
K - 0

C - 33
M - 85
Y - 37
K - 55

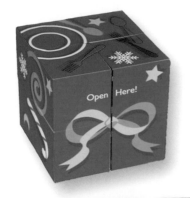

C - 0	C - 12	C - 71	C - 85	C - 40
M - 71	M - 91	M - 99	M - 16	M - 2
Y - 83	Y - 86	Y - 21	Y - 7	Y - 93
K - 0	K - 2	K - 7	K - 3	K - 1

design firm
Tom Fowler, Inc.
Norwalk, Connecticut
client
Pfizer

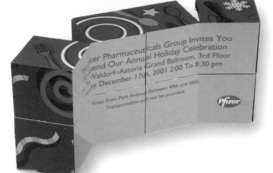

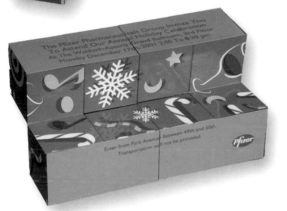

design firm
Greenfield/Belser Ltd.
Washington, D.C.
client
Local Initiatives Support Group

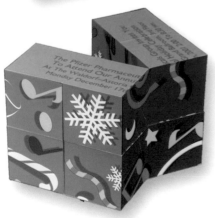

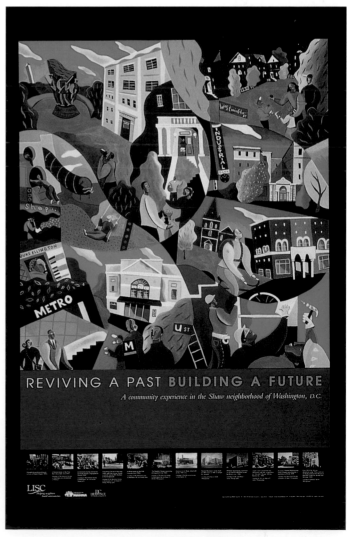

C - 33	C - 11	C - 17	C - 70	C - 99	C - 100
M - 100	M - 58	M - 12	M - 37	M - 1	M - 59
Y - 88	Y - 98	Y - 97	Y - 88	Y - 36	Y - 37
K - 15	K - 0	K - 3	K - 3	K - 0	K - 27

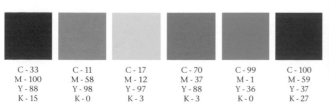

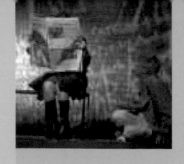

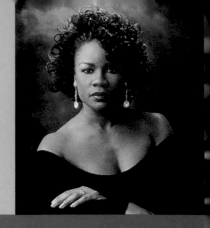

2002 • 2003

Your complete calendar to

THE **Performing Arts** *at Miami*

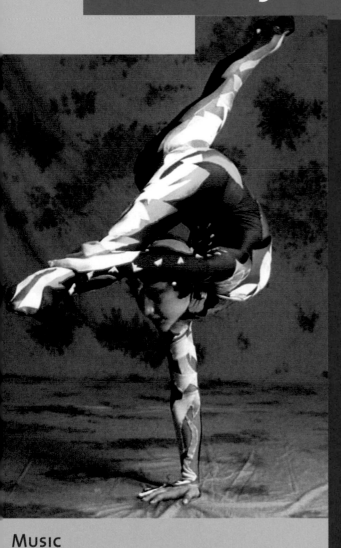

The best way
to experience the
THRILL *of a*
live performance is
to **BE THERE.**

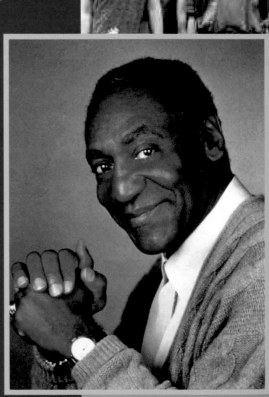

MUSIC
THEATRE
PERFORMING ARTS SERIES

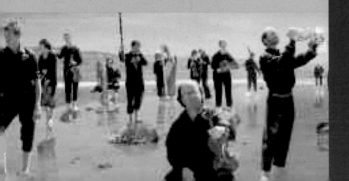

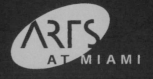

ARTS
AT MIAMI

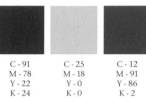

(opposite) *design firm*
Five Visual Communication and Design
West Chester, Ohio

C - 40	C - 95	C - 0	C - 0	C - 100	C - 83
M - 2	M - 95	M - 32	M - 84	M - 65	M - 11
Y - 93	Y - 14	Y - 92	Y - 89	Y - 0	Y - 21
K - 1	K - 4	K - 0	K - 0	K - 0	K - 2

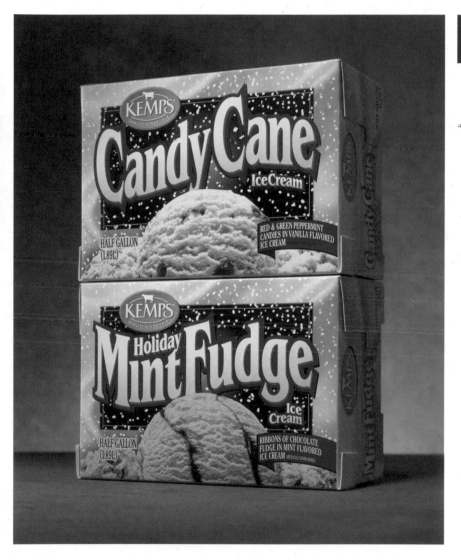

C - 91	C - 25	C - 12
M - 78	M - 18	M - 91
Y - 22	Y - 0	Y - 86
K - 24	K - 0	K - 2

design firm
Compass Design
Minneapolis, Minnesota

design firm
Greteman Group
Wichita, Kansas

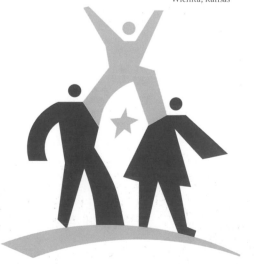

C - 18	C - 100
M - 0	M - 69
Y - 100	Y - 0
K - 18	K - 0

273

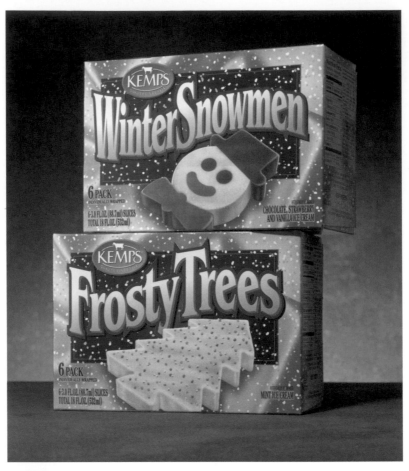

C - 60
M - 30
Y - 60
K - 25

C - 91
M - 78
Y - 22
K - 24

C - 25
M - 18
Y - 0
K - 0

C - 12
M - 91
Y - 86
K - 2

design firm
Compass Design
Minneapolis, Minnesota

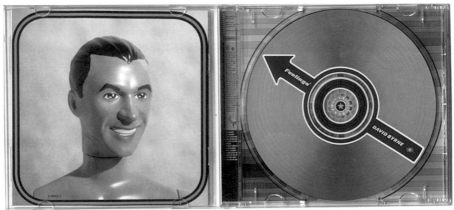

design firm
Sagmeister Inc.
New York, New York

C - 72
M - 15
Y - 67
K - 13

C - 1
M - 17
Y - 66
K - 0

C - 14
M - 76
Y - 35
K - 2

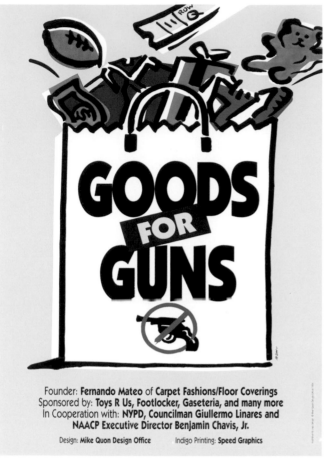

C - 6 M - 0 Y - 95 K - 0	C - 74 M - 49 Y - 0 K - 0

C - 24 M - 100 Y - 76 K - 15	C - 71 M - 24 Y - 100 K - 13	C - 0 M - 72 Y - 99 K - 0

design firm
Designation
New York, New York

design firm
Compass Design
Minneapolis, Minnesota

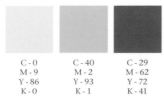

C - 0 M - 9 Y - 86 K - 0	C - 40 M - 2 Y - 93 K - 1	C - 29 M - 62 Y - 72 K - 41

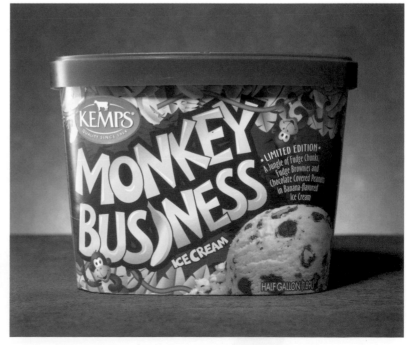

C - 100　　C - 97　　C - 12　　C - 2　　C - 21
M - 46　　M - 83　　M - 99　　M - 42　　M - 43
Y - 18　　Y - 15　　Y - 75　　Y - 88　　Y - 52
K - 12　　K - 17　　K - 18　　K - 2　　K - 15

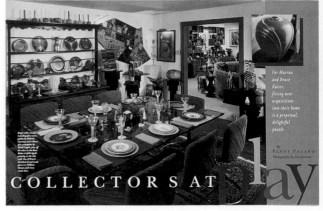

design firm
Dever Designs
Laurel, Maryland
client
AmericanStyle Magazine

design firm
LarsonLogosEtc
Rockford, Illinois

C - 1　　C - 100　　C - 77
M - 23　　M - 56　　M - 95
Y - 99　　Y - 1　　Y - 22
K - 0　　K - 34　　K - 0

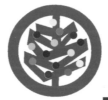

C - 1　　C - 100　　C - 0　　C - 85
M - 100　　M - 0　　M - 100　　M - 14
Y - 100　　Y - 91　　Y - 1　　Y - 1
K - 0　　K - 27　　K - 0　　K - 0

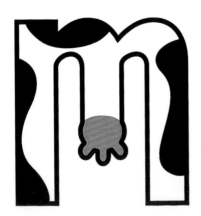

C - 1　　C - 97
M - 73　　M - 94
Y - 0　　Y - 95
K - 0　　K - 84

design firm
Supon Design Group
Washington, D.C.
client
M

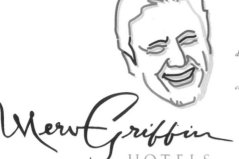

design firm
Mike Salisbury L.L.C.
Venice, California
client
Merv Griffin

C - 87	C - 66	C - 1	C - 3	C - 5
M - 38	M - 14	M - 15	M - 60	M - 80
Y - 33	Y - 69	Y - 93	Y - 87	Y - 75
K - 0	K - 0	K - 0	K - 0	K - 0

design firm
Mike Salisbury L.L.C.
Venice, California
client
Montana Eyes

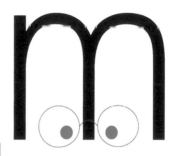

C - 95	C - 88	C - 16
M - 6	M - 80	M - 31
Y - 7	Y - 83	Y - 34
K - 0	K - 59	K - 0

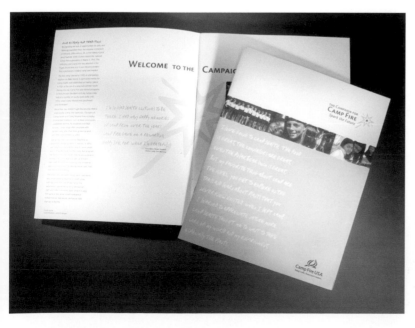

design firm
Belyea
Seattle, Washington
client
Campfire USA

C - 0	C - 74
M - 9	M - 45
Y - 69	Y - 0
K - 0	K - 21

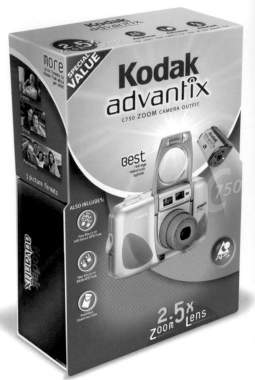

design firm
McElveney & Palozzi Design Group
Rochester, New York
client
Eastman Kodak Company

C - 0	C - 0	C - 74	C - 100
M - 100	M - 18	M - 3	M - 60
Y - 100	Y - 100	Y - 0	Y - 0
K - 0	K - 0	K - 0	K - 0

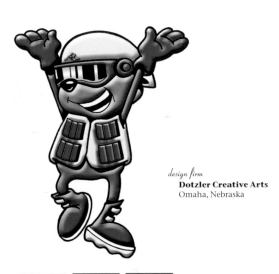

design firm
Dotzler Creative Arts
Omaha, Nebraska

C - 1	C - 100	C - 3
M - 0	M - 50	M - 87
Y - 87	Y - 0	Y - 90
K - 0	K - 16	K - 5

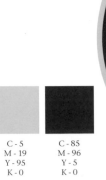

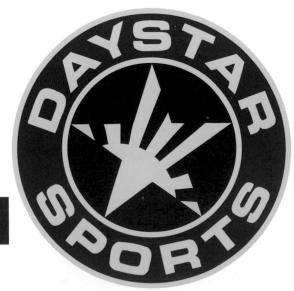

design firm
The Wecker Group
Monterey, California

C - 12	C - 5	C - 85
M - 92	M - 19	M - 96
Y - 96	Y - 95	Y - 5
K - 2	K - 0	K - 0

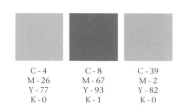

MICHAEL OSBORNE DESIGN

C - 4	C - 8	C - 39
M - 26	M - 67	M - 2
Y - 77	Y - 93	Y - 82
K - 0	K - 1	K - 0

design firm
Michael Osborne Design
San Francisco, California
client
Michael Osborne Design

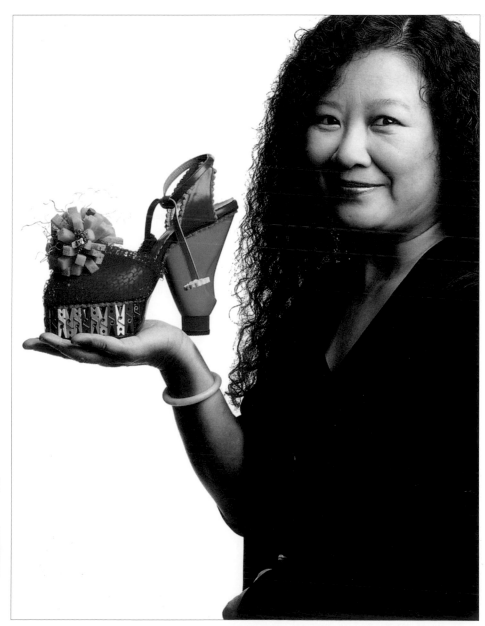

design firm
Cahan and Associates
San Francisco, California
client
Fine Arts Museum

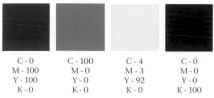

C - 0	C - 100	C - 4	C - 0
M - 100	M - 0	M - 3	M - 0
Y - 100	Y - 0	Y - 92	Y - 0
K - 0	K - 0	K - 0	K - 100

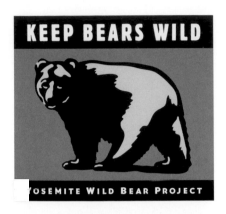

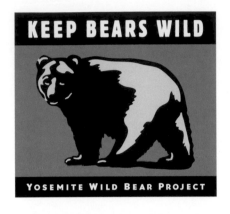

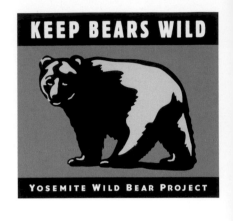

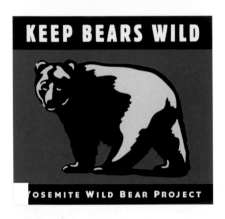

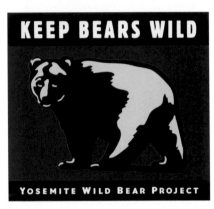

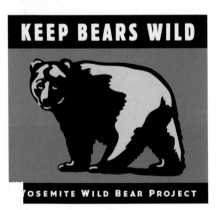

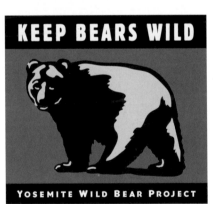

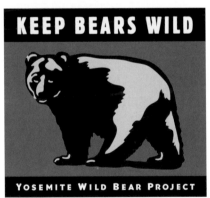

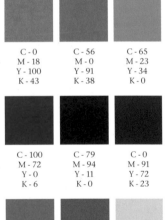

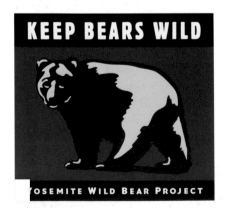

design firm
Michael Osborne Design
San Francisco, California
client
Yosemite Wild Bear Project

C - 0
M - 18
Y - 100
K - 43

C - 56
M - 0
Y - 91
K - 38

C - 65
M - 23
Y - 34
K - 0

C - 100
M - 72
Y - 0
K - 6

C - 79
M - 94
Y - 11
K - 0

C - 0
M - 91
Y - 72
K - 23

C - 0
M - 65
Y - 100
K - 0

C - 0
M - 56
Y - 100
K - 30

C - 0
M - 6
Y - 38
K - 18

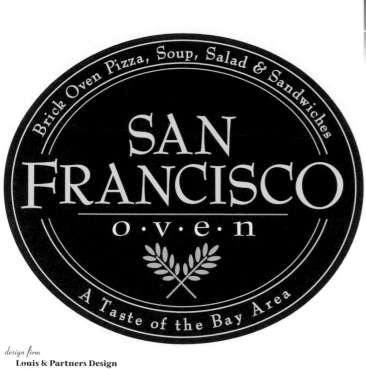

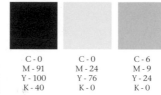

C - 0
M - 91
Y - 100
K - 40

C - 0
M - 24
Y - 76
K - 0

C - 6
M - 9
Y - 24
K - 0

design firm
Louis & Partners Design
Bath, Ohio

client
San Francisco Oven

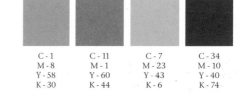

design firm
Hornall Anderson Design Works
Seattle, Washington

C - 1
M - 8
Y - 58
K - 30

C - 11
M - 1
Y - 60
K - 44

C - 7
M - 23
Y - 43
K - 6

C - 34
M - 10
Y - 40
K - 74

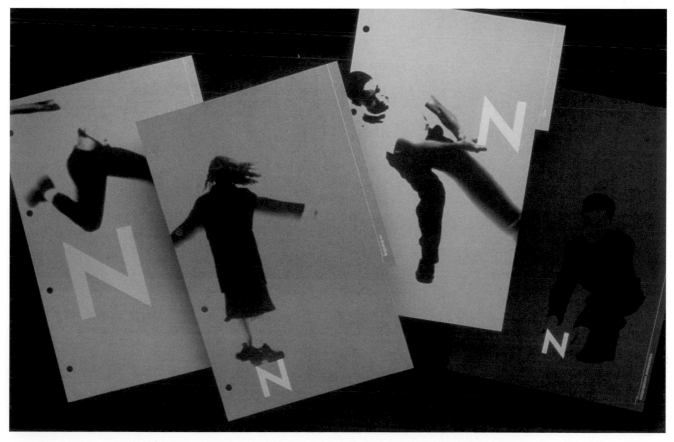

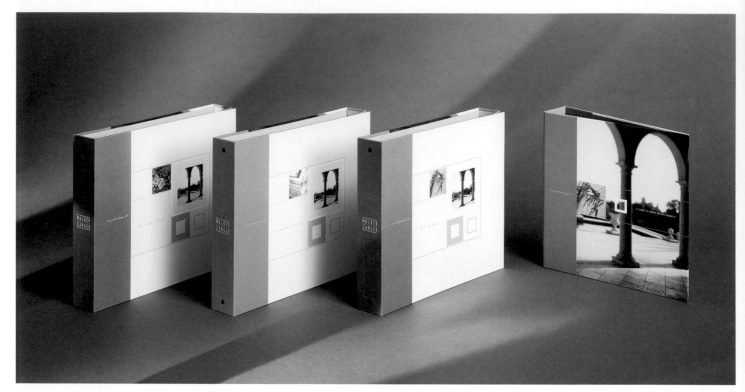

C - 35
M - 0
Y - 18
K - 51

C - 31
M - 28
Y - 47
K - 1

C - 2
M - 14
Y - 26
K - 38

C - 47
M - 43
Y - 44
K - 17

design firm
5D Studio
Malibu, California
client
Walker Zanger

design firm
**Hornall Anderson
Design Works**
Seattle, Washington

C - 0
M - 15
Y - 92
K - 26

C - 8
M - 76
Y - 55
K - 50

C - 57
M - 29
Y - 15
K - 47

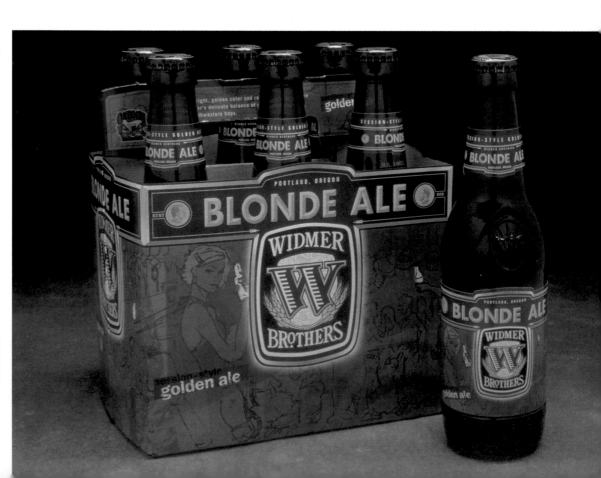

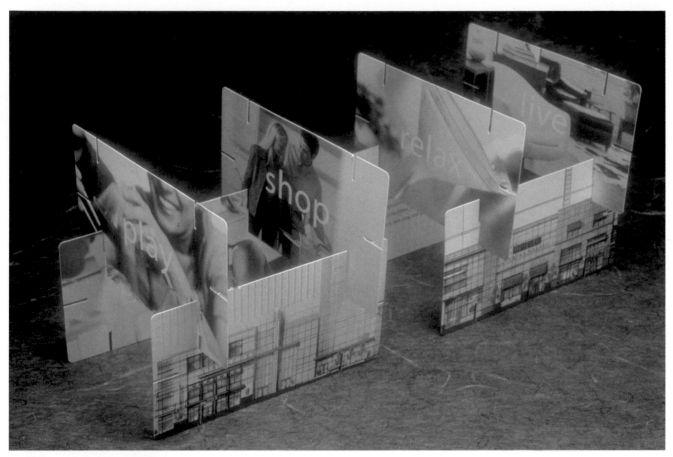

C - 2	C - 40	C - 5
M - 21	M - 24	M - 49
Y - 59	Y - 16	Y - 31
K - 44	K - 47	K - 60

design firm
Hornall Anderson Design Works
Seattle, Washington

design firm
Greteman Group
Wichita, Kansas

CITY

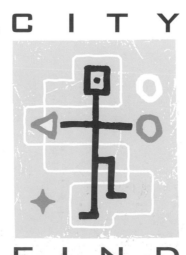

C - 57	C - 0	C - 12
M - 11	M - 0	M - 15
Y - 0	Y - 0	Y - 28
K - 18	K - 100	K - 2

FIND

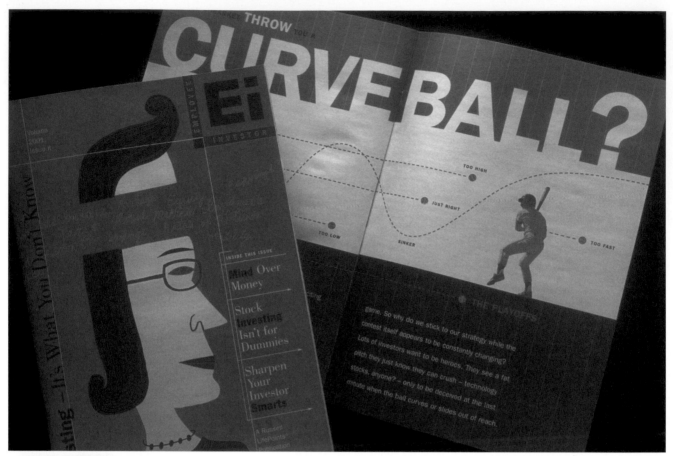

design firm
Hornall Anderson Design Works
Seattle, Washington

C - 20
M - 78
Y - 65
K - 42

C - 12
M - 62
Y - 81
K - 34

C - 0
M - 60
Y - 100
K - 20

C - 60
M - 0
Y - 100
K - 22570

design firm
Klündt Hosmer Design
Spokane, Washington
client
Spokane Public Schools

Spokane Public Schools
excellence for everyone

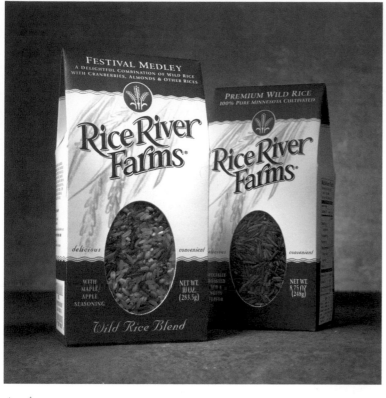

C - 26
M - 80
Y - 37
K - 19

C - 93
M - 70
Y - 0
K - 0

C - 68
M - 42
Y - 38
K - 40

design firm
Compass Design
Minneapolis, Minnesota

design firm
Compass Design
Minneapolis, Minnesota

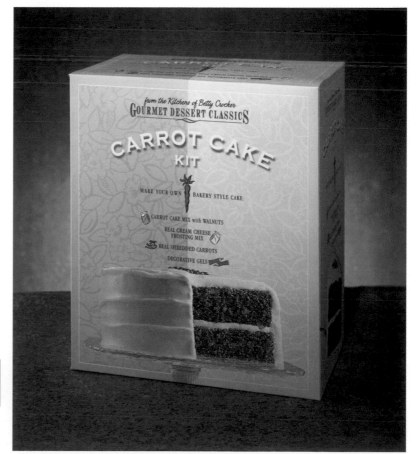

C - 42
M - 2
Y - 75
K - 1

C - 22
M - 14
Y - 46
K - 2

C - 0
M - 71
Y - 83
K - 0

C - 0   C - 0
M - 76   M - 5
Y - 76   Y - 20
K - 60   K - 0

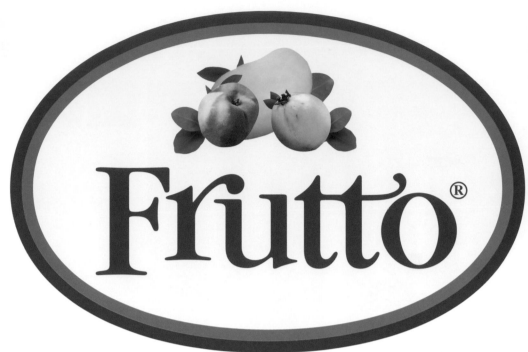

design firm
Praxis Diseñadores, S.C.
México City (Mexico)
client
Alegro Internacional

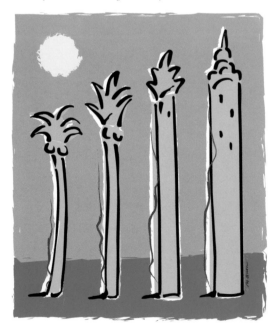

design firm
Designation
New York, New York

C - 1   C - 91   C - 62   C - 2
M - 31   M - 0   M - 3   M - 3
Y - 55   Y - 100   Y - 0   Y - 87
K - 0   K - 0   K - 0   K - 0

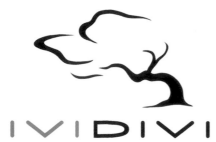

DIVIDIVI

C - 45   C - 0
M - 23   M - 0
Y - 49   Y - 0
K - 0   K - 100

design firm
Mike Salisbury L.L.C.
Venice, California
client
DiviDivi

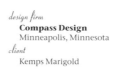

design firm
Compass Design
Minneapolis, Minnesota
client
Kemps Marigold

C - 99   C - 0
M - 33   M - 49
Y - 0   Y - 97
K - 2   K - 0

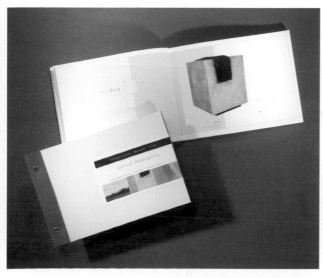

design firm
Belyea
Seattle, Washington
client
ColorGraphics

C - 31   C - 27   C - 41   C - 29
M - 15   M - 65   M - 23   M - 40
Y - 57   Y - 55   Y - 33   Y - 69
K - 3   K - 37   K - 5   K - 19

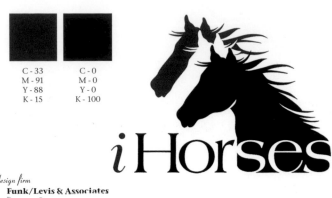

C - 33
M - 91
Y - 88
K - 15

C - 0
M - 0
Y - 0
K - 100

design firm
Funk/Levis & Associates
Eugene, Oregon
client
iHorses

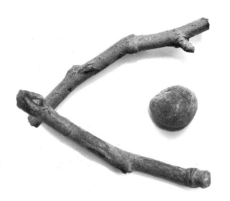

C - 0
M - 0
Y - 0
K - 100

C - 49
M - 37
Y - 38
K - 18

C - 33
M - 44
Y - 57
K - 21

design firm
Belyea
Seattle, Washington
client
Vue Lodge

vue
LODGE

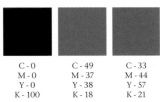

HERON HILL

design firm
McElveney & Palozzi Design Group
Rochester, New York
client
Heron Hill Winery

C - 8
M - 15
Y - 40
K - 0

C - 0
M - 0
Y - 0
K - 100

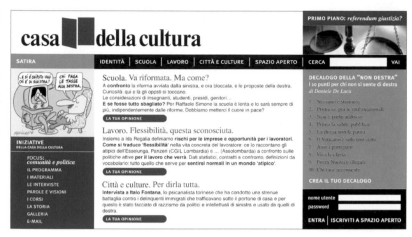

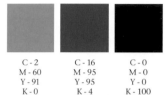

C - 2
M - 60
Y - 91
K - 0

C - 16
M - 95
Y - 95
K - 4

C - 0
M - 0
Y - 0
K - 100

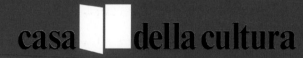

Riconoscerci come abitanti del pianeta. Prenderci cura del mondo in cui viviamo. Creare e difendere spazi aperti al confronto e alle differenze. Imparare il gioco della democrazia.

casa della cultura

Indignarci. Riscoprire il linguaggio elementare della meraviglia. Ascoltare oltre che affermare. Un percorso da fare insieme, alla ricerca dell'identità (perduta?) della sinistra.

design firm
Tangram Strategic Design
Novara (Italy)
client
Casa della Cultura

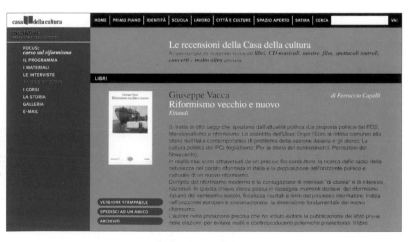

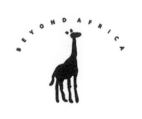

BEYOND AFRICA

C - 1	C - 29	C - 4	C - 0
M -54	M - 49	M - 29	M - 0
Y - 78	Y - 73	Y - 56	Y - 0
K - 0	K - 25	K - 1	K - 100

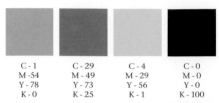

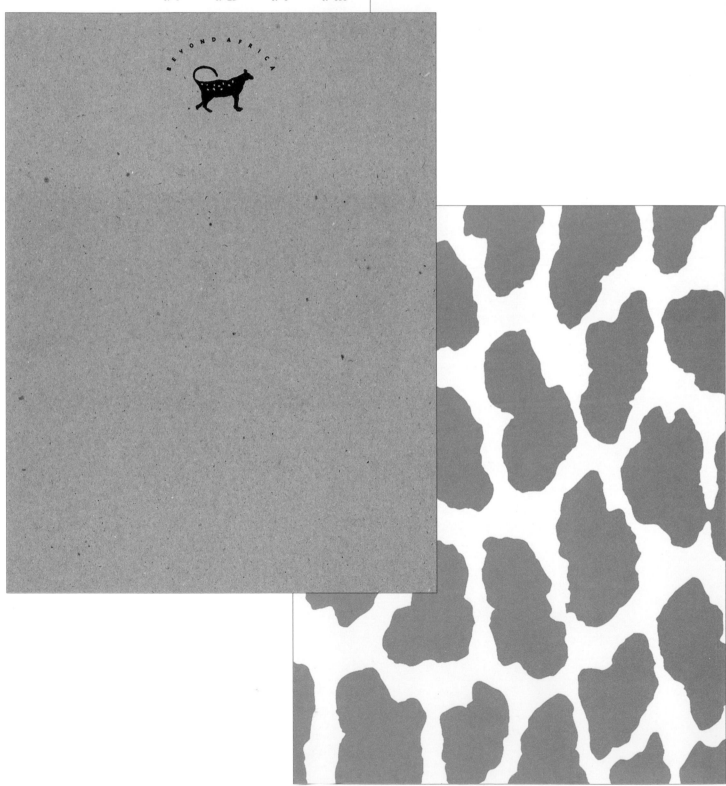

BEYOND AFRICA

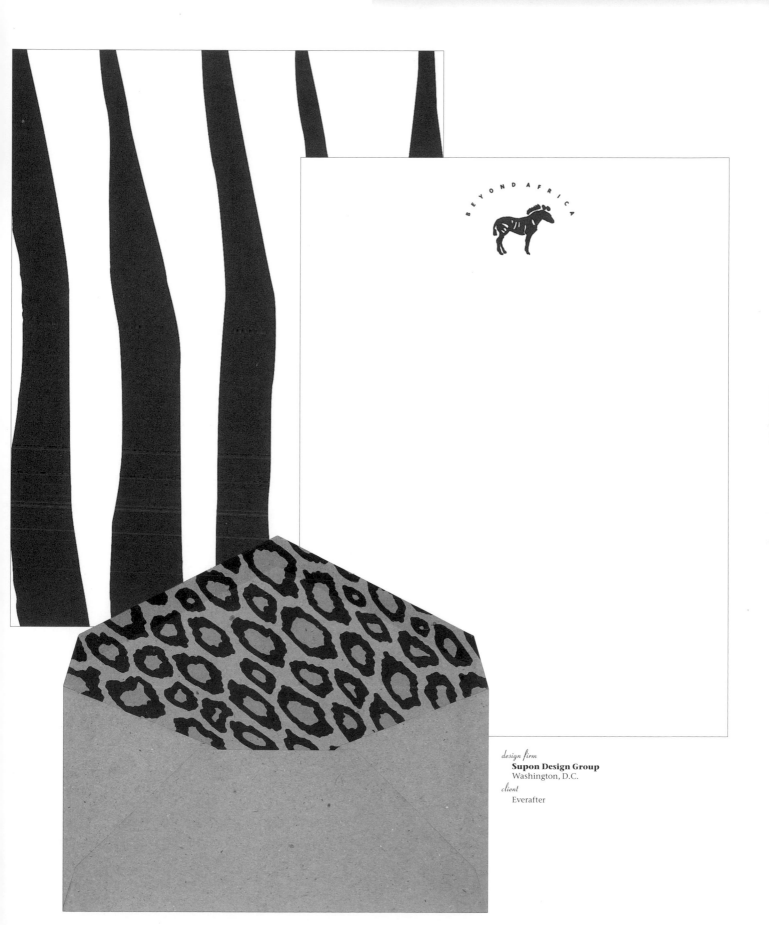

BEYOND AFRICA

design firm
Supon Design Group
Washington, D.C.
client
Everafter

C - 20
M - 70
Y - 80
K - 0

C - 80
M - 10
Y - 100
K - 0

C - 50
M - 40
Y - 50
K - 10

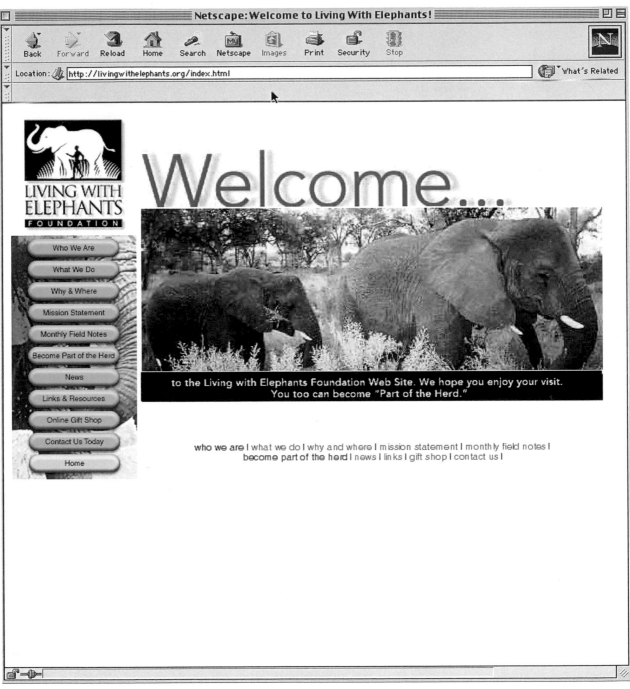

design firm
Tom Fowler, Inc.
Norwalk, Connecticut
client
Living with Elephants Foundation

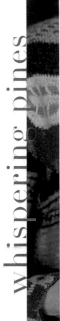

whispering pines

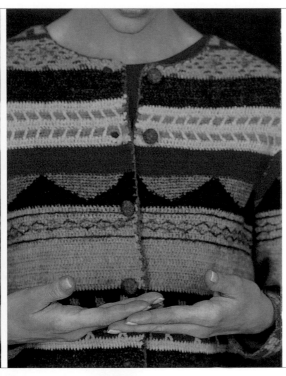

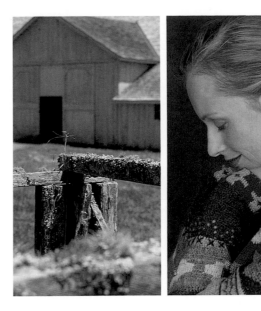

The world is not all angles and edges.

C - 0	C - 60	C - 10	C - 80
M - 90	M - 40	M - 20	M - 40
Y - 60	Y - 30	Y - 80	Y - 20
K - 25	K - 0	K - 10	K - 40

design firm
Leslie Evans Design Associates
Portland, Maine
client
Robert Scott—David Brooks

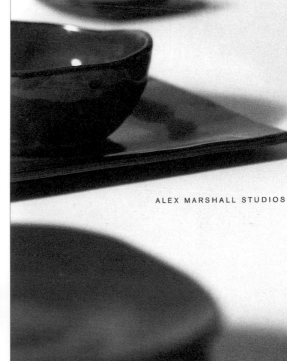

ALEX MARSHALL STUDIOS

design firm
Natalie Kitamura Design
San Francisco, California
client
Alex Marshall Studios

C - 20	C - 0
M - 90	M - 0
Y - 90	Y - 0
K - 20	K - 100

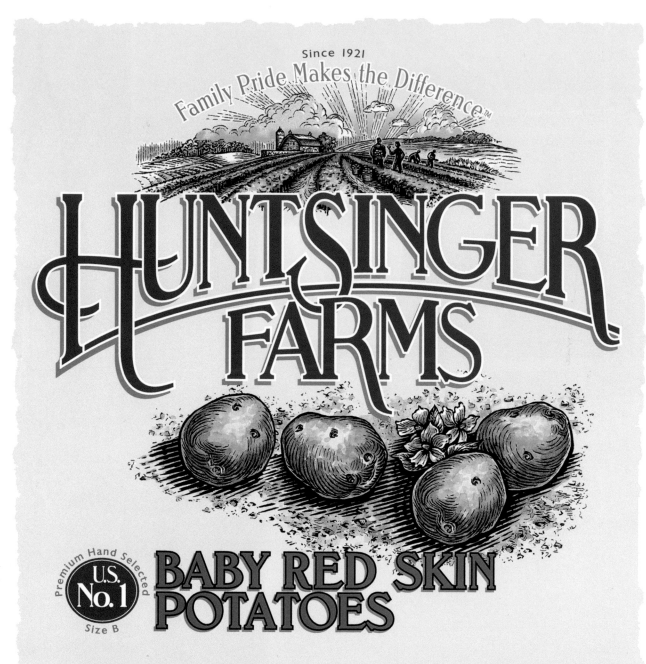

Since 1921

Family Pride Makes the Difference™

HUNTSINGER FARMS

Premium Hand Selected U.S. No. 1 Size B

BABY RED SKIN POTATOES

Packed by **Huntsinger Farms, Inc.**
Hegins, PA 17938

Net Wt 5 lb (2.27kg)

C - 20	C - 100	C - 10
M - 90	M - 20	M - 10
Y - 60	Y - 60	Y - 60
K - 20	K - 0	K - 0

design firm
Dean Design/Marketing Group
Lancaster, Pennsylvania
client
Huntsinger Farms

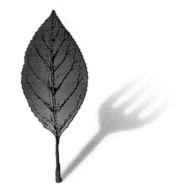

NEWLEAF

C - 79
M - 25
Y - 90
K - 34

C - 71
M - 28
Y - 73
K - 52

design firm
Conover
San Diego, California
client
SD Malkin

C - 100
M - 0
Y - 100
K - 40

C - 20
M - 75
Y - 100
K - 0

GEORGIA ORGANICS

design firm
B-Man Design
Atlanta, Georgia
client
Georgia Organics

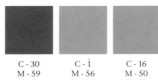

C - 30
M - 59
Y - 87
K - 44

C - 1
M - 56
Y - 95
K - 0

C - 16
M - 50
Y - 77
K - 6

design firm
AGC—Mktg. Comm. Dept.
Phoenix, Arizona
client
Deer Creek Golf Club at Meadow Ranch

DEER CREEK
GOLF CLUB
at Meadow Ranch

CAMPION WALKER
garden design

1044 PALMS
BOULEVARD
VENICE, CALIFORNIA
90291

❖

PHONE: 310 392 3535
FAX: 310 581 9405

design firm
Erbe Design
South Pasadena, California
client
Campion Walker

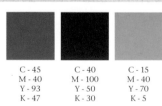

C - 45	C - 40	C - 15
M - 40	M - 100	M - 40
Y - 93	Y - 50	Y - 70
K - 47	K - 30	K - 5

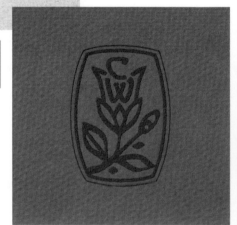

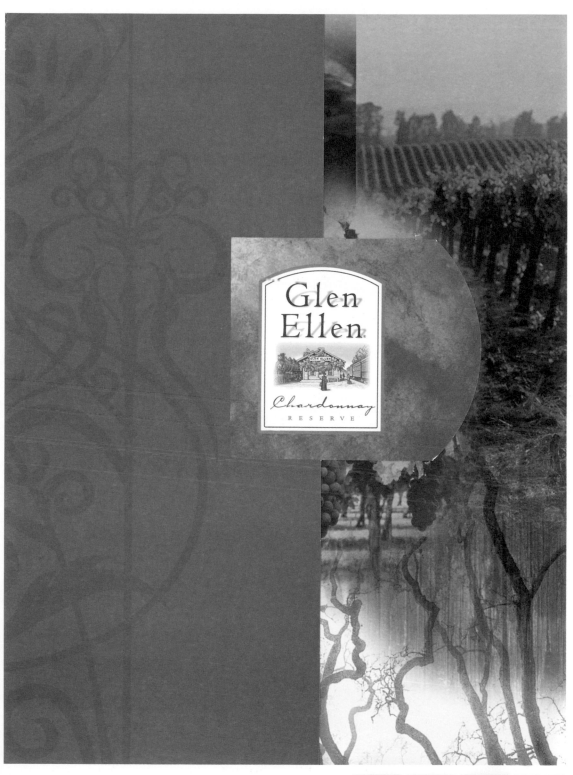

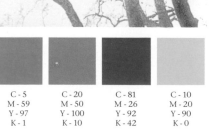

C - 5	C - 20	C - 81	C - 10
M - 59	M - 50	M - 26	M - 20
Y - 97	Y - 100	Y - 92	Y - 90
K - 1	K - 10	K - 42	K - 0

design firm
Halleck
Palo Alto, California
client
United Distillers & Vintners

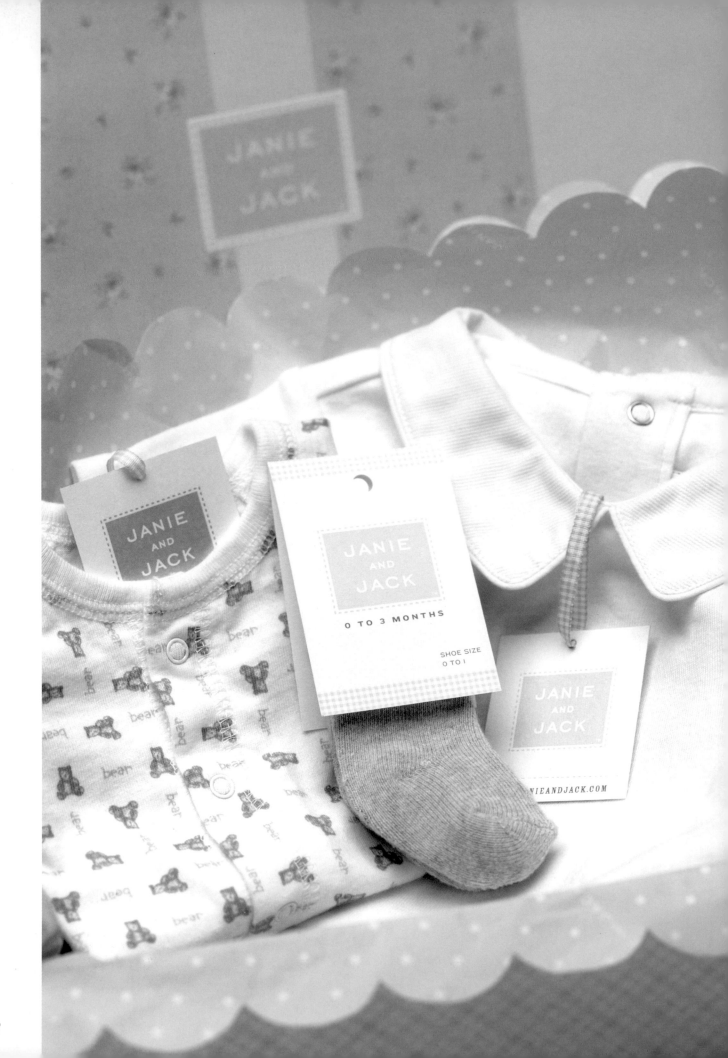

ReTReAT
Living the Spa Lifestyle

design firm
The Wecker Group
Monterey, California

C - 38
M - 2
Y - 26
K - 0

C - 38
M - 14
Y - 1
K - 0

C - 10
M - 4
Y - 3
K - 0

C - 9
M - 1
Y - 34
K - 0

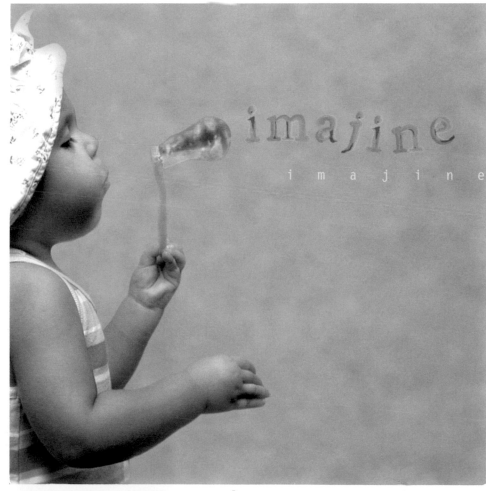

C - 3
M - 12
Y - 40
K - 0

C - 22
M - 23
Y - 4
K - 0

C - 0
M - 22
Y - 11
K - 0

C - 16
M - 4
Y - 26
K - 0

C - 28
M - 16
Y - 4
K - 1

C - 29
M - 1
Y - 17
K - 0

design firm
Im-aj Communications & Design, Inc.
West Kingston, Rhode Island

client
Im-aj Communications & Design, Inc.

(opposite) design firm
Michael Osborne Design
San Francisco, California

client
Janie and Jack

C - 13
M - 31
Y - 75
K - 0

C - 45
M - 27
Y - 53
K - 0

C - 19
M - 32
Y - 20
K - 0

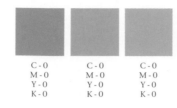

C - 0
M - 0
Y - 0
K - 0

C - 0
M - 0
Y - 0
K - 0

C - 0
M - 0
Y - 0
K - 0

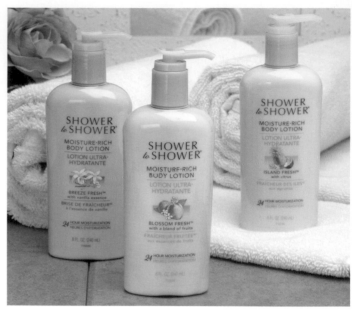

design firm
Bailey Design Group Inc.
Plymouth Meeting, Pennsylvania

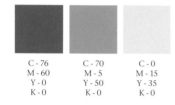

C - 76
M - 60
Y - 0
K - 0

C - 70
M - 5
Y - 50
K - 0

C - 0
M - 15
Y - 35
K - 0

water·color℠

A Southern Coastal Landscape. **FLORIDA**

design firm
David Carter Design Assoc.
Dallas, Texas
client
Arvida

C - 0
M - 0
Y - 0
K - 0

C - 0
M - 40
Y - 20
K - 10

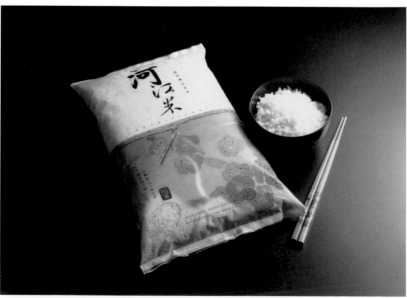

design firm
Ukulele Design Consultants Pte Ltd
Singapore (Singapore)
client
Ng Nam Bee Marketing Pte Ltd

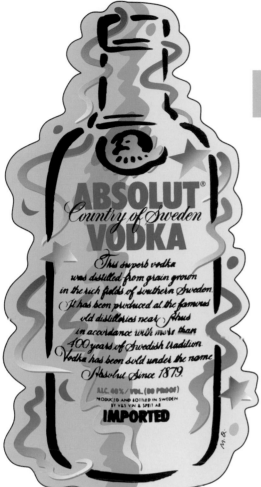

design firm
Designation
New York, New York

C - 63	C - 51	C - 1	C - 97	C - 0
M - 0	M - 81	M - 14	M - 56	M - 68
Y - 29	Y - 1	Y - 91	Y - 3	Y - 95
K - 0	K - 0	K - 0	K - 1	K - 0

C - 10	C - 0	C - 95
M - 50	M - 100	M - 75
Y - 90	Y - 100	Y - 35
K - 0	K - 0	K - 15

design firm
Interrobang Design Collaborative
Richmond, Virginia
client
Moodwax Candle Co.

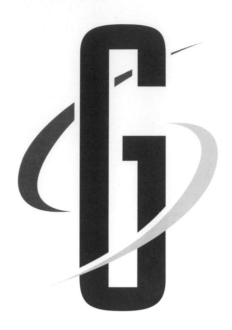

GRAPHICSOURCE
PRODUCTION/FULFILLMENT

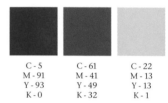

C - 5	C - 61	C - 22
M - 91	M - 41	M - 13
Y - 93	Y - 49	Y - 13
K - 0	K - 32	K - 1

design firm
Becker Design
Milwaukee, Wisconsin
client
Graphic Source

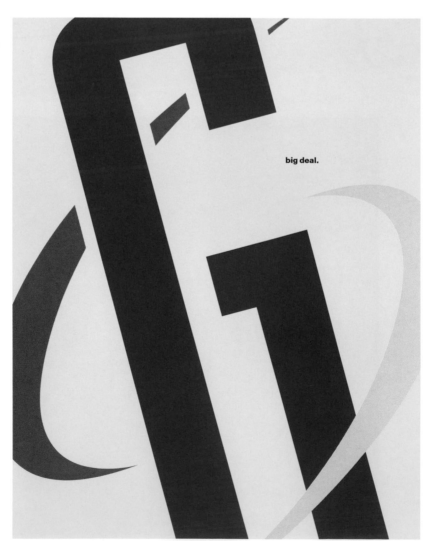

big deal.

C - 33
M - 19
Y - 18
K - 14

C - 30
M - 95
Y - 100
K - 33

design firm
Pearlfisher
London (England)

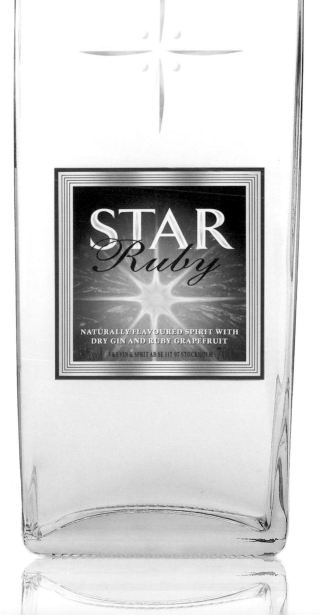

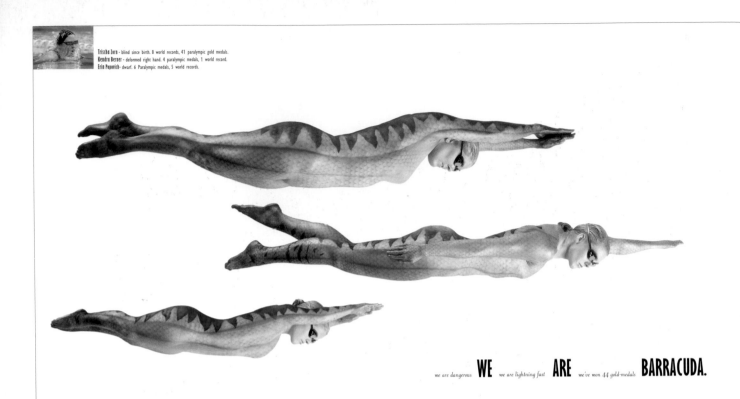

Trischa Zorn - blind since birth. 8 world records, 41 paralympic gold medals.
Kendra Berner - deformed right hand. 4 paralympic medals, 1 world record.
Erin Popovich - dwarf. 6 Paralympic medals, 5 world records.

we are dangerous **WE** we are lightning fast **ARE** we've won 44 gold-medals **BARRACUDA.**

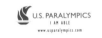

U.S. PARALYMPICS
I AM ABLE
www.usparalympics.com

A division of the US Olympic Committee

design firm
After Hours Creative
Phoenix, Arizona

C - 80   C - 56   C - 27
M - 67   M - 39   M - 18
Y - 38   Y - 18   Y - 7
K - 17   K - 3   K - 0

C - 49   C - 57   C - 100   C - 0
M - 1   M - 0   M - 0   M - 0
Y - 0   Y - 100   Y - 44   Y - 0
K - 0   K - 0   K - 0   K - 100

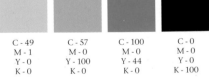

Intelsat

design firm
Addison
San Francisco, California
client
Intelsat

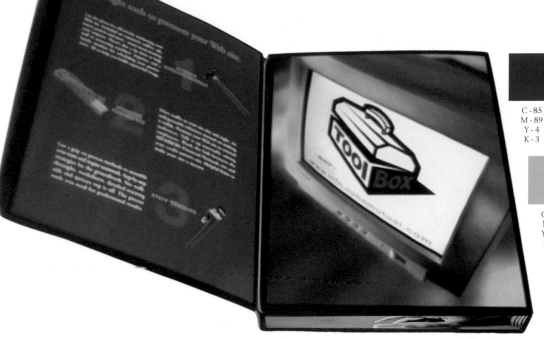

The right tools to promote your Web site.

C - 85	C - 55
M - 89	M - 82
Y - 4	Y - 18
K - 3	K - 18

C - 58	C - 13
M - 2	M - 95
Y - 35	Y - 43
K - 1	K - 14

design firm
Becker Design
Milwaukee, Wisconsin
client
ToolBox

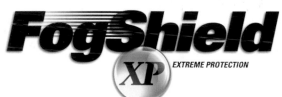

design firm
Sagmeister Inc.
New York, New York

design firm
McElveney & Palozzi Design Group
Rochester, New York
client
Bausch & Lomb

C - 12	C - 0
M - 1	M - 0
Y - 0	Y - 0
K - 1	K - 0

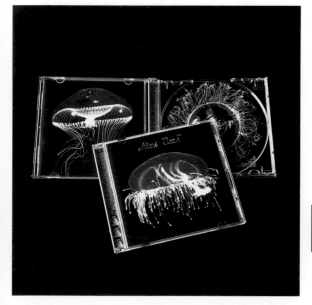

C - 93	C - 11	C - 82
M - 77	M - 99	M - 49
Y - 0	Y - 78	Y - 0
K - 0	K - 0	K - 0

design firm
McElveney & Palozzi Design Group
Rochester, New York
client
UNYCoR

C - 100
M - 0
Y - 18
K - 18

C - 100
M - 94
Y - 0
K - 6

C - 0
M - 0
Y - 0
K - 100

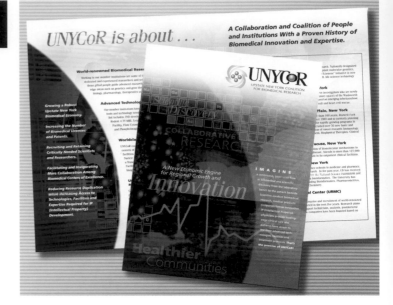

design firm
Stan Gellman Graphic Design
St. Louis, Missouri

C - 27
M - 53
Y - 99
K - 18

C - 22
M - 36
Y - 99
K - 3

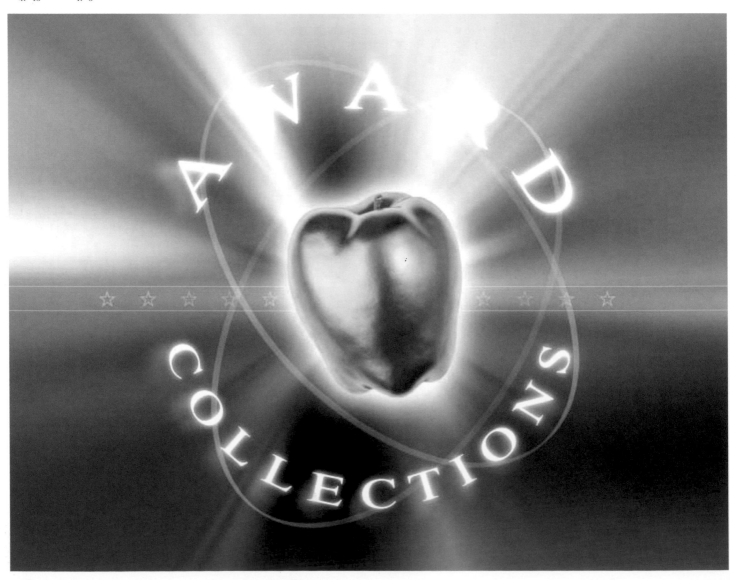

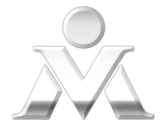

design firm
Dotzler Creative Arts
Omaha, Nebraska

M A R K E T P L A C E   V I S I O N

C - 0	C - 100
M - 2	M - 100
Y - 67	Y - 0
K - 1	K - 0

design firm
5D Studio
Malibu, California
client
Vecta

C - 40	C - 4	C - 1	C - 75
M - 23	M - 0	M - 82	M - 16
Y - 25	Y - 83	Y - 95	Y - 46
K - 12	K - 0	K - 15	K - 15

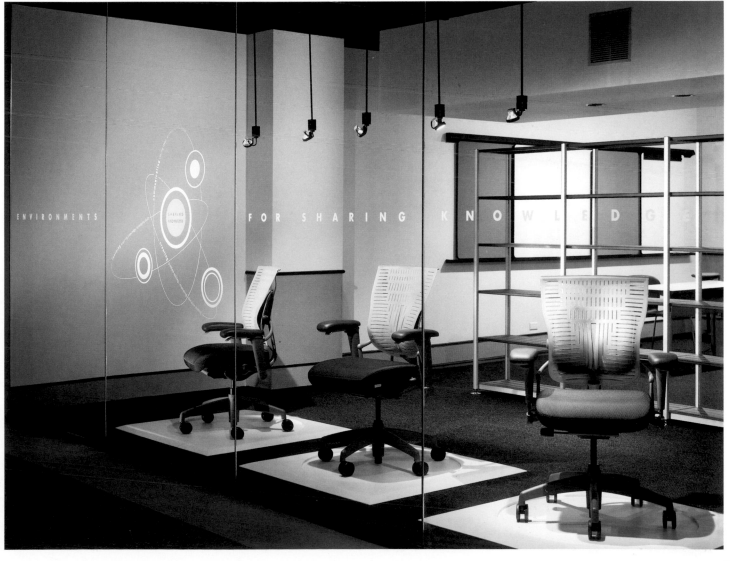

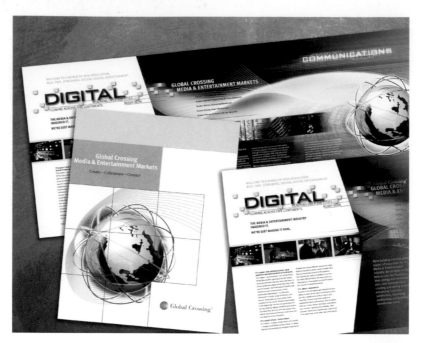

design firm
McElveney & Palozzi Design Group
Rochester, New York
client
Global Crossing

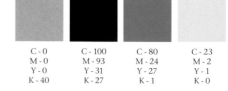

C - 0	C - 100	C - 80	C - 23
M - 0	M - 93	M - 24	M - 2
Y - 0	Y - 31	Y - 27	Y - 1
K - 40	K - 27	K - 1	K - 0

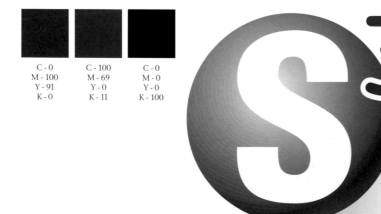

C - 0	C - 100	C - 0
M - 100	M - 69	M - 0
Y - 91	Y - 0	Y - 0
K - 0	K - 11	K - 100

S³

show. secure. sell.

design firm
Louis & Partners Design
Bath, Ohio
client
S3

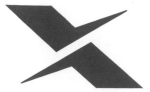

XELUS

design firm
McElveney & Palozzi Design Group
Rochester, New York

client
Xelus

C - 87
M - 54
Y - 5
K - 1

C - 0
M - 0
Y - 0
K - 0

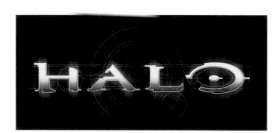

C - 67
M - 45
Y - 28
K - 0

C - 90
M - 94
Y - 90
K - 93

C - 07
M - 51
Y - 57
K - 16

design firm
Mike Salisbury L.L.C.
Venice, California

client
Bonsee Software

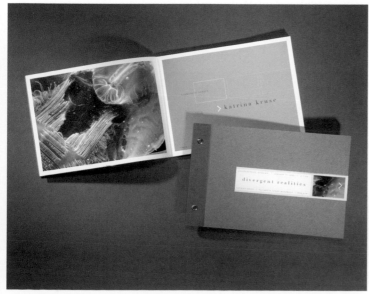

design firm
Belyea
Seattle, Washington

client
ColorGraphics

C - 14
M - 44
Y - 43
K - 2

C - 67
M - 40
Y - 31
K - 31

C - 38
M - 0
Y - 5
K - 0

C - 1
M - 58
Y - 73
K - 0

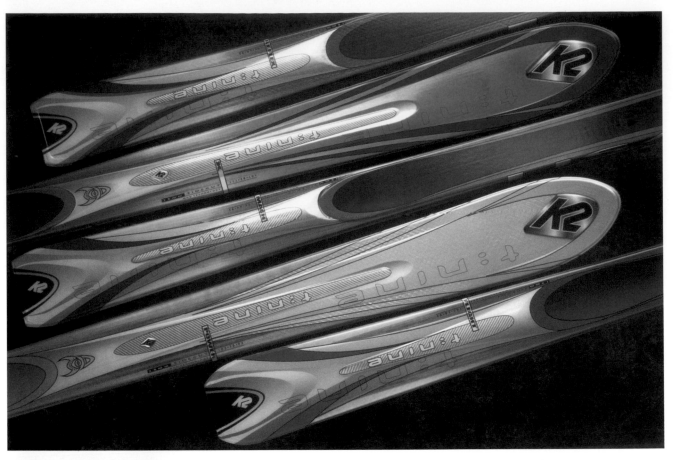

C - 60
M - 53
Y - 45
K - 44

C - 3
M - 93
Y - 77
K - 7

C - 80
M - 57
Y - 5
K - 5

design firm
Hornall Anderson Design Works
Seattle, Washington

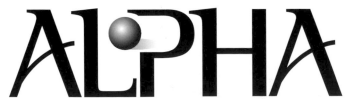

High-Shrink Solutions

C - 0
M - 75
Y - 75
K - 0

C - 0
M - 0
Y - 0
K - 100

design firm
Louis & Partners Design
Bath, Ohio
client
Alpha

C - 100   C - 33
M - 97   M - 19
Y - 2   Y - 18
K - 4   K - 14

design firm
Pearlfisher
London (England)

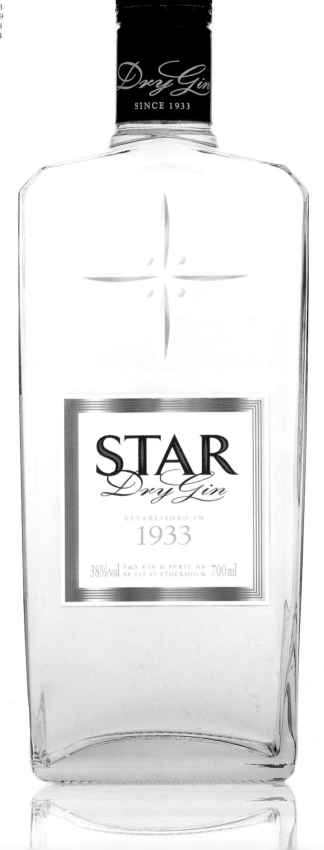

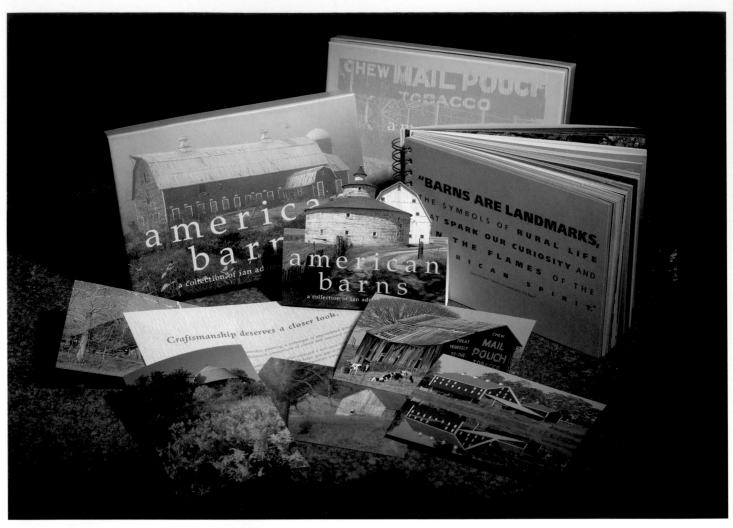

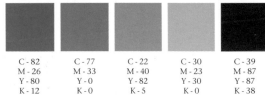

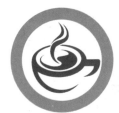

design firm
Louis & Partners Design
Bath, Ohio
client
Rohrich

C - 82	C - 77	C - 22	C - 30	C - 39
M - 26	M - 33	M - 40	M - 23	M - 87
Y - 80	Y - 0	Y - 82	Y - 30	Y - 87
K - 12	K - 0	K - 5	K - 0	K - 38

Cafe Bohéme
COFFEE HOUSE

C - 0	C - 72
M - 24	M - 15
Y - 100	Y - 0
K - 31	K - 56

design firm
Louis & Partners Design
Bath, Ohio
client
Café Bohéme

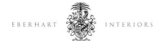

Kristen Eberhart Kottke

EBERHART INTERIORS

4385 Stone Canyon Drive
San Jose, California 95136

eberhartid@aol.com
p 408.229.0576 f 408.578.9958

EBERHART INTERIORS

EBERHART 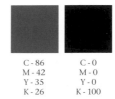 INTERIORS

C - 86
M - 42
Y - 35
K - 26

C - 0
M - 0
Y - 0
K - 100

design firm
Becker Design
Milwaukee, Wisconsin
client
Eberhart Interiors

4385 Stone Canyon Drive San Jose, California 95136 eberhartid@aol.com p 408.229.0576 f 408.578.9958

C - 100	C - 25	C - 27	C - 12	C - 0	C - 64	C - 5	C - 72	C - 0	C - 0
M - 68	M - 38	M - 100	M - 100	M - 0	M - 0	M - 60	M - 88	M - 19	M - 36
Y - 0	Y - 51	Y - 79	Y - 79	Y - 16	Y - 62	Y - 62	Y - 51	Y - 31	Y - 46
K - 25	K - 3	K - 24	K - 63	K - 54	K - 53	K - 15	K - 0	K - 5	K - 44

design firm
Bailey Design Group
Plymouth Meeting, Pennsylvania

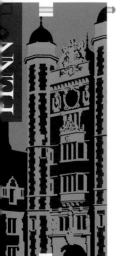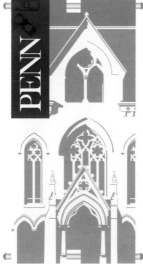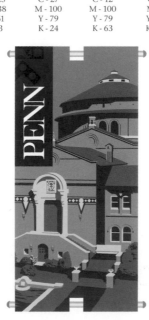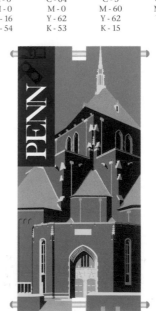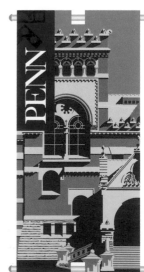

313

C - 61
M - 31
Y - 83
K - 54

C - 94
M - 81
Y - 25
K - 42

C - 4
M - 48
Y - 59
K - 1

C - 0
M - 89
Y - 93
K - 0

C - 84
M - 27
Y - 1
K - 1

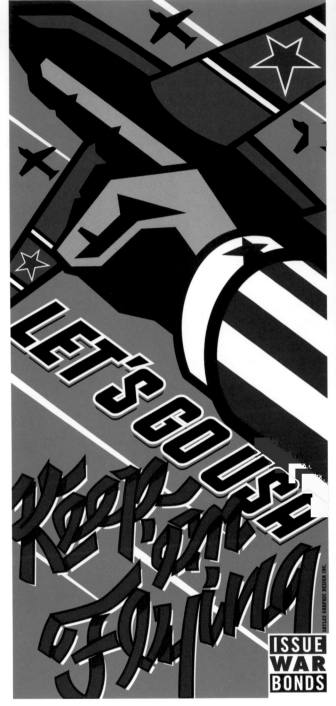

design firm
Sayles Graphic Design
Des Moines, Iowa
client
"Art Fights Back"

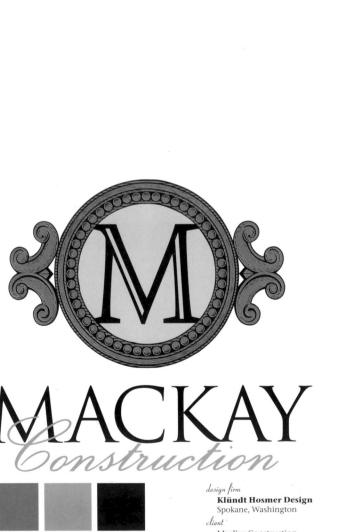

C - 18
M - 49
Y - 79
K - 12

C - 0
M - 6
Y - 91
K - 36

C - 0
M - 0
Y - 0
K - 100

design firm
Klündt Hosmer Design
Spokane, Washington
client
MacKay Construction

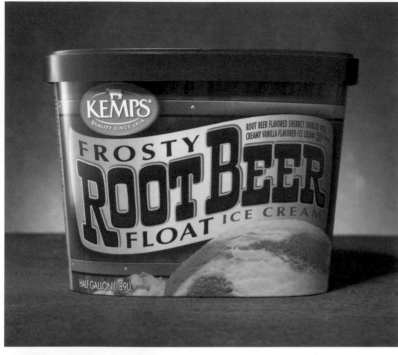

design firm
Compass Design
Minneapolis, Minnesota

design firm
Sayles Graphic Design
Des Moines, Iowa
client
"Art Fights Back"

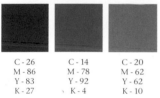

C - 26	C - 14	C - 20
M - 86	M - 78	M - 62
Y - 83	Y - 92	Y - 62
K - 27	K - 4	K - 10

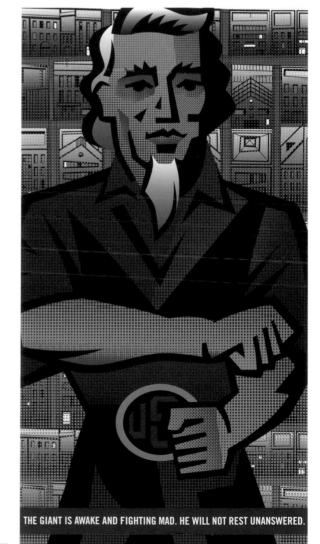

THE GIANT IS AWAKE AND FIGHTING MAD. HE WILL NOT REST UNANSWERED.

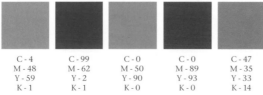

C - 4	C - 99	C - 0	C - 0	C - 47
M - 48	M - 62	M - 50	M - 89	M - 35
Y - 59	Y - 2	Y - 90	Y - 93	Y - 33
K - 1	K - 1	K - 0	K - 0	K - 14

admission is free

dinner
activities
music
prizes
museums

shuttle service
is provided
from each
hospital campus

note:
parking is limited
at museum center

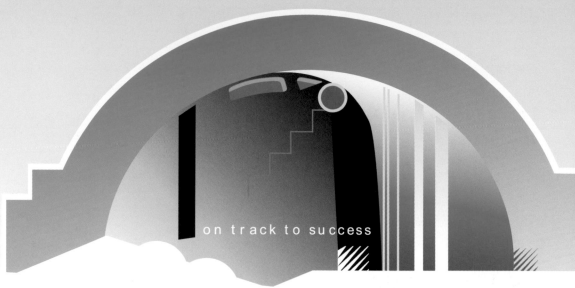

on track to success

march 7 & 8 **2002**

mercy health partners employee celebration

cincinnati museum center
6pm–midnight

look for your invitation in the mail

design firm
Five Visual Communication and Design
West Chester, Ohio

C - 72   C - 71   C - 22
M - 33   M - 99   M - 14
Y - 0   Y - 21   Y - 46
K - 1   K - 7   K - 2

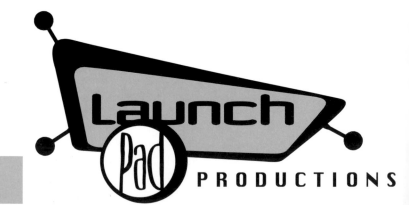

design firm
Klündt Hosmer Design
Spokane, Washington
client
Launch Pad

C - 0   C - 0
M - 0   M - 25
Y - 0   Y - 90
K - 100   K - 0

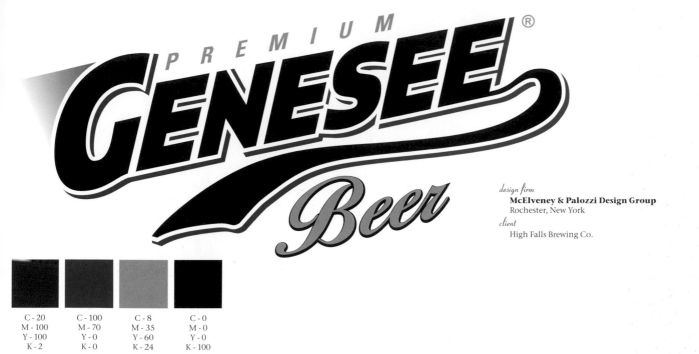

design firm
McElveney & Palozzi Design Group
Rochester, New York

client
High Falls Brewing Co.

C - 20	C - 100	C - 8	C - 0
M - 100	M - 70	M - 35	M - 0
Y - 100	Y - 0	Y - 60	Y - 0
K - 2	K - 0	K - 24	K - 100

design firm
Designation
New York, New York

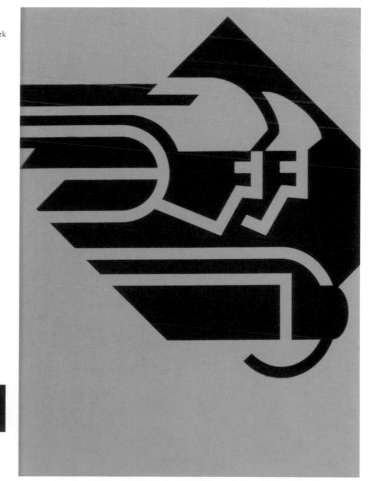

C - 1	C - 90
M - 41	M - 71
Y - 93	Y - 25
K - 0	K - 51

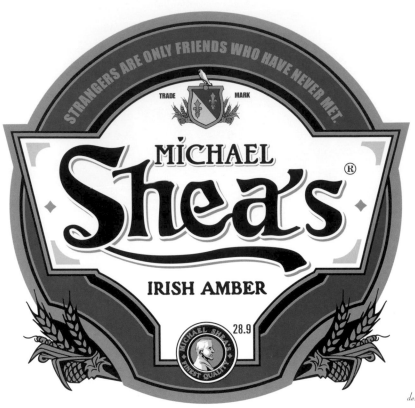

design firm
McElveney & Palozzi Design Group
Rochester, New York
client
High Falls Brewing Co.

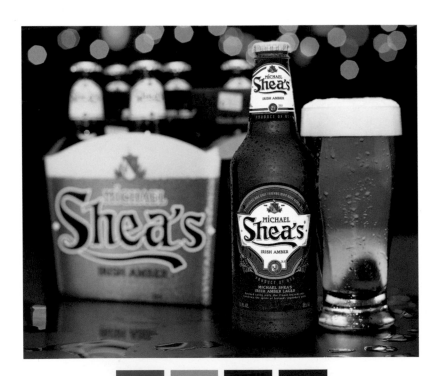

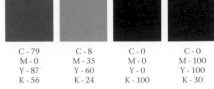

C - 79	C - 8	C - 0	C - 0
M - 0	M - 35	M - 0	M - 100
Y - 87	Y - 60	Y - 0	Y - 100
K - 56	K - 24	K - 100	K - 30

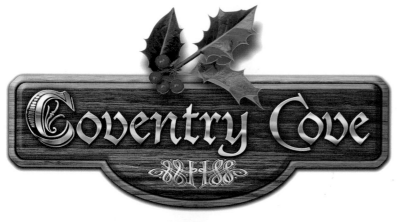

design firm
Armijo Design Office
Torrance, California

client
Lemax

C - 79	C - 4	C - 6	C - 24
M - 23	M - 89	M - 11	M - 54
Y - 89	Y - 86	Y - 64	Y - 71
K - 1	K - 4	K - 0	K - 0

C - 16	C - 24	C - 0
M - 88	M - 76	M - 50
Y - 67	Y - 95	Y - 85
K - 5	K - 18	K - 0

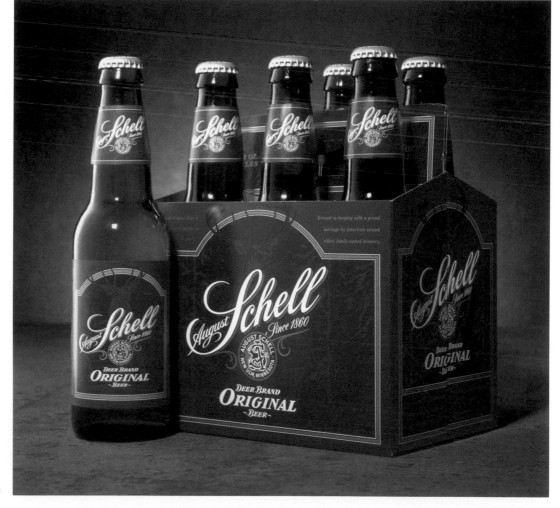

design firm
Compass Design
Minneapolis, Minnesota

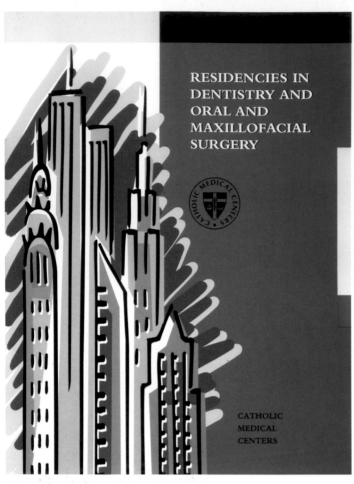

RESIDENCIES IN
DENTISTRY AND
ORAL AND
MAXILLOFACIAL
SURGERY

CATHOLIC
MEDICAL
CENTERS

C - 62
M - 20
Y - 67
K - 20

C - 77
M - 39
Y - 0
K - 0

C - 1
M - 84
Y - 95
K - 0

C - 37
M - 2
Y - 1
K - 0

design firm
Designation
New York, New York

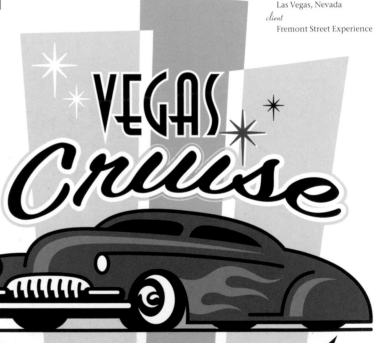

design firm
Brown & Partners
Las Vegas, Nevada
client
Fremont Street Experience

C - 3
M - 0
Y - 0
K - 22

C - 0
M - 75
Y - 100
K - 25

C - 100
M - 91
Y - 0
K - 44

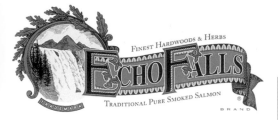

FINEST HARDWOODS & HERBS

TRADITIONAL PURE SMOKED SALMON

BRAND

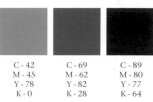

C - 42	C - 69	C - 89
M - 45	M - 62	M - 80
Y - 78	Y - 82	Y - 77
K - 0	K - 28	K - 64

design firm
Mark Oliver Inc.
Solvang, California
client
Ocean Beauty Seafood

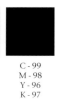

C - 92	C - 46	C - 99
M - 50	M - 51	M - 98
Y - 50	Y - 82	Y - 96
K - 48	K - 3	K - 97

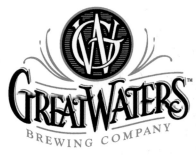

GREATWATERS™

BREWING COMPANY

design firm
Compass Design
Minneapolis, Minnesota
client
Great Waters Brewing Co.

C - 2	C - 35	C - 100	C - 54
M - 96	M - 12	M - 40	M - 44
Y - 78	Y - 19	Y - 0	Y - 24
K - 35	K - 31	K - 55	K - 76

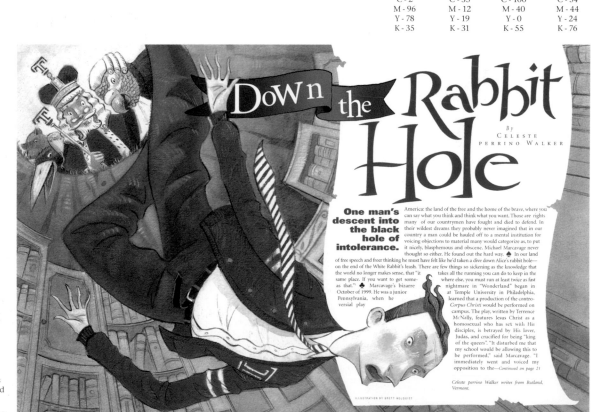

DoWn the Rabbit Hole

By
CELESTE PERRINO WALKER

One man's descent into the black hole of intolerance.

America: the land of the free and the home of the brave, where you can say what you think and think what you want. Those are rights many of our countrymen have fought and died to defend. In their wildest dreams they probably never imagined that in our country a man could be hauled off to a mental institution for voicing objections to material many would categorize as, to put it nicely, blasphemous and obscene. Michael Marcavage never thought so either. He found out the hard way. ♣ In our land of free speech and freer thinking he must have felt like he'd taken a dive down Alice's rabbit hole—on the end of the White Rabbit's leash. There are few things so sickening as the knowledge that the world no longer makes sense, that "it takes all the running you can do to keep in the same place. If you want to get some-where else, you must run at least twice as fast as that." ♣ Marcavage's bizarre nightmare in "Wonderland" began in October of 1999. He was a junior at Temple University in Philadelphia, Pennsylvania, when he learned that a production of the contro-versial play *Corpus Christi* would be performed on campus. The play, written by Terrence McNally, features Jesus Christ as a homosexual who has sex with His disciples, is betrayed by His lover, Judas, and crucified for being "king of the queers". "It disturbed me that my school would be allowing this to be performed," said Marcavage. "I immediately went and voiced my opposition to the—*Continued on page 21*

Celeste perrino Walker writes from Rutland, Vermont.

ILLUSTRATION BY BRETT HELQUIST

design firm
Dever Designs
Laurel, Maryland
client
Liberty Magazine

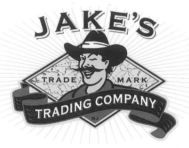

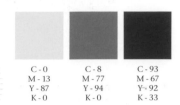

C - 0
M - 13
Y - 87
K - 0

C - 8
M - 77
Y - 94
K - 0

C - 93
M - 67
Y - 92
K - 33

design firm
Compass Design
Minneapolis, Minnesota
client
Jake's Trading Company

design firm
Dotzler Creative Arts
Omaha, Nebraska

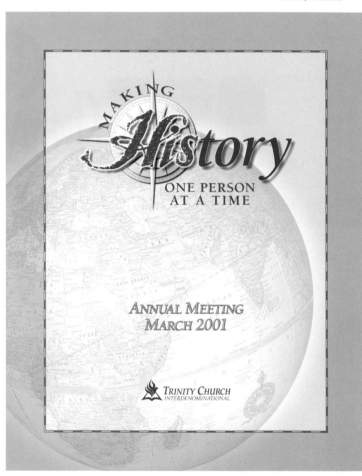

C - 98
M - 69
Y - 0
K - 3

C - 8
M - 98
Y - 92
K - 1

C - 0
M - 25
Y - 68
K - 23

design firm
Compass Design
Minneapolis, Minnesota

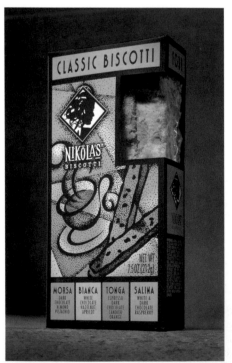

C - 0
M - 25
Y - 67
K - 0

C - 62
M - 51
Y - 49
K - 63

C - 13
M - 72
Y - 88
K - 3

322

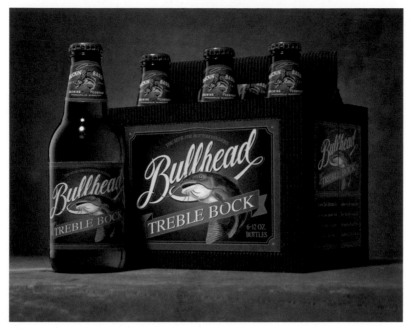

C - 34	C - 60	C - 13
M - 41	M - 53	M - 72
Y - 75	Y - 55	Y - 88
K - 25	K - 77	K - 3

design firm
Stan Gellman Graphic Design
St. Louis, Missouri

client
University of Illinois Foundation

C - 100	C - 27	C - 24
M - 86	M - 85	M - 31
Y - 29	Y - 97	Y - 66
K - 15	K - 25	K - 1

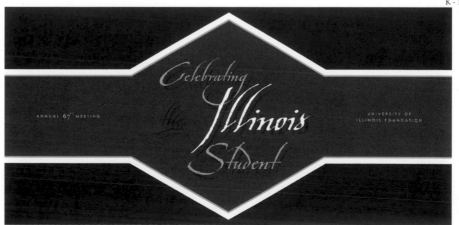

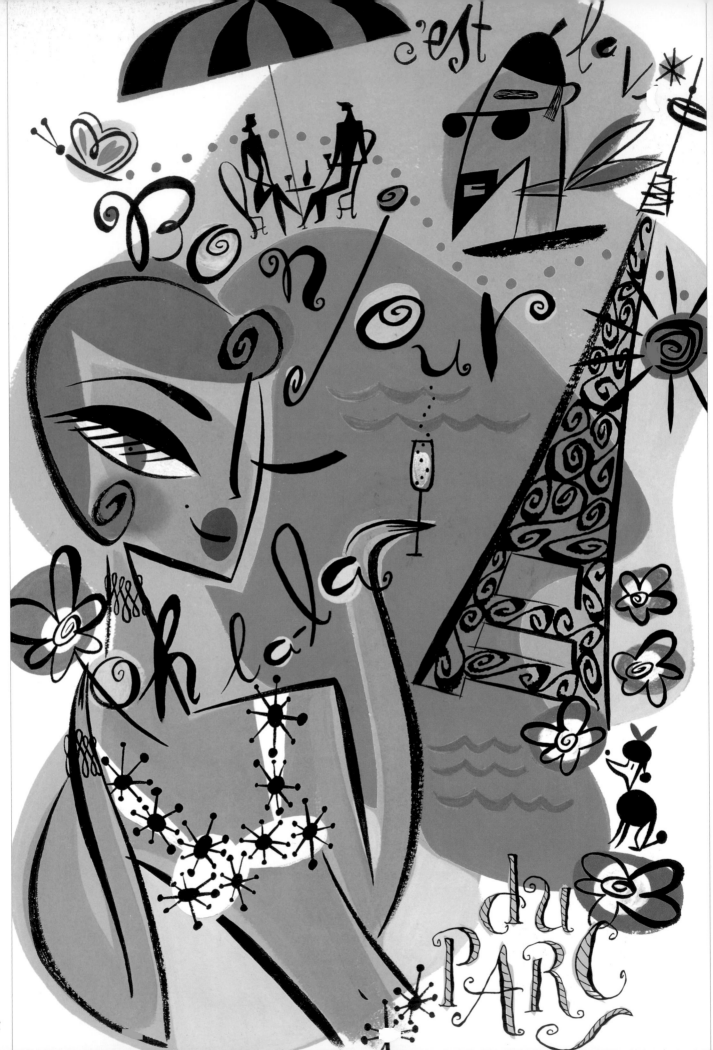

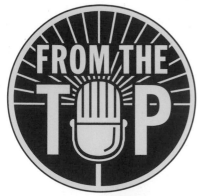

C - 2 M - 14 Y - 77 K - 0	C - 96 M - 78 Y - 3 K - 0

design firm
Corey McPherson Nash
Watertown, Massachusetts
client
Concert Productions

C - 2 M - 30 Y - 15 K - 1	C - 100 M - 100 Y - 20 K - 30	C - 20 M - 100 Y - 80 K - 0	C - 75 M - 10 Y - 0 K - 0

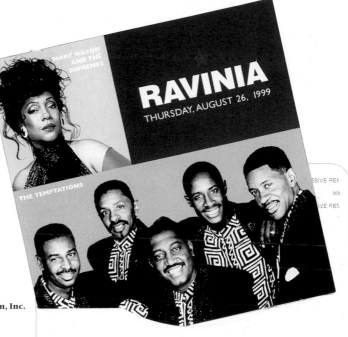

design firm
Connelly Design, Inc.
Chicago, Illinois
client
Arthur Anderson

(opposite) design firm
David Carter Design Assoc.
Dallas, Texas
client
Paris Casino Resort—Las Vegas

C - 0 M - 54 Y - 72 K - 0	C - 20 M - 58 Y - 3 K - 0	C - 45 M - 5 Y - 75 K - 0	C - 70 M - 19 Y - 20 K - 14

design firm
Louis & Partners Design
Bath, Ohio
client
San Francisco Oven

C - 43	C - 7	C - 41	C - 18
M - 38	M - 16	M - 50	M - 78
Y - 59	Y - 63	Y - 61	Y - 65
K - 5	K - 0	K - 11	K - 28

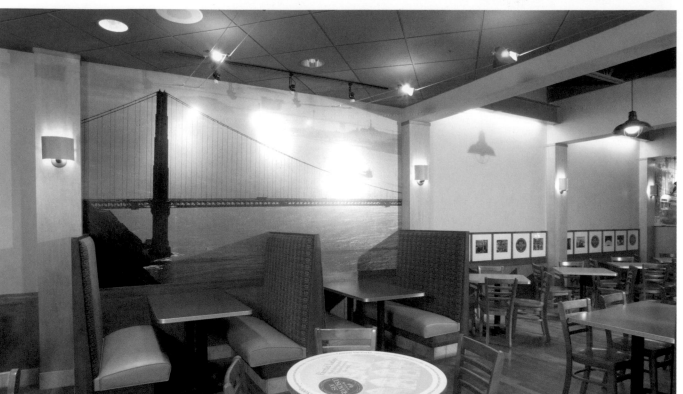

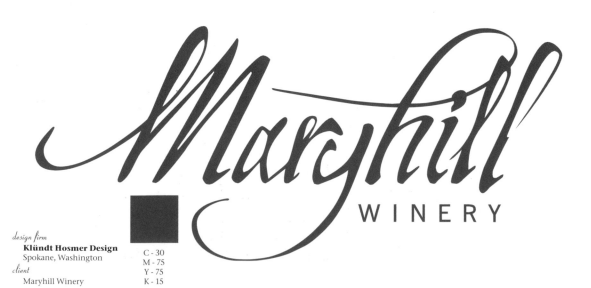

design firm
Klündt Hosmer Design
Spokane, Washington
client
Maryhill Winery

C - 30
M - 75
Y - 75
K - 15

C - 5	C - 3	C - 0
M - 92	M - 22	M - 0
Y - 80	Y - 57	Y - 0
K - 12	K - 0	K - 100

design firm
Slanting Rain Graphic Design
Logan, Utah

client
National Council on Education
for the Ceramic Arts

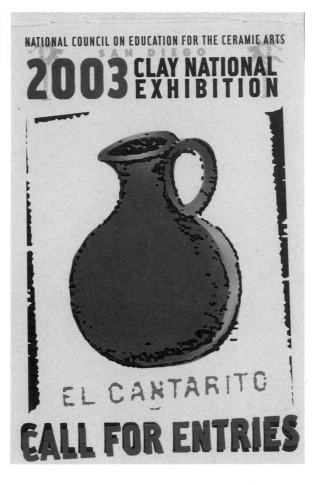

C - 27	C - 4	C - 51
M - 71	M - 6	M - 93
Y - 100	Y - 19	Y - 100
K - 17	K - 0	K - 61

design firm
Louis & Partners Design
Bath, Ohio

client
Belgium Iron Works

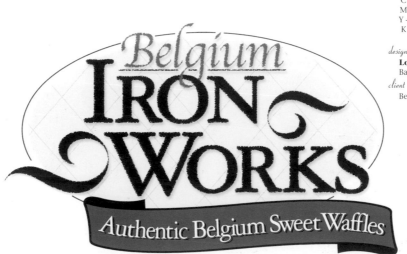

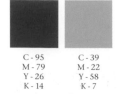

C - 95   C - 39
M - 79   M - 22
Y - 26   Y - 58
K - 14   K - 7

Barra

design firm
Addison
San Francisco, California
client
Barra Corp.

C - 32   C - 25   C - 56
M - 1   M - 63   M - 25
Y - 46   Y - 56   Y - 16
K - 1   K - 23   K - 13

design firm
Belyea
Seattle, Washington
client
ColorGraphics

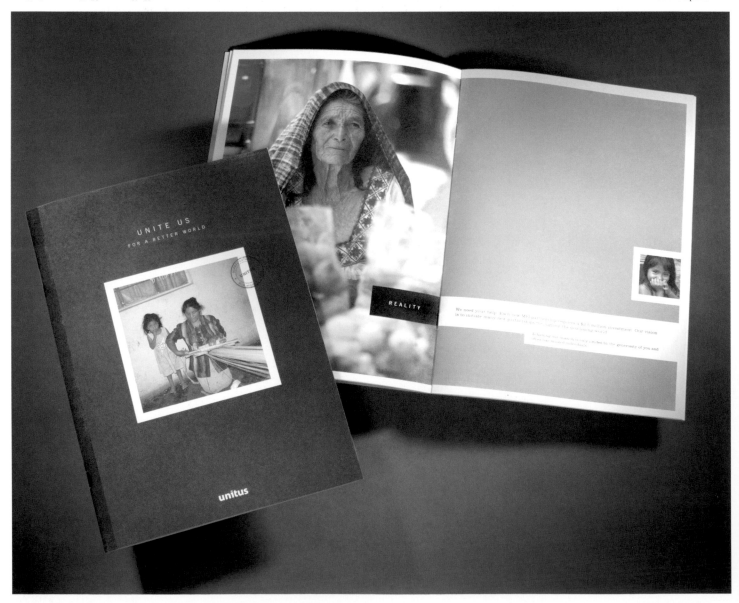

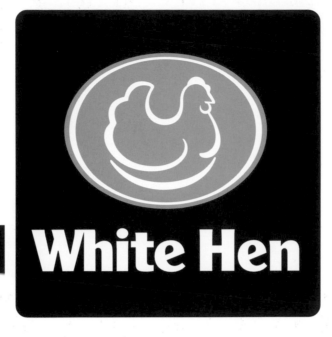

C - 5
M - 43
Y - 92
K - 0

C - 95
M - 79
Y - 36
K - 31

design firm
Addison
San Francisco, California
client
White Hen

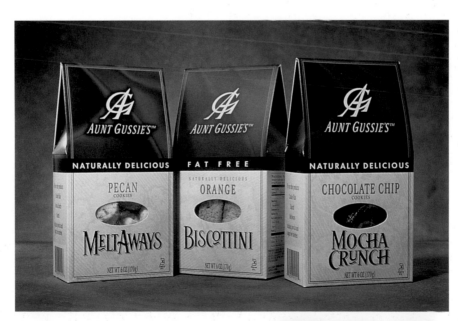

design firm
Compass Design
Minneapolis, Minnesota
client
Aunt Gussie's Cookies & Crackers

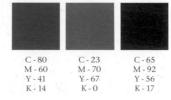

C - 80
M - 60
Y - 41
K - 14

C - 23
M - 70
Y - 67
K - 0

C - 65
M - 92
Y - 56
K - 17

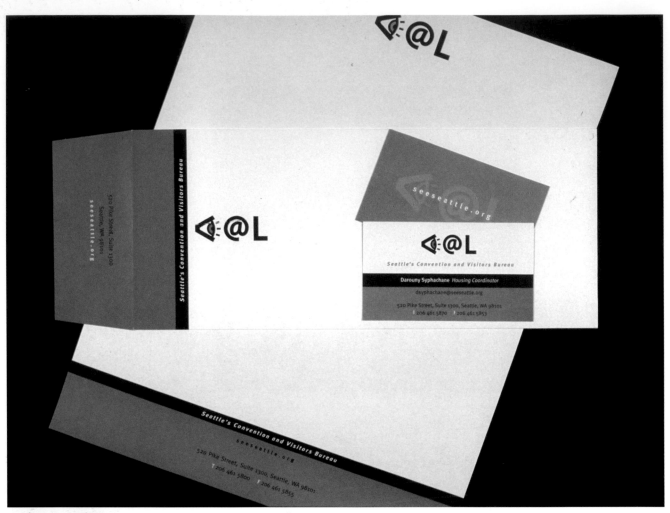

design firm
Hornall Anderson Design Works
Seattle, Washington

C - 47	C - 0
M - 47	M - 0
Y - 54	Y - 0
K - 25	K - 100

design firm
Brown & Partners
Las Vegas, Nevada
client
RS Development

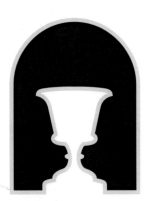

Canterra

AT THE VISTAS

C - 69	C - 4	C - 69
M - 100	M - 1	M - 100
Y - 0	Y - 0	Y - 0
K - 23	K - 18	K - 65

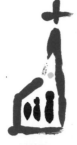

design firm
LarsonLogosEtc
Rockford, Illinois

client
Rockford Area Lutheran Ministries

C - 99	C - 0	C - 100
M - 0	M - 24	M - 100
Y - 83	Y - 98	Y - 1
K - 47	K - 0	K - 0

design firm
Phinney/Bischoff Design House
Seattle, Washington

client
Preston Gates & Ellis LLP

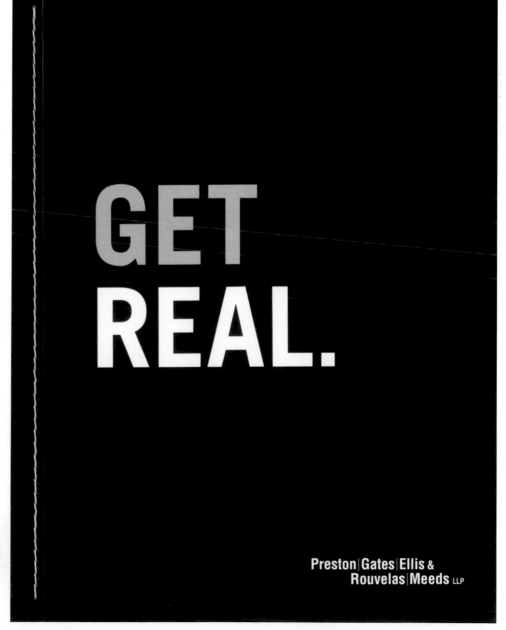

GET
REAL.

Preston|Gates|Ellis &
Rouvelas|Meeds LLP

C - 20	C - 0
M - 20	M - 0
Y - 40	Y - 0
K - 20	K - 100

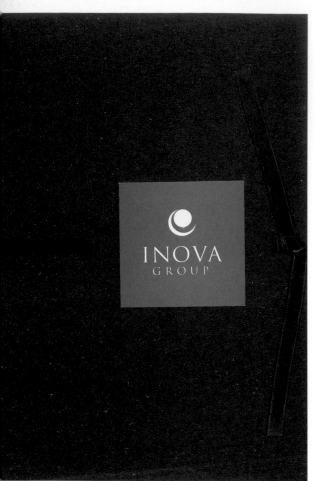

(opposite) design firm
Cahan and Associates
San Francisco, California
client
Fine Arts Museum

C - 0	C - 60	C - 40	C - 0
M - 70	M - 0	M - 0	M - 40
Y - 60	Y - 20	Y - 30	Y - 0
K - 30	K - 50	K - 20	K - 10

design firm
studioluscious
Columbus, Ohio
client
Inova Group

C - 60	C - 60
M - 50	M - 60
Y - 50	Y - 80
K - 0	K - 0

design firm
BET Weekend Magazine
Washington, D.C.
client
BET Publishing Group

C - 10	C - 15	C - 0
M - 100	M - 35	M - 10
Y - 70	Y - 55	Y - 20
K - 20	K - 10	K - 40

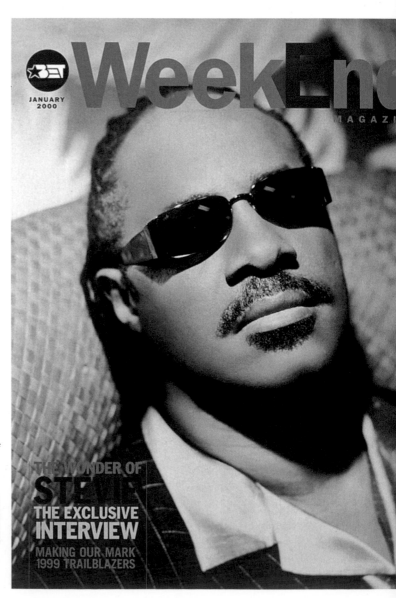

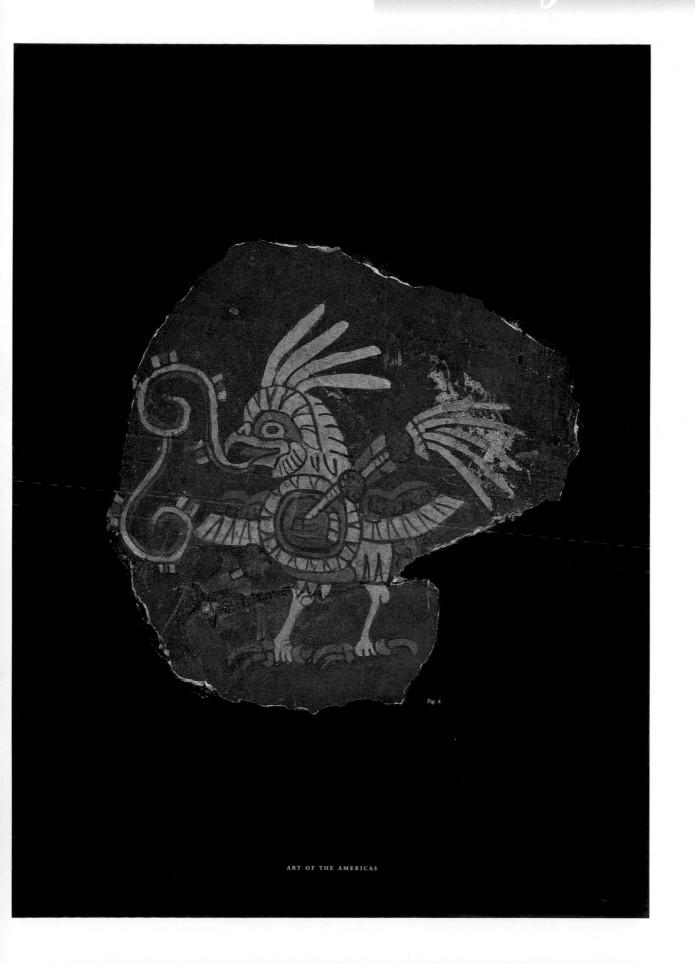

Fig. 6

ART OF THE AMERICAS

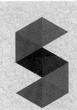

design firm
Wray Ward Laseter Advertising
Charlotte, North Carolina
client
SE Origami Festival

C - 27
M - 96
Y - 85
K - s9

C - 20
M - 35
Y - 20
K - 0

SOUTHEAST
ORIGAMI
PRODUCTIONS

Harvey Cohen
Executive Director

PO Box 2573
Charlotte, NC 28247
Direct 704.542.3991
Fax 704.544.9272

PO Box 2573 Charlotte, NC 28247 (704) 375-3692

SOUTHEASTORIGAMIPRODUCTIONS

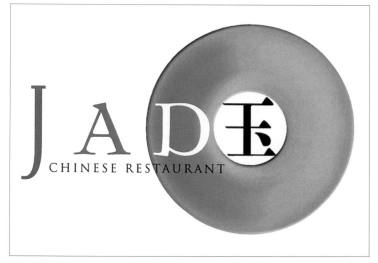

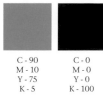

C - 90   C - 0
M - 10   M - 0
Y - 75   Y - 0
K - 5   K - 100

design firm
Design Objectives Pte Ltd
Singapore (Singapore)
client
The Fullerton Hotel, Singapore

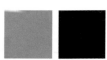

C - 10   C - 0
M - 50   M - 0
Y - 60   Y - 0
K - 20   K - 100

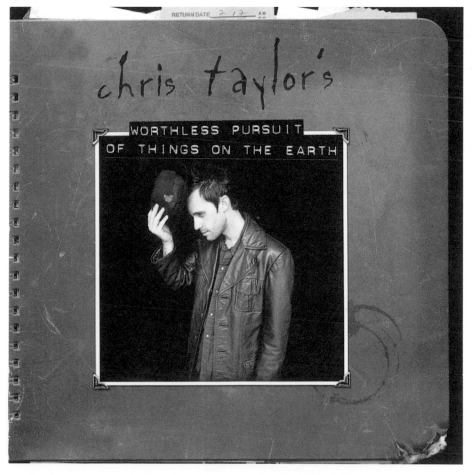

design firm
Toolbox Studios, Inc.
San Antonio, Texas
client
Rhythm House Records

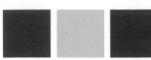

C - 12
M - 91
Y - 86
K - 2

C - 17
M - 12
Y - 97
K - 3

C - 26
M - 87
Y - 79
K - 21

2001
2002

The Contemporary
Arts Center

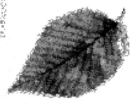

Education Programs & Exhibitions

CINCINNATI
Ohio

The
Contemporary
Arts Center

design firm
**Five Visual
Communication and Design**
West Chester, Ohio

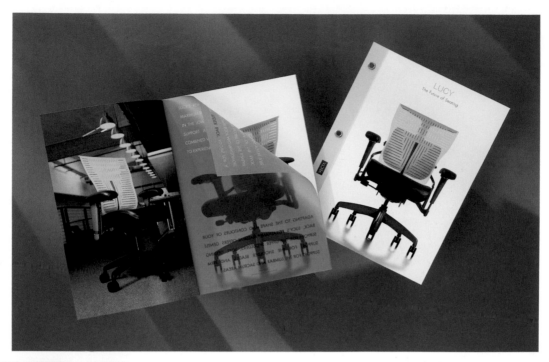

design firm
5D Studio
Malibu, California
client
Vecta

C - 19	C - 76	C - 27	C - 11
M - 20	M - 25	M - 85	M - 56
Y - 92	Y - 31	Y - 91	Y - 77
K - 0	K - 15	K - 33	K - 2

design firm
Greteman Group
Wichita, Kansas

C - 43	C - 0	C - 91
M - 0	M - 6	M - 60
Y - 15	Y - 43	Y - 0
K - 24	K - 0	K - 0

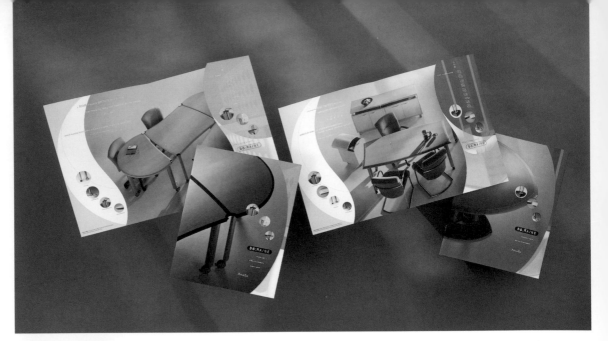

C - 22
M - 62
Y - 85
K - 13

C - 15
M - 40
Y - 79
K - 0

C - 27
M - 87
Y - 85
K - 33

C - 82
M - 73
Y - 67
K - 55

design firm
5D Studio
Malibu, California
client
Arcadia

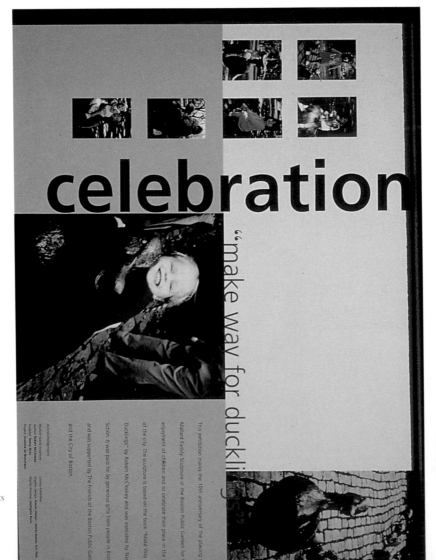

C - 71
M - 87
Y - 9
K - 10

C - 57
M - 24
Y - 64
K - 0

C - 14
M - 45
Y - 91
K - 0

C - 15
M - 18
Y - 70
K - 0

C - 41
M - 88
Y - 95
K - 11

design firm
Nassar Design
Brookline, Massachusetts
client
Boston Public Library

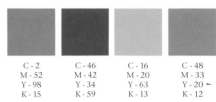

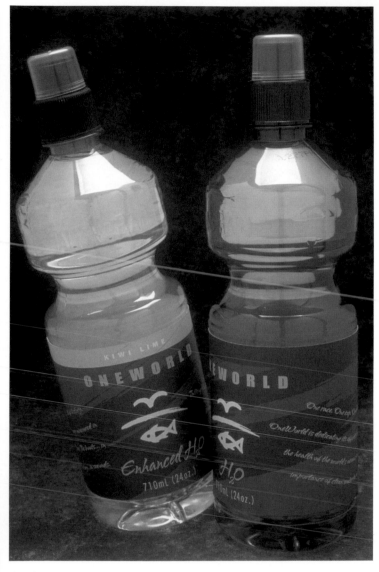

C - 2	C - 46	C - 16	C - 48
M - 52	M - 42	M - 20	M - 33
Y - 98	Y - 34	Y - 63	Y - 20
K - 15	K - 59	K - 13	K - 12

design firm
Hornall Anderson Design Works
Seattle, Washington

design firm
Compass Design
Minneapolis, Minnesota

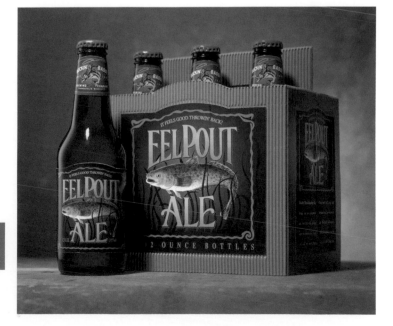

C - 33	C - 0	C - 45
M - 36	M - 24	M - 37
Y - 38	Y - 86	Y - 82
K - 10	K - 0	K - 38

C - 100   C - 78
M - 100   M - 27
Y - 22   Y - 84
K - 16   K - 17

design firm
Designation
New York, New York

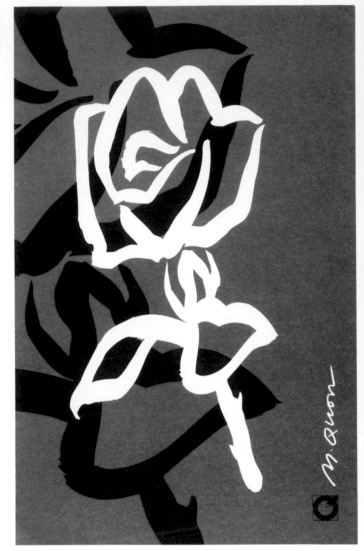

C - 100   C - 98   C - 84
M - 15   M - 82   M - 44
Y - 28   Y - 51   Y - 91
K - 7   K - 48   K - 31

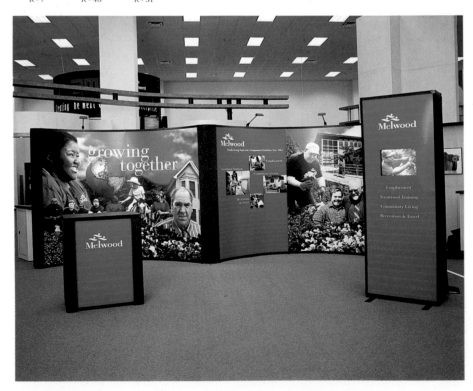

design firm
Dever Designs
Laurel, Maryland
client
Melwood

340

dever designs

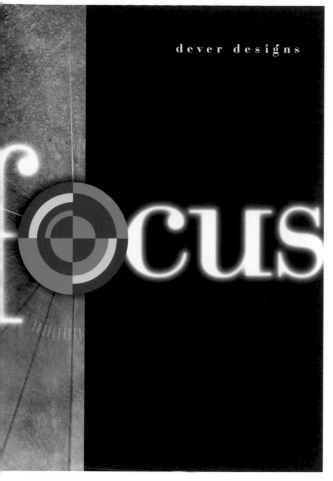

C - 40	C - 0	C - 100	C - 100	C - 100
M - 17	M - 17	M - 5	M - 74	M - 70
Y - 98	Y - 100	Y - 20	Y - 0	Y - 0
K - 19	K - 0	K - 0	K - 55	K - 0

design firm
Dever Designs
Laurel, Maryland
client
Dever Designs

design firm
Tom Fowler, Inc.
Norwalk, Connecticut
client
Honeywell Consumer Products

C - 1	C - 0	C - 81	C - 62
M - 97	M - 1	M - 1	M - 18
Y - 100	Y - 93	Y - 73	Y - 35
K - 19	K - 12	K - 42	K - 11

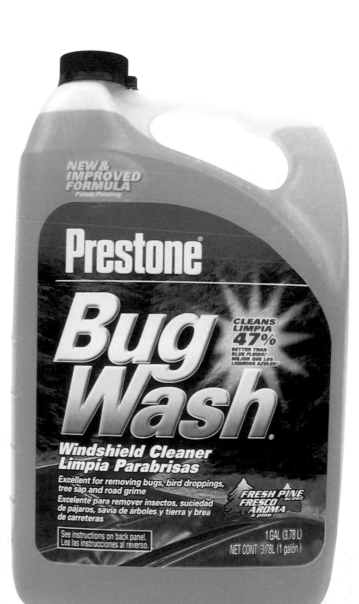

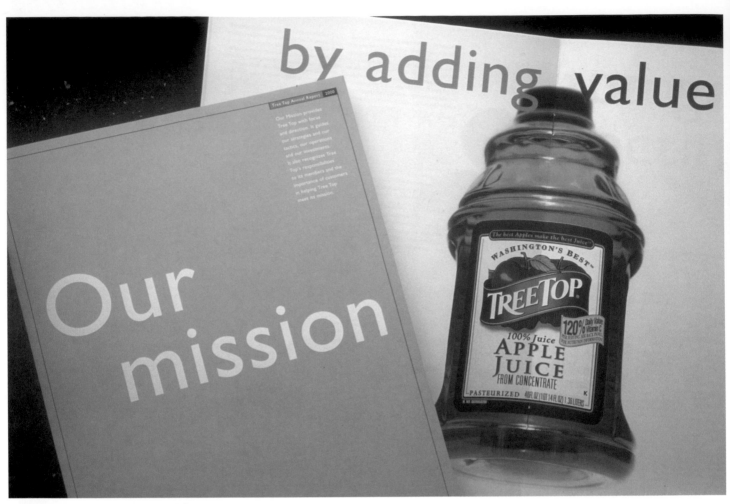

C - 42	C - 5	C - 10	C - 31
M - 21	M - 41	M - 84	M - 64
Y - 64	Y - 74	Y - 63	Y - 56
K - 26	K - 4	K - 16	K - 35

design firm
**Hornall Anderson
Design Works**
Seattle, Washington

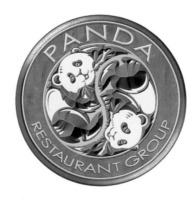

C - 59	C - 1	C - 36
M - 44	M - 22	M - 66
Y - 73	Y - 84	Y - 56
K - 3	K - 0	K - 3

design firm
Mike Salisbury L.L.C.
Venice, Caifornia
client
Panda Restaurant Group

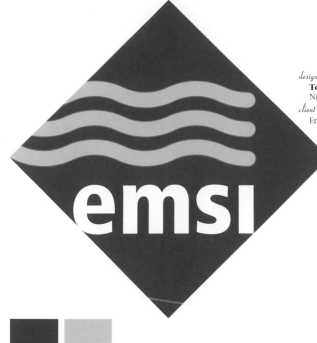

design firm
Tom Ventress Design
Nashville, Tennessee
client
Environmental Management Services Inc.

C - 100   C - 45
M - 60   M - 0
Y - 0   Y - 16
K - 0   K - 0

C - 100
M - 0
Y - 100
K - 0

design firm
LarsonLogosEtc
Rockford, Illinois
client
Village Bible Church

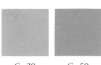

ACCESS MONTEREY PENINSULA

design firm
The Wecker Group
Monterey, California

C - 39   C - 50
M - 0   M - 22
Y - 100   Y - 0
K - 0   K - 0

BOMBARDIER

Contrails

A BOMBARDIER BUSINESS AIRCRAFT MAGAZINE   FALL 2002

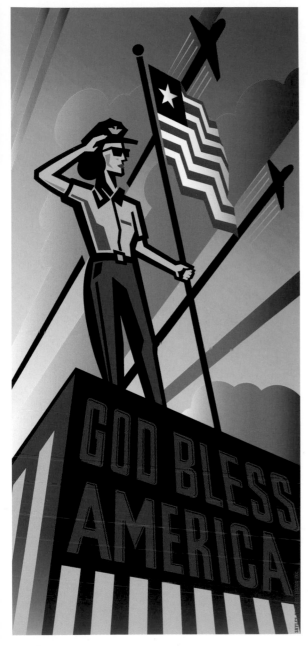

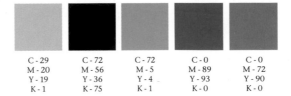

C - 29	C - 72	C - 72	C - 0	C - 0
M - 20	M - 56	M - 5	M - 89	M - 72
Y - 19	Y - 36	Y - 4	Y - 93	Y - 90
K - 1	K - 75	K - 1	K - 0	K - 0

design firm
Sayles Graphic Design
Des Moines, Iowa

client
"Art Fights Back"

C - 14	C - 90	C - 0
M - 100	M - 60	M - 0
Y - 100	Y - 0	Y - 0
K - 0	K - 0	K - 100

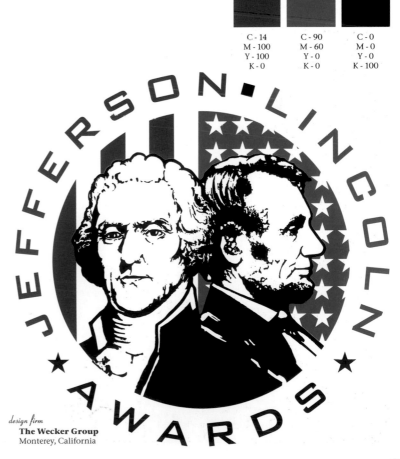

(opposite) design firm
Greteman Group
Wichita, Kansas

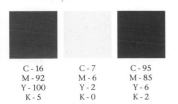

C - 16	C - 7	C - 95
M - 92	M - 6	M - 85
Y - 100	Y - 2	Y - 6
K - 5	K - 0	K - 2

design firm
The Wecker Group
Monterey, California

345

C - 100
M - 55
Y - 0
K - 0

C - 20
M - 100
Y - 70
K - 30

C - 0
M - 20
Y - 100
K - 0

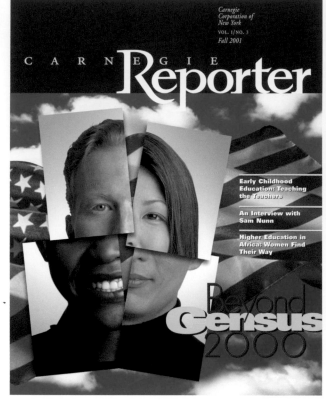

Carnegie
Corporation of
New York
VOL. 1/NO. 3
Fall 2001

CARNEGIE

Reporter

Early Childhood
Education: Teaching
the Teachers

An Interview with
Sam Nunn

Higher Education in
Africa: Women Find
Their Way

Beyond
Census
2000

design firm
Dever Designs
Laurel, Maryland
client
Carnegie Corporation of New York

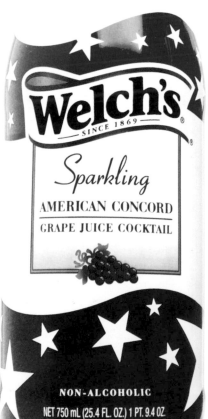

C - 0
M - 100
Y - 100
K - 1

C - 100
M - 94
Y - 2
K - 2

design firm
Bailey Design Group Inc.
Plymouth Meeting, Pennsylvania

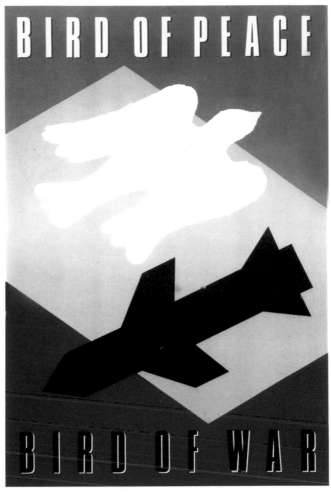

BIRD OF PEACE

BIRD OF WAR

C - 73
M - 29
Y - 76
K - 13

C - 19
M - 8
Y - 8
K - 0

C - 4
M - 99
Y - 100
K - 1

design firm
Designation
New York, New York

C - 61
M - 28
Y - 11
K - 7

C - 24
M - 94
Y - 84
K - 16

design firm
Dever Designs
Laurel, Maryland

client
National Air and
Space Museum

The spacesuit project team: from left, museum technician Samantha Gallagher, conservator Lisa Young, and museum specialist Amanda Young.

The deterioration of the Apollo suits is somewhat surprising to people because they were built to survive the harshest conditions in space, and you'd expect them to survive anything.
—LISA A. YOUNG, CONSERVATOR

SPACESUITS AND ARTIFACTS

In March 2000 the National Air and Space Museum's Division of Space History began a special two-year project to save artifacts of the Apollo Space Program. Funded by the Save America's Treasures grant program (a public-private partnership between the White House Millennium Council and the National Trust for Historic Preservation) and Hamilton Sundstrand (a United Technologies Company), museum specialist Amanda J. Young and conservator Lisa A. Young set out to accomplish four goals:
■ To document the condition of the spacesuits and to stabilize them for long-term storage and display.
■ To establish and maintain a Materials Advisory Group to research the issues inherent in the deterioration and preservation of the spacesuit collection.
■ To design, test, and implement procedures for the long-term storage of the collection.
■ To produce guidelines and standards for the storage, display, and preservation of spacesuits and make them available to other museums.

The project team established a priority list of suits for treatment, headed by the lunar suits, followed by the research and developmental suits, the flown mission suits, then training and non-flown suits. Work began with the lunar suits—including those custom-made for Neil A. Armstrong and Edwin E. "Buzz" Aldrin, Jr.'s historic Apollo 11 mission in July 1969, and that of Eugene A. Cernan

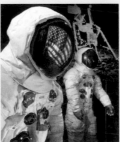

Neil Armstrong and Buzz Aldrin wore these spacesuits when they climbed down from their lunar module *Eagle* in July 1969 to become the first humans to walk on the Moon.

(Apollo 17), the "last man on the Moon," who, in 1972, explored the Moon in a lunar rover. They wrote condition reports for each suit, and over 260 components were examined and treated during this time. By targeting four areas of deterioration—the rubber components of suits and gloves, the PVC tubing, the interior and exterior zippers, and the anodized aluminum wrist and neck disconnects—the team established a baseline for each suit, which will make it easier to prioritize future conservation needs.

The suits were photographed in color to track visible changes over time. A colorimeter assessed color changes to the exterior fabrics of each suit, and they were evaluated with a CT scanner to record the relationships between interior layers of material. Having determined that flat storage

The spacesuit worn by astronaut Eugene Cernan, during the Apollo 10 mission, was treated as part of the Save America's Treasures project.

Amanda Young instructs student interns on how to write a condition report.

was detrimental, the staff designed and constructed a soft mannequin from polyethylene foam, polyester batting, and white nylon hose to fit inside each suit. Additionally, staff designed and constructed storage trays, and purchased a storage racking system to enable air to flow freely around the suits.

All these measures will extend the life of the collection, but according to Amanda Young, "These are extremely fragile artifacts, and the best we can currently hope for is to prevent or slow down further deterioration."

The results of the team's successful project can be found in "The Preservation, Storage, and Display of Spacesuits," by Lisa A. Young and Amanda J. Young, published as Report Number 5 in the National Air and Space Museum's Collections Care series.

Director's Report 111

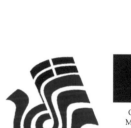

C - 92
M - 98
Y - 0
K - 3

C - 1
M - 98
Y - 64
K - 1

WASHINGTON
DC
CONVENTION & TOURISM
CORPORATION

design firm
Supon Design Group
Washington, D.C.

client
Washington D.C. Convention and Tourism Corporation

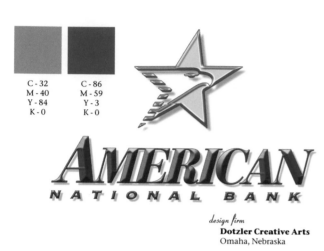

C - 32
M - 40
Y - 84
K - 0

C - 86
M - 59
Y - 3
K - 0

AMERICAN
NATIONAL BANK

design firm
Dotzler Creative Arts
Omaha, Nebraska

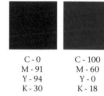

C - 0
M - 91
Y - 94
K - 30

C - 100
M - 60
Y - 0
K - 18

design firm
LarsonLogosEtc
Rockford, Illinois

client
St. Olaf College Viking Male Chorus

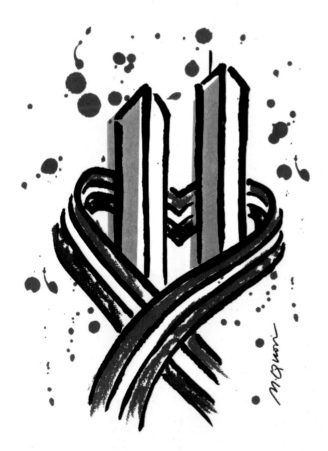

C - 22
M - 95
Y - 93
K - 1

C - 99
M - 80
Y - 11
K - 5

C - 45
M - 33
Y - 37
K - 1

design firm
Designation
New York, New York

design firm
Keiler & Company
Farmington, Connecticut
client
Connecticut Art Directors Club

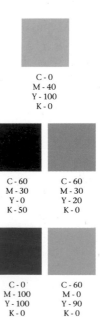

C - 0
M - 40
Y - 100
K - 0

C - 60
M - 30
Y - 0
K - 50

C - 60
M - 30
Y - 20
K - 0

C - 0
M - 100
Y - 100
K - 0

C - 60
M - 0
Y - 90
K - 0

design firm
5D Studio
Malibu, California
client
Vecta

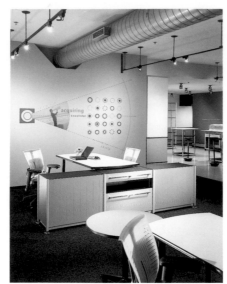

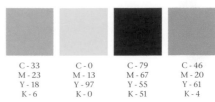

C - 33	C - 0	C - 79	C - 46
M - 23	M - 13	M - 67	M - 20
Y - 18	Y - 97	Y - 55	Y - 61
K - 6	K - 0	K - 51	K - 4

C - 13	C - 0	C - 14	C - 61
M - 4	M - 60	M - 53	M - 38
Y - 53	Y - 76	Y - 14	Y - 8
K - 40	K - 25	K - 55	K - 50

design firm
Hornall Anderson Design Works
Seattle, Washington

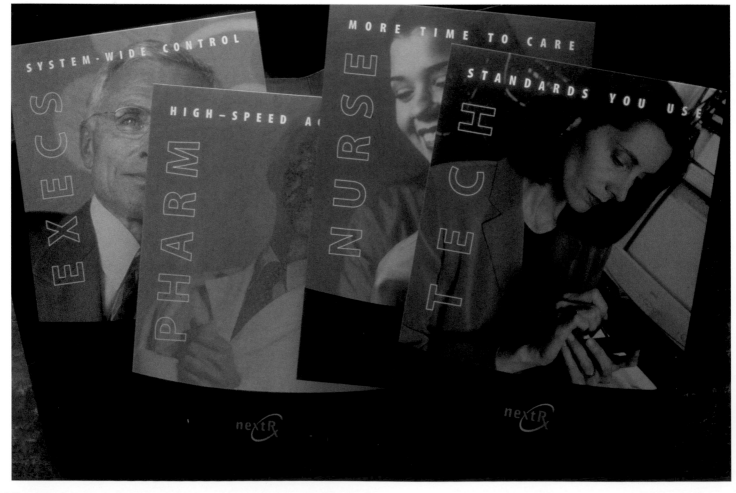

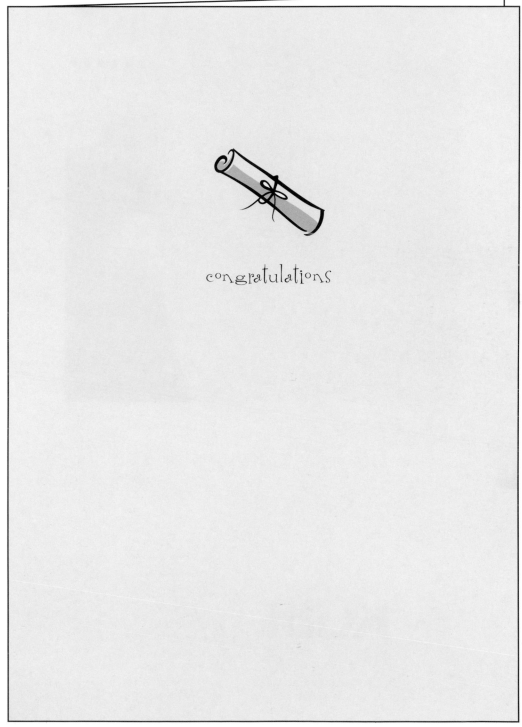

congratulations

design firm
After Hours Creative
Phoenix, Arizona

C - 4
M - 6
Y - 17
K - 11

C - 9
M - 13
Y - 38
K - 26

design firm
Dever Designs
Laurel, Maryland
client
National Air and Space Museum

C - 60
M - 30
Y - 0
K - 15

C - 0
M - 20
Y - 100
K - 0

C - 0
M - 80
Y - 100
K - 0

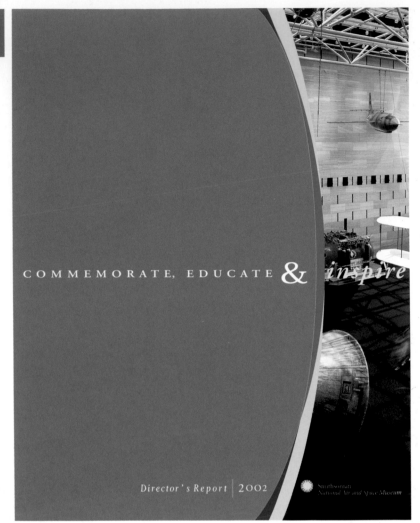

COMMEMORATE, EDUCATE & inspire

Director's Report | 2002

Smithsonian
National Air and Space Museum

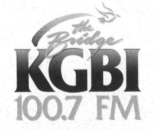

KGBI is a ministry of Grace University
www.GraceUniversity.edu

Tom Sommerville

*Director of Broadcasting
Grace University*

831 Pine Street
Omaha, NE 68108-3629

402-449-2900
Fax: 402-449-2825

Tom@TheBridge.fm
www.TheBridge.fm

design firm
Dotzler Creative Arts
Omaha, Nebraska

C - 16
M - 33
Y - 94
K - 11

C - 99
M - 75
Y - 0
K - 10

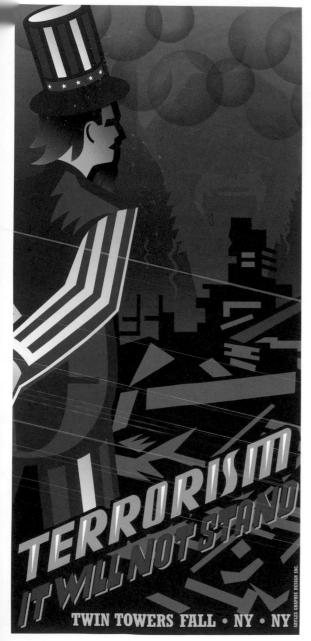

C - 100 | C - 99 | C - 25 | C - 0 | C - 57 | C - 0
M - 77 | M - 62 | M - 91 | M - 89 | M - 45 | M - 50
Y - 18 | Y - 2 | Y - 84 | Y - 93 | Y - 42 | Y - 90
K - 15 | K - 0 | K - 21 | K - 0 | K - 35 | K - 0

design firm
Sayles Graphic Design
Des Moines, Iowa

client
"Art Fights Back"

design firm
Sagmeister Inc.
New York, New York

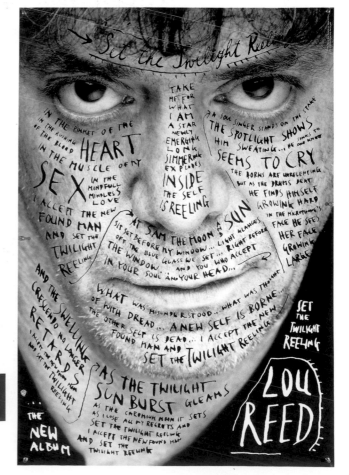

C - 50 | C - 99
M - 37 | M - 81
Y - 4 | Y - 52
K - 0 | K - 17

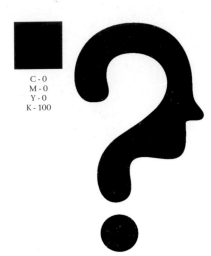

C - 0
M - 0
Y - 0
K - 100

design firm
Supon Design Group
Washington, D.C.
client
AdviceZone.com

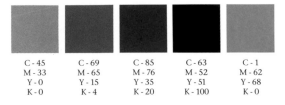

C - 45	C - 69	C - 85	C - 63	C - 1
M - 33	M - 65	M - 76	M - 52	M - 62
Y - 0	Y - 15	Y - 35	Y - 51	Y - 68
K - 0	K - 4	K - 20	K - 100	K - 0

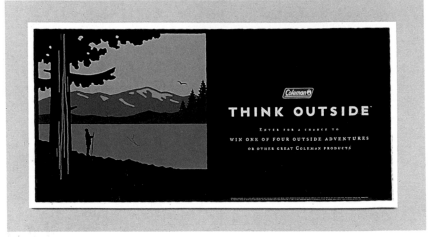

design firm
Clarion Marketing & Communications
Atlanta, Georgia
client
Coleman

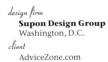

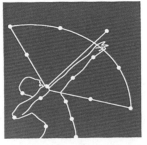

C - 76	C - 0
M - 33	M - 0
Y - 7	Y - 0
K - 0	K - 100

design firm
Supon Design Group
Washington, D.C.
client
OnPoint Digital, Inc.

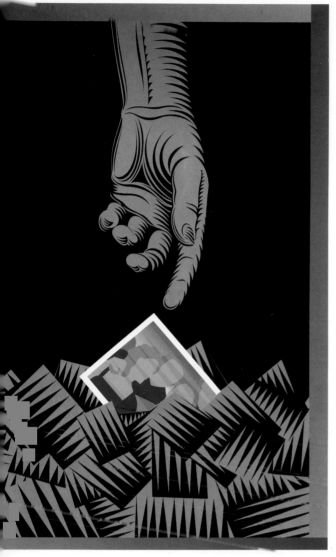

C - 0	C - 43	C - 99	C - 0	C - 0
M - 43	M - 43	M - 80	M - 0	M - 0
Y - 16	Y - 0	Y - 0	Y - 0	Y - 0
K - 0	K - 0	K - 0	K - 64	K - 100

design firm
Tom Fowler, Inc.
Norwalk, Connecticut
client
Connecticut Art Director's Club

design firm
Sam Smidt
Palo Alto, California
client
Healing Environments

C - 0
M - 0
Y - 0
K - 100

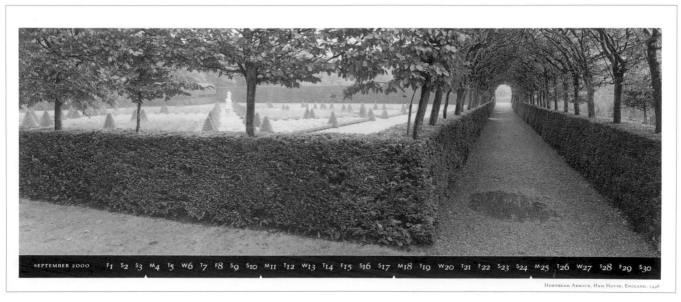

SEPTEMBER 2000 F1 S2 S3 M4 T5 W6 T7 F8 S9 S10 M11 T12 W13 T14 F15 S16 S17 M18 T19 W20 T21 F22 S23 S24 M25 T26 W27 T28 F29 S30

HORNBEAM ARBOUR, HAM HOUSE, ENGLAND, 1998

design firm
**Hornall Anderson
Design Works**
Seattle, Washington

C - 20
M - 30
Y - 47
K - 30

C - 5
M - 44
Y - 50
K - 3

C - 38
M - 34
Y - 30
K - 20

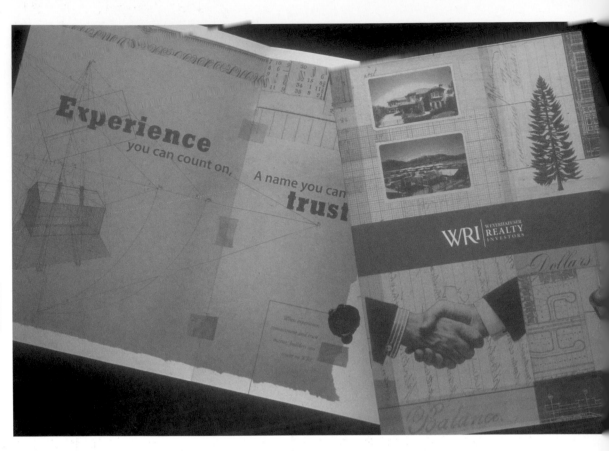

A FOOD
AFFAIR
CATERING

VAIL, CO

PERSONALIZED
CATERING
for
EVERY AFFAIR

P.O. BOX 3844
VAIL, COLORADO 81658
PHONE 970 477-1073

WECATER@MOUNTAINMAIL.NET

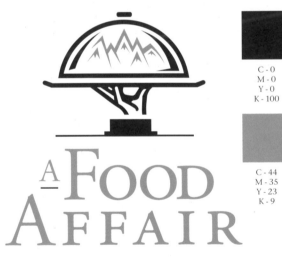

A FOOD
AFFAIR
CATERING

VAIL, CO

C - 0
M - 0
Y - 0
K - 100

C - 44
M - 35
Y - 23
K - 9

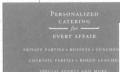

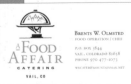

design firm
Becker Design
Milwaukee, Wisconsin
client
Food Affair

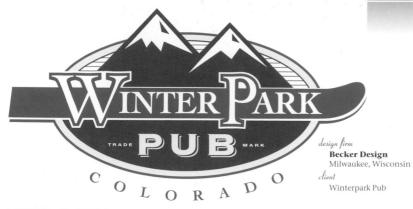

design firm
Becker Design
Milwaukee, Wisconsin
client
Winterpark Pub

C - 32	C - 93	C - 1
M - 83	M - 33	M - 8
Y - 76	Y - 85	Y - 27
K - 23	K - 23	K - 0

design firm
Belyea
Seattle, Washington
client
ColorGraphics

C - 32	C - 25	C - 56
M - 1	M - 63	M - 25
Y - 46	Y - 56	Y - 16
K - 1	K - 23	K - 13

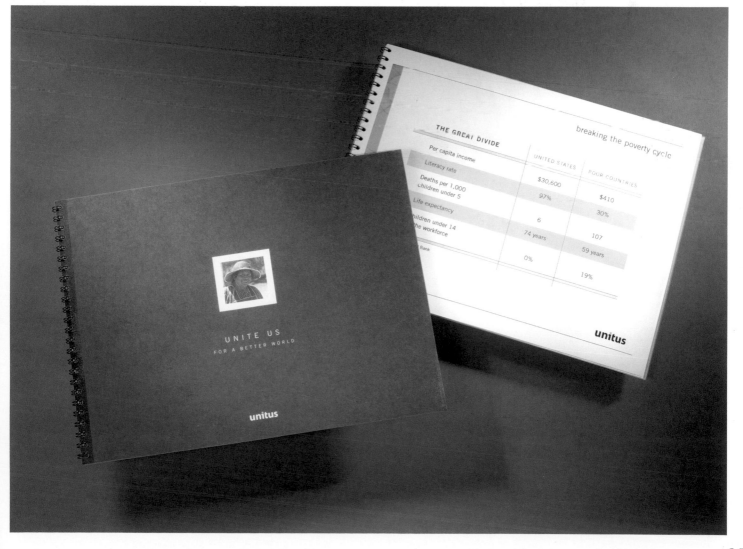

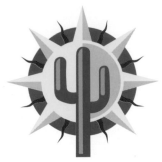

GAINEY SUITES HOTEL

design firm
The Wecker Group
Monterey, California
client
Gainey Suites Hotel

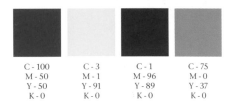

C - 100
M - 50
Y - 50
K - 0

C - 3
M - 1
Y - 91
K - 0

C - 1
M - 96
Y - 89
K - 0

C - 75
M - 0
Y - 37
K - 0

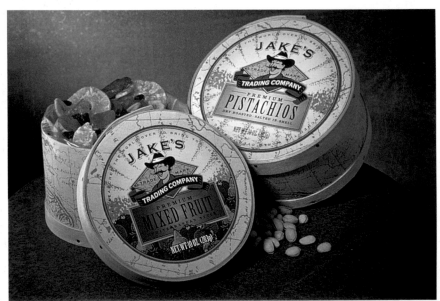

design firm
Compass Design
Minneapolis, Minnesota
client
Jake's Trading Co.

C - 0
M - 11
Y - 64
K - 0

C - 4
M - 65
Y - 98
K - 0

C - 19
M - 90
Y - 84
K - 4

C - 16
M - 27
Y - 33
K - 0

C - 2 M - 90 Y - 91 K - 0	C - 0 M - 23 Y - 94 K - 0	C - 40 M - 5 Y - 0 K - 0

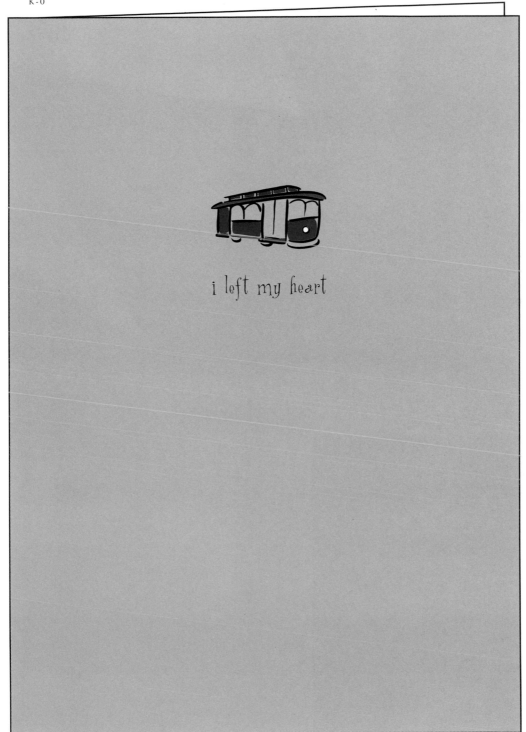

i left my heart

design firm
After Hours Creative
Phoenix, Arizona

design firm
Halleck
Palo Alto, California
client
St. Supery

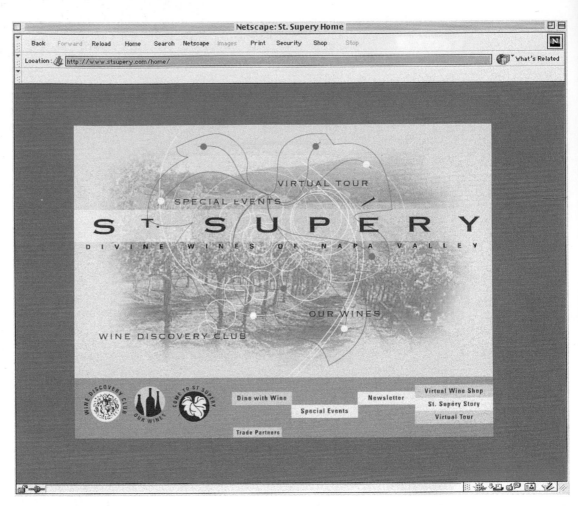

C - 20	C - 10	C - 10
M - 30	M - 10	M - 10
Y - 50	Y - 50	Y - 30
K - 40	K - 0	K - 10

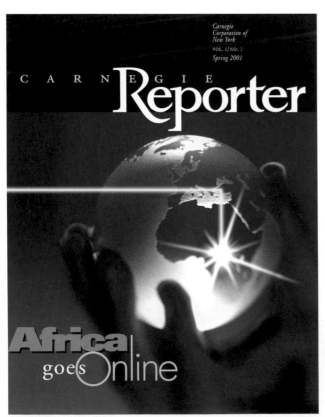

design firm
Dever Designs
Laurel, Maryland
client
Carnegie Corporation of New York

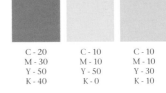

C - 0	C - 1	C - 19	C - 99	C - 100
M - 60	M - 1	M - 76	M - 75	M - 90
Y - 100	Y - 76	Y - 9	Y - 1	Y - 0
K - 0	K - 0	K - 17	K - 0	K - 35

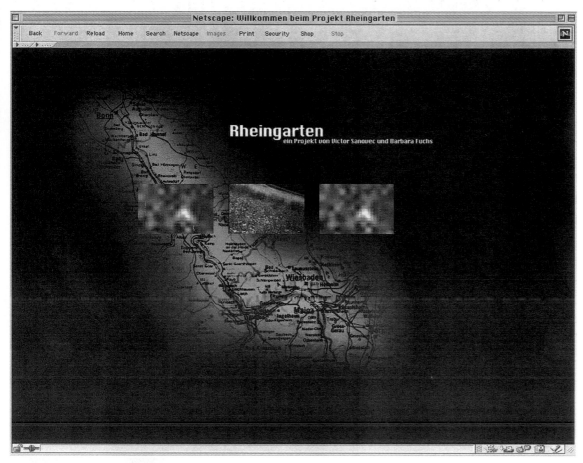

Back Forward Reload Home Search Netscape Images Print Security Shop Stop

Rheingarten
ein Projekt von Victor Sanovec und Barbara Fuchs

design firm
Sign Kommunikation GmbH
Frankfurt (Germany)
client
Victor Sanovec/Barbasa Fuchs

C - 80   C - 10   C - 0
M - 40   M - 0   M - 0
Y - 60   Y - 70   Y - 0
K - 0   K - 0   K - 100

C - 0   C - 0
M - 55   M - 0
Y - 100   Y - 0
K - 30   K - 100

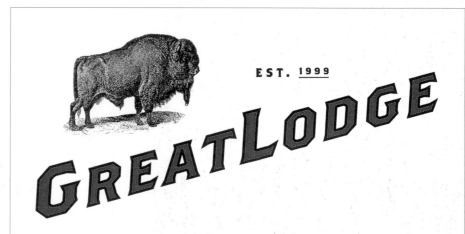

EST. 1999
GREATLODGE

design firm
Cahan and Associates
San Francisco, California
client
Greatlodge.com

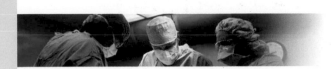

Coaptite is the most natural approach yet to the treatment of urinary incontinence. Where other materials are either short-lived or can produce acute reactions, Coaptite is a long-term solution compatible with the body's own chemistry.

The material is smooth, rounded, substantially spherical and 75 to 125 micron in size. Carefully controlled dispersion in the carrier gel facilitates easy injection. Coaptite particles readily flow through a very small 21 gauge needle, using standard 5 or 7 Fr cystoscopic injection catheters. In long-term performance, cells at the injection site grow directly on the surface of Coaptite particles, forming soft tissue identical to the surrounding area. Thus, Coaptite conforms to the body without reaction, isolation or migration.

The nature of Coaptite particles also offers other advantages:

> Skin testing is not required, allowing treatment to commence immediately.

> The small needle puncture minimizes loss of material at the injection site.

> Supplied in efficient 1cc syringes, Coaptite is cost-effective, requiring no special equipment such as injection guns or non-standard cystoscopes.

> Coaptite can be imaged using standard radiologic techniques. Treatment is optimized and the safety profile enhanced through verification that migration and absorption have not occurred.

COMPATIBLE WITH YOUR PRACTICE OF MEDICINE

Coaptite is not only compatible with the human body, it is also well-suited to the practice of medicine. From the design of the syringe to the formulation of the material, Coaptite has been developed to enhance your treatment of urinary incontinence. The syringe, unique to Coaptite, features wider flanges for better comfort and control. Even dispersion of Coaptite particles reduces mechanical effort and eliminates clumping. The product has a two-year shelf life with no special storage requirements. And Coaptite maintains familiarity, working with standard cystoscopic equipment.

The material advantages of Coaptite can assure patient comfort as well. Its biocompatibility alleviates concern about long-term effects, something which is unknown with silicone or polymer materials. As an outpatient procedure, augmentation with Coaptite allows for a quick recovery. And it does not preclude subsequent surgery if necessary.

The clinical evidence to date suggests that utilizing Coaptite as the initial approach may be the only approach most patients will ever need.

design firm
Becker Design
Milwaukee, Wisconsin

client
BioForm

C - 15
M - 5
Y - 40
K - 0

C - 30
M - 4
Y - 2
K - 0

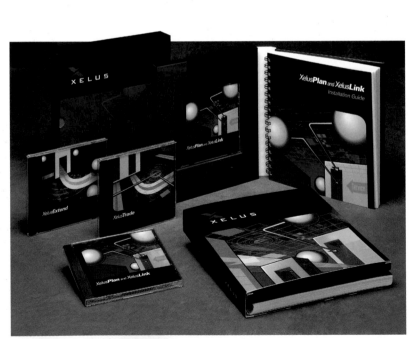

design firm
McElveney & Palozzi Design Group
Rochester, New York

client
Xelus

C - 87	C - 0	C - 75	C - 77	C - 4	C - 25
M - 54	M - 0	M - 16	M - 87	M - 10	M - 96
Y - 5	Y - 0	Y - 31	Y - 14	Y - 87	Y - 69
K - 1	K - 100	K - 2	K - 3	K - 0	K - 17

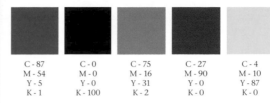

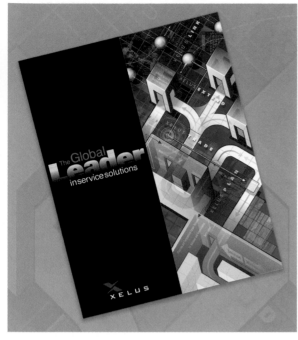

C - 87	C - 0	C - 75	C - 27	C - 4
M - 54	M - 0	M - 16	M - 90	M - 10
Y - 5	Y - 0	Y - 31	Y - 0	Y - 87
K - 1	K - 100	K - 2	K - 0	K - 0

design firm
McElveney & Palozzi Design Group
Rochester, New York

client
Xelus

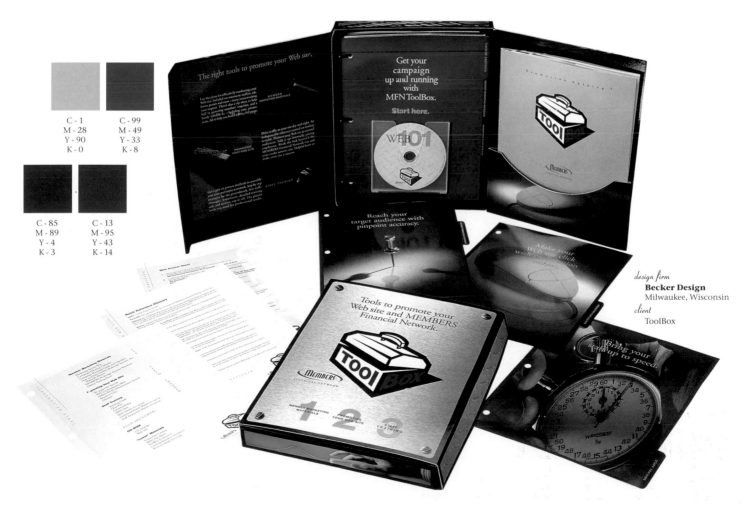

C - 1	C - 99
M - 28	M - 49
Y - 90	Y - 33
K - 0	K - 8

C - 85	C - 13
M - 89	M - 95
Y - 4	Y - 43
K - 3	K - 14

design firm
Becker Design
Milwaukee, Wisconsin

client
ToolBox

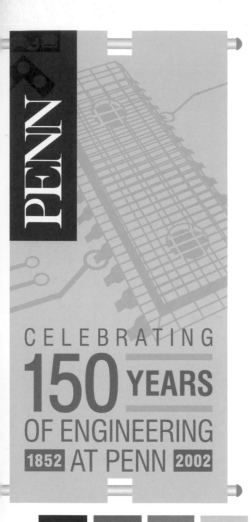
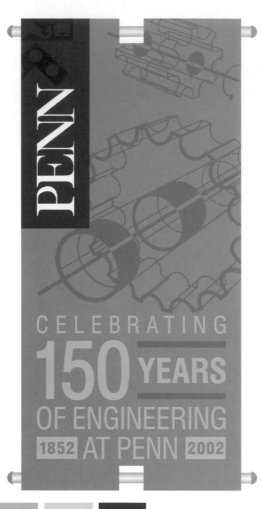
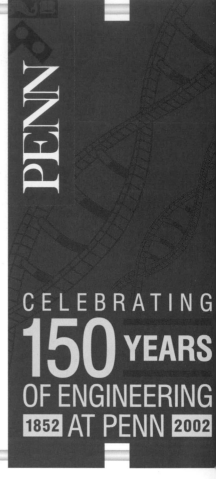

design firm
Bailey Design Group
Plymouth Meeting, Pennsylvania

C - 100	C - 75	C - 65	C - 0	C - 0	C - 0	C - 0
M - 68	M - 51	M - 35	M - 25	M - 35	M - 0	M - 100
Y - 0	Y - 0	Y - 0	Y - 100	Y - 100	Y - 50	Y - 100
K - 25	K - 0	K - 0	K - 0	K - 0	K - 20	K - 0

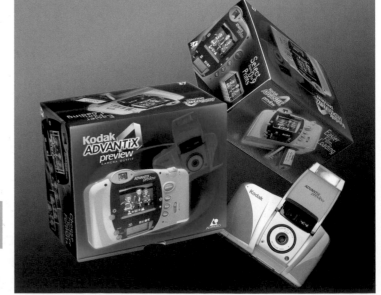

design firm
McElveney & Palozzi Design Group
Rochester, New York
client
Eastman Kodak Company

C - 100	C - 0	C - 32
M - 64	M - 18	M - 31
Y - 0	Y - 100	Y - 30
K - 0	K - 0	K - 0

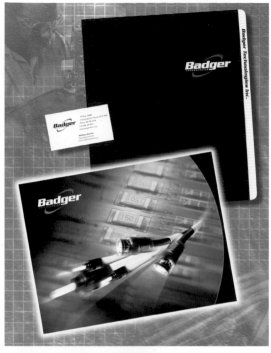

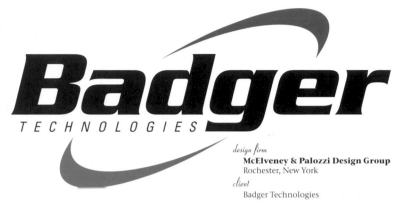

Badger
TECHNOLOGIES

design firm
McElveney & Palozzi Design Group
Rochester, New York
client
Badger Technologies

C - 0	C - 91	C - 0
M - 91	M - 43	M - 0
Y - 76	Y - 0	Y - 0
K - 6	K - 0	K - 100

design firm
Hornall Anderson Design Works
Seattle, Washington

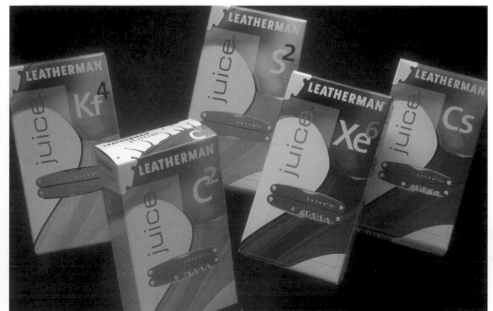

C - 29	C - 3	C - 66	C - 1
M - 12	M - 51	M - 49	M - 80
Y - 71	Y - 93	Y - 19	Y - 44
K - 56	K - 18	K - 38	K - 0

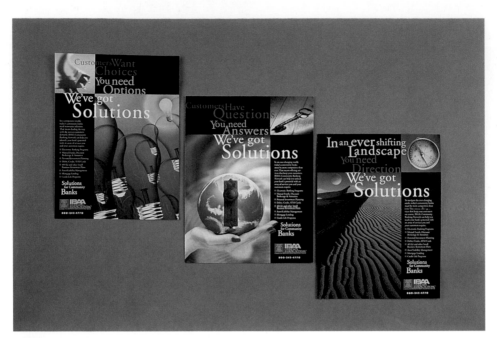

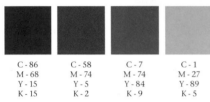

C - 86	C - 58	C - 7	C - 1
M - 68	M - 74	M - 74	M - 27
Y - 15	Y - 5	Y - 84	Y - 89
K - 15	K - 2	K - 9	K - 5

design firm
Dever Designs
Laurel, Maryland
client
Independent Bankers Association of America

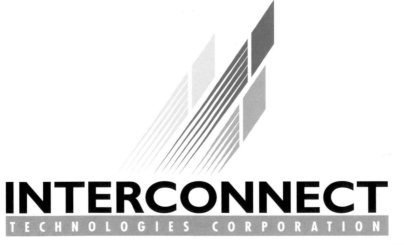

design firm
Imtech Communications
Berkeley, California
client
Interconnect Technologies Corp.

C - 2	C - 0	C - 0
M - 65	M - 0	M - 0
Y - 91	Y - 0	Y - 0
K - 0	K - 39	K -100

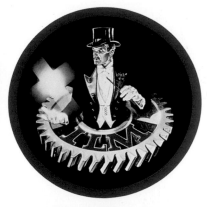

C - 88	C - 3	C - 68
M - 88	M - 98	M - 18
Y - 88	Y - 98	Y - 18
K - 78	K - 15	K - 0

design firm
Mike Salisbury L.L.C.
Venice, California
client
Bernie Yuman

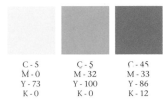

C - 5	C - 5	C - 45
M - 0	M - 32	M - 33
Y - 73	Y - 100	Y - 86
K - 0	K - 0	K - 12

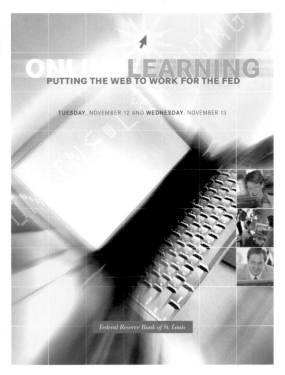

ONLINE LEARNING
PUTTING THE WEB TO WORK FOR THE FED

TUESDAY, NOVEMBER 12 AND WEDNESDAY, NOVEMBER 13

Federal Reserve Bank of St. Louis

design firm
Stan Gellman Graphic Design
St. Louis, Missouri
client
Federal Reserve Bank of St. Louis

C - 77	C - 1	C - 94	C - 93
M - 3	M - 96	M - 34	M - 94
Y - 91	Y - 89	Y - 7	Y - 2
K - 0	K - 0	K - 1	K - 0

design firm
Lane + Lane
Los Angeles, California
client
`OnlineLearning.net

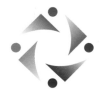 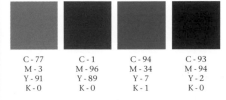

OnlineLearning.net

your source for continuing education online

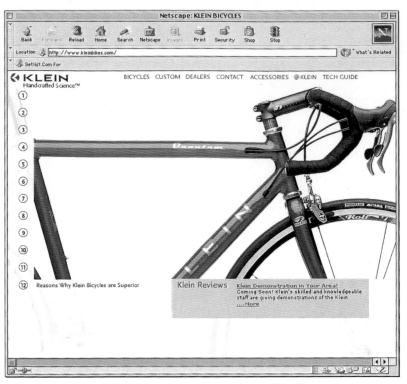

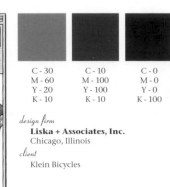

C - 30
M - 60
Y - 20
K - 10

C - 10
M - 100
Y - 100
K - 10

C - 0
M - 0
Y - 0
K - 100

design firm
Liska + Associates, Inc.
Chicago, Illinois

client
Klein Bicycles

design firm
Savage Design Group
Houston, Texas

client
Savage Design Group

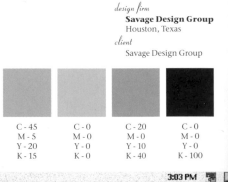

C - 45
M - 5
Y - 20
K - 15

C - 0
M - 0
Y - 0
K - 0

C - 20
M - 0
Y - 10
K - 40

C - 0
M - 0
Y - 0
K - 100

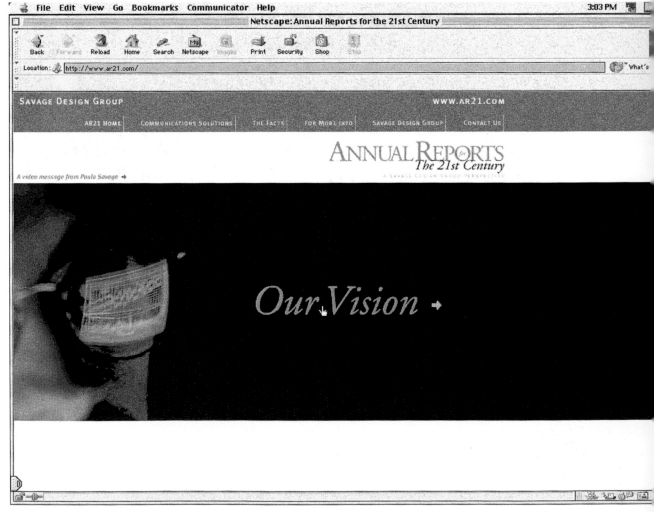

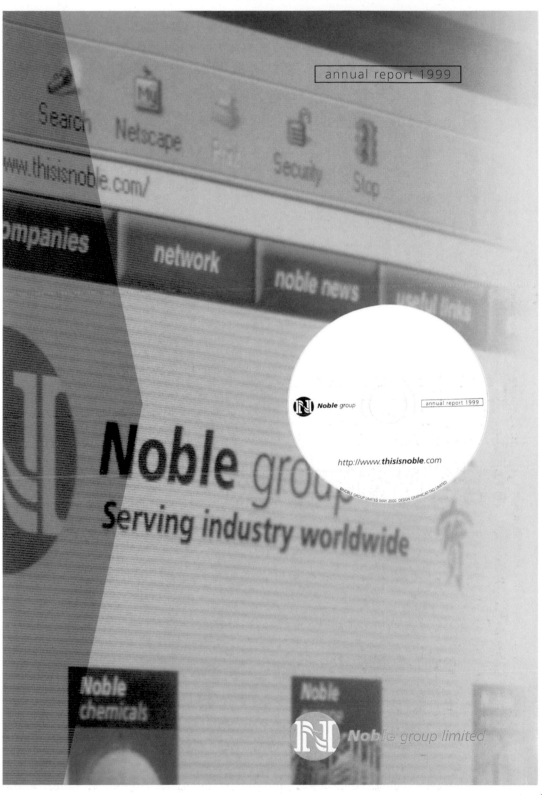

C - 34   C - 0
M - 29   M - 0
Y - 26   Y - 0
K - 5   K - 100

design firm
Graphicat Limited
Hong Kong, China
client
Noble Group Limited

369

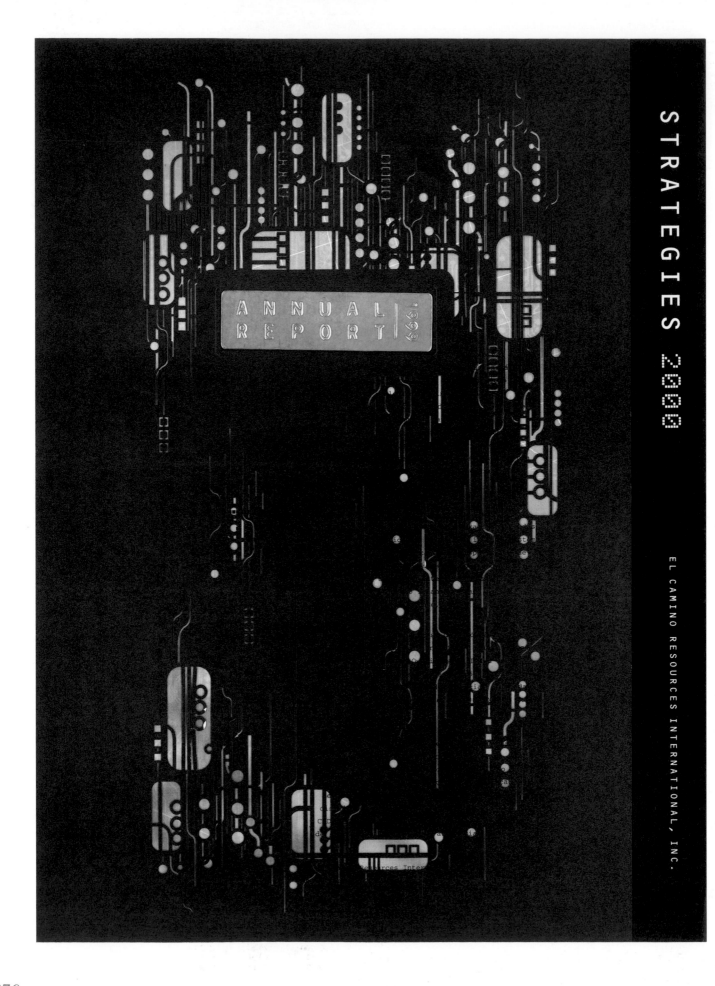

STRATEGIES 2000

EL CAMINO RESOURCES INTERNATIONAL, INC.

ANNUAL REPORT | 1999

(opposite) design firm
[i]e design
Studio City, California

client
El Camino Reserve

C - 5	C - 50	C - 0
M - 32	M - 67	M - 0
Y - 90	Y - 22	Y - 0
K - 0	K - 30	K - 100

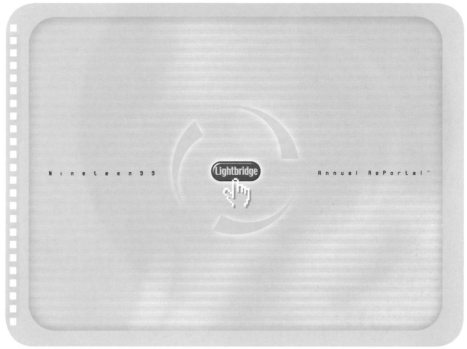

Nineteen99   Lightbridge   Annual RePortal™

design firm
Tepperman/Ray Associates, Inc.
Andover, Massachusetts

client
Lightbridge, Inc.

C - 0	C - 15
M - 20	M - 97
Y - 90	Y - 97
K - 0	K - 0

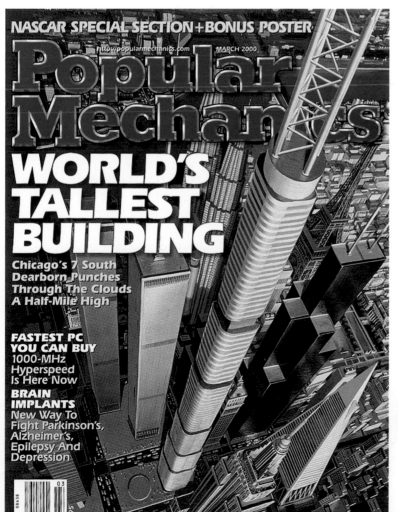

NASCAR SPECIAL SECTION + BONUS POSTER

http://popularmechanics.com   MARCH 2000

Popular Mechanics

WORLD'S TALLEST BUILDING

Chicago's 7 South Dearborn Punches Through The Clouds A Half-Mile High

FASTEST PC YOU CAN BUY
1000-MHz Hyperspeed Is Here Now

BRAIN IMPLANTS
New Way To Fight Parkinson's, Alzheimer's, Epilepsy And Depression

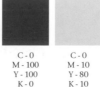

design firm
Popular Mechanics
New York, New York

client
Popular Mechanics

C - 0	C - 0	C - 20
M - 100	M - 10	M - 10
Y - 100	Y - 80	Y - 10
K - 0	K - 10	K - 10

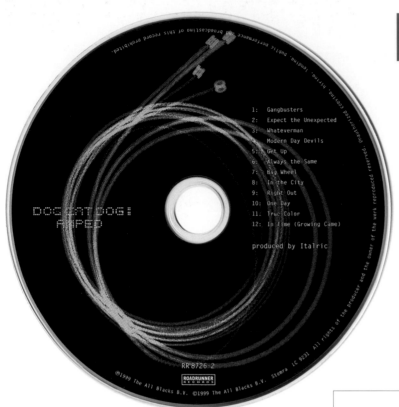

DOG EAT DOG: AMPED

1: Gangbusters
2: Expect the Unexpected
3: Whateverman
4: Modern Day Devils
5: Get Up
6: Always the Same
7: Big Wheel
8: In the City
9: Right Out
10: One Day
11: True Color
12: In Time (Growing Came)

produced by Italric

RR 8726-2

design firm
Kb.D
Hillsdale, New Jersey
client
Dog Eat Dog/Roadrunner Records

C - 100	C - 0
M - 50	M - 0
Y - 10	Y - 0
K - 10	K - 100

handspring™

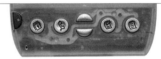

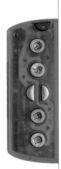

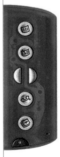

THERE'S MORE TO **VISOR™** THAN MEETS THE EYE

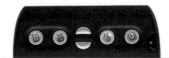

design firm
Mortensen Design
Mountain View, California
client
Handspring, Inc.

C - 0	C - 90	C - 100	C - 0
M - 40	M - 60	M - 20	M - 0
Y - 80	Y - 20	Y - 70	Y - 0
K - 10	K - 10	K - 20	K - 100

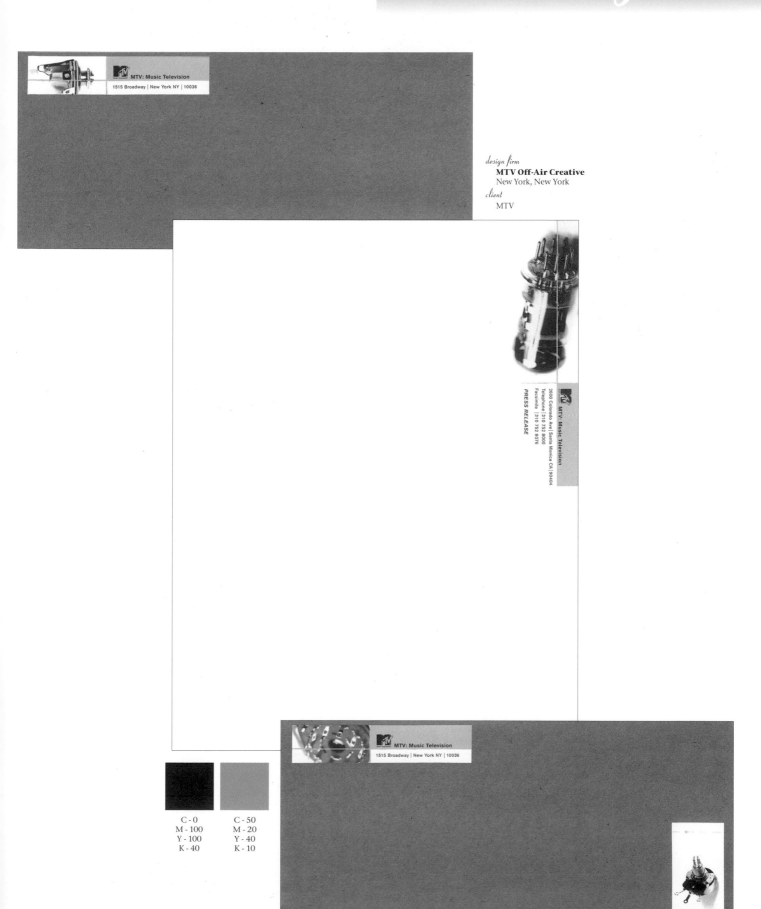

design firm
MTV Off-Air Creative
New York, New York
client
MTV

C - 0
M - 100
Y - 100
K - 40

C - 50
M - 20
Y - 40
K - 10

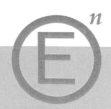

EPOS | endless possibilities productions inc.

1639 sixteenth street | santa monica | california 90404 | 310.581.2418 studio | www.epos-grd.com

C - 30	C - 55	C - 0	C - 100
M - 20	M - 100	M - 65	M - 5
Y - 80	Y - 15	Y - 80	Y - 5
K - 5	K - 30	K - 0	K - 0

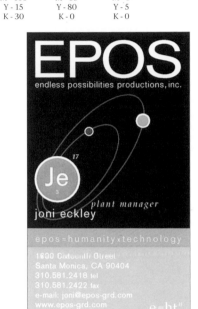

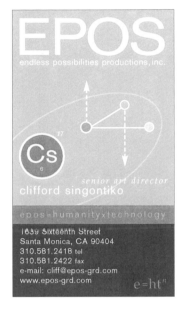

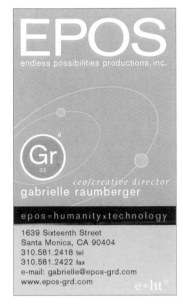

EPOS
endless possibilities productions, inc.

Je 17 3
plant manager
joni eckley

epos = humanity × technology

1600 Sixteenth Street
Santa Monica, CA 90404
310.581.2418 tel
310.581.2422 fax
e-mail: joni@epos-grd.com
www.epos-grd.com

$e = ht^n$

EPOS
endless possibilities productions, inc.

Cs 17 6
senior art director
clifford singontiko

epos = humanity × technology

1639 Sixteenth Street
Santa Monica, CA 90404
310.581.2418 tel
310.581.2422 fax
e-mail: cliff@epos-grd.com
www.epos-grd.com

$e = ht^n$

EPOS
endless possibilities productions, inc.

Gr 6 33
ceo/creative director
gabrielle raumberger

epos = humanity × technology

1639 Sixteenth Street
Santa Monica, CA 90404
310.581.2418 tel
310.581.2422 fax
e-mail: gabrielle@epos-grd.com
www.epos-grd.com

$e = ht^n$

E^n EPOS | endless possibilities productions inc.

1639 sixteenth street | santa monica | california 90404

design firm
EPOS, Inc.
Santa Monica, California
client
EPOS, Inc.

design firm
Agnew Moyer Smith, Inc.
Pittsburgh, Pennyslvania
client
The National Aviary

C - 57
M - 3
Y - 1
K - 0

C - 42
M - 2
Y - 75
K - 1

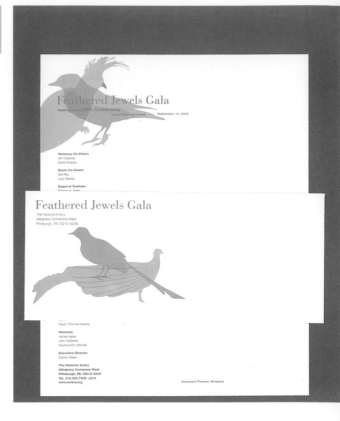

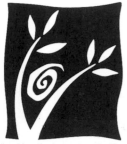

EUGENE
Parks and
Open Space

C - 98
M - 10
Y - 62
K - 0

C - 98
M - 75
Y - 0
K - 14

design firm
Funk/Levis & Associates
Eugene, Oregon
client
Eugene Parks & Open Spaces

design firm
designRoom Creative
Cleveland, Ohio
client
Euclid Hospital

C - 56
M - 29
Y - 76
K - 0

C - 33
M - 15
Y - 45
K - 0

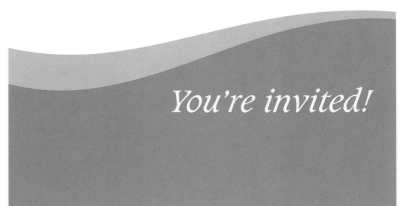

You're invited!

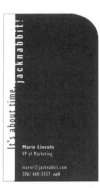

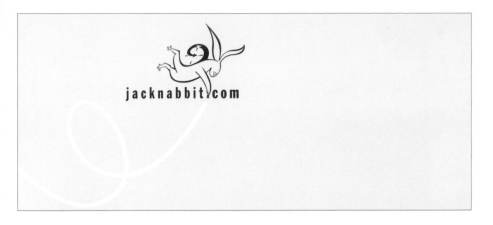

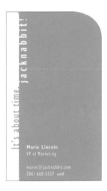

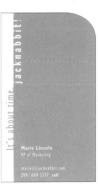

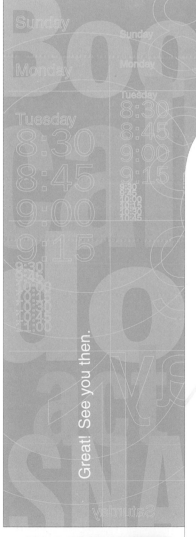

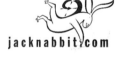

design firm
David Lemley Design
Seattle, Washington
client
jacknabbit.com

C - 5	C - 55	C - 100	C - 45
M - 5	M - 0	M - 5	M - 100
Y - 90	Y - 90	Y - 10	Y - 5
K - 0	K - 0	K - 0	K - 0

22605 SE 56th Street
Suite 250
Issaquah, Washington
98029

phone 425/ 557-8955
toll free 877-NABTIME
fax 425/ 557-8576

Appointime, Inc.

C - 49
M - 29
Y - 1
K - 0

C - 25
M - 2
Y - 53
K - 0

Protecting

your interests,

building

your investment.

2001 ANNUAL REPORT

design firm
Lawrence & Ponder Ideaworks
Newport Beach, California

client
Starbucks Coffee

design firm
Boller Coates & Neu
Chicago, Illinois

client
Hon Industries Inc.

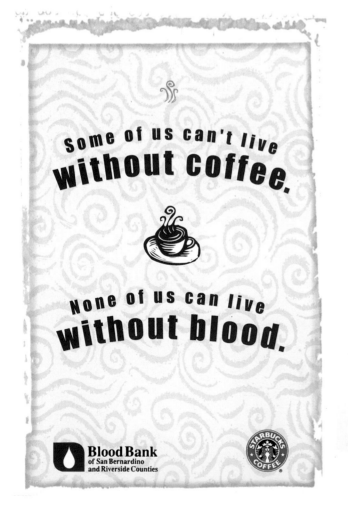

Some of us can't live **without coffee.**

None of us can live **without blood.**

Blood Bank of San Bernardino and Riverside Counties

C - 14
M - 1
Y - 1
K - 0

C - 22
M - 7
Y - 1
K - 0

C - 92
M - 82
Y - 1
K - 10

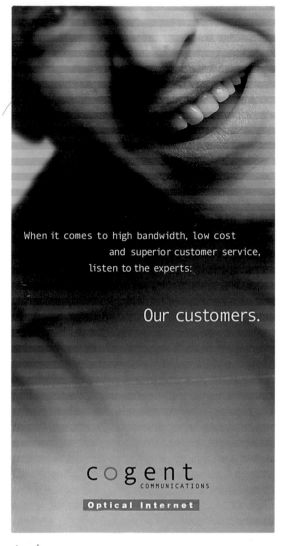

When it comes to high bandwidth, low cost
and superior customer service,
listen to the experts:

Our customers.

cogent
COMMUNICATIONS

Optical Internet

C - 86   C - 52
M - 58   M - 33
Y - 0   Y - 22
K - 0   K - 0

design firm
Don Schaaf & Friends, Inc.
Washington, D.C.
client
Cogent

design firm
Bernhardt Fudyma Design Group
New York, New York
client
Antigenics

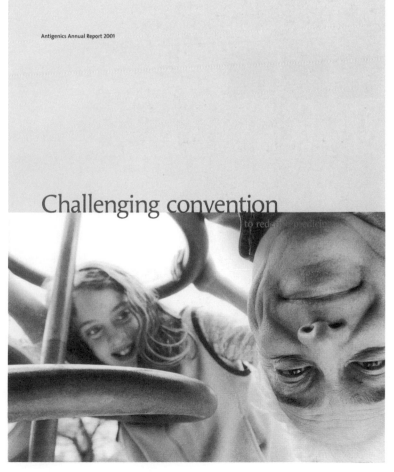

Antigenics Annual Report 2001

Challenging convention

C - 35   C - 36
M - 0   M - 26
Y - 13   Y - 25
K - 0   K - 0

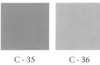

C - 70
M - 24
Y - 86
K - 25

C - 11
M - 98
Y - 86
K - 39

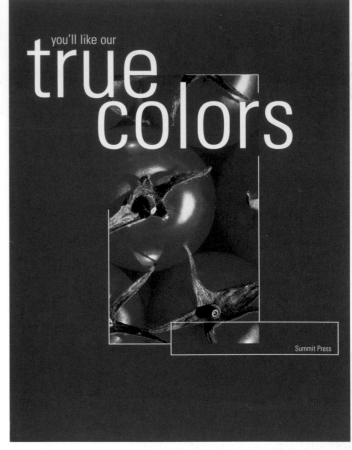

you'll like our
true
colors

Summit Press

design firm
Hull Creative Group
Boston, Massachusetts
client
Summit Press

C - 77
M - 66
Y - 26
K - 20

C - 0
M - 98
Y - 85
K - 4

C - 38
M - 79
Y - 84
K - 17

design firm
Kircher, Inc.
Washington, D.C.
client
International Association of
Amusement Parks and Attractions

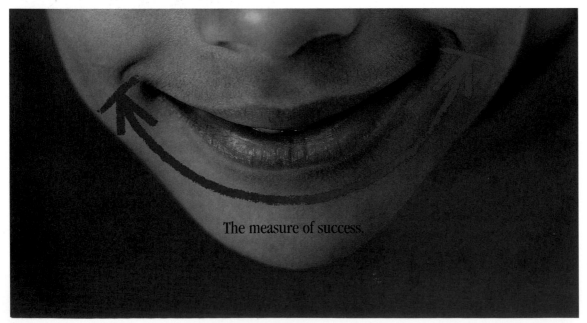

The measure of success.

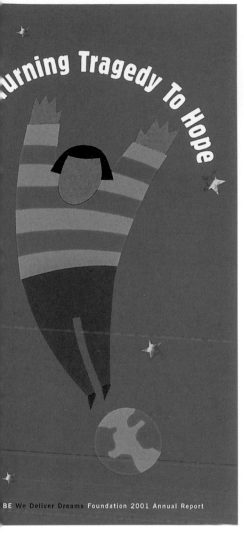

BE We Deliver Dreams Foundation 2001 Annual Report

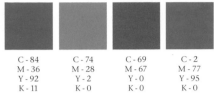

C - 84	C - 74	C - 69	C - 2
M - 36	M - 28	M - 67	M - 77
Y - 92	Y - 2	Y - 0	Y - 95
K - 11	K - 0	K - 0	K - 0

design firm
viadesign
San Diego, California
client
Mail Boxes Etc. Foundation

design firm
Rottman Creative Group, LLC
La Plata, Maryland
client
Rottman Creative Group, LLC

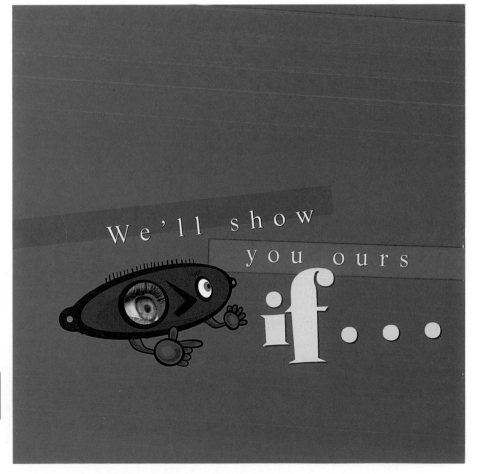

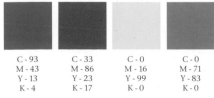

C - 93	C - 33	C - 0	C - 0
M - 43	M - 86	M - 16	M - 71
Y - 13	Y - 23	Y - 99	Y - 83
K - 4	K - 17	K - 0	K - 0

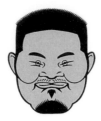

JAMES PETTUS
16 TIMBERLINE DRIVE FARMINGTON, CT 06032 USA
860.677.7116   jpet33@aol.com

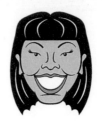

PATRICIA M. PETTUS
16 TIMBERLINE DRIVE FARMINGTON, CT 06032 USA
860.677.7116   patiopika@aol.com

C - 0   C - 98
M - 37   M - 95
Y - 48   Y - 95
K - 0   K - 90

design firm
Pettus Design
Farmington, Connecticut
client
James and Patricia Pettus

C - 0   C - 23
M - 0   M - 0
Y - 0   Y - 51
K - 100 K - 11

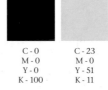

unitus

design firm
Belyea
Seattle, Washington
client
ColorGraphics

design firm
Hull Creative Group
Boston, Massachusetts
client
Dare Family Services

C - 33   C - 48
M - 85   M - 85
Y - 37   Y - 99
K - 55   K - 8

Dare
family services

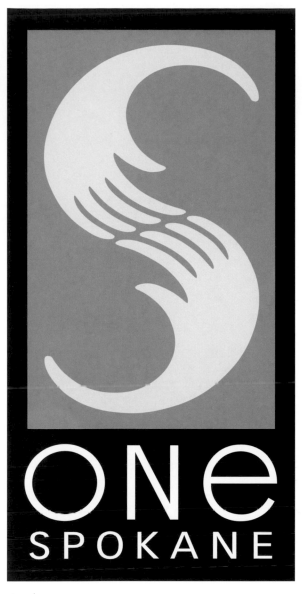

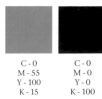

C - 0
M - 55
Y - 100
K - 15

C - 0
M - 0
Y - 0
K - 100

design firm
Klündt Hosmer Design
Spokane, Washington

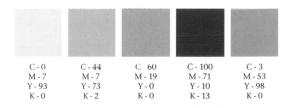

C - 0	C - 44	C - 60	C - 100	C - 3
M - 7	M - 7	M - 19	M - 71	M - 53
Y - 93	Y - 73	Y - 0	Y - 10	Y - 98
K - 0	K - 2	K - 0	K - 13	K - 0

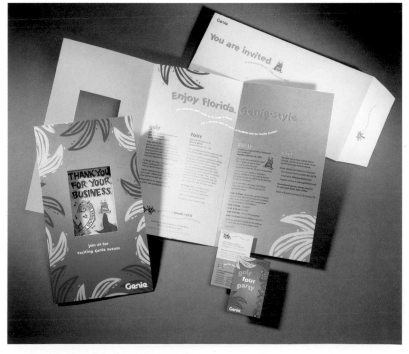

design firm
Belyea
Seattle, Washington
client
Genie Industries

Commissioning Editor: Madelene Hyde
Development Editor: Margaret Nelson
Project Manager: Maggie Johnson
Design: Stewart Larking
Illustration Manager: Jennifer Rose
Illustrator: Richard Tibbitts
Marketing Managers (UK/USA): Deborah Watkins for the UK and Veronica Short for US

COVER IMAGE
The micrograph on the cover shows Shigella
flexneri bound to Neutrophil Extracellular Traps (NETs),
a structure formed by neutrophil granulocytes that captures and kills pathogens.
Courtesy of Dr. Volker Brinkmann, Max Planck-Institut für Infektionsbiologie, Berlin.

DATE DUE

Mims' **Medical**
Microbiology

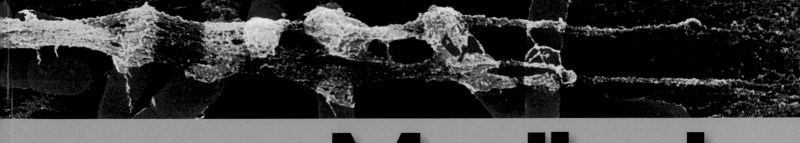

Mims' Medical Microbiology

Fifth Edition

Richard V Goering

BA MSc PhD
Professor and Chair
Department of Medical Microbiology
 and Immunology
Creighton University Medical Center
School of Medicine
Omaha, Nebraska USA

Hazel M Dockrell

BA (Mod) PhD
Professor of Immunology
Department of Infectious
 and Tropical Diseases
London School of Hygiene & Tropical
 Medicine
London, UK

Mark Zuckerman

BSc (Hons) MBBS MRCP MSc FRCPath
Consultant Virologist and Honorary Senior
 Lecturer
South London Specialist Virology Centre
King's College Hospital NHS
 Foundation Trust
King's College London School of Medicine
London, UK

Peter L Chiodini

BSc MBBS PhD FRCP FRCPath FFTM
RCPS (Glas)
Consultant Parasitologist
Hospital for Tropical Diseases
London
Honorary Professor
London School of Hygiene & Tropical
 Medicine
London, UK

Ivan M Roitt

DSc HonFRCP FRCPath FRS,
Hon Director
Middlesex Centre for Investigative
 & Diagnostic Oncology
School of Health & Social Sciences
Middlesex University
London, UK

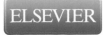

MIMS' MEDICAL MICROBIOLOGY (Main Edition)   ISBN: 978-0-7234-3601-0

MIMS' MEDICAL MICROBIOLOGY (International Edition)   ISBN: 978-0-8089-2440-1

British Library Cataloguing in Publication Data
A catalogue record for this book is available from the British Library

Library of Congress Cataloging in Publication Data
A catalog record for this book is available from the Library of Congress

Notices
Knowledge and best practice in this field are constantly changing. As new research and experience broaden our understanding, changes in research methods, professional practices, or medical treatment may become necessary.

Practitioners and researchers must always rely on their own experience and knowledge in evaluating and using any information, methods, compounds, or experiments described herein. In using such information or methods they should be mindful of their own safety and the safety of others, including parties for whom they have a professional responsibility.

With respect to any drug or pharmaceutical products identified, readers are advised to check the most current information provided (i) on procedures featured or (ii) by the manufacturer of each product to be administered, to verify the recommended dose or formula, the method and duration of administration, and contraindications. It is the responsibility of practitioners, relying on their own experience and knowledge of their patients, to make diagnoses, to determine dosages and the best treatment for each individual patient, and to take all appropriate safety precautions.

To the fullest extent of the law, neither the Publisher nor the authors, contributors, or editors, assume any liability for any injury and/or damage to persons or property as a matter of products liability, negligence or otherwise, or from any use or operation of any methods, products, instructions, or ideas contained in the material herein.

Printed in China

Last digit is the print number: 9 8 7 6 5 4 3 2 1

Preface

Medical Microbiology fifth edition continues the successful past approach of employing the dual viewpoints of basic science and system-based clinical application to present the conflict between infectious disease and host response. The title remains Mims' Medical Microbiology, recognizing the founding contribution of Cedric Mims to this work. Derek Wakelin, who played such a major part in earlier editions, has relinquished his role as a main author and we gratefully acknowledge his contribution.

This edition continues descriptive illustrations of 'Conflicts' in the introductory chapters as well as chapter-specific 'Lessons in Microbiology' and 'Key Facts' summaries. Discussion of microbial genomics, detection and diagnosis of infection, antimicrobial agents and chemotherapy, immune defence, tables, figures and the Pathogen Parade (now online-only) have all been updated. Chapter 32, Epidemiology and Control of Infectious Diseases, represents a total revision of text previously entitled Strategies for Control. Bibliographic references continue to include current Internet-based resources. Online access to interactive extras is provided via Elsevier's STUDENT CONSULT website (www.studentconsult.com) including chapter-specific questions and answers, mostly in USMLE format.

The contribution of molecular approaches to our understanding of pathogen–host response interaction has never been greater than it is today. The challenge is to incorporate this wealth of information into a logical and unified approach to the subject that is readable, exciting, and informative. We believe that is what the student will find in this new edition of Medical Microbiology.

Richard V Goering, Hazel M Dockrell, Mark Zuckerman,
Peter L Chiodini, Ivan M Roitt 2012

Acknowledgements

As in previous editions, we again express our sincere appreciation of the many colleagues who have helped in a variety of ways in the production of this text, particularly Mel Smith. Those who have kindly allowed us to use their illustrative material are duly acknowledged in the figure legends. We thank the Wellcome Institute for the History of Medicine for providing the portrait photographs used in the historical profiles. Other colleagues have patiently answered our questions and given valuable advice, ensuring accuracy and clarity as far as possible. Any remaining errors are entirely the responsibility of the authors. We would also like to thank the editorial and production staff of Elsevier, who have been unfailingly helpful and efficient.

RVG, HMD, MZ, PLC, IMR

Contributors

Dr Katharina Kranzer
Department of Clinical Research
Faculty of Infectious and
Tropical Diseases
London School of Hygiene &
Tropical Medicine
London, UK.

Student Consultants

Alison Bell
Queens' University Belfast
Belfast, UK
Year of Graduation 2013

Elizabeth Carr
University of St Andrews School of
Medicine
St Andrews, UK
Year of Graduation 2015

Terry Chen
Touro University Nevada College of
Osteopathic Medicine
Henderson, Nevada, USA
Year of Graduation 2014

Michael Cheng
David Geffen School of Medicine at UCLA
Los Angeles, California, USA
Year of Graduation 2012

Matthew Crowson
Dartmouth Medical School
Hanover, New Hampshire, USA
Year of Graduation 2013

Bernard Ho
St George's University of London
London, UK
Year of Graduation 2012

Contents

Contents

A contemporary approach to microbiology

INTRODUCTION

Microbes and parasites

The conventional distinction between 'microbes' and 'parasites' is essentially arbitrary

Microbiology is sometimes defined as the biology of microscopic organisms, its subject being the 'microbes'. Traditionally, clinical microbiology has been concerned with those organisms responsible for the major infectious diseases of humans and whose size makes them invisible to the naked eye. Thus, it is not surprising that the organisms included have reflected those causing diseases that have been (or continue to be) of greatest importance in those countries where the scientific and clinical discipline of microbiology developed, notably Europe and the USA. The term 'microbes' has usually been applied in a restricted fashion, primarily to viruses and bacteria. Fungi and protozoan parasites are included as relatively minor contributors, but in general they have been treated as the subjects of other disciplines (mycology and parasitology).

Although there can be no argument that viruses and bacteria are, globally, the most important pathogens, the conventional distinction between these as 'microbes' and the other infectious agents (fungi, protozoan, worm and arthropod parasites) is essentially arbitrary, not least because the criterion of microscopic visibility cannot be applied rigidly (Fig. Intro.1). Perhaps we should remember that the first 'microbe' to be associated with a specific clinical condition was a parasitic worm – the nematode *Trichinella spiralis* – whose larval stages are just visible to the naked eye (though microscopy is needed for certain identification). *T. spiralis* was first identified in 1835 and causally related to the disease trichinellosis in the 1860s. Equally, viruses and bacteria comprise only just over half of all human pathogen species (Table Intro.1).

THE CONTEXT FOR CONTEMPORARY MEDICAL MICROBIOLOGY

Many microbiology texts deal with infectious organisms as agents of disease in isolation, isolated both from other infectious organisms and from the biologic context in which they live and in which disease is caused. It is certainly convenient to list and deal with organisms group by group, to summarize the diseases they cause, and to review the forms of control available, but this approach produces a static picture of what is a dynamic relationship between the organism and its host.

Host response is the outcome of the complex interplay between host and parasite

Host response can be discussed in terms of pathologic signs and symptoms and in terms of immune control, but it is better treated as the outcome of the complex interplay between two organisms – host and parasite; without this dimension a distorted view of infectious disease results. It simply is not true that 'microbe + host = disease', and clinicians are well aware of this. Understanding why it is that most host–microbe contacts do not result in disease, and what changes so that disease does arise, is as important as the identification of infectious organisms and a knowledge of the ways in which they can be controlled.

We therefore continue to believe that our approach to microbiology, both in terms of the organisms that might usefully be considered within a textbook and also in terms of the contexts in which they and the diseases they cause are discussed, provides a more informative and more interesting picture of these dynamic interrelationships. There are many reasons for having reached this conclusion, the most important being the following:

- A comprehensive understanding now exists at the molecular level of the biology of infectious agents and of the host–parasite interactions that lead to infection and disease. It is important for students to be aware of this understanding so that they can grasp the connections between infection and disease within both individuals and communities and be able to use this knowledge in novel and changing clinical situations.
- It is now realized that the host's response to infection is a coordinated and subtle interplay involving the mechanisms of both innate and acquired resistance, and that these mechanisms are expressed regardless of the nature and identity of the pathogen involved. Our present understanding of the ways in which these mechanisms are stimulated and the ways in which they act is very sophisticated. We can now see that infection is a conflict between two organisms, with the outcome (resistance or disease) being critically dependent upon molecular interactions. Again, it is essential to understand the basis of this host–pathogen interplay if the processes of disease and disease control are to be interpreted correctly.

Emerging or re-emerging diseases continue to pose new microbiologic problems

Three other factors have helped to mould our opinion that a broader view of microbiology is needed to provide a firm basis for clinical and scientific practice:

- There is an increasing prevalence of a wide variety of opportunistic infections in patients who are hospitalized

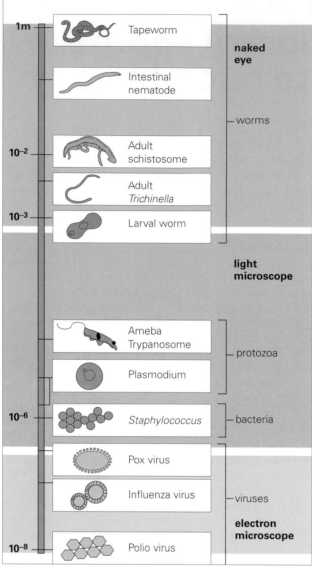

Figure Intro.1 Relative sizes of the organisms covered in this book.

Table Intro.1 Distribution of 1407 human pathogen species among the major groups of organisms (excluding arthropods)

Group	% of total
Viruses and prions	14–15
Bacteria	38–41
Fungi	22–23
Protozoa	4–5
Helminths	20

Data from average of multiple studies summarized by Smith, K.F. and Guegan, J-F, (2010) Changing geographic distributions of human pathogens. *Ann. Rev. Ecol. Evol.* 41:231–250.

or immunosuppressed. Immunosuppressive therapies are now more common, as are diseases in which the immune system is compromised – notably, of course, AIDS.

- Newly emerging disease agents continue to be identified, and old diseases, previously thought to be under control, re-emerge as causes of concern. Of the 1407 species identified as pathogenic for humans, 183 are regarded as emerging or re-emerging pathogens, almost half being viruses, some of animal origin (see Table Intro.1).
- Tropical infections are now of much greater interest. Clinicians see many tourists who have been exposed to the quite different spectrum of infectious agents found in tropical countries (at least 80 million people travel from resource-rich to resource-poor countries each year), and practicing microbiologists may be called upon to identify and advise on these organisms. There is also greater awareness of the health problems of the resource-poor world.

Thus, a broader view of microbiology is necessary; one that builds on the approaches of the past, but addresses the problems of the present and of the future.

MICROBIOLOGY PAST, PRESENT AND FUTURE

The demonstration in the nineteenth century that diseases were caused by infectious agents founded the discipline of microbiology. Although these early discoveries involved tropical parasitic infections as well as the bacterial infections common in Europe and the USA, microbiologists increasingly focused on the latter, later extending their interests to the newly discovered viral infections. The development of antimicrobial agents and vaccines revolutionized treatment of these diseases and raised hopes for the eventual elimination of many of the diseases that had plagued the human race for centuries. Those in the resource-rich world learned not to fear infectious disease and believed such infections would disappear in their lifetime. To an extent, this was realized; through vaccination, many familiar childhood diseases became uncommon, and those of bacterial origin were easily controlled by antibiotics. Encouraged by the eradication of smallpox during the 1970s, and the success of polio vaccines, the United Nations in 1978 announced programmes to obtain 'Health for All' by 2000. However, this optimistic picture has had to be re-evaluated.

Infectious diseases are still killers in the resource-rich world

Globally, infectious diseases cause more than 20% of all deaths and kill an increasing number in both the resource-rich and the resource-poor world. In the USA (and the picture is similar in Europe):

- deaths from HIV peaked at 50 000 in 1995, but still exceed 15 000 each year
- influenza with underlying respiratory and circulatory issues results in 15 000 deaths each year and affects millions
- some 3 to 4 million people carry hepatitis C virus, and ca. 12 000 develop life-threatening chronic liver disease
- drug-resistant tuberculosis (TB) is a major cause of concern, as are food-borne infections and healthcare-associated infections.

Infectious diseases are a major problem in the resource-poor world, particularly in children

The burden of infectious disease in the resource-poor world is increasing at an alarming rate, particularly in sub-Saharan Africa and SE Asia. Although sub-Saharan

Africa has only about 10% of the world's population, it has 67% of AIDS infections and a majority of all AIDS-related deaths, the highest HIV-TB co-infection rates and most of the global malaria burden. TB and HIV-AIDS are of increasing importance in SE Asia and the Pacific, where drug-resistant malaria is also common. Children younger than 5 years are most at risk from infectious diseases. Of the 8.1 million deaths in this age group recorded by WHO for the year 2009, at least half were due to infection such as acute respiratory infection and diarrheal diseases. The overwhelming majority of these infection-related deaths occurred in Africa, SE Asia and the Eastern Mediterranean. It is obvious that the prevalence and importance of infectious diseases in the resource-poor world are directly linked to poverty. The infectious diseases of most importance globally are shown in Table Intro.2.

Infections continue to emerge or re-emerge

On a world wide basis, between 1940 and 2004, 335 infectious diseases emerged in the human population for the first time. Since the 1970s, some familiar diseases, including TB, malaria, hepatitis, cholera and dengue, have re-emerged as major infections and more recently a number of new infectious agents have been identified (Table Intro.3), of which HIV is the most important. For many new diseases, there is no effective treatment. The economic cost of these diseases is enormous. For example, the total lifetime cost, including loss of productivity, for Americans diagnosed with AIDS is estimated to be greater than US$30 billion and in high-prevalence countries malaria consumes approximately 40% of public health spending. Successful eradication could therefore save very large sums, for example, an estimated US$20 billion from eradicating smallpox.

Modern lifestyles and technical developments facilitate transmission of disease

The reasons for the resurgence of infectious diseases are multiple. They include:

- New patterns of travel and trade (especially food commodities), new agricultural practices, altered sexual behaviour, medical interventions and overuse of antibiotics.
- The evolution of multi-drug resistant bacteria, such as MRSA, and their frequency in both healthcare and community settings have become major problems. The issue of antimicrobial resistance is compounded in resource-poor countries by inability or unwillingness to complete programmes of treatment, as seems to have happened with TB, and by the use of counterfeit drugs with, at best, partial action. The WHO estimates that globally 10% of antimicrobials (25% in resource-poor countries) are counterfeit, and a survey of seven African countries revealed that 20% to 90% of antimalarial drugs were substandard. In 2006, the WHO launched a new initiative to combat the lucrative business of counterfeit medical products including antibiotics and vaccines
- Breakdown of economic, social and political systems especially in the resource-poor world has weakened medical services and increased the effects of poverty and malnutrition.
- The dramatic increase in air travel over the last few decades has facilitated the spread of infection and increased the threat of new pandemics. The Spanish influenza pandemic in 1918 spread along railway and sea links. Modern air travel moves larger numbers of people more rapidly and more extensively and makes it possible for microbes to cross geographical barriers. The potential for spread of the SARS virus from Asia to Europe and North America provided a salutary reminder of these dangers.

What of the future?

Predictions based on data from the United Nations and the World Health Organization give a choice of optimistic, stable or pessimistic scenarios. Optimistically, the aging population, coupled with socioeconomic and medical advances, should see a fall in the problems posed by infectious disease, and a decrease in deaths from these causes from 34% of the global total in 1990 to 15% in 2020; HIV and TB would, however, still be responsible for a majority of deaths from infection. In 2009, 1.7 million people died of TB, 24% of whom were HIV positive, and 22% of the 1.8 million deaths in HIV-positive individuals were due to TB. The pessimistic view is that population growth in resource-poor countries, especially in urban populations, the increasing gap between rich and poor countries, and continuing changes in lifestyle will result in surges of infectious disease. Even in resource-rich countries, increasing drug resistance and a slowing of

Table Intro.2 Major infectious disease-related deaths worldwide*

Cause	Estimated number of deaths (millions)	Percent of total deaths
Lower respiratory tract infections	4.18	7.1
Diarrheal diseases	2.16	3.7
HIV/AIDS	2.04	2.5
Tuberculosis	1.46	2.5

*Data from WHO (2008).

Table Intro.3 Emerging diseases – examples of new infectious agents identified since the 1970s

Decade	Organisms
1980–1989	HTLV-1, HTLV-2, human herpes virus 6, HIV, hepatitis C, E. coli 0157, Borrelia burgdorferi, Helicobacter, toxin-producing Staph. aureus
1990–1999	Hanta virus, human herpes virus 8, hepatitis E-G, vCJD, Hendra virus, Nipah virus, Vibrio cholerae 0139, Cryptosporidium, Cyclospora
2000–present day	SARS associated coronavirus, epizootic avian influenza H5N1, HTLV-3, HTLV-4, xenotropic MuLV-related virus

HTLV, human T-cell lymphotropic virus; HIV, human immunodeficiency virus; vCJD, variant Creutzfeldt–Jakob disease; SARS, severe acute respiratory syndrome.

developments in new antimicrobials and vaccines will create problems in control. Added to these are three additional factors. These are:

- the emergence of new human infections such as a novel strain of influenza virus, or a new infection of wildlife origin
- climate change, with increased temperatures and altered rainfall adding to the incidence of vector-borne infection
- the threat of bioterrorism, with the possible deliberate spread of viral and bacterial infections.

The deliberate spread of anthrax through the US mail system in 2002 raised the frightening possibility that previously rare but potentially deadly infections might be deliberately spread to human populations with no acquired immunity or no history of vaccination. The range of organisms that could be used in this way includes exotic viruses (e.g. those causing haemorrhagic fevers and encephalitis), genetically modified organisms, or organisms such as smallpox, thought now to be extinct.

One thing is certain: whether optimistic or pessimistic scenarios prove true, microbiology will remain a critical medical discipline for the foreseeable future.

THE APPROACH ADOPTED IN THIS BOOK

The factors outlined above indicate the need for a text with a dual function:

1. It should provide an inclusive treatment of the organisms responsible for infectious disease.
2. The purely clinical/laboratory approach to microbiology should be replaced with an approach that will stress the biologic context in which clinical/laboratory studies are to be undertaken.

The approach we have adopted in this book is to look at microbiology from the viewpoint of the conflicts inherent in all host–pathogen relationships. We first describe the adversaries: the infectious organisms on the one hand, and the innate and adaptive defence mechanisms of the host on the other. The outcome of the conflicts between the two is then amplified and discussed system by system. Rather than taking each organism or each disease manifestation in turn, we look at the major environments available for infectious organisms in the human body, such as the respiratory system, the gut, the urinary tract, the blood and the central nervous system. The organisms that invade and establish in each of these are examined in terms of the pathologic responses they provoke. Finally, we look at how the conflicts we have described can be controlled or eliminated, both at the level of the individual patient and at the level of the community. We hope that such an approach will provide readers with a dynamic view of host–pathogen interactions and allow them to develop a more creative understanding of infection and disease.

KEY FACTS

- Our approach is to provide a comprehensive account of the organisms that cause infectious disease in humans, from the viruses to the worms, and to cover the biologic bases of infection, disease, host–pathogen interactions, disease control and epidemiology.

- The diseases caused by microbial pathogens will be placed in the context of the conflict that exists between them and the innate and adaptive defences of their hosts.

- Infections will be described and discussed in terms of the major body systems, treating these as environments in which microbes can establish themselves, flourish and give rise to pathologic changes.

The adversaries – microbes

Microbes as parasites

THE VARIETIES OF MICROBES

Prokaryotes and eukaryotes

A number of important and distinctive biologic characteristics must be taken into account when considering any organism in relation to infectious disease. One of these is the way in which the organism is constructed, particularly the way in which genetic material and other cellular components are organized.

All organisms other than viruses and prions are made up of cells

Viruses are not cells – they do have genetic material (DNA or RNA) but lack cell membranes, cytoplasm and the machinery for synthesizing macromolecules, depending instead upon host cells for this process. Conventional viruses have their genetic material packed in capsules. The agents (prions) which cause diseases such as Creutzfeldt–Jakob disease (CJD), variant CJD and kuru in humans, scrapie and bovine spongiform encephalopathy (BSE) in animals, appear to lack nucleic acid and consist only of infectious proteinaceous particles.

All other organisms have a cellular organization, their bodies being made up of single cells (most 'microbes') or of many cells. Each cell has genetic material (DNA) and cytoplasm with synthetic machinery, and is bounded by a cell membrane.

Bacteria are prokaryotes, all other organisms are eukaryotes

There are many differences between the two major divisions: prokaryotes and eukaryotes, of cellular organisms (Fig. 1.1). These include the following.

In prokaryotes:

- A distinct nucleus is absent.
- DNA is in the form of a single circular chromosome. Additional 'extrachromosomal' DNA is carried in plasmids.
- Transcription and translation can be carried out simultaneously.

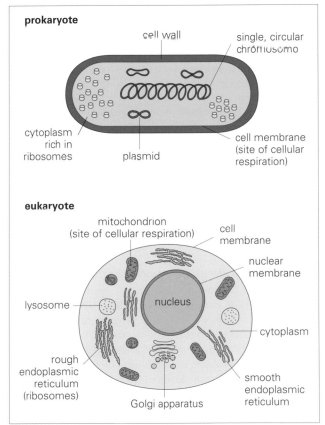

Figure 1.1 Prokaryote and eukaryote cells. The major features of cellular organization are shown diagrammatically.

In eukaryotes:

- DNA is carried on several chromosomes within a nucleus.
- The nucleus is bounded by a nuclear membrane.
- Transcription requires formation of messenger RNA (mRNA) and movement of mRNA out of the nucleus into the cytoplasm
- Translation takes place on ribosomes.
- The cytoplasm is rich in membrane-bound organelles (mitochondria, endoplasmic reticulum, Golgi apparatus, lysosomes) which are absent in prokaryotes.

Gram-negative bacteria have an outer lipopolysaccharide-rich layer

Another important difference between prokaryotes and the majority of eukaryotes is that the cell membrane (plasma membrane) of prokaryotes is covered by a thick protective cell wall. In Gram-positive bacteria, this wall, made of peptidoglycan, forms the external surface of the cell, while in Gram-negative bacteria there is an additional outer layer rich in lipopolysaccharides. These layers play an important role in protecting the cell against the immune system and chemotherapeutic agents, and in stimulating certain pathologic responses. They also confer antigenicity.

Microparasites and macroparasites

Microparasites replicate within the host

There is an important distinction between microparasites and macroparasites that overrides their differences in size. *Micro*parasites (viruses, bacteria, protozoa, fungi) replicate within the host and can, theoretically, multiply to produce a very large number of progeny, thereby causing an overwhelming infection. In contrast, *macro*parasites (worms, arthropods), even those that are microscopic, do not have this ability: one infectious stage matures into one reproducing stage, and, in most cases, the resulting progeny leave the host to continue the cycle. The level of infection is therefore determined by the numbers of organisms that enter the body. This distinction between microparasites and macroparasites has important clinical and epidemiologic implications.

The boundary between microparasites and macroparasites is not always clear. The progeny of some macroparasites do remain within the host, and infections can lead to the build-up of overwhelming numbers, particularly in immune-suppressed patients. The roundworms *Trichinella, Strongyloides stercoralis* and some filarial nematodes, and *Sarcoptes scabiei* (the itch mite), are examples of this type of parasite.

Organisms that are small enough can live inside cells

Absolute size has other biologically significant implications for the host–pathogen relationship, which cut across the divisions between micro- and macroparasites. Perhaps the most important of these is the relative size of a pathogen and its host's cells. Organisms that are small enough can live inside cells and, by doing so, establish a biologic relationship with the host that is quite different from that of an extracellular organism – one that influences both disease and control.

LIVING INSIDE OR OUTSIDE CELLS

The basis of all host–pathogen relationships is the exploitation by one organism (the pathogen) of the environment provided by another (the host). The nature and degree of exploitation varies from relationship to relationship, but the pathogen's primary requirement is a supply of metabolic materials from the host, whether provided in the form of nutrients or (as in the case of viruses) in the form of nuclear synthetic machinery. The reliance of viruses upon host synthetic machinery requires an obligatory intracellular habit: viruses must live within host cells. Some other groups of pathogens (*Chlamydia, Rickettsia*) also live only within cells. In the remaining groups of pathogens, different species have adopted either the intracellular or the extracellular habit, or, in a few cases, both. Intracellular microparasites other than viruses take their metabolic requirements directly from the pool of nutrients available in the cell itself, whereas extracellular organisms take theirs from the nutrients present in tissue fluids, or, occasionally, by feeding directly on host cells (e.g. *Entamoeba histolytica*, the organism associated with amoebic dysentery). Macroparasites are almost always extracellular (though *Trichinella* is intracellular), and many feed by ingesting and digesting host cells; others can take up nutrients directly from tissue fluids or intestinal contents.

Pathogens within cells are protected from many of the host's defence mechanisms

As will be discussed in greater detail in Chapter 13, the intracellular pathogens pose problems for the host that are quite different from those posed by extracellular organisms. Pathogens that live within cells are largely protected against many of the host's defence mechanisms while they remain there, particularly against the action of specific antibodies. Control of these infections depends therefore on the activities of intracellular killing mechanisms, short-range mediators or cytotoxic agents, although the latter may destroy both the pathogen and the host cell, leading to tissue damage. This problem, of targeting activity against the pathogen when it lives within a vulnerable cell, also arises when using drugs or antibiotics, as it is difficult to achieve selective action against the pathogen while leaving the host cell intact. Even more problematic is the fact that many intracellular pathogens live inside the very cells responsible for the host's immune and inflammatory mechanisms and therefore depress the host's defensive abilities. For example, a variety of viral, bacterial and protozoal pathogens live inside macrophages, and several viruses (including HIV) are specific for lymphocytes.

Intracellular life has many advantages for the pathogen. It provides access to the host's nutrient supply and its genetic machinery and allows escape from host surveillance and antimicrobial defences. However, no organism can be wholly intracellular at all times: if it is to replicate successfully, transmission must occur between the host's cells, and this inevitably involves some exposure to the extracellular environment. As far as the host is concerned, this extracellular phase in the development of the pathogen provides an opportunity to control infection through defence mechanisms such as phagocytosis, antibody and complement. However, transmission between cells can involve destruction of the initially infected cell and so contribute to tissue damage and general host pathology.

Living outside cells provides opportunities for growth, reproduction and dissemination

Extracellular pathogens can grow and reproduce freely, and may move extensively within the tissues of the body. However, they also face constraints on their survival and development. The most important is continuous exposure to components of the host's defence mechanisms, particularly antibody, complement and phagocytic cells.

The characteristics of extracellular organisms lead to pathologic consequences that are quite different from those associated with intracellular species. These are seen most dramatically with the macroparasites, whose sheer physical size, reproductive capacity and mobility can result in extensive destruction of host tissues. Many extracellular pathogens have the ability to spread rapidly through extracellular fluids or to move rapidly over surfaces, resulting in a widespread infection within a relatively short time. The rapid colonization of the entire mucosal surface of the small bowel by *Vibrio cholerae* is a good example. Successful host defence against extracellular parasites requires mechanisms that differ from those used in defence against intracellular parasites. The variety of locations and tissues occupied by extracellular parasites also poses problems for the host in ensuring effective deployment of defence mechanisms. Defence against intestinal parasites requires components of the innate and adaptive immune systems that are quite distinct from those effective against parasites in other sites, and those living in the lumen may be unaffected by responses operating in the mucosa. These problems in mounting effective defence are most acute where large macroparasites are concerned, because their size often renders them insusceptible to defence mechanisms that can be used against smaller organisms. For example, worms cannot be phagocytosed; they often have protective external layers, and can actively move away from areas where the host response is activated.

SYSTEMS OF CLASSIFICATION

Infectious diseases are caused by organisms belonging to a very wide range of different groups – prions, viruses, bacteria, fungi, protozoa, helminths (worms) and arthropods. Each has its own system of classification, making it possible to identify and categorize the organisms concerned. Correct identification is an essential requirement for accurate diagnosis and effective treatment. Identification is achieved by a variety of means, from simple observation to molecular analysis. Classification is being revolutionized by the application of genome sequencing. Many of the major pathogens in all categories have now been sequenced and this is allowing not only more precise identification but also a greater understanding of the interrelationships of members within each taxonomic group.

The approaches used vary between the major groups. For the protozoa, fungi, worms and arthropods, the basic unit of classification is the species, essentially defined as a group of organisms capable of reproducing sexually with one another. Species provide the basis for the binomial system of classification, used for eukaryote and some prokaryote organisms. Species are in turn grouped into a 'genus' (closely related but non-interbreeding species). Each organism is identified by two names, indicating the 'genus' and the 'species', respectively, for example, *Homo sapiens* and *Escherichia coli*. Related genera are grouped into progressively broader and more inclusive categories.

Classification of bacteria and viruses

The concept of 'species' is a basic difficulty in classifying prokaryotes and viruses, although the categories of genus and species are routinely used for bacteria. Classification of bacteria uses a mixture of easily determined microscopic, macroscopic and biochemical characteristics, based on size, shape, colour, staining properties, respiration and reproduction, and a more sophisticated analysis of immunologic and molecular criteria. The former characteristics can be used to divide the organisms into conventional taxonomic groupings, as shown for the Gram-positive bacteria in Figure 1.2 (see also Ch. 2).

Correct identification of bacteria below the species level is often vital to differentiate pathogenic and non-pathogenic forms

Correct treatment requires correct identification. For some bacteria, the important subspecies groups are identified on the basis of their immunologic properties. Cell wall, flagellar and capsule antigens are used in tests with specific antisera to define serogroups and serotypes (e.g. in salmonellae, streptococci, shigellae, *E. coli*). These tests are particularly useful for those organisms which grow poorly or not at all in vitro. Biochemical characteristics can be used to define other subspecies groupings (biotypes, strains, groups). For example, certain strains of *Staphylococcus aureus* release a β-haemolysin (causing red blood cells to lyse). Production of other toxins is also important in differentiating between groups, as in *E. coli*. Antibiotic susceptibility is also a useful technique for identification. Bacteria can also be classified below species level by their susceptibility to particular bacteriophage viruses. Phage typing is used, e.g. in differentiating between isolates of *Vibrio cholerae* and *Salmonella enterica* serovars.

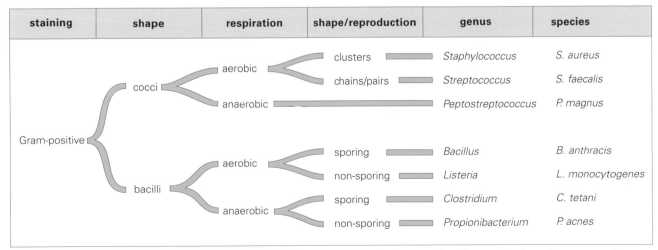

staining	shape	respiration	shape/reproduction	genus	species
Gram-positive	cocci	aerobic	clusters	*Staphylococcus*	*S. aureus*
			chains/pairs	*Streptococcus*	*S. faecalis*
		anaerobic		*Peptostreptococcus*	*P. magnus*
	bacilli	aerobic	sporing	*Bacillus*	*B. anthracis*
			non-sporing	*Listeria*	*L. monocytogenes*
		anaerobic	sporing	*Clostridium*	*C. tetani*
			non-sporing	*Propionibacterium*	*P. acnes*

Figure 1.2 How the structural and biologic characteristics of bacteria can be used in classification, taking Gram-positive bacteria as an example.

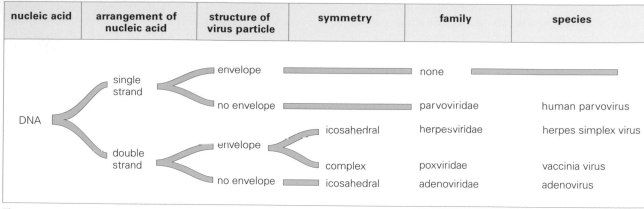

nucleic acid	arrangement of nucleic acid	structure of virus particle	symmetry	family	species
		envelope		none	
	single strand	no envelope		parvoviridae	human parvovirus
DNA		envelope	icosahedral	herpesviridae	herpes simplex virus
	double strand		complex	poxviridae	vaccinia virus
		no envelope	icosahedral	adenoviridae	adenovirus

Figure 1.3 How the characteristics of viruses can be used in classification, taking DNA viruses as an example.

Direct genetic approaches are also used in identification and classification such as the use of the polymerase chain reaction (PCR) and probes to detect organism-specific sentinel DNA sequences.

Classification of viruses departs even further from the binomial system

For viruses, families and, sometimes, genera are used, but there is much debate about the validity of the species concept for these organisms. Virus names draw on a wide variety of characteristics, e.g. size, structure, pathology, tissue location or distribution. Groupings are based on characteristics such as the type of nucleic acid present (DNA or RNA), the mode of replication, the symmetry of the virus particle (icosahedral, helical or complex) and the presence or absence of an external envelope, as shown for the DNA viruses in Figure 1.3 (see also Ch. 3). The equivalents of subspecies categories are also used, and indeed are more easily determined than species could be, given the peculiar biologic characteristics of viruses. These categories include serotypes, strains, variants and isolates and are determined primarily by serologic reactivity of virus material. The influenza virus, for example, can be considered as the equivalent of a genus containing three types (A, B, C). Identification can be carried out using the stable nucleoprotein antigen, which differs between the three types. The neuraminidase and haemagglutinin antigens are not stable and show variation within types. Characterization of these antigens in an isolate enables the particular variant to be identified, haemagglutinin (H) and neuraminidase (N) variants being designated by numbers, e.g. H5N1, the variant associated with fatal avian influenza (see Ch. 19). A further example is seen in adenoviruses, for which the various antigens associated with a component of the capsid can be used to define groups, types and finer subdivisions. The rapid rate of mutation shown by some viruses (e.g. HIV) creates particular problems for classification. The population present in a virus-infected individual may be genetically quite diverse and may best be described as a quasispecies – representing the average of the broad spectrum of variants present.

Classification assists diagnosis and the understanding of pathogenicity

Prompt identification of organisms is necessary clinically so that diagnoses can be made and appropriate treatments advised. To understand host–parasite interactions, however, not only should the identity of an organism be known, but as much as possible of its general biology; useful predictions can then be made about the consequences of infection. For these reasons, in subsequent chapters, we have included outline classifications of the important pathogens, accompanied by brief accounts of their structure (gross and microscopic), modes of life, molecular biology, biochemistry, replication and reproduction.

KEY FACTS

- Organisms that cause infectious diseases can be grouped into seven major categories: prions, viruses, bacteria, fungi, protozoa, helminths and arthropods.

- Identification and classification of these organisms is an important part of microbiology and essential for correct diagnosis, treatment and control.

- Each group has distinctive characteristics (structural and molecular make-up, biochemical and metabolic strategies, reproductive processes) which determine how the organisms interact with their hosts and how they cause disease.

- Many pathogens live within cells, where they are protected from many components of the host's protective responses.

The bacteria 2

Although free-living bacteria exist in huge numbers, relatively few species cause disease. The majority of these are well known and well studied; however, new pathogens continue to emerge and the significance of previously unrecognized infections becomes apparent. Good examples of the latter include infection with *Legionella*, the cause of Legionnaires' disease, coronavirus-associated severe acute respiratory syndrome (SARS), and gastric ulcers associated with *Helicobacter pylori* infection. Bacteria are single-celled prokaryotes, their DNA forming a long circular molecule, but not contained within a defined nucleus. Many are motile, using a unique pattern of flagella. The bacterial cell is surrounded by a complex cell wall and often a thick capsule. They reproduce by binary fission, often at very high rates, and show a wide range of metabolic patterns, both aerobic and anaerobic. Classification of bacteria uses both phenotypic and genotypic data. For clinical purposes, the phenotypic data are of most practical value, and rest on an understanding of bacterial structure and biology (see Fig. 32.15) Detailed summaries of members of the major bacterial groups are given in the Pathogen Parade (see online appendix).

STRUCTURE

Bacteria are 'prokaryotes' and have a characteristic cellular organization

The genetic information of bacteria is carried in a long, double-stranded (ds), circular molecule of DNA (Fig. 2.1). By analogy with eukaryotes (see Ch. 1), this can be termed a 'chromosome', but there are no introns; instead, the DNA comprises a continuous coding sequence of genes. The chromosome is not localized within a distinct nucleus; no nuclear membrane is present and the DNA is tightly coiled into a region known as the 'nucleoid'. Genetic information in the cell may also be extrachromosomal, present as small circular self-replicating DNA molecules termed plasmids. The cytoplasm contains no organelles other than ribosomes for protein synthesis. Although ribosomal function is the same in both pro- and eukaryotic cells, organelle structure is different. Ribosomes are characterized as 70S in prokaryotes and 80S in eukaryotes (the 'S' unit relates to how a particle behaves when studied under extreme centrifugal force in an ultracentrifuge). The bacterial 70S ribosome is specifically targeted by antimicrobials such as the aminoglycosides (see Ch. 33). Many of the metabolic functions performed in eukaryote cells by membrane-bound organelles such as mitochondria are carried out by the prokaryotic cell membrane. In all bacteria except mycoplasmas, the cell is surrounded by a complex cell wall. External to this wall may be capsules, flagella and pili. Knowledge of the cell wall and these external structures is important in diagnosis and pathogenicity and for understanding bacterial biology.

Bacteria are classified according to their cell wall as Gram-positive or Gram-negative

Gram staining is a basic microbiologic procedure for detection and identification of bacteria (see Ch. 32). The main structural component of the cell wall is a 'peptidoglycan'

Figure 2.1 Diagrammatic structure of a generalized bacterium.

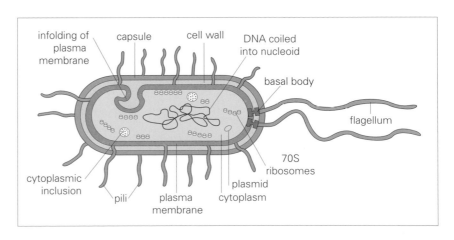

infolding of plasma membrane

capsule

cell wall

DNA coiled into nucleoid

basal body

flagellum

70S ribosomes

plasmid

cytoplasm

plasma membrane

pili

cytoplasmic inclusion

(mucopeptide or murein), a mixed polymer of hexose sugars (*N*-acetylglucosamine and *N*-acetylmuramic acid) and amino acids.

- In Gram-positive bacteria, the peptidoglycan forms a thick (20–80 nm) layer external to the cell membrane, and may contain other macromolecules.
- In Gram-negative species, the peptidoglycan layer is thin (5–10 nm) and is overlaid by an outer membrane, anchored to lipoprotein molecules in the peptidoglycan layer. The principal molecules of the outer membrane are lipopolysaccharides and lipoprotein (Fig. 2.2).

The polysaccharides and charged amino acids in the peptidoglycan layer make it highly polar, providing the bacterium with a thick hydrophilic surface. This property allows Gram-positive organisms to resist the activity of bile in the intestine. Conversely, the layer is digested by lysozyme, an enzyme present in body secretions, which therefore has bactericidal properties. Synthesis of peptidoglycan is disrupted by beta-lactam and glycopeptides antibiotics (see Ch. 33).

In Gram-negative bacteria, the outer membrane is also hydrophilic, but the lipid components of the constituent molecules give hydrophobic properties as well. Entry of hydrophilic molecules such as sugars and amino acids is necessary for nutrition and is achieved through special channels or pores formed by proteins called 'porins'. The lipopolysaccharide (LPS) in the membrane confers both antigenic properties (the 'O antigens' from the carbohydrate chains) and toxic properties (the 'endotoxin' from the lipid A component; see Ch. 17).

In the Gram-positive mycobacteria, the peptidoglycan layer has a different chemical basis for cross-linking to the lipoprotein layer, and the outer envelope contains a variety of complex lipids (mycolic acids). These create a waxy layer, which both alters the staining properties of these organisms (the so-called acid-fast bacteria) and gives considerable resistance to drying and other environmental factors. Mycobacterial cell wall components also have a pronounced adjuvant activity (i.e. they promote immunologic responsiveness).

External to the cell wall may be an additional capsule of high molecular weight polysaccharides (or amino acids in anthrax bacilli) that gives a slimy surface. This provides protection against phagocytosis by host cells and is important in determining virulence. With *Streptococcus pneumoniae* infection, only a few capsulated organisms can cause a fatal infection, but unencapsulated mutants cause no disease.

The cell wall is a major contributor to the ultimate shape of the organism, an important characteristic for bacterial identification. In general, bacterial shapes (Fig. 2.3) are categorized as either spherical (cocci), rods (bacilli) or helical (spirilla), although there are variations on these themes.

Many bacteria possess flagella

Flagella are long helical filaments extending from the cell surface, which enable bacteria to move in their environment. These may be restricted to the poles of the cell, singly (polar) or in tufts (lophotrichous), or distributed over the general surface of the cell (peritrichous). Bacterial flagella are quite different from eukaryote flagella, and the forces that result in movement are generated quite differently (being independent of adenosine triphosphate (ATP)). Motility allows positive and negative responses to chemical stimuli (chemotaxis). Flagella are built of protein components (flagellins), which are strongly antigenic. These antigens, the H antigens, are important targets of protective antibody responses.

Pili are another form of bacterial surface projection

Pili (fimbriae) are more rigid than flagella and function in attachment, either to other bacteria (the 'sex' pili) or to host cells (the 'common' pili). Adherence to host cells involves specific interactions between component molecules of the pili (adhesins) and molecules in host cell membranes. For example, the adhesins of *Escherichia coli* interact with fucose/mannose molecules on the surface of intestinal epithelial cells (see Ch. 22). The presence of many pili may help to prevent phagocytosis, reducing host resistance to bacterial infection. Although immunogenic, their antigens can be changed, allowing the bacteria to avoid immune recognition. The

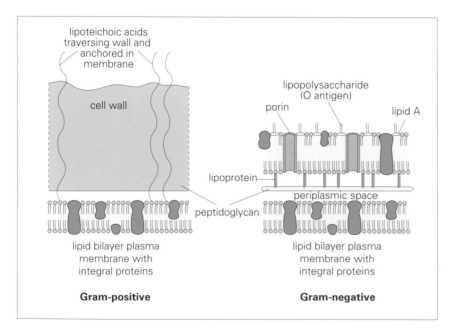

Figure 2.2 Construction of the cell walls of Gram-positive and Gram-negative bacteria.

Figure 2.3 The three basic shapes of bacterial cells.

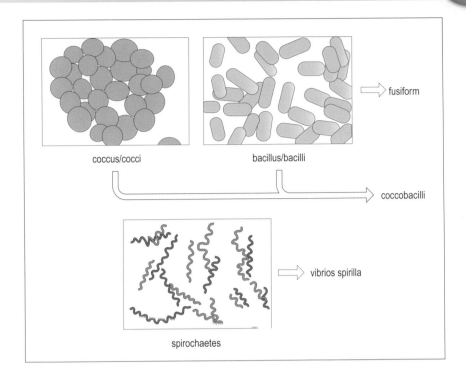

mechanism of 'antigenic variation' has been elucidated in the gonococci and is known to involve recombination of genes coding for 'constant' and 'variable' regions of pili molecules.

NUTRITION

Bacteria obtain nutrients mainly by taking up small molecules across the cell wall

Bacteria take up small molecules such as amino acids, oligosaccharides and small peptides across the cell wall. Gram-negative species can also take up and use larger molecules after preliminary digestion in the periplasmic space. Uptake and transport of nutrients into the cytoplasm is achieved by the cell membrane using a variety of transport mechanisms, including facilitated diffusion which utilizes a carrier to move compounds to equalize their intra- and extracellular concentrations, and active transport where energy is expended to deliberately increase intracellular concentrations of a substrate. Oxidative metabolism (see below) also takes place at the membrane–cytoplasm interface.

Some species require only minimal nutrients in their environment, having considerable synthetic powers, whereas others have complex nutritional requirements. *E. coli*, for example, can be grown in media providing only glucose and inorganic salts; streptococci, on the other hand, will grow only in complex media providing them with many organic compounds. Nevertheless, all bacteria have similar general nutritional requirements for growth which are summarized in Table 2.1.

All pathogenic bacteria are heterotrophic

All bacteria obtain energy by oxidizing preformed organic molecules (carbohydrates, lipids and proteins) from their environment. Metabolism of these molecules yields ATP as

Table 2.1 Major nutritional requirements for bacterial growth

Element	Cell dry weight (%)	Major cellular role
Carbon	50	Molecular 'building block' obtained from organic compounds or CO_2
Oxygen	20	Molecular 'building block' obtained from organic compounds, O_2 or H_2O; O_2 is an electron acceptor in aerobic respiration
Nitrogen	14	Component of amino acids, nucleotides, nucleic acids and coenzymes obtained from organic compounds and inorganic sources such as $NH4^+$
Hydrogen	8	Molecular 'building block' obtained from organic compounds, H_2O, or H_2; involved in respiration to produce energy
Phosphorus	3	Found in a variety of cellular components including nucleotides, nucleic acids, lipopolysaccharide (lps) and phospholipids; obtained from inorganic phosphates (PO_4^{3-})
Sulphur	1–2	Component of several amino acids and coenzymes; obtained from organic compounds and inorganic sources such as sulfates (SO_4^{2-})
Potassium	1–2	Important inorganic cation, enzyme cofactor, etc., obtained from inorganic sources

an energy source. Metabolism may be aerobic, where the final electron acceptor is oxygen, or anaerobic, where the final acceptor may be an organic or inorganic molecule other than oxygen.

- In aerobic metabolism (i.e. aerobic respiration), complete utilization of an energy source such as glucose produces 38 molecules of ATP.
- Anaerobic metabolism utilizing an inorganic molecule other than oxygen as the final hydrogen acceptor (anaerobic respiration) is incomplete and produces fewer ATP molecules than aerobic respiration.
- Anaerobic metabolism utilizing an organic final hydrogen acceptor (fermentation) is much less efficient and produces only two molecules of ATP.

Anaerobic metabolism, while less efficient, can thus be used in the absence of oxygen when appropriate substrates are available, as they usually are in the host's body. The requirement for oxygen in respiration may be 'obligate' or it may be 'facultative', some organisms being able to switch between aerobic and anaerobic metabolism. Those that use fermentation pathways often use the major product pyruvate in secondary fermentations by which additional energy can be generated. The interrelationship between these different metabolic pathways is illustrated in Figure 2.4.

The ability of bacteria to grow in the presence of atmospheric oxygen relates to their ability to enzymatically deal with potentially destructive intracellular reactive oxygen species (e.g. free radicals, anions containing oxygen, etc.) (Table 2.2). The interaction between these harmful compounds and detoxifying enzymes such as superoxide dismutase, peroxidase, and catalase is illustrated in Figure 2.5 (also see Ch. 9 and Box 9.2).

GROWTH AND DIVISION

The rate at which bacteria grow and divide depends in large part on the nutritional status of the environment. The growth and division of a single *E. coli* cell into identical 'daughter cells' may occur in as little as 20–30 min in rich laboratory media, whereas the same process is much slower (1–2 h) in a nutritionally depleted environment. Conversely, even in the best environment, other bacteria such as *Mycobacterium tuberculosis* may grow much more slowly, dividing every 24 h. When introduced into a new environment, bacterial growth follows a characteristic pattern depicted in Figure 2.6. After an initial period of adjustment (lag phase), cell division rapidly occurs, with the population doubling at a constant rate (generation time), for a period termed log or exponential phase. As nutrients

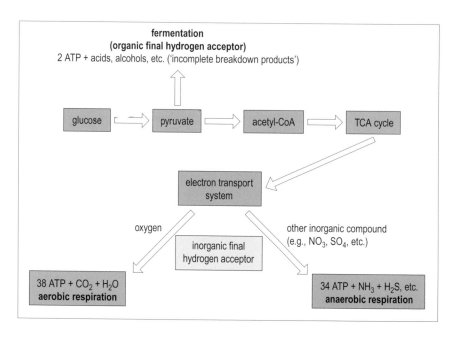

Figure 2.4 Catabolic breakdown of glucose in relationship to final hydrogen acceptor.

Table 2.2 Bacterial classification in response to environmental oxygen

Environmental oxygen			
Category	Present	Absent	Oxygen detoxifying enzymes (e.g. superoxide dismutase, catalase, peroxidase)
Obligate aerobe	Growth	No growth	Present
Microaerophile	Growth in low oxygen levels	No growth	Some enzymes absent; reduced enzyme concentration
Obligate anaerobe	No growth	Growth	Absent
Facultative (anaerobe/ aerobe)	Growth	Growth	Present

Figure 2.5 Interaction between oxygen detoxifying enzymes.

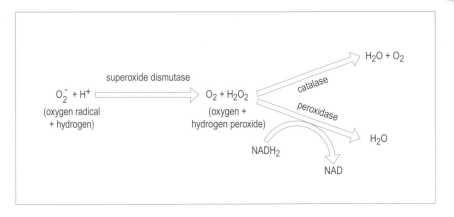

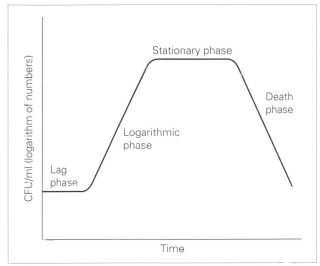

Figure 2.6 The bacterial growth curve. CFU, colony-forming units.

are depleted and toxic products accumulate, cell growth slows to a stop (stationary phase) and eventually enters a phase of decline (death).

A bacterial cell must duplicate its genomic DNA before it can divide

All bacterial genomes are circular, and their replication begins at a single site known as the origin of replication (termed OriC). A multienzyme replication complex binds to the origin and initiates unwinding and separation of the two DNA strands, using enzymes called helicases and topoisomerases (e.g. DNA gyrase). The separated DNA strands each serve as a template for DNA polymerase. The polymerization reaction involves incorporation of deoxyribonucleotides, which correctly base pair with the template DNA. Two characteristic replication forks are formed, which proceed in opposite directions around the chromosome. The two copies of the total genetic information (genome) produced during replication each comprise one parental strand and one newly synthesized strand of DNA.

Replication of the genome takes approximately 40 min in *E. coli*, so when these bacteria grow and divide every 20–30 min they need to initiate new rounds of DNA replication before an existing round of replication has finished. In such instances, daughter cells inherit DNA that has already initiated its own replication.

Replication must be accurate

Accurate replication is essential because DNA carries the information that defines the properties and processes of a cell. It is achieved because DNA polymerase is capable of proofreading newly incorporated deoxyribonucleotides and excising those that are incorrect. This reduces the frequency of errors to approximately one mistake (an incorrect base pair) per 10^{10} nucleotides copied.

Cell division is preceded by genome segregation and septum formation

The process of cell division (or septation) involves:

* segregation of the replicated genomes
* formation of a septum in the middle of the cell
* division of the cell to give separate daughter cells.

The septum is formed by an invagination of the cytoplasmic membrane and ingrowth of the peptidoglycan cell wall (and outer membrane in Gram-negative bacteria). Septation and DNA replication and genome segregation are not tightly coupled, but are sufficiently well coordinated to ensure that very few daughter cells do not have the correct complement of genomic DNA.

The mechanics of cell division result in reproducible cellular arrangements, when viewed by microscopic examination. For example, cocci dividing in one plane may appear chained (streptococci) or paired (diplococci), while division in multiple planes results in clusters (staphylococci). As with cell shape, these arrangements have served as an important characteristic for bacterial identification.

Bacterial growth and division are important targets for antimicrobial agents

Antimicrobials that target the processes involved in bacterial growth and division include:

* quinolones (ciprofloxacin and levofloxacin), which inhibit the unwinding of DNA by DNA gyrase during DNA replication
* the many inhibitors of peptidoglycan cell wall synthesis (e.g. beta-lactams such as the penicillins, cephalosporins and carbapenems, and glycopeptides such as vancomycin).

These are considered in more detail in Chapter 33.

GENE EXPRESSION

Gene expression describes the processes involved in decoding the 'genetic information' contained within a gene to produce a functional protein or RNA molecule.

Most genes are transcribed into messenger RNA (mRNA)

The overwhelming majority of genes (e.g. up to 98% in *E. coli*) are transcribed into mRNA, which is then translated into proteins. Certain genes, however, are transcribed to produce ribosomal RNA species (5S, 16S, 23S), which provide a scaffold for assembling ribosomal subunits; others are transcribed into transfer RNA (tRNA) molecules, which together with the ribosome participate in decoding mRNA into functional proteins.

Transcription

The DNA is copied by a DNA-dependent RNA polymerase to yield an RNA transcript. The polymerization reaction involves incorporation of ribonucleotides, which correctly base pair with the template DNA.

Transcription is initiated at promoters

Promoters are nucleotide sequences in DNA that can bind the RNA polymerase. The frequency of transcription initiation can be influenced by many factors, for example:

- the exact DNA sequence of the promoter site
- the overall topology (supercoiling) of the DNA
- the presence or absence of regulatory proteins that bind adjacent to and may overlap the promoter site.

Consequently, different promoters have widely different rates of transcriptional initiation (of up to 3000-fold). Their activities can be altered by regulatory proteins. Sigma factor (a component RNA polymerase) plays an important role in promoter recognition. The presence of several different sigma factors in bacteria enables sets of genes to be switched on simply by altering the level of expression of a particular sigma factor. This is particularly important in controlling the expression of genes involved in spore formation in Gram-positive bacteria.

Transcription usually terminates at specific termination sites

These termination sites are characterized by a series of uracil residues in the mRNA following an inverted repeat sequence, which can adopt a stem-loop structure (which forms as a result of the base-pairing of ribonucleotides) and interfere with RNA polymerase activity. In addition, certain transcripts terminate following interaction of RNA polymerase with the transcription termination protein, rho.

mRNA transcripts often encode more than one protein in bacteria

The bacterial arrangement seen for single genes (promoter-structural-gene-transcriptional-terminator) is described as monocistronic. However, a single promoter and terminator may flank multiple structural genes, a polycistronic arrangement known as an operon. Operon transcription thus results in polycistronic mRNA encoding more than one protein (Fig. 2.7). Operons provide a way of ensuring that protein subunits that make up particular enzyme complexes or are required for a specific biological process are synthesized simultaneously and in the correct stoichiometry. For example, the proteins required for the uptake and metabolism of lactose are encoded by the lac operon. Many of the

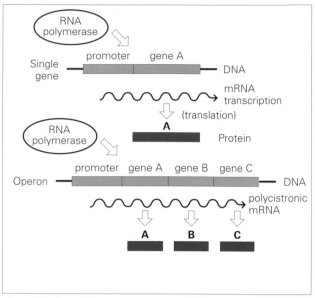

Figure 2.7 Bacterial genes are present on DNA as separate discrete units (single genes) or as operons (multigenes), which are transcribed from promoters to give, respectively, monocistronic or polycistronic messenger RNA (mRNA) molecules; mRNA is then translated into protein.

proteins responsible for the pathogenic properties of medically important microorganisms are likewise encoded by operons, for example:

- cholera toxin from *Vibrio cholerae*
- fimbriae (pili) of uropathogenic *E. coli*, which mediate colonization.

Translation

The exact sequence of amino acids in a protein (polypeptide) is specified by the sequence of nucleotides found in the mRNA transcripts. Decoding this information to produce a protein is achieved by ribosomes and tRNA molecules in a process known as translation. Each set of three bases (triplet) in the mRNA sequence corresponds to a codon for a specific amino acid. However, there is redundancy in the triplet code resulting in instances of more than one triplet encoding the same amino acid (i.e., also referred to as code degeneracy). Thus, a total of 64 codons encode all 20 amino acids as well as start and stop signal codons.

Translation begins with formation of an initiation complex and terminates at a STOP codon

The initiation complex comprises mRNA, ribosome and an initiator transfer RNA molecule (tRNA) carrying formylmethionine. Ribosomes bind to specific sequences in mRNA (Shine–Dalgarno sequences) and begin translation at an initiation (START) codon, AUG, which hybridizes with a specific complementary sequence (the anti-codon loop) of the initiator tRNA molecule. The polypeptide chain elongates as a result of movement of the ribosome along the mRNA molecule and the recruitment of further tRNA molecules (carrying different amino acids), which recognize the subsequent codon triplets. Ribosomes carry out a condensation reaction, which couples the incoming amino acid (carried on the tRNA) to the growing polypeptide chain.

Translation is terminated when the ribosome encounters one of three termination (STOP) codons: UGA, UAA or UAG.

Transcription and translation are important targets for antimicrobial agents

Such antimicrobial agents include:

- inhibitors of RNA polymerase, such as rifampicin
- a wide array of bacterial protein synthesis inhibitors including macrolides (e.g. erythromycin), aminoglycosides, tetracyclines, chloramphenicol, lincosamides, streptogramins, and oxazolidinones (see Ch. 33).

Regulation of gene expression

Bacteria adapt to their environment by controlling gene expression

Bacteria show a remarkable ability to adapt to changes in their environment. This is predominantly achieved by controlling gene expression, thereby ensuring that proteins are only produced when and if they are required. For example:

- Bacteria may encounter a new source of carbon or nitrogen and as a consequence switch on new metabolic pathways that enable them to transport and use such compounds.
- When compounds such as amino acids are depleted from a bacterium's environment the bacterium may be able to switch on the production of enzymes that enable it to synthesize the particular molecule it requires de novo.

Expression of many virulence determinants by pathogenic bacteria is highly regulated

This makes sense since it conserves metabolic energy and ensures that virulence determinants are only produced when their particular property is needed. For example, enterobacterial pathogens are often transmitted in contaminated water supplies. The temperature of such water will probably be lower than 25°C and low in nutrients. However, upon entering the human gut there will be a striking change in the bacterium's environment – the temperature will rise to 37°C, there will be an abundant supply of carbon and nitrogen and a low availability of both oxygen and free iron (an essential nutrient). Bacteria adapt to such changes by switching on or off a range of metabolic and virulence-associated genes.

The analysis of virulence gene expression is one of the fastest growing aspects of the study of microbial pathogenesis. It provides an important insight into how bacteria adapt to the many changes they encounter as they initiate infection and spread into different host tissues.

The most common way of altering gene expression is to change the amount of mRNA transcription

The level of mRNA transcription can be altered by altering the efficiency of binding of RNA polymerase to promoter sites. Environmental changes such as shifts in growth temperature (from 25°C to 37°C) or the availability of oxygen can change the extent of supercoiling in DNA, thereby altering the overall topology of promoters and the efficiency of transcription initiation. However, most instances of transcriptional regulation are mediated by regulatory proteins, which bind specifically to the DNA adjacent to or overlapping the promoter site and alter RNA polymerase binding and transcription. The regions of DNA to which regulatory proteins bind are known as operators or operator sites. Regulatory proteins fall into two distinct classes:

- those that increase the rate of transcription initiation (activators)
- those that inhibit transcription (repressors) (Fig. 2.8).

Genes subject to negative regulation bind repressor proteins. Genes subject to positive regulation need to bind activated regulatory protein(s) to promote transcription initiation.

The principles of gene regulation in bacteria can be illustrated by the regulation of genes involved in sugar metabolism

Bacteria use sugars as a carbon source for growth and prefer to use glucose rather than other less well-metabolized sugars. When growing in an environment containing both glucose and lactose, bacteria such as E. coli preferentially metabolize glucose and at the same time prevent the expression of the lac operon, the products of which transport and metabolize lactose (Fig. 2.9). This is known as catabolite repression. It occurs because the transcriptional initiation of the lac operon is dependent upon a positive regulator, the cAMP-dependent catabolite activator protein (CAP), which is only activated when cAMP is bound. When bacteria grow on glucose the cytoplasmic levels of cAMP are low and so CAP is not activated. CAP is therefore unable to bind to its DNA binding site adjacent to the lac promoter and facilitate transcription initiation by RNA polymerase. When the glucose is depleted, the cAMP concentration rises, resulting in the formation of activated cAMP–CAP complexes, which bind the appropriate site on the DNA, increasing RNA polymerase binding and transcription.

CAP is an example of a global regulatory protein that controls the expression of multiple genes; it controls the expression of over 100 genes in E. coli. All genes controlled by the same regulator are considered to constitute a regulon (see Fig. 2.8). In addition to the influence of CAP on the lac operon, the operon is also subject to negative regulation by the lactose repressor protein (LacI, see Fig. 2.9). LacI is encoded by the *lacI* gene, which is located immediately upstream of the lactose operon and transcribed by a separate promoter. In the absence of lactose, LacI binds specifically to the operator region of the lac promoter and blocks transcription. An inducer molecule, allolactose (or its non-metabolizable homologue, isopropylthiogalactoside–IPTG) is able to bind to LacI, causing an allosteric change in its structure. This releases it from the DNA, thereby alleviating the repression. The lac operon therefore illustrates the fine tuning of gene regulation in bacteria – the operon is switched on only if lactose is available as a carbon source for cell growth, but remains unexpressed if glucose, the cell's preferred carbon source, is also present.

Expression of bacterial virulence genes is often controlled by regulatory proteins

An example of such regulation is the production of diphtheria toxin by *Corynebacterium diphtheriae* (see Ch. 18), which is subject to negative regulation if there is free iron in the growth environment. A repressor protein, DtxR, binds iron and undergoes a conformational change that allows it to bind with high affinity to the operator site of the toxin gene and inhibit transcription. When C. diphtheriae grow in an environment with a very low concentration of iron (i.e. similar to that of human secretions), DtxR is unable to bind iron, and toxin production occurs.

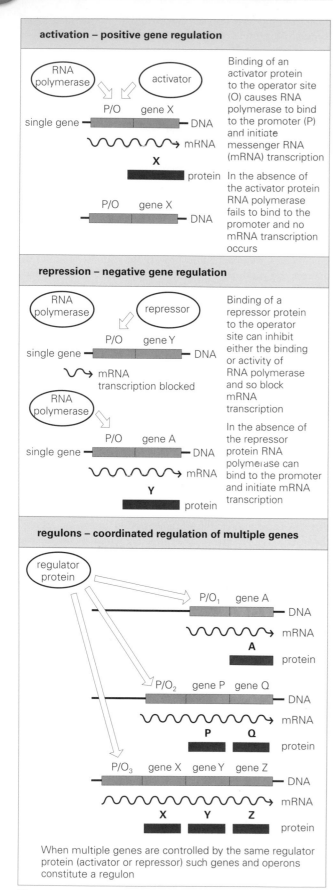

activation – positive gene regulation

Binding of an activator protein to the operator site (O) causes RNA polymerase to bind to the promoter (P) and initiate messenger RNA (mRNA) transcription

In the absence of the activator protein RNA polymerase fails to bind to the promoter and no mRNA transcription occurs

repression – negative gene regulation

Binding of a repressor protein to the operator site can inhibit either the binding or activity of RNA polymerase and so block mRNA transcription

In the absence of the repressor protein RNA polymerase can bind to the promoter and initiate mRNA transcription

regulons – coordinated regulation of multiple genes

When multiple genes are controlled by the same regulator protein (activator or repressor) such genes and operons constitute a regulon

Figure 2.8 Expression of genes in bacteria is highly regulated, enabling them to switch genes on or off in response to changes in available nutrients or other changes in their environment. Genes and operons controlled by the same regulator constitute a regulon.

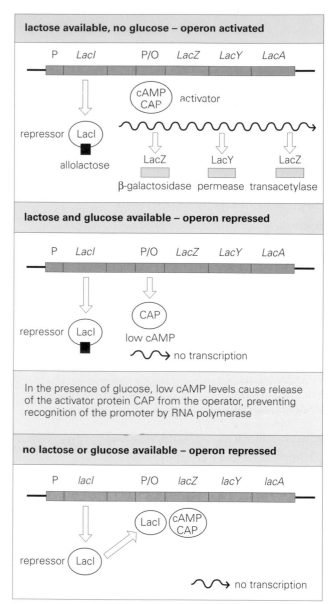

lactose available, no glucose – operon activated

lactose and glucose available – operon repressed

In the presence of glucose, low cAMP levels cause release of the activator protein CAP from the operator, preventing recognition of the promoter by RNA polymerase

no lactose or glucose available – operon repressed

Figure 2.9 Control of the lac operon. Transcription is controlled by the lactose repressor protein (LacI, negative regulation) and by the catabolite activator protein (CAP, positive regulation). In the presence of lactose as the sole carbon source for growth, the lac operon is switched on. Bacteria prefer to use glucose rather than lactose, so if glucose is also present the lac operon is switched off until the glucose has been used.

Many bacterial virulence genes are subject to positive regulation by 'two-component regulators'

These two-component regulators usually comprise two separate proteins (Fig. 2.10):

- one acting as a sensor to detect environmental changes (such as alterations in temperature)
- the other acting as a DNA-binding protein capable of activating (or repressing in some cases) transcription.

In *Bordetella pertussis*, the causative agent of whooping cough (see Ch. 19), a two-component regulator (encoded by the bvg locus) controls expression of a large number of virulence genes. The sensor protein, BvgS, is a cytoplasmic membrane-located histidine kinase, which senses environmental signals (temperature, Mg^{2+}, nicotinic acid), leading to an alteration in its autophosphorylating activity. In response to positive

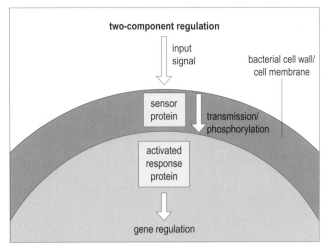

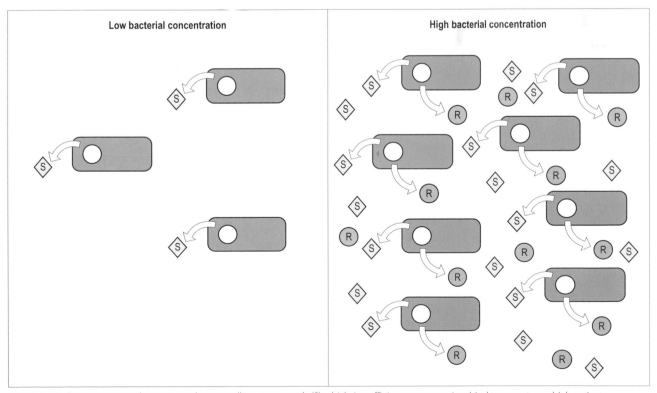

Figure 2.10 Two-component regulation is a signal transduction process that allows cellular functions to react in response to a changing environment. An appropriate environmental stimulus results in autophosphorylation of the sensor protein which, by a phosphotransfer reaction, activates the response protein which affects gene regulation.

regulatory signals such as an elevation in temperature, BvgS undergoes autophosphorylation and then phosphorylates, so activating the DNA-binding protein BvgA. BvgA then binds to the operators of the pertussis toxin operon and other virulence-associated genes and activates their transcription.

In *Staphylococcus aureus*, a variety of virulence genes are influenced by global regulatory systems, the best studied and most important of which is a two-component regulator termed accessory gene regulator (*agr*). Agr control is complex in that it serves as a positive regulator for exotoxins secreted late in the bacterial lifecycle (post-exponential phase) but behaves as a negative regulator for virulence factors associated with the cell surface.

Regulation of virulence genes often involves a cascade of activators

For example:

- In *B. pertussis*, BvgA appears to activate the expression of another regulatory protein, which in turn activates the expression of filamentous haemagglutinin, the major adherence factor produced by *B. pertussis*.
- The control of virulence gene expression in *V. cholerae* is under the control of ToxR, a cytoplasmic membrane-located protein, which senses environmental changes. ToxR activates both the transcription of the cholera toxin operon and another regulatory protein, ToxT, which in turn activates the transcription of other virulence genes such as toxin-co-regulated pili, an essential virulence factor required for colonization of the human small intestine.

In some instances the pathogenic activity of bacteria specifically begins when cell numbers reach a certain threshold

Quorum sensing is the mechanism by which specific gene transcription is activated in response to bacterial concentration. While quorum sensing is known to occur in a wide variety of microorganisms, a classic example is the production of biofilms by *Pseudomonas aeruginosa* in the lungs of cystic fibrosis (CF) patients. The production of these tenacious substances allows *P. aeruginosa* to establish serious long-term infection in CF patients which is difficult to treat (see Ch. 19;

Figure 2.11 Quorum sensing bacteria produce signalling compounds (S) which, in sufficient concentration, bind to receptors which activate transcription of specific response genes (R) (e.g. for biofilm production, etc.).

Fig. 19.22). As illustrated in Figure 2.11, when quorum-sensing bacteria reach appropriate numbers, the signalling compounds they produce are at sufficient concentration to activate transcription of specific response genes such as those related to biofilm production. Current research is aimed at better understanding the quorum-sensing process in hopes of finding approaches (e.g. inhibitory compounds) to interfere with this coordinated mechanism of bacterial virulence.

SURVIVAL UNDER ADVERSE CONDITIONS

Some bacteria form endospores

Certain bacteria can form highly resistant spores – endospores – within their cells, and these enable them to survive adverse conditions. They are formed when the cells are unable to grow (e.g. when environmental conditions change or when nutrients are exhausted), but never by actively growing cells. The spore has a complex multilayered coat surrounding a new bacterial cell. There are many differences in composition between endospores and normal cells, notably the presence of dipicolinic acid and a high calcium content, both of which are thought to confer the endospore's extreme resistance to heat and chemicals.

Because of their resistance, spores can remain viable in a dormant state for many years, re-converting rapidly to normal existence when conditions improve. When this occurs, a new bacterial cell grows out from the spore and resumes vegetative life. Endospores are abundant in soils, and those of the *Clostridium* and *Bacillus* are a particular hazard (Fig. 2.12). Tetanus and anthrax caused by these bacteria are both associated with endospore infection of wounds, the bacteria developing from the spores once in appropriate conditions.

MOBILE GENETIC ELEMENTS

The bacterial chromosome represents the primary reservoir of genetic information within the cell. However, a variety of additional genetic elements may also be present which are capable of independently moving to different locations within a cell or between cells (also termed horizontal gene transfer).

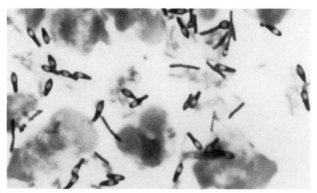

Figure 2.12 *Clostridium tetani* with terminal spores.

Many bacteria possess small, independently replicating (extrachromosomal) nucleic acid molecules termed plasmids and bacteriophages

Plasmids are independent, self-replicating, circular units of dsDNA, some of which are relatively large (60–120 kb) while others are quite small (1.5–15 kb). Plasmid replication is similar to the replication of genomic DNA, though there may be some differences. Not all plasmids are replicated bidirectionally – some have a single replication fork, others are replicated like a 'rolling circle'. The number of plasmids per bacterial cell (copy number) varies for different plasmids, ranging from 1 to 1000 copies/cell. The rate of initiation of plasmid replication determines the plasmid copy number; however, larger plasmids generally tend to have lower copy numbers than smaller plasmids. Some plasmids (broad host-range plasmids) are able to replicate in many different bacterial species, others have a more restricted host range.

Plasmids contain genes for replication, and in some cases for mediating their own transfer between bacteria (*tra* genes). Plasmids may additionally carry a wide variety of genes (up to 100 on larger plasmids) which can confer phenotypic advantages to the host bacterial cell.

Widespread use of antimicrobials has applied a strong selection pressure in favour of bacteria able to resist them

In the majority of cases, resistance to antimicrobials is due to the presence of resistance genes on conjugative plasmids (R plasmids; see Ch. 33). These are known to have existed before the era of mass antibiotic treatments, but they have become widespread in many species as a result of selection. R plasmids may carry genes for resistance to several antimicrobials. For example, the common R plasmid, R1, confers resistance to ampicillin, chloramphenicol, kanamycin, streptomycin and sulphonamides, and there are many others conferring resistance to a wide spectrum of antimicrobials. R plasmids can recombine so that individual plasmids can be responsible for new combinations of multiple drug resistance.

Plasmids can carry virulence genes

Plasmids may encode toxins and other proteins that increase the virulence of microorganisms. For example:

- The virulent enterotoxinogenic strains of *E. coli* that cause diarrhea produce one of two different types of plasmid-encoded enterotoxin. The enterotoxin alters the secretion of fluid and electrolytes by the intestinal epithelium (see Ch. 22).
- In *Staphylococcus aureus*, both an enterotoxin and a number of enzymes involved in bacterial virulence (haemolysin, fibrinolysin) are encoded by plasmid genes.

The production of toxins by bacteria, and their pathologic effects, is discussed in detail in Chapter 17.

Plasmids are valuable tools for cloning and manipulating genes

Molecular biologists have generated a wealth of recombinant plasmids to use as vectors for genetic engineering (Fig. 2.13). Plasmids can be used to transfer genes across species barriers so that defined gene products can be studied or synthesized in large quantities in different recipient organisms.

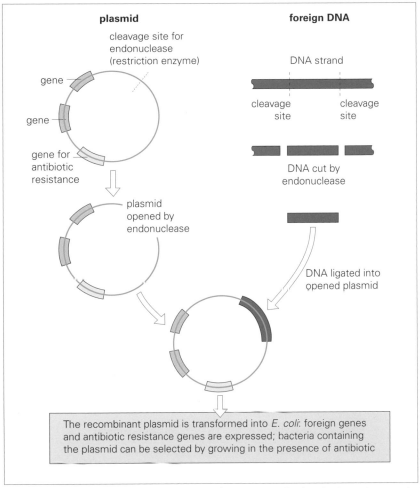

Figure 2.13 The use of plasmid vectors to introduce foreign DNA in *E. coli* – a basic step in gene cloning.

Bacteriophages are bacterial viruses that can survive outside as well as inside the bacterial cell

Bacteriophages differ from plasmids in that their reproduction usually leads to destruction of the bacterial cell. In general, bacteriophages consist of a protein coat or head (capsid), which surrounds nucleic acid which may be either DNA or RNA but not both. Some bacteriophages may also possess a tail-like structure which aids them in attaching to and infecting their bacterial host. As illustrated in Figure 2.14 for DNA-containing bacteriophages, the virus attaches and injects its DNA into the bacterium, leaving the protective protein coat behind. Virulent bacteriophages instigate a form of molecular mutiny to commandeer cellular nucleic acid and protein to produce new virus DNA and protein. Many new virus particles (virions) are then assembled and released into the environment as the bacterial cell ruptures (lyses), thus allowing the cycle to begin again.

While destruction of the host is always the direct consequence of virulent bacteriophage infection, temperate bacteriophages may exercise a 'choice'. Following infection, they may immediately reproduce in a manner similar to their virulent counterparts. However, in some instances they may insert into the bacterial chromosome. This process, termed lysogeny, does not kill the cell since the integrated viral DNA (now called a prophage) is quiescently carried and replicated within the bacterial chromosome. New characteristics may be expressed by the cell as a result of prophage presence (prophage conversion) which, in some instances, may increase bacterial virulence (e.g. the gene for diphtheria toxin resides on a prophage). Nevertheless, this latent state is eventually destined to end, often in response to some environmental stimulus inactivating the bacteriophage repressor which normally maintains the lysogenic condition. During this induction process, the viral DNA is excised from the chromosome and proceeds to active replication and assembly, resulting in cell lysis and viral release.

Whether virulent or temperate, bacteriophage infection ultimately results in death of the host cell which, given current problems with multiple resistance, has sparked a renewed interest in their use as 'natural' antimicrobial agents. However, a variety of issues related to dosing, delivery, quality control, etc. have impeded the use of 'bacteriophage therapy' in routine clinical practice.

Transposition

Transposable elements are DNA sequences that can jump (transpose) from a site in one DNA molecule to another in a cell. This movement does not rely on host-cell (homologous) recombination pathways which require extensive similarity between the resident and incoming DNA. Instead, movement involves short target sequences in the recipient DNA

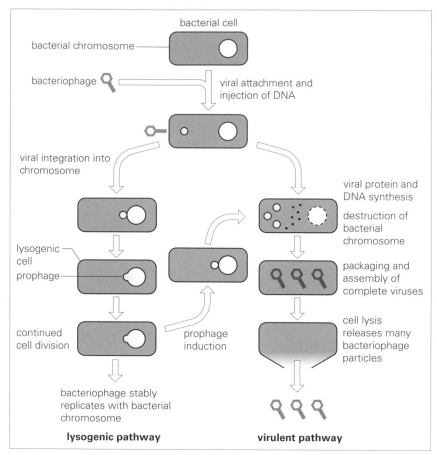

Figure 2.14 The life cycle of bacteriophages.

molecule where recombination/insertion is directed by the mobile element (site-specific recombination).

While plasmid transfer involves the movement of genetic information between bacterial cells, transposition is the movement of such information between DNA molecules. The most extensively studied transposable elements are those found in *E. coli* and other Gram-negative bacteria, although examples are also found in Gram-positive bacteria, yeast, plants and other organisms.

Insertion sequences are the smallest and simplest 'jumping genes'

Insertion sequence elements (ISs) are <2 kb in length and only encode functions such as the transposase enzyme, which is required for transposition from one DNA site to another. At the ends of ISs, there are usually short inverted repeat sequences (23 nucleotides long in IS1), which are also important in the process of locating and inserting into a DNA target (Fig. 2.15A). During the transposition process, a portion of the target sequence is duplicated, resulting in short direct repeat sequences (the same sequence in the same orientation) on each side of the newly inserted IS element. Many aspects of the target selection process remain unclear. While A/T-rich regions of DNA appear to be preferred, some ISs are highly selective, whereas others are generally indiscriminate. Transposition does not rely on enzymatic processes typically used by the cell for homologous recombination (recombination between highly related DNA molecules) and is thus termed 'illegitimate recombination'. The result

is a typically small number of ISs in bacterial genomes. In *E. coli*, IS1 is found in 6–10 copies; and five copies in IS2 and 3. Multiple IS copies serve an important function as 'portable regions of homology' throughout a bacterial genome where homologous recombination may occur between different DNA regions or molecules (e.g. chromosome and plasmid) carrying the same IS sequence. Two IS elements inserting relatively near to each other would allow the entire region to become transposable, further promoting the potential for genetic movement and exchange in bacterial populations.

Transposons are larger, more complex elements, which encode multiple genes

Transposons are >2 kb in size and contain genes in addition to those required for transposition (often encoding resistance to one or more antibiotics) (Fig. 2.15A). Furthermore, virulence genes, such as those encoding heat-stable enterotoxin from *E. coli*, have been found on transposons.

Transposons can be divided into two classes:

1. composite transposons, where two copies of an identical IS element flank antibiotic-resistance genes (kanamycin resistance in Tn5)
2. simple transposons, such as Tn3 (encoding resistance to beta-lactams).

ISs at the ends of composite transposons may be in either the same or inverted orientation (i.e. direct or indirect repeats). Although part of the composite transposon structure, the terminal IS elements are fully intact and capable of independent transposition.

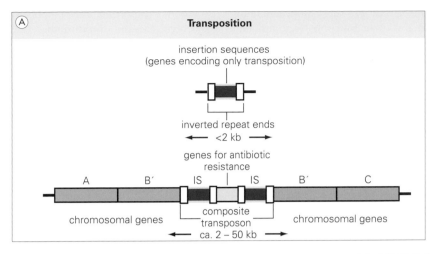

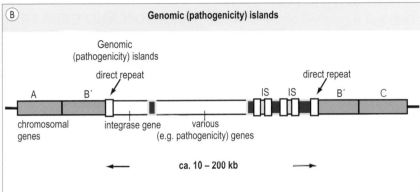

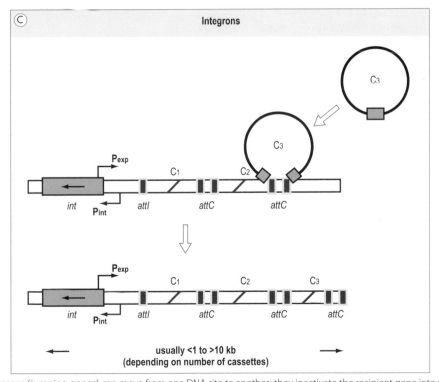

Figure 2.15 (A) Transposons (jumping genes) can move from one DNA site to another; they inactivate the recipient gene into which they insert. Transposons often contain genes which confer resistance to antibiotics. (B) Genomic islands are regions of DNA with 'signature sequences' (e.g. direct repeats) indicative of mobility. Their encoded functions increase bacterial fitness (e.g. pathogenicity). (C) Integrons are genetic regions into which independent open reading frames, also termed gene cassettes, can integrate and become functional (e.g. under control of the promoter P_{exp}). The integration process occurs by site-specific recombination between circular cassettes and their recipient integron, which is directed by an integrase gene (*intl*) with promoter P_{int} and an associated attachment site (*attl*).

Simple transposons move only as a single unit, containing genes for transposition and other functions (e.g. antibiotic resistance) with short, inversely oriented sequences (indirect repeats) at each end.

Mobile genetic elements promote a variety of DNA rearrangements which may have important clinical consequences

The ease with which transposons move into or out of DNA sequences means that transposition can occur:

- from host genomic DNA harbouring a transposon to a plasmid
- from one plasmid to another plasmid
- from a plasmid to genomic DNA.

Transposition onto a broad host-range conjugative plasmid can lead to the rapid dissemination of resistance among different bacteria. The transposition process (whether by ISs or transposons) can be deleterious if insertion occurs within, and disrupts, a functional gene. However, transpositional mutagenesis has been effectively utilized in the molecular biology laboratory to produce extremely specific mutations without the harmful secondary effects often seen with more generally acting chemical mutagens.

Other mobile elements also behave as portable cassettes of genetic information

Pathogenicity islands (Fig. 2.15B) are a special class of mobile genetic elements containing groups of coordinately controlled virulence genes, often with ISs, direct repeat sequences, etc. at their ends. Though originally observed in uropathogenic *E. coli* (encoding haemolysins and pili), pathogenicity islands have now been found in a number of additional bacterial species including *Helicobacter pylori*, *Vibrio cholerae*, *Salmonella* spp., *Staphylococcus aureus*, and *Yersinia* spp. Such regions are not found in non-pathogenic bacteria, may be quite large (up to hundreds of kilobases), and tend to be unstable (spontaneously lost). Differences in DNA sequence (G+C content) between such elements and their host genomes and the presence of transposon-like genes support speculation regarding their origin and movement from unrelated bacterial species. The term 'genomic island' has been given to DNA sequences similar to pathogenicity islands but lacking functional genes for movement.

Integrons are mobile genetic elements that are able to use site-specific recombination to acquire new genes in 'cassette-like' fashion and express them in a coordinated manner (Fig. 2.15C). Integrons lack terminal repeat sequences and certain genes characteristic of transposons but, similar to transposable elements, often carry genes associated with antibiotic resistance (see Fig. 33.5).

Another important type of mobile element includes staphylococcal cassette chromosomes (SCCs) such as SCC*mec*, which not only encodes methicillin resistance but also serves as a recombinational hot spot for the acquisition of other mobile sequences. SCCs influencing virulence and antimicrobial resistance include SCC*capI* encoding capsular polysaccharide I and SCC_{476} and SCCmercury conferring resistance to fusidic acid and mercury, respectively. The arginine catabolic mobile element (ACME) is a cassette-like element potentially contributing to the virulence of the important USA300 community-associated methicillin-resistant *Staphylococcus aureus* (MRSA) strain originally reported in the United States but now globally disseminated. An example of the interrelationship between the bacterial core genome and additional mobile genetic elements is depicted in Figure 2.16.

MUTATION AND GENE TRANSFER

Bacteria are haploid organisms, their chromosomes containing one copy of each gene. Replication of the DNA is a precise process resulting in each daughter cell acquiring an exact copy of the parental genome. Changes in the genome can occur by two processes:

- mutation
- recombination.

These processes result in progeny with phenotypic characteristics that may differ from those of the parent. This is of considerable significance in terms of virulence and drug resistance.

Mutation

Changes in the nucleotide sequence of DNA can occur spontaneously or under the influence of external agents

While mutations may spontaneously occur as a result of errors in the DNA replication process, a variety of chemicals (mutagens) bring about direct changes in the DNA molecule. A classic example of such an interaction involves compounds known as nucleotide-base analogues. These agents mimic normal nucleotides during DNA synthesis but are capable of multiple pairing with a counterpart on the opposite strand. While 5-bromouracil is considered a thymine analogue, for example, it may also behave as a cytosine, thus allowing the potential for a change from T-A to C-G in a replicating DNA duplex. Other agents may cause changes by inserting (intercalating) and distorting the DNA helix or by interacting directly with nucleotide bases to chemically alter them.

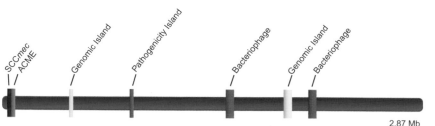

Figure 2.16 Linear depiction of the interrelationship between the USA300 MRSA core genome and key mobile genetic elements SCCmec, ACME, two different bacteriophages, two different genomic islands, and a pathogenicity island encoding antibiotic resistance and a variety of virulence factors.

2.87 Mb

Regardless of their cause, changes in DNA may generally be characterized as follows.

- Point mutations: changes in single nucleotides, which alter the triplet code. Such mutations may result in:
  - no change in the amino acid sequence of the protein encoded by the gene, because the different codons specify the same amino acid and are therefore silent mutations
  - an amino acid substitution in the translated protein (missense mutation), which may or may not alter its stability or functional properties
  - the formation of a STOP codon, causing premature termination and production of a truncated protein (nonsense mutation).
- More comprehensive changes in the DNA, which involve deletion, replacement, insertion or inversion of several or many bases. The majority of these changes are likely to harm the organism, but a few may be beneficial and confer a selective advantage through the production of different proteins.

Bacterial cells are not defenceless against genetic damage

Since the bacterial genome is the most fundamental molecule of identity in the cell, enzymatic machinery is in place to protect it against both spontaneously occurring and induced mutational damage. As illustrated in Figure 2.17, these DNA repair processes include the following:

- Direct repair which either reverses or simply removes the damage. This may be regarded as 'first line' defence. For example, abnormally linked pyrimidine bases in DNA (pyrimidine dimers) resulting from ultraviolet radiation are directly reversed by a light-dependent enzyme through a repair process known as photoreactivation.
- Excision repair where damage in a DNA strand is recognized by an enzymatic 'housekeeping' process and excised, followed by repair polymerization to fill the gap using the intact complementary DNA strand as a template. This is also a primary form of defence, since the goal is to correct damage before it encounters and potentially interferes with the moving DNA replication fork. Some of these housekeeping genes are also part of an inducible system (SOS repair), which is activated by the presence of DNA damage to quickly respond and effect repair.
- 'Second line' repair which operates when DNA damage has reached a point where it is more difficult to correct. When normal DNA replication processes are blocked, permissive systems may allow the interfering damage to be inaccurately corrected, allowing errors to occur but improving the probability of cell survival. In other

Figure 2.17 Mechanisms of DNA repair.

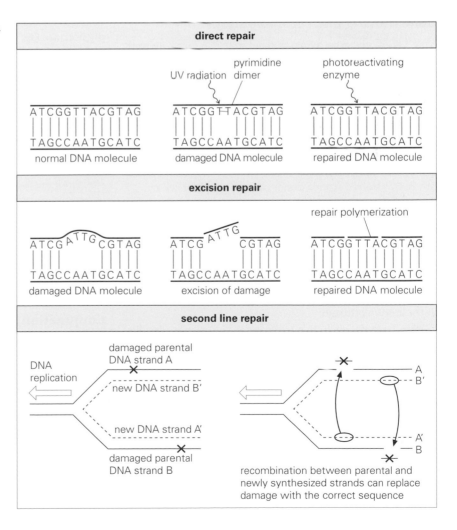

instances, where damage has passed the replication fork, post-replication or recombinational repair processes may 'cut and paste' to construct error-free DNA from multiple copies of the sequence found in parental and daughter strands.

Bacterial DNA repair has provided a model for understanding similar, more complex processes in humans

DNA repair mechanisms appear to be present in all living organisms as a defence against environmental damage. The study of these processes in bacteria has led to an important understanding of general principles that apply to higher organisms, including issues of cancer and aging in humans. For example, several human disorders are known to be DNA-repair related, including:

- xeroderma pigmentosum, characterized by extreme sensitivity to the sun, with great risk for development of a variety of skin cancers such as basal cell carcinoma, squamous cell carcinoma and melanoma
- Cockayne syndrome, characterized by progressive neurologic degeneration, growth retardation, and sun sensitivity not associated with cancer
- trichothiodystrophy, characterized by mental and growth retardation, fragile hair deficient in sulphur, and sun sensitivity not associated with cancer.

Gene transfer and recombination

New genotypes arise when genetic material is transferred from one bacterium to another. In such instances, the transferred DNA either:

- recombines with the genome of the recipient cell
- or is on a plasmid capable of replication in the recipient without recombination.

Recombination can bring about large changes in the genetic material, and since these events usually involve functional genes, they are likely to be expressed phenotypically. DNA can be transferred from a donor cell to a recipient cell by:

- transformation
- transduction
- conjugation.

Transformation

Some bacteria can be transformed by DNA present in their environment

Certain bacteria such as *Streptococcus pneumoniae*, *Bacillus subtilis*, *Haemophilus influenzae* and *Neisseria gonorrhoeae* are naturally 'competent' to take up DNA fragments from related species across their cell walls. Such DNA fragments may be present in the environment of the competent cell as a result of lysis of other organisms, the release of their DNA and its cleavage into smaller fragments. Once taken into the cell, chromosomal DNA must recombine with a homologous segment of the recipient's chromosome to be stably maintained and inherited. If the DNA is completely unrelated, the absence of homology prevents recombination and the DNA is degraded. However, plasmid DNA may be transformed into a cell and expressed without recombination. Thus,

transformation has served as a powerful tool for molecular genetic analysis of bacteria (Fig. 2.18).

Most bacteria are not naturally competent to be transformed by DNA, but competence can be induced artificially by treating cells with certain bivalent cations and then subjecting them to a heat shock at 42°C or by electric shock treatment (electroporation).

Prior to uptake by competent cells, DNA is extracellular, unprotected, and thus vulnerable to destruction by environmental extremes (e.g. DNA-degrading enzymes – DNases). Thus, it is the least important mechanism of gene transfer from the standpoint of clinical relevance (e.g. probability of transfer within a patient).

Transduction

Transduction involves the transfer of genetic material by infection with a bacteriophage

During the process of virulent bacteriophage replication (or temperate bacteriophages exercising the direct lysis option), other DNA in the cell (genomic or plasmid) is occasionally erroneously packaged into the virus head, resulting in a 'transducing particle', which can attach to and transfer the DNA into a recipient cell. If chromosomal, the DNA must be incorporated into the recipient genome by homologous recombination to be stably inherited and expressed. As with transformation, plasmid DNA may be transduced and expressed in a recipient without recombination. In either case, this type of gene transfer is known as generalized transduction (see Fig. 2.18).

Another form of transduction occurs with 'temperate' bacteriophages, since they integrate at specialized attachment sites in the bacterial genome. As these prophages prepare to enter the lytic cycle, they occasionally incorrectly excise from the site of attachment. This can result in phages containing a piece of bacterial genomic DNA adjacent to the attachment site. Infection of a recipient cell then results in a high frequency of recombinants where donor DNA has recombined with the recipient genome in the vicinity of the attachment site. Since this 'specialized transduction' is based on specific chromosome–prophage interaction, only genomic DNA, and not plasmids, is transferred by this process.

In contrast to transformation, transduced DNA is always protected, thus increasing its probability of successful transfer and potential clinical relevance. However, bacteriophages are extremely host-specific 'parasites' and therefore unable to move any DNA between bacteria of different species.

Conjugation

Conjugation is a type of bacterial 'mating' in which DNA is transferred from one bacterium to another

Conjugation is dependent upon the tra genes found in 'conjugative' plasmids which, among other things, encode instructions for the bacterial cell to produce a sex pilus – a tube-like appendage which allows cell-to-cell contact to insure the protected transfer of a plasmid DNA copy from a donor cell to a recipient (see Fig. 2.18). Since the tra genes take up genetic space, 'conjugative' plasmids are generally larger than non-conjugative ones.

Occasionally, conjugative plasmids such as the fertility plasmid (F plasmid or F factor) of *E. coli* integrate into the

Figure 2.18 Different ways in which genes can be transferred between bacteria. With the exception of plasmid transfer, donor DNA integrates into the recipient's genome by a process of either homologous or illegitimate (in the case of transposons) recombination.

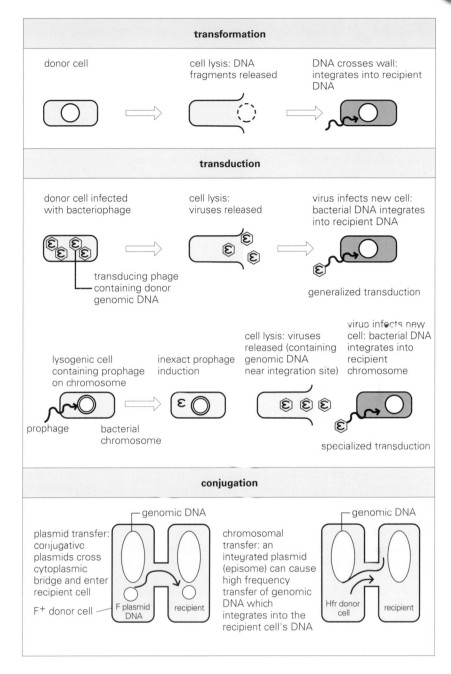

bacterial genome (e.g., facilitated by identical IS elements on both molecules as noted earlier), and such integrated plasmids are called episomes. When an integrated F episome attempts conjugative transfer, the duplication-transfer process eventually moves into regions of adjacent genomic DNA, which are carried along from the donor cell into the recipient. Such strains, in contrast to cells containing the unintegrated F plasmid, mediate high-frequency transfer and recombination of genomic DNA (Hfr strains). However, conjugation with Hfr donor cells does not result in complete transfer of the integrated plasmid. Thus, the recipient cell does not become Hfr and is incapable of serving as a conjugation donor. The circular nature of the bacterial genome and the relative 'map' positions of different genes were established using interrupted mating of Hfr strains.

When a non-conjugative plasmid is present in the same cell as a conjugative plasmid, they are sometimes transferred together into the recipient cell by a process known as mobilization. Conjugative transfer of plasmids with resistance genes has been an important cause of the spread of resistance to commonly used antibiotics within and between many bacterial species, since no recombination is required for expression in the recipient. Of all the mechanisms for gene transfer, this rapid and highly efficient movement of genetic information through bacterial populations is clearly of the highest clinical relevance.

THE GENOMICS OF MEDICALLY IMPORTANT BACTERIA

Advances in DNA sequencing techniques are leading to an ever-increasing number of bacterial pathogens for which the total genomic sequence is known (Box 2.1). This evolving database

Box 2.1 Representative Bacterial Pathogens whose Genomic Sequence is Largely Known

Acinetobacter baumannii, Bacillus anthracis, Bacteroides fragilis, Bartonella henselae, Bartonella quintana, Bordetella bronchiseptica, Bordetella parapertussis, Bordetella pertussis, Borrelia burgdorferi, Borrelia garinii, Brucella abortus, Brucella melitensis, Burkholderia cepacia, Burkholderia mallei, Burkholderia pseudomallei, Campylobacter jejuni, Chlamydia trachomatis, Chlamydophila pneumoniae, Chlamydophila psittaci, Clostridium botulinum, Clostridium difficile, Clostridium perfringens, Clostridium tetani, Corynebacterium diphtheriae, Coxiella burnetii, Enterobacter cloacae, Enterococcus faecalis, Enterococcus faecium, Escherichia coli, Francisella tularensis, Haemophilus ducreyi, Haemophilus influenzae, Helicobacter pylori, Klebsiella pneumoniae, Legionella pneumophila, Leptospira interrogans, Listeria monocytogenes, Moraxella catarrhalis, Mycobacterium avium, Mycobacterium bovis,
Mycobacterium leprae, Mycobacterium smegmatis, Mycobacterium tuberculosis, Mycoplasma genitalium, Mycoplasma pneumoniae, Neisseria gonorrhoeae, Neisseria meningitidis, Pasteurella multocida, Propionibacterium acnes, Proteus mirabilis, Pseudomonas aeruginosa, Rickettsia prowazekii, Rickettsia typhi Wilmington, Salmonella Dublin, Salmonella enterica Choleraesuis, Salmonella enteritidis, Salmonella paratyphi, Salmonella typhi, Salmonella typhimurium, Shigella boydii, Shigella dysenteriae, Shigella flexneri, Shigella sonnei, Staphylococcus aureus, Staphylococcus epidermidis, Streptococcus agalactiae, Streptococcus mutans, Streptococcus pneumoniae, Streptococcus pyogenes, Treponema pallidum, Ureaplasma urealyticum, Vibrio cholerae, Vibrio parahaemolyticus, Vibrio vulnificus, Yersinia enterocolitica, Yersinia pestis, Yersinia pseudotuberculosis

represents a powerful resource with enormous potential application for the understanding and treatment of infectious disease. At present, the utilization of this information is in its infancy; nevertheless, several instances where sequence-based information will be extremely useful in the study of clinically important microorganisms have already emerged, as described below.

Application of genomics facilitates identification

- Identification and classification. The genes encoding ribosomal RNA (16S, 23S and 5S) are typically found together in an operon where their transcription is coordinated (Fig. 2.19). This rDNA operon is found at least once and often in multiple copies distributed around the chromosome, depending on the bacterial species (*Borrelia burgdorferi* has one copy; *Staphylococcus aureus* has 5–6). While the rDNA operon contains many conserved sequences (identical in different bacterial species), a portion of the 16S- and 23S-encoding regions have been found to be species specific. In between them, an 'internally transcribed spacer' (ITS) region exhibits variability that may have utility in differentiating closely related bacterial isolates. Such information clearly has potential for future application in approaches to the rapid identification, classification and epidemiology of clinically important microorganisms (see Chs 31 and 36).
- Resistance to antimicrobial agents. Genes specifically mediating antimicrobial resistance are well known (see Ch. 33). However, total genome sequencing provides more detailed information to insure their detection and allows a global overview where multiple loci may interact to effect resistance. For example, methicillin

resistance in *Staphylococcus aureus* is influenced by a number of genes (e.g. mecA, femA, femB, murE, etc.) at different chromosomal locations.

- Molecular epidemiology. While a variety of phenotypic and genotypic methods have been employed to assess interrelationships in clinical isolates (see Ch. 36), epidemiologic analysis is now moving toward a more sequence-based approach. In contrast to earlier methods, sequence data are highly portable (internet transfer, etc.), less ambiguous (encoded entirely in the characters A, T, G and C, corresponding to the four bases adenine, thymine, guanine and cytosine, respectively), and easily stored in databases. In one approach, sequences from the internal regions of six or seven 'housekeeping' (essential) genes are compared to assess the epidemiologic relatedness of different isolates (multi-locus sequence typing, MLST). However, which chromosomal regions will ultimately provide the most epidemiologically relevant information in different bacterial pathogens will become clearer as additional genomes are sequenced.

Various approaches to the detection and utilization of genomic sequence information exist

Methods such as the polymerase chain reaction (PCR) and nucleic acid probes have clearly had a pivotal role in providing sequence-based answers to clinical microbiology questions (see Ch. 36). Nevertheless, the massive amounts of genomic sequence currently being generated have spawned innovative approaches aimed at extracting the maximum amount of information from the large databases which have been created.

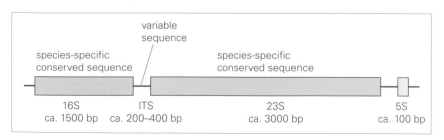

variable
sequence

species-specific
conserved sequence

species-specific
conserved sequence

| 16S | ITS | 23S | 5S |
| ca. 1500 bp | ca. 200–400 bp | ca. 3000 bp | ca. 100 bp |

Figure 2.19 Typical arrangement of the bacterial operon encoding ribosomal RNA. Sizes of the genes for 16S, 23S, 5S rRNA and the internally transcribed spacer (ITS) region are indicated in nucleotide base pairs (bp). Regions encoding sequences helpful for species identification or epidemiology are indicated.

DNA microarrays provide a means for the 'parallel processing' of genomic information

Traditionally, molecular biology has operated by analysing one gene in one experiment. While yielding important information, this approach is time consuming and does not afford ready access to the information (chromosomal organization and multiple-gene interaction) contained within genomic-sequence databases. Microarrays represent a new approach to this issue where information may be obtained from multiple queries simultaneously posed to a genomic-sequence database (parallel processing). DNA microarrays are based on the principles of nucleic hybridization (A pairs with T; G pairs with C). While there are a number of variations on the theme, the general format is the arrangement of samples (e.g. gene sequences) in a known matrix on a solid support (nylon, glass, etc.). Using specialized robotics, individual 'spots' may be less than 200 mm in diameter, allowing a single array (often called a DNA chip) to contain thousands of spots. Different fluorescently labelled probes of known sequence may then be simultaneously applied followed by monitoring to detect whether complementary binding has occurred.

At present, DNA microarrays are finding use in two main applications: identification of mutations and studies on gene expression

In a number of instances, specific point mutations are clinically important in pathogenic bacteria. Since these changes involve only one nucleotide base they are often referred to as single nucleotide polymorphisms (SNPs). Resistance to the quinolone class of antibiotics, for example, may result from a single base change within the bacterial gyrA gene (see Ch. 33). In the past, such mutations have been detected by PCR amplification of the desired gyrA region followed by DNA sequencing and analysis. As illustrated in Figure 2.20A, DNA microarrays allow gyrA amplicons from different

Figure 2.20 (A) Microarray detection of mutations and (B) analysis of gene expression.

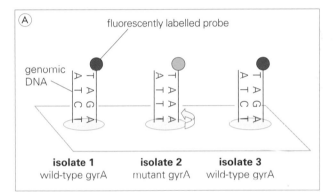

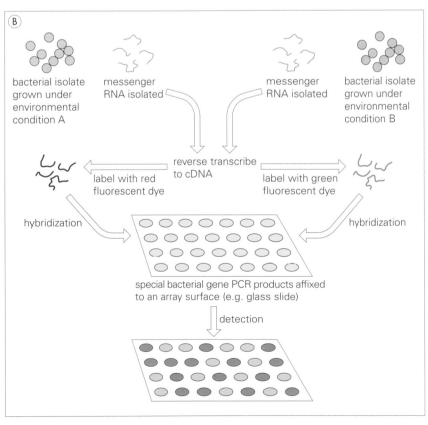

bacterial isolates to be applied to the same chip. Two gyrA probes (wild type, fluorescently labelled red; mutant, fluorescently labelled green) are applied to the array under conditions so stringent that only 100% homology will result in hybridization. In this way, the presence or absence of the specific mutation may be quickly and accurately assessed in a large number of isolates simultaneously.

Studies of gene expression are extremely important to the understanding of numerous bacterial processes, including virulence. For example, analysis might involve a comparison of gene expression (transcription) in an organism under different environmental conditions (Fig. 2.20B). In such an experiment, genomics can provide data allowing sequences from every known chromosomal gene of the organism to be applied to a unique position on the chip. Messenger RNA (the result of gene expression) may be isolated from the same bacteria grown under either environmental condition A or B. Using the enzyme reverse transcriptase in a process similar to that naturally employed by retroviruses (see Ch. 3), the mRNA is copied into complementary DNA (termed cDNA). Different fluorescent dyes (red or green) are bound to the A or B cDNA, respectively, which is then allowed to hybridize to complementary sequences on the chip. Array spots with red fluorescence will indicate genes expressed in environment A. Those appearing green will correspond to genes active in environment B, while yellow spots (red + green) will indicate genes active under both conditions.

Through innovative technologies such as DNA microarrays, and other approaches which may as yet only exist in an inquisitive mind, genomics will clearly play a major role in our understanding and treatment of infectious disease in the years ahead.

Major groups of bacteria

Detailed summaries of members of the major bacterial groups are given in the Pathogen Parade appendix available online.

 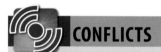

KEY FACTS

- Bacteria are prokaryotes. Their DNA is not contained within a nucleus and there are relatively few cytoplasmic organelles.

- The cell wall is a key structure in metabolism, virulence and immunity. Its staining characteristics define the two major divisions: the Gram-positive and Gram-negative bacteria. Flagella may be present and confer motility.

- Bacteria metabolize aerobically and anaerobically and can utilize a range of substrates.

- The bacterial cell walls and their reproductive processes are targets for antimicrobial agents.

- Transcription of bacterial DNA may involve single or multiple genes. The arrangement of promoter and terminal sequences flanking multiple genes forms an operon.

- Bacteria can regulate gene expression to optimize exploitation of their environment.

- Plasmids and bacteriophages are independently replicating extrachromosomal agents. Plasmids may carry genes that affect resistance to antimicrobials or virulence.

- Genetic material can be carried from one bacterium to another in several ways; this can result in the rapid spread of resistance to antimicrobials.

- Genomics is revolutionizing the study and the control of bacterial infections.

CONFLICTS

Bacteria have many ways of coming out top in the conflict with the host. A number produce highly resistant spores that can survive for long periods in the external world, increasing the chances of infection. Once in the host there are many ways of evading host responses. For example, some hide within cells, some have external surfaces that prevent host cells binding to them, others suppress host immunity. Perhaps the most significant advantage bacteria have in their conflict with the host is their ability to sidestep the antibiotics designed to inhibit or eliminate them. Either by mutation, facilitated by their rapid generation/duplication time, or by externally acquired genetic information they are able to engage in a game of 'cat and mouse', where repeated introduction of new and improved antimicrobial compounds is met with equally innovative mechanisms of resistance. A classic example of this interaction is seen with the Gram-positive bacterium *Staphylococcus aureus*. Although initially susceptible to penicillin, introduced in the 1950s, subsequent development and spread of resistant organisms rendered the antibiotic ineffective. This was countered with the introduction of methicillin in the 1980s leading to the development of methicillin-resistant *S. aureus* (MRSA) which has now been followed by isolates with resistance to the historically effective antibiotic, vancomycin. Unfortunately, a survival-of-the-fittest environment ensures the perpetuation of this conflict, underscoring the importance of the continued development of novel antimicrobial agents.

The viruses 3

Introduction

Viruses differ from all other infectious organisms in their structure and biology, particularly in their reproduction. Although viruses carry conventional genetic information in their DNA or RNA, they lack the synthetic machinery necessary for this information to be processed into new virus material. Viruses are metabolically inert and can replicate only after infecting a host cell and parasitizing the host's ability to transcribe and/or translate genetic information. Viruses infect every form of life. They cause some of the most common and many of the most serious diseases of humans. Some insert their genetic material into the human genome and can cause cancer. Others have the ability to remain latent in different cell types and then reactivate at any time but especially if the body is stressed. Viruses are difficult targets for antiviral agents as it is difficult to target only those cells infected by the virus. However, many can be controlled by vaccines.

Viruses share some common structural features

Viruses range from very small (poliovirus, at 30 nm) to quite large – vaccinia virus, at 400 nm, is as big as small bacteria). Their organization varies considerably between the different groups, but there are some general characteristics common to all:

- The genetic material, in the form of single-stranded (ss) or double-stranded (ds), linear or circular RNA or DNA, is contained within a coat or capsid, made up of a number of individual protein molecules (capsomeres).
- The complete unit of nucleic acid and capsid is called the 'nucleocapsid', and often has a distinctive symmetry depending upon the ways in which the individual capsomeres are assembled (Fig. 3.1). Symmetry can be icosahedral, helical or complex.
- In many cases, the entire virus particle or 'virion' consists only of a nucleocapsid. In others, the virion consists of the nucleocapsid surrounded by an outer envelope or membrane (Fig. 3.2). This is generally a lipid bilayer of host cell origin, into which virus proteins and glycoproteins are inserted.

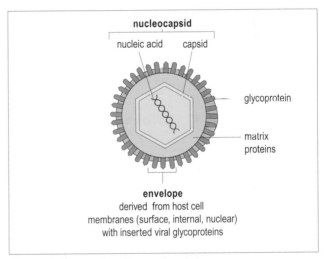

Figure 3.2 Construction of an enveloped virus.

The outer surface of the virus particle is the part that first makes contact with the membrane of the host cell

The structure and properties of the outer surface of the virus particle are therefore of vital importance in understanding the process of infection. In general, naked (envelope-free) viruses are resistant and survive well in the outside world; they may also be acid and bile-resistant, allowing infection through the gastrointestinal tract. Enveloped viruses are more susceptible to environmental factors such as drying, gastric acidity and bile. These differences in susceptibility influence the ways in which these viruses can be transmitted.

INFECTION OF HOST CELLS

The stages involved in infection of host cells are summarized in Figure 3.3 (see also Fig. 2.6).

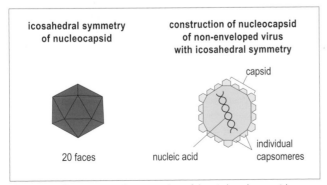

Figure 3.1 Symmetry and construction of the viral nucleocapsid.

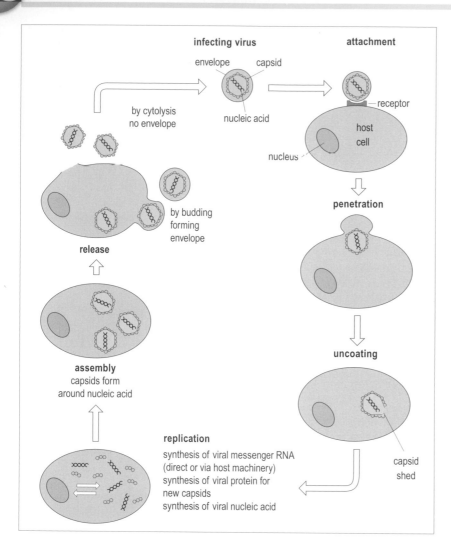

Figure 3.3 Stages in the infection of a host's cell and replication of a virus. Several thousand virus particles may be formed from each cell.

Virus particles enter the body of the host in many ways

The most common forms of virus transmission (Fig. 3.4; see Ch. 13) are:

- via inhaled droplets (e.g. rhinovirus, influenza viruses)
- in food or water (e.g. hepatitis A virus, noroviruses)
- by direct transfer from other infected hosts (e.g. HIV, hepatitis B virus)
- from bites of vector arthropods (e.g. yellow fever virus, West Nile virus).

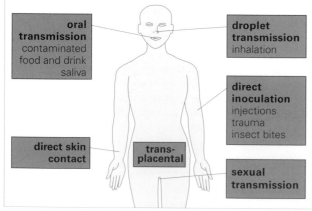

Figure 3.4 Routes by which viruses enter the body.

Viruses show host specificity and usually infect only one or a restricted range of host species. The initial basis of specificity is the ability of the virus particle to attach to the host cell

The process of attachment to, or adsorption by, a host cell depends on general intermolecular forces, then on more specific interactions between the molecules of the nucleocapsid (in naked viruses) or the virus membrane (in enveloped viruses) and the molecules of the host cell membrane. In many cases, there is a specific interaction with a particular host molecule, which therefore acts as a receptor. Influenza virus, for example, attaches by its haemagglutinin to a glycoprotein (sialic acid) found on cells of mucous membranes and on red blood cells; other examples are given in Table 3.1. Attachment to the receptor is followed by entry into the host cell.

Once in the host's cytoplasm the virus is no longer infective

After fusion of viral and host membranes, or uptake into a phagosome, the virus particle is carried into the cytoplasm across the plasma membrane. At this stage, the envelope and/or the capsid are shed and the viral nucleic acid released. The virus is now no longer infective: this 'eclipse phase' persists until new complete virus particles reform after replication. The way in which replication occurs is determined by the nature of the nucleic acid concerned.

Table 3.1 Viruses may use more than one receptor to gain entry into the host cell

Cell membrane receptors for virus attachment	
Virus	**Receptor molecule**
Influenza	Sialic acid receptor on lung epithelial cells and upper respiratory tract
Rabies	Acetylcholine receptor Neuronal cell adhesion molecule
HIV	CD4: Primary receptor CCR5 or CXCR4: chemokine receptors
Epstein–Barr virus	C3d receptor on B cells
Human parvovirus B19	P antigen on erythoid progenitor cells Ku80 antoantigen coreceptor
Hepatitis C virus	Epidermal growth factor receptor and ephrin receptor A2 are host co-factors for viral entry
Human rhinoviruses	Divided into two groups based on receptor binding: Major group: intercellular adhesion molecule 1 (ICAM-1) Minor group: very low density lipoprotein receptor (VLDL-R)

REPLICATION

Viruses must first synthesize messenger RNA (mRNA)

Viruses contain either DNA or RNA, never both. The nucleic acids are present as single or double strands in a linear (DNA or RNA) or circular (DNA) form. The viral genome may be carried on a single molecule of nucleic acid or on several molecules. With these options, it is not surprising that the process of replication in the host cell is also diverse. In viruses containing DNA, mRNA can be formed using the host's own RNA polymerase to transcribe directly from the viral DNA. The RNA of viruses cannot be transcribed in this way, as host polymerases do not work from RNA. If transcription is necessary, the virus must provide its own polymerases. These may be carried in the nucleocapsid or may be synthesized after infection.

RNA viruses produce mRNA by several different routes

In dsRNA viruses, one strand is first transcribed by viral polymerase into mRNA (Fig. 3.5). In ssRNA viruses, there are three distinct routes to the formation of mRNA:

1. Where the single strand has the positive (+) sense configuration (i.e. has the same base sequence as that required for translation), it can be used directly as mRNA.
2. Where the strand has the negative (–) sense configuration, it must first be transcribed, using viral polymerase, into a positive sense strand, which can then act as mRNA.
3. Retroviruses follow a completely different route. Their positive sense ssRNA is first made into a negative sense ssDNA, using the viral reverse transcriptase enzyme carried in the nucleocapsid, and dsDNA is then formed which enters the nucleus and becomes integrated into the host genome. This integrated viral DNA is then transcribed by host polymerase into mRNA.

Viral mRNA is then translated in the host cytoplasm to produce viral proteins

Once viral mRNA has been formed, it is translated using host ribosomes to synthesize viral proteins (Fig. 3.6). Viral mRNA, which is usually 'monocistronic' (i.e. has a single

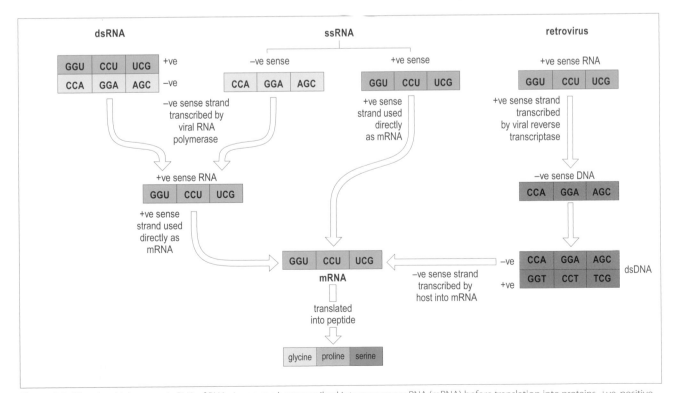

Figure 3.5 Ways in which genomic RNA of RNA viruses can be transcribed into messenger RNA (mRNA) before translation into proteins. +ve, positive sense; –ve, negative sense; ds, double stranded; ss, single stranded.

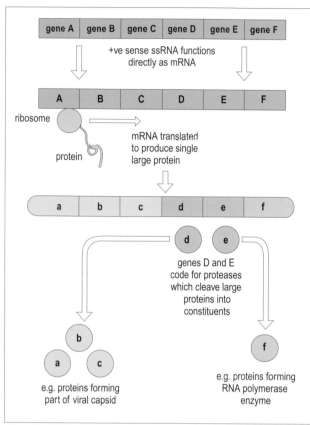

Figure 3.6 Translation and cleavage of viral proteins from messenger RNA (mRNA). +ve, positive sense; ss, single stranded.

coding region) can displace host mRNA from ribosomes so that viral products are synthesized preferentially. In the early phase, the proteins produced (enzymes, regulatory molecules) are those that will allow subsequent replication of viral nucleic acids; in the later phase, the proteins necessary for capsid formation are produced.

In viruses where the genome is a single nucleic acid molecule, translation produces a large multifunctional protein, a polyprotein, which is then cleaved enzymatically to produce a number of distinct proteins. In viruses where the genome is distributed over a number of molecules, several mRNAs are produced, each being translated into separate proteins. After translation, the proteins may be glycosylated, again using host enzymes.

Viruses must also replicate their nucleic acid

In addition to producing molecules for the formation of new capsids, the virus must replicate its nucleic acid to provide genetic material for packaging into these capsids. In positive sense ssRNA viruses such as poliovirus, a polymerase translated from viral mRNA produces negative sense RNA from the positive sense template, which is then transcribed repeatedly into more positive strands. Further cycles of transcription then occur, resulting in the production of very large numbers of positive strands, which are packaged into new particles using structural proteins translated earlier from mRNA (Fig. 3.7).

In negative sense ssRNA viruses (e.g. rabies virus), transcription by viral polymerase produces positive sense RNA strands from which new negative sense RNA is produced (Fig. 3.7). In the rabies virus, this replication occurs in the

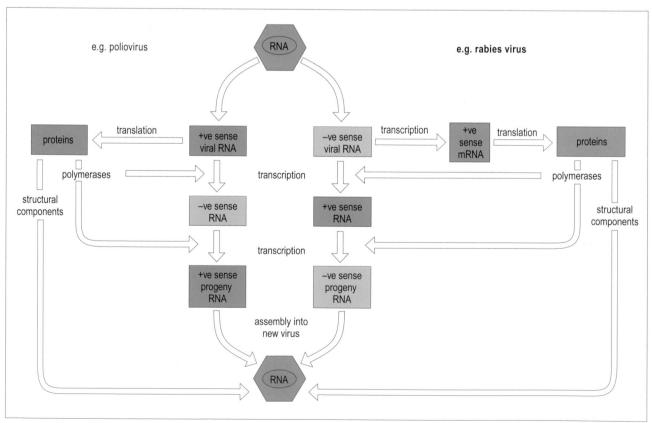

Figure 3.7 The ways in which genomic RNA of RNA viruses is replicated. +ve, positive sense; −ve, negative sense; mRNA, messenger RNA.

host cell cytoplasm, but in others (e.g. measles and influenza virus) replication takes place within the nucleus, large numbers of negative sense RNA molecules being transcribed for new particles.

Nucleic acid replication follows a similar pattern in dsRNA viruses (e.g. rotavirus) in that positive sense RNA strands are produced. These then act as templates in a subviral particle for the synthesis of new negative sense strands to restore the double stranded condition.

Replication of viral DNA occurs in the host nucleus – except for poxviruses, where it takes place in the cytoplasm

Viral DNA may become complexed with host histones to produce stable structures. With herpesviruses, mRNA translated in the cytoplasm produces a DNA polymerase that is necessary for the synthesis of new viral DNA; adenoviruses use both viral and host enzymes for this purpose. With retroviruses (e.g. HIV), synthesis of new viral RNA occurs in the nucleus, host RNA polymerase transcribing from the viral DNA that has become integrated into the host genome (see Fig. 3.5). Hepatitis B virus, a partially dsDNA virus, is unique in using a ssRNA intermediate transcribed from its DNA in order to synthesize new DNA. Retroviruses and hepatitis B are the only viruses affecting humans that have reverse transcriptase activity.

The final stage of replication is assembly and release of new virus particles

Assembly of virus particles involves the association of replicated nucleic acid with newly synthesized capsomeres to form a new nucleocapsid. This may take place in the cytoplasm or in the nucleus of the host cell. Enveloped viruses go through a further stage before release. Envelope proteins and glycoproteins, translated from viral mRNA, are inserted into areas of the host cell membrane (usually the plasma membrane). The progeny nucleocapsids associate specifically with the membrane in these areas, via the glycoproteins, and bud through it (Fig. 3.8). The new virus acquires the host cell membrane plus viral molecules as an outer envelope, and viral enzymes, such as the neuraminidase of influenza virus, may assist in this process (see details for influenza virus in Ch. 19). Host enzymes (e.g. cellular proteases) may cleave the initial large envelope proteins, a process that is necessary if the progeny viruses are to be fully infectious. In herpesviruses, acquisition of a membrane occurs as the nucleocapsids bud from the inner nuclear membrane. Release of enveloped viruses can occur without causing cell death so that infected cells continue to shed virus particles for long periods.

Insertion of viral molecules into the host cell membrane results in the host cell becoming antigenically different. Expression of viral antigens in this way is a major factor in the development of antiviral immune responses.

OUTCOME OF VIRAL INFECTION

Viral infections may cause cell lysis or be persistent or latent

In lytic infections, the virus goes through a cycle of replication, producing many new virus particles. These are released by cell lysis. This host cell destruction is the typical

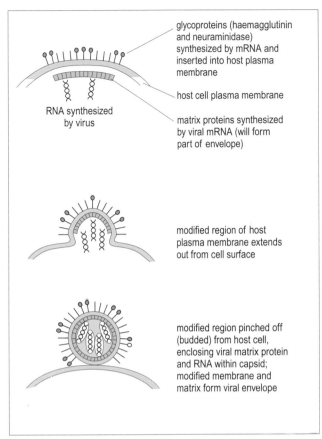

Figure 3.8 Release of enveloped RNA virus by budding through host cell membrane. Influenza A virus is shown in this example.

glycoproteins (haemagglutinin and neuraminidase) synthesized by mRNA and inserted into host plasma membrane

host cell plasma membrane

matrix proteins synthesized by viral mRNA (will form part of envelope)

RNA synthesized by virus

modified region of host plasma membrane extends out from cell surface

modified region pinched off (budded) from host cell, enclosing viral matrix protein and RNA within capsid; modified membrane and matrix form viral envelope

consequence of infection with polio or influenza viruses. With other infections, such as hepatitis B, the cell may remain alive and continue to release virus particles at a slow rate. These 'persistent' infections are of great epidemiologic importance, as the infected person may act as a symptomless carrier of the virus, providing a continuing source of infection (see Ch. 16). In both lytic and persistent infections, the virus undergoes replication. However, in latent infections, the virus remains quiescent, and the genetic material of the virus may:

- exist in the host cell cytoplasm (e.g. herpesvirus)
- be incorporated into the genome (retroviruses, hepatitis B).

Replication does not take place until some signal triggers a release from latency. The stimuli that result in release are not fully understood in all cases. In herpes simplex infection, stress can activate the virus, resulting in an active infection seen as cold sores.

Some viruses can 'transform' the host cell into a tumour or cancer cell

Lytic, persistent and latent infections involve essentially normal host cells, although cellular metabolic and regulatory processes can be severely disrupted. Some viruses, however, can 'transform' the host cell, malignant transformation being the change of a differentiated host cell into a tumour or cancer cell (see Ch. 17). Transformed cells show changes in morphology, behaviour and biochemistry. Controlled growth patterns and contact inhibition are lost, so that cells continue to divide and form random aggregations. They become invasive and can form tumours if injected into animals. However, not all transformed cells give rise to harmful tumours in vivo. Warts, for example, may be benign growths on the skin of the hands or feet caused by one group of papillomaviruses, or genital warts caused by a different group of specific papillomaviruses may lead to cervical cancer.

Cancer-inducing viruses are found in several different groups including both DNA and RNA viruses. They include the human T-cell lymphotropic virus type 1 (see below), the Epstein–Barr virus, papillomaviruses 16 and 18 and hepatitis B and C virus infections (see Ch. 17). Although the end results of transformation may be similar, the mechanisms involved vary between different viruses. However, all involve interference with the normal regulation of division and response to external growth-promoting and growth-inhibiting factors. These changes come about after viral nucleic acid is incorporated into the host genome. Finally, cancer is not always the result of some of these infections. Papillomaviruses are present in cervical cancer but additional cellular events are needed for most of the other viral infections to result in tumours.

For example, the Rous sarcoma virus is a retrovirus that causes cancer in chickens. 2011 was the hundredth anniversary of Francis Rous demonstrating that this chest tumour could be transmitted by giving tumour extracts that were cell-free to chickens related to the same brood. Transformation arises from the introduction into the host genome of a viral oncogene, v-src. This codes for an activated and overexpressed protein – tyrosine kinase, an enzyme involved in the phosphorylation of tyrosine residues in target proteins. This leads to some molecular events and changes in phenotype in transformed host cells and subsequent tumorigenesis as a result of the viral infection. A urokinase-type plasminogen activator (PLAU) gene is induced by v-src and highly up-regulated. PLAU is a protease enzyme that lyses fibrin and breaks down the extracellular matrix promoting cancer cell stickiness and spread

The first human tumour virus was discovered in 1964 when Epstein–Barr virus (EBV) was found by electron microscopic analysis of cells of a tumour called Burkitt's lymphoma seen in African patients.

More than 20 retroviral oncogenes are now known (Table 3.2). Of the retrovirus family, the human T-cell lymphotropic virus (HTLV type 1) is a cancer-causing virus in humans despite neither possessing a viral oncogene nor directly activating a cellular oncogene (see below). In contrast, HIV type 1 and 2 virus infections compromise the host's immune system, resulting in tumours associated

Table 3.2 Oncogenes, gene products, viruses known to carry them and associated human and animal diseases

Examples of retroviral oncogenes			
Class of gene product	**Oncogene**	**Virus**	**Disease**
Tyrosine kinases	*fms* *ros* *src* *yes*	FeLV ALV ALV ALV	Sarcoma
Serine/kinase threonine	*mos*	MuLV	Sarcoma
Growth factors	*sis*	FeLV	Sarcoma (platelet-derived growth factor)
Growth factor receptor	*erbB*	ALV	Erythroid leukeamia (epidermal growth factor)
Hormone receptor	*erbA*	ALV	Erythroid leukeamia (thyroid hormone)
GTP-binding proteins	Ha-*ras* Ki-*ras*	MuLV MuLV	Sarcoma Erythroid leukeamia
DNA-binding protein	*myb* *myc* *fos*	ALV ALV/FeLV MuLV	Myeloblast leukeamia Carcinoma Osteosarcoma
Examples of human oncogenic viruses			
	Onccogene	Virus	Disease
	HBx	Hepatitis B virus	Hepatocellular carcinoma
	LMP-1, BARF-1	Epstein–Barr virus	Burkitt's lymphoma, B-cell lymphoma, nasopharyngeal carcinoma
	vGPCR	Herpesvirus	Kaposi's sarcoma, primary effusion lymphoma
	E6, E7	Human papillomavirus	Cervical, anal and oral cancer
	T antigens	Merkel cell polyomavirus	Merkel cell carcinoma
	Tax	Human T-cell leukaemia lymphoma virus	Adult T-cell leukaemia/lymphoma

ALV/FeLV/MuLV, avian, feline and murine leukeamia viruses; GTP, guanosine triphosphate

HBx hepatitis B x gene, LMP-1 latent membrane protein-1, vGPCR virus G protein-coupled receptor.

with other viruses including EBV and Kaposi's sarcoma herpesvirus (KSHV) also known as human herpesvirus 8 (HHV-8). A larger number of retroviruses cause cancers in animals.

Tumour formation as a result of viral infection: direct and indirect mechanisms

Viruses associated with cancer may do so by direct means, by expressing viral oncogenes that transform the cell as mentioned above. Alternatively, they may do so indirectly by chronically infecting the cells resulting in inflammation and mutations that result in tumour formation. In addition, some virus infections including hepatitis B and C may produce various proteins that start oncogenic transformation of cells. New mechanisms are being detected by knocking out the action of certain genes and comparing the results with the control group.

Viral oncogenes have probably arisen from incorporation of host oncogenes into the viral genome during viral replication

Oncogenes are designated by short acronyms, preceded by 'v' if a viral oncogene is described (e.g. v-myc) or by 'c' for a cellular (host) oncogene (e.g. c-myc). DNA probes made from copies of the Rous sarcoma virus src oncogene have revealed complementary DNA in both infected and normal chicken cells, as well as in cancerous and normal human cells. This striking finding has since been repeated with many other retroviral oncogene sequences and it is now known that these can make up as much as 0.03–0.3% of the mammalian genome. Oncogene sequences have been identified in a wide variety of animals, from man to fruit flies, implying that they are conserved because of some valuable function. Which came first, host or viral oncogenes? The fact that host oncogenes contain introns, whereas viral oncogenes do not, and that their chromosomal positions are fixed, implies that they, and not the viral forms, are the original genes.

From what we now know about the gene products of viral oncogenes we can guess that cellular oncogenes (or 'proto-oncogenes') probably play an important role in host cell growth regulation. They may code for growth factors themselves, for cell surface receptor molecules that bind specific growth factors, for components of intracellular signalling systems, or for DNA-binding proteins that act as transcription factors.

The Rous sarcoma virus src oncogene is incorporated within the viral genome adjacent to the gene coding for viral envelope proteins (Fig. 3.9). Unlike other strongly transforming viruses, the Rous virus has all three genes (gag, pol and env) necessary for replication. In the others, termed 'defective' transforming viruses, incorporation of an oncogene results in deletion of genetic material in the regions coding for the pol and/or env genes, so preventing replication. This becomes possible only with help from genetically complete helper viruses.

Oncogenes can be carried from one cell to another within the same host or from one host to another. This can occur through 'vertical' transmission, from mother to offspring, through passage of viruses in gametes, across the placenta or in milk. It can also occur

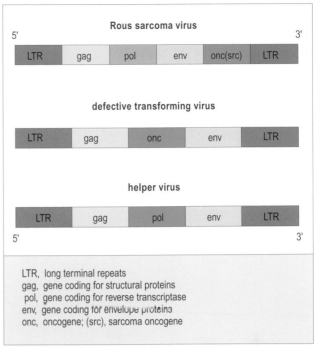

Figure 3.9 Rous sarcoma virus can transform the host cell and replicate because it has both the oncogene *src* and a complete genome. Some transforming viruses are defective – they carry the oncogene, but lack genes for full replication. Helper viruses can supply these genes.

by 'horizontal' transmission, the virus passing in, for example, saliva or urine (see Ch. 13).

Transformation of a cell occurs:

- when viral oncogenes are incorporated into the host genome (as in Rous sarcoma virus)
- when viral DNA is inserted near to a cellular oncogene.

The former may be due to mutations in the oncogene sequence while in the viral genome; single base changes in cellular oncogenes are known to confer the ability to transform normal cells. The latter may reflect altered expression of the host oncogene through disturbance of normal regulatory influences. Altered expression can occur whether the insertion is of a retroviral oncogene or of non-oncogenic viral DNA; it can also occur as a result of exposure to a variety of carcinogens. The products of cellular oncogenes are normally used in series to regulate cellular proliferation in a carefully controlled manner. Viral oncogene products or overexpressed cellular oncogene products short circuit and overload this complex control system, resulting in unregulated cell division.

MAJOR GROUPS OF VIRUSES

The classification of viruses into major groups (families) is based on a few simple criteria (Table 3.3 and the Pathogen Parade). These include:

- the type of nucleic acid in the genome
- the number of nucleic acid strands and their polarity
- the mode of replication
- the size, structure and symmetry of the virus particle.

Table 3.3 Summary of major families of viruses

Major groups of viruses

Virus family	Envelope present	Capsid symmetry	Particle size (nm)	DNA molecular weight (×10⁻⁶)	DNA/RNA structure	Medically important viruses
DNA viruses						
Parvoviridae	No	Icosahedral	18–26	2	ss linear	B19 virus
Papovaviridae	No	Icosahedral	45–55	3–5	ds circular supercoiled	Papilloma viruses Polyomavirus (JC, BK)
Adenoviridae	No	Icosahedral	70–90	23	ds linear	Adenoviruses
Hepadnaviridae	Yes	Icosahedral	42	1.5	ds incomplete, circular	Hepatitis B virus
Herpesviridae	Yes	Icosahedral	100ᵃ	100–150	ds linear	Herpes simplex virus Varicella-zoster virus Cytomegalovirus Epstein-Barr virus Human herpes virus (HHV)-6 Human herpes virus (HHV)-7 Human herpes virus (HHV)-8
Poxviridae	Yes	Complex	250×300	125–185	ds linear	Smallpox virus Vaccinia virus
RNA viruses						
Picornaviridae	No	Icosahedral	25–30	2–3	ss linear, non-segmented, +ve sense	Poliovirus, rhinovirus Hepatitis A virus Enteroviruses
Reoviridae	No	Icosahedral	75	15	ds linear, 10 segments	Reovirus, rotavirus Colorado tick fever
Togaviridae	Yes	Icosahedral	60–70	4	ss linear, non-segmented, +ve sense	Rubella virus Western equine encephalitis virus Chikungunya virus

Family	Envelope	Capsid symmetry	Size (nm)	Genome (kb)	Nucleic acid	Examples
Flaviviridae	Yes	?	40–60	3–4.4	ssRNA, +ve sense	Yellow fever virus Hepatitis C virus Dengue virus West Nile virus Japanese encephalitis virus
Retroviridae	Yes	Icosahedral	80–120	7[b]	ss linear, 2 segments, +ve sense	HIV types 1 and 2 Human cell lymphotropic virus types 1 and 2
Coronaviridae	Yes	Helical	120–160	5	ss linear, non-segmented, +ve sense	Coronavirus, SARS coronavirus (SARS CoV)
Caliciviridae	No	Icosahedral	35–40	2.6	ssRNA, +ve sense	Noroviruses (formerly SRSV or Norwalk-like viruses)
Orthomyxoviridae	Yes	Helical	80–120	4	ss linear, 8 segments, –ve sense	Influenza virus
Paramyxoviridae	Yes	Helical	120–250	6	ss linear, non-segmented –ve sense	Measles, mumps, parainfluenza, respiratory syncytial viruses
Rhabdoviridae	Yes	Helical	75×180	3–4	ss linear, non-segmented	Rabies virus
Arenaviridae	Yes	Helical	50–300	5	ss circular, 2 segments with cohesive ends, –ve sense	Lymphocytic choriomeningitis virus Lassa virus
Bunyaviridae	Yes	Helical	80–120	5	ss circular, 3 segments with cohesive ends, –ve sense	California encephalitis Sandfly fever viruses Crimean-Congo haemorrhagic fever virus Hantaan-like viruses Sin Nombre-like viruses
Filoviridae	Yes	Complex	80×14000	4.2	ssRNA, –ve sense	Marburg, Ebola virus

[a]The herpesvirus nucleocapsid is 100 nm, but the envelope varies in size; the entire virus can be as large as 200 nm in diameter.
[b]Retrovirus RNA contains two identical molecules of molecular weight 3.5×10^6. ss, single stranded; ds, double stranded. SARS, severe acute respiratory syndrome; SRSV, small round structured viruses.

35

KEY FACTS

- Viruses have RNA or DNA but absolutely depend on the host to process their genetic information into new virus particles.

- The outer surface of a virus (capsid or envelope) is essential for host cell contact and entry, and determines the capacity to survive in the outside world.

- Viruses are most often transmitted in droplets, in food and water or by intimate contact.

- Replication of viral RNA or DNA is a complex process, making use of host and/or viral enzymes.

- RNA of retroviruses becomes integrated into the host genome.

- New virus particles are released by cell lysis or by budding through the host cell membrane.

- Some viruses, such as herpesviruses, may become latent and require a trigger to resume replication; others replicate at a slow rate, persisting as a source of infection in symptomless carriers.

- A number of viruses transform the host cell, by interfering with normal cellular regulation, resulting in the development of a cancer cell. This may be the result of the activity of viral or cellular oncogenes.

CONFLICTS

Viruses have developed a cunning strategy as hardy infectious agents as, once they have infected the host cell, they may lie latent or integrate within the host cell chromosome and reactivate, potentially transmitting the infection to others. The host may not be too incapacitated, ensuring they can infect those susceptible. In addition, the host has to have a full immunosurveillance repertoire to suppress all these viruses waiting to step up to the plate. Once the defences are lowered by stress, immunosuppression or trauma, for example, active viral replication can occur.

Viruses may have a number of options with respect to receptors they can attach to and subsequently infect the host. They may be able to cross species barriers as well and not affect the reservoir host. With respect to transmissibility, their job description includes the ability to exist in blood and other body fluids, be aerosolized and to be carried by insect vectors.

To keep the host's immune system on its toes, most of the RNA viruses can subtly change their genetic make-up and drift away from the circulating strain, thus evading the immune response. Alternatively, they may have a number of genotypes with a different susceptibility to antiviral agents, are not cross-protective therefore ensuring a multivalent vaccine is required as a preventative measure, and are associated with a different clinical illness spectrum.

Viruses make full use of the cellular replicative machinery and therefore an antiviral agent has difficulty targeting the virus without affecting the host cell. As a result, most antiviral agents can adversely affect the host. This means that individuals taking certain antiviral agents have to be monitored carefully, as treatment can potentially lead to side effects including bone marrow suppression, renal toxicity and mitochondrial disorders.

What can the host do to offset all these advantages? Antiviral vaccines have been a major success, behavioural changes can limit the chances of infection and, increasingly, more precise chemotherapeutic targets are being identified.

The fungi 4

Introduction

Fungi are eukaryotes, but are quite distinct from plants and animals. Characteristically, they are multinucleate or multicellular organisms with a thick carbohydrate cell wall containing chitin, glucans, mannans and glycoproteins. They may grow as thread-like filaments (hyphae), but many other growth forms occur. Of these, the single-celled yeasts and the mushroom are most familiar. Fungi are ubiquitous as free-living organisms and are of enormous importance commercially in baking, brewing and in pharmaceuticals. Some form part of the body's normal flora, and others are common causes of local infections on skin and hair. A number of fungi are associated with significant disease and many of these are acquired from the external environment. Pathogenic species invade tissues and digest material externally by releasing enzymes; they also take up nutrients directly from host tissues. In recent years, invasive fungal disease has assumed much greater prominence in clinical practice as a result of the rise in number of severely immunocompromised patients. The study of fungi is known as mycology and fungal infections are known as mycoses.

MAJOR GROUPS OF DISEASE-CAUSING FUNGI

Importance of fungi in causing disease

There are more than 70 000 species of fungi but only about 300 are identified as pathogens in humans and animals. Some of these are cosmopolitan, others are found mainly in tropical regions. Some, those that infect superficially, cause only minor health problems but those that invade deeper tissues can be life threatening. These systemic forms have become much more serious problems as medical advances have taken place, e.g. immunosuppressive and antibiotic therapies, transplantation, invasive procedures and AIDS, such that opportunistic infections are now significant components of hospital-acquired infection.

Fungal pathogens can be classified on the basis of their growth forms or the type of infection they cause

Fungi were reclassified down to the level of order in 2007 following advances in fungal molecular taxonomy. Whilst this has no immediate effect on the practice of clinical microbiology, it will lead to greater understanding of the biology of the Kingdom Fungi and the diseases its members may cause.

Fungal pathogens may exist as branched filamentous forms or as yeasts (Fig. 4.1); some show both growth forms in their cycle and are known as dimorphic fungi. In filamentous forms (e.g. *Trichophyton*), the mass of hyphae forms a mycelium. Asexual reproduction results in the formation of sporangia, which are sacs that contain and then liberate the spores by which the fungus is dispersed; spores are a common cause of infection after inhalation. In yeast-like forms (e.g. *Cryptococcus*) the characteristic form is the single cell, which reproduces by division. Budding may also occur, with the bud remaining attached, forming pseudohyphae.

Dimorphic forms (e.g. *Histoplasma*) form hyphae at environmental temperatures, but occur as yeast cells in the body, the switch being temperature-induced. *Candida* is an important exception in the dimorphic group, showing the reverse and forming hyphae within the body.

Three types of infection (mycoses) are recognized:

- Superficial mycoses where the fungus grows on body surfaces (skin, hair, nails, mouth, vagina). Examples are tinea pedis (athlete's foot) and vaginal candidiasis (thrush).
- Subcutaneous mycoses where nails and deeper layers of the skin are involved. Examples are mycetoma (Madura foot) and sporotrichosis.
- Systemic or deep mycoses with involvement of internal organs. This category includes fungi capable of infecting individuals with normal immunity and the opportunistic fungi that cause disease in patients with compromised immune systems. Examples are histoplasmosis and systemic candidiasis.

The superficial mycoses are spread by person-to-person contact or from animal-to-human contact (e.g. from cats and dogs); the subcutaneous mycoses infect humans via the skin (e.g. following skin penetration in the case of mycetoma); the deep mycoses often result from the opportunistic growth of fungi in individuals with impaired immune competence and are primarily acquired via the respiratory tract (see Ch. 30), with intravenous lines an important portal of entry for *Candida*. Free-living fungi can also cause disease. This occurs indirectly when toxins produced by fungi are present in items used as food (e.g. aflatoxin, a carcinogen produced by *Aspergillus flavus*) or when their spores are inhaled, an immune response occurs and a hypersensitivity pneumonitis develops (allergic bronchopulmonary aspergillosis).

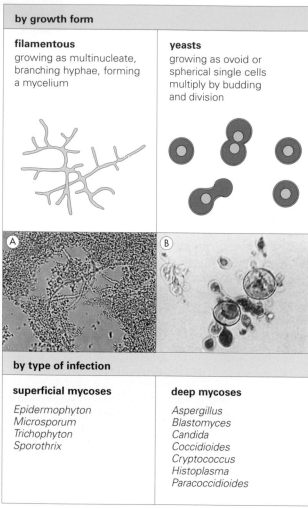

by growth form

filamentous	**yeasts**
growing as multinucleate, branching hyphae, forming a mycelium	growing as ovoid or spherical single cells multiply by budding and division

by type of infection

superficial mycoses	**deep mycoses**
Epidermophyton	Aspergillus
Microsporum	Blastomyces
Trichophyton	Candida
Sporothrix	Coccidioides
	Cryptococcus
	Histoplasma
	Paracoccidioides

Figure 4.1 Two ways to classify fungi that cause disease: by growth form and by type of infection. (A) Hyphae in skin scraping from ringworm lesion. (Courtesy of D.K. Banerjee.) (B) Spherical yeasts of *Histoplasma*. (Courtesy of Y. Clayton and G. Midgley.)

Many of the fungi that cause disease are normally free-living in the environment, but can survive in the body if acquired by inhalation or by entry through wounds. Some fungi are part of the normal flora (e.g. *Candida*) and are innocuous unless the body's defences are compromised, e.g. by underlying malignancy, diabetes mellitus or intravenous drug use. The filamentous forms grow extracellularly, but yeasts can survive and multiply within macrophages and neutrophils. Neutrophils can play a major role in controlling the establishment of invading fungi. Species that are too large for phagocytosis can be killed by extracellular factors released from phagocytes as well as by other components of the immune response. Some species, notably *Cryptococcus neoformans*, prevent phagocytic uptake because they are surrounded by a polysaccharide capsule (see Chs 24 and 30). Until, recently, *Pneumocystis*, an important opportunistic infection in AIDS patients, was classified as a protozoan, but it is now regarded as an atypical fungus. It attaches to lung cells (pneumocytes) and can give rise to a fatal pneumonia. Other pathogens previously thought to be protozoa may also turn out to be fungi, e.g. the microsporidia. The major groups of fungi causing human disease are shown in Table 4.1.

Control of fungal infection

The echinocandins inhibit glucan synthesis in the fungal cell wall. Below the fungal cell wall lies the plasma membrane or plasmalemma. Unlike human plasma membranes, where the dominant sterol is cholesterol, the fungal membrane is rich in ergosterol. Compounds that selectively bind to ergosterol can therefore be used as effective fungal agents. These include the polyenes nystatin and amphotericin B. The azoles (e.g. miconazole) and the allylamines (e.g. terbinafine) inhibit ergosterol synthesis. The pyrimidines (e.g. flucytosine) inhibit nucleic acid synthesis.

Table 4.1 Summary of fungi that cause important human diseases

Important fungal diseases				
Type	**Anatomic location**	**Representative disease**	**Causative organisms**	**Growth form**
Superficial	Hair shaft, dead layer of skin	Pityriasis versicolor, tinea nigra, piedra	*Trichosporon, Malassezia, Exophiala*	Y/F
Cutaneous	Epidermis, hair, nails	Tinea (ringworm)	*Microsporum, Trichophyton, Epidermophyton*	F
Subcutaneous	Dermis, subcutis	Sporotrichosis Mycetoma	*Sporothrix* several genera	Y[a] F
Systemic	Internal organs	Coccidioidomycosis Histoplasmosis Blastomycosis Paracoccioidomycosis	*Coccidioides Histoplasma Blastomyces Paracoccidioides*	Form[c] Y Y Y
Opportunistic	Internal organs	Cryptococcosis Candidiasis Aspergillosis Pneumocystis pneumonia	*Cryptococcus Candida Aspergillus Pneumocystis*	Y Y[b] F[a] N/A

[a]growth from the body;
[b]also forms pseudohyphae;
[c]*Coccidioides* has an unusual growth form with yeast-like endospores within a spherule; Y, yeast; F, filamentous; N/A, Y/F forms are not applicable.

KEY FACTS

- Fungi are distinct from plants and animals, have a thick chitin-containing cell wall, and grow as filaments (hyphae) or single-celled yeasts.

- Species causing disease may be acquired from the environment or occur as part of the normal flora.

- Infections may be located superficially, in cutaneous and subcutaneous sites, or in deep tissues.

- Infections are most serious in immunocompromised individuals.

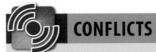

CONFLICTS

Fungi are versatile; the same species can be both free-living in the external environment and cause disease. Thus there is always a plentiful reservoir of infection. Fungi are physiologically versatile too, and can grow at a wide range of temperatures. Their reproductive stages (spores) are small, can be air-borne and easily inhaled. As they have a resistant chitinous coat, and may produce antiphagocytic factors, they can be difficult for innate defence systems to deal with. Once past the defences of the respiratory system many fungi change growth form and invade deeper tissues, often forming a network of elongate hyphae (e.g. in aspergillosis), which are even more difficult to defend against; indeed immunological responses may aggravate systemic pathology. The prevalence of infective stages in the environment and the ability of fungi to grow rapidly in the absence of effective defences makes fungal infection a major hazard for immunocompromised patients. The balance is further tipped in their favour by the difficulty in diagnosing deep-seated mycoses and by the toxicity to the host of some of the drugs used to treat them. Fortunately, immunologically competent individuals appear to deal well with what must be frequent exposure, although the potential for disease is always present.

The protozoa 5

Introduction

Protozoa are single-celled animals, ranging in size from 2 to 100 nm. Many species are free-living, but others are important parasites of humans. Some free-living species can infect humans opportunistically. Protozoa continue to multiply in their host until controlled by its immune response or by treatment and thus may cause particularly severe disease in immunocompromised individuals. Protozoal infections are most prevalent in tropical and subtropical regions, but also occur in temperate regions. Protozoa may cause disease directly (e.g. the rupture of red cells in malaria), but more often the pathology is caused by the host's response. Of all parasites, malaria presents the biggest and most severe global problem and kills >1.5 million people each year, mostly young children.

Protozoa can infect all the major tissues and organs of the body

Protozoa infect body tissues and organs as:

- intracellular parasites in a wide variety of cells (red cells, macrophages, epithelial cells, brain, muscle)
- extracellular parasites in the blood, intestine or genitourinary system.

The locations of the species of greatest importance are shown in Figure 5.1. Intracellular species obtain nutrients from the host cell by direct uptake or by ingestion of cytoplasm. Extracellular species feed by direct nutrient uptake or by ingestion of host cells. Reproduction of protozoa in humans is usually asexual, by binary or multiple division of growing stages (trophozoites). Sexual reproduction is normally absent or occurs in the insect vector phase of the life cycle, where present. *Cryptosporidium* is exceptional in undergoing both asexual and sexual reproduction in humans. Asexual reproduction gives the potential for a rapid increase in number, particularly where host defence mechanisms are impaired. For this reason some protozoa are most pathogenic in the very young (e.g. *Toxoplasma* in the fetus and in neonates). The AIDS epidemic has focused attention on a number of protozoa which give rise to opportunistic infections in immunocompromised individuals. These include *Cryptosporidium*, *Isospora* and members of the Microsporidia. New parasites continue to emerge, e.g. *Cyclospora cayetanensis*, a food-borne and water-borne cause of diarrhea, which became recognized in the early 1990s.

Protozoa have evolved many sophisticated strategies to avoid host responses

Extracellular species evade immune recognition of their plasma membrane. The interface between host and extracellular protozoa is the parasite's plasma membrane, and examples of strategies to avoid immune recognition of this surface include the following:

- Trypanosomes undergo repeated antigenic variation of surface antigens.
- Malaria parasites show polymorphisms in dominant surface antigens.
- Amoebae can consume complement at the cell surface.

Intracellular species evade host defence mechanisms. Although intracellular stages are removed from direct contact with antibody, complement and phagocytes, their antigens may be expressed at the surface of the host cell, which can then be a target for cytotoxic effectors. Survival within cells, particularly within macrophages (*Leishmania*, *Toxoplasma*), involves a variety of devices to evade or inactivate the harmful effects of intracellular enzymes or reactive oxygen and nitrogen metabolites.

Protozoa use a variety of routes to infect humans

Many extracellular protozoa are transmitted by ingestion of food or water contaminated with transmission stages such as cysts, but *Trichomonas vaginalis* is transmitted through sexual activity, and the trypanosomes by insect vectors. The most important intracellular species – *Plasmodium* and *Leishmania* – are also insect transmitted, but others (*Toxoplasma*) can be acquired by ingestion or from the mother in utero (Table 5.1).

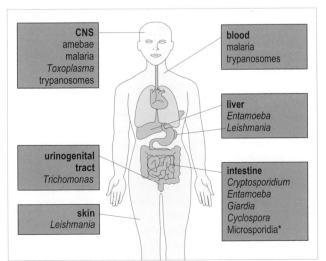

Figure 5.1 The occurrence of protozoan parasites in the body. *Can also occur in other sites. CNS, central nervous system.

41

Table 5.1 Summary of the location, transmission and diseases caused by protozoan parasites

Features of medically important protozoa			
Location	**Species**	**Mode of transmission**	**Disease**
Intestinal tract	*Entamoeba histolytica* *Giardia intestinalis* *Cryptosporidium* spp. *Isospora belli* *Cyclospora cayetanensis* Microsporidia	Ingestion of cysts in food or water	Amoebiasis Giardiasis Cryptosporidiosis Isosporiasis Cyclosporiasis Microsporidiosis
Urinogenital tract	*Trichomonas vaginalis*	Sexual	Trichomoniasis
Blood and tissue	*Trypanosoma* spp. *T. cruzi* *T. gambiense, T. rhodesiense*	Reduviid bug Tsetse fly	Trypanosomiasis, Chagas disease Sleeping sickness
	Leishmania spp. *L. donovani* complex *L. tropica, L. major, L. mexicana* *L. Viannia braziliensis*	Sand fly	Visceral leishmaniasis (kala-azar) Cutaneous leishmaniasis Mucosal leishmaniasis
	Plasmodium spp. *P. vivax, P. ovale, P. malariae* *P. falciparum, P.knowlesi*	*Anopheles* mosquito	Malaria
	Toxoplasma gondii	Ingestion of cysts in raw meat; contact with soil contaminated with cat faeces	Toxoplasmosis

KEY FACTS

- Protozoa are single-celled animals, occurring both as free-living organisms and as parasites. Both can cause disease in humans.

- The single most important protozoal disease is malaria, which causes some 1.5 million deaths each year.

- Protozoa live both outside and within cells, and have complex ways of avoiding the responses of their hosts.

- Most infections are acquired through ingestion of contaminated water or food, or via insect vectors. A few are transmitted from mother to fetus.

CONFLICTS

Malaria provides a good example of human–protozoan conflict. After a period in the liver, the malaria parasite spends all of its time inside the red cell. It grows, divides and releases new parasites by rupturing the red cell. At this stage, the parasite wins the conflict by hiding away inside a cell, a non-nucleated cell that cannot respond defensively. How can the host protect itself immunologically? It has a number of difficult choices. It can try to destroy the parasite inside the cell by producing toxic mediators or it can try to destroy the parasite and the cell together by targeting antibodies against antigens from the parasite that appear on the red cell surface, though the parasite presents a moving target as *P. falciparum* is adept at antigenic variation. Both of these are risky strategies. Toxic mediators can affect the host as well as the parasites, particularly if, as in *falciparum* malaria, the parasite-infected cells are lodged inside capillaries in vital organs. Destroying red cells can contribute to anaemia, and the by-products of destruction can also be toxic. A significant part of the pathology associated with malaria is therefore a cost of the host defending itself – game set and match to the parasite, although a dead host is of no further use to the parasite. Though treatment with antimalarials can be highly effective, if they are given late, the patient may still succumb as a result of complications despite clearance of parasites from the blood. Furthermore, the malaria parasite is adept at developing drug resistance, another example of the moving target.

The helminths and arthropods

6

Introduction

The term 'helminth' is used for all groups of parasitic worms. Three main groups are important in humans: the tapeworms (Cestoda), the flukes (Trematoda or Digenea) and the roundworms (Nematoda). The first two belong to the Platyhelminths or flatworms; the third are included in a separate phylum. Platyhelminths have flattened bodies with muscular suckers and/or hooks for attachment to the host. Nematodes (roundworms) have long cylindrical bodies and generally lack specialized attachment organs. Helminths are generally large organisms with a complex body organization. Although invading larval stages may measure only 100–200 μm, adult worms may be centimetres or even metres long. Infections are commonest in warmer countries, but intestinal species also occur in temperate regions. The arthropods are the largest and arguably most successful single group of animals. Those of most relevance to human disease are the insects, ticks and mites. Many of these have adapted to live on humans or use humans as sources of food (blood and tissue fluid). Linked with these feeding habits is the ability of many arthropods to transmit a very wide variety of microbial pathogens. Others, acting as intermediate hosts, may transmit helminth parasites when eaten, and yet other species can inflict dangerous bites and stings.

THE HELMINTHS

Transmission of helminths occurs in four distinct ways

Transmission routes are summarized in Figure 6.1. Infection can occur after:

- swallowing infective eggs or larvae via the faecal–oral route
- swallowing infective larvae in the tissues of another host
- active penetration of the skin by larval stages
- the bite of an infected blood-sucking insect vector.

The greater frequency of helminths in tropical and sub-tropical regions reflects the climatic conditions that favour survival of infective stages, the socioeconomic conditions that facilitate faecal–oral contact, the practices involved in food preparation and consumption, and the availability of suitable vectors. Elsewhere, infections are commonest in children, in individuals closely associated with domestic animals and in individuals with particular food preferences.

Many helminths live in the intestine, while others live in the deeper tissues. Almost all organs of the body can be parasitized. Flukes and nematodes actively feed on host tissues or on the intestinal contents; tapeworms have no digestive system and absorb predigested nutrients.

The majority of helminths do not replicate within the host, although certain tapeworm larval stages can reproduce asexually in humans. In most, sexual reproduction results in the production of eggs, which are released from the host in faecal material. In others, reproductive stages may accumulate within the host, but do not mature. The nematode *Strongyloides* and the tapeworm *Taenia solium* are exceptions in that eggs produced in the intestine can release infective larvae, which re-invade the body – the process of 'autoinfection'.

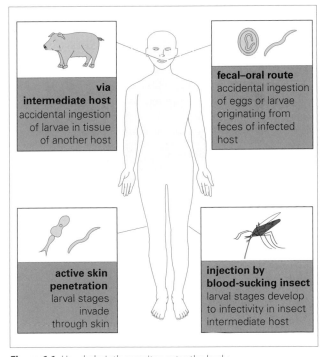

Figure 6.1 How helminth parasites enter the body.

via intermediate host
accidental ingestion of larvae in tissue of another host

fecal–oral route
accidental ingestion of eggs or larvae originating from feces of infected host

active skin penetration
larval stages invade through skin

injection by blood-sucking insect
larval stages develop to infectivity in insect intermediate host

The outer surfaces of helminths provide the primary host–parasite interface

In tapeworms and flukes, the surface is a complex plasma membrane, and in both there are protective mechanisms to prevent the host damaging the outer surface. The nematode outer surface is a tough collagenous cuticle, which, although antigenic, is largely resistant to immune attack. However, smaller larval stages may be damaged by host granulocytes and macrophages. Worms release large amounts of soluble antigenic material in their excretions and secretions, and this plays an important role both in immunity and pathology.

Life cycles

Many helminths have complex life cycles

In direct life cycles, reproductive stages produced by sexually mature adults in one host are released from the body and can develop directly to adult stages after infection of another host via the faecal–oral route (*Ascaris*) or by direct penetration (hookworms). Indirect cycles are those where reproductive stages must undergo further development in an intermediate host (tapeworms) or vector (filarial worms) before sexual maturity can be achieved in the final host.

The larvae of flukes and tapeworms must pass through one or more intermediate hosts, but those of nematodes can develop to maturity within a single host

Most flukes are hermaphrodites, except the schistosomes, which have separate sexes. The reproductive organs of tapeworms are replicated along the body (the strobila) in a series of identical segments or 'proglottids'. The terminal 'gravid' proglottids become filled with mature eggs, detach and pass out in the faeces. The eggs of both flukes and tapeworms develop into larvae that must pass through one or more intermediate hosts and develop into other larval stages before the parasite is again infective to humans. The tapeworm *Hymenolepis nana*, occasionally found in humans, is exceptional and can go through a complete cycle from egg to adult in the same host.

In nematodes, the sexes are separate. Most species liberate fertilized eggs, but some release early-stage larvae directly into the host's body. Development from egg or larva to adult can be direct and occur in a single host, or may be indirect, requiring development in the body of an intermediate host. Classification of nematodes is complex, and for practical purposes only two categories of human-specific nematodes are considered here:

- those that mature within the gastrointestinal tract, some of which may migrate through the body during development (e.g. *Ascaris*, hookworms, *Trichinella*, *Strongyloides*, *Trichuris*)
- those that mature in deeper tissues (e.g. the filarial nematodes).

In addition, humans can be infected with the larvae of species that mature in other hosts (e.g. the dog parasites *Toxocara canis* and *Ancylostoma brasiliense*).

Helminths and disease

Adult tapeworms are acquired by eating undercooked or raw meat containing larval stages

Tapeworms frequently infect humans, but are relatively harmless despite their potential for reaching a large size. Humans can also act as the intermediate hosts for certain species, and the development of larval stages in the body can cause severe disease (Table 6.1).

The most important flukes are those causing schistosomiasis

Several species of fluke can mature in humans, developing in the intestine, lungs, liver and blood vessels. The most important, both in terms of prevalence and pathology, are the blood flukes or schistosomes, the cause of schistosomiasis or bilharzia. Three main species, *Schistosoma haematobium*, *Schistosoma japonicum* and *Schistosoma mansoni*, infect many millions and are responsible for severe disease (Table 6.2). Like all flukes, schistosomes have an indirect life cycle

Table 6.1 Summary of the location, transmission and other hosts used by tapeworms that infect humans

Human tapeworm infections			
Species	**Acquired form**	**Other hosts**	**Site in humans**
Adult worms			
Taenia saginata	Larvae in beef	None	Intestine
Taenia solium	Larvae in pork	None	Intestine
Diphyllobothrium latum	Larvae in fish	Fish-eating mammals	Intestine
Hymenolepis nana	Eggs, or larvae in beetles	Rodents	Intestine
*Hymenolepis diminuta**	Larvae in insects	Rats, mice	Intestine
*Dipylidium caninum**	Larvae in fleas	Dogs, cats	Intestine
Larval worms			
Taenia solium (cysticercosis)	Eggs in food or water contaminated with human feces	Pigs	Brain, eyes
Echinococcus granulosus (hydatid disease)	Eggs passed by dogs	Sheep	Liver, lung, brain
*Echinococcus multilocularis**	Eggs passed by carnivores	Sheep	Liver
Pseudophyllidean tapeworms* (sparganosis)	Larvae in other hosts	Many vertebrates	Subcutaneous tissues, eyes
*Taenia multiceps**	Eggs passed by dogs	Sheep	Brain, eye, subcutaneous tissue

*Rare infections.

Table 6.2 Summary of the location and transmission of flukes that infect humans

Human fluke infections		
Species	**Acquired form**	**Site in humans**
Schistosoma haematobium *Schistosoma japonicum* *Schistosoma mansoni*	Penetration of skin by larval stages released from snails	Blood vessels of bladder Blood vessels of intestine Blood vessels of intestine
Clonorchis sinensis	Ingesting fish infected with larval stages	Liver
Fasciola hepatica	Ingesting vegetation (cress) with larval stages	Liver
Paragonimus westermani	Ingesting crabs infected with larval stages	Lungs

involving stages of larval development in the body of a snail, in this case aquatic snails. Humans become infected when they come into contact with water containing infective larvae released from the snails, the larvae penetrating through the skin. Other important species are *Clonorchis sinensis*, a liver fluke, and *Paragonimus westermani*, the lung fluke, transmitted by eating infected fish or crabs, respectively.

Certain nematodes that infect humans are highly specific; others are zoonoses

Several of the many species of nematode that infect humans are highly specific and can mature in no other host. Others have a much lower host specificity, being acquired acciden-

tally as zoonoses, with humans acting either as the intermediate or the final host after picking up infection from domestic animals or in food (Table 6.3).

Survival of helminths in their hosts

Many helminth infections are long lived, the worms surviving in their hosts for many years, despite living in parts of the body where there are effective immune defences. How this is achieved has been worked out in several species. Some, such as the schistosomes, disguise themselves from the immune system by acquiring host molecules on their outer surface, so they are less easily recognized as foreign invaders. Others actively suppress the host's

Table 6.3 Summary of the location and transmission of nematodes that infect humans

Human nematode infections		
Species	**Acquired by**	**Site in humans**
Transmitted person to person		
Ascaris lumbricoides	Ingestion of eggs	Small intestine
Enterobius vermicularis	Ingestion of eggs	Large intestine

Hookworms
   Ancylostoma duodenale
   Necator americanus
	Skin penetration by infective larvae
	Skin penetration by infective larvae
		Small intestine
		Small intestine

Strongyloides stercoralis	Skin penetration by infective larvae; autoinfection	Small intestine (adults), general tissues (larvae)
Trichuris trichiura	Ingestion of eggs	Large intestine
Transmitted person to person via arthropod vector		
Brugia malayi	Bite of mosquito carrying infective larvae	Lymphatics (adults), blood (larvae)
Onchocerca volvulus	Bite of *Simulium* fly carrying infective larvae	Skin (larvae, adults), eye (larva)
Wuchereria bancrofti	Bite of mosquito carrying infective larvae	Lymphatics (adults), blood (larvae)
Loa loa	Bite of deer-fly carrying infective larvae	Tissues
Zoonoses transmitted from animals		
Angiostrongylus cantonensis	Ingestion of larvae in snails, crustacea	CNS (larvae)
Anisakis simplex	Ingestion of larvae in fish	Stomach, small intestine (larvae)
Capillaria philippinensis	Ingestion of larvae in fish	Small intestine (adults, larvae)
*Toxocara canis**	Ingestion of eggs passed by dogs	Tissues, CNS (larvae)
*Trichinella spiralis**	Ingestion of larvae in pork, meat of wild mammals	Small intestine (adults), muscles (larvae)

*These species are the commonest in this group.

immune responses by releasing factors that interfere with, or divert, protective responses. The ability of worms to do this is being actively investigated as a potential therapeutic approach to the control of immunologically mediated conditions such as allergy and autoimmunity. It may one day be possible to protect patients at risk from these conditions by giving them a parasite infection!

THE ARTHROPODS

Arthropods cause disease directly by their feeding and indirectly by transmitting infections.

Many arthropods feed on human blood and tissue fluids

Blood feeders include mosquitoes, midges, biting flies, bugs, fleas and ticks. Some mites also feed in this way, chiggers, the larvae of trombiculid mites, being a familiar example. Contact may be temporary or permanent. Mosquitoes are temporary ectoparasites, feeding for only a few minutes; ticks feed for much longer. The head and body forms of the louse *Pediculus humanus*, and the crab louse *Phthirus pubis*,

spend almost all of their lives on humans, feeding on blood and reproducing on the body or in clothing. The scabies mite *Sarcoptes scabiei* lives permanently on humans, burrowing into the superficial layers of skin to feed and lay eggs. Heavy infections can build up, particularly on individuals with reduced immune responsiveness, causing a severe inflammatory condition (see Ch. 26).

Arthropod infestation carries the additional hazard of disease transmission

Arthropods transmit pathogens of all major groups, from viruses to worms and some (e.g. mosquitoes and ticks) transmit a wide variety of organisms (Table 6.4). The ability to transmit infections acquired from animals to humans poses a constant threat of acquiring zoonoses. Some vector-borne infections, such as yellow fever, have been known for centuries, whereas others, such as the viral encephalitides and Lyme disease, have been recognized more recently (1920s and 1975, respectively). Mosquito-transmitted West Nile virus has become a significant threat in North America, with sporadic cases and outbreaks reported from Europe (see Ch. 27).

Table 6.4 Summary of infectious diseases transmitted by arthropods

Infectious diseases transmitted by arthropods		
	Disease	**Arthropod vector**
Viruses		
Arboviruses	Dengue fever	Mosquitoes
	Yellow fever	Mosquitoes
	Encephalitides	Mosquitoes, ticks
	Hemorrhagic fevers	Ticks, mosquitoes
Bacteria		
Yersinia pestis	Plague	Fleas
Borrelia recurrentis	Relapsing fever	Soft ticks
Borrelia burgdorferi	Lyme disease	Hard ticks
Rickettsias		
R. prowazekii	Epidemic typhus	Lice, ticks
R. mooseri	Endemic (murine) typhus	Fleas
R. rickettsia	Spotted fever	Ticks
R. akari	Rickettsial pox	Mites
Protozoa		
Trypanosoma cruzi	American trypanosomiasis (Chagas disease)	Reduviid bugs
T.b. rhodesiense	African trypanosomiasis (sleeping sickness)	Tsetse flies
T.b. gambiense		
Plasmodium spp.	Malaria	Mosquitoes
Leishmania spp.	Leishmaniasis	Sandflies
Worms		
Wuchereria and *Brugia*	Lymphatic filariasis	Mosquitoes
Onchocerca	Onchocerciasis	*Simulium* flies

KEY FACTS

- Helminths are multicellular worms that parasitize many organs of the body, most commonly the gastrointestinal tract.

- Transmission may be direct, through swallowing infective stages or by larvae penetrating the skin, or indirect via intermediate hosts or insect vectors.

- The most serious helminth infection is schistosomiasis, caused by infection with blood flukes. The pathology is primarily due to hypersensitivity reactions to eggs as they pass through tissues.

- Arthropods of importance in human disease are those that feed on blood or body tissues (insects, ticks, mites) and those which transmit other infections, particularly viruses, bacteria and protozoa.

CONFLICTS

Helminths are typically large parasites, often covered by a protective outer layer, so they are difficult for the immune system to deal with – too big for phagocytosis or cytotoxic T cells and unaffected by direct antibody activity. They are often active and mobile and can move away from host defences, damaging host tissues as they do so. Many disguise their outer surfaces or produce immunosuppressive factors. Because they are long-lived and able to survive despite immune responses, they can produce chronic disease, either as a consequence of their activity or because of misdirected and pathological host immune responses. Reliance on direct infection through faecal–oral contact, or transmission by vectors, makes it difficult to avoid infection when climate and low standards of hygiene combine to tilt the balance in favour of the parasite. Treatment with anthelmintics works against many intestinal worms, but re-infection is almost routine in areas of poor sanitation, necessitating regular re-treatment programmes. Those living in the tissues are much more difficult to deal with, e.g. hydatid cysts may require major surgery as well as antiparasitic drugs, and there are still no effective drugs for the treatment of Guinea Worm.

Prions 7

Introduction

Prions are unusual infectious agents associated with a number of human, animal and fungal diseases. In humans they can cause degenerative changes in the brain: the transmissible spongiform encephalopathies. Kuru is the classic example of such a condition, epidemiological studies confirming human–human transmission. Prions lack a nucleic acid genome and are highly resistant to all conventional forms of disinfection processes. They are small proteinaceous particles that are modified forms of a normal cellular protein, and cause disease by converting normal protein into further abnormal forms. Prion-related conditions can arise endogenously by mutation (and be inherited) or be acquired exogenously during medical procedures or by ingestion of contaminated material. The prion diseases are part of a spectrum of neurodegenerative disorders in which soluble proteins are modified and accumulate as insoluble beta-sheet rich amyloid fibrils. The other neurogenerative disorders that include different types of dementia are not infectious but are sporadic or inherited, sharing a common pathogenesis. Endogenous sporadic Creutzfeldt–Jakob disease (CJD) has been known for some time as have Gerstmann–Sträussler–Scheinker disease, fatal familial insomnia and kuru. However, in the 1990s another form of this disease (variant CJD, vCJD) was associated with eating beef from cattle infected with the prion that causes bovine spongiform encephalopathy.

'ROGUE PROTEIN' PATHOGENESIS

Prions are unique infectious agents

There are a number of human and animal diseases – the spongiform encephalopathies – whose pathology is characterized by the development of large vacuoles in the CNS. These include kuru and Creutzfeldt–Jakob diseases (CJD) in humans, bovine spongiform encephalopathy (BSE) in cattle and scrapie in sheep. Sporadic CJD is the most common prion disease in humans worldwide and the incidence is approximately 1.5 per million people. For a long time, these diseases were thought to be caused by so-called unconventional slow viruses, but it is now known that the agents concerned are prions; small, proteinaceous infectious particles. Their characteristics include:

- small size (<100 nm, therefore filterable)
- lack of a nucleic acid genome
- extreme resistance to heat, disinfectants and irradiation (but susceptible to high concentrations of phenol, periodate, sodium hydroxide, sodium hypochlorite)
- slow replication – typically diseases have a long incubation period and usually appear late in life. Incubation periods of up to 35 years have been recorded in humans, but variant CJD can produce symptoms much more rapidly
- cannot be cultured in vitro
- do not elicit immune or inflammatory responses.

Prions are host-derived molecules

Studies on scrapie gave some insight into the nature of prions and their role in disease. The infectious agent is a host-derived 30–35 kDa glycoprotein (termed PrP^{Sc}, prion protein scrapie) that is associated with the characteristic intracellular fibrils seen in diseased tissue. PrP^{Sc} is derived from a naturally occurring cellular prion protein (PrP^c), expressed predominantly on the surface of nerve cells and coded by a single copy gene of unknown function (located on chromosome 20 in humans). Mice with the PrP^c gene disrupted are resistant to scrapie, and they show no gross abnormalities. The two proteins have a similar sequence, but differ in structure and protease resistance; PrP^{Sc} is globular and enzyme resistant; PrP^c is linear and enzyme susceptible. The association of PrP^{Sc} with PrP^c results in conversion of the latter into the abnormal form, the change being largely conformational, from alpha helices to beta-pleated sheets. Affected cells produce more PrP^c and the process is then repeated, the accumulating PrP^{Sc} aggregating into amyloid fibrils and plaques (Fig. 7.1). Replication can lead to very high titres of infectious particles and up to 10^8–10^9/g of brain tissue have been recorded.

Evidence that the interaction of PrP^{Sc} with PrP^c causes these events is based on extensive experiments in sheep and mice, the main conclusions being:

- Scrapie infectivity in material co-purifies with PrP^{Sc}.
- Purified PrP^{Sc} confers greater scrapie activity.
- Mice lacking the PrP^c gene do not develop disease when injected with prions.
- Introduction of a PrP transgene from a prion donor species (e.g. hamster) into a recipient species (e.g. mouse) facilitates cross-species transmission, suggesting that homology between the PrP genes of donor and recipient is the main molecular determinant of such transmission.
- In vitro, PrP^{Sc} can convert PrP^c into PrP^{Sc}, with the transfer of biochemical characteristics.

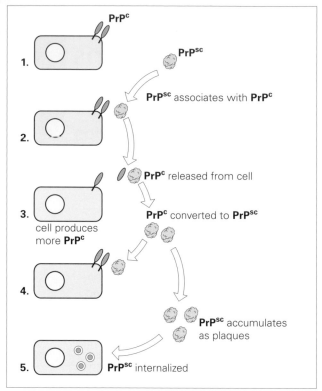

Figure 7.1 How prions may damage cells. (1) Normal cells express PrP^c at the cell membrane as linear proteins. (2) PrP^{sc} exists as a free globular glycoprotein, which can interact with PrP^c. (3) PrP^c is released from the cell membrane and is converted into PrP^{sc}. (4) Cells produce more PrP^c and the cycle is repeated. (5) PrP^{sc} accumulates as plaques, and is internalized by cells.

The development of scrapie in sheep shows strong genetic influences, some breeds being much more resistant than others, and similar genetic effects have been shown in mice. In humans, homozygosity for methionine at codon 129 of the prion protein gene is a major determinant of susceptibility to sporadic, iatrogenic and vCJD. There is also variation in prions, different strains being described. These combinations of host and prion variation result in a spectrum of disease onset and severity.

DEVELOPMENT, TRANSMISSION AND DIAGNOSIS OF PRION DISEASES

PrP is a modified host protein and the gene is located on chromosome 20. The normal form of the prion protein is referred to as PrP^c. PrP^{sc} is an abnormal isoform of PrP and accumulates in brain tissue. It only differs to PrP^c by having an increased beta-sheet content, which makes it more stable. In particular, it is quite resistant to proteolysis. The normally folded protein PrP^c is converted to an abnormal conformation by direct contact with the misfolded form PrP^{sc}. If the load of the latter increases it can lead to a rapid neurodegenerative phenotype. PrP^{sc} can be built into different structures and so these PrP^{sc} species can result in a variety of prion diseases such as sporadic CJD and two other human prion diseases: Gerstmann–Sträussler–Scheinker syndrome and fatal familial insomnia. There is some evidence that people have a

genetic predisposition for sporadic CJD. There is a naturally occurring polymorphism at codon 129 of the PrP^c gene on chromosome 20 and this codes for the amino acid methionine or valine. Compared with the unaffected population, people with sporadic CJD are many times more likely to be methione homozygous at this locus.

With the exception of those cases where prions arise by mutation, transmission and spread of prion disease requires exposure to the infective agent. Ways in which this could occur include eating contaminated food material, use of contaminated medical products (blood, hormone extracts, transplants), the introduction of prions from contaminated instruments during surgical procedures, as prions bind strongly to metal surfaces, and possibly mother–fetus transmission during pregnancy (although none of the hundreds of infants born to mothers with kuru developed the disease). The disease kuru was transmitted by eating the brains of dead humans in funeral rites, and vCJD is associated with eating contaminated beef products. In these cases, prions survive digestion and are taken up across the intestinal mucosa. They are then carried in lymphoid cells, eventually being transferred into neural tissues and entering the CNS.

Prions can cross species boundaries

Although prions from one species are more effective in transmitting disease to the same species, transmission can occur between different species (Fig. 7.2). The most serious example of this is the transfer of prions from cattle infected with BSE to humans through consumption of infected meat, which has been associated with outbreaks of vCJD. BSE itself arose as a result of transfer to cattle of prions from sheep infected with scrapie, and in 1996 it became clear that human vCJD and BSE were caused by the same prion strain. Unlike CJD itself, vCJD caused disease in younger individuals (14 years and upwards) with a much shorter incubation period. The number of human infections likely to arise from the UK epidemic of BSE in cattle (thought to have affected more than 2 million animals) is still controversial, though some believe the potential to be quite small. CJD surveillance was started in the United Kingdom in 1990 in order to identify the number of human infections arising from the UK epidemic of BSE in cattle that was thought to have affected more than 3 million animals. This estimate was based on the likely number of asymptomatic animals and the clinical diagnosis of BSE made in over 180 000 cattle. vCJD was first reported in the UK in 1996 by the National CJD Surveillance Unit. Those affected had a clinical and pathological phenotype distinct from sporadic CJD and were homozygous for methionine at codon 129. Again, this demonstrated a genetic predisposition for vCJD. vCJD is the only prion disease affecting humans that can be acquired from another species and is caused by BSE. This has also been shown by animal transmission studies in which the infectious agent associated with vCJD was shown to have the same biological properties as that causing BSE. Epidemiological studies suggest that the most likely route of transmission is the oral route, the affected individual having eaten beef contaminated with the BSE agent. PrP^{sc} has been found in the lymphoreticular system including the tonsils and spleen as well as neurological tissues and the prion may be carried in the blood by lymphocytes.

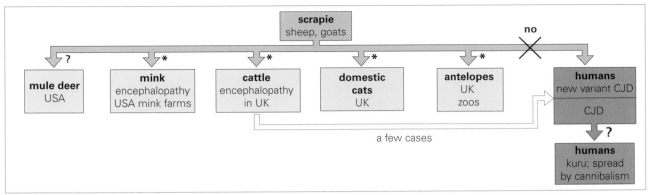

Figure 7.2 The spread of scrapie agents between species. Nearly all have been transmitted to laboratory rodents and primates. (*Infections transferred by scrapie-infected sheep materials present in foodstuff. Most of these infectious agents have mutations at amino acid residue 129 of the prion protein, which are thought to cause conversion of the protein into the pathogenic form.)

Overall, by July 2010, 220 people had developed vCJD in 11 countries around the world, 173 of whom were diagnosed in the UK. That number was much lower than predicted by mathematical modellers in the 1990s. As the incubation period can be very long, it is unclear how many people could be at risk and asymptomatic. Issues surrounding diagnostic tests include assay sensitivity and specificity, resulting in difficulty in comparing studies. A large study was carried out in the UK investigating more than 32 000 anonymized tonsil tissues for disease related prion protein referred to as PrP^{CJD} from people who underwent an elective tonsillectomy. Of these, 12 753 were from the 1961–1985 birth cohort that included the time most vCJD cases had arisen and 19,908 were from the 1986–95 cohort that would potentially have been exposed to BSE-contaminated meat products. PrP^{CJD} was not detected in any samples.

Prion diseases are difficult to diagnose

Because prions cannot be cultured, and since there is no immune response, prion disease in its early stages cannot be diagnosed easily. Clinical appearances usually indicate the probable occurrence of prion disease and this can be confirmed histologically post mortem. Tonsillar tissue is a good source of PrP^{Sc} in clinical cases and these prions can be identified by immunoblotting or immunohistochemistry. Tonsillar and other tissue homogenates can also be tested for the presence of the abnormal prion protein by enzyme immunoassays. These have been used in a number of studies and the development of diagnostic tests is important not only to make a diagnosis but also from a public health standpoint to prevent infection, as transmission by blood and blood products has been reported.

Lessons from Kuru

Kuru is a condition that was identified with cannibalistic behaviour in Papua New Guinea. There were more than 2700 infections between 1957 and 2004, the incubation period of the disease being estimated at more than 50 years. The fatality rate fell from over 200 per year in the late 1950s to 6 per year in the early 1990s. This reduction followed the prohibition of cannibalistic behaviour in the 1950s. A study investigating suspected kuru cases between 1996 and 2004 identified 11 infected individuals. The minimum estimated

incubation periods in this group ranged from 34 to 41 years, the range in males being from 39 to at least 56 years. Analysis of the prion protein gene (PRNP) showed that most patients with kuru were heterozygous at codon 129.

PREVENTION AND TREATMENT OF PRION DISEASES

Prion diseases are incurable

Although, as of 2012, there is neither an effective treatment nor vaccine, chemotherapeutic strategies involve stopping the conversion of the normal form of prion protein to the abnormal form PrP^{Sc}. Experimental studies in rodents demonstrated some protection when polyanionic and tricyclic compounds are given shortly after infection. Transgenic mouse models have helped elucidate the pathogenesis of human prion disease. Current understanding of the nature of the interactions between PrP^{Sc} and PrP^c may eventually offer some hope of regulating the development of disease by reducing or destabilizing the formation of PrP^{Sc}. Immunomodulation and mucosal immunization may be potential therapeutic and preventative approaches, especially as the alimentary tract is likely to be the main route of transmission.

KEY FACTS

- Prions are unusual infectious agents, causing diseases characterized by changes in the brain (spongiform encephalopathies) and motor disturbances.

- Prions are host-derived glycoproteins and lack a nucleic acid genome. They are extremely resistant to disinfection procedures.

- Transmission of prions is usually by ingestion of contaminated tissues, but can occur via medical procedures.

- Diseases caused by prions include kuru, Creutzfeldt–Jakob disease (CJD), variant CJD and bovine spongiform encephalopathy (BSE).

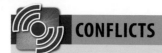

CONFLICTS

Of all the pathogens covered in this book, prions win the human–pathogen conflict. They are resistant to almost all disinfectant procedures and elicit minimal immune responses. They are never exposed to the outside world and cannot therefore be intercepted. They have no nucleic acids and no metabolic systems, so cannot be targeted by antimicrobial drugs. Prions can arise by mutation and hijack normal protein-folding control, producing abnormal molecules that are resistant to enzymes. Prions can cross from one species to another, and have crossed from animals to humans. Infection is therefore possible from meat-based food products. The presence of prions in meat is hard to detect; once ingested, prions can travel from the intestine to lymphoid and then to nervous tissues, ultimately causing profound and usually fatal changes in the CNS. Genetic characteristics of potential hosts seem to play an important role in determining the course of disease after exposure. Examples of prion-induced diseases are Creutzfeldt–Jakob disease (CJD); variant CJD (linked to 'mad cow disease'); and kuru. These diseases can be diagnosed but there is currently no effective treatment.

The host–parasite relationship

8

Introduction

The preceding chapters have focused primarily on organisms that are quite clearly disease agents. Small numbers may be found in healthy individuals, but their presence in large numbers is usually associated with pathologic changes. The organisms covered in the first section of this chapter may cause disease under certain circumstances (e.g. in the newborn or in stressed, traumatized or immunocompromised individuals), but usually coexist quite peacefully with their host. Many of these form what is termed the 'indigenous' or 'normal' flora of the body – a collection of species routinely found in the normal healthy individual and which, in some cases, are necessary for normal functioning of the human body. Their relationship with the host makes an interesting comparison with that of species that are considered as true parasites or pathogens and is discussed later in this chapter in the broader context of symbiotic relationships and the evolution of host–parasite relationships.

THE NORMAL FLORA

Why is it called the normal flora?

The term flora is used for the collective bacteria and other microorganisms in an ecosystem such as the human host. It has been estimated that humans have approximately 10^{13} cells in the body and something like 10^{14} bacteria associated with them, the majority in the large bowel. Members of groups such as viruses, fungi and protozoa are also regularly found in healthy individuals, but form only a minor component of the total population of resident organisms.

The organisms occur in those parts of the body that are exposed to, or communicate with, the external environment, namely the skin, nose and mouth and intestinal and urinogenital tracts. The main organisms found in these sites are shown in Figure 8.1. Internal organs and tissues are normally sterile.

The normal flora is acquired rapidly during and shortly after birth and changes continuously throughout life

The organisms present at any given time reflect the age, nutrition and environment of the individual. It is therefore difficult to define the normal flora very precisely because it is to a large extent environmentally determined. This is well illustrated by data from NASA astronauts who were rendered relatively bacteriologically sterile by antibiotic treatment before their space flights. It took only 6 weeks after the flight for their flora to re-populate, and the re-populating species were precisely those of their immediate neighbours. The bowel flora of children in developing countries is quite different from that of children in developed countries. In addition, breast-fed infants have lactic acid streptococci and lactobacilli in their gastrointestinal tract, whereas bottle-fed children show a much greater variety of organisms.

Different regions of the skin support different flora

Exposed dry areas are not a good environment for bacteria and consequently have relatively few resident organisms on the surface, whereas moister areas (axillae, perineum, between the toes, scalp) support much larger populations. *Staphylococcus epidermidis* is one of the commonest species, making up some 90% of the aerobes and occurring in densities of 10^3–10^4/cm^2; *Staphylococcus aureus* may be present in the moister regions.

Anaerobic diphtheroids occur below the skin surface in hair follicles, sweat and sebaceous glands, *Propionibacterium acnes* being a familiar example. Changes in the skin occurring during puberty often lead to increased numbers of this species, which can be associated with acne.

A number of fungi, including *Candida*, occur on the scalp and around the nails. They are infrequent on dry skin, but can cause infection in moist skinfolds (intertrigo).

Both the nose and mouth can be heavily colonized by bacteria

The majority of bacteria here are anaerobes. Common species colonizing these areas include streptococci, staphylococci, diphtheroids and Gram-negative cocci. Some of the aerobic bacteria found in healthy individuals are potentially pathogenic (e.g. *Staph. aureus, Streptococcus pneumoniae, Streptococcus pyogenes, Neisseria meningitidis*); *Candida* is also a potential pathogen.

The mucous membranes of the mouth can have the same microbial density as the large intestine, numbers approaching 10^{11}/g wet weight of tissue.

Dental caries is one of the most common infectious diseases in developed countries

The surfaces of the teeth and the gingival crevices carry large numbers of anaerobic bacteria. Plaque is a film of bacterial cells anchored in a polysaccharide matrix, which the organisms secrete. When teeth are not cleaned regularly, plaque

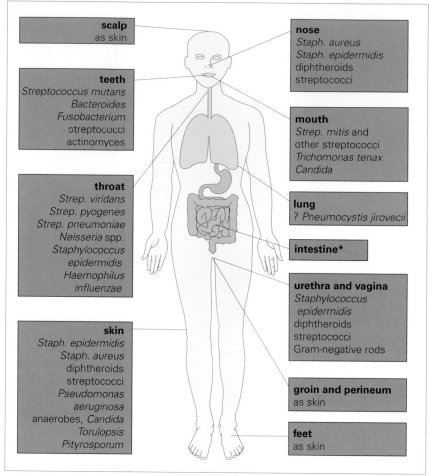

Figure 8.1 Examples of organisms that occur as members of the normal flora and their location on the body. (*Those found in the intestine are detailed in Fig. 8.2.)

can accumulate rapidly and the activities of certain bacteria, notably *Streptococcus mutans*, can lead to dental decay (caries), as acid fermented from carbohydrates can attack dental enamel. The prevalence of dental decay is linked to diet.

The pharynx and trachea carry their own normal flora

The flora of the pharynx and trachea may include both α- and β-haemolytic streptococci as well as a number of anaerobes, staphylococci (including *Staph. aureus*), *Neisseria* and diphtheroids. The respiratory tract is normally quite sterile, despite the regular intake of organisms by breathing. However, substantial numbers of clinically normal people may carry the fungus *Pneumocystis jirovecii* (previously known as *P. carinii*) in their lungs.

In the gut the density of microorganisms increases from the stomach to the large intestine

The stomach normally harbours only transient organisms, its acidic pH providing an effective barrier. However, the gastric mucosa may be colonized by acid-tolerant lactobacilli and streptococci. *Helicobacter pylori*, which can cause gastric ulcers (see Ch. 22), is carried without symptoms by large numbers of people, the bacterium being in mucus and neutralizing the local acidic environment. The upper intestine is only lightly colonized (10^4 organisms/g), but populations increase markedly in the ileum, where strep-

tococci, lactobacilli, enterobacteriaceae and *Bacteroides* may all be present. Bacterial numbers are very high (estimated at 10^{11}/g) in the large bowel, and many species can be found (Fig. 8.2). The vast majority (95–99%) are anaerobes, *Bacteroides* being especially common and a major component of faecal material; *E. coli* is also carried by most individuals. *Bacteroides* and *E. coli* are among the species capable of causing severe disease when transferred into other sites in the body. Harmless protozoans can also occur in the intestine (e.g. *Entamoeba coli*) and these can be considered as part of the normal flora, despite being animals.

The urethra is lightly colonized in both sexes, but the vagina supports an extensive flora of bacteria and fungi

The urethra in both sexes is relatively lightly colonized, although *Staph. epidermidis*, *Strep. faecalis* and diphtheroids may be present. In the vagina, the composition of the bacterial and fungal flora undergoes age-related changes:

- Before puberty, the predominant organisms are staphylococci, streptococci, diphtheroids and *E. coli*.
- Subsequently, *Lactobacillus aerophilus* predominates, its fermentation of glycogen being responsible for the maintenance of an acid pH, which prevents overgrowth by other vaginal organisms.

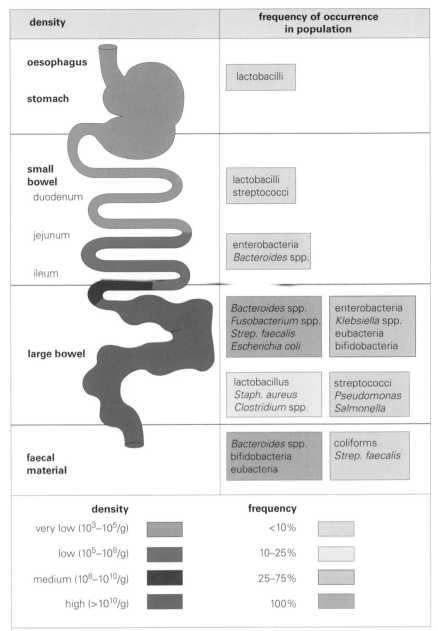

density	frequency of occurrence in population	
oesophagus **stomach**	lactobacilli	
small bowel duodenum	lactobacilli streptococci	
jejunum ileum	enterobacteria *Bacteroides* spp.	
large bowel	*Bacteroides* spp. *Fusobacterium* spp. *Strep. faecalis* *Escherichia coli*	enterobacteria *Klebsiella* spp. eubacteria bifidobacteria
	lactobacillus *Staph. aureus* *Clostridium* spp.	streptococci *Pseudomonas* *Salmonella*
faecal material	*Bacteroides* spp. bifidobacteria eubacteria	coliforms *Strep. faecalis*

density		frequency	
very low (10^3–10^5/g)		<10%	
low (10^5–10^8/g)		10–25%	
medium (10^8–10^{10}/g)		25–75%	
high (>10^{10}/g)		100%	

Figure 8.2 The longitudinal distribution, frequency of occurrence and densities of the bacteria making up the normal flora of the human gastrointestinal tract.

A number of fungi occur, including *Candida*, which can overgrow to cause the pathogenic condition 'thrush' if the vaginal pH rises and competing bacteria diminish. The protozoan *Trichomonas vaginalis* may also be present in healthy individuals.

Advantages and disadvantages of the normal flora

Some of the species of the normal flora are positively beneficial to the host

The importance of these species for health is sometimes revealed quite dramatically under stringent antibiotic therapy. This can drastically reduce their numbers to a minimum, and the host may then be over-run by introduced pathogens or by overgrowth of organisms normally present in small numbers. After treatment with clindamycin, overgrowth by *Clostridium difficile*, which survives treatment, can give rise to antibiotic-associated diarrhea or, more seriously, pseudomembranous colitis.

Ways in which the normal flora prevents colonization by potential pathogens include the following:

- Skin bacteria produce fatty acids, which discourage other species from invading.
- Gut bacteria release a number of factors with antibacterial activity (bacteriocins, colicins) as well as metabolic waste products that help prevent the establishment of other species.
- Vaginal lactobacilli maintain an acid environment, which suppresses growth of other organisms.
- The sheer number of bacteria present in the normal flora of the intestine means that almost all of the available ecologic niches become occupied; these species therefore out-compete others for living space.

Gut bacteria also release organic acids, which may have some metabolic value to the host; they also produce B vitamins and vitamin K in amounts that are large enough to be valuable if the diet is deficient. The antigenic stimulation provided by the intestinal flora helps to ensure the normal development of the immune system.

What happens when the normal flora is absent?

Germ-free animals tend to live longer, presumably because of the complete absence of pathogens, and develop no caries (see Ch. 18). However, their immune system is less well developed and they are vulnerable to introduced microbial pathogens. At the time of birth, humans are germ free, but acquire the normal flora during and immediately after birth, with the accompaniment of intense immunologic activity.

The disadvantages of the normal flora lie in the potential for spread into previously sterile parts of the body

This may happen:

- when the intestine is perforated or the skin is broken
- during extraction of teeth (when *Streptococcus viridans* may enter the bloodstream)
- when organisms from the perianal skin ascend the urethra and cause urinary tract infection.

Members of the normal flora are important causes of hospital-acquired infection when patients are exposed to invasive treatments. Patients suffering burns are also at risk.

Overgrowth by potentially pathogenic members of the normal flora can occur when the composition of the flora changes (e.g. after antibiotics) or when:

- the local environment changes (e.g. increases in stomach or vaginal pH)
- the immune system becomes ineffective (e.g. AIDS, clinical immunosuppression).

Under these conditions, the potential pathogens take advantage of the opportunity to increase their population size or invade tissues, so becoming harmful to the host. An account of diseases associated with such opportunistic infections is given in Chapter 30.

SYMBIOTIC ASSOCIATIONS

All living animals are used as habitats by other organisms; none is exempt from such invasion – bacteria are invaded by viruses (bacteriophages) and protozoans have their own flora and fauna – for example, amoeba are natural hosts for *Legionella pneumophila* infection. As evolution has produced larger, more complex and better regulated bodies, it has increased the number and variety of habitats for other organisms to colonize. The most complex bodies, those of birds and mammals (including humans), provide the most diverse environments, and are the most heavily colonized. Relationships between two species – interspecies associations or symbiosis – are therefore a constant feature of all life.

As the normal flora demonstrates, disease is not the inevitable consequence of interspecies associations between humans and microbes. Many factors influence the outcome of a particular association, and organisms may be pathogenic in one situation but harmless in another. To understand the microbiologic basis of infectious disease, host–microbe associations that can be pathogenic need to be placed firmly in the context of other symbiotic relationships, such as commensalism or mutualism, where the outcome for the host does not normally involve any damage or disadvantage.

Commensalism, mutualism and parasitism are categories of symbiotic association

All associations in which one species lives in or on the body of another can be grouped under the general term 'symbiosis' (literally 'living together'). Symbiosis has no overtones of benefit or harm and includes a wide diversity of relationships. Attempts have been made to categorize types of association very specifically, but these have failed because all associations form part of a continuum (Fig. 8.3). Three broad categories of symbiosis – commensalism, mutualism and parasitism – can be identified on the basis of the relative benefit obtained by each partner. None of these categories of association is restricted to any particular taxonomic group. Indeed, some organisms can be commensal, mutualist or parasitic depending upon the circumstances in which they live (Fig. 8.4).

Commensalism

In commensalism, one species of organism lives harmlessly in or on the body of a larger species

At its simplest, a commensal association is one in which one species of organism uses the body of a larger species as its physical environment and may make use of that environment to acquire nutrients.

Like all animals, humans support an extensive commensal microbial flora on the skin, in the mouth and in the alimentary tract. The majority of these microbes are bacteria, and their relationship with the host may be highly specialized, with specific attachment mechanisms and precise environmental requirements. Normally, such microbes are harmless, but they can become harmful if their environmental conditions change in some way (e.g. *Bacteroides*, *E. coli*, *Staphylococcus aureus*). Conversely, commensal microbes can benefit the host by preventing colonization by more pathogenic species (e.g. the intestinal flora), an interaction which could also be considered mutualistic. Thus, the normal definition of commensalism is not very exact, as the association can merge into mutualism or parasitism.

Mutualism

Mutualistic relationships provide reciprocal benefits for the two organisms involved

Frequently, the relationship is obligatory for at least one member, and may be for both. Good examples are the bacteria and protozoa living in the stomachs of domestic ruminants, which play an essential role in the digestion and utilization of cellulose, receiving in return both the environment and the nutrition essential for their survival. The dividing line between commensalism and mutualism can be hard to draw. In humans, good health and resistance to colonization by pathogens can depend upon the integrity of the normal commensal enteric bacteria, many of which are highly specialized for life in the human intestine, but there is certainly no strict mutual dependence in this relationship.

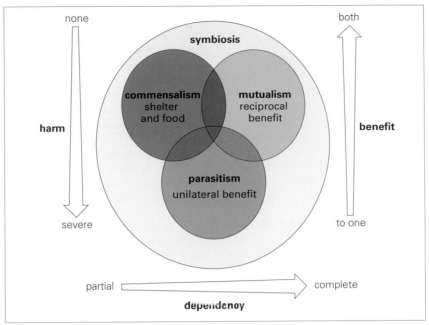

Figure 8.3 The relationships between symbiotic associations. Most species are independent of other species or rely on them only temporarily for food (e.g. predators and their prey). Some species form closer associations termed 'symbioses' and there are three major categories – commensalism, mutualism and parasitism – though each merges with the other and no definition separates one absolutely from the others.

commensalism – large intestine of man

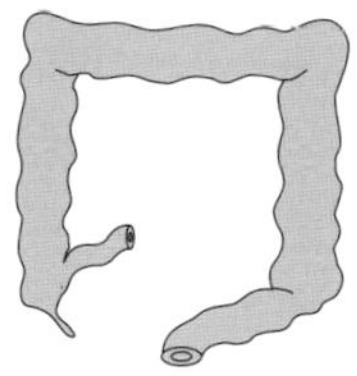

Bacteroides spp.

Host provides environment. Bacteria ferment digested food. Present in large numbers (10^{10}/g) but usually harmless. May be harmful if tissues damaged (surgery), gut flora changes (antibiotics), or immunity reduced

mutualism – rumen of cattle

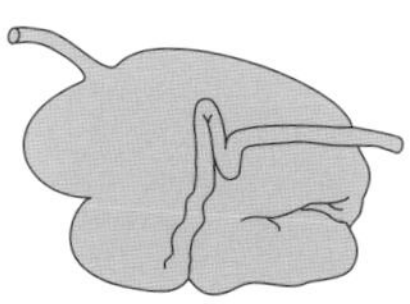

Bacteroides spp.

Host provides environment. Bacteria metabolize host food to fatty acids and gases. Host uses fatty acids as energy source

parasitism – large intestine of man

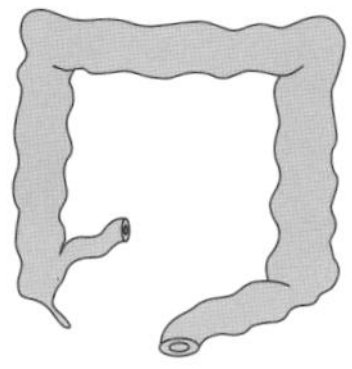

Entamoeba histolytica

Host provides environment. Protozoa feed on mucosa causing ulcers and dysentery

Figure 8.4 Examples of commensalism, mutualism and parasitism. These examples show how difficult it is to categorize any organism as entirely harmless, entirely beneficial or entirely harmful.

Parasitism

In parasitism, the symbiotic relationship benefits only the parasite

The terms 'parasites' and 'parasitism' are sometimes thought to apply only to protozoans and worms, but all pathogens are parasites. Parasitism is a one-sided relationship in which the benefits go only to the parasite, the host providing parasites with their physicochemical environment, their food, respiratory and other metabolic needs, and even the signals that regulate their development. Although parasites are thought of as necessarily harmful, this is a view coloured by human and veterinary clinical medicine, and by the results of laboratory experimentation. In fact, many 'parasites' establish quite innocuous associations with their natural hosts but may become pathogenic if there are changes in the host's health or they infect an unnatural host; the rabies virus, for example, coexists harmlessly with many wild mammals but can cause fatal disease in humans. This state of 'balanced pathogenicity' is sometimes explained as the outcome of selective pressures acting upon a relationship over a long period of evolutionary time. It may reflect selection of an increased level of genetically determined resistance in the host population and decreased pathogenicity in the parasite (as has happened with myxomatosis in rabbits). Alternatively, it may be the evolutionary norm, and 'unbalanced pathogenicity' may simply be the consequence of organisms becoming established in 'unnatural' (i.e. new) hosts. Thus, like the other categories of symbiosis, parasitism is impossible to define exclusively except in the context of clear-cut and highly pathogenic organisms. The belief that the ability to cause harm is a necessary characteristic of a parasite is difficult to sustain in any broader view (though it is a convenient assumption for those working with infectious diseases) and the reasons for this are discussed in more detail below.

THE CHARACTERISTICS OF PARASITISM

Many different groups of organisms are parasitic and all animals are parasitized

Parasitism as a way of life has been adopted by many different groups of organisms. Some groups, such as viruses, are exclusively parasitic (see below), but the majority include both parasitic and free-living representatives. Parasites occur in all animals, from the simplest to the most complex, and are an almost inevitable accompaniment of organized animal existence. We can see, then, that parasitism has been an evolutionary success; as a way of life, it must confer very considerable advantages.

Parasitism has metabolic, nutritional and reproductive advantages

The most obvious advantage of parasitism is metabolic. The parasite is provided with a variety of metabolic requirements by the host, often at no energy cost to itself, so it can devote a large proportion of its own resources to replication or reproduction. This one-sided metabolic relationship shows a broad spectrum of dependence, both within and between the various groups of parasites. Some parasites are totally dependent upon the host, while others are only partly dependent.

Viruses are completely dependent upon the host for all their metabolic needs

Viruses are at one extreme of the 'parasite dependency' spectrum. They are obligate parasites, possessing the genetic information required for production of new viruses, but none of the cellular machinery necessary to transcribe or translate this information, to assemble new virus particles or to produce the energy for these processes. The host provides not only the basic building blocks for the production of new viruses, but also the synthetic machinery and the energy required (Fig. 8.5). Retroviruses go one stage further in dependence, inserting their own genetic information into the host's DNA in order to parasitize the transcription process. Viruses therefore represent the ultimate parasitic condition and are qualitatively different from all other parasites in the nature of their relationship with the host.

The basis for the fundamental difference between viruses and other parasites is the difference between virus organization and the cellular organization of prokaryotic and eukaryotic parasites. Non-viral parasites have their own genetic and cellular machinery, and multi-enzyme systems for independent metabolic activity and macromolecular synthesis. The degree of reliance on the host for nutritional requirements varies considerably and follows no consistent pattern between the various groups, nor does it follow that smaller parasites tend to be more dependent; e.g. some of the largest parasites, the tapeworms, are wholly reliant upon the host's digestive machinery to provide their nutritional needs. All, of course, receive nutrition from the host but, whereas some use macromolecular material (proteins, polysaccharides) of host origin and digest it using their own enzyme systems, others rely on the host for the process of digestion as well, being able to take up only low molecular weight materials (amino acids, monosaccharides). Nutritional dependence may also include host provision of growth factors that the parasite is unable to synthesize itself. All internal parasites rely upon the host's respiratory and transport systems to provide oxygen, although some respire anaerobically in either a facultative or obligate manner.

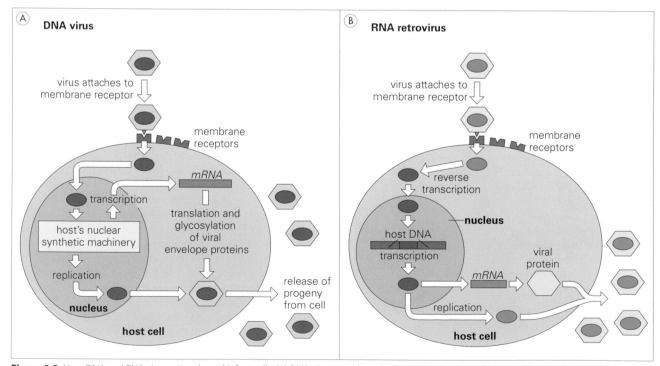

Figure 8.5 How DNA and RNA viruses invade and infect cells. (A) DNA viruses such as the herpes viruses have their own DNA, and use only the host's cellular machinery to make more DNA and more virus protein and glycoprotein. These are then reassembled into new virus particles before they are released from the cell. (B) RNA retroviruses (e.g. HIV) first make viral DNA, using their reverse transcriptase, insert this DNA into the host's genetic material so that viral RNA can be transcribed, and then translate some of the RNA into virus protein. The viral protein and RNA are then reassembled into new particles and released.

Parasite development can be controlled by the host

The advantage that parasitism confers in reproductive terms makes it vital to coordinate parasite development with the availability of suitable hosts. Indeed, one of the characteristic features of parasites is that their development may be controlled partly or completely by the host, the parasite having lost the ability to initiate or to regulate its own development. At its simplest, host control is limited to providing the cell surface molecules necessary for parasite attachment and internalization. Many parasites, from viruses to protozoa, rely on the recognition of such molecular signals for their entry into host cells, and this process provides the trigger for their replicative or reproductive cycles.

Other parasites, primarily the eukaryotes, require more comprehensive and sophisticated signals, often a complex of signals, to initiate and regulate their entire developmental cycle. The complexity of the signal required for development is one of the factors determining the specificity of the host–parasite relationship. Where the availability of one of the signals entails that parasite development can occur in only one species, host specificity is high. Where many host species are capable of providing the necessary signals for a parasite, specificity is low.

Disadvantages of parasitism

The most obvious disadvantage of parasitism arises from the fact that the host controls the development of the parasite. No development is possible without a suitable host, and many parasites will die if no host becomes available. For this reason, several adaptations have evolved to promote prolonged survival in the outside world and so maximize the chances of successful host contact (e.g. virus particles, bacterial spores, protozoan cysts and worm eggs). The prolific replication of parasites is another device to achieve the same end. Nevertheless, where parasites fail to make contact with a host, their powers of survival are ultimately limited. Adaptation to host signals can therefore have a reproductive cost (i.e. the loss of many potential parasites).

THE EVOLUTION OF PARASITISM

As so many organisms are parasitic and every group of animals is subject to invasion by parasites, the development of parasitism as a way of life must have occurred at an early stage in evolution and at frequent intervals thereafter. How this occurred is not fully understood, and it may well have been different in different groups of organisms. In many, parasitism most probably arose as a consequence of accidental contacts between organism and host. Of many such contacts, some would have resulted in prolonged survival and, under favourable nutritional circumstances, prolonged survival would have been associated with enhanced replication, giving the organism a selective advantage within the environment. Many parasites of humans and other mammals may have originated via the route of accidental contact, but it is clear that others have become adapted to these hosts after initially becoming parasitic in other species. For example, parasites of blood-feeding arthropods have ready access to the tissues of the animals on which the arthropods feed. Where the parasite becomes specialized for the non-arthropod host it may lose the ability to be transmitted by blood feeding. Where the arthropod host is retained in the life cycle the parasite is faced by competing demands for survival in each host, which probably explains why, for example, arboviruses are restricted to only a few families of RNA viruses and a single DNA virus, African swine fever virus.

Bacterial parasites evolved through accidental contact

In the case of bacteria, it is easy to see how accidental contact in environments rich in free-living bacteria could lead to successful invasion of external openings such as the mouth and eventual colonization of the gastrointestinal tract. Initially, the organisms concerned would have had to be facultative parasites, capable of life both within or outside host organisms (many pathogenic bacteria still have this property, e.g. *Legionella*, *Vibrio*), but selective pressures would have forced others into obligatory parasitism. Such events are of course speculative, but are supported by the close relationship of enteric bacteria such as *E. coli* with free-living photosynthetic purple bacteria.

Many bacterial parasites have evolved to live inside host cells

Bacteria that became parasitic by accidental contact would have lived outside host cells at first and would not have had the advantages of being intracellular. The evolution of the intracellular habit required further modifications to allow survival within host cells, but could easily have been initiated by passive phagocytic uptake. Subsequent survival of the microbe would depend upon the possession of surface or metabolic properties that prevented digestion and destruction by the host cell. The success of intracellular life can be measured not only by the large number of bacteria that have adopted this habit, but also by the extent to which some organisms have integrated their biology with that of the host cell. The endpoint of such integration is perhaps to be seen in the evolution of the eukaryote mitochondrion, which may have evolved from symbiotically associated heterotrophic purple bacteria (Fig. 8.6).

The pathway of virus evolution is uncertain

Clearly, parasitism by bacteria, which are undoubtedly ancient organisms (they can be traced back 3–5 billion years in the fossil record), depended upon the evolution of higher organisms to act as hosts. Whether the same is true of viruses is open to question, and depends upon whether viruses are considered primarily or secondarily simple. If viruses evolved from cellular ancestors by a process of secondary simplification, then parasitism must have evolved long after the evolution of prokaryotes and eukaryotes. If viruses are primitively non-cellular then it is possible that they became parasitic at a very early stage in the evolution of cellular life, at some point when, because of environmental change, independent existence became impossible. A third alternative is that viruses were never anything other than fragments of the nuclear material of other organisms and have in effect always been parasitic. Modern viruses may, in fact, have arisen by all three pathways.

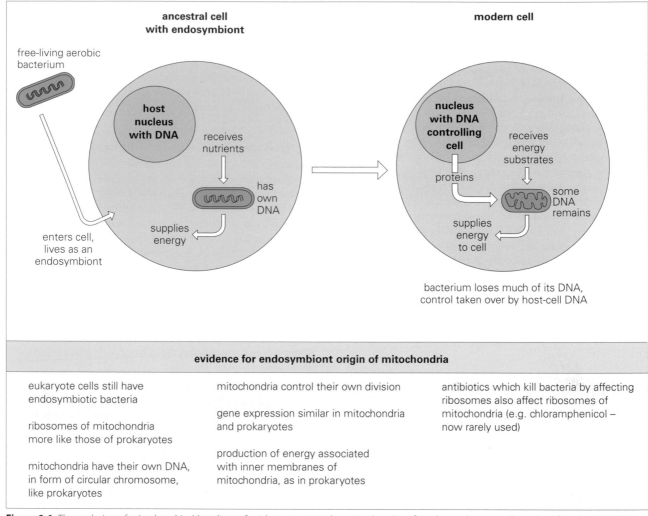

ancestral cell
with endosymbiont

modern cell

free-living aerobic
bacterium

host nucleus with DNA

receives nutrients

has own DNA

enters cell,
lives as an
endosymbiont

supplies
energy

nucleus with DNA controlling cell

receives energy substrates

proteins

some DNA remains

supplies energy to cell

bacterium loses much of its DNA,
control taken over by host-cell DNA

evidence for endosymbiont origin of mitochondria

eukaryote cells still have
endosymbiotic bacteria

ribosomes of mitochondria
more like those of prokaryotes

mitochondria have their own DNA,
in form of circular chromosome,
like prokaryotes

mitochondria control their own division

gene expression similar in mitochondria
and prokaryotes

production of energy associated
with inner membranes of
mitochondria, as in prokaryotes

antibiotics which kill bacteria by affecting
ribosomes also affect ribosomes of
mitochondria (e.g. chloramphenicol –
now rarely used)

Figure 8.6 The evolution of mitochondria. Many lines of evidence suggest that mitochondria of modern eukaryote cells evolved from bacteria that established symbiotic (mutualistic) relationships with ancestral cells.

Eukaryote parasites have evolved through accidental contact

The evolution of parasitism by eukaryotes is likely to have arisen much as it may have done in prokaryotes (i.e. through accidental contact and via blood-feeding arthropods). Examples can be found among protozoan and worm parasites to support this view:

- There are protozoa such as the free-living amoeba *Naegleria* which can opportunistically invade the human body and cause severe and sometimes fatal disease.
- There are several species of nematode worms that can live either as parasites or as free-living organisms, *Strongyloides stercoralis* being the most important in humans.
- It is likely that trypanosomes (the protozoans responsible for sleeping sickness) were primarily adapted as parasites of blood-feeding flies and only secondarily became established as parasites of mammals, though most retain the arthropod in their life cycle.

Parasite adaptations to overcome host inflammatory and immune responses

We can view the evolution of parasitism and the adaptations necessary for life within another animal as being exactly analogous to the adaptations necessary for life within any other specialized habitat: the environment in which parasites live is merely one of the many to which organisms have become adapted in evolution (comparable with life in soil, freshwater, salt water, decaying material and so on). However, it is always necessary to remember that in one major respect parasitism is quite different from any other specialist mode of life. This difference is that the environment in which a parasite lives, the body of the host, is not passive; on the contrary, it is capable of an active response to the presence of the parasite.

The attractiveness of animal bodies as environments for parasites means that hosts are under continual pressures from infection, and these pressures are increased when hosts live:

- close together
- in insanitary conditions
- in climates that favour the survival of parasite stages in the external world.

Pressure of infection has been a major influence in host evolution

Pressure of infection has been a major selective influence in evolution, and there is little doubt that it has been largely responsible for the development of the sophisticated inflammatory and immune responses we see in humans and other mammals. In evolutionary terms, all infection has its costs to the host because it diverts valuable resources from the activities of survival and reproduction; there has therefore been pressure to develop means of overcoming infection whether or not it causes disease. Of course, this is not the focus of clinical microbiology, which legitimately places emphasis on the costs of infection in terms of frank disease, but it should be remembered because it explains more fully the nature of the continuing battle between host and parasite – the former attempting to contain or destroy, the latter attempting to evade or suppress – and why the emergence of new, and the return of old, infectious diseases are a constant threat.

Parasites are faced not only with the problems of surviving within the environment they experience initially, but also of surviving in that environment as it changes in ways that are likely to be harmful to them. The inflammatory and immune responses that follow the establishment of infection are the most important means by which the host can control infections by those organisms able to penetrate its natural barriers and survive within its body. These responses represent formidable obstacles to the continued survival of parasites, forcing them to evolve strategies to cope with harmful changes in their environment. The successful parasite is therefore one that can cope with, or evade, the host's response in one of the ways shown in Table 8.1.

Table 8.1 Evasion strategies of parasites

Evasion strategies	
Strategy	**Example**
Elicit minimal response	Herpes simplex virus – survives in host cells for long periods in a latent stage – no pathology
Evade effects of response	Mycobacteria – survive unharmed in granulomas designed to localize and destroy infection
Depress host's response	HIV – destroys T cells; malaria – depresses immune responsiveness
Antigenic change	Viruses, spirochaetes, trypanosomes – all change target antigens so host response is ineffective
Rapid replication	Viruses, bacteria, protozoa – producing acute infections before recovery and immunity
Survival in weakly responsive individuals	Genetic heterogeneity in host population means some individuals respond weakly or not at all, allowing organism to reproduce freely; examples in all groups

All of these adaptations are known to exist within different groups of parasites and they are well documented in the case of some of the major human pathogens. Indeed, they are often the very reason why such organisms are major pathogens. Nevertheless, transmission and survival of many parasites depends upon the existence of particularly susceptible host individuals (e.g. children) to provide a continuing reservoir of infective stages.

Changes in parasites create new problems for hosts

From what has been said above, it can be appreciated that there is no such thing as a static host–parasite relationship, and that concepts of unchanging 'pathogenicity' or 'lack of pathogenicity' cannot be justified. Each relationship is an 'arms race'; changes in one member being countered by changes in the other. Quite subtle changes in either can completely change the balance of the relationship, towards greater or lesser pathogenicity, for example.

Perhaps the most important recent illustration of this situation is the dramatic and explosive appearance of HIV infections. This group of viruses was originally restricted to non-human primates, but changes in the virus have permitted extensive infections in humans. Similarly, changes in an avian influenza virus allowing human infection resulted in the major pandemic early in the twentieth century and the recent emergence of the new H1N1 flu in 2009 is another example; there is also current concern about the potential spread of avian virus such as H5N1. Of a different nature, but relevant to the general theme, is the acquisition of drug resistance in bacteria and protozoa (Fig. 8.7). Although the underlying genetic and metabolic changes do not by themselves influence pathogenicity, the expression of such changes in the face of intense and selective chemotherapy certainly does, so allowing overwhelming infection to occur. The problem of hospital-acquired MRSA infection is a perfect example.

Host adaptations to overcome changes in parasites

Changes in the host can also alter the balance of a host–parasite relationship. A particularly dramatic example is the intense selection for resistant genotypes in rabbit populations exposed to the myxomatosis virus, which took place concurrently with selection for reduced pathogenicity in the virus itself (see Ch. 12). There are no exactly equivalent examples in humans, but in evolutionary time there have been major selective influences on populations prompting changes to permit survival in the face of life-threatening infections. A good example is the selective pressure exerted by Falciparum malaria, which has been responsible for the persistence in human populations of many alleles associated with haemoglobinopathies (e.g. sickle cell haemoglobin). Although these abnormalities are detrimental to varying degrees, they persist because they are (or were) associated with resistance to malarial infection. One study has suggested that malaria has also changed the frequency of certain HLA antigens in areas where infection was severe, although this has not been confirmed elsewhere.

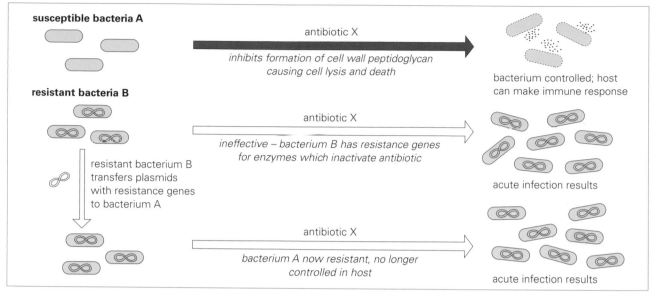

Figure 8.7 Antibiotic resistance in bacteria. The activity of many antibiotics can be blocked by bacterial enzymes coded for by genes located on cytoplasmic DNA in plasmids. The ability of bacteria to transfer plasmids between individual organisms means that strains or species previously susceptible to an antibiotic can acquire the ability to produce such enzymes and so gain antibiotic resistance directly from resistant organisms. These newly resistant forms are then differentially selected under antibiotic treatment, the susceptible individuals being deleted from the population. Primary antibiotic resistance also occurs through genetic mutations.

Social and behavioural changes can be as important as genetic changes in altering host–parasite relations

Social and behavioural changes can alter host–parasite relations both positively and negatively (Table 8.2). Although many bacterial infections of the intestine have declined in importance with changes in human lifestyle, there are other contemporary microbiologic problems in the resource-rich world whose onset can be traced directly to sociologic, environmental and even medical change (Table 8.2). A particularly

good example is disease arising from domestication of pets (e.g. toxoplasmosis) because it illustrates that human freedom from some infections arises primarily because of lack of contact with the organisms and not from any innate resistance to the establishment of the infection itself. Diseases arising from contact with infected animals or animal products (zoonotic infections) constitute a constant threat that can be realized by behavioural or environmental changes that alter established patterns of human–animal contact.

Table 8.2 Lifestyle changes and infectious diseases

Social and behavioral changes and infectious diseases	
The causes	**The results**
Altered environments (e.g. air conditioning)	Water in cooling systems provides growth conditions for *Legionella*
Changes in food production and food-handling practices	Intensive husbandry under antibiotic protection leads to drug-resistant bacteria; deep-freeze, fast-food and inadequate cooking allow bacteria and toxins to enter body (e.g. *Listeria*, *Salmonella*)
Routine use of antibiotics in medicine	Emergence of antibiotic-resistant bacteria as hazards to hospitalized patients (e.g. MRSA – methicillin-resistant *Staphylococcus aureus*)
Routine use of immunosuppressive therapy	Development of opportunistic infections in patients with reduced resistance (e.g. *Pseudomonas*, *Candida*, *Pneumocystis*)
Altered sexual habits	Promiscuity increases sexually transmitted diseases (e.g. gonorrhoea, genital herpes, AIDS)
Breakdown of filtration systems, overuse of limited water supplies	Transmission of animal infections leading to diarrheal and other infections (e.g. cryptosporidiosis, giardiasis, leptospirosis)
Increase in ownership of pets, particularly exotic species	Transmission of animal infections (e.g. *Chlamydia*, *Salmonella*, *Toxoplasma*, *Toxocara*)
Increased frequency of journeys to tropical and subtropical countries	Exposure to exotic organisms and vectors (e.g. malaria, viral encephalitides)

KEY FACTS

- The body is colonized by many organisms (the normal flora) which can be positively beneficial. They live on or within the body without causing disease, and play an important role in protecting the host from pathogenic microbes.

- The normal flora is predominantly made up of bacteria, but includes fungi and protozoa.

- Members of the normal flora can be harmful if they enter previously sterile parts of the body. They can be important causes of hospital-acquired infections.

- The usual relationship between the normal flora and the body is an example of beneficial symbiosis; parasitism (in the broad sense, covering all pathogenic microbes) is a harmful symbiosis.

- The biological context of host–parasite relationships, and the dynamics of the conflict between two species in this relationship, provide a basis for understanding the causes and control of infectious diseases.

- Changes in medical practice, in human behaviour and, not least, in infectious organisms, are broadening the spectrum of organisms responsible for disease.

The innate defences of the body

9

Introduction

In the preceding chapters, we have outlined some of the fundamental characteristics of the myriad types of microparasites and macroparasites that may infect the body. We now turn to consider the ways in which the body seeks to defend itself against infection by these organisms.

The body has both 'innate' and 'adaptive' immune defences

When an organism infects the body, the defence systems already in place may well be adequate to prevent replication and spread of the infectious agent, thereby preventing development of disease. These established mechanisms are referred to as constituting the 'innate' immune system. However, should innate immunity be insufficient to parry the invasion by the infectious agent, the so-called 'adaptive' immune system then comes into action, although it takes time to reach its maximum efficiency (Fig. 9.1). When it does take effect, it generally eliminates the infective organism, allowing recovery from disease.

The main feature distinguishing the adaptive response from the innate mechanism is that specific memory of infection is imprinted on the adaptive immune system, so that should there be a subsequent infection by the same agent, a particularly effective response comes into play with remarkable speed. It is worth emphasizing, however, that there is

close synergy between the two systems, with the adaptive mechanism greatly improving the efficiency of the innate response.

The contrasts between these two systems are set out in Table 9.1. On the one hand, the soluble factors such as lysozyme and complement, together with the phagocytic cells, contribute to the innate system, while on the other the lymphocyte-based mechanisms that produce antibody and T lymphocytes are the main elements of the adaptive immune system. Not only do these lymphocytes provide improved resistance by repeated contact with a given infectious agent, but the memory with which they become endowed shows very considerable specificity to that infection. For instance, infection with measles virus will induce a memory to that microorganism alone and not to another virus such as rubella.

DEFENCES AGAINST ENTRY INTO THE BODY

A variety of biochemical and physical barriers operate at the body surfaces

Before an infectious agent can penetrate the body, it must overcome biochemical and physical barriers that operate at the body surfaces. One of the most important of these is the skin, which is normally impermeable to the majority of infectious agents. Many bacteria fail to survive for long on the skin because of the direct inhibitory effects of lactic acid and fatty acids present in sweat and sebaceous secretions and the lower pH to which they give rise (Fig. 9.2). However, should there be skin loss, as can occur in burns, for example, infection becomes a major problem.

The membranes lining the inner surfaces of the body secrete mucus, which acts as a protective barrier, inhibiting the adherence of bacteria to the epithelial cells, thereby preventing them from gaining access to the body. Microbial and other foreign particles trapped within this adhesive mucus may be removed by mechanical means such as ciliary action, coughing and sneezing. The flushing actions of tears, saliva and urine are other mechanical strategies that help to protect the epithelial surfaces. In addition, many of the secreted body fluids contain microbicidal factors,

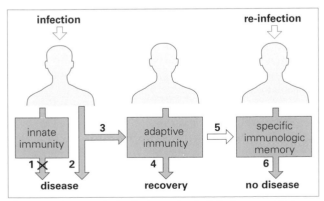

Figure 9.1 Innate and adaptive immunity. An infectious agent first encounters elements of the innate immune system. These may be sufficient (1) to prevent disease but if not, disease may result (2). The adaptive immune system is then activated (3) to produce recovery (4) and a specific immunologic memory (5). Following re-infection with the same agent, no disease results (6) and the individual has acquired immunity to the infectious agent.

Table 9.1 Comparison of innate and adaptive effector immune systems

	Innate immune system	Adaptive immune system
Major elements		
Soluble factors	Lysozyme, complement, acute phase proteins, e.g. C-reactive protein, interferon	Antibody
Cells	Phagocytes Natural killer cells	T lymphocytes
Response to microbial infection		
First contact	+	+ +
Second contact	+	+ + + +
	Non-specific; no memory Resistance not improved by repeated contact	Specific; memory Resistance improved by repeated contact

Innate immunity is sometimes referred to as 'natural', and adaptive as 'acquired'. There is considerable interaction between the two systems. 'Humoral' immunity due to soluble factors contrasts with immunity mediated by cells. Primary contact with antigen produces both adaptive and innate responses, but if the same antigen persists or is encountered a second time the specific adaptive response to that antigen is much enhanced.

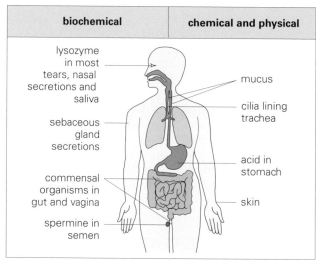

biochemical	chemical and physical

lysozyme in most tears, nasal secretions and saliva

mucus

cilia lining trachea

sebaceous gland secretions

acid in stomach

commensal organisms in gut and vagina

skin

spermine in semen

Figure 9.2 Exterior defences. Most of the infectious agents encountered by an individual are prevented from entering the body by a variety of biochemical and physical barriers. The body tolerates a variety of commensal organisms, which compete effectively with many potential pathogens.

e.g. the acid in gastric juice, spermine and zinc in semen, lactoperoxidase in milk, and lysozyme in tears, nasal secretions and saliva.

The phenomenon of microbial antagonism is associated with the normal bacterial flora of the body. These commensal organisms suppress the growth of many potentially pathogenic bacteria and fungi at superficial sites, first by virtue of their physical advantage of previous occupancy, especially on epithelial surfaces, second by competing for essential nutrients, or third by producing inhibitory substances such as acid or colicins. The latter are a class of bactericidins that bind to the negatively charged surface of susceptible bacteria and form a voltage-dependent channel in the membrane, which kills by destroying the cell's energy potential.

DEFENCES ONCE THE MICROORGANISM PENETRATES THE BODY

Despite the general effectiveness of the various barriers, microorganisms successfully penetrate the body on many occasions. When this occurs, two main defensive strategies come into play, based on:

- the mechanism of phagocytosis, involving engulfment and killing of microorganisms by specialized cells, the 'professional phagocytes'
- the destructive effect of soluble chemical factors, such as bactericidal enzymes.

Two types of professional phagocyte

Perhaps because of the belief that professionals do a better job than amateurs, the cells that shoulder the main burden of our phagocytic defences have been labelled 'professional phagocytes'. These consist of two major cell families, as originally defined by Elie Metchnikoff, the Russian zoologist (Box 9.1; Fig. 9.3):

- the large macrophages
- the smaller polymorphonuclear granulocytes, which are generally referred to as polymorphs or neutrophils because their cytoplasmic granules do not stain with haematoxylin and eosin.

As a very crude generalization, it may be said that the polymorphs provide the major defence against pyogenic (pus-forming) bacteria, while the macrophages are thought to be at their best in combating organisms capable of living within the cells of the host.

Macrophages are widespread throughout the tissues

Macrophages originate as bone marrow promonocytes, which develop into circulating blood monocytes (Fig. 9.4) and finally become the mature macrophages, which are widespread throughout the tissues and collectively termed the 'mononuclear phagocyte system' (Fig. 9.5). These macrophages are present throughout the connective tissue

Box 9.1   Lessons in Microbiology

Elie Metchnikoff (1845–1916)

This perceptive Russian zoologist can legitimately be regarded as the father of the concept of cellular immunity, in which it is recognized that certain specialized cells mediate the defence against microbial infections. He was intrigued by the motile cells of transparent starfish larvae and made the critical observation that a few hours after introducing a rose thorn into the larvae, the rose thorn became surrounded by the motile cells. He extended his investigations to mammalian leukocytes, showing their ability to engulf microorganisms, a process that he termed 'phagocytosis' (literally, eating by cells).

Because he found this process to be even more effective in animals recovering from an infection, he came to the conclusion that phagocytosis provided the main defence against infection. He defined the existence of two types of circulating phagocytes: the polymorphonuclear leukocyte, which he termed a 'microphage', and the larger 'macrophage'.

Although Metchnikoff held the somewhat polarized view that cellular immunity based upon phagocytosis provided the main, if not the only, defence mechanism against infectious microorganisms, we now know that the efficiency of the phagocytic system is enormously enhanced through cooperation with humoral factors, in particular antibody and complement.

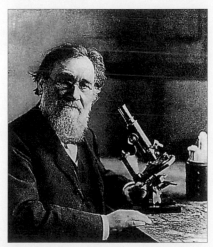

Figure 9.3 Elie Metchnikoff (1845–1916). (Courtesy of the Wellcome Institute Library, London.)

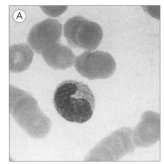
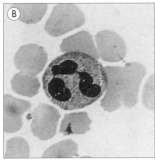

Figure 9.4 Phagocytic cells. (A) Blood monocyte and (B) polymorphonuclear neutrophil, both derived from bone marrow stem cells. (Courtesy of P.M. Lydyard.)

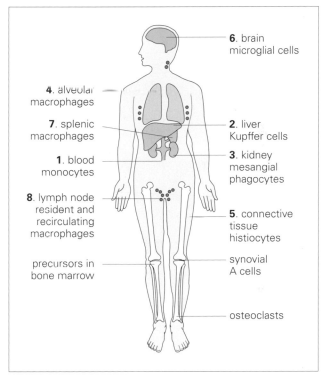

6. brain microglial cells

4. alveolar macrophages

7. splenic macrophages

1. blood monocytes

8. lymph node resident and recirculating macrophages

precursors in bone marrow

2. liver Kupffer cells

3. kidney mesangial phagocytes

5. connective tissue histiocytes

synovial A cells

osteoclasts

Figure 9.5 The mononuclear phagocyte system. Tissue macrophages are derived from blood monocytes, which are manufactured in the bone marrow. (The numbers relate to those in Fig. 9.6.)

(Fig. 9.8) related to the formidable array of different secretory proteins that these cells generate.

Polymorphs possess a variety of enzyme-containing granules

The polymorph is the dominant white cell in the bloodstream and, like the macrophage, shares a common haemopoietic stem cell precursor with the other formed elements of the blood. It has no mitochondria, but uses its abundant cytoplasmic glycogen stores for its energy requirements; therefore, glycolysis enables these cells to function under anaerobic conditions, such as those in an inflammatory focus. The polymorph is a non-dividing, short-lived cell, with a segmented nucleus; the cytoplasm is characterized by an array of granules, which are illustrated in Figure 9.9.

and are associated with the basement membrane of small blood vessels. They are particularly concentrated in the lung (alveolar macrophages), liver (Kupffer cells) and the lining of lymph node medullary sinuses and splenic sinusoids (Fig. 9.6), where they are well placed to filter off foreign material (Fig. 9.7). Other examples are the brain microglia, kidney mesangial cells, synovial A cells and osteoclasts in bone. In general, these are long-lived cells that depend upon mitochondria for their metabolic energy and show elements of rough-surfaced endoplasmic reticulum

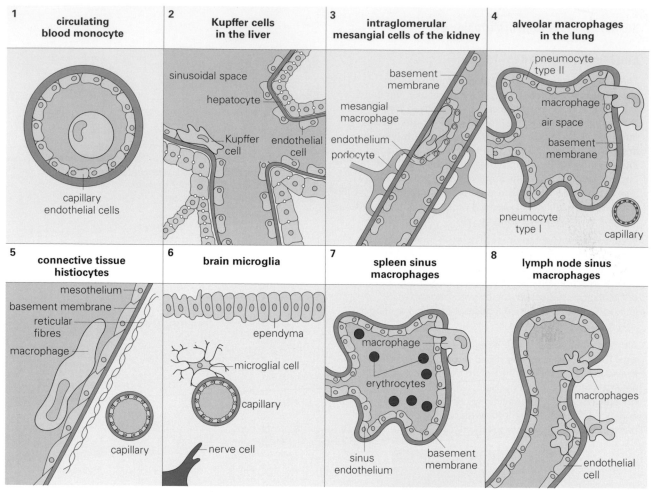

Figure 9.6 Tissue location of mononuclear phagocytes.

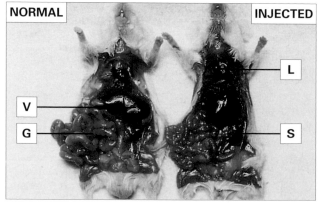

Figure 9.7 Localization of intravenously injected particles in the mononuclear phagocyte system. (*Right*) A mouse was injected with fine carbon particles and killed 5 min later. Carbon accumulates in organs rich in mononuclear phagocytes: lungs (L), liver (V), spleen (S) and areas of the gut wall (G). (*Left*) Normal organ colour shown in an uninjected control mouse. (Courtesy of P.M. Lydyard.)

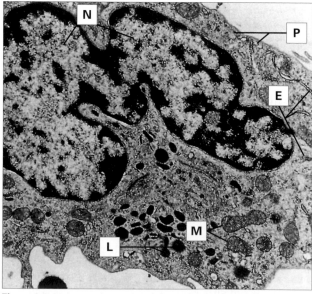

Figure 9.8 Monocyte (× 8000), with 'horseshoe' nucleus (N). Phagocytic and pinocytic vesicles (P), lysosomal granules (L), mitochondria (M) and isolated profiles of rough-surfaced endoplasmic reticulum (E) are evident. (Courtesy of B. Nichols; © Rockefeller University Press.)

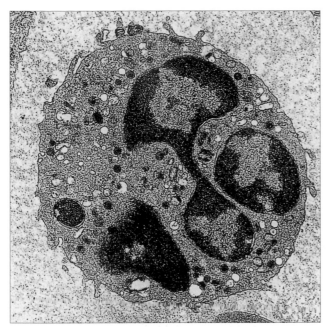

Figure 9.9 Neutrophil. The multi-lobed nucleus and primary azurophilic, secondary specific and tertiary lysosomal granules are well displayed. In some granules there is an overlap in the contents between azurophilic and secondary granules. Typical conventional lysosomes with acid hydrolase are also seen. (Courtesy of D. McLaren.)

Azurophil granules	Specific granules
0.5 μm	0.2 μm
1500/cell	3000/cell
Lysozyme	Lysozyme
Myeloperoxidase	Cytochrome b_{558}
Elastase	Alkaline phosphatase
Cathepsin G	Lactoferrin
Acid hydrolases	
Defensins	Vitamin B12 binding protein
BPI (bactericidal permeability increasing protein)	

Phagocytosis and killing

Phagocytes recognize pathogen-associated molecular patterns (PAMPs)

The first event in the uptake and digestion of a microorganism by the professional phagocyte involves the attachment of the microbe to the surface of the cell through the recognition of repeating pathogen-associated molecular patterns (PAMPs) on the microbe by pattern recognition receptors (PRRs) on the phagocyte surface (Fig. 9.10). A major subset of these PRRs belongs to the class of so-called 'Toll-like receptors' (TLRs) because of their similarity to the Toll receptor in the fruit fly, *Drosophila*, which, in the adult, triggers an intracellular cascade generating the expression of antimicrobial peptides in response to microbial infection. A series of cell surface TLRs acting as sensors for extracellular infections have been identified (Fig. 9.11) which are activated by microbial elements such as peptidoglycan, lipoproteins, mycobacterial lipoarabinomannan, yeast

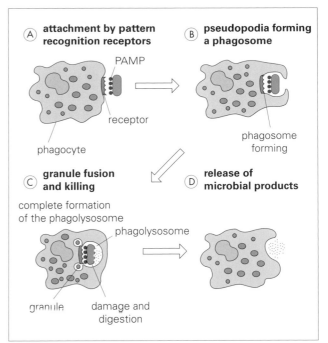

Figure 9.10 Phagocytosis. (A) Phagocytes attach to microorganisms (blue icon) via their cell surface receptors which recognize pathogen-associated molecular patterns (PAMPs) such as lipopolysaccharide. (B) If the membrane now becomes activated by the attached infectious agent, the pathogen is taken into a phagosome by pseudopodia, which extend around it. (C) Once inside the cell, the various granules fuse with the phagosome to form a phagolysosome. (D) The infectious agent is then killed by a battery of microbicidal degradation mechanisms, and the microbial products are released.

zymosan and flagellin. Other PRRs displayed by phagocytes include the cell bound 'C-type (calcium-dependent) lectins', of which the macrophage mannose receptor is an example, and 'scavenger receptors', which recognize a variety of anionic polymers and acetylated low density proteins. Examples of intracellular PAMPs are the unmethylated guanosine-cytosine (CpG) sequences of bacterial DNA and double-stranded RNA from RNA viruses.

The phagocyte is activated through PAMP recognition

The attached microbe may then signal through the phagocyte receptors to initiate the ingestion phase by activating an actin-myosin contractile system, which sends arms of cytoplasm around the particle until it is completely enclosed within a vacuole (phagosome; Fig. 9.12; see Fig. 9.10). Shortly afterwards, the cytoplasmic granules fuse with a phagosome and discharge their contents around the incarcerated microorganism.

The internalized microbe is the target for a fearsome array of killing mechanisms

As phagocytosis is initiated, the attached microbes also signal through one of the PRRs to engineer an appropriate defensive response to the different types of infection through a number of NFκB-mediated responses. This activation of a unique plasma membrane reduced nicotinamide adenine dinucleotide phosphate (NADPH) oxidase reduces oxygen to a series of powerful microbicidal agents, namely superoxide anion, hydrogen

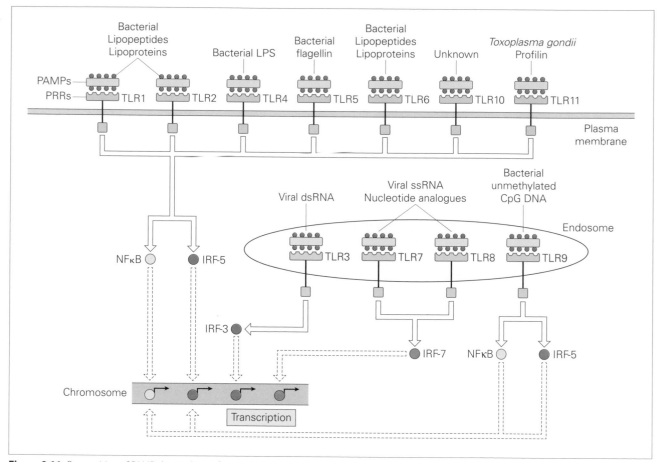

Figure 9.11 Recognition of PAMPs by a subset of pattern recognition receptors (PRRs) termed Toll-like receptors (TLRs). TLRs reside within plasma membrane or endosomal membrane compartments, as shown. All TLRs have multiple N-terminal leucine-rich repeats forming a horseshoe-shaped structure which acts as the PAMP-binding domain. Upon engagement of the TLR ectodomain with an appropriate PAMP (some examples are shown), signals are propagated into the cell that activate the nuclear factor kB (NFkB) and/or interferon regulated factor (IRF) transcription factors, as shown. NFkB and IRF transcription factors then direct the expression of numerous antimicrobial gene products such as cytokines and chemokines, as well as proteins that are involved in altering the activation state of the cell.

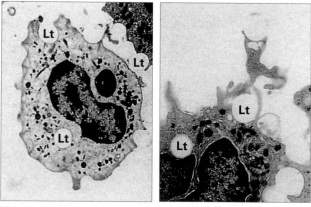

Figure 9.12 Electron micrographic study of phagocytosis. These two micrographs show human phagocytes engulfing latex particles (Lt). (A) × 3000; (B) × 4500. (Courtesy of C.H.W. Horne.)

peroxide, singlet oxygen and hydroxyl radicals (Box 9.2; see also Ch. 14). Subsequently, the peroxide, in association with myeloperoxidase, generates a potent halogenating system from halide ions, which is capable of killing both bacteria and viruses.

As superoxide anion is formed, the enzyme superoxide dismutase acts to convert it to molecular oxygen and hydrogen peroxide, but in the process consumes hydrogen

ions. Therefore initially there is a small increase in pH, which facilitates the antibacterial function of the families of cationic proteins derived from the phagocytic granules. These molecules damage microbial membranes by the proteolytic action of cathepsin G and by direct adherence to the microbial surface. The defensins have an amphipathic structure which allows them to insert into microbial membranes to form destabilizing voltage-regulated ion channels. These antibiotic peptides reach extraordinarily high concentrations within the phagosome and act as disinfectants against a wide spectrum of bacteria, fungi and enveloped viruses. Other important factors are:

- lactoferrin, which complexes iron to deprive bacteria of essential growth elements
- lysozyme, which splits the proteoglycan cell wall of bacteria
- nitric oxide, which can lead not only to iron seclusion but, together with its derivative, the peroxynitrite radical, can also be directly microbicidal.

The pH now falls so that the dead or dying microorganisms are extensively degraded by acid hydrolytic enzymes, and the degradation products released to the exterior.

NFkB activation can also lead to the release of proinflammatory mediators. These include the antiviral interferons,

Box 9.2 Antimicrobial Mechanisms in Phagocytic Vacuoles

Oxygen-independent antimicrobial mechanisms

Cathepsin G and elastase
Low molecular weight *defensins*
High molecular weight *cationic proteins*
Bactericidal *permeability-increasing protein* } Damage to microbial membranes

Lactoferrin Complex with iron
Lysozyme Splits proteoglycan
Acid hydrolases Degrade dead microbes

Oxygen-dependent antimicrobial mechanisms

Reaction Sequence Generated by NADPH Oxidase:

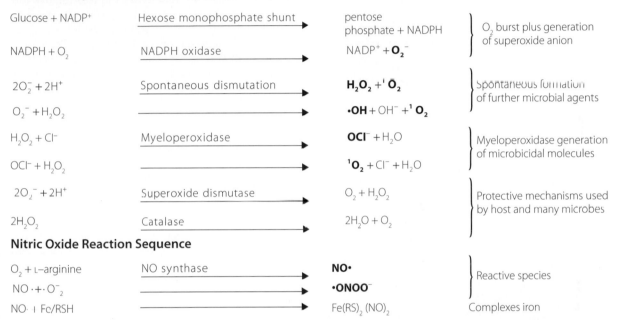

Glucose + NADP$^+$ → Hexose monophosphate shunt → pentose phosphate + NADPH

NADPH + O$_2$ → NADPH oxidase → NADP$^+$ + **O$_2^-$** } O$_2$ burst plus generation of superoxide anion

2O$_2^-$ + 2H$^+$ → Spontaneous dismutation → **H$_2$O$_2$ + ^{1}O$_2$**

O$_2^-$ + H$_2$O$_2$ → → **•OH + OH$^-$ + ^{1}O$_2$** } Spontaneous formation of further microbial agents

H$_2$O$_2$ + Cl$^-$ → Myeloperoxidase → **OCl$^-$ + H$_2$O**

OCl$^-$ + H$_2$O$_2$ → → **^{1}O$_2$ + Cl$^-$ + H$_2$O** } Myeloperoxidase generation of microbicidal molecules

2O$_2^-$ + 2H$^+$ → Superoxide dismutase → O$_2$ + H$_2$O$_2$

2H$_2$O$_2$ → Catalase → 2H$_2$O + O$_2$ } Protective mechanisms used by host and many microbes

Nitric Oxide Reaction Sequence

O$_2$ + L–arginine → NO synthase → **NO•**

NO• + •O$_2^-$ → → **•ONOO$^-$** } Reactive species

NO• + Fe/RSH → → Fe(RS)$_2$(NO)$_2$ Complexes iron

Microbicidal species in bold letters. Fe/RSH, a complex of iron with a general sulfhydryl molecule; Fe (RS)$_2$, oxidized Fe/RSH; O$_2^-$, superoxide anion; ^{1}O$_2$, singlet (activated) oxygen; •OH, hydroxyl free radical; NADPH, reduced nicotinamide adenine dinucleotide phosphate; NADP$^+$, oxidized NADPH; H$_2$O$_2$, hydrogen peroxide; OCl$^-$, hypochlorite anion; NO; nitric oxide; •ONOO$^-$, peroxynitrite radical.

the small protein *cytokines* interleukin-1β (IL-1β), IL-6, IL-12 and TNF (TNFα), which activate other cells through binding to specific receptors, and *chemokines* such as IL-8, which represent a subset of chemoattractant cytokines.

Microbial nucleotide breakdown products of infectious agents that have succeeded in gaining access to the interior of a cell can be recognized by the so-called NOD proteins and the typical CpG DNA motif which binds to the endosomal TLR9. Other endosomal Toll-like receptors, TLR3 and TLR7/8, are responsive to intracellular viral RNA sequences and engender production of antiviral interferon.

Phagocytes are mobilized and targeted onto the microorganism by chemotaxis

Phagocytosis cannot occur unless the bacterium first attaches to the surface of the phagocyte, and clearly this cannot happen unless both have become physically close to each other. There is therefore a need for a mechanism that mobilizes phagocytes from afar and targets them

onto the bacterium. Many bacteria produce chemical substances, such as formyl methionyl peptides, which directionally attract leukocytes, a process known as 'chemotaxis'. However, this is a relatively weak signalling system, and evolution has provided the body with a far more effective 'magnet' that uses a complex series of proteins collectively termed 'complement'.

Activation of the complement system

Complement resembles blood clotting, fibrinolysis and kinin formation in being a major triggered enzyme cascade system. Such systems are characterized by their ability to produce a rapid, highly amplified response to a trigger stimulus mediated by a cascade phenomenon in which the product of one reaction is the enzymic catalyst of the next. The most abundant and most central component is C3 (complement components are designated by the letter 'C' followed by a number), and the cleavage of this molecule is at the heart of all complement-mediated phenomena.

In normal plasma, C3 undergoes spontaneous activation at a very slow rate to generate the split product C3b. This is able to complex with another complement component, factor B, which is then acted upon by a normal plasma enzyme, factor D, to produce the C3-splitting enzyme C3bBb. This C3 convertase can then split new molecules of C3 to give C3a (a small fragment) and further C3b. This represents a positive feedback circuit with potential for runaway amplification; however, the overall process is restricted to a tick-over level by powerful regulatory mechanisms, which break the unstable soluble-phase C3 convertase into inactive cleavage products (Fig. 9.13).

In the presence of certain molecules, such as the carbohydrates on the surface of many bacteria, the C3 convertase can become attached and stabilized against breakdown. Under these circumstances, there is active generation of new C3 convertase molecules, and what is known as the 'alternative' complement pathway can swing into full tempo (see Ch. 10).

Complement synergizes with phagocytic cells to produce an acute inflammatory response

Activation of the alternative complement pathway with the consequent splitting of very large numbers of C3 molecules has important consequences for the orchestration of an integrated antimicrobial defense strategy (Fig. 9.14). Large numbers of C3b produced in the immediate vicinity of the microbial membrane bind covalently to that surface and act as opsonins (molecules that make the particle they coat more susceptible to engulfment by phagocytic cells; see below). This C3b, together with the C3 convertase, acts on the next component in the sequence, C5, to produce a small fragment, C5a which, together with C3a, has a direct effect on mast cells to cause their degranulation (Fig. 9.15). This results in the release not only of mediators of vascular permeability, but also of factors chemotactic for polymorphs (Table 9.2). The circulating equivalent of the tissue mast cell, the basophil, is shown in Figure 9.16.

The vascular permeability mediators increase the permeability of capillaries by modifying the intercellular forces between the endothelial cells of the vessel wall. This allows the exudation of fluid and plasma components, including more complement, to the site of the infection. These mediators (Table 9.2) also up-regulate molecules such as intercellular adhesion molecule-1 (ICAM-1) and endothelial cell leukocyte adhesion molecule-1 (ELAM-1), which bind to specific complementary molecules on the polymorphs and encourage them to stick to the walls of the capillaries, a process termed 'margination'.

The chemotactic factors, on the other hand, provide a chemical gradient which attracts marginated polymorphonuclear leukocytes from their intravascular location, through the walls of the blood vessels, and eventually leads them to the site of the C3b-coated bacteria that initiated the whole activation process. Polymorphs have a well-defined receptor for C3b on their surface, and as a result, the opsonized bacteria adhere very firmly to the surface of these newly arrived cells.

The processes of capillary dilation (erythema), exudation of plasma proteins and of fluid (oedema) due to hydrostatic and osmotic pressure changes, and the accumulation of neutrophils are collectively termed the 'acute inflammatory response', and result in a highly effective way of focusing phagocytic cells onto complement-coated microbial targets.

It also seems clear that the macrophage can be stimulated by certain bacterial toxins such as the lipopolysaccharides (LPS), by the action of C5a, and by the phagocytosis of C3b-coated bacteria, to secrete other potent mediators of acute inflammation, independently of the mast cell-directed pathway (Fig. 9.17).

C9 molecules form the 'membrane attack complex', which is involved in cell lysis

We have already introduced the idea that following the activation of C3 the next component to be cleaved is C5; the larger C5b fragment that results becomes membrane bound. This subsequently binds components C6, C7 and C8, which form a complex capable of inducing a critical conformational change in the terminal component C9. The unfolded C9 molecules become inserted into the lipid bilayer and polymerize to form an annular 'membrane attack complex' (MAC) (Figs 9.18, 9.19). This behaves as a transmembrane channel that is fully permeable to electrolytes and water; because of the high internal colloid osmotic pressure of cells, there is a net influx of sodium (Na^+) and this frequently leads to lysis.

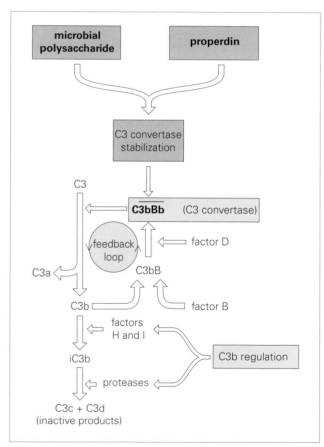

Figure 9.13 Activation of complement by microorganisms. C3b is formed by the spontaneous breakdown of C3 complexes with factor B to form C3bB which is split by factor D to produce a C3 convertase C3bBb, capable of further cleaving C3. The convertase is heavily regulated by factors H and I but can be stabilized on the surface of microbes and properdin. The horizontal bar indicates an enzymically active complex. iC3b, inactive C3b.

Figure 9.14 The defensive strategy of the acute inflammatory reaction initiated by bacterial activation of the alternative complement pathway. Activation of the C3bBb C3 convertase by the bacterium (1) leads to the generation of C3b (2) (which binds to the bacterium (3)), C3a and C5a (4), which recruit mast cell (MC) mediators. These in turn cause capillary dilation (5), exudation of plasma proteins (6), and chemotactic attraction (7) and adherence of polymorphs to the C3b-coated bacterium (8). Note that C5a itself is also chemotactic. The polymorphs are then activated for phagocytosis and the final kill (9).

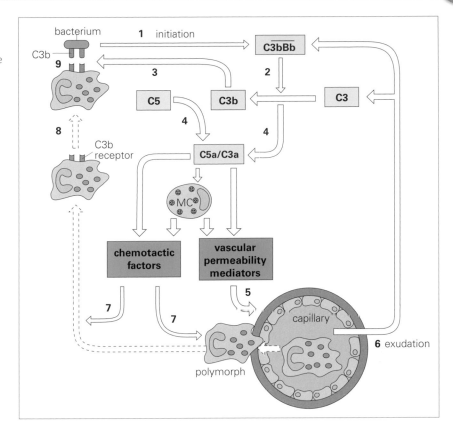

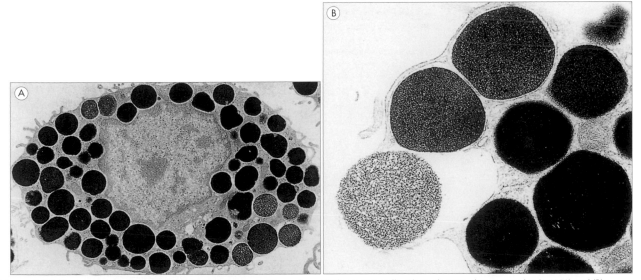

Figure 9.15 Electron micrographs of rat peritoneal mast cells. These show (A) the resting cell with its electron-dense granules (×6000) and (B) a granule in the process of exocytosis (×30 000). (Courtesy of T.S.C. Orr.)

Acute phase proteins

Certain proteins in the plasma, collectively termed 'acute phase proteins', increase in concentration in response to early 'alarm' mediators such as the cytokines interleukin-1 (IL-1), IL-6 and tumour necrosis factor (TNF), released as a result of infection or tissue injury. Many acute phase reactants such as mannose binding lectin and C-reactive protein (CRP) increase dramatically during inflammation (Fig. 9.20). Like the professional phagocytes, both use pattern recognition receptors to bind to molecular patterns on the pathogen (PAMPs), to generate defensive effector functions (Fig. 9.21). Other acute phase reactants show more moderate rises, usually less than fivefold (see Table 9.3). In general, these proteins are thought to have defensive roles.

Table 9.2 The major inflammatory mediators that control blood supply and vascular permeability or modulate cell movement

Inflammatory mediators		
Mediator	**Main source**	**Actions**
Histamine	Mast cells, basophils	Increased vascular permeability, smooth muscle contraction, chemokinesis
5-hydroxytryptamine (5HT – serotonin)	Platelets, mast cells (rodent)	Increased vascular permeability, smooth muscle contraction
Platelet activating factor (PAF)	Basophils, neutrophils, macrophages	Mediator release from platelets, increased vascular permeability, smooth muscle contraction, neutrophil activation
IL-8 (CXCL8)	Mast cells, endothelium, monocytes and lymphocytes	Polymorph and monocyte localization
C3a	Complement C3	Mast cell degranulation, smooth muscle contraction
C5a	Complement C5	Mast cell degranulation, neutrophil and macrophage chemotaxis, neutrophil activation, smooth muscle contraction, increased capillary permeability
Bradykinin	Kinin system (kininogen)	Vasodilation, smooth muscle contraction, increased capillary permeability, pain
Fibrinopeptides and fibrin breakdown products	Clotting system	Increased vascular permeability, neutrophil and macrophage chemotaxis
Prostaglandin E$_2$ (PGE$_2$)	Cyclo-oxygenase pathway, mast cells	Vasodilation, potentiates increased vascular permeability produced by histamine and bradykinin
Leukotriene B$_4$ (LTB$_4$)	Lipoxygenase pathway, mast cells	Neutrophil chemotaxis, synergizes with PGE$_2$ in increasing vascular permeability
Leukotriene D$_4$ (LTD$_4$)	Lipoxygenase pathway	Smooth muscle contraction, increasing vascular permeability

Other mediators are generated from the coagulation process. Chemotaxis refers to directed migration of granulocytes up the concentration gradient of the mediator, whereas chemokinesis describes randomly increased motility of these cells.
(Reproduced from Male D, Brostoff J, Roth DB, Roitt I. *Immunology*, 7th edition, 2006. Mosby Elsevier, with permission.)

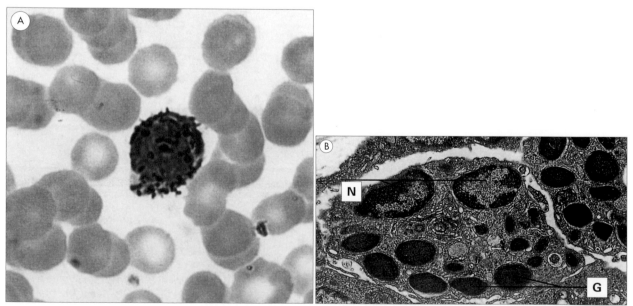

Figure 9.16 Morphology of the basophil. (A) This blood smear shows a typical basophil with its deep violet-blue granules. Wright's stain (× 1500). (B) Electron micrograph showing the ultrastructure of the basophil. Basophils in guinea pig skin showing the nuclei (N) and characteristic randomly distributed granules (G) (× 6000). (Courtesy of D. McLaren.)

Table 9.3 Acute phase proteins produced in response to infection in the human

Acute phase reactant	Function
Dramatic increases in concentration	
C-reactive protein	Fixes complement, opsonizes
Mannose binding lectin	Fixes complement, opsonizes
α_1 acid glycoprotein	Transports protein
Serum amyloid A protein	Complexes chondroitin sulphate
Moderate increases in concentration	
α_1 proteinase inhibitors	Inhibit bacterial proteases
α_1 anti-chymotrypsin	Inhibits bacterial proteases
Surfactant protein A	Binds influenza virus haemagglutinin
C3, C9, factor B	Increase complement function
Ceruloplasmin	O_2 scavenger
Fibrinogen	Coagulation
Angiotensin	Blood pressure
Haptoglobin	Binds haemoglobin
Fibronectin	Cell attachment

Other extracellular antimicrobial factors

There are many microbicidal agents that operate at short range within phagocytic cells, but also appear in various body fluids in sufficient concentration to have direct inhibitory effects on infectious agents. For example, lysozyme is present in fluids such as tears and saliva in amounts capable of acting against the proteoglycan wall of susceptible bacteria. Similarly, lactoferrin may appear in the blood in sufficient concentration to complex iron and deprive bacteria of this important growth factor. Whether agents that normally act over a short range, such as reactive oxygen metabolites or TNF (a cytotoxic molecule produced by macrophages and other cell types), can reach concentrations in the body fluids that are adequate to allow them to act at a distance from the cell producing them will be discussed in Chapter 14, particularly when considering the mechanisms by which the blood-borne forms of parasites such as malaria are attacked.

Interferons are a family of broad spectrum antiviral molecules

Interferons (IFNs) are widespread throughout the animal kingdom and are again discussed further in Chapter 14. They were first recognized by the phenomenon of viral interference, in which a cell infected with one virus is found to be resistant to superinfection by a second unrelated virus. Leukocytes produce many different α-interferons (IFNα),

Figure 9.17 A role for the macrophage (Mø) in the initiation of acute inflammation. Stimulation induces macrophage secretion of mediators. Blood neutrophils stick to the adhesion molecules on the endothelial cell and use them to provide traction as they force their way between the cells, through the basement membrane (with the help of secreted elastase) and up the chemotactic gradient. During this process they become progressively activated by neutrophil activating peptide-2 (NAP-2). PGE$_2$, prostaglandin E$_2$; LTB$_4$, leukotriene B$_4$; IL-1, interleukin-1; PMN, polymorphonuclear neutrophil; TNFα, tumour necrosis factor alpha; ELAM-1, endothelial cell leukocyte adhesion molecule-1; ICAM-1, intercellular adhesion molecule-1.

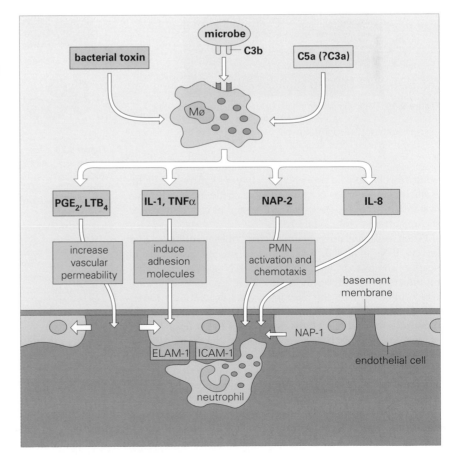

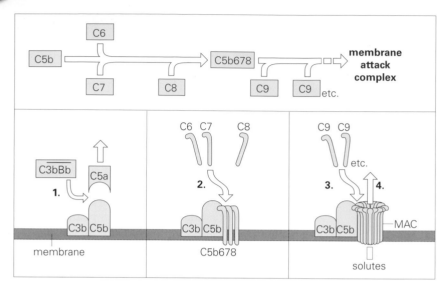

Figure 9.18 Assembly of the C5b-9 membrane attack complex (MAC). (1) Recruitment of a further C3b into the C3bBb enzymic complex generates a C5 convertase which cleaves C5a from C5 and leaves the remaining C5b attached to the membrane. (2) Once C5b is membrane bound, C6 and C7 attach themselves to form the stable complex C5b67, which interacts with C8 to yield C5b678. (3) This unit has some effect in disrupting the membrane, but primarily causes the polymerization of C9 to form tubules traversing the membrane. The resulting tubule is referred to as a MAC. (4) Disruption of the membrane by this structure permits the free exchange of solutes, which are primarily responsible for cell lysis.

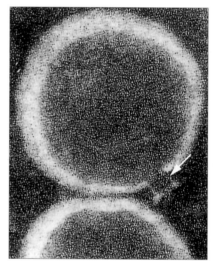

Figure 9.19 Electron micrograph of the MAC. The funnel-shaped lesion (*arrowed*) is due to a human C5b–9 complex that has been reincorporated into lecithin liposomal membranes (× 234 000). (Courtesy of J. Tranum-Jensen and S. Bhakdi.)

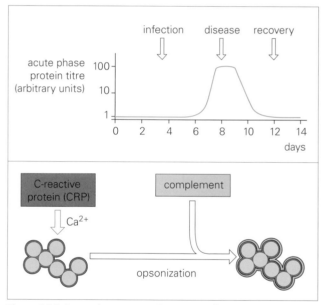

Figure 9.20 Acute phase proteins, here exemplified by C-reactive protein (CRP), are serum proteins that increase rapidly in concentration (sometimes up to 100-fold) following infection (graph). They are important in innate immunity to infection. CRP recognizes and binds in a calcium (Ca^{2+})-dependent fashion to molecular groups found on a wide variety of bacteria and fungi. In particular, it uses its pattern recognition to bind the phosphocholine moiety of pneumococci. The CRP acts as an opsonin and activates complement with all the associated sequelae. Mannose binding protein reacts not only with mannose but several other sugars, enabling it to bind to a wide variety of Gram-negative and -positive bacteria, yeasts, viruses and parasites, subsequently activating the complement system and phagocytic cells. The structurally related ficolins typically recognize PAMPs containing *N*-acetylglucosamine and can also activate the lectin complement pathway.

while fibroblasts and probably all cell types synthesize IFNβ. A third type (IFNγ) is not a component of the innate immune system and will be discussed in Chapter 10 as a member of the important cytokine family.

When cells are infected by a virus, they synthesize and secrete IFNs α and β, which bind to specific receptors on nearby uninfected cells. The bound IFN exerts its antiviral effect by facilitating the synthesis of two new enzymes, which interfere with the machinery used by the virus for its own replication. The mechanism of action of IFN is discussed more fully in Chapter 14; the net result is to set up a cordon of infection-resistant cells around the site of virus infection, so restraining its spread (Fig. 9.22). IFN is highly effective in vivo, as supported by experiments in which mice injected with an antiserum to murine IFN were found to be killed by several hundred times less virus than was needed to kill the controls. It should be emphasized, however, that IFN seems to play a significant role in recovery from, rather than prevention of, viral infections.

Extracellular killing

Natural killer cells attach to virally infected cells, allowing them to be differentiated from normal cells

There is a widely held view that viruses represent fragments of the genome of multicellular organisms that have achieved the ability to exist in an extracellular state. The small number of genes present in the viral genome, however, does not

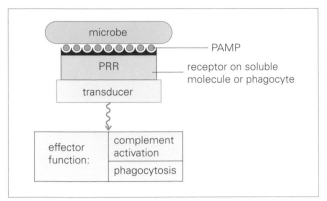

Figure 9.21 A major defensive strategy in which soluble factors, such as CRP (C reactive protein) and mannose binding protein, and professional phagocytes use their pattern recognition receptors (PRR) to bind to the pathogen-associated molecular patterns (PAMPs) on the microbial surface and signal through their transducer structures to initiate appropriate effector functions.

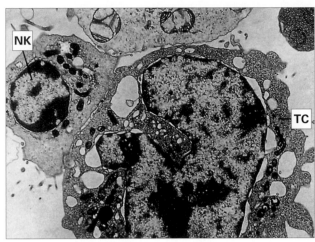

Figure 9.23 Electron micrograph of an NK cell killing a tumour cell (TC). NK cells bind to and kill IgG antibody-coated (see Fig. 10.13), and non-coated, tumour cells. It is essential for the membranes of the two cells to be closely apposed in order for the NK cell to deliver the 'kiss of death' (× 4500). (Courtesy of P. Lydyard.)

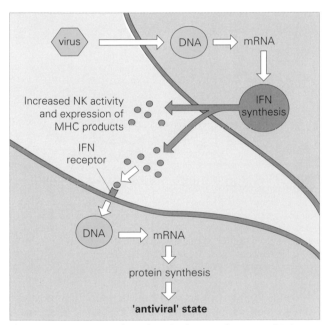

Figure 9.22 The action of interferon (IFN). Virus infecting a cell induces the production of IFNα/β. This is released and binds to IFN receptors on other cells. The IFN induces the production of antiviral proteins, which are activated if virus enters the second cell, and increased synthesis of surface MHC molecules which enhance susceptibility to cytotoxic T cells (cf. Ch. 10). NK, natural killer; MHC, major histocompatibility complex.

include those required for viral replication. Accordingly, it is essential for viruses to penetrate the cells of an infected host in order to subvert the cells' replicative machinery towards viral replication. Clearly, it is in the interests of the host to try to kill such infected cells before the virus has had a chance to reproduce. Natural killer (NK) cells are cytotoxic cells that appear to have evolved to carry out just such a task. These are large granular lymphocytes (LGLs) (Fig. 9.23) that recognize virus-infected or stressed cells and allow them to be differentiated from normal cells; this clever discrimination is mediated by activating receptors on the NK cells such as NKG2D that recognize ligands on the infected cell that are related to MHC Class I molecules, and inhibitory receptors

which bind to MHC Class I molecules on normal cells, generating signals that counteract those from the activating receptors. Activation of the NK cell results in the extracellular release of its granule contents into the space between the target and effector cells. These contents include perforin molecules, which resemble C9 in many respects, especially in their ability to insert into the membrane of the target cell and polymerize to form annular transmembrane pores, like the MAC. This permits the entry of another granule protein, granzyme B, which leads to death of the target cell by apoptosis (programmed cell death), a process mediated by a cascade of proteolytic enzymes termed caspases, which terminates with the ultimate fragmentation of DNA by a Ca-dependent endonuclease (Fig. 9.24).

Subsidiary mechanisms that can activate the caspase pathway include engagement of Fas on the target cell by the NK Fas ligand, and binding of tumour necrosis factor (TNF) released from the NK granules to surface receptors. TNF was first recognized as a product of activated macrophages known to be capable of killing certain other cells, particularly some tumour cells.

Yet a further mode of cytotoxicity can be turned on by the activated macrophage, involving the direct 'burning' of the surface of another cell by means of a stream of reactive oxygen intermediates, produced at the macrophage membrane by the respiratory oxygen burst, as discussed previously (see Box 9.2).

Eosinophils act against large parasites

It takes little imagination to realize that professional phagocytes are far too small to be capable of physically engulfing large parasites such as helminths. An alternative strategy, such as killing by an extracellular broadside of the type discussed above would seem to be a more appropriate form of defence. Eosinophils appear to have evolved to fulfil this role. These polymorphonuclear relatives of the neutrophil have distinctive cytoplasmic granules, which stain strongly with acidic dyes (Fig. 9.25) and have a characteristic ultrastructural appearance. A major

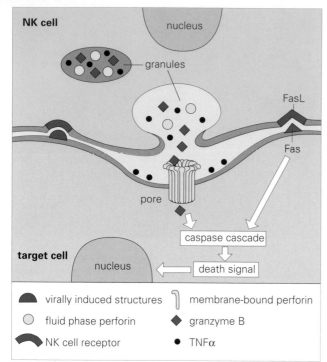

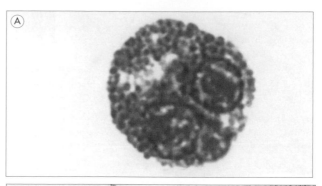

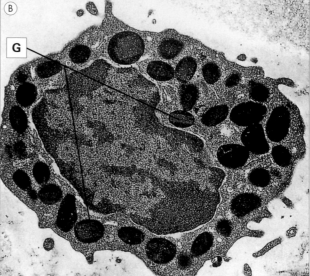

Figure 9.24 Schematic model of lysis of virally infected target cell by a natural killer (NK) cell. As the NK cell receptors bind to the surface of the virally infected cell, and if signals from activation receptors exceed those from the inhibitory receptors that recognize normal MHC Class I molecules, there is exocytosis of granules and release of cytolytic mediators into the intercellular cleft. A calcium (Ca^{2+})-dependent conformational change in the perforin enables it to insert and polymerize within the membrane of the target cell to form a transmembrane pore, which allows entry of granzyme B into the target cell, where it causes programmed cell death (apoptosis). A back-up cytolytic system using engagement of the Fas receptor with its ligand (FasL), can also trigger apoptosis as can binding of granule-derived tumour necrosis factor alpha (TNFα) to its receptor. Unlike the PRR-mediated activation of phagocytes by intracellular components – so-called danger-associated molecular patterns (DAMPs) – released on *necrotic* cell-death typically caused by tissue trauma, burns and other non-physiological stimuli, cells undergoing *apoptotic* death do not activate the immune system because they express surface molecules such as phosphatidyl serine which mark them out for phagocytic removal before they release their intracellular DAMPs.

Figure 9.25 The eosinophil granulocyte is capable of extracellular killing of parasites (e.g. worms) by releasing its granule contents. (A) Morphology of the eosinophil. This blood smear enriched for granulocytes shows an eosinophil with its multilobed nucleus and heavily stained cytoplasmic granules. Leishman's stain (×1800). (Courtesy of P. Lydyard.) (B) Electron micrograph showing the ultrastructure of a guinea pig eosinophil. The mature eosinophil contains granules (G) with central crystalloids (×8000). (Courtesy of D. McLaren.)

basic protein (MBP) has been identified in the core of the granule, while the matrix has been shown to contain an eosinophilic cationic protein, a peroxidase and a perforin-like molecule. Eosinophils have surface receptors for C3b and when activated generate copious amounts of active oxygen metabolites.

Many helminths can activate the alternative complement pathway but, although resistant to C9 attack, their coating with C3b allows adherence to the eosinophils through their C3b surface receptors. Once activated, the eosinophil launches its extracellular ammunition, which includes the release of major basic proteins and the cationic protein to damage the parasite membrane, with a possibility of a further 'chemical burn' from the oxygen metabolites and 'leaky pore' formation by the perforins.

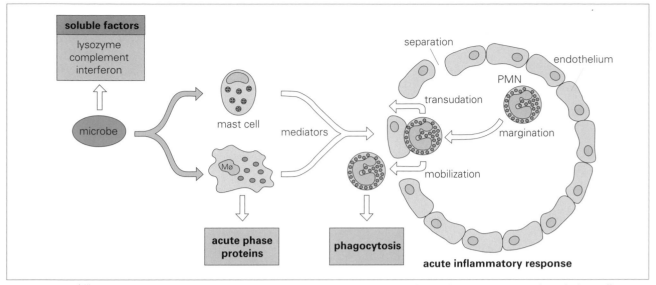

Figure 9.26 Mobilization of defensive components of innate immunity. Microbes, either through complement activation or through direct effects on macrophages, release mediators which increase capillary permeability to allow transudation of plasma bactericidal molecules, and chemotactically attract plasma polymorphs from the bloodstream to the infection site. PMN, polymorphonuclear neutrophil.

KEY FACTS

- The innate system of immune defence consists of a formidable barrier to entry and second-line defence by phagocytes and circulating soluble factors. Colonization of the body by normally non-pathogenic ('opportunistic') microorganisms occurs whenever there is a hereditary or acquired deficiency in any of these functions.

- The main phagocytic cells are polymorphonuclear neutrophils and macrophages. They adhere to the surface of the microbe by receptors which recognize pathogen-associated molecular patterns (PAMPs). This activates the engulfment process so that the organisms are taken inside the cell in a phagocytic vacuole which fuses with cytoplasmic granules. A formidable array of oxygen-dependent and oxygen-independent microbicidal mechanisms then comes into play.

- The complement system, a multicomponent triggered enzyme cascade, is used to attract phagocytic cells to the microbes and engulf them.

- The most abundant complement component, C3, is split by a convertase enzyme formed from its own cleavage product C3b and factor B and stabilized against breakdown caused by factors H and I through association with the microbial surface. As it is formed, C3b becomes covalently linked to the microorganism.

- The next most abundant component, C5, is activated to yield a small peptide, C5a, while residual C5b binds to the surface of the microorganism and assembles the terminal components C6–9 into a membrane attack complex (MAC), which is freely permeable to solutes and can lead to osmotic lysis. In addition, C5a is a potent chemotactic agent for polymorphs and greatly increases capillary permeability.

- C3a and C5a act on mast cells, causing the release of further mediators such as histamine, LTB_4 and TNFα, with effects on capillary permeability and adhesiveness and neutrophil chemotaxis. They also activate neutrophils, which bind to the C3b-coated microbes by their surface C3b receptors and then ingest them.

- The influx of polymorphs and increase in vascular permeability constitute the potent antimicrobial acute inflammatory response.

- Inflammation can also be initiated by tissue macrophages, which subserve a similar role to that of the mast cell since signalling by bacterial toxins C5a or by C3b-coated bacteria adhering to surface complement receptors on tissue macrophages causes the release of TNFα, LTB_4, PGE_2, the neutrophil chemotactic factor, IL-8, and a neutrophil-activating peptide.

- Other humoral defences include the acute phase proteins such as CRP, and the IFNs, which can block viral replication.

- Virally infected cells can be killed by NK cells, following increased recognition by activation receptors that overcomes inhibitory signals from normal MHC Class I recognition.

- Extracellular killing can also be effected by C3b-bound eosinophils, which may be responsible for the failure of many large parasites to establish a foothold in potential hosts.

- It is probably true to say that engulfment and killing by phagocytic cells is the mechanism used to dispose of the majority of microbes, and the mobilization and activation of these cells by orchestrated responses such as the acute inflammatory response (Fig. 9.26) is a key feature of innate immunity. However, not every organism is readily susceptible to phagocytosis or even to killing by complement or lysozyme, and this brings us to the role of the adaptive immune response, which is explored in Chapter 10.

Adaptive responses provide a 'quantum leap' in effective defence

10

Introduction

Infectious agents frequently find ways around the innate defences

In Chapter 9, we discussed the many ways in which the primary or innate defences of the body may counteract microbial infection. However, infectious agents frequently find ways around these defences, as there is a huge number of different microorganisms surrounding us and they have a powerful ability to mutate, e.g.:

- The surface of some microbes fails to activate the alternative complement pathway.
- Other microbes can activate the alternative complement pathway, but do so at the end of flagella, so that the membrane attack complex builds up at a site distant from the body of the organism and therefore causes no damage.
- In other cases, microorganisms taken into the body of the macrophage develop subterfuges that prevent the development of the awesome battery of microbicidal mechanisms that the macrophage normally expresses (see Ch. 16).
- Cells infected with certain viruses may prove to be resistant to the cytotoxic action of natural killer cells, or the viruses may be only weak stimulators of interferon, so that cell-to-cell transmission of the virus proceeds unchecked.
- Yet another microbial subterfuge is the production of bacterial toxins that can kill the phagocyte if not neutralized.

Adaptive responses act against microorganisms that overcome the innate defences

It is clear that the body needs to provide immune defences that can be 'tailor-made' to each individual variant of the different species of microorganisms. Ideally, these should link the organism directly into the various killing mechanisms of the innate system. In this chapter, we shall see how evolution has achieved this by inserting specific recognition sites on antibody molecules and on T cells. When an infectious agent enters the body, the lymphocytes respond to it and produce a reaction that is specific for that particular microorganism. Furthermore, the magnitude of this response increases with time, often to quite high levels, so that we speak of it as an 'adaptive' or 'acquired' response. We know that the body produces millions of different antibodies, which as a population are capable of recognizing virtually any pathogen that has arisen or might arise.

THE ROLE OF ANTIBODIES

The acute inflammatory response

Antibodies act as adaptors to focus acute inflammatory reactions

Antibodies are immunoglobulin molecules (Fig. 10.1, Table 10.1) which are synthesized by host B lymphocytes (so-called because they mature in the bone marrow; see Fig. 11.2) when they make contact with an infectious microbe, which acts as a foreign antigen (i.e. it *gen*erates *anti*bodies). Each antibody has two identical recognition sites that are complementary in shape to the surface of the foreign antigen and which enable it to bind with varying degrees of strength to that antigen. The recognition site is hypervariable in that antibodies of different antigen specificities each have a unique amino acid sequence in this region. This hypervariability is confined to three loops on the heavy and three on the light peptide chains, which make up the antibody molecule (Fig. 10.1) and are referred to as complementarity determining regions (CDRs) because they make complementary contact with the antigen. Thus, the amino acid sequences of these CDRs determine which antigen is recognized by a given antibody. Other sites on the antibody molecule are specialized for functions such as activating the complement system and inducing phagocytosis by macrophages and polymorphs (Fig. 10.2). Therefore, when a microbial antigen is coated with several of these adaptor antibody molecules, they induce complement fixation and phagocytosis, processes that the microbe may well have evolved to try and avoid. In this way, the reluctant microorganism becomes drawn into the innate defence mechanism of the acute inflammatory response. We will now examine the ways in which antibody can mediate these different phenomena.

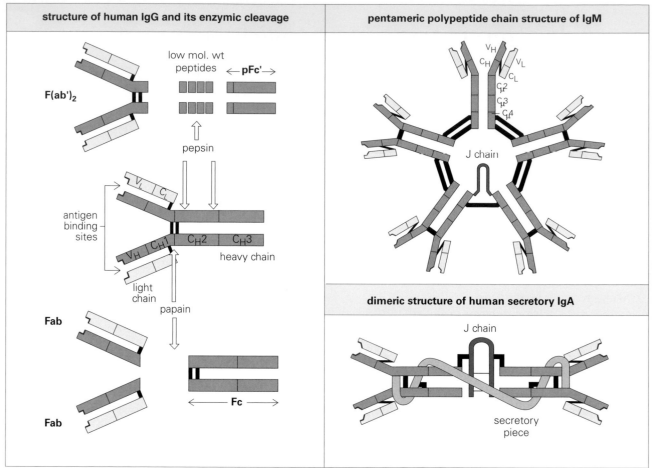

Figure 10.1 The structure of immunoglobulins. The basic structure of immunoglobulins is a unit consisting of two identical light polypeptide chains and two identical heavy polypeptide chains linked together by disulfide bonds (*black bars*). Each chain is made up of individual globular domains. Different antibodies have different V_L and V_H domains, the highly variable regions of the light and heavy chains, respectively. This hypervariability is confined to three loops on the V_L and three on the V_H domains. These make up the antigen-binding site (*highlighted in red*). In contrast, the remaining domains (C_L, C_H1, etc.) are relatively constant in amino acid structure. Cleavage of human immunoglobulin G (IgG) by pepsin induces a divalent antigen-binding fragment, $F(ab')_2$ and a pFc' fragment composed of two terminal C_H3 domains. Papain produces two univalent antigen binding fragments, Fab, and an Fc portion containing the C_H2 and C_H3 heavy chain domains. Polymerization of the basic immunoglobulin units to form IgM and IgA is catalysed by the J (joining) chain. The portion of the transporter (which transfers IgA across the mucosal cell to the lumen) which remains attached to the IgA is termed 'secretory piece'.

Table 10.1 Biologic properties of major immunoglobulin (Ig) classes in the human

Designation	IgG	[a]IgA	IgM	IgD	IgE
Major characteristics	Most abundant internal Ig	Protects external surfaces	Very efficient against bacteria	Mainly lymphocyte receptor	Initiates inflammation raised in parasitic infections; causes allergy symptoms
Antigen binding	+ +	+ +	+ +	+ +	+ +
Complement fixation (classical)	+ +	–	+ + +	+	–
Cross placenta	+ +	–	–	–	–
Fix to homologous mast cells and basophils	–	–	–	–	+ +
Binding to macrophages and polymorphs	+ + +	+	–	–	+

[a]Dimer in external secretion carries secretory piece; IgA dimer and IgM contain J chains.

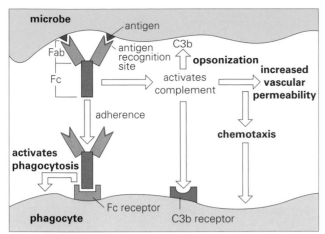

Figure 10.2 The antibody adaptor molecule. Antibodies (anti-foreign bodies) are produced by host lymphocytes on contact with invading microbes, which act as antigens (i.e. generate antibodies). Each antibody (see Fig. 10.1) has a recognition site (Fab) enabling it to bind antigen, and a backbone structure (Fc) capable of some secondary biologic action such as activating complement and phagocytosis. Thus, in the present case, antibody bound to the microbe activates complement and initiates an acute inflammatory reaction (cf. Fig. 9.14). The C3b generated fixes to the microbe and, together with the antibody molecules, facilitates adherence to Fc and C3b receptors on the phagocyte and thence microbial ingestion.

Antibody complexed with antigen activates complement through the 'classical' pathway

When antibody molecules bind an antigen, the resulting complex activates the first component of complement, C1, converting it into an esterase ($\overline{\text{C1qrs}}$). This initiates a second route of complement activation (Fig. 10.3) termed the 'classical' pathway, mainly because scientists discovered it before the 'alternative' pathway (see Ch. 9), although the evidence indicates that the alternative pathway is of greater antiquity in evolutionary terms. The activated first component splits off a small peptide from each of the succeeding components C4 and C2, the residual fragments forming a composite, the $\overline{\text{C4b2a}}$, complex. The $\overline{\text{C4b2a}}$ complex has the enzymatic ability or property of a C3 convertase. Being an enzyme, the $\overline{\text{C1qrs}}$ protease creates large numbers of the $\overline{\text{C4b2a}}$ convertase which itself also having proteolytic activity, cleaves many C3 molecules, this so-called *enzyme cascade* providing a mechanism for the striking amplification of the relatively few initial complement activation events. $\overline{\text{C4b2a}}$ has a similar function to the alternative pathway C3 convertase, $\overline{\text{C3bBb}}$, and the sequence of events following the splitting of C3 which generates an acute inflammatory response is indistinguishable from that occurring in the alternative pathway. C3a and C5a anaphylatoxins are formed, and C3b binds to the surface of the microbe–antibody complex (Fig. 10.4; compare Fig. 9.14). Subsequently, the later components are assembled into a membrane attack complex (MAC) (see Fig. 9.18), which may help to kill the microorganism if it has been focused onto a vulnerable site.

It is appropriate at this stage to recall the activation of complement by innate immune mechanisms involving the binding of mannose binding lectin (MBL) and C-reactive protein to carbohydrates on microbial surfaces (cf. Fig. 9.20), and it is noteworthy that both acute phase proteins activate the classical pathway albeit through different routes (Fig. 10.3).

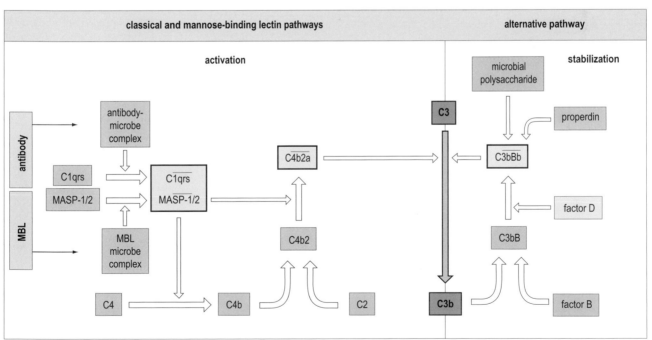

Figure 10.3 Comparison of the alternative classical and mannose binding lectin complement pathways. All converge with the formation of C3 convertase enzymes (*in heavily outlined boxes*) which split the dominant protein C3 into the C3b fragment, an event which is at the heart of the complement interactions. The complex of antibody with microbial antigen activates the first component of the 'classical' pathway (step 1) leading to cleavage of C3 through the $\overline{\text{C4b2a}}$, C3 convertase. Mannose binding lectin, when combined with microbial surface carbohydrate, associates with serine proteases MASP-1 and -2 which split C4 and C2, just like $\overline{\text{C1qrs}}$. In contrast, the activation of the 'alternative' pathway depends upon stabilization of the C3 convertase ($\overline{\text{C3bBb}}$) on the microbial surface produced by the feedback loop (cf. Fig. 9.13). The molecular units with protease activity are highlighted in green, the enzymatic domains showing considerable homology. Note that the acute phase protein, C-reactive protein, on binding to microbial phosphorylcholine, can trigger the classical pathway. An upper bar (—) indicates an active complex.

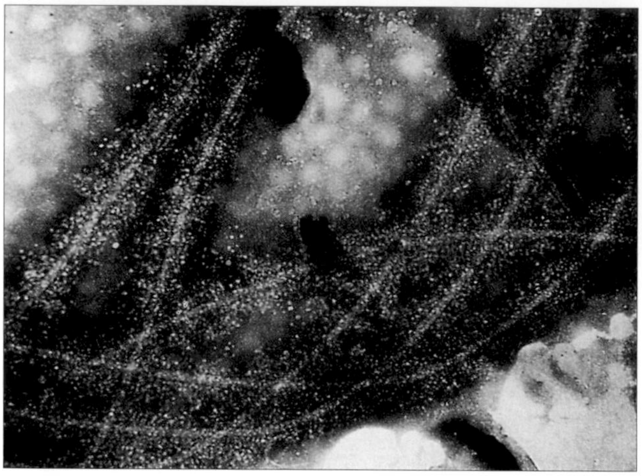

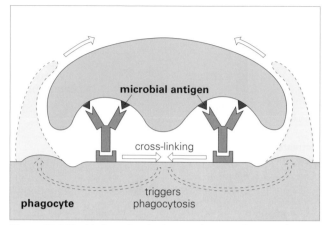

Figure 10.4 Electron microscopy of C3-coated salmonella flagella. The flagella have been incubated with anti-flagellum antibody and complement. The electron-dense material extending 30 nm on either side of each flagellum is believed to be C3b. The interpretation of this is that complement fixation by antibody results in a heavy macromolecular coating of C3b on biologic membranes to which complement has been fixed (×700 000). (Courtesy of A. Feinstein and E. Munn.)

The acute inflammatory reaction can also be initiated by antibody bound to mast cells

A specialized antibody, immunoglobulin E (IgE), has a backbone site with a high affinity for specific receptors on the surface of mast cells. When microbial antigen attaches to these cell-bound antibodies the surface receptors are cross-linked and transduce a signal to the interior of the cell. This signal leads to the release of mediators capable of increasing vascular permeability and inducing polymorph chemotaxis (Fig. 10.5).

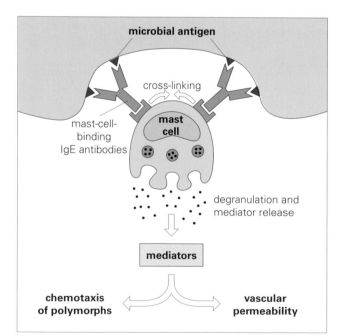

Figure 10.5 Degranulation of mast cells by interaction of microbial antigen with specific antibodies of the IgE class, which bind to special receptors on the mast cell surface. The cross-linking of receptors caused by this interaction leads to the release of mediators, which induce an increase in vascular permeability and attract polymorphs, i.e. they provoke an acute inflammatory reaction at the site of the microbial antigen.

Figure 10.6 The binding of a microbe to a phagocyte by more than one antibody cross-links the antibody receptors on the phagocyte surface and triggers phagocytosis of the microorganism, which is engulfed by the extending cytoplasmic projections.

Activation of phagocytic cells

Antigen–antibody complexes activate phagocytic cells

Other sites on the Fc backbone of certain types of antibody molecule bind to specialized Fc receptors on the surface of phagocytic cells. If there is more than one antibody in the antigen–antibody complex, these receptors are cross-linked, so inducing the cell to put out arms of cytoplasm, which enclose the complex in a phagocytic vacuole (Fig. 10.6). Note also that there is a 'bonus effect' of multivalent binding of reversible ligand-receptor links; for example, the association constant for a complex binding through two antibody molecules to the phagocyte is the product rather than the sum of the individual association constants.

Blocking microbial reactions

Antibodies block microbial interactions by combining with one of the reacting molecules

For example, an antibody directed against the influenza haemagglutinin will prevent the virus from attaching to its specific receptor on a cell, making it unable to infect that cell (Fig. 10.7). Likewise, antibodies to an essential transport molecule on a bacterial surface can prevent the uptake of that nutrient and cause a metabolic block. As a final example, an antibody to a bacterial toxin will prevent damage to the cells with which the toxin would otherwise interact.

THE ROLE OF T LYMPHOCYTES

Defence against intracellular organisms

The body has evolved an adaptive immune defence system based upon the T lymphocyte, so-called because it matures in the thymus gland. There are several specialized subsets of T cells (Table 10.2) but here we are concerned with those which provide a defence against viruses and many different species of microorganisms which can live within cells, where they are shielded from attack by antibody.

Figure 10.7 Because of its size, antibody can block interactions between (A) a virus and a cell, (B) a nutrient and a bacterium and (C) a toxin and a cellular receptor.

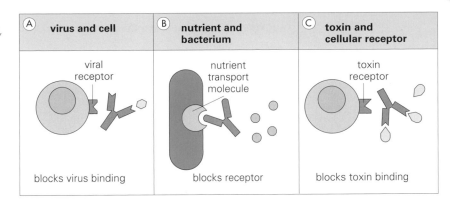

Table 10.2 Subpopulations of T cells

Type	Designation	ᵃ Markers	Recognize	Function
T-helper-1	Th1	αβTCR CD4	MHCI + peptide on dendritic (antigen-presenting) cells; macrophages	help macrophages to kill intracellular infection
T-helper-2	Th2	αβTCR CD4	MHCII + peptide on B-cells	help B cells to make antibody
T-helper-17	Th17	αβTCR CD4	MHCII + peptide	strongly proinflammatory
Cytotoxic T cells	Tc	αβTCR CD8	MHCGI + peptide on infected cells	kill virally infected cells before significant replication
γδ-T cells	γδ -T	γδTCR	certain microbial PAMPs; stressed epithelial DAMPs	mucosal protection against infection
Regulatory T cells	Treg	αβTCR CD4/8	see Fig. 11.16	regulate T cell responses

ᵃSee Table 11.1.

DAMPs, damage-associated molecular patterns; PAMPs, pathogen-associated molecular patterns; TCR, T cell receptor including the signal transduction complex CD3 (Fig. 10.9); MHC, major histocompatibility complex (Fig. 10.8). NKT cells have the cytotoxic functions of NK cells but express an invariant TCR which recognizes the MHC-like molecule CD1d.

Most T lymphocytes bind to peptide derived from intracellular organisms complexed with major histocompatibility complex

As microorganisms go through their various life cycles they sometimes die within the cells they infect. The proteins derived from these dead organisms and also newly synthesized viral proteins are fragmented by intracellular cytosolic enzymes ('processing') and the peptides are incorporated into cytoplasmic vacuoles where they bind to a molecule of the major histocompatibility complex (MHC) (Fig. 10.8). (MHC molecules were originally discovered because of their ability to bring about the most violent rejection of grafts interchanged between members of the same species.) We now know that one of their important functions is to act as cellular surface markers. Class I MHC molecules are present on virtually every cell in the body and can therefore be used as a marker indicating an instance of 'cell'. Class II MHC molecules appear mainly on macrophages and B cells.

A specialized T-cell receptor (TCR) on the T-lymphocyte surface (Fig. 10.9) is analogous to an antibody molecule in its ability to recognize foreign antigen. It resembles the immunoglobulin Fab portion in structure, with α and β chains instead of heavy and light chains, again with hypervariable loops to contact the antigen. However, unlike the antibody recognition site which interacts directly with a foreign antigen, the T-cell surface receptor is specialized for binding to the complex of MHC molecule and peptide derived from the processed intracellular organism. Thus, not only is the MHC a molecular signal for 'cell', but the foreign peptide is a signal that the cell has an intracellular microbe. Therefore, when the TCR recognizes these two moieties together, the T lymphocyte must be binding to an infected cell of a type indicated by the class of the MHC (see Table 10.2). The T lymphocyte then becomes activated and, depending upon its particular characteristics, sets off an effector mechanism to deal with the intracellular microorganisms, as explained below.

T lymphocytes help macrophages kill intracellular parasites

The task of recognizing macrophages that have unwelcome guests, such as listeria or tubercle bacilli living within them, falls mainly to a subset of lymphocytes called the Th1 T-helper cells (see Table 10.2). When a specific Th1 cell combines with a complex of class II MHC molecule and microbial peptide on the surface of an infected macrophage, the T cell is triggered to release macrophage activating factors, notably interferon gamma (IFNγ) (see Ch. 9). This unleashes previously suppressed microbicidal mechanisms within the macrophage, in particular the generation of NO radicals, so leading to the death of the intracellular parasites (Fig. 10.10). In general, Th1 cells evoke a chronic inflammatory response dominated by macrophages but, in addition, recent studies have revealed the powerful pro-inflammatory role of another subset, the Th17 cell.

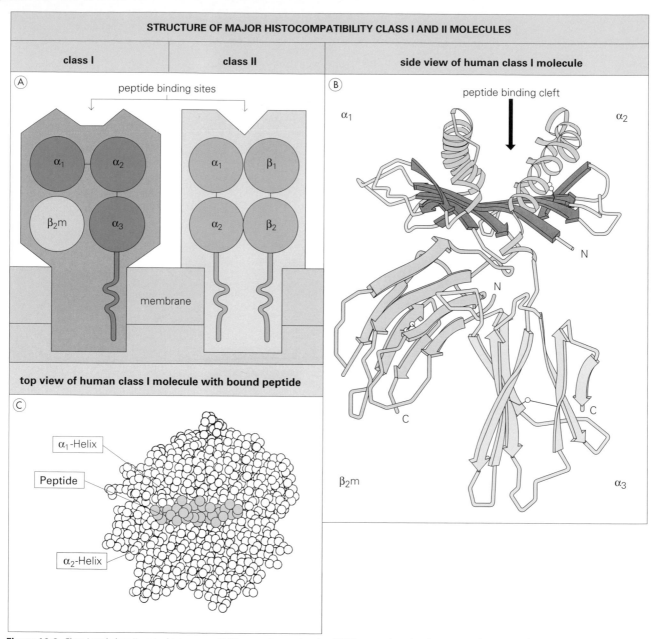

Figure 10.8 Class I and class II major histocompatibility complex molecules. (A) Diagram showing domains and transmembrane segments; the α-helices and β-pleated sheets are viewed end-on. (B) Side view of human class I molecule (HLA-A2) based on X-ray crystallographic structure showing the cleft and the typical immunoglobulin folding of the α$_3$ and β$_2$-microglobulin (β$_2$m) domains (four antiparallel β-strands on one face and three on the other). The strands making the β-pleated sheet are shown as thick gray arrows in the amino to carboxyl direction, α-helices are represented as helical ribbons. The inside facing surfaces of the two helices and the upper surface of the β-pleated sheet form a cleft which binds the peptide. (Adapted from: Bjorkman, P. I. et al. (1987) *Nature*; 329:512, with permission.) (C) Top view of a peptide bound tightly within the MHC class I cleft, in this case peptide 309–317 from HIV-1 reverse transcriptase bound to HLA-A2. This is the 'view' seen by the combining site of the T-cell receptor described below. (Based on Vignali, D. A. A. and Strominger, J. L. (1994) *The Immunologist*; 2:112, with permission.)

T lymphocytes inhibit intracellular replication of viruses

Cells infected with virus express complexes consisting of class I MHC and a virally derived peptide on their surface. These are recognized by the specific receptors on cytotoxic T (Tc) cells (Fig. 10.11), which are therefore led into close proximity to their virally infected target. The target cell is then killed by similar extracellular mechanisms to those described in Chapter 9. Since the virally derived peptides appear on the cell surface at a very early stage of infection, if the Tc cells kill the cell before the virus has had an opportunity to replicate significantly, the host has won an important battle. The natural killer (NK) cell fulfils a similar function to that of the Tc cell, but because it lacks the specialized receptors for recognizing the particular viral peptide in association with class I MHC, its chances of binding strongly to the surface of the infected target cell are much less than those of the Tc cell. However, it is of interest that not only can antibody binding

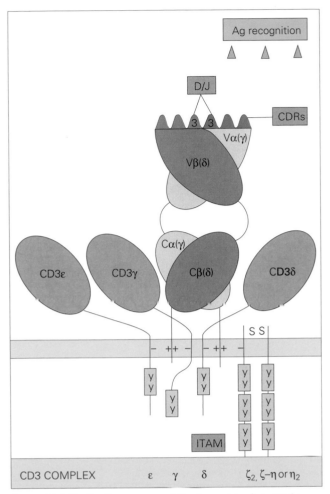

Figure 10.9 The T-cell receptor on αβ-T cells consists of an α and a β chain each composed of a variable (V) and a constant (C) domain resembling the immunoglobulin Fab antigen-binding fragment in structure. The highly variable (complementarity determining) regions (CDRs) on the variable domains contact the MHC-peptide antigen complex. This produces a signal which is transduced by the invariant CD3 complex composed of γ, δ, ε and ζ or η chains, through their cytoplasmic immune receptor tyrosine-based activation motifs (ITAM) which contact protein tyrosine kinases. γδ T cells (see below) have receptors composed of γ and δ chains as indicated in the figure.

to the target cell enhance NK cell potency (see Fig. 10.13) but both the Tc cell and the Th cell are capable of releasing IFNs, particularly IFNγ, which markedly improve the performance of the NK cell, so making a useful integrated system. An important additional responsibility of these IFNs is to render adjacent cells resistant to replication of viral particles, which gain entrance through intercellular transport mechanisms (Fig. 10.12).

EXTRACELLULAR ATTACK ON LARGE INFECTIOUS AGENTS

Defensive cells attack the antibody-coated surfaces of parasites

Where a parasite is demonstrably larger than a phagocytic cell, it is physically impossible for phagocytosis to occur. However, it is still possible for the defensive cells to deliver

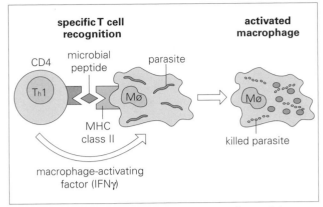

Figure 10.10 T-helper (Th1) cells trigger the killing of intracellular parasites within macrophages (Mφ). Recognition of the infected macrophage by the Th1 cell TCR results in lymphocyte activation with release of IFNγ. This then activates the macrophage, which turns on its microbicidal mechanisms to kill the intracellular parasite. Th17 helper cells subserve a similar role and are also thought to be a prominent factor in the pathogenesis of certain autoimmune disorders.

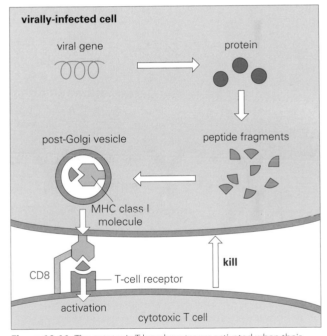

Figure 10.11 The cytotoxic T lymphocytes are activated when their specific cell surface receptors recognize an infected cell by binding to a surface MHC class I molecule that is associated with a peptide fragment derived from a degraded intracellular viral protein.

an extracellular attack on the surface of the parasite. This can occur through the phenomenon of 'antibody-dependent cellular cytotoxicity' (ADCC) in which effector cells bind through their surface receptors to antibody molecules coating the target cell (Fig. 10.13). The result of this interaction is to induce activation of the effector cell and the release of materials to damage the parasite target. Major cell types that indulge in this type of activity are:

- macrophages
- eosinophils
- NK cells.

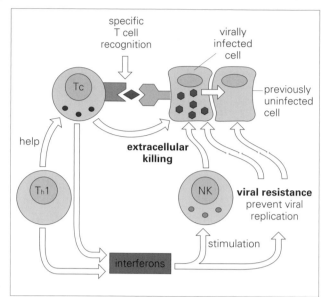

Figure 10.12 Cellular defences against viral infection. Cytotoxic T (Tc) cells specifically recognize surface MHC class I plus peptide derived from degraded viral protein and kill the infected cells before the virus replicates. Natural killer (NK) cells can do the same, though far less effectively; however, their activity is enhanced by interferons (IFNs) produced by Tc and Th1 cells. Local production of IFNs also prevents adjacent cells from becoming infected by intercellular viral transport.

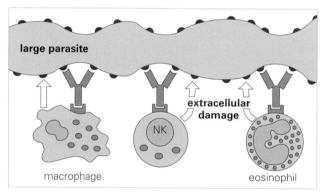

Figure 10.13 Antibody-dependent cellular cytotoxicity. Different effector cells bind to the parasite surface through their receptor for antibody and damage the parasite target. Macrophages burn the target cell surface by a stream of reactive oxygen intermediates generated by the respiratory oxygen burst, NK cells induce apoptosis by granzyme, TNF and Fas/FasL mechanisms, while eosinophils damage the target cell membrane by release of major basic protein, a perforin-like molecule and copious reactive oxygen metabolites. The antibodies mostly belong to the IgG class (see Fig. 10.1, Table 10.1).

LOCAL DEFENCES AT MUCOSAL SURFACES

The immune mechanisms involving the acute inflammatory response and T-cell-mediated systems operate well within the milieu of the body. It is worth examining, however, the special nature of the defences required to protect the body at the mucosal surfaces which face the exterior, for example in the lung and the gastrointestinal tract (Fig. 10.14).

The first line of defence aims to prevent the microbe from adhering to the mucosal surface. Adhesion to the mucosal

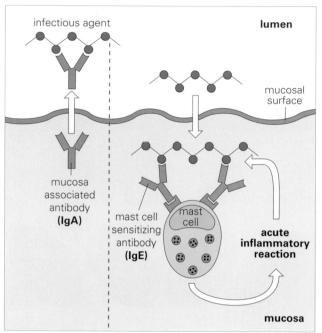

Figure 10.14 Defence of body mucosal surfaces. A specialized antibody associated with the mucosal surface – secretory immunoglobulin A (IgA) – is generated when mucosal IgA held as a dimer by J-chains (red in Fig. 10.1) is transported by the poly-Ig receptor across mucosal epithelium to the lumen where the major portion of the receptor remains bound to the IgA dimer as *secretory piece* and evidently protects the secretory IgA molecule from local adverse conditions. Secretory IgA blocks adherence of the microbe to the mucosa and hence entry into the body. An infectious agent gaining entrance to the body will fire IgE-sensitized mast cells, which cluster beneath the surface and generate a protective local acute inflammatory response by attracting complement-fixing antibodies, complement and polymorphs from the blood.

surface is a prerequisite for penetrating the body. To prevent this, there is the innate mechanism of mucus production. In addition, a special antibody, IgA, is synthesized by the lymphoid aggregates, some of which are organized (adenoids, tonsil, Peyer's patches), while others are less organized (lamina propria, lung, urinogenital tract). Together, these lymphoid aggregates constitute the mucosal-associated lymphoid tissue (MALT). The IgA is then actively transported by a carrier molecule, the so-called poly-Ig receptor, into the lumen and is associated with the mucosal surface in a high concentration where it continues to bear a portion of the carrier called 'secretory piece' (see Fig. 10.1). When coated with such IgA antibodies, the adhesion of infectious agents to the mucosa is greatly diminished, but they can still be captured by local macrophages with surface receptors for IgA. Mast cells tend to cluster in the submucosal region and, should a microorganism break through the mucosal barrier, it could encounter a mast cell that has bound the specialized IgE antibody to its surface; on reaction with this surface antibody, the mast cell is triggered to release mediators of the acute inflammatory reaction. By increasing vascular permeability, these mediators will bring about the flooding of the site with plasma proteins, including other classes of antibody and complement, while chemotactic agents will attract polymorphonuclear leukocytes.

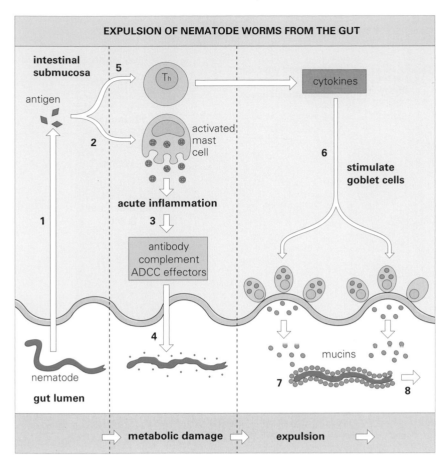

EXPULSION OF NEMATODE WORMS FROM THE GUT

Figure 10.15 Expulsion of nematode worms from the gut. Worm antigen (1) is thought to trigger an acute inflammatory reaction in the submucosa (2). This facilitates the recruitment of complement and possibly antibody-dependent cellular cytotoxicity (ADCC) effectors (3), which damage the parasite (4). Soluble factors (cytokines), released by antigen-specific triggering of T-helper cells (Th) (5), stimulate the secretion of mucins by goblet cells (6), which coat the worm (7) and aid its expulsion (8).

Larger parasites, such as nematodes, within the lumen of the gut pose special problems

It is thought that antigens derived from the nematode may penetrate the submucosal space and activate T and B cells and degranulate sensitized mast cells. The latter will produce an acute inflammation at the mucosal surface and almost certainly lead to an outflow of antibody, complement and probably effectors of ADCC into the lumen. In the lumen, the antibody, complement and effectors of ADCC can then interact with the parasite and inflict metabolic damage. In the meantime, the interaction with sensitized Th cells will lead to the release of soluble factors termed cytokines, which include a mediator capable of stimulating the goblet cells lining the intestinal villi. The goblet cells then release their mucins into the lumen where they coat the damaged parasite and facilitate expulsion from the body (Fig. 10.15).

A subset of T cells bearing $\gamma\delta$ receptors dominates the mucosal epithelium

In the human, T lymphocytes expressing $\alpha\beta$ receptors represent the large majority of T cells in the blood, but a subset composed of $\gamma\delta$ chains dominates the intestinal epithelium and skin. Unlike $\alpha\beta$ T cells, the $\gamma\delta$ subset can recognize antigen directly without the need for antigen processing. Heat shock proteins released from stressed or damaged cells are potent stimulators of $\gamma\delta$ T cells as are low molecular weight phosphate-containing non-proteinaceous antigens such as isopentenyl pyrophosphate and alkylamines which occur in a wide range of pathogens. $\gamma\delta$ T cells can also collaborate with mucosal epithelial cells expressing surface CD1 molecules (containing β_2 microglobulin but non-classical MHC-like chains) which have a hydrophobic cleft enabling them to present lipid and glycolipid microbial antigens such as lipoarabinomannan, the mycobacterial cell wall component.

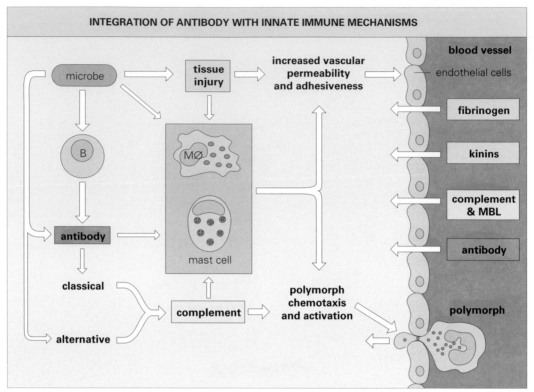

Figure 10.16 Integration of antibody with the innate immune mechanisms, leading to the production of a protective acute inflammatory reaction. The activated endothelial cells allow exudation of soluble proteins from the circulation and express accessory molecules, which aid the binding of the polymorphs to the capillary wall and their subsequent escape into the infected site. Mϕ, macrophage.

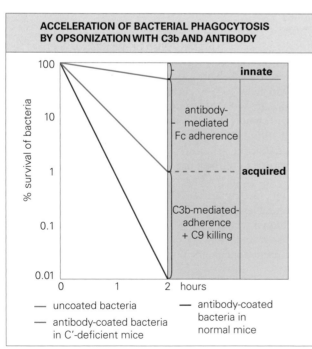

Figure 10.17 The slow rate of phagocytosis of uncoated bacteria (innate immunity) is increased many times by acquired immunity through coating with antibody and then C3b (opsonization). Killing may also take place through the C5–9 terminal complement components. This is a hypothetical but realistic situation; the natural proliferation of the bacteria has been ignored.

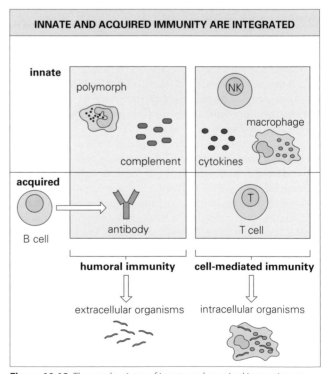

Figure 10.18 The mechanisms of innate and acquired immunity are integrated to provide the basis for humoral and cell-mediated immunity. Deficiencies of humoral immunity predispose to infection with extracellular organisms, and deficiencies of T-cell-mediated responses are associated primarily with intracellular infections.

KEY FACTS

- The evolution of the adaptive response has provided the body with a powerful series of mechanisms that extend and exploit the innate mechanisms of defence. Thus, this lymphocyte-mediated response greatly augments the innate defence against each particular infecting organism.

- In most cases, the effector mechanisms involve the innate systems of defence such as phagocytosis, complement activation and macrophage intracellular killing.

- Taking an overall view of the adaptive responses, humoral immunity mediated by antibody produced by B lymphocytes is effective in neutralizing bacterial toxins, and, by interacting with complement, mast cells and polymorphs, produces the acute inflammatory reaction (Fig. 10.16). This response is especially effective against extracellular microbes, and the 'quantum leap' provided by antibody in the clearance of extracellular bacteria from the blood is clearly shown in the example in Figure 10.17. The IgE-mediated acute inflammatory response and secreted IgA defend the mucosal surfaces against extracellular infections.

- In contrast, most T-cell-mediated responses are directed to intracellular organisms. The receptors on the majority of T cells are composed of α and β chains, each with a variable and constant domain resembling antibody Fab fragments. However, they recognize an infected cell as a target by binding to the surface major histocompatibility complex (MHC) molecule, which is a marker for a cell, linked to a peptide derived by degradation of intracellular microbial protein.

- $\alpha\beta$ T cells are divided into T-helper Th1, T-helper Th2, T-helper Th17, cytotoxic Tc cells and regulatory T cells. CD4 Th1 and Th17 cells recognize class II MHC on macrophages and produce soluble factors (cytokines), first chemotactic factors to attract, and second IFNγ, to activate phagocytic cells to switch on their intracellular antimicrobial mechanisms. CD4 Th2 cells recognize class II MHC on B cells and help them to produce antibody. CD8 Tc cells recognize MHC class I on most cells and are effective against viruses, killing virally infected targets and preventing the spread of virus through the local production of interferons. Tc cells can also be divided into subsets expressing either Th1- or Th2-type cytokine patterns. The different classes of regulatory cells which provide overall control of T-cell proliferation and, in particular, police the activity of any self-reacting T cells which have escaped elimination in the thymus are discussed in the next chapter (see Fig. 11.15 and Fig. 11.16). A subset expressing $\gamma\delta$ receptors dominates in the intestinal epithelium and skin and recognizes heat shock stress proteins and microbial non-proteinaceous phosphate-containing antigens without the need for antigen processing.

- Figure 10.18 emphasizes the close interactions between innate and acquired mechanisms leading to defence against extracellular microorganisms, on the one hand, and intracellular infections, on the other. In keeping with these concepts, deficiencies in humoral immunity from whatever cause, predispose the individual to infection by extracellular organisms, whereas defects in T-cell-mediated responses are primarily associated with intracellular infections.

- The first contact with antigen evokes a response that leaves behind a memory of the encounter so that the subsequent response to a second contact with antigen is more powerful and evolves more rapidly than on the first occasion. The cellular bases for these phenomena are explained in Chapter 11. The production of memory by a primary interaction with antigen provides the basis for vaccination, where the first contact is with an avirulent form of the microorganism or its component antigens.

- The other point to stress at this stage is the specificity of memory – infection with measles, for example, produces a subsequent immunity to that virus, but does not afford protection against an unrelated virus such as mumps.

The cellular basis of adaptive immune responses

11

Introduction

As we saw in a previous chapter, adaptive immune responses are generated by lymphocytes (Fig. 11.1), which are derived from stem cells differentiating within the primary lymphoid organs (bone marrow and thymus). From there, they colonize the secondary lymphoid tissues where they mediate the immune responses to antigens (Fig. 11.2). The lymph nodes are concerned with responses to antigens which are carried into them from the tissues, while the spleen is concerned primarily with antigens

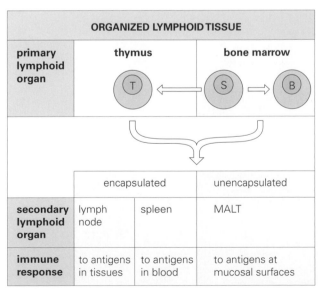

Figure 11.1 Lymphocytes and plasma cells. (1) Small B and T lymphocytes have a round nucleus and a high nuclear:cytoplasmic ratio. (2) A large granular lymphocyte with a lower nuclear:cytoplasmic ratio, an indented nucleus and azurophilic cytoplasmic granules. Fewer than 5% of T helper cells, and 30–50% of cytotoxic T cells, γδ T cells and natural killer (NK) cells have this morphology. (3) Antibody formed when B cells differentiate into plasma cells, here stained with fluoresceinated anti-human IgM (green) and rhodaminated anti-human IgG (red) showing extensive intracytoplasmic staining. Note that plasma cells produce only one class of antibody as the distinct staining reveals. (1 and 2, stained with Giemsa, courtesy of A. Stevens and J. Lowe; 3, adapted from: Zucker-Franklin A. et al. (1988) *Atlas of Blood Cells: Function and Pathology*, 2nd edn, Vol. 11, Milan: EE Ermes; Philadelphia: Lea and Febiger.)

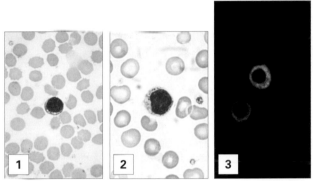

Figure 11.2 Organized lymphoid tissue. Stem cells (S) arising in the bone marrow differentiate into immunocompetent B and T cells in the primary lymphoid organs. These cells then colonize the secondary lymphoid tissues where immune responses are organized. MALT, mucosa-associated lymphoid tissue.

which reach it from the bloodstream (Fig. 11.3). Communication between these tissues and the rest of the body is maintained by a pool of recirculating lymphocytes which pass from the blood into the lymph nodes, spleen and other tissues and back to the blood by the major lymphatic channels such as the thoracic duct (Fig. 11.4). This traffic of lymphocytes between the tissues, the bloodstream and the lymph nodes enables antigen-sensitive cells to seek the antigen and to be recruited to sites at which a response is occurring. In addition, unencapsulated

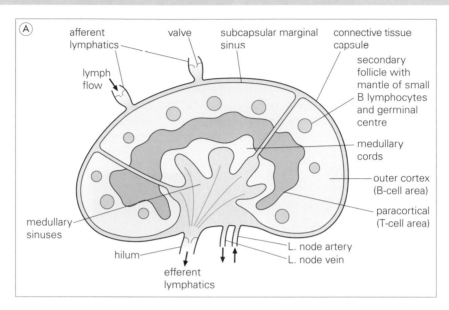

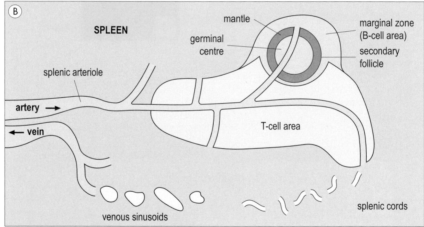

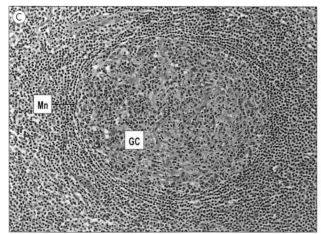

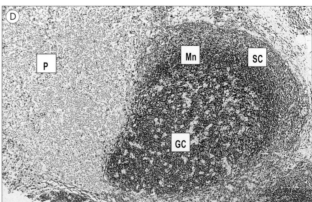

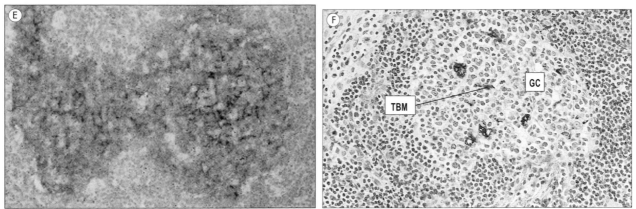

Figure 11.3 Structure of a lymph node and spleen. (A) Diagrammatic representation of section through a whole lymph node. The cortex is essentially a B-cell region where differentiation within the germinal centres of secondary follicles to antibody-forming plasma cells and memory cells occurs. (B) Diagrammatic representation of spleen showing B- and T-cell areas. (C) Structure of a secondary follicle. A large germinal centre (GC) is surrounded by the mantle zone (Mn). (D) Distribution of B cells in lymph node cortex. Immunochemical staining of B cells for surface immunoglobulin shows that they are concentrated largely in the secondary follicle, germinal centre (GC), mantle zone (Mn), and between the capsule and the follicle – the subcapsular zone (SC). A few B cells are seen in the paracortex (P), which contains mainly T cells. (E) Follicular dendritic cells in a secondary lymphoid follicle. This lymph node follicle is stained with enzyme-labelled monoclonal antibody to demonstrate follicular dendritic cells. (F) Germinal centre macrophages. Immunostaining for cathepsin D shows several macrophages localized in the germinal centre (GC) of a secondary follicle. These macrophages, which phagocytose apoptotic B cells, are called tingible body macrophages (TBM). (Courtesy of A. Stevens and J. Lowe; C–F reproduced from Male D, Brostoff J, Roth DB, Roitt I. *Immunology*, 7th edition, 2006. Mosby Elsevier, with permission.)

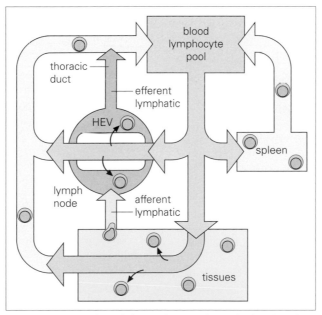

Figure 11.4 Lymphocyte traffic. The lymphocytes move through the circulation and enter the lymph nodes via the specialized endothelial cells of the postcapillary venules (HEVs). They leave through the efferent lymphatic vessels and pass through other nodes, finally entering the thoracic duct which empties into the circulation at the left subclavian vein (in humans). Lymphocytes enter the white pulp areas of the spleen in the marginal zones; they pass into the sinusoids of the red pulp and leave via the splenic vein. (Adapted from: Roitt, I. M., Brostoff, J., Male, D. (2002) *Immunology*, 6th edn. London: Elsevier Science.)

aggregates of lymphoid tissue termed 'mucosa-associated lymphoid tissue' or MALT, lie in the mucosal surface where they have the job of responding to antigens from the environment, particularly the heavy bacterial load in the intestine, by producing IgA antibodies for mucosal secretions. The lymphocytes which constitute the MALT system recirculate between these mucosal tissues using specialized homing receptors (Fig. 11.5).

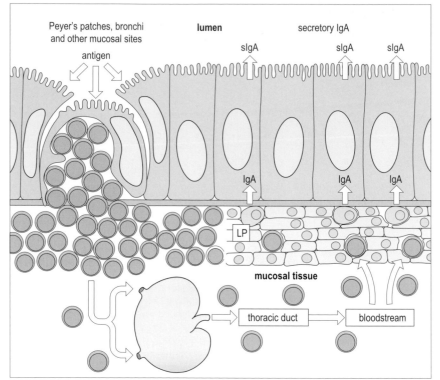

Figure 11.5 Mucosa-associated lymphoid tissue (MALT). Lymphoid cells which are stimulated by antigen in Peyer's patches (or the bronchi or another mucosal site) migrate via the regional lymph nodes and thoracic duct into the bloodstream and thence to the lamina propria (LP) of the gut or other mucosal surfaces which might be close to or distant from the site of priming. Thus lymphocytes stimulated at one mucosal surface may become distributed selectively throughout the MALT system. This is mediated through specific adhesion molecules on the lymphocytes and the mucosal high-walled endothelium of the postcapillary venules. (Adapted from: Roitt IM, Brostoff J, Male D. (2002) *Immunology*, 6th edn. London: Elsevier Science.)

B- AND T-CELL RECEPTORS

B and T cells can be distinguished by their surface markers

As they differentiate into populations with differing functions, B and T cells acquire molecules on their surface that reflect these specializations. It is possible to produce homogeneous antibodies of a single specificity, termed 'monoclonal antibodies', that can recognize such surface markers. When laboratories from all over the world compared the monoclonal antibodies they had raised, it was found that groups or clusters of monoclonal antibodies were each recognizing a common molecule on the surface of the lymphocyte. Each surface component so defined was referred to as a 'CD' molecule (Table 11.1), where CD refers to a 'cluster of differentiation'.

Each lymphocyte expresses an antigen receptor of unique specificity on its surface

Among the surface markers on the B and T cells referred to above are the receptors on the plasma membrane which are used to identify foreign antigens. B cells possess surface immunoglobulin, whereas the T-cell receptor (TCR) on the surface of the T lymphocyte acts as an antigen recognition unit (see Fig. 10.9). We now know that despite the very large number of different components that could be combined together in multiple ways to give a diversity of surface receptors, each B lymphocyte rearranges its germline genes coding for these receptors so that it selects one and only one of the specifici-

ties for each receptor polypeptide chain. It then expresses that receptor molecule on its surface (Fig. 11.6). Once this occurs, the other genes coding for these antigen receptors in the lymphocyte are no longer used. In other words, following this genetic rearrangement process, the lymphocyte becomes committed to the synthesis and expression of a single receptor type. An analogous process occurs in the rearrangement of the αβ and γδ genes coding for the TCR. Just as for B cells, each T cell expresses one and only one specific combination of receptor peptides, and therefore shows a single specificity to which it is committed for the whole of its lifespan.

CLONAL EXPANSION OF LYMPHOCYTES

Antigen selects and clonally expands lymphocytes bearing complementary receptors. As there are such a large number of different possible specificities that lymphocytes can express, perhaps of the order of millions, there must of necessity be only a relatively small number of particular specificities to which lymphocytes are committed. Thus, when a microbe invades the body, the total number of lymphocytes initially committed to recognizing the antigens that go to make up a particular microbe is relatively small, and must be expanded to provide a sufficient number to protect the host. Evolution has provided a masterful solution to this problem. When a microbe enters the body, its component antigens combine with only those B lymphocytes whose surface receptors are complementary to the shape of these antigens.

Table 11.1 Surface markers on B and T cells

Function/identity	*CD designation	B cells	T cells
Antigen receptors			
Surface immunoglobulin	–	+ +	–
T cell αβ, γδ	–	–	+ +
TCR signal transducer	CD3	–	+ +
Receptors for			
Leukocyte function antigen-3 (LFA-3)	CD2	–	+ +
MHC class II (T helpers)	CD4	–	+ +
MCH class I (cytotoxic T cells)	CD8	–	+ +
Complement (CR2)	CD21	+ +	–
Complement (CR1)	CD35	+ +	+
IgG (FcγIIR)	CDw32	+ +	–
IgE (FcεR)	CD23	+	–
Interleukin-2 (IL-2 α-chain)	CD25	act[a]	act[a]
CD40L	CD40	+ +	–
MHC			
Class I	–	+ +	+ +
Class II	–	+ +	act[a]
Other markers			+ +
Differentiation marker	CD5	Subset	Memory
Restricted leukocyte common antigen	CD45RO (man)	+	

[a]Activated cells and regulatory T cells (Tregs). IL, interleukin; MHC, major histocompatibility complex; TCR, T-cell receptor; Fc, dimer of immunoglobulin heavy chain excluding the Fab V_H and C_H1 domains in Fig. 10.1; CD40L, CD40 ligand (CD154).
*The CD marker is established by international consensus as identified by a given cluster of monoclonal antibodies.

The B cells that bind the antigen become activated and proliferate clonally under the influence of soluble growth factors termed cytokines (see section on Cytokines below) to form a large population of cells derived from the original (Fig. 11.7). The majority of these events occur within the lymphoid structure known as a germinal centre (see Fig. 11.3).

In the case of B cells, a large proportion of the clonally expanded lymphocytes become plasma cells (see Fig. 11.1), dedicated to the synthesis and secretion of antibodies. Since these plasma cells are derived from a parent cell that is already committed to the production of only one specific antibody, the final product is identical to the molecule that was posted on the surface of the original antigen-recognizing cell. Or at least almost so, because somatic mutation of the lymphocytes within the germinal centres which are synthesizing this antibody fine tunes the binding efficiency of the eventual product. The net result is that we have the production of large amounts of antibody which, like that on the surface of the parent cell, can combine with the invading antigen (Fig. 11.7).

A similar process of clonal selection and expansion occurs with T cells, producing a large number of T-cell effectors with the same specificity as the original parent cell; some of these cells release cytokines, whereas others have cytotoxic functions so that they act as effectors of T-cell-mediated immunity. One difference between T and B cells is that the T-cell receptors do not undergo further selection as a result of somatic mutation. Of crucial significance is the fact that in the case of both B and T cells, a fraction of the clonally expanded population differentiates into resting memory cells (Fig. 11.7). Thus, more cells are capable of recognizing the microbial antigen in any subsequent infection than in the initial virgin population that existed before the primary infection occurred. Human memory T cells can be identified by surface markers such as CD45RO, while memory B cells express CD27 and surface IgG, IgA or IgE.

THE ROLE OF MEMORY CELLS

Vaccination depends upon secondary immune responses being bigger and brisker than primary responses

In general, memory cells, as compared with naive cells, are more readily stimulated by a given dose of antigen. This occurs because they have greater combining power, in the case of B cells through mutation and selection during the primary response, and for T cells, which do not undergo affinity maturation, through increased expression of accessory adhesion molecules, CD2, LFA-1, LFA-3 and intercellular adhesion molecule-1 (ICAM-1), which enable the lymphocyte to bind more strongly to the specialized cells which present antigen. These factors, combined with the increased number of lymphocytes specific for a given antigen present in the memory pool produced by the primary response, result in a much stronger antibody or T-cell response on second contact with antigen. This provides the principle for vaccination (Fig. 11.8). The microbe or antigen to be used for vaccination is modified in such a way that it no longer produces disease or damage, but still retains the majority of its antigenic shapes. The primary response produced by the vaccination gives rise to a pool of memory cells, which can generate an abundant secondary response on subsequent contact with the antigen during a natural infection. Memory is usually long-lived, often extending over many years. There are many possible reasons for this: memory cells themselves may be innately long-lived or they may be sustained by gentle proliferation through subsequent contact with antigen present in reservoirs within the body or introduced by

DNA

V_H D J C_μ

5' ▬■▬■■▬■□ 3'   heavy chain genes

V_L J κ(λ)

5' ▬■▬■■▬ 3'   light chain genes

immature B cell

germline configuration of heavy and light chain DNA

DNA

V_H D J C_μ

■■■□

V_L J κ

■■■

differentiating B cell

with rearranged variable region receptor DNA

mRNA

V_H D J C_μ

■■■■

V_L J κ

■■■

IgM

sIgM$_m$

immunocompetent B cell

spliced transcribed RNA codes for individual IgM$_m$ monomer, which is expressed on the surface (sIgM$_m$) and displays the unique specific binding site for antigen

Figure 11.6 Differentiation events leading to the expression of unique IgM monomer sIgM on the surface of an immunocompetent B lymphocyte. There are of the order of 50 germline V_H genes encoding the major portion of the variable region, with 25 minigenes encoding the D segment and six, the J region. As the cell differentiates, V_H, D and J segments on one chromosome randomly fuse to generate lymphocytes with a very wide range of individual heavy chain variable domains. Variable region light chain domains are then formed by random V_L to J recombination. Finally, the variable and constant region genes respectively recombine to encode a single antibody molecule which is expressed on the mature B-cell surface as an sIgM antigen receptor. When activated for antibody production, the transmembrane segment of IgM, which normally holds the molecule on the surface is spliced out at the RNA stage and the soluble form of the IgM is secreted. Subsequently, heavy chain constant region gene switch can occur to generate the various immunoglobulin classes, IgG, IgA, etc. Leader sequences have been omitted for simplicity.

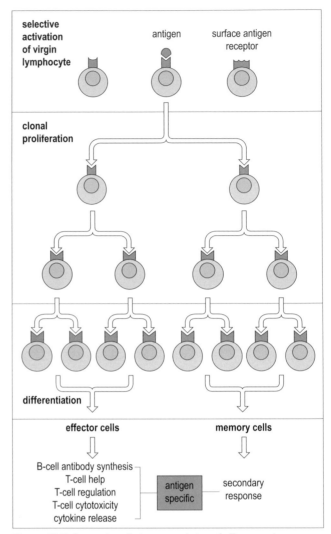

Figure 11.7 Generation of a large population of effector and memory cells by clonal proliferation after primary contact of B or T cell with antigen. A fraction of the progeny of the original antigen-reactive lymphocytes become non-dividing memory cells, whereas the others become the effector cells of humoral or cell-mediated immunity. Memory cells require fewer cycles before they develop into effectors, thus shortening the reaction time for the secondary response.

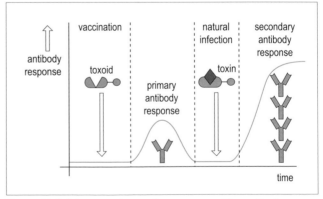

Figure 11.8 Primary and secondary responses. The antibody response on the second contact with antigen is more rapid and more intense. Therefore, following vaccination with a benign form of the antigen (in the example shown, a chemically modified form of tetanus toxin where the toxic element has been destroyed) to produce a primary response, subsequent contact with antigen in the form of a natural infection evokes the more efficient secondary response.

subclinical infection. An alternative mechanism in the case of T cells may be through stimulation by the cytokine IL-15 and in the case of B cells by anti-idiotypes (anti-antibodies produced in response to the combining region of the first antibody which may stimulate the memory B cells by 'tweaking' their surface receptors).

STIMULATION OF LYMPHOCYTES

T lymphocytes are activated by antigen presented on specialized cells

Naive T cells are potently stimulated by interdigitating dendritic cells (IDC), which are specialized antigen-presenting cells (APCs). Immature IDCs in the tissues take up antigen which is then processed and presented on the surface as a peptide complexed with MHC class II. The IDC migrates to the T-cell region of the draining lymph node, where it stimulates several T lymphocytes with which it makes contact through recognition of the MHC-peptide complex by the specific T-cell receptor, and by accessory interaction of the B7 co-stimulator with surface CD28 and by production of various cytokines which control the differentiation of distinct T-cell subsets (Fig. 11.9).

As noted above, primed T cells are more readily stimulated by antigen than naive cells, and in this case, macrophages can function as the antigen-presenting cell.

Some antigens stimulate B cells without the need for intervention by T lymphocytes

These so-called T-independent antigens are of two main types:

1. Antigens of the first type contain molecular features that enable them to stimulate a wide variety of B cells independently of their specific antigen receptors; they are therefore referred to as 'polyclonal activators'. Those B cells carrying surface receptors that recognize epitopes on the polyclonal activator attract the molecule to their surfaces and are preferentially stimulated relative to the remainder of the B-cell population (Fig. 11.10).

2. The second type of T-independent antigen involves repeating determinants presented on the surface of specialized macrophages located within the marginal zone associated with splenic secondary follicles with germinal centres or within the lymph node subcapsular sinus (see Fig. 11.3A, B), which can cross-link immunoglobulin receptors on the B cell and apparently stimulate the lymphocyte directly (Fig. 11.10).

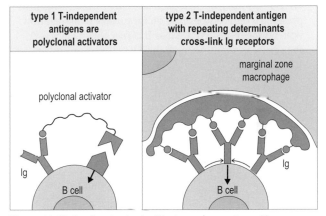

Figure 11.10 B-cell activation by T-independent antigens. The requirements for an antigen-presenting cell (APC) for type 2 antigens are still uncertain. Ig, immunoglobulin.

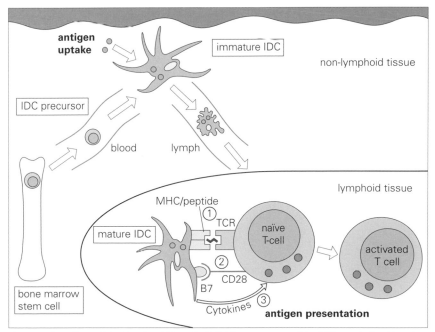

Figure 11.9 Migration and maturation of interdigitating dendritic cells (IDC). The precursors of the IDCs are derived from bone marrow stem cells. They travel via the blood to non-lymphoid tissues. These immature IDCs, e.g. Langerhans cells in skin, are specialized for antigen uptake. Subsequently, they travel via the afferent lymphatics to take up residence within secondary lymphoid tissues, where they express high levels of MHC class II and co-stimulatory molecules such as B7. These cells are highly specialized for the activation and differentiation of naive T cells which are effected through three signals: (1) TCR binding to MHC-peptide complex, (2) B7–CD28 co-stimulation and (3) cytokine release. (Reproduced with minor additions with permission from: Roitt, I. M. and Delves, P. J. (2001) *Roitt's Essential Immunology*, 10th edn. Oxford: Blackwell Science.)

One feature of both these types of T-independent antigen is that they give rise mainly to low-affinity IgM rather than IgG antibody responses and rarely induce a memory response.

Antibody production frequently requires T-cell help

The majority of antigens will stimulate B cells only if they have the assistance of T-lymphocyte helper (Th) cells. The sequence of events is as follows:

- In stage 1, the antigen is processed by an antigen-presenting cell and primes a Th cell with a complementary receptor on its surface as described above.
- In stage 2, a B cell with surface receptors complementary to an epitope on the original antigen captures the antigen on its receptor, internalizes it and, after processing, also presents a derived peptide on its surface in association with endogenous MHC class II molecules. This is the complex against which the Th cell was originally primed, and recognition of the processed antigen by the primed Th cell and of CD40 by the co-stimulatory CD40L causes activation of the B cell, with subsequent activation, proliferation and maturation (Fig. 11.11).

It should be noted that although the Th cell recognizes a processed determinant of the antigen, the B cell is programmed to make only antibody with the same specificity as its surface receptor, and therefore the antibodies that finally result will be directed against the epitope on the antigen recognized by the B-cell surface receptor.

B cells proliferate, are selected for high affinity and differentiate into plasma cell precursors and memory cells in the germinal centres.

Histological features of the important centre for antibody formation, the germinal centre, were presented in Figure 11.3. In essence, the germinal centre consists of a dark zone and a light zone: the dark zone is the site where one or a few B cells enter the primary lymphoid follicle and undergo active proliferation leading to clonal expansion. These B cells are termed 'centroblasts' and undergo a process of 'somatic hypermutation', which leads to the generation of cells with a wide range of affinities for antigen. In the light zone, B cells ('centrocytes') encounter the antigen on the surface of follicular dendritic cells (see Fig. 11.3E) and only those cells with higher affinity for antigen survive. Cells with mutated antibody receptors of lower affinity die by apoptosis and are phagocytosed by germinal centre macrophages.

Selected centrocytes interact with germinal centre CD4+ Th cells and undergo 'class switching' (i.e. replacement of their originally expressed immunoglobulin heavy chain constant region genes by another class – for instance IgM to IgG, IgA or IgE – which subserve different functions (cf. Table 10.1).

The selected germinal centre B cells differentiate into 'memory B cells' or 'plasma cell' precursors and leave the germinal centre (Fig. 11.12).

CYTOKINES

Cytokines are soluble intercellular communication factors in the immune response

Interactions between the APC, the CD4 Th cell and the B cell are effected by the recognition of processed antigen in association with MHC class II molecules by the TCR and by cognate co-stimulatory surface interactions, B7/CD28 and CD40L/CD40, respectively, as indicated in Figure 11.11. Following this recognition process, the cells become activated and proliferate by releasing soluble factors termed cytokines (Table 11.2), which react with appropriate complementary surface receptors on the target cell. For example, in the activated T cell, the gene encoding the IL-2 receptor (IL-2R) is derepressed and the IL-2R molecule is expressed on the surface of the lymphocytes. A subpopulation of Th cells is also induced to synthesize IL-2, which acts as a growth factor for T cells by combining with the IL-2R, causing proliferation (see Fig. 11.7).

Cytokine production helps to define T-helper subsets (cf. Table 10.2)

Helper T-cell clones generated by antigenic stimulation can be divided into three main types with distinct cytokine secretion phenotypes (Fig. 11.13). This makes biological sense in that Th1 cells producing cytokines such as IFNγ would be especially effective against intracellular infections with viruses and organisms which grow in macrophages, while Th2 cells are very good helpers for B cells and would

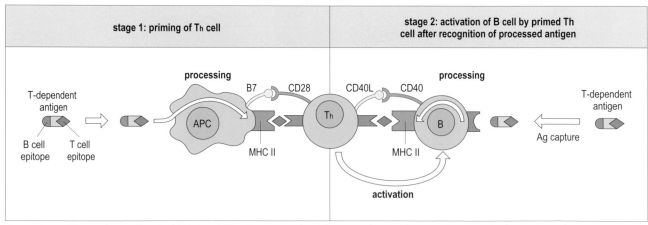

Figure 11.11 The mechanism by which T-helper (Th) cells are primed and then stimulate B cells to synthesize antibody to T-dependent antigens with the help of the cognate co-stimulatory pairs B7/CD28 and CD40L/CD40. See text for a detailed description of the sequence of events. Ag, antigen; APC, antigen-presenting cell; MHC, major histocompatability complex; CD40L, CD40 ligand.

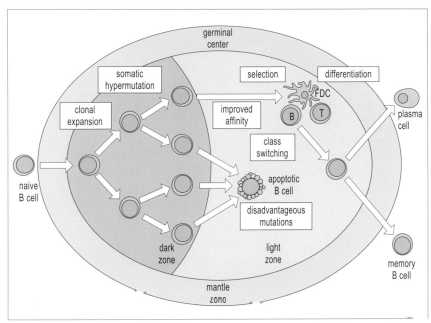

Figure 11.12 Structure and function of the germinal center. One or a few B cells (founder cells) in the dark zone proliferate actively. This proliferation leads to clonal expansion and is accompanied by somatic hypermutation of the immunoglobulin V region genes. B cells with the same specificity, but various affinities, are therefore generated. In the light zone, B cells with disadvantageous mutations or with low affinity undergo apoptosis (Fig. 11.3F) and are phagocytosed by macrophages. Cells with appropriate affinity encounter the antigen on the surface of the follicular dendritic cells (FDCs) and, with the help of CD4⁺ T cells, undergo class switching, leaving the follicle as memory B cells or plasma cells precursors. (Reproduced from Male D, Brostoff J, Roth DB, Roitt I. *Immunology*, 7th edition, 2006. Mosby Elsevier, with permission.)

Table 11.2 Known cytokines (hormones of the immune system) and their actions

Factor	Source	Actions
IL-1 α/β	Macrophages	Acute phase proteins
IL-2	T cells	T-cell proliferation
IL-3	T cells	Pluripotent growth
IL-4	T cells	B-cell proliferation and IgE selection, Th1 suppression
IL-5	T cells	B-cell growth, IgA and eosinophil differentiation
IL-6	T cells	B-cell differentiation, induce acute phase proteins
IL-7	T cells	B- and T-cell proliferation
IL-8	T cells	Chemotaxis and activation of PMN
IL-9	T cells	Mast cell growth
IL-10	T cells	Inhibition of Th1 cytokine production
IL-11	BM stromal cells	Osteoclast formation, CSF inhibits proinflammatory cytokine production
IL-12	Monocytes, Mφ	Induction of Th1 cells
IL-13	T cells	Inhibits mononuclear phagocyte inflammation: proliferation and differentiation of B cells
IL-14	T cells	Proliferation of activated B cells, inhibits Ig secretion
IL-15	Antigen-presenting cells	Proliferation of T-, NK and activated B cells; maintenance of T-memory cells
IL-16	CD8⁺ T cells and eosinophils	Chemotaxis of CD4 T cells
IL-17	CD4⁺ T cells	Proinflammatory; stimulates production of cytokines including TNFα, IL-1β, IL-6, IL-8, G-CSF
IL-18	Macrophages	Induces IFNγ production by T cells; enhances NK cytotoxicity
IL-21	Th cells	NK differentiation; B activation; T cell co-stimulation induces acute phase reactants
IL-22	T cells	Inhibits IL-4 production by Th 2; induces production of antimicrobial proteins by epithelial cells
IL-23	Dendritic cells	Induces proliferation and IFNγ production by Th1 T cell; induces proliferation of memory cells
IFNα	Leukocytes	Antiviral, stimulates IL-12 production and NK cells, induction MHC class I, anti-proliferative
IFNβ	Fibroblasts, epithelia	Antiviral, induction MHC class I, anti-proliferative
IFNγ	T cells, NK cells	Antiviral, activation of macrophages, inhibition of Th 2 cells, MHC class I and II induction
TNFα	Monocytes, T cells	Cytotoxicity, cachexia, fever

Continued

Table 11.2 Known cytokines (hormones of the immune system) and their actions—cont'd

Factor	Source	Actions
Lymphotoxin (TNFβ)	T cells	Cytotoxicity, cachexia, fever
TGFβ	T cells/macrophages	Inhibits activation of NK and T cells, macrophages; inhibits proliferation of B and T cells, promotes wound healing
GM-CSF	T cells	Growth of granulocytes and monocytes
G-CSF	Macrophages	Growth of granulocytes
M-CSF	Macrophages	Growth of monocytes
MIF	T cells, macrophages	Migration inhibition and activation of macrophages
Steel factor	BM stromal cells	Stem cell division (c-*kit* ligand)

BM, bone marrow; G-CSF, granulocyte colony stimulating factor; GM-CSF, granulocyte-macrophage colony stimulating factor; IFN, interferon; IL, interleukin; M-CSF, macrophage colony stimulating factor; NK, natural killer cell; PMN, polymorphonuclear lymphocyte; TGF, transforming growth factor; TNFβ, tumour necrosis factor β.

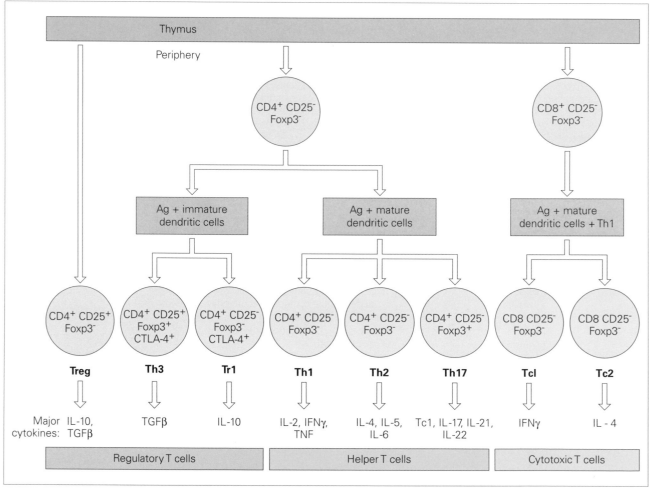

Figure 11.13 Differentiation of thymus-derived T cells into effector subsets and their major secretory cytokine patterns. The various cytokines are listed in Table 11.2. IL-10 is not listed; although classed as a Th2 cytokine in the mouse, it is produced by Th1 and Th2 cells in the human. γδ T cells differentiate as a distinct line from double negative (CD4⁻ CD8⁻) thymic precursors as do NKT cells. Activation of naive cells to become effectors is always accompanied by generation of memory cells. CD25, IL-2 receptor α-chain; Foxp3, forkhead/winged helix transcription factor, mutations in which lead to dysregulation and autoimmunity; CTLA-4, a down-regulatory factor which binds the B7 co-stimulator (see Fig. 11.9).

seem to be adapted for defence against parasites which are vulnerable to IL-4-switched IgE, IL-5-induced eosinophilia and IL-3/4-stimulated mast cell proliferation. The skewing of phenotype towards the extreme Th1/Th2 patterns occurs during the immune response and is partly determined by the nature of the antigen stimulus. There is mutual antagonism between these two subsets in that IL-4 down-regulates Th1 cells and IFNγ suppresses the activity of Th2 lymphocytes. The third helper subset, Th17, secretes powerfully proinflammatory cytokines, and worthy of note is the production of IL-22 which stimulates epithelial cells to produce microbicidal proteins active against bacteria and fungi. It now appears that these cells play a prominent role in the pathogenesis of several autoimmune disorders, but that is another

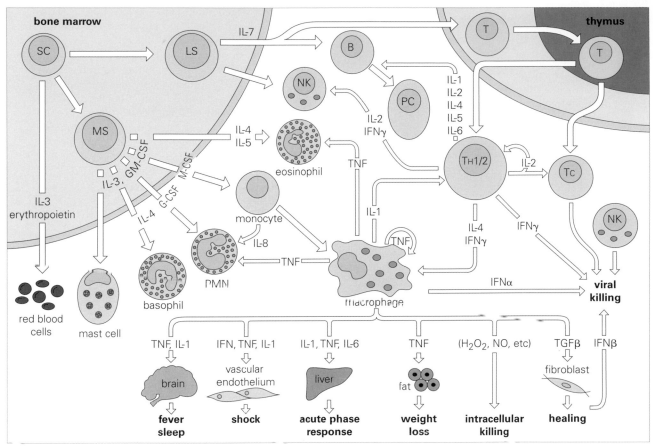

Figure 11.14 Cellular interactions mediated by cytokines. As described above, T-helper (Th) cells tend to skew into three major subsets: Th1, producing interleukin-2 (IL-2) and interferon-γ (IFNγ), which activate macrophage-mediated chronic inflammatory reactions; Th2, producing IL-4, IL-5 and IL-6, which act to support B-cell antibody responses and Th17 secreting proinflammatory cytokines including IL-22 which stimulate the production of bactericidal and fungicidal proteins by epithelial cells (space and a desire not to further complicate the diagram have precluded Th17 inclusion in the figure). G-CSF, granulocyte colony stimulating factor; GM-CSF, granulocyte-macrophage colony stimulating factor; H₂O₂, hydrogen peroxide; LS, lymphoid stem cell; M-CSF, macrophage colony stimulating factor; MS, myeloid stem cell; NK, natural killer cell; NO, nitric oxide; PC, plasma cell; PMN, polymorphonuclear lymphocyte; SC, stem cell; Tc, cytotoxic T cell; TGFβ, transforming growth factor beta; TNF, tumour necrosis factor. (Adapted from: Playfair, J. H. L. (2001) *Immunology at a glance*, Oxford: Blackwell Science.)

story. Attention has been drawn to the existence of regulatory T-cell subsets which can mediate immunosuppressive effects and have been implicated in the maintenance of self-tolerance (see below). Figure 11.14 shows the broad sweep of the cytokine network and the involvement of many different cell types.

The recruitment of the different cells participating in the immune response to the optimal anatomical location is mediated by a very large number of relatively low molecular weight chemoattractant cytokines, termed chemokines, which act through surface receptors on their target cell. Families of chemokines are based on the spacing of conserved cysteine (C) residues. Thus, α-chemokines have a CXC structure and β-chemokines a CC structure. The receptors for the CXC chemokines are designated CXCR1, CXCR2 and so on and of course receptors for CC chemokines are CCR1 etc. Until recently, most chemokines had a descriptive name and acronym such as macrophage chemotactic protein (MCP-1), now designated CCL2, meaning it is a ligand for the CCR receptor family. Other prominent chemokines include IL-8 (now CXCL8), which potently attracts neutrophils, and RANTES (now CCL5), a general attractant for T, NK and dendritic cells plus monocytes, eosinophils and basophils to inflammatory

sites, and which binds to CCR5, a co-receptor used in the entry of macrophage-tropic strains of HIV-1 into cells.

REGULATORY MECHANISMS

Unlimited expansion of clones must be checked by regulatory mechanisms

Once lymphocyte clones are activated by antigen, they clearly cannot be allowed to go on dividing indefinitely, otherwise they would completely fill the body of the host. There are therefore several mechanisms regulating the expansion of these dividing lymphocytes.

One of the most important factors controlling the immune response is the concentration of antigen. There is, of course, a distinct evolutionary advantage in a system where the immune response is switched on by antigen and switched off when the antigen is no longer present. It is perhaps not surprising then that selective processes have guided the production of such a system in which the immune response is antigen-driven through the direct effect of antigen on the lymphocyte receptors. As the antigen is eliminated by metabolic catabolism and by clearance through the immune response, the stimulus to the immune system disappears.

Antibody itself has feedback potential

Immunoglobulin M (IgM) produced early in the response has a positive feedback, stimulating the response in its fledgling stages. In contrast, IgG in sufficient concentrations produces negative feedback and acts to down-regulate the immune response partly by antigen removal and, significantly, by cross-linking antigen bound to B-cell surface receptors with the down-regulatory IgG Fc receptor (FcγRIIB) through the V_H and Fc domains on the IgG specific antibody molecule respectively (Fig. 11.15).

Immune responses can be controlled by regulatory T cells

These cells function to prevent T cells, and by implication also B cells, from getting out of hand when responding to antigen and act to prevent autoimmunity by maintaining self-tolerance (see Fig. 11.17). They do not prevent initial T-cell activation but inhibit sustained responses and prevent chronic and potentially damaging immunopathology. Suppression is largely mediated through secretion of IL-10 and/or TGFβ.

A naturally occurring population of regulatory CD4+ cells (Tregs) expressing high levels of CD25 and the transcription

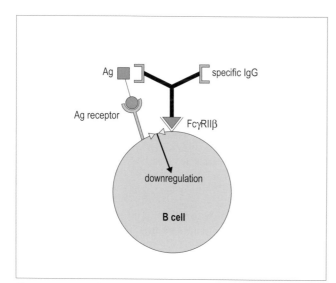

Figure 11.15 B-cell downregulation. The inhibitory FcγRIIB receptor is activated by the cross-linking through feedback IgG antibody and specific antigen as shown.

factor Foxp3 is generated in the thymus (see Fig. 11.13), and suppresses T-helper cells by direct cell–cell contact. Their role in the maintenance of self-tolerance is revealed by the development of autoimmunity induced by experimental depletion of this subset, or by mutations in the *Foxp3* gene. Induced Th3 and Tr1 cells are generated in the periphery by contact with antigen-pulsed immature dendritic cells and suppress T helpers by TGFβ or IL-10 cytokines, respectively.

An overview of the factors regulating immune responses is presented in Figure 11.16.

TOLERANCE MECHANISMS

Tolerance mechanisms prevent immunologic self-reactivity

To avoid reaction against the body's own components, it is essential for the immune system to develop non-reactivity or 'tolerance' to self molecules. In essence, it is thought that cells that are autoreactive are:

- eliminated by some form of clonal deletion
- made anergic early in the life of the cell
- sometimes silenced through T-regulatory cells later in life (Fig. 11.17).

T cells are more readily tolerized than B cells at a given antigen concentration

There is extremely good evidence that self molecules in the thymus can lead to the deletion or 'anergy' of the specific T-cell clone, although autoreactive T cells will survive if the concentration of MHC/self-peptide on the appropriate antigen-presenting cell is too low. B cells in contact with a relatively high concentration of self proteins are also subject to clonal deletion or anergy, but there is less need to tolerize other B cells in the sense that autoreactive B cells directed to thymus-dependent antigens will be unable to respond (helpless) if the corresponding Th cells to that molecule have been tolerized, be it through clonal deletion or suppression by T regulators (Fig. 11.17).

Unresponsiveness will also result if self components cannot be seen or recognized by the immune system. This may occur because over a long period of time the repertoire has lost the genes giving rise to autoreactive receptors. However, even if autoreactive T cells are present, they will not be activated if the self antigen (sAg) is anatomically secluded or is not presented

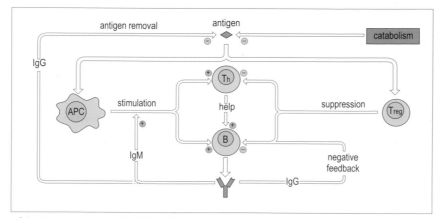

Figure 11.16 Regulation of the immune response. T help for cell-mediated immunity is subject to similar regulation. APC, antigen-presenting cell.

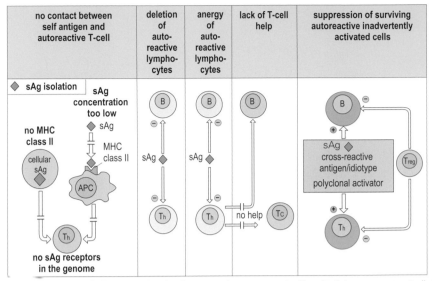

Figure 11.17 Mechanisms of self-tolerance. Self antigens (sAg) will not stimulate autoreactive Th cells if they are anatomically isolated, or if there is too low a concentration of processed peptide-major histocompatibility complex class II (MHC II) molecules, or if there is no MHC II on the cell. Both B and T cells can be silenced by clonal deletion or made anergic (still living, but unresponsive) by contact with self antigen. Too low a concentration of presented sAg will fail to silence differentiating immature lymphocytes bearing the cognate receptors, leading to the survival of populations of autoreactive T and B cells. Th cells are the most readily tolerized population, and surviving autoreactive B cells and cytotoxic T (Tc) cells cannot function without T-cell help. Furthermore, inadvertent stimulation of surviving autoreactive cells may be checked by regulatory T cells (Treg). Cells that are dead, unreactive or suppressed are shown in grey. APC, antigen-presenting cell. (Modified from: Delves P. J. et al. (2006) *Roitt's Essential Immunology*, 11th edn. Oxford: Blackwell Science.)

in processed form in combination with MHC class II molecules in adequate concentrations. Therefore, they will also be unable to react with processed sAg presented on the surface of cells that do not express class II. Since most cells express class I molecules, it seems reasonable to assume that the cytotoxic T (Tc) cells capable of reacting against cells expressing processed intracellular components have been deleted, are helpless or are suppressed. As mentioned above, the development of autoimmunity following deletion of the CD4+25+ population and normalization after restoration of this subset strongly suggest that autoreactive cells arising through inadvertent stimulation can be monitored and controlled by these regulatory T cells.

KEY FACTS

- Each lymphocyte expresses either antibody or a TCR with a single specificity for antigen.

- A lymphocyte bearing a complementary antibody or TCR on its surface will bind antigen, be activated, proliferate to form a clone, and differentiate into antibody-forming cells or effectors of cell-mediated immunity, and also form a large pool of memory cells.

- Second contact with antigen stimulates the pool of memory cells to produce a larger and faster response than the primary reaction. Therefore, vaccination with a benign form of the antigen prepares the individual for an effective response on second contact with the antigen during a natural infection.

- Many antigens require T-cell help before they can activate B cells, and subsequent proliferation is mediated by a variety of soluble cytokines.

- Unlimited expansion of clones is restricted by antigen concentration, antibody feedback, regulatory T cells and apoptosis.

- Reactivity to self is prevented by a variety of tolerance mechanisms.

The conflicts

Background to the infectious diseases

Introduction

Vertebrates have been continuously exposed to microbial infections throughout their hundreds of millions of years of evolution. Disease or death was the penalty for inadequate defences. Therefore they have developed:

- highly efficient methods for recognizing foreign invaders
- effective inflammatory and immune responses to restrain the growth and spread of foreign invaders and to eliminate them from the body.

The fundamental bases of these defences have been described in Chapters 9 and 10. If these defences were completely effective, microbial infections would be scarce and terminated rapidly, as microorganisms would not be allowed to persist in the body for long periods.

Microbes rapidly evolve characteristics that enable them to overcome the host's defences

Microorganisms faced with the antimicrobial defences of the host species have evolved and developed a variety of characteristics that enable them to bypass or overcome these defences and carry out their obligatory steps for survival (Table 12.1). Unfortunately, microorganisms evolve with extraordinary speed in comparison with their hosts. This is partly because they multiply much more rapidly, the generation time of an average bacterium being 1h or less compared with about 20 years for the human host. Rapid evolutionary change is also favoured in bacteria that can hand over genes (carried on plasmids) directly to other bacteria, including unrelated bacteria. Antibiotic resistance genes, for instance, can then be transferred rapidly between species. This rapid rate of evolution ensures that microbes are always many steps ahead of the host's antimicrobial defences. Indeed, if there are possible ways around the established defences, microorganisms are likely to have discovered and taken advantage of them. Infectious microorganisms therefore owe their success to this ability to adapt and evolve, exploiting weak points in the host's defences, as outlined in Table 12.2 and Figures 12.1, 12.2. The host, in turn, has had to respond to such strategies by slowly improving defences, adding extra features, and having multiple defence mechanisms with overlap and a good deal of duplication.

HOST–PARASITE RELATIONSHIPS

The speed with which host adaptive responses can be mobilized is crucial

Every infection is a race between the capacity of the microorganism to multiply, spread and cause disease and the ability of the host to control and finally terminate the infection (Fig. 12.1). For instance, a 24-h delay before an important

Table 12.1 Successful infectious microorganisms must take certain obligatory steps

Obligatory steps for infectious microorganisms		
Step	Requirement	Phenomenon
Attachment ± entry into body	Evade natural protective and cleansing mechanisms	Entry (infection)
Local or general spread in the body	Evade immediate local defences	Spread
Multiplication	Increase numbers (many will die in the host, or en route to new hosts)	Multiplication
Evasion of host defences	Evade immune and other defences long enough for the full cycle in the host to be completed	Microbial answer to host defences
Shedding from body (exit)	Leave body at a site and on a scale that ensures spread to fresh hosts	Transmission
Cause damage in host	Not strictly necessary but often occurs[a]	Pathology, disease

[a]The last step, causing damage in the host, is not strictly necessary, but a certain amount of damage may be essential for shedding. The outpouring of infectious fluids in the common cold or diarrhea, for instance, or the trickle from vesicular or pustular lesions, is required for transmission to fresh hosts.

Table 12.2 Host defences and microbial evasion strategies: mechanical and other barriers

Host's defences and the microbes' answer

	Defence	Microbial answer	Mechanism	Example
Mechanical and other barriers	Microbe rinsed away from epithelial surface by host secretions (plus ciliary activity in respiratory tract)	Bind firmly to epithelial surface	Surface molecule on microbe attaches to 'receptor' molecule on host epithelial cell	Influenza, rhinovirus, *Chlamydia*, gonococci
		Interfere with ciliary activity	Produce ciliotoxic/ciliostatic molecule	*Bordetella pertussis*, pneumococci, *Pseudomonas*
	Host cell membranes as barrier to microbe	Traverse host cell membrane	Fusion protein in viral envelope	Influenza, HIV
		Suffer up-take by phagocyte and resist killing	See below	See below
		Enter cell by active penetration	Microbial enzymes mediate cell penetration	Trypanosomes, *Toxoplasma gondii*
Phagocytic and immediate host defences	Microbe ingested and killed by phagocyte	Interfere with function (e.g. chemotaxis) of phagocyte or kill it (before or after phagocytosis)	Release leukocidins, antiphagocytic haemolysins, etc.	Staphylococci, streptococci, *Shigella*, *E. coli*, *Pseudomonas*
		Inhibit phagocytosis	Microbial outer wall or capsule impedes phagocytosis	Pneumococci, *Treponema pallidum*, *H. influenza*
		Inhibit phagosome–lysosome fusion	Sulphatides of *M. tuberculosis* inhibit fusion	*M. tuberculosis*
		Interfere with signal transduction in macrophage	Induction of SOCS* proteins	*Toxoplasma gondii*
		Resist killing and multiply in phagocyte	Unknown; may involve exit from phagosome (*Listeria*)	*Brucella* spp., *Listeria monocytogenes*, measles, dengue viruses
	Host molecules (lactoferrin, transferrin etc.) restrict availability of free iron needed by microbe	Microbe competes with host for iron	Microbe possesses avidly iron-binding siderophores	Pathogenic *Neisseria*, *E. coli*, *Pseudomonas*
	Complement activated with antimicrobial effects	Interfere with alternate pathway complement activation	Fully sialylated bacterial surface	K antigen of *E. coli*, Group B meningococci
		Inactivate complement components	Production of an elastase	*Pseudomonas aeruginosa*
		Interfere with complement-mediated phagocytosis	C3b receptor on microbe competes with that on phagocyte and complement access blocked	*Candida albicans*, *Toxoplasma gondii*, M protein of *Strep. pyogenes*
	Infected host produces interferons to inhibit virus replication	Induce a poor interferon response	Core antigen of hepatitis B suppresses IFNβ production	Hepatitis B, rotaviruses
		Insensitive to interferons	Prevent activation of interferon-induced enzymes	Adenovirus

Immune defences			
Infected host produces antibody	Destroy antibody	Bacterium liberates IgA protease	Gonococci, *H. influenzae*, streptococci
	Fail to induce protective antibody	Infection of follicular dendritic cells	Scrapie agents
	Display Fc receptor on microbial surface	Antibody bound to microbe in upside down position	Staphylococci (Protein A), trypanosomes, certain streptococci, herpes simplex virus, cytomegalovirus
	Microbial antigen (polysaccharide) projects beyond microbial surface	C activation occurs away from microbial surface and C-mediated damage is thus avoided	Gram-negative bacteria
	Avoid immune recognition	Acquire coating of host molecules	Hydatid disease, schistosomiasis
Infected host produces antimicrobial cell-mediated immune response	Invade T cells, and interfere with their function or kill them	Virus envelope molecule binds to CD4 on helper T-cell surface	HIV
	Switch on T cells or B cells non-specifically, non-productively	Polyclonal activation of T cells by release of T-cell mitogens	EB virus, *Mycoplasma pneumoniae*, staphylococcal toxins
	Induce regulatory T cells	Suppress beneficial immunity	*Bordetella pertussis*, *Mycobacterium tuberculosis*, *Helicobacter pylori*, HIV
Antimicrobial immune response recognizes infected cells and destroys them, or secretes cytokines with antimicrobial effects	Microbe in cells fails to display microbial antigens on cell surface	Antiviral antibody modulates and removes viral antigens	Measles
		Viral antigens not synthesized	Herpes simplex virus latent in sensory neurons
		Virus inhibits transport of MHC class I molecules to cell surface thus avoiding recognition by CD8 T cell	Cytomegalovirus, adenovirus
Antimicrobial immune responses	Infect glands or epithelial surfaces relatively inaccessible to circulating antibody or immune cells	Virus has tropism for cells in glands or on surfaces	Cytomegalovirus, rabies virus (salivary glands)
	Suppress immune responses	Invade immune cells	HIV, measles
	Vary microbial antigens in individual host, or during spread in host community	Switch on different surface antigens	*Trypanosoma* spp., *Borrelia recurrentis*
		Mutation, genetic recombination	Influenza virus, streptococci, gonococci
	Alter balance between Th1 (cell-mediated) and Th2 (antibody) responses	Induce non-protective rather than protective type of response	Lepromatous leprosy, *M. tuberculosis*

Microbes evolve fast and are generally one step ahead in this ancient conflict, but it must be remembered that the antimicrobial defences themselves represent the host's answer to invading microbes. Although inflammation is not listed as a host defence in its own right, many of these defences depend on local inflammation. Inflammation (see Ch. 9) means an increased blood supply and the delivery of antibodies, complement, immune cells and phagocytes to the site of infection. In the days before antibiotics, people applied hot poultices to staphylococcal boils and abscesses so as to increase the amount of inflammation and hasten recovery. Microbes that interfere with the action of complement or with chemotaxis (staphylococci, streptococci, *Pseudomonas aeruginosa*, herpes simplex viruses) will thereby tend to reduce inflammation.

* SOCS Suppressor of cytokine signalling.

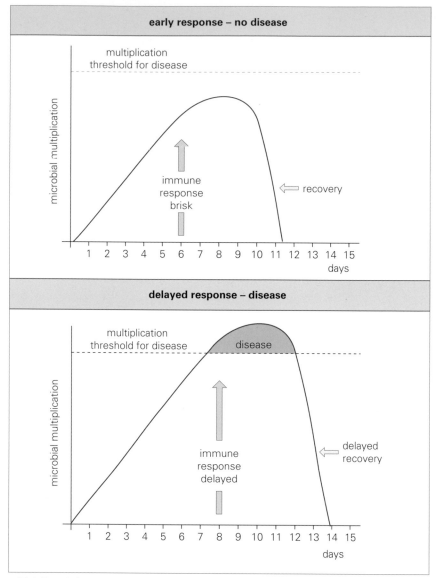

Figure 12.1 Every infection is a race. Delays in mobilizing host adaptive defences can lead to disease or death.

host response comes into operation can give a decisive advantage to a rapidly growing microorganism. From the host's point of view, it may allow enough damage to cause disease. More importantly, from the microbe's point of view, it may give the microbe the opportunity to be shed from the body in larger amounts or for an extra day or two. A microbe that achieves this will be rapidly selected for in evolution.

Adaptation by both host and parasite leads to a more stable balanced relationship

The picture of conflict between host and parasite, usually and appropriately described in military terms, is central to an understanding of the biology of infectious disease. As with military conflicts, adaptation on both sides (Box 12.1) tends to lessen the damage and incidence of death in the host population, leading to a more stable and balanced relationship. The successful parasite gets what it can from the host without causing too much damage, and in general, the more ancient the relationship, the less the damage. Many microbial parasites, not only the normal flora (see Ch. 8), but also polioviruses, meningococci

and pneumococci and others, live for the most part in peaceful coexistence with their human host.

Some microorganisms remain at body surfaces, perhaps spreading locally, but failing to invade deeper tissues. These include the common cold viruses, wart viruses, mycoplasmas and skin fungi. Often the disease is mild, but severe illness can occur when powerful toxins are produced and act either locally (cholera) or at distant sites (diphtheria).

Infecting microorganisms can gain entry and cause disease in four ways (Fig. 12.3). There are:

- microorganisms with specific mechanisms for attaching to, or penetrating, the body surfaces of normal healthy hosts (most viruses and certain bacteria)
- microorganisms introduced into normal healthy hosts by biting arthropods (e.g. malaria, plague, typhus, yellow fever)
- microorganisms introduced into otherwise normal healthy hosts via skin wounds or animal bites (clostridia, rabies, *Pasteurella multocida*)

Box 12.1 Lessons in Microbiology

Myxomatosis

Myxomatosis provides a well-studied classic example of the evolution of an infectious disease unleashed on a highly susceptible population. Myxomavirus, which is spread mechanically by mosquitoes, normally infects South American rabbits (*Sylvilagus brasiliensis*), but they remain perfectly well, developing only a virus-rich skin swelling at the site of the mosquito bite. The same virus in the European rabbit (*Oryctolagus cuniculus*) causes a rapidly fatal disease.

Myxomavirus was successfully introduced into Australia in 1950 as an attempt to control the rapidly increasing rabbit population. Initially, more than 99% of infected rabbits died (Fig. 12.2), but then two fundamental changes occurred:

1. New, less lethal strains of virus appeared and replaced the original strain. This occurred because rabbits infected with these strains survived for longer and their virus was therefore more likely to be transmitted.

2. The rabbit population changed its character, as those that were genetically more susceptible to the infection were eliminated. In other words, the virus selected out the more resistant host, and the less lethal virus strain proved to be a more successful parasite. If the rabbit population had been eliminated, the virus would also have died out, but the host–parasite relationship quite rapidly settled down to reach a state of better balanced pathogenicity, and by the 1970s only about half the rabbits died from infection. Australian rabbits have since faced a new threat, a calicivirus introduced from Europe, which spreads by contact and causes a lethal haemorrhagic disease.

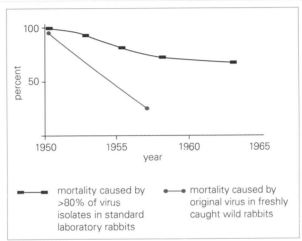

Figure 12.2 Myxomatosis is the best-studied example of the appearance of a highly lethal microbe in a host population that gradually settles down to a state of more balanced pathogenicity. *Vibrio cholerae* has progressed in this direction, and perhaps HIV is destined to tread the same path.

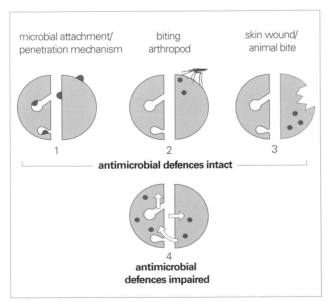

Figure 12.3 Four types of microbial infection can be distinguished. (The diagrams show a schematic representation of the body surfaces of a host, similar to that in Fig. 13.1.) Surface or systemic defences of the host can be impaired in a variety of ways.

• microorganisms able to infect a normal healthy host only when surface or systemic defences are impaired (see Ch. 30) – as occurs with burns, insertion of foreign bodies (cannulas and catheters), urinary tract infections in men (stones, enlarged prostate, see Ch. 20), bacterial pneumonia following initial viral damage (post-influenza) or depressed immune responses (immunosuppressive drugs or diseases such as AIDS).

CAUSES OF INFECTIOUS DISEASES

More than 100 microbes commonly cause infection

Humans are host to many different microorganisms. In addition to the scores of microbes that form the normal flora, there are more than 100 that quite commonly cause infection, some of them remaining in the body for many years afterwards, and several hundred others that are responsible for less common infections. Against this rich background of parasitic activity, how do we prove that a certain microorganism is the culprit in a given disease? In some instances (anthrax, cholera, tetanus), the causative microorganism is identified and incriminated at an early

Box 12.2 Lessons in Microbiology

Robert Koch (1843–1910)

In 1876, while in general practice in Berlin, Robert Koch (Fig. 12.4) isolated the anthrax bacillus, and became the first to show a specific organism as the cause of a disease. In 1882, he discovered *Mycobacterium tuberculosis* as the cause of tuberculosis. He then went on to lead the 1883 expedition to Egypt and India, and discovered the cause of cholera: *Vibrio cholerae*.

Koch was the founder of the 'germ theory' of disease, which maintained that certain diseases were caused by a single species of microbe. In 1890, he set out his 'postulates' as ground rules. New techniques were necessary to meet the exacting requirements of the postulates, and Koch became the first to grow bacteria in 'colonies', initially on potato slices and later, with his pupil Petri, on solid gelatin media.

Koch himself could not reproduce cholera in animals, however, and not all microbes could be cultivated. His neat rules therefore had to be modified. Nevertheless, he brought order and clarity to medicine – until then diseases were attributed to miasmas or mists, to punishments from the Gods or devils, or to unfortunate conjunctions of the stars and planets. However, there was resistance to his ideas. A distinguished Munich physician, Max Von Petternkofer, believed that he had put paid to the new theory when he drank a pure culture of *V. cholerae* and suffered no more than mild diarrhea!

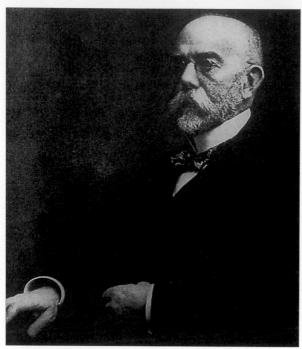

Figure 12.4 Robert Koch (1843–1910).

stage, but in the case of glandular fever and viral hepatitis it is not so easy.

Koch's postulates to identify the microbial causes of specific diseases

In 1890, Robert Koch (Box 12.2) set out as 'postulates' the following criteria he felt to be necessary for a microorganism to be accepted as the cause of a given disease:

- The microbe must be present in every case of the disease.
- The microbe must be isolated from the diseased host and grown in pure culture.
- The disease must be reproduced when a pure culture is introduced into a non-diseased-susceptible host.
- The microbe must be recoverable from an experimentally infected host.

In the early days of microbiology, Koch's postulates brought a welcome clarity. The germ theory of disease causation had only recently been set out following Koch's classic studies on anthrax (1876) and tuberculosis (1882), and methods for isolating microbes in pure culture and identifying them were only just being developed. However, modifications were needed in order to include certain bacterial diseases and the new world of viral diseases. The microbe could not always be grown in the laboratory (*Treponema pallidum*, wart viruses), and for certain microbes: hepatitis B, Epstein–Barr virus (EBV), there were (initially) no susceptible animal species. The criteria were modified, therefore, on several occasions to accommodate these problems and finally reformulated by A.S. Evans in 1976.

Conclusions about causation are now reached using enlightened common sense

Nowadays, with our vastly increased technology and understanding of infection, those attempts to make lists and apply rigid criteria may seem old fashioned. Perhaps we can now reach conclusions about causation using common sense. For instance, we recognize that diseases sometimes do not appear until many years after a specific infection (subacute sclerosing panencephalitis, Creutzfeldt–Jakob disease; see Ch. 24). Molecular genetic techniques may now identify previously uncultivable causative organisms. The polymerase chain reaction was used to amplify and sequence small amounts of mRNA from the bowel of patients with Whipple's disease, a rare multisystem disorder. A unique 16s mRNA was identified, belonging to a previously uncharacterized, uncultivable bacterium, *Tropheryma whippelii*. Nevertheless, grey areas remain, especially in diseases of possible or probable microbial aetiology where the microbe does not act alone. Co-factors or genetic and immunologic factors in the host may play a vital part. Examples include:

- the cancers associated with viruses (hepatitis B, genital wart viruses, EBV)
- diseases of possible microbial origin where a number of different microbes may be involved (post-viral fatigue syndrome, exacerbations of multiple sclerosis)
- diseases that might be infectious, but occur in only a very small proportion of genetically predisposed individuals (rheumatoid arthritis, juvenile diabetes mellitus).

Possible problems in assigning disease aetiology

Finally, there are two interesting possibilities that could give problems in assigning disease aetiology, although neither has yet been shown to apply to human disease:

- First, in some infections, the DNA of the causative virus is integrated into the genome of the host, and is transmitted vertically. It therefore behaves as a genetic attribute. This is known to occur, for instance, with mammary tumour virus in mice.
- Second, the causative microbe triggers off the disease process and then disappears completely from the body and is no longer detectable. This is known to be the case in the cerebellar hypoplasia occurring in hamsters and cats after intrauterine infection with parvovirus. There are no known examples in humans.

THE BIOLOGIC RESPONSE GRADIENT

It is uncommon for a microbe to cause exactly the same disease in all infected individuals

Hence, a physician must be able to make a diagnosis when only some of the possible signs and symptoms are present. The exact clinical picture depends upon many variables such as infecting dose and route, age, sex, presence of other microbes, nutritional status and genetic background. Infections such as measles or cholera give a fairly consistent disease picture, but others such as syphilis cause such a wide spectrum of pathology that Sir William Osler (1849–1919) stated that 'He who knows syphilis, knows medicine'.

There is great variation not only in the nature, but also in the severity of clinical disease. Many infections are asymptomatic in >90% individuals, the clinically characterized illness applying to only an occasional unfortunate host (Table 12.3). This illness can be mild or severe. Asymptomatically infected individuals are important because, although they develop immunity and resistance to reinfection, they are not identified, move normally in the community and can infect others. Clearly, there is little point in isolating a clinically infected patient when there is a high frequency of asymptomatically infected individuals in the community. This phenomenon can be represented as an iceberg (Fig. 12.5).

Table 12.3 The likelihood of developing clinical disease often depends upon age and sex

Frequency of clinically apparent disease	
Infection	**Approximate % with clinically apparent disease[a]**
Pneumocystis jirovecii[b]	0
Poliomyelitis (child)	0.1–1.0
Epstein–Barr virus (1–5 year old child)	1.0[c]
Rubella	50
Influenza (young adult)	60
Whooping cough Typhoid Anthrax	>90
Malaria (1–5 year old child)	25
Adult	2
Gonorrhoea (adult male) Measles	99
HIV[d] Rabies	100

When there is a lengthy incubation period, the proportion with clinical disease may increase with time, from a few percent to (nearer) 100% in the case of HIV.

[a] On primary infection
[b] formerly *P. carinii*
[c] 30–75% in young adults
[d] Some individuals infected with HIV can maintain high CD4 counts and very low viral loads for >5 years, and are called 'long-term non-progressors' or 'controllers', with a few individuals called 'elite controllers' controlling progression to disease for >20 years.

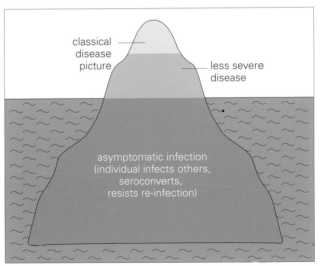

Figure 12.5 The 'iceberg' concept of infectious disease.

KEY FACTS

- Faced with host defences (see Chs 9,10), the microbes (see Chs 1–7) have developed mechanisms to bypass them, and in turn the host defences have had to be modified, although slowly, in response.

- There is a conflict between the microbe and host, and every infectious disease is the result of this ancient battle. Details of the host–microbe conflict are given in Chs 12–17, an outline of diagnostic methods in Ch. 31, and a central account of infectious diseases according to the body systems involved in Chs 18–30.

- Speed matters. Every infection is a race between microbial replication and spread and the mobilization of host responses.

- Microorganisms can infect in four main ways, depending upon whether host defences are intact or impaired.

- It is sometimes difficult to incriminate a specific microbe as the cause of a disease.

- Microbes do not necessarily produce the same disease in all infected individuals. A biologic response gradient causes a spectrum that can range from an asymptomatic to a lethal infection.

Entry, exit and transmission

Introduction

Microorganisms must attach to, or penetrate, the host's body surfaces

The mammalian host can be considered as a series of body surfaces (Fig. 13.1). To establish themselves on or in the host, microorganisms must either attach to, or penetrate, one of these body surfaces. The outer surface, covered by skin or fur, protects and isolates the body from the outside world, forming a dry, horny, relatively impermeable outer layer. Elsewhere, however, there has to be more intimate contact and exchange with the outside world. Therefore, in the alimentary, respiratory and urogenital tracts, where food is absorbed, gases exchanged and urine and sexual products released, respectively, the lining consists of one or more layers of living cells. In the eye, the skin is replaced by a transparent layer of living cells, the conjunctiva. Well-developed cleansing and defence mechanisms are present at all these body surfaces, and entry of microorganisms always has to occur in the face of these natural mechanisms. Successful microorganisms therefore possess efficient mechanisms for attaching to, and often traversing, these body surfaces.

Receptor molecules

There are often specific molecules on microbes that bind to receptor molecules on host cells, either at the body surface (viruses, bacteria) or in tissues (viruses). These receptor molecules, of which there may be more than one, are not present for the benefit of the virus or other infectious agent; they have specific functions in the life of the cell. Very occasionally, the receptor molecule is present only in certain cells, which are then uniquely susceptible to

infection. Examples include the CD4 molecule and the CCR5 beta-chemokine receptor for HIV, the C3d receptor (CR_2) for Epstein–Barr virus, and alpha-dystroglycan seems to act as receptor for *M. leprae* in Schwann cells (the same receptor can be used by arenaviruses). In these cases, the presence of the receptor molecule determines microbial tropism and accounts for the distinctive pattern of infection. Receptors are therefore critical determinants of cell susceptibility, not only at the body surface, but in all tissues. After binding to the susceptible cell, the microorganism can multiply at the surface (mycoplasma, *Bordetella pertussis*) or enter the cell and infect it (viruses, chlamydia; see Ch. 15).

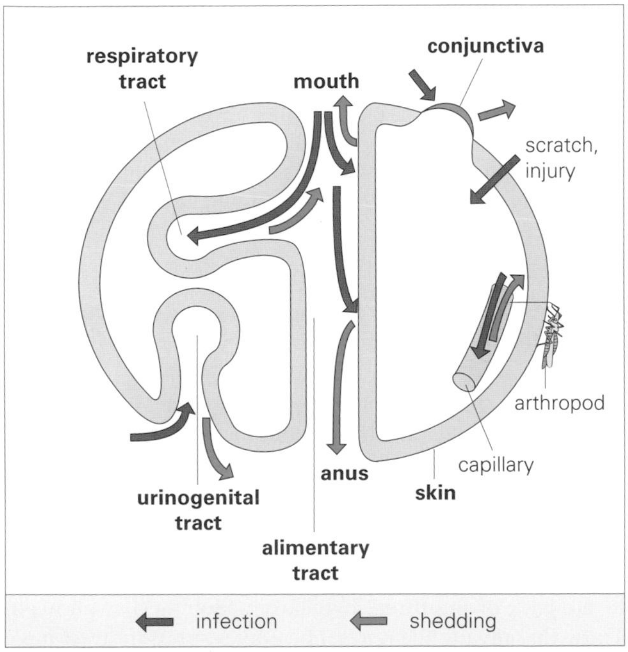

Exit from the body

Microorganisms must also exit from the body if they are to be transmitted to a fresh host. They are either shed in large numbers in secretions and excretions or are available in the blood for uptake, for example by blood-sucking arthropods or needles.

SITES OF ENTRY

Skin

Microorganisms gaining entry via the skin may cause a skin infection or infection elsewhere

Microorganisms which infect or enter the body via the skin are listed in Table 13.1. On the skin, microorganisms other than residents of the normal flora (see Ch. 8) are soon inactivated, especially by fatty acids (skin pH is about 5.5), and probably by substances secreted by sebaceous and other glands, and certain peptides formed locally by keratinocytes protect against invasion by group A streptococci. Materials

Figure 13.1 Body surfaces as sites of microbial infection and shedding.

Table 13.1 Microorganisms that infect via the skin

Microorganism	Disease	Comments
Arthropod-borne viruses	Various fevers	150 distinct viruses, transmitted by bite of infected arthropod
Rabies virus	Rabies	Bite from infected animals
Human papillomaviruses	Warts	Infection restricted to epidermis
Staphylococci	Boils	Commonest skin invaders
Rickettsia	Typhus, spotted fevers	Infestation with infected arthropod
Leptospira	Leptospirosis	Contact with water containing infected animals' urine
Streptococci	Impetigo, erysipelas	Concurrent pharyngeal infection in one-third of cases
Bacillus anthracis	Cutaneous anthrax	Systemic disease following local lesion at inoculation site
Treponema pallidum and *T. pertenue*	Syphilis, yaws	Warm, moist skin susceptible
Yersinia pestis, Plasmodia	Plague, malaria	Bite from infected rodent flea or mosquito
Trichophyton spp. and other fungi	Ringworm, athlete's foot	Infection restricted to skin, nails, hair
Ancylostoma duodenale (or *Necator americanus*)	Hookworm	Silent entry of larvae through skin of, e.g. foot
Filarial nematodes	Filariasis	Bite from infected mosquito, midge, blood-sucking fly
Schistosoma spp.	Schistosomiasis	Larvae (cercariae) from infected snail penetrate skin during wading or bathing

Some remain restricted to the skin (papillomaviruses, ringworm), whereas others enter the body after growth in the skin (syphilis) or after mechanical transfer across the skin (arthropod-borne infections, schistosomiasis).

produced by the normal flora of the skin also protect against infection. Skin bacteria may enter hair follicles or sebaceous glands to cause styes and boils, or teat canals to cause staphylococcal mastitis.

Several types of fungi (the dermatophytes) infect the non-living keratinous structures (stratum corneum, hair, nails) produced by the skin. Infection is established as long as the parasites' rate of downward growth into the keratin exceeds the rate of shedding of the keratinous product. When the latter is very slow, as in the case of nails, the infection is more likely to become chronic.

Wounds, abrasions or burns are more common sites of infection. Even a small break in the skin can be a portal of entry if virulent microorganisms such as streptococci, water-borne leptospira or blood-borne hepatitis B virus are present at the site. A few microbes, such as leptospira or the larvae of *Ancylostoma* and *Schistosoma*, are able to traverse the unbroken skin by their own activity.

Biting arthropods

Biting arthropods such as mosquitoes, ticks, fleas and sandflies (see Ch. 27) penetrate the skin during feeding and can thus introduce infectious agents or parasites into the body. The arthropod transmits the infection and is an essential part of the life cycle of the microorganism. Sometimes the transmission is mechanical, the microorganism contaminating the mouth parts without multiplying in the arthropod. In most cases, however, the infectious agent multiplies in the arthropod and, as a result of millions of years of adaptation, causes little or no damage to that host. After an incubation period, it appears in the saliva or faeces and is transmitted during a blood feed. The mosquito, for instance, injects saliva directly into host tissues as an anticoagulant, whereas the human body louse defecates as it feeds, and *Rickettsia*

rickettsii, which is present in the faeces, is introduced into the bite wound when the host scratches the affected area.

The conjunctiva

The conjunctiva can be regarded as a specialized area of skin. It is kept clean by the continuous flushing action of tears, aided every few seconds by the windscreen wiper action of the eyelids. Therefore, the microorganisms that infect the normal conjunctiva (chlamydia, gonococci) must have efficient attachment mechanisms (see Ch. 25). Interference with local defences due to decreased lacrimal gland secretion or conjunctival or eyelid damage allows even non-specialist microorganisms to establish themselves. Contaminated fingers, flies, or towels carry infectious material to the conjunctiva, examples including herpes simplex virus infections leading to keratoconjunctivitis or chlamydial infection resulting in trachoma. Antimicrobial substances in tears, including lysozyme, an enzyme, and certain peptides have a defensive role.

Respiratory tract

Some microorganisms can overcome the respiratory tract's cleansing mechanisms

Air normally contains suspended particles, including smoke, dust and microorganisms. Efficient cleansing mechanisms (see Chs 18 and 19) deal with these constantly inhaled particles. With about 500–1000 microorganisms/m^3 inside buildings, and a ventilation rate of 6 l/min at rest, as many as 10 000 microorganisms/day are introduced into the lungs. In the upper or lower respiratory tract, inhaled microorganisms, like other particles, will be trapped in mucus, carried to the back of the throat by ciliary action, and swallowed. Those that invade the normal healthy respiratory tract have developed specific mechanisms to avoid this fate.

Interfering with cleansing mechanisms

The ideal strategy is to attach firmly to the surfaces of cells forming the mucociliary sheet. Specific molecules on the organism (often called adhesins) bind to receptor molecules on the susceptible cell (Fig. 13.2). Examples of such respiratory infections are given in Table 13.2.

Inhibiting ciliary activity is another way of interfering with cleansing mechanisms. This helps invading microorganisms establish themselves in the respiratory tract. *B. pertussis*, for instance, not only attaches to respiratory epithelial cells, but also interferes with ciliary activity, while other bacteria (Table 13.3) produce various ciliostatic substances of generally unknown nature.

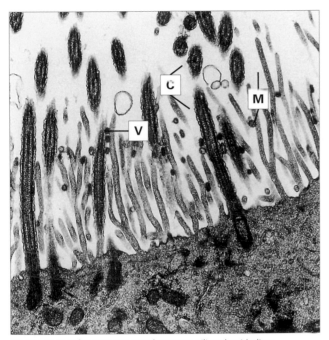

Figure 13.2 Influenza virus attachment to ciliated epithelium. Influenza virus particles (V) attached to cilia (C) and microvilli (M). Electron micrograph of thin section from organ culture of guinea pig trachea 1 h after addition of the virus. (Courtesy of R.E. Dourmashkin.)

Avoiding destruction by alveolar macrophages

Inhaled microorganisms reaching the alveoli encounter alveolar macrophages, which remove foreign particles and keep the air spaces clean. Most microorganisms are destroyed by these macrophages, but one or two pathogens have learnt either to avoid phagocytosis or to avoid destruction after phagocytosis. Tubercle bacilli, for instance, survive in the macrophages, and respiratory tuberculosis is thought to be initiated in this way. Inhalation of as few as 5–10 bacilli is enough. The vital role of macrophages in antimicrobial defences is dealt with more thoroughly in Chapter 14. Alveolar macrophages are damaged following inhalation of toxic asbestos particles and certain dusts, and this leads to increased susceptibility to respiratory tuberculosis.

Gastrointestinal tract

Some microorganisms can survive the intestine's defences of acid, mucus and enzymes

Apart from the general flow of intestinal contents, there are no particular cleansing mechanisms in the intestinal tract, except insofar as diarrhea and vomiting can be included in this category. Under normal circumstances, multiplication of resident bacteria is counterbalanced by their continuous passage to the exterior with the rest of the intestinal contents. Ingestion of a small number of non-pathogenic bacteria, followed by growth in the lumen of the alimentary canal, produces only relatively small numbers within 12–18h, the normal intestinal transit time.

Infecting bacteria must attach themselves to the intestinal epithelium (Table 13.4) if they are to establish themselves and multiply in large numbers. They will then avoid being carried straight down the alimentary canal to be excreted with the rest of the intestinal contents. The concentration of microorganisms in faeces depends on the balance between the production and removal of bacteria in the intestine. *Vibrio cholerae* (Figs 13.3, 13.4) and rotaviruses both establish specific binding to receptors on the surface of intestinal epithelial cells. For *V. cholerae*, establishment in surface mucus may be sufficient for infection and pathogenicity. The fact that certain microbes infect mainly the large bowel

Table 13.2 Microbial attachment in the respiratory tract

Microorganisms	Disease	Microbial adhesion	Receptor on host cell
Influenza A virus	Influenza	Haemagglutinin	Sialyloligosaccharides
Rhinovirus	Common cold	Capsid protein	ICAM-1 (CD54)
Coxsackie A viruses	Common cold, oropharyngeal vesicles	Capsid protein	Integrin or ICAM-1
Parainfluenza virus type 1, respiratory syncytial virus	Respiratory illness	Envelope protein	Sialoglycolipids
Mycoplasma pneumoniae	Atypical pneumonia	Mediated by the terminal organelle, a membrane bound extension of the mycoplasma infected cell	Neuraminic acid
Haemophilus influenzae *Strep. pneumoniae* *Klebsiella pneumoniae*	Respiratory disease	Surface molecule	Carbohydrate sequence in glycolipid
Measles virus	Measles	Haemagglutinin	CD46

ICAM-1, intercellular adhesion molecule-1; CD46, membrane cofactor protein involved in complement regulation; integrins, family of adhesion receptors (e.g. laminin receptor) expressed on many cell types.

Table 13.3 Interference with ciliary activity in respiratory infections

Cause	Mechanisms	Importance
Infecting bacteria interfere with ciliary activity (*B. pertussis, H. influenzae, P. aeruginosa, M. pneumoniae*)	Production of ciliostatic substances (tracheal cytotoxin from *B. pertussis*, at least two substances from *H. influenzae*, at least seven from *P. aeruginosa*)	+ +
Viral infection	Ciliated cell dysfunction or destruction by influenza, measles	+ + +
Atmospheric pollution (automobiles, cigarette smoking)	Acutely impaired mucociliary function	? +
Inhalation of unhumidified air (indwelling tracheal tubes, general anaesthesia)	Acutely impaired mucociliary function	+
Chronic bronchitis, cystic fibrosis	Chronically impaired mucociliary function	+ + +

Although microbes can actively interfere with ciliary activity (first item), a more general impairment of mucociliary function also acts as a predisposing cause of respiratory infection.

Table 13.4 Microbial attachment in the intestinal tract

Microorganism	Disease	Attachment site	Mechanism
Poliovirus	Poliomyelitis	Intestinal epithelium	Viral capsid protein reacts with specific receptor on cell (CD155[a])
Rotavirus	Diarrhea	Intestinal epithelium	Viral outer capsid proteins binds to sialic acid-containing oligosaccharide receptor on cell
Vibrio cholera *Escherichia coli* (certain strains) *Salmonella typhi*	Cholera Diarrhea Enteric fever	Intestinal epithelium	Specific bacterial molecule (adhesin)[b] binds to fucose/mannose receptor on cell
Shigella spp.	Dysentery	Colonic epithelium	Lpa molecule on bacteria binds to integrin on host cell[c]
Giardia lamblia	Diarrhea	Duodenal, jejuna epithelium	Protozoa bind to mannose-6 phosphate on host cell; also have mechanical sucker
Entamoeba histolytica	Dysentery	Colonic epithelium	Lectin on surface of amoebae binds to asialofetuin on host cell
Ancylostoma duodenale	Hookworm	Intestinal epithelium	Buccal capsule

[a]CD155 is immunoglobulin-like and of unknown function in the normal cell.
[b]Often on pili or fimbriae (e.g. up to 200 pili, each bearing adhesins, on *E. coli*).
[c]After attachment *Shigella* (and other pathogenic bacteria) induces epithelial cell to engulf it.

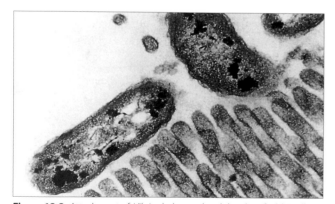

Figure 13.3 Attachment of *Vibrio cholerae* to brush border of rabbit villus. Thin section electron micrograph (×10 000). (Courtesy of E.T. Nelson.)

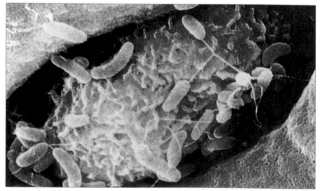

Figure 13.4 Adherence of *Vibrio cholerae* to M cells in human ileal mucosa. (Courtesy of T. Yamamoto.)

(*Shigella* spp.) or small intestine (most salmonellae, rotaviruses) indicates the presence of specific receptor molecules on mucosal cells in these sections of the alimentary canal.

Infection sometimes involves more than mere adhesion to the luminal surface of intestinal epithelial cells. *Shigella*

flexneri, for example, can only enter these cells from the basal surface. Initial entry occurs after uptake by M cells, and the bacteria then invade local macrophages. This gives rise to an inflammatory response with an influx of polymorphs, which in turn causes some disruption of the epithelial barrier.

Bacteria can now enter on a larger scale from the intestinal lumen and invade epithelial cells from below. The bacteria enhance their entry by exploiting the host's inflammatory response.

Crude mechanical devices for attachment

Crude mechanical devices are used for the attachment and entry of certain parasitic protozoans and worms. *Giardia lamblia*, for example, has specific molecules for adhesion to the microvilli of epithelial cells, but also has its own microvillar sucking disk. Hookworms attach to the intestinal mucosa by means of a large mouth capsule containing hooked teeth or cutting plates. Other worms (e.g. *Ascaris*) maintain their position by 'bracing' themselves against peristalsis, while tapeworms adhere closely to the mucus covering the intestinal wall, the anterior hooks and sucker playing a relatively minor role for the largest worms. A number of worms actively penetrate into the mucosa as adults (*Trichinella*, *Trichuris*) or traverse the gut wall to enter deeper tissues (e.g. the embryos of *Trichinella* released from the female worm and the larvae of Echinococcus hatched from ingested eggs).

Mechanisms to counteract mucus, acids, enzymes and bile

Successful intestinal microbes must counteract or resist mucus, acids, enzymes and bile

Mucus protects epithelial cells, perhaps acting as a mechanical barrier to infection. It may contain molecules that bind to microbial adhesins, therefore blocking attachment to host cells. It also contains microbe-specific secretory IgA antibodies, which protect the immune individual against infection. Motile microorganisms (*V. cholerae*, salmonellae and certain strains of *E. coli*) can propel themselves through the mucus layer and are therefore more likely to reach epithelial cells to make specific attachments; *V. cholerae* also produces a mucinase, which probably helps its passage through the mucus.

Non-motile microorganisms, in contrast, rely on random and passive transport in the mucus layer.

As might be expected, microorganisms that infect by the intestinal route are often capable of surviving in the presence of acid, proteolytic enzymes and bile. This also applies to microorganisms shed from the body by this route (Table 13.5).

All organisms infecting by the intestinal route must run the gauntlet of acid in the stomach. *Helicobacter pylori* has evolved a specific defence (Box 13.1). The fact that tubercle bacilli resist acid conditions favours the establishment of intestinal tuberculosis, but most bacteria are acid sensitive and prefer slightly alkaline conditions. For instance, volunteers who drank different doses of *V. cholerae* contained in 60 mL saline showed a 10 000-fold increase in susceptibility to cholera when 2 g of sodium bicarbonate was given with the bacteria. The minimum disease-producing dose was 10^8 bacteria without bicarbonate and 10^4 bacteria with bicarbonate. Similar experiments have been carried out in volunteers with *Salmonella typhi*, and the minimum infectious dose of 1000–10 000 bacteria was again significantly reduced by the ingestion of sodium bicarbonate. Infective stages of protozoa and worms resist stomach acid because they are protected within cysts or eggs.

When the infecting microorganism penetrates the intestinal epithelium (*Shigella*, *S. typhi*, hepatitis A and other enteroviruses) the final pathogenicity depends upon:

- subsequent multiplication and spread
- toxin production
- cell damage
- inflammatory and immune responses.

Microbial exotoxin, endotoxin and protein absorption

Microbial exotoxins, endotoxins and proteins can be absorbed from the intestine on a small scale. Diarrhea generally promotes the uptake of protein, and absorption of

Table 13.5 Microbial properties that aid success in the gastrointestinal tract

Property	Examples	Consequence
Specific attachment to intestinal epithelium	Poliovirus, rotavirus, *Vibrio cholerae*	Microorganism avoids expulsion with other gut contents and can establish infection
Motility	*V. cholerae*, certain *E. coli* strains	Bacteria travel through mucus and are more likely to reach susceptible cell
Production of mucinase	*V. cholerae*	May assist transit through mucus (neuraminidase)
Acid resistance	*Mycobacterium tuberculosis*	Encourages intestinal tuberculosis (acid labile microorganisms depend on protection in food bolus or in diluting fluid) increased susceptibility in individuals with achlorhydria
	Helicobacter pylori	Establish residence in stomach
	Enteroviruses (hepatitis A, poliovirus, coxsackieviruses, echoviruses)	Infection and shedding from gastrointestinal tract
Bile resistance	*Salmonella*, *Shigella*, enteroviruses	Intestinal pathogens
	Enterococcus faecalis, *E. coli*, *Proteus*, *Pseudomonas*	Establish residence
Resistance to proteolytic enzymes	Reoviruses in mice	Permits oral infection
Anaerobic growth	*Bacteroides fragilis*	Most common resident bacteria in anaerobic environment of colon

Box 13.1 Lessons in Microbiology

How to survive stomach acid: the neutralization strategy of *Helicobacter pylori*

This bacterium was discovered in 1983, and was shown to be a human pathogen when two courageous doctors, Warren and Marshall in Perth, Western Australia, drank a potion containing the bacteria and developed gastritis. The infection spreads from person to person by the gastro–oral or fecal–oral route, and 150 years ago, nearly all humans were infected as children. Today, in countries with improved hygiene, this is put off until later in life, until at the age of 50 more than half of the population have been infected. The clinical outcome includes peptic ulcer, gastric cancer and gastric mucosa-associated lymphoid tissue (MALT) lymphoma and host, bacterial and environmental factors are thought to be involved. Genetic susceptibility is implicated in both acquiring and clearing *H. pylori* (HP) infection. After being eaten, the bacteria have a number of strategies resulting in adaptation to the host gastric mucosa having attached by special adhesins to the stomach wall. These include host mimicry leading to evasion of the host response and genetic variation. Most microbes (e.g. *V. cholerae*) are soon killed at the low pH encountered in the stomach. *H. pylori*, however, protects itself by releasing large amounts of urease, which acts on local urea to form a tiny cloud of ammonia round the invader. The attached bacteria induce apoptosis in gastric epithelial cells, as well as inflammation, dyspepsia and occasionally a duodenal or gastric ulcer, so that treatment of these ulcers is by antibiotics rather than merely antacids. Some 90% of duodenal ulcers are due to HP infection, and the rest to aspirin or NSAIDs. The bacteria do not invade tissues, and they stay in the stomach for years, causing asymptomatic chronic gastritis. Up to 3% of infected individuals develop chronic active gastritis and progress to intestinal metaplasia which can lead to stomach cancer. *H. pylori* was the third bacterium for which the entire genome was sequenced; several gene products have been characterized and key developments include understanding the genetic variation of genes encoding the outer membrane proteins and host adaptation.

protein also takes place more readily in the infant, which in some species needs to absorb antibodies from milk. As well as large molecules, particles the size of viruses can also be taken up from the intestinal lumen. This occurs in certain sites in particular, such as those where Peyer's patches occur. Peyer's patches are isolated collections of lymphoid tissue lying immediately below the intestinal epithelium, which in this region is highly specialized, consisting of so-called M cells (see Fig. 13.4). M cells take up particles and foreign proteins and deliver them to underlying immune cells with which they are intimately associated by cytoplasmic processes.

Urogenital tract

Microorganisms gaining entry via the urogenital tract can spread easily from one part of the tract to another

The urogenital tract is a continuum, so microorganisms can spread easily from one part to another, and the distinction between vaginitis and urethritis, or between urethritis and cystitis, is not always easy or necessary (see Chs 20 and 21).

Vaginal defences

The vagina has no particular cleansing mechanisms, and repeated introductions of a contaminated, sometimes pathogen-bearing foreign object (the penis), makes the vagina particularly vulnerable to infection, forming the basis for sexually transmitted diseases (see Ch. 21). Nature has responded by providing additional defences. During reproductive life, the vaginal epithelium contains glycogen due to the action of circulating estrogens, and certain lactobacilli colonize the vagina, metabolizing the glycogen to produce lactic acid. As a result, the normal vaginal pH is about 5.0, which inhibits colonization by all except the lactobacilli and certain other streptococci and diphtheroids. Normal vaginal secretions contain up to 10^8/mL of these commensal bacteria. If other microorganisms are to colonize and invade they must either have specific mechanisms for attaching to vaginal or cervical mucosa or take advantage of minute local injuries during coitus (genital warts, syphilis) or impaired defences (presence of tampons, estrogen imbalance). These are the microorganisms responsible for sexually transmitted diseases.

Urethral and bladder defences

The regular flushing action of urine is a major urethral defence, and urine in the bladder is normally sterile.

The bladder is more than an inert receptacle, and in its wall there are intrinsic, but poorly understood, defence mechanisms. These include a protective layer of mucus and the ability to generate inflammatory responses and produce secretory antibodies and immune cells.

Mechanism of urinary tract invasion

The urinary tract is nearly always invaded from the exterior via the urethra, and an invading microorganism must first and foremost avoid being washed out during urination. Specialized attachment mechanisms have therefore been developed by successful invaders (e.g. gonococci, Fig. 13.5). A defined peptide on the bacterial pili binds to a syndecan-like proteoglycan on the urethral cell, and the cell is then induced to engulf the bacterium. This is referred to as parasite-directed endocytosis and also occurs with chlamydia.

The foreskin is a handicap in genitourinary infections. This is because sexually transmitted pathogens often remain in the moist area beneath the foreskin after detumescence, giving them increased opportunity to invade. All sexually transmitted infections are more common in uncircumcised males.

Intestinal bacteria (mainly *E. coli*) are common invaders of the urinary tract, causing cystitis. The genitourinary anatomy is a major determinant of infection (Fig. 13.6). Spread to the bladder is no easy task in the male, where the flaccid

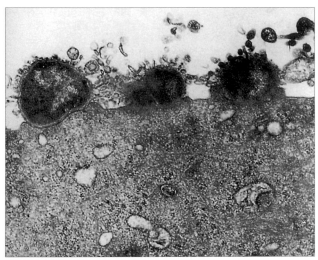

Figure 13.5 Adherence of gonococci to the surface of a human urethral epithelial cell. (Courtesy of P.J. Watt.)

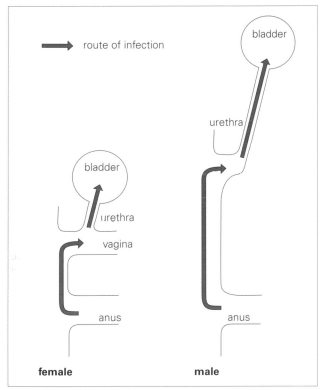

Figure 13.6 The female urinogenital tract is particularly vulnerable to infection with faecal bacteria, mainly because the urethra is shorter and nearer to the anus.

urethra is 20 cm long. Therefore, urinary infections are rare in males unless organisms are introduced by catheters or when the flushing activity of urine is impaired (see Ch. 20). The foreskin causes trouble, again, in urinary tract infection by faecal bacteria. These infections are more common in uncircumcised infants because the prepuce may harbour faecal bacteria on its inner surface.

Things are different in females. Not only is the urethra much shorter (5 cm), but it is also very close to the anus (Fig. 13.6), which is a constant source of intestinal bacteria. Urinary infections are about 14 times more common in women, and at least 20% of women have a symptomatic

urinary tract infection at some time during their life. The invading bacteria often begin their invasion by colonizing the mucosa around the urethra and probably have special attachment mechanisms to cells in this area. Bacterial invasion is favoured by the mechanical deformation of the urethra and surrounding region that occurs during sexual intercourse, which can lead to urethritis and cystitis. Bacteriuria is about 10 times more common in sexually active women than in nuns.

Oropharynx

Microorganisms can invade the oropharynx when mucosal resistance is reduced

Commensal microorganisms in the oropharynx are described in Chapter 18.

Oropharyngeal defences

The flushing action of saliva provides a natural cleansing mechanism (about 1 L/day is produced, needing 400 swallows), aided by masticatory and other movements of the tongue, cheek and lips. On the other hand, material borne backwards from the nasopharynx is firmly wiped against the pharynx by the tongue during swallowing, and microbes therefore have an opportunity to enter the body at this site. Additional defences include secretory IgA antibodies, antimicrobial substances such as lysozyme, the normal flora, and the antimicrobial activities of leukocytes present on mucosal surfaces and in saliva.

Mechanisms of oropharyngeal invasion

Attaching to mucosal or tooth surfaces is obligatory for both invading and resident microorganisms. For instance, different types of streptococci make specific attachments via lipoteichoic acid molecules on their pili to the buccal epithelium and tongue (resident *Streptococcus salivarius*), to teeth (resident *Strep. mutans*), or to pharyngeal epithelium (invading *Strep. pyogenes*).

Factors that reduce mucosal resistance allow commensal and other bacteria to invade, as in the cases of gum infections caused by vitamin C deficiency, or of *Candida* invasion (thrush) promoted by changed resident flora after broad-spectrum antibiotics. When salivary flow is decreased for 3–4 h, as between meals, there is a fourfold increase in the number of bacteria in saliva (see Ch. 18). In dehydrated patients, salivary flow is greatly reduced and the mouth soon becomes overgrown with bacteria. As at all body surfaces, there is a shifting boundary between good behaviour by residents and tissue invasion according to changes in host defences.

EXIT AND TRANSMISSION

Microorganisms have a variety of mechanisms to ensure exit from the host and transmission

Successful microbes must leave the body and then be transmitted to fresh hosts. Highly pathogenic microbes (e.g. Ebola virus, *Legionella pneumophila*) will have little impact on host populations if their transmission from person to person is uncommon or ineffective. Nearly all microbes are shed from body surfaces, this being the route of exit to the outside world. Some, however, are extracted from inside the body by vectors, e.g. the blood-sucking arthropods that transmit

Table 13.6 Types of infection and their role in transmission

Type of infection	Host defences	Microbial evasion mechanism	Examples	Value of evasion mechanism in transmission
Respiratory tract	Mucociliary clearance	Adhere to epithelial cells, interfere with ciliary action	Influenza virus, pertussis	Essential
	Alveolar macrophage	Replicate in alveolar macrophage	*Legionella*, tuberculosis	Essential
Intestinal tract	Mucus, peristalsis	Adhere to epithelial cells	Rotavirus, *Salmonella*	Essential
	Acid, bile	Resist acid, bile	Poliovirus	Essential
Liver	Kupffer cells and endothelial cells	Localize in sinusoid, bypass Kupffer cells and endothelial cells	Hepatitis viruses	Essential: Microbe from liver → bile → gut (hepatitis A); Microbe from liver → blood (hepatitis B virus, yellow fever)
Reproductive tract	Flushing action of urine and sexual secretions, mucosal defences	Adhere to urethral/vaginal epithelial cells	Gonococcus, *Chlamydia*	Essential
Urinary tract	Flushing action of urine	Adhere to urethral/epithelial cells	*E. coli*	No value
		Reach urine from tubular epithelium	Polyomavirus	Valuable
Central nervous system	Enclosed in bony 'box' of skull and vertebral column	Reach CNS via nerves or blood vessels that enter skull or vertebral column	Bacterial meningitis, viral encephalitis (e.g. rabies)	No value (except rabies)
Skin, mucosa	Layers of constantly shed cells (mucosa)	Invade skin/mucosa from below	Varicella, measles	Essential
	Dead keratinized cell layers (skin)	Infect basal epidermal layer	Papillomaviruses	Essential
		Infect via minor abrasions	Staphylococci, streptococci	Essential
		Penetrate intact skin	Schistosomiasis, ancyclostomiases, leptospirosis	Essential
Vascular system	Skin	Infection of microbe by biting vector, replication in blood cells or in vascular endothelial cells	Malaria, yellow fever	Essential

For each type of host defence, the successful microbe has an answer, which may or may not be important for transmission.

yellow fever, malaria and filarial worms. Table 13.6 lists the types of infection and their role in the transmission of the microbe and provides a summary of the host defences and the ways in which they are evaded. Transfer from one host to another forms the basis for the epidemiology of infectious disease (see Ch. 31).

Transmission depends upon three factors:

- the number of microorganisms shed
- the microorganism's stability in the environment
- the number of microorganisms required to infect a fresh host (the efficiency of the infection).

Number of microorganisms shed

Obviously, the more virus particles, bacteria, protozoa and eggs that are shed, the greater the chance of reaching a fresh host. There are, however, many hazards. Most of the

shed microorganisms die, and only an occasional one survives to perpetuate the species.

Stability in the environment

Microorganisms that resist drying spread more rapidly in the environment than those that are sensitive to drying (Table 13.7). Microorganisms also remain infectious for longer periods in the external environment when they are resistant to thermal inactivation. Certain microorganisms have developed special forms (e.g. clostridial spores, amoebic cysts) that enable them to resist drying, heat inactivation and chemical insults, and this testifies to the importance of stability in the environment. If still alive, microorganisms are more thermostable when they have dried. Drying directly from the frozen state (freeze-drying) can make them very resistant to environmental temperatures. The fact that spores and cysts are dehydrated accounts for much of their stability. Microorganisms that are

Table 13.7 Microbial resistance to drying as a factor in transmission

Stability on drying	Examples	Consequence
Stable	Tubercle bacilli Staphylococci	Spread more readily in air (dust, dried droplets)
	Clostridial spores Anthrax spores Histoplasma spores	Spread readily from soil
Unstable	Neisseria meningitidis Streptococci Bordetella pertussis Common cold viruses Influenza virus Measles virus	Require close (respiratory) contact
	Gonococci HIV Treponema pallidum	Require close (sexual) contact
	Polioviruses Hepatitis A Vibrio cholerae Leptospira	Spread via water, food
	Yellow fever virus Malaria Trypanosomes	Spread via vectors (i.e. remain in a host)
	Larvae/eggs of worms	Need moist soil (except pinworms)

Microbes that are already dehydrated such as spores and artificially freeze-dried viruses are also more resistant to thermal inactivation. Spores can survive for years in soil.

sensitive to drying depend for their spread on close contact, vectors, or contamination of food and water for spread.

Number of microorganisms required to infect a fresh host

The efficiency of the infection varies greatly between microorganisms, and helps explain many aspects of transmission. For instance, volunteers ingesting 10 *Shigella dysenteriae* bacteria (from other humans) will become infected, whereas as many as 10^6 *Salmonella* spp. (from animals) are needed to cause food poisoning. The route of infection also matters. A single tissue culture infectious dose of a human rhinovirus instilled into the nasal cavity causes a common cold, and although this dose contains many virus particles, about 200 such doses are needed when applied to the pharynx. As few as 10 gonococci can establish an infection in the urethra, but many thousand times this number are needed to infect the mucosa of the oropharynx or rectum.

Other factors affecting transmission

Genetic factors in microorganisms also influence transmission. Some strains of a given microorganism are therefore more readily transmitted than others, although the exact mechanism is often unclear. Transmission can vary independently of the ability to do damage and cause disease (pathogenicity or virulence).

Activities of the infected host may increase the efficiency of shedding and transmission. Coughing and sneezing are reflex activities that benefit the host by clearing foreign material from the upper and lower respiratory tract, but they also benefit the microorganism. Strains of microorganism that are more able to increase fluid secretions or irritate respiratory epithelium will induce more coughing and sneezing than those less able and will be transmitted more effectively. Similar arguments can be applied to the equivalent intestinal activity: diarrhea. Although diarrhea eliminates the infection more rapidly (prevention of diarrhea often prolongs intestinal infection), from the microbe's point of view it is a highly effective way of contaminating the environment and spreading to fresh hosts.

TYPES OF TRANSMISSION BETWEEN HUMANS

Microorganisms can be transmitted to humans by humans, vertebrates and biting arthropods. Transmission is most effective when it takes place directly from human to human. The most common worldwide infections are spread by the respiratory, faecal–oral or venereal routes. A separate set of infections are acquired from animals, either directly from vertebrates (the zoonoses) or from biting arthropods. Infections acquired from other species are either not transmitted or transmit very poorly from human to human. Types of transmission are illustrated in Figure 13.7.

Transmission from the respiratory tract

Respiratory infections spread rapidly when people are crowded together indoors

An increase in nasal secretions with sneezing and coughing promotes effective shedding from the nasal cavity. In a sneeze (Fig. 13.8) up to 20 000 droplets are produced, and during a common cold, for instance, many of them will contain virus particles.

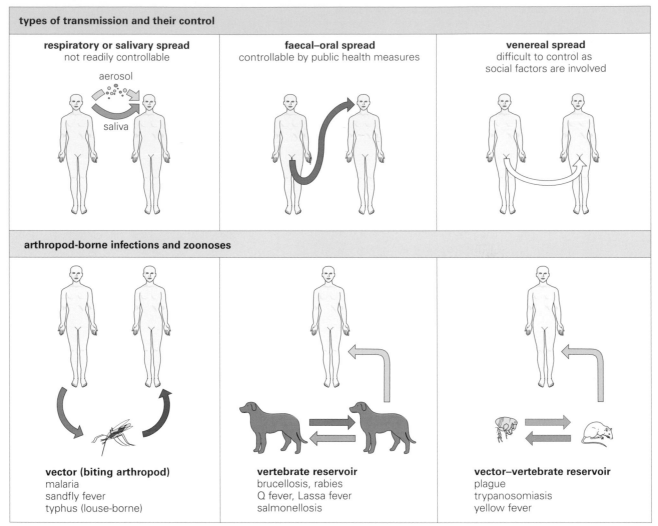

types of transmission and their control

| **respiratory or salivary spread** not readily controllable | **faecal–oral spread** controllable by public health measures | **venereal spread** difficult to control as social factors are involved |

aerosol

saliva

arthropod-borne infections and zoonoses

vector (biting arthropod)
malaria
sandfly fever
typhus (louse-borne)

vertebrate reservoir
brucellosis, rabies
Q fever, Lassa fever
salmonellosis

vector–vertebrate reservoir
plague
trypanosomiasis
yellow fever

Figure 13.7 Types of transmission and their control. Arthropod-borne infections and zoonoses can be controlled by controlling vectors or by controlling animal infection; there is virtually no person-to-person transmission of these infections (except for pneumonic plague, see Ch. 28).

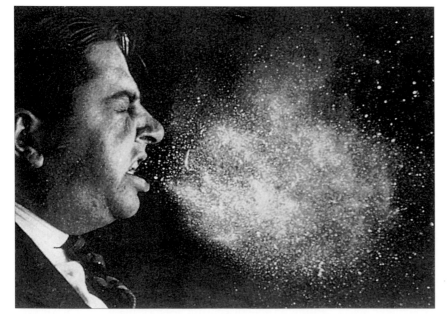

Figure 13.8 Droplet dispersal following a violent sneeze. Most of the 20 000 particles seen are coming from the mouth. (Reprinted with permission from: Moulton F. R. (ed.) (1942) *Aerobiology*. American Association for the Advancement of Science.)

A smaller number of microorganisms (hundreds) are expelled from the mouth, throat, larynx and lungs during coughing (whooping cough, tuberculosis). Talking is a less important source of air-borne particles, but does produce them, especially when the consonants 'f, p, t and s' are used. It is surely no accident that many of the most abusive words in the English language begin with these letters, so that a spray of droplets (possibly infectious) is delivered with the abuse!

The size of inhaled droplets determines their initial localization. The largest droplets fall to the ground after travelling approximately 4 m, and the rest settle according to size. Those 10 μm or so in diameter can be trapped on the nasal mucosa. The smallest (1–4 μm diameter) are kept suspended for an indefinite period by normal air movements, and particles of this size are likely to pass the turbinate baffles in the nose and reach the lower respiratory tract.

When people are crowded together indoors, respiratory infections spread rapidly – for example, the common cold in schools and offices and meningococcal infections in military recruits. This is perhaps why respiratory infections are common in winter. The air in ill-ventilated rooms is also more humid, favouring survival of suspended microorganisms such as streptococci and enveloped viruses. Air conditioning is another factor, as the dry air leads to impaired mucociliary activity. Respiratory spread is, in one sense, unique. Material from one person's respiratory tract can be taken up almost immediately into the respiratory tract of other individuals. This is in striking contrast to the material expelled from the gastrointestinal tract, and helps explain why respiratory infections spread so rapidly when people are indoors.

Handkerchiefs, hands and other objects can carry respiratory infection such as common cold viruses from one individual to another, although coughs and sneezes provide a more dramatic route. Transmission from the infected conjunctiva is referred to in Chapter 25.

The presence of receptors (see Table 13.2) and local temperature as well as initial localization can determine which part of the respiratory tract is infected. For instance, it can be assumed that rhinoviruses arrive in the lower respiratory tract on a large scale, but fail to grow there because, like leprosy bacilli, they prefer the cooler temperature of the nasal mucosa.

Transmission from the gastrointestinal tract

Intestinal infection spreads easily if public health and hygiene are poor

The spread of an intestinal infection is assured if public health and hygiene are poor, the microbe appears in the faeces in sufficient numbers and there are susceptible individuals in the vicinity. Diarrhea gives it an additional advantage, and the key role of diarrhea in transmission has been referred to above. During most of human history, there has been a large-scale recycling of faecal material back into the mouth, and this continues in resource-poor countries. The attractiveness of the faecal–oral route for microorganisms and parasites is reflected in the great variety that are transmitted in this way.

Intestinal infections have been to some extent controlled in resource-rich countries. The great public health reforms of the nineteenth century led to the introduction of adequate sewage disposal and a supply of purified water. For instance, in England 200 years ago, there were no flushing toilets and no sewage disposal and much of the drinking water was contaminated. Cholera and typhoid spread easily, and in London, the Thames became an open sewer. Today, as in other cities, a complex underground disposal system separates sewage from drinking water. Intestinal infections are still transmitted in resource-rich countries, but via food and fingers rather than by water and flies. Therefore, although each year in the UK there are dozens of cases of typhoid acquired on visits to resource-poor countries, the infection is not transmitted to others.

The microorganisms that appear in faeces usually multiply in the lumen or wall of the intestinal tract, but there are a few that are shed into bile. For instance, hepatitis A enters bile after replicating in liver cells.

Transmission from the urogenital tract

Urogenital tract infections are often sexually transmitted

Urinary tract infections are common, but most are not spread via urine. Urine can contaminate food, drink and living space. Examples of some infections that are spread by urine are listed in Table 13.8.

Table 13.8 Human infections transmitted via urine

Infection	Details	Value in transmission
Schistosomiasis	Parasite eggs excreted in bladder	+ + +
Typhoid	Bacterial persistence in bladder scarred by schistosomiasis	+
Polyomavirus infection	Commonly excreted in urine	?
Cytomegalovirus infection	Commonly excreted in infected children	?
Leptospirosis	Infected rats and dogs excrete bacteria in urine	+ +
Lassa fever (and South American haemorrhagic fevers)	Persistently infected rodent excretes virus in urine	+ + +

Schistosomiasis is the major infection transmitted in this way, the eggs undergoing development in snails before reinfecting humans. Viruses are shed in the urine after infecting tubular epithelial cells in the kidney.

Sexually transmitted infections (STIs)

Microorganisms shed from the urogenital tract are often transmitted as a result of mucosal contact with susceptible individuals, typically as a result of sexual activity. If there is a discharge, organisms are carried over the epithelial surfaces and transmission is more likely. Some of the most successful sexually transmitted microorganisms (gonococci, chlamydia) therefore induce a discharge. Other microorganisms are transmitted effectively from mucosal sores (ulcers), e.g. *Treponema pallidum* and herpes simplex virus. The human papillomaviruses are transmitted from genital warts or from foci of infection in the cervix where the epithelium, although apparently normal, is dysplastic and contains infected cells (see Ch. 21).

The transmission of STIs is determined by social and sexual activity. Changes in the size of the human population and way of life have had a dramatic effect on the epidemiology of STIs. More opportunities to have sexual encounters have arisen due to increasing population density, increased movement of people, the decline of the idea that sexual activity is sinful and the knowledge that STIs are treatable and pregnancy is avoidable. In addition, the contraceptive pill has favoured the spread of STIs by discouraging the use of mechanical barriers to conception. Condoms have been shown to reliably retain herpes simplex virus, HIV, chlamydia and gonococci in simulated coital tests of the syringe and plunger type (see Ch. 21).

STIs are, however, transmitted with far less speed and efficiency than respiratory or intestinal infections. Influenza can be transmitted to a multitude of others during 1 h in a crowded room, or a rotavirus to a score of children during a morning at kindergarten, but STIs can only spread to each person by a separate sexual act. Promiscuity is therefore essential. Frequent sexual activity is not enough without promiscuity because those in a stable partnership can do no more than infect each other. The increased general level of promiscuity in society, together with the huge numbers of sexual partners of certain individuals, such as prostitutes, has led to a dramatic rise in the incidence of STIs.

As almost all mucosal surfaces of the body can be involved in sexual activity, microorganisms have had increasing opportunity to infect new body sites. The meningococcus, a nasopharyngeal resident, has therefore sometimes been recovered from the cervix, the male urethra, and the anal canal, while occasionally gonococci and chlamydia infect the throat and anal canal. The possibilities are illustrated in all their complexity in Figure 13.9, apparently limited only by anatomic considerations. It is no surprise that genito–oro–anal contacts have sometimes allowed intestinal infections such as salmonella, giardia, hepatitis A virus, shigella, and pathogenic amoebae to spread directly between individuals despite good sanitation and sewage disposal.

Semen as a source of infection

It might be expected that semen is involved in the transmission of infection, and this is the case in viral infections of animals such as blue tongue and foot and mouth disease. In humans, cytomegalovirus that is shed from the oropharynx is also often present in large quantities in semen, and the

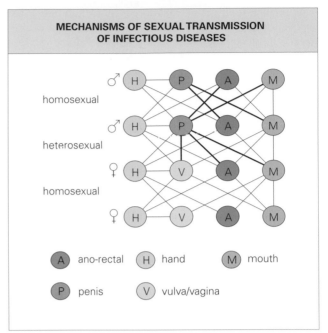

Figure 13.9 The mechanisms of sexual transmission of infection. (Redrawn from: Wilcox R. R. (1981) The rectum as viewed by the venereologist. *Br J Ven Dis* 1981; 57:1–6.)

fact that it is also recoverable from the cervix suggests that it is sexually transmitted. Hepatitis B virus and HIV are also present in semen.

Perinatal transmission

The female genital tract can also be a source of infection for the newborn child (see Ch. 23). During passage down an infected birth canal, microorganisms can be wiped onto the conjunctiva of the infant or inhaled, leading to a variety of conditions such as conjunctivitis, pneumonia and bacterial meningitis.

Transmission from the oropharynx

Oropharyngeal infections are often spread in saliva

Saliva is often the vehicle of transmission. Microorganisms such as streptococci and tubercle bacilli reach saliva during upper and lower respiratory tract infections, while certain viruses infect the salivary glands and are transmitted in this way. Paramyxovirus, herpes simplex virus, cytomegalovirus and human herpesvirus type 6 are shed into saliva. In young children, fingers and other objects are regularly contaminated by saliva, and each of these infections is acquired by this route. Epstein–Barr virus is also shed into saliva, but is transmitted less effectively, perhaps because it is present only in cells or in small amounts. In resource-rich countries, people often escape infection during childhood, and become infected as adolescents or adults during the extensive salivary exchanges (mean 4.2 mL/h) that accompany deep kissing (see Ch. 18). Saliva from animals is the source of a few infections, and these are included in Table 13.9.

Table 13.9 Human infections transmitted via saliva

Microorganism	Comments
Herpes simplex, paramyxovirus	Infection generally during childhood
Cytomegalovirus, Epstein–Barr virus	Adolescent/adult infection is common
Rabies virus	Shed in saliva of infected dogs, wolves, jackals, vampire bats
Pasteurella multocida	Bacteria in upper respiratory tract of dogs, cats appear in saliva and are transmitted via bites, scratches
Streptobacillus moniliformis	Present in rat saliva and infects humans (rat bite fever)

Transmission from the skin

Skin can spread infection by shedding or direct contact

Dermatophytes (fungi such as those that cause ringworm) are shed from skin and also from hair and nails, the exact source depending on the type of fungus (see Ch. 26). Skin is also an important source of certain other bacteria and viruses, as outlined in Table 13.10.

Shedding to the environment

The normal individual sheds desquamated skin scales into the environment at a rate of about 5×10^8/day, the rate depending upon physical activities such as exercise, dressing and undressing. The fine white dust that collects on indoor surfaces, especially in hospital wards, consists largely of skin scales. Staphylococci are present, and different individuals show great variation in staphylococcal shedding, but the reasons are unknown.

Transmission by direct contact or by contaminated fingers is much more common than following release into the environment, and microorganisms transmitted in this way include potentially pathogenic staphylococci and human papillomaviruses.

Transmission in milk

Milk is produced by a skin gland. Microorganisms are rarely shed into human milk, and examples include HIV, cytomegalovirus and human T-cell lymphotropic virus 1 (HTLV-1), but milk from cows, goats and sheep can be important sources of infection (Table 13.11). Bacteria can be introduced into milk after collection.

Transmission from blood

Blood can spread infection via arthropods or needles

Blood is often the vehicle of transmission. Microorganisms and parasites spread by blood-sucking arthropods (see below) are effectively shed into the blood. Infectious agents present in blood (hepatitis B and C viruses, HIV) are also transmissible by needles, either in transfused blood or when contaminated needles are used for injections or intravenous drug misuse. Intravenous drug misuse is a well-known factor in the spread of these infections. In addition, at least 12000 million injections are given each year, worldwide, about 1 in 10 of them for vaccines. Unfortunately, in parts of the resource-poor world, disposable syringes tend to be used more than once, without

Table 13.10 Human infections transmitted from the skin

Microorganism	Disease	Comments
Staphylococci	Boils, carbuncles, neonatal skin sepsis	Pathogenicity varies, skin lesions or nose picking are common sources of infection
Treponema pallidum	Syphilis	Mucosal surfaces more infectious than skin
Treponema pertenue	Yaws	Regular transmission from skin lesions
Streptococcus pyogenes	Impetigo	Vesicular (epidermal) lesions crusting over, common in children in hot, humid climates
Staphylococcus aureus	Impetigo	Less common; bullous lesions, especially in newborn
Dermatophytes	Skin ringworm	Different species infect skin, hair, nails
Herpes simplex virus	Herpes simplex, cold sore	Up to 10^6 infectious units/ml of vesicle fluid
Varicella-zoster virus	Varicella, zoster	Vesicular skin lesions occur but transmission is usually respiratory[a]
Coxsackievirus A16	Hand, foot and mouth disease	Vesicular skin lesions but transmission faecal and respiratory
Papillomaviruses	Warts	Many types[b]
Leishmania tropica	Cutaneous leishmaniasis	Skin sores are infectious
Sarcoptes scabei	Scabies	Eggs from burrow transmitted by hand (also sexually)

[a]Except in zoster, where a localized skin eruption occurs and the respiratory tract is generally unaffected.
[b]Generally direct contact, but plantar warts are commonly spread following contamination of floors.

Table 13.11 Human infections transmitted via milk

Microorganism	Type of milk	Importance in transmission
Cytomegalovirus	Human	–
HIV	Human	+
HTLV-1	Human	+
Brucella	Cow, goat, sheep	+ +
Mycobacterium bovis	Cow	+ +
Coxiella burnetii (Q fever)	Cow	+
Campylobacter jejuni	Cow	+ +
Salmonella spp. *Listeria monocytogenes* *Staphylococcus* spp. *Streptococcus pyogenes* *Yersinia enterocolitica*	Cow	+

Human milk is rarely a significant source of infection. All microbes listed are destroyed by pasteurization.

being properly sterilized in between ('If it still works, use it again'). To prevent this, the World Health Organization (WHO) encouraged the use of syringes in which, for instance, the plunger cannot be withdrawn once it has been pushed in.

Blood is also the source of infection in transplacental transmission and this generally involves initial infection of the placenta (see Ch. 23).

Vertical and horizontal transmission

Vertical transmission takes place between parents and their offspring

When transmission occurs directly from parents to offspring via, e.g. sperm, ovum, placenta (Table 13.12), milk or blood, it is referred to as vertical. This is because it can be represented as a vertical flow down a page (Fig. 13.10), just like a family pedigree. Other infections, in contrast, are said to be horizontally transmitted, with an individual infecting other individuals by contact, respiratory or faecal–oral spread. Vertically transmitted infections can be subdivided as shown in

Table 13.12 Human infections transmitted via the placenta

Transplacental transmission of infection	
Microorganism	**Effect**
Rubella virus, cytomegalovirus	Placental lesion, abortion, stillbirth, malformation
HIV	Childhood HIV and AIDS
Hepatitis B virus	Antigen carriage in infant, but most of these infections are perinatal or postnatal
Treponema pallidum	Stillbirth, congenital syphilis with malformation
Listeria monocytogenes	Meningoencephalitis
Toxoplasma gondii	Stillbirth, CNS disease

Table 13.13. Strictly speaking, these infections are able to maintain themselves in the species without spreading horizontally, as long as they do not affect the viability of the host. Various retroviruses are known to maintain themselves vertically in animals (e.g. mammary tumour virus in milk, sperm and ovum of mice), but this does not appear to be important in humans, except possibly for HTLV-1, where milk transfer is important. There are, however, many retrovirus sequences present in the normal human genome known as endogenous retroviruses. These DNA sequences are too incomplete to produce infectious virus particles, but can be regarded as amazingly successful parasites. In addition, some of them may confer benefit, for example, by coding for proteins that help coordinate early stages of fetal development. They presumably do no harm and survive within the human species, watched over, conserved and replicated as part of our genetic constitution.

TRANSMISSION FROM ANIMALS

Humans and animals share a common susceptibility to certain pathogens

Humans live in daily contact, directly or indirectly, with a wide variety of other animal species, both vertebrate and invertebrate, not only sharing a common environment, but also a common susceptibility to certain pathogens. The degree to which animal contacts transmit infection depends upon the type of environment (urban/rural, tropical/temperate, hygienic/insanitary) and on the nature of the contact. Close contact is made with vertebrate animals used for food or as pets, and with invertebrate animals adapted to live or feed on the human body. Less intimate contact is made with many other species, which nevertheless may transmit pathogens equally well. For convenience, animal-transmitted infections can be divided into two categories:

- those involving arthropod and other invertebrate vectors
- those transmitted directly from vertebrates (zoonoses).

More detailed accounts of these infections are given in Chapters 27 and 28.

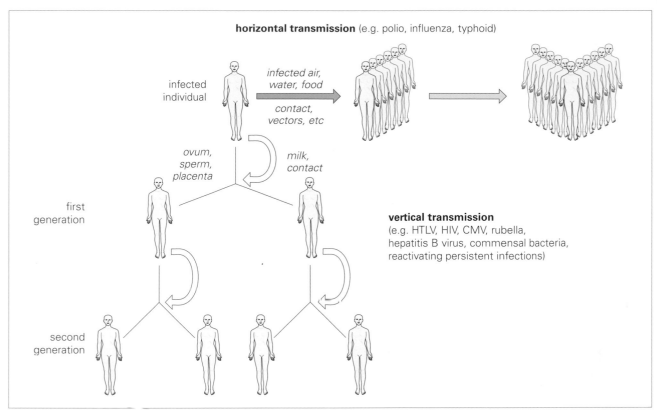

Figure 13.10 Vertical and horizontal transmission by infection. Most infections are transmitted horizontally, as might be expected in crowded human populations. Vertical transmission becomes more important in small isolated communities (see Ch. 17). CMV, cytomegalovirus; HTLV, human T-cell lymphotropic virus.

Table 13.13 Types of vertical transmission

Type	Route	Examples
Prenatal	Placenta	Rubella; cytomegalovirus; syphilis; toxoplasmosis
Perinatal	Infected birth canal	Gonococcal/chlamydial conjunctivitis; hepatitis B
Postnatal	Milk or direct contact	Cytomegalovirus; hepatitis B virus; HIV, HTLV-1
Germline	Viral DNA sequences in human genome	Many ancient retroviruses

HTLV, human T-cell lymphotropic virus.

Invertebrate vectors

Insects, ticks and mites – the bloodsuckers – are the most important vectors spreading infection

By far the most important vectors of disease belong to these three groups of arthropods. Many species are capable of transmitting infection, and a wide range of organisms is transmitted (Table 13.14). In the past, insects have been responsible for some of the most devastating epidemic diseases, for example, fleas and plague and lice and typhus. Even today, one of the world's most important infectious diseases, malaria, is transmitted by the *Anopheles* mosquito. The distribution and epidemiology of these infections are determined by the climatic conditions that allow the vectors to breed and the organism to complete its development in their bodies. Some diseases are therefore purely tropical and subtropical, for example, malaria, sleeping sickness and yellow fever, while others are much more widespread, e.g. plague and typhus.

Passive carriage

Insects may carry pathogens passively on their mouth parts, on their bodies, or within their intestines. Transfer onto food or onto the host occurs directly as a result of the insect feeding, regurgitating or defecating. Many important diseases, such as trachoma, can be transmitted in this way by common species such as houseflies and cockroaches.

Blood-feeding species have mouth parts adapted for penetrating skin in order to reach blood vessels or to create small pools of blood (Fig. 13.11). The ability to feed in this way provides access to organisms in the skin or blood. The mouth parts can act as a contaminated hypodermic needle, carrying infection between individuals.

Biologic transmission

This is much more common, the blood-sucking vector acting as a necessary host for the multiplication and development of the pathogen. Almost all of the important infections (listed in Table 13.14) are transmitted in this way. The pathogen is

Table 13.14 Arthropod-borne pathogens. Mosquitoes are a major source of infection. (Note that, with the exception of pneumonic plague, none is transmitted from human to human.)

Arthropod-borne pathogens			
Arthropods	**Pathogens**	**Types**	**Diseases**

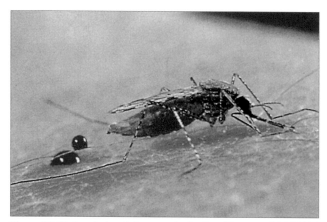

		Flaviviruses	Yellow fever, dengue, febrile diseases, encephalitides
		Bunyaviruses	Haemorrhagic fevers
		Yersinia	Plague, tularemia
		Rickettsias	Q fever, spotted fevers, typhus, rickettsial pox
		Spirochaetes	Relapsing fever, Lyme disease
		Trypanosomes	Sleeping sickness, Chagas' disease
		Leishmania	Leishmaniasis
		Plasmodium	Malaria
		Plasmodium nematodes	Lymphatic filariases, loiasis, onchocerciasis

The arthropods listed (connected to Viruses, Bacteria, Protozoa, Helminths):

Insects
- Houseflies
- Sandflies
- Mosquitoes
- Blackflies
- Lice
- Fleas
- Hemiptera bugs
- Midges
- Tabanids

Acarids
- Ticks
- Mites

Pathogens: Viruses, Bacteria, Protozoa, Helminths

Figure 13.11 Female *Anopheles* mosquito feeding. (Courtesy of C.J. Webb.)

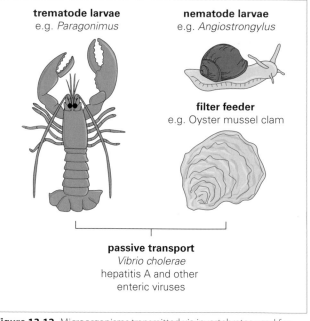

trematode larvae
e.g. *Paragonimus*

nematode larvae
e.g. *Angiostrongylus*

filter feeder
e.g. Oyster mussel clam

passive transport
Vibrio cholerae
hepatitis A and other
enteric viruses

Figure 13.12 Microorganisms transmitted via invertebrates used for food. Filter-feeding molluscs living in estuaries near sewage outlets are a common source of infection.

reintroduced into the human host, after a period of time, at the next blood meal. Transmission can be by direct injection, usually in the vector's saliva (malaria, yellow fever), or by contamination from faeces or regurgitated blood deposited at the time of feeding (typhus, plague).

Other invertebrate vectors spread infection either passively or by acting as an intermediate host

Many invertebrates used for food convey pathogens (Fig. 13.12). Perhaps the most familiar are the shellfish (molluscs and crustacea) associated with food poisoning and acute gastroenteritis. These filter feeders accumulate viruses and bacteria in their bodies, taking them in from contaminated waste, and transferring them passively. In other cases, the relationship between the pathogen and the invertebrate is much closer. Many parasites, especially worms, must undergo part of their development in the invertebrate before being able to infect a human. Humans are infected when they eat the invertebrate (intermediate) host. Dietary habits are therefore important in infection.

Aquatic molluscs (snails) are necessary intermediate hosts for schistosomes – the blood flukes. They become infected by

larval stages, which hatch from eggs passed into water in the urine or faeces of infected people. After a period of development and multiplication, large numbers of infective stages (cercariae) escape from the snails. These can rapidly penetrate through human skin, initiating the infection that will result in adult flukes occupying visceral blood vessels (see Ch. 30).

Transmission from vertebrates

Many pathogens are transmitted directly to humans from vertebrate animals

Strictly, the term zoonoses can apply to any infection transmitted to humans from infected animals, whether this is direct (by contact or eating) or indirect (via an invertebrate vector). Here, however, zoonoses are used to describe infections of vertebrate animals that can be transmitted directly. Many pathogens are transmitted in this way (Table 13.15) by a variety of different routes including contact, inhalation, bites, scratches, contamination of food or water and ingestion as food.

The epidemiology of zoonoses depends upon the frequency and the nature of contact between the vertebrate and the human hosts. Some are localized geographically, being dependent, for example, on local food preferences. Where these involve eating uncooked animal products such as fish or amphibia, a variety of parasites (especially tapeworms and nematodes) can be acquired. Others are associated with occupation; for example, if this involves contact with raw animal products (butchers in the case of toxoplasmosis and Q fever) or frequent contact with domestic stock (farm workers in the case of brucellosis and dermatophyte fungi). In urban areas, zoonoses are most likely to be acquired by eating or drinking infected animal products or by contact with dogs, cats and other domestic pets.

Domestic pets or pests?

Dogs and cats are the most common domestic pets, and both are reservoirs of infection for their owners (Fig. 13.13). The pathogens concerned are spread by contact, bites and scratches, by vectors, and by contamination with faecal material. Major infections transmitted in these ways include:

- toxocariasis from dogs
- toxoplasmosis from cats.

Both are almost universal in their distribution.

Humans may acquire hydatid disease from tapeworm eggs passed in dog faeces where dogs are used for herding domestic animals and have access to infected carcasses. In rural areas of many countries this has been, or remains, an important infection.

Many species of birds are kept as pets and some can pass on serious infections to those in contact with them. Contact is usually through inhalation of infected particulate material. Perhaps the most important of these is psittacosis caused by

Table 13.15 Zoonoses: human infections transmitted directly from vertebrates (birds and mammals)

Pathogens	Vertebrate vector	Diseases
Viruses		
Arenaviruses	Mammals	Lassa fever, lymphocytic choriomeningitis, Bolivian haemorrhagic fever
Poxviruses	Mammals	Cowpox, orf
Rhabdoviruses	Mammals	Rabies
Bacteria		
Bacillus anthracis	Mammals	Anthrax
Brucella	Mammals	Brucella
Chlamydia	Birds	Psittacosis
Leptospira	Mammals	Leptospirosis (Weil's disease)
Listeria	Mammals	Listeriosis
Salmonella	Birds, mammals	Salmonellosis
Mycobacterium tuberculosis	Mammals	Tuberculosis
Fungi		
Cryptococcus	Birds	Meningitis
Dermatophytes	Mammals	Ringworm
Protozoa		
Cryptosporidium	Mammals	Cryptosporidiosis
Giardia	Mammals	Giardiasis
Toxoplasma	Mammals	Toxoplasmosis
Helminths		
Ancylostoma	Mammals	Hookworm disease
Echinococcus	Mammals	Hydatid disease
Taenia	Mammals	Tapeworms
Toxocara	Mammals	Toxocariasis (visceral larval migrans)
Trichinella	Mammals	Trichinellosis

A few virus infections acquired from animals (SARS, influenza A H5N1 virus) show poor transmission from person to person, but they may at any time change and develop the capacity for efficient transmission.

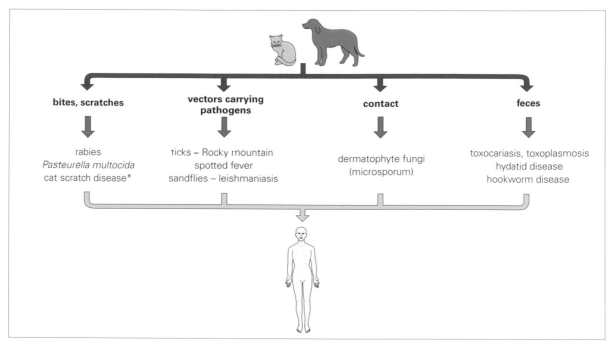

Figure 13.13 Man's best friends? Zoonoses transmitted from dogs and cats. (*A benign infection, with skin lesions and lymphadenopathy, shown to be due to a bacterium, *Bartonella henselae*)

Chlamydophila (formerly *Chlamydia*) *psittaci*, which despite the common name 'parrot fever' can be acquired from many avian species.

The recent trend in resource-rich countries towards keeping unusual or exotic pets (especially reptiles, exotic birds and mammals) raises new risks of zoonotic infection. Many reptiles, for example, pass human-infective *Salmonella* spp. in their droppings. Exotic birds and mammals can carry a range of viruses that could be transmitted under the correct conditions. Diagnosis of infections under these circumstances can be difficult if the physician does not know of the existence of such pets.

KEY FACTS

- To establish infection in the host, microbes must attach to, or pass across, body surfaces.

- Many microbes have developed chemical or mechanical mechanisms to attach themselves to the surface of the respiratory, urogenital or alimentary tracts. In the skin, they generally depend upon entry via small wounds or arthropod bites.

- Microbes must exit from the body after replication in order to be transmitted to fresh hosts. This also takes place across body surfaces.

- Efficient shedding of microbes from the skin or respiratory, urogenital or alimentary tracts, or delivery into the blood or dermal tissues for uptake during arthropod feeding, are vital stages in their life cycles.

- Many human infections come from animals, either directly (zoonoses) or indirectly (via blood-sucking arthropods), and the incidence of these infections depends upon exposure to infected animals or arthropods.

Immune defences in action

Introduction

The barrier effects of the skin and mucous membranes and their adjuncts such as cilia have already been referred to (see Ch. 9). We now turn to the back-up mechanisms called rapidly into play when an organism has penetrated these barriers – namely, complement, the phagocytic and cytotoxic cells, and a variety of cytotoxic molecules. While they lack the dramatic specificity and memory of adaptive (i.e. lymphocyte-based) immune mechanisms, these natural defences are vital to survival – particularly in invertebrates, where they are the only defence against infection (adaptive responses only evolved with the earliest vertebrates).

In addition to these non-specific mechanisms, the immune system enables the specific recognition of antigens by T and B cells as part of adaptive immunity. Broadly speaking, antibodies are particularly important in combating infection by extracellular microbes, particularly pyogenic bacteria, while T-cell immunity is required to control intracellular infections with bacteria, viruses, fungi or protozoa. Their value is illustrated by the generally disastrous results of defects in T and/or B cells, or their products, discussed in more detail in Chapter 30. This chapter gives examples of how these different types of immunity contribute to the body's defences against microbes.

Antimicrobial peptides protect the skin against invading bacteria

A number of proteins that are expressed at epithelial surfaces, and by polymorphonuclear leukocytes (PMNs), can have a direct antibacterial effect. These include β-defensins, dermicidins and cathelicidins. Defensins form 30–50% of neutrophil granules, and disrupt the lipid membranes of bacteria. Dermicidin is made by sweat glands and secreted into sweat; it is active against *E. coli*, *Staphylococcus aureus* and *Candida albicans*. The precursor cathelicidin protein is cleaved into two peptides, one of which, LL37, is not only toxic to microorganisms but also binds LPS. Mice whose PMNs and keratinocytes are unable to make cathelicidin become susceptible to infection with group A streptococcus. Cathelicidin also plays a role in immunity to *M. tuberculosis*, through its action on vitamin D.

An interesting innate defence mechanism is the formation of neutrophil extracellular traps or NETS. Neutrophil serine proteinases such as cathepsin G, neutrophil elastase and proteinase 3 can be exocytosed by neutrophils to form neutrophil extracellular traps with chromatin that bind both Gram-positive and Gram-negative bacteria (Fig. 14.1) Of course, the bacteria can fight back, in this case through secreting DNAases or by having capsules to prevent entrapment.

Lysozyme is one of the most abundant antimicrobial proteins in the lung. Genetically engineered transgenic mice that had a lot more lysozyme activity than control mice in their bronchoalveolar lavage were much better at killing group B streptococci, and *Pseudomonas aeruginosa* (Fig. 14.2).

COMPLEMENT

The alternative pathway and lectin binding pathways of complement activation are part of the early defence system

The basic biology of the complement system and its role in inducing the inflammatory response and promoting chemotaxis, phagocytosis and vascular permeability have been described in Chapter 9. Here we are concerned with its ability to directly damage microorganisms as part of the early response to infection. Contrary to what might be expected from the dramatic lysis of many kinds of bacteria in the test tube, the action of complement in vivo is restricted mainly to the *Neisseria*. Patients deficient in C5, C6, C7, C8 or C9 are unable to eliminate gonococci and meningococci, with the increased risk of developing septicaemia or becoming a carrier.

It should be emphasized that only the alternative pathway of complement activation or the mannan-binding lectin pathway form part of this natural 'early defence' system. Activation through the classical pathway occurs only after an antibody response has been made. It is not surprising to learn, therefore, that the alternative pathway appears to have evolved first.

ACUTE PHASE PROTEINS AND PATTERN RECOGNITION RECEPTORS

C-reactive protein is an antibacterial agent produced by liver cells in response to cytokines

Among the acute phase proteins produced in the course of most inflammatory reactions, C-reactive protein (CRP) is particularly interesting in being an antibacterial agent, albeit

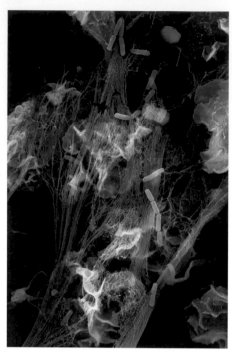

Figure 14.1 Neutrophil extracellular traps can trap bacteria. These chromatin-containing complexes can trap bacteria such as *Shigella* (illustrated). (Photograph courtesy of Dr. Volker Brinkmann, Max Planck Institute for Infection Biology, Berlin.)

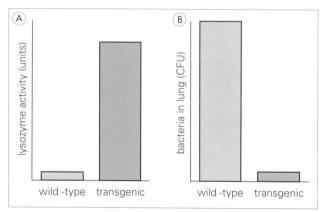

Figure 14.2 Transgenic mice making greater amounts of lysozyme are more resistant to infection with *Pseudomonas aeruginosa*. (A) The transgenic mice made 18-fold more lysozyme than the wild-type control mice. (B) The transgenic mice showed much greater killing of *Pseudomonas aeruginosa* in the lungs following intratracheal infection than the wild-type mice. (Redrawn with data from Akinbi, H.T. et al. (2000) Bacterial killing is enhanced by expression of lysozyme in the lungs of transgenic mice. *J Immunol* 165:5760–5766.)

phase proteins are produced in increased amounts early in infection and have not just antimicrobial activity but can act as opsonins, antiproteases, play an immunomodulatory role or be involved in the fibrinolytic or anticoagulant pathways. For example, many of the complement components are acute phase proteins. Those with a role in protection against infection are also termed pattern recognition receptors, such as mannose-binding lectin. Some acute phase proteins such as lipopolysaccharide binding protein may reduce pathology by binding toxic bacterial products such as lipopolysaccharide.

Macrophages can recognize bacteria as foreign using Toll-like receptors

Another family of surface receptors, called Toll-like receptors, on macrophages and other cells, bind conserved microbial molecules such as lipopolysaccharide (LPS) (endotoxin), bacterial DNA, double-stranded RNA or bacterial flagellin. Pattern recognition receptors recognize these repeated structures (pathogen-associated molecular patterns, see Ch. 9) and this leads to release of proinflammatory cytokines such as tumour necrosis factor alpha (TNFα), IL-1 and IL-6. Signalling through the Toll-like receptors also leads to the increased expression of major histocompatibility complex (MHC) molecules and of co-stimulatory molecules, thus enhancing antigen presentation and usually leading to the activation of T-helper 1 (Th1) cells. It was recently suggested that a number of rare single nucleotide polymorphisms within the TLR4 gene (TLR4 binds endotoxin) were more common in people with meningococcal disease compared with controls.

Microbes in the cytosol of a cell can also be recognized as foreign, using another family of pattern recognition receptors, called nucleotide-binding and oligomerization leucine-rich repeat receptors (NLR). Some NLRs can sense bacterial or viral DNA, leading to activation of inflammasomes, which are complexes of proteins, ultimately leading to the secretion of IL-1β and other proinflammatory cytokines. NLRs can also induce a process called autophagy, in which normal cytoplasmic contents are degraded after fusion with autolysosmes.

Collectins and ficolins

Collectins are proteins that bind to carbohydrate molecules expressed on bacterial and viral surfaces. This results in cell recruitment, activation of the alternative complement cascade, and macrophage activation. Two collectins, the surfactant proteins A and D, are able to directly inhibit bacterial growth and opsonize bacteria, leading to phagocytosis and activation of complement. Surfactant protein A, has been shown to play a role in the innate defence of the lung against infection with group B streptococci. Mice deficient in surfactant protein A were much more susceptible to infection, developing greater pulmonary infiltration and dissemination of bacteria to the spleen, compared with those able to produce the collectin. Polymorphisms in the surfactant A and D genes have also been linked to susceptibility to respiratory syncytial virus (RSV), as these surfactants act as opsonins for the virus.

Mannose-binding lectin (MBL) is another collectin found in serum. Binding of MBL to carbohydrates containing

of very restricted range. CRP is a pentameric β-globulin, somewhat resembling a miniature version of IgM (molecular weight 130000 compared with 900000 for IgM). It reacts with phosphorylcholine in the wall of some streptococci and subsequently activates both complement and phagocytosis. CRP is produced by liver cells in response to cytokines, particularly interleukin-6 (IL-6, see Ch. 11), and levels can rise as much as 1000-fold in 24h – a much more rapid response than that of antibody (see Ch. 9). Therefore, CRP levels are often used to monitor inflammation, for example, in rheumatic diseases. Most of the other acute mannose on microorganisms leads to complement activation, through the mannan-binding lectin pathway. Bacteria opsonized by MBL bind to the C1q receptor on macrophages, leading to phagocytosis. Many individuals have low serum concentrations of MBL due to mutations in the MBL gene or its promoter. A recent study of children with malignancies showed that MBL deficiency increased the duration of infections. Lung surfactant proteins A and D, and MBL, bind to the surface spikes or S protein of the SARS virus (see Ch. 19), and so people with low MBL genotypes may be at increased risk of SARS infection.

Ficolins are plasma proteins with a similar structure to collectins, and bind N-acetyl glucosamine and lipotechoic acid from the cell walls of Gram-positive bacteria.

FEVER

A raised temperature almost invariably accompanies infection (see Ch. 29). In many cases, the cause can be traced to the release of cytokines such as IL-1 or IL-6, which play important roles in both immunity and pathology (see Ch. 11). However, the interesting question as to whether the raised temperature itself is useful to the host remains unresolved.

It is probably unwise to generalize about the benefit or otherwise of fever

Several microorganisms have been shown to be susceptible to high temperature. This was the basis for the 'fever therapy' of syphilis by deliberate infection with blood-stage malaria, and the malaria parasite itself may also be damaged by high temperatures, though it is obviously not totally eliminated. In general, however, one would predict that successful parasites were those that were adapted to survive episodes of fever; indeed the 'stress' or 'heat-shock' proteins produced by both mammalian and microbial cells in response to stress of many kinds, including heat, are thought to be part of their protective strategy. On the other hand, several host immune mechanisms might also be expected to be more active at slightly higher temperatures: examples are complement activation, membrane function, lymphocyte proliferation and the synthesis of proteins such as antibody and cytokines.

NATURAL KILLER CELLS

Natural killer cells are a rapid but non-specific means of controlling viral and other intracellular infections

Natural killer (NK) cells provide an early source of cytokines and chemokines during infection, until there is time for the activation and expansion of antigen-specific T cells. NK cells can provide an important source of interferon-gamma (IFNγ) during the first few days of infection. NK cell cytokine production can be induced by monokines such as IL-12 and IL-18 that are in turn induced by macrophages in response to LPS or other microbial components. As well as IFNγ, NK cells can make TNFα and, under some conditions, the down-regulatory cytokine IL-10. Some tissues like the gut need their own special populations of NK-like cells. NK-like cells express some but not all the usual NK cell markers – but they do make large amounts of the cytokine IL-22, which helps defend the gut against certain intestinal pathogens.

NK cells can also act as cytotoxic effector cells, lysing host cells infected with viruses and some bacteria, as they make both cytotoxic granules and perforin. They recognize their targets by means of a series of activating and inhibitory receptors that are not antigen-specific. The inhibitory receptors recognize the complex of MHC class I and self peptide; if both this inhibitory receptor and another NK-cell-activating receptor are engaged, the NK cell will not be activated. However, if there is insufficient MHC class I on the cell surface, the inhibitory receptor is not engaged and the NK cell is activated to kill the target cell. This is an effective strategy, as some viruses inhibit MHC class I expression on the cells they infect. NK cells are therefore a more rapid but less specific means of controlling viral and other intracellular infections. The importance of NK cells is highlighted by the ability of mice lacking both T and B cells (severe combined immunodeficiency, SCID) to control some virus infections, and humans with NK cell defects are also susceptible to certain viruses (Table 14.1).

NK cells form a bridge between the innate and adaptive immune responses, and their function may be enhanced by components of adaptive immunity. Some recent work even suggests that some NK cells can show some immunological memory, so perhaps their full functions are not yet fully appreciated!

PHAGOCYTOSIS

Phagocytes engulf, kill and digest would-be parasites

Perhaps the greatest danger to the would-be parasite is to be recognized by a phagocytic cell, engulfed, killed and digested (Fig. 14.3). A description of the various stages of phagocytosis is given in Chapter 9. Phagocytes (principally macrophages) are normally found in the tissues where invading microorganisms are more likely to be encountered. In addition, phagocytes present in the blood (principally the PMNs) can be rapidly recruited into the tissues when and where required. Only about 1% of the normal adult bone marrow reserve of 3×10^{12} PMNs is present in the blood at any one time, representing a turnover of about 10^{11} PMNs/day. Most macrophages remain within the tissues, and well under 1% of our phagocytes are present in the blood as monocytes. PMNs are short lived, but macrophages can live for many years (see below).

Table 14.1 Natural killer cells play an important role in controlling infections

Infections where NK cells have been shown to help control infection	
Human	**Mouse**
Human cytomegalovirus (HCMV; human herpesvirus 5)	Mouse cytomegalovirus (MCMV)
Vesicular stomatitis virus (VSV)	Herpes simplex virus
Herpes simplex virus (HSV)	Vaccinia virus
Human papilloma virus (HPV)	Influenza virus

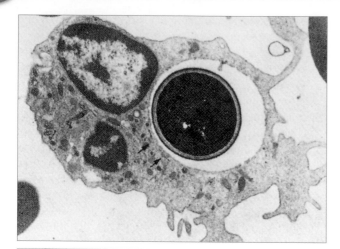

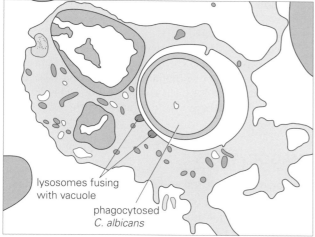

lysosomes fusing
with vacuole

phagocytosed
C. albicans

Figure 14.3 (A) Electron micrograph and (B) diagrammatic representation of neutrophil containing phagocytosed *Candida albicans* (× 7000). (Courtesy of H. Valdimarsson.)

Intracellular killing by phagocytes

Phagocytes kill organisms using either an oxidative or a non-oxidative mechanism

The mechanisms by which phagocytes kill the organisms they ingest are traditionally divided into oxidative and non-oxidative, depending upon whether the cell consumes oxygen in the process. Respiration in PMNs is non-mitochondrial and anaerobic, and the burst of oxygen consumption, the so-called 'respiratory burst' (Fig. 14.4) that accompanies phagocytosis represents the generation of microbicidal reactive oxygen intermediates (ROIs).

Oxidative killing

Oxidative killing involves the use of ROIs

The importance of ROIs in bacterial killing was revealed by the discovery that PMNs from patients with chronic granulomatous disease (CGD) did not consume oxygen after phagocytosing staphylococci. Patients with CGD have one of three kinds of genetic defect in a PMN membrane enzyme system involving nicotinamide adenine dinucleotide phosphate (NADPH) oxidase, *PHOX* (see Ch. 30). The normal activity of this system is the progressive reduction of atmospheric oxygen to water with the production of ROIs such as the superoxide ion, hydrogen peroxide and free hydroxyl radicals, all of which can be extremely toxic to microorganisms (Table 14.2).

CGD patients are unable to kill staphylococci and certain other bacteria and fungi, which consequently cause deep chronic abscesses. They can, however, deal with catalase-negative bacteria such as pneumococci because these produce, and do not destroy, their own hydrogen peroxide in sufficient amounts to interact with the cell myeloperoxidase, producing the highly toxic hypochlorous acid. The defective PMNs from CGD patients can be readily identified in vitro by their failure to reduce the yellow dye nitroblue tetrazolium to a blue compound (the 'NBT test', see Ch. 31).

The way in which ROIs actually kill microorganisms is controversial

ROIs can damage cell membranes (lipid peroxidation), DNA and proteins (including vital enzymes), but in some cases it may be the altered pH that accompanies the generation of ROIs that does the damage. Killing of some bacteria and fungi (e.g. *E. coli*, *Candida*) occurs only at an acid pH, while killing of others (e.g. staphylococci) occurs at an alkaline pH. There may also be a need for protease activity

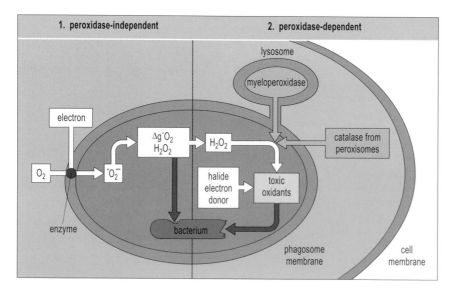

Figure 14.4 Oxygen-dependent microbicidal activity during the respiratory burst. The enzyme NADPH oxidase in the phagosome membrane reduces oxygen by the addition of electrons to form superoxide anion ($^{\bullet}O_2^{-}$). This can then give rise to hydroxyl radicals ($^{\bullet}OH$), singlet oxygen ($\Delta g'O_2$) and H_2O_2, all of which are potentially toxic. If lysosome fusion occurs, myeloperoxidase or in some cases, catalase from peroxisomes, acts on peroxides in the presence of halides to generate toxic oxidants such as hypohalite. NADPH, nicotinamide adenine dinucleotide phosphate. (Reproduced from: Male, D., Brostoff, J., Roth, D.B., Roitt, I. (2006) *Immunology*, 7th edn. Mosby Elsevier, with permission.)

Table 14.2 Some organisms killed by reactive oxygen and nitrogen species

Bacteria	Fungi	Protozoa
Staphylococcus aureus	Candida albicans	Plasmodium
E. coli	Aspergillus	Leishmania (nitric oxide)
Serratia marcescens		

(e.g. cathepsins, elastase), with enzyme solubilization occurring as a result of the influx of H+ and K+ into the phagocytic vesicle.

Cytotoxic lipids prolong the activity of ROIs

As already mentioned, one of the targets of the toxic ROIs is lipid in cell membranes. ROIs are normally extremely short lived (fractions of a second), but their toxicity can be greatly prolonged by interaction with serum lipoproteins to form lipid peroxides. Lipid peroxides are stable for hours and can pass on the oxidative damage to cell membranes, both of the parasite (e.g. malaria-infected red cell) and of the host (e.g. vascular endothelium). The cytotoxic activity of normal human serum to some blood trypanosomes has been traced to the high-density lipoproteins, and in cotton rats to a macroglobulin.

Non-oxidative killing

Non-oxidative killing involves the use of the phagocyte's cytotoxic granules

Oxygen is not always available for killing microorganisms; indeed, some bacteria grow best in anaerobic conditions (e.g. the *Clostridia* of gas gangrene), and oxygen would in any case be in short supply in a deep tissue abscess or a TB granuloma. Phagocytic cells therefore contain a number of other cytotoxic molecules. The best studied are the proteins in the various PMN granules (Table 14.3), which act on the contents of the phagosome as the granules fuse with it. Note that the transient fall in pH accompanying the respiratory burst enhances the activity of the cationic microbicidal proteins and defensins. Neutrophil serine proteinases have homology to the cytotoxic granzymes released by cytotoxic T cells.

Another phagocytic cell, the eosinophil, is particularly rich in cytotoxic granules (Table 14.3). The highly cationic (i.e. basic) contents of these granules give them their characteristic acidophilic staining pattern. Five distinct eosinophil cationic proteins are known and seem to be particularly toxic to parasitic worms, at least in vitro. Because of the enormous difference in size between parasitic worms and eosinophils, this type of damage is limited to the outer surfaces of the parasite. The eosinophilia typical of worm infections is presumably an attempt to cope with these large and almost indestructible parasites. Both the production and level of activity of eosinophils is regulated by T cells and macrophages and mediated by cytokines such as interleukin 5 (IL-5) and tumour necrosis factor alpha (TNFα).

Monocytes and macrophages also contain cytotoxic granules. Unlike PMNs (Table 14.4), macrophages contain little or no myeloperoxidase, but secrete large amounts of lysozyme. Lysozyme is an antibacterial molecule maintained at a concentration of about 30 mg/mL in serum, though this concentration can increase to as high as 800 mg/mL in rare cases of monocytic leukaemia. Macrophages are extremely sensitive to activation by bacterial products (e.g. LPS) and T-cell products, e.g. IFNγ. Activated macrophages have a greatly enhanced ability to kill both intracellular and extracellular targets.

Nitric oxide

A major secreted product of the activated macrophage is nitric oxide (NO), one of the reactive nitrogen intermediates (RNIs) generated during the conversion of arginine to citrulline by arginase. NO is strongly cytotoxic to a variety of cell types, and RNIs are generated in large amounts during infections (e.g. leishmaniasis, malaria). Arginase can also cause damage by leading to a deprivation of arginine, which is an essential amino acid for some viruses (e.g. herpes simplex) and parasites (e.g. the liver fluke *Schistosoma*).

Table 14.3 Contents of polymorphonuclear leukocyte (PMN) and eosinophil granules

PMN and eosinophil granule contents		
PMN		**Eosinophil**
Primary (azurophil)	**Specific (heterophil)**	**Cationic**
Myeloperoxidase	Lysozyme	Peroxidase
Acid hydrolases	Lactoferrin	Cationic proteins
Cathepsins G, B, D	Alkaline phosphatase	ECP
Defensins	NADPH oxidase	MBP
BPI	Collagenase	Neurotoxin
Cationic proteins	Histaminase	Lysophospholipase
Lysozyme		

BPI, bactericidal permeability increasing protein; ECP, eosinophil cationic protein; MBP, major basic protein; NADPH, nicotinamide adenine dinucleotide phosphate.

Table 14.4 The major phagocytic cells – PMNs and macrophages – differ in a number of important respects

Polymorphonuclear leukocytes and macrophages compared		
	PMN	**Macrophage**
Site of production	Bone marrow	Bone marrow
Duration in marrow	14 days	54 h
Duration in blood	7–10 h	20–40 h (monocyte)
Average life span	4 days	Months–years
Numbers in blood	$(2.5–7.5) \times 10^9$/L	$(0.2–0.8) \times 10^9$/L
Marrow reserve	10 × blood	
Numbers in tissues	(Transient)	100 × blood
Principal killing mechanisms	Oxidative, non-oxidative	Oxidative, nitric oxide, cytokines
Activated by	TNFα, IFNγ, GM-CSF, microbial products	TNFα, IFNγ, GM-CSF, microbial products (e.g. LPS)
Important deficiencies	CGD Myeloperoxidase Chemotactic Chediak–Higashi	Lipid storage diseases
Major secretory products	Lysozyme	Over 80, including: lysozyme, cytokines (TNFα, IL-1), complement factors

CGD, chronic granulomatous disease; GM-CSF, granulocyte-macrophage colony-stimulating factor; IFN, interferon; IL, interleukin; LPS, lipopolysaccharide; TNFα, tumour necrosis factor alpha.

CYTOKINES

Cytokines contribute to both infection control and infection pathology

Early studies with supernatants from cultures of lymphocytes and macrophages revealed a family of non-antigen-specific molecules with diverse activities, which were involved in cell-to-cell communication. These are now collectively known as 'cytokines'. They play many crucial roles in protection against infectious diseases. The way in which these molecules acquired their sometimes rather misleading names, and the bewildering overlap of function between molecules of quite different structure, are described in detail in Chapter 11.

Cytokines are of importance in infectious disease for two contrasting reasons:

- They can contribute to the control of infection.
- They can contribute to the development of pathology.

The latter harmful aspect, of which TNFα in septic shock is a good example, is discussed in Chapter 17. The beneficial effects can be direct or more often indirect via the induction of some other antimicrobial process.

Interferons

The best-established antimicrobial cytokines are the interferons (IFNs) (Table 14.5). The name is derived from the demonstration in 1957 that virus-infected cells secreted

Table 14.5 Human interferons (IFNs)

Human interferons			
	IFNα	**IFNβ**	**IFNγ**
Alternative name	'Leukocyte' IFN	'Fibroblast' IFN	'Immune' IFN
Principal source	All cells	All cells	T lymphocytes (NK cells)
Inducing agent	Viral infection (or dsRNA)	Viral infection (or dsRNA)	Antigen (or mitogen)
Number of species	22[a]	1	1
Chromosomal location of gene(s)	9	9	12
Antiviral activity	+ + +	+ + +	+
Immunoregulatory activity Macrophage action MHC I up-regulation MHC II up-regulation	– + –	– + –	+ + + +

dsRNA, double stranded ribonucleic acid; MHC, major histocompatibility complex.
[a] Each species coded by a different gene.

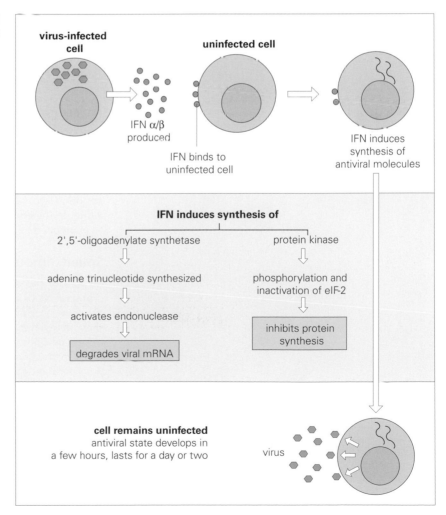

a molecule that interfered with viral replication in bystander cells. IFNs of all three types (α, β and γ) interact with specific receptors on most cells, one for α and β and another for γ, following which they induce an antiviral state via the generation of at least two types of enzyme: a protein kinase and a 2′,5′-oligoadenylate synthetase. Both of these enzymes result in the inhibition of viral RNA translation and therefore of protein synthesis (Fig. 14.5).

IFNα and IFNβ constitute a major part of the early response to viruses

IFNα and IFNβ (type I interferons) are produced rapidly within 24 h of infection, and constitute a major part of the early response to viruses.

Type I IFNs can also inhibit virus assembly at a later stage (e.g. retroviruses), while many of the other effects of IFN contribute to the antiviral state, for example, by the enhancement of cellular MHC expression and the activation of NK cells and macrophages (Fig. 14.6). Unlike cytotoxic T cells, IFN normally inhibits viruses without damaging the host cell. Although best known for their antiviral activity, type I IFNs have recently been shown to be induced by, and active against, infections with a wide range of organisms, including rickettsia, mycobacteria and several protozoa. A recent study of gene expression in patients with tuberculosis identified that many genes induced by type I interferons as well as by type II IFNγ were activated.

In animal experiments, treatment with antibodies to IFNα greatly increases susceptibility to viral infection; treatment with IFNα has proved useful for some human virus infections, notably chronic hepatitis B (see Ch. 22).

IFNγ (type II, immune interferon) is mainly a T-cell product and is therefore produced later, although, as discussed above, an early IFNγ response may be mounted by NK cells. The role of IFNγ is discussed further under T cells, below. Some intracellular organisms (e.g. *Leishmania*) can counteract the effect of IFNγ on MHC expression, thereby facilitating their own survival.

Other cytokines

TNFα production can be good or bad

A striking example of a potentially useful role for TNFα in infection is illustrated by what happened when a humanized antibody against tumour necrosis factor alpha was used to treat patients with rheumatoid arthritis and Crohn's disease. A number of treated patients developed tuberculosis soon after starting therapy (Fig. 14.7); others developed *Listeria*, *Pneumocystis* or *Aspergillus* infections. Patients should now be tested for latent tuberculosis before starting treatment with the tumour necrosis blocking antibody. However, TNF is also thought to contribute to the pathology of tuberculosis, as well as that of malaria (see Ch. 12). This illustrates the often confusing role that cytokines play

Figure 14.5 The molecular basis of type I interferon (IFN) action. eIF-2, eukaryotic initiation factor 2.

virus-infected cell

uninfected cell

IFN α/β produced

IFN binds to uninfected cell

IFN induces synthesis of antiviral molecules

IFN induces synthesis of

2′,5′-oligoadenylate synthetase

adenine trinucleotide synthesized

activates endonuclease

degrades viral mRNA

protein kinase

phosphorylation and inactivation of eIF-2

inhibits protein synthesis

cell remains uninfected
antiviral state develops in a few hours, lasts for a day or two

virus

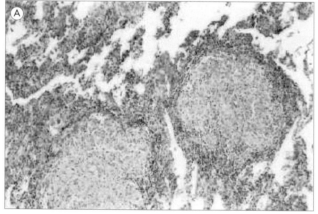

Figure 14.6 The multiple activities of interferons (IFNs) in viral immunity. MHC, major histocompatibility complex; NK, natural killer.

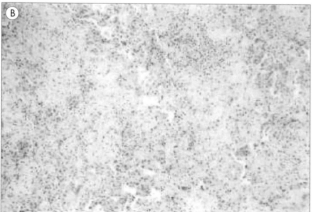

Figure 14.7 Photomicrographs of lung specimens from patients with tuberculosis (A) who did not (×100) or (B) who did (×100) receive Infliximab, a humanized antibody to TNFα. In the patient without Infliximab treatment, the well-formed granuloma shows little necrosis; in the patient with anti-TNF treatment, there is minimal granuloma formation but much fibrosis and inflammation. (Reproduced from Keane, J. et al. (2001) Tuberculosis associated with infliximab, a tumor necrosis factor alpha-neutralizing agent. *N Engl J Med* 345:1098–1104, with permission.)

in infectious diseases of all kinds – 'enough is enough' and 'too much is dangerous' seem to be the rules for these powerful molecules. Paradoxically, TNF concentration is raised in HIV infection and has been found to enhance the replication of HIV in T cells – a 'positive feedback' with worrying potential. The role of T-cell-derived cytokines such as IFNγ in immunity to infection is discussed below.

ANTIBODY-MEDIATED IMMUNITY

The key property of the antibody molecule is to bind specifically to antigens on the foreign microbe. In many cases, this is followed by secondary binding to other cells or molecules of the immune system (e.g. phagocytes, complement). These are discussed below, but first some general features that influence the effectiveness of the antibody response should be mentioned.

Speed, amount and duration

Because of the cell interactions involved and the need for proliferation of a small number of specific precursor lymphocytes, a primary antibody response can be dangerously slow in reaching protective levels. The classic example, before penicillin, was lobar pneumonia, where the race between bacterial multiplication and antibody production was 'neck-and-neck' for about 1 week, at which point one side or the other dramatically won. Nowadays, of course, vaccines and antibiotics have intervened to improve the patient's chances. Experiments with specially bred lines of mice suggest that the speed and size of an antibody response is under the control of a large number of genes, and the same is undoubtedly true in humans.

The rate of replication of the microorganism must also be considered. Replication rates, as indicated by doubling times (see Ch. 15) vary from <1h (most viruses, many bacteria) to days or even weeks (mycobacteria, *T. pallidum*). Microorganisms tend to grow more slowly in vivo than in vitro, which shows that the host environment is generally hostile. When the incubation period is only a few days (e.g. rhinovirus, rotavirus, cholera) the antibody response is too slow to affect the initial outcome, and rapidly produced cytokines such as interferons are more important.

Generally speaking, the antibody response continues as long as antigen is present, although some down-regulation may occur in very prolonged responses, presumably in an effort to limit immunopathology (see Ch. 17). The lifelong immunity that follows many virus infections may often be due to regular boosting by viruses in the community, but sometimes (e.g. yellow fever) there is no obvious boost yet antibodies persist for decades. Such persistence of immunological memory may be due to the non-specific stimulation of memory B and T cells by cytokines during responses to other antigens, a process called bystander activation.

Affinity

It seems self-evident that a higher antigen-binding affinity would render antibody more useful, and passive protection experiments have confirmed this. Affinity is determined by both the germline antibody gene pool and somatic mutation in individual B lymphocytes, and appears to be under genetic control that is separate from that controlling the total amount of antibody made. A tendency towards a low antibody affinity to the tetanus toxoid vaccine has been found in some subjects, particularly those with predominantly IgG4 responses, and there is strong evidence from mouse experiments that failure to develop high-affinity antibody responses can predispose to immune complex disease.

Antibody classes and subclasses (isotypes)

The different Fc portions of the antibody molecule are responsible for most of the differences in antibody function (see Ch. 10). Switching from one to another while preserving the same Fab portion allows the immune system to 'try out' different effector mechanisms against the microbial invader. This flexibility is not total. For example, T-independent antigens such as some polysaccharides induce only IgM antibodies, T cells being required for the switch to IgG, IgA or IgE. IgG antipolysaccharide responses tend to be mainly IgG2, whereas antiprotein IgG is mainly IgG1. The poor development of IgG2 in children below the age of about 2 years explains their lack of response to bacteria with polysaccharide capsules (e.g. *Strep. pneumoniae*, *Haemophilus influenzae*), and considerable effort is being made to produce vaccines that would induce other subclasses of IgG. Antibodies to viruses are predominantly IgG1 and IgG3, and to helminths, IgG4 and IgE, while antigens encountered via the digestive tract induce mainly IgA, the only type of antibody that can function in the protease-rich intestinal environment; T cells and cytokines also play important roles in these isotype preferences.

Blocking and neutralizing effects of antibody

Simple binding of antibody molecules to a microbial surface is often enough to protect the host. It may physically interfere with the receptor interaction necessary for microbial entry (e.g. of a virus into a cell) or with the binding of a toxin to its host receptor. This is the basis of many life-saving vaccines against viruses or bacterial toxins.

Blocking of attachment and entry can be effective against all organisms that use specific attachment sites, whether viral, bacterial or protozoal (see Ch. 16). An important exception is those organisms that parasitize the macrophage, such as the virus of dengue fever; here the presence of a low concentration of IgG antibody can actually enhance infection by promoting attachment to Fc receptors (see below).

A more subtle blocking effect of antibody is interference with essential surface components of the parasite, particularly if these are enzymes or transport molecules. Needless to say, the successful parasite takes steps to protect such components whenever possible, as described in Chapter 16.

Immobilization and agglutination

Immunoglobulin antibodies, particularly the large, pentameric IgM, are the same order of size as some of the smaller viruses, and larger than the thickness of a bacterial flagellum (Fig. 14.8), so the simple physical attachment of antibody can considerably restrict the activities of motile organisms. In addition, the multivalent design of the antibody molecules enables it to link together two or more organisms, as can readily be demonstrated in the bacterial agglutination tests (Fig. 14.9). The protective value of agglutination in vivo is hard to assess; once clumped, most organisms are probably rapidly phagocytosed, but clumps of still motile trypanosomes can be seen in the blood of infected animals with enough serum antibodies. Agglutination reactions in vitro are very useful in diagnosis (see Ch. 31).

Lysis

Lysis of bacteria in the presence of complement provides another convenient assay for the presence of antibody. However, lysis probably plays a major protective role in only a restricted range of infections, notably those caused by *Neisseria* and some viruses (see Ch. 17).

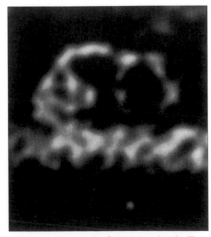

Figure 14.8 Electron micrograph of an IgM molecule. The crab-like configuration is due to cross-linkage with a single flagellum. As an independent molecule, it adopts a 'star-line' configuration. (Courtesy of A. Feinstein.)

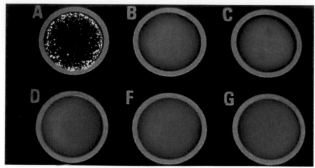

Figure 14.9 Bacterial agglutination. Agglutination of group A streptococcus with latex particles coated with anti-group A antibodies. (Courtesy of D.K. Banerjee.)

Opsonization

Whether by the direct binding of the immunoglobulin CH2 and CH3 regions to Fc receptors, or via the activation of complement to allow C3b to bind to its receptor, opsonization represents the most important overall function of the antibody molecule. Telling evidence for this is the general similarity in the effects on the patient of defects in antibody, complement (up to and including C3) and phagocytic cells (see Ch. 30). It is estimated that the rate of phagocytosis is enhanced by up to 1000-fold by antibody and complement acting together (Fig. 14.10). Lobar pneumonia due to *Strep. pneumoniae* again provides a good example: IgG antibody against the capsule allows neutrophils to phagocytose the organisms, converting overnight a lung virtually solid with fluid, fibrin and phagocytic cells into the normal breathing apparatus. Note that the later complement components C5–9 are not required, so that deficiencies of these do not predispose to bacterial infection in general (see Ch. 30). Of course, the effectiveness of opsonization depends on the phagocytic cell being capable of finishing off the ingested organism. This is not the case, however, with organisms that inhibit or avoid the normal intracellular killing processes, of which mycobacteria are a typical example (see Ch. 16).

Antibody-dependent cellular cytotoxicity

In the case of larger organisms (worms being the most obvious example), phagocytosis is clearly not a possibility. However, several types of cell, having made contact with the

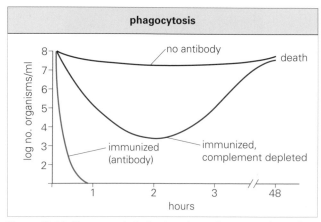

Figure 14.10 Phagocytosis. Antibody and complement accelerate the clearance of pneumococci from the blood of mice.

parasite through antibody and Fc receptors in the same way as phagocytes do, can inflict damage extracellularly. These include most conventional phagocytes as well as eosinophils and platelets. It must be said that virtually all the evidence for this kind of mechanism comes from experiments done in vitro, and here again it is extremely difficult to assess their role in vivo.

Indeed, the precise way in which antibody protects against infection is, in the majority of cases, still unknown. For example, the enormous production of IgA in the intestine, which may amount to half of all antibody produced in the body, suggests the vital importance of mucosal protection, and yet deficiency of IgA is relatively common and not particularly serious.

Table 14.6 gives some examples of common infections normally controlled by antibody. Once again, it must be emphasized that the presence of antibody by no means denotes a protective role. It may be directed against irrelevant or noncritical microbial antigens, or the infection may be of a type that is not controlled by antibody, as with many intracellular infections (tuberculosis, typhoid, herpes virus). The best indication of the value of antibody comes from antibody-deficiency syndromes (Ch. 30).

CELL-MEDIATED IMMUNITY

T cells form the second main component of the adaptive immune response (Chs 10 and 11). Some act by producing cytokines that induce macrophage activation or help antibody production, others by their direct cytotoxic action on infected target cells. In both cases, the T cell needs to 'see' the combination of specific peptide and MHC molecule that is recognized by its T-cell receptor. Some examples of the importance of antibody and cell-mediated immunity in resistance to systemic infections are given in Table 14.6.

T-cell immunity correlates with control of bacterial growth in leprosy

In leprosy, there is a spectrum of disease, ranging from the paucibacillary tuberculoid form to the multibacillary lepromatous disease. *M. leprae*-specific T-cell immunity, as measured by lymphocyte proliferation, secretion of Th1 cytokines such as IFNγ, or delayed-type hypersensitivity skin testing, is found in patients with tuberculoid leprosy, but absent in patients with lepromatous leprosy. The value of T-cell stimulation leading to macrophage activation and bacterial killing is clearly illustrated by experiments in which lepromatous leprosy patients' skin lesions were injected with IFNγ. This resulted in an influx of T cells and macrophages into the skin lesions, and a reduction in the number of bacteria. Another good example of the protective role of IFNγ and Th1 immunity is seen in animal models of *Leishmania* infection: i.e. some mouse strains such as C57BL/6 are resistant to disease, controlling the infection and making a good Th1 cytokine response, whereas other susceptible strains such as BALB/c cannot control parasite growth and fail to make IFNγ (Table 14.7).

Further evidence for the protective effects of IFNγ

The protective effects of making IFNγ, which then binds to its specific receptor on macrophages and induces macrophage activation and the production of antimicrobial molecules,

Table 14.6 Antibody and cell-mediated immunity (CMI) in resistance to systemic infections

Antibody and CMI in resistance to systemic infections		
Type of resistance	**Antibody**	**CMI**
Recovery from primary infection	Yellow fever, polioviruses, coxsackieviruses Streptococci, staphylococci *Neisseria meningitides* *Haemophilus influenza* *Candida* spp. *Giardia lamblia* Malaria[a]	Poxviruses: e.g. ectromelia (mice), vaccinia (humans) Herpes-type viruses: herpes simplex, varicella-zoster, cytomegalovirus LCM virus (mice) Tuberculosis Leprosy Systemic fungal infections Chronic mucocutaneous candidiasis[b]
Resistance to re-infection	Nearly all viruses including measles, most bacteria	Tuberculosis Leprosy
Resistance to reactivation of latent infection		Varicella-zoster, cytomegalovirus, Herpes simplex, tuberculosis, *Pneumocystis jiroveci*[c]

Either antibody or CMI is known to be the major factor in these examples. But in many other infections there is no information, and sometimes both types of immunity are important. LCM lymphocytic choriomeningitis.
[a]Protection is incomplete and short-lived.
[b]Both Th1 and Th17 cells may be involved
[c]Formerly *P. carinii*.

Table 14.7 Cytokine production in the spleens of mice infected with *Leishmania major*

Protective influence of IFNγ in *Leishmania* infection			
Mouse strain	**Phenotype**	**IFNγ**	**Production of IL-4**
C57BL/6	Resistant	+	−
BALB/c	Susceptible	−	+

The resistant phenotype (C57BL/6 mice) was associated with the production of the Th1 cytokine IFNγ, whereas the susceptible phenotype was associated with the production of the Th2 cytokine IL-4.
(From Heinzel, F.P. et al. (1989) Reciprocal expression of interferon gamma or interleukin 4 during the resolution or progression of murine leishmaniasis. *J Exp Med* 169:59, with permission.)

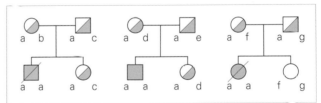

Figure 14.11 Genetic mutations in the IFNγ receptor cause susceptibility to mycobacterial infections. Three Maltese families had children who were susceptible to atypical mycobacterial infection (solid symbols), two of whom died (slashed symbols). Individuals with carrier status are shown with half-filled symbols. All of the affected children were homozygous for the disease locus a on chromosome 6q22-q23, with a point mutation in the gene for the IFNγ receptor. This mutation introduces a stop codon resulting in a non-functional truncated protein. (From: Newport, M.J. et al. (1996) A mutation in the interferon-gamma-receptor gene and susceptibility to mycobacterial infection. *N Engl J Med* 335:1941–1949, with permission. © Massachusetts Medical Society.)

are illustrated very clearly by the consequences of a failure in IFNγ synthesis or of binding to its receptor. Mice in which the gene for IFNγ has been inactivated ('knocked-out') become very susceptible to intracellular infections. Rare individuals with mutations in the genes for the IFNγ receptor have been identified. Such individuals are susceptible to infections with mycobacteria, or to disseminated infections following BCG vaccination (Fig. 14.11).

Some bacteria evade protective Th1 responses by inducing antigen-specific regulatory T cells. *Bordetella pertussis* infection induces regulatory T cells specific for its filamentous haemagglutinin and pertactin. These regulatory T cells produce IL-10 which then suppresses Th1 immunity.

Human IFNγ and IFNα are now used to treat a number of infections (Table 14.8).

Cytokine signatures

During viral infections, the pattern or signature of cytokines produced by T cells may vary with clearance of infection, or antigen load during a chronic infection (Fig. 14.12).

For example, primary infection with HIV or CMV induces mainly IFNγ-producing T cells; in influenza IL-2-producing cells predominate after viral clearance; chronic viral infection such as EBV or HIV in non-progressors seem to lead to a mixed IFNγ and IL-2 signature, but with progressive HIV infection and a higher antigen load this shifts to dominant IFNγ production. The balance between effector T cells and resting memory T cells will also change from acute to chronic disease with HIV. Healthy people have balanced populations of naive, effector and memory T cells in both the CD4 and CD8 compartments; in acute HIV, the effector CD8 T cells expand, but with chronic infection the naive and memory CD4 T cells are lost.

Th17 T cells

The division of CD4 T cells into Th1 and Th2 T cells has aided our understanding of immunity to many infections. However, another CD4 subset making IL-17, and so called

Table 14.8 Examples of the therapeutic use of cytokines in infectious diseases in humans

Cytokine	Organisms	Comments
IFNα	Hepatitis B, Hepatitis C	Pegylated formulation; for HCV usually given with ribavirin/protease inhibitors
	Human herpesvirus 8	Intralesional injection of Kaposi's sarcoma plaques
	Human papillomavirus	Intralesional therapy for genital lesions
IFNγ	Hepatitis B	Pegylated formulation
	M. tuberculosis	Aerosolized treatment given on trial basis to patients with drug-resistant TB and atypical mycobacteria
	Cryptococcus neoformans	Combined with standard antifungal therapy in a phase II trial with a trend towards improved outcomes
	General	Given to patients with chronic granulomatous disease to prevent bacterial and fungal infections

The evidence of benefit for some of these treatments is stronger than for others. The main clinical use of a cytokine is the treatment of patients with chronic granulomatous disease with IFNγ to prevent bacterial and fungal infections.

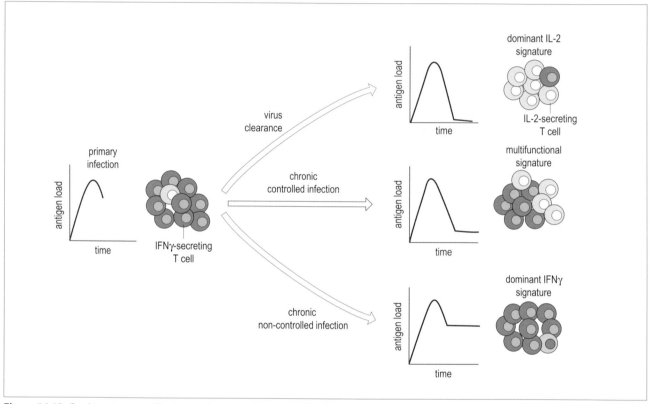

Figure 14.12 Cytokine signatures. The balance between virus-specific T cells secreting IFNγ (purple cells) and T cells secreting IL-2 (yellow cells) is shown for different types of viral infection, illustrated by the small graphs of antigen load over time. Acute infections such as primary HIV-1 or CMV have a high antigen load; following clearance of virus with an infection such as influenza the antigen load falls and IL-2-producing cells predominate; in a chronic controlled infection such as EBV, chronic CMV or HIV-1 in long-term non-progressors there is production of both IL-2 and IFNγ-secreting T cells, and in chronic infection with high antigen load such as progressive HIV-1 infection, IFNγ-producing cells predominate. (Redrawn from: Pantaleo, G., Harari, A. (2006) Functional signatures in antiviral T-cell immunity for monitoring virus-associated diseases. *Nat Rev Immunol* 6:417–423.)

Th17, and induced by the cytokine IL-23, contributes to antimicrobial immunity. Th17 cells play a role in immunity against a number of bacterial infections including *Klebsiella pneumoniae, E. coli, Staph. aureus, Listeria monocytogenes* and *Candida albicans*. One way in which IL-17 works is by inducing neutrophil recruitment. Some patients with chronic mucocutaneous candidiasis have signalling defects leading to problems with production of Th17 cells and increased susceptibility to *Candida*. IL-17 along with IL-22 may also help restrict tissue damage during episodes of inflammation.

Is a positive delayed-type hypersensitivity skin test an indicator of immunity?

The most widely used test of T-cell immunity in humans is the delayed-type hypersensitivity (DTH) skin test, in which induration induced by the intradermal injection of antigen is measured 2–3 days later. Such tests can be used to screen for T-cell anergy, e.g. by using candidin, as most individuals will have been exposed to *Candida*. The most widely used skin test is the Mantoux skin test using antigens from *M. tuberculosis*. However, this test is neither diagnostic nor a correlate of immunity. Unfortunately, many of the antigens in the purified protein derivative of *M. tuberculosis* used as the antigen in this test are cross-reactive with those in other mycobacteria, including BCG and non-tuberculous environmental mycobacteria. This means that skin test positivity may be found in BCG-vaccinated subjects, and in people not exposed to *M. tuberculosis* itself. Nevertheless, those with a large skin test response are at increased risk of developing tuberculosis, showing that strong T-cell responses can be induced during disease progression and that a strongly positive skin test can indicate infection rather than immunity. More specific interferon-gamma release assays that measure IFNγ release in response to antigens present in *M. tuberculosis* and not found in BCG or most environmental mycobacteria are now available.

Cytotoxic T lymphocytes kill by inducing 'leaks' in the target cell

The well-known cytotoxic T lymphocyte (CTL) is unusual in that both antigen-specific recognition and killing of the target are carried out by the same cell. The recognition step, involving an antigenic fragment that becomes associated with a class I MHC molecule, is discussed in Chapter 10, and displays the high degree of specificity characteristic of adaptive responses. The killing mechanism, however, is relatively non-specific. It appears to involve the induction of 'leaks' or pores in the target cell membrane by the insertion of perforin, a 66 kDa molecule that is structurally and functionally similar to the terminal complement component C9 (80 kDa; Fig. 14.13). Other molecules, including granzymes and cytokines such as TNFα, may also be involved, and their effects may be either direct or indirect. Target cell death may be due to:

- leakage
- induction of apoptosis: a 'suicide' programme built into all cells and induced by Fas/FasL interactions, granzymes and TNFα.

These mechanisms are thought to operate principally against virus-infected cells, but some cells infected with other intracellular parasites, including mycobacteria (e.g. *M. leprae* in Schwann cells) and even protozoa (e.g. *Theileria parva* in lymphocytes) may also be susceptible. Most cytotoxic T cells are CD8-positive, recognizing MHC class-I-restricted peptide epitopes, but cytotoxicity can also be mediated by CD4 T cells and by γδ T cells. CD8 T cells are activated in some bacterial infections such as tuberculosis, where the microbe or its antigens may escape into the cytoplasm. CD8 activation may also result from a process called cross-priming, where bacterial antigens taken up by a dendritic cell are processed not only for MHC class II but also for MHC class I presentation. In some cases, apoptotic blebs released by apoptotic infected macrophages may be taken up by the dendritic cells. The lysis of an infected target cell may not always kill the intracellular microbe, but its release from its hideaway may lead to phagocytosis and subsequent killing by a more highly activated macrophage (Fig. 14.14).

Another interesting recent finding is that not all CD8 T cells can act as effector cytotoxic T cells. More human CD8 T cells express the granule protease granzyme A than the pre-formed effector molecule perforin. In HIV infection, two-thirds of the CD8 T cells express granzymes but only one-third express perforin. This may explain why virus-infected cells escape killing by antigen-specific CD8 T cells in HIV infection.

A summary of cytotoxic molecules made by cells involved in both natural and adaptive immunity is given in Table 14.9.

RECOVERY FROM INFECTION

The everyday concept of an infectious disease is one where the patient is ill for a period of days to months and then recovers. In some cases, they are subsequently immune to the disease. In such circumstances, one can be fairly certain

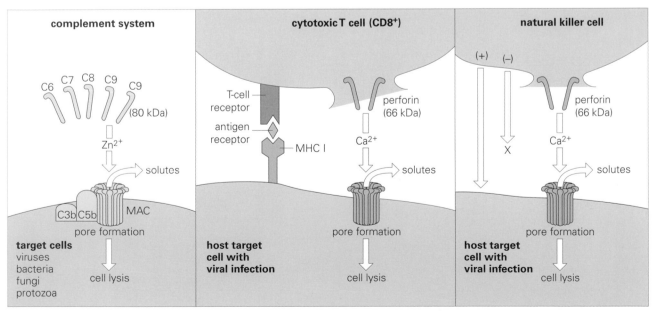

Figure 14.13 Comparison of the lytic mechanisms of cytotoxic cells and the complement system. Ca²⁺, calcium; MAC, membrane attack complex; MHC, major histocompatability complex; Zn²⁺, zinc.

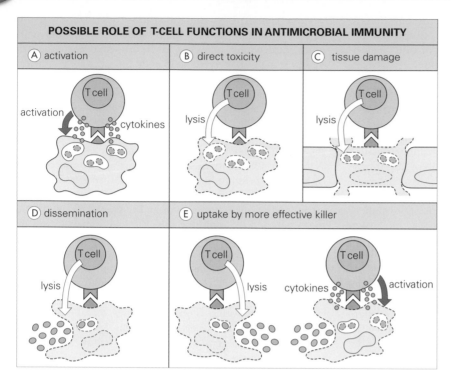

POSSIBLE ROLE OF T-CELL FUNCTIONS IN ANTIMICROBIAL IMMUNITY

(A) activation

(B) direct toxicity

(C) tissue damage

(D) dissemination

(E) uptake by more effective killer

Figure 14.14 Possible roles for T cells in immunity to intracellular microbes. (A) The T cell activates intracellular killing mechanisms by secretion of cytokines such as IFNγ, e.g. in a macrophage. (B) The T cell directly kills cell and parasite. (C) The T cell destroys vital tissue in the process of killing the parasite. (D) By lysing cells the T cell allows still-living parasites to disseminate. (E) Parasites released in this way may be phagocytosed by a more effective host cell. (Redrawn from: Kaufmann, S.H. (1989) In vitro analysis of the cellular mechanisms involved in immunity to tuberculosis. *Rev Infect Dis* 11(Suppl 2):S448–S454.)

Table 14.9 Some important cytotoxic molecules that operate against infectious organisms

Cytotoxic molecules		
Host component		
Major cell source	**Molecule**	**Effective against**
Liver cells	Complement C1–3	Bacteria, fungi
Macrophage	Complement C5–9	*Neisseria* Streptococci
Macrophage, neutrophil, eosinophil	Reactive oxygen intermediates (plus peroxidase)	Bacteria, fungi, malaria
Macrophage	Lysozyme Interferon (α, β) Tumor necrosis factor Reactive nitrogen intermediates	Gram-positive bacteria Viruses Viruses, bacteria, malaria Leishmania, malaria
Neutrophil	Defensins Cathepsins Lactoferrin	Bacteria, fungi Bacteria, fungi Bacteria, yeasts
Eosinophil	Cationic proteins	Schistosome worms
T lymphocyte	Cytokines Perforins Granzymes Granulysin	Viruses, some bacteria, fungi, protozoa Bacteria, fungi
Natural killer cell	Perforins Granzymes Granulysin	Viruses Bacteria, fungi
Liver, fat	High density lipoprotein Low density lipoprotein (oxidized)	Trypanosomes Malaria
Kidney	Urea	Bacteria

that adaptive (lymphocyte-based) mechanisms have been at work, since: (1) the existence of disease symptoms implies that natural defence mechanisms, which act rapidly, did not succeed in eliminating the parasite; (2) a period of days or weeks is typical of the time that adaptive immune mechanisms take to reach maximal levels; and (3) subsequent immunity is a sign of the immunological memory exclusive to lymphocytes, which possess the ability to specifically recognize antigens, to proliferate into clones, and to survive as memory cells. Thus, the older individuals are, the better they are adapted to the environment, until old age begins to weaken the immune system itself.

In the early stages of an infection, however, adaptive immunity can appear somewhat clumsy and ineffective. Since the lymphocytes are programmed to recognize the shapes of antigenic epitopes, they cannot distinguish virulent from harmless parasites, and must rely on recognizing "danger" signals – nor can they 'know' which type of immune response will be most effective. Often, one mechanism is responsible for recovery and another for resistance to re-infection (e.g. cytotoxic cells and interferon in recovery from measles, antibody in prevention of a second attack). In many infections, there is still controversy as to which of the numerous responses that can be detected are useful, harmful or neutral. The reason for an individual's failure to recover from, or to suffer from, an infection can also be hard to pinpoint. If the infection is one from which most people recover (e.g. measles), or from which they do not suffer at all (e.g. *Pneumocystis*), an immunodeficiency should be considered (see Ch. 30). Infections that are rapidly fatal in normal individuals (e.g. Lassa fever) are frequently those to which the human immune system has not been exposed, since they are normally maintained in animals and only accidentally infect humans (see Zoonoses, Ch. 28). But if the infection normally runs a prolonged course without either being eliminated or killing the host, the parasite can be considered to be successful, and this success will be due to one or more survival strategies. These are the subject of Chapter 16.

Nutrition may have more subtle effects on immunity to infection

Even if an immunodeficiency state is not present, other factors may affect how a person copes with an infection. For example, during starvation or malnutrition, concentrations of the hormone leptin (which is produced by adipocytes and among other functions induces PMN activation) fall. Mice fasted for 2 days had higher numbers of *Strep. pneumoniae* in their lungs than normally fed animals, but if the fasted animals were given leptin, the number of PMNs in the lungs increased and the bacterial counts fell (Fig. 14.15). Leptin-deficient mice are highly susceptible to bacterial infections such as *Klebsiella* and *Listeria*. However, being obese is not good either – it is worth noting that obese people seem to be more susceptible to many more types of infections than those of a normal weight.

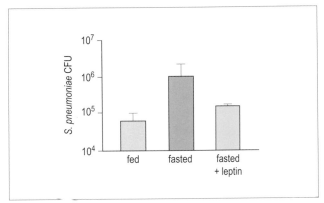

Figure 14.15 Leptin can restore host defence against Strep. pneumoniae in fasted mice. Colony-forming units (CFU) of bacteria in the lung were measured after normal feeding (orange column), in animals fasted for 48 h (purple column), or fasted but given leptin (blue column), 24 h after infection with *Strep. pneumoniae*. (Redrawn from: Mancuso, P. et al. (2006) Leptin corrects host defense defects after acute starvation in murine pneumococcal pneumonia. *Am J Respir Crit Care Med* 173:212–218.)

KEY FACTS

- Protection against infectious organisms that penetrate the outer barriers of the skin and mucous membranes is mediated by a variety of early defence mechanisms, which constitute innate immunity.

- These early defence mechanisms occur more rapidly but are less specific than the adaptive mechanisms based on lymphocyte (T and B cell) responses.

- Important early defence mechanisms include the acute phase response, the complement system, IFNs, phagocytic cells and NK cells. Together, these act as a first line of defence during the initial hours or days of infection.

- Adaptive immunity, mediated by antibody and T cells, is responsible for recovery from infection in many cases, although these mechanisms take days to weeks to reach peak efficiency.

- Sometimes, as in the common viral infections, cell-mediated immunity is responsible for recovery from infection, and antibody for the maintenance of immunity.

- Failure to recover from infection may be due to some deficiency of host immunity or to successful evasion strategies used by the microorganism.

Spread and replication

Introduction

An infection may be a surface infection or a systemic infection

Many successful microorganisms multiply in epithelial cells at the site of entry on the body surface, but fail to spread to deeper structures or through the body. Local spread takes place readily on a fluid-covered mucosal surface, often aided by ciliary action, and large-scale movements of fluid spread the infection to more distant areas on the surface. This is obvious in the gastrointestinal tract. In the upper respiratory tract, high 'winds' (coughing, sneezing) can splatter infectious agents onto new areas of mucosa, or into the openings of sinuses or the middle ear, while the gentler downward trickle of mucus during sleep may seed an infectious agent into the lower respiratory tract. As a result, large areas of the body surface can be involved within a few days, with shedding to the exterior. There is not enough time for a primary immune response to be generated, and therefore non-adaptive responses – interferon, natural killer cells – are more important in controlling the infection. These surface infections therefore show a 'hit-and-run' pattern. In contrast, other microorganisms spread systemically through the body via lymph or blood. They often undergo a complex or stepwise invasion of various tissues before reaching the final site of replication and shedding to the exterior (e.g. measles, typhoid). Surface and systemic infections and their consequences are compared in Figure 15.1.

Figure 15.1 Surface and systemic infections. IFN, interferon; NK, natural killer.

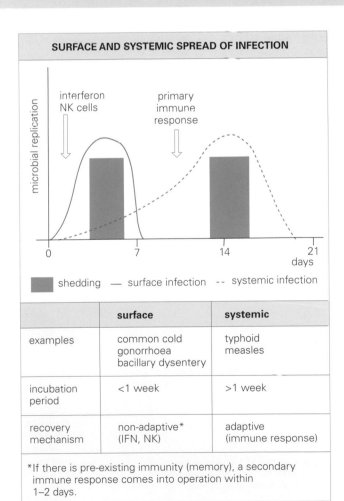

SURFACE AND SYSTEMIC SPREAD OF INFECTION

	surface	**systemic**
examples	common cold gonorrhoea bacillary dysentery	typhoid measles
incubation period	<1 week	>1 week
recovery mechanism	non-adaptive* (IFN, NK)	adaptive (immune response)

*If there is pre-existing immunity (memory), a secondary immune response comes into operation within 1–2 days.

FEATURES OF SURFACE AND SYSTEMIC INFECTIONS

A variety of factors determine whether an infection is a surface or a systemic infection

What prevents surface infections from spreading more deeply? Why do the microbes that cause systemic infections leave the relatively safe haven of the body surface to spread through the body, where they will bear the full onslaught of host defences? These are important questions. For instance, what are the factors that persuade meningococci residing harmlessly on the nasal mucosa to invade deeper tissues, reach the blood and meninges, and cause meningitis (see Ch. 24)? The answer is not known.

Temperature is one factor that can restrict microbes to body surfaces. Rhinovirus infections, for instance, are restricted to the upper respiratory tract because they are temperature sensitive, replicating efficiently at 33°C, but not at the temperatures encountered in the lower respiratory tract (37°C). *Mycobacterium leprae* is also temperature sensitive, which accounts for its replication being more or less limited to nasal mucosa, skin and superficial nerves.

The site of budding is a factor that can restrict viruses to body surfaces. Influenza and parainfluenza viruses invade surface epithelial cells of the lung, but are liberated by budding from the free (external) surface of the epithelial cell, not from the basal layer from where they could spread to deeper tissues (Fig. 15.2).

Many microorganisms are obliged to spread systemically because they fail to spread and multiply at the site of initial infection, the body surface. In the case of measles or typhoid, there is, for unknown reasons, next to no replication at the site of initial respiratory or intestinal infection. Only after spreading through the body systemically are large numbers of microorganisms delivered back to the same surfaces, where they multiply and are shed to the exterior. Other microorganisms need to spread systemically because they have committed themselves to infection by one route, while major replication and shedding occurs at a different site. The microbe must reach the replication site, and there is then no need for extensive replication at the site of initial infection. For instance, mumps and hepatitis A viruses infect via the respiratory and alimentary routes, respectively, but must spread through the body to invade and multiply in salivary glands (mumps) and liver (hepatitis A).

In systemic infections, there is a stepwise invasion of different tissues of the body

This stepwise invasion is illustrated in Figure 15.3, and such infections include measles (Fig. 15.4) and typhoid (Fig. 15.5). Although the final sites of multiplication may be essential for microbial shedding and transmission (e.g. measles), they are sometimes completely unnecessary from this point of view (e.g. meningococcal meningitis, paralytic poliomyelitis).

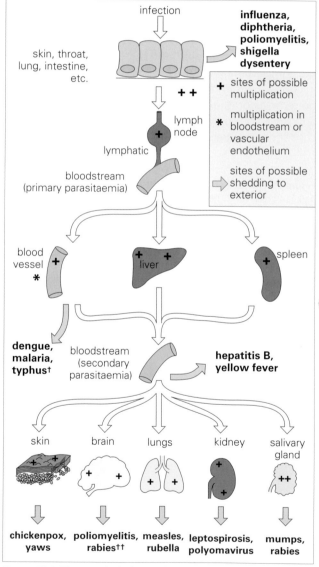

Figure 15.3 The spread of infection throughout the body. Bone marrow and muscle are possible sources for secondary parasitaemia in addition to blood vessels, liver and spleen. †In dengue, malaria and typhus, multiplication occurs in blood cells or vascular endothelium. ††Poliovirus invades the brain and spinal cord from the blood, but is not shed from these sites, whereas rabies invades and later travels from brain to salivary glands via peripheral nerves.

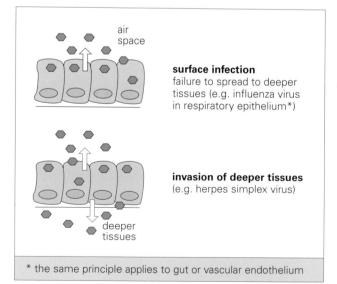

surface infection
failure to spread to deeper tissues (e.g. influenza virus in respiratory epithelium*)

invasion of deeper tissues
(e.g. herpes simplex virus)

* the same principle applies to gut or vascular endothelium

Figure 15.2 Topography of virus release from epithelial surfaces can determine the pattern of infection.

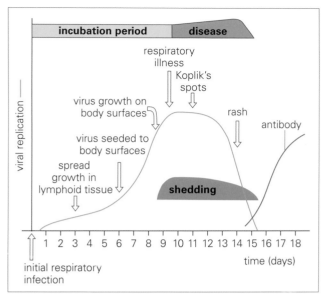

Figure 15.4 The pathogenesis of measles. Virus invades body surfaces from the blood, traversing blood vessels to reach surface epithelium first in the respiratory tract where there are only 1–2 layers of epithelial cells and then in mucosae (Koplik's spots) and finally in the skin (rash).

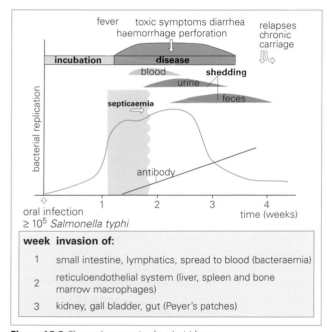

week	invasion of:
1	small intestine, lymphatics, spread to blood (bacteraemia)
2	reticuloendothelial system (liver, spleen and bone marrow macrophages)
3	kidney, gall bladder, gut (Peyer's patches)

Figure 15.5 The pathogenesis of typhoid fever.

These microbes are not shed to the exterior after multiplying in the meninges or spinal cord.

For the microbe, systemic spread is fraught with obstacles, and a major encounter with immune and other defences is inevitable. Microorganisms have therefore been forced to develop strategies for bypassing or countering these defences (see Ch. 16).

Rapid replication is essential for surface infections

The rate of replication of the infecting microorganism is of central importance, and doubling times vary from 20 min to several days (Table 15.1). Hit-and-run (surface) infections need to replicate rapidly, whereas a microorganism that divides

every few days (e.g. *Mycobacterium tuberculosis*) is likely to cause a slowly evolving disease with a long incubation period. Microorganisms nearly always multiply faster in vitro than they do in the intact host, as might be expected if host defences are performing a useful function. In the host, microorganisms are phagocytosed and killed and the supply of nutrients may be limited. The net increase in numbers is slower than in laboratory cultures where microbes are not only free from attack by host defences, but also every effort has been made to supply them with optimal nutrients, susceptible cells, and so on.

MECHANISMS OF SPREAD THROUGH THE BODY

Spread to lymph and blood

Invading microbes encounter a variety of defences on entering the body

After traversing the epithelium and its basement membrane at the body surface, invading microbes face the following defences:

- tissue fluids containing antimicrobial substances (antibody, complement).
- local macrophages (histiocytes). Subcutaneous and submucosal macrophages are a threat to microbial survival.
- the physical barrier of local tissue structure. Local tissues consist of various cells in a hydrated gel matrix; although viruses can spread by stepwise invasion of cells, invasion is more difficult for bacteria, and those that spread effectively sometimes possess special spreading factors (e.g. streptococcal hyaluronidase).
- the lymphatic system. The rich network of the lymphatic system soon conveys microorganisms to the battery of phagocytic and immunologic defences awaiting them in the local lymph node (Fig. 15.6). Macrophages, strategically placed in the marginal and other lymph sinuses, constitute an efficient filtering system for lymph.

Table 15.1 Replication rates of different microorganisms

Microorganisms	Situation	Mean doubling time
Most viruses	In cell[a]	<1 h
Many bacteria, e.g. *Escherichia coli*, staphylococci	In vitro	20–30 min
Salmonella typhimurium	In vitro / In vivo	30 min / 5–12 h
Mycobacterium tuberculosis	In vitro / In vivo	24 h / Many days
Mycobacterium leprae[b]	In vivo	2 weeks
Treponema pallidum[b]	In vivo	30 h
Plasmodium falciparum	In vitro/in vivo (erythrocyte or hepatic cell)	8 h

[a]But some viruses show greatly delayed replication or delayed spread from cell to cell.
[b]But cannot be cultivated in vitro.

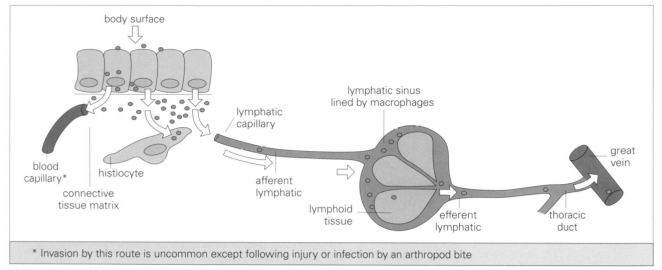

Figure 15.6 Microbial invasion and spread to lymph and blood. Microbes (or other particles) beneath surface epithelium readily enter local lymphatics.

The infection may be halted at any stage, but by multiplying locally or in lymph nodes and by evading phagocytosis, the microorganism can ultimately reach the bloodstream. Therefore, a minor injury to the skin, followed by a red streak (inflamed lymphatic) and a tender, swollen local lymph node are classic signs of streptococcal invasion. Most bacteria cause a great deal of inflammation when they invade in this way. In the early stages, lymph flow increases, but eventually, if there is enough inflammation and tissue damage in the node itself, the flow of the lymph may cease. In contrast, viruses and other intracellular microorganisms often invade lymph and blood silently and asymptomatically during the incubation period; this is facilitated when they infect monocytes or lymphocytes without initially damaging them.

Spread from blood

The fate of microorganisms in the blood depends upon whether they are free or associated with circulating cells

Viruses or small numbers of bacteria can enter the blood without causing a general body disturbance. For instance, transient bacteraemia are fairly common in normal individuals (e.g. they may occur after defecation or brushing teeth), but the bacteria are usually filtered out and destroyed in macrophages lining the liver and spleen sinusoids. Under certain circumstances, the same bacteria have a chance to localize in less well-defended sites, such as congenitally abnormal heart valves in the case of viridans streptococci causing infective endocarditis, or in the ends of growing bones in the case of *Staphylococcus aureus* osteomyelitis.

If microorganisms are free in the blood, they are exposed to body defences such as antibodies and phagocytes. However, if they are associated with circulating cells, these cells can protect them from host defences and carry them around the body. For example, many viruses, such as Epstein–Barr virus (EBV) and rubella, and intracellular bacteria (*Listeria*, *Brucella*) are present in lymphocytes or monocytes and, if not damaged or destroyed, these 'carrying cells' protect and transport them. Malaria infects erythrocytes.

On entering the blood, microorganisms are exposed to macrophages of the reticuloendothelial system (see Ch. 9). Here, in the sinusoids, where blood flows slowly, they are often phagocytosed and destroyed. But certain microorganisms survive and multiply in these cells (*Salmonella typhi*, *Leishmania donovani*, yellow fever virus). The microorganism may then:

- spread to adjacent hepatic cells in the liver (hepatitis viruses), or splenic lymphoid tissues (measles virus)
- re-invade the blood (*S. typhi*, hepatitis viruses).

Each circulating microorganism invades characteristic target organs and tissues

If uptake by reticuloendothelial macrophages is not complete within a short time, or if large numbers of microorganisms are present in the blood, there is an opportunity for localization elsewhere in the vascular system. Why each circulating microorganism invades characteristic target organs and tissues (Table 15.2) is not completely understood, but may be due to:

- specific receptors for the microorganism, leading to localization on the vascular endothelium of certain target organs
- random localization in organs throughout the body, only some of them being suitable for subsequent colonization and replication
- accumulation of circulating microbes in sites where there is local inflammation, because of the slower flow and sticky endothelium in inflamed vessels.

After localization and organ invasion, the replicating microbe is shed from the body if the organ has a surface with access to the outside world (see Fig. 15.3). It may also be shed back into the bloodstream, either directly or via the lymphatic system.

Spread via nerves

Certain viruses spread via peripheral nerves from peripheral parts of the body to the central nervous system and vice versa

Tetanus toxin reaches the central nervous system (CNS) by this route. Rabies, herpes simplex virus (HSV) and varicella-zoster virus (VZV) travel in axons (see Chs 13

Table 15.2 Circulating microorganisms that invade organs via small blood vessels

Microbe	Disease	Principal organs invaded[a]
Viruses		
Hepatitis B	Hepatitis B	Liver
Rubella	Congenital rubella	Placenta (fetus)
Varicella-zoster virus	Chickenpox	Skin, respiratory tract
Polio	Poliomyelitis	Brain, spinal cord
Mumps	Mumps	Parotid, mammary glands
Bacteria		
Rickettsia rickettsi	Rocky Mountain spotted fever	Skin
Treponema pallidum	Secondary syphilis	Skin, mucosae
Neisseria meningitidis	Meningitis	Meninges
Protozoa		
Trypanosoma cruzi	Chagas disease	Heart, skeletal muscle
Plasmodium spp.	Malaria	Liver
Helminths		
Schistosoma spp. (larvae)	Schistosomiasis	Veins of bladder, bowel
Ascaris lumbricoides (larvae)	Ascariasis	Lung
Ancylostoma duodenale (larvae)	Hookworm	Lung

[a]In liver, sinusoids; elsewhere, capillaries, venules.

and 24) and although the rate is slow, being accounted for by axonal flow (up to 10 mm/h), this movement is important in the pathogenesis of these infections. Rabies not only reaches the CNS largely by peripheral nerves, but takes the same route from the CNS when it invades the salivary glands. Few, if any, host defences are in a position to control this type of viral spread once nerves are invaded. Routes of invasion of the CNS are illustrated in Figure 15.7.

An uncommon route of spread to the CNS is via olfactory nerves with axons terminating on olfactory mucosa. For instance, certain free-living amoebae (e.g. *Naegleria* spp.) found in sludge at the bottom of freshwater pools may take this route and cause meningoencephalitis in swimmers (see Ch. 24). Viruses and bacteria in the nasopharynx (e.g. meningococci, poliovirus) generally spread to the CNS via the blood.

Spread via cerebrospinal fluid

Once microorganisms have crossed the blood–cerebrospinal barrier, they spread rapidly in the cerebrospinal fluid spaces

Such microorganisms can then invade neural tissues (echoviruses, mumps virus) as well as multiply locally (*Neisseria meningitidis*, *Haemophilus influenzae*, *Streptococcus pneumoniae*) and possibly infect ependymal and meningeal cells.

Spread via other routes

Rapid spread from one visceral organ to another can take place via the pleural or peritoneal cavity

Both the pleural and peritoneal cavities are lined by macrophages, as if in expectation of such invasion, and the peritoneal cavity contains an antimicrobial armoury, consisting of

Figure 15.7 Routes of microbial invasion of the central nervous system. CSF, cerebrospinal fluid.

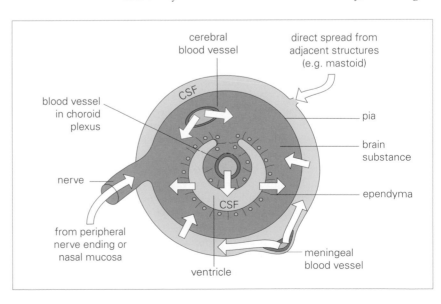

the omentum (the 'abdominal policeman'), and many lymphocytes, macrophages and mast cells. Injury or disease in an abdominal organ provides a source of infection for peritonitis, as do chest wounds or lung infections for pleurisy.

GENETIC DETERMINANTS OF SPREAD AND REPLICATION

The pathogenicity of a microorganism is determined by the interplay of a variety of factors

These factors are referred to in Chapters 12 and 16. A distinction is sometimes made between pathogenicity and virulence: virulence implies a quantitative measure of pathogenicity. For instance, it can be expressed as the number of organisms necessary to cause death in 50% of individuals: lethal dose 50 (LD50). Nearly all pathogenicity factors are controlled by host and microbial genes. It has long been known that there are host genetic influences on susceptibility to infectious disease, and that mutations in microorganisms affect their pathogenicity. A number of these genetic factors have been revealed by the application of molecular genetics techniques, and as a result it is increasingly possible to identify the specific gene products involved. Progress has also been made, though with greater difficulty, in understanding the mode of action of these gene products.

Genetic determinants in the host

The ability of a microorganism to infect and cause disease in a given host is influenced by the genetic constitution of the host

At a relatively gross level, some human pathogens either do not infect other species or infect only closely related primates (e.g. measles, trachoma, typhoid, hepatitis B, warts), whereas others infect a very wide range of hosts (rabies, anthrax). Also, within a given host species, there are genetic determinants of susceptibility. The best examples are found in animals, but there are examples for human disease (see below).

One example at the molecular level is the sickle cell gene and susceptibility to malaria. Malaria merozoites (see Ch. 27) parasitize red blood cells and metabolize haemoglobin, freeing haem and using globin as a source of amino acids. The sickle cell gene causes a substitution of the amino acid valine for glutamic acid at one point in the b-polypeptide chain of the haemoglobin molecule. The new haemoglobin (haemoglobin S) becomes insoluble when reduced, and precipitates inside the red cell envelope, distorting the cell into the shape of a sickle. In homozygous individuals, there are two of these genes and the individual has the disease sickle cell anaemia, because the red cells are so fragile they sickle under normal circumstances. But in the heterozygote (sickle cell trait), the gene is less harmful, and provides resistance to severe forms of falciparum malaria, which ensures its selection in endemic malarial regions. The gene would be eliminated from populations after 10–20 generations unless it conferred some advantage. Restriction endonuclease analyses of the gene in Indian and West African populations have revealed that it arose independently in these malarious countries. Homozygotes, however, show increasing sus-

ceptibility to other infections, particularly *Strep. pneumoniae*, as a result of splenic dysfunction following repeated splenic infarcts.

Other examples are individuals whom are nonsecretors of ABO blood groups, due to homozygosity for a fucosyltransferase 2 (FUT2) variant that is critical for AB antigen synthesis, who are completely resistant to norovirus infections that cause diarrhea. Almost total resistance to HIV-1 infection and new variant Creutzfeldt–Jakob disease is seen in individuals homozygous for a 32-base pair deletion in the CCR5 chemokine receptor gene and those homozygous for valine at codon 129 of the prion protein gene, respectively.

Susceptibility often operates at the level of the immune response

A poor immune response to a given infection can lead to increased susceptibility to disease, whereas an immune response that is too vigorous may lead to immunopathologic disease (see Ch. 17). Of particular importance are the major histocompatibility complex (MHC) genes on chromosome 6, coding for MHC class II (HLA DP, DQ, DR) antigens and controlling specific immune responses (see Chs 10 and 11). For example, susceptibility to leprosy (see Ch. 26) is strongly influenced by MHC class II genes. People with the HLA DR3 antigen are more susceptible to tuberculoid leprosy, whereas those with HLA DQ1 are more susceptible to lepromatous leprosy.

Studies of identical twins (Box 15.1) provide evidence that genetic determinants affect susceptibility to tuberculosis. The present-day European population shows considerable resistance to this disease. During the great epidemics of pulmonary tuberculosis in Europe in the seventeenth, eighteenth and nineteenth centuries, genetically susceptible individuals were weeded out. In 1850, mortality rates in Boston, New York, London, Paris and Berlin were over 500/100 000, but with improvements in living conditions these fell to 180/100 000 by 1900, and they have fallen even more since then. However, previously unexposed populations, especially in Africa and the Pacific Islands, show much greater susceptibility to respiratory tuberculosis. In the Plains Indians living in the Qu'Appelle Valley reservation in Saskatchewan, Canada, in 1886, tuberculosis spread through the body to infect glands, bones, joints and meninges, giving a death rate of 9000/100 000.

Genetic determinants in the microbe

Virulence is often coded for by more than one microbial gene

Virulence is determined by numerous factors such as adhesion, penetration into cells, antiphagocytic activity, production of toxins and interaction with the immune system. Consequently, different genes and gene products are involved in different ways and at different stages in pathogenesis.

Under natural circumstances, microorganisms are constantly undergoing genetic change (i.e. mutations). The single-stranded RNA viruses in particular show very high mutation rates. Mutations affecting surface antigens undergo rapid selection in the host under immune pressure (antibody, cell-mediated immunity), as in the case of the

Box 15.1   Lessons in Microbiology

Genetically determined susceptibility to infection

There are several classic examples of susceptibility to infectious disease determined by unidentified but presumably genetic factors in the human host.

The Lubeck disaster due to vaccination with virulent tubercle bacilli

In Lubeck, Germany, between December 1929 and April 1930, three oral doses of living virulent tubercle bacilli, instead of attenuated (vaccine) bacilli were inadvertently given to 251 infants < 10 days old. There were 72 deaths, 135 developed clinical tuberculosis but recovered and were alive and well 12 years later, while 44 became tuberculin-positive but remained well. Each received the same inoculum, and it seems likely that the differences in outcome were largely due to genetic factors in the host. This disaster was a setback for early BCG enthusiasts. Dr George Deycke, in whose laboratory the contaminated batch of BCG had been produced (but never tested for virulence before use), was tried, found guilty of manslaughter and injury by negligence, and sent to prison, together with the Director of Lubeck Health Office.

A military misfortune due to contamination of yellow fever vaccine with hepatitis B virus

In 1942, >45 000 US military personnel were vaccinated against yellow fever, but were inadvertently injected at the same time with hepatitis B virus present as a contaminant in the human serum used to stabilize the vaccine. There were 914 clinical cases of hepatitis, of which 580 were mild, 301 moderate and 33 severe. Even with a given batch of vaccine, the incubation period varied in the range 10–20 weeks. Serologic tests were not then available, so the number of subclinical infections is unknown. In this case, both physiologic and genetic influences on susceptibility may have played a part.

Identical twins are affected similarly by respiratory tuberculosis

A study of tuberculosis in twins when at least one twin had the disease showed that, for identical twins, the other twin was affected in 87% of cases. With non-identical twins, the equivalent figure was only 26%. In addition, the identical twins had a similar type of clinical disease.

---

rapidly evolving M proteins of streptococci, and the capsid proteins of picornaviruses. In addition, genetic changes in bacteria are often due to acquisition or loss of genetic elements such as integrins, pathogenicity islands, transposons and plasmids (see Chs 2 and 33).

Changes in the virulence of a microorganism take place during artificial culture in the laboratory. For instance, in the classic procedure for obtaining a live vaccine (see Ch. 34), a microorganism is repeatedly grown (passaged) in vitro, and this generally leads to reduced pathogenicity in the host. The new strain is then referred to as 'attenuated' (Table 15.3).

Our understanding of the genetic basis for microbial pathogenicity has advanced due to genetic manipulation techniques such as cloning and site-specific mutagenesis. For instance, by introducing or deleting/inactivating genome segments, the virulence genes can be identified. Examples are shown in Table 15.4. Major advances in genomics including rapid DNA sequencing and sophisticated computer programs for DNA analysis have also made major contributions to our understanding of virulence genes and conditions affecting their expression. This has allowed sequencing of the entire genome for many infectious agents (bacteria and viruses). This information has facilitated the assignment of virulence functions to specific loci and greatly improved our understanding of the way microorganisms sense and respond to the host environment (e.g. two-component regulation and quorum sensing; Figs 2.10 and 2.11, respectively).

OTHER FACTORS AFFECTING SPREAD AND REPLICATION

Various other factors have an influence on susceptibility to infectious disease (Table 15.5). In most cases, it is not known whether this involves differences in microbial spread and replication or differences in host immune and inflammatory responses. Infections in hosts with immunologic and other defects are described in Chapter 33.

The brain can influence immune responses

When stress (a loosely used word) is associated with malnutrition or crowding, it may be difficult to disentangle the separate influences of these various factors on susceptibility to infection, as in the case of tuberculosis. The brain can, however, influence immune responses, acting via the hypothalamus, pituitary and adrenal cortex. It has long been known that glucocorticoids, which have powerful actions on immune cells, are needed for resistance to infection and trauma. A shortage of glucocorticoids, as in Addison's disease, or an excess, as with steroid therapy, results in increased susceptibility to infection (Table 15.5). In addition, the brain, the endocrine and the immune systems often use the same molecular messengers: cytokines, peptide hormones, neurotransmitters. Neural cells, for instance, have receptors for interferons and for interleukins IL-1, IL-2, IL-3, and IL-6, and thymic lymphocytes can produce prolactin and growth hormone. Immune–neuroendocrine cross-talk now has molecular respectability and provides an acceptable basis for the influence of the brain on immunity and infectious disease.

Table 15.3 Examples of attenuation of pathogens following repeated passage in vitro

Pathogen	Passage	Attenuated (live) product
Mycobacterium bovis	10 years of repeated passage in glycerin-bile-potato medium	Bacille Calmette–Guérin (BCG) vaccine
Rubella virus	27 passages in human diploid cells	Rubella vaccine (Wistar RA 27/3)

Table 15.4 Examples of the molecular basis of microbial pathogenicity

Microorganism	Gene or gene product	Effect on virulence
Streptococcus pyogenes	M protein; 60 mm long coiled coil extending from bacterial cell wall with N terminal hypervariable domain Amino acid sequence overlap with host components (myosin, tropomyosin, keratin, etc.)	Antiphagocytic role; inhibits opsonization; exact mechanism unknown Autoimmune complication
Yersinia enterocolitica	Invasion (inv) gene codes for 92 kDa protein on bacterial surface	Required for uptake of bacteria into epithelial cells and macrophages of Peyer's patches
Shigella spp.	Ipa B (invasion plasmid antigen B) gene	Mediates lysis of vacuolar membrane and escape of bacteria into cytoplasm of colonic epithelial cells[a]
Leishmania donovani	Arg-Gly-Asp sequence of gp63 surface protein	Binds to C3b receptor on macrophage and thereby infects this cell
Neisseria gonorrhoeae	Genes for proteins of pili (fimbriae) and for certain outer membrane proteins	Proteins mediate attachment to mucosal cells, independent control of each gene makes *N. gonorrhoeae* the 'master chameleon', altering its surface antigens to evade host immune responses
Herpes simplex virus type 1	Gene for envelope glycoprotein C (gC)	gC acts as receptor for C3b, blocking the classical pathway and enabling virus or virus-infected cell to resist lysis by complement plus antibody
Helicobacter pylori CagA	Cag pathogenicity island encoding 40 genes including cagA gene	Transportation of protein into stomach epithelial cells activates the epidermal growth factor receptor (EGFR) resulting in altered cellular signal transduction and gene expression associated with ulcer formation

[a]*Shigellae* enter the gut wall via M cells in Peyer's patches, then invade colonic epithelial cells from basolateral surfaces. In this, as in other bacterial infections, invasiveness depends upon coordinated expression of many different genes.

Table 15.5 Host factors influencing susceptibility to infectious diseases

Factor	Example	Alteration in susceptibility	Mechanism
Pregnancy	Hepatitis E virus Urinary infections	More lethal outcome Pyelonephritis more ommon	?Increased metabolic burden for liver in pregnancy/immune response Reduced peristalsis in ureter
Malnutrition	Measles	More severe; more lethal	Vitamin A deficiency; depressed CMI
Age	Respiratory syncytial virus Mumps, chickenpox, Epstein–Barr virus infection	More severe; more lethal in infant More severe in adult	Small diameter of airways ?Increased immunopathology
Atmospheric pollution	Raised sulphur dioxide levels Silicosis	Excess acute respiratory disease Increased susceptibility to tuberculosis	?Interference with mucociliary defences ?Damage to lung macrophages
Foreign bodies	Necrotic bone fragments Necrotic tissues	Chronic osteomyelitic more common Increased susceptibility to *Clostridium perfringens*	Antimicrobial defences less effective in necrotic tissue Anaerobic necrotic tissues favour bacterial growth
Stress, hormones	Glucocorticoid production: *Decreased* (Addison's disease) *Increased* (steroid therapy)	Increased susceptibility to infection Increased susceptibility to infection	Hypersensitivity to inflammatory/immune responses? Reduction in protective immune/inflammatory responses

CMI, cell-mediated immunity.

KEY FACTS

- Infections restricted to the body surfaces (e.g. common cold, shigella dysentery) have shorter incubation periods than systemic infections (e.g. measles, typhoid), and adaptive (immune) host responses tend to be less important.

- Microbes with a slow growth rate (e.g. *M. tuberculosis*) tend to cause diseases which evolve slowly.

- Spread through the body takes place primarily via lymph and blood. The fate of circulating microbes depends upon whether they are free or present in circulating blood cells.

- Uptake by reticuloendothelial cells in liver and spleen focuses infection into these organs, but specific localization in the vascular bed of other organs (e.g. mumps virus in salivary glands, meningococci in meninges) is not understood.

- Viruses can spread in either direction along nerve axons, and this is important in the pathogenesis of recurrent herpes simplex virus infection, zoster and rabies.

- Pathogenicity and virulence are strongly influenced by genetic factors in the host (e.g. tuberculosis in identical twins) and by genetic factors in the microbe (e.g. sickle cell trait in falciparum malaria).

- Our understanding of virulence has been greatly enhanced by advances in molecular biology which have allowed sequence analysis of entire microbial genomes and a clearer view of microbial response to the host environment.

Parasite survival strategies and persistent infections

16

Introduction

The most common infectious organisms have developed 'answers' to host defences

So far, we have concentrated on the battery of mechanisms available to the host, both natural and adaptive, to keep out and destroy the parasite. Powerful as these are, they are obviously not 100% effective; otherwise healthy people would never have infections. In fact, most of the common infectious organisms described in this book have developed 'answers' to host defences because their ability to survive as human parasites has depended upon this. They successfully infect humans and are of concern to the physician precisely because they have developed strategies for evading or actively interfering with host defences.

Strategies to evade natural non-adaptive defences such as the phagocyte

These include the following:

- *Killing or avoiding being killed by phagocytes*. Successful parasites have evolved numerous ingenious antiphagocytic devices. Antiphagocytic devices (Fig. 16.1) range from killing or inhibiting the phagocyte itself, via more subtle ways of eluding contact, to protection against intracellular death allowing the microorganism to survive within the phagocyte – a very serious challenge to the host.
- *Interfering with ciliary action* (see Fig. 13.3).
- *Interfering with the activation of complement*. Microorganisms can acquire or mimic complement regulators, actively inhibit complement components, or enzymatically destroy complement components. A variety of microbes can bind complement regulators, including *E. coli*, streptococci and *Candida albicans*. The smallpox and vaccinia viruses produce proteins that mimic host complement regulators. *Staph. aureus*, streptococci, herpes simplex virus, *Schistosoma* and *Trypanosoma* express complement inhibitors. Proteases that destroy complement components are produced by *Pseudomonas*, *Serratia marcescans* and *Schistosoma mansoni*. Other strategies are to physically block complement lysis – the insertion of the C567 complex is prevented by the long side chains of the cell wall polysaccharides of smooth strains of *Salmonellae* and by the capsules of staphylococci, which do not activate complement, and the cell wall of Gram-positive bacteria prevents lysis by the complement membrane attack complex (Fig. 16.2). However, some pathogens take the opposite approach, choosing to enter host cells by exploiting opsonization with complement components – HIV-1 and *Mycobacterium tuberculosis* exploit the CR3 receptor in this way.
- *Producing iron-binding molecules*. Nearly all bacteria need iron, but the host's iron-binding proteins such as transferrin limit the availability of this element.

Accordingly, certain bacteria (e.g. *Neisseria*) produce their own powerful iron-binding proteins to circumvent the shortage
- *Blocking interferons*. Host cells respond to double-stranded DNA (dsRNA) from infecting microbes (including all viruses), by forming interferons alpha and beta. These are produced rapidly, within 24-h, after infection and are part of the non-adaptive response. Certain viruses are either poor inducers of interferons (hepatitis B) or produce molecules that block the action of interferons in cells (hepatitis B, HIV, adenoviruses, Epstein–Barr virus, vaccinia virus). Interferon gamma (IFNγ), an essential part of the adaptive response, is also affected.

Strategies to evade adaptive defences

Strategies to evade adaptive defences are more sophisticated than those for evading innate defences

The success of microbes in evading or interfering with adaptive (immune) defences is discussed in this chapter. The strategies involved are more sophisticated than those for evading innate defences, because lymphocytes are programmed so that their cell receptors can recognize virtually any shape (B cells) or amino acid sequence (T cells), provided it is not identical to self. For example:

- The polysaccharide capsules of bacteria prevent non-immune contact between phagocytes and the bacterial cell wall, but are quickly recognized as foreign by B-cell surface receptors (immunoglobulin), leading to the formation of antibody with consequent opsonization and phagocytosis of the bacteria
- Many microorganisms such as bacteria and fungi can resist intracellular destruction by macrophages, but their peptides are presented in association with major histocompatibility complex (MHC) molecules on the macrophage surface, and their presence is detected by T cells. A new set of cytotoxic and other immune mechanisms is then brought into action.

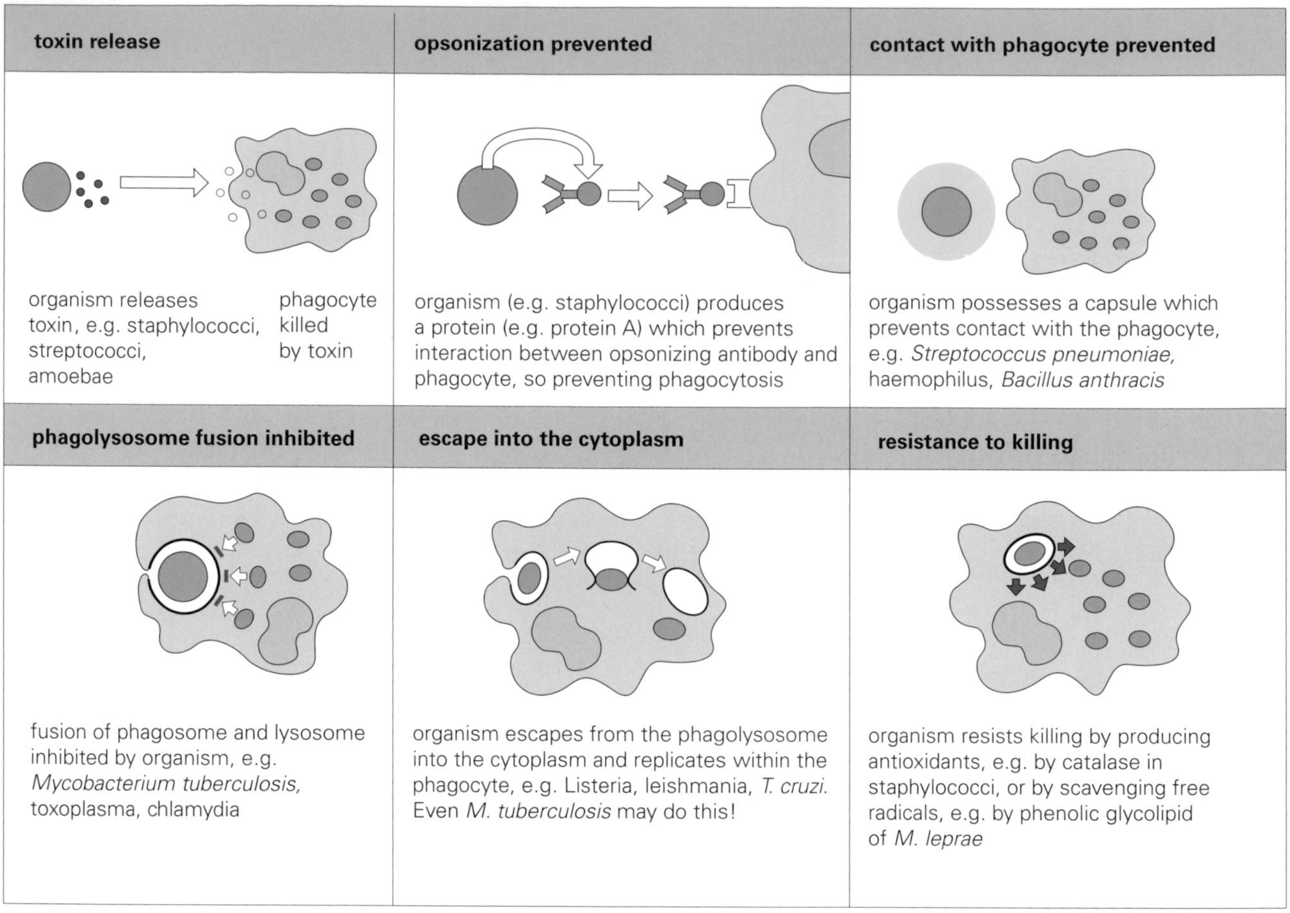

toxin release	opsonization prevented	contact with phagocyte prevented
organism releases toxin, e.g. staphylococci, streptococci, amoebae — phagocyte killed by toxin	organism (e.g. staphylococci) produces a protein (e.g. protein A) which prevents interaction between opsonizing antibody and phagocyte, so preventing phagocytosis	organism possesses a capsule which prevents contact with the phagocyte, e.g. *Streptococcus pneumoniae*, haemophilus, *Bacillus anthracis*
phagolysosome fusion inhibited	escape into the cytoplasm	resistance to killing
fusion of phagosome and lysosome inhibited by organism, e.g. *Mycobacterium tuberculosis*, toxoplasma, chlamydia	organism escapes from the phagolysosome into the cytoplasm and replicates within the phagocyte, e.g. Listeria, leishmania, *T. cruzi*. Even *M. tuberculosis* may do this!	organism resists killing by producing antioxidants, e.g. by catalase in staphylococci, or by scavenging free radicals, e.g. by phenolic glycolipid of *M. leprae*

Figure 16.1 Various mechanisms adopted by microorganisms to avoid phagocytosis.

In both these examples, the lymphocytes are behaving like a highly specialized and sharply observant secret police force in contrast to the everyday activities of the more pedestrian macrophages.

PARASITE SURVIVAL STRATEGIES

Parasite survival strategies can take as many forms as there are parasites, but they can be usefully classified according to the immune component that is evaded and the means selected to do this (see Ch. 12). As a result, the microbe is able to undergo what are often quite lengthy periods of growth and spread during the incubation period before being shed and transmitted to the next host, as occurs in hepatitis B and tuberculosis. Shedding of the microbe for just a few extra days after clinical recovery gives more extensive transmission in the community, and this is a worthwhile result for the microbe.

Viruses are particularly good at thwarting immune defences

Viruses are able to thwart immune defences for a number of reasons:

- Their invasion of tissues and cells is often 'silent'. Unlike most bacteria, they do not form toxins, and as long as they do not cause extensive cell destruction there is no sign of illness until the onset of immune and inflammatory responses, sometimes several weeks after infection, as occurs in hepatitis B virus and EBV infections.

- Viruses such as rubella virus, wart viruses, hepatitis B virus and EBV can infect cells for long periods without adverse effects on cell viability.

Some microbes are able to persist in the host

Certain microbes are able to remain (persist) in the host for many years, often for life. From the microbe's point of view, persistence is worthwhile only if shedding occurs during the persistence. Persistent microbes fall into two categories:

- those that are shed more or less continuously, such as the Epstein–Barr virus (EBV) into saliva, hepatitis B virus into blood, and eggs into faeces in various helminth infections
- those that are shed intermittently, such as herpes simplex virus (HSV), polyomaviruses, typhoid bacilli, tubercle bacilli and malaria parasites.

Virus latency is a type of persistence and is based on an intimate molecular relationship with the infected cell. The viral genome continues to be present in the host without producing antigens or infectious material, and only does so very occasionally, when the virus reactivates (becomes patent) (Box 16.1).

Strategies for evading host defences cause a rapid 'hit-and-run' infection

One evasion strategy for microorganisms is to cause a rapid 'hit-and-run' infection. The microbe invades, multiplies and is shed within a few days, before adaptive immune defences have had time to come into action. Infections of the body surfaces (rhinoviruses, rotaviruses) come into this category. Otherwise,

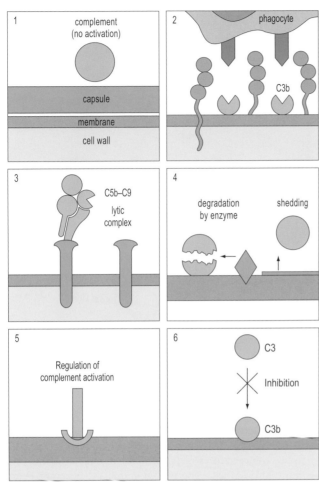

Figure 16.2 Bacteria avoid complement-mediated damage by a variety of strategies. (1) An outer capsule or coat prevents complement activation. (2) An outer surface can be configured so that complement receptors on phagocytes cannot obtain access to fixed C3b. (3) Surface structures can be expressed that divert attachment of the lytic complex (MAC) from the cell membrane. (4) Membrane-bound enzyme can degrade fixed complement or cause it to be shed. (5) Complement inhibitors can be captured onto the surface. (6) Direct inhibition of the C3 and C5 convertases blocks complement activation. (Panels 1–4 reproduced from: Male, D., Brostoff, J., Roth, D.B., Roitt, I. (2006) *Immunology*. Mosby Elsevier, with permission.)

the principal strategies employed by parasites to elude the lymphocyte (as discussed in the following pages) are:

- concealment of antigens
- antigenic variation
- immunosuppression.

Concealment of antigens

A spy in a foreign country can conceal his presence from the police by hiding, by never venturing out of doors, or by adopting the disguise of a native. Parasites have the same choices. Places to hide include the interior of host cells (though the MHC molecules act as 'informers' for this compartment, picking up and transporting microbial peptides to the cell surface where they will be recognized) and particular sites in the body where lymphocytes do not normally circulate ('privileged sites', the equivalent of 'no-go' areas).

Remaining inside cells without their antigens being displayed on the surface prevents recognition

If a microbe can remain inside cells without allowing its antigens to be displayed on the cell surface, it will remain unrecognized ('incognito') as far as immune defences are concerned. Even if specific antibody and T-cell responses have been induced, the microbe inside such a cell is unaffected. Persistent latent viruses such as HSV in sensory neurones behave in this way. During reactivation, of course, re-exposure and boosting of immune defences is inevitable.

Other strategies are possible. Several viruses (HIV in macrophages, coronaviruses) display their proteins 'secretly' on the walls of intracellular vacuoles instead of at the cell surface, and bud into these vacuoles. Adenoviruses have taken more active steps to avoid antigen display. One of the adenoviral proteins (E19) combines with class I MHC molecules and prevents their passage to the cell surface so that infected cells are not recognized by cytotoxic T cells.

Colonizing privileged sites keeps the microbe out of reach of circulating lymphocytes

The vast numbers of microbes that colonize the skin and the intestinal lumen, together with those that are shed

---

Box 16.1   Lessons in Microbiology

Trail of illness from a slippery cook

In 1901, Mary Mallon, from Long Island, New York, took a job as cook with a family in New York City. Soon afterwards, the family washerwoman and a visitor to the house became ill with enteric fever (typhoid). Mary moved to another job and a few weeks later all seven family members plus two of the servants went down with enteric fever. Similar infections followed her movements as a cook and in 1906 the authorities tried to dissuade her from such work. She was indignant at the suggestion that she was carrying a dangerous germ, knowing that she was healthy, and failed to keep promises to have regular checks and give up work. She was suspicious of officials and aggressive, on one occasion advancing towards the questioner brandishing a carving knife. She was later arrested and put in an isolation hospital. After appealing to the US Supreme Court, she was released in 1910 with promises not to work as a cook. Then in 1914 typhoid epidemics broke out in a hospital and in

a sanatorium where she had worked as a cook. She was traced, living under a false name, and in the interests of public safety, she was detained permanently on North Brother Island, where she died in 1938. In her cooking career she had been responsible for about 200 cases of typhoid in eight different families and had started seven epidemics of the disease. Her favourite recipe, an iced peaches dessert, may have been a good source of infection.

Mary had recovered fully from an attack of typhoid earlier in life, but she had gallstones and this enabled the bacteria to persist in her gallbladder for many years, appearing intermittently in the faeces. About 5% of cases become carriers, either in gallbladder or urinary bladder, and they play a central role as foci of infection. Nowadays, Mary would have to have acquired her original infection in a region such as the Indian subcontinent where typhoid is endemic. Each year, there are up to 22 million typhoid cases worldwide, 300 of which are in the USA, most being travellers to the Indian subcontinent (see also Ch. 22).

directly into external secretions, are effectively out of reach of circulating lymphocytes. They are exposed to secretory antibodies, which although able to bind to the microbe (e.g. influenza virus) and render it less infectious, are generally unable to kill the microbe or control its replication in or on the epithelial surface (Figs 16.3, 16.4). A local inflammatory response, however, can enhance host defences.

Within the body, it is more difficult to avoid lymphocytes and antibodies, but certain sites are safer than others. These include the central nervous system, joints, testes and placenta. Here, lymphocyte circulation is less intense, and access of antibodies and complement is more restricted. However, as soon as inflammatory responses are induced, then lymphocytes, monocytes and antibodies are rapidly delivered and the site loses its privilege.

Additional privileged sites can be created by the infectious organism itself. A good example is the hydatid cyst that develops in liver, lung or brain around growing colonies of the tapeworm *Echinococcus granulosus* (Fig. 16.5), inside which the worms can survive even though the blood of the host contains protective levels of antibody.

Perhaps the most highly privileged site of all is host DNA, and this is occupied by the retroviruses. Retroviral RNA is transcribed by the reverse transcriptase into DNA as a necessary part of the replicative cycle, and this then becomes integrated into the DNA of the host cell (see Ch. 21). Once integrated, and as long as there is no cell damage and viral products are not expressed on the cell surface where they

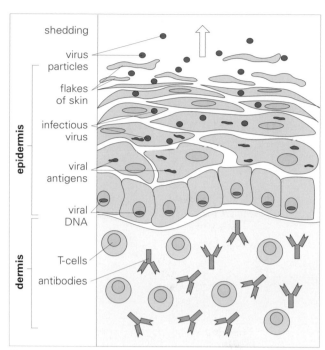

Figure 16.4 Wart virus replication in epidermis – a privileged site? Cell differentiation such as keratinization controls virus replication, and as a result virus matures when it is physically removed from immune defences.

can be recognized by immune defences, the virus enjoys total anonymity. This is what makes complete cure and complete removal of virus from a patient infected with HIV such a daunting task. The intragenomic site becomes even more privileged if the egg or sperm is infected. The viral genome will then be present in all embryonic cells and transferred from one generation to another as if it were the host's own DNA. Luckily, this does not happen with HIV or with human T-cell lymphotropic virus (HTLV) 1 and 2. However, the 'endogenous' retroviruses of humans present in profusion as DNA sequences in our genome, but not expressed as antigens, come into this category. They are part of our inheritance. This surely represents the ultimate, the final logical step in parasitism, at the borderline between infection and heredity.

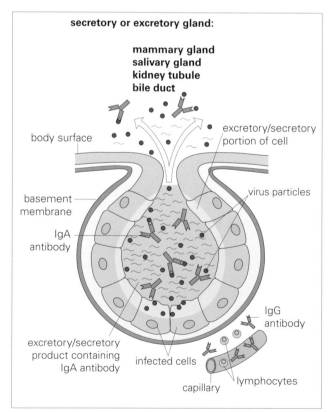

Figure 16.3 Viral infection of cell surfaces facing the external world. Infection of the surface epithelium of, for instance, a secretory or excretory gland allows direct shedding of the virus to the exterior, as well as avoidance of host immune defences.

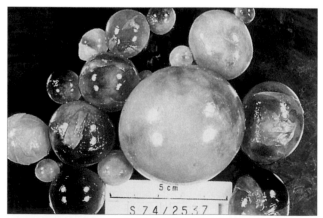

Figure 16.5 Hydatid cysts. Multiple, thin-walled, fluid-filled cysts in a surgical specimen. The lung is a common site. Growing within a cyst is a survival strategy for *Echinococcus granulosus*. (Courtesy of J.A. Innes.)

Mimicry sounds like a useful strategy, but does not prevent the host from making an antimicrobial response

If the microbe can in some way avoid inducing an immune response, this can be regarded as a 'concealment' of its antigens. One method is by mimicking host antigens, as such self antigens are not recognized as foreign. Numerous examples are known of parasite-derived molecules that resemble those of the host (Table 16.1). In the case of viral proteins, mimicry based on amino acid sequence homology (sharing of 8–10 consecutive amino acids) is seen to be common when computer comparisons are made between viral and host proteins. Perhaps the most celebrated example, however, is the cross-reaction between group A beta-haemolytic streptococci and human myocardium. This cross-reaction underlies the development of rheumatic heart disease, following repeated streptococcal infection because of antibody made against the cross-reacting determinant meromyosin (Fig. 16.6). The fact that the host makes such autoantibodies shows that in this case mimicry does not protect the bacteria. The conclusion is that, although mimicry sounds like a useful strategy for microbes and occurs quite frequently, it is probably an accident rather than a sinister microbial strategy. It does not prevent the host from making an antimicrobial and autoimmune response.

Microbes can conceal themselves by taking up host molecules to cover their surface

This is illustrated in Table 16.1. A superb example of this is the blood fluke *Schistosoma*, as the schistosomula acquire a surface coat of host blood group glycolipids and MHC antigens from the plasma. Such a parasite must indeed be virtually invisible even to a lymphocyte. For unknown reasons, however, this strategy is essentially restricted to worms.

The uptake of immunoglobulin molecules by the microbe seems to be a more widespread phenomenon. A number of viruses and bacteria produce Fc receptors, which

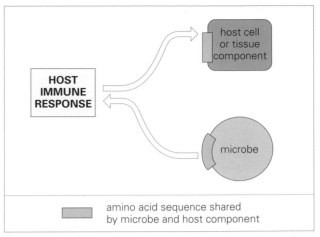

Figure 16.6 Molecular mimicry by the microbe can induce host cell damage, for example rheumatic heart disease following streptococcal infection is caused by antibodies reacting with meromyosin, the cross-reacting determinant.

are displayed on their surface and bind immunoglobulin molecules of all specificities in an immunologically useless upside-down position (Fig. 16.7, and see below). This prevents the access of specific antibodies or T cells to the microbe or the infected cell.

Immune modulation

Modulation of the host immune response by the microbe can prevent this response being an effective one. An alternative strategy for the microbe is to avoid inducing an immune response or to induce a poor response. There are five possible methods:

- infection during early embryonic life
- the production of large quantities of the microbial antigen or of antigen–antibody complexes

Table 16.1 Some examples of mimicry or uptake of host antigens by parasites

Microbe's strategy	Parasite	Corresponding host antigen
Mimicry	Epstein–Barr virus	Human fetal thymus[a]
	Streptococci	Cardiac muscle (meromyosin)
	Mycobacterium tuberculosis	65 kDa heat shock protein
	Neisseria meningitidis	Embryonic brain, vitronectin
	Treponema	Cardiolipin[b]
	Mycoplasma pneumoniae	Erythrocytes[c]
	Plasmodium falciparum	Spondin[d]
	Trypanosoma cruzi	Heart myosin, nerve
	Schistosoma	Glutathione transferase
Antigen uptake	*Neisseria meningitides*	Vitronectin
	Haemophilus influenzae	Vitronectin
	Cytomegalovirus	β_2-microglobulin
	Schistosoma	Glycolipids, HLA I, HLA II
	Filarial nematodes	Albumin
	Ascaris	Blood group antigens

[a]Also cross-reacts with erythrocytes of certain species and is the basis for the Paul Bunnell (heterophil antibody) test.
[b]Basis for Wasserman-type antibody test for syphilis.
[c]Basis for cold agglutinin test, but may result from damage to erythrocytes rather than direct mimicry.
[d]The homologous malaria protein thrombospondin-related anonymous protein (TRAP) shares sequence with the circumsporozoite protein that mediates binding to hepatocytes. HLA, human leukocyte antigen; Ig, immunoglobulin.

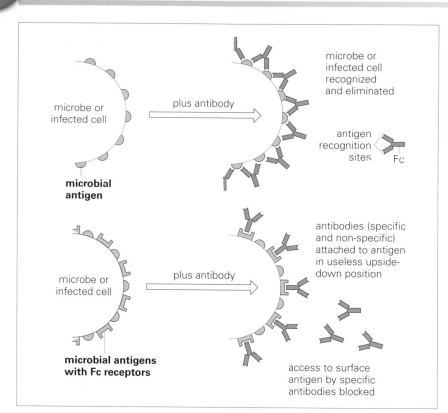

Figure 16.7 The production of Fc receptors is of some benefit to microbes, for example staphylococci, streptococci, herpes simplex virus, varicella-zoster virus and cytomegalovirus.

- exploiting 'gaps' in the host's immune repertoire
- upsetting the balance between antibody and cell-mediated immune responses – between T-helper cell (Th) 1 and 2 responses
- inducing immune responses that down-regulate or suppress protective immunity.

Infection during early embryonic life

Before development of the immune system, a time when antigens present are regarded as 'self', infection could possibly result in immune tolerance. However, in the case of intrauterine infection with cytomegalovirus (CMV), rubella virus and syphilis, the fetus does eventually produce IgM antibody, which is detectable in umbilical cord blood, but cell-mediated responses are more seriously impaired. Children with congenital CMV or rubella fail to develop lymphoproliferative responses to CMV or rubella antigens and consequently take years to clear the virus from the body (see Ch. 23). In some cases, infection in the neonatal period is more likely to result in tolerance than infection in later life. Therefore, neonatal infection with hepatitis B virus frequently results in permanent carriage of the virus, though the mechanism is unknown.

Production of large quantities of microbial antigen or antigen–antibody complexes

Large quantities of microbial antigen or antigen–antibody complexes circulating in the body can cause immune tolerance to that antigen. Anergy, as evidenced by normal antibody but depressed cell-mediated immune responses to the invading microbe, is seen in disseminated coccidioidomycosis and cryptococcosis, and in visceral and diffuse cutaneous leishmaniasis, in each case associated with large amounts of microbial antigen in the circulation.

Exploiting 'gaps' in the host's immune repertoire

There are likely to be certain peptides to which the host makes a poor immune response, based on the nature of the host's MHC class II molecules. These represent genetically determined 'gaps' in the host's immune repertoire, and microbes, as they evolve, might be expected to match these peptides. In other words, microbes may be constantly 'probing' the immune repertoire of the host, seeking out weaknesses. European populations today may have more resistant immune repertoires selected following the deaths of so many young adults from tuberculosis in the nineteenth century.

Upsetting the balance between Th1 and Th2 responses

Resistance to infection often depends upon a suitable balance between Th1 and Th2 responses (see Ch. 10). Good defence against tuberculosis and herpesviruses needs cell-mediated immunity, whereas antibody is required for good defence against polioviruses or *Streptococcus pneumoniae*. In active tuberculosis, T cells making IL-4 can be detected, with a reduction in the beneficial Th1 cytokine response. By inducing an ineffective type of response a microbe can promote its own survival.

An altered Th1:Th2 balance can also alter the phenotype of macrophages. In helminth infections, as well as allergy, Th2 cytokines such as IL-4 and IL-13 induce alternatively activated macrophages (classically activated macrophages are those activated by IFNγ). Alternatively activated macrophages are thought to play a role in worm expulsion from the gut.

Regulatory T cells

Some bacteria evade protective Th1 responses by inducing antigen-specific regulatory T cells. *Bordetella pertussis* infection induces regulatory T cells specific for its filamentous haemagglutinin and pertactin. These regulatory T cells produce IL-10, and thus suppress Th1 immunity to two vital bacterial components which help the bacteria attach to host cells. Regulatory T cells are induced by many other bacteria and even by some helminth antigens. (Other types of immunomodulation caused by microbes, e.g. superantigen production, are described below, see 'Immunosuppression'.)

ANTIGENIC VARIATION

Reverting to the metaphor of a spy in foreign territory, there is another way to confuse the enemy and that is by repeated changes in appearance. The African trypanosome, the causative organism of sleeping sickness, does this, and so do a wide range of viruses, bacteria and protozoa. Antigenic variation can occur:

- during the course of infection in a given individual
- during spread of the microbe through the host community (Fig. 16.8).

As a strategy for evading host immune responses, antigenic variation depends upon variation occurring in antigens whose recognition is involved in protection. Antigenic variation is common as the microbe passes through the host community and it tends to be more important in longer-lived hosts, such as humans in whom microbial survival is favoured by multiple re-infections during the lifetime of a given individual. Also, it is more common in infections limited to respiratory or intestinal epithelium where the incubation period is <1 week and the microbe can commonly infect, multiply and be shed from the body before a significant secondary immune response is generated. During systemic infections (e.g. measles, mumps, typhoid), the incubation period is longer and secondary responses have more opportunity to come into action and control an infection by an antigenic variant. Accordingly, antigenic variation is not an important feature of these systemic infections.

At the molecular level, there are three main mechanisms for antigenic variation:

- mutation
- recombination
- gene switching.

The best known example of mutation is the influenza virus

As the influenza virus spreads through the community there are repeated mutations in the genes coding for haemagglutinin and neuraminidase (see Ch. 19), causing small antigenic changes that are sufficient to reduce the effectiveness of B- and T-cell memory built up in response to earlier infections. This is called 'antigenic drift'. Human rhinoviruses and enteroviruses are evolving rapidly and show a similar drift. Antigenic drift could account for the wealth of antigenic types of staphylococci, streptococci and pneumococci. During earlier poliovirus epidemics, mutations occurred at the rate of about two base substitutions per week, some of them involving the main antigenic sites on the virus. HIV (see Ch. 21) undergoes antigenic drift, but in this case it occurs during infection of a given individual, which helps to explain the difficulties experienced by the immune system in controlling this infection. Mutations affecting the epitopes recognized by cytotoxic T (Tc) cells are the source of 'escape mutants'.

The classic example of recombination involves influenza A virus

More extensive and sudden alterations in antigens can take place by the exchange of genetic material between two different microbes. The classic example is genetic 'shift' in influenza A virus (Fig. 16.9; and see Ch. 19). When human and avian virus strains recombine, a completely new strain of influenza A virus suddenly emerges, brandishing a haemagglutinin or neuraminidase of avian origin. This new virus, not previously experienced by the present population, gives rise to an influenza pandemic. The 2009/2010 'swine flu' epidemic which originated in Mexico spread rapidly and was caused by a H1N1 virus – segments of its genome were identified in flu isolates almost 20 years earlier but reassortment led to the new pandemic strain (Fig. 16.9). Surprisingly, new evidence suggests that the 1918 Spanish flu pandemic may not have been caused by antigenic shift, but by an avian flu that became able to infect humans.

Gene switching was first demonstrated in African trypanosomes

Gene switching represents the most dramatic form of antigenic variation and was first demonstrated in the African trypanosomes, *Trypanosoma gambiense* and *T. rhodesiense* (see Ch. 27). These organisms carry genes for about 1000 quite distinct surface molecules known as variant-specific glycoproteins, which cover almost the entire surface and are immunodominant. The trypanosome can switch from the use of one gene to another, much as a B cell does with the immunoglobulin heavy chain-constant genes. The effect on the host is a sequence of unrelated infections at approximately weekly

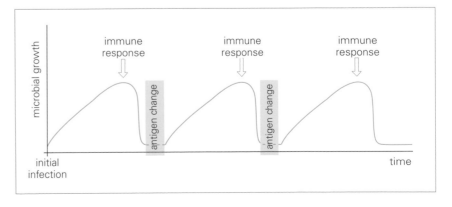

Figure 16.8 Antigenic variation as a microbial strategy. The change in antigens may take place in the originally infected individual, enabling the microbe to undergo renewed growth (e.g. trypanosomiasis, relapsing fever – see Ch. 27) or it may take place as the microbe passes through the host population, enabling it to re-infect a given individual (e.g. influenza).

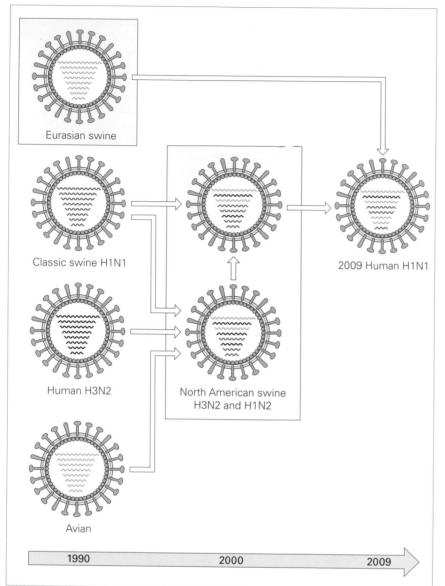

Eurasian swine

Classic swine H1N1

Human H3N2

Avian

North American swine
H3N2 and H1N2

2009 Human H1N1

1990   2000   2009

Figure 16.9 The major surface antigens of influenza virus are haemagglutinin and neuraminidase. Haemagglutinin is involved in attachment to cells, and antibodies to haemagglutinin are protective. Antibodies to neuraminidase are much less effective. The influenza virus can change its antigenic properties slightly (antigenic drift) or radically (antigenic shift). Pandemics can arise when there is antigenic shift with reassortment of genes. The diagram shows the origins of the 2009 pandemic influenza A (H1N1). The official influenza antigen nomenclature is based on the type of haemagglutinin (H_1, H_2, etc.) and neuraminidase (N_1, N_2, etc) expressed on the surface of the virion. Note that, although new strains replace old strains, the internal antigens remain largely unchanged. (Redrawn from Trifonof V. et al., *N Engl J Med* (2009) 361: 115–119.)

intervals. This enables the trypanosome to persist while the immune system is constantly trying to catch up with it. The main stimulus for each gene switch is possibly the antibody response itself, but the exact mechanism is not clear. About 10% of the trypanosome genome consists of surface coat genes, but this is a worthwhile investment for the parasite.

Gene switching is thought to result in the relapsing persistent course of certain infections

Gene switching is also thought to be responsible for the relapsing persistent course of certain other infections, including that by *Borrelia recurrentis* (relapsing fever) and brucellosis. It is also important in gonorrhoea, not because of antigenic variation, but because changes in bacterial properties are desirable at different stages of the infection. For instance, attachment to urethral epithelium is vital early in infection by *Neisseria gonorrhoeae*, but attachment to phagocytes is less desirable. Hence, there is a switching of genes coding for the pilin and outer membrane proteins that mediate attachment. However, gonococci also show

great antigenic variation as they circulate through the host community, and this is achieved by genetic rearrangements and recombinations in the repertoire of pilin genes.

IMMUNOSUPPRESSION

Many virus infections cause a general temporary immunosuppression

A large variety of microorganisms cause immunosuppression in the infected host. The mechanism is generally not understood, but it often involves invasion of the immune system by the microbe – in other words, 'to evade, invade'. As a subversive strategy this makes sense, but the extent to which the microbe benefits is often debatable. The host shows a depressed immune response to antigens of the infecting microbe (antigen-specific suppression) or, more commonly, both to antigens of the infecting microbe and unrelated antigens. HIV is one of the most spectacular, but by no means the only microbe that interferes with the immune system in this way (Table 16.2). HIV causes death of CD4+ T cells, resulting in a disastrous loss of T-cell function.

Table 16.2 Depressed immune responses in microbial infections

Parasite	Feature of immunosuppression	Mechanism
Viruses		
HIV	↓Ab ↓CMI, long-lasting	↓CD4[a] T cells Immunosuppressive molecule (gp41) ↓antigen presentation by infected APC Polyclonal activation of B cells
Epstein–Barr virus	↓CMI, temporary	Includes polyclonal activation of infected B cells[a]
Measles	↓CMI, temporary[b]	Differentiation blocked in infected T and B cells
Cytomegalovirus	↓CMI, temporary	Unknown; very occasional infection of mononuclear cells
Varicella-zoster virus, mumps	↓CMI, temporary	Infection of T cells
Bacteria		
M. leprae (lepromatous leprosy)	↓CMI	Polyclonal activation of B cells, production of IL-4 and IL-10
Protozoa		
Trypanosoma *Plasmodia* *Toxoplasma* *Leishmania*	↓Ab ↓CMI	Regulatory T cells, production of IL-10, ↓T cell proliferation Regulatory T cells, ↓antigen presentation ↓CD4 T cells, IFNγ Production of IL-10 and TGFβ

In most cases, the mechanisms are unclear, but possible important factors are listed. [a]For HIV, the depressed responses are seen later, after initial neutralizing antibody and cytotoxic cell responses. There are at least nine possible mechanisms involved in HIV immunosuppression, but decreased numbers of CD4+ T cells is probably the most important.
[b]Also, the BCRF-1 gene of the virus codes for an IL-10-like molecule that enhances antibody rather than protective CMI responses.
[c]Patients with a positive tuberculin skin test become temporarily negative during measles infection. Measles also stops macrophages producing IL-12, a molecule needed for the Th1-type (protective) immune response. Ab, antibody; CMI, cell mediated immunity; APC, antigen-presenting cell.

Clearly it would benefit the microbe if most responses to its own but not to other antigens were suppressed, but this is uncommon. However, a general immunosuppression, as long as it is temporary, might give the microbe enough time to grow, spread and be shed before being eliminated. This is what happens in many virus infections. A lasting general immunosuppression would be detrimental to the microbe because susceptibility to other infections would cause unnecessary damage to the host species. From this point of view, HIV has certainly overstepped the mark.

Different microbes have different immunosuppressive effects

Immunosuppression by microbes often involves actual infection of immune cells:

- T cells (HIV, measles)
- B cells (EBV)
- macrophages (HIV, CMV, leishmania)
- dendritic cells (HIV).

This may result in impaired cell function, such as blocking of cell division, blocking of release of interleukin 2 (IL-2) or other cytokines, or in cell death.

Additional immunosuppressive actions taken by microbes include the release of immunosuppressive molecules. For instance, the gp41 polypeptide formed by HIV acts as an 'immunologic anaesthetic', temporarily blocking T-cell function. Other microbes (poxviruses, herpesviruses, *T. cruzi*) release molecules that interfere with the action of complement or with immunologically important cytokines such as IL-2, IFNs (see above) or tumour necrosis factor (TNF).

Certain microbe toxins are immunomodulators

A particularly dramatic form of immune interference is practised by the staphylococci. Many strains liberate exotoxins (staphylococcal enterotoxin, epidermolytic toxin and toxic shock syndrome toxin) that are responsible for disease. At first sight, producing these toxins seems to be of no advantage to the staphylococci, but it is now recognized that they have extremely powerful immunomodulatory actions – they are the most potent T-cell mitogens known, and act at picomolar concentrations. They function as 'superantigens' and, after binding to class II MHC molecules on antigen-presenting cells, act as polyclonal activators of T cells (Fig. 16.10). A large proportion (2–20%) of all T cells then respond by dividing and releasing cytokines; only 0.001–0.01% are capable of doing this in response to a regular antigen.

It would be logical to presume that these toxins, which are coded for by plasmids, were acquired by the parasite to upset immune responses and therefore to help in the eternal battle with host defences. As if to confirm this, it has been found that similar molecules are produced by certain streptococci and mycoplasmas.

Possible mechanisms by which the staphylococcal toxins may interfere with immune defences include:

- excessive local liberation of cytokines by activated cells, upsetting the delicate balance of immune regulation
- killing of T cells or other immune cells
- diversion of T cells of all specificities into immunologically unproductive activity by polyclonal activation.

Less dramatic polyclonal activation is seen in many other infections. Microbes may cause polyclonal activation of B cells as well as T cells, e.g. in EBV and HIV infections, and this can be interpreted as an 'immunodiversion' by the infecting

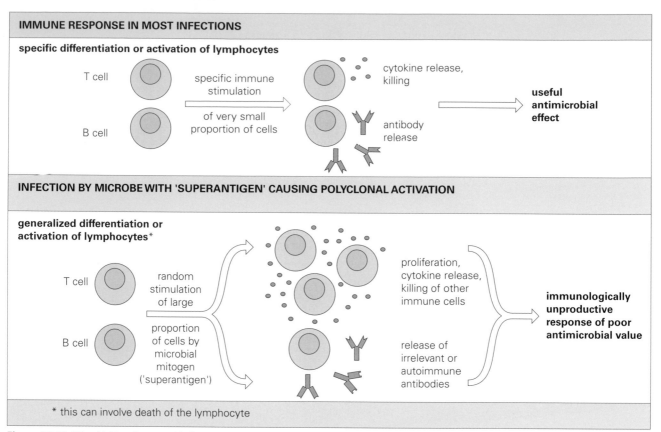

Figure 16.10 Microbial interference with the immune system by production of T- or B-cell superantigens (polyclonal activators).

microbe, or in the case of EBV as production of a supply of B cells in which the virus can grow. One consequence is that a range of 'irrelevant', sometimes autoimmune, antibodies are formed (e.g. heterophil antibodies in EBV infection).

Successful microbes often interfere with signalling between immune cells, with cytotoxic T-cell recognition or with host apoptotic responses

Many microbes interfere with host molecules such as cytokines, chemokines, MHC, and apoptotic and complement receptors, all of which are essential components of host defence. Many DNA viruses code for fake molecules or fake cell receptors for the host molecules, and this disrupts the antimicrobial response. Herpes simplex virus (HSV) produces a molecule, gC (glycoprotein C), that functions as a receptor for C3b. It is present on the virus particle and on the infected cell and interferes with complement activation, protecting both the virus and the infected cell from destruction by antibody and complement.

EB virus produces a homologue of IL-10, which favours a humoral rather than the more protective CMI response induced by IL-12. Virulent strains of *Mycobacterium tuberculosis* induce IL-10 production by infected macrophages, which again favours the infecting microbe. Furthermore, *M. tuberculosis*, as well as other intracellular organisms (*Leishmania major*, *Histoplasma capsulatum*) inhibit IL-12 production by the infected macrophages. T cells are therefore not activated by IL-12 to form IFNγ, and the immune response is again pushed away from the protective Th1 pattern.

Adenoviruses and herpesviruses reduce MHC class I expression on infected cells so that cytotoxic T cells fail to recognize such cells. Other viruses (rotaviruses, adenoviruses) interfere with the production or action of interferons.

A strategy useful for one microbe is not necessarily good for others. For example, a local cell infected with a virus can commit suicide by undergoing apoptosis, a useful defence if it takes place before virus replication is complete. Accordingly, certain viruses (HSV, EBV, HIV) code for proteins that interfere with apoptosis, permitting long-term infection of the cell. Other viruses, however, such as measles, induce apoptosis, as do certain bacteria (*Shigella flexneri*, *Salmonella*) after encountering macrophages, enabling them to escape destruction. It may be useful to induce apoptosis in one cell but not in another. Thus, HIV inhibits apoptosis in the infected immune cell, but induces apoptosis in neighbouring uninfected cells.

Some microbes interfere with the local expression of the immune response in tissues

Some microbes do not interfere with the development of an immune response, but actively interfere with its expression in tissues. For instance *N. gonorrhoeae*, *Strep. pneumoniae* and many strains of *Haemophilus influenzae* liberate a protease that cleaves human IgA antibody. These bacteria are residents or invaders of mucosal surfaces where IgA antibodies operate, and the ability to produce such an enzyme seems unlikely to be mere coincidence.

An equally worthwhile local interference, practised by so many different infectious agents that it is likely to be significant, is the production by the microbe of Fc receptor molecules (see Fig. 16.7). The best-known example is protein A, a cell wall protein excreted from virulent staphylococci that inhibits the phagocytosis of antibody-coated bacteria. Certain herpesviruses (HSV, varicella-zoster virus (VZV), CMV) code for molecules that act as Fc receptors for IgG, and streptococci produce an Fc receptor for IgA, as shown in Figure 16.7.

Table 16.3 Examples of persistent infections in humans

Microorganism	Site of persistence	Infectiousness of persistent microorganism	Consequence	Shedding of microorganism to exterior
Viruses				
Herpes simplex	Dorsal root ganglia	−	Activation, cold sore	+
	Salivary glands	+	Not known	+
Varicella-zoster	Dorsal root ganglia	−	Activation, zoster	+
Cytomegalovirus	Lymphoid tissue	−	Activation ± disease	+
Epstein–Barr virus	Lymphoid tissue	−	Lymphoid tumour	−
	Epithelium	−	Nasopharyngeal carcinoma	−
	Salivary glands	+	Not known	+
Hepatitis B and C	Liver (virus shed into blood)	+	Chronic hepatitis: liver cancer	+
Adenoviruses	Lymphoid tissue	−	None known	+
Polyomaviruses BK and JC (humans)	Kidney	−	Activation (pregnancy, immunosuppression)	+
T-cell leukaemia viruses	Lymphoid and other tissues	±	Late leukaemia, neurologic disease	−
Paramyxovirus	Brain	±	Subacute sclerosing panencephalitis	−
HIV	Lymphocytes, macrophages	+	Chronic disease	+
Chlamydia				
Chlamydia trachomatis	Conjunctiva	+	Chronic disease and blindness	+
Rickettsia				
Rickettsia prowazekii	Lymph node	?	Activation	+
Bacteria				
Salmonella typhi	Gall bladder	+	Intermittent shedding in urine, faeces	+
	Urinary tract			
Mycobacterium tuberculosis	Lung or lymph nodeless (macrophages?)	?	Activation, (immunosuppression, old age)	+
Treponema pallidum	Disseminated	±	Chronic disease	−
Parasites				
Plasmodium vivax	Liver	?	Activation, clinical malaria	+
Toxoplasma gondii	Lymphoid tissue, muscle, brain	±	Activation, neurological disease	−
Trypanosoma cruzi	Blood, macrophages	±	Chronic disease	−
Schistosome mansoni	Gut	+	Chronic disease	Eggs
Filaria	Lymphatics, lymph nodes	+	Chronic disease	+

Shedding to the exterior takes place either directly, for example via skin lesions, saliva or urine, or indirectly via the blood (hepatitis B, malaria).

Other examples include the production by *Pseudomonas* of an elastase that inactivates the C3b and C5a components of complement and hence tends to inhibit opsonic and other host defence functions of complement.

Unfortunately, although the above phenomena look convincingly like microbial adaptations for upsetting host defences, it is not always easy to prove that this is the case.

PERSISTENT INFECTIONS

Persistent infections represent a failure of host defences

One way of looking at persistent infections (Table 16.3) is to regard them as failures of host defences. Host defences are designed to control microbial growth and spread and to eliminate the microbe from the body. The microbe may persist:

- in a flagrantly defiant infectious form, as with hepatitis B in the blood or the schistosome in the blood vessels of the alimentary tract or bladder

- in a form with low or partial infectivity, for instance adenoviruses in the tonsils and adenoids
- in a metabolically altered state, such as *M. tuberculosis*
- in a completely non-infectious form, often without producing any microbial antigens. Latent virus infections are classic examples of this type of persistence. In the case of HSV, viral DNA persists for many years, probably for life, in sensory neurones in the dorsal root ganglia.

The molecular basis for viral latency has still not been elucidated. It involves special adaptations by the virus to the state of latency – in the case of HSV and VZV, there is very limited transcription of viral RNA in infected neurones, known as 'latency-associated transcripts'. The viral genome is not integrated with host DNA, and instead of being linear it is circular, and exists in free episomal form.

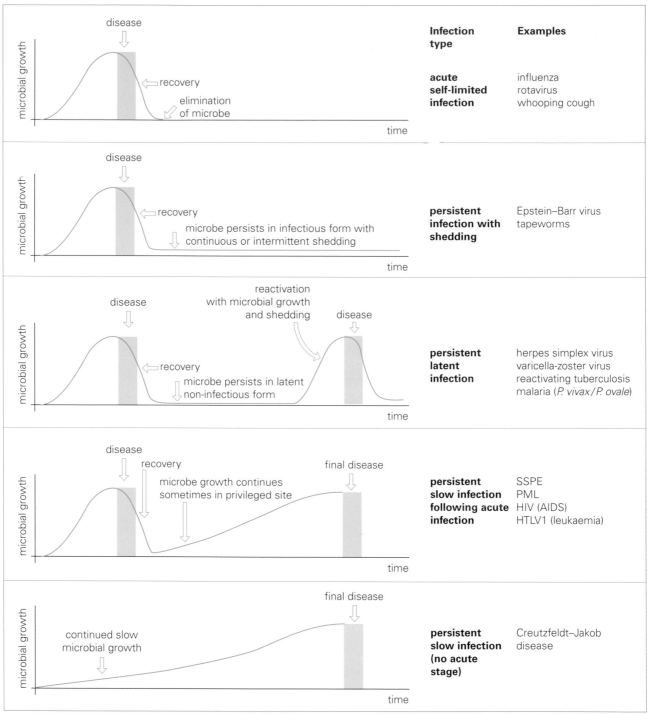

Figure 16.11 Patterns of acute and persistent infections. For some microbes (e.g. CMV, tuberculosis), the distinction between persistence in infectious form and true latency is not clear. HTLV1, human T-cell leukaemia virus 1; PML, progressive multifocal leukoencephalopathy; SSPE, subacute sclerosing panencephalitis.

Latent infections can become patent

Latent infections are so-called because they can become patent. This is where they become of immense medical interest, and the legacy of latent herpesvirus infections in humans is described in Chapter 26. Different patterns of persistent infections are illustrated in Figure 16.11, and they are important for four main reasons:

1. They can be reactivated.

2. They are sometimes associated with chronic disease, as in the case of chronic hepatitis B infections, subacute sclerosing panencephalitis following measles, and AIDS.

3. They are sometimes associated with cancers, such as hepatocellular carcinoma with hepatitis B virus, and Burkitt's lymphoma and nasopharyngeal carcinoma with EBV.

4. From the microbial viewpoint, they enable the infectious agent to persist in the host community (Box 16.2).

Box 16.2 Lessons in Microbiology

Persistence is of survival value for the microbe

Persistence without any further shedding, as occurs in subacute sclerosing panencephalitis and progressive multifocal leukoencephalopathy (see Ch. 24), is of no survival value, but there are obvious advantages if the microbe is also shed, either continuously or intermittently. This is especially true when the host species consists of small isolated groups of individuals (Fig. 16.12). Measles, for instance, is not normally a persistent infection. It only infects humans, does not survive for long outside the body and has nowhere else to go (i.e. there is no animal reservoir). Without a continued supply of fresh susceptible humans, the virus could not maintain itself and would become extinct. There has to be, at all times, someone acutely infected with measles. From studies of island communities it is clear that you need a minimum of about 500 000 humans to maintain measles without reintroduction from outside. In Palaeolithic times, when humans lived in small, isolated groups, measles could not have existed in its present form.

In contrast, persistent and latent infections are admirably adapted for survival under these circumstances. VZV can maintain itself in a community of < 1000 individuals. Children get chickenpox, the virus persists in latent form in sensory neurones, and later in life the virus reactivates to cause shingles. By this time, a new generation of susceptible individuals has appeared and the shingles vesicles provide a fresh source of virus.

Serologic studies show that the viral infections prevalent in small, completely isolated Indian communities in the Amazon basin are persistent or latent (e.g. due to adenoviruses, polyomaviruses, papillomaviruses, herpesviruses) rather than non-persistent (e.g. due to influenza, measles, poliovirus). The same principles apply to non-viral infections. Those present in small communities are either persistent/latent (typhoid, respiratory tuberculosis) or have an animal reservoir for maintenance of the microbe.

non-persistent microbe (e.g. measles)

small community

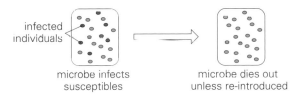

microbe infects susceptibles → microbe dies out unless re-introduced

large community

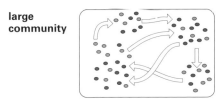

microbe infects susceptibles, spreads through community causing repeated outbreaks as fresh susceptibles appear

persistent microbe (e.g. varicella-zoster virus)

small community

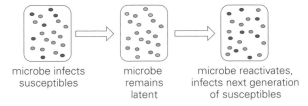

microbe infects susceptibles → microbe remains latent → microbe reactivates, infects next generation of susceptibles

Figure 16.12 Persistence is a microbial survival strategy.

Reactivation of latent infections

Reactivation is clinically important in immunosuppressed individuals

Reactivation occurs in immunocompromised patients, and is of major clinical importance in those immunosuppressed as a result of chronic disease or infection (AIDS), tumours (leukaemias, lymphomas), or in those immunosuppressed by the physician following transplantation (Table 16.4). Reactivation also occurs during naturally occurring periods of immunocompromise, the most important of these being pregnancy and old age. From the microbe's point of view, latency is an adaptation that allows reactivation with renewed growth and shedding of the infectious agent during these naturally occurring periods.

Features of reactivation in herpesvirus infections are described in Chapters 21 and 26. We still know very little about reactivation mechanisms at the molecular level, as might be expected in view of our ignorance about the latent state itself. Latency is often thought of as a period when the microbe is in deep sleep. However, recent experiments suggest it may be a more active state. For example, *M. tuberculosis* needs to make certain proteins to keep itself in a latent state. Other products – called resuscitation promoting factors – may be needed to wake up latent *M. tuberculosis*.

It is useful to distinguish two stages in reactivation

The first event (stage A) in reactivation (Fig. 16.13), the resumption of viral activity in the latently infected cell, is the most mysterious stage. In the case of HSV, this can be triggered by sensory stimuli arriving in the neurone (from skin areas responding to sunlight) and also by certain fevers (i.e. during other infections) or by hormonal influences. Little more than this is known.

Table 16.4 Reactivation of persistent infections

Circumstance	Infectious agent	Site of shedding
Old age	Varicella-zoster virus	Skin vesicles
	Mycobacterium tuberculosis	Lung
Pregnancy	Polyomaviruses (BK, JC)	Urine
	Cytomegalovirus	Cervix
	Herpes simplex virus 2	Cervix
	Epstein–Barr virus	Saliva
Leukaemias, lymphomas (e.g. Hodgkin's disease)	Varicella-zoster virus	Skin vesicles
	Polyomavirus	CNS (PML)[a]
Post-transplant immunosuppression	Herpes simplex virus	Skin/mucosal lesions
	Varicella-zoster virus	Skin vesicles
	Wart viruses	Skin
	Cytomegaloviruses	Viraemia, pneumonitis[a]
	Epstein–Barr virus	Saliva
	Hepatitis B,C	Blood
	Polyomavirus (BK)	Urine
HIV infection	*Pneumocystis jiroveci*[b]	Lung[a]
	Toxoplasma gondii	CNS[a]
	Varicella-zoster virus	Skin vesicles
	Herpes simplex virus	Skin/mucosal lesions
	Mycobacterium tuberculosis	Lung
	Polyomavirus (JC)	CNS (PML)[a]

[a]No shedding from these sites.
[b]Formerly *P. carinii*. PML, progressive multifocal leukoencephalopathy.

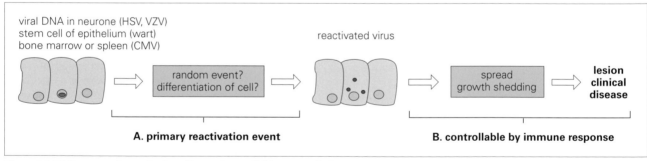

Figure 16.13 Two stages in reactivation of latent viruses. CMV, cytomegalovirus.

The second event (stage B) involves the spread and replication of the reactivated virus. HSV must travel down the sensory axon to the skin or mucosal surface, infect and spread in subepithelial tissues and then in the epithelium, finally forming a virus-rich vesicle (>1 million infectious units/mL of vesicle fluid). All this takes at least 3–4 days. Stage B is less mysterious than stage A and can be controlled by the immune system. Therefore, cold sores may be associated with poor lymphocyte responses to HSV antigens, and zoster with declining cell-mediated responses (specifically to VZV antigens) in old people.

Stage A probably occurs more frequently than stage B, because immune defences often arrest the process during stage B before final production of the lesion. Hence, as many

as 10–20% of HSV reactivation episodes are thought to be 'non-lesional' with burning, tingling and itching at the site, but no signs of a cold sore. Also, zoster may involve no more than the sensory prodrome associated with virus reactivation and replication in sensory neurones; skin lesions are prevented by host defences.

Reactivation of EBV and CMV with appearance of the virus in saliva (EBV) or blood (CMV) is generally asymptomatic. In immunologically deficient individuals, however, reactivation may progress to cause clinical disease: either hepatitis and pneumonitis in the case of CMV or the rarer hairy tongue leukoplakia due to EBV (see Ch. 30).

KEY FACTS

- Many successful parasites have adopted strategies for evading immune responses. These enable them to stay in the body long enough to complete their business of infection and shedding to fresh hosts. Some parasites persist indefinitely in the body.

- Mechanisms of immune evasion include:

  - concealing parasite antigens from the host (staying inside host cells, infecting 'privileged sites')

  - changing parasite antigens, either in the infected individual (trypanosomiasis) or during spread through the host population (influenza)

  - direct action on immune cells (e.g. HIV on CD4+ T cells) or on immune signalling systems (e.g. production of fake cytokine molecules)

  - local interference with immune defences (production of IgA proteases, Fc receptors).

- During persistent infections, the microbe may continue to multiply and be able to infect others (HIV, hepatitis B).

- Alternatively, during persistent infections, the microbe enters into a latent state and later in life reactivates with renewed multiplication and the ability to infect others (herpesviruses, *M. tuberculosis*).

Pathologic consequences of infection

Introduction

Symptoms of infections are produced by the microorganisms or by the host's immune responses

Symptoms that appear rapidly after the acquisition of an infection are usually due to the direct action of the invading microbe by what it secretes. Thus a virus in a cell may cause metabolic 'shut-down' or lyse the cell. Bacteria, however, provoke most of their acute effects by releasing toxins, but may also cause distress by inducing inflammation. The inflammatory response is, of course, an important component of host protection, vascular permeability being vital for the rapid mobilization of cells such as neutrophils, and serum components such as complement and antibody. Inflammation is therefore intrinsically a healthy sign, and it is interesting that some virulent bacteria (e.g. staphylococci) can, to some extent, inhibit the inflammatory response.

Often, however, pathologic changes are secondary to the activation of immunologic mechanisms that are normally thought of as protective. These may involve innate or the adaptive immune system or, more usually, both (Fig. 17.1). Tissue damage resulting from adaptive immune responses is usually referred to as 'immunopathology' and is quite common in infectious diseases, particularly those that are chronic and persistent. The immunologic basis of these mechanisms of tissue damage is described in Chapter 11.

Certain viruses can cause permanent malignant change in cells as a result of direct, indirect and a mixture of both mechanisms. Seven viruses that infect humans cause up to 15% of human cancers around the world. These include HTLV type 1 (lymphomas, leukaemias), Epstein–Barr virus (nasopharyngeal carcinoma and Burkitt's lymphoma), human papillomaviruses (cervical cancer), hepatitis B and C virus infections (liver cancer), HIV (immunosuppression leads to the development of cancers associated with KSHV and EBV) and Merkel cell polyomavirus (Merkel cell carcinoma of the skin). Co-factors may be involved. Immunization programmes focusing on hepatitis B and human papillomaviruses will reduce the incidence of liver and cervical cancer, respectively.

PATHOLOGY CAUSED DIRECTLY BY MICROORGANISM

Direct effects may result from cell rupture, organ blockage or pressure effects

Organisms that multiply in cells and subsequently spread usually do so by rupturing the cell. Many viruses and some intracellular bacteria and protozoa behave in this way (Table 17.1). It is important to realize that many others do not. For example, viruses or bacteria may remain latent (e.g. herpes simplex virus and varicella-zoster virus in nerve ganglia, and *Mycobacterium tuberculosis* in macrophages), and many viruses can bud from a cell without disrupting it. The type of cell infected may also have an influence on survival of the organism. Thus although HIV causes lysis of CD4 T cells, macrophages are more resistant to lysis, perhaps because the virus activates the NFκB pathway, and so virus may persist within intracytoplasmic compartments. Other direct effects include:

- blockage of major hollow viscera by worms
- blockage of lung alveoli by dense growth of, e.g. *Pneumocystis*
- mechanical effects of large cysts (e.g. hydatid).

Exotoxins are a common cause of serious tissue damage, especially in bacterial infection

The parasite may actively secrete 'exotoxins' (Table 17.2). In some cases, these are clearly part of its strategy for entry, spread or defence against the host, but sometimes they seem to be of little or no benefit to the parasite.

Most exotoxins are proteins and are often coded not by the bacterial DNA, but in plasmids (e.g. *E. coli*) or phages (e.g. botulism, diphtheria, scarlet fever). In some cases, they consist of two or more subunits, one of which is required for binding and entry to the cell while the other switches on or inhibits some cellular function.

Powerful toxins are generally secreted from extracellular microbes. Microbes that multiply in cells cannot afford to cause serious damage at too early a stage, and such toxins therefore tend to be less prominent in intracellular infections due to *Mycobacteria*, *Chlamydia* or *Mycoplasma*. For example, leprosy patients with lepromatous disease can live with huge bacterial loads for many years. Although many toxins can kill host cells, lower concentrations may be important by causing dysfunction in immune or phagocytic cells. For example, concentrations of streptolysin well below the cell-killing level will inhibit leukocyte chemotaxis, and the

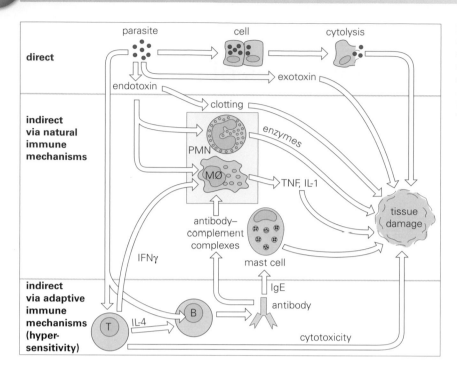

Figure 17.1 Pathologic effects of infection: a general scheme. Infectious parasitic organisms can cause disease directly (top) or indirectly via overactivation of various immune mechanisms, either natural (middle) or adaptive (bottom). IFN, interferon; IL, interleukin; Mφ, macrophage; PMN, polymorphonuclear leukocyte; TNF, tumour necrosis factor.

Table 17.1 Organisms that directly damage tissue

Organism	Cell or tissue damaged	Mechanism
Viruses		
Poliovirus	Neurones	Cytopathic
Rhinovirus	URT mucosa	
HIV	CD4 T cells, macrophages	
Coxsackievirus	Pancreatic β cells, heart cells	
Rotavirus	Enterocytes	
Bacteria		
Streptococcus mutans	Teeth	Acid production
Mycobacteria	Macrophages	Damaged macrophage releases cytokines
Fungi		
Histoplasma	Macrophages	Damaged macrophage releases cytokines
Protozoa		
Plasmodium	Erythrocytes	Damaged erythrocyte removed
Helminths		
Ascaris	Intestinal occlusion	Mechanical
	Biliary occlusion	Mechanical, inflammation
Echinococcus	Hydatid cyst	Pressure effects

Many organisms directly damage or destroy the tissues they infect. This is especially common with cytopathic viruses. URT, upper respiratory tract.

staphylococcal enterotoxin and epidermolytic toxins also have immunomodulatory activity at exceedingly low (nanogram to picogram) levels.

Inactivation of toxins without altering antigenicity results in successful vaccines

Toxins can often be inactivated (e.g. by formaldehyde) without altering their antigenicity, and the resulting toxoids are among the most successful of all vaccines (see Ch. 34), the classic examples being diphtheria and tetanus toxoids.

Toxins are generally more highly conserved in their structure than the surface antigens of the organism secreting them. This allows for more effective cross-immunity and explains, for example, why scarlet fever (caused by streptococcal erythrotoxin) usually occurs only once, while streptococcal infections recur almost indefinitely.

Mode of action of toxins and consequences

These can be considered under five headings (Fig. 17.2).

Table 17.2 Important exotoxins in disease

Organism	Exotoxin	Tissue damaged	Action	Disease
Bacteria				
Clostridium tetani	Tetanus toxin	Neurones	Spastic paralysis	Tetanus
Clostridium perfringens	α-toxin	Erythrocytes, platelets, leukocytes, endothelium	Cell lysis	Gas gangrene
Clostridium botulinum	Neurotoxin	Nerve-muscle junct on	Flaccid paralysis	Botulism
Corynebacterium diphtheriae	Diphtheria toxin	Throat, heart, peripheral nerve	Inhibits protein synthesis	Diphtheria
Shigella dysenteriae	Enterotoxin	Intestinal mucosa	Destroys mucosal cells	Dysentery
E. coli	Enterotoxin	} Intestinal epithelium	} Fluid loss from intestinal cells	Gastroenteritis
Vibrio cholerae	Enterotoxin			Cholera
Staphylococcus aureus	α-haemolysin	Red and white cells (via cytokines)	Hemolysis	Abscesses
	Leucocidin	Leukocytes	Destroys leukocytes	
	Enterotoxins*	Intestinal cells	Induces vomiting, diarrhea	Food poisoning
	TSST1	T cells	Release of cytotoxins	Toxic shock syndrome
	Epidermolytic	Epidermis	Destroys skin desmosomal proteins	Scalded skin syndrome
Streptococcus pyogenes	Streptolysin O and S	Red and white cells	Haemolysis	Haemolysis, pyogenic lesions
	Erythrogenic	Skin capillaries	Skin rash	Scarlet fever
Bacillus anthracis	Cytotoxin	Lung	Pulmonary oedema	Anthrax
Bordetella pertussis	Pertussis toxin	Trachea	Kills epithelium	Whooping cough
Legionella pneumophila	Numerous	Neutrophils	Cell lysis	Legionnaires' disease
Listeria monocytogenes	Hemolysin	Leukocytes, monocytes	Cell lysis	Listeriosis
Pseudomonas aeruginosa	Exotoxin A	Cells	Cell lysis	Various infections
Fungi				
Aspergillus fumigatus	Aflatoxin	Liver	Carcinogenic	?Liver damage/cancer[a]
Protozoa				
Entamoeba histolytica	Enterotoxin	Colonic epithelium	Cell lysis	Amoebic dysentery

Many bacteria and a few other organisms damage host tissues by secreting exotoxins. Some bacterial exotoxins are among the most powerful toxins known. Vaccination, by inducing antibody, is often very effective in protection.

Staphylococcus aureus has 5 enterotoxins, SEA, SEB, SEC, SED and SEE. TSST1, toxic shock syndrome toxin. Staphylococcal entertoxins and TSST-1 are superantigens that activate T cells expressing particular Vβ genes in their T cell receptors.

[a] In turkeys and pigs from *A. fumigatus* contaminated ground nuts but not so far in humans.

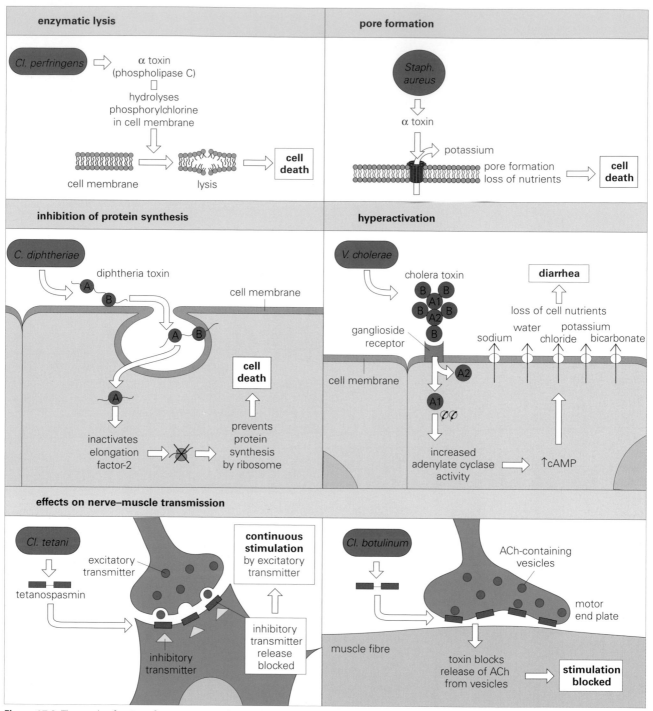

Figure 17.2 The mode of action of some exotoxins. Bacterial toxins act in a variety of ways. Often the toxin is a two-chain molecule, one chain being concerned with entry into cells while the other has inhibitory activity against some vital function. ACh, acetylcholine; cAMP, cyclic adenosine monophosphate; C, *Corynebacterium*; Cl, *Clostridium*; Staph, *Staphylococcus*; V, *Vibrio*.

Bacteria may produce enzymes to promote their survival or spread

A number of bacteria release enzymes that break down the tissues or the intercellular substances of the host, allowing the infection to spread freely. Among these enzymes are hyaluronidase, collagenase, DNase and streptokinase. Some staphylococci release a coagulase, which deposits a protective layer of fibrin onto and around the cells, thus localizing them.

Toxins may damage or destroy cells and are then known as haemolysins

Cell membranes can be damaged enzymatically by lecithinases or phospholipases, or by insertion of pore-forming molecules, which destroy the integrity of the cell. The collective term for such toxins is 'haemolysins', although many cells other than red blood cells can be affected. Both staphylococci and streptococci produce pore-forming toxins; pseudomonads release enzymatic haemolysins. The staphylococcal alpha-haemolysin is secreted as a soluble monomer but binds to a membrane protein to form a heptamer, making a beta-barrel pore in the membrane.

Toxins may enter cells and actively alter some of the metabolic machinery

Characteristically, these toxin molecules have two subunits. The A subunit is the active component, while the B subunit is a binding component needed to interact with receptors on the cell membrane. When binding occurs, the A subunit, or the whole toxin-receptor complex, is taken into the cell by endocytosis, and the A subunit becomes activated. Two well-studied toxins of this type are those of diphtheria (see Ch. 18) and cholera.

Diphtheria toxin blocks protein synthesis

Diphtheria toxin is synthesized as a single polypeptide and binds by the B subunit to target cells (Fig. 17.2). The polypeptide is partially cleaved and then the entire toxin-receptor complex is internalized. The A subunit then splits off and passes into the cytosol, where it inactivates the transfer of amino acids from transfer RNA to the polypeptide chain during translation of mRNA by ribosomes. It does this by catalysing attachment of adenosine diphosphate (ADP) ribose to the elongation protein (ADP ribosylation), effectively blocking protein synthesis.

Cholera toxin results in massive loss of water from intestinal epithelial cells

Cholera toxin is released as a complex of five B subunits surrounding the A subunit. The latter is cleaved into two fragments: A1 and A2, held by disulfide bonds. The B subunits bind to ganglioside receptors on intestinal epithelial cells, leading to internalization of the A subunits, which then separate from one another (Fig. 17.2). The A1 portion then ADP-ribosylates one of the regulatory molecules involved in the production of cyclic adenosine monophosphate (cAMP). As a result, the regulatory molecule is unable to turn off cAMP production. The increased levels of cAMP in the cell change the sodium/chloride flux across the cell membrane, resulting in a massive outflow of water and electrolytes from the cell and causing the profuse diarrhea of cholera. The exotoxins of *E. coli* and salmonella have similar actions, as does pertussis toxin.

Tetanus and botulinum toxins are among the most potent affecting nerve impulses

These toxins are extremely potent and active at low doses. Tetanus and botulinum toxins have the characteristic A + B structure, the B subunit binding to ganglioside receptors on nerve cells. The internalized A subunit of tetanus is carried by axonal transport from the point of production to the central nervous system (CNS), where it interferes with synaptic transmission in inhibitory neurones by blocking neurotransmitter release. This allows the excitatory transmitter to continuously stimulate the motor neurones, causing spastic paralysis. Botulinum toxin enters the body via the intestine, escaping digestion and crossing the gut wall. The toxin affects peripheral nerve endings at the neuromuscular junction, blocking presynaptic release of acetylcholine. This prevents muscle contraction, causing flaccid paralysis.

Toxins as magic bullets

An interesting offshoot of the two-subunit structure of toxins is that by changing the specificity of the part responsible for attachment, the specificity of the toxin for a particular cell type can be changed. An example is the plant toxin ricin – the A subunit can be attached to a monoclonal antibody to make it a specific poison for tumour cells. The same strategy could obviously be used against parasites if desired.

DIARRHEA

Diarrhea is an almost invariable result of intestinal infections

Diarrhea is one of the major causes of death in children worldwide, with rotavirus as the main culprit (see Ch. 22). In industrialized regions, bacterial pathogens such as *Campylobacter* and non-typhoidal *Salmonella* are increasingly important, and *Clostridium difficile* can be a problem in hospitals, particularly in the elderly. Diarrhea can be considered as:

- a means for the host to rid itself rapidly of the infectious organism
- a means for the infection to spread to other hosts.

Diarrhea is a feature of a wide range of organisms, but in only a few cases is the exact mechanism understood. While toxins are often the cause (e.g. cholera, shigella), microbial invasion and damage to epithelial cells may also be important. The pathophysiology, with changes in electron transport or loss of enterocytes, has been elucidated in some cases. Many of the organisms causing diarrhea can be 'picked up' from food, but the term 'food poisoning' is usually reserved for those cases where toxins are already present in the food rather than being generated during the growth of organisms in the intestine (Fig. 17.3). As would be expected, 'food poisoning' causes symptoms earlier – that is, hours after exposure rather than days (Table 17.3). Some viral infections, such as *Norovirus*, sometimes referred to as causing 'winter vomiting disease', cause outbreaks of diarrhea and vomiting, particularly in closed groups or communities – such as in hospitals or on cruise ships; in the UK in 2009/2010 there were 1888 reported hospital outbreaks, of which 1538 led to ward closures.

PATHOLOGIC ACTIVATION OF NATURAL IMMUNE MECHANISMS

Overactivity can damage host tissues

The very potent natural immune mechanisms discussed in Chapter 14 have inbuilt safety as far as specificity is concerned. They have had to evolve in the constant presence of the host's 'self' antigens, to which they do not therefore respond. However, they are not so well controlled quantitatively, and there are many cases when overactivity not only damages an invading parasite, but also damages innocent host tissues. The expression of natural immunity often causes a certain amount of inflammation – and this can be severe, with tissue damage. Complement, polymorphs and tumour necrosis factor (TNF) play important roles.

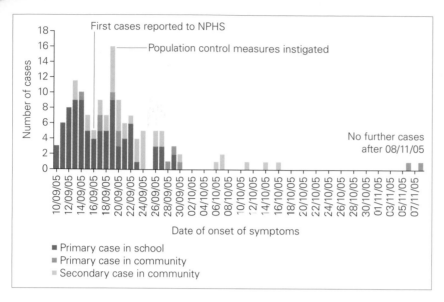

Figure 17.3 Outbreak of bloody diarrhea caused by Verocytotoxin-producing *E. coli* O157 in South Wales, in 2005. The first cases had all eaten school dinners containing cooked meats from a single supplier. Of the total 157 reported cases, 65% were in school-aged children. Thirty-one people were admitted to hospital and one child died. NPHS National Public Health Service (Data from: The Public Inquiry into the September 2005 Outbreak of *E. coli* O157 in South Wales. Chairman H. Pennington, March 2009. http://wales.gov.uk/ecolidocs/3008707/reporten.pdf?skip=1&lang=en)

Table 17.3 Infectious causes of diarrhea

	Onset	Source
Food poisoning (due to pre-formed toxin in food)		
Staphylococcus aureus	1–6 h	Cream, meat, poultry
Clostridium perfringens	8–20 h	Reheated meat
Clostridium botulinum	12–36 h	Canned food
Bacillus cereus	1–20 h	Reheated foods
Intestinal infections		
Rotavirus	2–5 days	Contact
Norovirus	1–2 days	Contact (faecal–oral)
Salmonella	1–2 days	Eggs
Clostridium difficile	1–2 days	Faecal–oral
Shigella	1–4 days	Faecal–oral
Campylobacter	1–4 days	Poultry, domestic animals
Vibrio cholerae	2 days	Faecal–oral
Escherichia coli	1–4 days	Food
Yersinia enterocolitica	days–weeks	Pets (e.g. dogs)
Giardia lamblia	1–2 weeks	⎱ Contaminated water
Entamoeba histolytica	days–weeks	⎰
Cryptosporidium	⎱ days–weeks	⎱ Faecal–oral, opportunistic (e.g. in AIDS)
Isospora belli	⎰	⎰

Worldwide, infectious diarrhea is the major cause of infant mortality.

Microbial endotoxin activates the immune system and induces cytokines, causing a bewildering variety of biologic effects (Fig. 17.4). At the clinical level, it can be responsible for septic shock.

Endotoxins are typically lipopolysaccharides

'Endotoxins' of bacteria and other microorganisms have a deceptively similar name to exotoxins, but are profoundly different in their significance. Unlike exotoxins, these are integral parts of the microbial cell wall and are normally released only when the cell dies. Endotoxins are particularly characteristic of Gram-negative bacteria. A typical lipopolysaccharide (LPS) endotoxin is composed of:

- a conserved lipid portion (lipid A) inserted into the cell wall, responsible for much of the toxic activity
- a conserved core polysaccharide

- the highly variable O-polysaccharide, responsible for the serologic diversity which is a feature of organisms such as salmonellae and shigellae.

LPSs stimulate an extraordinary range of host responses – or perhaps one should say a wide range of responses have evolved to respond to LPSs. These include LPS binding protein (the LPS–LPS binding protein complex then binds to CD14 on macrophages and dendritic cells) and TLR4 (see Ch. 9). In the words of Lewis Thomas, 'when we sense lipopolysaccharide, we are likely to turn on every defence at our disposal' (Fig. 17.4). Evidently, the body needs to be aware of invading Gram-negative bacteria at the earliest possible stage.

Clinically, the most important effects of LPS are:

- fever
- vascular collapse (or shock).

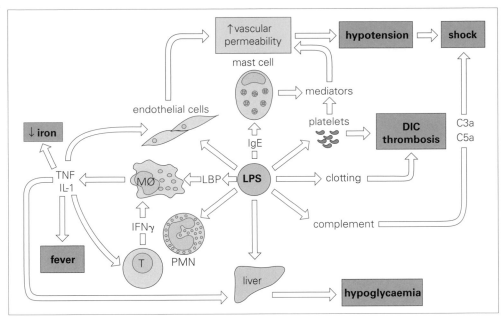

Figure 17.4 The many activities of bacterial endotoxin. Lipopolysaccharide (LPS) activates almost every immune mechanism as well as the clotting pathway and, as a result, LPS is one of the most powerful immune stimuli known. DIC, disseminated intravascular coagulation; IFN, interferon; IL, interleukin; LBP, LPS binding protein; Mφ, macrophage; PMN, polymorphonuclear leukocyte; TNF, tumour necrosis factor.

As mentioned in Chapter 14, fever may benefit host or parasite, or both, and is currently considered to be mainly due to the action of two cytokines, interleukin 1 (IL-1) and tumour necrosis factor (TNF), on the hypothalamus. Both these cytokines are produced by macrophages in response to LPS (and to analogous molecules from other organisms, see below and Box 17.1).

Endotoxin shock is usually associated with systemic spread of organisms

The commonest example of endotoxin (or 'septic') shock is septicaemia with Gram-negative bacteria such as *E. coli* or *Neisseria meningitidis*. However, many other organisms also release molecules that stimulate TNFα and/or IL-1 production (Table 17.4) and therefore function in part like LPS, although they are more or less unrelated in structure. In the 'toxic shock syndrome' of young women with staphylococcal infections of the genital tract, toxic shock syndrome toxin (TSST1) is the mediator; it acts as a superantigen, activating a large proportion of all T cells (up to 1 in 5, see Ch. 16) that express particular Vβ genes in their T cell receptors. Activating an enormous number of T cells produces enough cytokines to cause the toxic effect.

Septic shock, however, is a complex phenomenon, and other bacterial components, such as peptidoglycans, may also play a part. Disseminated intravascular coagulation (DIC),

---

Box 17.1 Lessons in Microbiology

Is it a cold – or is it flu?

The common cold is usually caused by a rhinovirus, or a coronavirus. Real influenza, caused by the influenza virus usually has a more sudden onset and the combination of fever and a cough has a predictive value of around 80%. But what causes the symptoms of sore throat, sneezing, nasal discharge and nasal congestion?

Sore throat symptoms are thought to be caused by prostaglandins and bradykinin acting on sensory nerve endings in the airway. Sneezing is triggered by inflammatory mediators in the nose and nasopharynx acting on the trigeminal nerves. The plasma-rich exudate that forms part of the nasal discharge can change from clear to yellow/green during an upper respiratory infection. The colour reflects the recruitment of leukocytes into the airway lumen. If large numbers of leukocytes are present, the green protein myeloperoxidase found in the azurophil granules of neutrophils gives the discharge a green colour. Nasal

congestion occurs later in infection, when inflammatory mediators such as bradykinin cause the large veins in the nasal epithelium to dilate. Common cold viruses do not cause such damage to the airway epithelium and infection may not create a cough – but influenza usually causes serious damage to the respiratory epithelium. Fever is mainly caused by the interleukins IL-1 and IL-6. It also seems that cytokines are responsible for muscle aches and pains, by causing the breakdown of muscle proteins. Of course, TNF was originally called cachexin, because of its ability to cause muscle wasting or cachexia.

Sometimes, in past flu epidemics, such as the Spanish flu epidemic in 1918, people died very quickly, within a few days of infection – which seems too fast for secondary infections to be responsible. Reconstructed viruses with the same haemagglutinin and neuraminidase seem to cause severe inflammation and it is possible that excessive cytokine release, in a 'cytokine storm', caused the pathology.

Table 17.4 Important endotoxins and functionally related molecules that induce TNF

Organisms	Toxin
Bacteria	
Gram-negative	
Salmonella	
Shigella	} LPS
Escherichia coli	
Neisseria meningitidis	
Gram-positive	
Staphylococcus aureus	TSST1
Mycobacteria	Lipoarabinomannan
Bordetella pertussis	Endotoxin
Fungi	
Yeasts	Zymosan
Protozoa	
Plasmodium	Phospholipids (exoantigens)

Most endotoxins are lipopolysaccharides (LPS) and exert their main effects by stimulating cytokine release. TSST1, toxic shock syndrome toxin. LPS can also induce the secretion of other cytokines such as Interleukin-1.

hypoglycaemia and cardiovascular failure are all features of septic shock. In streptococcal infections, the culprits are pyrogenic (erythrogenic) exotoxins released by the bacteria.

The involvement of cytokines in the pathogenesis of shock is by no means a purely academic concern, because it suggests the possibility of treatment by antagonists of a small number of cytokines (e.g. by monoclonal antibodies or inhibitors), rather than by antibodies to the toxins themselves, which are of enormous antigenic diversity. This idea is discussed further in Chapter 35.

The cytokine most closely linked to disease is TNF

Raised concentrations of TNFα in the serum have been shown to correlate with severity in patients with meningococcal septicaemia and with *Plasmodium falciparum* malaria.

However, animal experiments indicate that, in such cases, TNFα probably synergizes with other cytokines such as IL-1 and interferon-gamma (IFNγ), to produce its full effects. In meningococcal disease, TNFα concentrations in blood and cerebrospinal fluid (CSF) can change independently, the former being raised in septicaemia and the latter in meningitis; it therefore appears that the production and/or effects of TNFα can be restricted to a particular body compartment.

In some cases, it may be worth suppressing inflammation with steroids; e.g. a randomized trial in which dexamethasone was given to patients with acute bacterial meningitis showed that corticosteroid reduced mortality. The immune system itself also tries to control inflammation during sepsis by producing anti-inflammatory mediators such as IL-10 and TGFβ.

There may also be strain differences in the ability of bacteria to induce inflammation; *Haemophilus influenzae* strains isolated from patients with chronic obstructive pulmonary disease exacerbations induce more inflammation than colonizing strains not associated with the worsening of symptoms (Fig. 17.5).

Complement is involved in several tissue-damaging reactions

The activation of complement is a vital part of immunity to many bacteria, viruses and protozoa (see Ch. 14). Complement can, however, be involved in tissue-damaging reactions, e.g. immune complex disease, which also involves antibody and, usually, polymorphonuclear leukocytes (PMNs). Complement also plays an important role in the acute inflammatory response by generating the chemotactic factors C3a and C5a (see Ch. 9). Animal experiments suggest that C5a contributes to cardiac problems during sepsis, as it binds to C5a receptors on cardiomyocytes (cardiomyocytes are also damaged by LPS itself and by inflammatory cytokines such as IL-1β, TNFα and IL-6).

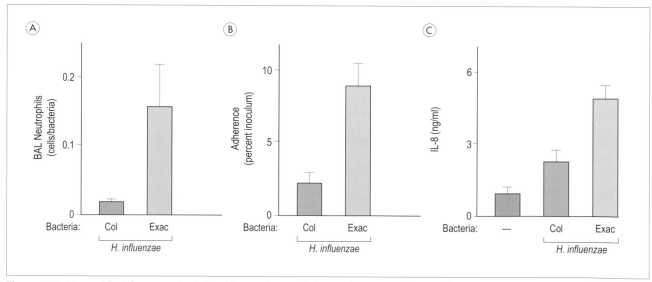

Figure 17.5 *Haemophilus influenzae* strains isolated from patients with chronic obstructive pulmonary disease (COPD) induce more inflammation than colonizing strains not associated with worsening of symptoms. *H. influenzae* strains from patients with COPD exacerbations (Exac) induce greater numbers of neutrophils (A), more adherence to airway epithelial cells (B) and more IL-8 (C) than isolates associated with colonization (Col). BAL, bronchoalveolar lavage. (Redrawn from: Chin, C. L. et al. (2005) *Haemophilus influenzae* from patients with chronic obstructive pulmonary disease exacerbation induce more inflammation than colonizers. *Am J Respir Crit Care Med* 172:85–91.)

Direct activation of complement by LPS may contribute to the shock induced by toxic amounts of this endotoxin, in which the levels of complement components (e.g. C3) drop profoundly; this response appears to involve both the classic and the alternative pathways, which are activated by the lipid and polysaccharide components, respectively. C3a and C5a are produced in large amounts, and there is frequently a severe decrease in the number of PMNs because of aggregation of these cells, adherence to vessel walls, and their activation to release toxic molecules, both oxidative and non-oxidative. When this occurs in the pulmonary capillaries, severe pulmonary oedema may result – the 'adult respiratory distress syndrome' (ARDS).

Disseminated intravascular coagulation is a rare but serious feature of bacterial septicaemia

Disseminated intravascular coagulation (DIC) can be a feature of bacterial (e.g. meningococcal) septicaemia, but is also seen in some virus infections such as Ebola fever (Ch. 28). The relative contributions of immune complexes, platelets, and direct activation of the clotting pathway via the effect of LPS on Hageman factor remain controversial. For example, the haemorrhagic phenomena of yellow fever are probably secondary to coagulation defects due to the extensive liver damage, whereas in dengue ('haemorrhagic') fever it has been suggested that there is immune complex deposition in blood vessels. However, in all these haemorrhagic syndromes the role of cytokines such as TNF also needs to be considered.

Mast cell degranulation in response to LPS is usually secondary to IgE antibody formation

Some insect venoms, however, may be able to activate mast cells directly, and reactions of this kind are called 'anaphylactoid'.

PATHOLOGIC CONSEQUENCES OF THE IMMUNE RESPONSE

Overreaction of the immune system is known as 'hypersensitivity'

Adaptive immune responses are vital to defence against infection, as witnessed by the increased susceptibility to infectious disease of immunodeficient patients (see Ch. 30). The antimicrobial effects of lymphocyte responses act mainly by focusing or enhancing non-specific effector mechanisms (see Ch. 10). This may, however, also enhance the pathologic effects outlined above. The tissue-damaging effects of hypersensitivity are referred to as 'immunopathologic'. Coombs and Gell classified hypersensitivity into four types in 1958, based on the immunologic mechanism underlying the tissue damaging reaction.

Each of the four main types of hypersensitivity can be of microbial or non-microbial origin

Hypersensitivity of microbial origin includes some of the most serious of these responses (Table 17.5). Organisms of many sorts can be involved, but one common feature is that the infection is prolonged, with continuous or repeated antigenic stimulation.

Type I hypersensitivity

These reactions are often called 'immediate', as they can occur within minutes, when the allergen triggers the degranulation of mast cells pre-coated with specific IgE antibodies.

Allergic reactions are a feature of worm infections

The most dramatic allergic (type I) reaction is that following the rupture of a hydatid cyst. Slow leakage of worm antigens ensures that the patient's mast cells are sensitized with specific IgE, and the massive flood of antigens on rupture may cause acute fatal anaphylaxis, with vascular collapse and pulmonary oedema. Even the small amount of antigen used in diagnostic skin tests can have this effect, although this is rare.

Another worm associated with high levels of IgE is *Ascaris*, but here the pathologic consequences are mainly respiratory, with eosinophilic infiltrates and asthmatic episodes corresponding to passage of the parasite through the lung. The itching rashes characteristic of helminth infections when the worms die in the skin are probably also of this type, an example being 'swimmer's itch' due to animal or avian schistosomes.

Why allergic reactions are such a feature of worm infections is not really clear, but they may be due to some feature of the antigens; in addition, it has been suggested that IgE plays a role in protection against worms. One would hope so, as in all other respects this class of antibody appears to be nothing but a nuisance.

Type II hypersensitivity

Type II reactions are mediated by antibodies to the infectious organism or autoantibodies

Strictly speaking, type II reactions are mediated by antibody (usually IgG) leading to cytotoxicity, either extracellular or intracellular (e.g. after phagocytosis). Antibody binds to the cell and, if complement is activated, the cell is lysed. Cytotoxicity by T cells is considered under type IV reactions. An important distinction can be made between antibodies to the (foreign) infectious organism and autoantibodies; the former kill host cells because they display foreign antigens, whereas the latter bind to unaltered host antigens, and both types of response occur in infectious disease (see Table 17.5). In the latter case, of course, the interesting question is why autoantibodies should be formed during infection, and several mechanisms have been postulated for this. However, the whole question of autoimmunity remains highly controversial.

In blood-stage malaria, microbial antigens attach themselves to host cells

It has been shown that the haemolytic anaemia of blood-stage malaria is due not to autoantibody, as previously thought, but to antibodies to parasite-derived antigens that have been picked up by red cells. In some cases, it may be the antigen–antibody complex that binds to the cell. A similar reaction can occur following quinine treatment of *Plasmodium falciparum* malaria – blackwater fever.

Antimyocardial antibody of group A β-haemolytic streptococcal infection is the classic autoantibody triggered by infection

This reaction is due to the presence of the same cross-reacting carbohydrate antigen on the bacterium and the myocardium. However, as more protein sequences are obtained and

Table 17.5 Hypersensitivity of microbial origin

Coombs and Gell classification	Principal mechanism	Examples
Type I (allergic/anaphylactic)	IgE, mast cells	Helminths *Ascaris* Hydatid (ruptured cyst) ? Viral skin rash ? Upper respiratory tract Viral infections
Type II (cytotoxic)	IgG to surface antigens Complement Cytotoxic cells	Virus infected cells Malaria infected erythrocytes Autoantibodies in: *Mycoplasma* Streptococci *Trypanosoma cruzi*
Type III (immune complex-mediated)	Immune complexes Complement PMN	In tissues: Allergic alveolitis Actinomycosis In blood vessels: Glomerulonephritis Malaria Streptococci Hepatitis B Syphilis
Type IV (cell-mediated)	T lymphocytes Cytokines Macrophages (and other non-specific cells)	Granuloma Tuberculosis Leprosy (tuberculoid) Schistosomiasis (eggs) *Histoplasma* Mononuclear infiltration ± cell damage in many virus infections (i.e. tissue delayed-type hypersensitivity responses) with CD4 and CD8 T cell cytokines and macrophages playing roles Viral rashes
Autoimmunity	Cross-reaction with host Polyclonal B cell activation	Streptococcal myocarditis African trypanosomiasis

All four classic types of hypersensitivity can be induced by infectious organisms, types II and III being the most commonly encountered. Note that some mechanisms mediating hypersensitivity also take part in protective immunity. PMN, polymorphonuclear leukocyte.

compared, numerous other similar examples have come to light, and it is possible that cross-reaction between microbial and human antigens may underlie a number of diseases of currently unknown origin. Whether this mimicry of host antigens has any survival value to the microbe is discussed in Chapter 16.

Type III hypersensitivity

Immune complexes cause disease when they become lodged in tissues or blood vessels

Immune complexes cause pathology if they are made in excess, if they are not removed properly from the circulation and if they deposit in tissues.

The formation of immune complexes can lead to phagocytosis and removal of antigen, but also to complement activation. Complications occur when the complexes escape removal by the phagocytes of the reticuloendothelial system and become lodged in the tissues or blood vessels, attracting complement and neutrophils. Release of lysosomal enzymes then results in local damage, which is particularly serious in small blood vessels, especially in the renal glomeruli. Immune complex disease is a major cause of both acute and

chronic glomerulonephritis, and the majority of cases are probably the result of infection. There is also an important group in which autoantigen–autoantibody complexes are responsible (e.g. DNA–anti-DNA in systemic lupus erythematosus), but even these may ultimately be the consequence of a viral infection.

Like most other immunopathologic conditions, immune complex deposition is usually a feature of chronic infection (e.g. malaria). However, a persistent antigenic stimulus is not the only prerequisite, indicated by the fact that the most serious form of malarial nephropathy is found in *Plasmodium malariae* (quartan) malaria, which progresses despite successful treatment of the infection, while the nephropathy of *P. falciparum* (malignant tertian) malaria typically recovers after the infection has been cured. Predisposing factors may include a poor antibody response (in terms of amount or affinity), a particular tendency of the antigen itself to bind to vascular endothelium, or inhibition of the normal function of phagocytes or complement in removing circulating complexes.

Acute glomerulonephritis occurs as a serious complication of streptococcal infection (see Ch. 18) and is at least partly due to localization in glomeruli of immune complexes containing streptococcal antigens (see Fig. 17.7). Polymorph infiltration and alterations in the basement membrane cause leakage of albumin, even red cells, into the urine. The glomerulonephritis appears a few weeks after the infection has been terminated. When complexes are deposited over a long period (malarial nephropathy), the mesangial cell intrusions and fusion of foot processes cause a more irreversible impairment of glomerular function (chronic glomerulonephritis).

Occupational diseases associated with inhalation of fungi are the classic examples of immune complex deposition in the tissues

Immune complex deposition in the tissues, made famous by the work of Arthus on antigens injected into the skin of animals with pre-existing antibody (mainly IgG), manifests as a combination of thrombosis in small blood vessels and necrosis in the tissues due to PMN degranulation (Fig. 17.6). Perhaps the best-studied examples are the occupational diseases associated with inhalation of fungi (e.g. farmer's lung, pigeon-fancier's disease, maple bark stripper's disease) in which chronic inflammation of the lung can lead to a state of destruction and fibrosis known as 'extrinsic allergic alveolitis', an unfortunate name since classic (IgE-mediated) allergy does not seem to be involved.

Another well-known model of immune complex disease is serum sickness

Serum sickness follows repeated injections of foreign protein, leading to circulating complexes, which deposit in the kidneys (Fig. 17.7), skin and joints. This was common in the pre-antibiotic days of passive serotherapy with horse serum for diphtheria (see Ch. 35). It is also a possible complication of treatment with murine monoclonal antibodies. As giving such blocking antibodies is an increasingly attractive approach to many conditions, the antibodies are now genetically engineered so that as much of the molecule as possible is humanized.

Type IV hypersensitivity

Cell-mediated immune responses invariably cause some tissue destruction, which may be permanent

Despite the examples of antibody-mediated tissue damage discussed above, the antibody response generally achieves its purpose in eliminating invading organisms without any trace of damage to the host. Cell-mediated (type IV) responses are not quite so sure-footed, in that the activation of both T cells and macrophages invariably causes some tissue destruction, which may be reparable if not too prolonged, but can also lead to fibrosis and even calcification with serious permanent loss of tissue.

Confusion has occurred due to the use of a number of terms to describe and subdivide type IV responses. Some reflect actual pathologic conditions, while others describe the results of diagnostic skin tests, and none corresponds exactly to the processes by which cell-mediated immunity protects against infection (Table 17.6).

From the medical viewpoint, granuloma formation is the most important type IV response

The cell-mediated response to microbial antigen is responsible for granuloma formation and plays a major role in diseases such as tuberculosis, tuberculoid leprosy, lymphogranuloma inguinale, and in *Toxocara* infection. The complex involvement of the cytokine network in type IV responses poses certain paradoxes. For example, the tendency of some granulomas to undergo necrosis (e.g. caseation in tuberculosis) whereas others do not (e.g. leprosy, sarcoidosis) may be explained in terms of the different pattern of cytokines involved. TNF, often in association with some microbial products, is especially likely to cause necrosis through its effects on vascular endothelium, which probably accounts for much of its antitumour activity.

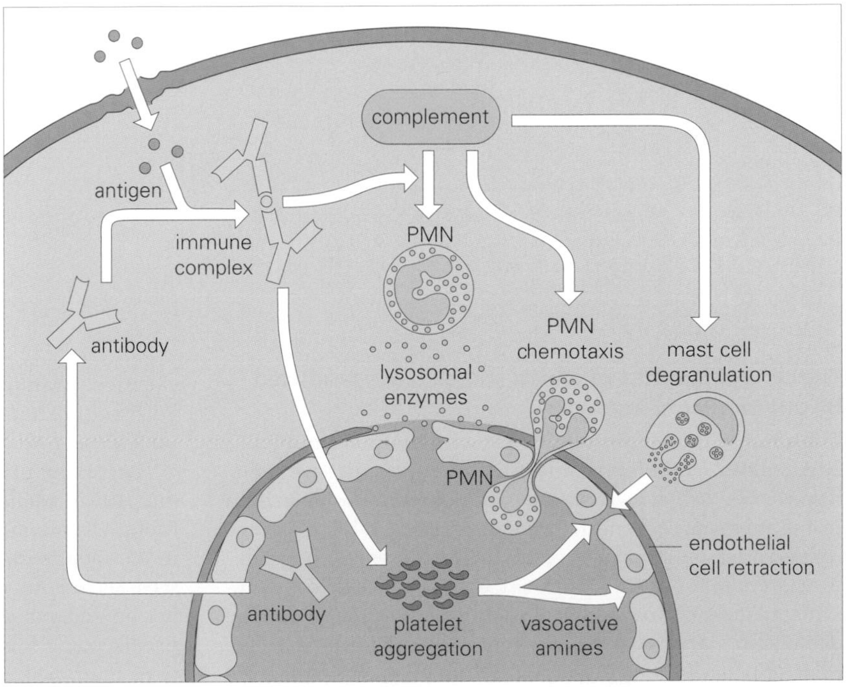

Figure 17.6 The Arthus reaction. Microbial antigens that enter the tissues (e.g. fungal particles in the lung) encounter antibody and form immune complexes. These activate complement and initiate chemotaxis of polymorphonuclear leukocytes (PMNs), and degranulation of these and tissue mast cells. The resulting inflammatory response is further potentiated by damage induced by PMN-derived lysosomal enzymes.

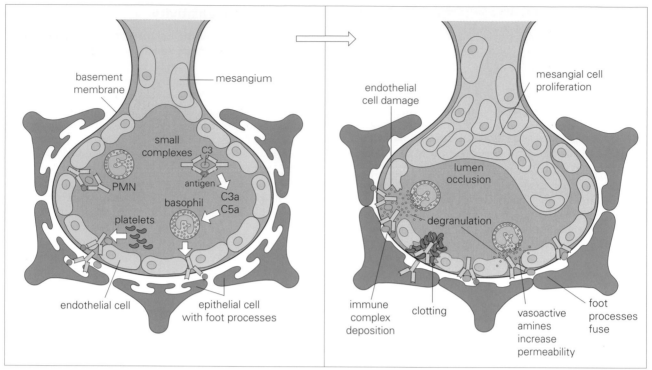

Figure 17.7 Glomerulonephritis caused by immune complex-mediated tissue damage. Type III hypersensitivity results in the deposition of immune complexes in the blood vessel walls, particularly at sites of high pressure, filtration or turbulence such as the kidney. Large complexes deposit on the glomerular basement membrane, while small ones pass through the basement membrane and then deposit on the epithelial side of the glomerulus. PMN, polymorphonuclear leukocyte.

Table 17.6 Cell-mediated immunity in protection and disease

Cell-mediated responses			
Immune cells or molecules	**Protective effect against**	**Pathologic effect**	**Skin test**
Cytotoxic T cells (CD8)	Virus infections *Theileria*, (Mycobacteria)[a]	Local tissue loss	
Basophils, T cells	?	Inflammation	24 h (Jones–Mote)
T cells (CD4) Macrophages Cytokines Giant cells Epithelioid cells Eosinophils	Intracellular organisms Viruses Bacteria Fungi Protozoa Worms	Mononuclear cell infiltration Granuloma Fibrosis Calcification	} Delayed/tuberculin type (>2 days)

The nomenclature of cell-mediated immune responses is complicated. Although often described in terms of skin tests, their real significance is related to protective and/or pathologic reactions in the tissues.
[a]A role for CD8 T cells in protection against *M. tuberculosis* has been proposed.

The clinical features of schistosomiasis are produced by cell-mediated immunity

The price paid for protective cell-mediated immunity is particularly well illustrated by the helminth disease schistosomiasis. *Schistosoma mansoni* (the blood fluke) lays eggs in the mesenteric venous system, some of which become lodged in small portal vessels in the liver. Strong cell-mediated reactions to secreted enzymes lead to granulomatous reactions around each egg, resulting in egg destruction and sparing of liver parenchyma from the toxic effects of the egg enzymes. However, the coalescent calcified granulomas ultimately cause portal cirrhosis, with portal hypertension, oesophageal varices and haematemesis (see Ch. 22).

The rather unexpected effect of malnutrition in reducing the incidence and severity of certain diseases (e.g. typhus, malaria) may be attributable to a reduction in immunopathology, though in the majority of diseases (e.g. measles, meningococcal infection, tuberculosis), the reverse is true. Indeed, poor nutrition is regarded as a major factor predisposing to the greater severity of many common infections in tropical countries.

Antibodies can also cause enhancement of pathology, as in dengue

Most cases of dengue haemorrhagic fever occur in people who get a second infection with the dengue virus. Antibody binding to the virus leads to greater internalization of virus, through Fc binding. The viral load falls as the fever falls, but this is when the most severe symptoms and pathology appear, including leakage of plasma from capillaries, haemorrhage and shock.

SKIN RASHES

A variety of skin rashes have an immunologic origin

The ways in which infections can affect the skin are detailed in Chapter 26, but here it should be mentioned that some rashes are considered to be immunologically mediated. For example, the characteristic skin rash of measles is absent in children with T-cell deficiency (e.g. thymic aplasia or DiGeorge syndrome), who instead develop a fatal systemic infection, indicating that the skin lesions are T-cell mediated and represent some form of successful cell-mediated immunity. In contrast, if children with T-cell deficiency are vaccinated with live vaccinia virus, they develop an inexorable spreading skin lesion, which is clearly a direct and not an immunopathologic effect.

Table 17.7 lists the more common skin conditions of immunologic origin in which an infectious organism is thought to be involved. (Further details can be found in Ch. 26.)

The SARS coronavirus caused lung immunopathology and T-cell loss

The SARS coronavirus killed over 750 people in the 2002/3 epidemic. The lungs of patients with SARS viral pneumo-nia show diffuse damage to the alveoli, with the presence of multinucleate giant cells and many macrophages (Figure 17.8). The virus could also be found in other organs such as the intestine, liver and kidney of patients. The virus multiplies slowly at first, with a gradual increase in viral titre over the first 10 days. This suggests that the virus evades the innate immune response, possibly by failing to induce IFNα and IFNβ.

During the acute phase of infection, lymphopenia occurs with loss of both CD4 and CD8 T cells. However, it was a puzzle as to how this could happen, as T cells do not

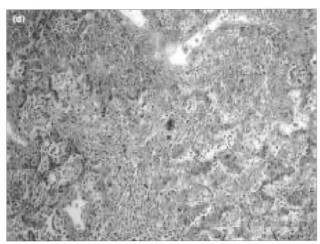

Figure 17.8 Pathology of SARS. The figure shows organizing diffuse alveolar damage, with giant cell formation in a patient who died of SARS. (Courtesy of John Nicholls, Department of Pathology, The University of Hong Kong; taken from Lau, Y. L. and Peris, J. S. (2005) Pathogenesis of severe acute respiratory syndrome. *Curr Opin Immunol* 17:404, with permission).

Table 17.7 Skin rashes and their immunologic basis

Organism	Disease	Character	Pathogenic basis
Viruses			
Measles	Measles	Maculopapular rash	} T cells; immune complexes; allergy
Rubella	German measles	Maculopapular rash	
Varicella-zoster	Chickenpox/zoster	Vesicular rash	Viral cytopathic
Hepatitis B	Hepatitis B	Urticarial	Immune complexes
Bacteria			
Streptococcus pyogenes	Scarlet fever	Erythematous rash	Erythrogenic toxin
Treponema pallidum	Syphilis	} Disseminated infectious rash in secondary stage	Immune complexes
Treponema pertenue	Yaws		
Salmonella typhi	Typhoid, enteric fever	Sparse rose spots	} Immune complexes
Neisseria meningitidis	Meningitis, spotted fever	Petechial or maculopapular lesions	
Mycobacterium leprae	Tuberculoid leprosy	Hypopigmented skin lesions	T cells, macrophages
Rickettsia prowazeki and others	Typhus	Maculopapular or haemorrhagic rash	Thrombosis
Fungi			
Dermatophytes	Dermatophytid or allergic rash		Immune complexes?
Blastomyces dermatitidis	Blastomycosis	Papule or pustule developing into granuloma	Hypersensitivity to fungal antigens, T cells
Protozoa			
Leishmania tropica	Cutaneous leishmaniasis	Papules ulcerating to form crusted infectious sores	T cells, macrophages

Many skin rashes represent immunologic reactions occurring in the skin. It is suspected that several skin diseases of unknown origin are in fact caused by viruses, either directly or indirectly.

express the angiotensin-converting enzyme 2, which is the functional receptor for the SARS virus. The answer seems to be that T-cell apoptosis is caused by proteins expressed by the virus.

The hygiene hypothesis – are we too clean?

Allergic diseases are more common than they used to be, and it has been proposed that this may be because most of us now grow up in an environment that is too clean. The hygiene hypothesis proposes that if we are exposed to a range of bacterial and viral infections in infancy, this may prevent the development of more harmful allergies by promoting a bias towards Th1 cytokine production. A more informative name might be 'microbial exposure deficiency hypothesis'. Certainly, people living in Africa seem to have had more exposure to antigens, age for age, than those living in Europe, as they have more memory T cells and fewer naive T cells. Slightly surprisingly, it also seems that infections with helminths, which promote copious Th2 responses, also protect against development of atopy, possibly because they out-compete the allergen-specific IgE on the mast cells. Other factors, such as innate immunity and regulatory T cells that act to reduce harmful immune responses that cause immunopathology, may be involved.

VIRUSES AND CANCER

A variety of RNA and DNA viruses can cause permanent malignant changes within cells (Table 17.8). Such malignant transformation by these 'tumour viruses' has been extensively studied. An account of proviruses and oncogenes (genes causing malignancy) is included in Chapter 3. However, only a small number of human cancers have been shown to be associated with such tumour viruses (Table 17.9). Some of these include cancers associated with HIV and AIDS and are caused by the resulting immunosuppression and loss of immune control over members of the γ-herpesvirus family such as HHV-8 and EBV. There are latent and lytic components to their life cycles. Few genes are expressed in latent infections, allowing the virus to reside in specific sites with the potential

Table 17.8 Malignant transformation

Changes	Details
Morphology	Loss of shape; rounding
Growth, contact	Decreased adhesion to surface
	Loss of contact inhibition of growth and movement
	Increased ability to grow from a single cell
	Increased ability to grow in suspension
	Capacity for continued growth (immortalization)
Cellular properties	DNA synthesis induced
	Chromosomal changes
	Appearance of new antigens (viral or cellular in origin)
Biochemical properties	Loss of fibronectin
	Reduced cAMP

These changes occur when tumour viruses cause transformation of cultured cells. Many of these changes are obviously relevant for tumour production in vivo. cAMP, cyclic adenosine monophosphate.

for reactivation and setting up the environment for infected cells to undergo malignant change. The virus can disseminate in the lytic stage by release from infected cells. Some of the genes expressed can also promote tumour development. This part of the viral replicative cycle may be of more importance in virus-associated malignancy.

Human T-cell lymphotropic virus type 1 (HTLV-1) is associated with adult T-cell leukaemia/lymphoma

HTLV-1 and HTLV-2 are retroviruses that have no oncogenes (see Ch. 3). HTLV-1 proviral DNA is detectable in the cellular DNA of individuals with adult T-cell leukaemia/lymphoma (ATLL). Although reported around the world, HTLV-1 infection is endemic in Southern Japan, the Caribbean islands, West and Central Africa and parts of South America. Less

Table 17.9 Viruses and human cancer

Viruses	Cancer	Strength of association	Viral genome in cancer cells	Cofactor
Epstein–Barr virus	Burkitt's lymphoma	++	+	Malaria
	Nasopharyngeal carcinoma	++	+	Nitrosamines
	Hodgkin's disease	–	–	–
Human papillomavirus	Cervical cancer	++	+	? cigarettes ? HSV2
	Skin cancer	±	+	? UV light
Hepatitis B virus	Liver cancer	++	+	? Aflatoxin
Hepatitis C virus	Liver cancer	++	–	? Hepatocyte regeneration
HTLV-1	T-cell leukaemia	++	+	–
HSV-2	Cervical cancer	±	±	–

Many viruses transform cells in culture, but only a few are important in human cancer. The associations are strongly supported by studies of naturally occurring or experimentally induced cancers in animals. HTLV, human T-cell lymphotropic virus; HSV, herpes simplex virus; UV, ultraviolet.

is known about the geographic distribution of HTLV-2, which can be isolated from hairy T-cell leukaemia but has no association with malignancy. This virus can be found in certain Amerindian tribes and is associated with neurological and other chronic inflammatory conditions.

The carcinogenic nature of HTLV-1 is not due to activation of a cellular oncogene, but is due to the Tax accessory gene product enhancing transcription of host genes involved in cell division. This transactivation by *Tax* and stimulation of T-cell proliferation by HTLV-1 are thought to be central to oncogenesis. Adult T-cell leukemia/lymphoma (ATLL) cells contain the integrated HTLV-1 proviral DNA but the latter is not transcribed very actively. The TAX oncoprotein may cause precancerous cell proliferation, and HBZ, another oncoprotein, may maintain cell transformation. These infections are described in more detail in Chapter 26.

Epstein–Barr virus (EBV) is associated with nasopharyngeal carcinoma and lymphoma including post-transplant lymphoproliferative disease

Epstein–Barr virus is closely linked with the development of nasopharyngeal carcinoma (NPC) (see Ch. 18), which is common in Southern China and other parts of Asia (12–30 cases/100 000 people/year), less common in parts of North Africa, and rare elsewhere in the world. The reason for this restricted geographic distribution is unknown. There is no convincing evidence for specific carcinogenic EBV strains, but these effects could be due to the presence locally of co-carcinogens such as nitrosamines in salted fish. EBV DNA can be demonstrated in the cancer cells, but the precise mechanism for tumorigenicity is unknown; cellular oncogenes have not been implicated. People at high risk of developing NPC show high IgA titres to EBV capsid antigen a year or more before clinical symptoms appear.

Epstein–Barr virus is associated with Burkitt's lymphoma

Burkitt's lymphoma, a tumour of immature B cells, occurs in parts of East Africa, such as Uganda, and in Papua New Guinea in 6–14-year-old children, especially boys. EBV DNA is present in the tumour cells, but most of the many copies of the EBV gene are not integrated into the host cell DNA. The tumour is probably caused by the action of EBV on B cells, causing them to proliferate and making activation of cellular oncogenes more likely. The cellular oncogene c-*myc* is translocated from chromosome 8 to the immunoglobulin heavy chain locus on chromosome 14, where it is expressed. As a result of this, the B cell may be prevented from entering the resting stage. There is also down-regulation of adhesion and human leukocyte antigen (HLA) molecules, so that the EBV-containing cells, which are normally subject to immune control, develop into tumour cells. The Burkitt's lymphoma cells also show other chromosomal abnormalities, but their role in tumorigenesis is unclear.

The fact that EBV is a common worldwide infection, whereas Burkitt's lymphoma, like NPC, is strikingly localized geographically, points once again to the involvement of local co-factors, perhaps chemical or infectious co-carcinogens. Malaria is a recognized co-factor in Burkitt's lymphoma, possibly having a role in altering the balance of the host's immune response.

Epstein–Barr virus is also associated with Hodgkin's lymphoma and lymphomas in immunosuppressed individuals

Epstein–Barr virus has been shown to be associated with classical Hodgkin's lymphoma, in particular that seen in childhood and older adulthood. In addition, bearing in mind that cytotoxic T cells police EBV infection, the T-cell surveillance function is reduced in situations where the host is immunosuppressed, resulting in uncontrolled lymphoproliferation. This can be altered in EBV-driven post-transplant lymphoproliferative diseases by reducing the immunosuppression, although a consequence can be graft rejection. Other treatment is usually required, involving targeted monoclonal antibodies and cytotoxic chemotherapy.

EBV-associated primary cerebral lymphoma may occur in HIV-infected individuals. About 3% of patients with AIDS develop non-Hodgkin's lymphomas, 20% of these occurring in the brain. The role of HIV is mostly indirect and is related to immunosuppression or B-cell activation. About 30% of AIDS-related lymphomas are Burkitt's lymphomas.

Certain human papillomavirus infections are associated with cervical cancer

Papillomavirus infection is associated with a number of epithelial hyperproliferative diseases. The viral life cycle is intertwined with the host keratinocyte cells' differentiation cycles. After small epithelial abrasions in skin or mucosal surfaces, these cells in the basal skin layer are exposed to HPV and the viral DNA becomes episomal and replicates with the host DNA using host synthetic machinery.

There are clear associations between the development of cervical cancer and infection with certain of the 77 distinct genotypes of human papillomavirus (HPV; see Chs 3, 21 and 26). They account for more than 80% of cervical cancers. Penile, vulval and rectal cancers are also associated with these types of HPV. Those at high risk include types 16 and 18, and those with low risk types 6 and 11. The latter cause cervical lesions but have a lower risk of progression to malignancy. HPV vaccine programmes were started in 2009 (see Ch. 34).

In most primary and metastatic cancer cells, the HPV genomes are present in integrated form (i.e. within the host genome), and certain viral oncoprotein genes referred to as E6 and E7 are transcribed and translated. Integration occurs at different chromosomal locations and the E6 and E7 open reading frames seem to be involved in transformation of epithelial cells and in maintenance of the transformed state, probably by binding to and inactivating tumour-suppressing cellular proteins concerned with regulation of the cell cycle. E6 is involved in turnover of p53, a tumour suppressor protein, and E7 binds and inactivates the retinoblastoma proteins. Both of these activities are critical in HPV-induced oncogenesis and result in genome instability, accumulation of oncogene mutations, uncontrolled cell growth and eventually cancer. Cervical cancer is an uncommon sequel to infection with these strains of HPV, and co-carcinogens such as cigarette smoke and herpes simplex virus (HSV) have been implicated.

Human papillomavirus infection is associated with squamous cell carcinoma of the skin

It is possible that ultraviolet light acts as a co-carcinogen, as is known to be the case with papillomaviruses and skin cancers in sheep and cattle. People with the rare autosomal recessive disease epidermodysplasia verruciformis are infected with up to 20 different but less common types of HPV, and 35% of patients develop multiple squamous cell carcinomas (SCC) of the skin. Of these tumours, 90% contain HPV-5 or HPV-8 DNA. These HPV types may act as co-carcinogens with ultraviolet light or immunosuppression in the development of non-melanoma skin cancers, the most common form of skin tumours in populations with fair skin.

HPVs may also play a role in the genesis of 90% of the skin cancers that appear in immunosuppressed organ transplant recipients, and cutaneous warts are common in these patients. In addition, there are reports that skin cancers in healthy individuals may be associated with HPV infection.

With respect to head and neck SCC, there are reports demonstrating the association of HPV-16 with SCC in the oral cavity and oropharynx and some evidence for HPV-18 resulting in oral cavity SCC.

Hepatitis B and hepatitis C viruses are major causes of hepatocellular carcinoma

The results, in sequential order, of chronic active hepatitis (CAH) include hepatocyte necrosis, chronic inflammation, cytokine production, fibrosis and finally cirrhosis. Therefore, CAH is a major driver for the development of hepatocellular carcinoma (HCC).

Individuals with active hepatitis B infections are 20-fold more likely to develop HCC than uninfected individuals. The oncogenic process depends on a number of predisposing factors that are both viral and host derived (Fig. 17.9). HCC is the outcome of chronic necroinflammatory liver disease associated with higher levels of HBV replication as well as the host immune response. Moreover, some HBV mutant strains and specific genotypes may be associated with HCC development. Integrated HBV sequences found in the HCC tumour cells may activate cellular oncogenes that encode proteins linked with controlling cell signalling, proliferation and viability, such as the *myc* family. Chronic inflammation, associated with increased liver cell proliferation, induces several rearrangements of the integrated HBV genome that

can generate chromosomal instability. Moreover, there is evidence for the involvement of occult HBV infections, in which hepatitis B surface antigen cannot be detected but HBV DNA is integrated in the hepatocytes. Finally, HBV and HCV co-infection may act in concert with chronic alcohol consumption in liver carcinogenesis.

HCC is more common in certain parts of the world, such as Africa and South-East Asia, and this may be due to the presence of co-carcinogens (e.g. aflatoxin). However, the closely related hepadnavirus of woodchucks (Box 17.2) causes the same tumour in these animals in the apparent absence of co-carcinogens.

The mechanism by which hepatitis C virus (HCV) causes HCC is considered to be indirect, as HCV sequences are not integrated into tumour cells. It is thought that the persistent hepatocyte damage and inflammation in HCV carriers, together with the effects of cytokines on the development of fibrosis and hepatocyte proliferation, results in HCC. It is also thought that HCV may have a direct action via specific viral proteins interacting with host cell factors modulating pathways such as cell signalling and proliferation and apoptosis that result in malignant transformation of liver cells. Once cirrhosis is established, there is a 1–4% risk of HCC. In addition, HCV is associated with mixed cryoglobulinaemia, a lymphoproliferative disorder that can develop into B-cell non-Hodgkin's lymphoma.

Several DNA viruses can transform cells in which they are unable to replicate

In addition, the viral genome is sometimes integrated into the host cell genome. Extensive studies have been carried out with the conclusion that despite high oncogenicity

---

Box 17.2 Lessons in Microbiology

The many faces of hepatitis B

Classic epidemiologic studies on hepatitis B virus in Taiwan showed two things. First, 90% of those infected in infancy became carriers, as did 23% of those infected at 1–3 years, but only 3% of those infected as university students. Second, among 3454 carriers of HBsAg, there were 184 cases of hepatocellular carcinoma, whereas there were only 10 cases among 19 253 non-carriers. Some 80% of all liver cancers are due to hepatitis B.

Worldwide, there are about 350 million carriers of this virus and, therefore, with liver cancer causing up to 2 million deaths each year, hepatitis B virus is second only to tobacco as a human carcinogen.

The mechanism of carcinogenesis is not clear. Nearly all human cancers show chromosomal integration of the virus, but there is great variation in integration site and in the number of copies of the viral genome.

Very similar viruses infect woodchucks, ground squirrels and Pekin ducks. In Northwest USA, 30% of woodchucks are carriers and most develop liver cancer in later life. In this host, the virus infects not only liver cells but also lymphoid cells in the spleen, peripheral blood and thymus, and pancreatic acinar cells and bile duct epithelium.

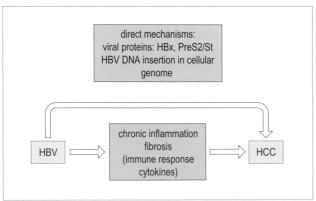

Figure 17.9 Development of hepatocellular carcinoma (HCC).

Figure 17.10 Activities of the vGPCR protein in HHV-8. The constitutively active viral G-protein-coupled receptor (vGPCR) of HHV-8 may promote the development of Kaposi's sarcoma by means of a variety of mechanisms. Signalling by vGPCR activates Akt, an activated protein kinase which directly induces cell transformation. The vGPCR also results in the production of a variety of other factors, including the nuclear factor (NF)-κB-dependent factors interleukin-8, growth-related protein α (GRO-α), interleukin-6, interleukin-1β and tumour necrosis factor alpha (TNFα); AP-1-dependent basic fibroblast growth factor (bFGF); platelet-derived growth factor B (PDGF-B); and placental growth factor (PIGF). Some, but not all, studies have found that vGPCR induces secretion of vascular endothelial growth factor (VEGF) and there is evidence that this secretion may be mediated by hypoxia-inducible factor (HIF). Also, vGPCR up-regulates the expression of the VEGF receptors 1 and 2 (VEGFR-1 and VEGFR-2, respectively). PIGF, VEGF and other factors can act in an autocrine or paracrine fashion to promote Kaposi's sarcoma. (Redrawn from: Yarchoan, R. (2006) Key role for a viral lytic gene in Kaposi's sarcoma. *N Engl J Med* 355:1383–1385, with permission.)

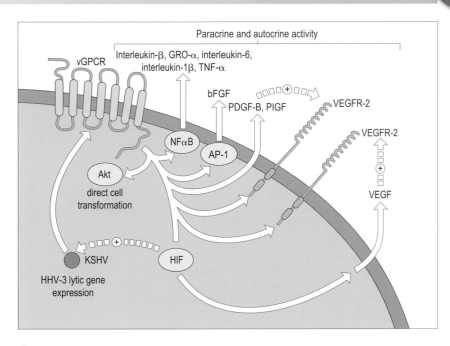

in vitro and in laboratory animals, these viruses do not seem to be important in human cancer. For instance:

- Human adenoviruses transform cells in culture and cause sarcomas experimentally in hamsters. About 10% of the adenovirus genome integrates, and the T antigen is expressed. However, adenoviruses are not associated with human cancer.
- Polyomavirus (Latin: *poly*, many; *oma*, tumours), a mouse papovavirus, and simian vacuolating virus 40 (SV40), a monkey papovavirus, both cause tumours in experimentally inoculated hamsters. The viral DNA is integrated into tumour cells, and T antigens are expressed. Are these viruses, or their human equivalents (BK and JC viruses), linked with human cancers? An incident occurred about 30 years ago, when thousands of children were accidentally inoculated with SV40 virus present in certain batches of poliovirus vaccine. The formalin inactivation procedure had failed to kill the SV40 virus present in the monkey kidney cells in which the polio vaccine had been grown. There was, however, no consequent increase in tumour incidence in the SV40-infected individuals. Nevertheless, evidence is accumulating that JC, BK and SV40 viruses associated with certain cancers of the brain, with certain lymphomas and with other tumours. However, a causative role has not been established.

Kaposi's sarcoma is caused by HHV-8

Kaposi's sarcoma (KS) is a multicentric tumour that involves massive proliferation of endothelial cells. It is 300 times more common among patients with AIDS than among other immunosuppressed groups, but is seen almost entirely in those who acquired HIV by sexual contact. It was identified in 1994 from a lesion in an individual with AIDS-associated KS. Human herpesvirus 8 (HHV-8), referred to originally as the Kaposi's sarcoma-associated herpesvirus (KSHV), appears to be sexually transmitted and is present in the tumours.

HHV-8 latently infects most tumour cells in lymphomas and KS. As a result, they are resistant to antiviral drugs targeting herpesviruses in the lytic cycle of replication. Novel treatment strategies are being investigated that induce HHV-8 to enter the lytic part of the life cycle leading to apoptosis of HHV-8 infected cells. It has been demonstrated that one of the HHV-8 lytic genes encodes the viral G-protein-coupled receptor (vGPCR), a constitutively active cellular chemokine receptor. vGPCR signalling can result in cell proliferation, the production of angiogenic factors and, in an animal model, can lead to KS-like lesions (Fig. 17.10). Moreover, there are indirect mechanisms involved in oncogenesis relating to altered T-cell responses and HHV-8 immunoregulation.

The incidence of KS has fallen sharply in HIV-infected individuals after the advent of highly active antiretroviral therapy (HAART), an element of which is thought to be due to direct activity on KS by these agents.

HHV-8 is also associated with benign and malignant lymphomatous conditions, namely multicentric Castleman's disease and primary effusion lymphoma, respectively.

Bacteria associated with cancer

The association between *Helicobacter pylori* and stomach and duodenal cancer, including gastric mucosa-associated lymphoid tissue (MALT) lymphoma, is referred to in Chapter 22. It is thought that a number of inflammatory reactions are triggered as a result of *H. pylori* colonizing the stomach mucosa leading to chronic atrophic gastritis (CAG). This sets off a cascade of mucosal changes resulting in intestinal metaplasia, dysplasia and carcinoma. The question is whether there are other environmental or genetic co-factors involved in oncogenesis. The tumour is associated with chronic inflammation secondary to *H. pylori* colonization, but it is thought that the bacterium alone is not sufficient for cancer to develop.

KEY FACTS

- Tissue damage or disease can be caused by infectious organisms in several ways.

- Infectious organisms may destroy cells directly (e.g. cytopathic viruses), release toxins that destroy cells or their cellular function (e.g. staphylococcus or tetanus toxins), overstimulate normal defence systems (e.g. LPS) or stimulate excessive or prolonged adaptive responses.

- Such effects of infectious organisms on defence systems may be antibody- or T-cell-mediated and are collectively known as 'hypersensitivity reactions' or 'immunopathology'.

- Some viruses have been shown to be involved in the initiation of tumours, with the viral genome being found in the cancer cells. The restricted geographic distribution of some of these tumours may be due to the local presence of co-carcinogens.

Clinical manifestation and diagnosis of infections by body system

THE CLINICAL MANIFESTATIONS OF INFECTION

A system of classification is essential in order to describe the diversity of infectious diseases. In Chapters 18–26, infections are classified according to the body system primarily involved at the clinical level. For example, rhinoviruses specifically cause infection of the upper respiratory tract, and bacillary or amoebic dysentery are gastrointestinal tract infections. Other infections characteristically cause damage predominantly to one part of the body, although other parts may be affected. Therefore, tuberculosis is considered in Chapter 19 (lower respiratory tract infections) and typhoid in Chapter 22 (gastrointestinal tract infections), these being the sites primarily affected, but there may be dissemination to other sites. Finally, some microbes can be grouped together with others acquired in the same way, even though more than one system may be involved. Examples are syphilis and HIV, which are dealt with in Chapter 21 (sexually transmitted diseases) and rubella in Chapter 23 (obstetric and perinatal infections).

The systems approach is useful because it includes infections caused by a wide variety of microbes on the basis of the clinical syndrome produced. As with any system of classification, however, there are grey areas and overlaps. Referral to the Appendix, where definitive accounts of the most important infectious organisms are given, will help clarify any ambiguities.

Chapters 27 and 28 deal with those infections that cannot be readily pigeonholed into systems. These include multisystem infections (i.e. infections that are not obviously localized to any one system of the body). Many multisystem infections are also multihost in that they can be transmitted:

- from person to person by an intermediate vector (usually an arthropod), their distribution depending upon climate, ecology and the presence of adequate numbers of the required arthropod (see Ch. 27)
- directly to humans from other vertebrates, in which case they are known as 'zoonoses' (see Ch. 28), with distributions ranging from highly restricted (Rocky Mountain spotted fever, Lassa fever) to widespread (Q fever, leptospirosis).

Finally, there are two further disease groupings, founded on clinical presentation:

- those presenting as 'fevers of unknown origin' (see Ch. 29)
- those seen in the compromised host (see Ch. 30).

The latter category has become increasingly important because of the large number of patients whose defences are impaired as a result of disease (cystic fibrosis, diabetes mellitus), infection (HIV/AIDS), immunosuppressive therapy (transplant patients) or other causes (e.g. burns, catheters).

Upper respiratory tract infections

18

Introduction

The mucociliary system and the flushing action of saliva are defences against upper respiratory tract infection

The air we inhale contains millions of suspended particles, including microorganisms, most of which are harmless. However, the air may contain large numbers of pathogenic microorganisms if someone is near an individual with a respiratory tract infection. Efficient cleansing mechanisms (see Chs 9 and 13) are therefore vital components of the body's defence against infection of both the upper and lower respiratory tract. Infection takes place against the background of these natural defence mechanisms, and it is then appropriate to ask why the defences have failed. For the upper respiratory tract, the flushing action of saliva is important in the oropharynx and the mucociliary system in the nasopharynx traps invaders. As on other surfaces of the body (see Ch. 8), a variety of microorganisms live harmoniously in the upper respiratory tract and oropharynx (Table 18.1); they colonize the nose, mouth, throat and teeth and are well adapted to life in these sites. Normally they are well-behaved guests, not invading tissues and not causing disease. However, as in other parts of the body, resident microorganisms can cause trouble when host resistance is weakened.

The upper and lower respiratory tracts form a continuum for infectious agents

We distinguish between upper and lower respiratory tract infections, but the respiratory tract from the nose to the alveoli is a continuum as far as infectious agents are concerned (Fig. 18.1). There may, however, be a preferred 'focus' of infection (e.g. nasopharynx for coronaviruses and rhinoviruses); but parainfluenza viruses, for instance, can infect the nasopharynx to give rise to a cold, as well as the larynx and trachea resulting in laryngotracheitis (croup), and occasionally the bronchi and bronchioles (bronchitis, bronchiolitis or pneumonia).

Two useful generalizations can be made about upper and lower respiratory tract infections:

1. Although many microorganisms are restricted to the surface epithelium, some spread to other parts of the body before returning to the respiratory tract, oropharynx, salivary glands (Table 18.2).
2. Two groups of microbes can be distinguished: 'professional' and 'secondary' invaders.

Professional invaders are those that successfully infect the normally healthy respiratory tract (Table 18.3). They generally possess specific properties that enable them to evade local host defences, such as the attachment mechanisms of respiratory viruses (Table 18.4). Secondary invaders only cause disease when host defences are already impaired (Table 18.3).

RHINITIS

Rhinoviruses and coronaviruses together cause more than 50% of colds

Viruses are the most common invaders of the nasopharynx, and a great variety of types (Table 18.4) are responsible for the symptoms referred to as the common cold. They induce a flow of virus-rich fluid which is called rhinorrhoea from the nasopharynx, and when the sneezing reflex is triggered, large numbers of virus particles are discharged into the air. Transmission is therefore by aerosol and also by virus-contaminated hands (see Ch. 13). Most of these viruses possess surface molecules that bind them firmly to host cells or to cilia or microvilli protruding from these cells. As a result, they are not washed away in secretions and are able to initiate infection in the normally healthy individual. Virus progeny from the first-infected cell then spread to neighbouring cells and via surface secretions to new sites on the mucosal surface. After a few days, damage to epithelial cells and the secretion of fluid containing inflammatory mediators such as bradykinin lead to common cold-type symptoms (Fig. 18.2).

Common cold virus infections are diagnosed by clinical appearance

In view of the large variety of viruses and because common colds are generally mild and self-limiting with no systemic spread in healthy individuals, determining the aetiology may only be helpful from an epidemiological perspective. Diagnosis becomes important when the lower respiratory tract is involved, as for instance with influenza viruses or in children with respiratory syncytial virus (RSV) infection. The diagnosis can be made using a number of different methods that include detecting viral antigens in exfoliated cells in samples such as nasopharyngeal aspirates or throat swabs using:

- immunofluorescence techniques (see Fig. 19.5)
- or by detecting viral genomic material using molecular methods such as the polymerase chain reaction (PCR) or microarrays
- or by virus isolation in cell culture

Alternatively, collecting an acute and convalescent serum sample and looking for a rise in virus-specific antibodies can confirm the diagnosis retrospectively.

199

Table 18.1 The normal flora of the respiratory tract

Type of resident[a]	Microorganism
Common residents (>50% of normal people)	Oral streptococci *Neisseria* spp. *Branhamella* Corynebacteria *Bacteroides* Anaerobic cocci (*Veillonella*) Fusiform bacteria[b] *Candida albicans*[b] *Streptococcus mutans* *Haemophilus influenzae*
Occasional residents (<10% of normal people)	*Streptococcus pyogenes* *Streptococcus pneumoniae* *Neisseria meningitidis*
Uncommon residents (<1% normal people)	*Corynebacterium diphtheria* *Klebsiella pneumoniae* *Pseudomonas* ⎱ Especially *E. coli* ⎰ after antibiotic *C. albicans* ⎰ treatment
Residents in latent state in tissues:[c] Lung Lymph nodes, etc. Sensory neurone/glands connected to mucosae	*Pneumocystis jirovecii*[d] *Mycobacterium tuberculosis* Cytomegalovirus (CMV) Herpes simplex virus Epstein–Barr virus

[a]All except tissue residents are present in the oronasopharynx or on teeth.
[b]Present in mouth; also *Entamoeba gingivalis*, *Trichomonas tenax*, micrococci, *Actinomyces* spp.
[c]All except *M. tuberculosis* are present in most humans.
[d]Formerly *P. carinii*.

Due to the increased sensitivity in detecting respiratory viruses by PCR, together with automated sample extraction and detection methods, many laboratories use molecular methods for making a diagnosis using combined nose and throat swab samples.

Treatment of the common cold is symptomatic

It is often said that a common cold will resolve in 48 h if vigorous treatment with anticongestants, analgesics and antibiotics is undertaken. There are no vaccines to protect against the common cold viruses as the vaccines would have to be polyvalent to cover this antigenically diverse group of viruses, and treatment is for the most part symptomatic.

PHARYNGITIS AND TONSILLITIS

About 70% of acute sore throats are caused by viruses

Microorganisms that cause sore throats (acute pharyngitis) are listed in Table 18.5. Those viruses that infect the upper respiratory tract inevitably encounter the submucosal lymphoid tissues that form a defensive ring around the oropharynx (see Fig. 18.1). The throat becomes sore either because the overlying mucosa is infected or because of inflammatory and immune responses in the lymphoid tissues themselves. Adenoviruses are common causes, often infecting the conjunctiva as well as the pharynx to cause pharyngoconjunctival fever. Epstein–Barr virus (EBV) and cytomegalovirus (CMV) multiply locally in the pharynx (Fig. 18.3), and herpes simplex virus (HSV) and certain coxsackie A viruses multiply in the oral mucosa to produce a painful local lesion or ulcer. Certain enteroviruses (e.g. coxsackie A16) can cause

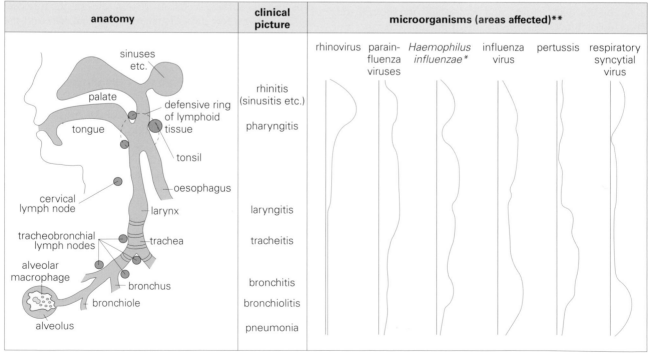

Figure 18.1 The respiratory tract as a continuum. * Asymptomatic nasopharyngeal colonization is common. ** Magnitude of rhinitis, laryngitis, etc. is shown by area between black and blue lines.

Table 18.2 Two types of respiratory infection

Type	Examples	Consequences
Restricted to surface	Common cold viruses Influenza *Streptococci* in throat *Chlamydia* (conjunctivitis) Diphtheria Pertussis *Candida albicans* (thrush)	Local spread Local (mucosal) defences important Adaptive (immune) response sometimes too late to be important in recovery Short incubation period (days)
Spread through body	Measles, mumps, rubella EBV, CMV *Chlamydophila psittaci*[a] Q fever *Cryptococcosis*	Little or no lesion at entry site Microbe spreads through body, returns to surface for final multiplication and shedding, e.g. salivary gland (mumps, CMV, EBV), respiratory tract (measles) Adaptive immune response important in recovery Longer incubation period (weeks)

After entry via the respiratory tract, microbes either stay on the surface epithelium or spread through the body.
[a]Formerly *Chlamydia psittaci*; CMV, cytomegalovirus; EBV, Epstein–Barr virus.

Table 18.3 The two types of respiratory invader – professional or secondary

Type	Requirement	Examples
Professional invaders (infect healthy respiratory tract)	Adhesion to normal mucosa (in spite of mucociliary system)	Respiratory viruses (influenza, rhinoviruses) *Streptococcus pyogenes* (throat) *Strep. pneumoniae* *Chlamydia* (psittacosis, chlamydial conjunctivitis and pneumonia, trachoma)
	Ability to interfere with cilia	*Bordetella pertussis, M. pneumoniae, Strep. pneumoniae* (pneumolysin)
	Ability to resist destruction in alveolar macrophage	*Legionella, Mycobacterium tuberculosis*
	Ability to damage local (mucosal, submucosal) tissues	*Corynebacterium diphtheriae* (toxin), *Strep. pneumoniae* (pneumolysin)
Secondary invaders (infect when host defences impaired)	Initial infection and damage by respiratory virus (e.g. influenza virus)	*Staphylococcus aureus; Strep. pneumoniae,* pneumonia complicating influenza
	Local defences impaired (e.g. cystic fibrosis)	*Staph. aureus, Pseudomonas*
	Chronic bronchitis, local foreign body or tumour	*Haemophilus influenzae, Strep. pneumoniae*
	Depressed immune responses (e.g. AIDS, neoplastic disease)	*Pneumocystis jirovecii,* cytomegalovirus, *M. tuberculosis*
	Depressed resistance (e.g. elderly, alcoholism, renal or hepatic disease)	*Strep. pneumoniae, Staph. aureus, H. influenzae*

additional vesicles on the hands and feet and in the mouth (hand, foot and mouth disease; Fig. 18.4).

Cytomegalovirus infection

Cytomegalovirus can be transmitted by saliva, urine, blood, semen and cervical secretions

Cytomegalovirus is the largest human herpesvirus (Fig. 18.5) and is species specific; humans are the natural hosts. Cytomegalovirus refers to the multinucleated cells, which together with the intranuclear inclusions, are characteristic responses to infection with this virus. CMV was originally called 'salivary gland' virus and is transmitted by saliva and other secretions. In addition, CMV can be transmitted by sexual contact, as semen and cervical secretions may also contain this virus, and by blood

transfusions (although leukodepletion reduces the risk significantly) and organ transplants from CMV antibody-positive donors. The CMV load will be high in the urine from babies with congenital CMV infection and careful hand washing and disposal of nappies will reduce the risk of transmission to susceptible individuals. CMV can be detected in breast milk, but this is of doubtful significance in transmission.

Cytomegalovirus infection is often asymptomatic, but can reactivate and cause disease when cell-mediated immunity (CMI) defences are impaired

After clinically silent infection in the upper respiratory tract, CMV spreads locally to lymphoid tissues and then systemically in circulating lymphocytes and monocytes to involve lymph nodes and the spleen. The infection then localizes in

Table 18.4 Common cold viruses and their mechanisms of attachment

Virus	Types involved	Attachment mechanism	Disease
Rhinoviruses (>100 types)[a]	Several at any given time in the community	Capsid protein binds to ICAM-1 type molecule on cell[b]	Common cold
Coxsackie virus A (24 types)[c]	Especially A21	Capsid protein binds to ICAM-1 type molecule on cell[b]	Common cold; also oropharyngeal vesicles (herpangina) and hand, foot and mouth disease (A16)
Influenza virus	Several	Haemagglutinin binds to neuraminic acid-containing glycoprotein on cell tract	May also invade lower respiratory tract
Parainfluenza virus (4 types)	1,2,3,4	Viral envelope protein binds to glycoside on cell	May also invade larynx
Respiratory syncytial virus	2 types	G protein on virus attaches to receptor on cell	May also invade lower respiratory tract
Coronaviruses (several types)	All	Viral envelope protein binds to glycoprotein receptors on cell	Common cold; severe acute respiratory syndrome
Adenovirus (41 types)	5–10 types	Penton fibre binds to cell receptor	Mainly pharyngitis; also conjunctivitis, bronchitis
Echovirus (34 types)	4,9,11,20,25		Common cold

[a]A given type shows little or no neutralization by antibody against other types.
[b]ICAM-1: intercellular adhesion molecule expressed on a wide variety of normal cells; member of immunoglobulin superfamily, coded on chromosome 19.
[c]Coxsackie virus A9 binds to vitronectin, an integrin protein; types 1 and 8 bind to very-late-activating antigen-2 (an integrin) and 6,7,12,21 to decay-accelerating factor (CD55) on cell.

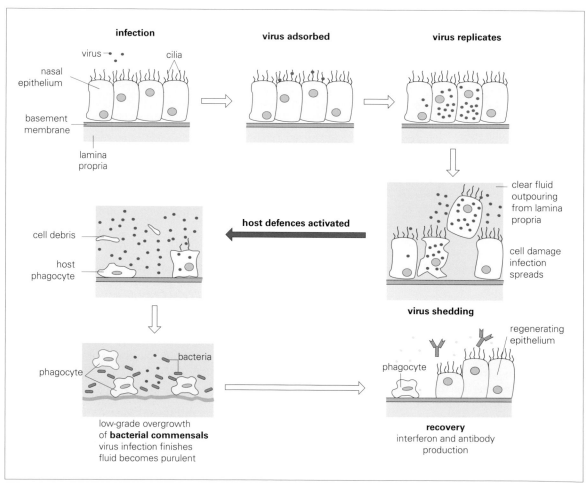

Figure 18.2 The pathogenesis of the common cold. For simplification, the epithelium is represented as one cell thick.

Table 18.5 Microorganisms that cause acute pharyngitis

Organisms	Examples	Comments
Viruses	Rhinoviruses, coronaviruses	A mild symptom in the common cold
	Adenoviruses (types 3,4,7,14,21)	Pharyngoconjunctival fever
	Parainfluenza viruses	More severe than common cold
	Influenza viruses, cytomegalovirus	Not always present
	Coxsackie A and other enteroviruses	Small vesicles (herpangina)
	Epstein–Barr virus	Occurs in 70–90% of glandular fever patients
	Herpes simplex virus type 1	Can be severe, with palatal vesicles or ulcers
Bacteria	*Streptococcus pyogenes*	Causes 10–20% of cases of acute pharyngitis; sudden onset; mostly in 5–10-year-old children
	Neisseria gonorrhoeae	Often asymptomatic; usually via orogenital contact
	Corynebacterium diphtheriae	Pharyngitis often mild, but toxic illness can be severe
	Haemophilus influenzae	Epiglottis
	Borrelia vincentii plus fusiform bacilli	Vincent's angina; commonest in adolescents and adults

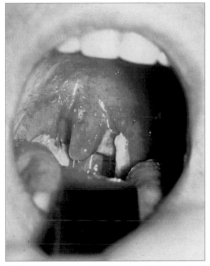

Figure 18.3 Infectious mononucleosis caused by Epstein–Barr virus. The tonsils and uvula are swollen and covered in white exudate. There are petechiae on the soft palate. (Courtesy of J.A. Innes.)

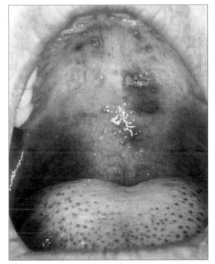

Figure 18.4 Ulcers on the hard palate and tongue in hand, foot and mouth disease due to coxsackie A virus. (Courtesy of J.A. Innes.)

epithelial cells in salivary glands and kidney tubules, and in cervix, testes and epididymis, from where the virus is shed to the outside world (Table 18.6).

Infected cells may be multinucleated or bear intranuclear inclusions, but pathologic changes are minor. The virus inhibits T-cell responses, and there is a temporary reduction in their immune reactivity to other antigens.

Although specific antibodies and CMI responses are generated, these fail to clear the virus (see Ch. 16), which often continues to be shed in saliva and urine for many months. The infection is, however, eventually controlled by CMI mechanisms, although infected cells remain in the body throughout life and can be a source of reactivation and disease when CMI defences are impaired.

CMV owes its success in our species to its ability to evade immune defences. For instance, it presents a poor target for cytotoxic T (Tc) cells by interfering with the transport of

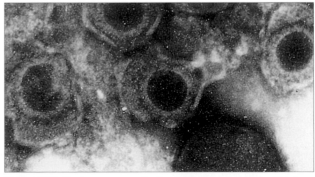

Figure 18.5 Electron micrograph of cytomegalovirus particles. This is the largest human herpes virus, with a diameter of 150–200 nm, and a dense DNA core. (Courtesy of D.K. Banerjee.)

Table 18.6 The effects of cytomegalovirus (CMV) infection

Site of infection	Result	Comment
Salivary glands	Salivary transmission	Via kissing and contaminated hands
Tubular epithelium of kidney	Virus in urine	Probable role in transmission by contaminating environment
Cervix, testis/epididymis	Sexual transmission	Up to 10^7 infectious doses/ml of semen in an acutely infected male
Lymphocytes, macrophages	Virus spread through body via infected cells Mononucleosis may occur Immunosuppressive effect	Probable site of persistent infection
Placenta, fetus	Congenital abnormalities	Greatest damage in fetus after primary maternal infection rather than reactivation

CMV is a 'well-behaved parasite', causing little or no damage to the host unless it infects the fetus or placenta to cause congenital abnormalities or it reactivates following depressed cell-mediated immunity (post-transplant, immunosuppression) to cause viraemia, fever, hepatitis or pneumonia.

major histocompatibility complex (MHC) class I molecules to the cell surface (see Ch. 10), and it induces Fc receptors on infected cells (see Ch. 16).

Cytomegalovirus infection can cause fetal malformations and pneumonia in immunodeficient patients

In the natural host, the human infant or child, CMV causes no illness, and in general it causes a mild illness in adults. However, as with all infections, there is a spectrum of clinical disease ranging from asymptomatic to severely ill. A glandular fever-type illness can occur in adolescents which is similar to Epstein–Barr virus (EBV) infection, with fever, lethargy and abnormal lymphocytes and mononucleosis in blood smears. Primary infection during pregnancy allows the spread of virus from the blood to the placenta and then to the fetus, resulting in symptomatic CMV infection at birth in 18%, and detection of other sequelae in 25% by just under 5 years of age, as described in Chapter 23. Reactivation of infection during pregnancy also occurs, which may be asymptomatic at birth but up to 8% will have symptoms by 5 years of age. CMV is second only to Down's syndrome as a cause of mental retardation in babies.

In immunodeficient patients such as bone marrow or solid organ transplant recipients (see Ch. 30), CMV infection can cause an interstitial pneumonitis with infiltrating infected mononuclear cells. Other sites affected include the CNS, with focal cerebral 'micronodular' lesions with infected mononuclear cells, together with a variety of other complications, including retinitis in HIV-infected individuals with AIDS. This was a major complication before the advent of highly active antiretroviral therapy (HAART). In addition, the gastrointestinal tract may be involved, with a colitis and hepatitis.

Clinical diagnosis of primary infection is rarely possible, because it is often asymptomatic. However, in symptomatic immunocompetent individuals, the diagnosis is made by detecting CMV IgM in blood samples. In those with possible CMV pneumonitis, a bronchoalveolar lavage sample is collected by passing a bronchoscope into the lungs and collecting washings, and CMV antigen or CMV DNA detection methods are used to make the diagnosis. Multinucleated cells or cells with prominent intranuclear inclusions may be seen in lung biopsy material. CMV IgM and IgG serology is available but is unlikely to be of diagnostic help in immunosuppressed patients. The management of post-transplant recipients involves CMV DNA monitoring of whole blood or plasma samples and giving pre-emptive therapy, having detected a CMV viraemia (see Ch. 30).

Antiviral treatment options in CMV infection

While ganciclovir, foscarnet or cidofovir are effective treatments, aciclovir is ineffective. These antiviral drugs reduce viral replication, do not eliminate the virus and can be used in specific clinical situations as pre-emptive therapy (see Ch. 30). As CMV pneumonitis is an immunopathological disease, CMV specific or human normal immunoglobulin is given in addition to the antiviral agent to potentially block the Tc-cell response to pneumocytes expressing the target antigens.

Prevention of CMV infection

There is no vaccine, but trials of live, inactivated and recombinant vaccines have been carried out. Bearing in mind that it is the second most common cause of mental retardation in babies, immunization is a major consideration once a number of practical issues have been resolved. The results of a recombinant CMV glycoprotein B vaccine trial reported in 2011 involving solid organ transplant recipients suggested that antibody levels generated in response to vaccine led to reduced viraemia and duration of antiviral use. Transmission can be reduced in various settings by avoiding contact between congenitally infected children and susceptible pregnant women or maintaining good hand hygiene if this is not possible. Blood for transfusion of newborns, and solid organ and bone marrow transplants, should preferably come from CMV antibody-negative donors.

Epstein–Barr virus infection

Epstein–Barr virus is transmitted in saliva

Epstein–Barr virus (EBV), like CMV, is species specific. EBV is structurally and morphologically identical to other herpesviruses (see Ch. 3), but is antigenically distinct. Major antigens include the viral capsid antigen (VCA) and the EBV-associated nuclear antigens (EBNA) that are used in diagnostic tests. Humans are the natural hosts.

EBV is transmitted by the exchange of saliva, for instance during kissing, and is a ubiquitous infection. In resource-poor countries, infection probably occurs via close contact

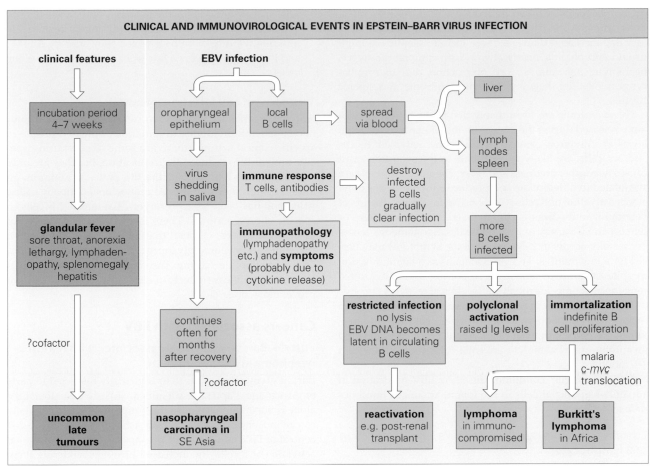

Figure 18.6 Clinical and immunovirologic events in Epstein–Barr virus (EBV) infection in adolescents or adults. A milder, often subclinical infection, occurs in children.

in early childhood and is subclinical. Elsewhere, infection occurs in two peaks at 1–6 years and 14–20 years of age, and in most cases, causes illness.

The clinical features of EBV infection are immunologically mediated

Clinical and immunologic events in EBV infection are illustrated in Figure 18.6. EBV replicates in B lymphocytes, after making a specific attachment to the C3d receptor (CD21) on these cells, and also in certain epithelial cells. The pathogenesis of the disease and the clinical features can be accounted for on this basis. Virus is shed in saliva from infected epithelial cells and possibly lymphocytes in salivary glands, and from the oropharynx, with clinically silent spread to B lymphocytes in local lymphoid tissues and elsewhere in the body (lymph nodes, spleen).

T lymphocytes respond immunologically to the infected B cells (outnumbering the latter by about 50 to 1) and appear in peripheral blood as 'atypical lymphocytes' (Fig. 18.7). Much of the disease is attributable to an immunologic civil war, as specifically activated T cells respond to the infected B cells. In the naturally infected infant or small child, these immune responses are weak and there is generally no clinical disease. Older children, however, become unwell, and young adults especially develop infectious mononucleosis or glandular fever 4–7 weeks after initial infection. This is characterized by fever, sore throat (see Fig. 18.3), often

with petechiae on the hard palate, lymphadenopathy and splenomegaly, with anorexia and lethargy as prominent features. Hepatitis may occur, with mild elevations of hepatocellular enzymes in 90% of cases and jaundice in 9%. Splenic rupture may occur.

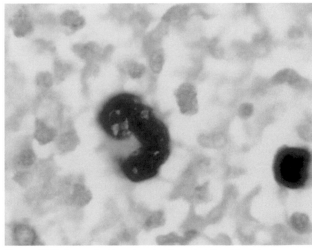

Figure 18.7 An atypical lymphocyte characteristic of Epstein–Barr virus infection. (From Valbuena et al: Classical Hodgkin lymphoma arising in the rectum, *Annals of Diagnostic Pathology* 9:38-42, 2005.)

Complications are seen in about 1% of acute EBV infections and may be due to virus invading the tissue or to immune-mediated damage. These include aseptic meningitis and encephalitis, nearly always with complete recovery, haemolytic anaemia, airway obstruction due to oropharyngeal swelling, haemophagocytic syndrome and splenic rupture.

The symptoms are presumably due to the action of cytokines released during the intense immunologic activity. High levels of interferon-gamma, produced by activated T cells and NK cells, are likely to contribute to the symptoms as it causes headache, tiredness and fever. The infected B cells are stimulated to differentiate and produce antibodies; this polyclonal activation of B cells is responsible for the production of heterophil antibodies (reacting with erythrocytes of sheep or horses) and a variety of autoantibodies. Spontaneous recovery usually occurs in 2–3 weeks, but the symptoms may persist for a few months. The virus remains as a latent infection in spite of antibody and CMI responses, and saliva often remains infectious for months after clinical recovery.

The autoantibodies produced in response to EBV infection include IgM antibodies to erythrocytes (cold agglutinins), which are present in most cases. About 1% of cases develop an autoimmune haemolytic anaemia, which subsides within 1–2 months.

A 'hairy tongue' condition caused by EBV replication in squamous epithelial cells in the tongue occurs in immunodeficient patients.

Epstein–Barr virus remains latent in a small proportion of B lymphocytes

Epstein–Barr virus is well equipped to evade immune defences (see Ch. 16). It acts against complement and interferon, and produces a fake interleukin 10 (IL-10) molecule that interferes with the action of the host's own IL-10 (an important immunoregulatory cytokine). EBV also prevents apoptosis (lysis) of infected cells, and the boldness of its strategy has enabled it to take up permanent residence within the immune system.

EBV DNA is present in episomal form in a small proportion of B lymphocytes, and a few copies may be integrated into the cell genome. Later in life, immunodeficiency can lead to reactivation of infection so that EBV reappears in the saliva, usually with no clinical symptoms.

Laboratory tests for diagnosing infectious mononucleosis should include viral capsid antigen IgM detection

Infectious mononucleosis is diagnosed clinically by the characteristic syndrome and the appearance of palatal petechiae in the throat. Laboratory diagnosis is made by detecting VCA IgM in the serum. However, there are other tests that help and these include:

- demonstrating atypical lymphocytes, comprising up to 30% of nucleated cells, in a blood smear. A number of viral infections cause an atypical lymphocytosis; therefore this is not specific to EBV.
- demonstrating heterophil antibodies to horse (or sheep) erythrocytes in the 'monospot' test. These are present in 90% of cases, but may not be detected in those less than 14 years of age and the response is short lived.

- EBV-specific antibody is the mainstay of diagnosis, in particular detecting VCA IgM indicates current infection. VCA IgG can be detected soon after VCA IgM and EBNA IgG appears a few weeks later after symptom onset.

Treatment of EBV infection is limited

Antiviral agents are not used to treat EBV-infected immunocompetent individuals. In immunosuppressed people in specific clinical settings there are some data on using specific antivirals to reduce viral replication, but they are only effective in the lytic part of the life cycle. In addition, an anti-CD20 receptor humanized monoclonal antibody called rituximab has been used to target EBV-infected B cells in specific clinical settings. There is no licensed vaccine, but placebo-controlled clinical trials have been carried out involving an envelope glycoprotein subunit vaccine and a CD8 T-cell peptide vaccine. The subunit vaccine was shown to have a significant effect on clinical disease but did not prevent infection.

Cancers associated with EBV

Epstein–Barr virus is closely associated with Burkitt's lymphoma in African children

Burkitt's lymphoma (Fig. 18.8) is virtually restricted to parts of Africa and Papua New Guinea, so it is clear that EBV alone is not enough to cause the lymphoma. The most likely co-carcinogen is malaria, which acts by weakening T-cell control of EBV infection and perhaps by causing polyclonal activation of B cells, the increased turnover rendering them more susceptible to neoplastic transformation.

Epstein–Barr virus is closely associated with other B-cell lymphomas in immunodeficient patients

For example, B-cell lymphomas occur in 1–10% of solid organ transplant recipients, especially children, when primary EBV infection occurs post-transplantation. EBV

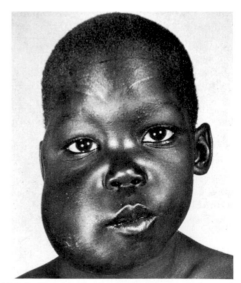

Figure 18.8 Burkitt's lymphoma affecting the maxilla in an African child. (Courtesy I. Magrath, MD, Bethesda, Md. From Zitelli B, Davis H: *Atlas of Pediatric Physical Diagnosis*, 2007, Mosby Elsevier.)

DNA and RNA transcripts are found in the tumour cells, which also show a translocation of the *c-myc* oncogene on chromosome 8 to the immunoglobulin heavy chain locus on chromosome 14 (see Ch. 17). Post-transplant lymphoproliferative disorders (PTLD) are due to uncontrolled B-cell proliferation. In addition, there is the rare X-linked lymphoproliferative disease (XLP) that is associated with EBV infection. This inherited disorder involves mutations in the gene that codes for the signalling lymphocyte activation molecule associated protein. The latter is key to B-cell activation of T cells and NK cells which control EBV-infected B cells. Therefore, individuals with this X-linked disorder can develop fatal infectious mononucleosis and lymphomas and it can only be prevented by having an allogeneic bone marrow transplant.

Epstein–Barr virus infection is also closely associated with nasopharyngeal carcinoma

Nasopharyngeal carcinoma (NPC) is a very common cancer in China and South-East Asia. EBV DNA is detectable in the tumour cells, and a co-carcinogen, possibly ingested nitrosamines from preserved fish, is likely. Host genetic factors controlling human leukocyte antigens (HLA) and immune responses may confer susceptibility to NPC.

Bacterial infections

Bacteria responsible for pharyngitis include:

- *Strep. pyogenes* (group A β-haemolytic, Fig. 18.9), the commonest and most important to diagnose because it can lead to complications (see below), but can be readily treated with penicillin
- *Corynebacterium diphtheriae*
- *Haemophilus influenzae* (type B), which occasionally causes severe epiglottitis with obstruction of the airways, especially in young children
- *Borrelia vincentii* together with certain fusiform bacilli, which can cause throat or gingival ulcers
- *Neisseria gonorrhoeae*.

Each of these types of bacteria attach to the mucosal surface, sometimes invading local tissues.

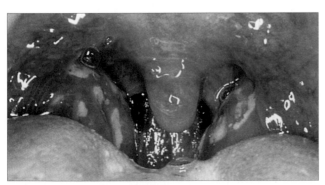

Figure 18.9 Streptococcal tonsillitis due to group A β-haemolytic *Streptococcus pyogenes* with intense erythema of the tonsils and a creamy-yellow exudate. (Courtesy of J.A. Innes.)

Complications of *Strep. pyogenes* infection

Complications of *Strep. pyogenes* throat infection include quinsy, scarlet fever, rheumatic fever, rheumatic heart disease and glomerulonephritis

These complications are important enough to be listed separately, although most are uncommon in resource-rich countries where there is good access to medical care and probably less exposure to streptococci. The complications include:

- Peritonsillar abscess ('quinsy') is an uncommon complication of untreated streptococcal sore throat.
- Otitis media, sinusitis, mastoiditis (see below) is caused by local spread of *Strep. pyogenes*.
- Scarlet fever. Certain strains of *Strep. pyogenes* produce an erythrogenic toxin coded for by a lysogenic phage. The toxin spreads through the body and localizes in the skin to induce a punctate erythematous rash (scarlet fever; Fig. 18.10). The tongue is initially furred, but later red. The rash begins as facial erythema and then spreads to involve most of the body except the palms and soles. The face is generally flushed with circumoral pallor. The rash fades over the course of 1 week and is followed by

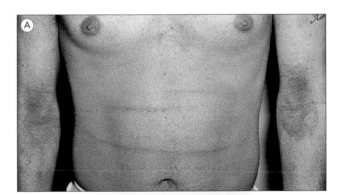

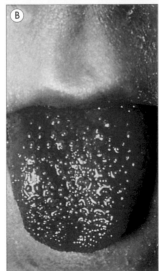

Figure 18.10 Scarlet fever. (A) Punctate erythema is followed by peeling for 2–3 weeks. (From James et al: Andrews' Diseases of the Skin, 2006, Saunders Elsevier.) (B) The tongue is furred at first and then becomes raw with prominent papillae. (Courtesy of W.E. Farrar.)

extensive desquamation. The skin lesions themselves are not serious, but they signal infection by a potentially harmful streptococcus, which in pre-antibiotic days could sometimes spread through the body to cause cellulitis and septicaemia.

- Rheumatic fever. This is an indirect complication. Antibodies formed to antigens in the streptococcal cell wall cross-react with the sarcolemma of human heart, and with tissues elsewhere. Granulomas are formed in the heart (Aschoff's nodules), and 2–4 weeks after the sore throat the patient (usually a child) develops myocarditis or pericarditis, which may be associated with subcutaneous nodules, polyarthritis and, rarely, chorea. Chorea is a disease of the central nervous system resulting from streptococcal antibodies reacting with neurones.

- Rheumatic heart disease. Repeated attacks of *Strep. pyogenes* with different M types can lead to damage to the heart valves. Certain children have a genetic predisposition to this immune-mediated disease. If a primary attack is accompanied by rising or high antistreptolysin O (ASO) antibody levels, future attacks must be prevented by penicillin prophylaxis throughout childhood. In many developing countries, rheumatic heart disease is the most common type of heart disease.

- Acute glomerulonephritis. Antibodies to streptococcal components combine with them to form circulating immune complexes, which are then deposited in glomeruli, together, probably, with autoantibodies to glomerular components. Here, the complement and coagulation systems are activated, resulting in local inflammation. Blood appears in the urine (red cells, protein) and there are signs of an acute nephritis syndrome (oedema, hypertension) 1–2 weeks after the sore throat. ASO antibodies are usually elevated. Only four to five of the 65 M types of *Strep. pyogenes* give rise to this condition, and repeated infection with different 'nephritogenic' types is unlikely. Penicillin prophylaxis is therefore not given. In contrast to rheumatic fever, second attacks are rare.

Diagnosis

A laboratory diagnosis is not generally necessary for pharyngitis and tonsillitis

There are many possible viral causes of pharyngitis and tonsillitis, and the clinical condition is generally not serious enough to seek laboratory help. The diagnosis of EBV or CMV infection is helped by detecting a lymphocytosis and atypical lymphocytes in a blood film. EBV is distinguished from CMV by detecting VCA IgM, although the less specific tests such as the Paul–Bunnell or monospot test may be used, whereas CMV diagnosis is made by detecting CMV IgM. HSV is readily isolated or the DNA detected in swabs from the lesions sent to the laboratory, but clinical diagnosis is usually adequate. Bacteria are identified by culturing throat swabs (see Ch. 32). It is especially important to diagnose *Strep. pyogenes* infection by culture because of the possible complications (see above) and because, unlike *Strep. pneumoniae*, it remains

susceptible to penicillin. Resistance to erythromycin and tetracycline, however, is increasing. Although during the winter months up to 16% of schoolchildren carry group A streptococci in the throat without symptoms, treatment is recommended.

PAROTITIS

Mumps virus is spread by airborne droplets and infects the salivary glands

There is only one serotype of this single-stranded RNA paramyxovirus. It spreads by airborne droplets, salivary secretions and possibly urine. Close contact is necessary, for example, at school, as the peak incidence is at 5–14 years of age. However, susceptible adults are at risk of complications of mumps such as orchitis.

After entering the body, the primary site of replication is the epithelium of the upper respiratory tract or eye. The virus spreads, undergoing further multiplication in local lymphoid tissues (lymphocytes and monocytes) and reticuloendothelial cells. After approximately 7–10 days the virus enters the blood, a primary viraemia, and localizes in salivary and other glands and body sites including the central nervous system, testis, pancreas and ovary (Fig. 18.11) and is excreted in the urine. Infected cells lining the parotid ducts degenerate and finally, after an incubation period of 16–18 days, the inflammation, with lymphocyte infiltration and often oedema, results in disease. After a prodromal period of malaise and anorexia lasting 1–2 days, the parotid gland becomes painful, tender and swollen, and is sometimes accompanied by submandibular gland involvement (Fig. 18.12). This is the classic sign of mumps, and parotitis is the most common clinical sign. Other sites may be invaded, with clinical consequences such as inflammation of the testis and pancreas, resulting respectively in orchitis and pancreatitis (Table 18.7). CMI as well as antibody responses appear, and the patient usually recovers within 1 week. There is life-long resistance to reinfection.

Laboratory diagnosis is made:

- by detecting viral RNA in throat swabs, cerebrospinal fluid (CSF) or urine or by isolating virus in cell culture
- by detecting mumps-specific IgM antibody.

Treatment and prevention

There is no specific treatment, but mumps is prevented by using the attenuated live virus vaccine, which is safe and effective. This is usually given in combination with measles and rubella vaccines (MMR vaccine).

Combined MMR has been a controversial issue in the UK after autism and bowel disorders were reported as being possibly associated with immunization. However, despite a series of epidemiological studies showing no association with immunization, there was a fall in MMR uptake rates and subsequent outbreaks of mumps and measles around the UK. These rates had improved by 2011; however, increasing numbers of outbreaks of measles were seen in other parts of Europe.

Figure 18.11 The pathogenesis of mumps. Understanding the pathogenesis of this infection helps to explain the disease picture, sites of shedding and the complications that can arise, but little is known about the events that occur during the first week of infection.

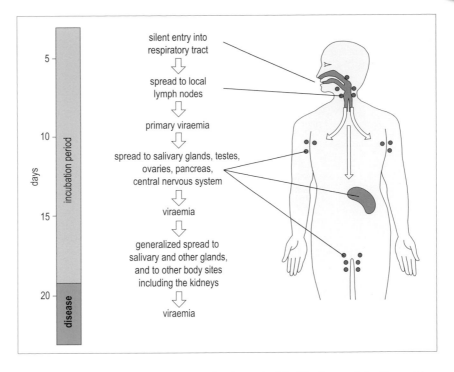

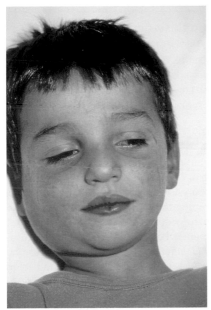

Figure 18.12 Enlarged submandibular glands in a child with mumps. (From Heumann et al: *Klinische Infektiologie*, 2008, Elsevier.)

OTITIS AND SINUSITIS

Otitis and sinusitis can be caused by many viruses and a range of secondary bacterial invaders

Many viruses are capable of invading the air spaces associated with the upper respiratory tract (sinuses, middle ear, mastoid). Mumps virus or respiratory syncytial virus (RSV), for instance, can cause vestibulitis or deafness, which is generally temporary. The range of secondary bacterial invaders is the same as for other upper respiratory tract infections, i.e. *Strep. pneumoniae* and *H. influenzae* and sometimes anaerobes, such as *Bacteroides fragilis*. Brain abscess is a major complication (see Ch. 24). Blockage of the Eustachian (auditory) tube or the opening of sinuses, caused by allergic swelling of the mucosa, prevents mucociliary clearance of infection, and the local accumulation of inflammatory bacterial products causes further swelling and blockage.

Acute otitis media

Common causes of acute otitis media are viruses, *Strep. pneumoniae* and *H. influenzae*

This condition is extremely common in infants and small children, partly because the eustachian (auditory) tube is open more widely at this age. A study in Boston showed that 83% of 3-year-olds had had at least one episode, and 46% had had three or more episodes since birth. At least 50% of the attacks are viral in origin (especially RSV), and the bacterial invaders are nasopharyngeal residents, most commonly *Strep. pneumoniae* or *H. influenzae*, and sometimes *Strep. pyogenes* or *Staph. aureus*. There may be general symptoms, and acute otitis media should be considered in any child with unexplained fever, diarrhea or vomiting. The ear drum shows dilated vessels with bulging of the drum at a later stage (Fig. 18.13). Fluid often persists in the middle ear for weeks or months ('glue ear'), regardless of therapy, and contributes to impaired hearing and learning difficulties in infants and small children.

If acute attacks are inadequately treated, there may be continued infection with a chronic discharge through a perforated drum and impaired hearing. This is 'chronic suppurative otitis media'.

Otitis externa

Causes of otitis externa are *Staph. aureus*, *Candida albicans* and Gram-negative opportunists

Infections of the outer ear can cause irritation and pain, and must be distinguished from otitis media. In contrast to the middle ear, the external canal has a bacterial flora similar

Table 18.7 Clinical consequences of mumps virus invasion of different body tissues

Site of growth	Result	Comment
Salivary glands	Inflammation, parotitis Virus shed in saliva (from 3 days before to 6 days after symptoms)	Often absent; can be unilateral
Meninges Brain	Meningitis Encephalitis } Up to 7 days after parotitis	Common (in about 10% cases) Less common; complete recovery is the rule, deafness is a rare complication
Kidney	Virus present in urine	No clinical consequences
Testis, ovary	Epididymo-orchitis; rigid tunica albuginea around testis make orchitis more painful and more damaging in male	Common in adults (20% in adult males); often unilateral; not a significant cause of sterility
Pancreas	Pancreatitis	Rare complication (possible role in juvenile diabetes mellitus)
Mammary gland	Virus detectable in milk; mastitis in 10% post-pubertal females	
Thyroid	Thyroiditis	Rare
Myocardium	Myocarditis	Rare
Joints	Arthritis	Rare

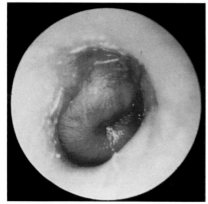

Figure 18.13 Acute otitis media with bulging ear drum. (Courtesy of M. Chaput de Saintonge.)

to that of the skin (staphylococci, corynebacteria and, to a lesser extent, propionibacteria), and the pathogens responsible for otitis media are rarely found in otitis externa. The warm moist environment favours *Staph. aureus*, *Candida albicans* and Gram-negative opportunists such as *Proteus* and *Pseudomonas aeruginosa*.

Ear drops containing polymyxin or other antibiotics are usually an effective treatment.

Acute sinusitis

The aetiology and pathogenesis of acute sinusitis are similar to those of otitis media. Clinical features include facial pain and localized tenderness. It may be possible to identify the causative bacteria by microscopy and culture of pus aspirated from the sinus, but sinus puncture is not often carried out. In addition, as is the case for otitis media, the patient can be treated empirically with ampicillin or amoxicillin, or with the newer oral cephalosporins (e.g. cefixime) to deal with beta-lactamase-producing organisms.

ACUTE EPIGLOTTITIS

Acute epiglottitis is generally due to *H. influenzae* capsular type B infection

Acute epiglottitis is most often seen in young children. For unknown reasons, *H. influenzae* capsular type B spreads from the nasopharynx to the epiglottis, causing severe inflammation and oedema. There is usually a bacteraemia.

Acute epiglottitis is an emergency and necessitates intubation and treatment with antibiotics

Acute epiglottitis is characterized by difficulty in breathing because of respiratory obstruction and, until the airway has been secured by intubation, extreme care must be taken when examining the throat in case the swollen epiglottis is sucked into the oedematous airway and causes total obstruction. Treatment is begun immediately with antibiotics effective against *H. influenzae* (cefotaxime, chloramphenicol). The clinical diagnosis is confirmed by isolating bacteria from the blood and possibly the epiglottis. The *H. influenzae* type B (Hib) vaccine greatly reduces the frequency of this and other infections due to *H. influenzae* type B.

Respiratory obstruction due to diphtheria (see below) is rare in resource-rich countries, but the characteristic false membrane and local swelling can extend from the pharynx to involve the uvula.

ORAL CAVITY INFECTIONS

Saliva flushes the mouth and contains a variety of antibacterial substances

The oral cavity is continuous with the pharynx, but is dealt with separately because of the presence of teeth, which are subject to a particular set of microbiologic problems. The normal mouth contains commensal microorganisms, some of which are to a large extent restricted to the mouth (see Table 18.1). Most of them make specific attachments to teeth or mucosal surfaces and are shed into the saliva as they multiply. The litre or so of saliva secreted each day mechanically flushes the mouth. It also contains secretory antibodies, polymorphs, desquamated mucosal cells and antibacterial substances such as lysozyme and lactoperoxidase. When salivary flow is decreased for a few hours, as between meals, there is a fourfold increase in the number of bacteria in saliva, and, in dehydrated patients or in severe illnesses such as typhoid or pneumonia, the mouth becomes foul because of microbial overgrowth.

Oral candidiasis

Changes in the oral flora produced by broad-spectrum antibiotics and impaired immunity predispose to thrush

The presence of commensal bacteria in the mouth makes it difficult for invading microorganisms to become established, but changes in oral flora upset this balance. For instance, prolonged administration of broad-spectrum antibiotics allows the normally harmless *C. albicans* to flourish, penetrating the epithelium with its pseudomycelia, and causing thrush. Oral thrush (candidiasis, Fig. 18.14) is also seen when immunity is impaired, as in HIV infection and malignancy, and occasionally in newborn infants and the elderly. It sometimes spreads to involve the oesophagus. The diagnosis is readily confirmed by Gram stain and culture of scraped material, which shows large Gram-positive budding yeasts.

Topical antifungal agents (e.g. nystatin or clotrimazole) or oral fluconazole (see Ch. 33) are effective treatments for thrush, together with attention to any predisposing factors.

Another example of the shifting boundary between harmless coexistence and tissue invasion by resident microbes is seen with vitamin C deficiency, which reduces mucosal resistance and allows residents to cause gum infections.

Caries

In the USA and Western Europe, 80–90% of people are colonized by *Streptococcus mutans*, which causes dental caries

The microorganisms specifically adapted for life on teeth form a film called dental plaque on the tooth surface. This is a complex mass containing about 10^9 bacteria/g embedded in a polysaccharide matrix (Fig. 18.15). The film, visible as a red layer when a dye such as Erythrocin is taken

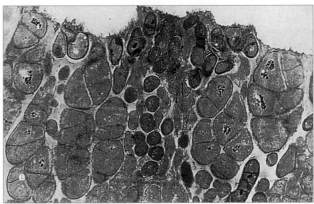

Figure 18.15 Dental plaque on the deep surface of a child's tooth. e, enamel. (×20 000) (Courtesy of H.N. Newman.)

into the mouth, is largely removed by thorough brushing, but re-establishes itself within a few hours. The clean teeth become covered with salivary glycoproteins to which certain streptococci (especially *Strep. mutans* and *Strep. sobrinus*) become attached and multiply. In the USA and Western Europe, 80–90% of people are colonized by *Strep. mutans*. *Strep. mutans* itself synthesizes glucan (a sticky high molecular weight polysaccharide) from sucrose and this forms a matrix between these streptococci. Certain other bacteria, including anaerobic filamentous fusobacteria and actinomycetes, are also present. When the teeth are not cleaned for several days, plaque becomes thicker and more extensive – a tangled forest of microorganisms.

The bacteria in plaque use dietary sugar and form lactic acid, which decalcifies the tooth locally. Proteolytic enzymes from the bacteria help to break down other components of the enamel to give rise to a painful cavity in the tooth (caries). Infection may then spread into the pulp of the tooth to form a pulp or root abscess, and from here to the maxillary or mandibular spaces.

The pH in an active caries lesion may be as low as 4.0. Therefore, caries usually develops in crevices on the tooth when suitable bacteria (*Strep. mutans*) are in the plaque and there is a regular supply of sucrose. It may legitimately be regarded as an infectious disease – one of the most prevalent infectious diseases in resource-rich countries due to closely placed bacteria-coated teeth and a sugary, often fluoride-deficient, diet.

Periodontal disease

Actinomyces viscosus, *Actinobacillus* and *Bacteroides* spp. are commonly involved in periodontal disease

A space (the gingival crevice) readily forms between the gums and tooth margin, and it may be considered as an oral backwater. It contains polymorphs, complement, IgG and IgM antibodies, and easily becomes infected. Gingival crevices normally contain an average of 2.7×10^{11} microbes/g, and 75% of them are anaerobes. Bacteria such as *Actinomyces viscosus*, *Actinobacillus* and *Bacteroides* spp. are commonly involved. In periodontal disease, the space enlarges to become a 'pocket', with local inflammation, an increasing number of polymorphs and a serum exudate. The inflamed gum bleeds readily and later recedes, while

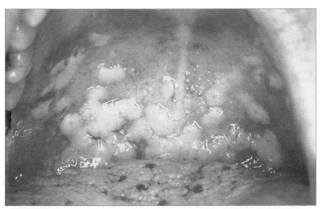

Figure 18.14 Oral candidiasis. (Courtesy of J.A. Innes.)

the multiplying bacteria cause halitosis. Finally, the structures supporting the teeth are affected, with reabsorption of ligaments and weakening of bone, causing the teeth to loosen. Periodontal disease with gingivitis is almost universal, although its severity varies greatly. It is a major cause of tooth loss in adults.

KEY FACTS

- The respiratory tract from the nose to the alveoli is a continuum, and any given microbe can cause disease in more than one segment.

- Some respiratory infections are restricted to the surface epithelium (influenza, diphtheria, pertussis), while others spread throughout the body (measles, rubella, mumps, CMV, EBV).

- 'Professional' invaders infect the healthy respiratory tract (e.g. common cold viruses, influenza viruses, mumps,

CMV, EBV, *M. tuberculosis*), whereas 'secondary' invaders cause disease when host defences are impaired (e.g. *Staph. aureus, Pneumocystis jiroveii, Pseudomonas*).

- Common diseases of the teeth and neighbouring structures – caries, periodontal disease – are of microbial aetiology.

- Diphtheria is a life-threatening disease caused by a biochemically defined bacterial toxin, and is completely preventable by vaccination.

Lower respiratory tract infections

Introduction

Although the respiratory tract is continuous from the nose to the alveoli, it is convenient to distinguish between infections of the upper and lower respiratory tract, even though the same microorganisms might be implicated in infections of both. Infections of the upper respiratory tract and associated structures are the subject of Chapter 18. Here, we discuss infections of the lower respiratory tract. These infections tend to be more severe than infections of the upper respiratory tract, and the choice of appropriate antimicrobial therapy is important and may be life saving.

LARYNGITIS AND TRACHEITIS

Parainfluenza viruses are common causes of laryngitis

Viral infections of the upper respiratory tract may spread downwards to involve the larynx and the trachea. Usually the cause is a parainfluenza virus, but sometimes it is RSV, influenza virus or an adenovirus. Diphtheria (see below) may involve the larynx or trachea.

In adults, laryngeal infection (laryngitis) and tracheitis cause hoarseness and a burning retrosternal pain. The larynx and trachea have non-expandable rings of cartilage in the wall, and are easily obstructed in children, due to the narrow passages, leading to hospital admission. Swelling of the mucous membrane may lead to a dry cough and inspiratory stridor ('crowing') known as croup. Bacteria such as group A streptococci, *Haemophilus influenzae* and *Staphylococcus aureus* are less common causes of laryngitis and tracheitis.

DIPHTHERIA

Diphtheria is caused by toxin-producing strains of *Corynebacterium diphtheriae* and can cause life-threatening respiratory obstruction

Diphtheria is now rare in resource-rich countries due to widespread immunization with toxoid (see Ch. 34), but it is still common in resource-poor countries. Non-toxigenic strains occur in the normal pharynx, but bacteria producing the extracellular toxin (exotoxin; see Ch. 2) must be present to cause disease. They can colonize the pharynx (especially the tonsillar regions), the larynx, the nose and occasionally the genital tract, and in the tropics or in indigent people with poor skin hygiene, the skin.

Adhesion is mediated by pili or fimbriae covalently attached to the bacterial cell wall. The bacteria multiply locally without invading deeper tissues or spreading through the body. The toxin destroys epithelial cells and polymorphs, and an ulcer forms, which is covered with a necrotic exudate forming a 'false membrane'. This soon becomes dark and malodorous, and bleeding occurs on attempting to remove it. There is extensive inflammation and swelling (Fig. 19.1) and the cervical lymph nodes may be enlarged to give a 'bull neck' appearance.

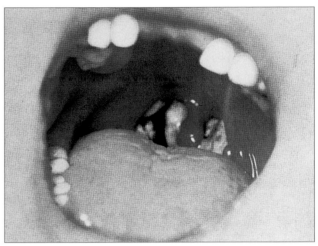

Figure 19.1 Pharyngeal diphtheria. Characteristic diphtheria 'false membrane' in a child, with local inflammation. (Courtesy of Norman Begg.)

Nasopharyngeal diphtheria is the most severe form of the disease. When the larynx is involved, it can result in life-threatening respiratory obstruction. Anterior nasal diphtheria is a mild form of the disease if it occurs on its own, because the toxin is less well absorbed from this site, and a nasal discharge may be the main symptom. The patient will, however, be highly infectious.

Diphtheria toxin can cause fatal heart failure and a polyneuritis

The toxin (Box 19.1 and Fig. 19.2) is absorbed into the lymphatics and blood, and has several effects:

- Constitutional upset, with fever, pallor, exhaustion.
- Myocarditis, usually within the first 2 weeks. Electrocardiographic changes are common and cardiac failure can occur. If this is not lethal, complete recovery is usual.
- Polyneuritis, which may occur after the onset of illness, due to demyelination. It may, for instance, affect the 9th cranial nerve, resulting in paralysis of the soft palate and regurgitation of fluids.

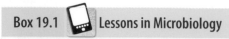
Diphtheria toxin

The genes encoding toxin production are carried by a temperate bacteriophage which, during the lysogenic phase, is integrated into the bacterial chromosome. The toxin is synthesized as a single polypeptide (molecular weight 62 000; 535 amino acids) consisting of:

- fragment B (binding) at the carboxy terminal end, which attaches the toxin to the host cells (or to any eukaryotic cell)

- fragment A (active) at the amino terminal end, which is the toxic fragment.

Toxic fragment A is only formed by protease cleavage and reduction of disulfide bonds after cellular uptake of the toxin. Fragment A inactivates elongation factor-2 (EF-2) by adenosine diphosphate (ADP) ribosylation and thereby inhibits protein synthesis (Fig. 19.2). Prokaryotic and mitochondrial protein synthesis is not affected because a different EF is involved. A single bacterium can produce 5000 toxin molecules/h and the toxic fragment is so stable within the cell that a single molecule can kill a cell. For unknown reasons, myocardial and peripheral nerve cells are particularly susceptible.

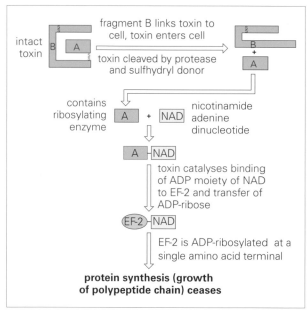

Figure 19.2 Mechanism of action of diphtheria toxin. ADP, adenosine diphosphate; EF-2, elongation factor-2.

Diphtheria is managed by immediate treatment with antitoxin and antibiotic

Diphtheria is a life-threatening disease, and clinical diagnosis is a matter of urgency. As soon as the diagnosis is suspected clinically, the patient is isolated to reduce the risk of the toxigenic strain spreading to other susceptible individuals, and antitoxin treatment is started. The antitoxin is produced in horses, and tests for hypersensitivity to horse serum should be carried out. Penicillin or erythromycin

is given as well. Laryngeal diphtheria may result in an obstructed airway and require a tracheotomy to assist with respiration.

The diagnosis is confirmed in the laboratory by isolation and identification of the organism (Ch. 32) and demonstrating toxin production by a gel-diffusion precipitin reaction (Elek test). PCR can be carried out in some reference laboratories to detect the *tox* gene responsible for producing the toxin.

Contacts may need chemoprophylaxis or immunization

Contacts of diphtheria patients should be tested for carriage of toxigenic *C. diphtheriae* and if necessary be given chemoprophylaxis or immunization. Toxigenic bacteria may be carried and transmitted by asymptomatic convalescents or by apparently healthy individuals.

Diphtheria is prevented by immunization

Diphtheria has almost disappeared from resource-rich countries as a result of the immunization of children with a safe, effective toxoid vaccine (see Ch. 34). However, the disease reappears when immunization is neglected. In 1990, epidemics began in the Russian Federation, and by 1994, all 15 of the newly independent states of the former Soviet Union were involved, with 157 000 reported cases by 1997. The World Health Organization (WHO) website reported in 2011 that the incidence of diphtheria ranged from 0.5–1/100 000 population in Armenia, Estonia, Lithuania and Uzbekistan, to 27–32/100 000 in Russia and Tajikistan. Case fatality rates ranged from 2–3% in Russia to 17–23% in Azerbaijan, Georgia and Turkmenistan. Worldwide, in 2004, the World Health Organization estimated there were 5000 deaths and in 2009, 857 cases were reported.

WHOOPING COUGH

Whooping cough is caused by the bacterium *Bordetella pertussis*

Whooping cough or pertussis is a severe disease of childhood. *Bordetella pertussis* is confined to humans and is spread from person to person by airborne droplets. The organisms attach to, and multiply in, the ciliated respiratory mucosa, but do not invade deeper structures. Surface components such as filamentous haemagglutinin and fimbrial agglutinogens play an important role in specific attachment to respiratory epithelium.

B. pertussis infection is associated with the production of a variety of toxic factors

Some of these toxic factors affect inflammatory processes, while others damage ciliary epithelium. They are:

- Pertussis toxin, which resembles diphtheria and other toxins (see Chs 17 and 18) in being a subunit toxin with an active (A) unit and a binding (B) unit. The A unit is an adenosine diphosphate (ADP)-ribosyl transferase, which catalyses the transfer of ADP-ribose from nicotinamide adenine dinucleotide (NAD) to host cell proteins. The functional consequence of this is a disruption of signal transduction to the affected cell, but the toxin probably has other effects on the cell surface as well.

- Adenylate cyclase toxin, which is a single peptide that can enter host cells and cause them to increase their cyclic adenosine monophosphate (cAMP) to supraphysiologic levels. In neutrophils, this results in an inhibition of defence functions such as chemotaxis, phagocytosis and bactericidal killing. This toxin may also be responsible for the haemolytic properties of *B. pertussis*.
- Tracheal cytotoxin, which is a cell wall component derived from the peptidoglycan of *B. pertussis* that specifically kills tracheal epithelial cells (see Ch. 2).
- Endotoxin, which differs from the classic endotoxin of other Gram-negative rods, but has functional similarities and may play a role in the pathogenesis of infection.

B. pertussis infection is characterized by paroxysms of coughs followed by a 'whoop'. After an incubation period of 7–10 days (range 5–21 days), *B. pertussis* infection is manifest first as a catarrhal illness with little to distinguish it from other upper respiratory tract infections. This is followed up to 1 week later by a dry non-productive cough, which becomes paroxysmal. A paroxysm is characterized by a series of short coughs producing copious mucus, followed by a 'whoop', which is a characteristic sound produced by an inspiratory gasp of air. Despite the severity of the cough, the symptoms are confined to the respiratory tract, and lobar or segmental collapse of the lungs can occur (Fig. 19.3).

Complications include central nervous system (CNS) anoxia, exhaustion and secondary pneumonia due to invasion of the damaged respiratory tract by other pathogens.

The early clinical picture is non-specific, and the true diagnosis may not be suspected until the paroxysmal phase. The organisms can be isolated on suitable media from throat swabs or on 'cough plates' (see Ch. 32), but they are fastidious and do not survive well outside the host's environment.

Whooping cough is managed with supportive care and erythromycin

Supportive care is of prime importance. Infants are at greatest risk of complications, and admission to hospital should be considered for children less than 1 year of age. For specific antibacterial treatment to be effective it must penetrate the respiratory mucosa and inhibit or kill the infecting organism. Treatment with macrolide antibiotics such as erythromycin, clarithromycin or azithromycin is recommended. Although the treatment is often only started when the disease is recognized in the paroxysmal phase, it does appear to reduce its severity and duration. It also reduces the bacterial load in the throat, thereby helping to reduce both the infectivity of the patient and the risk of secondary infections.

Prophylaxis with macrolide antibiotics of close contacts of active cases is helpful in controlling the spread of infection.

Whooping cough can be prevented by active immunization

For many years, a whole cell vaccine comprising a killed suspension of *B. pertussis* cells was used, combined with purified diphtheria and tetanus toxoids and administered as 'DPT' or 'triple' vaccine. Although an effective vaccine, there were major concerns about side effects. These included fever, malaise and pain at the site of administration in up to 20% of infants; convulsions, thought to be associated with the vaccine in about 0.5% of vaccinees; and encephalopathy and permanent neurologic sequelae associated with vaccination, with an estimated rate of 1 in 100 000 vaccinations (<0.001%).

Concern about side effects led to a marked fall in uptake of the vaccine and subsequently to a marked increase in the incidence of whooping cough (see Ch. 31).

Acellular pertussis vaccines became the dominant vaccine preparation as they provide the same or better protection against whooping cough and cause fewer side effects as they are highly purified with much reduced levels of endotoxin compared with whole cell vaccines. The acellular vaccines contain pertussis toxoid and other bacterial components, including the filamentous haemagglutinin and fimbriae, and are given in combination with other vaccines such as diphtheria, tetanus, polio and *Haemophilus influenzae* type B. In 2008, about 82% of all infants worldwide received three doses of pertussis vaccine. WHO estimated that global pertussis immunization prevented about 687 000 deaths that year and that about 16 million cases of pertussis occurred worldwide. Ninety-five per cent were in resource-poor countries and whooping cough led to about 195 000 childhood deaths.

ACUTE BRONCHITIS

Acute bronchitis is an inflammatory condition of the tracheobronchial tree, usually due to infection

Causative agents include rhinoviruses and coronaviruses, which also infect the upper respiratory tract, and lower tract pathogens such as influenza viruses, adenoviruses and *Mycoplasma pneumoniae*. Secondary bacterial infection with *Streptococcus pneumoniae* and *Haemophilus influenzae* may also play a role in pathogenesis. The degree of damage to the respiratory epithelium varies with the infecting agent:

- With influenza virus infection, it may be extensive and leave the host prone to secondary bacterial invasion (post-influenza pneumonia; see below).
- With *Mycoplasma pneumoniae* infection, specific attachment of the organism to receptors on the bronchial

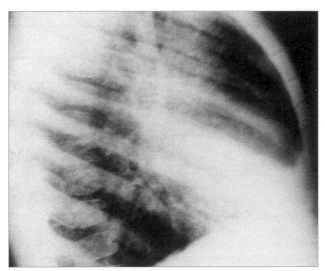

Figure 19.3 Chest radiograph showing patchy consolidation and collapse of the right middle lobe in whooping cough. (Courtesy of J.A. Innes.)

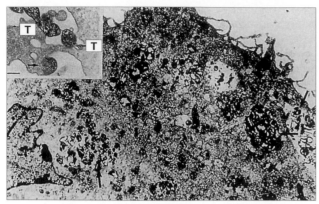

Figure 19.4 Opsonized *Mycoplasma pneumoniae* cells (arrowed) phagocytosed by an alveolar macrophage (bar, 2 μm). The insert shows *M. pneumoniae* cells adhering with the tip organelle (T) to macrophage surfaces. (From Jacobs E. *Rev Med Microbiol* 2:83–90, © 1991.)

mucosal epithelium (Fig. 19.4) and the release of toxic substances by the organism results in sloughing of affected cells. There is a 4-yearly epidemic cycle that normally occurs 2 years after the Olympic Games. A dry cough is the most prominent presentation, and treatment is largely symptomatic. However, it can cause pneumonia and complications involving other organs, such as hepatitis, encephalitis, arthralgia, skin lesions and haemolytic anaemia. Treatment involves antibiotics such as tetracyclines or macrolides.

ACUTE EXACERBATIONS OF CHRONIC BRONCHITIS

Infection is only one component of chronic bronchitis

Chronic bronchitis is a condition characterized by cough and excessive mucus secretion in the tracheobronchial tree that is not attributable to specific diseases such as bronchiectasis, asthma or tuberculosis. Infection appears to be only one component of the syndrome, the others being cigarette smoking and inhalation of dust or fumes from the workplace. Bacterial infection does not appear to initiate the disease, but is probably significant in perpetuating it and in producing the characteristic acute exacerbations. *Streptococcus pneumoniae* and unencapsulated strains of *Haemophilus influenzae* are the organisms most frequently isolated, but interpretation of the significance of their presence in sputum is difficult because they are also commonly found in the normal throat flora and can therefore contaminate expectorated sputum. Other bacteria such as *Staphylococcus aureus* and *Mycoplasma pneumoniae* are less commonly associated with infection and exacerbation. Viruses are frequent causes of acute infection.

Antibiotic therapy may be helpful in the treatment of acute exacerbations, although its efficacy is difficult to assess.

BRONCHIOLITIS

Around 75% of bronchiolitis presentations are caused by respiratory syncytial virus infection

Bronchiolitis is a disease restricted to childhood, and usually to children less than 2 years of age. The bronchioles of a young child have such a fine bore that if their lining cells are swollen by inflammation the passage of air to and from the alveoli can be severely restricted. Infection results in necrosis of the epithelial cells lining the bronchioles and leads to peribronchial infiltration, which may spread into the lung fields to give an interstitial pneumonia (see below). As many as 75% of these infections are caused by respiratory syncytial virus (RSV) and the other 25% are also of viral aetiology, although *Mycoplasma pneumoniae* is implicated occasionally.

RESPIRATORY SYNCYTIAL VIRUS INFECTION

Respiratory syncytial virus is the most important cause of bronchiolitis and pneumonia in infants

Respiratory syncytial virus (RSV) is a typical paramyxovirus, and two major strains have been identified: group A and group B. Its surface spikes bear G protein (not haemagglutinin or neuraminidase) for attachment to the cell, and fusion (F) protein. The latter initiates viral entry by fusing the viral envelope to the cell membrane, and also fuses host cells to form syncytia.

RSV infection is transmitted by droplets and to some extent by hands. Outbreaks occur each winter, and during the RSV season, infection can spread in hospitals as well as in the community. Nearly all individuals have been infected by 2 years of age. About 1 in every 100 infants with RSV bronchiolitis or pneumonia requires admission to hospital.

Respiratory syncytial virus infection can be particularly severe in young infants

After inhalation, the virus establishes infection in the nasopharynx and lower respiratory tract. Clinical illness appears after an incubation period of 4–5 days. The illness can be particularly severe in young infants, with peak mortality at 3 months of age, the virus invading the lower respiratory tract by direct surface spread to cause bronchiolitis or pneumonia. Young infants develop a cough, rapid respiratory rate and cyanosis. In young children and adults, however, the virus is restricted to the upper respiratory tract, causing a less severe common cold-type illness. Otitis media is quite common. Secondary bacterial infection is rare.

The manifestations of RSV infection appear to have an immunopathologic basis

Maternal antibodies in the infant react with virus antigens, perhaps with the liberation of histamine and other mediators from the host's cells. In early trials, a killed vaccine was used and, during subsequent natural RSV infection, the vaccinees had more frequent and severe lower respiratory tract disease compared with unimmunized children, supporting an immune-mediated pathogenesis.

Neutralizing antibodies are formed, at lower levels in younger infants, but cell-mediated immunity (CMI) is needed to terminate the infection. The virus continues to be shed from the lungs of children lacking CMI for many months. Apparently healthy children may continue to show depressed pulmonary function or wheeze even 1–2 years after apparent recovery.

Recurrent infections are common, but are less severe. The reason for recurrence, which is also a feature of parainfluenza virus infection, is unknown.

Respiratory syncytial virus RNA is detectable in throat swab specimens, and ribavirin is indicated for severe disease

Molecular methods, such as PCR, used to detect RSV RNA in throat swab specimens, have a higher diagnostic sensitivity than immunofluorescence (Fig. 19.5) or enzyme-linked immunosorbent assay (ELISA) methods (see Ch. 32), detecting RSV-specific antigens in smears of exfoliated cells obtained by nasopharyngeal aspiration. However, virus isolation is less helpful due to the time taken to detect a cytopathic effect, and success depends on inoculating respiratory secretions as soon as possible into cell cultures.

In most children, treatment is supportive, involving rehydration, bronchodilators and, if needing admission to hospital, oxygen. The antiviral agent ribavirin, given as an aerosol, has been used successfully in a number of clinical settings, including children with severe infection and immunosuppressed individuals at risk of severe disease. A monoclonal antibody, palivizumab, can be used as prophylaxis to prevent RSV infection in infants less than 2 years old at risk of severe disease such as those with chronic lung disease, congenital heart disease or those born at less than 32 weeks of age. At present, there is no vaccine available.

HANTAVIRUS PULMONARY SYNDROME (HPS)

The reservoir host for Sin Nombre virus (SNV), a New World hantavirus, is the deer mouse found commonly in North America. In 1993, individuals were infected in southwest USA and developed severe cardiopulmonary disease. HPS followed flu-like symptoms as viral invasion of the pulmonary capillary endothelium led to fluid pouring into the lungs due to increased vascular permeability, and at least 26 deaths were reported secondary to pulmonary oedema, hypotension and cardiogenic shock. The route of transmission is by inhaling SNV-infected rodent faeces, saliva or urine. The Old World hantaviruses cause haemorrhagic fever with renal syndrome. The pathogenesis of both diseases is thought to involve aberrant immune responses by SNV-infected endothelial cells that are also involved in regulating vascular permeability. By 2009, 510 individuals with HPS had been reported in the USA, with a 35% mortality rate.

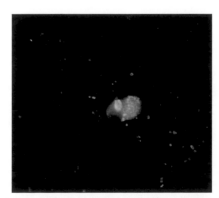

Figure 19.5 Immunofluorescent preparation from the nasopharynx showing respiratory syncytial virus-infected cells (bright green). (Courtesy of H. Stern.)

Ribavirin treatment may be successful if initiated at an early stage in the disease course.

PNEUMONIA

Pneumonia has long been known as 'the old person's friend' as it is the most common cause of infection-related death in the USA and Europe. It is caused by a wide range of microorganisms giving rise to indistinguishable symptoms. The challenge lies not in the clinical diagnosis of pneumonia, except perhaps in children, in whom it may be more difficult to diagnose, but in the laboratory identification of the microbial cause.

Microorganisms reach the lungs by inhalation, aspiration or via the blood

Microorganisms gain access to the lower respiratory tract by inhalation of aerosolized material or by aspiration of the normal flora of the upper respiratory tract. The size of inhaled particles is important in determining how far they travel down the respiratory tract; only those less than about 5 mm in diameter reach the alveoli. Less frequently, the lungs become seeded with organisms as a result of spread via the blood from other infected sites. Healthy individuals are susceptible to infection by a range of pathogens possessing adhesins, which allow the pathogens to attach specifically to the respiratory epithelium. In addition, people with impaired defences, for example, if immunocompromised, with preceding viral damage, or with cystic fibrosis, may develop infections with organisms that do not cause infections in health. An example is *Pneumocystis jirovecii*, an important cause of pneumonia in individuals with AIDS.

The respiratory tract has a limited number of ways in which it can respond to infection

The host's response can be defined by the pathologic and radiologic findings, but the terms can be confusing because they are applied differently in different situations. However, four descriptive terms are in common use (Fig. 19.6):

- Lobar pneumonia refers to involvement of a distinct region of the lung. The polymorph exudate formed in response to infection clots in the alveoli and renders them solid. Infection may spread to adjacent alveoli until constrained by anatomic barriers between segments or lobes of the lung. Thus one lobe may show complete consolidation.
- Bronchopneumonia refers to a more diffuse patchy consolidation, which may spread throughout the lung as a result of the original pathologic process in the small airways.
- Interstitial pneumonia involves invasion of the lung interstitium and is particularly characteristic of viral infections of the lungs.
- Lung abscess, sometimes referred to as necrotizing pneumonia, is a condition in which there is cavitation and destruction of the lung parenchyma.

The outcomes common to all these conditions are respiratory distress resulting from the interference with air exchange in the lungs, and systemic effects as a result of infection in any part of the body.

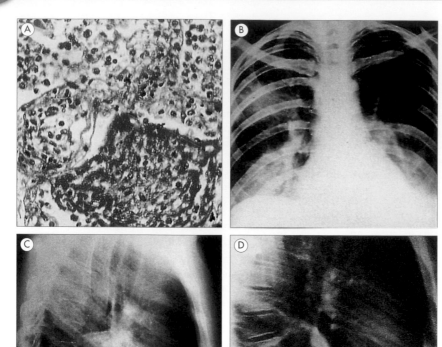

Figure 19.6 Four types of pneumonia. (A) Pneumococcal lobar pneumonia, showing consolidated alveoli filled with neutrophils and fibrin. (H&E stain) (Courtesy of I.D. Starke and M.E. Hodson.) (B) Mycoplasma bronchopneumonia, with patchy consolidation in several areas of both lungs. (Courtesy of J.A. Innes.) (C) Interstitial pneumonia due to influenza virus. (Courtesy of I.D. Starke and M.E. Hodson.) (D) Lung abscess, showing an abscess cavity in the lower lobe of the right lung. (Courtesy of J.A. Innes.)

A wide range of microorganisms can cause pneumonia

Age is an important determinant (Table 19.1):

- Most childhood pneumonia is caused either by viruses or by bacteria invading the respiratory tract secondary to viral infection, e.g. after measles infection. Neonates born to mothers with genital *Chlamydia trachomatis* infection may develop a chlamydial interstitial pneumonitis (see Ch. 21) resulting from colonization of the respiratory tract during birth.
- In the absence of an underlying disorder such as cystic fibrosis, pneumonia is unusual in older children. Children and young adults with cystic fibrosis are very prone to lower respiratory tract infection, caused characteristically by *Staphylococcus aureus*, *Haemophilus influenzae* and *Pseudomonas aeruginosa*.

Table 19.1 Causes of pneumonia related to age

Children	Adults
Mainly viral (e.g. respiratory syncytial virus, parainfluenza) or bacterial secondary to viral respiratory infection (e.g. after measles)	Bacterial causes more common than viral
Neonates may develop interstitial pneumonitis caused by *Chlamydia trachomatis* acquired from the mother at birth	Aetiology varies with age, underlying disease, occupational and geographic risk factors

Pneumonia in children is more often viral in origin or bacterial secondary to a viral respiratory infection. In adults, bacterial pneumonia is more common.

- The cause of pneumonia in adults depends upon a number of risk factors such as age, underlying disease and exposure to pathogens through occupation, travel or contact with animals.

Pneumonia acquired in hospital tends to be caused by a different spectrum of organisms, particularly Gram-negative bacteria. The causative agents of adult pneumonia are summarized in Figure 19.7. Although clinical and epidemiologic clues help to suggest the likely cause, microbiologic investigations are essential to confirm the diagnosis and ensure optimal antimicrobial therapy.

Viral pneumonias show a characteristic interstitial pneumonia on chest radiography more often than bacterial pneumonias (see Fig. 19.6C), and for the sake of clarity are described separately below. Infections with RSV have been described earlier in this chapter, and opportunist pathogens, such as *Pneumocystis jirovecii*, associated specifically with pneumonia in the immunocompromised, are described in Chapter 30.

BACTERIAL PNEUMONIA

Streptococcus pneumoniae is the classic bacterial cause of acute community-acquired pneumonia

In the past, 50–90% of pneumonias were caused by *Streptococcus pneumoniae* (the 'pneumococcus'), but the relative importance of this pathogen has decreased and it now causes only 25–60% of cases (Table 19.2). *Haemophilus influenzae* is estimated to be the cause of 5–15% of cases, but the true incidence is difficult to determine because this

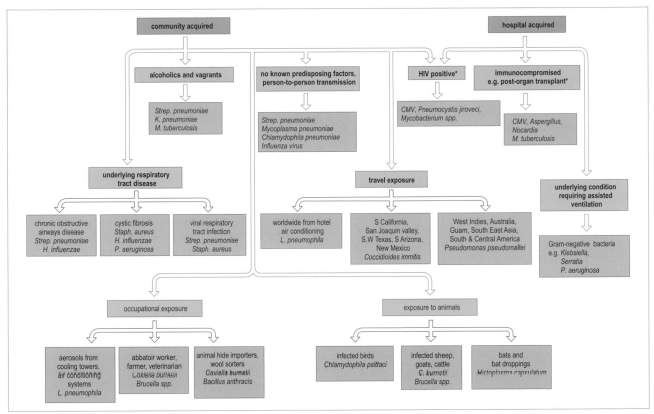

Figure 19.7 Many pathogens are capable of causing pneumonia in adults, and the aetiology is related to risk factors such as the exposure to pathogens through occupation, travel and contact with animals. The elderly are more likely to be infected and tend to have a more severe illness than young adults. * These infections are often reactivating endogenous infections rather than community or hospital acquired. C., *Coxiella*; CMV, cytomegalovirus; H., *Haemophilus*; K., *Klebsiella*; L., *Legionella*; M., *Mycobacterium*; P., *Pseudomonas*; Staph., *Staphylococcus*; Strep., *Streptococcus*.

Table 19.2 Common causes of pneumonia in community-based studies in three countries

Pathogen	Percentage[a] of cases for which a pathogen was identified		
	Sweden	**Denmark**	**Canada**
Streptococcus pneumoniae	66	26	11
Legionella pneumophila	4	30	5
Mycoplasma and Chlamydia	9	8	10
Haemophilus influenzae	13	32	8
Moraxella catarrhalis	3	0	1
Staphylococcus aureus	0	7	6
Viral cause (not specified)	15	13	21

[a]Note that more than one possible cause was isolated from some patients, therefore accounting for totals >100%. Despite the numerous possible pathogens, the vast majority of infections are caused by just a few. *Streptococcus pneumoniae* is the classic cause of lobar pneumonia, but its incidence has been declining in recent years in comparison with the incidence of the so-called atypical causes of pneumonia such as *Mycoplasma* and *Legionella*. (Data from T.J. Marrie et al. and S.S. Pederson.)

organism frequently colonizes the upper respiratory tract of bronchitic patients (see above).

A variety of bacteria cause primary atypical pneumonia

When penicillin, an effective antibiotic treatment for pneumococcal infection, became widely available, a significant proportion of cases of pneumonia failed to respond to this treatment and were labelled 'primary atypical pneumo-

nia'. 'Primary' refers to pneumonia occurring as a new event, not secondary to influenza, for example, and 'atypical' to the fact that *Strep. pneumoniae* is not isolated from sputum from such patients, the symptoms are often general as well as respiratory, and the pneumonia fails to respond to penicillin or ampicillin. The causes of atypical pneumonia include *Mycoplasma pneumoniae*, *Chlamydophila* (formerly *Chlamydia*) *pneumoniae* and *Chlamydophila* (formerly *Chlamydia*) *psittaci*, *Legionella pneumophila* and

Coxiella burnetii. The relative importance of these pathogens varies in different studies (Table 19.2). Infection with *Chlamydophila pneumoniae* is common. About 50% of adults have antibodies, and in the USA it causes up to 300 000 cases of pneumonia each year in adults. *Mycoplasma pneumoniae* and *Chlamydophila pneumoniae* appear to be solely human pathogens, whereas *Chlamydophila psittaci* and *Coxiella burnetii* are acquired from infected animals, and *Legionella pneumophila* is acquired from contaminated environmental sources (see Fig. 19.7).

Moraxella catarrhalis (previously *Branhamella catarrhalis*) is recognized increasingly as a cause of pneumonia, particularly in patients with carcinoma of the lung or other underlying lung disease. Other aetiologic agents of pneumonia associated with particular underlying diseases, occupations or exposure to animals and travel are summarized in Figure 19.7 and described in other chapters. It is important to note that a causative organism is not isolated in up to 35% of lower respiratory tract infections.

Patients with pneumonia usually present feeling unwell and with a fever

Signs and symptoms of a chest infection include:

- chest pain, which may be pleuritic in nature (pain on inspiration)
- a cough, which may produce sputum
- shortness of breath (dyspnoea).

Some infections result in symptoms confined mainly to the chest, whereas others such as Legionnaires' disease caused by *Legionella pneumophila* have a much wider systemic involvement, and the patient may present with mental confusion, diarrhea and evidence of renal or liver dysfunction. However, the distinction between localized and systemic symptoms is not usually reliable enough for an accurate diagnosis.

Chest examination may reveal abnormal crackling sounds, called 'rales', and evidence of consolidation, even before changes become evident on radiography.

Patients with pneumonia usually have shadows in one or more areas of the lung

The chest radiograph is an important adjunct to the clinical diagnosis. Patients with pneumonia usually have shadows indicating consolidation (see above for descriptions of lobar, broncho- and interstitial pneumonia). However, careful interpretation is required to differentiate between infection and non-infective processes such as tumours.

Pneumonia is the most common cause of death from infection in the elderly

It is also an important cause of death in the young and previously healthy. Complications of infection include spread of the infecting organisms:

- directly to extrapulmonary sites such as the pleural space, giving rise to empyema (see below)
- indirectly, via the blood to other parts of the body.

For example, the majority of patients with pneumococcal pneumonia have positive blood cultures, and pneumococcal meningitis not infrequently follows pneumonia in the elderly.

Sputum samples are best collected in the morning and before breakfast

Microscopic examination and culture of expectorated sputum remain the mainstays of respiratory bacteriology, despite doubts about the value of these procedures. Collection of sputum is non-invasive, but more invasive techniques, such as transtracheal aspiration, bronchoscopy and bronchoalveolar lavage and open lung biopsy, may yield more useful results.

Sputum samples are best collected in the morning because sputum tends to accumulate while the patient is lying in bed, and before breakfast to reduce contamination by food particles and bacteria from food. It is important that the specimen submitted for examination is truly sputum and not simply saliva. A physiotherapist can be of great assistance to ill patients who may be unable to cough unaided.

The usual laboratory procedures on sputum specimens from patients with pneumonia are Gram stain and culture

Examination of the Gram-stained sputum (see Ch. 32) can give a presumptive diagnosis within minutes if the film reveals a host response in the form of abundant polymorphs and the putative pathogen, e.g. Gram-positive diplococci characteristic of *Streptococcus pneumoniae* (Fig. 19.8). The presence of organisms in the absence of polymorphs is suggestive of contamination of the specimen rather than infection, but it is important to remember that immunocompromised patients may not be able to mount a polymorph leukocyte response. Also, remember that the causative agents of atypical pneumonia, with the exception of *Legionella pneumophila* (Fig. 19.9), will not be seen in Gram-stained smears.

Standard culture techniques will allow the growth of the bacterial pathogens such as *Streptococcus pneumoniae*, *Staphylococcus aureus*, *Haemophilus influenzae* and *Klebsiella pneumoniae* and other non-fastidious Gram-negative rods. Special media or conditions are required for the causative agents of atypical pneumonia, including *Legionella pneumophila* (Fig. 19.9).

Rapid non-cultural techniques have been applied successfully to the diagnosis of pneumococcal pneumonia. Detection of pneumococcal antigen by agglutination of antibody-coated latex particles (see Ch. 32) can be used with both sputum

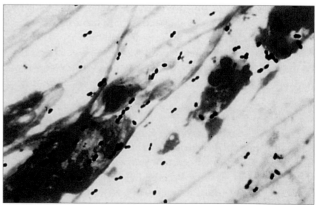

Figure 19.8 Gram-stained smears of sputum can help the physician make a rapid diagnosis if, like this, they contain abundant Gram-positive diplococci characteristic of pneumococci, as well as polymorphs. However, many of the important causes of pneumonia will not be stained by Gram stain.

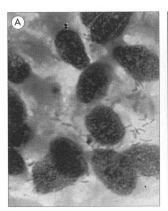
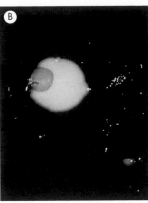

Figure 19.9 *Legionella pneumophila*. (A) Gram stain of a bronchial biopsy specimen in a patient with fulminant Legionnaires' disease. (Courtesy of S. Fisher-Hoch.) (B) Culture plate showing white colonies on buffered charcoal yeast extract medium. (Courtesy of I. Farrell.)

and urine specimens, as antigen is excreted in the urine. Use of this technique means the result is available within 1 h of receipt of the specimen, but antibiotic susceptibility tests cannot be performed unless the organisms are isolated.

Microbiologic diagnosis of atypical pneumonia is usually confirmed by serology

As mentioned above, several important causes of pneumonia will not be revealed in Gram-stained sputum smears and cannot be grown on simple routine culture media. For these reasons, the diagnosis is usually confirmed by serologic tests rather than by culture. In some infections, IgM, antigen or genome detection is being used to make the diagnosis at an early stage. The classic techniques involve detection of a single high titre of specific antibodies, or preferably demonstration of a rising titre between the acute and convalescent phase of the disease, but the diagnosis is often made retrospectively. The important serologic tests are shown in Table 19.3.

Pneumonia is treated with appropriate antimicrobial therapy

Once the cause of the pneumonia has been identified, selection of the appropriate antimicrobial therapy is relatively straightforward (Table 19.4), though the incidence of penicillin and other antibiotics resistance in pneumococci has increased in some countries.

The choice of treatment is more difficult when sputum is not produced or does not reveal the pathogen. It is therefore important to take a full history and use invasive diagnostic techniques if appropriate to help establish the cause.

Prevention of pneumonia involves measures to minimize exposure, and pneumococcal immunization post-splenectomy and for those with sickle cell disease

Respiratory infections are usually transmitted by airborne droplets, so person-to-person spread is virtually impossible to prevent, although less crowding and better ventilation help to reduce the chances of acquiring infection. Infections acquired from sources other than humans may be more amenable to prevention, for example, by avoiding contact with sick animals (Q fever) or birds (psittacosis). The contamination of cooling systems and hot water supplies by *Legionella* has been the subject of intense study, and regulations are now in force in the UK and elsewhere to provide guidance for maintenance engineers.

Immunization is available for a few respiratory pathogens. A pneumococcal vaccine incorporating the polysaccharide capsular antigens of the most common types of *Strep. pneumoniae* is recommended for those at particular risk, e.g. post-splenectomy or individuals with sickle cell disease who are unable to deal effectively with capsulate organisms.

VIRAL PNEUMONIA

Viruses can invade the lung from the bloodstream as well as directly from the respiratory tract

Many viruses cause pneumonia (Table 19.5) and, as with viral infections of the upper respiratory tract, generally accomplish infection in the face of normal host defences. Perfectly healthy individuals are susceptible, and most of these viruses have surface molecules that attach specifically to the respiratory epithelium. RSV can cause pneumonia in infants and is described earlier in this chapter.

Even when viruses of this group do not themselves cause pneumonia, they may damage respiratory defences, laying the ground for secondary bacterial pneumonia. Sometimes the virus fails to spread significantly to air spaces, but remains in interstitial tissues to cause interstitial pneumonitis. An example is cytomegalovirus (CMV) pneumonitis in immunodeficient patients, particularly bone marrow transplant recipients.

PARAINFLUENZA VIRUS INFECTION

As with RSV, parainfluenza viruses are most likely to cause lower respiratory tract disease, croup and pneumonia, in children.

Table 19.3 Serological diagnosis of 'atypical' pneumonia

Pathogen	Test
Mycoplasma pneumoniae	Complement fixation test (CFT), IgM by latex agglutination or ELISA
Legionella pneumophila	Urinary antigen test or rapid microagglutination test
Chlamydophila pneumonia *Chlamydophila psittaci*	Microimmunofluorescence or ELISA using species-specific antigens
Coxiella burnetii	CFT (phase I and phase II antigens)

Several of the bacterial causes of pneumonia are difficult to grow in the laboratory, so examination of the patient's serum for specific antibodies is the usual method of diagnosis. It is always better to demonstrate a rising titre between acute- and convalescent-phase sera than to rely on a single sample. ELISA, enzyme-linked immunosorbent assay.

Table 19.4 Antibacterial agents for pneumonia

Initial treatment of community-acquired pneumonia	
First choice	Ampicillin + erythromycin
Unless clinical picture clearly indicates lobar pneumonia; if so	Ampicillin
Pneumonia secondary to viral respiratory tract infection	Ampicillin + flucloxacillin
Pneumonia in chronic bronchitis	Co-amoxiclav or cefuroxime
Pneumonia in an alcoholic, drug user or a patient who may have aspirated	Ampicillin + gentamicin
Treatment of choice when pathogen has been identified	
Streptococcus pneumoniae	Ampicillin or penicillin (erythromycin if allergic to beta-lactams)
Mycoplasma pneumoniae *Legionella pneumoniae* *Chlamydophila pneumoniae* *Chlamydophila psittaci* *Coxiella burnetii*	Erythromycin
Staphylococcus aureus	Flucloxacillin
Haemophilus influenzae	Ampicillin[a], augmentin or cefuroxime
Klebsiella pneumoniae	Gentamicin, chloramphenicol or ciprofloxacin

Penicillin (or ampicillin) remains the agent of choice for pneumococcal infections as long as the isolates are susceptible. Penicillin-resistant pneumococci now occur in many countries, and in some it is no longer safe to assume susceptibility to penicillin (or ampicillin). Many of the resistant strains are still susceptible to cephalosporins, and in countries with a high incidence of resistance, these agents may replace penicillin, at least until the results of antibiotic susceptibility are known. It is important to recognize that penicillin (and ampicillin and cephalosporins) is not active against the other common causes of pneumonia. Therefore, a combination is often recommended for initial therapy.
[a]If non-beta-lactamase producer.

Table 19.5 Viral pneumonia

Virus	Clinical condition	Comments
Influenza A or B	Primary viral pneumonia or pneumonia associated with secondary bacterial infection	Pandemics (type A) and epidemics (type A or B); increased susceptibility in elderly or in certain chronic diseases; antivirals and vaccine available
Parainfluenza (types 1–4)	Croup, pneumonia in children < 5 years of age; upper respiratory illness (often subclinical) in older children and adults	Antiviral (ribavirin) available but is of limited effectiveness vaccines not available
Measles	Secondary bacterial pneumonia common; primary viral (giant cell) pneumonia in those with immunodeficiency	Adult infection rare but severe; King and Queen of Hawaii both died of measles when they visited London in 1824; antivirals and vaccine available
Respiratory syncytial virus	Bronchiolitis (infants); common cold syndrome (adults)	Peak mortality in 3–4 month old infants; secondary bacterial infection rare; antivirals available
Adenovirus	Pharyngoconjunctival fever, pharyngitis, atypical pneumonia (military recruits)	Vaccines not available, cidofovir or ribavirin could be used in specific clinical settings
Cytomegalovirus	Interstitial pneumonitis	In immunocompromised patients (e.g. bone marrow transplant recipients); antivirals and immunoglobulin available
Varicella-zoster virus	Pneumonia in young adults suffering primary infection	Uncommon; recognized 1–6 days after rash; lung lesions may eventually calcify; antivirals and vaccine available

Several different groups of viruses cause infection of the lower respiratory tract, particularly in children. Some, such as influenza and measles, leave the patient particularly susceptible to secondary bacterial infection.

There are four types of parainfluenza viruses with differing clinical effects

The surface spikes of parainfluenza viruses are composed of haemagglutinin plus neuraminidase on one type of spike and fusion proteins on another. The four types of virus have different antigens. After infection by respiratory droplets, these viruses spread locally on respiratory epithelium.

Parainfluenza viruses 1–3 cause pharyngitis, croup, otitis media, bronchiolitis and pneumonia. Croup is seen in children less than 5 years of age, and consists of acute laryngotracheobronchitis with a harsh cough and hoarseness. Parainfluenza virus 4 is less common and generally causes a common-cold-type illness.

Real-time PCR methods detecting parainfluenza RNA in throat swabs have revolutionized the diagnosis of these and other respiratory virus infections due to the increased sensitivity and time to diagnosis using these tests. Virus-specific antigens can be detected in cells from respiratory washings, and virus culture can be carried out, in settings where molecular analysis is not available. Ribavirin may be given in severe infections or in immunosuppressed individuals but there is no vaccine.

ADENOVIRUS INFECTION

Adenoviruses cause about 5% of acute respiratory tract illness overall

There are 41 antigenic types of adenovirus, some of which cause upper respiratory tract infections such as pharyngoconjunctival fever and sore throat (see Ch. 18) and lower respiratory tract infections. Adenovirus respiratory tract infections generally cause non-specific symptoms in children less than 5 years of age. As maternal antibody wanes, lower respiratory tract illnesses become more frequent, especially with adenovirus 7.

Types 3, 4 and 7 have caused outbreaks of respiratory illness ranging from pharyngitis to atypical pneumonia in military recruits, with crowding and stress as possible co-factors.

Recovery is generally uneventful, but adenoviruses may persist in the body, because they can be recovered from at least 50% of surgically removed tonsils. An enteric-coated vaccine for types 4 and 7 has been used to prevent outbreaks of infection in military recruits. In 2011, the FDA approved a new version of this vaccine that was planned to be offered to all military trainees in the USA.

HUMAN METAPNEUMOVIRUS

Human metapneumovirus (hMPV), discovered in Holland in 2001, is a respiratory pathogen closely related to RSV, peaks in the winter months and accounts for up to 15% of respiratory tract infections. It is associated with a spectrum of illness from mild infection to bronchiolitis and pneumonia. Symptoms may include a fever, runny nose, cough, sore throat and wheeze. Infection occurs in infants and young children, with some reports that by 5 years of age most children have had an hMPV infection. In addition, hMPV has also been detected in older children and adults, suggesting that reinfection may occur. Archived sera have been tested and it seems that humans have been exposed to hMPV for at least 50 years.

HUMAN BOCAVIRUS

Human bocavirus (HBoV), discovered in 2005, is a member of the Parvoviridae subfamily. A report from Sweden compared the results of testing 258 children with lower respiratory tract infections with, and 282 without, a diagnosis. HBoV was detected by PCR in samples from 17 children (3.1%), 14 of whom were negative for other respiratory viruses and the children had lower respiratory tract symptoms. The remainder had two RSV and one adenovirus co-infection. The virus has been detected in faecal and serum samples and as a co-infection in respiratory samples. The clinical importance of HBoV has been difficult to determine, especially as it can be detected in ill as well as healthy control subjects. However, when quantifying the HBoV load, it has been shown to be significantly higher in those patients with HBoV alone compared with those co-infected.

INFLUENZA VIRUS INFECTION

Influenza viruses are classic respiratory viruses and cause endemic, epidemic and pandemic influenza

The structure of a typical orthomyxovirus single-stranded RNA is shown in Figure 19.10, and the budding process in Figure 19.11.

There are three types of influenza virus: A, B and C

The internal ribonucleoprotein (RNP) is a group-specific antigen that distinguishes influenza A, B and C viruses:

- Influenza A viruses cause epidemics and occasionally pandemics, and there is an animal reservoir, notably in birds.
- Influenza B viruses only cause epidemics and do not involve animal hosts.
- Influenza C viruses do not cause epidemics and give rise to only minor respiratory illness.

The influenza virus envelope has haemagglutinin and neuraminidase spikes

These are shown in Figure 19.10. In the case of influenza A, the haemagglutinin (H) and neuraminidase (N) are type-specific antigens and are used to characterize different strains of influenza A virus (Table 19.6). Circulating strains are H3N2, H1N1 and H1N2. In giving the full nomenclature, the influenza type, the location and year of isolation is also included (e.g. A/Philippines/82/H3N2).

The single-stranded RNA genome is segmented, and these segments can be reassorted during virus replication to give a progeny virus with a novel combination of H and N antigens when virus particles of more than one strain infect a cell simultaneously.

Influenza viruses undergo genetic change as they spread through the host species

These changes are of two types:

1. *Antigenic drift*. Small mutations affecting the H and N antigens occur constantly. When changes in these antigens enable the virus to multiply significantly in individuals with immunity to preceding strains, the new subtype can reinfect the community. Antigenic drift is seen with all types of influenza.

2. *Antigenic shift*. Less commonly, and only with influenza A, there is a sudden major change referred to as shift, in the antigenicity of the H or N antigens. This is based on recombination between different virus strains when they infect the same cell. The major change in H or N means that the new strain can spread through populations immune to pre-existing strains and the stage is set for a new pandemic (Table 19.6). Associated with the change in H and N are other genetic changes, which may or may not confer increased pathogenicity or change the ability to spread rapidly from person to person.

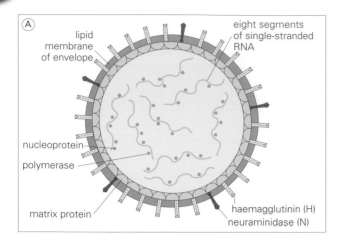

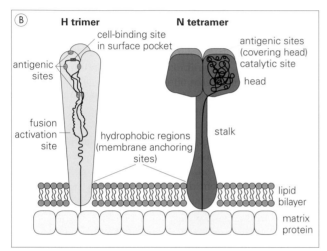

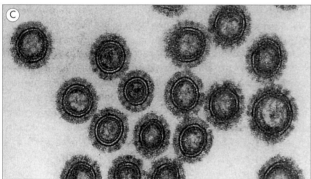

Figure 19.10 The influenza A virus particle (A), with detail enlarged (B) to show surface haemagglutinin (H) and neuraminidase (N). Each particle has approximately 500 H spikes, which bind to the host cell and fuse the viral envelope to the cell's plasma membrane to initiate infection, and approximately 100 N spikes, which release the virus from the cell surface. Nucleoprotein and polymerase proteins are closely associated with RNA segments to form ribonucleoprotein (RNP). The N tetramer is propeller-shaped as viewed from the end. Detail of only one unit of H trimer and N tetramer is shown. The three-dimensional structure is known from X-ray crystallographic analysis. Electron micrograph (C) shows sectioned influenza virus particles. ×300 000. (Courtesy of D. Hockley.)

Influenza is a highly infectious, acute viral infection that has affected both humans and animals over the centuries. It was so named after an outbreak of a respiratory disease in Italy in the fifteenth century that was thought to have developed under the influence of the stars.

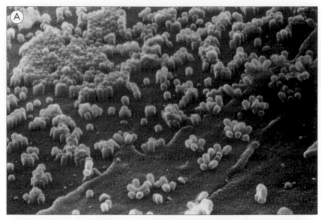

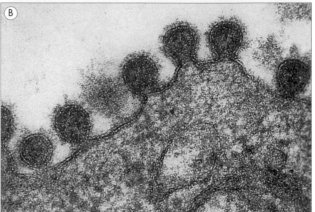

Figure 19.11 Influenza virus budding from the surface of an infected cell. (A) Scanning electron micrograph (×27 000). (B) In section (×350 000). (Courtesy of D. Hockley.)

The mixing vessel hypothesis for the production of new influenza strains came about as a result of influenza A viruses infecting pigs, horses, seals and other mammals, and the ability of the virus to reassort. For example, pigs in some countries live in the same dwellings as the farmers, allowing the potential mixing of influenza viruses and emergence of new strains.

The 1918 Spanish influenza pandemic (H1N1) was estimated to have led to 50–100 million deaths around the world and was followed in 1957 and 1968 by the less severe Asian (H2N2) and Hong Kong (H3N2) influenza pandemics, respectively. These were examples of antigenic shift, whereas antigenic drift resulted in frequent epidemics between the pandemic years. In 1976, there was a swine influenza scare in Fort Dix, USA, and in 1997, 18 people in Hong Kong became ill having had an H5N1 avian influenza A virus infection. Six of the infected people subsequently died. The outbreak ceased after public health authorities ordered the slaughter of all live chickens in Hong Kong.

Five human infections were reported in 1999 in Hong Kong and South China with the avian influenza A virus, H9N2. There was neither evidence of wider spread nor human-to-human transmission with either strain although it had circulated widely among birds in Hong Kong and China (Fig. 19.12). WHO has reported avian influenza A (H5N1) virus infections with a 60% mortality,

Table 19.6 Pandemic human influenza viruses

Type	Subtype[a]	Year	Clinical severity	Prototype virus
A	H3N2 (?)	1889	Moderate	⎫ Designation based on serologic studies, 1918 H1N1 virus
	H1N1 (avian)[b]	1918	Severe	⎭ sequenced from viruses not isolated
	H2N2 (Asian)	1957	Severe	A/Japan/57/H2N2
	H3N2 (Hong Kong)[c]	1968	Moderate	A/Hong Kong/68/H3N2
	H1N1	1977	Mild	A/USSR/77
	H1N1	2009	Mild	H1N1 virus sequenced
B	None	1940	Moderate	B/Lee/40
C	None	1947	Very mild	C/Taylor/47

Novel strains of virus arising in one continent spread rapidly to other continents, causing outbreaks during appropriate times of the year (winter months in temperate climates). There is a World Health Organization global surveillance system for influenza involving more than 100 laboratories in 79 different countries. New strains affecting humans include H5N1, an avian strain which caused 18 infections in humans in Hong Kong in 1997, and by 2006, there were 229 infections in 10 countries that resulted in 131 deaths; and H9N2, an avian strain which caused 5 infections in humans in Hong Kong and South China.
[a]Antigenic shift in influenza A virus is shown by the appearance of a novel combination of H and N antigens.
[b]Reports suggest that this virus was derived from an avian source. In a remarkable experiment, viral RNA was extracted from the lung tissue of someone who died in the 1918 pandemic and was buried in the permafrost and also from formalin-fixed lung tissue. This allowed the 1918 viral genome to be reconstructed.
[c]Amino acid and base sequence analysis suggest that recombination between H3N8 (from ducks) and H2N2 gave rise to H3N2.

mostly in children and young adults, with 560 cases and 330 deaths worldwide between 2003 and 2011. Most infections have been documented especially in Indonesia and Vietnam, but also in Asia, Africa, the Pacific and a few in Europe.

Another avian influenza virus, H7N7, is highly pathogenic in birds and may be more transmissible between humans. During an outbreak of highly pathogenic avian influenza in Holland in 2003, an H7N7 virus infected 86 poultry workers and three family members who had no contact with chickens. They developed conjunctivitis and/or flu-like symptoms. A veterinarian who handled infected chickens died of pneumonia and acute respiratory distress.

The 16 antigenically distinct H subtypes (H1–16) of influenza A virus reservoirs include wild birds, especially waterfowl. These include the H5 and H7 subtypes. There are nine N subtypes (N1–9). Outbreaks of H5N1 avian influenza in migratory waterfowl, domestic poultry, and humans in Asia have occurred. Over time, the host range has increased, with

Figure 19.12 Deaths due to avian flu. Hong Kong, 1997–2003; Thailand, 2004–2005. (Redrawn from: Fauci AS. Pandemic influenza threat and preparedness. *Emerg Infect Dis* 2006; 12:73–7.)

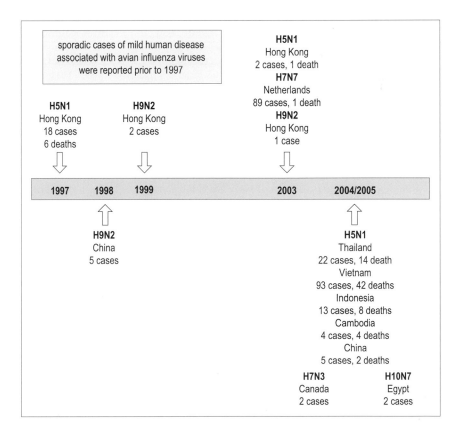

infections in waterfowl, ferrets, members of the cat family and humans. The virus has become more virulent, as seen by the mortality rate in the human population together with neurological clinical features.

Descriptive molecular epidemiology has shown that the precursor of the 1997 Hong Kong H5N1 virus was first seen in geese in 1996 in Guangdong, China. In turn, the goose virus had RNA segments from influenza viruses found in quail and the N segment from a duck virus. Subsequent evolution of the goose virus resulted in a predecessor of the Z genotype that caused the death of many waterfowl in Hong Kong nature parks and infected humans in that area in 2002. The Z genotype then predominated and spread across South-East Asia and killed, or resulted in culling of, millions of domestic fowl.

The 1918 pandemic H1N1 strain is believed to have resulted from spontaneous mutations in an avian H1N1 virus after sequence analysis was carried out on viral RNA recovered from people who had died and had been buried in the Scandinavian permafrost. However, the other pandemic viruses mentioned above, including the 2009 pandemic H1N1 strain, were due to genetic reassortment of the viral segmented RNA genomes after a host was infected by avian and human influenza A viruses at the same time.

In April 2009, there were reports from Mexico and the USA, in southern California, of a respiratory illness caused by a novel swine influenza A H1N1 virus. These were worrying times as it was thought that the new influenza virus could cause a pandemic with high morbidity and mortality. Pandemic influenza response plans had been developed and refined in many countries for the expected and overdue influenza outbreak. Viral sequence analysis showed that it was composed of a combination of genes most closely related to North American and Eurasian swine-lineage H1N1 influenza viruses. Exposure to pigs was not seen when investigating those infected. In addition, the new virus was circulating among humans and not among pig herds. Within weeks there were reports of people with influenza in a number of American states and also Canada and other parts of the world. The influenza pandemic alert was raised to phase 4 on the basis of human-to-human spread and outbreaks in the community. This became phase 5 by the end of April and countries started to activate their pandemic response plans as the pandemic had started. Diagnostic real-time polymerase chain reaction (PCR) tests were developed in days in order to confirm the diagnosis and a vaccine virus chosen for high-yield preparation in case it was needed. National stockpiles of antiviral drugs (oseltamivir and zanamivir) and personal protective equipment were activated

By June 2009, WHO changed its alert level to pandemic phase 6 as pandemic H1N1 was reported in more than 70 countries and community outbreaks were happening globally. This virus contained gene reassortments from Eurasian and North American swine influenza, North American avian influenza and North American human influenza virus infections. The seasonal aspect of influenza virus infections had altered as laboratories experienced huge workloads over the northern hemisphere summer months.

Confirmed and probable infections occurred mainly among 5–24-year-olds. Mostly older children and young adults were admitted to hospital as well as those in the at-risk groups identified in previous influenza pandemics, including women who were pregnant. In addition, increased risk of complications was seen in obese people and those with chronic neurological conditions. There were few influenza infections seen in the 65 year and older age groups, which was unusual. Studies showed that children and young adults had no pre-existing cross-reactive antibody to the 2009 H1N1 influenza virus compared with over 30% of adults 60 years of age or older who had been exposed previously.

Networks were set up worldwide to ensure that the experiences managing influenza-infected individuals in critical care facilities and elsewhere in the southern hemisphere were shared and lessons learnt. In addition, the circulating influenza viruses were monitored closely for any antigenic variation as well as the development of antiviral resistance. Influenza-infected patients on critical care units in acute respiratory failure received mechanical ventilation with intermittent positive-pressure ventilation in which the lungs receive air enriched with oxygen at high pressure. However, another technique called extracorporeal membrane oxygenation (ECMO) treatment improved recovery by providing gas exchange outside the body using heart–lung bypass equipment and obviating the deleterious effects of providing direct oxygenation at high pressure.

Across the northern hemisphere, the 2009 H1N1 influenza A summer activity peaked and declined during the summer but levels of influenza activity remained above normal with small community outbreaks. On 10 August 2010, the WHO International Health Regulations (IHR) Emergency Committee declared an end to the 2009 H1N1 pandemic globally.

There was concern about a second wave of infection and preparations were made to offer the recently prepared vaccine to specific groups of individuals, those at-risk and healthcare workers. The anticipated second wave started in the autumn and the amount of influenza activity fell quite quickly and remained at lower levels until the spring.

The WHO Global Influenza Surveillance and Response System monitoring circulating influenza viruses detected an avian influenza A H5N1 virus that was reported as H5N1 clade 2.3.2.1 that circulated in poultry in parts of Asia in February 2011. This was not detected in humans and was not seen as a public health threat, more as a marker of the continual evolution of these viruses.

Epidemics and pandemics are due to the appearance of new strains of viruses so that a given individual is regularly reinfected with different strains. This is in contrast to viruses that undergo minimal antigenic variation (monotypic viruses), such as measles or mumps, for which one infection confers life-long immunity. Monitoring avian influenza viruses such as H5N1 and H7N7 is therefore critical in determining their potential to become more pathogenic and spread. Reassortment between H5N1 or H7N7 and human H1N1 or H3N2 influenza viruses may result in efficient transmissibility together with retention of viral pathogenicity. An influenza pandemic could then evolve.

Transmission of influenza is by droplet inhalation

Influenza infections occur throughout the world. Except in the tropics, the infection is almost entirely restricted to the coldest months of the year. This is largely because, during cold weather, people spend more time inside buildings with limited air space, which favours transmission by droplet inhalation, and perhaps also because of decreased host resistance. Influenza activity within a community is reflected not only in the numbers of people becoming ill and consulting doctors, but also in excess mortality due to acute respiratory disease, such as pneumonia, which particularly affects the elderly (Fig. 19.13).

With respect to the avian influenza viruses, they are spread by movement of poultry and poultry products, live poultry markets and unhygienic practices, and backyard flocks that are not controlled.

The initial symptoms of influenza are due to direct viral damage and associated inflammatory responses. The virus enters the respiratory tract in droplets and attaches to sialic acid receptors on epithelial cells via the H glycoprotein of the virus envelope. Just 1–3 days after infection, the cytokines liberated from damaged cells and from infiltrating leukocytes cause symptoms such as chills, malaise, fever and muscular aches. There are also respiratory symptoms such as a runny nose and cough. Most people feel better within 1 week. The direct viral damage and associated inflammatory responses can be severe enough to cause bronchitis and interstitial pneumonia.

Influenzal damage to the respiratory epithelium predisposes to secondary bacterial infection

Secondary bacterial invaders include staphylococci, pneumococci and *Haemophilus influenzae*. Life-threatening influenza is often due to secondary bacterial infection, especially with *Staphylococcus aureus*, the viral infection being brought under control by antibody and cell-mediated immune responses to the infecting virus. Although antiviral antibodies may not be detected within the serum for 1–2 weeks, they are produced at an earlier stage, but are complexed with viral antigens in the respiratory tract.

Mortality due to secondary bacterial pneumonia is higher in apparently healthy individuals over 60 years of age and in those with impaired resistance due to, for example, chronic cardiorespiratory disease or renal disease. Pregnant women are also more vulnerable.

Rarely, influenza causes CNS complications

Central nervous system (CNS) complications include meningitis, encephalomyelitis and polyneuritis. These appear to be indirect immunopathologic complications rather than due to CNS invasion by the virus. Guillain–Barré syndrome, a polyneuropathy with proximal, distal or generalized motor weakness, occurred as a significant but rare (1/100 000) sequel to the widespread vaccination of citizens in the USA with inactivated H3N2 influenza virus in 1976. However, subsequent vaccines have not been associated with this syndrome.

During influenza epidemics a diagnosis can generally be made clinically

Rapid diagnosis can be made by collecting samples from the respiratory tract, such as throat swabs that can be tested by real-time PCR for influenza viral RNA, and the viruses can be typed simultaneously. Antiviral resistance can also be detected using PCR as well as sequence analysis. Alternatively, if these methods are not available, influenza-infected cells can be detected using immunofluorescence techniques, but nasopharyngeal aspirates are usually required to improve the yield of cellular material for testing. Virus isolation can also be used but there may be a delay of

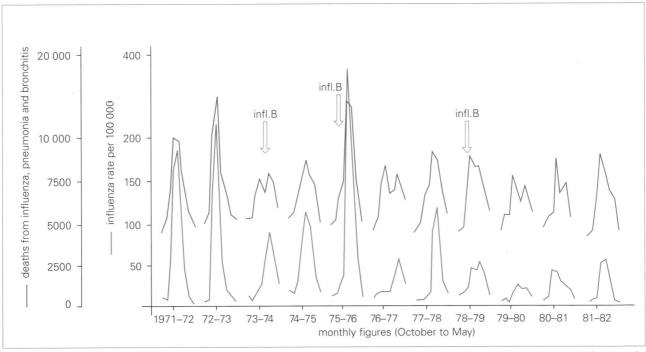

Figure 19.13 Outbreaks of influenza within a community are reflected by a general increase in deaths from acute respiratory disease. Notifications of new cases of clinical influenza are paralleled by an increase in deaths attributed to influenza, pneumonia and bronchitis. Monthly figures from October to May for England and Wales (1971–83) are shown. The peaks are due to the spread of different strains of influenza A (H3N2 and H1N1) and influenza B (arrows) viruses in the community. (Data from the Office of Population, Censuses and Surveys.)

at least 7 days until identification. Finally, a rise in specific antibodies can be detected by complement fixation test or ELISA (see Ch. 32) in paired serum samples, taken within a few days of illness and 7–10 days later. However, this is only helpful retrospectively.

Vaccines and antiviral agents can be used to prevent influenza

The aim of immunization is to help prevent infection, and those at risk of complications from influenza infection should be offered vaccine before the 'flu season'.

Influenza virus vaccines in regular use are:

- those consisting of egg-grown virus, which are then purified, formalin-inactivated and extracted with ether
- the less reactogenic purified H and N antigens prepared from virus that has been disrupted ('split') by lipid solvents.

Studies investigating the protective efficacy of cell culture-derived influenza virus vaccines have demonstrated similar results to the egg-grown virus vaccine. Influenza A (H3N2 and H1N1 strains) and influenza B are included in the vaccine. The exact virus strains are reviewed annually in relation to the viruses circulating the previous year. The vaccines are given by parenteral injection, and provide protection against disease in up to 70% of individuals for about 1 year. Vaccination of individuals at high risk, especially those over 65 years of age and those with chronic cardiopulmonary disease, is recommended. It might be expected that the respiratory route would be a better way of inducing respiratory immunity, and live attenuated virus vaccines administered intranasally have been investigated.

The antiviral agents rimantadine and amantadine are M2 ion channel blockers, stop hydrogen ion efflux by altering the pH as they are basic compounds and affect intracellular viral uncoating. They only inhibit the replication of influenza A viruses and were superseded in 1999 by the neuraminidase inhibitors, zanamivir and oseltamivir, which act on both influenza A and B. Oseltamivir (Tamiflu) is easier to administer as it is given orally as opposed to zanamivir that is given by inhaler. These antivirals can reduce the severity of the infection, but should be given within 1–2 days of disease onset. They have also been shown to be effective when used for prophylaxis if given within 48 hours of symptom onset.

Oseltamivir resistance has been widely reported and transmission of oseltamivir resistance has occurred without direct selective drug pressure. This did not affect virulence or viral replication. During the 2009 influenza A H1N1 pandemic, intravenous oseltamivir and zanamivir preparations were made available together with peramivir and laninamivir, also NA inhibitors that had been developed, the latter has a longer half-life.

Finally, another therapeutic option from last century involved using hyperimmune plasma made from blood collected from human donors who had recovered from the 1918 Spanish influenza pandemic. This was given to patients with severe influenza infections who subsequently recovered. Some individuals with severe pandemic H1N1 infections recovered, having received hyperimmune plasma infusions collected from individuals with pandemic H1N1 infection or from vaccinated donors.

With an eye to a future pandemic, nations have been developing stockpiles of anti-influenza drugs that include oseltamivir. New drug targets focusing on entry, replication, and maturation as well as novel approaches to rapid vaccine production are being investigated.

Culling domestic poultry has contained the spread of the H5N1 virus. However, rapid detection and increased biosecurity together with the use of vaccines are critical in controlling the infection. In addition, after the SARS-associated coronavirus (SARS CoV) outbreak (see next section) there are questions as to what lessons were learnt for any future influenza epidemic or pandemic. The problem is that influenza viruses are more easily transmitted than SARS CoV. Together with the reduced transmissibility, early detection and containment that were successful in controlling the SARS CoV may not be effective in preventing an influenza pandemic.

SEVERE ACUTE RESPIRATORY SYNDROME-ASSOCIATED CORONAVIRUS INFECTION

An outbreak of severe respiratory disease with no identifiable cause was reported from Guangdong Province in the People's Republic of China in November 2002. The agent spread to mainly parts of east and southeast Asia, as well as Toronto in Canada, and was eventually reported in 30 countries. The WHO issued a global health alert in March 2003 concerning severe acute respiratory syndrome (SARS). The main symptoms were high fever > 38°C, cough, shortness of breath or difficulty in breathing. Chest X-rays consistent with pneumonia were also seen. Close contact with someone infected with the SARS agent was the highest risk of the infection spreading from person to person and occurred mostly in family members and hospital staff caring for SARS patients. The incubation period was generally between 2 and 7 days, with a 10-day maximum.

The SARS-associated coronavirus (SARS CoV), a new member of the coronavirus family, was identified by virus isolation in cell culture and electron microscopy in conjunction with molecular methods. Diagnostic methods included PCR detection and serology. The rapid identification of the SARS-associated coronavirus, implementation of infection control on a scale not seen previously involving face masks, checking for fever in the community and at airports, which resulted in rapid isolation on detecting symptom onset, international scientific networking, and immediate availability of data set a global standard for investigation of disease outbreaks.

By July 2003, just slightly more than 4 months since the virus began moving between countries via international air travel, WHO reported that all known chains of person-to-person transmission of the SARS virus had been broken. The largest outbreaks occurred in mainland China, with 5327 cases and 348 deaths, and Hong Kong, where 1755 cases and 298 deaths were reported. Overall, there were 8437 SARS diagnoses in 29 countries and nearly 10% case fatality rate. The predecessor of the SARS-associated coronavirus crossed species barriers over the years when changes in the viral reservoir and humans' eating habits resulted in an ability to transmit to, and between, humans. In China, the quality of the food is considered to be best if it is prepared freshly from live animals in wet-markets found close to residential areas. In addition, eating a range of exotic wild animals, including bats and civet cats, is popular in south China as it is thought to improve both health and sexual performance. Although the natural reservoir for the SARS-CoV has not been discovered, a number of SARS-CoV-like viruses have been detected in various wildlife species including Himalayan masked palm civet cats, Chinese ferret badgers, raccoon dogs and horseshoe bats. Angiotensin-converting enzyme 2 (ACE2) is the SARS-CoV receptor on host cells that binds the viral spike protein. With respect to transmissibility, it is interesting to note that there is a large difference in the binding affinity of the palm civet and human SARS-CoV strains spike proteins to the human ACE2 receptor despite there being only four amino acid differences between them. Sequencing studies have shown that during the outbreaks various genes evolved quite rapidly in the animal reservoirs, which would have improved the transmissibility between animals and humans and between humans as well (Fig. 19.14).

From a management perspective, the relatively poor transmissibility of the virus spreading mainly by respiratory droplets over a short distance was helpful in controlling infections.

However, transmission also occurred by direct and indirect contact with respiratory secretions, faeces or infected animals. The virus was shown to be stable at room temperature, surviving for up to 2 days on surfaces and up to 4 days in faeces. Protection was afforded by face masks, including the N95 masks. SARS-CoV spread more efficiently in hospitals, especially in intensive care unit settings, and clusters of cases occurred in hotel and apartment buildings in Hong Kong. Attack rates as high as 50% or more were seen. Isolation of infected individuals and stringent infection control measures were observed.

Laboratory diagnosis was carried out using methods including SARS-CoV RNA detection by PCR in clinical specimens including respiratory samples and faeces.

No specific antiviral treatment was available, although ribavirin was used to treat some individuals, although little effect was seen in vitro. Corticosteroids damped down the effect of virally induced cytokine responses that could damage lung tissue. Interferons were reported to inhibit the virus. Intriguingly, some reports suggested some antiretroviral therapies might help, such as protease inhibitors, and further work has focused on these agents and looks promising.

Finally, with regard to potential vaccines and the correlates of protection, neutralizing antibodies are found in convalescent human serum. As these antibodies to the viral spike protein prevent virus entry and neutralize virus infectivity in vitro, whole inactivated virus and recombinant protein vaccines have been developed that elicit neutralizing antibody responses. These have been shown to prevent SARS although cell-mediated immunity may also assist viral clearance and disease resolution.

MEASLES

Secondary bacterial pneumonia is a frequent complication of measles in developing countries

Measles is dealt with in detail as a multisystem infection in Chapter 26. It is mentioned here because:

- It can cause 'giant cell' pneumonia in those with impaired immune responses.
- The virus replicates in the lower respiratory tract and, under certain circumstances, causes sufficient damage to lead to secondary bacterial pneumonia.

Secondary bacterial pneumonia is now uncommon in resource-rich countries, but is a frequent complication among children in resource-poor countries, and measles remains a major cause of death in childhood. Depressed immune responsiveness, inadequate vaccination programmes, malnutrition (especially vitamin A) and poor medical care to deal with complications tip the host–parasite balance markedly in favour of the virus.

After an incubation period of 10–14 days, symptoms include fever, a runny nose, conjunctivitis and cough. Koplik's spots and then the characteristic rash appear 1–2 days later. The virus replicates in the epithelium of the nasopharynx, middle ear and lung, interfering with host defences and enabling bacteria such as pneumococci, staphylococci and meningococci to establish infection. Pneumonia generally results in those with measles being admitted to hospital, but otitis media is also common. Virus replication continues unchecked in children with severely impaired cell-mediated immune responses, giving rise to a giant cell pneumonia, which is a rare and usually fatal manifestation (Fig. 19.15). Other complications are referred to in Chapter 26, and the neurologic complications in Chapter 24.

Measles is diagnosed clinically, but detection of specific IgM responses, measles viral RNA detection and virus isolation are helpful.

Antibiotics are needed for secondary bacterial complications of measles, but the disease can be prevented by immunization

If severe, ribavirin treatment is available, but antibiotics are needed for bacterial complications. Children with severe measles generally have very low levels of serum retinol; recovery is hastened and death is made less likely when they are given 400 000 IU vitamin A.

Measles is prevented by a highly effective, live, attenuated vaccine, given with mumps and rubella vaccines

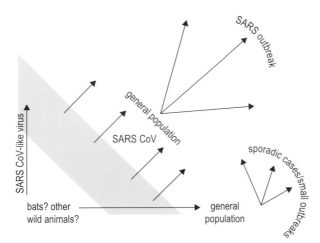

Figure 19.14 Chinese wet-markets and SARS. (Redrawn from Woo PC et al. Infectious diseases emerging from Chinese wet-markets: zoonotic origins of severe respiratory viral infections. Curr Opin Infect Dis 2006; 19:401–7.)

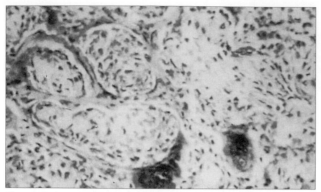

Figure 19.15 Lung biopsy in measles pneumonia showing inflammatory cell infiltrate, proliferation of the alveolar lining cells and large, darkly staining, multinucleate giant cells. (H&E stain.) (Courtesy of I.D. Starke and M.E. Hodson.)

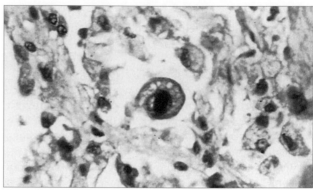

Figure 19.16 Owl's eye inclusion body in cytomegalovirus infection. Large numbers of virus particles accumulate in the nucleus of the enlarged infected cell to produce a single dense inclusion. (H&E stain.) (Courtesy of I.D. Starke and M.E. Hodson.)

(MMR, see Ch. 34). Since immunization began, the number of cases has declined by 70%. In the USA, after a rise to nearly 30 000 cases in 1990, the number fell to 488 (47 of them imported) in 1996. It was planned to eliminate the disease in the Americas by the year 2000, by which time a group of scientists convened by the Centers for Disease Control (CDC) decided that measles was no longer endemic in the USA. The WHO is hoping for global eradication by 2010–2015. However, due to an unfounded MMR vaccine scare in the UK, the number of individuals with measles rose considerably due to a fall in vaccine uptake. Before the vaccine was available in the 1960s, there were 135 million cases and 7–8 million deaths each year worldwide. Measles is still a killer, but deaths had already been reduced to an estimated 164 000 a year by 2008.

CYTOMEGALOVIRUS INFECTION

Cytomegalovirus (CMV) infection can cause an interstitial pneumonitis in immunocompromised patients

As discussed in Chapter 18, the virus does not normally replicate in respiratory epithelium or cause respiratory illness; but in immunocompromised patients, in particular bone marrow transplant recipients, it can give rise to an interstitial pneumonia. CMV monitoring in specific groups of immunosuppressed patients is critical, especially in the first few months post transplantation. In a number of different types of sample, CMV DNA can be detected and quantified, the virus can be isolated, and characteristic inclusions demonstrated in lung tissue (Fig. 19.16).

TUBERCULOSIS

Tuberculosis is one of the most serious infectious diseases of the resource-poor world

Tuberculosis kills about 3 million people and infects almost 9 million others every year wherever poverty, malnutrition and poor housing prevail. It affects the apparently healthy as well as being a serious disease of the immunocompromised, and has become particularly obvious in patients with AIDS. Tuberculosis is primarily a disease of the lungs, but may

spread to other sites or proceed to a generalized infection ('miliary' tuberculosis). It is also referred to in Chapters 20, 24 and 26.

Tuberculosis is caused by *Mycobacterium tuberculosis*

Other species of mycobacteria, referred to as atypical mycobacteria, mycobacteria other than tuberculosis (MOTT) or non-tuberculous mycobacteria (NTM) also cause infection in the lungs (Table 19.7).

Table 19.7 Mycobacteria associated with human disease

Species	Clinical disease
Slow growers[a]	
M. tuberculosis	Tuberculosis
M. bovis	Bovine tuberculosis
M. leprae	Leprosy
M. avium[b]	⎱ Disseminated infection in AIDS
M. intracellulare[b]	⎰ patients
M. kansasii	Lung infections
M. marinum	Skin infections and deeper infections (e.g. arthritis, osteomyelitis) associated with aquatic activity
M. scrofulaceum	Cervical adenitis in children
M. simiae	Lung, bone and kidney infections
M. szulgai	Lung, skin and bone infections
M. ulcerans	Skin infections
M. xenopi	Lung infections
M. paratuberculosis	? Association with Crohn's disease
Rapid growers[a]	
M. fortuitum	Opportunist infections with introduction of organisms into deep subcutaneous tissues; usually associated with trauma or invasive procedures
M. chelonae	

Many species of mycobacteria are associated with occasional disease, but the major pathogens of the genus are *M. tuberculosis*, *M. bovis* and *M. leprae*.
[a]Slow growers require > 7 days for visible growth from a dilute inoculum; rapid growers require < 7 days from a dilute inoculum.
[b]*M. avium* complex; recent studies show that the two species are distinct. Of the *M. avium* complex, serotypes 1–6 and 8–11 are assigned to *M. avium*, serotypes 7,12–17,19,20 and 25 assigned to *M. intracellulare*.

Infection is acquired by inhalation of *Mycobacterium tuberculosis* in aerosols and dust. Airborne transmission of tuberculosis is efficient because infected people cough up enormous numbers of mycobacteria, projecting them into the environment, where their waxy outer coat (see Ch. 2) allows them to withstand drying and therefore survive for long periods of time in air and house dust.

The pathogenesis of tuberculosis depends upon the history of previous exposure to the organism

In primary infection, i.e. infection in individuals encountering *Mycobacterium tuberculosis* for the first time, the organisms are engulfed by the alveolar macrophages in which they can both survive and multiply. Non-resident macrophages are attracted to the site, ingest the mycobacteria and carry them via the lymphatics to the local hilar lymph nodes. In the lymph nodes, the immune response, predominantly a CMI response, is stimulated. The CMI response is detectable 4–6 weeks after infection by introducing purified protein derivative (PPD) of *Mycobacterium tuberculosis* into the skin. A positive result is shown by local induration and erythema, 48–72 h later.

The CMI response helps to curb further spread of *Mycobacterium tuberculosis*

However, some *Mycobacterium tuberculosis* organisms may have already escaped to set up foci of infection in other body sites. Sensitized T cells release lymphokines that activate macrophages and increase their ability to destroy the mycobacteria. The body reacts to contain the organisms within 'tubercles', which are small granulomas consisting of epithelioid cells and giant cells (Fig. 19.17). The lung lesion plus the enlarged lymph nodes is often called the Ghon or primary complex. After a time, the material within the granulomas becomes necrotic and caseous or cheesy in appearance.

The tubercles may heal spontaneously, become fibrotic or calcified, and persist as such for a lifetime in people who are otherwise healthy. They will show up on a chest radiograph as radiopaque nodules (Fig. 19.18). However, in a small percentage of people with primary infection, and particularly in the immunocompromised, the mycobacteria are not contained within the tubercles, but invade the

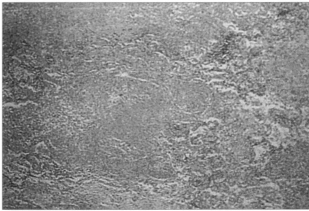

Figure 19.17 Histopathology showing dense inflammatory infiltration, granuloma formation and caseous necrosis in pulmonary tuberculosis. (Courtesy of R. Bryan.)

bloodstream and cause disseminated disease ('miliary' tuberculosis, Fig. 19.19).

Secondary tuberculosis is due to reactivation of dormant mycobacteria, and is usually a consequence of impaired immune function resulting from some other cause such as malnutrition, infection (e.g. AIDS), chemotherapy for treatment of malignancy, or corticosteroids for the treatment of inflammatory diseases.

Tuberculosis illustrates the dual role of the immune response in infectious disease

On the one hand, the CMI response controls the infection and, when it is inadequate, the infection disseminates or reactivates. On the other hand, nearly all the pathology and disease is a consequence of this CMI response, as *Mycobacterium tuberculosis* causes little or no direct or toxin-mediated damage.

Reactivation occurs most commonly in the apex of the lungs. This site is more highly oxygenated than elsewhere, allowing the mycobacteria to multiply more rapidly to produce caseous necrotic lesions, which spill over into other sites in the lung, and from where organisms spread to more distant sites in the body.

Figure 19.18 Chest radiographs of (A) primary tuberculosis, showing the Ghon focus in the lower left lung, and (B) post-primary pulmonary tuberculosis showing advanced disease. (Courtesy of J.A. Innes.)

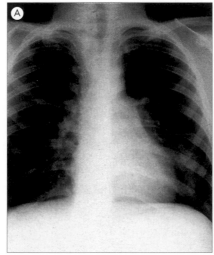
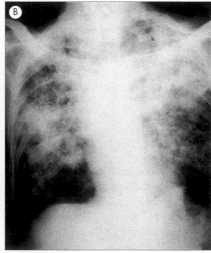

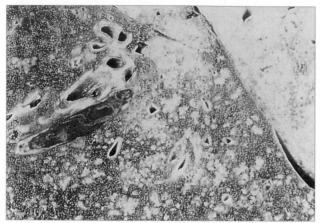

Figure 19.19 Miliary tuberculosis. Gross specimen of lung showing the cut surface covered with white nodules, which are the miliary foci of tuberculosis. (Courtesy of J.A. Innes.)

Primary tuberculosis is often asymptomatic

In contrast to pneumonia, which is usually an acute infection, the onset of tuberculosis is insidious, the infection proceeding for some time before the patient becomes sufficiently ill to seek medical attention. Primary tuberculosis is usually mild and asymptomatic and in 90% of cases does not proceed further. However, clinical disease develops in the remaining 10%.

Mycobacteria have the ability to colonize almost any site in the body. The clinical manifestations are variable: fatigue, weight loss, weakness and fever are all associated with tuberculosis. Infection in the lungs characteristically causes a chronic productive cough, and the sputum may be blood-stained as a result of tissue destruction. Necrosis may erode blood vessels, which can rupture and cause death through haemorrhage.

Complications of *Mycobacterium tuberculosis* infection arise from local spread or dissemination

The organism may disseminate via the lymphatics and bloodstream to other parts of the body. This usually occurs at the time of primary infection, and in this way chronic foci are established, which may proceed to necrosis and destruction in, for example, the kidney. Alternatively, spread may be by extension to a neighbouring part of the lung, for instance when a tubercle erodes into a bronchus and discharges its contents, or into the pleural cavity, resulting in a pleural effusion.

Although the number of cases of pulmonary tuberculosis has been declining in resource-rich countries since the beginning of the twentieth century, hastened by the advent of specific antimicrobial drugs, the incidence of extrapulmonary tuberculosis has stayed roughly constant for many years and therefore makes up a greater proportion of the tuberculosis caseload in resource-rich countries than in resource-poor countries.

The Ziehl–Neelsen stain of sputum can provide a diagnosis of tuberculosis within 1 h, whereas culture can take 6 weeks

A diagnosis of tuberculosis is suggested by the clinical signs and symptoms referred to above, supported by characteristic changes on chest radiography (see Fig. 19.18) and positive skin test reactivity in the tuberculin (Mantoux) test. These tests are confirmed by microscopic demonstration of acid-fast rods and culture of *Mycobacterium tuberculosis*. Microscopic examination of a smear of sputum stained by Ziehl–Neelsen's method or by auramine (see Ch. 32) often reveals acid-fast rods (Fig. 19.20). This result can be obtained within 1 h of receipt of the specimen in the laboratory. This is important because *Mycobacterium tuberculosis* can take up to 6 weeks to grow in culture, although radiometric methods may reduce the time required for detection, and therefore confirmation of the diagnosis is necessarily delayed. Rapid non-culture tests to detect *Mycobacterium tuberculosis* (e.g., using the polymerase chain reaction [PCR, see Ch. 32]; the new automated Xpert MTB-RIF molecular test) are becoming increasingly available. Further tests are required to identify the mycobacterial species and to establish susceptibility to antituberculosis drugs.

Specific antituberculosis drugs and prolonged therapy are needed to treat tuberculosis

Mycobacteria are innately resistant to most antibacterial agents, and specific antituberculosis drugs have to be used; these are reviewed in Chapter 33. The key features of treatment are the use of:

- combination therapy – usually three drugs such as isoniazid, rifampicin, ethambutol to prevent emergence of resistance
- prolonged therapy – minimum 6 months period which is necessary to eradicate these slow-growing intracellular organisms.

The number of strains resistant to the first-line antituberculosis drugs has increased and has stimulated health agencies to monitor treatment more carefully (e.g. DOTS, directly observed treatment, short-course) and rekindled research interest in finding new agents. Extensively, drug resistant TB, referred to as XDR tuberculosis, has been described in strains in Asia, the Americas and Europe. Between 2000 and 2004, a survey of 17 000 TB isolates from these areas revealed that 2% of multidrug resistant (MDR) TB was also XDR. In an outbreak in an HIV-infected population attending a rural hospital in South Africa, 24% of MDR TB was also resistant to at least three of the six

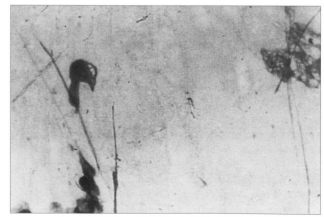

Figure 19.20 Pulmonary tuberculosis. Sputum preparation showing pink-stained, acid-fast tubercle bacilli. (Ziehl•Neelsen stain.) (Courtesy of J.A. Innes.)

classes of second-line agents. A high mortality rate within a median of 25 days was reported. It seems that this is not a single strain and may arise regularly in many different places due to badly managed care, i.e. non-compliance and poor prescribing practices, and disease control. As a result, methods detecting drug resistant TB at the point of care, together with new antituberculosis agents and strategies to reduce transmission, need to be established.

Tuberculosis is prevented by improved social conditions, immunization and chemoprophylaxis

The steady decline in incidence of tuberculosis since the beginning of the twentieth century, and before specific preventive measures were available, underlines the importance of improvements in social conditions in the prevention of this and many other infectious diseases. However, there has been an increase in the number of cases associated with AIDS; in some countries in the resource-poor world, HIV infection and AIDS are threatening to overwhelm tuberculosis control programmes.

Immunization with a live attenuated BCG (bacille Calmette–Guérin) vaccine, has been used effectively in situations where tuberculosis is prevalent. Immunization, which confers positive skin test reactivity, does not prevent infection, but it allows the body to react quickly to limit proliferation of the organisms. In areas where there is a low prevalence of disease, immunization has been largely replaced by chemoprophylaxis.

Prophylaxis with isoniazid for 1 year is recommended for people who have had close contact with a case of tuberculosis. It is also advocated for individuals who show recent conversion to skin test positivity, when it is essentially early treatment of subclinical infection rather than prophylaxis.

CYSTIC FIBROSIS

Individuals with cystic fibrosis are predisposed to develop lower respiratory tract infections

Cystic fibrosis is the most common lethal inherited disorder among Caucasians, with an incidence of approximately 1 in 2500 live births. The disease is characterized by pancreatic insufficiency, abnormal sweat electrolyte concentrations and production of very viscid bronchial secretions. The latter tend to lead to stasis in the lungs and this predisposes to infection.

P. aeruginosa colonizes the lungs of almost all 15–20-year-olds with cystic fibrosis

The respiratory mucosa of individuals with cystic fibrosis presents a different environment for potential pathogens from that found in healthy individuals, and the common infecting organisms and the nature of infections differ from other lung infections. These invaders include:

- *Staph. aureus*, which causes respiratory distress and lung damage, but can be well controlled by specific antistaphylococcal chemotherapy
- *Pseudomonas aeruginosa*, which is the pathogen of paramount importance (see below)
- in recent years *P. cepacia*, another member of the genus *Pseudomonas*, which has become an increasing problem

- *H. influenzae*, typically non-encapsulated strains, which may be found in association with *Staph. aureus* and *P. aeruginosa*; their pathogenic significance is unclear, but they appear to contribute to respiratory exacerbations.

P. aeruginosa infection is uncommon in those under 5 years of age, but colonizes the lungs of almost all patients aged 15–20 years, often encouraged by its intrinsic resistance to antistaphylococcal agents. Early in the course of infection, normal colony types are grown from sputum cultures, but as infection progresses, the organism changes to a highly mucoid form, almost mimicking the mucoid secretions of the patient (Fig. 19.21). These mucoid forms are thought to grow in microcolonies in the lung, but most of the lung damage is due to immunologic responses to the organisms and to the alginate, which forms the mucoid material (Fig. 19.22). *P. aeruginosa* rarely invades beyond the lung even in the most severely infected individuals.

Although specific antibacterial chemotherapy can reduce the symptoms of infection and improve the quality of life, infections, particularly with *P. aeruginosa* and *P. cepacia*, are impossible to eradicate and are frequently a cause of death. Heart–lung transplantation is a successful alternative treatment for some patients.

LUNG ABSCESS

Lung abscesses usually contain a mixture of bacteria including anaerobes

This is a suppurative infection of the lung, sometimes referred to as 'necrotizing pneumonia'. The most common predisposing cause is aspiration of respiratory or gastric secretions as a result of altered consciousness. The infection is therefore endogenous in origin and cultures often reveal a mixture of bacteria, with anaerobes such as *Bacteroides* and *Fusobacterium* playing an important role (Fig. 19.23).

Patients with lung abscesses may be ill for at least 2 weeks before presentation, with possible swinging fever, and usually produce large amounts of sputum, which, if foul smelling, gives a strong hint of the presence of anaerobes and often suggests the diagnosis. Most diagnoses are made from chest radiographs (see Fig. 19.7D) and the cause confirmed by microbiologic investigation.

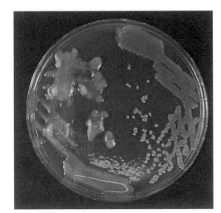

Figure 19.21 *Pseudomonas aeruginosa* isolated from the sputum of patients with cystic fibrosis characteristically grows in a very mucoid colonial form, shown here on the left of the picture, with the normal colonial form on the right for comparison.

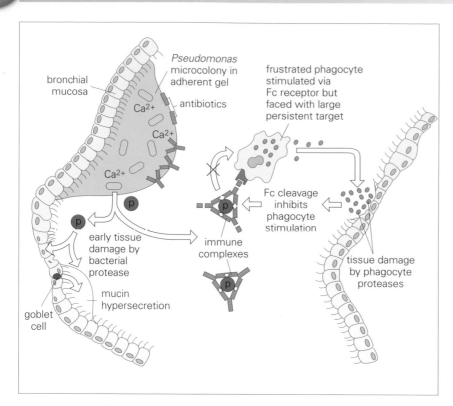

Figure 19.22 *Pseudomonas* infection in the lung of cystic fibrosis is chronic, but rarely invasive beyond the bronchial mucosa. The organisms are thought to grow in microcolonies embedded in a calcium (Ca^{2+})-dependent mucoid alginate gel, which contains DNA and tracheobronchial mucin, and attaches to the bronchial mucosa. This protects the organisms from the host defences and provides a physical and electrolyte barrier to antibiotics. Much of the damage to tissue is thought to be due to the slow release of bacterial proteases (which disrupt the mucosa and cause mucin hypersecretion), immunopathologic mechanisms exacerbated by the size, antigenicity and persistence of the alginate matrix, and the indirect action of immune complexes associated with *Pseudomonas antigens* (p). Tissue damage is also caused by phagocyte proteases. Intermittent exacerbations can be explained by the cleavage of the Fc of immune complexes by these proteases and consequent inhibition of further phagocyte stimulation. (Redrawn from Govan JRW. *Rev Med Microbiol* 1:19–28, © 1990.)

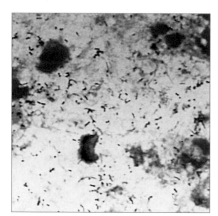

Figure 19.23 Gram stain of pus from a lung abscess showing Gram-positive cocci and both Gram-negative and Gram-positive rods. (Courtesy of J.R. Cantey.)

Treatment of lung abscess should include an anti-anaerobic drug and last 2–4 months

Because of the likely presence of anaerobes, a suitable anti-anaerobic agent such as metronidazole should be part of the treatment regimen, and treatment may be needed for 2–4 months to prevent relapse. If diagnosis and treatment are delayed, infection may spread to the pleural space, giving rise to empyema (see below).

Pleural effusion and empyema

Up to 50% of patients with pneumonia have a pleural effusion

Pleural effusions arise in a variety of different diseases. Sometimes the organisms infecting the lung spread to the pleural space and give rise to a purulent exudate or 'empyema'.

Pleural effusions can be demonstrated radiologically, but detection of empyema can be difficult, particularly in a patient with extensive pneumonia.

Aspiration of pleural fluid provides material for microbiologic examination, and *Staph. aureus*, Gram-negative rods and anaerobes are commonly involved.

Treatment should be directed at drainage of pus, eradication of infection and expansion of the lung.

FUNGAL INFECTIONS

Disease associated with fungal infection is most commonly seen in patients with defective immunity, either as a consequence of immune suppressive treatment or of concomitant disease. A number of species can cause opportunistic infections, and two are of particular importance: *Aspergillus fumigatus* and *Pneumocystis jirovecii* (formerly *P. carinii*).

Aspergillus

The most important species are *Aspergillus fumigatus* and *Aspergillus flavus*.

Aspergillus can cause allergic bronchopulmonary aspergillosis, aspergilloma or disseminated aspergillosis

The genus *Aspergillus* contains many species and these are ubiquitous in the environment. They do not form part of the normal flora. Their spores are regularly inhaled without harmful consequences, but some species, notably *A. fumigatus*, are able to cause a range of diseases, including:

- Allergic bronchopulmonary aspergillosis (ABPA), which is, as its name suggests, an allergic response to the presence of *Aspergillus* antigen in the lungs and occurs in patients with asthma. ABPA occurs in some 10% of cystic fibrosis patients.

- Aspergilloma in patients with pre-existing lung cavities or chronic pulmonary disorders. *Aspergillus* colonizes a cavity and grows to produce a fungal ball, a mass of entangled hyphae – the aspergilloma (Fig. 19.24). In this case, fungi do not invade the lung tissue, but the presence of a large aspergilloma can cause respiratory problems. Aspergillomas can be related, however, to chronic pulmonary aspergillosis where invasion of lung tissue does occur.
- Disseminated disease in the immunosuppressed patient when the fungus spreads from the lungs.

Invasive aspergillosis carries a high mortality as treatment is very difficult due to the limited number and toxic nature of antifungal agents active against *Aspergillus* (see Ch. 33) plus the lack of functional host defences. Treatment is with an intravenous lipid formulation of amphotericin B. Voriconazole or caspofungin are alternatives. A primary aim of therapy is to improve the neutrophil count.

Pneumocystis jirovecii (formerly *P. carinii*)

Pneumocystis pneumonia is an important opportunistic infection in AIDS

P. jiroveciii is a fungus commonly found in immunocompetent humans and in rodents. There is strong host specificity, so *Pneumocystis* infection of humans is not a zoonosis. Infection probably spreads by droplet though airborne transmission has only been directly demonstrated in animal models. Disease occurs in debilitated and immune-deficient individuals. Before the advent of highly active antiretroviral therapy (HAART), a high proportion of AIDS patients developed *Pneumocystis* pneumonia, which could be fatal.

Pneumocystis occurs as three developmental forms, the trophozoite, up to 5 μm diameter, precyst and cyst. Spores are released when the cysts rupture. Disease is associated with an interstitial pneumonitis, with plasma cell infiltration. Infections of internal organs other than the lung (e.g. lymph nodes, spleen, liver) have also been reported at post-mortem examination.

Treatment is dealt with in Chapter 30.

PARASITIC INFECTIONS

A variety of parasites localize to the lung or involve the lung at some stage in their development

Such parasites include:

- Nematodes such as *Ascaris, Strongyloides* and the hookworms (see Chs 6 and 22), which migrate through the lungs as they move to the small intestine, breaking out of the capillaries around the alveoli to enter the bronchioles. The damage caused by this process, and the development of inflammatory responses, can lead to a transient pneumonitis with cough, wheeze, dyspnoea and pulmonary infiltrates.
- Schistosome larvae, which may cause mild respiratory symptoms as they migrate through the lungs (see Chs 6 and 22). Heavy acute infections may produce pneumonitis with poorly defined nodular lesions or reticulonodular appearances.
- The microfilariae of filarial nematodes such as *Wuchereria* or *Brugia*, which appear in the peripheral circulation with a regular diurnal or nocturnal periodicity, their appearance coinciding with the time at which the vector blood-sucking insects are likely to feed. Outside these periods, the larvae become sequestered in the capillaries of the lung. Under certain conditions, as yet undefined, and in certain individuals, the presence of the larvae triggers a condition known as 'tropical pulmonary eosinophilia' (TPE or Weingarten's syndrome). This is characterized by the onset over several months of cough, dyspnoea and wheeze, worse at night and marked peripheral blood eosinophilia. Microfilariae are absent from the peripheral blood. Antifilarial antibody tests are strongly positive. Chest X-ray examination shows bilateral fine nodular or reticulonodular shadowing.
- *Ascaris* and *Strongyloides* infections, which may also trigger a pulmonary eosinophilia, although the condition is distinct from TPE.
- *Echinococcus granulosus* infection, which leads to the development of hydatid cysts in a proportion (20–30%) of cases due to localization of the larvae of the tapeworm in the lungs (see Chs 6 and 22). These cysts may reach a considerable size, causing respiratory distress, largely as a consequence of the mechanical pressure exerted on

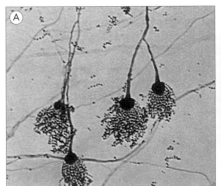
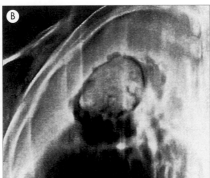
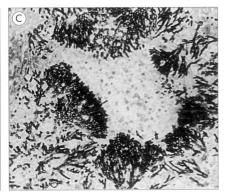

Figure 19.24 *Aspergillus fumigatus*. (A) Lactophenol cotton blue stained preparation showing the characteristic conidiophores. (B) Aspergilloma. Tomogram showing fungus ball contained within the lung cavity, outlined by air space. (Courtesy of J.A. Innes.) (C) Invasive aspergillosis. Histologic section showing fungal hyphae invading the lung parenchyma and blood vessels. (Grocott stain.) (Courtesy of C. Kibbler.)

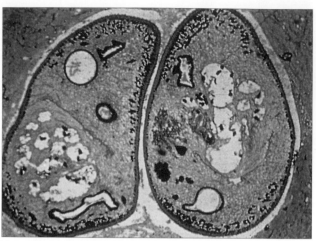

Figure 19.25 Two adult *Paragonimus* contained within a fibrous cyst in the lung. (Courtesy of H. Zaiman.)

lung tissue. Spontaneous rupture may occur and result in acute anaphylaxis.

- *Entamoeba histolytica* infection, which may rarely involve the lung.
- *Paragonimus westermani*, the oriental lung fluke, which is the most important example of one of the very few adult parasites that live in the lung, infecting an estimated 22 million people, mainly in Asia. Infection is acquired by eating crustaceans containing the infective metacercariae. These migrate from the intestine across the body cavity and penetrate into the lungs. The adults develop within fibrous cysts, which connect with the bronchi to provide an exit for the eggs (Fig. 19.25). Infections cause chest pain and difficulty in breathing, and can cause bronchopneumonia when large numbers of parasites are present. Single lesions can be confused with lung cancer, tuberculosis and fungal lesions. Praziquantel is an efficient anthelmintic for paragonimiasis.

KEY FACTS

- Although continuous from nose to alveoli, the respiratory tract is divided into 'upper' and 'lower' from the viewpoint of infection.

- Infections in the lower respiratory tract are spread by the airborne route (except parasites), are acute or chronic, tend to be severe and may be fatal without correct treatment. They are caused by a wide range of organisms – usually bacteria or viruses, but also fungi and parasites.

- Bronchitis, an inflammatory condition of the tracheobronchial tree, is usually chronic with acute exacerbations associated with infection by viruses and bacteria. The disease is characterized by cough and excessive mucus production, and the diagnosis is clinical. Antibiotics are often given, but their efficacy is uncertain.

- Bronchiolitis, usually caused by RSV, is acute and severe in young children. RSV causes outbreaks in the community and in hospitals. The disease has an immunopathologic basis, and specific treatment (ribavirin) may be considered. No vaccine is available.

- Pneumonia is caused by a variety of pathogens depending upon the patients' age, previous or underlying disease, and occupational and geographic factors. Correct microbiologic diagnosis is essential to optimize therapy. Mortality from pneumonia remains significant.

- *B. pertussis* colonizes the ciliated respiratory epithelium causing the specifically human infection whooping cough. Pertussis toxin and other toxic factors are important for virulence. Diagnosis is clinical, alerted by the characteristic paroxysmal cough. Supportive care is paramount; antibiotics play a peripheral role. Prevention by immunization is effective, and new safer vaccines are becoming available.

- Influenza viruses cause endemic, epidemic and pandemic infections as a result of the capacity of the virus for antigenic drift and shift. The disease is acute in onset and can be clinically severe. Viral damage to the respiratory mucosa predisposes to secondary bacterial pneumonia. Antiviral agents are available. Immunization is important, but needs to be kept up to date due to the frequent antigenic changes in the circulating virus.

- Tuberculosis, a major killer, is becoming more common because of its association with AIDS. Infection is usually chronic. Primary infection with *M. tuberculosis* results in a localized pulmonary lesion, while secondary disease arises from reactivation as a result of an impairment of immune function. Clinical diagnosis is supported by demonstrating the acid-fast *M. tuberculosis* in sputum. Effective treatment is available, but long courses of drug combinations are essential. Chemoprophylaxis and BCG immunoprophylaxis are important in prevention.

- *Aspergillus* causes disease in the lung ranging from invasive disease in the immunocompromised to allergic conditions in the otherwise healthy. Effective treatment is difficult because of the limited number of active antifungals and lack of host defences.

- Cystic fibrosis is an inherited disease that predisposes to a particular pattern of lung disease characterized by infection with *P. aeruginosa*. Infection can be controlled by antibacterials, but rarely eradicated.

- Various species of parasites pass through or localize in the lungs at some stage in their life cycle. Damage is limited unless the parasite load is high, and is usually immunopathologic in nature.

Urinary tract infections

20

Introduction

Urinary tract infections are common, especially among women

The urinary tract is one of the most common sites of bacterial infection, particularly in females; 20–30% of women have recurrent urinary tract infections (UTIs) at some time in their life. UTIs in men are less common and primarily occur after 50 years of age. Although the majority of infections are acute and short-lived, they contribute to a significant amount of morbidity in the population. Severe infections result in a loss of renal function and serious long-term sequelae. In females, a distinction is made between cystitis, urethritis and vaginitis, but the genitourinary tract is a continuum and the symptoms often overlap.

ACQUISITION AND ETIOLOGY

Bacterial infection is usually acquired by the ascending route from the urethra to the bladder

The infection may then proceed to the kidney. Occasionally, bacteria infecting the urinary tract invade the bloodstream to cause septicaemia. Less commonly, infection may result from haematogenous spread of an organism to the kidney, with the renal tissue being the first part of the tract to be infected.

From an epidemiological viewpoint, UTIs occur in two general settings: community-acquired and hospital (nosocomially)-acquired, the latter most often being associated with catheterization. Hospital-acquired UTIs, while less common than community acquired, contribute significantly (ca. 40%) to overall nosocomial infection rates.

The Gram-negative rod *Escherichia coli* is the commonest cause of ascending UTI

Other members of the Enterobacteriaceae are also implicated (Fig. 20.1). *Proteus mirabilis* is often associated with urinary stones (calculi), probably because this organism produces a potent urease, which acts on urea to produce ammonia, rendering the urine alkaline. *Citrobacter, Klebsiella, Enterobacter, Proteus,* and *Pseudomonas aeruginosa* are more frequently found in hospital-acquired UTI because their resistance to antibiotics favours their selection in hospital patients (see Ch. 36).

Among the Gram-positive species, *Staphylococcus saprophyticus* has a particular propensity for causing infections, especially in young sexually active women. *Staphylococcus epidermidis* and *Enterococcus* species are more often associated with UTI in hospitalized patients (especially those with AIDS), where multiple antibiotic resistance can cause treatment difficulties. In some instances, capnophilic species (organisms that grow better in air enriched with carbon dioxide), including corynebacteria and lactobacilli, have been implicated as possible causes of UTI. Obligate anaerobes are very rarely involved.

When there has been haematogenous spread to the urinary tract, other species may be found, e.g. *Salmonella typhi, Staphylococcus aureus* and *Mycobacterium tuberculosis* (renal tuberculosis).

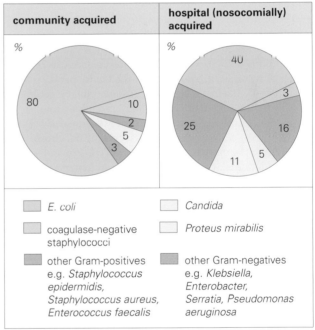

community acquired	hospital (nosocomially) acquired
% 80 10 2 5 3	% 40 3 16 25 11 5

☐ *E. coli*

☐ coagulase-negative staphylococci

☐ other Gram-positives e.g. *Staphylococcus epidermidis, Staphylococcus aureus, Enterococcus faecalis*

☐ *Candida*

☐ *Proteus mirabilis*

☐ other Gram-negatives e.g. *Klebsiella, Enterobacter, Serratia, Pseudomonas aeruginosa*

Figure 20.1 Common causes of urinary tract infection. The percentages of infections caused by different bacteria in outpatients and hospital inpatients are shown. *E. coli* is by far the commonest isolate in both groups of patients, but note the difference in the percentage of infections caused by other Gram-negative rods. These isolates often carry multiple antibiotic resistance and colonize patients in hospital, especially those receiving antibiotics.

Viral causes of UTI appear to be rare, although there are associations with haemorrhagic cystitis and other renal syndromes

Certain viruses may be recovered from the urine in the absence of urinary tract disease and include:

- The human polyomaviruses, JC and BK, enter the body via the respiratory tract, spread through the body and infect epithelial cells in the kidney tubules and ureter, where they establish latency with persistence of the viral genome. About 35% of kidneys from healthy individuals contain polyomavirus DNA sequences. However, during normal pregnancy, the viruses may reactivate asymptomatically, with the appearance of large amounts of virus in the urine. Reactivation also occurs in immunocompromised patients (see Ch. 30) and may lead to haemorrhagic cystitis.

- High titres of cytomegalovirus (CMV) and rubella may be shed asymptomatically in the urine of congenitally infected infants (see Ch. 23).
- In contrast to asymptomatic shedding, some serotypes of adenovirus have been implicated as a cause of haemorrhagic cystitis.
- The rodent-borne hantavirus responsible for Korean haemorrhagic fever infects capillary blood vessels in the kidney and can cause a renal syndrome with proteinuria.
- Finally, a number of other viruses can infect the kidneys, including mumps and HIV.

Urine samples are commonly investigated by virus isolation, immunological and genomic detection methods.

Very few parasites cause UTIs

Other causes of UTI include:

- The fungi *Candida* spp. and *Histoplasma capsulatum*.
- The protozoan *Trichomonas vaginalis* (see Ch. 21), which can cause urethritis in both males and females, but is most often considered as a cause of vaginitis.
- Infections with *Schistosoma haematobium* (see Ch. 27), which result in inflammation of the bladder and commonly haematuria. The eggs penetrate the bladder wall, and in severe infections large granulomatous reactions can occur and the eggs may become calcified. Bladder cancer is associated with chronic infections, although the mechanism is uncertain. Obstruction of the ureter as a result of egg-induced inflammatory changes can also lead to hydronephrosis.

PATHOGENESIS

A variety of mechanical factors predispose to UTI

Anything that disrupts normal urine flow or complete emptying of the bladder or facilitates access of organisms to the bladder will predispose an individual to infection (Fig. 20.2). The shorter female urethra is a less effective deterrent to infection than the male urethra (see Ch. 13). Sexual intercourse facilitates the movement of organisms up the urethra, particularly in females, so the incidence of UTI is higher among sexually active women than among celibate women. Preceding bacterial colonization of the periurethral area of the vagina is perhaps important (see below).

In male infants, UTIs are more common in the uncircumcised, and this is associated with colonization of the inside of the prepuce and urethra with faecal organisms.

Pregnancy, prostatic hypertrophy, renal calculi, tumours and strictures are the main causes of obstruction to complete bladder emptying

Increased volumes of post-void residual urine are associated with a greater likelihood of infection. Infection, superimposed on urinary tract obstruction, may lead to ascent of infection to the kidney and rapid destruction of renal tissue.

Loss of neurologic control of the bladder and sphincters (e.g. in spina bifida, paraplegia or multiple sclerosis), and the resultant large residual volume of urine in the bladder, causes a functional obstruction to urine flow, and such patients are particularly prone to recurrent infections.

Vesicoureteral reflux (reflux of urine from the bladder cavity up the ureters, sometimes into the renal pelvis or parenchyma) is common in children with anatomic abnormalities of the urinary tract and may predispose to ascending infection and kidney damage. Reflux may also occur in

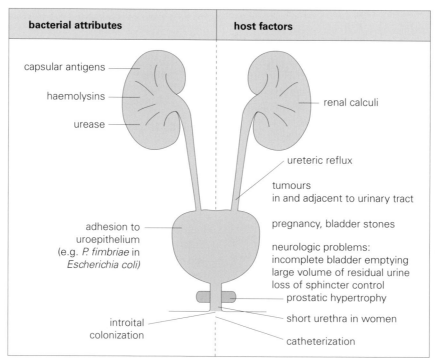

bacterial attributes	host factors

- capsular antigens
- haemolysins
- urease
- renal calculi
- ureteric reflux
- tumours in and adjacent to urinary tract
- adhesion to uroepithelium (e.g. *P. fimbriae* in *Escherichia coli*)
- pregnancy, bladder stones
- neurologic problems: incomplete bladder emptying large volume of residual urine loss of sphincter control
- prostatic hypertrophy
- introital colonization
- short urethra in women
- catheterization

Figure 20.2 Bacterial attributes and host factors favouring urinary tract infection (UTI). Abnormalities of the urinary tract tend to predispose to infection. Bacterial adherence factors have been studied in detail, but relatively little is known about other bacterial virulence factors in UTI.

association with infection in children without underlying abnormalities, but tends to disappear with age.

Clinical studies including reports that pyelonephritis (infection of the kidney) is commonly found in people with diabetes mellitus at post-mortem suggest an increased propensity for UTI in individuals with diabetes mellitus. People with diabetes mellitus may have more severe UTIs, and if diabetic neuropathy interferes with normal bladder function, persistent UTIs are common.

Catheterization is a major predisposing factor for UTI

During insertion of the catheter, bacteria may be carried directly into the bladder and, while in situ, the catheter facilitates bacterial access to the bladder either via the lumen of the catheter or by tracking up between the outside of the catheter and the urethral wall (Fig. 20.3). The catheter disrupts the normal bladder's protective function action and allows bacteria to get a foothold. Thus, duration of catheterization is directly associated with increased probability of infection (i.e. risk of UTI increases by about 3–10% each day of catheterization).

A variety of virulence factors are present in the causative organisms

The conflict between host and parasite in the urinary tract has been discussed in Chapter 13. Most urinary tract pathogens originate in the faecal flora, but only the aerobic and facultative species such as *E. coli* possess the attributes required to colonize and infect the urinary tract. The ability to cause infection of the urinary tract is limited to certain serogroups of *E. coli* such as O (semantic) serotypes (e.g. O1, O2, O4, O6, O7 and O75) and K (capsular) serotypes (e.g. K1, K2, K3, K5, K12 and K13). These serotypes differ from those associated with gastrointestinal tract infection (see Ch. 22), which has led to use of the term 'uropathogenic *E. coli*' (UPEC). The success of these strains is attributable to a variety of genes in chromosomal pathogenicity islands (see Ch. 2) which are not found in faecal *E. coli*. For example, UPEC typically contains genes associated with colonization of the periurethral areas. A prime example is the adhesion known as *P. fimbriae* (pyelonephritis-associated pili (PAP)), which allows UPEC to specifically adhere to urethral and bladder epithelium. Studies with other species of urinary tract pathogens have confirmed the presence of similar adhesins for uroepithelial cells (Fig. 20.4).

Other features of *E. coli* which appear to assist in the localization of organisms in the kidney and in renal damage include:

- The capsular acid polysaccharide (K) antigens are associated with the ability to cause pyelonephritis and are known to enable *E. coli* strains to resist host defences by inhibiting phagocytosis.
- Haemolysin production by *E. coli* is linked with the capacity to cause kidney damage; many haemolysins act more generally as membrane-damaging toxins.

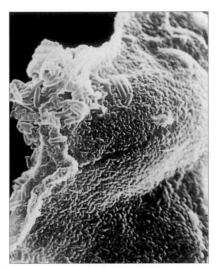

Figure 20.4 Scanning electron micrograph showing bacteria attached to an exfoliated uroepithelial cell from a patient with acute cystitis. (Courtesy of T.S.J. Elliot and the editor of *British Journal of Urology*.)

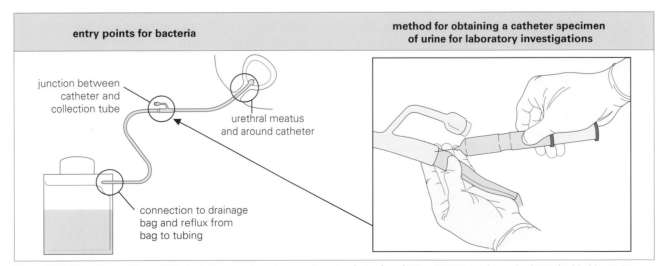

entry points for bacteria	method for obtaining a catheter specimen of urine for laboratory investigations

junction between catheter and collection tube

urethral meatus and around catheter

connection to drainage bag and reflux from bag to tubing

Figure 20.3 The urinary catheter. Catheterization is an important predisposing factor for infection. Bacteria can be pushed into the bladder as the catheter is inserted and, while the catheter is in place, bacteria reach the bladder by tracking up between the outside of the catheter and the urethra. Contamination of the catheter drainage system by bacteria from other sources can also result in infection. Specimens of bladder urine for laboratory investigations can be collected from catheterized patients as shown. The second port (above) is for putting fluids into the bladder. Urine from the drainage bag should not be tested because it may have been standing for several hours.

The production of urease by organisms such as *Proteus* spp. has been correlated with their ability to cause pyelonephritis and stones.

The healthy urinary tract is resistant to bacterial colonization

With the exception of the urethral mucosa, the urinary tract usually eliminates microorganisms rapidly and efficiently (see Ch. 13). The pH, chemical content and flushing mechanism of urine help to dispose of organisms in the urethra. Although urine is a good culture medium for most bacteria, it is inhibitory to some, and anaerobes and other species (non-haemolytic streptococci, corynebacteria and staphylococci), which comprise most of the normal urethral flora, do not readily multiply in urine.

Although the inflammatory response to urinary tract infection involves leukocytic, chemokine, and cytokine response, the role of humoral immunity in the host's defence against infection of the urinary tract is poorly understood. After infection of the kidney, IgG and secretory IgA antibodies can be detected in urine but do not appear to protect against subsequent infection. Infection of the lower urinary tract is usually associated with a low or undetectable serologic response, reflecting the superficial nature of the infection; the bladder and urethral mucosa are rarely invaded in UTIs.

CLINICAL FEATURES AND COMPLICATIONS

Acute lower UTIs cause dysuria, urgency and frequency

Acute infections of the lower urinary tract are characterized by a rapid onset of:

- dysuria (burning pain on passing urine)
- urgency (the urgent need to pass urine)
- frequency of micturition.

However, UTIs in the elderly and those with indwelling catheters are usually asymptomatic.

The urine is cloudy due to the presence of pus cells (pyuria) and bacteria (bacteriuria), and may contain blood (haematuria). Examination of urine specimens in the laboratory is essential to confirm the diagnosis. Patients with genital tract infections such as vaginal thrush or chlamydial urethritis may present with similar symptoms (see Ch. 21).

Pyuria in the absence of positive urine cultures can be due to chlamydiae or tuberculosis and is also seen in patients receiving antibacterial therapy for UTI, as the bacteria are inhibited or killed by the antibacterial agent before the inflammatory response dies away.

Recurrent infections of the lower urinary tract occur in a significant proportion of patients. They may be:

- relapses, caused by the same strain of organism
- reinfections by different organisms.

Recurrent infections can result in chronic inflammatory changes in the bladder, prostate and periurethral glands.

Acute bacterial prostatitis causes systemic symptoms (fever) and local symptoms (perineal and low back pain, dysuria and frequency)

Acute bacterial prostatitis may arise from ascending or haematogenous infection, and people lacking the antibacterial substances normally present in prostatic fluid are perhaps more susceptible. Chronic bacterial prostatitis, however, although usually caused by *E. coli*, is difficult to cure and can be a source of relapsing infection within the urinary tract.

Upper UTIs

Although it may be important to know whether an infection is restricted to the bladder (lower urinary tract) or has ascended to the upper urinary tract and kidney, there are no satisfactory methods for distinguishing the two other than by examining urine directly from the ureter by ureteric catheterization.

Pyelonephritis causes a fever and lower urinary tract symptoms

Patients with pyelonephritis (infection of the kidney, Fig. 20.5) present with lower urinary tract symptoms and usually have a fever. Staphylococci are a common cause and renal abscesses are generally present. Recurrent episodes of pyelonephritis result in a loss of function of renal tissue, which may in turn cause hypertension, itself a cause of renal damage. Infection associated with stone formation can result in obstruction of the renal tract and septicaemia.

Haematuria is a feature of endocarditis and a manifestation of immune complex disease, as well as a result of infections of the kidney, and its presence warrants careful investigation. Pyuria may be associated with kidney infection by *M. tuberculosis*. This organism cannot be grown by normal urine culture methods and therefore the patient may appear to have a sterile pyuria.

Asymptomatic infection (i.e. significant numbers of bacteria in the urine in the absence of symptoms, see below) can be detected only by screening urine samples in the laboratory. It is important in instances such as:

- pregnant women and young children, where failure to treat may result in chronic renal damage
- people undergoing instrumentation of the urinary tract, in whom bacteriuria may proceed to bacteraemia
- the elderly and those with diabetes (both risk factors for asymptomatic bacteriuria).

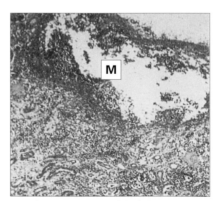

Figure 20.5 Histologic appearance of the kidney in acute pyelonephritis, showing the intense inflammatory reaction and microabscesses (M). (H&E stain.) (Courtesy of M.J. Wood.)

LABORATORY DIAGNOSIS

A key feature is the detection of significant bacteriuria.

Infection can be distinguished from contamination by quantitative culture methods

In health, the urinary tract is sterile, although the distal region of the urethra is colonized with commensal organisms, which may include periurethral and faecal organisms. As urine specimens are usually collected by voiding a specimen into a sterile container, they become contaminated with the periurethral flora during collection. Infection can be distinguished from contamination by quantitative culture methods. Bacteriuria is defined as 'significant' when a properly collected midstream urine (MSU) specimen is shown to contain over 10^5 organisms/mL. Infected urine usually contains only a single bacterial species. Contaminated urine usually has < 10^4 organisms/mL and often contains more than one bacterial species (Fig. 20.6). Distinguishing infection from contamination when counts are 10^4–10^5 organisms/mL can be difficult. Careful collection and rapid transport of urine specimens to the laboratory are essential (see below and Ch. 32).

It is important to recognize that the criteria for 'significant bacteriuria' do not apply to urine specimens collected from catheters or nephrostomy tubes or by suprapubic aspiration directly from the bladder, in which any number of organisms may be significant because the specimen is not contaminated by periurethral flora. In addition, infection of sites in the urinary tract below the bladder, and by organisms that are not members of the normal faecal flora, may not lead to the presence of significant numbers in the urine.

The usual urine specimen for microbiologic examination is an MSU sample

An MSU sample should be collected into a sterile wide-mouthed container after careful cleansing of the labia or glans with soap (not antiseptic) and water, and after allowing the first part of the urine stream to be voided, as this helps to wash out contaminants in the lower urethra. After suitable instruction, the majority of adult patients can collect satisfactory samples with minimum supervision, though collection may be difficult for elderly and bedridden patients and consideration should be given to these difficulties when interpreting results.

Collection of MSU samples from babies and young children is difficult. 'Bag urine' may be collected by sticking a plastic bag to the perineum in girls or to the penis in boys, but such specimens are frequently heavily contaminated with faecal organisms. These problems can be overcome by suprapubic aspiration of urine directly from the bladder (Fig. 20.7).

Urine specimens should be transported to the laboratory with minimum delay because urine is a good growth medium for many bacteria and multiplication of organisms in the specimen between collection and culture will distort the results (see Ch. 32).

Ideally, samples should be collected before antimicrobial therapy is started. If the patient is receiving, or has received, therapy within the previous 48 h, this should be stated clearly on the request form.

For patients with a catheter, a catheter specimen of urine is used for microbiologic examination

Patients should not be catheterized simply to obtain a urine sample. Urine is obtained from patients who have a catheter in situ by withdrawing a sample with a syringe and needle from the catheter tube as shown in Figure 20.3. Urine that has been standing in the catheter drainage bag for hours is unsuitable for testing because the organisms may have multiplied to give much greater numbers than those present in the patient.

Special urine samples are required to detect *M. tuberculosis* and *Schistosoma haematobium*

These include:

* three early morning urine samples on consecutive days for *M. tuberculosis*; these do not require the same precautions during collection as an MSU sample, because the culture technique prohibits the growth of organisms other than mycobacteria
* the last few millilitres of a urine sample collected early afternoon after exercise for detection of *S. haematobium*.

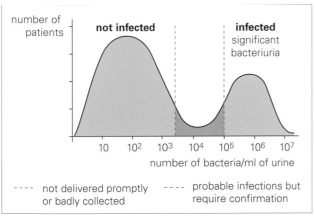

number of patients

not infected

infected
significant bacteriuria

number of bacteria/ml of urine

- - - - not delivered promptly or badly collected

- - - - probable infections but require confirmation

Figure 20.6 Significant bacteriuria. Voided specimens of urine are rarely sterile because the urine is contaminated with organisms from the periurethral area during collection. Even well-collected specimens from healthy individuals may contain up to 10^3 bacteria/mL of urine. A count of 10^5 bacteria/mL is considered a reliable indicator of infection. However, there are various reasons why lower counts may sometimes be significant (e.g. acute dysuria, ureteral obstruction, etc.).

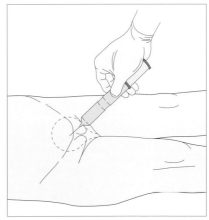

Figure 20.7 Suprapubic aspiration of bladder urine. Urine samples can be collected directly from the bladder by insertion of a needle. This method is useful in young children from whom it is difficult to obtain uncontaminated midstream urine specimens.

Laboratory investigations

Urine specimens should be examined macroscopically and microscopically and should be cultured by quantitative or semiquantitative methods, as summarized in Chapter 32.

Microscopic examination of urine allows a rapid preliminary report

Bacteria may be seen on microscopy when present in the specimen in large numbers. However, they are not necessarily indicative of infection, but may indicate that the specimen has been poorly collected or left at room temperature for a prolonged period of time.

The presence of red and white blood cells, although abnormal, is not necessarily indicative of UTI. Haematuria may be present in association with:

- infection of the urinary tract and elsewhere (e.g. bacterial endocarditis)
- renal trauma
- calculi
- urinary tract carcinomas
- clotting disorders
- thrombocytopenia.

Occasionally, red blood cells may contaminate urine specimens of menstruating women.

White blood cells are present in the urine in very small numbers (e.g. <10/mL) in health; a count of over 10/mL is considered abnormal, but is not always associated with bacteriuria. Sterile pyuria is an important finding and may reflect:

- concurrent antibiotic therapy
- other diseases such as neoplasms or urinary calculi
- infection with organisms not detected by routine urine culture methods.

Renal tubular cells, seen in the urine of aspirin-misusers, may be confused with white blood cells. Urinary casts are also indicative of renal tubular damage.

A laboratory diagnosis of significant bacteriuria requires quantification of the bacteria

Conventional culture methods produce results within 18–24 h, but rapid methods (e.g. based on bioluminescence, turbidimetry, leukocyte esterase/nitrate reductase test, etc.) are also available. In some laboratories, direct antibiotic susceptibility tests may be initiated upon detecting abnormal numbers of white blood cells or bacteria on microscopy, so that both culture and susceptibility results are available within 24 h.

Interpretation of the significance of bacterial culture results depends upon a variety of factors

These factors relate to:

- *collection* – specimen collection must be carried out properly.
- *storage* – the urine must be cultured within 1 h of collection or held at 4°C for not more than 18 h before culture.
- *antibiotic treatment* – in a patient receiving antibiotics, smaller numbers of organisms may be significant and may represent an emerging resistant population; simple laboratory methods are available to detect antibacterial substances.
- *fluid intake* – the patient may be taking more or less fluid than usual, and this will clearly influence the quantitative result.
- *the specimen* – the quantitative guidelines are valid for MSU specimens; they do not apply to catheter specimens, suprapubic aspirates or nephrostomy samples.

TREATMENT

Depending on clinical evaluation of the patient and local antimicrobial resistance trends, uncomplicated UTI is typically treated with an oral antibacterial for 3 days

Uncomplicated UTI (cystitis) generally resolves spontaneously within 4 weeks in up to 40% of patients; however, treatment with antibacterial agents reduces symptoms and ensures bacterial eradication. Oral antimicrobial chemotherapy is generally administered twice a day for 3 days, depending upon the drug and clinical evaluation of the patient. The commonly prescribed agents are shown in Table 20.1. The choice of agent should be based on the results of susceptibility tests. However, for uncomplicated UTIs in patients in the community, therapy is often 'best guess', at least until

Table 20.1 Oral antibacterials for urinary tract infections (UTIs)

Examples of common oral antibacterials for urinary tract infections		
Antibacterial	**Class of agent**	**Comments**
Trimethoprim	Antimetabolite/nucleic-acid synthesis inhibitor	Incidence of resistant strains increasing
Co-trimoxazole	Combination of trimethoprim with sulphamethoxazole (also antimetabolite nucleic-acid synthesis inhibitor)	One of the most common 'first-line' therapeutic approaches; may be useful in 'blind' treatment but more toxic than trimethoprim alone; resistance also an issue
Nitrofurantoin	Urinary antiseptic	For uncomplicated UTI caused by *E. coli* and *Staphylococcus saprophyticus*; not active in alkaline pH (therefore not useful for *Proteus* infections)
Ciprofloxacin, norfloxacin, ofloxacin, etc.	Quinolone	Very broad spectrum; not highly active against enterococci; increasing resistance an issue

Several different classes of antibacterial are available in oral formulations and suitable for treatment of UTI. Nitrofurantoin is useful only for lower UTIs as it does not achieve adequate serum and tissue concentrations to treat upper UTIs.

laboratory results are available. This requires a knowledge of the likely pathogens and their antibiotic susceptibility patterns in the locality. Follow-up cultures should be carried out after treatment has been completed (at least 2 days later) to confirm eradication of the infecting organism. In addition to antibacterial therapy, the patient should be advised to drink large volumes of fluid to help the normal flushing process.

Children and pregnant women with asymptomatic bacteriuria should be treated with antibacterials and followed-up to check for eradication of the infection. Instrumentation of the urinary tract should be delayed in patients with significant bacteriuria until appropriate treatment has rendered the urine sterile.

Complicated UTI (pyelonephritis) should be treated with a systemic antibacterial agent

The organism should be known to be susceptible to the antibacterial, and systemic treatment should continue until the signs and symptoms subside. It can then be replaced by oral therapy. The usual length of treatment is at least 10 days, but longer treatment may be necessary to sterilize the kidney.

Hospital-acquired infections or recurrent infections, particularly in catheterized patients, may be caused by antibiotic-resistant organisms, and the agent of choice will depend upon the antibacterial susceptibility pattern. If possible, the catheter should be removed, as eradication of infection is extremely difficult to achieve in catheterized patients, and some would advocate treatment only when the patient complains of symptoms or before invasive procedures. Guidelines for catheter care and for the prevention of catheter-associated UTIs are shown in Box 20.1.

Infections acquired by haematogenous spread require specific antibacterial therapy, as described in Chapter 33 for tuberculosis, Chapter 22 for *S. typhi*, Chapter 26 for *Staph. aureus* and Chapter 27 for schistosomiasis.

Box 20.1 Guidelines For Catheter Care

- Avoid catheterization whenever possible.
- Keep duration of catheterization to a minimum.
- Use intermittent rather than continuous catheterization when feasible.
- Insert catheters with good aseptic technique.
- Use a closed sterile drainage system.
- Maintain a gravity drain.
- Use topical antiseptics around the meatus in women.
- Wash hands before and after inserting catheters and collecting specimens, and after emptying drainage bags.
- Catheters that drain into open collecting vessels are highly conducive to infection. Thus, closed drainage systems are now used in most hospitals, but even then, bacteriuria occurs in a significant number of patients.

PREVENTION

Many of the features of the pathogenesis of UTI and host predispositions are not clearly understood

Recurrent infections in otherwise healthy women can be prevented by regularly emptying the bladder. This washes bacteria out of the urinary tract and is particularly important following intercourse. The prophylactic use of antibiotics may also prevent recurrent infections, but in the presence of underlying abnormalities, there is a tendency to select antibiotic-resistant strains, which subsequently cause infections that are more difficult to treat.

Infection in catheterized patients is very common, but can be reduced by good catheter care procedures (Box 20.1, see Ch. 36). Catheterization should be avoided if possible or kept to a minimum duration.

KEY FACTS

- UTIs are among the commonest bacterial infections, especially in women.
- Most UTIs are acute episodes without sequelae.
- UTIs are usually endogenously acquired, with colonizing bacteria ascending the urinary tract from the periurethral area. *E. coli* is the predominant pathogen; other Gram-negative rods are also responsible, especially in hospitalized patients. Viruses are not important causes of UTI.
- Structural or mechanical factors in the host, or catheterization, predispose to infection.
- Bacterial attributes such as adhesions and capsular polysaccharides may be important in the development of UTI. Specific toxins are not implicated, but haemolysins (cytotoxins) may be.
- Lower UTI usually presents with acute frequency and dysuria. Asymptomatic infection is common in pregnancy and in children. Infection is recurrent in a significant proportion of people.
- Pyelonephritis (upper UTI) has a more severe presentation than lower UTI, with fever and loin pain; recurrent infection results in renal damage.
- Bacteriologic confirmation of the diagnosis requires quantitative methods. Pyuria also implies infection.
- Short-course treatment with oral antibacterials is effective for lower UTI; pyelonephritis needs longer treatment, often commencing with systemically administered drugs.
- Hospital-acquired UTI is often caused by multiple-resistant Gram-negative bacteria, and treatment should be based on the results of antibiotic susceptibility tests.

Sexually transmitted infections

Introduction

Sexually transmitted infections usually cause diseases

In some instances, sexually transmitted infections (STIs) may not result in overt disease symptoms, such as in the early stages of HIV infection and asymptomatic gonorrhoea in females. This is particularly concerning since people with asymptomatic or unreported STIs are unlikely to receive treatment, thus facilitating further cycles of infection and spread. While STIs are of major medical importance throughout the world, HIV infection has had the greatest global impact, estimated to affect nearly 35 million people by 2009. In addition to HIV, new cases of other STIs occur globally with alarming frequency (hundreds of millions of new cases) each year.

The incidence of most STIs is increasing

This is typified by the situation in the UK where, in 2009, 482 700 new STD cases were reported by genitourinary medicine clinics, an increase of over 12 000 from the previous year. A similar situation exists in other countries, including the USA. The reasons for this increase include:

- increasing density and mobility of human populations
- the difficulty of engineering changes in human sexual behaviour
- the absence of vaccines for almost all STIs.

The last two factors may change. There is evidence of changes in male homosexual behaviour, leading to decreased transmission of some STIs in this group, and vaccines for infections such as human papillomavirus have been developed.

HIV infection and AIDS have overshadowed other STIs with immense impact as a highly lethal infectious disease. Measuring plasma HIV-1 RNA load, CD4 counts and percentage, together with antiretroviral resistance and tropism testing by sequence analysis have become mainstays in the management of HIV infection with regard to monitoring disease progress and response to antiretroviral therapy in resource-rich countries.

The most common STIs are listed in Table 21.1. Table 21.2 gives examples of the strategies used by the microorganisms to overcome host defences.

STIs AND SEXUAL BEHAVIOUR

The general principles of entry, exit and transmission of the microorganisms that cause STIs are set out in Chapter 13.

The spread of STIs is inextricably linked with sexual behaviour

There are therefore many more opportunities for controlling STIs than, for instance, respiratory infections. Infected but asymptomatic individuals play an important role, and important determinants are promiscuity and sexual practices involving contact between different orifices and mucosal surfaces (see Ch. 13). For example, transmission between heterosexuals or male homosexuals can take place following oral or anal intercourse. The gonococcus, for instance, causes pharyngitis and proctitis, although it infects stratified squamous epithelium less readily than columnar epithelium. As described more fully in Chapter 31, calculations regarding the number of infected secondary cases resulting from each primary STD case depends on a variety of behavioural factors since the number of sexual partners acquired by a given individual, i.e. the level of promiscuity, varies considerably. Those who have many sexual partners are both more likely to acquire and to transmit infection and play a key role in the persistence of such infections in the community of sexually active individuals. People with many sexual partners are therefore an obvious target for treatment and education about safer sex practices (e.g. condom use, etc.)

Various host factors influence the risk of acquiring an STI

It is not surprising that the type of sexual activity is important or that genital lesions or ulcers increase the risk of acquiring infections such as HIV. Other factors are less well understood, such as the numerous observations that uncircumcised men have a higher risk of infection.

STIs do not necessarily occur singly, and the possibility of multiple infections must always be borne in mind. For instance, syphilis can accompany gonorrhoea, and there is evidence that genital herpes may be reactivated during an attack of gonorrhoea.

SYPHILIS

Syphilis is caused by the spirochete *Treponema pallidum*

Treponema pallidum is closely related to the treponemes that cause the non-venereal infections of pinta and yaws (Table 21.3; Fig. 21.1). *T. pallidum* has a worldwide distribution, and syphilis remains a serious problem not only in resource-rich countries but especially in resource-poor areas, due to the serious sequelae and the risk of congenital infection. Although syphilis rates in the USA fell to an all-time

Table 21.1 The most common sexually transmitted infections (STIs)

Organism	Disease	Comment	Treatment
Papillomaviruses (types 6, 11, 16 and 18)	Genetic warts, dysplasias	Vaccines available	Podophyllin, cryotherapy
Chlamydia trachomatis	D-K serotypes (non-specific urethritis); L serotypes (lymphogranuloma venereum)	Most common STD in the U.S.; urethritis very common; lymphogranuloma venereum primarily in resource poor countries	Azithromycin, doxycycline
Candida albicans	Vaginal thrush	Predisposing factors	Nystatin, fluconazole
Trichomonas vaginalis	Vaginitis, urethritis	Often asymptomatic; causes ca. 50% of curable vaginal infections worldwide	Metronidazole
Herpes simplex virus types 1 and 2	Genital herpes	Problem of latency and reactivation	Acyclovir, valacyclovir, famciclovir
Neisseria gonorrhoeae	Gonorrhoea	2nd most common STD in the U.S.; incidence under reported; quinolone resistance common	Cephalosporin (e.g., ceftriaxone)
HIV	AIDS	Worldwide problem	Antiretrovirals (e.g., AZT)
Treponema pallidum	Syphilis	Decreasing incidence in resource-rich countries	Penicillin
Hepatitis B virus	Hepatitis	Vaccine available	Lamivudine, tenofovir, interferon alpha
Haemophilus ducreyi	Chancroid	Mainly tropical	Azithromycin, ceftriaxone
Sarcoptes scabiei	Genital scabies	Human mite burrows into upper skin layer	Permethrin cream
Phthirus pubis	Pubic lice	#1 louse infestation in US adults	Permethrin cream

Table 21.2 Strategies adopted by sexually transmitted microorganisms to combat host defences

Host defences	Microbial strategies	Examples
Integrity of mucosal surface	Specific attachment mechanism	Gonococcus or chlamydia to urethral epithelium
Urine flow (for urethral infection)	Specific attachment; induce own uptake and transport across urethral epithelial surface in phagocytic vacuole	Gonococcus
	Infection of urethral epithelial or subepithelial cells	Herpes simplex virus (HSV), chlamydia
Phagocytes (especially polymorphs)	Induce negligible inflammation	Treponema pallidum, mechanism unclear, perhaps poorly activates alternative complement pathway due to sialic acid coating
	Resist phagocytosis	Gonococcus (capsule) T. pallidum (absorbed fibronectin)
Complement	C3d receptor on microbe binds C3b/d and reduces C3b/d-mediated polymorph phagocytosis	Candida albicans
Inflammation	Induce strong inflammatory response, yet evade consequences	Gonococcus, C. albicans, HSV, chlamydia
Antibodies (especially IgA)	Produce IgA protease	Gonococcus
Cell-mediated immune response (T cells, lymphokines, natural killer cells, etc.)	Antigenic variation; allows re-infection of a given individual with an antigenic variant	Gonococcus, chlamydia
	Poorly understood factors cause ineffective cell-mediated immune response	T. pallidum, HIV

Table 21.3 Spiral organisms of medical importance

Family	Genus	Species	Subspecies	Disease
Spirochaetaceae	*Treponema*	*Pallidum* *Pallidum* *Carateum*	*Pallidum* *Pertenue*	Syphilis Yaws Pinta
	Borrelia	*Recurrentis* *Burgdorferi*		Relapsing fever Lyme disease
Leptospiraceae	*Leptospira*	*Interrogans*	(Serovar) *Icterohaemorrhagiae*	Leptospirosis (Weil's disease)

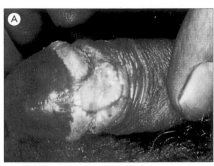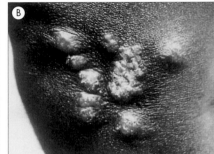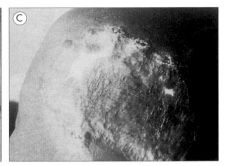

Figure 21.1 (A) Typical penile chancre of primary syphilis. (Courtesy of R.D. Catterall.) (B) Yaws and (C) pinta are endemic in tropical and subtropical countries and are spread by direct contact. (Courtesy of P.J. Cooper and G. Griffin.)

low in 2000, the incidence has since increased with a 70% greater risk in men during the past 5 years. A similar trend has also been seen in the UK.

T. pallidum enters the body through minute abrasions on the skin or mucous membranes. Transmission of *T. pallidum* requires close personal contact because the organism does not survive well outside the body and is very sensitive to drying, heat and disinfectants. Horizontal spread (see Ch. 13) occurs through sexual contact, and vertical spread via transplacental infection of the fetus (see Ch. 23).

Local multiplication leads to plasma cell, polymorph and macrophage infiltration, with later endarteritis. The bacteria multiply very slowly, and the average incubation period is 3 weeks.

Classically, *T. pallidum* infection is divided into three stages

The three classical stages of syphilis are primary, secondary and tertiary syphilis (Table 21.4). However, not all patients go through all three stages; a substantial proportion remains permanently free of disease after suffering the primary or secondary stages of infection. The lesion of primary syphilis is illustrated in Figure 21.1. The secondary stage may be followed by a latent period of some 3–30 years, after which the disease may recur – the tertiary stage. Unlike most bacterial pathogens, *T. pallidum* can survive in the body for many years despite a vigorous immune response. It has been suggested that the healthy treponeme evades recognition and elimination by the host by maintaining a cell surface rich in lipid. This layer is antigenically unreactive and the antigens are only uncovered in dead and dying organisms when the host is then able to respond. Tissue damage is mostly due to the host response.

Despite many years of effort, *T. pallidum* still cannot be cultivated in the laboratory in artificial media. It has therefore been difficult to study possible virulence factors at a molecular level, although a variety of genes have been cloned, the entire chromosome has been sequenced, and major proteins have been characterized.

An infected woman can transmit *T. pallidum* to her baby in utero

Congenital syphilis is acquired after the first 3 months of pregnancy. The disease may manifest as:

- serious infection resulting in intrauterine death
- congenital abnormalities, which may be obvious at birth
- silent infection, which may not be apparent until about 2 years of age (facial and tooth deformities).

Laboratory diagnosis of syphilis

As *T. pallidum* cannot be grown in vitro, laboratory diagnosis hinges on microscopy and serology.

Microscopy

Exudate from the primary chancre should be examined by either:

- dark-field microscopy immediately after collection
- ultraviolet (UV) microscopy after staining with fluorescein-labelled antitreponemal antibodies.

The organisms have tightly wound, slender coils with pointed ends and are sluggishly motile in unstained preparations. *T. pallidum* is very thin (about 0.2 mm in diameter, compared with *E. coli*, which is about 1 mm) and cannot be seen in Gram-stained preparations. Silver impregnation stains can be used to demonstrate the organisms in biopsy material.

Serology

Serologic tests for syphilis are the mainstay of diagnosis. They are divided into non-specific and specific tests for the detection of antibodies in patients' serum.

Table 21.4 The pathogenesis of syphilis

Stage of disease	Signs and symptoms	Pathogenesis
Initial contact ↓ 2–10 weeks (depends on inoculum size)	Primary chancre[a] at site of infection	Multiplication of treponemas at site of infection; associated host response
Primary syphilis ↓ 1–3 months	Enlarged inguinal nodes, spontaneous healing	Proliferation of treponemas in regional lymph nodes
Secondary syphilis ↓ 2–6 weeks	Flu-like illness; myalgia, headache, fever; mucocutaneous rash[a]; spontaneous resolution	Multiplication and production of lesion in lymph nodes, liver, joints, muscles, skin and mucous membranes
Latent syphilis ┊ 3–30 years		Treponemas dormant in liver or spleen Re-awakening and multiplication of treponemas
Tertiary syphilis	Neurosyphilis; general paralysis of the insane, tabes dorsalis Cardiovascular syphilis; aortic lesions, heart failure Progressive destructive disease	Further dissemination and invasion and host response (cell-mediated hypersensitivity) Gummas in skin, bones, testis

A feature of *Treponema pallidum* infection is its chronic nature, which seems to involve a delicately balanced relationship between pathogen and host.
[a]Chancre: Initially a papule; forms a painless ulcer; heals without treatment within 2 months. Live treponemas can be seen in dark-ground microscopy of fluid from lesions; patient highly infectious.

Non-specific tests (non-treponemal tests) for syphilis are the VDRL and RPR tests

The term non-specific is used because the antigens are not treponemal in origin, but are from extracts of normal mammalian tissues. Cardiolipin, from beef heart, allows the detection of anti-lipid IgG and IgM formed in the patient in response to lipoidal material released from cells damaged by the infection, as well as to lipids in the surface of *T. pallidum*. The two tests in common use today are:

- the Venereal Disease Research Laboratory (VDRL) test
- the rapid plasma reagin (RPR) test.

Both are available in kit form.

Non-specific tests show up as positive within 4–6 weeks of infection (or 1–2 weeks after the primary chancre appears) and decline in positivity in tertiary syphilis or after effective antibiotic treatment of primary or secondary disease. Therefore, these tests are useful for screening. However, they are non-specific and may give positive results in conditions other than syphilis (biologic false positives, Table 21.5). All positive results should therefore be confirmed by a specific test. However, treatment (e.g. especially during the primary and secondary stages) tends to result in seroreversion to these tests. Thus, with confirmed disease (see below), these tests can provide at least an indication of therapeutic efficacy.

Table 21.5 Serologic tests for syphilis and conditions associated with false-positive results

Test	Conditions associated with false-positive results
Non-specific (non-treponemal) VDRL RPR	Viral infection, collagen vascular disease, acute febrile disease, post-immunization, pregnancy. leprosy, malaria, drug misuse
Specific (non-treponemal) FTA-ABS TP-PA TPHA	Diseases associated with increased or abnormal globulins, lupus erythematosus, Lyme disease, autoimmune disease, diabetes mellitus, alcoholic cirrhosis, viral infections, drug misuse, and pregnancy

FTA-ABS, fluorescent treponemal antibody absorption test; MHA-TP, microhaemagglutination assay for *T. pallidum*; RPR, rapid plasma reagin test; TPHA, *T. pallidum* haemagglutination test; TP-PA, *T. pallidum* particle agglutination test; VDRL, Venereal Disease Research Laboratory test.

Commonly used specific tests for syphilis are the treponemal antibody test, FTA-ABS test and the MHA-TP

These tests use recombinant proteins or treponemal antigens extracted from *T. pallidum*. Tests in common use include:

- enzyme-linked immunosorbent assays which detect IgM and IgG
- the fluorescent treponemal antibody absorption (FTA-ABS, Fig. 21.2) test in which the patient's serum is first absorbed with non-pathogenic treponemes to remove cross-reacting antibodies before reaction with *T. pallidum* antigens
- the microhaemagglutination assay for *T. pallidum* (MHA-TP).

These tests should be used to confirm that a positive result with a non-specific test is truly due to syphilis. Also, because they become positive earlier in the course of the disease, they can be used for confirmation when the clinical picture is strongly indicative of syphilis. They tend to remain positive for many years and may be the only positive test in patients with late syphilis. However, they remain positive after appropriate antibiotic treatment and cannot therefore be used as indicators of therapeutic response. They can also give false-positive reactions (see Table 21.5).

Confirmation of a diagnosis of syphilis depends upon several serologic tests

Positive serologic test results for babies born to infected mothers may represent passive transfer of maternal antibody or the baby's own response to infection. These two possibilities can be distinguished by testing for IgM and retesting at 6 months of age, by which time maternal antibody levels have waned. Antibody titres remain elevated in babies with congenital syphilis.

At present, several serologic tests are needed to confirm a diagnosis of syphilis. None of these tests distinguishes syphilis from the non-sexually transmitted treponematoses, yaws and pinta. Western blot assays using whole *T. pallidum* cells as antigen are an important newer confirmatory test.

Treatment

Penicillin is the drug of choice for treating people with syphilis and their contacts

Penicillin is very active against *T. pallidum* (see Table 21.1). For patients who are allergic to penicillin, treatment with doxycycline should be given. Only penicillin therapy reliably treats the fetus when administered to a pregnant mother.

Prevention of secondary and tertiary disease depends upon early diagnosis and adequate treatment. Contact tracing with screening and treatment is also important. Several STIs may be present in one patient concurrently, and patients with other STIs should be screened for syphilis.

Congenital syphilis is completely preventable if women are screened serologically early in pregnancy (<3 months) and those who are positive are treated with penicillin.

GONORRHOEA

Gonorrhoea is caused by the Gram-negative coccus *Neisseria gonorrhoeae* (the 'gonococcus')

This bacterium is a human pathogen and does not cause natural infection in other animals. Therefore its reservoir is human and transmission is direct, usually through sexual contact, from person to person. The organism is sensitive to drying and does not survive well outside the human host, so intimate contact is required for transmission. It is thought that a woman has a 50% chance of becoming infected after a single sexual intercourse with an infected man, while a man has a 20% chance of acquiring infection from an infected woman.

Asymptomatically infected individuals (almost always women, see below) form the major reservoir of infection. Infection may also be transmitted vertically from an infected mother to her baby during childbirth. Infection in babies is usually manifest as ophthalmia neonatorum (see Ch. 23).

The gonococcus has special mechanisms to attach itself to mucosal cells

The usual site of entry of gonococci into the body is via the vagina or the urethral mucosa of the penis, but other sexual practices may result in the deposition of organisms in the throat or on the rectal mucosa. Special adhesive mechanisms (Fig. 21.3) prevent the bacteria from being washed away by urine or vaginal discharges. Following attachment, the gonococci rapidly multiply and spread through the cervix in women, and up the urethra in men. Spread is facilitated by various virulence factors (Fig. 21.3), although the organisms do not possess flagella and are non-motile. Production of an IgA protease helps to protect them from the host's secretory antibodies.

Host damage in gonorrhoea results from gonococcal-induced inflammatory responses

The gonococci invade non-ciliated epithelial cells, which internalize the bacteria and allow them to multiply within intracellular vacuoles, protected from phagocytes and antibodies. These vacuoles move down through the cell and fuse with the basement membrane, discharging their bacterial contents into the subepithelial connective tissues. *Neisseria gonorrhoeae* does not produce a recognized exotoxin. Damage to the host results from inflammatory responses elicited by the organism (e.g. lipopolysaccharide and other cell wall components; see Ch. 2). Persistent untreated infection can result in chronic inflammation and fibrosis.

Infection is usually localized, but in some cases bacteria isolates (e.g. resistant to the bactericidal action of serum, etc.) can invade the bloodstream and so spread to other parts of the body.

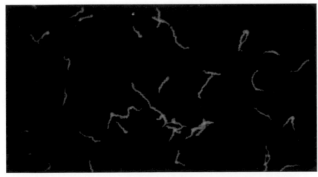

Figure 21.2 The fluorescent treponemal antibody absorption test for syphilis. Antibody in the patient's serum binds to bacteria and is visualized by a fluorescent dye.

virulence factors

peptidoglycan

pilus aids attachment to human mucosal epithelium; contains constant and hypervariable regions—analogous to immunoglobulins (Igs)— that contribute to antigenic diversity in gonococci

Por proteins form pores through outer membrane; antigenic; specific serotypes associated with virulence

Opa proteins assist binding to epithelial cells

LOS lipooligosaccharide (endotoxin activity)

cytoplasmic membrane

Rmp proteins inhibit 'cidal' activity of serum

IgA protease core contains enzyme; released by cell to destroy IgA1

capsule resists phagocytosis, unless antibody present

Figure 21.3 The spread of *Neisseria gonorrhoeae* is facilitated by various virulence factors. Changes in the surface structure of the gonococcus render the organism avirulent.

Gonorrhoea is initially asymptomatic in many women, but can later cause infertility

Symptoms develop within 2–7 days of infection and are characterized:

- in the male by urethral discharge (Fig. 21.4) and pain on passing urine (dysuria)
- in the female by vaginal discharge.

At least 50% of all infected women have only mild symptoms or are completely asymptomatic. They do not therefore seek treatment and will continue to infect others. Asymptomatic infection, however, is not the usual course of events in men. Women may not be alerted to their infection unless or until complications arise, such as:

- pelvic inflammatory disease (PID)
- chronic pelvic pain
- infertility resulting from damage to the fallopian tubes.

Ophthalmia neonatorum is characterized by a sticky discharge (see Fig. 23.5).

Gonococcal infection of the throat may result in a sore throat (see Ch. 18), and infection of the rectum also results in a purulent discharge.

In men, local complications of urethral infection are rare (Fig. 21.5). Invasive gonococcal disease is much more common in infected women than in men, but prompt treatment is important in containing local infection. The common occurrence of asymptomatic infection in women is an important factor in the occurrence of complications (i.e. the infection is

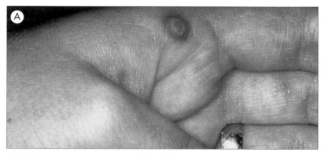

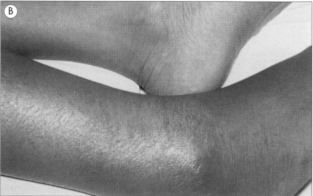

Figure 21.5 Local and systemic complications of gonococcal infection. (A) Skin lesions start as erythematous papules, which often become pustular and haemorrhagic with necrotic centres. (Courtesy of J.S. Bingham.) (B) Septic arthritis of the ankle with marked erythema and swelling of the ankle and leg. (Courtesy of T.F. Sellers, Jr.)

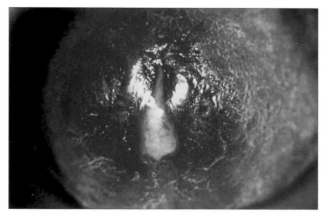

Figure 21.4 Gonococcal urethritis. Typical purulent meatal discharge with inflammation of the glans. (Courtesy of J. Clay.)

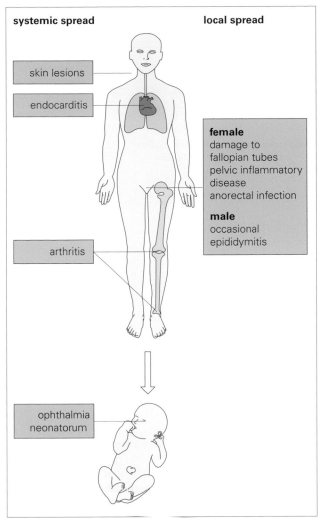

systemic spread

skin lesions

endocarditis

arthritis

ophthalmia neonatorum

local spread

female
damage to
fallopian tubes
pelvic inflammatory
disease
anorectal infection

male
occasional
epididymitis

Figure 21.6 Local and systemic spread of gonococcal infection and complications.

unrecognized and untreated). In 10–20% of untreated women, infection spreads up the genital tract to cause pelvic inflammatory disease (PID) and damage to the fallopian tubes.

Disseminated infection occurs in 1–3% of women, but is less common in men (see above and Fig. 21.6). It is a function not only of the strain of gonococcus (see above), but also host factors (e.g. about 5% of people with disseminated infection have deficiencies in the late-acting components of complement (C5–C8)).

A diagnosis of gonorrhoea is made from microscopy and culture of appropriate specimens

Urethral and vaginal discharges and other specimens where indicated are used for microscopy and culture. Although a purulent discharge is characteristic of local gonococcal infection, it is not possible to distinguish reliably between gonococcal discharge and that caused by other pathogens such as *Chlamydia trachomatis* on clinical examination.

With experience, the finding of Gram-negative intracellular diplococci in a smear of urethral discharge from a symptomatic male patient is a highly sensitive and specific test for the diagnosis of gonorrhoea.

Culture is essential in the investigation of infection in women and asymptomatic men, and for specimens taken from sites other than the urethra. Specimens from symptomatic men should also be cultured:

- to confirm the identity of the isolate; misinterpretation of microscopy or culture results can cause severe distress and may result in litigation
- to perform antibiotic susceptibility tests (see Ch. 32)
- to aid in the distinction between treatment failure and reinfection.

Because of the organism's sensitivity to drying, cultures should be made on warmed selective (i.e. modified Thayer Martin) and non-selective (chocolate blood agar) medium to insure recovery. Inoculation into appropriate transport medium is required if transfer to the laboratory will be delayed (no more than 48 h). Blood cultures should be collected if disseminated disease is suspected, and joint aspirates may yield positive cultures.

Serologic tests are unsatisfactory. Commercial nucleic acid-based approaches (specific probes, amplification, etc.) are now available, providing reliable results within a few hours.

Antibacterials used to treat gonorrhoea are cefixime or ceftriaxone

The antibacterial agents of choice are shown in Table 21.1. Penicillinase-producing *N. gonorrhoeae* were first observed in 1976 with increasing resistance that has severely compromised the effective treatment of gonorrhoea in many parts of the world, especially SE Asia. Resistance to fluoroquinolones has also occurred. Since patients with gonorrhoea may also be infected with chlamydia (see below), treatment regimens often include a combination of agents targeting both organisms (e.g. ceftriaxone and doxycycline, respectively). Early treatment of a significant proportion of sexually promiscuous patients achieves a striking reduction in the duration of infectiousness and transmission rates. Prophylactic use of antibacterials has no effect in preventing sexually-acquired gonorrhoea, but the application of antibacterial eye drops to babies born to mothers with gonorrhoea or suspected gonorrhoea is effective. Infection can be prevented by the use of condoms.

Follow-up of patients and contact tracing are vital to control the spread of gonorrhoea. At present, effective vaccines are not available, but the possibility of using some of the pilus proteins or other outer membrane components of the gonococcal cell as antigens has been under investigation. However, immunization may prevent symptomatic disease without preventing infection, and the dangers of asymptomatic infection have been discussed above.

Repeated infections can occur with strains of bacteria with different pilin proteins (e.g. antigenic variation; see Ch. 16).

CHLAMYDIAL INFECTION

C. trachomatis serotypes D–K cause sexually transmitted genital infections

The chlamydiae are very small bacteria that are obligate intracellular parasites. They have a more complicated life cycle than free-living bacteria because they can exist in different forms:

- The elementary body (EB) is adapted for extracellular survival and for initiation of infection.
- The reticulate body (RB) is adapted for intracellular multiplication (Fig. 21.7).

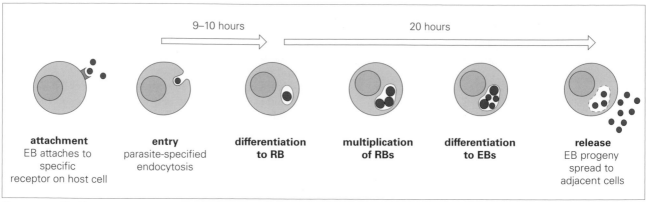

Figure 21.7 The life cycle of *Chlamydia*. EB, elementary body; RB, reticulate body.

Table 21.6 Medically important species of *Chlamydiaceae*

Species	Serotype	Natural host	Disease in humans
Chlamydia trachomatis	A, B, C D–K L1, L2, L3	Humans Humans Humans	Trachoma Cervicitis, urethritis, proctitis, conjunctivitis, pneumonia (in neonates) Lymphogranuloma venereum
Chlamydophila psittaci	Primarily A	Birds and non-human mammals	Pneumonia
Chlamydophila pneumoniae	?	Humans	Acute respiratory disease

Chlamydia trachomatis is the species associated with sexually transmitted disease.

Traditionally, three species of Chlamydia were recognized: *C. trachomatis*, *C. psittaci* and *C. pneumoniae*. However, the latter two have been moved to the genus, *Chlamydophila* (Table 21.6). *Chlamydophila psittaci* and *Chlamydophila pneumoniae* infect the respiratory tract and have been discussed in Chapter 19. The species *Chlamydia trachomatis* can be subdivided into different serotypes (also known as serovars) and these have been shown to be linked characteristically with different infections:

- Serotypes A, B and C are the causes of the serious eye infection trachoma (see Ch. 25).
- Serotypes D–K are the cause of genital infection and associated ocular and respiratory infections (Table 21.7).
- Serotypes L1, L2 and L3 cause the systemic disease lymphogranuloma venereum (LGV) (see below).

Table 21.7 Clinical syndromes and complications caused by *C. trachomatis*, serotypes D–K

Infection in	Clinical syndromes	Complications
Men	Urethritis, epididymitis, proctitis, conjunctivitis	Systemic spread, Reiter's syndrome[a]
Women	Urethritis, cervicitis, bartholinitis, salpingitis, conjunctivitis	Ectopic pregnancy, infertility, systemic spread: perihepatitis arthritis dermatitis
Neonates	Conjunctivitis	Interstitial pneumonitis

[a]Urethritis, conjunctivitis, polyarthritis, mucocutaneous lesions.

C. trachomatis serotypes D–K have a worldwide distribution, whereas the distribution of LGV serotypes is more restricted.

The majority of infections are genital and are acquired during sexual intercourse. Asymptomatic infection is common, especially in women. Ocular infections in adults are probably acquired by autoinoculation from infected genitalia or by ocular–genital contact. Ocular infections in neonates are acquired during passage through an infected maternal birth canal, and the infant is also at risk of developing *C. trachomatis* pneumonia (see Ch. 19).

Chlamydiae enter the host through minute abrasions in the mucosal surface

They bind to specific receptors on the host cells and enter the cells by 'parasite-induced' endocytosis (see Ch. 13). Once inside the cell, fusion of the chlamydia-containing vesicle with lysosomes is inhibited by an incompletely understood mechanism and the EB begins its developmental cycle (Fig. 21.7). Within 9–10 h of cell invasion, the EBs differentiate into metabolically active RBs, which divide by binary fission and produce fresh EB progeny. These are then released into the extracellular environment within a further 20 h.

The clinical effects of *C. trachomatis* infection appear to result from cell destruction and the host's inflammatory response

The released EBs invade adjacent cells or cells distant from the site of infection if carried in lymph or blood.

Growth of *C. trachomatis* serotypes D–K seems to be restricted to columnar and transitional epithelial cells, but serotypes L1, L2 and L3 cause systemic disease (LGV). The site of infection determines the nature of clinical disease (see Table 21.7). Genital tract infection with serotypes D–K is locally asymptomatic in most women, but usually symptomatic in men.

Laboratory tests are essential to diagnose chlamydial urethritis and cervicitis

Chlamydial urethritis and cervicitis cannot be reliably distinguished from other causes of these conditions on clinical grounds alone. The methods traditionally available include cell culture and direct antigen detection.

Most infected patients develop antibodies, but serology is unreliable for diagnostic purposes. As chlamydiae are obligate intracellular parasites, traditional identification by isolation must be performed by growth in cell cultures. When this approach is available, the specimen is suspended in fluid and centrifuged on to a monolayer of tissue culture (McCoy) cells pretreated with cycloheximide, which enhances the uptake of chlamydiae. After 48–72 h, *C. trachomatis* forms characteristic cytoplasmic inclusions, which stain with iodine because they contain glycogen (Fig. 21.8) or can be visualized with immunofluorescent stains.

C. trachomatis can be detected directly on microscopy using the direct fluorescent antibody test

C. trachomatis can be detected directly in smears of clinical specimens made on microscope slides stained with fluorescein conjugated monoclonal antibodies and viewed by UV microscopy – the direct fluorescent antibody (DFA) test. The EBs stain as bright yellow-green dots (Fig. 21.9). Results can be obtained within a few hours. Compared with culture, this method is extremely specific, but often not sensitive enough for asymptomatic infections. Chlamydial antigens can also be detected in specimens using an enzyme-linked immunosorbent assay (ELISA), but this test also suffers from reduced sensitivity in asymptomatic patients.

A variety of nucleic acid-based tests are commercially available for chlamydial detection

Nucleic acid probe and amplification-based tests are capable of directly detecting *C. trachomatis* in specimens from infected individuals (e.g. cervix, urethra, urine, etc.). As mentioned previously, these commercially available kits can provide rapid (2–4 h) and specific detection of both *N. gonorrhoeae* and *Chlamydia* DNA, which is important since patients are often co-infected with both organisms. These quick and

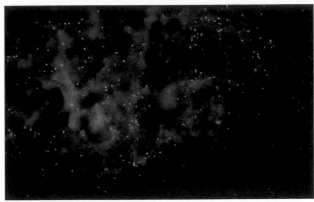

Figure 21.9 Direct fluorescent antibody test for *Chlamydia trachomatis*. Elementary bodies can be seen as bright yellow-green dots under the ultraviolet microscope. (Courtesy of J.D. Treharne.)

accurate molecular approaches are increasingly used as the preferred test for the detection of these organisms.

Chlamydial infection is treated or prevented with doxycycline or azithromycin

It is important to remember that chlamydiae are not susceptible to the beta-lactam antibiotics, which are important for the treatment of gonorrhoea and syphilis. It is recommended that patients receiving treatment for gonorrhoea also be treated with doxycycline or azithromycin for possible concurrent chlamydial infection (see Table 21.1). In addition, patients with clinically diagnosed chlamydial genital infections, their sexual contacts and babies born to infected mothers should be treated. Erythromycin should be used for babies.

Prevention depends upon recognizing the importance of asymptomatic infections. Early diagnosis and treatment of cases and of their sexual partners is important in order to avoid complications and reduce opportunities for transmission. Remember that STIs are not mutually exclusive, and patients may have concurrent infections with quite different pathogens.

OTHER CAUSES OF INGUINAL LYMPHADENOPATHY

Genital infections are common causes of inguinal lymphadenopathy (swelling of lymph nodes in the groin) among sexually active people. Syphilis and gonorrhoea have been discussed above. Lymphogranuloma venereum (LGV), chancroid and donovanosis are more common in tropical and subtropical countries than in Europe and the USA but may be imported by travellers who have acquired the disease through sexual contact in these areas.

Lymphogranuloma venereum (LGV)

Lymphogranuloma venereum is caused by *C. trachomatis* serotypes L1, L2 and L3

Lymphogranuloma venereum (LGV) is a serious disease especially common in Africa, Asia and South America. It occurs sporadically in Europe, Australia and North America, particularly among homosexual males. The prevalence

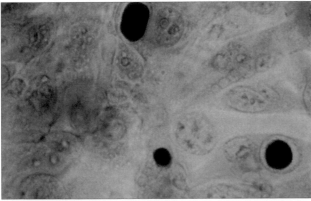

Figure 21.8 Chlamydial inclusion bodies stained dark brown with iodine.

appears to be higher among males than females, probably because symptomatic infection is more common in men.

Lymphogranuloma venereum is a systemic infection involving lymphoid tissue and is treated with doxycycline or erythromycin

The clinical picture can be contrasted with the more restricted infection seen with *C. trachomatis* serotypes D–K (see above). The primary lesion is an ulcerating papule at the site of inoculation (after an incubation period of 1–4 weeks) and may be accompanied by fever, headache and myalgia. The lesion heals rapidly, but the chlamydiae proceed to infect the draining lymph nodes, causing characteristic inguinal buboes (Fig. 21.10), which gradually enlarge. Chlamydiae may disseminate from the lymph nodes via the lymphatics to the tissues of the rectum to cause proctitis. Other systemic complications include fever, hepatitis, pneumonitis and meningoencephalitis. The infection may resolve untreated, but:

- Abscesses may form in lymph nodes, which suppurate and discharge through the skin.
- Chronic granulomatous reactions in lymphatics and neighbouring tissues can eventually give rise to fistula in ano or genital elephantiasis.

Cell culture methods are available (see above), but the chlamydial isolation rate is reported to be low (24–30%). Historically, the 'Frei' skin test was used in diagnosis involving intradermal injection of the LGV antigen. However, the test is no longer used due to a lack of reliability and sensitivity in early disease and it lacks specificity because the Frei antigen is only genus specific. As discussed above, nucleic acid-based tests are also available. Treatment with doxycycline or erythromycin (see Table 21.1) is recommended. Pregnant women and children under 9 years of age should be treated with erythromycin.

Chancroid (soft chancre)

Chancroid is caused by *Haemophilus ducreyi* and is characterized by painful genital ulcers

Infection by the Gram-negative bacterium *Haemophilus ducreyi* is manifest as painful non-indurated genital ulcers and local lymphadenitis (Fig. 21.11). Note the difference between this and the chancre of primary syphilis, which is painless, but the ulcers may be confused with those of

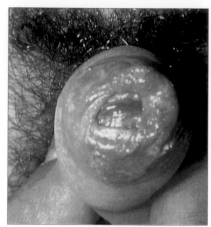

Figure 21.11 Chancroid. Several irregular ulcers on the prepuce. (Courtesy of L. Parish.)

genital herpes, though they are usually larger and have a more ragged appearance. While the disease is endemic in some areas of the USA, cases generally tend to occur in distinct outbreaks. However, in Africa and Asia chancroid is the commonest cause of genital ulcers. Epidemiologic information is important because the diagnosis is usually clinical as the organism is difficult to grow in the laboratory. Chancroid may also be confused with donovanosis (see below).

Chancroid is diagnosed by microscopy and culture and treated with azithromycin, ceftriaxone, erythromycin or ciprofloxacin

Gram-stained smears of aspirates from the ulcer margin or enlarged lymph node characteristically show large numbers of short Gram-negative rods and chains, often described as having a 'school of fish' appearance, within or outside polymorphs. Aspirates should be cultured on a rich medium (GC agar with 1–2% haemoglobin, 5% fetal bovine serum, 10% CVA and vancomycin, 3 μg/mL) at 33°C in 5–10% carbon dioxide. *H. ducreyi* will not tolerate higher temperatures. Growth is slow, and it may take 2–9 days for colonies to appear. Treatment with a macrolide (e.g. erythromycin or azithromycin) or ceftriaxone (see Table 21.1) is generally recommended.

Donovanosis

Donovanosis is caused by *Calymmatobacterium granulomatis* and is characterized by genital nodules and ulcers

Donovanosis (granuloma inguinale or granuloma venereum) is rare in temperate climates, but common in tropical and subtropical regions such as the Caribbean, New Guinea, India and central Australia. The infection is characterized by nodules, almost always on the genitalia, which erode to form granulomatous ulcers that bleed readily on contact. The infection may extend and the ulcers may become secondarily infected. The pathogen is a Gram-negative rod, traditionally called *Calymmatobacterium granulomatis*. However, genomic analysis has placed this organism into the genus *Klebsiella* (i.e. *Klebsiella granulomatis*); however, some literature continues to use the *C. granulomatis*

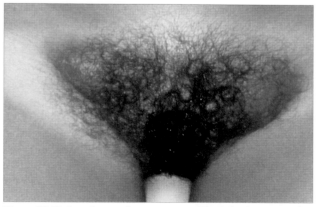

Figure 21.10 Lymphogranuloma venereum. Bilateral enlargement of inguinal glands. (Courtesy of J.S. Bingham.)

designation. The bacteria invade and multiply within mononuclear cells and are liberated when the cells rupture.

Donovanosis is diagnosed by microscopy and treated with doxycycline

The diagnosis of donovanosis is made by examining a smear from the lesion stained with Wright's or Giemsa stain. 'Donovan bodies' appear as clusters of blue- or black-stained organisms in the cytoplasm of mononuclear cells. Treatment with doxycycline, azithromycin or co-trimoxazole is recommended.

MYCOPLASMAS AND NON-GONOCOCCAL URETHRITIS

Mycoplasma hominis, M. genitalium, and *Ureaplasma urealyticum* may be causes of genital tract infection

Although *Mycoplasma pneumoniae* has a proven role in the causation of pneumonia (see Ch. 19), the role of *M. hominis, M. genitalium* and *Ureaplasma urealyticum* (which metabolizes urea; also called 'T strains') in STIs is less certain. These organisms frequently colonize the genital tracts of healthy sexually active men and women. They are less common in sexually inactive populations, which supports the view that they may be sexually transmitted. It is difficult to prove that they cause infection of the genital tract, but *M. genitalium* may cause non-gonococcal urethritis, *M. hominis* may cause PID, postabortal and postpartum fevers, and pyelonephritis. *U. urealyticum* has also been associated with non-gonococcal urethritis and prostatitis.

M. hominis, M. genitalium, and *U. urealyticum* are treated with either doxycycline or azithromycin (some Ureaplasmas are tetracycline resistant) which is also the treatment for chlamydial infections.

OTHER CAUSES OF VAGINITIS AND URETHRITIS

Candida infection

Candida albicans causes a range of genital tract diseases, which are treated with oral or topical antifungals

These vary from mild superficial, localized infections in an otherwise healthy individual to disseminated, often fatal infections in the immunocompromised. This yeast is a normal inhabitant of the female vagina, but in some women and in circumstances which are not clearly understood, the candidal load increases and causes an intensely irritant vaginitis with a cheesy vaginal discharge. This may be accompanied by urethritis and dysuria and may present as a urinary tract infection (see Ch. 20). The diagnosis can be confirmed by microscopy and culture of the discharge (Fig. 21.12).

Treatment with an oral antifungal such as fluconazole or a topical preparation such as nystatin is recommended, but recurrence is frequent in a small proportion of women. *Balanitis* (inflammation of the glans penis) is seen in approximately 10% of male partners of females with *vulvovaginal candidiasis*, but urethritis is uncommon in men and is rarely symptomatic.

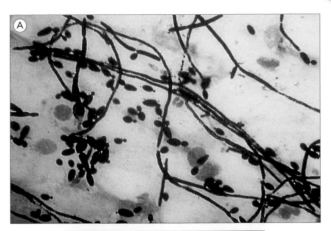

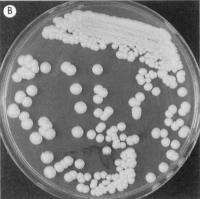

Figure 21.12 *Candida albicans.* (A) Light microscopic appearance and (B) culture of vaginal discharge.

Trichomonas infection

Trichomonas vaginalis is a protozoan parasite and causes vaginitis with copious discharge

Trichomonas vaginalis inhabits:

- the vagina in women
- the urethra (and sometimes the prostate) in men.

It is transmitted during sexual intercourse. In women, heavy infections cause vaginitis with a characteristic copious foul-smelling discharge, though the infection may be asymptomatic in some females. There is an associated increase in the vaginal pH. The infection should be distinguished from bacterial vaginosis (see below) by microscopic examination of the discharge, which shows actively motile trophozoites (Fig. 21.13). *Trichomonas* may be cultured from a vaginal

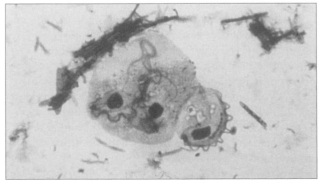

Figure 21.13 Motile trophozoites in vaginal discharge in *T. vaginalis* infection. (Giemsa stain.) (Courtesy of R. Muller.)

(not cervical) swab and nucleic acid detection can be used for diagnosis though it is not yet generally available.

Metronidazole is recommended for symptomatic *T. vaginalis* infections. Tinidazole may also be used but belongs to the same class of compounds as metronidazole, so there is a need for orally active alternative agents.

In men, *Trichomonas vaginalis* is rarely symptomatic, but sometimes causes a mild urethritis. Regular sexual partners of symptomatic women should be treated at the same time to prevent reinfection.

Bacterial vaginosis

Bacterial vaginosis is associated with *Gardnerella vaginalis* plus anaerobic infection and a fishy-smelling vaginal discharge

This non-specific vaginitis is a syndrome in women characterized by at least three of the following signs and symptoms:

- excessive malodorous vaginal discharge
- vaginal pH > 4.5
- presence of clue cells (vaginal epithelial cells coated with bacteria, Fig. 21.14)
- a fishy amine-like odour.

There is a significant increase in the numbers of *G. vaginalis* in the vaginal flora and a concomitant increase in the numbers of obligate anaerobes such as *Bacteroides*.

G. vaginalis is consistently found in association with vaginosis, but is also found in 20–40% of healthy women. It is generally present in the urethra of male partners of women with vaginosis, indicating that it can be sexually transmitted. *G. vaginalis* has also been isolated from blood cultures from women with postpartum fever.

G. vaginalis has had a chequered taxonomic history, being first classified as a haemophilus, then as a corynebacterium, reflecting the fact that it tends to be Gram-variable (sometimes appearing Gram-negative, sometimes Gram-positive). It grows in the laboratory on human blood agar in a moist atmosphere enriched with carbon dioxide. The organism is treated with oral metronidazole. Species of the genus *Mobiluncus* appear to be related to *G. vaginalis* and have also been implicated in vaginosis.

The pathogenesis of bacterial vaginosis is still unclear, but appears to be related to factors that disrupt the normal acidity of the vagina and the equilibrium between the different constituents of the normal vaginal flora. Whether any of these or other unknown factors are sexually transmissible is unclear.

GENITAL HERPES

Herpes simplex virus (HSV)-2 is the most common cause of genital herpes, but HSV-1 is being detected more frequently

Herpes simplex virus (HSV) is a ubiquitous infection of humans worldwide. HSV-1 is generally transmitted via saliva, causing primary oropharyngeal infection in children, and cold sores occur after virus reactivation. However, HSV-2 emerged as a result of independent transmission by the venereal route. HSV-2 shows biologic and antigenic differences from HSV-1 and can be distinguished by molecular typing methods as well as older techniques such as immunofluorescence. There is little cross-immunity. Although originally recovered from separate sites, orogenital sexual practices have obscured the topographic difference between the strains, so that HSV-1 and HSV-2 can be recovered from oral and genital sites. HSV-2 is one of the most common STIs and it has been estimated that there are over 500 million individuals with HSV-2 globally. In the USA, a Centers for Disease Control (CDC) survey from 2005–2008 reported that HSV-2 antibody was detected in 16% of the study population, greater among females. One of the worrying aspects surrounding HSV-2 is that most people do not know that they have an HSV-2 infection as up to 75% may not have symptoms and therefore will not realize that they may transmit this infection. Finally, HSV-2 infection can result in a twofold increased risk of developing HIV infection. This is likely to be due to breaches in the mucosal barrier as a result of the HSV ulcers.

Genital herpes is characterized by ulcerating vesicles that can take up to 2 weeks to heal

The primary genital lesion on the penis or vulva is seen 3–7 days after infection. It consists of vesicles that soon break down to form painful shallow ulcers (Fig. 21.15). Local lymph nodes are swollen, and there may be constitutional symptoms including fever, headache and malaise. Occasionally the lesions are on the urethra, causing dysuria or pain on micturition. Healing takes up to 2 weeks, but the virus in the lesion travels up sensory nerve endings to establish latent infection in dorsal root ganglion neurones (see Ch. 24). From this site it can reactivate, travel down nerves to the same area, and cause recurrent lesions ('genital cold sores').

Aseptic meningitis or encephalitis occurs in adults as a rare complication, and spread of infection from mother to infant at the time of delivery can give rise to neonatal disseminated herpes or encephalitis.

Genital herpes is generally diagnosed from the clinical appearance, and acyclovir can be used for treatment

Herpes simplex virus DNA can be detected in vesicle fluid or ulcer swabs. More classic techniques involved virus isolation and subsequently typing the isolate by immunofluorescence using type-specific monoclonal antibodies. Recurrent genital infection is more frequent with HSV-2; therefore typing is of help in determining the prognosis.

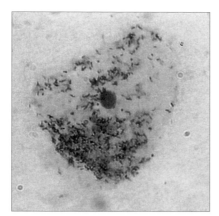

Figure 21.14 Clue cells in bacterial vaginosis.

Figure 21.15 Genital herpes. Vesicles (A) on the penis and (B) in the perianal area and vulva. Those on the labia minora and fourchette have ruptured to reveal characteristic herpetic erosions. (Courtesy of J.S. Bingham.)

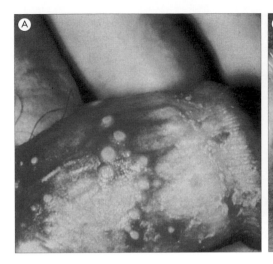

The cytopathic effect is characteristic and is generally seen within 1–2 days post-inoculation, with ballooning degenerating cells and multinucleate giant cells. HSV DNA detection methods which include type differentiation may be used, and have a much greater sensitivity than virus isolation. A number of antivirals, including oral acyclovir, valaciclovir and famciclovir can be used for treatment of severe or early lesions, and acyclovir may need to be given intravenously if there are systemic complications. Recurrent attacks are troublesome, and treatment options include starting an antiviral when prodromal symptoms occur or alternatively taking 6–12 months low-dose acyclovir or one of the alternative agents to stop or at least reduce the frequency of recurrences.

HUMAN PAPILLOMAVIRUS INFECTION

There are over 120 distinct types of human papillomaviruses, all infecting skin or mucosal surfaces, and the DNA of each showing less than 50% cross-hybridization with that of others. These are evidently ancient viral associates of humans that have evolved extensively, and many of the different types are adapted to specific regions of the body.

Many papillomavirus types are transmitted sexually and cause genital warts

Warts (*condylomata acuminata*) appear on the penis, vulva and perianal regions (Fig. 21.16) after an incubation period of 1–6 months (see Ch. 26). They may not regress for many months and can be treated with podophyllin. The lesion on the cervix is a flat area of dysplasia visible by colposcopy as a white plaque (Fig. 21.17) after the local application of 5% acetic acid. Because of their association with cervical cancer, especially types 16 and 18, cervical lesions are best removed by laser or loop excision.

HUMAN IMMUNODEFICIENCY VIRUS

Human immunodeficiency virus (HIV) is a retrovirus (Table 21.8), so-called because this single-stranded RNA virus contains a *pol* gene that codes for a reverse transcriptase (Latin: *retro*, backwards).

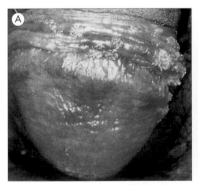
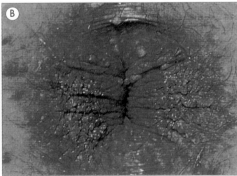
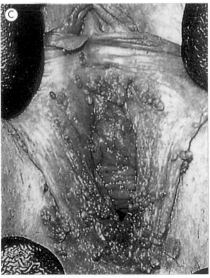

Figure 21.16 Genital warts. (A) Warts on the penis are usually multiple, and on the shaft are often flat and keratinized. (B) Warts in the perianal area often extend into the anal canal. (C) Warts in the vulvoperineal area can enlarge dramatically and extend into the vagina. (Courtesy of J.S. Bingham.)

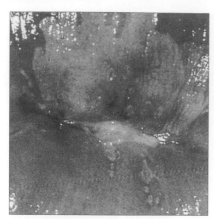

Figure 21.17 Cervical dysplasia caused by papillomavirus should be removed by laser. (Courtesy of A. Goodman.)

Acquired immune deficiency syndrome (AIDS) was first recognized in 1981 in the USA

In 1981, the Communicable Disease Center, Atlanta, USA, noted an increase in requests to use pentamidine for *Pneumocystis carinii* (now classified as *P. jirovecii*) infection in previously well individuals who also suffered severe infections by other normally harmless microorganisms. These included *C. albicans* oesophagitis, mucocutaneous HSV, toxoplasma CNS infection or pneumonia, and cryptosporidial enteritis; Kaposi's sarcoma was also often present. Patients had evidence of impaired immune function, as shown by skin test anergies, and depletion of CD4-positive T-helper (Th) lymphocytes. This immunodeficiency syndrome appearing in an individual without a known cause such as treatment with immunosuppressive drugs was referred to as 'acquired immune deficiency syndrome' (AIDS). An internationally agreed definition of AIDS soon followed. Epidemics subsequently occurred in San Francisco, New York and other cities in the USA, and in the UK and Europe a few years later.

Human immunodeficiency virus, the causative virus of AIDS, was isolated from blood lymphocytes in 1983

It was recognized as belonging to the lentivirus (slow virus) group of retroviruses and related to similar agents in monkeys and to visnavirus in sheep and goats. The structure of the viral particle and its genome are illustrated in Figure 21.18 and its replication mechanism in Figures 21.19 and 21.20.

Virus replication is regulated by at least six genes. The replication cycle is often halted after integration of the provirus so that the infection remains latent in the cell. The tat and rev genes function as transactivating factors, and can increase production of viral RNAs and proteins when latently infected cells are:

- stimulated to differentiate (e.g. Th cells by antigen)
- stimulated by infection with certain other viruses such as HSV or cytomegalovirus (CMV).

Human immunodeficiency virus infection probably started in Africa in the 1950s, and 35 million people worldwide were infected by 2009

The molecular biologic evidence (in terms of nucleic acid sequence) indicates that both HIV-1 and the closely related HIV-2 seen in West Africa probably arose from closely related primate viruses. HIV-1 is separated into three groups, namely M (main), N (new) and O (outlier). The M group comprises the HIV-1 subtypes A to J, with the N and O groups focused in western central Africa. The geographical prevalence of the subtypes differs, with subtype B being most common in North America and Europe, and the non-B strains such as A and C being found more frequently in Africa. However, with increasing travel the subtype distribution is changing and, together with the potential for mixed or superinfections, i.e. an HIV-infected individual becoming infected with another strain, and viral recombination events, other subtypes are being seen such as the circulating recombinant forms (CRF). These may be important in having different rates of disease progression.

Table 21.8 Human retroviruses

Virus	Comment
HTLV1	Endemic in West Indies and SW Japan; transmission via blood, human milk; can cause adult T-cell leukaemia, and HTLV1-associated myelopathy, also known as tropical spastic paraparesis
HTLV2	Uncommon, sporadic occurrence; transmission via blood; can cause hairy T-cell leukaemia and neurological disease
HIV-1, HIV-2	Transmission via blood, sexual intercourse; responsible for AIDS. HIV-2 West African in origin, closely related to HIV-1 but antigenically distinct
Human foamy virus	Causes foamy vacuolation in infected cells; little is known of its occurrence or pathogenic potential
Human placental virus(es)	Detected in placental tissue by electron microscopy and by presence of reverse transcriptase
Human genome viruses	Nucleic acid sequences representing endogenous retroviruses are common in the vertebrate genome, often in well-defined genetic loci; acquired during evolutionary history; not expressed as infectious virus; function unknown; perhaps should be regarded as mere parasitic DNA

Human T-cell lymphotropic virus (HTLV)1, HTLV2, HIV-1 and HIV-2 have been cultivated in human T cells in vitro. The human placental and genome viruses are not known as infectious agents. Retroviruses are also common in cats (FAIDS), monkeys (MAIDS), mice (mouse leukaemia) and other vertebrates. ARC, AIDS-related complex.

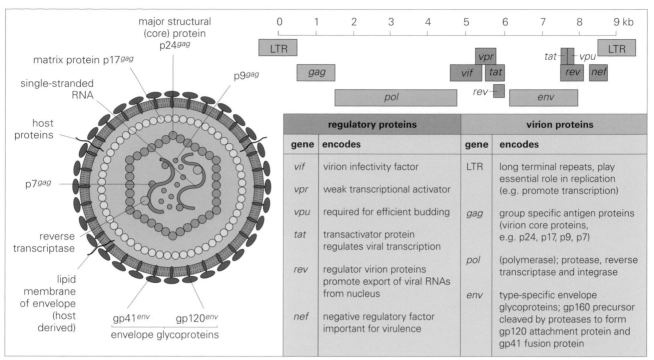

Figure 21.18 The structure and genetic map of HIV. The *rev* and *tat* genes are divided into non-contiguous pieces and the gene segments spliced together in the RNA transcript. Occasional host proteins such as major histocompatibility complex (MHC) molecules are present in the envelope. (p) is protein and (gp) is glycoprotein. About 10^9 HIV-1 particles are produced each day at the peak of infection, and this, together with the low fidelity of reverse transcriptase, means that new virus variants are always appearing. Mutations are seen especially in *env* and *nef* genes. Any one patient contains many variants, and drug resistant and immune-resistant mutants emerge. There are also macrophage-tropic and T-cell-tropic populations of virus and syncytium-inducing and non-syncytium-inducing populations, with effects on disease progression. By genetic analysis, HIV-1 strains are subdivided into group M (most HIV-1 isolates), which contains at least 10 subtypes (A–J) differing in geographic distribution, and groups N and O (African). The degree of cross-immunity between these strains is not clear.

HIV-1 may have been present in humans in central Africa for many years, but in the late 1970s it began to spread rapidly (Fig. 21.21), possibly with changed biologic properties, as a result of increased transmission following major socioeconomic upheavals and migrations of people from central to east Africa. Female prostitutes and male soldiers and workers travelling around the country played a major part. The disease soon appeared in Haiti and the USA, followed by Europe and Australasia.

In the late 1980s, HIV began to appear in Asian countries, beginning with Thailand, and by 1995 explosive spread was based on heterosexual transmission, with high infection rates in female sex workers and transmission among users of injected drugs in Asia.

Worldwide by the end of 2009, about 35 million adults and children were infected with HIV including:

- 22.5 million in sub-Saharan Africa
- 5 million in South, South-East and East Asia
- 1.4 million in Eastern Europe and Central Asia
- 1.5 million in North America
- 0.8 million in Western and Central Europe.

Nearly 3 million people were newly infected in 2009, and 1.8 million died as a result of HIV infection that year.

In 2010, the UNAIDS global report stated that there had been a stabilization in the growth of the global AIDS epidemic. HIV incidence, that is, the number of new infections, had been falling since the late 1990s as had the AIDS-related

mortality figures. It was estimated that when comparing the data from 1999 to 2009, the incidence had fallen in 2009 by 19% to 2.6 million newly infected individuals, having peaked in 1997. Over the same time period, there was a 25% fall in new HIV infections in 33 countries, 22 of which were in sub-Saharan Africa, but a 25% increase was seen in 7 other countries, including parts of North and Central Asia (source: http://www.unaids.org/globalreport/Global_report.htm).

Human immunodeficiency virus mainly infects cells bearing the CD4 cell surface antigen and also requires chemokine co-receptors

The HIV transmission route for more than 80% of adults involves mucosal surfaces, in particular cervicovaginal, penile and rectal. The remainder may be infected by intravenous or percutaneous routes. The window period for detecting the virus is 7–21 days, as HIV multiplies in the mucosa and draining lymphoreticular tissues. The first targets are CD4 receptor-bearing cells that include Th cells, Langerhans cells and other dendritic cells and microglia (Figs 21.22, 21.23). Monocyte-derived macrophages are not as good targets compared with the others. The CD4 molecule acts as a high-affinity binding site for the viral gp120 envelope glycoprotein. Productive replication and cell destruction does not occur until the Th cell is activated. Th cell activation is greatly enhanced not only in attempts to respond to HIV antigens, but also as a result of the secondary microbial infections seen

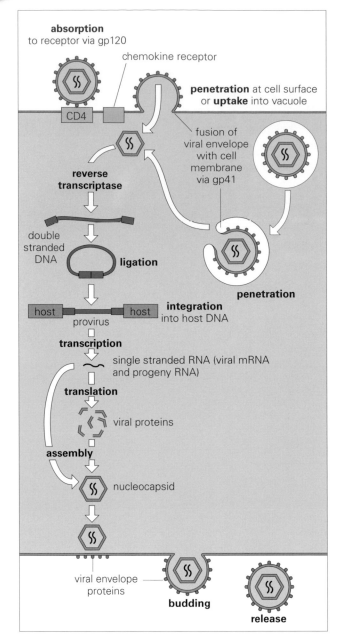

absorption
to receptor via gp120

chemokine receptor

CD4

penetration at cell surface
or **uptake** into vacuole

fusion of
viral envelope
with cell
membrane
via gp41

**reverse
transcriptase**

double
stranded
DNA

ligation

penetration

host host **integration**
into host DNA

provirus

transcription

single stranded RNA (viral mRNA
and progeny RNA)

translation

viral proteins

assembly

nucleocapsid

viral envelope
proteins

budding

release

Figure 21.19 The HIV replication cycle. The virus enters the cell either by fusion with the cell membrane at the cell surface or via uptake into a vacuole and release within the cell.

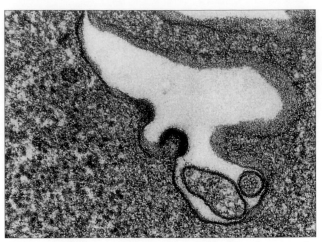

Figure 21.20 Electron micrograph showing HIV budding from the cell surface before release. (Courtesy of D. Hockley.)

using the CXCR4 alpha-chemokine receptor. Cell susceptibility to infection is therefore affected by the levels of these chemokine co-receptors; for example, their expression may be up-regulated by opportunistic infections.

Productive infection of resting CD4 T cells in the lympho-reticular system of the gastrointestinal tract occurs. These cells express integrin receptors, viral attachment molecules, as well as Th cell surface markers, and HIV-1 infection rapidly expands with a rise in HIV-1 RNA levels at the same time as the irreversible depletion of reservoirs of Th cells. A latency state is soon established with the formation of persistent lymphoid tissue viral reservoirs.

At first the immune system fights back against HIV infection, but then begins to fail

During the first few months virus-specific CD8-positive T cells are formed and reduce the viraemia which is referred to as the HIV load. This is followed by the appearance of neutralizing antibodies. Even so, up to 10^{10} infectious virus particles and up to 10^9 infected lymphocytes are produced daily. Then the immune system begins to suffer gradual damage, and the number of circulating CD4-positive T cells steadily falls and the HIV load rises. Nearly all infected CD4-positive T cells are in lymph nodes. The cell-mediated immune responses to viral antigens, as judged by lympho-proliferation, weaken, whereas responses to other antigens are normal. Perhaps the virus initially engineers a specific suppression of protective responses to itself. Eventually, the patient loses the battle to replace lost T cells, and the number falls more rapidly. Skin test delayed-type hypersensitivity (DTH) responses are absent, natural killer (NK) cell and cytotoxic T-cell (Tc) activity is reduced, and there are various other immunologic abnormalities, including polyclonal activation of B cells. Functional changes in T lymphocytes – reduced responses to mitogens, reduced interleukin 2 (IL-2) and interferon-gamma (IFNγ) production – are also seen. As AIDS develops, responses to HIV and unrelated antigens are further depressed. The immune system has lost control. Plasma HIV-1 RNA load measurements have been shown to predict clinical outcome and are used in clinical management to help determine disease stage and progression as well as antiretroviral therapy response.

in patients. Monocytes and macrophages, Langerhans cells and follicular dendritic cells also express the CD4 molecule and are infected, but are not generally destroyed, potentially acting as a reservoir for infection. Langerhans cells, for example dendritic cells in the skin and genital mucosa, may be the first cells infected. Later in the disease, there is a remarkable disruption of histologic pattern in lymphoid follicles as a result of the breakdown of follicular dendritic cells.

HIV-1 enters host cells by binding the viral gp120 to the CD4 receptor and a chemokine co-receptor on the host cell surface. The CCR5 beta-chemokine receptor is important in establishing the infection. Those people with CCR5 gene deletions are resistant to infection. On the other hand, disease progression has been associated with HIV variants

Figure 21.21 Early spread of HIV infection (now worldwide). HIV-1 may have been present in central Africa for many years before increased migration and socioeconomic upheaval caused it to begin spreading in the late 1970s. Outside Africa, most infections occurred in men.

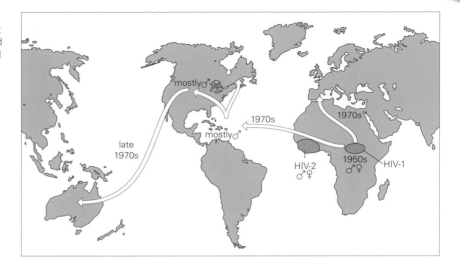

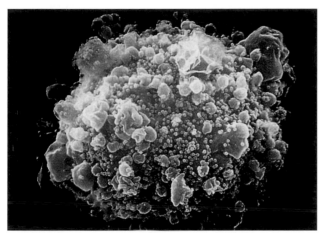

Figure 21.22 Scanning electron micrograph of an HIV-infected Th cell. (×20 000). (Courtesy of D. Hockley.)

The exact mechanism of the immunosuppression in HIV infection is still unclear

The following factors need to be considered:

- Th cells directly killed by virus
- Th cells induced to commit suicide (apoptosis, programmed cell death) by virus
- Th cells made vulnerable to immune attack by Tc cells
- T-cell replenishment impaired by damage to the thymus and lymph nodes and by infection of stem cells
- defects in antigen presentation associated with infection of dendritic cells
- immunosuppressive virus-coded molecules (gp120, gp41).

The host response is further handicapped by the high rate of viral evolution assisted by the lack of a reverse transcriptase proofreading function. The virus exists as a quasispecies, in other words the infection comprises a number of heterogeneous strains. Some of the variants show resistance to currently circulating Tcs (i.e. are immune escape variants). Others show increased pathogenicity.

Before the advent of highly active antiretroviral therapy the immunosuppression was permanent, the patient

remained infectious, the virus persisted in the body and death was due to opportunist infections and tumours.

HIV-2 appears to be transmitted less easily than HIV-1, probably because the viral load is lower, and the progression to AIDS is slower. HIV-2 is endemic in West Africa, and has spread to Portugal and parts of India.

Routes of transmission

In resource-rich countries, homosexual men have so far been the group most vulnerable to HIV infection and AIDS, especially the passive partner in anal intercourse. Infection is transmitted primarily from male to male and from male to female (Fig. 21.24), although not very efficiently compared with other STIs. Transmission from female to male, however, is a common and well-established feature of HIV in Africa and Asia. In randomly selected rural communities in parts of central and east Africa, up to 40% of the population is infected with HIV, mostly young adults.

Heterosexual transmission has not so far been as important in resource-rich as in resource-poor countries

One explanation for the greater heterosexual spread in resource-poor countries is that other STIs are more common, causing ulcers and discharges, which are sources of infected lymphocytes and monocytes. Genital ulcers are associated with a fourfold increase in the risk of infection. Also, viral strains from Asia and sub-Saharan Africa have been shown to infect Langerhans cells in genital mucosa more easily than do other strains. It is not clear whether HIV can infect males by the urethra or whether pre-existing genital skin breaks are necessary. As with other STIs, uncircumcised males are more likely to be infected.

HIV can also be transmitted vertically from infected mothers to their babies, but the infant is not infected in 55–85% of pregnancies, the upper limit being associated with avoiding breastfeeding. Overall, the infant is infected in about 20% of pregnancies in utero and intrapartum. The transmission rate peri- and postnatally is around 11–16%, the higher end of the range depending on whether the child has been breastfed for up to 24 months. In resource-rich countries, antenatal HIV screening, offering antiretroviral drugs

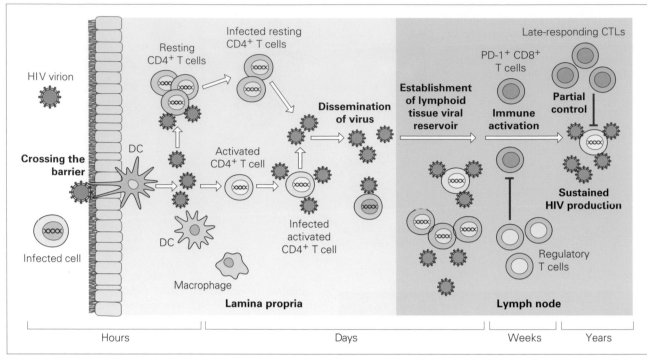

Figure 21.23 Phases of infection following exposure to human immunodeficiency virus (HIV). Infection begins with transmission across a mucosal barrier, either by a cell-free virus, infected cell, or virion attached to dendritic cells (DCs) or Langerhans cells (LCs). Early low-level propagation probably occurs in partially activated CD4⁺ T cells, followed by massive propagation in activated CD4⁺ T cells of the gut-associated lymphoid tissue lamina propria. Dissemination of HIV to other secondary lymphoid tissues and establishment of stable tissue viral reservoirs ensue. Immune response lags behind the burst of viraemia and provides only partial control of viral replication. Abbreviations: CTL, cytotoxic T lymphocyte; PD-1, programmed death 1. (Redrawn from Moir, S. et al: Pathogenic mechanisms of HIV disease, *Annu Rev Pathol Mech Dis* 6:223–248, 2011.)

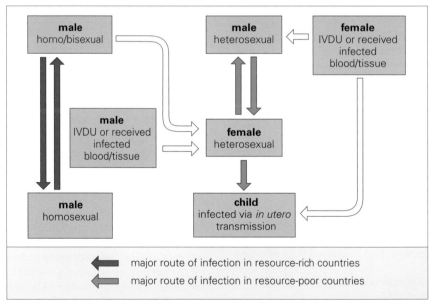

Figure 21.24 Major routes of transmission of HIV. Although the heterosexual route of transmission has so far been well established only in resource-poor countries, there is evidence that this route is becoming more important in the resource-rich countries. IVDU, intravenous drug user.

during pregnancy and caesarean section delivery, avoiding breastfeeding, and giving antiretroviral drugs to the newborn infant have reduced the risk of HIV transmission to the child. In resource-poor countries it has been shown that giving one dose of one antiretroviral drug to both mother and child reduced HIV transmission by 47%.

By the end of 2009, there were around 370 000 children newly infected with HIV, a fall of 24% from 2004.

Nineteen per cent fewer children died from AIDS-related illnesses than the estimated 320 000 who died in 2004.

Haemophiliacs who have received contaminated blood products have also been infected, though less commonly, as well as have injecting drug users. As with other blood-borne virus infections, using contaminated needles can lead to infection, i.e. in tattooing, body piercing and acupuncture.

Finally, healthcare workers are at risk of HIV infection after sustaining needlestick or mucous membrane splash injuries involving an HIV-infected source. The risk of infection is approximately 1 in 400 and is dependent on a number of factors, including depth of the injury and amount of blood to which the recipient has been exposed. Wearing protective clothing such as gloves and goggles is part of universal precautions to avoid exposure.

Development of disease

Primary HIV infection may be accompanied by a mild mononucleosis-type illness

Signs and symptoms of the mild mononucleosis-type illness associated with HIV infection include fever, malaise and lymphadenopathy. A maculopapular rash may also occur. Antibody responses can be detected in a few weeks, and Tc cells are formed. The acute infection and rapid, widespread viral dissemination is followed by a chronic asymptomatic stage. Viral replication is reduced in line with the immune response, and the individual usually remains well. The duration of this stage is dependent on a number of factors including the viral phenotype, host immune response and use of antiretroviral therapy (Fig. 21.25). Infected cells are, however, still present, and at a later stage the infected individual may develop weight

loss, fever, persistent lymphadenopathy, oral candidiasis and diarrhea. Further viral replication takes place until finally, some years after initial infection, full-blown AIDS develops (Fig. 21.26).

Progression to AIDS

Viral invasion of the CNS, with self-limiting aseptic meningoencephalitis as the most common neurological picture, occurs in early infection.

A progressive HIV-associated encephalopathy is seen in individuals with AIDS and is characterized by multiple small nodules of inflammatory cells; most of the infected cells appear to be microglia or infiltrating macrophages. These cells express the CD4 antigen, and it has been suggested that infected monocytes carry the virus into the brain, but the picture is complicated by the various persistent infections that are activated and give rise to their own CNS pathology. These include infections by HSV, varicella-zoster virus (VZV), *Toxoplasma gondii*, JC virus (progressive multifocal leukoencephalopathy, PML) and *Cryptococcus neoformans*.

HIV exercises complex control over its own replication (see Fig. 21.19). Replication is also affected by responses to other infections, which act as antigenic stimuli, and some of them directly as transactivating agents.

Some patients, especially in Africa, develop a wasting disease ('slim' disease), possibly due to unknown intestinal infections or infestations, and perhaps also to the direct effects of the virus infecting cells of the intestinal wall.

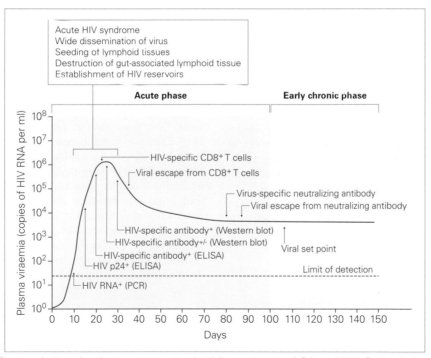

Figure 21.25 Kinetics of immunologic and virologic events associated with human immunodeficiency (HIV) infection during acute and early chronic phases. The schematic represents the sequence of events, including the appearance of viral antigens, HIV-specific antibodies, and HIV-specific CD8+ T cells during the acute and early chronic phases of infection. HIV reservoirs are established during the acute phase of infection soon after emergence of plasma viraemia. Throughout the acute phase of infection, characterized by massive virus replication and high levels of plasma viraemia, an acute HIV syndrome develops in the majority of infected individuals, and the virus rapidly spreads to various lymphoid organs, causing extensive depletion of CD4+ T cells. Although anti-HIV immunity, including virus-specific CD8+ T cells and antibodies, develops during the acute phase of infection, escape viral mutants rapidly emerge. Abbreviations: ELISA, enzyme-linked immunosorbent assay; PCR, polymerase chain reaction. (Redrawn from Moir, S. et al: Pathogenic mechanisms of HIV disease, *Annu Rev Pathol Mech Dis* 6:223–248, 2011.)

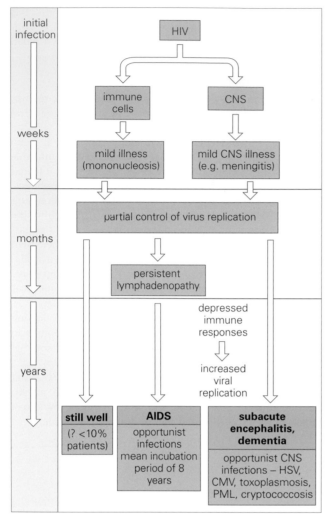

Figure 21.26 The clinical features and progression of untreated HIV infection. CMV, cytomegalovirus; CNS, central nervous system; HSV, herpes simplex virus; PML, progressive multifocal leukoencephalopathy.

AIDS, symptomatic disease, consists of a large spectrum of microbial diseases acquired or reactivated as a result of the underlying immunosuppression due to HIV (Fig. 21.27; Table 21.9). The disease picture of AIDS is therefore an indirect result of infection with HIV.

Before the advent of antiretroviral therapy, one study in New York reported a mortality rate of 80%, 5 years after the onset of the disease, and the average survival time after hospital admission was 242 days.

Treatment

Antiretroviral therapy results in a dramatic improvement in disease prognosis

In the 1990s, a range of antiretroviral therapies was introduced which included the nucleoside reverse transcriptase inhibitors (NRTIs), non-nucleoside reverse transcriptase inhibitors (NNRTIs) and protease inhibitors (PIs). These were developed further over the next two decades in terms of new drugs in all classes and combinations. In 2003, a fusion inhibitor was added to the list and by 2009 two other classes were available, an integrase inhibitor and chemokine receptor antagonist (see Ch. 33 for more detail).

In combination with two NRTIs, the NNRTI or PI drugs have had a dramatic effect on progression to AIDS and led to the term highly active antiretroviral therapy (HAART). One drawback is the number of important side effects of the drugs, including mitochondrial toxicity and altered fat distribution known as lipodystrophy. Treatment compliance with certain drugs is a problem because of the side effects and the number and frequency of pills taken each day. This is important, as missing any doses can lead to the development of drug resistance, thus limiting treatment options. Improved monitoring using plasma HIV load measurements and CD4 counts and percentages has shown the success of HAART, with rapid falls in plasma HIV load and rises in CD4 cells seen after initiating therapy. HIV is found in various compartments of the body including the CSF and genital tract. Antiretroviral drugs may not penetrate these sites, resulting in a high viral load detectable in semen despite suppression of the plasma HIV load. As a result of improved diagnosis, surveillance, prevention and use of HAART, the number of AIDS-related deaths among children and adults worldwide was stable at 1.8 million in 2001 and 2009.

Development of antiretroviral resistance and cross-resistance is a feature

Plasma HIV-1 RNA load is a good indicator of viral replication, and failure of antiretroviral therapy is seen by a rise in viral load. Antiretroviral resistance testing and therapeutic drug monitoring are part of clinical management. Drug resistance testing may be carried out when the plasma HIV-1 load is not suppressed whilst on antiretroviral therapy. Specific mutations in the reverse transcriptase and protease regions of plasma virus, associated with reduced susceptibility to one or more antiretroviral drugs, have been identified by nucleic acid sequencing, known as genotypic analysis. Some drug resistance mutations confer resistance to more than one drug of the same class, whereas others appear unique to specific drugs.

Transmission of drug-resistant HIV is an important issue. Drug resistance mutations were detected in around 16% of samples tested between 2001 and 2006 from antiretroviral therapy naive adults infected with HIV in the UK. The prevalence of drug-resistant viruses in newly infected individuals will depend on factors such as whether the individual was infected by someone failing on antiretroviral therapy, this being less likely in those infected in resource-poor regions. Baseline antiretroviral drug resistance testing is part of the management guidelines in many countries before starting treatment, as infection with a drug-resistant virus may affect the efficacy of subsequent therapy.

Treatment of AIDS involves prophylaxis and treatment of opportunist infections as well as using antiretrovirals

Depending on the CD4 count, prophylaxis is given for specific opportunistic infections such as *Pneumocystis jirovecii* and *Cryptococcus neoformans*. When opportunist infections are diagnosed, they are treated appropriately, for example co-trimoxazole or pentamidine with or without steroids for *P. jirovecii*, ganciclovir for CMV, and fluconazole or amphotericin for *C. neoformans* infection.

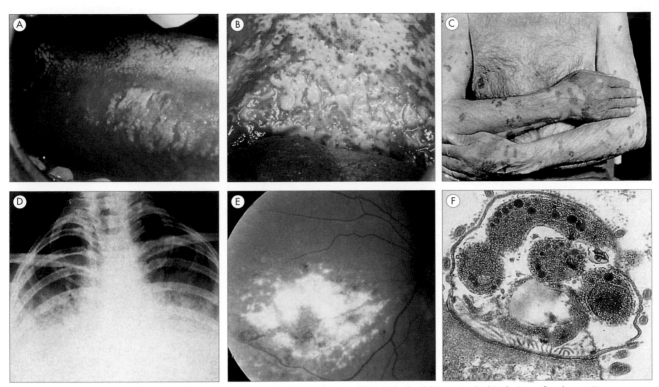

Figure 21.27 Opportunist infections and tumours associated with HIV infection. (A) Hairy leukoplakia – raised white lesions of oral mucosa, predominantly along the lateral aspect of the tongue, due to Epstein–Barr virus infection. (Courtesy of H.P. Holley.) (B) Extensive oral candidiasis. (Courtesy of W.E. Farrar.) (C) Kaposi's sarcoma – brown pigmented lesions on the upper extremities. (Courtesy of E. Sahn.) (D) Pneumocystis pneumonia, with extensive infiltrates in both lungs. (Courtesy of J.A. Innes.) (E) Cytomegalovirus retinitis showing scattered exudates and haemorrhages, with sheathing of vessels. (Courtesy of C.J. Ellis.) (F) Cryptosporidiosis – electron micrograph showing mature schizont with several merozoites attached to intestinal epithelium. (Courtesy of W.E. Farrar.)

Table 21.9 Opportunist infections and tumours in AIDS

Viruses	Disseminated CMV (including retina, brain, peripheral nervous system, gastrointestinal tract) HSV (lungs, gastrointestinal tract, CNS, skin) JC virus (brain – PML) EBV (hairy leukoplakia, primary cerebral lymphoma)
Bacteria[a]	Mycobacteria (e.g. *Mycoplasma avium*, *M. tuberculosis* – disseminated, extrapulmonary) *Salmonella* (recurrent, disseminated) septicaemia
Protozoa	*Toxoplasma gondii* (disseminated, including CNS) *Cryptococcus neoformans* (CNS) Histoplasmosis (disseminated, extrapulmonary) *Coccidioides* (disseminated, extrapulmonary)
Tumours	Kaposi's sarcoma[b] B cell lymphoma (e.g. in brain, some are EBV induced)
Other	Wasting disease (cause unknown) HIV encephalopathy

[a]Also pyogenic bacteria (e.g. *Haemophilus, Streptococcus, Pneumococcus*) causing septicaemia, pneumonia, meningitis, osteomyelitis, arthritis, abscesses, etc.; multiple or recurrent infections, especially in children.
[b]Associated with HHV-8, an independently-transmitted agent; 300 times as frequent in AIDS as in other immunodeficiencies. AIDS is defined as the presence of antibodies to HIV plus one of the conditions in this table. CMV, cytomegalovirus; CNS, central nervous system; EBV, Epstein–Barr virus; HSV, herpes simplex virus; PML, progressive multifocal leukoencephalopathy.

Laboratory tests

Laboratory tests for HIV infection involve both serological and molecular analysis

Acquired immune deficiency syndrome (AIDS) is a clinical definition; in the presence of antibodies to HIV, any of the conditions listed in Table 21.9, regardless of the presence of other causes of immunodeficiency, indicate AIDS. The range and complexity of tests used for HIV-1 and -2 screening, diagnosis of infection, and monitoring disease progression and response to therapy have increased dramatically.

Viral replication occurs during the incubation period, during which time the viral genome and, briefly, viral p24 antigen but not the host's antibody response may be detected.

HIV-1 and -2 diagnostic tests can be divided into antibody detection, combined antibody and antigen detection, antigen detection, and genome detection. The last can be divided into qualitative HIV-1 proviral DNA and quantitative HIV-1 RNA detection. In addition, antiretroviral drug resistance assays are becoming part of standard management.

Initially, an HIV-1 and -2 antibody/antigen combination assay which includes antibody and p24 antigen is carried out (see Ch. 32). These assays have been developed to reduce the diagnostic window period. Assay reactivity is confirmed using an alternative HIV test format on the original unseparated sample stored in the laboratory. This is to ensure that a specimen separation error has not occurred. HIV type differentiation may be carried out using an immunoblot, where the antigens are coated on nitrocellulose strips. A positive result is confirmed on a further blood sample, to ensure that the original sample had not been mislabelled at collection.

HIV-1 RNA or proviral DNA tests may be carried out on plasma and whole blood samples, respectively, if it is difficult to make a diagnosis because low level reactivity is detected when the serum sample is tested and the result is indeterminate, or the patient may have a seroconversion illness and the screening tests are negative.

Part of monitoring HIV-1-infected individuals on or off antiretroviral therapy involves measuring the plasma HIV-1 RNA load, which can be quantified using several commercial or in-house assays using different methods. The main assay formats are based on reverse transcription polymerase chain reaction (RT-PCR), branched DNA signal amplification, and RNA transcription isothermal amplification.

In addition, part of the laboratory portfolio involves antiretroviral resistance genotypic analysis by automated DNA sequencing. This is a costly, specialized test, and the interpretation of the results may be complicated.

Diagnosis of HIV infection in newborn infants can be difficult because passively acquired maternal IgG will be detected in the first 12 months after birth. Reference laboratories may have virus-specific IgM and IgA in-house tests, which would signify in utero infection (see Ch. 23), as part of their test portfolio. Samples from infants are tested at various time intervals up to 12–24 months for p24 antigen, HIV-1 RNA and/or HIV-1 proviral DNA, and HIV antibody to assess their HIV status.

Measures to control spread

Many resource-rich countries have taken measures to reduce the spread of HIV

Up to 2010, the number of new HIV infections fell by nearly 20%. HIV prevalence fell by more than 25% among young people in 15 of the most severely affected countries after this group adopted safer sexual practices. In addition, 53% of HIV-positive pregnant women received treatment to prevent transmission of the virus to their child in 2009 compared with 35% in 2007. In resource-rich countries such as the UK compared with Africa and Asia, most new infections in 2009 involved men who have sex with men (MSM) (Figure 21.28).

The risk of transmitting HIV via blood and blood products is reduced considerably by donor screening programmes, in addition to other blood-borne viruses, and heat treatment, respectively. Those at risk of infection are advised not to donate. Heat treatment of factor VIII is a further precaution

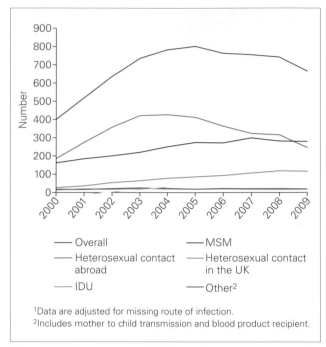

Figure 21.28 Number of new HIV diagnoses[1] by prevention group, UK: 2000–2009. Data are adjusted for missing route of infection. [2]Includes mother to child transmission and blood product recipient. (Data from Health Protection Agency Health Protection Report Volume 4 Number 47 Published on: 26 November 2010 HIV in the United Kingdom : 2010 Report.)

before this product is used to treat haemophiliac patients. HIV has a delicate outer envelope and is highly susceptible to heat and chemical agents. HIV is inactivated under pasteurization conditions and also by hypochlorites, even at concentrations as low as 1 in 10 000 ppm; 2.5% glutaraldehyde and ethyl alcohol are also effective against the virus.

The main effort in the prevention of HIV infection concerns mass public education programmes. These involve advice to change sexual behaviour and the use of barrier contraceptives such as condoms. The problem of transmission between injecting drug users is being tackled in some areas by measures that were originally controversial, such as the free distribution of clean needles and syringes.

The importance of reducing transmission rates is discussed in Chapter 31. The biggest risk for the future in resource-rich countries is that heterosexual transmission becomes more common. Unfortunately, the determinants of heterosexual transmission are not understood, but the means for prevention are nevertheless clear – condoms and change in sexual behaviour. Public health educational programmes have been presented by various types of media in order to reduce the incidence of all STIs.

Vaccination

There are a number of challenges in developing a successful vaccine against HIV infection

More than 50 vaccine regimens have undergone clinical trials since 1999. However, only four transferred to test-of-concept or efficacy trials. The prospects are limited for a number of reasons including viral antigenic variation and sequence diversity, slow neutralizing antibody response to HIV infection, viral evasion of immune responses and establishment of latent viral reservoirs. Various subunit envelope glycoproteins, whole killed virus vaccines, plasmid DNA vaccines and virus vectors to carry HIV antigens have been investigated and tested. Trials have been carried out in animal (monkey) models and also humans.

The aim is to prevent infection or reduce the HIV load and clinical progression post infection. The immune correlates of protection have yet to be well defined and are critical in order to protect against infection. Two vaccine candidates involved in efficacy studies were an envelope gp120 protein vaccine that resulted in type-specific but not broadly reactive neutralizing antibody responses and a replication-incompetent adenovirus vector expressing HIV-1 gag, pol and nef gene products. The latter resulted in cellular immune responses in most recipients. However, the vaccine was neither protective nor reduced HIV loads post infection. The fact that there is a successful killed virus vaccine for a feline retrovirus (feline leukaemia), and that a similar vaccine protects monkeys from simian AIDS does, however, give some hope for the development of an HIV vaccine.

To prevent sexual transmission, mucosal immunity is needed, and this is likely to come from a mucosally administered vaccine. The major route of HIV 1 transmission is via mucosal surfaces. Worldwide, the cervical and vaginal mucosa are the major portals but the rectal mucosa is the more common route in North America and Europe. Penile foreskin increases the risk of HIV transmission due to the high density of HIV target Langerhans cells in addition to the inner mucosal surface not being keratinized. Circumcision has been shown to reduce the risk of transmission. Macaque SIV infection models have shown additional mucosal routes of entry, suggesting that HIV infection might also be transmitted through oropharyngeal and upper gastrointestinal mucosa. A T-cell vaccine would need to induce a long-lasting mucosal immune response that includes mucosal neutralizing IgA and IgG antibody and T-cell responses. Mucosal CD8+ CTLs would limit infection and subsequent HIV viraemia as well as clearance of viral reservoirs in the gut mucosa.

OPPORTUNIST STIs

Opportunist STIs include salmonellae, shigellae, hepatitis A, *Giardia intestinalis* and *Entamoeba histolytica* infections

Although STIs are classically transmitted during heterosexual intercourse, they can also be transmitted whenever two mucosal surfaces are brought together. Anal intercourse allows the transfer of microorganisms from penis to rectal mucosa or to anal and perianal regions. Gonococcal or papillomavirus lesions, for instance, may occur in any of these sites. A few microorganisms (hepatitis B, HIV) are transmitted more often across rectal mucosa. If there is oral–anal contact, a variety of intestinal pathogens are given the opportunity to spread as STIs and can then be regarded as 'opportunistic STIs'. These include salmonellae, shigellae, hepatitis A virus, *Giardia intestinalis* and *Entamoeba histolytica* (see Ch. 22). Together with chronic infections such as CMV and cryptosporidiosis, they contribute to intestinal symptoms and diarrhea in AIDS patients.

Hepatitis B virus is often transmitted sexually

Hepatitis B virus is detectable in semen, saliva and vaginal secretions. HBV transmission, like HIV, is more likely when genital areas are ulcerated or contaminated with blood (e.g. menstrual blood). Hepatitis B transmission among MSMs parallels the transmission of HIV, with passive anal intercourse as a high-risk factor. Hepatitis D transmission can only follow hepatitis B as it is a defective virus that needs HBsAg to replicate. Hepatitis C is less commonly transmitted sexually; <5% of long-term sexual partners are infected.

ARTHROPOD INFESTATIONS

Infection with the pubic or crab louse causes itching and is treated with permethrin shampoo

The 'crab louse', *Phthirus pubis*, is distinct from the other human lice, *Pediculus humanus humanus* and *Pediculus humanus capitis*. The crab louse is well adapted for life in the genital region, clinging tightly to the pubic hairs (see Ch. 6). Occasionally, hairs on the eyebrows or in the axilla are colonized. It takes up to 10 blood feeds a day and this causes itching at the site of the bites. Eggs called 'nits' are seen attached to the pubic hairs, and the characteristic lice, up to 2 mm long, are visible (often at the base of a hair) under a hand lens or by microscopy. Infestation is common, e.g. there are more than 10 000 cases/year in the UK.

Treatment is by the application of permethrin cream or aqueous phenothrin.

Genital scabies is also treated with permethrin cream

Sarcoptes scabiei (see Ch. 26) may cause local lesions on the genitalia, and can thus be sexually transmitted. Patients may have evidence of scabies elsewhere on the body, with burrows between the fingers or toes. Genital scabies is also treated with permethrin cream.

KEY FACTS

- Microorganisms transmitted by the sexual route in humans include representatives from all groups apart from the rickettsiae and helminths.

- STIs are found in the general community rather than being confined only to high-risk groups.

- Genital herpes, warts, chlamydial urethritis, and gonorrhoea are by far the most common of all the STIs, but HIV infection has had a major impact, eclipsing all the other well-known STIs because it is usually eventually lethal.

- Except for hepatitis and human papillomavirus there are no vaccines for these infections, but antimicrobial chemotherapy is often available.

- At present, the best method of control is prevention.

- Transmission depends upon human behaviour, which is notoriously difficult to influence.

- Long intervals between the onset of infectiousness and disease increase the chances of transmission.

Gastrointestinal tract infections

22

Introduction

Ingested pathogens may cause disease confined to the gut or involve other parts of the body

Ingestion of pathogens can cause many different infections. These may be confined to the gastrointestinal tract or are initiated in the gut before spreading to other parts of the body. In this chapter, we consider the important bacterial causes of diarrheal disease and summarize the other bacterial causes of food-associated infection and food poisoning. Viral and parasitic causes of diarrheal disease are discussed, as well as infections acquired via the gastrointestinal tract and causing disease in other body systems, including typhoid and paratyphoid fevers, listeriosis and some forms of viral hepatitis. For clarity, all types of viral hepatitis are included in this chapter, despite the fact that some are transmitted by other routes of infection. Infections of the liver can also result in liver abscesses, and several parasitic infections cause liver disease. Peritonitis and intra-abdominal abscesses can arise from seeding of the abdominal cavity by organisms from the gastrointestinal tract. Several different terms are used to describe infections of the gastrointestinal tract; those in common use are shown in Box 22.1.

A wide range of microbial pathogens is capable of infecting the gastrointestinal tract, and the important bacterial and viral pathogens are listed in Table 22.1. They are acquired by the faecal–oral route, from faecally contaminated food, fluids or fingers.

For an infection to occur, the pathogen must be ingested in sufficient numbers or possess attributes to elude the host defences of the upper gastrointestinal tract and reach the intestine (Fig. 22.1; see also Ch. 13). Here they remain localized and cause disease as a result of multiplication and/or toxin production, or they may invade through the intestinal mucosa to reach the lymphatics or the bloodstream (Fig. 22.2). The damaging effects resulting from infection of the gastrointestinal tract are summarized in Box 22.2.

Box 22.1 Terms Used to Describe Gastrointestinal Tract Infections

As well as many colloquial expressions, several different clinical terms are used to describe infections of the gastrointestinal tract. Diarrhea without blood and pus is usually the result of enterotoxin production, whereas the presence of blood and/or pus cells in the faeces indicates an invasive infection with mucosal destruction.

- Gastroenteritis
  - A syndrome characterized by gastrointestinal symptoms including nausea, vomiting, diarrhea and abdominal discomfort
- Diarrhea
  - Abnormal faecal discharge characterized by frequent and/or fluid stool; usually resulting from disease

of the small intestine and involving increased fluid and electrolyte loss
- Dysentery
  - An inflammatory disorder of the gastrointestinal tract often associated with blood and pus in the faeces and accompanied by symptoms of pain, fever, abdominal cramps; usually resulting from disease of the large intestine
- Enterocolitis
  - Inflammation involving the mucosa of both the small and large intestine

---

Food-associated infection versus food poisoning

Infection associated with consumption of contaminated food is often termed 'food poisoning', but 'food-associated infection' is a better term. True food poisoning occurs after consumption of food containing toxins, which may be chemical (e.g. heavy metals) or bacterial in origin (e.g. from

Clostridium botulinum or *Staphylococcus aureus*). The bacteria multiply and produce toxins within contaminated food. The organisms may be destroyed during food preparation, but the toxin is unaffected, consumed and acts within hours. In food-associated infections, the food may simply act as a vehicle for the pathogen (e.g. *Campylobacter*) or provide conditions in which the pathogen can multiply to produce numbers large enough to cause disease (e.g. *Salmonella*).

Table 22.1 Important bacterial and viral pathogens of the gastrointestinal tract

Pathogen	Animal reservoir	Food-borne	Water-borne
Bacteria			
Escherichia coli	+?	+ (EHEC)	+ (ETEC)
Salmonella	+	+ + +	+
Campylobacter	+	+ + +	+
Vibrio cholerae	–	+	+ + +
Shigella	–	+	–
Clostridium perfringens	+	+ + +	–
Bacillus cereus	–	+ +	–
Vibrio para-haemolyticus	–	+ +	–
Yersinia enterocolitica	+	+	–
Viruses			
Rotavirus	–	–	–
Noroviruses (previously known as SRSV or Norwalk-like viruses)	–	+ +	+

Many different pathogens cause infections of the gastrointestinal tract. Some are found in both humans and animals, while others are strictly human parasites. This difference has important implications for control and prevention. EHEC, enterohaemorrhagic (verotoxin-producing) *E. coli*; ETEC, enterotoxigenic *E. coli*; SRSV, small round structured viruses.

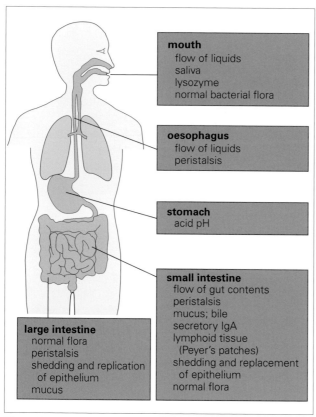

mouth
flow of liquids
saliva
lysozyme
normal bacterial flora

oesophagus
flow of liquids
peristalsis

stomach
acid pH

small intestine
flow of gut contents
peristalsis
mucus; bile
secretory IgA
lymphoid tissue
(Peyer's patches)
shedding and replacement
of epithelium
normal flora

large intestine
normal flora
peristalsis
shedding and replication
of epithelium
mucus

Figure 22.1 Every day we swallow large numbers of microorganisms. Because of the body's defence mechanisms, however, they rarely succeed in surviving the passage to the intestine in sufficient numbers to cause infection.

DIARRHEAL DISEASES CAUSED BY BACTERIAL OR VIRAL INFECTION

Diarrhea is the most common outcome of gastrointestinal tract infection

Infections of the gastrointestinal tract range in their effects from a mild self-limiting attack of 'the runs' to severe, sometimes fatal, diarrhea. There may be associated vomiting,

fever and malaise. Diarrhea is the result of an increase in fluid and electrolyte loss into the gut lumen, leading to the production of unformed or liquid faeces and can be thought of as the method by which the host forcibly expels the pathogen (and in doing so, aids its dissemination). However, diarrhea also occurs in many non-infectious conditions, and an infectious cause should not be assumed.

In the resource-poor world, diarrheal disease is a major cause of mortality in children

In the resource-poor world, diarrheal disease is a major cause of morbidity and mortality, particularly in young children. In the resource-rich world, it remains a very common complaint, but is usually mild and self-limiting except in the very young, the elderly and immunocompromised patients. Most of the pathogens listed in Table 22.1 are found throughout the world, but some, such as *Vibrio cholerae*, have a more limited geographic distribution. However, such infections can be acquired by travellers to these areas and imported into their home countries.

Many cases of diarrheal disease are not diagnosed, either because they are mild and self-limiting and the patient does not seek medical attention, or because medical and laboratory facilities are unavailable, particularly in resource-poor countries. It is generally impossible to distinguish on clinical grounds between infections caused by the different pathogens. However, information about the patient's recent food and travel history, and macroscopic and microscopic examination of the faeces for blood and pus can provide helpful clues. A precise diagnosis can only be achieved by laboratory investigations. This is especially important in outbreaks, because of the need to instigate appropriate epidemiologic investigations and control measures.

Bacterial causes of diarrhea

Escherichia coli

E. coli is one of the most versatile of all bacterial pathogens. Some strains are important members of the normal gut flora in humans and animals (see Ch. 2), whereas others possess

Figure 22.2 Infections of the gastrointestinal tract can be grouped into those that remain localized in the gut and those that invade beyond the gut to cause infection in other sites in the body. In order to spread to a new host, pathogens are excreted in large numbers in the faeces and must survive in the environment for long enough to infect another person directly or indirectly through contaminated food or fluids.

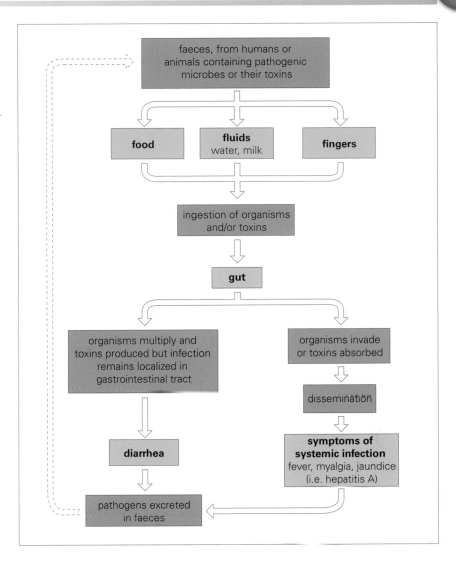

Box 22.2 — Damage Resulting from Infection of The Gastrointestinal Tract

- Pharmacologic action of bacterial toxins, local or distant to site of infection, e.g. cholera, staphylococcal food poisoning

- Local inflammation in response to superficial microbial invasion, e.g. shigellosis, amoebiasis

- Deep invasion to blood or lymphatics; dissemination to other body sites, e.g. Hepatitis A, enteric fevers

- Perforation of mucosal epithelium after infection, surgery or accidental trauma, e.g. peritonitis, intra-abdominal abscesses.

Infection of the gastrointestinal tract can cause damage locally or at distant sites.

There are six distinct groups of *E. coli* with different pathogenetic mechanisms

Initially, all diarrhea-associated *Escherichia coli* were termed enteropathogenic *E. coli* (EPEC). However, greater insight into mechanisms of pathogenicity has led to specific group designations: enteropathogenic *E. coli* (EPEC), enterotoxigenic *E. coli* (ETEC), enterohaemorrhagic *E. coli* (EHEC), enteroinvasive *E. coli* (EIEC), enteroaggregative *E. coli* (EAEC), and diffuse-aggregative *E. coli* (DAEC).

Enteropathogenic *E. coli* (EPEC) do not appear to make any toxins

They do produce bundle-forming pili (Bfp), intimin (an adhesin) and an associated protein (translocated intimin receptor, Tir). These virulence factors allow bacterial attachment to epithelial cells of the small intestine, leading to disruption of the microvillus (an 'attaching–effacing' mechanism of action; Table 22.2; Fig. 22.3) leading to diarrhea (Table 22.3).

Enterotoxigenic *E. coli* (ETEC) possess colonization factors (fimbrial adhesins)

These bind the bacteria to specific receptors on the cell membrane of the small intestine (Table 22.2; Fig. 22.4). These organisms produce powerful plasmid-associated

virulence factors that enable them to cause infections in the intestinal tract or at other sites, particularly the urinary tract (see Ch. 20). Strains that cause diarrheal disease do so by several distinct pathogenic mechanisms and differ in their epidemiology (Table 22.2).

Table 22.2 Characteristics of *Escherichia coli* strains causing gastrointestinal infections

Pathogenic group	Epidemiology	Laboratory diagnosis*
Enteropathogenic *E. coli* (EPEC)	EPEC strains belong to particular O serotypes Cause sporadic cases and outbreaks of infection in babies and young children Importance in adults less clear	Isolate organisms from faeces Determine serotype of several colonies with polyvalent antisera for known EPEC types *Adhesion to tissue culture cells can be demonstrated by a fluorescence actin staining test* *DNA-based assays for detection of attachment (virulence) factors*
Enterotoxigenic *E. coli* (ETEC)	Most important bacterial cause of diarrhea in children in resource-poor countries Most common cause of traveller's diarrhea Water contaminated by human or animal sewage may be important in spread	Isolate organisms from faeces Tests commercially available for immunologic detection of toxins from culture supernatants *Gene probes specific for LT and ST genes available for detection of ETEC in faeces and in food and water samples*
Enterohaemorrhagic (verotoxin-producing) *E. coli* (EHEC)	Serotype O157 most important EHEC in human infections Outbreaks and sporadic cases occur worldwide Food and unpasteurized milk important in spread May cause haemolytic-uremic syndrome (HUS)	Isolate organisms from faeces Proportion of EHEC in fecal sample may be very low (often <1% of *E. coli* colonies) Usually sorbitol non-fermenters *Shiga toxin production and associated genes detected by biological, immunological and nucleic-acid based assays*
Enteroinvasive *E. coli* (EIEC)	Important cause of diarrhea in areas of poor hygiene Infections usually food-borne; no evidence of animal or environmental reservoir	Isolate organisms from faeces *Test for enteroinvasive potential in tissue culture cells or nucleic-acid-based assays for invasion-associated genes*
Enteroaggregative *E. coli* (EAEC) Diffuse-aggregative *E. coli* (DAEC)	Characteristic attachment to tissue culture cells Cause diarrhea in children in resource-poor countries Role of toxins uncertain	*Tissue culture assays for aggregative or diffuse adherence*

E. coli is a major cause of gastrointestinal infection, particularly in resource-poor countries and in travellers. There is a range of pathogenic mechanisms within the species, resulting in more or less invasive disease.
*Specialized tests are given in italics. LT, heat-labile enterotoxin; ST, heat-stable enterotoxin.

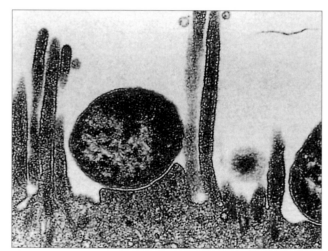

Figure 22.3 Electron micrograph of enteropathogenic *E. coli* adhering to the brush border of intestinal mucosal cells with localized destruction of microvilli. (Courtesy of S. Knutton.)

enterotoxins which are characterized as being either heat labile (LT) or heat stable (ST):

- Heat-labile enterotoxin LT-I is very similar in structure and mode of action to cholera toxin produced by *V. cholerae*, and infections with strains producing LT-I can mimic cholera, particularly in young and malnourished children (Table 22.3).

- Other ETEC strains produce heat-stable enterotoxins (STs) in addition to or instead of LT. STs have a similar but distinct mode of action to that of LT. ST_A activates guanylate cyclase activity, causing an increase in cyclic guanosine monophosphate, which results in increased fluid secretion. Immunoassays are commercially available for the identification of ETEC (Table 22.2).

Enterohaemorrhagic *E. coli* (EHEC) isolates produce a verotoxin

The verotoxin (i.e. toxic to tissue cultures of 'vero' cells) is essentially identical to *Shiga* (*Shigella*) toxin. After attachment to the mucosa of the large intestine (by the 'attaching– effacing' mechanism also seen in EPEC), the produced toxin has a direct effect on intestinal epithelium, resulting in diarrhea (Table 22.3). EHEC cause haemorrhagic colitis (HC) and haemolytic-uraemic syndrome (HUS). In HC, there is destruction of the mucosa and consequent haemorrhage; this may be followed by HUS. Verotoxin receptors have been identified on renal epithelium and may account for kidney involvement. While there are many serotypes of EHEC, the most common is O157:H7.

Enteroinvasive *E. coli* (EIEC) attach specifically to the mucosa of the large intestine

They invade the cells by endocytosis by using plasmid-associated genes. Inside the cell, they lyse the endocytic vacuole, multiply and spread to adjacent cells, causing

Table 22.3 The clinical features of bacterial diarrheal infection

Pathogen	Incubation period	Duration	Symptoms			
			Diarrhea	Vomiting	Abdominal cramps	Fever
Salmonella	6 h–2 days	48 h–7 days	Watery	+	+	+
Campylobacter	2–11 days	3 days–3 weeks	Bloody	−	+	+
Shigella	1–4 days	2–3 days	Bloody	−	+	+
Vibrio cholerae	2–3 days	up to 7 days	Watery	+	+	−
Clostridium perfringens	8 h–1 day	12 h–1 day	Watery	−	+	−
Bacillus cereus Diarrheal Emetic	8 h–12 h 15 min–4 h	12 h–1 day 12 h–2 days	Watery Watery	− +	+ +	− −
Yersinia enterocolitica	4–7 days	1–2 weeks	Bloody	−	+	+
Enteropathogenic *E. coli* (EPEC)	1–2 days	weeks	Watery	+	+	+
Enterotoxigenic *E. coli* (ETEC)	1–7 days	2–6 days	Watery	+	+	−
Enterohaemorrhagic *E. coli* (EHEC)	3–4 days	5–10 days	Bloody	+	+	−
Enteroinvasive *E. coli* (EIEC)	1–3 days	7–10 days	Bloody	+	+	+

It is difficult, if not impossible, to determine the likely cause of a diarrheal illness on the basis of clinical features alone, and laboratory investigations are essential to identify the pathogen.

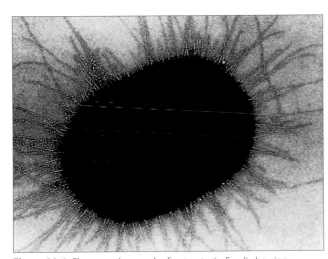

Figure 22.4 Electron micrograph of enterotoxin *E. coli*, showing pili necessary for adherence to mucosal epithelial cells. (Courtesy of S. Knutton.)

tissue destruction, inflammation, necrosis and ulceration, resulting in blood and mucus in stools (Tables 22.2, 22.3).

Enteroaggregative *E. coli* (EAEC) derive their name from their characteristic attachment pattern to tissue culture cells

The pattern is an aggregative or 'stacked brick' formation. These organisms act in the small intestine to cause persistent diarrhea, especially in children in resource-poor countries. Their aggregative adherence ability is due to plasmid-associated fimbriae. EAEC also produce heat-labile toxins

(an enterotoxin and a toxin related to *E. coli* haemolysin) but their role in diarrheal disease is uncertain.

Diffuse-aggregative *E. coli* (DAEC) produce an alpha haemolysin and cytotoxic necrotizing factor 1

They are also known as diffuse-adherent or cell-detaching *E. coli*. Their role in diarrheal disease, especially in young children, is incompletely understood and somewhat controversial, with some studies reporting no association.

EPEC and ETEC are the most important contributors to global incidence of diarrhea, while EHEC is more important in resource-rich countries

The diarrhea produced by *E. coli* varies from mild to severe, depending upon the strain and the underlying health of the host. ETEC diarrhea in children in resource-poor countries may be clinically indistinguishable from cholera. EIEC and EHEC strains both cause bloody diarrhea (Table 22.3). Following EHEC infection, HUS is characterized by acute renal failure (Fig. 22.5), anaemia and thrombocytopenia, and there may be neurologic complications. HUS is the most common cause of acute renal failure in children in the UK and USA. Although *E. coli* O157:H7 is the most commonly recognized serotype involved in HUS, *E. coli* 0104:H4, that had not been reported as causing an outbreak previously, caused a significant outbreak of HUS and bloody diarrhea in 15 countries across Europe in 2011. Over several months starting in May 2011, 860 individuals with HUS and over 3000 with bloody diarrhea were reported in Germany, many of whom had laboratory confirmed *E. coli* 0104:H4 infection. More than 50 people died and the likely vehicle was sprouted beans imported from the Middle East.

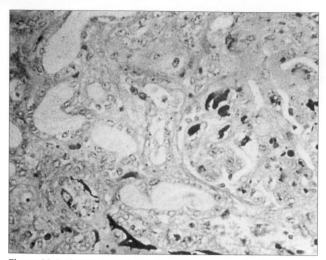

Figure 22.5 Verotoxin-producing *E. coli* infection, showing fibrin 'thrombi' in glomerular capillaries in haemolytic–uraemic syndrome. (Weigert stain.) (Courtesy of H.R. Powell.)

Specific tests are needed to identify strains of pathogenic *E. coli*

Because *E. coli* is a member of the normal gastrointestinal flora, specific tests are required to identify strains that may be responsible for diarrheal disease. These are summarized in Table 22.2. Infections are more common in children and are also often travel-associated, and these factors should be considered when samples are received in the laboratory. It is important to note that specialized tests beyond routine stool cultures are required to identify specific diarrhea-associated *E. coli* types. Such tests are not ordinarily performed with uncomplicated diarrhea, which is usually self-limiting. However, concern regarding EHEC (e.g. bloody diarrhea) has led most laboratories in resource-rich countries to screen for *E. coli* O157:H7.

Antibacterial therapy is not indicated for *E. coli* diarrhea

Specific antibacterial therapy is not indicated. Fluid replacement may be necessary, especially in young children. Treatment of HUS is urgent and may involve dialysis.

Provision of a clean water supply and adequate systems for sewage disposal are fundamental to the prevention of disease. Food and unpasteurized milk can be important vehicles of infection, especially for EIEC and EHEC, but there is no evidence of an animal or environmental reservoir.

Salmonella

Salmonellae are the most common cause of food-associated diarrhea in many resource-rich countries

However, in some countries such as the USA and UK, they have been relegated to second place by *Campylobacter*. Like *E. coli*, the salmonellae belong to the family Enterobacteriaceae. Historically, salmonella nomenclature has been somewhat confusing, with more than 2000 serotypes defined on the basis of differences in the cell wall (O) and flagellar (H) antigens (Kauffmann–White scheme). However, DNA hybridization studies indicate that there are only two species, the most important of which, for human infection,

is *Salmonella enterica*. To simplify discussion and comparison, past convention has been to replace this species name with the serotype designation. While technically incorrect (the serotype is not a species), this practice is helpful when discussing interrelationships between different isolates, e.g. in epidemiologic analysis when tracing the source of an outbreak. This convention is thus followed here to maintain continuity with other scientific literature.

All salmonellae except for *Salmonella typhi* and *S. paratyphi* are found in animals as well as humans. There is a large animal reservoir of infection, which is transmitted to humans via contaminated food, especially poultry and dairy products (Fig. 22.6). Water-borne infection is less frequent. Salmonella infection is also transmitted from person to person, and secondary spread can therefore occur, for example, within a family after one member has become infected after consuming contaminated food.

Salmonellae are almost always acquired orally in food or drink that is contaminated

Diarrhea is produced as a result of invasion by the salmonellae of epithelial cells in the terminal portion of the small intestine (Fig. 22.7). Initial entry is probably through uptake by M cells (the 'antigenic samplers' of the bowel) with subsequent spread to epithelial cells. A similar route of invasion occurs in *Shigella*, *Yersinia* and reovirus infections. The bacteria migrate to the lamina propria layer of the ileocaecal region, where their multiplication stimulates an inflammatory response, which both confines the infection to the gastrointestinal tract and mediates the release of prostaglandins. These in turn activate cyclic adenosine monophosphate (cAMP) and fluid secretion, resulting in diarrhea.

Species of *Salmonella* that normally cause diarrhea (e.g. *S. enteritidis*, *S. choleraesuis*) may become invasive in patients with particular predispositions (e.g. children, immunocompromised patients or those with sickle cell anaemia). The organisms are not contained within the gastrointestinal tract, but invade the body to cause septicaemia; consequently, many organs become seeded with salmonellae, sometimes leading to osteomyelitis, pneumonia or meningitis.

In the vast majority of cases, *Salmonella* spp. cause an acute but self-limiting diarrhea, though in the young and the

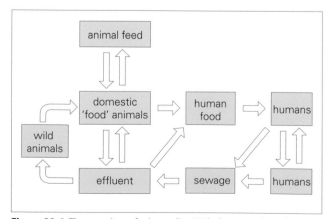

Figure 22.6 The recycling of salmonellae. With the exception of *Salmonella typhi*, salmonellae are widely distributed in animals, providing a constant source of infection for humans. Excretion of large numbers of salmonellae from infected individuals and carriers allows the organisms to be 'recycled'.

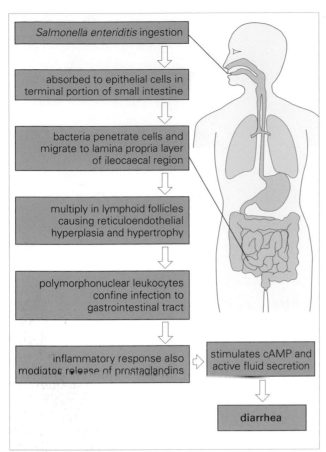

Figure 22.7 The passage of salmonellae through the body. The vast majority of salmonellae cause infection localized to the gastrointestinal tract and do not invade beyond the gut mucosa. cAMP, cyclic adenosine monophosphate.

The flowchart reads:
- *Salmonella enteriditis* ingestion
- absorbed to epithelial cells in terminal portion of small intestine
- bacteria penetrate cells and migrate to lamina propria layer of ileocaecal region
- multiply in lymphoid follicles causing reticuloendothelial hyperplasia and hypertrophy
- polymorphonuclear leukocytes confine infection to gastrointestinal tract
- inflammatory response also mediates release of prostaglandins → stimulates cAMP and active fluid secretion
- diarrhea

elderly the symptoms may be more severe. Vomiting is also common with enterocolitis, while fever is usually a sign of invasive disease (Table 22.3). *S. typhi* and *S. paratyphi* invade the body from the gastrointestinal tract to cause systemic illness and are discussed in a later section.

Salmonella diarrhea can be diagnosed by culture on selective media

The methods for culturing faecal specimens on selective media are summarized in the Appendix. The organisms are not fastidious and can usually be isolated within 24 h, although small numbers may require enrichment in selenite broth before culture. Preliminary identification can be made rapidly, but the complete result, including serotype, takes at least 48 h.

Fluid and electrolyte replacement may be needed for salmonella diarrhea

Diarrhea is usually self-limiting and resolves without treatment. Fluid and electrolyte replacement may be required, particularly in the very young and the elderly. Unless there is evidence of invasion and septicaemia, antibiotics should be positively discouraged because they do not reduce the symptoms or shorten the illness, and may prolong excretion of salmonellae in the faeces. There is some evidence that symptomatic treatment with drugs that reduce diarrhea has the same adverse effect.

Salmonellae may be excreted in the faeces for several weeks after a salmonella infection

Figure 22.6 illustrates the problems associated with the prevention of salmonella infections. The large animal reservoir makes it impossible to eliminate the organisms, and preventive measures must therefore be aimed at 'breaking the chain' between animals and humans, and from person to person. Such measures include:

- maintaining adequate standards of public health (clean drinking water and proper sewage disposal)
- education programmes on hygienic food preparation.

Following an episode of salmonella diarrhea, an individual can continue to carry and excrete organisms in the faeces for several weeks. Although in the absence of symptoms, the organisms will not be dispersed so liberally into the environment, thorough handwashing before food handling is essential. People employed as food handlers are excluded from work until three specimens of faeces have failed to grow salmonella.

Campylobacter

Campylobacter infections are among the most common causes of diarrhea

Campylobacter spp. are curved or S-shaped Gram-negative rods (Fig. 22.8). They have long been known to cause diarrheal disease in animals, but are also one of the most common causes of diarrhea in humans. The delay in recognizing the importance of these organisms was due to their cultural requirements, which differ from those of the enterobacteria as they are microaerophilic and thermophilic (growing well at 42°C); they do not therefore grow on the media used for isolating *E. coli* and salmonellae. Several species of the genus *Campylobacter* are associated with human disease, but *Campylobacter jejuni* is by far the most common. *Helicobacter pylori*, previously classified as *Campylobacter pylori*, is an important cause of gastritis and gastric ulcers (see below).

As with salmonellae, there is a large animal reservoir of *Campylobacter* in cattle, sheep, rodents, poultry and wild birds. Infections are acquired by consumption of contaminated food, especially poultry, milk or water. Studies have shown an association between infection and consumption of milk from bottles with tops that have been pecked

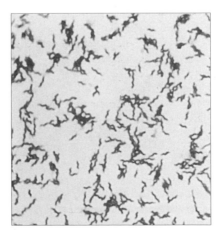

Figure 22.8 *Campylobacter jejuni* infection. Gram stain showing Gram-negative, S-shaped bacilli. (Courtesy of I. Farrell.)

by wild birds. Household pets such as dogs and cats can become infected and provide a source for human infection, particularly for young children. Person-to-person spread by the faecal–oral route is rare, as is transmission from food handlers.

Campylobacter diarrhea is clinically similar to that caused by other bacteria such as salmonella and *shigella*

The gross pathology and histologic appearances of ulceration and inflamed bleeding mucosal surfaces in the jejunum, ileum and colon (Fig. 22.9) are compatible with invasion of the bacteria, but the production of cytotoxins by *C. jejuni* has also been demonstrated. Invasion and bacteraemia are not uncommon, particularly in neonates and debilitated adults.

The clinical presentation is similar to that of diarrhea caused by salmonellae and *shigella*, although the disease may have a longer incubation period and a longer duration. The key features are summarized in Table 22.3.

Cultures for *Campylobacter* should be set up routinely in every investigation of a diarrheal illness

The methods are described in the Appendix, but it is important to note that the media and conditions for growth differ from those required for the enterobacteria. Growth is often somewhat slow compared with that of the enterobacteria, but a presumptive identification should be available within 48 h of culture.

Erythromycin is used for severe *Campylobacter* diarrhea

Macrolide antibiotics such as erythromycin can be used in diarrheal disease that is severe enough to warrant treatment. Invasive infections may require treatment with an additional antibiotic such as a quinolone or an aminoglycoside.

The preventive measures for salmonella infections described above are equally applicable to the prevention of *Campylobacter* infections, but there are no requirements for the screening of food handlers because contamination of food by this route is very uncommon.

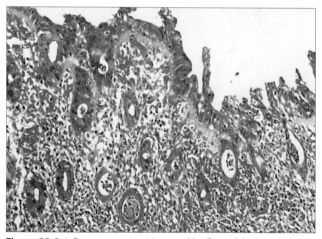

Figure 22.9 Inflammatory enteritis caused by *Campylobacter jejuni*, involving the entire mucosa, with flattened atrophic villi, necrotic debris in the crypts and thickening of the basement membrane. (Cresyl-fast violet stain.) (Courtesy of J. Newman.)

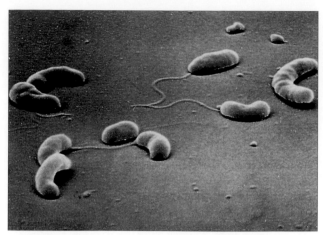

Figure 22.10 Scanning electron micrograph of *Vibrio cholerae* showing comma-shaped rods with a single polar flagellum ($\times$ 13 000). (Courtesy of D.K. Banerjee.)

Cholera

Cholera is an acute infection of the gastrointestinal tract caused by the comma-shaped Gram-negative bacterium *V. cholerae* (Fig. 22.10). The disease has a long history characterized by epidemics and pandemics. The last cases of cholera acquired in the UK were in the nineteenth century following the introduction of the bacterium by sailors arriving from Europe, and in 1849 Snow published his historic essay *On the Mode of Communication of Cholera*.

Cholera flourishes in communities with inadequate clean drinking water and sewage disposal

The disease remains endemic in SE Asia and parts of Africa and South America. Unlike salmonellae and *Campylobacter*, *V. cholerae* is a free-living inhabitant of fresh water, but causes infection only in humans. Asymptomatic human carriers are believed to be a major reservoir. The disease is spread via contaminated food; shellfish grown in fresh and estuarine waters have also been implicated. Direct person-to-person spread is thought to be uncommon. Therefore, cholera continues to flourish in communities where there is absent or unreliable provision of clean drinking water and sewage disposal. Cases still occur in resource-rich countries (e.g. the Gulf Coast of Louisiana and Texas in the USA), but high standards of hygiene mean that secondary spread should not occur.

V. cholerae serotypes are based on somatic (O) antigens

Serotype O1 is the most important and is further divided into two biotypes: classical and El Tor (Fig. 22.11). The El Tor biotype, named after the quarantine camp where it was first isolated from pilgrims returning from Mecca, differs from classical *V. cholerae* in several ways. In particular, it causes only mild diarrhea and has a higher ratio of carriers to cases than classic cholera; carriage is also more prolonged, and the organisms survive better in the environment. The El Tor biotype, which was responsible for the seventh pandemic, has now spread throughout the world and has largely displaced the classic biotype.

In 1992, a new non-O1 strain (O139) arose in south India. It spread rapidly, infected O1-immune individuals, caused

Figure 22.11 *Vibrio cholerae* serotype O1, the cause of cholera, can be subdivided into different biotypes with different epidemiologic features, and into sero-subgroups and phage types for the purposes of investigating outbreaks of infection. Although *V. cholerae* is the most important pathogen of the genus, other species can also cause infections of both the gastrointestinal tract and other sites.

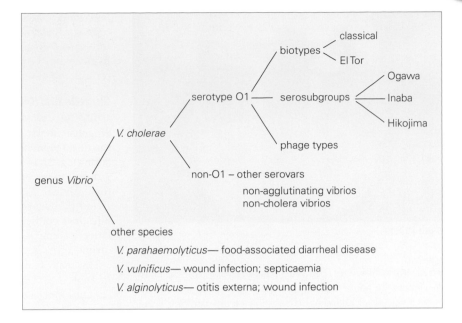

genus *Vibrio*

V. cholerae

serotype O1

biotypes
— classical
— El Tor

serosubgroups
— Ogawa
— Inaba
— Hikojima

phage types

non-O1 – other serovars
non-agglutinating vibrios
non-cholera vibrios

other species

V. parahaemolyticus— food-associated diarrheal disease

V. vulnificus— wound infection; septicaemia

V. alginolyticus— otitis externa; wound infection

epidemics, and was the eighth pandemic strain of cholera. *V. cholerae* O139 appeared to have originated from the El Tor O1 biotype when the latter acquired a new O (capsular) antigen by horizontal gene transfer from a non-O1 strain. This provided the recipient strain with a selective advantage in a region where a large part of the population was immune to O1 strains.

Other species of *Vibrio* cause a variety of infections in humans (Fig. 22.11). *V. parahaemolyticus* is another cause of diarrheal disease, but this is usually much less severe than cholera (see below).

The symptoms of cholera are caused by an enterotoxin

The symptoms of cholera are entirely due to the production of an enterotoxin in the gastrointestinal tract (see Ch. 17). However, the organism requires additional virulence factors to enable it to survive the host defences and adhere to the intestinal mucosa. These are illustrated in Figure 22.12 (see also Ch. 13).

The clinical features of cholera are summarized in Table 22.3. The severe watery non-bloody diarrhea is known as rice water stool because of its appearance (Fig. 22.13) and can result in the loss of 1 L of fluid every hour. It is this fluid loss and the consequent electrolyte imbalance that results in marked dehydration, metabolic acidosis (loss of bicarbonate), hypokalaemia (potassium loss) and hypovolaemic shock resulting in cardiac failure. Untreated, the mortality from cholera is 40–60%; rapidly instituted fluid and electrolyte replacement reduces the mortality to <1%.

Culture is necessary to diagnose sporadic or imported cases of cholera and carriers

In countries where cholera is prevalent, diagnosis is based on clinical grounds, and laboratory confirmation is rarely sought. It is worth remembering that ETEC infection can resemble cholera in both its severity and the management of infected individuals, as fluid and electrolyte replacement are of paramount importance. The methods are given in the Appendix.

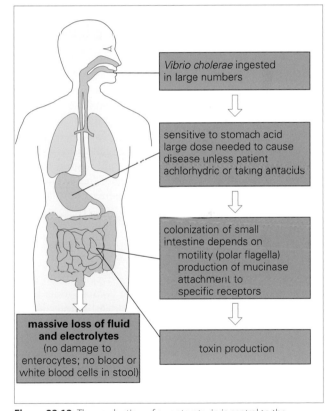

Vibrio cholerae ingested in large numbers

sensitive to stomach acid large dose needed to cause disease unless patient achlorhydric or taking antacids

colonization of small intestine depends on
motility (polar flagella)
production of mucinase
attachment to
specific receptors

toxin production

massive loss of fluid and electrolytes
(no damage to enterocytes; no blood or white blood cells in stool)

Figure 22.12 The production of an enterotoxin is central to the pathogenesis of cholera, but the organisms must possess other virulence factors to allow them to reach the small intestine and to adhere to the mucosal cells.

Prompt rehydration with fluids and electrolytes is central to the treatment of cholera

Oral or intravenous rehydration may be used. Antibiotics are not necessary, but tetracycline may be given, as some evidence indicates that this reduces the time of excretion of *V. cholerae* thereby reducing the risk of transmission.

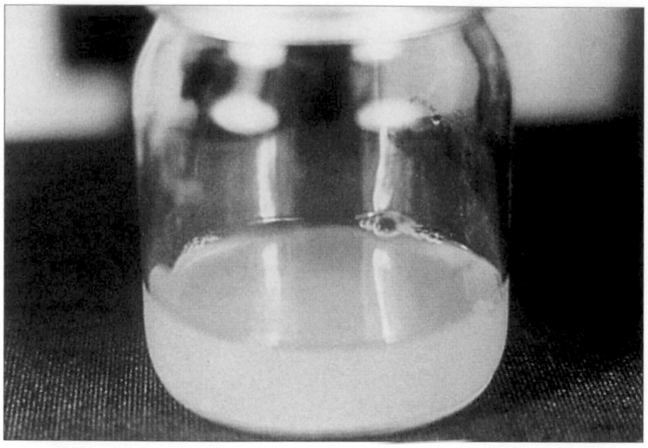

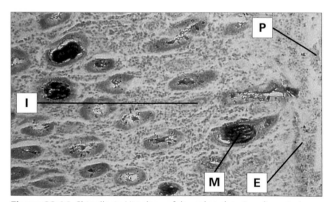

Figure 22.13 Rice water stool in cholera. (Courtesy of A.M. Geddes.)

There have, however, been reports of tetracycline-resistant *V. cholerae* in some areas.

As with other diarrheal disease, a clean drinking water supply and adequate sewage disposal are fundamental to the prevention of cholera. As there is no animal reservoir, it should in theory be possible to eliminate the disease. However, carriage in humans, albeit for only a few weeks, occurs in 1–20% of previously infected patients, making eradication difficult to achieve.

Cholera vaccines are not recommended for most travellers

A killed whole-cell vaccine is available and is given parenterally, but is effective in only about 50% of those vaccinated, with protection lasting for only 3–6 months. It is no longer recommended by the World Health Organization (WHO) for travellers to cholera-endemic areas, although it may be required in certain countries. Oral vaccines (not available in the USA) appear to provide somewhat better protection.

Shigellosis

Symptoms of *Shigella* infection range from mild to severe depending upon the infecting species

Shigellosis is also known as bacillary dysentery (in contrast to amoebic dysentery; see below) because in its more severe form it is characterized by an invasive infection of the mucosa of the large intestine, causing inflammation and resulting in the presence of pus and blood in the diarrheal stool. However, symptoms range from mild to severe depending upon the species of *Shigella* involved and on the underlying state of health of the host. There are four species:

- *Shigella sonnei* causes most infections at the mild end of the spectrum.
- *Shigella flexneri* and *S. boydii* usually produce more severe disease.
- *Shigella dysenteriae* is the most serious.

Shigellosis is primarily a paediatric disease. When associated with severe malnutrition it may precipitate complications such as the protein deficiency syndrome 'kwashiorkor'. Like *V. cholerae*, shigellae are human pathogens without an animal reservoir, but unlike the vibrios, they are not found in the environment, being spread from person to person by the faecal–oral route and less frequently by contaminated food

and water. Shigellae appear to be able to initiate infection from a small infective dose (10–100 organisms) and therefore spread is easy in situations where sanitation or personal hygiene may be poor (e.g. refugee camps, nurseries, daycare centres and other residential institutions).

Shigella diarrhea is usually watery at first, but later contains mucus and blood

Shigellae attach to, and invade, the mucosal epithelium of the distal ileum and colon, causing inflammation and ulceration (Fig. 22.14). However, they rarely invade through the gut wall to the bloodstream. *S. dysenteriae* produce a (Shiga) toxin similar to that associated with enterohaemorrhagic *E. coli* (EHEC; see above), which can cause damage to the intestinal epithelium and glomerular endothelial cells, the latter leading to kidney failure (haemolytic-uraemic syndrome, HUS; see above).

The main features of shigella infection are summarized in Table 22.3. Diarrhea is usually watery initially, but later contains mucus and blood. Lower abdominal cramps can be severe. The disease is usually self-limiting, but dehydration can occur, especially in the young and elderly. Complications can be associated with malnutrition (see above).

Antibiotics should only be given for severe shigella diarrhea

Rehydration may be indicated. Antibiotics, especially those that also decrease intestinal motility, should not be given except in severe cases. Plasmid-mediated resistance is common, and antibiotic susceptibility tests should be performed on shigella isolates if treatment is required.

Education in personal hygiene and proper sewage disposal are important. Infected individuals may continue to excrete shigellae for a few weeks, but longer-term carriage is unusual; therefore, with adequate public health measures and no animal reservoir, the disease is potentially eradicable.

Other bacterial causes of diarrheal disease

The pathogens described in the previous sections are the major bacterial causes of diarrheal disease. Salmonella and *Campylobacter* infections and some types of *E. coli* infections are most often food-associated, whereas cholera is more often water-borne and shigellosis is usually spread by direct

Figure 22.14 Shigellosis. Histology of the colon showing disrupted epithelium covered by pseudomembrane and interstitial infiltration. Mucin glands have discharged their contents and the goblet cells are empty. E, epithelium; I, interstitial infiltration; M, mucin in glands; P, pseudomembrane (colloidal iron stain). (Courtesy of R.H. Gilman.)

faecal–oral contact. Other bacterial pathogens that cause food-associated infection or food poisoning are described below.

V. parahaemolyticus and Yersinia enterocolitica are food-borne Gram-negative causes of diarrhea

V. parahaemolyticus is a halophilic (salt-loving) vibrio that contaminates seafood and fish. If these foods are consumed uncooked, diarrheal disease can result. The mechanism of pathogenesis is still unclear. Most strains associated with infection are haemolytic due to production of a heat-stable cytotoxin and have been shown to invade intestinal cells (in contrast to *V. cholerae*, which is non-invasive and cholera toxin, which is not cytotoxic).

The clinical features of infection are summarized in Table 22.3. The methods used for the laboratory diagnosis of *V. parahaemolyticus* infection are given in the Appendix (e.g. special media for cultivation). Prevention of infection depends upon cooking fish and seafood properly.

Yersinia enterocolitica is a member of the Enterobacteriaceae and is a cause of food-associated infection especially among infants and particularly in colder parts of the world. The reason for this geographic distribution is unknown, but it has been speculated that it is because the organism prefers to grow at temperatures of 22–25°C. *Y. enterocolitica* is found in a variety of animal hosts including rodents, rabbits, pigs, sheep, cattle, horses and domestic pets. Transmission to humans from household dogs has been reported. The organism survives and multiplies, albeit more slowly, at refrigeration temperatures (48°C) and has been implicated in outbreaks of infection associated with contaminated milk as well as other foods.

The mechanism of pathogenesis is unknown, but the clinical features of the disease result from invasion of the terminal ileum, necrosis in Peyer's patches and an associated inflammation of the mesenteric lymph nodes (Fig. 22.15). The presentation, with enterocolitis and often mesenteric adenitis, can easily be confused with acute appendicitis, particularly in children. The clinical features are summarized in Table 22.3. The laboratory diagnosis is outlined in the

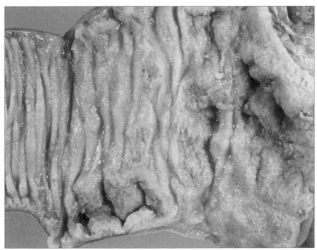

Figure 22.15 *Yersinia enterocolitica* infection of the ileum, showing superficial necrosis of the mucosa and ulceration. (Courtesy of J. Newman.)

Appendix. As with *V. parahaemolyticus*, an indication of a suspicion of yersinia infection is useful so that the laboratory staff can process the specimen appropriately.

Clostridium perfringens and Bacillus cereus are spore-forming Gram-positive causes of diarrhea

The Gram-negative organisms described in the previous sections invade the intestinal mucosa or produce enterotoxins, which cause diarrhea. None of these organisms produces spores. Two Gram-positive species are important causes of diarrheal disease, particularly in association with spore-contaminated food. These are *Clostridium perfringens* and *Bacillus cereus*.

Cl. perfringens is associated with diarrheal diseases in different circumstances, and the pathogenesis is summarized in Figure 22.16:

- Enterotoxin-producing strains are a common cause of food-associated infection.
- Much more rarely, β-toxin-producing strains produce an acute necrotizing disease of the small intestine, accompanied by abdominal pain and diarrhea. This form occurs after the consumption of contaminated meat by people who are unaccustomed to a high-protein diet and do not have sufficient intestinal trypsin to destroy the toxin. It is traditionally associated with the orgiastic pig feasts enjoyed by the natives of New Guinea, but also occurred in people released from prisoner-of-war camps.

The clinical features of the common type of infection are shown in Table 22.3. The laboratory investigation of suspected *Cl. perfringens* infection is outlined in the Appendix. The organism is an anaerobe and grows readily on routine laboratory media. Enterotoxin production can be demonstrated by a latex agglutination method.

Antibacterial treatment of *Cl. perfringens* diarrhea is rarely required. Prevention depends on thorough reheating of food before serving, or preferably avoiding cooking food too long before consumption.

Cl. perfringens is also an important cause of wound and soft tissue infections, as described in Chapter 26.

Bacillus cereus spores and vegetative cells contaminate many foods, and food-associated infection takes one of two forms:

- diarrhea resulting from the production of enterotoxin in the gut
- vomiting due to the ingestion of enterotoxin in food.

Two different toxins are involved, as illustrated in Figure 22.17. The clinical features of the infections are summarized in Table 22.3. Laboratory confirmation of the diagnosis requires specific media as described in the Appendix. The emetic type of disease may be difficult to assign to *B. cereus* unless the incriminated food is cultured.

As with *Cl. perfringens*, prevention of *B. cereus* food-associated infection depends upon proper cooking and rapid consumption of food. Specific antibacterial treatment is not indicated.

Antibiotic-associated diarrhea – *Clostridium difficile*

Clostridium difficile infection is the most commonly diagnosed bacterial cause of hospital-acquired infectious diarrhea in resource-rich countries.

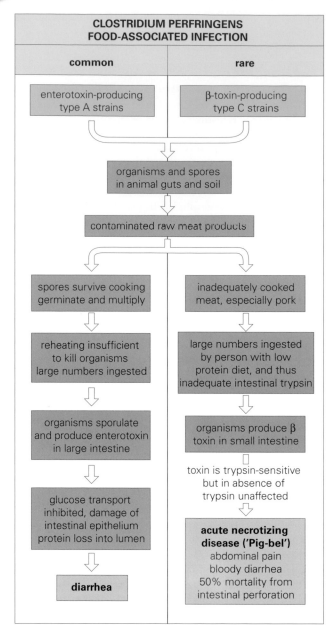

CLOSTRIDIUM PERFRINGENS FOOD-ASSOCIATED INFECTION

common	rare
enterotoxin-producing type A strains	β-toxin-producing type C strains

organisms and spores in animal guts and soil

contaminated raw meat products

spores survive cooking germinate and multiply	inadequately cooked meat, especially pork
reheating insufficient to kill organisms large numbers ingested	large numbers ingested by person with low protein diet, and thus inadequate intestinal trypsin
organisms sporulate and produce enterotoxin in large intestine	organisms produce β toxin in small intestine
glucose transport inhibited, damage of intestinal epithelium protein loss into lumen	toxin is trypsin-sensitive but in absence of trypsin unaffected
diarrhea	**acute necrotizing disease ('Pig-bel')** abdominal pain bloody diarrhea 50% mortality from intestinal perforation

Figure 22.16 *Clostridium perfringens* is linked with two forms of food-associated infection. The common, enterotoxin-mediated infection (left) is usually acquired by eating meat or poultry that has been cooked enough to kill vegetative cells, but not spores. As the food cools, the spores germinate. If reheating before consumption is inadequate (as it often is in mass catering outlets), large numbers of organisms are ingested. The rare form associated with β-toxin-producing strains (right) causes a severe necrotizing disease.

Treatment with broad-spectrum antibiotics can be complicated by antibiotic associated *Cl. difficile* diarrhea

All the infections described so far arise from the ingestion of organisms or their toxins. However, diarrhea can also arise from disruption of the normal gut flora. Even in the early days of antibiotic use, it was recognized that these agents affected the normal flora of the body as well as attacking the pathogens. For example, orally administered tetracycline disrupts the normal gut flora, and patients sometimes become recolonized not with the usual facultative

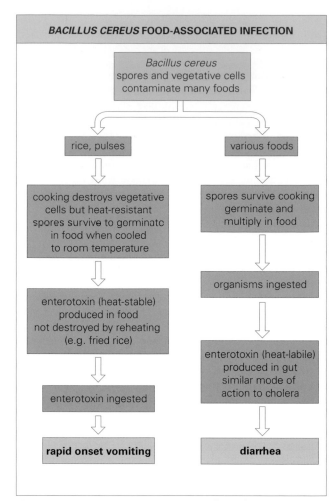

***BACILLUS CEREUS* FOOD-ASSOCIATED INFECTION**

Bacillus cereus spores and vegetative cells contaminate many foods

rice, pulses	various foods
cooking destroys vegetative cells but heat-resistant spores survive to germinate in food when cooled to room temperature	spores survive cooking germinate and multiply in food
enterotoxin (heat-stable) produced in food not destroyed by reheating (e.g. fried rice)	organisms ingested
enterotoxin ingested	enterotoxin (heat-labile) produced in gut similar mode of action to cholera
rapid onset vomiting	**diarrhea**

Figure 22.17 *Bacillus cereus* can cause two different forms of food-associated infection. Both involve toxins.

Gram-negative anaerobes but with *Staphylococcus aureus*, causing enterocolitis, or with yeasts such as *Candida*. Soon after clindamycin was introduced for therapeutic use, it was found to be associated with severe diarrhea in which the colonic mucosa became covered with a characteristic fibrinous pseudomembrane (pseudomembranous colitis; Fig. 22.18). However, clindamycin is not the cause of the condition; it merely inhibits the normal gut flora and allows

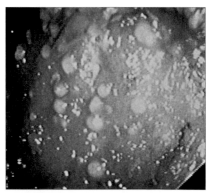

Figure 22.18 Antibiotic-associated colitis due to *Clostridium difficile*. Sigmoidoscopic view showing multiple pseudomembranous lesions. (Courtesy of J. Cunningham.)

Cl. difficile to multiply. This organism is commonly found in the gut of children and to a lesser extent in adults, but can also be acquired from other patients in hospital by cross-infection. *Cl. difficile* is a spore former and survives in the environment as it is resistant to heat and acid, for example. The spores contaminate the environment and become vegetative bacteria that can be transmitted between patients on the wards. In common with other clostridia, *Cl. difficile* produces exotoxins, two of which have been characterized: one is a cytotoxin and the other an enterotoxin that cause haemostasis and tissue necrosis in the colon, resulting in diarrhea.

Toxin A and toxin B are encoded within a short chromosomal segment carried by pathogenic strains of *Cl. difficile*, referred to as the pathogenicity locus, as is a regulatory gene *tcdC*. There is also a binary toxin encoded by two chromosomal genes separate from the chromosomal pathogenicity locus. One gene mediates cell surface binding and intracellular translocation and the other causes cell death.

An emergent epidemic *Cl. difficile* variant strain called *Cl. difficile* 027 has been shown to produce more toxin A and toxin B than most hospital strains. A study reported that the binary toxin genes were associated with partial deletions in the *tcdC* gene that down-regulates the toxin A and B genes, and that severe *Cl. difficile*-associated diarrhea was significantly associated with them. Finally, *Cl. difficile* 027 was associated with much higher levels of toxins A and B than in other strains. This strain detected in the USA, Canada, the UK and other parts of Europe is not only highly transmissible but causes more severe disease in individuals in both hospitals and the community. It has been associated with higher case fatality rates, with some infected individuals requiring a colectomy and intensive care unit support, and has also been shown to be more resistant to the fluoroquinolone antibiotics than other strains.

Although initially associated with clindamycin, *Cl. difficile* diarrhea has since been shown to follow therapy with many other broad-spectrum antibiotics; hence the term antibiotic-associated diarrhea or colitis. The infection is often severe and may require treatment with the anti-anaerobic agent metronidazole, or with oral vancomycin. However, the emergence of vancomycin-resistant enterococci, probably originating in the gut flora, has led to the recommendation that oral vancomycin be avoided wherever possible (see Ch. 33).

Viral diarrhea

Over 3 million infants die of gastroenteritis each year, and viruses are the most common cause

Non-bacterial gastroenteritis and diarrhea are usually caused by viruses. Infection is seen in all parts of the world, especially in infants and young children (Fig. 22.19). Its impact is staggering, as in parts of Asia, Africa and Latin America more than 3 million infants die of gastroenteritis each year, and children may have a total of 60 days of diarrhea in each year. It has a major effect on nutritional status and growth. In the USA, about 200 000 children under 5 years of age are hospitalized each year because of infectious gastroenteritis.

Although viruses appear to be the most common causes of gastroenteritis in infants and young children, viral gastroenteritis is not distinguishable clinically from other types of gastroenteritis. The viruses are specific to humans,

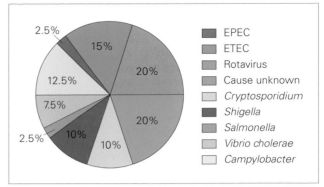

Figure 22.19 Diarrheal disease is a major cause of illness and death in children in resource-poor countries. This illustration shows the proportion of infections caused by different pathogens. Note that in as many as 20% of infections, a cause is not identified, but many of these are likely to be viral. EPEC, enteropathogenic *E. coli*; ETEC, enterotoxigenic *E. coli*. (Data from the WHO.)

and infection follows the general rules for faecal–oral transmission. Oral transmission of non-bacterial gastroenteritis was first demonstrated experimentally in 1945, but it was not until 1972 that viral particles were identified in faeces by electron microscopy. It has been difficult or impossible to cultivate most of these viruses in cell culture.

Rotaviruses

These are morphologically characteristic viruses (Fig. 22.20) named after the Latin word *rota* meaning a wheel, with a genome consisting of 11 separate segments of double-stranded RNA. Different rotaviruses infect the young of many mammals, including children, kittens, puppies, calves, foals and piglets, but it is thought that viruses from one host species occasionally cross-infect another. There are at least two human serotypes.

Replicating rotavirus causes diarrhea by damaging transport mechanisms in the gut

The incubation period is 1–2 days. After virus replication in intestinal epithelial cells there is an acute onset of vomiting, which is sometimes projectile, and diarrhea which

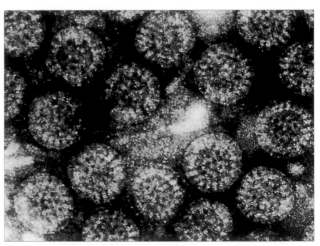

Figure 22.20 Rotavirus. The virus particles (65 nm in diameter) have a well-defined outer margin and capsules radiating from an inner core to give the particle a wheel-like (hence 'rota') appearance. (Courtesy of J.E. Banatvala.)

lasts from 4 to 7 days. The replicating virus damages transport mechanisms in the gut, and loss of water, salt and glucose causes diarrhea (Fig. 22.21). Infected cells in the intestine are destroyed, resulting in villous atrophy. The villi, long finger-like projections, become flattened, resulting in the loss of both the surface area for absorption and the digestive enzymes, and raised osmotic pressure in the gut lumen causes diarrhea. There is no inflammation or loss of blood. Exceedingly large numbers of virus particles, 10^{10}–10^{11}/g, appear in the faeces. For unknown reasons, respiratory symptoms such as cough and coryza are quite common. The disease is more severe in infants in resource-poor countries.

Infection is most common in children under 2 years of age, and has a seasonal pattern, being most frequent in the cooler months of the year in temperate climates. IgA antibodies in colostrum give protection during the first 6 months of life. Outbreaks are sometimes seen in nurseries. Older children are less susceptible to infection, nearly all of them having developed antibodies, but occasional infections occur in adults.

Rotaviruses are well-adapted intestinal infectious agents. As few as 10 ingested particles can cause infection, and by generating diarrhea laden with enormous quantities of infectious particles, together with their stability in the environment, these organisms have ensured their continued transmission and survival.

Rotavirus infection is confirmed by viral RNA or antigen detection

Laboratory diagnosis is generally not available in resource-poor countries, but during the acute stages, the diagnosis is made by detecting viral RNA or antigen using PCR or ELISA methods, respectively (see Ch. 32). The characteristic 65-nm particles can be seen in faecal samples by electron microscopy. They show cubic symmetry and an outer capsid coat arranged like the spokes of a wheel (Fig. 22.20).

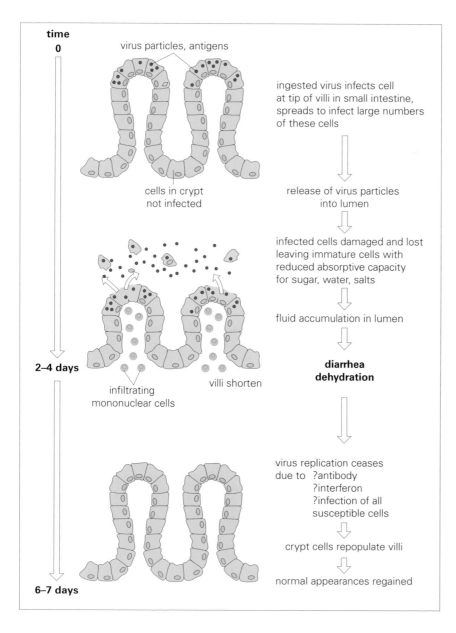

Figure 22.21 The pathogenesis of rotavirus diarrhea. This may differ with other viral infections of the gastrointestinal tract.

time
0

virus particles, antigens

cells in crypt not infected

ingested virus infects cell at tip of villi in small intestine, spreads to infect large numbers of these cells

release of virus particles into lumen

infected cells damaged and lost leaving immature cells with reduced absorptive capacity for sugar, water, salts

fluid accumulation in lumen

2–4 days

infiltrating mononuclear cells

villi shorten

diarrhea dehydration

virus replication ceases due to ?antibody
?interferon
?infection of all susceptible cells

crypt cells repopulate villi

normal appearances regained

6–7 days

Fluid and salt replacement can be life-saving in rotavirus diarrhea

Dehydration occurs readily in infants, and fluid and salt replacement orally or intravenously can be life-saving. There are no antiviral agents available, but a variety of live attenuated oral vaccines have undergone successful trials. In 2006, the US Food and Drug Administration (FDA) announced the approval of a live, oral vaccine for use in preventing rotavirus gastroenteritis in infants.

Other viruses

Other viruses causing diarrhea in humans include caliciviruses, astroviruses, adenoviruses and coronaviruses

Caliciviruses are 27 nm in diameter, single-stranded RNA viruses. They include the noroviruses, previously known as the small round structured viruses (SRSV) or Norwalk-like viruses (NLV) that cause 'winter vomiting disease' and sapoviruses. They have not yet been cultivated in vitro and cause gastroenteritis when fed to adult volunteers. One of the first identified norovirus outbreaks was in a school in Norwalk, Ohio, in 1969. Infection is common in older children and adults. These viruses are highly infectious, spread rapidly and nosocomial infection is common. The incubation period is 12–72 h. In up to 50% of cases there may be chills, headache, myalgia or fever as well as nausea, abdominal pain, vomiting and diarrhea. Recovery may occur within 24–48 h but may take longer. Noroviruses bind to cell surface carbohydrates of the ABH histo-blood group antigens and some strains have different binding affinities for different patterns of these antigens. In addition, these antigens are expressed to varying degrees in different individuals, resulting in some people being resistant to infection with specific norovirus strains. Laboratory diagnosis, important in outbreaks and for epidemiologic studies, is usually by PCR, electron microscopy or ELISA. Viruses in this group are often implicated in diarrhea associated with food- or waterborne routes occurring after eating sewage-contaminated shellfish such as cockles or mussels. In particular, noroviruses are a major cause of gastroenteritis in healthcare settings and many outbreaks have been reported in crowded environments such as cruise ships. Noroviruses show a high level of variability, resulting in both limited cross-protection between strains and reduced immunity in the population. In addition, due to this diversity, diagnostic assays have to be modified in order to optimize detection, and vaccine design either has to involve a cross-protective component or the development of a multivalent vaccine.

Astroviruses are 28-nm single-stranded RNA viruses of which five serotypes are known and have characteristic five- or six-pointed star patterns. Most infections occur in childhood and are mild. Adenoviruses are unenveloped, 70–80-nm double-stranded DNA viruses of which types 40 and 41 are associated with gastroenteritis. Types 40 and 41 can only be grown in specialized cell culture lines. They are second to rotaviruses as a cause of acute diarrhea in young children in temperate climates. The role of coronaviruses and human bocavirus infections in causing gastroenteritis is uncertain.

Although outbreaks of gastroenteritis often have a viral aetiology it may be difficult to be sure about the exact role of a given virus when it is identified in faeces, as there are a number of viruses that replicate in the gastrointestinal tract, enteroviruses, for example, which are not associated with acute diarrheal illness.

FOOD POISONING

In this chapter, the term 'food poisoning' is restricted to the diseases caused by toxins elaborated by contaminating bacteria in food before it is consumed (see above). The emetic toxin of *B. cereus* fits this definition, as do the diseases associated with the consumption of *Staph. aureus* enterotoxin and *Cl. botulinum* toxin.

Staphylococcus aureus

Eight different enterotoxins are produced by different strains of *Staph. aureus*

Twenty two serologically distinct enterotoxins have been reported to be produced by strains of *Staph. aureus*, the best understood of which are enterotoxins A–E (Table 22.4). All are heat stable and resistant to destruction by enzymes in the stomach and small intestine. Their mechanism of action is incompletely understood; however, similar to the TSST-1 toxin of toxic shock syndrome (see Ch. 26), they generally behave as superantigens (see Ch. 16), binding to major histocompatibility complex (MHC) class II molecules, which results in T-cell stimulation. Their effect on the central nervous system results in severe vomiting within 3–6 h of consumption. Diarrhea is not a feature, and recovery within 24 h is usual.

Up to 50% of *Staph. aureus* strains produce enterotoxin, and food (especially processed meats) is contaminated by human carriers. The bacteria grow at room temperature and release toxin. Subsequent heating may kill the organisms, but the toxin is stable. Often there are no viable organisms detectable in the food consumed, but enterotoxin can be detected by a latex agglutination test.

Botulism

Exotoxins produced by *Cl. botulinum* cause botulism

Botulism is a rare but serious disease caused by the exotoxin of *Cl. botulinum*. The organism is widespread in the environment, and spores can be isolated readily from soil samples and from various animals including fish. Seven serologically distinct toxins have been identified, but only four, A, B, E,

Table 22.4 Staphylococcal enterotoxins

Enterotoxin	
A	Most commonly associated with food poisoning
B	Associated with staphylococcal enterocolitis (rare)
C	Rare ⎫ Associated with
D	Second most common ⎬ contaminated
	Alone or in combination with A ⎭ milk products
E	Rare
TSST-1	Toxic shock syndrome toxin, not food-associated

Staphylococcus aureus produces at least eight immunologically distinct enterotoxins, the most important of which are listed here. Strains may produce one or more of the toxins simultaneously. Enterotoxin A is by far the most common in food-associated disease.

and less frequently F, are associated with human disease. While not destroyed by digestive enzymes, the toxins are inactivated after 30 min at 80°C. The toxins are ingested in food (often canned or reheated) or produced in the gut after ingestion of the organism; they are absorbed from the gut into the bloodstream and then reach their site of action, the peripheral nerve synapses. The action of the toxin is to block neurotransmission (see Ch. 17).

Infant botulism is the most common form of botulism

There are three forms of botulism:

1. food-borne botulism
2. infant botulism
3. wound botulism.

In food-borne botulism, toxin is elaborated by organisms in food, which is then ingested. In infant and wound botulism, the organisms are, respectively, ingested or implanted in a wound, and multiply and elaborate toxin in vivo. Infant botulism has been associated with feeding babies honey contaminated with *Cl. botulinum* spores.

The clinical disease is the same in all three forms and is characterized by flaccid paralysis leading to progressive muscle weakness and respiratory arrest. Intensive supportive treatment is urgently required, and complete recovery may take many months. Improvements in supportive care have reduced the mortality from around 70% to approximately 10%, but the disease, although rare, remains life-threatening. In addition, since botulinum toxin is one of the most potent biological toxins known, there is concern regarding its potential use as an agent of biowarfare.

Laboratory diagnosis of botulism involves injecting faecal and food samples into mice

Laboratory diagnosis depends largely upon demonstrating the presence of toxin or culturing the bacteria. However, a bioassay may need to be used if serum is available, whereby the serum would be injected into mice that have been protected with botulinum antitoxin or left unprotected. Culture of faeces or wound exudate for *Cl. botulinum* as well as toxin detection by polymerase chain reaction (PCR)-based assays for toxin sequences and ELISA (see Ch. 32) tests for functional toxin activity.

Polyvalent antitoxin is recommended as an adjunct to intensive supportive therapy for botulism

Since botulinum toxins are antigenic, they can be inactivated and used to produce antitoxin in animals. When botulism is suspected, antitoxin should be promptly administered along with supportive care, which may include mechanical ventilation (due to difficulty in breathing) and intravenous and nasogastric nutritional support (due to difficulty in swallowing). Antibiotics are generally used only for treatment of secondary infections.

It is not practicable to prevent food becoming contaminated with botulinum spores, so prevention of disease depends upon preventing the germination of spores in food by:

- maintaining food at an acid pH
- storing food at <4°C
- destroying toxin in food by heating for 30 min at 80°C.

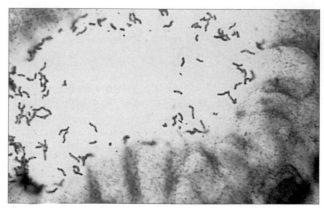

Figure 22.22 *Helicobacter pylori* gastritis. Silver stain showing numerous spiral-shaped organisms adhering to the mucosal surface. (Courtesy of A.M. Geddes.)

HELICOBACTER PYLORI AND GASTRIC ULCER DISEASE

Helicobacter pylori is associated with most duodenal and gastric ulcers

It is now well established that the Gram-negative spiral bacterium *H. pylori* is associated with over 90% of duodenal ulcers and 70–80% of gastric ulcers (Fig. 22.22). *H. pylori* does not appear to play a role in gastroesophageal reflux disease (GERD) or non-ulcer dyspepsia, most commonly presenting with persistent or recurrent pain in the upper abdomen in the absence of structural evidence of disease. Diagnosis may be made on the basis of histologic examination of biopsy specimens, although the non-invasive urea breath test (*H. pylori* produces large amounts of urease) is the most rapid means of detecting the organism's presence. Faecal *Helicobacter pylori* antigen testing is another non-invasive test. *H. pylori* can be cultured in the laboratory, but is difficult to grow.

The mechanism of pathogenicity is still being elucidated but involves a number of virulence factors, including a cytotoxin, acid-inhibiting protein, adhesins, urease (which aids survival in the acidic environment) and other factors which disrupt the gastric mucosa. Eradication of *H. pylori* to promote the remission and healing of ulcers requires combination therapy such as a proton pump inhibitor and two antibiotics such as clarithromycin and amoxicillin (see Ch. 33). However, studies suggesting that *H. pylori* may actually provide protection from some oesophageal and gastric cancers have led to active discussion regarding whether the organism should be eliminated from asymptomatic patients. It has been postulated that *H. pylori* interferes with the secretion of gastric acid that is associated with GERD, which in turn may precede oesophageal cancer. It is particularly confusing as it has also been associated with the development of stomach ulcers and cancer.

The interrelationship between *H. pylori* and gastric disease is thus complex and remains to be further clarified.

PARASITES AND THE GASTROINTESTINAL TRACT

Many species of protozoan and worm parasites live in the gastrointestinal tract, infecting some 3.5 billion people worldwide. Only a few are a frequent cause of serious pathology (Fig. 22.23) and these will form the focus of this part of the chapter.

Figure 22.23 Gastrointestinal parasites of humans. The majority of these infections are found in resource-poor countries, but all species also occur in the resource-rich world and some have come to prominence because of their association with AIDS. The most important parasite species are highlighted in bold type.

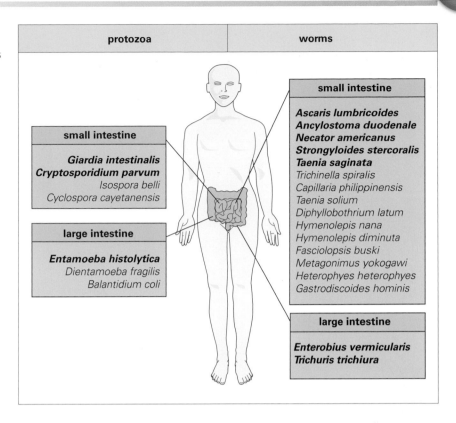

protozoa	worms

small intestine

Giardia intestinalis
Cryptosporidium parvum
Isospora belli
Cyclospora cayetanensis

large intestine

Entamoeba histolytica
Dientamoeba fragilis
Balantidium coli

small intestine

Ascaris lumbricoides
Ancylostoma duodenale
Necator americanus
Strongyloides stercoralis
Taenia saginata
Trichinella spiralis
Capillaria philippinensis
Taenia solium
Diphyllobothrium latum
Hymenolepis nana
Hymenolepis diminuta
Fasciolopsis buski
Metagonimus yokogawi
Heterophyes heterophyes
Gastrodiscoides hominis

large intestine

Enterobius vermicularis
Trichuris trichiura

Transmission of intestinal parasites is maintained by the release of life cycle stages in faeces

The different life cycle stages include cysts, eggs and larvae. In most cases new infections depend either directly or indirectly on contact with faecally derived material, infection rates therefore reflecting standards of hygiene and levels of sanitation. In general, the stages of protozoan parasites passed in faeces are either already infective or become infective within a short time. These parasites are therefore usually acquired by swallowing infective stages in faecally contaminated food or water. Worm parasites, with two major exceptions (pinworm and the dwarf tapeworm), produce eggs or larvae that require a period of development outside the host before they become infective. Transmission routes are more complex here:

- Some species are acquired through food or water contaminated with infective eggs or larvae, or are picked up directly via contaminated fingers.
- Some have larvae that can actively penetrate through the skin, migrating eventually to the intestine.
- Others are acquired by eating animals or animal products containing infective stages.

The symptoms of intestinal infection range from very mild, through acute or chronic diarrheal conditions associated with parasite-related inflammation, to life-threatening diseases caused by spread of the parasites into other organs of the body. Most infections fall into the first of these categories.

Protozoan infections

Three species are of particular importance:

- *Entamoeba histolytica*
- *Giardia intestinalis*
- *Cryptosporidium parvum*.

All three can give rise to diarrheal illnesses, but the organisms have distinctive features that allow a differential diagnosis to be made quite easily (Fig. 22.24). Other intestinal protozoa of concern, particularly in immunosuppressed patients, include *Cyclospora cayetanensis*, *Isospora belli* and the microsporidia.

Entamoeba histolytica

Entamoeba histolytica infection is particularly common in subtropical and tropical countries

For many years, it was considered that infections with *E. histolytica* could be asymptomatic or pathogenic, with dysentery a key symptom when the amoebae invaded the mucosa. Two species are involved: *E. histolytica* being invasive and *E. dispar* being non-invasive. *E. histolytica* occurs worldwide, but is most often found in subtropical and tropical countries, where the prevalence may exceed 50%. The trophozoite stages of the amoebae live in the large intestine on the mucosal surface. Reproduction of these stages is by simple binary fission, and there is periodic formation of resistant encysted forms, which pass out of the body. These cysts can survive in the external environment and act as the infective stages. Infection occurs when food or drink is contaminated either by infected food handlers or as a result of inadequate sanitation. Transmission can also take place as a result of anal sexual activity. The cysts pass intact through the stomach when swallowed and excyst in the small intestine, each giving rise to four progeny. These adhere to the epithelial cells and damage them by phagocytosis and cytolysis. They can invade the mucosa and feed on host tissues including red blood cells, giving rise to amoebic colitis.

E. histolytica infection may cause mild diarrhea or severe dysentery

Infections with *E. dispar* are asymptomatic. Invasion of the mucosa by *E. histolytica* may produce small localized superficial ulcers or involve the entire colonic mucosa with the

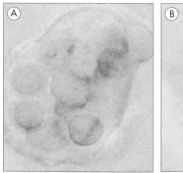
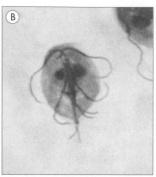
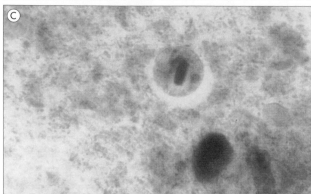
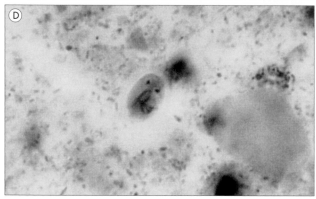

Figure 22.24 Protozoan infections of the gastrointestinal tract. (A) *Entamoeba histolytica*. Trophozoite found in the acute stage of the disease, which often contains ingested red blood cells. (B) *Giardia intestinalis* trophozoite associated with acute infection in humans. (Courtesy of D.K. Banerjee.) (C) Cyst of *E. histolytica*, with only one of the four nuclei visible. The broad chromatid bar is a semicrystalline aggregation of ribosomes. (H&E stain). (D) Oval cyst of *G. intestinalis* showing two of the four nuclei. (Iron haematoxylin stain.) (Courtesy of R. Muller and J.R. Baker.)

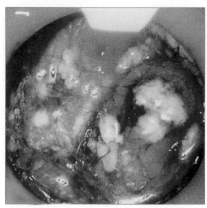

Figure 22.25 Amoebic colitis. Sigmoidoscopic view showing deep ulcers and overlying purulent exudate. (Courtesy of R.H. Gilman.)

Table 22.5 Features of bacillary and amoebic dysentery

	Bacillary	**Amoebic**
Organism	Shigella	Entamoeba
Polymorphs and macrophages in stool	Many	Few
Eosinophils and Charcot–Leyden crystals in stool	Few or absent	Often present
Organisms in stool	Many	Few
Blood and mucus in stool	Yes	Yes

E. histolytica infection can be diagnosed in asymptomatic patients from the presence of characteristic four-nucleate cysts in the stool

These cysts may be infrequent in light infections, and repeated stool examination is necessary. Care must be taken to differentiate *E. histolytica* from other non-pathogenic species that might be present (Fig. 22.26). Trophozoites can be found in cases of dysentery (when the stools are loose and wet), but they are fragile and deteriorate rapidly; specimens should therefore be preserved before examination. ELISA tests are available, as is a triage panel assay that can distinguish between *E. histolytica/E. dispar Cryptosporidium parvum* and *Giardia intestinalis*. Differentiation of *E. histolytica* from *E. dispar* requires immunological tests or PCR.

Acute *E. histolytica* infection can be treated with metronidazole or tinidazole

Recovery from infection is usual, and there is some immunity to reinfection. Metronidazole or tinidazole kill amoebic trophozoites in both intestinal and extraintestinal sites of infection and result in rapid clinical improvement, but relapse of the infection may occur unless a second antiamoebic agent is given to eradicate amoebae from the gut lumen. Examples are diloxanide furoate or paromomycin. Prevention of amoebiasis in the community requires the same approaches to hygiene and sanitation as those adopted for bacterial infections of the intestine.

formation of deep confluent ulcers (Fig. 22.25). The former causes a mild diarrhea, whereas more severe invasion leads to 'amoebic dysentery', which is characterized by mucus and blood in the stools. Dysenteries of amoebic and bacillary origin can be distinguished by a number of features (Table 22.5).

Complications include perforation of the intestine, leading to peritonitis, and extraintestinal invasion. Trophozoites can spread via the blood to the liver, with the formation of an abscess, and may secondarily extend to the lung and other organs. Rarely, abscesses spread directly and involve the overlying skin.

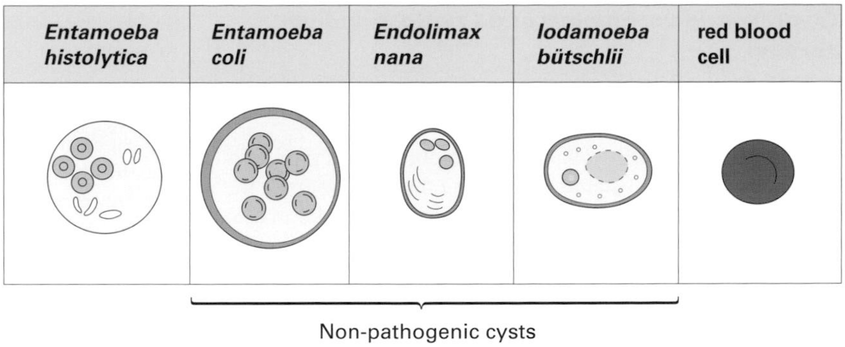

Figure 22.26 Characteristics of cysts (size and number of nuclei) are used to differentiate pathogenic from non-pathogenic protozoa. A red blood cell is shown for comparison.

Entamoeba histolytica	Entamoeba coli	Endolimax nana	Iodamoeba bütschlii	red blood cell

Non-pathogenic cysts

Giardia intestinalis

Giardia was the first intestinal microorganism to be observed under a microscope. It was discovered by Anton van Leeuwenhoek in 1681, using the microscope he had invented to examine specimens of his own stool. It has a global distribution and is a frequent cause of traveller's diarrhea. *Giardia* is the most commonly diagnosed intestinal parasite in the USA, having been detected in both drinking and recreational water. There is confusion over nomenclature, and the species infecting humans is also commonly referred to as *G. lamblia*, and sometimes as *G. duodenalis* (human).

Like *Entamoeba*, *Giardia* has only two life cycle stages

The two life cycle stages are the flagellate (four pairs of flagella) binucleate trophozoite and the resistant four-nucleate cyst. The trophozoites live in the upper portion of the small intestine, adhering closely to the brush border of the epithelial cells by specialized attachment regions (Fig. 22.27). They divide by binary fission and can occur in such numbers that they cover large areas of the mucosal surface. Cyst formation occurs at regular intervals, each cyst being formed as one trophozoite rounds up and produces a resistant wall. Cysts pass out in the stools and can survive for several weeks under optimum conditions. Infection occurs when the cysts are swallowed, usually as a result of drinking contaminated water. The minimum infective dose is very small: 10–25 cysts.

Epidemics of giardiasis have occurred when public drinking supplies have become contaminated, but smaller outbreaks have been traced to drinking from rivers and streams that

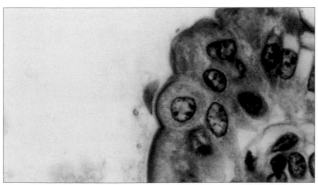

Figure 22.27 Trophozoite of *Giardia intestinalis* attached to the mucosal surface of the small intestine. (Iron haematoxylin stain.) (Courtesy of R. Muller and J.R. Baker.)

have been contaminated by wild animals. Apart from water-borne transmission, *Giardia* can be passed from person to person, especially within families, with food-borne transmission being rare. *Giardia* may also be transmitted sexually among homosexual men. The genus *Giardia* is widely distributed in mammals, and there is suggestive evidence for cross-infection between certain animal hosts (e.g. beaver) and humans. Much of this is circumstantial, but case reports provide more direct evidence.

Mild *Giardia* infections are asymptomatic, more severe infections cause diarrhea

The diarrhea may be:

- self-limiting, with 7–10 days being the usual course
- chronic, and develop into a serious condition, particularly in patients with deficient or compromised immunologic defences.

It is thought to arise from inflammatory responses triggered by the damaged epithelial cells and from interference with normal absorptive processes. Characteristically, the stools are loose, foul-smelling and often fatty.

Diagnosis of *Giardia* infection is based on identifying cysts or trophozoites in the stool

Repeated examination is necessary in light infections, when concentration techniques improve the chances of finding cysts. Duodenal intubation or the use of recoverable swallowed capsules and threads may aid in obtaining trophozoites directly from the intestine. Alternatives to microscopic methods are increasingly available, including faecal antigen ELISA tests with good specificity, immunochromatographic tests in cassette form, and PCR in some centres.

Giardia infection can be treated with a variety of drugs

Metronidazole and tinidazole are commonly used. Nitazoxanide or albendazole are alternatives and mepacrine hydrochloride is sometimes used. Community measures for prevention include the usual concerns with hygiene and sanitation, and improved treatment of drinking water supplies (largely filtration and chlorination) where these are suspected as a source. Care in drinking from potentially contaminated natural waters is also indicated.

Cryptosporidium hominis and Cryptosporidium parvum

The protozoan genus Cryptosporidium is widely distributed in many animals

Awareness of *Cryptosporidium* as an important cause of diarrhea in humans was established during the early years of the AIDS epidemic, although similar parasites were known to be widely distributed in many animals. There are two major species, *C. hominis* causing human infection, and *C. parvum* primarily infecting animals (including cattle), though cross-infection to humans does occur. The parasite has a complex life cycle, going through both asexual and sexual phases of development in the same host. Transmission requires ingestion of a minimum of 10 or so of the resistant oocyst stage (4–5 mm in diameter) in faecally contaminated material (Fig. 22.28). In the small intestine, the cyst releases infective sporozoites, which invade the epithelial cells, remaining closely associated with the apical plasma membrane. Here they form schizonts, which divide to release merozoites, and these then re-invade further epithelial cells. Eventually, a sexual phase occurs and oocysts are released. Transmission probably occurs most often via drinking water contaminated by oocysts, either from other humans or from animals. In 1993, *Cryptosporidium* caused a massive outbreak of watery diarrhea affecting 403 000 people in Milwaukee, USA. It was transmitted through the public water supply and probably originated from cattle.

Cryptosporidial diarrhea ranges from moderate to severe

Symptoms of infection with *Cryptosporidium* range from moderate diarrhea to more severe profuse diarrhea that is self-limiting in immunocompetent individuals (lasting 15–40 days), but can become chronic in immunocompromised patients. Cryptosporidiosis is a common infection in people with AIDS. In individuals with CD4+ T-cell counts <100/mm³ diarrhea is prolonged, may become irreversible, and can be life-threatening.

Routine faecal examinations are inadequate for diagnosing cryptosporidial diarrhea

Concentration techniques and special staining (e.g. modified Ziehl–Neelsen stain) are necessary to recover and identify the oocysts. Direct immunofluorescence and antigen detection ELISA tests are also used. PCR is available in reference centres and is becoming more widely available.

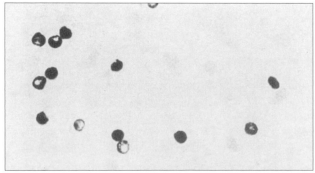

Figure 22.28 Cryptosporidium oocysts in faecal specimen. (Courtesy of S. Tzipori.)

In general, only immunocompromised patients need antiparasitic treatment for cryptosporidial diarrhea

Highly active antiretroviral therapy (HAART) in individuals with AIDS infected with *Cryptosporidium* has been reported to improve the diarrhea symptoms. This may be due to the protease inhibitors used in combination therapy interfering directly with the cryptosporidial proteases involved in the protozoal life cycle. In addition, HAART results in lowering of the HIV load and immune reconstitution. Paromomycin reduces oocyst output but does not clear infection. Nitazoxanide is effective in HIV-negative patients but is only partially active in those co-infected with HIV. Public health measures are similar to those outlined for controlling giardiasis, although *Cryptosporidium* is more resistant to chlorination. Some water treatment facilities deploy an additional ozonation step to inactivate cryptosporidia.

Cyclospora, Isospora and the Microsporidia

Cyclospora, like *Isospora belli* and *Cryptosporidium*, is a coccidian parasite, whose life cycle stages take place in epithelial cells of the mucosa. *Cyclospora* and *Isospora* have only been found in humans, unlike other coccidia that are zoonotic.

Cyclospora cayetanensis, identified in 1994, is one of the causes of diarrhea in travellers, but it can also be acquired from contaminated imported food; for example, Guatemalan raspberries were thought to be the cause of five diarrheal outbreaks in the USA in the years 1995 to 2000. Diarrhea can be prolonged and is severe in immunosuppressed individuals. Trimethoprim-sulphamethoxazole (co-trimoxazole) treatment is effective. Ciprofloxacin is partially effective.

AIDS patients infected with *Isospora belli* may show particularly severe symptoms, persistent diarrhea causing weight loss and even death. Treatment is with co-trimoxazole.

Infections with microsporidia, an unusual group, have also become recognized as a cause of diarrhea in AIDS and other immunosuppressed patients. *Enterocytozoon bieneusi* is the commonest cause, although *Encephalitozoon intestinalis* also occurs. Transmission appears to be direct. Albendazole treatment is effective against *Encephalitozoon intestinalis* but has disappointing activity against *Enterocytozoon bieneusi*. Where possible, immune reconstitution is the mainstay of treatment.

'Minor' intestinal protozoa

The human intestine may harbour a large number of protozoa, many of which appear to be quite harmless. Some have a questionable role in disease: these include *Blastocystis hominis*, *Dientamoeba fragilis* and *Sarcocystis hominis*.

Worm infections

The most important intestinal worms clinically are the nematodes known as 'soil-transmitted helminths'

Soil-transmitted helminths fall into two distinct groups:

- *Ascaris lumbricoides* (large roundworm) and *Trichuris trichiura* (whipworm), in which infection occurs by swallowing the infective eggs
- *Ancylostoma duodenale* and *Necator americanus* (hookworms) and *Strongyloides stercoralis*, which infect by active skin penetration by infective larvae which then undertake a systemic migration through the lungs to the intestine.

With the exception of *Trichuris* all the soil-transmitted nematodes inhabit the small bowel.

The pinworm or threadworm *Enterobius vermicularis* is probably the commonest intestinal nematode in resource-rich countries and is the least pathogenic. The females of this species, which live in the large bowel, release infective eggs onto the perianal skin. This causes itching, and transmission usually occurs directly from contaminated fingers, but the eggs are also light enough to be carried in dust.

The soil-transmitted helminths are commonest in the warmer resource-poor countries. About one-quarter of the world's population carry these worms, children being the most heavily infected section of the population. Transmission is favoured where there is inadequate disposal of faeces, contamination of water supplies, use of faeces (night-soil) as fertilizer, or low standards of hygiene (see below). Vast numbers of eggs are released in the lifetime of each female (tens of thousands by *Trichuris* and *Ancylostoma* and hundreds of thousands by *Ascaris*).

Life cycle and transmission

Female *Ascaris* and *Trichuris* lay thick-shelled eggs in the intestine, which are expelled with faeces and hatch after being swallowed by another host

The thick-shelled eggs of *Ascaris* and *Trichuris* are shown in Figure 22.29. The eggs require incubation for several days at optimum conditions (warm temperature, high humidity) for the infective larvae to develop. Once this occurs, the eggs remain infective for many weeks or months, depending upon the local microclimate. After being swallowed, the eggs hatch in the intestine, releasing the larvae. Those of *Ascaris* penetrate the gut wall and are carried in the blood through the liver to the lungs, climbing up the bronchi and trachea before being swallowed and once again reaching

the intestine. The adult worms live freely in the gut lumen, feeding on intestinal contents. In contrast, *Trichuris* larvae remain within the large bowel, penetrating into the epithelial cell layer, where they remain as they mature.

Adult female hookworms lay thin-shelled eggs that hatch in the faeces shortly after leaving the host

A hookworm egg is shown in Figure 22.29. The larvae of these hookworms (*A. duodenale* and *N. americanus*) feed on bacteria until infective, and then migrate away from the faecal mass. Infection takes place when larvae come into contact with unprotected skin (or additionally, in the case of *Ancylostoma*, are swallowed). They penetrate the skin, migrate via the blood to the lungs, climb the trachea and are swallowed. Adult worms attach by their enlarged mouths to the intestinal mucosa, ingest a plug of tissue, rupture capillaries and suck blood.

The adult female *Strongyloides* lays eggs that hatch in the intestine

The life cycle of *Strongyloides* is similar to that of hookworms, but shows some important differences. The adult worm exists as a parthenogenetic female that lays eggs into the mucosa. These eggs hatch in the intestine and the released larvae usually pass out in the faeces (Fig. 22.29). Development outside the host can follow the hookworm pattern, with the direct production of skin-penetrating larvae, or may be diverted into the production of a complete free-living generation, which then produces infective larvae. Under certain conditions, and particularly when the host is immunocompromised, *Strongyloides* larvae can re-invade before they are voided in the faeces. This process of autoinfection can give rise to the severe clinical condition known as disseminated strongyloidiasis, also known as hyperinfection, which is often complicated by Gram-negative bacterial septicaemia. All soil-transmitted helminths are relatively long-lived (several months to years), but authenticated cases show that *Strongyloides* infections can persist for more than 30 years, presumably through continuous internal autoinfection.

Clinical features

In most individuals, worm infections produce chronic mild intestinal discomfort rather than severe diarrhea or other conditions. Infections may lead to hypersensitivity responses and can also reduce responses to vaccination. Each parasite has a number of characteristic pathologic conditions linked with it.

Large numbers of adult *Ascaris* worms can cause intestinal obstruction

The migration of *Ascaris* larvae through the lungs can cause severe respiratory distress (pneumonitis), and this stage is often associated with pronounced eosinophilia. Intestinal stages of infection can cause abdominal pain, nausea and digestive disturbances. In children with a suboptimal nutritional intake, these disturbances can contribute to clinical malnutrition. Large numbers of adult worms can cause a physical blockage in the intestine, and this may also occur as worms die following chemotherapy. Intestinal worms tend to migrate out of the intestine, often up the bile duct, causing cholangitis. Perforation of the intestinal wall can also occur. Worms have occasionally been reported in unusual locations, including the orbit of the eye and the (male) urethra.

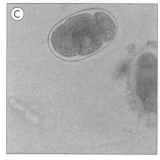
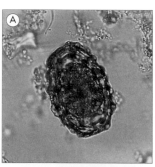
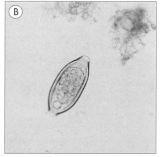
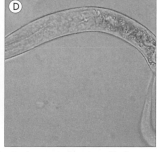

Figure 22.29 Eggs and larvae of intestinal nematodes passed in faeces. (A) Egg of *Ascaris* (fertile). (B) Egg of *Trichuris*. (C) Egg of hookworm. The embryo continues to divide in the faecal sample and may be at the 16- or 32-cell stage by the time the sample is examined. (D) Larva of *Strongyloides stercoralis*. (Courtesy of J.H. Cross.)

Ascaris is highly allergenic, and infections often give rise to symptoms of hypersensitivity which may persist for many years after the infection has been cleared.

Moderate to severe *Trichuris* infection can cause chronic diarrhea

As with all intestinal worms, children are the members of the community most heavily infected with *Trichuris*. Although previously regarded as of little clinical significance, research has shown that moderate to heavy infections in children can cause a chronic diarrhea (Fig. 22.30), reflected in impaired nutrition and retarded growth. Occasionally, heavy infections lead to prolapse of the rectum.

Hookworm disease can result in iron-deficiency anaemia

Invasion of hookworm larvae through the skin and lungs can cause a dermatitis and pneumonitis, respectively. The blood-feeding activities of the intestinal worms can lead to an iron-deficiency anaemia if the diet is inadequate. Heavy infections cause a marked debility and growth retardation.

Strongyloidiasis can be fatal in immunosuppressed people

Heavy intestinal infection with strongyloidiasis causes persistent and profuse diarrhea with dehydration and electrolyte imbalance. Profound mucosal changes can also lead to a malabsorption syndrome, which is sometimes confused with tropical sprue. People with diseases that suppress immune function, such as AIDS and cancer, or who are being treated with immunosuppressive drugs are susceptible to the development of disseminated strongyloidiasis. Invasion of the body by many thousands of autoinfective larvae can be fatal. Gram-negative bacterial septicaemia or meningitis can ensue.

The most common sign of pinworm (threadworm) infection is anal pruritus. Occasionally, this is accompanied by mild diarrhea. Migrating worms sometimes invade the appendix and have been linked with appendicitis. Invasion of the vagina has been reported in female children.

Laboratory diagnosis

All five of the soil-transmitted species can be diagnosed by finding eggs or larvae in the fresh stool, and direct smears or concentration techniques can be used. Acute infections with *Ascaris*, hookworms and *Strongyloides* are often accompanied by a marked blood eosinophilia. Although this is not diagnostic, it is a strong indicator of worm infection. Enzyme immunoassays can be used to detect *Strongyloides* antibody and has a 90% sensitivity of detection. However, there is cross-reactivity with IgG made against other nematode infections and one cannot determine whether the infection occurred recently or in the past.

The eggs of *Ascaris*, *Trichuris* and hookworms are characteristic

These eggs are shown in Figure 22.29 and are easily recognizable. Identification of the species of hookworm requires culture of the stool to allow the eggs to hatch and the larvae to mature into the infective third stage. The presence of adult *Ascaris* can sometimes be confirmed directly by radiography (Fig. 22.31).

The presence of larvae in fresh stools is diagnostic of *Strongyloides* infection.

Pinworm infection is diagnosed by finding eggs on perianal skin

Although adult pinworms sometimes appear in the stools, the eggs are seldom seen because they are laid directly onto the perianal skin (Fig. 22.32). They can be found by wiping this area with a piece of clear adhesive tape (the 'Scotch tape' test) and examining the tape under the microscope.

Treatment and prevention

Enterobius is treated with mebendazole or piperazine; *Ascaris* with mebendazole or piperazine; hookworm with mebendazole or albendazole; *Trichuris* with mebendazole or albendazole. *Strongyloides* requires treatment with ivermectin; thiabendazole is also effective, but is less well tolerated by the patient. At the community level, prevention can be achieved through improved hygiene and sanitation, making sure that faecal material is disposed of properly.

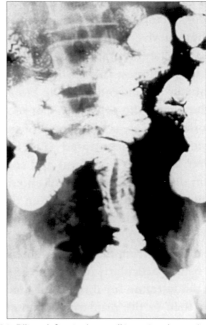

Figure 22.31 Filling defect in the small intestine due to the presence of *Ascaris*, seen on a radiograph after a barium meal. (Courtesy of W. Peters.)

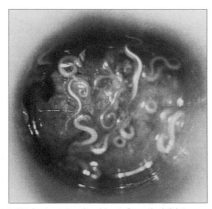

Figure 22.30 Trichuriasis in a healthy, infected, child. Proctoscopic view showing numerous adult *Trichuris trichiura* attached to the intestinal mucosa. (Courtesy of R.H. Gilman.)

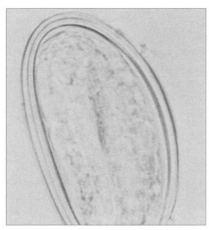

Figure 22.32 Egg of *Enterobius* on perianal skin. (Courtesy of J.H. Cross.)

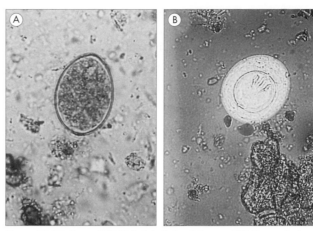

Figure 22.34 Eggs of (A) *Diphyllobothrium latum* and (B) *Hymenolepis nana*. (Courtesy of R. Muller and J.R. Baker.)

Other intestinal worms

Many other worm species can infect the intestine, but most are uncommon in resource-rich countries

Of the human tapeworms:

- The beef tapeworm *Taenia saginata*, transmitted through infected beef, is the most widely distributed. However, infection is usually asymptomatic, apart from the nausea felt on passing the large segments. Diagnosis involves finding these segments or the characteristic eggs in the stool (Fig. 22.33).
- *Diphyllobothrium latum*, the fish tapeworm, is widely distributed geographically, but infection is restricted to individuals eating raw or undercooked fish carrying the infective larvae. The eggs of this species have a terminal 'lid' and are the diagnostic stage in the stool (Fig. 22.34).
- *Hymenolepis nana*, the dwarf tapeworm, occurs primarily in children, infection occurring directly by swallowing eggs (Fig. 22.34). This worm has the ability to undergo autoinfection within the host's intestine, so that a large number of worms can build up rapidly, leading to diarrhea and some abdominal discomfort.

All these tapeworms can be removed by praziquantel or niclosamide.

Intestinal symptoms (predominantly diarrhea and abdominal pain) are also associated with infections by the nematode *Trichinella spiralis*, which is better known clinically for the pathology caused by the blood-borne muscle phase (see Chs 26 and 28). Infection with the two species of schistosome associated with mesenteric blood vessels (*Schistosoma japonicum* and *S. mansoni*) can also cause symptoms of intestinal disease. As the eggs pass through the intestinal wall, they cause marked inflammatory responses, granulomatous lesions form, and diarrhea may occur in the early acute phase. Heavy chronic *S. mansoni* infection is associated with inflammatory polyps in the colon, while severe involvement of the small bowel is more common with *S. japonicum*.

SYSTEMIC INFECTION INITIATED IN THE GASTROINTESTINAL TRACT

We opened this chapter by noting that infections acquired by the ingestion of pathogens could remain localized in the gastrointestinal tract or could disseminate to other organs and body systems. Important examples of disseminated infection are the enteric fevers and viral hepatitis types A and E. Listeriosis also appears to be acquired via the gastrointestinal tract. For the sake of clarity and convenience, other types of viral hepatitis will also be discussed in this chapter.

Enteric fevers: typhoid and paratyphoid

The term 'enteric fever' was introduced in the last century in an attempt to clarify the distinction between typhus (see Ch. 27) and typhoid. For many years these two diseases had been confused, as the common root of their names suggests (typhus, a fever with delirium; typhoid, resembling typhus), but even before the causative agents were isolated (typhoid caused by *S. typhi* and typhus caused by *Rickettsia* spp.), it was pointed out that it was 'just as impossible to confuse the intestinal lesions of typhoid with the pathologic findings of typhus as it was to confuse the eruptions of measles with the pustules of smallpox'. In fact, enteric fevers can be caused by *S. typhi* and three additional salmonella species, but the name 'typhoid' has stuck.

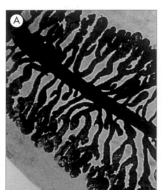
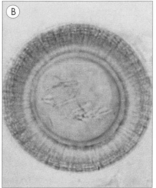

Figure 22.33 *Taenia saginata*. (A) Gravid proglottid stained with India ink to show numerous side branches. (B) Egg containing six-hooked (hexacanth) larva. (Courtesy of R. Muller and J.R. Baker.)

S. typhi, and paratyphi types S. paratyphi A, S. schottmuelleri (previously named S. paratyphi B), and S. hirschfeldii (previously named S. paratyphi C) cause enteric fevers

These species of *Salmonella* are restricted to humans and do not have a reservoir in animals. Therefore, spread of the infection is from person to person, usually through contaminated food or water. After infection, people can carry the organism for months or years, providing a continuing source from which others may become infected. Typhoid Mary, a cook in New York City in the early 1900s, is one such example. She was a long-term carrier who succeeded in initiating at least 10 outbreaks of the disease (see Ch. 16, Box 16.1).

The salmonellae multiply within, and are transported around, the body in macrophages

After ingestion, the salmonellae that survive the antibacterial defences of the stomach and small intestine penetrate the gut mucosa through the Peyer's patches, probably in the jejunum or distal ileum (Fig. 22.35). Once through the mucosal barrier, the bacteria reach the intestinal lymph nodes, where they survive and multiply within macrophages. They are transported in the macrophages to the mesenteric lymph nodes and thence to the thoracic duct and are eventually discharged into the bloodstream. Circulating in the blood, the organisms can seed many organs, most importantly in areas where cells of the reticuloendothelial system are concentrated (i.e. the spleen, bone marrow, liver and Peyer's patches). In the liver, they multiply in Kupffer cells. From the reticuloendothelial system, the bacteria re-invade the blood to reach other organs (e.g. kidney). The gallbladder is infected either from the blood or from the liver via the biliary tract, the bacterium being particularly resistant to bile. As a result, *S. typhi* enters the intestine for a second time in much larger numbers than on the primary encounter and causes a strong inflammatory response in Peyer's patches, leading to ulceration, with the danger of intestinal perforation.

Rose spots on the upper abdomen are characteristic, but absent in up to half of patients with enteric fever

After an incubation period of 10–14 days (range 7–21 days), the disease has an insidious onset with non-specific symptoms of fever and malaise accompanied by aches and

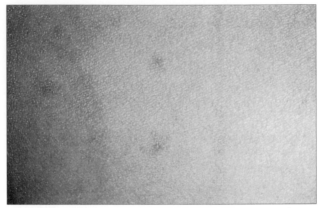

Figure 22.36 Rose spots on the skin in typhoid fever. (Courtesy of W.E. Farrar.)

respiratory symptoms, and may resemble a flu-like illness (see Ch. 15). Diarrhea may be present, but constipation is just as likely. At this stage, the patient often presents with a fever of unknown origin (FUO; see Ch. 29). In the absence of treatment, the fever increases and the patient becomes acutely ill. Rose spots – erythematous maculopapular lesions that blanch on pressure (Fig. 22.36) – are characteristic on the upper abdomen, but may be absent in up to half of patients. They are transient and disappear within hours to days. Without treatment, an uncomplicated infection lasts 4–6 weeks.

Before antibiotics, 12–16% of patients with enteric fever died, usually of complications

The complications can be classified into:

- those secondary to the local gastrointestinal lesions (e.g. haemorrhage and perforation; Fig. 22.37)
- those associated with toxaemia (e.g. myocarditis, hepatic and bone marrow damage)
- those secondary to a prolonged serious illness
- those resulting from multiplication of the organisms in other sites, causing meningitis, osteomyelitis or endocarditis.

Before antibiotics became available, 12–16% of patients died, usually of complications occurring in the third or fourth week of the disease. Relapse after an initial recovery was also common.

One to three per cent of patients with enteric fever become chronic carriers

Patients usually continue to excrete *S. typhi* in the faeces for several weeks after recovery, and 1–3% become chronic carriers, which is defined as *S. typhi* excretion in faeces or urine for 1 year after infection. Chronic carriage is more common in women, in older patients and in those with underlying disease of the gallbladder (e.g. stones) or urinary bladder (e.g. schistosomiasis).

Diagnosis of enteric fever depends upon isolating S. typhi or paratyphi types using selective media

Diagnosis cannot be made on clinical grounds alone, although the presence of rose spots in a febrile patient is highly suggestive. Samples of blood, faeces and urine should be cultured on selective media. An antibody response to

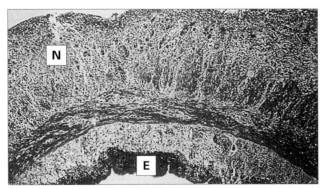

Figure 22.35 Typhoid. Section of ileum showing a typhoid ulcer with a transmural inflammatory reaction, focal areas of necrosis (N) and a fibrinous exudate (E) on the serosal surface (H&E stain). (Courtesy of M.S.R. Hutt.)

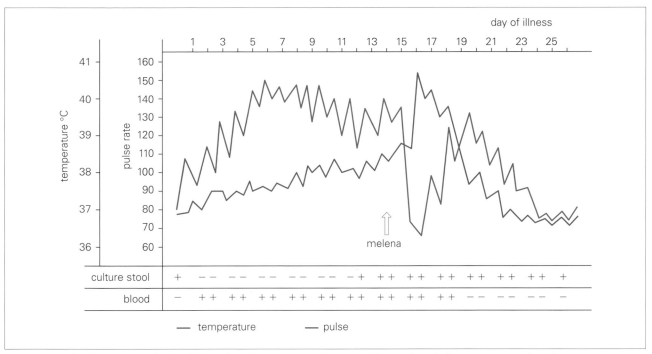

Figure 22.37 The clinical course of typhoid fever. Chart of temperature, pulse rate and bacteriologic findings in a patient whose illness was complicated by massive haemorrhage. (Courtesy of H.L. DuPont.)

infection can be detected by an agglutination test (Widal test), but non-specific cross-reaction with other enterobacteria may also cause an increase in H and O antibody levels. Interpretation of the results is complicated and depends on knowing the normal antibody titres in the population and whether the patient has been vaccinated. A demonstration of a rising titre between acute- and convalescent-phase sera is more useful than examination of a single sample. At best, the results confirm the microbiologic diagnosis, at worst they are misleading.

Antibiotic treatment should be started as soon as enteric fever is diagnosed

Ciprofloxacin or ceftriaxone followed by cefixime have been effectively used in antimicrobial chemotherapy, which should continue for at least 1 week after the patient's temperature has returned to normal. Some antibiotics appear active in vitro, but do not achieve a clinical cure, presumably because they do not reach the bacteria in their intracellular location. Isolates of *S. typhi* resistant to a variety of antimicrobial agents have been reported.

Prevention of enteric fever involves public health measures, treating carriers and vaccination

Breaking the chain of spread of infection from person to person depends upon good personal hygiene, adequate sewage disposal and a clean water supply. These conditions exist in the resource-rich world, where outbreaks of enteric fever are rare but still occur.

Typhoid carriers are a public health concern and should be excluded from employment involving food handling. Every effort should be made to eradicate carriage by antibiotic treatment, and if this is unsuccessful, removal of the gallbladder (the most common site of carriage) should be considered.

A single-dose injectable vaccine (Typhim Vi) which contains capsular polysaccharide antigen and an oral, live-attenuated, vaccine (strain Ty21a) are available and recommended for travellers to resource-poor countries. However, with both vaccines protection is complete in only 50–80% of recipients.

Listeriosis

Listeria infection is associated with pregnancy and reduced immunity

Listeria monocytogenes is a Gram-positive coccobacillus that is widespread among animals and in the environment. It is a food-borne pathogen, associated particularly with uncooked foods such as pâté, contaminated milk, soft cheeses and coleslaw. Studies of cases involving unpasteurized milk suggest that fewer than one thousand organisms may cause disease, and the ability of the organism to multiply, albeit slowly, at refrigeration temperatures allows an infective dose to accumulate in goods stored in this way. Even then, the population at risk appears primarily to be:

- pregnant women, with the possibility of infection of the baby in the uterus or during birth
- immunocompromised individuals including those with cancer, AIDS, on immunosuppressive drugs
- elderly individuals.

The disease usually presents as meningitis (see Ch. 24).

Viral hepatitis

An alphabetical litany of viruses directly target the liver, from hepatitis A to E

Hepatitis means inflammation and damage to the liver, and has differing aetiologies including non-infectious multisystemic conditions and drug toxicity as well as infectious agents. The latter include viruses and less commonly bacteria (e.g. *Leptospira* spp.), and other microorganisms. There is a broad spectrum of clinical illness ranging from asymptomatic, symptomatic with malaise, anorexia, nausea, abdominal pain and jaundice, to acute life-threatening liver failure, which is rare. Jaundice is a clinical term for the yellow tinge to the skin, sclera and mucous membranes. This is a result of liver cell damage which means that the liver cannot transport bilirubin into the bile, causing increased bilirubin levels in the body fluids. More than half of the liver must be damaged or destroyed before liver function fails. Regeneration of liver cells is rapid, but fibrous repair, especially when infection persists, can lead to permanent damage called cirrhosis. Cirrhosis results in a small, shrunken liver with poor function.

At least six different viruses are referred to as hepatitis viruses (Table 22.6), and generally they cannot be distinguished clinically. However, hepatitis A and E viruses are transmitted by the faecal–oral route and do not result in a carrier state; both infections resolve. In contrast, hepatitis B, D (delta), and C are transmitted by similar routes involving blood-contaminated equipment, although sexual transmission of hepatitis B is much more common than in hepatitis C, and all can lead to chronic carriage. Some agents have been reported that were thought to be involved in the spectrum of what is referred to as non-A–E hepatitis. However, there is no evidence that the GB, hepatitis G and TT viruses infect the liver directly, the liver being affected as a bystander. Other viruses also cause hepatitis as part of a disease syndrome and are dealt with in other chapters. Dramatic elevations of serum aminotransferase concentration (alanine aminotransferase, ALT; aspartate aminotransferase, AST) are characteristic of acute viral hepatitis. Specific laboratory tests to make the serological diagnosis of hepatitis A, B, D, C and E virus infections are available, as are PCR tests to detect and quantify the hepatitis B and C virus load in those with chronic infections. With the exception of hepatitis A and B there are no licensed vaccines, and specific antiviral treatments with and without immunomodulators are available for hepatitis B and C.

Hepatitis A

This disease is caused by hepatitis A virus (HAV), a single-stranded unenveloped RNA virus that has its own genus *Hepatovirus* in the Picornaviridae family. There is only one serotype, and the virus is endemic worldwide.

HAV is transmitted by the faecal–oral route

Virus is excreted in large amounts in faeces (10^8 infectious doses/g) and spreads from person to person by close contact (poor hand hygiene), by intimate contact (anal intercourse) or by contamination of food or water. The incubation period is 3–5 weeks, with a mean of 4 weeks; virus is present in faeces 1–2 weeks before symptoms appear and during the first week (sometimes also the second and third week) of the illness. Person-to-person transmission can lead to outbreaks in places such as schools and camps, and viral contamination of water or food is a common source of infection (Fig. 22.38). In resource-poor countries up to 90% of children have been infected by 5 years of age, whereas in resource-rich countries up to 20% of young adults have been infected. The latter figure used to be higher but is mostly a result of improved sanitation and less overcrowding.

Clinically, hepatitis A is milder in young children than in older children and adults

After infection, the virus enters the blood from the gastrointestinal tract, where it may replicate. It then infects liver cells, passing into the biliary tract to reach the intestine and appears in faeces (Fig. 22.39). Relatively small amounts of virus enter the blood at this stage. Events during the rather lengthy incubation period are poorly understood, but liver cells are damaged, and this is thought to be due to direct viral action. Common clinical manifestations are fever, anorexia, nausea and vomiting; jaundice is more common in adults. The illness generally has a more sudden onset than hepatitis B. The best laboratory method for diagnosis is to detect HAV-specific IgM antibody in serum.

Pooled human normal immunoglobulin (HNIG) contains antibody to HAV and will prevent or attenuate infection if given as pre- or post-exposure prophylaxis. There is no antiviral therapy, but an effective formaldehyde-inactivated vaccine should be offered to a number of groups at particular risk of infection. These include travellers to HAV-endemic countries, sewage workers, child daycare centre staff, institutional care workers, male homosexuals, and individuals with chronic liver disease. The vaccine is used

Table 22.6 The main viruses causing hepatitis in humans

Virus	Virus classification	Type of virus	Mode of infection	Incubation period	Other comments
Hepatitis A (HAV)	Hepatovirus	ssRNA	Faecal–oral	2–4 weeks	No carrier state
Hepatitis B (HBV)	Hepadnavirus	dsDNA	Blood-borne, sexual	6 weeks–6 months	Carriage associated with liver cancer
Hepatitis C (HCV)	Flavivirus	ssRNA	Blood-borne	2 months	Carriage associated with liver cancer
Hepatitis D (HDV)	Deltavirus	ssRNA	From blood	2–12 weeks	Needs concurrent hepatitis B virus infection
Hepatitis E (HEV)	Calicivirus	ssRNA	Faecal–oral	6–8 weeks	Common in Far East, no carrier state
Yellow fever	Flavivirus	ssRNA	Mosquito	3–6 days	No person-to-person spread, no carrier state

Other viruses causing hepatitis include Epstein–Barr virus (mild hepatitis in 15% of infected adults and adolescents), cytomegalovirus and rarely herpes simplex virus, while intrauterine infection with rubella or cytomegalovirus causes hepatitis in the newborn. ds, double-stranded; ss, single-stranded.

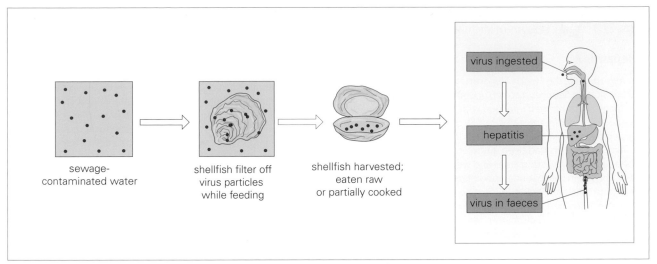

Figure 22.38 Contamination of shellfish by hepatitis A virus (HAV) can lead to human infection.

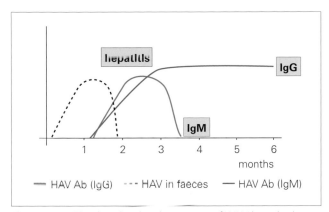

Figure 22.39 The clinical and virologic course of HAV. Ab, antibody.

alone or together with HNIG in certain situations in the post-exposure setting providing it can be given to contacts within 14 days of the onset of jaundice in the infected individual.

Hepatitis E

Hepatitis E virus (HEV) spreads by the faecal–oral route

This disease, also known as enteric non-A-non-B hepatitis, is caused by a small single-stranded RNA virus, and shares similarities with the caliciviruses. It has been classified in the genus *Hepevirus* in the family Hepeviridae, with four genotypes and one serotype.

Genotypes 1 and 2 have been involved in epidemics in resource-poor countries and infect humans only, and genotypes 3 and 4 infect humans and other animals in both resource-rich and -poor settings and are zoonoses. The virus is excreted in faeces and spreads by the faecal–oral route. It is the major cause of sporadic (up to 60%) as well as epidemic hepatitis in Asia, in the latter due to water-borne routes of transmission. In addition, there are sporadic cases in resource-rich countries.

HEV has been identified in a variety of animals, especially pigs, rabbits, chickens and sika deer and they constitute a probable reservoir for infection. Hepatitis E is likely to be another example of a zoonotic infection and experimental data showing the potential for transmission between pigs

and humans have been reported. In Japan, eating under-cooked pig liver and uncooked meats has been identified as a source of infection. The incubation period is 6–8 weeks. The disease is generally mild, but is severe in pregnant women, with a high mortality, up to 20% during the third trimester, due to fulminant hepatitis. The virus is eliminated from the body on recovery and there are no carriers. The diagnosis is made using serological tests to detect HEV-specific IgM. The 3-D crystal structure of the HEV capsid protein has been determined, which will lead to potential vaccines and antiviral agents. Two recombinant vaccines have undergone successful clinical trials.

Hepatitis B

This disease is caused by hepatitis B virus (HBV) infections, a hepadna (hepatitis DNA) virus (Box 22.3) containing a partially double-stranded circular DNA genome and three important antigens: HB surface antigen, HB core antigen and HBe antigen (Fig. 22.40; Table 22.7). HBe antigen is a soluble component secreted by the virus core, is expressed on the hepatocyte surface, and is targeted by the host immune system. Infection with a given strain of HBV confers resistance to all strains, but antigenic variation occurs. The four serological subtypes (adw, adr, ayw and ayr) have been superseded by the genetic classification in which the eight genotypes A to H have been determined. These can influence the clinical outcome of infection and response to antiviral treatment, and are useful in epidemiologic studies.

HB surface antigen can be found in blood and other body fluids

HBV can be transmitted by various routes, including:

- sexual intercourse
- vertically from mother to child (intrauterine, peri- and postnatal infection; see Ch. 23)
- via blood and blood products, blood-contaminated needles and equipment which may be used by injecting drug users
- in association with tattooing, body-piercing and acupuncture, again due to reusing needles which may be contaminated by blood.

Box 22.3 Lessons in Microbiology

Hepatitis A

In August 1988, the Florida Department of Health and Rehabilitation Services traced 61 people who had suffered serologically confirmed infection with HAV. These individuals resided in five different states, but 59 of them had eaten raw oysters from the same growing areas in Bay County coastal waters. The oysters had been gathered illegally from outside the approved harvesting areas and were contaminated with HAV. The mean incubation period of the disease was 29 days (range 16–48 days). Probable sources of faecal contamination near the oyster beds included boats with inappropriate sewage disposal systems and discharge from a local sewage treatment plant that contained a high concentration of faecal coliforms.

Hepatitis B

One of the largest outbreaks of hepatitis B virus infections in Europe occurred in London in 1998. A patient went to an alternative medicine clinic and was treated with a technique called autohaemotherapy. This involved mixing a small sample of the patient's blood with saline, then injecting the blood and saline mixture into her buttocks or acupuncture points. She subsequently developed acute hepatitis B and the public health doctors were contacted and an investigation started having identified the practices in the clinic that could have resulted in her becoming jaundiced.

A lookback exercise involving 352 patients who had attended the clinic between January 1997 and February 1998 and four staff was carried out. Evidence of exposure to hepatitis B was found in samples from 57 (16%) of this group. Hepatitis B surface antigen was detected in blood samples collected from a total of 33 patients and staff, 23 of whom had acute hepatitis B. Molecular analysis revealed that 30 (91%) samples had identical nucleotide sequences and were part of a large community outbreak of hepatitis B. Five patients were chronic hepatitis B carriers, one of whom was the likely source of infection, with the vehicle being the contaminated saline in a vial that was used to mix the blood on a number of occasions for the other patients involved in the outbreak.

This demonstrated once again that only single-use vials must be used in healthcare settings, together with the benefits in those countries that offer universal immunization against hepatitis B to their populations.

Hepadnaviruses

Hepadnaviruses are also found in woodchucks, ground squirrels and Pekin ducks. In each case, the infection persists in the body, with HBsAg-like particles in the blood and chronic hepatitis and liver cancer as sequelae. These viruses often infect non-hepatic cells. In northeast USA, for instance, 30% of woodchucks carry their own type of hepadnavirus and most develop liver cancer by later life. The virus replicates not only in liver cells, but also in lymphoid cells in the spleen, peripheral blood and thymus and in pancreatic acinar cells and bile duct epithelium.

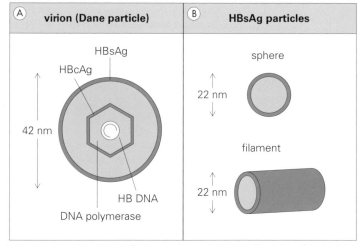
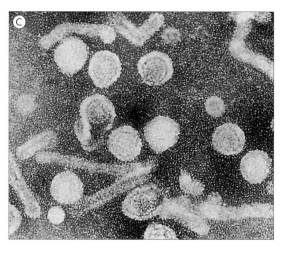

Figure 22.40 During acute infection, and in some carriers there are 10^6–10^7 infectious (Dane) particles/mL of serum (A), and as many as 10^{12} HB surface antigen (HBsAg) particles/mL (B). (C) Electron micrograph showing Dane particles and HBsAg particles. (Courtesy of J.D. Almeida.)

Transmission has been reported in healthcare settings such as renal units and has been associated with blood contaminated haemodialysis equipment. This has been reduced dramatically since the introduction of regular HB surface antigen (HBsAg) monitoring of patients and disposable dialysis cartridges. In addition, incidents have been reported involving HBV transmission from hepatitis B carrier healthcare workers (HCWs) to their patients while carrying out exposure-prone procedures, such as cardiothoracic surgery, due to intraoperative needlestick injuries resulting in blood-to-blood contact. Hepatitis B immunization and HBsAg screening of HCWs reduces the incidence of these transmission events. Blood and organ donors are also screened for HBsAg and HB core antibody in many counties worldwide, reducing the potential for transmission to recipients.

The number of HBV carriers worldwide is estimated to be over 350 million, and they play a major role in transmission. The HBV carrier prevalence is estimated to be up

Table 22.7 Characteristics of hepatitis B virus (HBV) antigens (Ag) and antibodies (Ab)

HBsAg	Envelope (surface) antigen of HBV particle also occurs as free particles (spheres and filaments) in blood; indicates infectivity of blood
HBsAb	Antibody to HBsAg; provides immunity; appears late (not in carriers)
HBcAg	Antigen in core of HBV
HBcAb	Antibody to HBcAg; appears early
HBeAg	Antigen derived from core; indicates high transmissibility
HBeAb	Antibody to the soluble component of core

to 0.5% in north, west and central Europe, North America and Australia, up to 0.7% in east Europe, the Mediterranean littoral, Central and South America, Russia and southwest Asia, and up to 20% in southeast Asia, sub-Saharan Africa and China. In countries where infant and childhood infection is common (possibly because there is a high carrier rate in mothers), overall carrier rates are higher.

HBV is not directly cytopathic for liver cells, and the pathology is largely immune mediated

After entering the body, the virus reaches the blood, then the liver, where the result is inflammation and necrosis. Much of the pathology is immune mediated, as infected liver cells are attacked by virus-specific cytotoxic T cells. The incubation period ranges from 6 weeks to 6 months, the median being 2.5 months.

As liver damage increases, clinical signs of hepatitis appear (Fig. 22.41); the disease is generally more severe than hepatitis A. The immune response slowly becomes effective, virus replication is curtailed, and eventually, although sometimes not for many months, the blood becomes non-infectious.

Certain groups of people are more likely to become carriers of hepatitis B

People with a more vigorous immune response to the infection clear the virus more rapidly, but tend to suffer a more severe illness. However, about 10% of infected adults fail to eliminate the virus from the body, and become carriers. The blood remains infectious, often for life, and although continuing liver damage can cause chronic hepatitis, the damage is often so mild that the carrier remains in good health. Certain groups of people are more or less likely to become carriers, as follows:

- Immunodeficient patients develop a milder disease due to the effect of reducing the host response to the infection, but are more likely to become carriers.
- There is a marked age-related effect. For example, in a study carried out in Taiwan, 90–95% of perinatally infected infants became carriers compared with 23% of those infected at 1–3 years of age and only 3% of those infected as university students.
- Gender is another factor, with males being more likely to become carriers.

Complications of hepatitis B are cirrhosis and hepatocellular carcinoma

Complications of hepatitis B include:

- Cirrhosis, as a result of chronic active hepatitis. This is an irreversible form of liver injury which may lead to primary hepatocellular carcinoma.
- Hepatocellular carcinoma is one of the 10 most common cancers worldwide. Hepatitis B carriers are 200 times more likely to develop liver cancer than non-carriers. This is not seen until 20–30 years after the infection. The cancer cells contain multiple integrated copies of HBV DNA and this could be the carcinogenic factor (see Ch. 17).

Serological tests are used in the diagnosis of HBV infection

HBsAg appears in the serum during the incubation period in the form of infectious Dane particles (see Fig. 22.41). The characteristic serological picture in an acute HBV infection includes the detection of HBsAg, HB core IgM and HBe antigen. The HBsAg concentration generally falls and finally disappears during recovery and convalescence. As HBsAg disappears, the HB core IgM level wanes over the next 3 months, HB core total antibody (IgM and IgG) is detected but is almost all IgG by this stage, and HB surface antibody

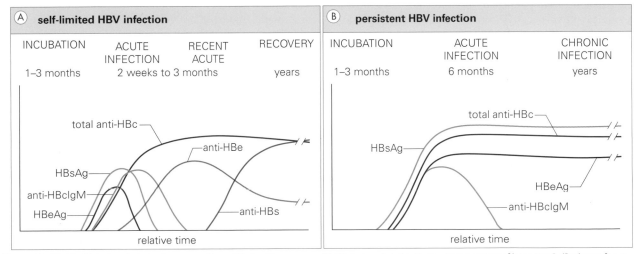

Figure 22.41 (A) Clinical and virologic course of hepatitis B, with recovery. (B) Clinical and virologic course in a carrier of hepatitis B. (Redrawn from: Farrar, W.E., Wood M.J., Innes, J.A. et al. (1992) *Infectious Diseases*, 2nd edn. London: Mosby International.)

Table 22.8 Interpretation of hepatitis B virus serological results

	Acute hepatitis B	Hepatitis B carrier	Hepatitis B carrier	Past hepatitis B	Hepatitis B vaccine response
HBsAg*	+	+	+	–	–
HB core antibody (total)	+	+	+	+	–
HB core IgM	+	–	–	–	–
HB e antibody	–	+	–	+	–
HBe antigen	+	–	+	–	–
HB surface antibody	–	–	–	+	+

*always confirm by neutralization if positive.

becomes detectable. Therefore, evidence of past infection will give the following serological profile (Table 22.8): HBsAg negative, HB core total antibody positive and HB surface antibody positive. HBV carriage is defined by detecting HBsAg in blood for a period of 6 months after the acute infection. When HBe antigen is detected, there are large amounts of virus in the blood and the carrier is considered to be of high infectivity, and when it disappears HBe antibody may become detectable. HBe antibody-positive carriers are considered to be of low infectivity. However, HBV DNA load is becoming a more useful marker of infectivity as mutations have been detected in the region encoding the e antigen which result in absence of e antigen production yet infectious virus is still assembled. They are known as pre-core mutant viruses. Therefore, these patients will be HBe antigen negative and HBe antibody positive but could be highly infectious.

Antiviral therapy is available

Two classes of drugs used to treat hepatitis B virus infections are pegylated interferon and nucleotide/nucleoside analogues. Management of HBV carriers has been revolutionized with the advent of oral antiviral therapy, in particular lamivudine (3TC), adefovir, entecavir, emtricitabine and tenofovir. Previously, therapy with interferon α2b, an immunomodulator, was used, but only 30% of selected patients achieved sustained responses. In addition, interferon (IFN) treatment has significant side effects. However, the better pharmacokinetics of pegylated interferon α2a has improved the results with respect to sustained response after treatment has been discontinued, especially in the e antigen-positive carriers. Better responses to IFN are seen in females under 50 years old, infected in adulthood with HBV genotype A or B, with a lower HBV DNA load and alanine aminotransferase more than twice the upper limit of normal. Moreover, with the range of antivirals available, courses of treatment are available that depend on a number of factors related to the virus as well as the stage of liver disease. For example, entecavir or tenofovir can be used if lamivudine resistance develops, which it does in 70% of those treated after 5 years.

Hepatitis B infection can be prevented by immunization

The original vaccine was produced in 1981 and consisted of purified HBsAg, prepared from the plasma of carriers, which was chemically treated to kill any contaminating viruses. The current vaccine is genetically engineered

HBsAg produced in yeast or mammalian cells. Three injections of vaccine over a 6-month period give good protection in over 90% of healthy adults. Immunization is recommended, especially for those who may be exposed to blood or blood products, such as receiving multiple transfusions or dialysis patients, all healthcare workers, sexual contacts of individuals with acute or chronic hepatitis B, and injecting drug users. One problem is that up to 10% of healthy individuals fail to produce the protective HB surface antibody, even when re-immunized. This could be due to genetically determined defects in the immune repertoire or because of the induction of immune suppressor cells.

After accidental exposure to infection, hepatitis B immunoglobulin (HBIG) can be used to provide immediate passive protection. This is prepared from the serum of individuals with high titres of HB surface antibody. It may also be used together with hepatitis B vaccine to prevent transmission to children of HBV-carrier mothers.

Hepatitis C

Hepatitis C virus was the most common cause of transfusion-associated non-A-non-B viral hepatitis

Hepatitis C virus (HCV) was discovered in 1989 as the cause of 90–95% of cases of transfusion-associated non-A-non-B hepatitis. It is a single-stranded RNA virus related to the flaviviruses and pestiviruses. The discovery of HCV was a tour de force in molecular virology. The viral RNA was extracted from blood, a complementary DNA (cDNA) clone was made, and viral antigen produced. Serum from individuals with non-A-non-B hepatitis was then tested for the presence of antibody to the viral antigen. The introduction of first-generation HCV antibody screening tests between 1990 and 1992, and subsequent improvement in sensitivity and specificity of these assays and genome detection methods, has resulted in a massive reduction in transfusion-associated HCV infection. It is estimated that more than 170 million people worldwide are infected with HCV.

HCV transmission routes share similarities with hepatitis B

HCV is present in blood, and transmission routes include blood and blood products, blood-contaminated needles and equipment which may be used by injecting drug users, and in association with tattooing, body-piercing and acupuncture, again due to reusing potentially blood-contaminated needles from other clients. Transmission has been reported in healthcare settings such as renal units because of contaminated dialysis equipment and other fomites, including gloves. Although the introduction of regular HCV monitoring of patients and disposable dialysis cartridges has helped in infection control, transmission has also occurred by other routes, probably often involving contaminated gloves worn by HCWs, which are not changed between patients. In addition, there have been incidents involving HCV transmission from HCV carrier HCWs carrying out exposure-prone procedures on their patients, such as intraoperative needlestick injuries resulting in blood-to-blood contact during cardiothoracic surgery. Unlike hepatitis B, HCV transmission is uncommon vertically, from mother to infant, and by sexual intercourse. There may be other methods of spread, as the route of transmission is unknown in up to 40% of infected individuals.

The HCV envelope binds to the hepatocyte cell surface membrane allowing viral entry, probably by endocytosis. Some of the HCV proteins interfere with the host response and other evasive measures include the high degree of genetic diversity due to the high error rate of RNA replication.

Six HCV genotypes and multiple subtypes have been identified. Genotype determination is predictive of antiviral therapy response, genotype 1 being associated with poor response. Viral and host factors affect the disease progression rate, with high HCV load in blood, genotype, and the degree of viral heterogeneity referred to as the quasispecies, being associated with more rapid progression. Viral clearance is associated with both the development and persistence of strong HCV-specific cytotoxic T-cell and helper T-cell responses. Being infected with one genotype does not protect against the others; therefore multiple infections are possible, thus making the production of a cross-protective vaccine more difficult.

About 75–85% of HCV-infected individuals develop chronic HCV

The incubation period is 2–4 months, with a mean of 7 weeks. Subclinical infection is the rule, with mild disease occurring in about 10% of individuals. Virus is often detectable in the blood after recovery from the acute illness, and carriers are a source of infection. Up to 2% of apparently healthy individuals in the USA have HCV antibody, and as a result, between 2.7 and 3.9 million people have an active infection. About 75–85% of HCV-infected individuals will develop chronic HCV and 10–15% will progress to cirrhosis within the first 20 years, with a resultant 1–4% risk per year of liver cancer in those with established cirrhosis. It is also a leading indication for liver transplantation. The rate of chronic HCV infection depends on the infected individual's age, gender, ethnicity and immune response.

Diagnostic tests for HCV infection involve serological assays to detect HCV antibody, qualitative and quantitative HCV RNA detection methods and genotype analysis. HCV RNA is present in approximately 70% of individuals with HCV antibody.

Treatment with pegylated IFNα and ribavirin is the standard of care

The aim of treatment is a sustained virological response (SVR) which means that HCV RNA cannot be detected 6 months after completing a course of treatment. Antiviral therapy with ribavirin has made a huge impact on the management of HCV infection, used in combination with pegylated interferon alpha. Originally, IFNα monotherapy resulted in up to 40% initial response rates, but under 20% were sustained responses. Treatment with pegylated IFNα, in which polyethylene glycol is attached to interferon and extends the half-life and duration of activity, and ribavirin has resulted in an SVR in 45% of patients with genotype 1 or 4 infections (48 weeks' treatment) and 80% of those with genotype 2 or 3 (24 weeks' treatment). Combining pegylated interferon and ribavirin with viral protease inhibitors such as telaprevir or boceprevir improves the SVR rates in the more difficult to treat HCV infections. No vaccine is available.

Hepatitis D

Hepatitis D virus can only multiply in a cell infected with HBV

This is caused by hepatitis D virus (HDV or delta virus), which has a very small, circular, single-stranded RNA genome and is a defective virus, so-named because it can successfully multiply in a cell only when the cell is infected with HBV at the same time. When HDV buds from the surface of a liver cell it acquires an envelope consisting of HBsAg (Fig. 22.42). The HBs envelope makes the 35–37-nm virus particle infectious by attaching it to hepatic cells.

Spread of HDV is similar to that of HBV and HBC

Infected blood contains very large amounts of virus (up to 10^{10} infectious doses/mL in experimentally infected chimpanzees), and spread is similar to that of the other parenterally transmitted hepatitis viruses.

HDV infection may occur at the same time as an HBV infection, and the resulting disease is often more severe than with HBV alone. Alternatively, HDV superinfection of an HBV carrier may occur, which may accelerate the course of the chronic hepatitis-B-related liver disease. Infection is uncommon in the UK and USA, but common in the Mediterranean littoral, parts of South America and Africa. Worldwide, HDV infection may occur in approximately 5% of HBV carriers.

The diagnosis is made by serological tests for HD antigen ('delta' antigen) or HD IgM and IgG. HBsAg will also be present.

There is no HDV-specific vaccine, but successful hepatitis B immunization prevents infection with hepatitis D.

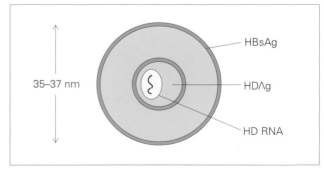

Figure 22.42 Structure of hepatitis D virus in serum. Ag, antigen.

Viral hepatitis, the rest of the alphabet

After the discovery of HCV, a small percentage of hepatitis infections known to be transmitted by blood transfusion have yet to be attributed to a virus infection, although hepatitis G virus referred to as GB virus C, transfusion transmitted virus or Torque Teno virus (TTV) and SENV 25–28 have been detected in individuals with post-transfusion hepatitis. There are even more human hepatitis viruses waiting to be discovered.

Parasitic infections affecting the liver

Few protozoa affect the liver. Some worms live there as adults and others migrate through the liver to reach other locations.

Inflammatory responses to the eggs of *Schistosoma mansoni* result in severe liver damage

Liver pathology in parasitic infections is most severe in *S. mansoni* infection. Although the worms spend only a relatively short time in the liver before moving to the mesenteric vessels, eggs released by the females can be swept by the bloodstream into the hepatic circulation and be filtered out in the sinusoids. The inflammatory response to these trapped eggs is the primary cause of the complex changes that result in hepatomegaly, fibrosis and the formation of varices (Fig. 22.43).

Whereas schistosomiasis is widespread in tropical and subtropical regions, other parasitic infections affecting the liver are much more restricted in their distribution (e.g. clonorchiasis, fascioliasis, hydatid disease).

In Asia, infections with the human liver fluke *Clonorchis sinensis* are acquired by eating fish infected with the metacercarial stage. Juvenile flukes released in the intestine move up the bile duct and attach to the duct epithelium, feeding on the cells and blood and tissue fluids. In heavy infections, there is a pronounced inflammatory response, and proliferation and hyperplasia of the biliary epithelium, cholangitis, jaundice and liver enlargement are possible consequences. Chronic infection with *Clonorchis sinensis* or *Opisthorchis viverrini* is a recognized cause of intrahepatic cholangiocarcinoma.

A number of animal liver flukes can also establish themselves in humans. These include species of *Opisthorchis* (in Asia and Eastern Europe) and the common liver fluke *Fasciola hepatica*. In general, the symptoms associated with these infections are similar to those described for *C. sinensis*.

The larval stages of the dog tapeworm *Echinococcus granulosus* can develop in humans when the eggs are swallowed. Larvae from the eggs move from the intestine into the body and frequently develop into large hydatid cysts (cystic echinococcosis) in the liver. These can be diagnosed on scans as large cavities. Apart from pressure damage to

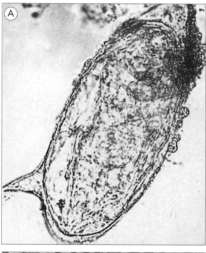
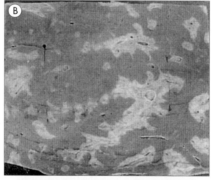
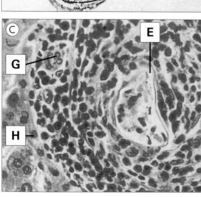
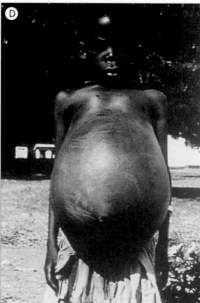

Figure 22.43 The portal fibrosis of *Schistosoma mansoni* is the end result of huge numbers of granulomas formed around worm eggs deposited in the liver. In the related *Schistosoma haematobium* infection, a similar process occurs in the wall of the bladder. (A) Egg of *S. mansoni* (× 400). (Courtesy of R. Muller.) (B) Pipe-stem fibrosis in the liver as a result of coalescent calcified granulomas. (Courtesy of R. Muller.) (C) Cellular reaction around an egg in the liver. E, egg containing miracidium; G, giant cell; H, hepatic cell. (Courtesy of R. Muller.) (D) Clinical schistosomiasis with massive hepatosplenomegaly and ascites due to portal obstruction. (Courtesy of G. Webbe.)

surrounding tissues, rupture of the cysts leads to secondary cysts and may cause anaphylaxis. Cysts can be removed surgically or treated with benzimidazole drugs. *E. multilocularis*, acquired from eggs passed by wild carnivores, develops in the liver not as cysts but as a ramifying mass resembling a carcinoma (alveolar echinococcosis). *E. multilocularis* is treated by radical excision plus benzimidazole therapy. Inoperable cysts require life-long drug therapy. Liver transplantation is sometimes used.

Other parasitic infections associated with liver pathology are malaria, leishmaniasis, ascariasis and extraintestinal amoebiasis, which causes liver abscesses.

Liver abscesses

Despite the name, an amoebic liver abscess does not consist of pus

E. histolytica can move from the gastrointestinal tract and cause disease in other sites, including the liver (see above). However, the term 'amoebic liver abscess' is not strictly accurate because the lesion formed in the liver consists of necrotic liver tissue rather than pus. True liver abscesses – walled-off lesions containing organisms and dead or dying polymorphs (pus) – are frequently polymicrobial, containing a mixed flora of aerobic and anaerobic bacteria (Fig. 22.44). Lesions caused by *E. granulosus* in hydatid disease can become secondarily infected with bacteria. The source of infection may be local to the lesion or another body site, but is usually undiagnosed. Broad-spectrum antimicrobial therapy is required to cover both aerobes and anaerobes.

Biliary tract infections

Infection is a common complication of biliary tract disease

Although infection is not often the primary cause of disease in the biliary tract, it is a common complication. Many patients with gallstones obstructing the biliary system develop infective complications caused by organisms from the normal gastrointestinal flora such as enterobacteria and anaerobes. Local infection can result in cholangitis and subsequent liver abscesses or invade the bloodstream to cause septicaemia and generalized infection. Removing the underlying obstruction in the biliary tree is a prerequisite to successful therapy. Antibacterial therapy is usually broad spectrum, covering both aerobes and anaerobes.

Peritonitis and intra-abdominal sepsis

The peritoneal cavity is normally sterile, but is in constant danger of becoming contaminated by bacteria discharged through perforations in the gut wall arising from trauma (accidental or surgical) or infection. The outcome of peritoneal contamination depends upon the volume of the inoculum (1 mL of gut contents contains many millions of microorganisms), and the ability of the local defences to wall off and destroy the microorganisms.

Peritonitis is generally classified as primary (without apparent source of infection) or secondary (e.g. due to perforated appendicitis, ulcer, colon)

Peritonitis usually begins as an acute inflammation in the abdomen which may progress to the formation of localized intra-abdominal abscesses. In general, the aetiologic agents responsible for primary and secondary peritonitis and intraperitoneal abscesses are different. Spontaneous bacterial peritonitis (SBP) is most commonly associated with cirrhosis of the liver. SBP is typically due to Gram-negative enteric bacteria, most commonly *E. coli*. Secondary peritonitis and intra-abdominal abscesses more often involve a mixture of organisms, especially the Gram-negative anaerobe *Bacteroides fragilis*. *Mycobacterium tuberculosis* and *Actinomyces* can also cause intraperitoneal infection (Fig. 22.45). In the absence of appropriate antibiotic therapy, infections are frequently fatal, and even with appropriate treatment the mortality remains at 1–5%. Empiric antibiotic therapy for SBP commonly involves third-generation cephalosporins (see Ch. 33) with re-evaluation when culture results are available. Initial antimicrobial treatment of secondary peritonitis must especially target the Gram-negative anaerobe *B. fragilis* (e.g. metronidazole) and Gram-negative aerobic pathogens (e.g. third-generation cephalosporins, etc.) as well as taking steps to eliminate the source of contamination. Mycobacterial infection requires specific antituberculosis therapy (see Ch. 33), while actinomycosis responds well to prolonged treatment with penicillin.

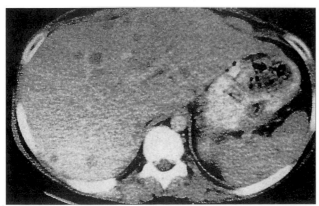

Figure 22.44 Multiple pyogenic liver abscesses due to *Pseudomonas aeruginosa*. (Courtesy of N. Holland.)

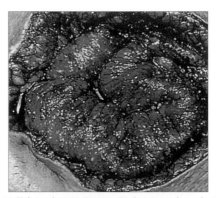

Figure 22.45 Tuberculous peritonitis. Oedematous bowel with multiple lesions on the peritoneal surface. (Courtesy of M. Goldman.)

KEY FACTS

- Diarrheal disease is a major cause of morbidity and mortality in the resource-poor world. A wide range of diverse microbes cause infections of the gastrointestinal tract. Diarrhea, the most common symptom, ranges from mild and self-limiting to severe with consequent dehydration and death.

- Gastrointestinal pathogens are transmitted by the faecal–oral route. They may invade the gut, causing systemic disease (e.g. typhoid), or multiply and produce locally acting toxins and damage only the gastrointestinal tract (e.g. cholera). The number of organisms ingested and their virulence attributes are critical factors in determining whether infection becomes established.

- Microbiologic diagnosis is usually impossible without laboratory investigations, but the patient's history, including food and travel history, provides useful pointers.

- The major bacterial causes of diarrhea are *E. coli*, salmonellae, *Campylobacter*, *V. cholerae* and shigellae. Other less common causes include *Cl. perfringens*, *B. cereus*, *V. parahaemolyticus* and *Y. enterocolitica*. Food poisoning (i.e. the ingestion of bacterial toxins in food) is caused by *Staph. aureus* and *Cl. Botulinum*.

- *E. coli* is the major bacterial cause of diarrhea in resource-poor countries and of traveller's diarrhea. Distinct groups within the species (ETEC, EHEC, EPEC and EIEC) have different pathogenic mechanisms – some are invasive, others toxigenic.

- Salmonellae and *Campylobacter* are common in resource-rich countries, have large animal reservoirs and spread via the food chain. Both cause disease by multiplication in the gut and the production of locally acting toxins.

- *V. cholerae* and shigellae have no animal reservoirs, and the diseases are potentially eradicable. Transmission is prevented by good hygiene, clean drinking water and hygienic disposal of faeces. The pathogenesis of cholera depends upon production of cholera enterotoxin, which acts on the gastrointestinal mucosal cells. In contrast, *Shigella* invades the mucosa, causing ulceration and bloody diarrhea, symptoms similar to those of amoebic dysentery.

- *H. pylori* is associated with gastritis and duodenal ulcers. Removal of the bacterium by combination treatment with antibiotics and proton pump inhibitors reduces symptoms and encourages healing.

- Disruption of the normal bacterial flora of the gut (usually due to antibiotic treatment) allows organisms normally absent or present in small numbers (e.g. *Cl. difficile*) to multiply and cause antibiotic-associated diarrhea.

- Viral gastroenteritis causes appalling morbidity and mortality, especially in young children in the resource-poor world. The chief culprits are the rotaviruses, which are specific to humans, spread by the faecal–oral route and restrict their multiplication to the gastrointestinal epithelial cells, which they destroy. Very small numbers can initiate infection and multiply in the gut to produce enormous numbers for excretion and transmission to new hosts.

- Ingestion of food or water contaminated with *S. typhi* or *paratyphi* types can result in the systemic infection enteric (typhoid) fever. These pathogens invade the gut mucosa and are ingested by, and survive in, macrophages. They are transported via the lymphatics to the bloodstream from whence they seed many organs and give the characteristic multisystem disease. Positive diagnosis depends upon culture of the organism. Specific antibiotic therapy is required and specific prevention is achievable through immunization.

- Hepatitis is usually caused by viruses (e.g. hepatitis A–E). Hepatitis A and E are transmitted by the faecal–oral route and the rest by contaminated blood or the sexual route. Infection with HBV and HCV often leads to chronic hepatitis and can result in liver cancer.

- Many protozoa and worms live in the intestine, but relatively few cause severe diarrhea. Important protozoa are *E. histolytica*, *G. intestinalis* and *Cryptosporidium*, which are acquired by ingestion of infective cysts in faecally contaminated food or water. Important worms are *Ascaris*, *Trichuris*, *Strongyloides* and hookworm. They have more complex routes of transmission, with the eggs or larvae requiring a development period outside the human host.

- Parasitic infections involving the liver include infections by *Schistosoma mansoni* in the tropics and subtropics, and *Clonorchis sinensis*, the human liver fluke, in Asia. Other parasitic infections with important liver pathology include malaria, leishmaniasis, extraintestinal amoebiasis, hydatid disease and ascariasis.

- Infection of the biliary tree is usually secondary to obstruction. The normal intestinal flora causes mixed infections, which may extend to produce liver abscesses and septicaemia.

- Peritonitis and intra-abdominal sepsis follow contamination of the normally sterile abdominal cavity with intestinal microbes. The presentation is acute, and infection can be fatal. Antibiotic therapy against both aerobic and anaerobic bacteria is essential.

Obstetric and perinatal infections

23

Introduction

During pregnancy, a novel set of tissues potentially susceptible to infection appear, including the fetus, the placenta and the lactating mammary glands. The placenta acts as an effective barrier, protecting the fetus from most circulating microorganisms, and the fetal membranes shield the fetus from microorganisms in the genital tract. Perforation of the amniotic sac, for instance, at a late stage of pregnancy, often results in fetal infection.

During pregnancy, certain infections in the mother can be more severe than usual (malaria, hepatitis) or latent viruses such as herpes simplex virus (HSV) and cytomegalovirus (CMV) can reactivate and infect the fetus, and after delivery the raw uterine tissue is susceptible to streptococcal and other pathogens, causing puerperal sepsis.

The fetus, once infected via the placenta, is highly susceptible, but may survive certain pathogens and develop congenital abnormalities; examples include: rubella, CMV, *Toxoplasma gondii* and *Treponema pallidum*. Bacteria from the vagina, such as group B streptococci, can cause neonatal septicaemia, meningitis and death, and a birth canal infected with *Neisseria gonorrhoeae* or *Chlamydia trachomatis* inoculates the infant to cause neonatal conjunctivitis. Maternal genital HSV infection can cause more serious neonatal disease and is underreported.

Maternal HIV infection often causes abortion, prematurity and low birth weight. In resource-poor countries or where maternal infection is undiagnosed, up to 40% of infants are infected, about one-third in utero and two-thirds perinatally from maternal blood or milk. Maternal blood may also transmit hepatitis B and C viruses, and milk can be a source of human T-cell lymphotropic virus type 1 (HTLV-1) infection.

Here, we describe infections that occur during pregnancy and around the time of birth, and discuss their effects on the mother, the fetus and the neonate.

INFECTIONS OCCURRING IN PREGNANCY

Immune and hormonal changes during pregnancy worsen or reactivate certain infections

The fetus may be considered as an immunologically incompatible transplant that must not be rejected by the mother. Reasons for the failure to reject the fetus include:

- the absence or low density of major histocompatibility complex (MHC) antigens on placental cells
- a covering of antigens with blocking antibody
- subtle defects in the maternal immune responses.

A severe or generalized immunosuppression in the mother would be undesirable because it would mean potentially disastrous susceptibility to infectious disease. Certain infections, however, are known to be more severe (Table 23.1), and certain persistent infections reactivate during pregnancy (Table 23.2). The hormonal changes that accompany pregnancy can also increase susceptibility. The picture is further complicated when there is malnutrition, which in itself impairs host defences by weakening immune responses, decreasing metabolic reserves and interfering with the integrity of epithelial surfaces.

The fetus has poor immune defences

Once the fetus is infected, it is exquisitely susceptible because:

- IgM and IgA antibodies are not produced in significant amounts until the second half of pregnancy.
- There is no IgG antibody synthesis.
- Cell-mediated immune responses are poorly developed or absent, with inadequate production of the necessary cytokines.

Indeed, if the fetus were able to generate a vigorous response to maternal antigens, a troublesome graft-versus-host reaction could be unleashed.

Most microorganisms have sufficient destructive activity to kill the fetus once it is infected, leading to spontaneous abortion or stillbirth. Here, our interests focus on the few microorganisms that are capable of more subtle, non-lethal effects. They overcome the placental barrier by infecting it so that the infection then spreads to the fetus. They can then interfere with fetal development or cause lesions so that a live but damaged baby is born.

CONGENITAL INFECTIONS

Intrauterine infection may result in death of the fetus or congenital malformations

After primary infection during pregnancy, certain microorganisms enter the blood, establish infection in the placenta, and then invade the fetus. The fetus sometimes dies, leading

303

Table 23.1 The effect of pregnancy on the severity of infectious disease

Infection	Comments
Malaria	? Depressed cell-mediated immunity
Viral hepatitis	The viral load may fluctuate due to immunomodulation in pregnancy
Influenza	Higher mortality during pandemics
Poliomyelitis	Paralysis more common
Urinary tract infection	Cystitis; pyelonephritis more common; atony of bladder and ureter leads to less effective flushing, emptying
Candidiasis	Vulvovaginitis
Listeriosis	Influenza-like illness
Coccidioidomycosis	Leading cause of maternal mortality in endemic areas in SW USA and Latin-America

Table 23.2 Reactivation of persistent infections during pregnancy

Infection	Phenomenon
Cytomegalovirus	Increased shedding from cervix, virus in milk of nursing mother
Herpes simplex virus	Increased replication in cervical region

to abortion, but when the infection is less severe, as in the case of a relatively non-cytopathic virus, or when it is partially controlled by the maternal IgG response, the fetus survives. It may then be born with a congenital infection, often showing malformations or other pathologic changes. The infant is generally small and fails to thrive. It produces specific antibodies, but often, for instance with CMV, fails to generate an adequate virus-specific cell-mediated immune response, remaining infected for a long period. Hence, the lesions may progress after birth. It is a striking feature of these infections that they are generally mild or unnoticed by the mother.

Important causes of congenital infections are shown in Table 23.3. Viruses that induce fetal malformations (i.e. act as teratogens) share certain characteristics with other teratogens such as drugs or radiation (Table 23.4). The fetus tends to show similar responses (e.g. hepatosplenomegaly, encephalitis, eye lesions, low birth weight) to different infectious agents, and the diagnosis is difficult on purely clinical grounds. Most of these infections, HSV, rubella, CMV and syphilis, can also, at times, kill the fetus. They generally follow primary infection of the mother during pregnancy, so their incidence depends upon the proportion of non-immune females of childbearing age.

Routine antenatal screening for rubella antibody, treponemal antibody (which includes syphilis, yaws, pinta or bejel, which cannot be identified individually by serology), hepatitis B surface antigen and HIV antibody is being carried out to differing degrees worldwide. These tests help identify women who are infected with hepatitis B or HIV, infected or have been exposed in the past to treponemal infections, the most important of which is syphilis in this setting, or are susceptible to rubella.

Routine screening programmes lead to clinical management issues for both the mother and child. For example, HIV

Table 23.3 Maternal infections that are transmitted to the fetus

Microorganism	Effects
Rubella virus	Congenital rubella
Cytomegalovirus (CMV)	Congenital CMV, deafness, mental retardation
Human immunodeficiency virus (HIV)	Congenital infection, childhood AIDS; about 1 in 5 infants born to infected mothers are infected in utero[a]
Varicella-zoster virus (VZV)	Skin lesions; musculoskeletal, CNS abnormalities when fetus infected before 20 weeks. After later infection childhood zoster a common sequel[b]
Herpes simplex virus (HSV)	Neonatal HSV infection, often disseminated. Much higher risk when maternal infection primary rather than recurrent, infection in utero is rare
Hepatitis B virus	Congenital hepatitis B, persistent infection[a,c]
Parvovirus B19	After maternal infection 5–10% fetuses lost (abortion, hydrops fetalis)
Treponema pallidum	Congenital syphilis, classical syndrome
Toxoplasma gondii	Congenital toxoplasmosis
Listeria monocytogenes	Congenital listeriosis, pneumonia, septicaemia, meningitis[b]
Mycobacterium leprae	Congenital infection common in mothers with lepromatous leprosy

Congenitally infected babies may be symptomless, especially in cytomegalovirus infection. They are often small, fail to thrive or show detectable abnormalities later in childhood. In all cases, the baby remains infected, often for long periods, and may infect others.
[a]This figure is for resource-poor countries with no intervention (no antiretroviral drugs, no caesarean section, or avoidance of breastfeeding).
[b]Infection also occurs during and immediately after birth.
[c]Protection of newborn by hepatitis B vaccine plus specific immunoglobulin.

Table 23.4 Comparison between teratogenic viruses and other teratogens

	Viral teratogens (e.g. rubella)	Other teratogens (e.g. drugs, radiation)
Critical stages of susceptibility during pregnancy (organogenesis)	+	+
Fetal death a possible outcome	+	+
Maternal effects minimal or absent	+	+
Cause retarded fetal growth	+	+
Increase in frequency of naturally occurring abnormalities	–	+
Influence of genetic factors in mother/fetus	–	+

diagnosis will lead to consideration of antiretroviral therapy for the mother and, immediately on birth, the child, offering a caesarean section delivery, and advising against breastfeeding to reduce the risk of vertical transmission. In addition, the child will then be followed up for at least 12 months using sensitive tests to determine whether HIV has been transmitted vertically. Diagnosis of chronic hepatitis B infection will result in determination of the maternal level of infectivity, and subsequently offering an accelerated course of hepatitis B vaccine alone or, if the mother is highly infectious, vaccine and HBV-specific immunoglobulin to the baby. In addition, there are antiviral drugs for chronic hepatitis B that might be offered, together with long-term follow-up, to the mother. Rubella-susceptible women are offered rubella immunization postnatally. Women found to have been exposed to treponemal infection in pregnancy are offered antibiotic treatment and the baby is followed up for the first year using serology to identify active infection, as congenital syphilis can result from earlier untreated infection of the mother. In the case of CMV, which is not part of routine antenatal screening in the UK and USA, for example, a primary infection, reinfection or reactivation of the latent virus during pregnancy can lead to fetal infection (see next section).

The likelihood of fetal infection is increased when the mother develops a poor immune response, when the concentration of infectious agents in her blood is high (primary or secondary syphilis, *e* antigen positive hepatitis B carrier, HIV), or in a primary infection.

There is no good evidence to suggest that maternal mumps, influenza or poliovirus infection during pregnancy leads to harmful effects in the fetus, but the human parvovirus (see Ch. 26) occasionally causes fetal damage or death in 5–10% of cases following maternal infection in early pregnancy. The infected fetus develops severe anaemia with ascites and hepatosplenomegaly (hydrops fetalis) as the virus infects progenitor erythroid stem cells. Intrauterine exchange blood transfusion is used to manage hydrops fetalis.

Congenital rubella

The fetus is particularly susceptible to rubella infection when maternal infection occurs during the first 3 months of pregnancy

At this time, the heart, brain, eyes and ears are being formed and the infecting virus interferes with their development. If the fetus survives, it may show certain abnormalities (Fig. 23.1). Not all fetuses are affected; in one study, detectable congenital defects were seen in 15% of cases when maternal rubella occurred in the first month of pregnancy, 25% in the second month, 18% in the third month and 7% in the fourth month. The figure for the first month is relatively low because fetal death is a common sequel at this stage.

Congenital rubella can affect the eye, heart, brain and ear

Clinical manifestations of congenital rubella include low birth weight and eye (Fig. 23.2) and heart lesions. Effects on the brain and ears may not become detectable until later in childhood, in the form of mental retardation and deafness. Up to 80% of infected infants eventually suffer from deafness. About 25% of congenitally infected children develop insulin-dependent diabetes mellitus later in life (the virus replicates in the pancreas), but rubella is a very uncommon cause of this disease. There is 15% mortality in infants showing signs of infection at birth, often associated with hypogammaglobulinaemia.

Fetal rubella IgM is found in cord and infant blood

Infected fetuses produce their own IgM antibody to rubella virus, which can be detected in cord and infant blood. Maternal IgG antibodies are also present and together with interferons help control the spread of infection in the fetus. Virus can be isolated from the infant's throat or urine. The infant sheds virus into the throat and urine for several months and can infect susceptible individuals. Rubella virus RNA detection may be carried out in specific centres in order to assist with the diagnosis.

Congenital rubella can be prevented by vaccination

Vaccination with live attenuated rubella virus is given during childhood, usually with the combined MMR (mumps, measles and rubella) vaccine (see Ch. 34). Pregnancy is a contraindication to vaccination, as it is a live vaccine, and the only safe time during reproductive life is the immediate postpartum period. This is an interesting example of a vaccine that is given to protect an as yet non-existent individual (the future fetus), the infection being only subclinical or mild in the mother. Until effective vaccines became available in the late 1960s (Box 23.1), rubella was an important cause of congenital heart disease, deafness, blindness and mental retardation. The virus continues to circulate in the community and damage fetuses in countries with less extensive rubella vaccination programmes.

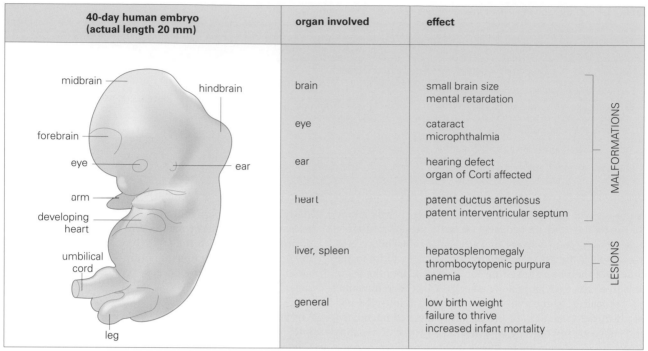

40-day human embryo (actual length 20 mm)	organ involved	effect	
	brain	small brain size mental retardation	MALFORMATIONS
	eye	cataract microphthalmia	MALFORMATIONS
	ear	hearing defect organ of Corti affected	MALFORMATIONS
	heart	patent ductus arteriosus patent interventricular septum	MALFORMATIONS
	liver, spleen	hepatosplenomegaly thrombocytopenic purpura anemia	LESIONS
	general	low birth weight failure to thrive increased infant mortality	

Labels on embryo diagram: midbrain, hindbrain, forebrain, eye, ear, arm, developing heart, umbilical cord, leg

Figure 23.1 Organ involvement and effects in congenital rubella.

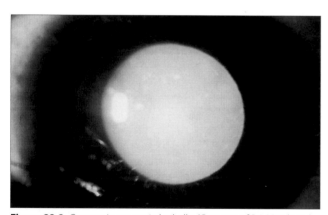

Figure 23.2 Cataract in congenital rubella. (Courtesy of R.J. Marsh and S. Ford.)

Congenital CMV infection

Mothers with a poor T-cell proliferative response to CMV antigens are more likely to infect their fetus

After primary maternal infection during pregnancy, about 40% of fetuses are infected, and 5% of these show signs at birth. It is not known whether the fetus is especially vulnerable at certain stages of pregnancy. The fetus is also infected following CMV reactivation during pregnancy in women with previous CMV exposure, but fetal damage is then uncommon. As many as 1–2% of infants born in the USA are infected, and up to about 10% of these are symptomatic, with up to 1 million infectious doses of virus present per millilitre of urine. However, the incidence of congenital CMV infection is likely to be an underestimate worldwide. In large cohorts of pregnant women studied it has been shown that 2% develop a primary CMV infection, but over 95% were asymptomatic. Of those women with a primary infection in the first trimester, up to 30% of babies may develop central nervous system (CNS) sequelae including sensorineural hearing loss. Although the percentage is much reduced if the maternal infection is later in pregnancy, a degree of CNS damage still occurs. However, the relationship between a first trimester infection and outcome is much clearer in rubella infections than with CMV. In CMV reactivation or reinfection, partial control of the infection by maternal antibody under these circumstances means that the baby may be infected but not affected, although a small percentage become symptomatic over the next couple of years. The frequency and outcome of congenital CMV infections in reactivation or reinfection in pregnancy is still not well understood. However, the incidence of symptomatic congenital CMV infections has been reported to be similar in pregnant women with primary infections and reactivations or reinfections.

Clinical features of congenital CMV include mental retardation, choroidoretinitis and optic atrophy, hearing defects, hepatosplenomegaly, thrombocytopenic purpura and anaemia (Fig. 23.3). Deafness and mental retardation may not be detectable until later in childhood.

Diagnosis is by detecting CMV-specific IgM antibodies in infant blood within 3 weeks of delivery, and by detecting and quantifying CMV DNA in the blood or urine during this period. Virus can also be isolated from throat swab or urine samples. Live attenuated vaccines have been investigated (AD169 and Towne strains), and in preliminary studies no-one who became pregnant after vaccination transmitted the virus to the infant.

Antiviral drugs such as ganciclovir and valganciclovir can be considered in managing symptomatic babies with congenital CMV infection.

Box 23.1 Lessons in Microbiology

Rubella and the fetus

Dr Norman McAllister Gregg (1892–1966) was ophthalmic surgeon to the Royal Alexandra Hospital for Children in Sydney, and during the Second World War, he noticed what he called an 'epidemic' of congenital cataract in infants. He went further and made the astute observation that all the mothers had suffered from rubella during early pregnancy. There were 78 infants with cataract, and 68 of the mothers had a history of rubella in early pregnancy. Many of the infants had heart defects, were small, and two-thirds of them had microphthalmia. He published his findings in 1941, providing the first clear demonstration that an environmental factor could cause congenital malformations. It is a striking feature of the infection that, whereas the fetus suffers cruel malformations, the mother shows little or no signs of illness. We now know that several other viruses, notably CMV, can do this, as well as factors such as thalidomide and folate deficiency. Later studies on rubella revealed that congenitally infected infants also developed deafness and brain defects. Survivors were followed up until 1991 when they were 50, and other abnormalities have been observed, including the development of diabetes by the age of 25 years and certain vascular abnormalities.

It was not until 1962 that the causative virus was isolated and grown in cell culture. A rubella epidemic in the USA in 1964–1965 left in its wake 20 000 infants with the congenital rubella syndrome. By the late 1960s, an effective live virus vaccine was available, and congenital rubella is now seen only when vaccination cover is poor. The fetus is exquisitely vulnerable to rubella during the first trimester of pregnancy. This is the critical stage in embryonic development when key organs (heart, ear, eye, brain) are being formed, and although the virus does no damage to the cells in which it grows, it interferes with mitosis. Interference with programmed mitosis in these major organs causes the malformations, vasculitis playing a part. The fetus is good at repairing damage but it cannot at a later stage compensate for the failure in basic organ development. The antimitotic action of the virus also means that the total number of cells in the body is reduced, and this is why the rubella-infected infants are smaller. The rubella virus remains in infected organs such as the lens and brain for more than 1 year, but eventually there is an adequate cell-mediated immune response and the virus is eliminated.

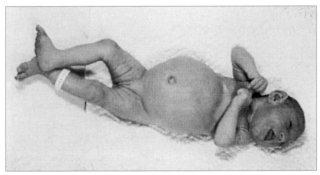

Figure 23.3 Microcephaly with associated severe psychomotor retardation and hepatosplenomegaly in congenital cytomegalovirus infection. (Courtesy of W.E. Farrar.)

Congenital syphilis

As a result of routine serologic screening for syphilis in antenatal clinics and treatment with penicillin (see Ch. 21), congenital syphilis is now rare, but is more common in resource-poor countries. Clinical features in the infant include rhinitis (snuffles), skin and mucosal lesions, hepatosplenomegaly, lymphadenopathy, and abnormalities of bones, teeth and cartilage (saddle-shaped nose). Pregnancy often masks the early signs of syphilis, but the mother will have serological evidence of treponemal infection, and treponemal IgM will be detected in the fetal blood. Vertical transmission most commonly takes place after 4 months of gestation; therefore treatment of the mother before the fourth month of pregnancy should prevent fetal infection.

Congenital toxoplasmosis

Acute asymptomatic infection by *Toxoplasma gondii* during pregnancy can cause fetal malformation

Approximately 35% of healthy adults have serological evidence of previous *Toxoplasma gondii* infection. Clinical features of congenital toxoplasmosis in the infant include convulsions, microcephaly, chorioretinitis, hepatosplenomegaly and jaundice, with later hydrocephaly, mental retardation and defective vision (see Ch. 25). There are often no detectable abnormalities at birth, but signs (e.g. chorioretinitis; see Fig. 25.5) generally appear within a few years. The incidence of fetal infection and damage (leading to abortion, stillbirth or disease in the newborn) increases from 14% when maternal infection is in the first trimester to 59% when in the third trimester. Damage is more severe the earlier in pregnancy infection is contracted.

Toxoplasma-specific IgM antibodies may be detected in cord blood. Treatment of a pregnant woman or an infected infant is with spiramycin or (with care to avoid toxicity) sulphadiazine plus pyrimethamine plus folinic acid.

There is no vaccine. Prevention is by avoidance of primary infection which occurs via ingesting cysts from cat faeces or lightly cooked meat during pregnancy.

Congenital HIV infection

In resource-poor countries, approximately one-quarter of infants born to mothers with HIV are infected: about one-third of these in utero and the rest perinatally

Clinically, congenital HIV infection manifests as poor weight gain, susceptibility to sepsis, developmental delays, lymphocytic pneumonitis, oral thrush, enlarged lymph nodes, hepatosplenomegaly, diarrhea and pneumonia, and some infants develop encephalopathy and AIDS by 1 year of age. Since most infections take place during late pregnancy or during delivery, transmission rates are reduced by lowering the HIV load by offering antiretroviral drugs during pregnancy, especially during the last trimester or during labour, carrying out an elective caesarean section, and avoiding breastfeeding.

IgG antibodies present in the neonatal blood sample may be maternal in origin and can persist for at least 1 year. The mainstay of laboratory diagnosis therefore involves detection of HIV-1 proviral DNA or HIV-1 RNA by polymerase chain reaction (PCR), although these tests may not be positive until several months after birth, in conjunction with HIV antibody and antigen detection using the combination assay.

Congenital and neonatal listeriosis

Maternal exposure to animals or foods infected with *Listeria* can lead to fetal death or malformations

Listeria monocytogenes is a small Gram-positive rod, which is motile and beta-haemolytic. It is distributed worldwide in a great variety of animals including cattle, pigs, rodents and birds, and the bacteria occur in plants and in soil. *Listeria* can grow at regular refrigeration temperatures (e.g. 3–4 C). Transmission to humans is by:

- contact with infected animals and their faeces
- consumption of unpasteurized milk or soft cheeses or contaminated vegetables.

In the USA, there are about 2000 reported cases of listeriosis each year; about one-third of them in newborn infants. Faecal carriage is uncommon, except in contacts of cases.

L. monocytogenes in the pregnant woman causes a mild influenza-like illness or is asymptomatic, but there is a bacteraemia which leads to infection of the placenta and then the fetus. This may cause abortion, premature delivery, neonatal septicaemia or pneumonia with abscesses or granulomas. The infant can also be infected shortly after birth, for instance, from other babies or from hospital staff, and this may lead to a meningitic illness.

L. monocytogenes is isolated from blood cultures, cerebrospinal fluid (CSF) or newborn skin lesions.

Treatment is with ampicillin, which may need to be combined with gentamicin to achieve a bactericidal effect. There are no vaccines.

Pregnant women should avoid exposure to infected material, but the exact source of infection is generally unknown.

INFECTIONS OCCURRING AROUND THE TIME OF BIRTH

Effects on the fetus and neonate

The routes of infection in the fetus and neonate are shown in Figure 23.4

Viral infections (e.g. rubella, CMV) are generally less damaging to the fetus when the maternal infection occurs late in pregnancy. Primary infection with varicella-zoster virus (VZV) in the first 20 weeks of pregnancy can lead to limb deformities and other severe lesions in the newborn. HSV

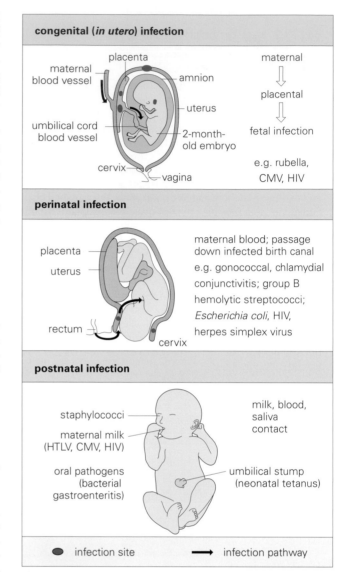

Figure 23.4 Routes of infection in the fetus and neonate. CMV, cytomegalovirus; HIV, human immunodeficiency virus; HTLV, human T-cell lymphotropic virus.

infection in this setting is underdiagnosed and can lead to neonatal morbidity and mortality.

Bacterial infections originating from the vagina and perineum late in pregnancy, especially those occurring when the fetal membranes have been ruptured for more than 1–2 days, may result in chorioamnionitis, maternal fever, premature delivery and stillbirth. Infants of low birth weight (<1500 g) tend to be more severely affected. Bacteria involved include:

- group B haemolytic streptococci; 10–30% of pregnant women are colonized in the rectum or vagina
- *E. coli*
- *Klebsiella*
- *Proteus*
- *Bacteroides*
- staphylococci
- *Mycoplasma hominis*.

These infections may also be acquired after delivery to give later-onset disease.

Neonatal septicaemia often progresses to meningitis

Bacterial meningitis (see Table 24.5) is frequently fatal unless treated. Clinical diagnosis is difficult because the infant shows generalized signs such as respiratory distress, poor feeding, diarrhea and vomiting, but early diagnosis is essential and emergency treatment is required. 'Blind' antibiotic treatment should be started as soon as cerebrospinal fluid (CSF) (Gram stain and culture) and blood samples have been taken.

Fetal infection with herpes simplex must be considered in a baby who is acutely ill within a few weeks of birth

Fetal infection during labour results from direct contact with the infecting microorganism as the fetus passes down an infected birth canal (Table 23.5). For instance, cutaneous lesions of herpes simplex may develop 1 week after delivery, with generalized infection and severe CNS involvement. Approximately 80% of mothers with primary HSV infection (only about 10% with recurrent HSV) have cervical lesions and about a third of their infants are infected. Babies <4 weeks of age may present with neonatal HSV as acutely ill and 'septic' but classically there are three well-defined clinical presentations. Those with infection affecting the skin, eye and/or mouth (SEM); encephalitis with or without skin involvement; and disseminated disease involving the lungs, liver, central nervous system, adrenal glands and SEM. The diagnosis may be missed as neonatal HSV infection may present without skin lesions in up to 39% of babies. Therefore, there must be a low threshold for considering this diagnosis and acyclovir therapy should be started as soon as possible. Treatment could be started at the same time as samples are collected for HSV DNA detection that include swabs of the SEM and vesicles, if present, EDTA whole blood samples and cerebrospinal fluid. Morbidity and mortality rates are higher in those with encephalitis and disseminated disease.

Gonococci (Fig. 23.5), chlamydia or staphylococci (see Ch. 25) can infect the eye to cause ophthalmia neonatorum. Infection with group B streptococci generally occurs at this time.

In countries with high hepatitis B carrier rates, maternal blood is a major source of infection during or shortly after birth. More than 90% of infants from carrier mothers become infected and then carry the virus. This is preventable by giving the vaccine plus specific immunoglobulin to the newborn. Hepatitis C, in contrast, is not usually transmitted in this way, and <5% of children with carrier mothers are infected.

Human milk may contain rubella virus, CMV, human T-cell lymphotropic virus (HTLV) and HIV. The amount of virus detectable in milk is low and, except in the case of HTLV and HIV, milk is not thought to be an important source of infection. However, it makes sense to pasteurize milk in human milk banks, just as we pasteurize cows' milk.

Effects on the mother

Puerperal sepsis is prevented by aseptic techniques

After delivery (or abortion), a large area of damaged vulnerable uterine tissue is exposed to infection. Puerperal sepsis (childbed fever) was a major cause of maternal death in Europe in the nineteenth century. In 1843, Oliver Wendell Holmes made the unpopular suggestion that it was carried on the hands of doctors, and 4 years later, Ignaz Semmelweiss in Vienna showed how it could be prevented if doctors and midwives washed their hands before attending a woman in labour and practiced aseptic techniques. This is because:

- Group A beta-haemolytic streptococci were the major culprits and came from the nose, throat or skin of hospital attendants.
- Other possible organisms include anaerobes such as *Clostridium perfringens* or *Bacteroides*, *E. coli* and group B streptococci and originate from the mother's own faecal flora.

Puerperal sepsis carried a mortality rate of up to 10% until the 1930s, but, like septic abortion, is now uncommon in resource-rich countries. Predisposing factors include premature rupture of the membranes, instrumentation and retained fragments of membrane or placenta. High vaginal swabs and blood cultures should be taken if there is postnatal pyrexia or an offensive discharge.

Other neonatal infections

Infection may be transmitted to the newborn infant during the first 1–2 weeks after birth, rather than during delivery as follows:

- Group B beta-haemolytic streptococci and Gram-negative bacilli (see above) acquired by cross-infection in the nursery can still cause serious infection at this time, often with meningitis (see Ch. 24).

Table 23.5 Neonatal infections acquired during passage down an infected birth canal

Infectious agent	Site of infection	Phenomenon
Neisseria gonorrhoeae	Conjunctiva	Neonatal conjunctivitis (ophthalmia neonatorum)
Chlamydia trachomatis	Conjunctiva, respiratory tract	Neonatal conjunctivitis (ophthalmia neonatorum), neonatal pneumonia
Herpes simplex virus	Skin, eye, mouth	Neonatal herpetic infection[a]
Genital papillomavirus	Respiratory tract	Laryngeal warts in young children
Group B streptococci[b], Gram-negative bacilli (*E. coli* etc.)	Respiratory tract	Septicaemia; death if not treated
Candida albicans	Oral cavity	Neonatal oral thrush

[a]Although preventable by caesarean section, it is often difficult to detect maternal genital infection; infants can be treated prophylactically with acyclovir.
[b]Up to 30% of women carry these bacteria in the vagina or rectum.

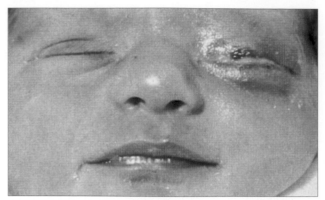

Figure 23.5 Gonococcal ophthalmia neonatorum. Signs appear 2–5 days after birth. The inflammation and oedema are more severe than with chlamydia infection. (Courtesy of J.S. Bingham.)

- Herpes simplex virus from cold sores or herpetic whitlows of attending adults.
- *Staphylococci* from the noses and fingers of adult carriers may cause staphylococcal conjunctivitis or 'sticky eye' (see Ch. 25), skin sepsis in the neonate, and sometimes the staphylococcal 'scalded skin' syndrome (Fig. 23.6) due to a specific 'epidermolytic' staphylococcal toxin.

During the first 1–2 weeks of life, the nose of the neonate becomes colonized with *Staphylococcus aureus*, which can enter the nipple during feeding to cause a breast abscess. These infections are preventable if hospital staff pay vigorous attention to handwashing and aseptic techniques.

If hygienic practices are poor, the umbilical stump, especially in resource-poor countries, may be infected with *Clostridium tetani*, usually because instruments used to cut the cord are contaminated with bacterial spores, resulting in

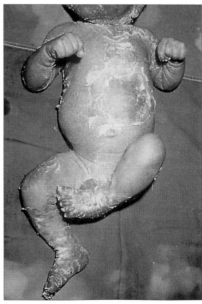

Figure 23.6 Staphylococcal scalded skin syndrome. There are large areas of epidermal loss where bullae have burst. (Courtesy of L. Brown.)

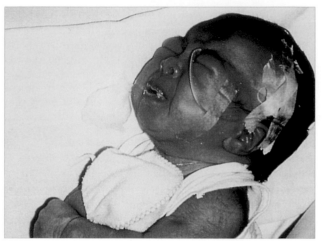

Figure 23.7 Tetanus. Risus sardonicus in a newborn infant. (Courtesy of W.E. Farrar.)

neonatal tetanus (Fig. 23.7). It can be prevented by immunizing mothers with tetanus toxoid.

In resource-poor countries, gastroenteritis is an important problem during the neonatal period as well as during infancy.

Diarrhea leading to water and electrolyte depletion is particularly serious in low birth weight infants. Causative agents include strains of *E. coli* and salmonellae rather than rotaviruses (Ch. 22). Breastfeeding gives some protection by supplying specific antibodies and other less well-characterized protective factors.

KEY FACTS

- During pregnancy, certain infections (coccidioidomycosis, influenza) can be more severe than usual, and there can be reactivation of certain persistent infections (HSV, CMV).

- A few infections are able to pass to the fetus via the placenta and cause damage. These infections are generally mild or subclinical in the mother (rubella, CMV, toxoplasmosis), but this is not always the case (syphilis).

- Once infected, the fetus may die, but if the baby survives it may be born with the infection (HIV, toxoplasmosis), often showing characteristic malformations (rubella, syphilis).

- Infection of the infant during birth or shortly afterwards can cause local disease (conjunctivitis due to gonococci or chlamydia) or occasionally severe life-threatening illness (*E. coli* meningitis, herpes simplex virus or group B streptococcal infection).

- Life-threatening bacterial infection of the mother via the postpartum uterus (puerperal sepsis) used to be common but is now rare in resource-rich countries.

Central nervous system infections

24

Introduction

Central nervous system infections are usually blood-borne or infectious agents invading via peripheral nerves

The brain and spinal cord are protected from mechanical pressure or deformation by enclosure in rigid containers, the skull and vertebral column, which also act as barriers to the spread of infection. The blood vessels and nerves that traverse the walls of the skull and vertebral column are the main routes of invasion. Blood-borne invasion is the most common route of infection, for example, by polioviruses or *Neisseria meningitidis*. Invasion via peripheral nerves is less common; examples include herpes simplex, varicella-zoster and rabies viruses. Local invasion from infected ears or sinuses, local injury or congenital defects such as spina bifida, also occurs, while invasion from the olfactory tract leading to amoebic meningitis is rare.

Here, we discuss the main routes of central nervous system invasion by microorganisms (see also Ch. 13) and the body's response, followed by a more detailed discussion of the diseases that result.

INVASION OF THE CENTRAL NERVOUS SYSTEM

Natural barriers act to prevent blood-borne invasion

Blood-borne invasion takes place across:

- the blood–brain barrier to cause encephalitis
- the blood–cerebrospinal fluid (CSF) barrier to cause meningitis (Fig. 24.1).

The blood–brain barrier consists of tightly joined endothelial cells surrounded by glial processes, while the brain–CSF barrier at the choroid plexus consists of endothelium with fenestrations, and tightly joined choroid plexus epithelial cells. Microbes can traverse these barriers by:

- growing across, infecting the cells that comprise the barrier
- being passively transported across in intracellular vacuoles
- being carried across by infected white blood cells.

Examples of each route are seen in viral infections. Poliovirus, for instance, invades the central nervous system (CNS) across the blood–brain barrier. After oral ingestion of virus, a complex stepwise series of events leads to CNS invasion (Fig. 24.2). Poliovirus also invades the meninges after localizing in vascular endothelial cells, and can cross the blood–CSF barrier. Mumps virus behaves in the same way, as do circulating *Haemophilus influenzae*, meningococci or pneumococci. Once infection has reached the meninges and CSF, the brain substance can in turn be invaded if the infection crosses the pia. In poliomyelitis, for instance, a meningitic phase often precedes encephalitis and paralysis.

CNS invasion, however, is a rare event because most microorganisms fail to pass from blood to the CNS across the natural barriers. A large variety of viruses can grow and cause disease if introduced directly into the brain, but circulating viruses generally fail to invade, and CNS involvement by polio, mumps, rubella or measles viruses is seen in only a very small proportion of infected individuals. The factors that determine such CNS invasion are unknown.

Invasion of the CNS via peripheral nerves is a feature of herpes simplex, varicella-zoster and rabies virus infections

Herpes simplex virus (HSV) and varicella-zoster virus (VZV) present in skin or mucosal lesions (see Ch. 26), travel up axons using the normal retrograde transport mechanisms that can move virus particles (as well as foreign molecules such as tetanus toxin) at a rate of about 200 mm/day, to reach the dorsal root ganglia. Rabies virus, introduced into muscle or subcutaneous tissues by the bite of a rabid animal, infects muscle fibres and muscle spindles after the virus binds to the nicotinic acetylcholine receptor. It then enters peripheral nerves and travels to the CNS, to reach glial cells and neurones, where it multiplies.

THE BODY'S RESPONSE TO INVASION

CSF cell counts increase in response to infection

The response to invading viruses is reflected by an increase in lymphocytes, mostly T cells, and monocytes in the CSF (Table 24.1). A slight increase in protein also occurs, the CSF remaining clear. This condition is termed 'aseptic' meningitis. The response to pyogenic bacteria shows a more spectacular and more rapid increase in polymorphonuclear leukocytes and proteins (Fig. 24.3), so that the CSF becomes visibly turbid. This condition is termed 'septic' meningitis. Certain slower growing or less pyogenic microorganisms induce less dramatic changes, such as in tuberculous or listerial meningitis.

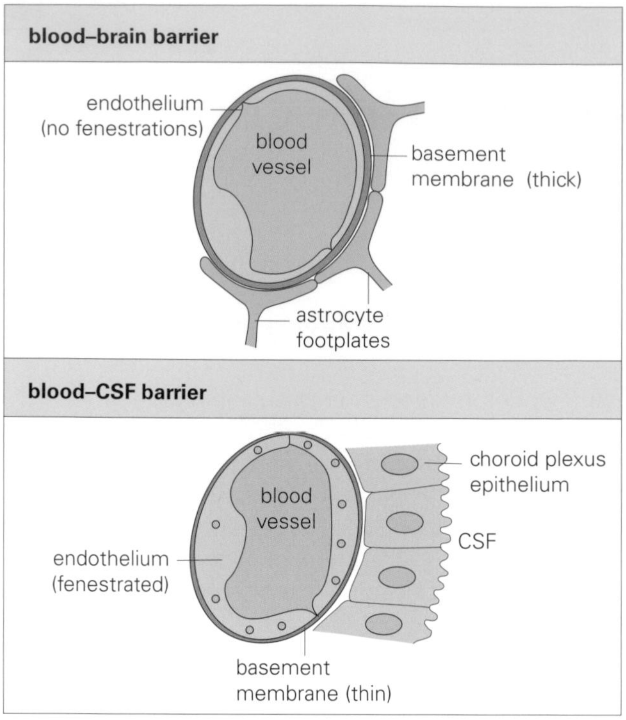

blood–brain barrier

endothelium (no fenestrations)

blood vessel

basement membrane (thick)

astrocyte footplates

blood–CSF barrier

blood vessel

choroid plexus epithelium

CSF

endothelium (fenestrated)

basement membrane (thin)

Figure 24.1 Structures of the blood–brain and blood–cerebrospinal fluid (CSF) barriers.

The pathologic consequences of CNS infection depend upon the microorganism

In the CNS itself, viruses can infect neural cells, sometimes showing a marked preference. Polio and rabies viruses, for instance, invade neurones, whereas JC virus invades oligo-dendrocytes. Because there is very little extracellular space, spread is mostly direct from cell to cell along established nervous pathways. Invading bacteria and protozoa generally induce more dramatic inflammatory events, which limit local spread so that infection is soon localized to form abscesses.

Viruses induce perivascular infiltration of lymphocytes and monocytes, sometimes, as in the case of polio, with direct damage to infected cells. (The pathogenesis of viral encephalomyelitis is shown later, in Fig. 24.7.) Associated immune responses not only to viral, but also often to host CNS components, play a part in postvaccinial encephalitis. Infiltrating B cells produce antibody to the invading microorganism, and T cells react with microbial antigens to release cytokines that attract and activate other T cells and macrophages. The pathologic condition evolves over the course of several days and occasionally, when partly controlled by host defences, over the course of years, e.g. subacute sclerosing panencephalitis (SSPE) caused by measles, which has both a virological and immunological pathogenesis. Bacteria cause more rapidly evolving pathologic changes, with local responses to bacterial antigens and toxins playing an important part.

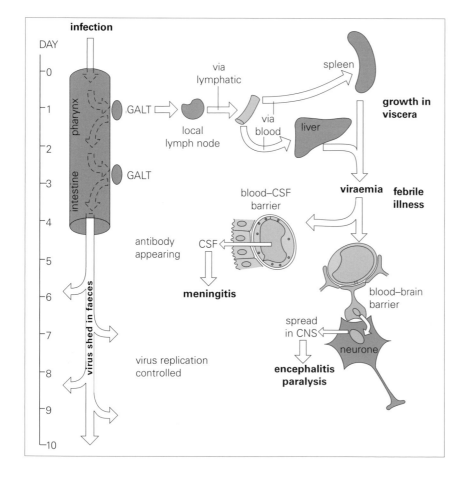

Figure 24.2 The mechanism of central nervous system (CNS) invasion by poliovirus. CSF, cerebrospinal fluid; GALT, gut-associated lymphoid tissue.

Table 24.1 Changes in cerebrospinal fluid (CSF) in response to invading microbes

	Cells/ml	Protein (mg/dL)	Glucose (mg/dL)	Causes
Normal	0–5	15–45	45–85	
Septic (purulent) meningitis	200–20 000 (mainly neutrophils)	High (>100)	<45	Bacteria, amoebae, brain abscess
Aseptic[a] meningitis or meningoencephalitis	100–1000 (mainly mononuclear)	Moderately high (50–100)	Normal[b]	Viruses, tuberculosis, leptospira, fungi, brain abscess, partly treated bacterial meningitis

[a]Aseptic because the CSF is sterile on regular bacteriologic culture.
[b]Low (<45) in the case of tuberculosis, fungi, leptospira.

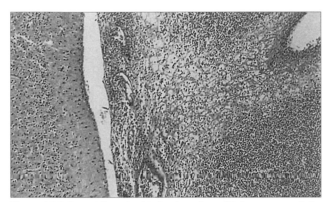

Figure 24.3 Bacterial meningitis. Exudate of acute inflammatory cells in the subarachnoid space (H&E stain). (Courtesy of P. Garen.)

In all cases, a degree of inflammation and oedema that would be trivial in striated muscle, skin or liver may be life-threatening when it occurs in the vulnerable 'closed box' containing the leptomeninges, brain and spinal cord. It may be several weeks after clinical recovery before cellular infiltrations are removed and histologic appearances are restored to normal.

CNS invasion only rarely assists in the transmission of infection

From the point of view of a parasitic microorganism that needs to be transmitted to a fresh host, invasion of the CNS is generally foolish because it damages the host. The only occasions on which it makes sense are:

• When dorsal root ganglion neurones are invaded as an essential step in establishing latency (HSV and VZV). This gives a mechanism for reactivation and further episodes of shedding from mucosal or skin lesions.
• In the case of rabies (see below), where CNS invasion in the animal host is necessary for two reasons. First, it enables the virus to spread from the CNS down peripheral nerves to the salivary glands, from which transmission takes place. Second, invasion of the limbic system of the brain causes a change in behaviour of the infected animal so that it becomes less retiring, more aggressive and more likely to bite, thus transmitting the infection. Invasion of the limbic system can be regarded as a fiendish strategy on the part of rabies virus to promote its own transmission and survival.

MENINGITIS

Bacterial meningitis

Acute bacterial meningitis is a life-threatening infection, needing urgent specific treatment

Bacterial meningitis is more severe, but less common, than viral meningitis and may be caused by a variety of agents (Table 24.2). Prior to the 1990s, *Haemophilus influenzae* type b (Hib) was responsible for most cases of bacterial meningitis. However, the introduction of the Hib vaccine into childhood immunization regimens has lowered overall Hib incidence in favour of *Neisseria meningitidis* and *Streptococcus pneumoniae*, which are now responsible for most bacterial meningitis. These three pathogens have several virulence factors in common (Table 24.3), including possession of a polysaccharide capsule (Table 24.4).

Meningococcal meningitis

Neisseria meningitidis is carried by about 20% of the population, but higher rates are seen in epidemics

Neisseria meningitidis is a Gram-negative diplococcus which closely resembles *N. gonorrhoeae* in structure (see Ch. 21), but with an additional polysaccharide capsule that is antigenic and by which the serotype of *N. meningitidis* can be recognized. The bacteria are carried asymptomatically in the population, up to 20% depending on geographic location, and are attached by their pili to the epithelial cells in the nasopharynx. Invasion of the blood and meninges is a rare and poorly understood event. The known virulence factors are summarized in Table 24.3. People possessing specific complement-dependent bacterial antibodies to capsular antigens are protected against invasion. Those with C5–C9 complement deficiencies show increased susceptibility to bacteraemia (as they do to *N. gonorrhoeae* bacteraemia; see Ch. 21). Young children who have lost the antibodies acquired from their mother, and adolescents who have not previously encountered the infecting serotype, and therefore have no type-specific immunity, are those most often infected.

Person-to-person spread takes place by droplet infection, and is facilitated by other respiratory infections, often viral, that cause increased respiratory secretions. Thus, conditions of overcrowding and confinement such as prisons, military barracks and college dormitories contribute to the frequency of infection in populations. During outbreaks of meningococcal meningitis, which most frequently occur in late winter and early spring, the carrier rate may reach 60–80%. Specific serotypes associated with infection

Table 24.2 The important causative agents of non-viral meningitis, their treatment and prevention

Pathogen	Treatment[a]	Prevention
Neisseria meningitidis	Penicillin (or chloramphenicol)	Rifampicin prophylaxis for close contacts; polysaccharide vaccine (poor protection against group B)
Haemophilus influenzae	Ampicillin[b], ceftriaxone or cefotaxime (or chloramphenicol)	Polysaccharide vaccine against type b (Hib)
Streptococcus pneumoniae	Penicillin[c] (or ceftriaxone or chloramphenicol)	Prompt treatment of otitis media and respiratory infections; polyvalent (23 serotypes) polysaccharide vaccine
Escherichia coli (and other coliforms), group B streptococci	Gentamicin + cefotaxime or ceftriaxone (or chloramphenicol)[b]	No vaccines available
Listeria monocytogenes	Penicillin or ampicillin + gentamicin	No vaccines available
Mycobacterium tuberculosis	Isoniazid and rifampin and pyrazinamide ± streptomycin	BCG vaccination; isoniazid prophylaxis for contacts recommended in USA
Cryptococcus neoformans	Amphotericin B and flucytosine	No vaccines available

[a]Treatment should be initiated immediately and the susceptibility of the infecting isolate confirmed in the laboratory.
[b]If isolate is shown to be susceptible (10–20% of isolates are resistant because they produce a plasmid coded beta-lactamase).
[c]In areas of high prevalence of penicillin resistant pneumococci initial treatment with ceftriaxone may be advised until susceptibility of isolate is known. BCG, bacille Calmette–Guérin.

Table 24.3 Virulence factors in bacterial meningitis

Virulence factor	Bacterial pathogen		
	Neisseria meningitidis	*Haemophilus influenzae*	*Streptococcus pneumoniae*
Capsule	+	+	+
IgA protease	+	+	+
Pili	+	+	−
Endotoxin	+	+	−
Outer membrane proteins	+	+	−

Table 24.4 Polysaccharide capsules are important virulence factors in the pathogenesis of bacterial meningitis

Pathogen	Capsule	Important type	Vaccine
Neisseria meningitidis	Polysaccharide	A, B, C, Y, W-135	Good for A and C; poor for B
Haemophilus influenzae	Polysaccharide	B	Hib vaccine for < 1 year olds
Streptococcus pneumoniae	Polysaccharide	Many	Pneumovax: 23-valent most common types
Group B streptococcus	Polysaccharide rich in sialic acid	(Ia, Ib, II) III in neonatal meningitis	? Future
Escherichia coli		KI in meningitis	? Future

exhibit some geographic variation. However, serotypes B, C and Y tend to predominate in more resource-rich countries, whereas serotypes A and W-135 are more common in less developed regions. Available vaccines target serotypes A, C, Y and W-135 but not B (Table 24.4). The UK was the first country to introduce the meningitis C conjugate vaccine. It has been part of routine childhood immunization since November 1999. The UK Department of Health recommends that all first-year university and college students and others between 20 and 24 years old should be immunized against meningitis C. The US Centers for Disease Control guidance is similar.

Group B meningococcal disease is diagnosed in more than 50% of meningitis cases; however, vaccine development has been hindered because a potential target, the group B capsule, is an autoantigen. Vaccines have been prepared using the bacterial outer membrane and recombinant proteins which may be protective.

Clinical features of meningococcal meningitis include a haemorrhagic skin rash

After an incubation period of 1–3 days, the onset of meningococcal meningitis is sudden with a sore throat, headache, drowsiness and signs of meningitis which include

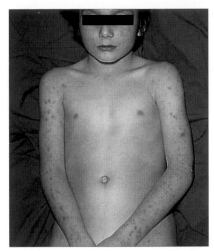

Figure 24.4 Meningococcal septicaemia showing a mixed petechial and maculopapular rash on the extremities and exterior surfaces. (Courtesy of W.E. Farrar.)

fever, irritability, neck stiffness and photophobia. There is often a haemorrhagic skin rash with petechiae, reflecting the associated septicaemia (Fig. 24.4). In about 35% of patients, this septicaemia is fulminating, with complications due to disseminated intravascular coagulation, endotoxaemia and shock, and renal failure. In the most severe cases there is an acute Addisonian crisis, with bleeding into the brain and adrenal glands referred to as Waterhouse–Friedrichsen syndrome. Mortality from meningococcal meningitis reaches 100% if untreated, but remains around 10% even if treated. In addition, serious sequelae such as permanent hearing loss may occur in some survivors (Table 24.5).

A diagnosis of acute meningitis is usually suspected on clinical examination

Laboratory identification of the bacterial cause of acute meningitis is essential so that appropriate antibiotic therapy can be given and prophylaxis of contacts initiated. Preliminary microscopy results involving white cell counts and Gram staining for bacteria should be available within an hour of receipt of the CSF sample in the laboratory. Results of culture of CSF and blood should follow after 24 h (see Ch. 32). Molecular diagnosis of meningococcal infection can also be carried out, and may be of clinical assistance as early treatment saves lives, but makes culture of viable organisms from specimens more difficult.

Serology is not helpful in the diagnosis because the infection is too acute for an antibody response to be detectable. Bacterial meningitis is a medical emergency and antibiotic therapy (penicillin or ampicillin) must be instigated if the diagnosis is suspected (Table 24.2).

Close contacts in the family, referred to as 'kissing contacts', should be given single-dose ciprofloxacin. Note that penicillin is not used for prophylaxis because it does not eliminate nasopharyngeal carriage of meningococci. Rifampicin used to be recommended but it is associated with rapid induction of resistance, has to be taken for a longer time period and interacts with oral contraceptives.

Haemophilus meningitis

Type b *H. influenzae* causes meningitis in infants and young children

H. influenzae is a Gram-negative coccobacillus. 'Haemophilus' means 'blood-loving', and the name 'influenzae' was given because it was originally thought to be the cause of influenza, but is now known to be a common secondary invader in the lower respiratory tract. There are six types (a–f) of *H. influenzae*, distinguishable serologically by their capsular polysaccharides:

- Unencapsulated strains are common and are present in the throat of most healthy people.
- The capsulated type b, a common inhabitant of the respiratory tract of infants and young children (where it may cause infection: see Ch. 18), very occasionally invades the blood and reaches the meninges.

Maternal antibody protects the infant up to 3–4 months of age, but as it wanes, there is a 'window of susceptibility' until the child produces his/her own antibody. Anticapsular antibodies are good opsonins (see Ch. 14), which allow the bacteria to be phagocytosed and killed, but children do not generally produce them until 2–3 years of age, possibly because these antibodies are T independent. In addition to the capsule, *H. influenzae* has several other virulence factors, as shown in Table 24.3.

Acute *H. influenzae* meningitis is commonly complicated by severe neurologic sequelae

The incubation period of *H. influenzae* meningitis is 5–6 days, and the onset is often more insidious than that of meningococcal or pneumococcal meningitis (Table 24.5). The condition is less frequently fatal, but, as with meningococcal infection, serious sequelae such as hearing loss, delayed language development, and mental retardation and seizures may occur (Table 24.5).

Table 24.5 Clinical features of bacterial meningitis

Pathogen	Host (patient)	Important clinical features	Mortality[a]	Sequelae[a,b]
Neisseria meningitidis	Children and adolescents	Acute onset (6–24 h); skin rash	7–10	<1
Haemophilus influenzae	Children < 5 years of age	Onset often less acute; (1–2 days)	5	9
Streptococcus pneumoniae	All ages, but especially children < 2 years of age and elderly	Acute onset may follow pneumonia and/or septicaemia in elderly	20–30	15–20

[a]As percentage of treated cases.
[b]Major central nervous system deficit; in addition, up to 10% of patients develop deafness.

General diagnostic features are the same as for meningococcal meningitis, as explained above. For laboratory diagnosis, see Chapter 32. It is important to note that the organisms may be difficult to see in Gram-stained smears of CSF, particularly if they are present in small numbers.

H. *influenzae* type b (Hib) vaccine is effective for children from 2 months of age

General features of treatment are referred to above under meningococcal meningitis; details are summarized in Table 24.2. An effective Hib vaccine, suitable for children 2 months of age and upwards, is available. Rifampicin prophylaxis is recommended for close contacts of patients with invasive Hib disease.

Pneumococcal meningitis

Streptococcus pneumoniae is a common cause of bacterial meningitis, particularly in children and the elderly

Strep. pneumoniae was first isolated more than 100 years ago but relatively little is known about its virulence attributes apart from its polysaccharide capsule (Tables 24.3, 24.4), and the pneumococcus remains a major cause of morbidity and mortality. (Pneumococcal respiratory tract infections are reviewed in Ch. 19.)

Strep. pneumoniae is a capsulate Gram-positive coccus carried in the throats of many healthy individuals. Invasion of the blood and meninges is a rare event, but is more common in the very young (<2 years of age), in the elderly, in those with sickle cell disease, in debilitated or splenectomized patients and following head trauma. Susceptibility to infection is associated with low levels of antibodies to capsular polysaccharide antigens: antibody opsonizes the organism and promotes phagocytosis, thereby protecting the host from invasion. However, this protection is type specific and there are more than 85 different capsular types of *Strep. pneumoniae*.

The clinical features of pneumococcal meningitis are generally worse than with *N. meningitidis* and *H. influenzae* and are summarized in Table 24.5. The general diagnostic features are the same as for meningococcal meningitis described above. Details are referred to in Chapter 32.

Treatment and prevention of pneumococcal meningitis are summarized in Table 24.2. Since penicillin-resistant pneumococci have been observed worldwide, attention must be paid to the antibiotic susceptibility of the infecting strain, and empiric chemotherapy usually involves a combination of vancomycin and either cefotaxime or ceftriaxone.

An effective heptavalent protein-conjugate pneumococcal vaccine is available which the US Centers for Disease Control recommends for all children from 2 to 23 months of age (i.e. to be given with other recommended childhood vaccines) and for older children (24–59 months) who are at high risk (e.g. sickle cell disease, HIV infection, chronic illness or weakened immune systems) for serious pneumococcal infection. The older 23-valent polysaccharide vaccine remains available for children older than 5 years of age.

Listeria monocytogenes meningitis

Listeria monocytogenes causes meningitis in immunocompromised adults

Listeria monocytogenes is a Gram-positive coccobacillus and an important cause of meningitis in immunocompromised adults, especially in renal transplant and cancer patients. It also causes intrauterine infections and infections of the newborn, as summarized in Chapter 23. *L. monocytogenes* is less susceptible than *Strep. pneumoniae* to penicillin, and the recommended treatment is a combination of penicillin or ampicillin with gentamicin.

Neonatal meningitis

In general, neonates, especially those with low birth weight, are at increased risk for meningitis because of their immature immunological status. This is illustrated by problems with, for example, humoral and cellular immunity, phagocytic capability and inefficient alternative complement pathway. This is especially true as a result of medical advances that have contributed to the increased survival of pre-term infants.

Although mortality rates due to neonatal meningitis in resource-rich countries are declining, the problem is still serious

Neonatal meningitis can be caused by a wide range of bacteria, but the most frequent are group B haemolytic streptococci (GBS) and *E. coli* (Table 24.6; see also Ch. 23). This may occur by routes such as nosocomial infection. However, the infant may also be infected from the mother. For example, with women vaginally colonized by GBS, the infant may swallow maternal secretions such as infected amniotic fluid during delivery.

Neonatal meningitis often leads to permanent neurologic sequelae such as cerebral or cranial nerve palsy, epilepsy, mental retardation or hydrocephalus. This is partly because the clinical diagnosis of meningitis in the neonate is difficult, perhaps with no more specific signs than fever, poor feeding, vomiting, respiratory distress or diarrhea. In addition, due to the possible range of aetiological agents, 'blind' antibiotic therapy in the absence of susceptibility tests may not be optimal, and adequate penetration of the antibiotic into the CSF is also an issue.

Tuberculous meningitis

Patients with tuberculous meningitis always have a focus of infection elsewhere, but approximately 25% may have no clinical or historic evidence of such an infection. In > 50% of cases, meningitis is associated with acute miliary tuberculosis (Fig. 24.5). In areas with a high prevalence of tuberculosis, meningitis tends to be most commonly seen in children from 0 to 4 years of age. However, in areas where tuberculosis is less frequent, most meningitis cases are in adults.

Tuberculous meningitis usually presents with a gradual onset over a few weeks

There is a gradual onset of generalized illness beginning with malaise, apathy and anorexia and proceeding within a few weeks to photophobia, neck stiffness and impairment of consciousness. Occasionally, the onset is much more rapid and may be mistaken for a subarachnoid haemorrhage. The variability of presentation means that the clinician needs

Table 24.6 Group B streptococci are a major cause of neonatal meningitis

	At or soon after birth	In the nursery
	Early onset disease	**Late onset disease**
	Group B streptococci (*Streptococcus agalactiae*) are normal inhabitants of the female genital tract and may be acquired by the neonate	
Age	<7 days	1 week–3 months
Risk factors	Heavily colonized mother lacking specific antibody Premature rupture of membranes Pre-term delivery Prolonged labour, obstetric complications	Lack of maternal antibody Exposure to cross-infection from heavily colonized babies Poor hygiene in nursery
Type of disease	Generalized infection including bacteraemia, pneumonia and meningitis	Predominantly meningitis
Type of group B streptococcus	All serotypes but meningitis mostly due to type III	90% type III
Outcome	Approximately 60% fatal; serious sequelae in many survivors	Approximately 20% fatal
Treatment	Take blood and CSF for culture Treat on suspicion Gentamicin and ampicillin or cefotaxime/ceftriaxone	Treat on suspicion Take blood and CSF for culture Gentamicin and ampicillin or cefotaxime/ceftriaxone
Prevention	Antibiotic treatment does not reliably abolish carriage in mother; not recommended 'Blind' treatment of sick baby who has risk factors Future: ?? immunize antibody-negative females of child-bearing age	Good hygiene practices in nursery Do not allow mothers to handle other babies

CSF, cerebrospinal fluid.

Figure 24.5 The association between acute miliary tuberculosis and meningitis. (* Leads to miliary tuberculosis (Latin: *milium*, millet seed – each tubercle resembles a millet seed). Miliary tuberculosis also occurs in the lungs and elsewhere.

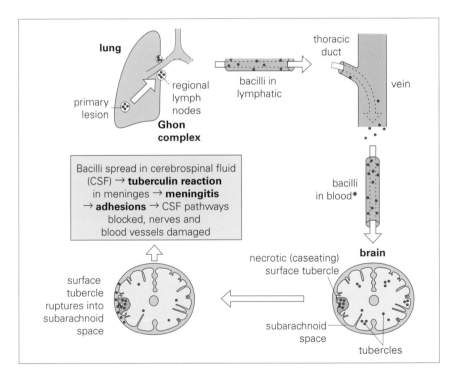

to maintain an awareness of possible tuberculous meningitis to make the diagnosis. A delay in making the diagnosis and in starting appropriate antimicrobial therapy (Table 24.2) results in serious complications and sequelae.

Spinal tuberculosis is uncommon now except in resource-poor countries; bacteria in the vertebrae destroy the intervertebral disks to form epidural abscesses. These compress the spinal cord and lead to paraplegia.

Fungal meningitis

Cryptococcus neoformans and *Coccidioides immitis* can invade the blood from a primary site of infection in the lungs and thence to the brain to cause meningitis. *Cryptococcus* has a marked tropism for the CNS and is the major cause of fungal meningitis. *C. neoformans* occurs as two varieties, each with two serotypes.

Cryptococcus neoformans meningitis is seen in patients with depressed cell-mediated immunity

It therefore occurs in individuals with AIDS and other immunosuppressive conditions. The onset is usually slow, over days or weeks. The capsulate yeasts can be seen in Indian ink-stained preparations of cerebrospinal fluid (CSF) (Fig. 24.6) and can be cultured (see Ch. 32). Antigen detection is also a useful diagnostic tool and evidence of a decline in antigen and an increase in antibody levels in the CSF can be used as a measure of successful therapy. Treatment with the antifungal drugs amphotericin B and flucytosine in combination is recommended, the former penetrating poorly into CSF.

Coccidioides immitis infection is common in particular geographic locations

These locations are notably southwest USA, Mexico and South America. CNS infection occurs in < 1% of infected individuals, but is fatal unless treated. It may be part of the generalized disease or may represent the only extrapulmonary site. The organisms are rarely visible in the CSF, and cultures are positive in < 50% of cases, but the diagnosis can be made by demonstrating complement-fixing antibodies in the serum. Treatment with amphotericin B, fluconazole or miconazole is recommended.

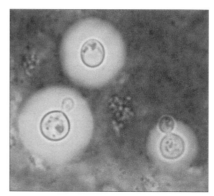

Figure 24.6 *Cryptococcus neoformans* in Indian ink-stained preparation of cerebrospinal fluid sediment. (Courtesy of A.E. Prevost.)

Protozoal meningitis

The free-living amoeba *Naegleria* can multiply in stagnant fresh water in warm countries, especially in the sludge at the bottom of lakes and swimming pools. If inhaled, they can reach the meninges via the olfactory tract and cribriform plate. Primary amoebic meningoencephalitis caused by *Naegleria* affects healthy individuals with no obvious defect in immunity. The disease shows a rapid onset, and the mortality rate is high.

Acanthamoeba spp. are widespread in the environment. They more commonly affect those who are already unwell or immunocompromised and are thought to enter via the skin or the respiratory tract. *Acanthamoeba* causes a chronic condition (granulomatous amoebic encephalitis).

Balamuthia mandrillaris is found in soil or stagnant water and humans become infected by inhalation of cysts or direct contamination of skin. Cases have been reported in patients with a variety of underlying medical conditions but also in immunocompetent individuals. Infection of the CNS produces encephalitis with raised protein, lymphocytic CSF and normal or low CSF glucose.

Under the microscope, *Naegleria* appear as slowly motile amoebae on careful examination of a fresh wet sample of CSF. *Acanthamoeba* are rarely seen in the CSF but can be visualized in brain biopsies. They also grow well in cultures prepared from tissue biopsies. Diagnosis of *Balamuthia* infection is by histopathology of biopsy samples, serology and PCR on brain tissue or CSF. Treatment is not fully satisfactory. Amphotericin B, with miconazole and rifampin, has been used for *Naegleria*; a variety of drugs have been used for *Acanthamoeba*. Two survivors of *Balamuthia* infection received a combination of albendazole and itraconazole.

Viral meningitis

Viral meningitis is the most common type of meningitis

It is a milder disease than bacterial meningitis, with headache, fever and photophobia, but less neck stiffness. The CSF is clear in the absence of bacteria, and the cells are mainly lymphocytes, although polymorphonuclear leukocytes may be present in the early stages (Table 24.1). The causes of viral meningitis are listed in Table 24.7 and before the advent of molecular-based methods of detection, viruses were isolated from the CSF in < 50% of cases.

Table 24.7 Causes of viral meningitis

Virus	Virus group	Comments
Herpes simplex virus	Alpha herpesvirus	May follow genital infection with HSV-2
Mumps	Paramyxovirus	A quite common complication
Lymphocytic choriomeningitis	Arenavirus	Uncommon infection from urine of mice, hamsters carrying the virus
Enteroviruses including coxsackievirus, echovirus and poliovirus	Picornaviruses (enterovirus group)	Commonly seen, especially due to echoviruses
Japanese encephalitis	Togavirus	India, South East Asia, Japan
Eastern and Western equine encephalitis	Togavirus	East and West USA
Louping Ill	Togavirus	Scotland
HIV	Retrovirus	May occur early after infection

There are five groups of human enteroviruses which include the echoviruses, coxsackie group A and B viruses, and the three types of polioviruses. Enteroviruses are common causes of seasonal aseptic meningitis. In contrast to bacterial meningitis, viral meningitis usually has a benign course, and complete recovery is the rule.

ENCEPHALITIS

Encephalitis is usually caused by viruses, but there are many cases where the infectious aetiology is not identified

The causes and pathogenesis of viral encephalitis are shown in Table 24.8 and Figure 24.7. Approximately 700 cases of viral encephalitis occur annually in England with a 7% mortality rate and substantial morbidity including physical, cognitive and behavioural difficulties. It is thought that the annual costs of illness caused by encephalitis to the United States health service amounts to around US$630 million.

Characteristically, there are signs of cerebral dysfunction, as the substance of the brain is affected, unlike meningitis where the lining of the brain is inflamed. Someone with an encephalitic illness will present with abnormal behaviour, seizures and altered consciousness, often with nausea, vomiting and fever.

Up to 85% of individuals diagnosed with encephalitis globally are of unknown aetiology. Emerging viruses that can cause encephalitis include the Nipah virus, bat lyssaviruses, and avian influenza A H5N1 virus infections. Immune-mediated forms of encephalitis, including voltage-gated potassium channel and N-methyl-D-aspartate (NMDA) receptor antibody-associated encephalitis, must be considered in the differential diagnosis as they have a similar presentation as infectious causes.

Preventative measures include measles, mumps and rubella immunization. In addition, antiviral drugs are used to treat herpes simplex and varicella-zoster virus encephalitis and immunomodulation for the immune-mediated encephalitides including acute disseminated encephalomyelitis (ADEM) or other immune-mediated encephalitides.

Toxoplasma gondii and *C. neoformans* can also cause life-threatening encephalitis or meningoencephalitis. This is particularly likely in those with defective cell-mediated immunity, and cerebral malaria as a complication of *Plasmodium falciparum* infection is frequently fatal. Encephalitis may occur in Lyme disease (*Borrelia burgdorferi*) and Legionnaires' disease (*Legionella pneumophila*), but the relative importance of bacterial invasion, bacterial toxins and immunopathology is unknown.

HSV encephalitis (HSE) is the most common form of severe sporadic acute focal encephalitis

It is thought that the incidence of HSE in the USA is about 1/250 000 to 500 000 population per year. A distinction is made between HSV infections of the CNS during the

Table 24.8 Infectious causes of encephalitis

Cause	Infectious agent	Comments
Viruses (sporadic occurrence)	Herpes simplex virus Mumps Varicella-zoster virus Cytomegalovirus Rabies Louping ill HIV	Infant and adult forms distinguished Much less common than meningitis A rare complication of ophthalmic zoster In utero and in immunosuppressed (e.g. AIDS) 55 000 deaths/year, in Asia and Africa One of tick-borne encephalitis virus complex (others cause Russian spring–summer encephalitis etc.) Subacute encephalitis (often together with other central nervous system infections)
Viruses (may be outbreaks)	Polio and other enteroviruses Eastern and western equine encephalitis St Louis encephalitis virus Japanese encephalitis virus Californian encephalitis virus	Uncommon; may be spastic paralysis Mosquito-borne togaviruses Mosquito-borne bunyavirus
Slow viruses	Rubella Measles JC virus (progressive multifocal leukoencephalopathy)	Infection in utero (microcephaly etc.) or subacute sclerosing panencephalitis (SSPE)-type disease SSPE following uncomplicated measles after interval of up to 10 years Usually in immunocompromised, especially in AIDS
Atypical agents of scrapie group (non-viral)	Prions	Creutzfeldt–Jakob disease (CJD) and kuru in humans; incubation period up to 20 years; 'spongiform' encephalopathy
Postvaccinal or postinfectious	?	Occurs as a rare complication 2–3 weeks after exposure to certain viruses (e.g. measles) or vaccines; strong autoimmune component
Protozoa and fungi	*Toxoplasma gondii* *Cryptococcus neoformans* *Plasmodium falciparum* *Trypanosoma* spp.	Encephalitis a rare complication Meningoencephalitis Cerebral malaria Sleeping sickness in Africa
Bacteria	*Treponema pallidum* *Mycoplasma pneumoniae* *Borrelia burgdorferi*	Rare Rare Uncommon

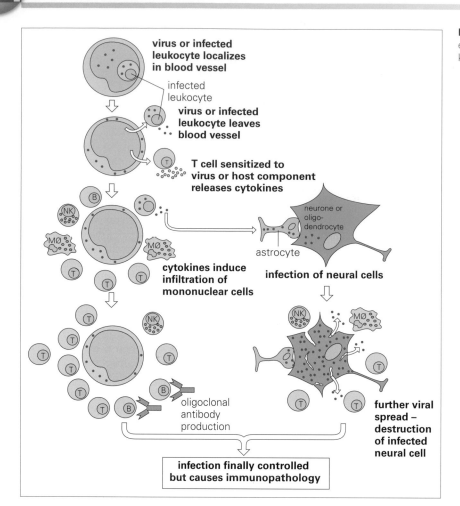

virus or infected leukocyte localizes in blood vessel

infected leukocyte

virus or infected leukocyte leaves blood vessel

T cell sensitized to virus or host component releases cytokines

neurone or oligo-dendrocyte

astrocyte

cytokines induce infiltration of mononuclear cells

infection of neural cells

oligoclonal antibody production

further viral spread – destruction of infected neural cell

infection finally controlled but causes immunopathology

Figure 24.7 The pathogenesis of viral encephalomyelitis. Mϕ, macrophage; NK, natural killer cell.

neonatal period and those in older children and adults. Neonates may acquire a primary and disseminated infection with a diffuse encephalitis after vaginal delivery from a mother shedding HSV-2 in the genital tract. Most HSE seen in older children and adults is due to HSV-1, of which most are due to virus reactivation in the trigeminal ganglia (see Ch. 15), the infection then passing back to the temporal lobe of the brain, and the minority are due to a primary infection. About 30% of HSE is seen in people < 20 years old, and 50% in the over-50 age range.

Herpetic skin or mucosal lesions may be present. The diagnosis is indicated by finding temporal lobe enhancement using CT and MRI scans (Fig. 24.8). HSV DNA detection should be carried out on a CSF sample using PCR. An electroencephalogram (EEG) may also be helpful. The 70% mortality rate in untreated patients is greatly reduced by early and prolonged treatment with intravenous aciclovir. The 21-day treatment course is important, as relapse can occur.

Other herpesviruses less commonly cause encephalitis

With VZV, encephalitis generally occurs as a sequel to reactivation, and with cytomegalovirus (CMV) either during primary infection in utero (see Ch. 21) or reactivation as a complication of immunodeficiency, for example, in AIDS. HHV-6 encephalitis has also been reported in immunosuppressed patients. Finally, B virus is a *Cercopithecine* herpesvirus of macaque monkeys that does not really affect the animal but can cause a severe and fatal encephalitis in

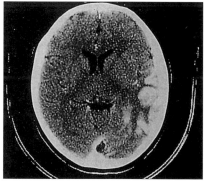

Figure 24.8 Herpes simplex encephalitis. Computerized tomographic scan showing enhancement of gyral structures in the left temporal lobe and associated cerebral oedema. (Courtesy of J. Curé.)

humans when bitten or scratched by an infected monkey. The wound should be cleaned immediately and antiviral prophylaxis is recommended.

Enteroviral infections

Poliovirus used to be a common cause of encephalitis

In the great 1916 polio epidemic in New York City, 9000 cases of paralysis were reported, nearly all in children < 5 years of age. CNS disease occurs in < 1% of those infected. After an initial 1–4 days of fever, sore throat and malaise, meningeal

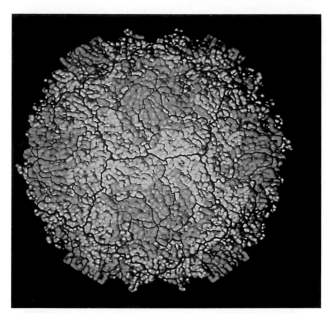

Figure 24.9 Computer graphic model of the surface of a poliovirus based on X-ray diffraction studies. The capsid protein subunits visible on the surface of the virus particle are viral protein 1 (VP1) in blue, VP2 in green and VP3 in grey. (Courtesy of A.J. Olson, Research Institute of Scripps Clinic, La Jolla, California.)

signs and symptoms appear, followed by involvement of motor neurones and paralysis (see Fig. 24.2).

There are successful vaccines; the structure (Fig. 24.9) and replication of the virus are better understood, and efforts to eradicate the disease by 2002 had driven the incidence of polio to its lowest point in history. The disease is completely preventable by vaccination (see Ch. 31) and has been disappearing in resource-rich countries since vaccination programmes were first carried out in the 1950s (Fig. 24.10). The Global Polio Eradication Initiative reduced the number of polio-endemic countries from 20 to 10 between 2000 and 2001. By 2010, a 95% and 94% fall in the number of children paralysed by polio in Nigeria and India were reported,

respectively, together with a 92% decline in polio cases due to type 3 wild poliovirus (WPV3) globally. Imported wild poliovirus transmission was also interrupted in all countries that reported reinfections in 2009. The fall in PV transmission in these countries and WPV3 worldwide was due to a new bivalent oral polio vaccine and new ways of delivering the vaccine. However, an outbreak of paralytic polio occurred in Tajikistan and the Democratic Republic of Congo in 2010 due to importation of wild PV.

There are three serologic (antigenic) types of poliovirus, with little cross-reaction between them, so that antibody to each type is necessary for protection. At least 75% of paralytic cases are due to type 1 polioviruses.

Enterovirus-71-associated hand, foot and mouth epidemic resulted in a high rate of neurologic complications

Other enteroviruses such as coxsackieviruses and echoviruses occasionally cause meningoencephalitis. However, in 1998, there was a large outbreak of enterovirus 71 (EV71) hand, foot and mouth (HFMD) infection in Taiwan, in which most of the 405 patients were children under 5 years of age, with a mortality rate of 19%. The most severely affected children had brainstem involvement, and many were left with permanent neurological sequelae. Treatment is supportive and there is no vaccine. Since then, EV71, having been identified in Guangdong province in the People's Republic of China and having caused epidemics in south China, several epidemics have been reported in the middle or north of China, such as in Anhui, Shandong, Shanghai, and Beijing. Overall, 488 955 HFMD cases were reported nationwide, including 126 fatal cases in 2008.

Paramyxoviral infections

Mumps virus is a common cause of mild encephalitis

Asymptomatic CNS invasion may be common because there are increased numbers of cells in the CSF in about 50% of patients with parotitis. However, meningitis and encephalitis are often seen without parotitis.

Figure 24.10 The incidence of paralytic poliomyelitis in the USA from 1951 to 2000.

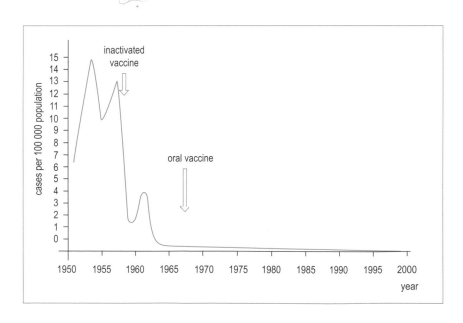

Nipah virus encephalitis, a zoonotic paramyxovirus infection

In 1998, an outbreak of encephalitis with a high mortality rate was reported among pig farm workers in Malaysia. In total, there were 105 deaths among 265 patients with Nipah virus encephalitis. At first attributed to Japanese encephalitis, the clinical, epidemiologic and virologic characteristics showed that the virus was a paramyxovirus which was transmitted to humans by close contact with infected pigs, probably by aerosol. The outbreak was ended by culling more than 1 million infected or exposed pigs in the local and surrounding regions in Malaysia. The island flying fox, *Pteropus hypomelanus*, a fruit bat, is the natural reservoir for the virus and the virus can be found in the urine and saliva of infected bats. The pigs were infected having eaten food contaminated by fruit bat secretions. Human-to-human transmission can also play an important role in Nipah virus transmission.

Rabies encephalitis

More than 55 000 people die of rabies worldwide each year

- Rabies occurs in more than 150 countries and territories.
- Wound cleansing and immunization within a few hours after contact with a suspect rabid animal can prevent the onset of rabies and death.
- Every year, more than 15 million people worldwide receive a post-exposure preventive regimen to avert the disease – this is estimated to prevent 327 000 rabies deaths annually.

The causative agent of rabies is a rhabdovirus, a bullet-shaped single-stranded RNA virus. The *Lyssavirus* genus sits within the Rhabdoviridae family and there are seven genotypes: genotype 1 occurs worldwide and is the classic rabies virus, genotypes 2, 3 and 4 are the African Lagos, Mokola and Duvenhage bat viruses, respectively, genotypes 5 and 6 are the European bat *Lyssaviruses* (EBLV) 1 and 2, respectively, and genotype 7 is the Australian bat *Lyssavirus*.

The virus is excreted in the saliva of infected dogs, foxes, jackals, wolves, skunks, raccoons and vampire and other bats, and transmission to humans follows a bite or salivary contamination of other types of skin abrasions or wounds. The infection is eventually fatal, although the course of the disease varies considerably between species. If an apparently healthy dog is still healthy 15 days after biting a human, rabies is extremely unlikely. However, the virus may be excreted in the dog's saliva before the animal shows any clinical signs of disease.

The virus can infect all warm-blooded animals. Rabies from vampire bats causes more than 1 million deaths per year in cattle in Central and South America. Dogs are the source of more than 99% of human rabies deaths and are involved in most of the 55 000 cases of human rabies that occur in the world each year. In all the mainland masses, the infection maintains itself in non-human mammalian hosts; islands such as Australia, Great Britain, Japan, Hawaii, most of the Caribbean islands and also Scandinavia, are free of rabies because of strict controls over the importation of animals such as dogs and cats, although this is changing. Since the development of the Channel Tunnel linking the UK and the rest of Europe, a number of rabies infections occurred associated with contact with bats. Thirty different bat species have been identified in Europe, a number of which carry EBVL 1 or 2. They are distinct from rabies genotype 1 infections in foxes, dogs and other terrestrial animals. In the USA, the incidence of human rabies has been falling since the 1940s and 1950s, when most cases followed exposure to infected dogs. Since then, the source has more often been non-domesticated animals such as skunks, raccoons and bats, or exposure to dogs in other countries.

Raccoon rabies spread slowly northwards from Florida in the 1950s, and in the 1980s caused an explosive epidemic in Virginia, Maryland and the District of Columbia. This outbreak was due to the importation of raccoons from infected areas for sporting purposes.

The incubation period in humans is generally 4–13 weeks, although it may occasionally be as long as 6 months, possibly due to a delay in virus entry into peripheral nerves. The virus travels up peripheral nerves and, in general, the further the bite is from the CNS, the longer the incubation period. For instance, a bite on the foot leads to a longer incubation period than a bite on the face.

While the virus is travelling up the axons of motor or sensory neurones, there is no detectable antibody or cell-mediated immune response, possibly because antigen remains sequestered in infected muscle cells. Hence, passively administered rabies immunoglobulin may be given during the incubation period.

Once in the brain, the virus spreads from cell to cell until a large proportion of neurones are infected, but there is little cytopathic effect, even when viewed by electron microscopy, and almost no cellular infiltration. The striking symptoms of this disease are largely due to dysfunction rather than visible damage to infected cells. The change in behaviour of infected animals results from virus invasion of the limbic system.

Clinical features of rabies include muscle spasms, convulsions and hydrophobia

After developing a sore throat, headache, fever and discomfort at the site of the bite, the patient becomes excited, with muscle spasms and convulsions. Involvement of the muscles of swallowing when attempting to drink water gave the old name for rabies, hydrophobia, as the symptoms are sometimes precipitated by the mere sight of water.

Once rabies has developed it is fatal, death occurring following cardiac or respiratory arrest. Paralysis is often a major feature of the disease. One or two patients treated in intensive care units have recovered, but with serious neurologic sequelae.

Rabies can be diagnosed by detecting viral antigen or RNA

Laboratory diagnosis can be made by the detection of viral antigen by immunofluorescence or using PCR to detect rabies viral RNA in skin biopsies, corneal impression smears or brain biopsy. Characteristic intracytoplasmic inclusions called Negri bodies are seen in neurones (Fig. 24.11). There is no treatment except supportive care.

Many countries have developed vaccination programmes for domestic dogs, e.g. France, and in Canada and elsewhere, wild foxes have been vaccinated by dropping food

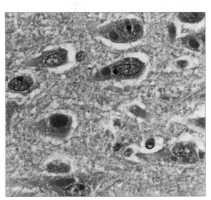

Figure 24.11 Multiple cytoplasmic Negri bodies in pyramidal neurones of the hippocampus in rabies. (Courtesy of P. Garen.)

baited with live virus vaccine from the air. For the rabies-free countries, constant vigilance at borders and strict quarantine regulations are necessary to prevent the introduction of infected animals. In 1886, there were 36 human rabies deaths in England, 11 of them in London. As recently as 1906, rabies was still endemic in England, and there were deaths due to rabies in the deer in Hampton Court Park, London.

After exposure to a possibly infected animal, immediate preventive action should be taken

This action includes:

- prompt cleaning of the wound (alcoholic iodine, debridement)
- confirmation of whether or not the animal is rabid (clinical observation of suspected dogs, histologic observation of the brain of other suspected species)
- administration of human rabies immunoglobulin (RIG) to ensure prompt passive immunization; RIG is infiltrated intramuscularly around the wound site
- active immunization with killed diploid cell-derived rabies virus (see Ch. 34). The chances of preventing the disease are greater when vaccination is started as early as possible after infection. Vaccine and RIG must never be administered at the same anatomical site.

Togavirus meningitis and encephalitis

Numerous arthropod-borne togaviruses can cause meningitis or encephalitis

These togaviruses are listed in Tables 24.7 and 24.8, and sometimes cause outbreaks of infection. In different parts of the world, different mammals, birds or even reptiles act as reservoirs and there are a variety of arthropod (mosquito and tick) vectors. Usually, <1% of humans infected develop neurologic disease (see Ch. 27). There may be a febrile illness, but asymptomatic infection is common. In California, for instance, western equine encephalomyelitis (WEE) virus and St Louis encephalitis (SLE) virus are prevalent and transmitted by the mosquito *Culex tarsalis*; a WEE vaccine is available, but only for horses.

Japanese encephalitis virus infection is common in India and can result in a mortality of more than 50% in older age groups; a vaccine for humans has been developed.

West Nile virus, another emerging viral cause of encephalitis

In 1999, an epidemic of viral encephalitis was reported in New York City, leading to 62 patients with encephalitis, seven of whom died. Meningoencephalitis was rare in the younger age groups and more common in those over 50 years of age. Originally thought to be due to St Louis encephalitis (SLE), once again the clinical, epidemiologic and virologic characteristics resulted in the correct identification of West Nile virus infection, as there had been an epidemic of deaths among wild and other birds which are the avian reservoir of SLE but are not usually killed by the virus. West Nile virus belongs to the Japanese encephalitis serogroup of flaviviruses that includes SLE, had not been seen in the western hemisphere but was well recognized in Africa and the Middle East. West Nile virus is primarily an infection of birds and culicine mosquitoes, with humans and horses acting as incidental hosts. Since 1999, the virus has been successfully dispersed by migratory birds and has spread through most of the USA. Transmission has also been reported in four organ transplant recipients having received organs from one donor with West Nile viraemia antemortem.

The diagnosis can be made by detecting West Nile viral RNA or an IgM response in serum and/or CSF samples. Treatment is supportive, there is no vaccine, and prevention includes mosquito control programmes.

HIV meningitis and encephalitis

HIV can cause subacute encephalitis, often with dementia

HIV (see Ch. 21) often invades the CNS shortly after initial infection, resulting in an increase in cells in the CSF and a mild meningitic illness. At a later stage, and quite independently of the disease picture that results from immune deficiency, a subacute encephalitis may develop, often with dementia. This is sometimes difficult to distinguish from the neurologic disease caused by microorganisms such as *T. gondii*, *C. neoformans*, cytomegalovirus and JC virus. JC virus, a polyomavirus, occasionally invades oligodendrocytes in immunodeficient people, particularly in AIDS, and eventually gives rise to progressive multifocal leukoencephalopathy (PML). In HIV-related dementia, the brain is shrunken, with enlarged ventricles and vacuolation of myelin tracts. HIV mainly infects macrophages and microglia in the CNS, and because the clinical disease is more severe than might be expected from the pathologic changes, additional pathogenic mechanisms have been proposed. For instance, there are amino acid sequence similarities between the HIV envelope protein *gp120* and certain transmitter molecules, so that HIV-derived molecules could block the action of natural neurotransmitters. Highly active antiretroviral therapy has reduced the severity of HIV-associated neurocognitive disorders (HAND). However, their prevalence remains high. This will be improved by using blood–brain barrier-penetrating drugs, possibly at an earlier stage, treating other possible causes including other medical conditions that affect neural function as well as proinflammatory processes, free radical formation and apoptosis. HAND is correlated with long-term central nervous system inflammation.

Viral myelopathy

A number of viral infections can cause inflammation of the spinal cord, a myelitis. Acute myelitis may result in symmetrical symptoms if it transverses the spinal cord. These will include motor weakness and sensory loss, for example. The symptoms will be asymmetrical if only part of the spinal cord is involved. When the anterior horn cells of the cord are affected by polio, coxsackie, enterovirus 71 and West Nile virus infection, the symptoms are motor and result in acute flaccid paralysis. A number of herpesviruses including HSV, CMV, EBV and VZV have been associated with a myelitis. Post-infectious causes have also been reported.

Chronic myelopathy can be caused by HTLV-1 infection and patients present with tropical spastic paraparesis (TSP), also called HAM (HTLV-1-associated myopathy). HIV-1 infection is also part of the differential diagnosis.

Post-vaccinial and post-infectious encephalitis

Encephalitis following viral infection or vaccination possibly has an autoimmune basis

Encephalitis very occasionally occurs 1–2 weeks after an apparently normal measles virus infection, and even less commonly after varicella. It is also seen after *Mycoplasma* infection and various influenza-like illnesses. The infectious agent is generally not recoverable from the CNS, and the perivascular infiltration, sometimes with demyelination, suggests an autoimmune pathogenesis. A similar condition occurs after administration of brain-derived inactivated rabies vaccine, which is now obsolete, and after other immunizations with non-infectious materials. The clinical picture resembles experimental allergic encephalitis, and is probably due to autoimmune responses triggered by the infection or by the injected material.

An analogous inflammatory demyelinating condition of the peripheral nervous system called Guillain–Barré syndrome has been associated with a variety of viral infections, as well as with immunization with non-infectious material. In 1976, most adults in the USA were given inactivated influenza virus vaccine, which resulted in a small but highly significant number of cases of Guillain–Barré syndrome.

In addition, rubella or measles virus invades the CNS, but virus growth is slow, often incomplete, and partially controlled by host defences (see Ch. 11); clinical disease appears after an incubation period of up to 10 years. For instance:

- In otherwise uncomplicated measles, CNS invasion can take place and eventually result in SSPE.
- Rubella very occasionally causes a similar disease to SSPE but, more commonly, like CMV, it invades the brain of the fetus, interfering with development to cause mental retardation.

NEUROLOGIC DISEASES OF POSSIBLE VIRAL AETIOLOGY

It has often been suggested that certain neurologic diseases of unknown origin, including multiple sclerosis, amyotrophic lateral sclerosis, Parkinson's disease, schizophrenia and senile dementia, have a viral origin. Although so far there is no definitive evidence for this, it is possible that viruses and other infectious agents may, at times, trigger dangerous autoimmune-type responses in the CNS.

SPONGIFORM ENCEPHALOPATHIES CAUSED BY SCRAPIE-TYPE AGENTS

Scrapie-type agents are closely associated with host-coded prion protein

Scrapie-type agents infect a variety of mammals, including humans, and are transmissible to laboratory rodents or primates. They show a number of remarkable biological characteristics; their molecular biology is now well described and experiments in laboratory mice have revealed much about their interaction with host tissues (see Ch. 7). Disease is characterized by the appearance of a spongiform appearance of nervous tissues, caused by vacuolation and plaque formation. Infections in animals seem to have originated from sheep and goats with scrapie (see Fig. 7.2), which has been present in Europe for 200–300 years. Affected animals itch and scrape themselves against posts for relief.

CNS DISEASE CAUSED BY PARASITES

The CNS is an important target in toxoplasmosis

Although congenitally acquired *Toxoplasma gondii* is initially generalized, it may become localized in the CNS. Damage to the eye is the most common consequence (see Ch. 25), but the brain may also be affected, with hydrocephalus and intracerebral calcification. In the days before the advent of highly active antiretroviral therapy, toxoplasmosis was an important cause of death in AIDS patients, with encephalitis and toxoplasma abscess due to necrosis as contributory causes.

Cerebral malaria is a major killer

The life cycle of *Plasmodium falciparum* shows an unusual feature in that red blood cells containing the asexual stages (asexual stages are in humans; sexual stages are in mosquitoes, see Ch. 27) adhere to the walls of capillaries. When this occurs in the brain, cerebral malaria may result, and this is an important cause of mortality in African children. Fever is followed by a variety of symptoms, including convulsions and coma, and these lead rapidly to death if not treated. Artemisinin combination therapy is replacing quinine as the treatment of choice for severe malaria. Coma is reversible, mostly without residual neurologic deficit, when treatment is successful.

Toxocara infection can result in granuloma formation in the brain and retina

The cat and dog roundworms *Toxocara cati* and *Toxocara canis* infect humans, usually children, when *Toxocara* eggs derived from kitten or puppy faeces are ingested (see Ch. 6). After ingestion by humans, the eggs hatch and the larvae migrate from the gut to the liver, lung, eye (see Ch. 25), brain, kidney and muscles. However, as humans are dead-end hosts for these parasites, they cannot reach full maturity. Granulomas form around the larvae, which in the brain may cause convulsions, and in the eye a tumour-like mass can cause retinal detachment and eventually blindness. Peripheral blood eosinophilia is rarely seen in ocular toxocariasis.

Serum can be tested by ELISA for antibodies to *Toxocara* excretory–secretory antigen, but may give false-negative results in ocular toxocariasis. Antibody detection in ocular vitreous fluid samples is more sensitive. The disease is prevented by de-worming puppies and kittens, and by reducing the contamination by dog excreta of children's play areas. Anthelmintic therapy is not given in ocular toxocariasis. Corticosteroids and appropriate ophthalmic surgery are the mainstays of therapy.

Cystic hydatid disease is characterized by cyst formation, potentially in any organ but most commonly in the liver

Cystic hydatid disease is caused by the tapeworm *Echinococcus granulosus* (see Chs 6 and 22) which has a worldwide distribution, especially in sheep-rearing areas. When humans ingest eggs from infected dogs, the embryos emerge, migrate through the gut to the portal blood vessels, and subsequently develop into hydatid cysts. These may occur in any organ but are found especially in the liver and, less commonly, in the lungs, brain and kidney. Disease is caused by local pressure from the cyst, and sometimes hypersensitivity reactions to hydatid antigens. Neurologic symptoms include nausea and vomiting, seizures and altered mental status.

Hydatid disease is diagnosed by detecting serum antibody to hydatid antigens and, specifically for CNS involvement, by CT or MRI scanning, to demonstrate the presence of cysts (Fig. 24.12). Hydatid cysts in the CNS require surgical removal, with special care to avoid cyst rupture, plus adjunctive therapy with albendazole.

The disease is prevented by interrupting the natural dog–sheep, dog–goat, or other carnivore–herbivore transmission cycle.

Cysticercosis is characterized by cyst formation in the brain and eye

Cysticercosis results from infection with the larval stage of *Taenia solium*, a human tapeworm. The eggs present in human faeces infect pigs, which develop cysts in muscle tissue ('measly pork') and are a source of further human infection. Humans ingest eggs in material contaminated with human faeces, often from another person rather than from a tapeworm infection of their own, which explains why vegetarians can contract cysticercosis. After passing through the gut wall, the parasite develops into cysts, usually in skeletal muscle, but also and more importantly in the brain (Fig. 24.13) or eye, causing convulsions or, if very

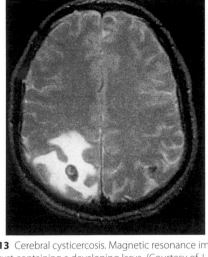

Figure 24.13 Cerebral cysticercosis. Magnetic resonance imaging scan showing a cyst containing a developing larva. (Courtesy of J. Curé.)

heavily infected, cysticercotic encephalopathy. Diagnosis is by detecting specific antibody in serum or CSF (interestingly, there is a higher positivity rate in serum than in CSF), and visualizing cysts, preferably by MRI scan. Treatment is with albendazole or praziquantel under corticosteroid cover.

BRAIN ABSCESSES

Brain abscesses are usually associated with predisposing factors

Since the development of antibiotics, brain abscesses have become rare and usually follow surgery or trauma, chronic osteomyelitis of neighbouring bone, septic embolism or chronic cerebral anoxia. They are also seen in children with congenital cyanotic heart disease in whom the lungs fail to filter off circulating bacteria. Acute abscesses are caused by various bacteria, generally of oropharyngeal origin, including anaerobes. There is usually a mixed bacterial flora. Chronic abscesses may be due to *Mycobacterium tuberculosis* or *C. neoformans*. In immunosuppressed patients, opportunistic infection may occur with fungi and protozoan aetiologic agents.

Brain abscesses are diagnosed clinically and by CT and MRI brain scans. If an abscess is suspected, lumbar puncture is contraindicated but, if performed, generally shows raised CSF cells and proteins (see Table 24.1). Treatment

Figure 24.12 Echinococcosis. (A) Cerebral angiography showing displacement of vessels by a large frontal mass. (B) Cyst removed from patient in (A). (Courtesy of H. Whitwell.)

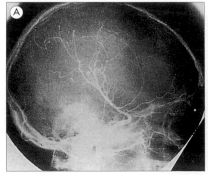
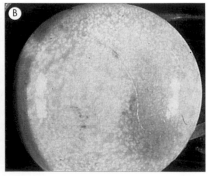

Table 24.9 Infections causing chronic meningitis or brain abscess

Bacterial	
Tuberculosis	*Mycobacterium tuberculosis*
Syphilis	*Treponema pallidum*
Brucellosis	*Brucella abortus*
Lyme disease	*Borrelia burgdorferi*
Nocardiosis[a]	*Nocardia asteroides*
Actinomycosis[a]	*Actinomyces fumigatus*
Fungal	
Cryptococcosis	*Cryptococcus neoformans*
Coccidioidomycosis	*Coccidioides immitis*
Histoplasmosis	*Histoplasma capsulatum*
Candidiasis	*Candida albicans*
Blastomycosis[a]	*Blastomyces dermatitidis*
Parasitic	
Toxoplasmosis[a]	*Toxoplasma gondii*
Cysticercosis[a]	*Taenia solium*

[a]Disease manifest as brain abscess.

is by surgical drainage if the abscess is well encapsulated, and antibiotics should be given for at least 1 month. Other infections that may manifest as chronic meningitis or brain abscess are summarized in Table 24.9.

TETANUS AND BOTULISM

Several bacteria release toxins that act on the nervous system (see Ch. 17), but do not themselves invade the CNS. In the case of *Clostridium tetani* and *Clostridium botulinum*, the major clinical impact is neurologic.

Tetanus

Cl. tetani toxin is carried to the CNS in peripheral nerve axons

Tetanus spores are widespread in soil and originate from the faeces of domestic animals. The spores enter a wound, and if necrotic tissue or the presence of a foreign body permits local and anaerobic growth of bacteria, the toxin tetanospasmin (see Ch. 17) is produced. All strains of *Cl. tetani* produce the same toxin. The wound can be anything from a small gardener's scratch or cut to that seen in a large automobile or battlefield injury. However, in as many as 20% of cases, there is no history of injury. Infection of the umbilical stump can cause neonatal tetanus, which killed nearly 5000 infants in 2009 worldwide (compared with nearly 30 000 in 1989), especially in resource-poor countries (see Ch. 23).

The toxin is carried in peripheral nerve axons and probably in the blood to the CNS, where it binds to neurones and blocks the release of inhibitory mediators in spinal synapses, causing overactivity of motor neurones. It can also pass up sympathetic nerve axons and lead to overactivity of the sympathetic nervous system.

Clinical features of tetanus include muscle rigidity and spasms

After a period of 3–21 days, but sometimes longer, there are exaggerated reflexes, muscle rigidity and uncontrolled muscle spasms. Lockjaw (trismus) is due to contraction of jaw muscles. Dysphagia, *risus sardonicus* (a sneering appearance), neck stiffness and opisthotonos (especially in neonatal tetanus; see Ch. 23) are also seen. Muscle spasms may lead to injury and eventually there is respiratory failure. Tachycardia and sweating can result from effects on the sympathetic nervous system. Mortality is up to 50%, depending on the severity and quality of treatment.

The diagnosis is clinical. Organisms are rarely isolated from the wound, and only a small number of bacteria are needed to form enough toxin to cause disease.

Human antitetanus immunoglobulin should be given as soon as tetanus is suspected clinically

The wound should be excised if necessary and penicillin given to inhibit bacterial replication. Muscle relaxants are used and, if necessary, respiratory support in an intensive care unit.

Immunization with toxoid prevents tetanus, the effects of the vaccine lasting for 10 years after the last dose. Thus, tetanus represents a vaccine-preventable disease that is unique in not being communicable but, instead, acquired from the environment as a result of exposure to *Cl. tetani* spores. Wounds should be cleaned, necrotic tissue and foreign bodies removed, and a tetanus toxoid booster given. Those with badly contaminated wounds should also be given tetanus immunoglobulin and penicillin.

In resource-poor countries, routine immunization of women with tetanus toxoid and improved hygienic birth practices are having a significant impact in reducing the rates of neonatal tetanus.

Botulism

Spores of *Cl. botulinum* are widespread in soil and contaminate vegetables, meat and fish. When foods are canned or preserved without adequate sterilization (often at home), contaminating spores survive and can germinate in the anaerobic environment, leading to the formation of toxin.

Cl. botulinum toxin blocks acetylcholine release from peripheral nerves

Preformed botulinus toxin is ingested, then absorbed from the gut into the blood (see Ch. 22). It acts on peripheral nerve synapses by blocking the release of acetylcholine (see Ch. 17). It is therefore a type of food poisoning that affects the motor and autonomic nervous systems. Sometimes spores contaminate a wound and the toxin is then absorbed from this site. If the organism is ingested by infants, in the honey smeared on pacifiers, for instance, it can multiply in the gut and produce the toxin, causing infant botulism.

Clinical features of botulism include weakness and paralysis

After an incubation period of 2–72 h, there is descending weakness and paralysis, with dysphagia, diplopia, vomiting, vertigo and respiratory muscle failure. There is no abdominal pain, diarrhea or fever. Infants develop generalized weakness ('floppy babies'), but usually recover.

Botulism is treated with antibodies and respiratory support

A diagnosis of botulism is mainly clinical. The toxin can be demonstrated in contaminated food and occasionally in the patient's serum.

Since the specific *Cl. botulinum* strain(s) responsible are normally unknown, trivalent antitoxin (for type A, B and E toxins) must be given promptly together with respiratory support. The mortality is < 20%, depending upon the success of the respiratory support.

Prevention is by avoiding imperfectly sterilized canned or preserved food. Contaminated cans are often swollen due to the release of gas by clostridial enzymes. Home-preserved foods are often incriminated, but fruit, with its acidic pH, usually prevents the development of the spores. The toxin is heat labile and is destroyed by adequate cooking, for example, boiling for 10 min. The spores can, however, survive boiling for 3–5 h.

KEY FACTS

- Microbial invasion of the CNS is uncommon, due to the presence of the blood–brain and blood–CSF barriers, which limit the spread of infection

- Once infectious agents have traversed these barriers, they generally cause neurologic disease by involving the meninges (meningitis) or the brain substance (encephalitis).

- Viral aetiology of meningitis is most common, followed by bacterial meningitis, with cerebral abscesses and viral encephalitis as rarities. The spinal cord (in myelitis) or peripheral nerves (in neuritis) are occasionally affected.

- Disease results from interference with the function of infected nerve cells (e.g. rabies), from direct damage to infected nerve cells (e.g. poliomyelitis), or from the inflammatory sequel to CNS invasion (e.g. bacterial meningitis, viral encephalitis).

- Because the anatomically defined compartments of the nervous system are adjacent or interconnected, more than one of them can be involved in a given infectious disease.

- CNS disease is sometimes seen in the helminth infections toxocariasis, hydatid disease and cysticercosis.

- CNS disease can also result when bacterial neurotoxins reach the CNS either from extraneural sites of growth (tetanus) or from contaminated food (botulism).

Infections of the eye

25

Introduction

Because the outer surface of the eye is exposed to the external world, it is easily accessible to infective organisms. The conjunctiva is particularly susceptible. Not only is it a vulnerable epithelial surface, it is covered by the eyelids, which create a warm, moist, enclosed environment in which contaminating organisms can quickly establish and set up a focus of infection. The eyelids and tears protect the external surfaces of the eye, both mechanically and biologically; any interference with their function increases the chance of a pathogen becoming established.

Eyelid infections are generally due to *Staphylococcus aureus*, with involvement of the lid margins, causing blepharitis, and eyelid glands or follicles causing styes or hordeolums.

The conjunctiva can be invaded by other routes, such as the blood or nervous system. The deeper tissues of the eye can also be invaded from within, particularly by protozoan and worm parasites. Differentiating between the different causes of conjunctivitis on the basis of clinical signs and symptoms can be difficult.

CONJUNCTIVITIS

A wide variety of viruses and bacteria can cause conjunctivitis or pinkeye (Table 25.1). Conjunctivitis can start in one eye and then progress to the other. The eye will be red, irritated and there will be a lot of tear fluid. A sticky discharge is likely to be secondary to a bacterial infection. Some infections are common in children and resolve quickly, others are potentially more serious. Keratoconjunctivitis from adenovirus, herpes simplex virus or varicella-zoster virus infection can result in severe damage. An acute haemorrhagic conjunctivitis is highly contagious and outbreaks have been reported around the world. It presents as a pink eye, fast-onset eye pain with tear formation and light sensitivity or photophobia. It can follow infection with enterovirus 70 and coxsackievirus A24.

Chlamydial infections

Different serotypes of *Chlamydia trachomatis* cause inclusion conjunctivitis and trachoma

To establish infection on the conjunctiva, microorganisms must avoid being rinsed and wiped away in tears. The best way of achieving this is to have a specific mechanism of attachment to conjunctival cells. *Chlamydia*, for example, has surface molecules that bind specifically to receptors on host cells. This is one of the reasons that, of all the organisms infecting the conjunctiva (Table 25.1), they are among the most successful. There are eight different serotypes of *Chlamydia trachomatis* responsible for inclusion conjunctivitis (D–K) (Fig. 25.1) and another four serotypes responsible for trachoma (A, B, Ba and C), which, globally, is the most important eye infection in the world.

Eight million people worldwide are visually impaired because of trachoma

Approximately 84 million people worldwide are affected by trachoma. Of these, about 8 million have some degree of visual impairment and the disease accounts for more than 3% of the world's blindness. Trachoma is endemic in resource-poor countries where prevalence rates in pre-school children can reach 60–90%. Trachoma was known in ancient Egypt 4000 years ago, and tweezers to remove in-turned eyelashes (Fig. 25.2) have been found in royal tombs. Transmission of *C. trachomatis* is by contact, for example, by contaminated flies, fingers and towels.

Trachoma itself is the result of chronic repeated infections (Fig. 25.2), which are especially prevalent when there is poor access to water, preventing regular washing of the hands and face. Under these circumstances, chlamydial infection is frequently spread from one conjunctiva to another and this can be referred to as 'ocular promiscuity', comparable with the spread of genital secretions in non-specific urethritis (see Ch. 21). Some chlamydial serotypes can infect the urogenital tract (see Ch. 21) as well as the conjunctiva, and the conjunctiva or lungs of a newborn infant may become infected after passage down an infected birth canal (see Ch. 23). In this situation, systemic treatment with erythromycin is generally needed.

Chlamydial infections are treated with antibiotic and prevented by face washing

Laboratory diagnosis of chlamydial infections (see Chs. 21 and 32) can be carried out using conjunctival fluid or scrapings. Point-of-care tests for rapid diagnosis in the field are available but there are issues regarding sensitivity. Treatment is with topical or oral antibiotics (e.g. azithromycin, doxycycline, etc.). Because infection and reinfection are

Table 25.1 Microbial infections of the conjunctiva

Organism	Comments
Adenovirus	Especially types 3, 7, 8, 19
Measles virus	Infection of conjunctiva via blood
Herpes simplex virus	Virus reactivating in ophthalmic division of trigeminal ganglia causes corneal lesion (dendritic ulcer)
Varicella-zoster virus	May involve conjunctiva
Enterovirus 70, coxsackievirus A24	Acute haemorrhagic conjunctivitis
Chlamydia trachomatis Types A–C Types D–K	Cause of trachoma and commonly blindness Cause of inclusion conjunctivitis; infection via fingers, or in newborn via birth canal
Neisseria gonorrhoeae	Infection of newborn via birth canal
Staphylococcus aureus *Streptococcus pneumoniae* *Haemophilus influenzae*	Cause eyelid infection (styes) and 'sticky eye' in neonates

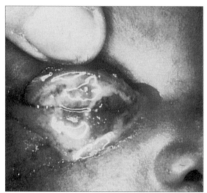

Figure 25.1 Chlamydial conjunctivitis is the most common form of neonatal conjunctivitis. (Courtesy of G. Ridgway.)

facilitated by overcrowding, shortage of water and abundant fly populations, the disease can be prevented by improvements in standards of hygiene. In many areas with high rates of endemic trachoma, disease leading to blindness has been sharply reduced or eliminated by socioeconomic development and specific intervention steps (e.g. face washing). This has led the World Health Organization to establish an international alliance for the global elimination of blinding trachoma by the year 2020.

In spite of many decades of research, there are still no vaccines for chlamydial infections. This is partly because immunopathology itself makes a major contribution to the disease, and vaccine-induced immune responses could be harmful.

Other conjunctival infections

In resource-rich countries, conjunctivitis is caused by a variety of bacteria

Several bacteria (especially *Haemophilus influenzae*, *Staphylococcus aureus*, and *Streptococcus pneumoniae*) can cause conjunctivitis (Fig. 25.3).

Infection by *Neisseria gonorrhoeae* is a hazard of birth through an infected birth canal, and can result in a severe purulent condition. It is seen on the first or second day of life (ophthalmia neonatorum) and requires urgent treatment with ceftriaxone (penicillin resistance is widespread). *Staph. aureus* also produces infections in newborns as well as in adults. The eyes of infants may be invaded by this organism if the organism is transferred from the child's own body or from an infected adult. Despite vaccine development, *Haemophilus influenzae* continues to be a significant cause of conjunctivitis in children since the strains are non-typeable (nonencapsulated).

Direct infection of the eye may be associated with wearing contact lenses

Excessive wearing of contact lenses can lead to a reduction in the effectiveness of the eye's defence mechanisms, allowing pathogens to become established, but more likely hazards are the use of contaminated eye drops or cleaning solutions and the insertion of contaminated lenses. A number of bacteria can be transmitted directly in this way. Species of the free-living amoeba *Acanthamoeba* can multiply in unchanged lens cleaning fluids and be transferred when the lens is inserted, causing corneal ulceration. Diagnosis is by microscopy and culture of corneal scrapings. PCR can be used to type isolates.

Conjunctival infection may be transmitted by the blood or nervous system

Several organisms invade the superficial tissues of the eye after transport through the blood or, in the case of herpes simplex virus (HSV), by movement along the trigeminal nerve. Reactivation of this virus can result in the development of a keratitis with the formation of dendritic ulcers (Fig. 25.4). The keratitis can lead to corneal scarring with new blood vessel formation, neovascularization, resulting in loss of sight. Antiviral drugs such as aciclovir and famciclovir, combined with steroid treatment, may be effective. However, if uncontrolled, corneal transplantation may be necessary. Varicella-zoster virus may cause conjunctivitis

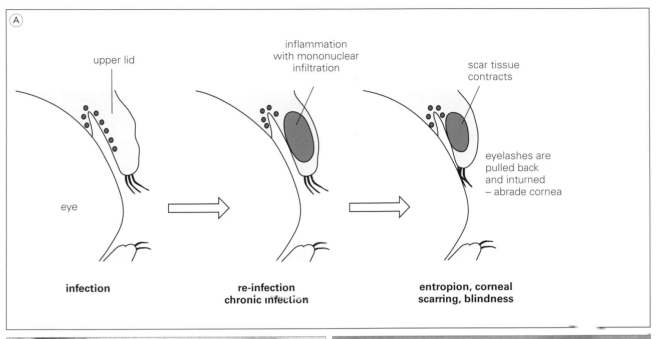

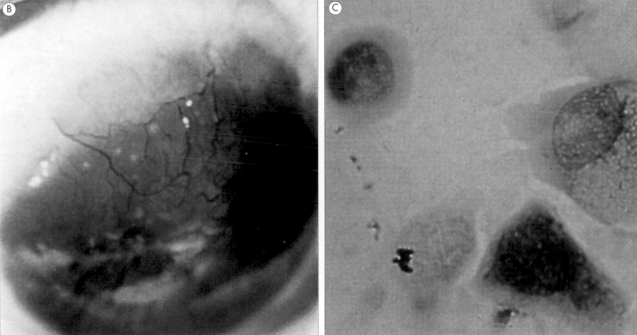

Figure 25.2 *Chlamydia trachomatis* and blindness. The pathogenesis is outlined in (A). Scarring of the cornea (B) results from long-standing ocular trachoma. (Courtesy of R.C. Barnes.) Giemsa stain of an ocular scraping from trachoma (C) shows *C. trachomatis* as an intracellular inclusion. (Courtesy of G. Ridgway.)

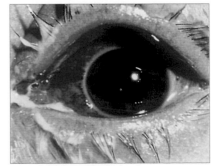

Figure 25.3 Purulent discharge in bacterial conjunctivitis is often associated with infections by *Streptococcus pneumoniae*, *Haemophilus influenzae* or *Staphylococcus aureus*. (Courtesy of M. Tapert.)

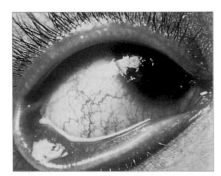

Figure 25.4 Herpes simplex virus (HSV) keratitis. Dendritic ulcers, seen here on the cornea, are common in recurrent HSV infections. (Courtesy of M.J. Wood.)

Table 25.2 Infections of the deep layers of the eye

Organism	Disease	Route of infection
Rubella virus	Cataracts, microphthalmia	Infection in utero
Cytomegalovirus	Chorioretinitis	Infection in utero; may occur in AIDS and other immunocompromised individuals
Pseudomonas aeruginosa	Serious inner eye infection	After trauma; foreign bodies in eye; eye operations; bacteria can contaminate eye drops
Toxoplasma gondii (toxoplasmosis)	Chorioretinitis	Infection in utero
Echinococcus granulosus (hydatid disease)	Distortion of the eye by growth of larval tapeworm in hydatid cyst	Transmission by eggs passed by dogs
Toxocara canis (ocular toxocariasis)	Chorioretinitis, posterior pole granuloma, blindness	Transmission by eggs passed by dogs
Onchocerca volvulus (river blindness)	Sclerosing keratitis, chorioretinitis	Larvae transmitted by blood-feeding *Simulium* flies

associated with chickenpox or as a secondary infection. Overall, viral conjunctivitis is most commonly caused by adenovirus infections. Many years ago, due to the strong occupational association, shipyard eye was the name given to adenoviral conjunctivitis seen in shipbuilders and other workers exposed to the risk of eye injuries that could then result in an adenovirus infection. These viruses also cause pharyngoconjunctival fever, which includes, as one might expect, pharyngitis, fever and an acute follicular conjunctivitis that clears within a few weeks.

INFECTION OF THE DEEPER LAYERS OF THE EYE

The spectrum of organisms causing disease in the deeper layers of the eye is wider than that associated with the conjunctiva (Table 25.2).

Entry into the deeper layers occurs by many routes

Trauma to the eye may result in the opportunistic establishment of a *Pseudomonas aeruginosa* infection, giving rise to serious inner eye infection. This organism may also be introduced via contaminated eye drops. Congenital syphilis produces a retinopathy with quiescent lesions, and keratitis may appear in later life. Secondary syphilis is also associated with ocular inflammation.

Rubella virus and cytomegalovirus (CMV) may invade the fetal eye in utero, the former causing cataracts and microphthalmia, the latter a severe chorioretinitis. CMV can also cause chorioretinitis in AIDS patients, although highly active antiretroviral therapy has resulted in a large reduction of eye disease (see Fig. 21.26E). Ocular complications have been reported in patients with West Nile virus infection.

Toxoplasmosis

Toxoplasma gondii infection can cause retinochoroiditis leading to blindness

Infection with this protozoan is widespread in adults and children (see Ch. 5), and is normally acquired by swallowing oocysts released by infected cats (the definitive host) or by eating meat containing tissue cysts. Women who become infected in pregnancy may transmit the infection to the fetus,

as tachyzoites can cross the placenta. Tissue cysts can form in the retina of the fetus and undergo continuous proliferation, producing progressive lesions, particularly when levels of immunity are low. These lesions may also involve the choroid (Fig. 25.5) and lead ultimately to blindness. One or both eyes may be affected.

Infection is not serious unless:

- acquired in utero, when the organism invades all tissues, especially the central nervous system (CNS)
- acquired (or reactivated) under immunosuppression.

Damage to the eye occurs both in congenital (Fig. 25.5) and in postnatally acquired toxoplasmosis and may present at any age. Ocular toxoplasmosis may present years after the initial infection, whether congenital or acquired postnatally, and can be more serious in the elderly population.

Parasitic worm infections

Toxocara canis larvae cause an intense inflammatory response and can lead to retinal detachment

Larval tapeworms (e.g. the hydatid cyst stage of *Echinococcus granulosus* transmitted by eggs passed from infected dogs) occasionally enter the eye, with growth of the cysts causing severe mechanical damage. Invasion by migratory larvae of the nematode *Toxocara canis* is more common. This parasite occurs naturally in the intestines of dogs, releasing thick-shelled resistant eggs into the environment. The eggs can

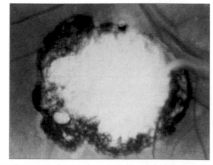

Figure 25.5 Congenital toxoplasmosis. Fundal photograph showing the scar of healed chorioretinitis. (Courtesy of M.J. Wood.)

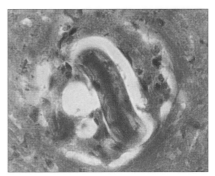

Figure 25.6 *Toxocara.* Granuloma in the posterior pole of an infected eye. The larval nematode is clearly visible in the centre of the granuloma. (Courtesy of D. Spalton.)

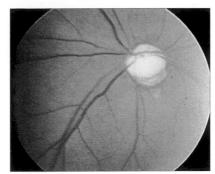

Figure 25.7 Onchocerciasis. Sclerosis of the choroidal vessels caused by invading microfilaria of *Onchocerca volvulus*. (Courtesy of J. Anderson.)

hatch if swallowed by humans, the larvae initiating, but failing to complete, their customary migration through the tissues. In the canine host, migration results in the worms re-entering the intestine where they mature. In humans, larvae can enter almost any organ, often the CNS or eye (Fig. 25.6), triggering an intense eosinophilic inflammatory response. In the eye, *Toxocara* larvae may lead to posterior uveitis, localized retinal granuloma, traction bands and retinal detachment. The misdiagnosis of retinal granuloma as retinoblastoma has led to enucleation. Serology on serum samples may give false-negative results in ocular toxocariasis; serology may need to be performed on vitreous samples to make the diagnosis. Anthelmintic treatment is not routinely given as it may lead to worsening of inflammation; corticosteroids are used to suppress the inflammatory response. Laser photocoagulation has also been used to destroy *Toxocara* larvae.

Onchocerca volvulus infection causes 'river blindness' and is transmitted by *Simulium* flies

Onchocerca volvulus infection, the cause of 'river blindness' in Africa and Central America, is transmitted by biting *Simulium* flies, which take up microfilariae larvae from the skin of infected hosts and reintroduce the larvae after they have further developed to become infective, at a future feed. Adult worms live in subcutaneous nodules, and are comparatively harmless. The microfilariae, released by the females in enormous numbers, induce intense inflammatory reactions in the skin (see Ch. 26). The larvae migrate through the subcutaneous tissue, and invasion of the eye has been particularly common in certain regions of Africa as well as Central America.

The inflammatory responses in the eye cause a number of pathologic changes, which may affect both the anterior and posterior chambers (Fig. 25.7). These include:

- punctate and sclerosing keratitis
- iridocyclitis
- chorioretinitis
- optic atrophy.

The disease is called river blindness because the *Simulium* flies develop in fast flowing rivers, and people living near these sites are most affected. In the past, blindness rates have reached 40% of the adult population in endemic areas, but vector control and especially ivermectin treatment have dramatically reduced the incidence of new infections in many African countries. Unfortunately, the blindness is irreversible.

KEY FACTS

- The external surfaces of the eye are vulnerable to infection. It is protected by the eyelids and by factors such as lysozyme in tears.

- It can be difficult to make a diagnosis regarding the aetiology of conjunctivitis on clinical signs and symptoms alone.

- The consequences of eye infection are always potentially serious given that sight is dependent upon the presence of an intact transparent cornea.

- Microbes infecting the conjunctiva have specific attachment mechanisms.

- Inflammatory responses, though 'designed' to limit invasion and repair damage, can irreversibly damage conjunctival and corneal surfaces.

- Relatively few organisms invade the retina, and those that do are potentially sight-threatening.

- Some of the most serious infection-related diseases of the eye involve invasion by protozoan or helminth parasites. The diagnosis then often follows rather than precedes the development of visual impairment.

Infections of the skin, soft tissue, muscle and associated systems

26

Introduction

Healthy intact skin protects underlying tissues and provides excellent defence against invading microbes

The microbial load of normal skin is kept in check by various factors, as shown in Box 26.1. Alterations in these factors (e.g. prolonged exposure to moisture) upset the ecologic balance of the commensal flora, and predispose to infection.

A small number of microbes cause diseases of muscle, joints or the haemopoietic system. Invasion of these sites is generally from the blood, but the reason for localization to particular tissues is often obscure. Circulating microbes tend to localize in growing or damaged bones (acute osteomyelitis) and in damaged joints, but we do not know why coxsackieviruses or *Trichinella spiralis* invade muscle. On the other hand, some viruses infect a given target cell, and plasmodia invade erythrocytes because they have specific attachment sites for these cells.

Box 26.1 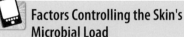 **Factors Controlling the Skin's Microbial Load**

- the limited amount of moisture present
- acid pH of normal skin
- surface temperature < optimum for many pathogens
- salty sweat
- excreted chemicals such as sebum, fatty acids and urea
- competition between different species of the normal flora.

The number of bacteria on the skin vary from a few hundred/cm² on the arid surfaces of the forearm and back, to tens of thousands/cm² on the moist areas, such as the axilla and groin. This normal flora plays an important role in preventing 'foreign' organisms from colonizing the skin, but it too needs to be kept in check.

Infections of the skin

In addition to being a structural barrier, the skin is colonized by an array of organisms which forms its normal flora. The relatively arid areas of the forearm and back are colonized with fewer organisms, predominantly Gram-positive bacteria and yeasts. In the moister areas, such as the groin and the armpit, the organisms are more numerous and more varied and include Gram-negative bacteria. The normal flora of the skin plays an important role, as does the normal flora in other body sites, in defending the surface from 'foreign invaders'.

An appreciation of the structure of the skin helps in understanding the different sorts of infection to which the skin and its underlying tissues are prone (Fig. 26.1). If organisms breach the stratum corneum the host defences are mobilized, the epidermal Langerhans cells elaborate cytokines, neutrophils are attracted to the site of invasion, and complement is activated via the alternative pathway.

Microbial disease of the skin may result from any of three lines of attack

These lines of attack are:

- breach of intact skin, allowing infection from the outside
- skin manifestations of systemic infections, which may arise as a result of blood-borne spread from the infected focus to the skin or by direct extension (e.g. draining sinuses from actinomycotic lesions, or necrotizing anaerobic infection from intra-abdominal sepsis)
- toxin-mediated skin damage due to production of a microbial toxin at another site in the body (e.g. scarlet fever, toxic shock syndrome).

The sequence of events in the pathogenesis of mucocutaneous lesions caused by bacterial, fungal and viral infections is outlined in Figure 26.2. Breaches in the skin range from microscopic to major trauma, which may be accidental (e.g. lacerations or burns) or intentional (e.g. surgery). Hospitalized patients are liable to other skin breaches (e.g. pressure sores and intravenous catheter insertions), which may become infected (see Ch. 36). Infections in compromised individuals such as patients with burns are discussed in Chapter 30. Here, we will consider primary infections of the skin and underlying soft tissues, together with mucocutaneous lesions resulting from certain systemic viral infections. Examples of systemic bacterial and fungal infections that cause mucocutaneous lesions are summarized in Table 26.1.

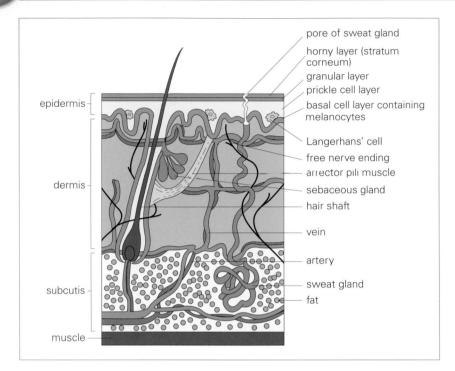

Figure 26.1 Infection of the skin and soft tissue can be related to the anatomy of the skin. Pathogens usually enter the lower layers of the epidermis and dermis only after the skin surface has been damaged.

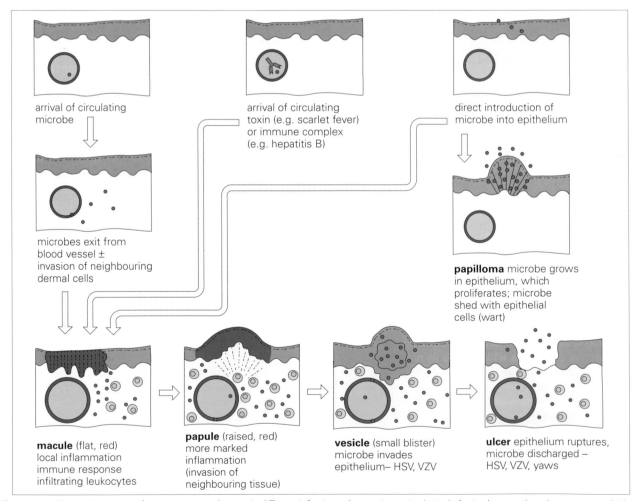

Figure 26.2 The pathogenesis of mucocutaneous lesions. In different infections, the starting point (arrival of microbe or toxin or immune complex) and the final picture (e.g. maculopapular rash, vesicle) will be different. HSV, herpes simplex virus; VZV, varicella-zoster virus.

Table 26.1 Skin manifestations of systemic infections caused by bacteria and fungi

Organism	Disease	Skin manifestation
Salmonella typhi, *Salmonella schottmuelleri*	Enteric fever	'Rose spots' containing bacteria
Neisseria meningitidis	Septicaemia, meningitis	Petechial or maculopapular lesions containing bacteria
Pseudomonas aeruginosa	Septicaemia	Ecthyma gangrenosum, skin lesion pathognomonic if infected by this organism
Treponema pallidum *Treponema pertenue*	Syphilis Yaws	Disseminated infectious rash seen in secondary stage of disease, 2–3 months after infection
Rickettsia prowazekii *Rickettsia typhi* *Rickettsia rickettsii*	Typhus Spotted fever	Macular or haemorrhagic rash
Streptococcus pyogenes	Scarlet fever	Erythematous rash caused by erythrogenic toxin
Staphylococcus aureus	Toxic shock syndrome	Rash and desquamation due to toxin
Blastomyces dermatitidis *Cryptococcus neoformans*	Blastomycosis Cryptococcosis	Papule or pustule develops into granuloma lesions containing organisms Papule or pustule, usually on face or neck

Skin lesions are often associated with systemic infection with particular bacteria and fungi. The lesions may provide useful diagnostic aids. Sometimes they are a site from which organisms are shed.

BACTERIAL INFECTIONS OF SKIN, SOFT TISSUE AND MUSCLE

These can be classified on an anatomic basis

The classification depends upon the layers of skin and soft tissue involved, although some infections may involve several components of the soft tissues:

- *Abscess formation.* Boils and carbuncles are the result of infection and inflammation of the hair follicles in the skin (folliculitis).
- *Spreading infections.* Impetigo is limited to the epidermis and presents as a bullous, crusted or pustular eruption of the skin. Erysipelas involves the blocking of dermal lymphatics and presents as a well-defined, spreading erythematous inflammation, generally on the face, legs or feet, and often accompanied by pain and fever. If the focus of infection is in the subcutaneous fat, cellulitis, a diffuse form of acute inflammation is the usual presentation.
- *Necrotizing infections.* Fasciitis describes the inflammatory response to infection of the soft tissue below the dermis. Infection spreads, often with alarming rapidity, along the fascial planes causing disruption of the blood supply. Gangrene or myonecrosis may follow infection associated with ischaemia of the muscle layer. Gas resulting from the fermentative metabolism of anaerobic organisms may be palpable in the tissues (gas gangrene).

The common causative organisms are shown in Table 26.2. Note that the same pathogen (e.g. *Streptococcus pyogenes*) can cause different infections in different layers of the skin and soft tissue.

Table 26.2 Direct entry into skin of bacteria and fungi

Structure involved	Infection	Common cause
Keratinized epithelium	Ringworm	Dermatophyte fungi (*Trichophyton*, *Epidermophyton* and *Microsporum*)
Epidermis	Impetigo	*Streptococcus pyogenes* and/or *Staphylococcus aureus*
Dermis	Erysipelas	*Strep. pyogenes*
Hair follicles	Folliculitis Boils (furuncles) Carbuncles	*Staph. aureus*
Subcutaneous fat	Cellulitis	*Strep. pyogenes*
Fascia	Necrotizing fasciitis	Anaerobes and microaerophiles, usually mixed infections
Muscle	Myonecrosis gangrene	*Clostridium perfringens* (and other clostridia)

Direct introduction of bacteria or fungi into the skin is the most common route of skin infection. Infections range from mild, often chronic, conditions such as ringworm to acute and life-threatening fasciitis and gangrene. Relatively few species are involved in the common infections.

Staphylococcal skin infections

Staphylococcus aureus is the most common cause of skin infections and provokes an intense inflammatory response

Staphylococcus aureus causes minor skin infections such as boils or abscesses as well as more serious postoperative wound infection. Infection may be acquired by 'self-inoculation' from a carrier site (e.g. the nose) or acquired by contact with an exogenous source, usually another person. People who are nasal carriers of virulent *Staph. aureus* may suffer from recurrent boils, but an inoculum of about 100 000 organisms is thought to be required in the absence of a wound or foreign body. *Staph. aureus* can also cause serious skin disease due to toxin production (scalded skin syndrome, toxic shock syndrome; see below). In addition, skin and soft tissue infections caused by community-associated, methicillin-resistant *Staph. aureus* strains (CA-MRSA) are of increasing incidence and concern (see Ch. 36).

A boil begins within 2–4 days of inoculation, as a superficial infection in and around a hair follicle (folliculitis; Fig. 26.3). In this site, the organisms are relatively protected from the host defences, multiply rapidly and spread locally. This provokes an intense inflammatory response with an influx of neutrophils. Fibrin is deposited, and the site is walled off. Abscesses typically contain abundant yellow creamy pus formed by the massive number of organisms and necrotic white cells. They continue to expand slowly, eventually erode the overlying skin, 'come to a head' and drain. Drainage inwards can result in seeding of the staphylococci to underlying body sites to cause serious infections such as peritonitis, empyema or meningitis.

Staph. aureus infections are often diagnosed clinically and treatment includes drainage and antibiotics

Staph. aureus is the most common cause of boils, and diagnosis is made on clinical grounds. Isolation and further characterization of the infecting staphylococcus in hospital patients and staff are important in the investigation of hospital infections (see Ch. 36).

Treatment involves drainage and this is usually sufficient for minor lesions, but antibiotics may be given in addition when the infection is severe and the patient has a fever. Most *Staph. aureus* are beta-lactamase producers, but methicillin-susceptible *Staph. aureus* (MSSA) can be treated with enzyme-stable penicillins such as nafcillin. Isolates resistant to these compounds (i.e. methicillin-resistant *Staph. aureus* (MRSA); see Ch. 33) may be treated with vancomycin, linezolid, quinopristin-dalfoprisin, or daptomycin. Treatment with these agents does not necessarily eradicate carriage of the staphylococci.

Recurrent infections may be treated in nasal carriers of *Staph. aureus* with nasal creams containing antibiotics. For example, mupirocin has been used successfully for carriers of methicillin-resistant staphylococci (see Ch. 36). Good skin care and personal hygiene should be encouraged.

Staphylococcal scalded skin syndrome is caused by toxin-producing *Staph. aureus*

This condition, also known as 'Ritter's disease' in infants and 'Lyell's disease' or 'toxic epidermal necrolysis' in older children, occurs sporadically and in outbreaks. It is caused by strains of *Staph. aureus* producing a toxin known as 'exfoliatin' or 'scalded skin syndrome toxin'. The initial skin lesion may be minor, but the toxin causes destruction of the intercellular connections and separation of the top layer of the epidermis. Large blisters are formed, containing clear fluid, and within 1 or 2 days, the overlying areas of skin are lost (Fig. 26.4), leaving normal skin underneath. The baby is irritable and uncomfortable, but rarely severely ill. However, treatment should take into account the risk of increased loss of fluid from the damaged surface, and fluid replacement may be needed. As mentioned above, antimicrobial chemotherapy would employ beta-lactamase stable penicillins (e.g. nafcillin) against MSSA, whereas vancomycin, linezolid, quinopristin-dalfoprisin, or daptomycin would be used for MRSA.

Toxic shock syndrome is caused by toxic shock syndrome toxin-producing *Staph. aureus*

This systemic infection came to prominence through its association with tampon use by healthy women, but it is not confined to women and can occur as a result of *Staph. aureus* infection at non-genital sites (e.g. a wound). Toxic shock syndrome (TSS) involves multiple organ systems and is characterized by fever, hypotension and a diffuse macular

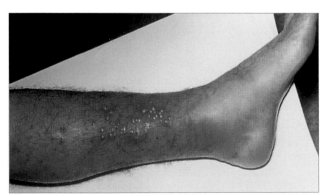

Figure 26.3 Folliculitis. A superficial infection is shown here localized in the hair follicles on the leg. The boils contain creamy-yellow pus and masses of bacteria. *Staphylococcus aureus* is the most common cause. (Courtesy of A. du Vivier.)

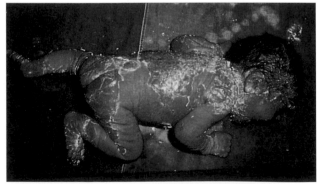

Figure 26.4 Scalded skin syndrome results from infection of the skin with strains of *Staphylococcus aureus* producing a specific toxin, which destroys the intercellular connections in the skin, resulting in large areas of desquamation. The appearance may be confused with a burn. (Courtesy of A. du Vivier.)

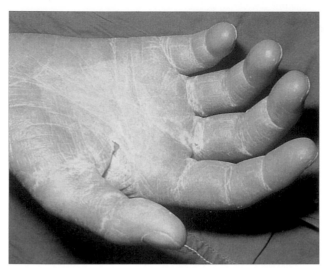

Figure 26.5 Toxic shock syndrome results from systemic infection with *Staphylococcus aureus*, but has skin manifestations in the form of desquamation, particularly of the palm and soles. (Courtesy of M.J. Wood.)

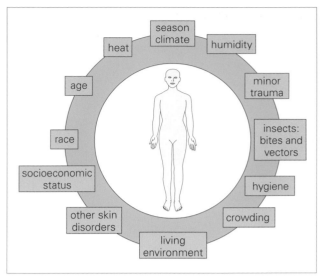

Figure 26.6 Various factors are involved in the development of streptococcal skin infections. Particular M types of *Streptococcus pyogenes* have a predilection for skin, but various factors predispose the host (usually a child) to infection. Mixed infections with *Staphylococcus aureus* are also common.

erythematous rash followed by desquamation of the skin, particularly on the soles and palms (Fig. 26.5). TSS is caused by exotoxins of *Staph. aureus*, most commonly TSST1, which behaves as a superantigen (stimulating T-cell proliferation and cytokine release; see Ch. 16). While the prevalence of TSS in the USA is currently estimated at <200 cases/year, >90% of adults carry antibodies to TSST1. Treatment of TSS includes steps to open the infected site (e.g. drainage), fluid replacement and antistaphylococcal chemotherapy.

Streptococcal skin infections

Streptococcal skin infections are caused by *Strep. pyogenes* (group A streptococci)

Streptococcal impetigo develops independently of streptococcal upper respiratory tract infection, and although up to 35% of patients carry the same strain in their nose or throat, colonization may well occur after the skin has become infected. The organisms are acquired through contact with other people with infected skin lesions and may first colonize and multiply on normal skin before invasion through minor breaks in the epithelium and the development of lesions. The various risk factors involved in the development of streptococcal impetigo are shown in Figure 26.6. *Strep. pyogenes* may also cause erysipelas, an acute deeper infection in the dermis. About 5% of patients with erysipelas go on to develop bacteraemia which carries a high mortality if untreated. As discussed previously, impetigo may also be caused by *Staph. aureus* and occasionally presents in more extreme bullous form (i.e. bullous impetigo) as blisters resembling localized scalded skin syndrome (see above).

Strep. pyogenes possesses certain surface proteins (M and T) which are antigenic. The species can be subdivided (typed) on the basis of these antigens, and it has been recognized that certain M and T types are associated with skin infection (and these differ from the types associated with sore throats). T proteins play no known role in virulence, and their function is unknown. M proteins are important virulence factors because they inhibit opsonization and confer on the bacterium resistance to phagocytosis. A variety of additional factors contribute to the virulence of the organism, such as lipoteichoic acid

(LTA; a component of the Gram-positive cell wall) and F protein, which facilitate binding to epithelial cells.

Clinical features of streptococcal skin infections are typically acute

They develop within 24–48h of skin invasion and trigger a marked inflammatory response as the host attempts to localize the infection (Fig. 26.7 and Fig. 26.8). *Strep. pyogenes* elaborates a number of toxic products and enzymes, such as hyaluronidase, which help the organism to spread in tissue. Lymphatic involvement is common, resulting in lymphadenitis and lymphangitis.

Lysogenic strains of *Strep. pyogenes* produce pyrogenic exotoxins (SPE; formally called erythrogenic toxins). As with TSST1 in *Staph. aureus* (discussed previously), these toxins are

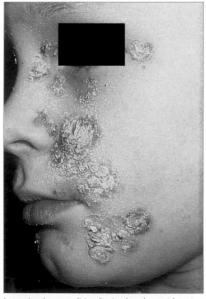

Figure 26.7 Impetigo is a condition limited to the epidermis, with typically yellow, crusted lesions. It is commonly caused by *Streptococcus pyogenes* either alone or together with *Staphylococcus aureus*. (Courtesy of M.J. Wood.)

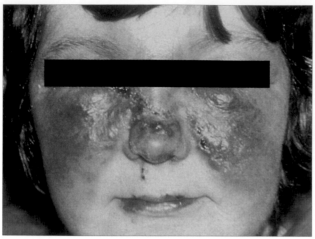

Figure 26.8 Erysipelas. Infection with *Streptococcus pyogenes* involves the dermal lymphatics and gives rise to a clearly demarcated area of erythema and induration. When the face is involved, there is often a typical 'butterfly-wing' rash, as shown here. (Courtesy of M.J. Wood.)

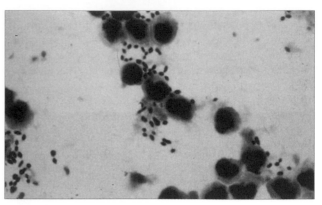

Figure 26.9 Gram-positive cocci in pus.

superantigens with a potent influence on the immune system. The toxins (e.g. SPEA, B, and C) also act on skin blood vessels to cause the diffuse erythematous rash of scarlet fever, which may occur with streptococcal pharyngitis. *Strep. pyogenes* may also cause a form of toxic shock syndrome which has been especially associated with the production of the SPEA.

M protein is a major virulence factor in *Strep. pyogenes* with over 100 types, some of which (e.g. M49) are specifically associated with diseases such as acute glomerulonephritis

Acute glomerulonephritis (AGN) occurs more often after skin infections than after infections of the throat (see Ch. 18). It is characterized by the deposition of immune complexes on the basement membrane of the glomerulus but the precise role of the streptococcus in the causation is still unclear (see Ch. 17); 10–15% of individuals infected with a nephritogenic strain will develop AGN about 2–3 weeks after the primary infection. Most people recover completely, and recurrence after a subsequent streptococcal infection is rare. Rheumatic fever (see Ch. 18) very rarely follows skin infections with *Strep. pyogenes*.

Streptococcal skin infections are usually diagnosed clinically and treated with penicillin

Gram stains of pus from vesicles in impetigo show Gram-positive cocci, and culture reveals *Strep. pyogenes* sometimes mixed with *Staph. aureus* (Fig. 26.9). In erysipelas, skin cultures are often negative, although culture of fluid from the advancing edge of the lesion may be successful.

Penicillin is the drug of choice, although erythromycin, newer macrolides, or an oral cephalosporin may be used for penicillin-allergic patients. However, the prevalence of resistance (e.g. to erythromycin) in streptococci is increasing, and these drugs are not effective in mixed infections with *Staph. aureus*. Severe infections may require hospitalization.

Impetigo is prevented by improving the host factors associated with acquisition of the disease, as illustrated in Figure 26.6. Since AGN rarely recurs on subsequent streptococcal infection, long-term prophylaxis with penicillin is not indicated (in contrast to the long-term prophylaxis following rheumatic fever; see Ch. 18).

Cellulitis and gangrene

Cellulitis is an acute spreading infection of the skin that involves subcutaneous tissues

Cellulitis extends deeper than erysipelas and usually originates either from superficial skin lesions such as boils or ulcers or following trauma. It is rarely blood-borne, but conversely it may lead to bacterial invasion of the bloodstream. Infection develops within a few hours or days of trauma and quickly produces a hot red swollen lesion (Fig. 26.10). Regional lymph nodes are enlarged and the patient suffers malaise, chills and fever.

The great majority of cases of cellulitis are caused by *Strep. pyogenes* and *Staph. aureus*. Occasionally, in patients who have had particular environmental exposure, other organisms may be implicated. For example, *Erysipelothrix rhusiopathiae* is associated with cellulitis in butchers and fishmongers, while *Vibrio vulnificus* and *Vibrio alginolyticus* may complicate traumatic wounds acquired in saltwater environments.

The pathogen causing cellulitis is isolated in only 25–35% of cases, and initial therapy should cover streptococci and staphylococci. Attempts can be made to confirm the clinical diagnosis by culture of:

- aspirates from the advancing edge of the cellulitis
- the site of trauma (if present)
- skin biopsies
- blood.

Treatment should be initiated on the basis of the clinical diagnosis because of the rapid progression of the disease, particularly when caused by *Strep. pyogenes*.

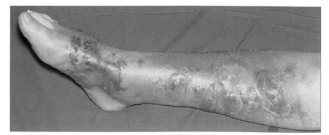

Figure 26.10 When the focus of infection is in the subdermal fat, cellulitis – a severe and rapidly progressive infection – is the typical presentation. Large blisters and scabs may also be present on the skin surface. (Courtesy of M.J. Wood.)

Anaerobic cellulitis may develop in areas of traumatized or devitalized tissue

Such damaged tissue is associated with surgical or traumatic wounds or is found in ischaemic extremities. Diabetic patients are particularly prone to anaerobic cellulitis of their feet (Fig. 26.11). The causative organisms depend upon the circumstances of the trauma: infections in the lower parts of the body are most often caused by organisms from the faecal flora whereas wounds from human bites are infected with oral organisms. Foul-smelling discharge, marked swelling and gas in the tissues are characteristic of anaerobic cellulitis, and a mixture of organisms is usually cultured from the wound. Treatment needs to be aggressive to halt the spread of infection, and both antibiotics and surgical debridement are required. Osteomyelitis (see below) is a common sequela.

Synergistic bacterial gangrene is a relentlessly destructive infection

This rare infection is caused by a mixture of organisms, typically *microaerophilic streptococci* and *Staph. aureus*. The gangrene most commonly follows surgery in the groin or genital area, starting at the site of a drain or suture. Cellulitis develops in the surrounding skin and extends rapidly (within hours), leaving a black necrotic centre. The condition is often fatal, and treatment requires radical excision of the necrotic area and systemic antibiotic therapy.

Necrotizing fasciitis, myonecrosis and gangrene

Necrotizing fasciitis is a frequently fatal mixed infection caused by anaerobes and facultative anaerobes

Although apparently resembling synergistic bacterial gangrene, necrotizing fasciitis is a much more acute and highly toxic infection, causing widespread necrosis and undermining of the surrounding tissues, such that the underlying destruction is more widespread than the skin lesion (Fig. 26.12). Necrotizing fasciitis has been most prominently linked by the popular media with *Strep. pyogenes*, where it has been frequently termed 'flesh-eating bacteria'. However, the infection may be caused by a variety of other organisms, especially including MRSA. Patients with necrotizing fasciitis deteriorate rapidly and frequently die. Radical excision of all necrotic fascia is an essential part of therapy, along with antibiotics given both locally to the wound and systemically.

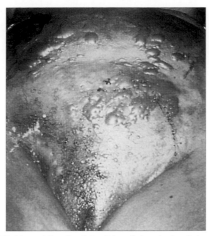

Figure 26.12 Necrotizing fasciitis of the abdominal wall. In patients such as this, infection can be seen rapidly spreading from its origin and causing deep and widespread necrosis. Complete debridement and intensive antimicrobial therapy is required, but the condition is often fatal. (Courtesy of W.M. Rambo.)

Traumatic or surgical wounds can become infected with *Clostridium* species

Clostridium tetani gains access to the tissues through trauma to the skin, but the disease it produces is entirely due to the production of a powerful exotoxin (see Ch. 17).

Gas gangrene or *clostridial myonecrosis* can be caused by several species of *clostridia*, but *Clostridium perfringens* is the most common. The organism and its spores are found in the soil and in human and animal faeces, and can therefore gain access to traumatized tissues by contamination from these sources. Infection develops in areas of the body with poor blood supply (anaerobic), and the buttocks and perineum are common sites, particularly in patients with ischaemic vascular disease or peripheral arteriosclerosis. The organisms multiply in the subcutaneous tissues, producing gas and an anaerobic cellulitis, but a characteristic feature of clostridial infection is that the organisms invade deeper into the muscle, where they cause necrosis and produce bubbles of gas, which can be felt in the tissue and sometimes seen in the wound (Fig. 26.13). The infection proceeds very rapidly and causes acute pain. Much of the damage is due to the

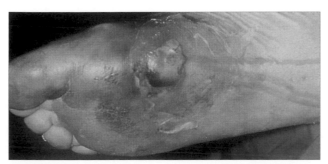

Figure 26.11 Severe progressive cellulitis of the foot. Such cellulitis is usually caused by anaerobic bacteria or a mixture of aerobes and anaerobes and is a particular problem in diabetic patients with peripheral vascular and neuropathic damage. (Courtesy of J.D. Ward.)

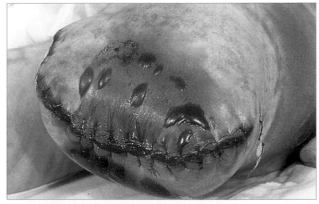

Figure 26.13 Gas gangrene caused by *Clostridium perfringens*. Organisms from the fecal flora may contaminate a wound and grow and multiply in poorly perfused (anaerobic) tissue. Infection spreads rapidly, and gas can be felt in the tissue and seen on radiographs. (Courtesy of J. Newman.)

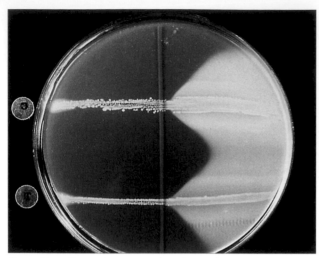

Figure 26.14 The Nagler reaction. *Clostridium perfringens* produces alpha toxin, which is a lecithinase. If the organism is grown on a medium containing egg yolk (lecithin), enzyme activity can be detected as opacity around the line of growth (right). If anti-alpha toxin is applied to the surface of the plate before inoculation of the organism, the action of the toxin is inhibited (left). This test can be used to confirm the identity of a clostridial isolate.

production by *Cl. perfringens* of a lecithinase (also known as alpha toxin), which hydrolyses the lipids in cell membranes, resulting in cell lysis and death (Fig. 26.14). The presence of dead and dying tissue further compromises the blood supply, and the organisms multiply and produce more toxin and more damage. Other extracellular enzymes may also play a role in helping the clostridia to spread. If the toxin escapes from the affected area and enters the bloodstream, there is massive haemolysis, renal failure and death.

Amputation may be necessary to prevent further spread of clostridial infection

Because of the rapid progression and fatal outcome of this type of clostridial infection, gangrenous areas require immediate surgery to excise all the affected tissue, and amputation may be necessary. Although some reports suggest that anti-alpha toxin may help if given early enough, antitoxin treatment is not generally viewed as effective, while treatment in a hyperbaric oxygen chamber, where available, may be helpful (i.e. oxygenation of tissue) in some cases.

Antibiotics (e.g. penicillin) are adjuncts to, not replacements for, surgical debridement.

Prevention of infection is of foremost importance. Wounds should be cleansed and debrided early to remove dead and poorly perfused tissue, which the anaerobes favour. Prophylactic antibiotics should be given preoperatively to patients having elective surgery of body sites liable to contamination with faecal flora (see Chs 33 and 36).

Propionibacterium acnes and acne

P. acnes go hand in hand with the hormonal changes of puberty which result in acne

An increased responsiveness to androgenic hormones leads to increased sebum production plus increased keratinization and desquamation in pilosebaceous ducts. Blockage of ducts turns them into sacs in which *P. acnes* and other members of the normal flora (e.g. micrococci, yeasts, staphylococci)

multiply. *P. acnes* acts on sebum to form fatty acids and peptides which, together with enzymes and other substances released from bacteria and polymorphs, cause the inflammation (Fig. 26.15). Comedones are greasy plugs composed of a mixture of keratin, sebum and bacteria and capped by a layer of melanin (blackheads in popular terminology) (Fig. 26.16).

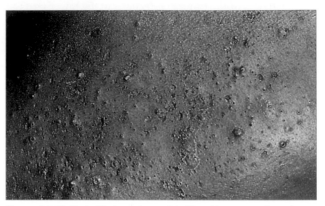

Figure 26.15 Typical lesions of acne. 'blackheads' are seen when plugs of keratin block the pilosebaceous duct. (Courtesy of A. du Vivier.)

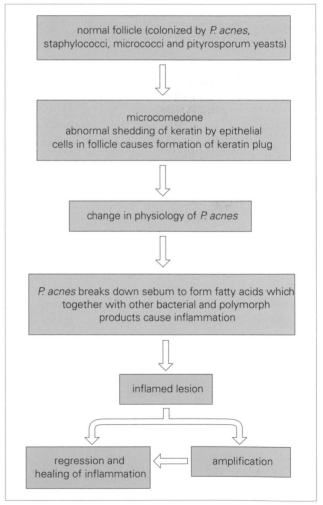

Figure 26.16 The proposed mechanism of the pathogenesis of acne. Hormonal changes in the host initiate the formation of comedones from normal follicles and thereby change the environment of *Propionibacterium acnes* and its physiologic properties. *P. acnes* is also known to be an immunostimulator.

Treatment of acne includes long-term administration of oral antibiotics

The antibiotics used to treat acne are usually one of the tetracyclines, or erythromycin. Other treatments include skin care, keratolytics and, in severe cases, synthetic vitamin A derivatives such as isotretinoin. Orally administered antibiotics reduce the surface numbers of *P. acnes* with a concomitant lowering of the free fatty acids, which act as skin irritants, which result from the activity of bacterial enzymes on sebum. Acne can be a problem for teenagers, but often disappears in older age groups as the sebaceous follicles become less active.

Other Gram-positive rods related to *P. acnes*, such as corynebacteria and brevibacteria, can also cause skin infections.

MYCOBACTERIAL DISEASES OF THE SKIN

Leprosy

Leprosy is decreasing in incidence but still remains a concern

Leprosy has been recognized since biblical times, but in the past, the word was a generic term applied to several different diseases and also implying 'moral uncleanliness'. Leprosy is thought to have spread to Europe in the sixth century, and by the thirteenth century there were some two hundred leper hospitals in England. Over the centuries that followed, leprosy declined in incidence, and by the fifteenth century was no longer endemic in England; in contrast tuberculosis was on the increase. Now leprosy is rare in the UK and USA and the WHO estimates that the number of new cases worldwide has decreased about 18% per year (2005–2009) with approximately 245 000 new cases detected in 2009. However, the disease still represents a significant problem in SE Asia, Africa and the Americas.

Leprosy is caused by *Mycobacterium leprae*

Mycobacterium leprae was discovered in 1873 by G.A. Hansen, who identified it as the first bacterial agent capable of causing human disease. Leprosy (Hansen's disease) appears to be confined to humans. *M. leprae* is found in nine-banded armadillos, chimpanzees and mangabey monkeys; however, epidemiologic studies have not demonstrated a significant link between this carriage and human disease. Transmission of infection is directly related to overcrowding and poor hygiene and occurs by direct contact and aerosol inhalation. Relatively few organisms are shed from skin lesions, but nasal secretions of patients with lepromatous leprosy are laden with *M. leprae*. Arthropod vectors may play a role in transmission. Leprosy is not highly contagious, and prolonged exposure to an infected source is necessary; it seems that children living under the same roof as an open case of leprosy are most at risk. Ironically, because the lesions of leprosy are more obvious, patients were in the past excluded from the community and gathered in leper colonies, whereas tuberculosis is much more contagious, but people with tuberculosis were not shunned.

The clinical features of leprosy depend upon the cell-mediated immune response to *M. leprae*

M. leprae cannot be grown in artificial culture media, and little is known about its mechanism of pathogenicity. Two animal models have been used: infection in the armadillo and in the footpads of mice. The organism grows better at temperatures below 37°C, hence its concentration in the skin and superficial nerves, and it grows extremely slowly; in the mouse footpad the generation time is 11–13 days. Likewise in humans, the incubation period may be many years.

M. leprae grows intracellularly, typically within skin histiocytes and endothelial cells and the Schwann cells of peripheral nerves. The immune response is all important in deciding the type of disease.

M. leprae shares many pathobiologic features with *M. tuberculosis*, but the clinical manifestations of the diseases are quite different. After an incubation period of several years, the onset of leprosy is gradual and the spectrum of disease activity is very broad depending upon the presence or absence of a cell-mediated immune (CMI) response to *M. leprae* (Fig. 26.17). At one end of the spectrum is tuberculoid leprosy (TT), characterized by blotchy red lesions with anaesthetic areas on the face, trunk and extremities (Fig. 26.18). There is palpable thickening of the peripheral nerves because the organisms multiply in the nerve sheaths. The local anaesthesia renders the patient prone to repeated trauma and secondary bacterial infection. This disease state is equivalent to secondary tuberculosis (see Ch. 19), with a vigorous CMI response leading to phagocytic destruction of bacteria, and exaggerated allergic responses. TT carries a better prognosis than lepromatous leprosy (LL) and in some patients is self-limiting, but in others may progress across the spectrum towards LL.

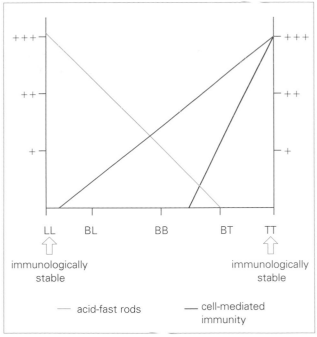

Figure 26.17 Immunologic responses in leprosy. In tuberculoid leprosy (TT) the patient is capable of mounting an effective cell-mediated immune (CMI) response, which makes it possible for macrophages to destroy the organisms and contain the infection. At the other extreme, in lepromatous leprosy (LL) the patient is incapable of producing a CMI response and the organisms multiply unhindered. These patients have many acid-fast rods in their skin and nasal secretions, and are much more infectious than TT patients. Borderline lepromatous (BL), borderline borderline (BB), and borderline tuberculoid (BT) responses are found between these extremes.

343

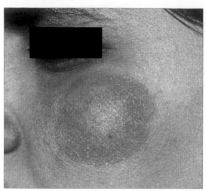

Figure 26.18 Tuberculoid leprosy – a characteristic dry blotchy lesion on the face, but the diagnosis needs to be confirmed by microscopic examination of skin biopsy (see Fig. 26.21). (Courtesy of the Institute of Dermatology.)

In LL, there is extensive skin involvement with large numbers of bacteria in affected areas. As the disease progresses there is loss of eyebrows, thickening and enlargement of the nostrils, ears and cheeks, resulting in the typical leonine (lion-like) facial appearance (Fig. 26.19). There is progressive destruction of the nasal septum, and the nasal mucosa is loaded with organisms (Fig. 26.20). This form of the disease is equivalent to miliary tuberculosis (see Ch. 19) with a weak CMI response and many extracellular organisms

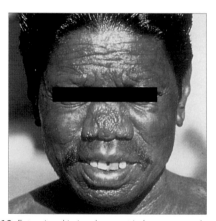

Figure 26.19 Extensive skin involvement in lepromatous leprosy results in a characteristic leonine appearance. (Courtesy of D.A. Lewis.)

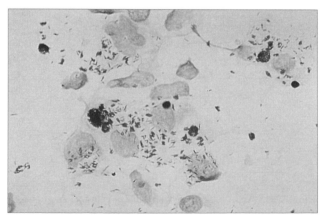

Figure 26.20 In lepromatous leprosy, the nasal mucosa is packed with *Mycobacterium leprae*, seen here in an acid-fast stain (Ziehl–Neelsen) of nasal scrapings. (Courtesy of I. Farrell.)

visible in the lesions. The gross deformities characteristic of late disease result primarily from infectious destruction of the nasomaxillary facial structures, and secondarily from pathologic changes in the peripheral nerves predisposing to repeated trauma of the hands and feet and subsequent superinfection with other organisms.

Whether a patient develops TT or LL may in part be genetically determined. Patients with intermediate forms of the disease may progress to either extreme.

M. leprae are seen as acid-fast rods in nasal scrapings and lesion biopsies

Alertness to the possibility of leprosy when confronted with a patient with dermatologic, neurologic or multisystem complaints is of fundamental importance. Although the majority of cases are in people who are not native to Europe or the USA, the diagnosis should also be considered in those who have worked in endemic areas.

Nasal scrapings and biopsies of skin lesions should be stained by Ziehl–Neelsen or auramine stain to demonstrate acid-fast rods. In LL these are numerous, but in TT few if any organisms are seen, but the appearance of granulomas is sufficiently typical to allow the diagnosis to be made (Fig. 26.21). Remember that, in contrast to *M. tuberculosis*, the organism cannot be grown in vitro.

Treatment

Leprosy is treated with dapsone given as part of a multidrug regimen to avoid resistance

If the disease is diagnosed early and treatment initiated promptly the patient has a much better prognosis. Dapsone (see Ch. 33) had long been the mainstay of therapy, but multidrug therapy is now used because of dapsone resistance:

* For LL, triple therapy with dapsone, rifampin and clofazimine is given for a minimum of 2 years and may be lifelong or until all skin scrapings and biopsies are negative for acid-fast rods.
* For TT, a combination of dapsone and rifampin for 6 months is recommended, the rationale being that in this form of disease there are many fewer organisms and therefore less chance of emergence of resistant mutants.

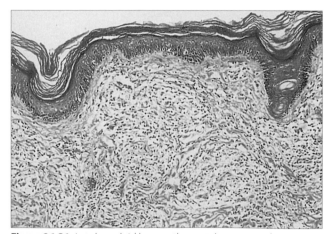

Figure 26.21 In tuberculoid leprosy, the organisms are much sparser but characteristic granulomas form in the dermis, as shown in this histologic preparation. (Courtesy of C.J. Edwards.)

As a result of multidrug therapy, which is reasonably cheap, well tolerated and effects a complete cure, steady progress is being made towards the elimination of leprosy as a public health problem.

Destruction of the organisms by effective antimicrobial therapy may result in an inflammatory response, erythema nodosum leprosum, which may be severe and, occasionally, fatal. Treatment with corticosteroids or thalidomide may be indicated.

Vaccination with bacille Calmette–Guérin (BCG) has been used in countries with high incidence where potential protection outweighs negative factors such as a positive skin test. Vaccination is not useful for immunocompromised individuals.

Other mycobacterial skin infections

Mycobacterium marinum, M. ulcerans and *M. tuberculosis* also cause skin lesions

Mycobacterium marinum and *M. ulcerans* are two slow-growing mycobacterial species that prefer cooler temperatures and cause skin lesions. As its name suggests, *M. marinum* is associated with water and marine organisms. Human infections follow trauma, often minor such as a graze acquired while climbing out of a swimming pool or while cleaning out an aquarium, which becomes contaminated with mycobacteria from the wet environment. After an incubation period of 2–8 weeks, initial lesions appear as small papules, which enlarge and suppurate and may ulcerate. Histologically, the lesions are granulomas and hence the name 'swimming pool granuloma' or 'fish-tank granuloma' (Fig. 26.22). Sometimes the nodules follow the course of the draining lymphatic and produce an appearance that may be mistaken for sporotrichosis (see below).

M. ulcerans causes chronic, relatively painless cutaneous ulcers known as 'Buruli ulcers'. This disease is prevalent in Africa and Australia, but is rarely seen elsewhere.

Tuberculosis of the skin is exceedingly uncommon. Infection can occur by direct implantation of *M. tuberculosis* during trauma to the skin (lupus vulgaris) or may extend to the skin from an infected lymph node (scrofuloderma).

FUNGAL INFECTIONS OF THE SKIN

Fungal infections may be confined to the very outermost layers of the skin and hair shafts or penetrate into the keratinized layers of the epidermis, nails and hair (the superficial and cutaneous mycoses); others develop in the dermal layers (subcutaneous mycoses). In addition, some systemic fungal infections acquired by the air-borne route have skin manifestations (see Table 26.1).

Superficial and cutaneous mycoses

These are some of the most common infections in humans. Superficial infections of the skin and hair (pityriasis versicolor, tinea nigra, black and white piedras) mainly cause cosmetic problems; cutaneous infections (ringworm, tineas) caused by the dermatophyte fungi are more significant. The important causative agents are the superficial yeast *Malassezia furfur* and the cutaneous dermatophytes *Epidermophyton*, *Trichophyton* and *Microsporum*.

Pityriasis versicolor

M. furfur is the cause of pityriasis or tinea versicolor

The yeast *M. (Pityrosporum) furfur* is a common skin inhabitant. The change from commensalism to pathogenicity appears to be associated with the phase change from yeast to hyphal forms of the fungus, but the stimulus for this is unknown. Infections are usually confined to the trunk or proximal parts of the limbs and are associated with hypo- or hyperpigmented macules that coalesce to form scaling plaques. The lesions are not usually itchy and in some patients, they resolve spontaneously.

Malassezia yeasts are also thought to be involved in the pathogenesis of seborrhoeic dermatitis and dandruff.

Diagnosis of pityriasis versicolor can be confirmed by direct microscopy of scrapings

Direct microscopy of scrapings shows characteristic round yeast forms (Fig. 26.23), and treatment with a topical azole antifungal (see below) or with selenium sulphide (2.5%) lotion is appropriate.

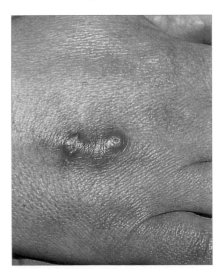

Figure 26.22 Fish-tank granuloma caused by *Mycobacterium marinum* infection of a lesion acquired while cleaning out a fish tank. (Courtesy of M.J. Wood.)

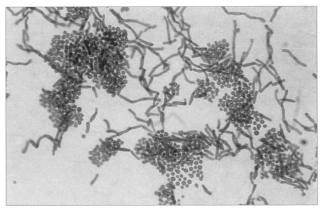

Figure 26.23 Infected skin scales stained to show the thick-walled yeast forms of *Malassezia furfur* and the short angular hyphae. (Courtesy of Y. Clayton and G. Midgley.)

Cutaneous dermatophytes

- ### Dermatophyte infections are acquired from many sources and are spread by arthrospores

Species of dermatophytes are described as anthropophilic, zoophilic or geophilic depending upon their primary source (human, animal or soil). The species concerned differ in their geographic distribution, in their predilection for different body sites and in the degree of host response elicited in humans. The source of an infection determines its route of transmission to humans and, to some extent, its distribution in human populations (Fig. 26.24), although population movements are changing established patterns. For example, for a time immigration from Latin America replaced *Microsporum audouinii* by *Trichophyton tonsurans* as the common cause of tinea capitis in the USA, but the latter (which responds poorly to treatment) is now again predominant.

The anthropophilic species are the most common causes of dermatophyte infections. In temperate countries, *Trichophyton verrucosum* from cattle, *T. mentagrophytes* from rodents, and

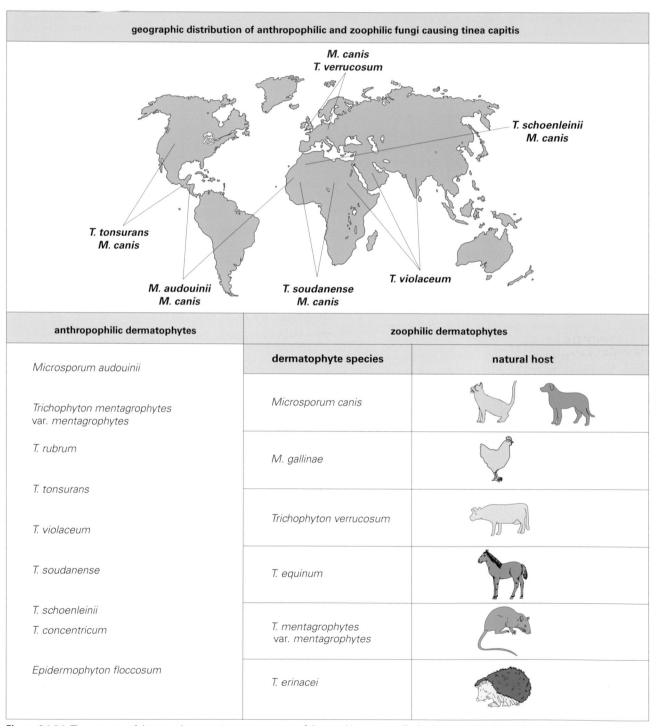

geographic distribution of anthropophilic and zoophilic fungi causing tinea capitis

M. canis
T. verrucosum

T. schoenleinii
M. canis

T. tonsurans
M. canis

M. audouinii
M. canis

T. soudanense
M. canis

T. violaceum

anthropophilic dermatophytes	zoophilic dermatophytes	
	dermatophyte species	**natural host**
Microsporum audouinii	*Microsporum canis*	
Trichophyton mentagrophytes var. *mentagrophytes*		
T. rubrum	*M. gallinae*	
T. tonsurans		
T. violaceum	*Trichophyton verrucosum*	
T. soudanense	*T. equinum*	
T. schoenleinii		
T. concentricum	*T. mentagrophytes* var. *mentagrophytes*	
Epidermophyton floccosum	*T. erinacei*	

Figure 26.24 Three genera of dermatophytes are important causes of disease: *Microsporum*, *Trichophyton* and *Epidermophyton*. Within each genus there are anthropophilic, zoophilic and geophilic species. The natural host and therefore distribution of anthropophilic species varies. *Microsporum gypseum* is the geophilic species of importance.

Microsporum canis from cats and dogs, are the most common zoophilic causes of human infection. Geophilic species such as *Microsporum gypseum* are uncommon causes of human disease, but are seen in people who have appropriate exposure, such as gardeners and agricultural workers. Zoophilic and geophilic species tend to cause a greater inflammatory response than anthropophilic species.

Infections are spread by contact with arthrospores, the thick-walled vegetative cells formed by dermatophyte hyphae (Fig. 26.25), which can survive for months. In anthropophilic and zoophilic species, these are shed from the primary host in skin scales and hair.

Dermatophytes invade skin, hair and nails

The dermatophytes are keratin-loving organisms and invade the keratinized structures of the body (i.e. skin, hair and nails). The arthrospores adhere to keratinocytes, germinate and invade. The Latin word *tinea* (meaning a maggot or grub) or 'ringworm' is used for these infections because they were originally thought to be caused by a worm-like parasite. Thus, tinea capitis affects the hair and skin of the scalp, tinea corporis the body, tinea cruris the crotch, tinea manuum the hands, tinea unguium the nails and tinea pedis the feet (Fig. 26.26).

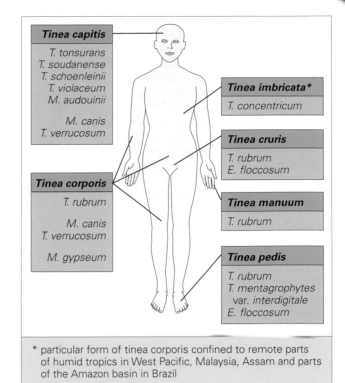

* particular form of tinea corporis confined to remote parts of humid tropics in West Pacific, Malaysia, Assam and parts of the Amazon basin in Brazil

Figure 26.26 Tinea (or ringworm) is the disease of skin, hair and nails caused by dermatophyte fungi. Different species have predilections for different body sites. E., *Epidermophyton*; M., *Microsporum*; T., *Trichophyton*.

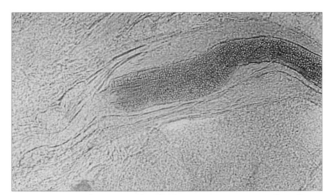

Figure 26.25 Arthrospores of *Trichophyton tonsurans* in an infected hair shaft. These thick-walled spores are the form in which infection is spread. They can survive in the environment for weeks or months before infecting a new host. (Courtesy of A.E. Prevost.)

The typical lesion is an annular or serpentine scaling patch with a raised margin. The main symptom is itching, but this is variable in degree. The skin is often dry and scaly and sometimes cracks (e.g. between the toes in tinea pedis), while infections of hair cause hair loss (Fig. 26.27). The degree of associated inflammation varies with the infecting species, usually being greater with zoophilic than with anthropophilic species. Individuals also differ in their susceptibility to infection, but the factors determining these differences are not clearly understood. Similarly, dermatophyte species differ in their ability to elicit an immune response; some, such as *Trichophyton rubrum*, cause chronic or relapsing conditions,

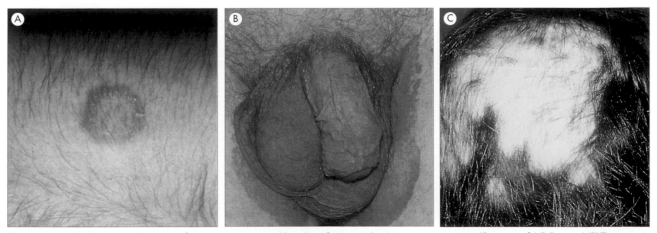

Figure 26.27 (A) Classic annular lesion of tinea corporis, caused here by infection with a *Microsporum* species. (Courtesy of A.E. Prevost.) (B) Tinea cruris or 'jock itch' is a scaly rash on the thighs; the scrotum is usually spared. (Courtesy of M.J. Wood.) (C) Tinea capitis is characterized by scaling on the scalp and hair loss. Some dermatophytes fluoresce under ultraviolet light, and this can be an aid to diagnosis. (Courtesy of M.H. Winterborn.)

whereas other species induce long-term resistance to reinfection. In some patients, circulating fungal antigens give rise to immunologically mediated hypersensitivity phenomena in the skin (e.g. erythema or vesicles) known as dermatophytid reactions. When the skin becomes cracked and macerated as a result of infection, it is liable to superinfection with other organisms such as Gram-negative bacteria in moist sites.

Very rarely, dermatophytes invade the subcutaneous tissues via the lymphatics, causing granulomas, lymphoedema and draining sinuses. Further extension to sites such as the liver and brain may be fatal.

Most dermatophyte species fluoresce under ultraviolet light

This feature can be used as a diagnostic aid, particularly for tinea capitis, in the clinic. Laboratory diagnosis depends upon culture of scrapings or clippings from lesions on Sabouraud agar or other agars to which inhibitory agents (antibiotics/cycloheximide) have been added to provide some selectivity (Fig. 26.28). Dermatophytes infecting hair show a characteristic distribution, which may be helpful for identification:

- Some, such as most *Microsporum* species, form arthrospores on the outside of the hair shaft (ectothrix infections).
- The majority of *Trichophyton* infections form arthrospores within the hair shaft (endothrix infection, Fig. 26.29).

Confirmation of identity depends upon the colonial and microscopic characteristics of the fungi cultured on Sabouraud agar (Fig. 26.30). Growth may take up to 2 weeks, but identification is not difficult and is useful for determining the source of infection.

Dermatophyte infections are treated topically if possible

A range of agents is available for topical treatment (see Ch. 33), both antifungals (e.g. miconazole) and keratolytic agents such as Whitfield's ointment (a mixture of salicylic and benzoic acids). However, infections of nails and hair are better treated by oral antifungal drugs. Terbinafine or itraconazole are now used in preference to griseofulvin. These newer agents may give a cure rate of 70–80% for nail infections.

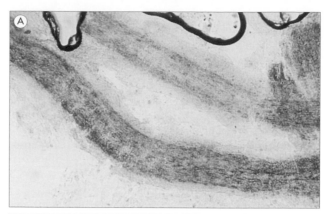

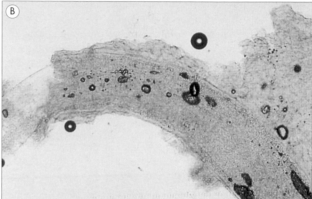

Figure 26.29 Dermatophytes may form arthrospores within the hair shafts (endothrix infection) as shown in (A) and less commonly outside the shaft (ectothrix infection) as shown in (B). (Courtesy of Y. Clayton and G. Midgley.)

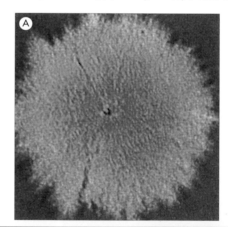

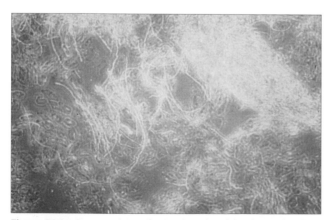

Figure 26.28 Dermatophyte infection. Samples of skin, hair and nails need to be 'cleared' by treatment with potassium hydroxide before examining under the microscope for the presence of fungal hyphae. (Courtesy of R.Y. Cartwright.)

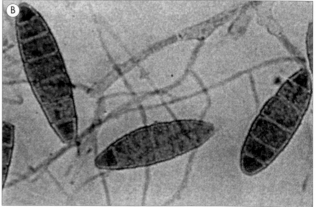

Figure 26.30 (A) Macroscopic growth (colony) and (B) microscopic preparation showing the macroconidia of *Microsporum gypseum*.

Candida and the skin

Candida requires moisture for growth

The relative dryness of most areas of skin limits the growth of fungi such as *Candida* that require moisture. *Candida* is found in low numbers on healthy intact skin, but rapidly colonizes damaged skin and intertriginous sites (opposed skin sites which are often moist and become chafed, Fig. 26.31). *Candida* also colonizes the oral and vaginal mucosa and overgrowth may result in disease in these sites (thrush, see Ch. 21). However, a substantial lowering of host resistance (e.g. neutropenia) is necessary for *Candida* to invade deeper subcutaneous tissue, and disseminated candidiasis does not often originate from skin infection unless there is instrumentation through infected areas (see Ch. 30).

Subcutaneous mycoses

Subcutaneous fungal infections can be caused by a number of different species

Lesions usually develop at sites of trauma (a thorn, a bite) where the fungus becomes implanted. With the exception of sporotrichosis, subcutaneous fungal infections are rare, but similar diseases can be caused by certain bacteria such as *Actinomyces* and atypical mycobacteria, and therefore it is important to establish the aetiology in order to select optimal therapy. The fungi involved are difficult to eradicate with antifungal agents, and surgical intervention, in the form of excision or amputation, is often required.

Sporotrichosis is a nodular condition caused by *Sporothrix schenckii*

Sporothrix schenckii is a saprophytic fungus that is widespread in nature in soil, on rose and berberis bushes, tree bark and sphagnum moss. Infection is acquired through trauma (e.g. a thorn) and is an occupational hazard for people such as farmers, gardeners and florists. A small papule or subcutaneous nodule develops at the site of trauma 1 week to 6 months after inoculation, and infection spreads, producing a series of secondary nodules along the lymphatics that drain the site (Fig. 26.32). Diagnosis is made by culture of drained or aspirated material onto Sabouraud agar; serological tests are available. Azole drugs are highly effective and, where available, itraconazole or fluconazole have replaced treatment with oral potassium iodide.

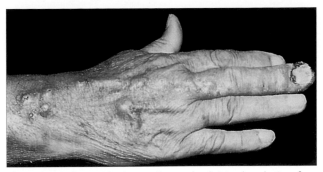

Figure 26.32 *Sporotrichosis* spreading up the draining lymphatics of the hand following a primary infection in the nailbed of the third finger. (Courtesy of T.F. Sellers, Jr.)

Disseminated disease can occur following cutaneous or pulmonary infection with *S. schenckii*. It is more common in compromised patients such as those with underlying carcinoma or sarcoidosis, but many cases occur in people in whom no underlying disease is recognized. Treatment with amphotericin B is indicated, and the prognosis is often poor.

Other species causing subcutaneous infections include *Cladosporium* and *Phialophora* (chromoblastomycosis), *Pseudallescheria* and *Madurella* (mycetoma).

Systemic fungal infections with skin manifestations include blastomycosis, coccidioidomycosis and cryptococcosis

Skin lesions are the most common presenting symptom of blastomycosis, a disease endemic in Central and North America and Africa and caused by *Blastomyces dermatitidis*. Infection is acquired by aspiration of the fungal spores and spreads from the primary site in the lung. Blastomycosis can be a systemic disease in apparently immunologically normal hosts (Fig. 26.33). It also causes disease in horses and dogs.

Other systemic infections that may have skin manifestations are those caused by *Coccidioides immitis* and *Cryptococcus neoformans*.

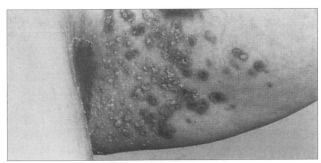

Figure 26.31 *Candida* infection of the skin. Here, infection has occurred between two apposing skin surfaces, which provide a suitably moist environment for this yeast to multiply. (Courtesy of A. du Vivier and St Mary's Hospital.)

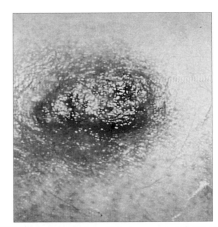

Figure 26.33 Typical skin lesion of blastomycosis. Infection is acquired by the respiratory route, and the primary site of infection is the lung. However, in chronic blastomycosis the skin is the most common extrapulmonary site of infection. (Courtesy of K.A. Riley.)

PARASITIC INFECTIONS OF THE SKIN

The skin is a major route of entry for parasites, which may:

- penetrate directly (e.g. schistosomes, hookworm)
- be injected by blood-feeding vectors.

Many of these parasites leave the skin almost immediately as they progress through their life cycle, but some remain there and others may become trapped. A few parasites actually exit from the body through the skin (e.g., release of Guinea worm larvae). Pathologic responses to parasites associated with the skin range from mild to disablingly severe. Some species causing severe conditions are described briefly below.

Leishmaniasis may be cutaneous or mucosal (formerly termed mucocutaneous)

Two major disease complexes caused by the protozoans *Leishmania* affect the skin and both are transmitted by the bite of sandfly vectors:

- The cutaneous leishmaniases, which occur in both the Old World (Asia, Africa, Southern Europe) and New World (Central and South America), include conditions ranging from localized self-healing ulcers to non-curing, disseminated lesions similar to leprosy in appearance.
- In the New World, mucosal leishmaniasis occurs when the parasite in the skin invades mucosal surfaces (nose, mouth), giving rise to chronic disfiguring conditions. Leishmaniasis is discussed in detail in Chapter 27.

Schistosome infection can cause a dermatitis

Transmission of schistosome infection to humans is achieved by active skin penetration by larvae (cercariae) released into fresh water by the snail intermediate host (see Ch. 27). This stage of infection can give rise to a dermatitis known as swimmers' itch. It may also be produced by the cercariae of bird schistosomes and is relatively common where natural water used for recreation is populated with aquatic birds. It is a frequent problem in lakes in North America. Topical anti-inflammatory treatments are effective therapy.

Cutaneous larval migrans is characterized by itchy inflammatory hookworm larvae trails

Human hookworms (the nematodes *Ancylostoma* and *Necator*) invade the body through the skin, the infective larvae burrowing into the dermis and then migrating via the blood to eventually reach the intestine. Invasion may cause dermatitis (known as ground itch) and this becomes more severe upon repeated infection. Humans, however, can also be invaded by the larvae of the cat and dog species of *Ancylostoma*. Infection is acquired when exposed skin comes into contact with soil that has been contaminated by animals carrying the adult worms in their intestines. Eggs in the faeces hatch to produce the infective larvae, which remain viable for prolonged periods. As the human host is foreign for these species, the larvae fail to escape from the dermis after invasion, and may live for some time, migrating parallel to the skin and leaving intensely itchy sinuous inflammatory trails (creeping eruption), which are easily visible at the surface (Fig. 26.34). Treatment is with topical thiabendazole paste or oral ivermectin.

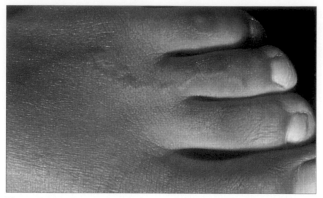

Figure 26.34 Cutaneous larval migrans (creeping eruption), showing the raised inflammatory track left by the invading hookworm larvae. (Courtesy of A. du Vivier.)

Onchocerciasis is characterized by hypersensitivity responses to larval antigens

Onchocerciasis is also known as river blindness. The adult stages of *Onchocerca volvulus* live for many years in subcutaneous nodules. Female worms release live microfilariae, which migrate away from the nodules, remaining largely in the dermal layers. They can invade the eye, causing river blindness (see Ch. 25). The slow build-up of parasite numbers and the development of a hypersensitivity response to the antigens released by living and dying larvae give rise to inflammatory skin conditions. In the early stages, these appear as erythematous papular rashes accompanied by intense itching. Later, there is skin thickening, elasticity is lost, and excessive wrinkling occurs and depigmentation is also common. The microfilariae can be killed by ivermectin treatment, but the skin changes, once advanced, are irreversible. Dermal inflammatory condition and secondary bacterial infection are not uncommon during infection with lymphatic filarial nematodes.

Arthropod infections

Some flies, mainly in the tropics and subtropics, have larvae that develop within the skin

Myiasis is a condition associated with invasion of the body by the larvae (maggots) of dipteran flies such as *Dermatobia*. Several species of fly have a cycle in which the larvae feed and grow in the skin of a mammal, just below the surface, escaping before or after pupation to continue their life cycle and lead ultimately to the release of adult forms. Female flies lay eggs or larvae directly onto the skin, and larvae may then invade wounds or natural orifices. The activities and feeding of the larvae cause intense painful reactions, and large lesions may develop. A number of these species have been found in humans, and infections have been recorded in many countries, although primarily in tropical and subtropical regions. Treatment involves removal of the larvae, alleviation of symptoms and prevention of secondary bacterial infection.

There is a revival of interest in using maggots of non-myiasis species to remove necrotic tissue from wounds, their secretions also preventing bacterial contamination.

Certain ticks, lice and mites live on blood or tissue fluids from humans

Some feed non-selectively on humans, the normal hosts being animals; other species are human specific. The feeding processes and the inevitable release of saliva, give rise to skin irritation, which becomes more intense as the body responds immunologically to the proteins present in the saliva. Prolonged feeding, as practiced by ticks, may leave painful lesions in the skin, which can become secondarily infected. Species such as lice and scabies mites, which spend the greater part or the whole of their lives on the human body, can cause severe skin conditions when populations accumulate. These conditions arise from:

- the activity of the arthropods themselves
- their production of excreta
- the oozing of blood and tissue fluids from the feeding sites
- the host's inflammatory reaction.

Pediculosis – infection with head and body lice of the genus *Pediculus* – can, when severe, give rise to encrusting inflammatory masses in which fungal infections may establish. Good personal hygiene prevents infestation; use of insecticidal creams, lotions, shampoos and powders containing malathion or carbaryl helps to clear the insects directly.

The scabies mite has a more intimate contact with the human host than lice, living its whole life in burrows within the skin. The female lays eggs into these burrows, and so the area of infection can spread to cover large areas of the body from the original site, which is usually on the hands or wrists (Fig. 26.35; see Ch. 21). Infection causes a characteristic rash with itching, and secondary infections may follow scratching. Very heavy infections may develop in immunocompromised individuals or in people who are unable to care adequately for themselves. Under these conditions, there is extensive thickening and crusting of the skin (Norwegian scabies). Treatment with permethrin or malathion is recommended; benzyl benzoate can also be used on unbroken skin but is less effective. Oral ivermectin may be required in addition to topical therapy for Norwegian scabies.

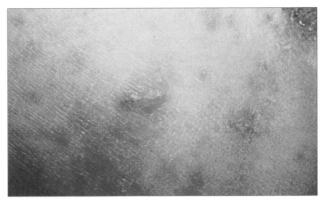

Figure 26.35 A characteristic cutaneous burrow in scabies. (Courtesy of M.J. Wood.)

MUCOCUTANEOUS LESIONS CAUSED BY VIRUSES

Mucocutaneous lesions caused by viruses can be divided into:

- those in which the virus remains restricted to the body surface at the site of initial infection
- those in which the virus causes mucocutaneous lesions after spreading systemically through the body (Table 26.3).

The infections that spread systemically can in turn be divided into:

- those in which the skin lesions (vesicular) are sites of virus replication and are infectious
- those in which the skin lesions (maculopapular) are non-infectious and immunologically mediated, although the virus can be shed from other sites.

The skin rash has a characteristic distribution in many infectious diseases, but with the exception of zoster, the reason for this is unknown.

Table 26.3 Mucocutaneous lesions caused by viruses

Virus	Lesion	Virus shedding from lesion
No systemic spread		
Papilloma (wart)	Common wart; plantar wart; genital wart	+
Molluscum contagiosum (poxvirus)	Fleshy papule	+
Orf (poxvirus from sheep, goats)	Papulovesicular	+
Systemic spread		
Herpes simplex, varicella-zoster	Vesicular (neural spread and latency)	+
Coxsackievirus A (9, 16, 23)	Vesicular, in mouth (herpangina)	+
Coxsackievirus A16	Vesicular (hand, foot and mouth disease)	+
Parvovirus B19	Facial maculopapular (erythema infectiosum)	–
Human herpesvirus 6	Exanthem subitum (roseola infantum)	–
Measles	Maculopapular skin rash	–
Rubella, echoviruses (4, 6, 9, 16)	Maculopapular not distinguishable clinically	–
Dengue and other arthropod transmitted viruses	Maculopapular	–

The pathogenesis of these diseases is illustrated in Figure 26.2. Papillomas and vesicular lesions are generally sites of virus shedding. The distribution as well as the nature of the lesion can be important in diagnosis (e.g. varicella), but many maculopapular rashes are clinically indistinguishable.

Rashes are particular features of human infection and are rare in animals. This is because human skin is naked and is a turbulent, highly reactive tissue in which immune and inflammatory events are clearly visible. Rashes cause discomfort and may be painful but they may be very helpful for the clinician who needs to make a diagnosis. The veterinarian is less privileged because the skin of most other mammals is largely covered with fur, and skin lesions generally involve hairless areas such as udders, scrotums, ears, prepuces, teats, noses or paws, which have the human properties of thickness, sensitivity and vascular reactivity.

Papillomavirus infection

Over 120 different types of papillomavirus can infect humans and are species specific

Papillomaviruses are 55 nm in diameter, icosahedral, double-stranded DNA viruses and cause skin papillomas (warts). The 70 different types that can infect humans show <50% cross-hybridization of DNA, although not all types are common. Human papillomaviruses (HPV) are species specific and distinct from animal papillomaviruses. They are highly adapted to human skin and mucosa and are ancient associates of our species; therefore, for most of the time they cause little or no disease. They show some adaptation to definite sites on the body:

- At least 40 types, including HPV 6, 11, 16 and 18, can infect the anogenital tract and other mucosal areas and are sexually transmitted.
- HPV 1 and 4 tend to cause plantar warts.
- HPV 2, 3 and 10 cause warts on the knees and fingers.

Papillomaviruses are generally transmitted by direct contact, but they are stable and can also be spread indirectly. For instance, plantar warts can be acquired from contaminated floors or from the non-slip surfaces at the edges of swimming pools, and in a given individual warts can be spread from one site to another by shaving.

Papillomavirus infects cells in the basal layers of skin or mucosa and are tissue tropic

After entering the body via surface abrasions, the virus infects cells in the basal layers of the skin or mucosa (see Fig. 26.2). There is no spread to deeper tissues. Virus replication is slow and is critically dependent on the differentiation of host cells. Viral DNA is present in basal cells, but viral antigen and infectious virus are produced only when the cells begin to become squamified and keratinized as they approach the surface. The infected cells are stimulated to divide and finally, 1–6 months after initial infection, the mass of infected cells protrudes from the body surface to form a visible papilloma or wart (Fig. 26.36). There is marked proliferation of prickle cells, and vacuolated cells are present in the more superficial layers. Warts can be:

- filiform with finger-like projections
- flat topped
- flat because they grow inwards due to external pressure (plantar warts)
- a cauliflower-like protuberance (e.g. genital warts)
- a flat area of dysplasia on the cervix.

Immune responses eventually bring virus replication under control and, several months after infection, the wart regresses.

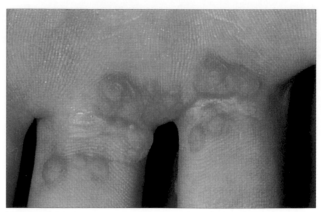

Figure 26.36 Common warts (papillomas) on the hand. (Courtesy of M.J. Wood.)

Antibodies are demonstrable, but CMI responses are more important in recovery. Viral DNA remains in a latent state in the basal cell layer, infecting an occasional stem cell, and is therefore retained within the layer as epidermal cells differentiate and are shed from the surface. When patients are subsequently immunocompromised (e.g. post-transplant) crops of warts may result from reactivation of latent virus in the skin.

Papillomavirus infections are associated with cancer of the cervix, vulva, penis, rectum, head, and neck

Human papillomavirus infections are associated with nearly 4% of all cancers. The association between genital warts and cancer of the cervix, vulva, penis and rectum is referred to in Chapter 17. Infection with specific genital HPVs causes invasive cervical cancer. There is a rare autosomal recessive disease, epidermodysplasia verruciformis, characterized by multiple warts containing many different HPV types which are not normally seen causing skin warts and immunologic defects. Warts may undergo malignant change (squamous cell carcinomas) in nearly 30% of these patients, usually in sun-exposed sites.

Diagnosis of papillomavirus infection is clinical and there are many treatments

Wart viruses cannot be cultivated in the laboratory, and serologic tests are mainly of epidemiological, rather than diagnostic, use. HPV DNA detection methods can be used to examine samples not only for the HPV type but also to quantify the viral load.

Many treatments have been used for warts, some of them doubtless seeming effective because skin warts eventually disappear without treatment. Treatments of skin warts include the application of karyolytic agents such as salicylic acid and destruction of wart tissue by cryotherapy, freezing with dry ice (solid carbon dioxide) or with liquid nitrogen. The latter is the most commonly used and most effective treatment. Genital intraepithelial lesions, especially cervical, can lead to malignant disease, and treatment to eliminate the infection may involve laser therapy, loop excision, and surgery. Immunomodulating and antiviral agents such as imiquimod and topical cidofovir, respectively, have been used in certain clinical settings.

Molluscum contagiosum is an umbilicated lesion caused by a poxvirus

The poxvirus infects epidermal cells to form a fleshy lesion, often with an umbilicated centre (Fig. 26.37). It only infects humans and is spread by contact, or in the case of genital lesions, by sexual intercourse. There are two antigenically distinct types. Poxvirus particles can be seen by electron microscopy (see Ch. 3).

Orf is a papulovesicular lesion caused by a poxvirus

Orf (contagious pustular dermatitis) is an uncommon infection of the epidermis and is acquired by direct contact with infected sheep or goats. There is a papulovesicular lesion, generally on the hands, which may ulcerate. It is a clinical diagnosis and can be confirmed by electron microscopy.

Herpes simplex virus infection

Herpes simplex virus infection is universal and occurs in early childhood

Herpes simplex virus (HSV) is a medium-sized (120 nm) double-stranded DNA virus of the herpesvirus group. Two types, HSV-1 and HSV-2, are distinguishable antigenically. They cause a wide variety of clinical syndromes, the basic lesion being an intraepithelial vesicle, from which the virus is shed. Infection is usually transmitted from the saliva or cold sores of other individuals and frequently by kissing.

Clinical features of HSV infection are vesicles and latency

After infection, the virus replicates in cells in the oral mucosa and forms virus-rich vesicles. The patient suffers at most a mild febrile illness. The vesicles ulcerate and become coated with a whitish-grey slough (Fig. 26.38).

During the primary infection, virus particles enter sensory nerve endings in the lesion and are transported to the dorsal root (trigeminal) ganglion, where they initiate latent infection in sensory neurones (see Ch. 16). The lesion resolves as antibody and CMI responses develop. The latent virus remains in the sensory ganglion for life, and under certain circumstances can reactivate and spread down sensory nerves to cause cold sores at the site of the original infection (Fig. 26.39).

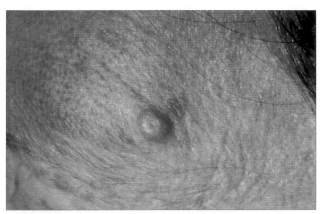

Figure 26.37 Single umbilicated lesion in *molluscum contagiosum*. (Courtesy of M.J. Wood.)

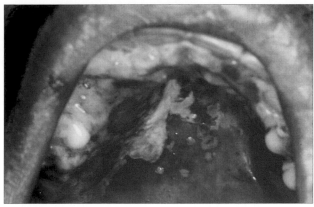

Figure 26.38 Primary herpes simplex virus infection. There are shallow ulcers with white exudate on the palate and gums. (Courtesy of J.A. Innes.)

Primary infection can also occur in:

- the eye, to cause conjunctivitis and keratitis, often with vesicles on the eyelids (see Ch. 25)
- the finger, to cause herpetic whitlow
- other skin sites following direct contact with infected individuals where there is rubbing or trauma, for instance in rugby football ('scrum pox') or in wrestlers ('herpes gladiatorum')
- the genital tract (see Ch. 21). Although HSV-2 arose as a sexually transmitted variant of HSV-1, the sites infected by the two types are now less clearly distinct.

Serious complications associated with HSV infection include:

- herpetic infection of eczematous skin areas leading to severe disease in young children (Fig. 26.40)
- acute necrotizing encephalitis following either primary infection or reactivation (see Ch. 24)
- neonatal infection acquired from the genital tract of the mother (see Ch. 23)
- primary or reactivating HSV infection in immunocompromised individuals, causing very severe disease (see Ch. 30).

Herpes simplex virus reactivation is provoked by a variety of factors

In healthy individuals, HSV reactivation is provoked by:

- certain febrile illnesses (e.g. common cold, pneumonia)
- direct sunlight
- stress
- trauma
- menstruation
- immunocompromise.

Reactivation is more severe in immunocompromised patients (see Ch. 30).

A sensory prodrome in the affected area which may include feeling pins and needles, pain, burning, and itching precedes the appearance of the lesion and is due to virus activity in sensory neurones. The lesion, a so-called 'cold sore', generally occurs around the mucocutaneous junctions in the nose or mouth (Fig. 26.41). Less commonly, when the ophthalmic branch of the trigeminal ganglion is involved, the lesion is a dendritic ulcer of the cornea. Large amounts of virus are shed in the cold sore, which scabs over and heals over the course of about 1 week. Occasionally, the sensory

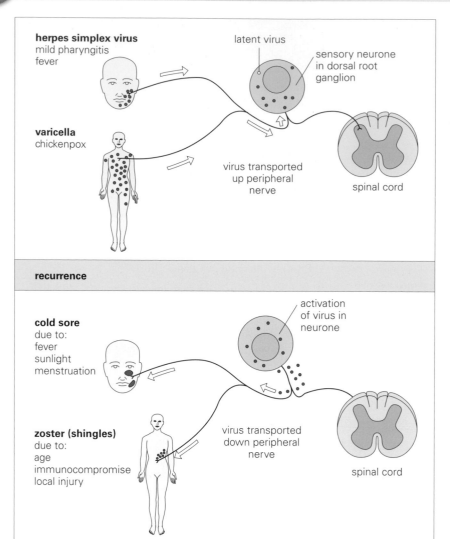

Figure 26.39 Pathogenesis of cold sores and zoster. In both herpes simplex virus and varicella-zoster virus infections the virus in mucocutaneous nerve endings travels up the axon to reach the sensory neurones, where it becomes latent. Recurrences are due to reactivation of the virus within the neurone to become infectious followed by passage of virus down the axon to mucocutaneous site(s) and local spread and replication to form clinical lesion(s).

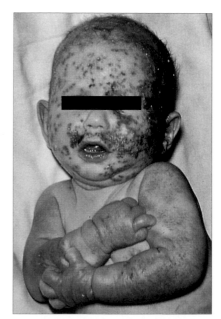

Figure 26.40 Eczema herpeticum due to herpes simplex virus infection in an infant. (Courtesy of M.J. Wood.)

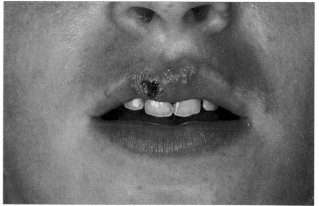

Figure 26.41 Recurrent herpes simplex virus vesicles on the mucocutaneous margin of the lip. (Courtesy of A. du Vivier.)

prodrome occurs without proceeding to a cold sore (see also varicella-zoster virus recurrence below).

Herpes simplex virus is readily isolated from vesicle fluid, and infection is treated with aciclovir

Herpes simplex virus is also readily isolated from saliva, conjunctival fluid and lesions at affected sites. The majority of samples sent to hospital laboratories are from genital lesions, and the virus causes a distinct cytopathic effect when isolated in the laboratory using cell culture lines such as human embryo lung. However, high-sensitivity molecular-based techniques have improved the diagnosis of HSV infection by detecting HSV types 1 and 2 DNA in a variety of samples and have replaced virus culture in many laboratories around the world.

Aciclovir revolutionized the treatment of HSV infection (see Ch. 33) and can be used either topically or systemically. It is relatively non-toxic and acts specifically in virus-infected cells. Recurrent herpetic eruptions have been successfully treated with low doses of aciclovir given twice daily for 6 to 12 months, at which time treatment can be stopped and the frequency of recurrent infection reassessed.

Other antiviral treatment options include valaciclovir and famciclovir. Aciclovir must be given intravenously when treating severe HSV infections such as herpes simplex encephalitis or disseminated HSV infection in immunocompromised individuals. Alternative antivirals such as ganciclovir, foscarnet or cidofovir may be used when antiviral resistance is being considered.

Varicella-zoster virus (VZV) infection

Varicella-zoster virus causes chickenpox (varicella) and zoster (shingles) and is highly infectious

Varicella-zoster virus is a medium-sized (100–200 nm in diameter) double-stranded DNA virus of the herpesvirus group and is morphologically indistinguishable from HSV. There is only one serologic type. The virus grows more slowly than HSV and is not released from the infected cell. Infection is by inhalation of droplets from respiratory secretions and saliva, or by direct contact from skin lesions. Primary infection with VZV causes varicella (chickenpox). Immunity develops and prevents reinfection (a second attack of varicella), but the virus persists in the body, and later in life, after reactivation, causes zoster (shingles). Nearly all humans in resource-rich countries are infected during childhood, but there are many areas of the world where the incidence of chickenpox in children is low, e.g. Africa and the Caribbean islands. The vesicles are an important source of varicella in the community (see Ch. 16).

Varicella is characterized by crops of vesicles that develop into pustules and then scab over

After primary infection, the virus passes across surface epithelium in the respiratory tract to infect mononuclear cells, and is then carried to lymphoid tissues. There are no symptoms and no detectable lesions at the site of entry into the body. The virus slowly replicates in lymphoreticular tissues for about 1 week, and then enters the blood in association with mononuclear cells and is seeded out to epithelial sites. These are mainly the respiratory tract and the skin, but also include the mouth, often the conjunctiva, and probably also the alimentary and urogenital tracts. In the skin, for unknown reasons, the trunk, face and scalp are especially involved. At these epithelial sites, the virus exits from small blood vessels, infecting subepithelial and finally epithelial cells. Multinucleated giant cells with intranuclear inclusions are present in the lesions. In the oropharynx and respiratory tract, the virus reaches the surface and is shed to the exterior

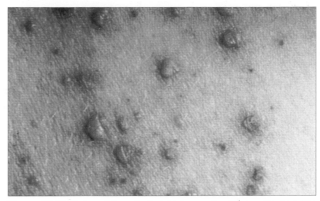

Figure 26.42 Early rash in varicella (chickenpox), with macules, papules and vesicles. (Courtesy of M.J. Wood.)

to infect other individuals about 2 weeks after initial infection. In the skin, it takes a day or two longer, and it is at this stage, when the characteristic varicella vesicles appear in a centripetal distribution, that a clinical diagnosis can be made (Fig. 26.42) The mean incubation period is 14 days (range 10–23 days).

The patient remains well until a day or two before the rash, when there may be slight fever and malaise, but the illness is usually mild and often unnoticed. The vesicles appear first on the trunk, then on the face and scalp, and less commonly, on the arms and legs. They often come in 'crops' over the course of several days and all stages of lesions occur simultaneously, then develop into pustules, break down, and scab over. The lesions are deeper than with HSV, and scarring is more common. Lesions in the mouth may be painful.

Varicella is usually more severe and more likely to cause complications in adults

The skin lesions of varicella can become infected with staphylococci or streptococci to produce secondary impetigo, but varicella in a child is characteristically a very mild illness. The main complications are:

- interstitial pneumonia, which can be detected radiologically, although it is often subclinical, in up to 20% of adults with varicella; secondary bacterial pneumonia can also occur
- CNS involvement, which may consist of a lymphocytic meningitis or an encephalomyelitis (see Ch. 24).

Thrombocytopenia can occur, but it is usually symptomless. In immunocompromised patients, particularly children with leukaemia, varicella can be a life-threatening disease.

After primary infection during pregnancy the virus may infect the fetus (see Ch. 23), but maternal antibody is present by then and the infection is generally without serious consequences. Congenital varicella syndrome is seen in up to 1–2% if maternal infection occurs in the first or second trimester. Clinical features include skin scarring, hypoplastic limbs, and other stigmata involve the eyes and brain. When the mother is infected a few days before or after delivery, the infant is exposed without the protection of maternal antibody and can suffer a serious disease. Passive immunization with varicella-zoster immune globulin (VZIG) may prevent or attenuate the infection in the infant.

Zoster results from reactivation of latent VZV

During primary infection, VZV in mucocutaneous lesions enters sensory nerve endings and establishes latent infection in sensory neurones in dorsal root ganglia (see Fig. 26.39). Later in life, reactivation can occur to cause zoster in the dermatome, the area of skin supplied by that nerve, at the site of the reactivation. Thoracic dermatomes are most commonly affected because these are the most common sites for the original varicella lesions. Zoster is unilateral because the reactivation is a localized event in a single dorsal root ganglion. Zoster therefore originates from inside the body and is not directly acquired from either varicella or zoster in other individuals. During reactivation in sensory neurones (see Fig. 26.39), there is paraesthesia and pain. Pain may be severe and precedes the development of the erythematous rash in which virus-rich vesicles appear (Fig. 26.43) by several days. It takes a few days for the virus to travel down peripheral nerves and multiply in the skin. Fever and malaise may accompany the rash. Sometimes, the immune response controls the reactivating virus before skin lesions have had time to form, and in this case, the sensory phenomena occur without the skin eruption.

Conditions that predispose to zoster include:

- Increasing age. Although zoster is very occasionally seen in childhood, its incidence increases with increasing age, rising from 3/1000 per year in 50–59-year-olds to 10/1000 per year in 80–89-year-olds.
- Immunocompromise due to leukaemia, lymphoma, AIDS, solid organ transplant or other drug-induced immunosuppression.
- Trauma or tumours affecting the brain or spinal cord.

The skin areas affected by zoster reflect the distribution of the original varicella rash, as might be expected from its pathogenesis (see Fig. 26.39). Hence, the trunk is most commonly involved. Ophthalmic zoster involving the upper eyelid, forehead and scalp is a particularly unpleasant manifestation, which can be sight-threatening.

Postherpetic neuralgia is a common complication of zoster

In the healthy host, postherpetic neuralgia (also known as zoster-associated pain, ZAP) is common, especially in the elderly. The pain, which can be severe early in the illness, continues for up to several months after the lesions have resolved. It is difficult to treat, although antiviral agents reduce the incidence, duration and severity of ZAP if started as soon as possible after zoster occurs.

Zoster may be severe in immunocompromised patients. A few days after the localized eruption, the virus, with inadequate control by cell-mediated immunity, spreads via the blood to produce skin and visceral lesions throughout the body. Haemorrhagic complications and pneumonia may occur.

Laboratory diagnosis of VZV

It is a clinical diagnosis that can be assisted by carrying out molecular tests to detect VZV DNA in swabs from the vesicles or alternative tests less widely used including immunofluorescence tests on skin lesion scrapings using VZV-specific monoclonal antibodies or by isolating VZV in cell culture, although the cytopathic effect may take a couple of weeks. Herpesvirus particles can be seen by electron microscopy in vesicle fluid, but are indistinguishable from other herpesviruses, and in particular HSV, which also causes vesicular lesions. Past infection is determined by detecting VZV IgG by enzyme-linked immunosorbent assay (ELISA) or other methods. A VZV IgM result may be helpful if the skin lesions have healed and the diagnosis needs to be made for clinical reasons.

Treatment of varicella and zoster infection

Varicella-zoster virus is much less sensitive than HSV to acyclovir, but this drug, or the more readily bioavailable valaciclovir or famciclovir, can be used orally to treat varicella and zoster. Treatment is often not considered, as chickenpox is thought of as a mild infection that causes little discomfort. However, varicella can cause complications in adolescents and adults, and antiviral treatment should be offered, especially as new lesion formation, viral shedding and symptoms will be reduced. Severe infections must be treated with intravenous acyclovir, especially in high-risk groups. VZIG contains a high titre of human antibody to the virus, and is used to prevent varicella in susceptible individuals at risk of complications (e.g. immunocompromised patients) after exposure. Varicella skin lesions may be treated with calamine lotion to relieve itching and to prevent scratching and secondary infection.

A live attenuated vaccine is licensed in a number of countries, and universal childhood immunization was started in the USA in 1995.

Rashes caused by coxsackieviruses and echoviruses

Coxsackieviruses and echoviruses cause a variety of exanthems (skin rashes)

Sometimes, such infections are accompanied by an enanthem (lesions on internal epithelial surfaces such as the

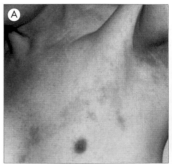
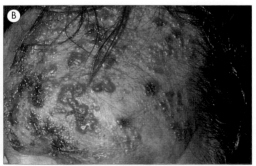

Figure 26.43 Zoster rash. (A) A band of faint erythema, an early sign of shingles, along an intercostal nerve. (B) Rash affecting the ophthalmic division of the trigeminal nerve. (Courtesy of M.J. Wood.)

oral cavity). These infections are generally seen in young children, are not usually distinguishable on clinical examination, and are not severe. These viruses are also responsible for illnesses affecting the CNS (see Ch. 24), the upper respiratory tract (see Ch. 18), and striated and heart muscle (see below).

Coxsackievirus A lesions are usually vesicular and occur mostly on the buccal mucosa and the tongue. Most children complain of a sore mouth or tongue and there is slight fever. When vesicular lesions are also seen on the skin, principally on the hands and feet, the condition is called 'hand, foot and mouth disease' (Fig. 26.44). The virus is present in the lesions, and coxsackievirus A16 is the most common cause.

Maculopapular rashes resembling rubella and often occurring in the summer are common manifestations of some coxsackie A and echovirus infections.

Rashes caused by human parvovirus B19

Parvovirus B19 causes slapped cheek syndrome

Parvoviruses are very small (22 nm in diameter) single-stranded DNA viruses. The defective parvoviruses require a helper (adeno-) virus to replicate, and are called 'adeno-associated viruses'; there are four serotypes and infection is common, but they have not been implicated in any human disease. However, parvovirus B19 grows in mitotically active cells and causes a febrile illness in children with a characteristic maculopapular rash on the face ('slapped cheek syndrome'). The condition is referred to as 'erythema infectiosum' and sometimes 'fifth disease', it being the fifth of the six common exanthematous infections recognized by nineteenth-century physicians.

Symptomless parvovirus B19 infection is common and spreads by respiratory droplets

Nearly 50% of the population has had parvovirus B19 in the past. The virus grows in haemopoietic cells in the bone marrow, and although this normally causes no more than a temporary and barely detectable fall in haemoglobin levels, it can lead to serious consequences in those with chronic anaemia. In children with sickle cell anaemia, for instance, the effect on erythropoiesis may cause an aplastic crisis. The virus can also cause arthralgia when it infects adults. Laboratory diagnosis is made by testing sera for parvovirus B19-specific IgM. Molecular tests may be used to detect B19 DNA in fetal blood when hydrops fetalis is suspected. Parvovirus B19 cannot be isolated in cell culture.

Rashes caused by human herpesviruses 6 and 7 (HHV-6 and -7)

Human herpesviruses-6 is present in the saliva of over 85% of adults and causes roseola infantum

Human herpesviruses-6 and -7 were discovered in 1986 and 1990, respectively, the preceding five HHVs being HSV-1, HSV-2, VZV, CMV and EBV. Both infections are prevalent globally and occur in most of the population in the first 2 years of life. HHV-6 replicates in T and B cells and also in the oropharynx, from where it is shed into saliva. The virus persists in the body after initial infection. There are two HHV-6 variants, namely HHV-6A and 6B. Their tissue distribution differs in that HHV-6B can be detected in blood, saliva and in brain tissue whereas 6A occurs more often in the lungs and skin.

HHV-6B is the cause of exanthem subitum (also called *roseola infantum*), a very common acute febrile illness in infants and young children. After an incubation period of about 2 weeks, children develop a high fever which lasts for 3–5 days. The disease is mild, and within 2 days of the fever subsiding a maculopapular rash is seen (Fig. 26.45). HHV-6B is also associated with about 30% of febrile fits in children and HHV-6 encephalitis has been reported in bone marrow transplant recipients.

Human herpesviruses -7 is acquired slightly later in early childhood

Human herpesviruses-7 has been isolated from CD4-positive T cells. Infection occurs later than HHV-6 during infancy and early childhood. Persistence in the saliva and exanthem subitum have been reported with HHV-7.

Human herpesviruses-8 is associated with all forms of Kaposi's sarcoma skin lesions

After a number of epidemiologic reports, it had been thought that a transmissible agent was involved in the development of Kaposi's sarcoma (KS), a skin malignancy more common in some Mediterranean areas and parts of Africa in addition to AIDS-associated KS. A number of molecular technology developments allowed the identification of KS-associated

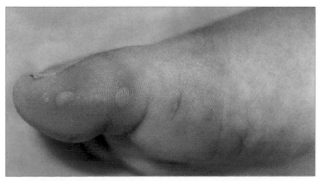

Figure 26.44 Vesicular lesions on the foot in hand, foot and mouth disease. (Courtesy of M.J. Wood.)

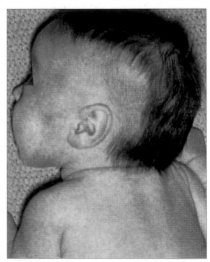

Figure 26.45 Maculopapular rash in roseola infantum. (Courtesy of M.J. Wood.)

herpesvirus (KSHV), also known as HHV-8, in 1994 in the endothelial cells of KS lesions. It is not a ubiquitous infection and has also been associated with two other rare malignancies, primary effusion lymphoma and multicentric Castleman's disease. Transmission is mostly via saliva, and interactions between defective cellular immune responses, the endothelial system and KSHV result in the pathogenesis of KS.

It is a clinical diagnosis. The incidence of AIDS-associated KS has dropped since the advent of highly active antiretroviral therapy. In addition, retrospective studies have shown that ganciclovir and foscarnet treatment has resulted in a reduction of KS lesions.

SMALLPOX

Smallpox (variola) was a major scourge of humankind for at least 3000 years. It was caused by a poxvirus and spread from person to person by contact with skin lesions and via the respiratory tract. The disease was severe, with a generalized rash (Fig. 26.46), and was fatal in up to 40% of cases, depending upon the strain of virus.

Global smallpox eradication was officially certified in December 1979

During the first part of the twentieth century, smallpox was largely eradicated from Oceania, North America and Europe by widespread vaccination, as originally developed by Edward Jenner (see Ch. 34), using a live

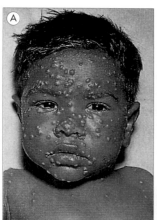
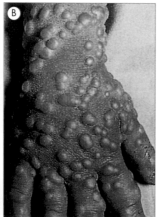
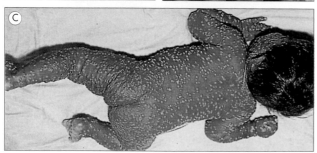

Figure 26.46 Smallpox. A–C These pictures were used as smallpox recognition cards by the World Health Organization during its smallpox eradication campaign. After upper respiratory tract infection, the virus reached the skin, where it replicated to cause a widespread vesiculopustular rash, with later scarring, especially on the face. The fatality rate was up to 40%, depending on the age of the host and the strain of the virus. (Courtesy of the World Health Organization.)

attenuated strain of virus (vaccinia virus), together with strict controls at frontiers. In 1967, the WHO started a campaign to eradicate smallpox from the world, focusing on South America, Africa, India and Indonesia, making use of vaccination, surveillance and containment of cases. Despite such daunting difficulties as cultural barriers, warfare and transport to remote areas, the campaign was successful. Occasional cases had continued to occur in the USA until the 1940s, and in 1974, there were 218 000 cases worldwide, mostly in Asia, but the last case was recorded in Somalia in October 1977. The total cost to the WHO was about US$150 million.

Global eradication of smallpox was possible for a variety of reasons

These reasons are as follows:

- There were no subclinical infections, so cases could be readily identified.
- The virus was eliminated from the body on recovery, with no carriers.
- Humans were the only host (no animal reservoir).
- An effective vaccine was available.

For a few years there were concerns about monkeypox, a simian disease caused by a similar virus and acquired by contact with infected monkeys in Africa. It is, however, poorly transmitted from human to human. However, over 80 people were believed to have contracted monkeypox in the USA in 2003. This was thought to be due to contact with infected prairie dogs. Concerns about the use of smallpox by bioterrorists have resulted in countries making contingency plans for the potential threat, which include the stockpiling of smallpox vaccine.

MEASLES

Measles has several special features, as follows:

- Nearly all infected individuals become unwell and develop disease. This is in contrast to most other viral infections, in which a significant proportion of individuals undergo an asymptomatic or subclinical infection.
- The disease is so characteristic that a clinical diagnosis can nearly always be made without the need for laboratory help. We can recognize measles as described 1000 years ago by the Arabian physician, Rhazes.
- There is only one antigenic type of measles virus.
- After infection, there is complete resistance to reinfection, which is probably lifelong. Second attacks are almost unknown.
- Measles is highly infectious, and nearly all susceptible children contract the disease on exposure. Until recently, measles was regarded as a routine inescapable part of childhood, and more than 99% of individuals were infected until immunization programmes were developed.
- There is a striking contrast between measles in wellnourished children with good access to medical care (i.e. in resource-rich countries) and measles under conditions of malnutrition or starvation or with poor medical services (i.e. resource-poor countries, Table 26.4).

Table 26.4 The clinical impact of measles depends upon the host

Site of virus growth	Well-nourished child; good medical care	Malnourished child; poor medical care
Lung	Temporary respiratory illness	Life-threatening pneumonia
Ear	Otitis media quite common	Otitis media more common, more severe
Oral mucosa	Koplik's spots	Severe ulcerating lesions
Conjunctiva	Conjunctivitis	Severe corneal lesions, secondary bacterial infection, blindness may result
Skin	Maculopapular rash	Haemorrhagic rashes may occur ('black measles')
Intestinal tract	No lesions	Diarrhea – exacerbates malnutrition, halts growth, impairs recovery
Urinary tract	Virus detectable in urine	No known complications
Overall impact	Serious disease in a small proportion of those infected	Major cause of death in childhood (estimated 1 million deaths/year worldwide)

Measles is a much more serious disease in malnourished children with poor access to medical care. The same epithelial surfaces are infected more extensively and with more serious sequelae.

Aetiology and transmission

Measles outbreaks occur every few years in unvaccinated populations

The basic virology of this paramyxovirus is described in Chapter 3 and it is transmitted by respiratory droplets. Although the virus is soon inactivated as it dries on surfaces, it is more stable in droplets suspended in the air. In unvaccinated populations, outbreaks tend to occur every few years when the number of susceptible children reaches a high enough level. There were a number of measles outbreaks in Europe in 2011, some of which were large, including more than 7000 cases in France, that resulted in further immunization campaigns in a number of countries.

Clinical features of measles include respiratory symptoms, Koplik's spots and a rash

The inhaled virus enters the body at unknown sites in the upper or lower respiratory tract or conjunctiva and spreads to subepithelial and local lymphatic tissues, without causing detectable lesions or symptoms. During the next few days, there is a primary viraemia and the virus slowly spreads and multiplies in lymphoid tissues elsewhere in the body, including the spleen and the respiratory tract. There is then a secondary viraemia around 5 days after the initial infection and the virus disseminates to a variety of epithelial sites including the skin, kidney, and bladder. Clinical signs soon appear in the respiratory tract where there are only one or two layers of epithelial cells to traverse. The patient is well until 9–10 days after infection and then develops an acute respiratory illness with a runny nose, fever and cough. Conjunctivitis is also a feature, and as a result of the large amounts of virus being shed in respiratory secretions, the patient is highly infectious. The diagnosis may be suspected during this prodromal illness, especially after known exposure to measles. It takes a day or two longer for the foci of infection at mucosal and skin surfaces to cause lesions. Koplik's spots, pathognomonic of measles, appear inside the cheek (Fig. 26.47), and shortly afterwards the maculopapular rash (Fig. 26.48) is seen, first on the face, then spreading down the body to the extremities.

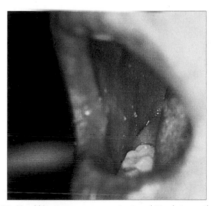

Figure 26.47 Koplik's spots seen as minute white dots on the inflamed buccal mucosa of a patient with measles. (Courtesy of M.J. Wood.)

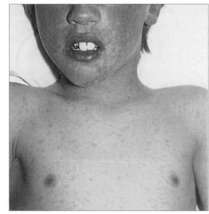

Figure 26.48 Maculopapular rash on the face and trunk of a patient with measles. (Courtesy of M.J. Wood.)

Measles rash results from a cell-mediated immune response

Antibodies are formed, but a cell-mediated immune (CMI) response is needed to control the virus in the lungs and elsewhere. Without it, the virus continues to multiply and gives rise to giant cell pneumonia (see Ch. 19). The CMI response is also responsible for the skin lesions, which are not seen in patients with serious defects in this type of immunity.

Children with agammaglobulinaemia, on the other hand, have a normal course of disease, develop normal immunity, and can be protected by vaccination. In uncomplicated cases, recovery is rapid.

During measles, as in a variety of other acute infections, there are temporary defects in immune responses to unrelated antigens. For instance, at about the time the rash appears, individuals who are known to be tuberculin-positive give negative skin test responses to tuberculin. This returns to normal in about 1 month. During the 'virgin-soil' epidemic, when measles reappeared after a long absence in Southern Greenland, in 1953, and adults as well as children were infected, there was increased mortality in those previously infected with tuberculosis.

Complications of measles are particularly likely among children in resource-poor countries

Complications of measles include:

- opportunistic bacterial superinfections, which are quite common, especially otitis media and pneumonia, as a result of virus damage to respiratory surfaces
- a primary measles virus pneumonia (giant cell pneumonia), which is seen in patients with serious CMI response defects
- encephalitis, which occurs in about 1 in 1000 cases (see Ch. 24)
- very rarely, subacute sclerosing panencephalitis (SSPE). This develops 1–10 years after apparent recovery from acute infection.

Children in countries where there is poor medical care and malnutrition develop a more serious disease (see Table 26.4), especially during famine. This is attributable to:

- poor local mucosal defences, which can be improved by vitamin A administration
- impaired immune defences due to protein–calorie malnutrition, with the added impact of measles virus-induced immunosuppression
- poor medical services, with less ready availability of antibiotics to control secondary infection
- high levels of bacterial contamination of the environment
- exposure to a larger virus dose – a possible factor if others with severe measles shed larger amounts of virus from the respiratory tract.

Diagnosis, treatment and prevention

Measles is usually diagnosed clinically; ribavirin can be used as antiviral treatment if clinically indicated and there is a safe and effective vaccine

Although the clinical diagnosis should be clear, the rash is similar to a number of other viral exanthems which affect the same age group. In addition, with the success of the vaccine, the incidence of measles infection has fallen and it is less likely that healthcare workers will see children with measles in resource-rich countries. Therefore, the measles virus RNA or IgM assay is helpful in confirming the diagnosis either on blood or saliva samples. Virus isolation in cell culture is rarely necessary. Complicated measles infection can be treated with ribavirin.

A live attenuated vaccine has been available since 1963. It is effective, safe and long-lasting, and is combined with mumps and rubella vaccines (MMR vaccine; see Ch. 34). Before a vaccine became available, measles killed 7–8 million children each year worldwide. By 1996, this was reduced to 1 million, and the WHO/UNICEF initiatives included applying the mass immunization programmes used in the Americas and Europe to resource-poor countries.

RUBELLA

Rubella virus infection causes a multisystem infection, but its main impact is on the fetus

There is only one serotype of this single-stranded RNA toga-virus, and its principal impact is on the fetus (see Ch. 23). It is transmitted by droplet infection, and is less contagious than measles, but more so than mumps.

After entering the body via the upper respiratory tract, the virus replicates for a period in local lymphoid tissues, followed by spread to the spleen and to lymph nodes elsewhere in the body. One week after infection further multiplication in these tissues leads to viraemia and localization of virus in the respiratory tract and skin, and sometimes the placenta, joints and kidney. The pathogenesis of rubella is outlined in Figure 26.49, and the clinical consequences of infection in various tissues of the body are shown in Table 26.5.

After an incubation period of 14–21 days, there is a mild disease, with fever, malaise and an irregular maculopapular

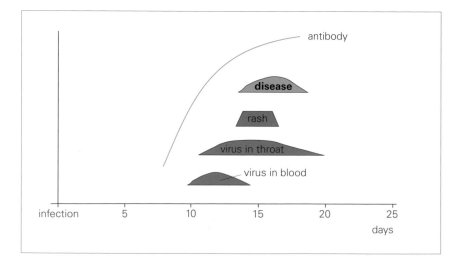

Figure 26.49 The pathogenesis of rubella. Rubella is generally a very mild, often subclinical infection, but it can cause arthritis and has a major impact when it infects the fetus.

Table 26.5 Clinical consequences of rubella virus invasion of different body tissues

Site of virus growth	Result	Comment
Respiratory tract	Virus shedding but symptoms minimal (mild sore throat, coryza, cough)	Patient infectious 5 days before to 3 days after symptoms
Skin	Rash	Often fleeting, atypical; immunopathology involved (Ag-Ab complexes)
Lymph nodes	Lymphadenopathy	More common in posterior triangle of neck or behind ear
Joints	Mild arthralgia, arthritis	Immunopathology involved (circulating immune complexes)
Placenta/fetus	Placentitis, fetal damage	Congenital rubella

rash lasting 3 days. Enlarged lymph nodes are often evident behind the ear, but the infection is commonly subclinical.

Rubella is diagnosed serologically; there is no treatment, but there is a vaccine

Clinical diagnosis of rubella is sometimes possible but should be confirmed in the laboratory. Laboratory diagnosis is made by demonstrating rubella-specific IgM antibodies (see Ch. 32). Virus isolation from the throat is rarely indicated – virus isolation requires specialized cell lines, and indirect methods are needed to demonstrate its growth. Viral RNA can be detected in samples from different sites.

There is no antiviral treatment. A live attenuated rubella vaccine that is safe and effective is given by injection, generally in combination with measles and mumps vaccines (MMR vaccine). Prevention of congenital rubella is referred to in Chapter 23.

The maculopapular rashes seen in certain arthropod-borne virus infections (e.g. dengue) and in zoonotic virus infections (e.g. Marburg disease) are referred to in Chapters 27 and 28. A maculopapular rash may be seen in the prodromal stage of hepatitis B virus infection (see Ch. 22) and is immune complex mediated.

OTHER INFECTIONS PRODUCING SKIN LESIONS

Other bacterial, fungal and rickettsial infections produce a variety of rashes or other skin lesions

Most of these are referred to elsewhere in this book, and they are listed in Table 26.1. Rashes in rickettsial infections are often striking, as in the case of Rocky Mountain spotted fever or typhus (see Ch. 27). Most rickettsia invade vascular endothelial cells and are shed into the blood to infect blood-sucking arthropod vectors. Invasion of vascular endothelial cells in the skin provides the basis for the skin rash but is not a source of direct shedding to the exterior.

KAWASAKI SYNDROME

Kawasaki syndrome is an acute vasculitis and is probably caused by superantigen toxins

The Kawasaki syndrome is a childhood illness that occurs in genetically susceptible hosts with dysregulated T-cell activation after exposure to infectious triggers. Patients, who are generally under 4 years of age, develop fever, conjunctivitis and a rash. There is dryness and redness of the lips and red palms and soles with some oedema, desquamation of fingertips, often arthralgia and myocarditis, which gives a case mortality of about 2%. The basic pathology is an acute multisystemic vasculitis, and 20% of untreated patients develop coronary artery aneurysms. The disease is more common in those of Asian ethnicity, but occurs worldwide. There is no clear evidence for person-to-person transmission and the disease is endemic with seasonal fluctuations and outbreaks. It is thought to be of infectious origin, and the mechanism of immune activation may be due to either an antigen or superantigen such as the toxins (see Ch. 16) of *Staph. aureus* or *Strep. pyogenes*. A superantigen is a group of proteins that can stimulate many T cells by attaching to part of the T-cell receptor in association with the MHC class II molecules without needing antigen processing.

Treatment, with intravenous immunoglobulin and aspirin reduces the incidence of coronary artery damage and prevents the aneurysms if given early enough.

VIRAL INFECTIONS OF MUSCLE

Viral myositis, myocarditis and pericarditis

Some viruses, particularly coxsackievirus B, cause myocarditis and myalgia

A cytotoxic effect is seen in animal models after viral attachment to the cellular receptors found in cardiac myocytes and macrophages. Group B, and to a lesser extent group A, coxsackieviruses and certain enteroviruses are the main viral causes of acute myocarditis and pericarditis. There is a slight male predominance in myocarditis and both myocarditis and pericarditis can be mistaken for myocardial infarction, yet the prognosis is good and complete recovery is the rule. There is also evidence for persistent infection linked with chronic myocarditis and chronic dilated cardiomyopathy. The most common cause of viral myocarditis in infants is the coxsackievirus B group, and it may be rapid in onset and fatal. These infections are transmitted by the faecal–oral route and occasionally from pharyngeal secretions. Ingested coxsackieviruses spread from the pharynx or gastrointestinal mucosa to the lymphatics and then to the blood. Invasion of striated muscles, heart or pericardium takes place across small blood vessels and results in acute inflammation. In the heart and pericardium, this gives rise to dyspnoea, pain in the chest, and sometimes mimics a myocardial infarction.

Coxsackievirus may be isolated from throat swabs, faecal specimens or occasionally pericardial fluid. Alternatively, viral RNA detection methods may be used, for example in-situ hybridization on endomyocardial biopsy tissue. Mumps and influenza are less common causes of myocarditis or pericarditis. Rubella (see Ch. 23) can cause myocarditis and associated congenital lesions in the fetus.

Group B coxsackieviruses also cause pleurodynia or epidemic myalgia. This condition is sometimes called 'Bornholm disease', after the Danish island where there was an extensive outbreak in 1930. There is pain and inflammation involving intercostal or abdominal muscles.

Influenza (especially influenza B in children) can cause pain and tenderness in muscles, but it is not known whether this is associated with viral invasion of muscle. Myalgias are also seen in dengue and in rickettsial and other febrile infections and are probably caused by circulating cytokines.

Laboratory diagnosis in these settings can be difficult, as serology and virus isolation can only give circumstantial evidence for association between that virus infection and a specific organ. Direct detection methods in affected tissue may be more helpful.

The antiviral drug pleconaril has been used to treat enterovirus infections. However, it is no longer in production. There are no specific vaccines for coxsackievirus infections. The mainstay of treatment involves medical management of acute heart failure. This can involve mechanical circulatory support and extracorporeal membrane oxygenation (ECMO) in some clinical situations.

Postviral fatigue syndrome

It has been difficult to establish postviral fatigue syndrome as a clinical entity

The postviral fatigue syndrome or chronic fatigue syndrome is sometimes referred to as myalgic encephalomyelitis, but this is inappropriate because there is no evidence for CNS pathology. It consists of:

- chronic and severe muscle weakness, lasting at least 6 months, often as a sequel to an acute febrile illness
- severe tiredness
- less regularly associated symptoms such as depression, headache and anxiety.

It is more reliably identified when the first two symptoms appear in a previously healthy individual with no history of psychosomatic illness. Several viruses have been suggested as causes. There have been repeated claims for the role of coxsackie B viruses, based on antibody tests and on the detection of a virus-specific protein in the serum of patients, but these results have not been widely confirmed, and the picture remains unclear. A small proportion of cases appear to be due to chronic infection with Epstein–Barr virus (EBV). Occasional reports have associated the condition with HHV-6 as well as other viruses. It has also been suggested that it is due to 'allergic reactions' triggered by virus infections.

In 2009, a gammaretrovirus called xenotropic murine leukaemia virus (XMRV) was detected in peripheral blood mononuclear cells from nearly 67% of people with chronic fatigue syndrome compared to 4% of healthy controls.

However, the association was not confirmed in other studies and it was thought that the genomic sequences detected were actually part of the enzymes used in the PCR process.

PARASITIC INFECTIONS OF MUSCLE

Relatively few protozoan or helminth parasites invade muscle tissues and cause serious disease. Three of the more common are described here to illustrate the variety of organisms and the range of pathology.

Trypanosoma cruzi infection

Trypanosoma cruzi is a protozoan and causes Chagas disease

Chagas disease is also known as American trypanosomiasis (see Ch. 27). The disease is restricted to Central and South America, where it affects an estimated 10–12 million people. It is a zoonosis, and *Trypanosoma cruzi* has been isolated from more than 150 species of mammal. The parasite is carried by blood-sucking reduviid bugs, which deposit infective trypomastigote stages on to the skin as they defecate while feeding. If these are rubbed into mucous membranes or wounds, the parasites penetrate cells, transform into amastigotes and proliferate. The infected cells then burst, liberating trypomastigotes, and a local lesion is formed. The parasite is dispersed around the body to reinvade other cells. Major sites of infection include the CNS, intestinal myenteric plexus, reticuloendothelial system and cardiac muscle.

Chagas disease is complicated by cardiac conduction disorders, ventricular aneurysm formation or heart failure many years later

Chagas disease may be asymptomatic from the outset or occur as an acute febrile phase, with intense inflammatory changes, followed by a chronic phase that may produce no apparent damage (indeterminate phase), or progress to cause damage years later. In the chronic phase, there is gradual tissue destruction with autoimmune damage playing an important role. The parasite invades the myofibrils of the heart (see Fig. 27.15) causing myocarditis, and muscle fibrils and Purkinje fibres may be replaced by fibrous tissue. As a result of the conduction defects this causes, the heart enlarges, there are cardiac arrhythmias, and heart failure can occur.

Benznidazole or nifurtimox are used to treat the acute phase and some cases in the indeterminate or chronic phase. These drugs are available from the World Health Organization. Posaconazole has been used in individual cases. At time of writing, no vaccine is available, and prevention of infection is the most important measure.

Taenia solium infection

The larval stages of *Taenia solium* invade body tissues

Tapeworms are intestinal parasites, but the larval stages of several species may invade deeper tissues. The most important of these are:

- *Echinococcus granulosus* (which causes hydatid disease, see Chs 24 and 28)
- the pork tapeworm *Taenia solium*.

Humans acquire *T. solium* infection by eating under-cooked infected pig meat in which the cysticercus larvae are found as small, bladder-like structures in the muscle tissue. These larvae are digested out in the intestine and mature into the adult tapeworm, which may reach a length of several metres. *T. solium* eggs released in human faeces and ingested by a pig hatch in the pig intestine and release larvae which cross the intestinal wall and are carried via the blood to muscle. *T. solium* is unusual in that its eggs can hatch directly in the human intestine. In areas of poor sanitation, this may result from accidental swallowing of water or food contaminated with eggs. If hatching occurs, larvae can invade and form cysticerci in human muscle or, much more seriously, in the CNS. Cysts in muscle eventually become calcified and can be seen on radiography (Fig. 26.50). Muscle infection is not serious, being largely asymptomatic. Infections are common in many parts of the world, particularly South and Central America and Asia. Avoidance of undercooked pork products is the safest precaution against developing pork tapeworm, whereas good sanitation and good personal hygiene practice are required to avoid ingesting eggs and thus developing cysticercosis.

Trichinella spiralis infection

The larvae of *Trichinella spiralis* invade striated muscle

This nematode has many unique features. It is able to infect almost any warm-blooded animal, and has a life cycle in which a complete generation (infective stage to infective stage) develops within the body of a single host. Transmission depends upon the ingestion of muscle tissue containing viable infective larvae. As far as humans are concerned, the commonest route of transmission is through infected pig meat, but many other meat sources have been known to transmit infection (e.g. bear, boar, horse). Infections occur worldwide. When infected undercooked meat is eaten, the larvae are digested out in the small intestine and develop rapidly into the adult worms. These live in the mucosa, each female releasing about one thousand newborn larvae directly into the intestinal tissues, from where they are carried in blood or lymph around the body. Eventually, the larvae penetrate striated muscles and mature into the infective stage, transforming muscle cells into a parasite-sustaining nurse cell (see Fig. 28.10).

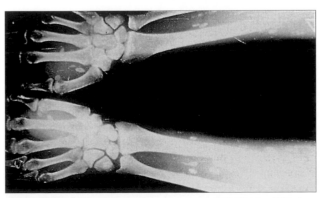

Figure 26.50 Radiograph showing numerous calcified cysts of *Taenia solium* in the forearms. (Courtesy of R. Muller and J.R. Baker.)

Light infections are asymptomatic, but the migration and penetration of the larvae is associated with inflammatory reactions, which can be severe and life-threatening when a person is heavily infected. Various symptoms are associated with this phase, of which fever, muscle pains, weakness and eosinophilia are characteristic. Myocarditis may also occur, although the parasite does not develop in the heart.

Diagnosis by symptoms usually occurs after the parasites have invaded the muscles and treatment then is difficult. Albendazole or mebendazole are used. Adjunctive corticosteroids are given in severely symptomatic cases.

Sarcocystis

Sarcocystis is a rare muscle parasite

The cyst stages of *Sarcocystis*, a protozoan related to *Toxoplasma*, are occasionally reported in human muscles.

JOINT AND BONE INFECTIONS

Joints and bones will be considered separately for convenience, but joint lesions often spread to involve neighbouring bone, and vice versa (e.g. in tuberculosis).

Reactive arthritis, arthralgia and septic arthritis

Arthralgia and arthritis occur in a variety of infections and are often immunologically mediated

Examples of such infections are outlined in Table 26.6. Joints can become infected by the haematogenous route or directly following trauma or surgery, but in many cases the condition is immunologically mediated rather than due to microbial invasion of the joint. The microbe responsible is at a distant site in the body and causes a 'reactive arthritis'. Reactive arthritis and arthralgia occur after certain enteric bacterial infections, and the arthralgia in rubella and hepatitis B infections is of similar origin. In this type of arthritis, more than one joint is usually affected.

Ankylosing spondylitis is associated with *Klebsiella* infection, and it has been suggested that the antigenic similarity between *Klebsiella* and HLA B27 antigens provokes a cross-reactive immune response that causes the disease. So far, there is no evidence that rheumatoid arthritis is caused by either viruses or other microbes.

Circulating bacteria sometimes localize in joints, especially following trauma

Such bacterial localization can then cause a suppurative (septic) arthritis. Generally, a single joint is involved. Joints are very susceptible, particularly if they are already damaged, for instance by rheumatoid arthritis, or if a prosthesis has been inserted. Knees are most commonly affected, followed by hips, ankles (see Fig. 21.5B) and elbows. Signs include a fever, joint pain, limitation of movement and swelling, and usually a joint effusion. Bacteria can be isolated from the joint fluid or seen in the centrifuged deposit, and the commonest organism is *Staph. aureus*. Sometimes the source of the circulating bacteria is obvious (e.g. a septic skin lesion), but often no source is apparent.

Table 26.6 Arthralgia and arthritis in infectious diseases

Infectious agent	Comments
Viral arthritis	
Hepatitis B	Occurs in prodromal period; due to circulating immune complexes
Rubella	Especially in young women, often follows live virus vaccine
Mumps	Unusual; mostly in men
Ross River and other togaviruses	Mosquito-transmitted infections in Australia (Ross River) and Africa
Parvovirus	May follow adult infection
Reactive arthritis	
Campylobacter, Yersinia, salmonellae, shigellae, *Chlamydia trachomatis* (Reiter's syndrome[a])	'Post-infectious' arthritis, HLA B27-associated, no bacterial invasion of joint, immune mediated
Septic arthritis	
Staphylococcus aureus	Commonest cause of suppurative arthritis
Streptococci (Group A and B)	Common in adults and children
Haemophilus influenzae	Occurrence in children has decreased with *H. influenzae* vaccine
Neisseria gonorrhoeae	May affect multiple joints
Mycobacterium tuberculosis	Often with bone lesions, especially weight bearing joints and bones
Borrelia burgdorferi	Arthritis a late feature of Lyme disease
Gram-negative bacilli	Neonates, the elderly, patients with immune deficiency disorders
Sporothrix schenckii	Fungal infection of joints; increased risk with HIV infection

[a]Urethritis, arthritis, uveitis, mucocutaneous lesions; complicates a small percentage of cases of chlamydial urethritis.

Osteomyelitis

Bone can become infected by adjacent infection or haematogenously

As with joints, infection of bones can be by the direct route (e.g. from a nearby focus of infection, after fractures, after orthopaedic surgery) or from circulating microbes. The commonest cause of haematogenous osteomyelitis is *Staph. aureus*, but when infection is from a neighbouring site it is generally mixed, with Gram-negative rods and occasionally anaerobes also present. There seems to be no equivalent to reactive arthritis, in which inflammation is due to infection at a distant site.

Acute osteomyelitis typically involves the growing end of a long bone, where sprouting capillary loops adjacent to epiphyseal growth plates promote the localization of circulating bacteria. It therefore tends to be a disease of children and adolescents, and may follow non-penetrating injury to the bone.

Osteomyelitis results in a painful tender bone lesion and a general febrile illness.

Osteomyelitis is treated with antibiotics and sometimes surgery

The infection is diagnosed from blood cultures taken before the start of antimicrobial therapy or, if there is an open lesion, from a bone biopsy. Periosteal reaction and bone loss may be visible radiologically (Fig. 26.51). Treatment is begun on a 'most likely' basis (e.g. nafcillin for MSSA, see above) as soon as microbiologic samples have been taken.

Osteomyelitis can become chronic, especially when there are necrotic bone fragments to act as a continued source of infection. Surgical intervention for debridement and drainage, as well as prolonged courses of antibiotics, may be necessary.

Tuberculosis may affect the spine, the hip, the knee and the bones of the hands and feet, and in resource-rich countries

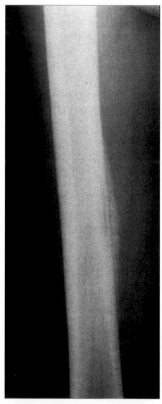

Figure 26.51 Acute staphylococcal osteomyelitis in the femur of a 24-year-old woman. There is a well-defined periosteal reaction in relation to the midshaft of the femur and an underlying lucency. (Courtesy of A.M. Davies.)

is particularly seen in immigrants from the Indian subcontinent. Constitutional disturbances are often absent, but the site is generally painful and pressure from a tuberculous abscess in the spine can cause paraplegia.

INFECTIONS OF THE HAEMOPOIETIC SYSTEM

Many infectious agents cause changes in circulating blood cells

Examples of such agents include:

- *Bordetella pertussis*, which causes lymphocytosis
- EBV and cytomegalovirus infections, which cause mononucleosis
- *Plasmodium* spp. which cause anaemia and thrombocytopenia.

A smaller number of infectious agents act directly on cells in the bone marrow (human parvovirus) or cause malignant transformation of lymphocytes, for example, human T-cell lymphotropic virus (HTLV) type 1. The range of possibilities is summarized in Table 26.7. HTLV-1 and HTLV-2 are mentioned in Chapters 21 and 24, but are described more fully below.

Human T-lymphotropic virus-1 infection

Human T-lymphotropic virus -1 is mainly transmitted by maternal milk

Human T-lymphotropic virus -1 was first isolated in 1980 from a patient with adult T-cell leukaemia (ATLL). Infection is widespread, especially in certain islands in the West Indies and Japan, where 5–15% of the population are infected, and also in South America and parts of Africa. Transmission is primarily via maternal milk, less effectively via sexual intercourse, and by blood-contaminated equipment in injecting drug users.

Human T-lymphotropic virus -1 infects T cells, and up to 5% of those infected develop T-cell leukaemia

Human T-lymphotropic virus-1 infects T cells and persists. The tax gene product, a transcriptional activator protein, stimulates transcription of host genes controlling production of interleukin 2 (IL-2), IL-2 receptor and other molecules, thus affecting cell replication. Infected T cells proliferate, and if in addition there are certain chromosomal abnormalities, malignant transformation takes place.

Clinically, the patient develops a mild febrile disease with lymphadenopathy. The skin is often involved, with nodule and plaque formation, and pleural effusion or aseptic meningitis can occur. There is also increased susceptibility to opportunist infections such as *Pneumocystis jirovecii* and *Strongyloides stercoralis*. Depressed delayed hypersensitivity responses to tuberculin are associated. Polymyositis has been described. Up to 5% of infected individuals eventually develop T-cell leukaemia, which has a high and rapid mortality rate, and a similar proportion progress to 'tropical' spastic paraparesis (TSP), also known as HTLV-associated myelopathy (HAM), in which there is primary demyelination (see Ch. 24). Neural cells do not appear to be infected, and it is not known how the virus causes a neurologic disease.

Detection of HTLV-1 and HTLV-2-specific antibody is based on serological methods with type differentiation by immunoblot. Antiretroviral agents other than protease inhibitors have been shown to inhibit viral replication and are under investigation as part of the management of individuals with ATLL or TSP. Other treatments have been examined with limited success. HTLV infection can be transmitted by

Table 26.7 Examples of microbes affecting blood cells or haemopoiesis

Microbe	Disease	Effect	Mechanism
Plasmodium spp. *Babesia* spp.	Malaria Babesiosis (uncommon, tick-borne)	Anaemia	Replication in erythrocytes
Bartonella bacilliformis	Oroya fever[a] (rare, sandfly transmitted, occurs in Peru)		
Ehrlichia spp. (*Rickettsiae*)	Human ehrlichiosis (tick transmitted in Southern USA and Japan)	Leucopenia, thrombocytopenia	Replication in leukocytes
Human parvovirus	Erythema infectiosum	Temporary fall in haemoglobin levels Aplastic crisis (individual with chronic anaemia)	Replication in erythropoietic cells
Colorado tick fever virus	Colorado tick fever	No effect on survival of infected erythrocytes	
Human T-cell lymphotropic virus HTLV-1, HTLV-2	T-cell leukaemia, lymphoma	Malignant transformation of infected T cells	Replication in T cells
HIV[b]	AIDS	Immunosuppression	Infection of CD4-positive T cells
Epstein–Barr virus (EBV)	Infectious mononucleosis	Thrombocytopenia, anaemia	Autoantibody to platelets, erythrocytes
Cytomegalovirus (CMV)	Congenital CMV complication of adult infection	Anaemia, thrombocytopenia	Infection of, or autoantibody to, erythrocytes, platelets

[a] A cutaneous form (Verrugas) also occurs; in 1885 a Peruvian medical student, Daniel Carrion, demonstrated the common bacterial origin by inoculating himself with infected blood from the cutaneous form of the disease and developing Oroya fever. [b] Many other viruses infect immune cells and depress immune responses less dramatically (e.g. CMV, measles).

HTLV antibody-positive individuals and they should not donate blood or organs. HTLV antibody screening of blood donors is now included in many countries.

Human T-lymphotropic virus-2 infection

Human T-lymphotropic virus-2 was first isolated in 1982 from a patient with T-cell hairy leukaemia, although it is not the usual cause of this condition. HTLV-2 is closely related to HTLV-1, is transmitted by similar routes and has been reported in injecting drug users and native Amerindian tribes in North, Central and South America. It has been associated with a number of neurological conditions including occasional reports of myelopathy.

KEY FACTS

- The intact skin is an invaluable barrier that defends the body against invasion.

- A wide range of organisms is associated with skin infection and disease.

- Bacteria, fungi and viruses usually gain access through breaches of the barrier caused by trauma.

- Some parasites initiate their own penetration into the skin (hookworm, schistosomes).

- Other microbes are introduced into the skin by arthropod vectors.

- Once in the skin, microbes cause local infections or disseminate through the body to distant sites.

- Pathogens may be acquired by other routes, disseminate in the body and then localize in the skin or cause toxic or immunopathologic manifestations in the skin.

- Superficial infections of the skin are among the commonest human infections (boils, impetigo, warts, acne, ringworm).

- Invasion of pathogens deeper into dermal and subdermal tissues may produce severe infections that can be rapidly fatal, as in gangrene, or slow but progressive deformation and destruction, as in leprosy.

- Infections of muscle usually arise from invasion from the outside, whereas infections of joints are more often blood-borne.

- Bone infections may arise either by local spread from an infected joint or as a result of haematogenous seeding.

- Bone marrow cells or leukocytes may be invaded by viruses that interfere with haemopoiesis (parvovirus), cause malignant transformation (HTLV-1), or interfere with the immune system (EBV, HIV).

Vector-borne infections

Introduction

A number of important human diseases, caused by organisms ranging from viruses to worms, are transmitted by blood-feeding arthropods. These vectors inject the organisms into humans as they take a blood meal. Two classes of arthropods make the major contribution to disease transmission, the six-legged insects and the eight-legged ticks and mites. Arthropod-transmitted infections are commonest in warmer countries, but occur worldwide. Of these, malaria is undoubtedly the most important. This chapter will also cover schistosomiasis, a major tropical disease, which is often described as vector-transmitted, but the aquatic snail 'vectors' are more accurately referred to as intermediate hosts.

Transmission of disease by vectors

In sparsely populated areas, transmission by insects is an effective means of spread

Disease transmission by insects has major implications for the host, the vector and the parasite. To consider the parasite first, it requires the organism to be present in the right place (in the blood) and at the right time (some insects, for example, bite only at night). Blood is an inhospitable environment, and this may require quite subtle evasion mechanisms for parasite survival. In addition, the conditions found in the vector are likely to be very different from those in the human host, and the parasite may have to make a remarkably complex transition in a short time. With the larger protozoal and helminth parasites, this transition often involves clearly visible changes in appearance and is responsible for much of the complicated nomenclature of parasite life cycles. Since some insect vectors have lifespans hardly longer than those of their parasites, there is considerable wastage due to death of the vector before the parasite has matured to the infective stage for humans. A difference of a few days in a mosquito's lifespan can make an enormous difference to the effectiveness of malaria transmission, and indeed this simple factor is believed to underlie much of the difference between the African pattern of endemic infection and the Indian pattern of sporadic epidemics. However, what may be lost from wastage is more than compensated for by the increased distances over which spread of the parasite can occur.

Vector transmission of disease means that the disease may be controlled by controlling the vector and is, for instance, a major reason why malaria is not endemic in many European countries, where it used to be common.

A potential advantage of this type of transmission for the host is that it is sometimes possible to immunize specifically against the stages infective to humans or those responsible for infecting the vector transmission stages of the parasite. Again, malaria can serve as an example – vaccines against the sporozoites, gametocytes and gametes having been clearly shown to block transmission in animal models. Once transmission is blocked, there is a mathematically calculable possibility that the disease will die out. A vaccine against sporozoites has shown promising activity in protecting African children from *falciparum* malaria.

ARBOVIRUS INFECTIONS

Arboviruses are arthropod-borne viruses

A wide range of about 500 different viruses is transmitted by arthropods such as ticks, mosquitoes and sandflies. These arboviruses multiply in the arthropod vector, and for each virus there is a natural cycle involving vertebrates (various birds or mammals) and arthropods. The virus enters the arthropod when the latter takes a blood meal from the infected vertebrate, and passes through the gut wall to reach the salivary gland where replication takes place. Once this has occurred, 1–2 weeks after ingesting the virus, the arthropod becomes infectious, and can transmit the virus to another vertebrate during a blood meal. Certain arboviruses that infect ticks are also transmitted directly from adult tick to egg (transovarial transmission), so that future generations of ticks are infected without the need for a vertebrate host.

Only a small number of arboviruses are important causes of human disease

Arboviruses tend to replicate in vascular endothelium, the central nervous system (CNS), skin and muscle, and are therefore multisystem infections. They are generally named after the clinical disease (e.g. yellow fever) or the place where they were first discovered (e.g. Rift Valley fever, Japanese encephalitis). A few (e.g. Ross River virus in Australia and the Pacific and Chikungunya virus in Africa and Asia) cause arthritis.

The human stage of the virus cycle may be essential (urban yellow fever, dengue), there being no other vertebrate host, or it may be 'accidental' from the virus's point of view, with humans acting as 'dead end' hosts who do not form a necessary part of the natural cycle (e.g. equine encephalitides, West Nile virus).

Yellow fever

Yellow fever virus is transmitted by mosquitoes and is restricted to Africa, Central and South America and the Caribbean

Yellow fever virus is a flavivirus, and there is only one antigenic type. It was taken to the Americas by the early slave traders, and the first recorded case was in Yucatan in 1640. Yellow fever virus is transmitted by two different cycles:

- from human to human by the mosquito *Aedes aegypti*; which is well-adapted to breeding around human habitations; the infection can be maintained in this way as 'urban' yellow fever
- from infected monkeys to humans by mosquitoes such as *Haemagogus*. This is 'jungle' yellow fever and is seen in Africa and South America.

Yellow fever is not transmitted directly from human to human by day-to-day contact, but transmission from ill patients to healthcare workers has been reported, notably after needlestick injury.

Clinical features of yellow fever may be mild, but in 10% to 20% of cases classic yellow fever with liver damage occurs, which can prove fatal

The virus enters dermal tissues or blood vessels at the site of a mosquito bite and spreads through the body, infecting vascular endothelium and liver. After an incubation period of 3–6 days, there is a sudden onset of fever, headache and muscular aches. Although mild cases occur, prostration and shock are not uncommon, and severe liver damage may result in death. Coagulation defects (largely due to prothrombin deficiency) cause haemorrhage into the gastrointestinal tract (manifest as haematemesis and melena) and elsewhere. Renal damage is also seen, with proteinuria and occasionally tubular necrosis. The case mortality rate is in the range of 5–50%.

The diagnosis is usually clinical; there is no specific treatment, but there is a vaccine

The virus can be isolated from blood during the acute stage, and a post-mortem diagnosis can be made from the severe mid-zonal changes and acidophilic inclusion bodies seen in the liver. Virus-specific IgM antibodies are detectable after a week.

The best prevention is to give the live attenuated 17D yellow fever vaccine to those who may be exposed. Protection lasts at least 10 years, and vaccination is necessary for entry into and travel through endemic areas. The international health regulations permit a state to require a valid certificate of vaccination from a traveller from an endemic area to another country where the right mosquitoes are present but the disease does not occur (e.g. from tropical Africa to India). Vaccines based on recombinant DNA technology have been developed. As with all arthropod-borne infections, control of arthropod vectors (insecticides, attention to breeding sites) and reduced exposure (insect repellents, mosquito nets) are also important.

Dengue fever

Dengue virus is transmitted by mosquitoes and occurs in SE Asia, the Pacific area, India, South and Central America

Dengue is one of the most rapidly re-emerging arbovirus diseases, with between 50 and 100 million cases each year. Dengue virus is a flavivirus with four antigenic subtypes. The mosquito *A. aegypti* is the principal human vector. The virus also circulates in monkeys and can be transmitted by mosquitoes to cause 'jungle' dengue in humans, a disease analogous to jungle yellow fever.

Dengue fever may be complicated by dengue haemorrhagic fever/dengue shock syndrome

Dengue virus replicates in monocytes and possibly in vascular endothelium. After an incubation period of 4–8 days, there is malaise, fever, headache, arthralgia, nausea and vomiting, and sometimes a maculopapular or erythematous rash. Recovery may be followed by prolonged fatigue and/or depression.

Dengue haemorrhagic fever/dengue shock syndrome (DHF/DSS) is a particularly severe form of the disease. In the past, mortality rates were high, but with prompt access to expert hospital care, a fatality rate of below 1% can be achieved. The pathogenesis of this syndrome is shown in Figure 27.1. After an earlier attack of dengue, antibodies are formed that are specific for that serotype. On subsequent infection with a different serotype, the antibodies bind to the virus and not only fail to neutralize it (as might be expected for a different subtype), but actually enhance its ability to infect monocytes. The Fc portion of the virus-bound immunoglobulin molecule attaches to Fc receptors on monocytes, and entry into the cell by this route increases the efficiency of infection. Infection of increased numbers of monocytes results in an increased release of cytokines into the circulation (see Ch. 17) and this leads to vascular damage, shock and haemorrhage, especially into the gastrointestinal tract and skin. Similar 'enhancing' antibodies are formed in many other virus infections, but it is only in dengue haemorrhagic fever that they are known to play a pathogenic role. A number of other factors can influence the course of dengue infection, including age and dengue virus strain virulence.

There is no antiviral therapy for dengue fever. Treatment is supportive. The World Health Organization has published a revised dengue case classification based on the presence or absence of warning signs in order to improve patient care (see bibliography).

There is no currently licensed dengue vaccine. A suitable vaccine must be tetravalent to avoid the danger that a vaccine could induce the type of antibody associated with DHF/DSS. Candidate live attenuated tetravalent vaccines are undergoing field testing.

Chikungunya virus infection (CHIKV)

Chikungunya is an arbovirus transmitted mainly by *Aedes aegypti*. The disease is present in Africa and Asia and resulted in an outbreak in Italy in 2007. The illness is similar to dengue but polyarthritis is very common and retro-orbital pain rare in CHIKV.

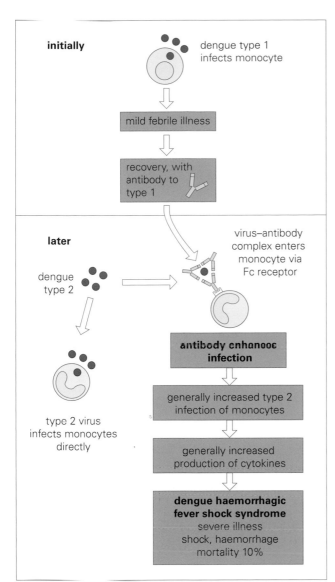

initially

dengue type 1
infects monocyte

mild febrile illness

recovery, with
antibody to
type 1

later

dengue
type 2

virus–antibody
complex enters
monocyte via
Fc receptor

type 2 virus
infects monocytes
directly

**antibody enhanced
infection**

generally increased type 2
infection of monocytes

generally increased
production of cytokines

**dengue haemorrhagic
fever shock syndrome**
severe illness
shock, haemorrhage
mortality 10%

Figure 27.1 The pathogenesis of dengue haemorrhagic shock syndrome. There are four serotypes of dengue virus. Types 1 and 2 are illustrated as examples. Antibody to type 1 binds to type 2 without preventing infection with type 2.

Arbovirus encephalitis

The encephalitic arboviruses only occasionally cause encephalitis

Six of the ten encephalitic arboviruses listed in Table 27.1 cause disease in the USA, and although most infections are subclinical or mild, fatal encephalitis can occur. The viruses replicate in the CNS, but a cell-mediated immune response to infection makes a major contribution to the encephalitis. Vaccines against Western equine encephalitis (WEE), Eastern equine encephalitis (EEE) and Venezuelan equine encephalitis (VEE), each of which may cause disease in horses, have been used for laboratory workers. A Japanese encephalitis vaccine is also available and is used in the UK for the occasional at-risk traveller. Laboratory diagnosis is carried out in special centres, occasionally by virus isolation, but more commonly by demonstrating a rise in specific antibody.

Prior to the mid-1990s, West Nile virus, which is transmitted from infected birds by *Culex* mosquitoes and for which humans are considered to be dead-end hosts, was not considered a major public health problem, but viral changes then resulted in cases with severe neurologic disease. The virus, which had not previously been reported from the Western hemisphere, was recorded in New York in 1999 and since then has spread widely in the USA, Canada, Mexico and the Caribbean. In 2006, the CDC reported a total of more than 1500 human cases in the USA and more than 150 blood donors with the virus. By 2010, it was reported to have caused more than 25 000 cases, 12 000 of whom had severe neurologic disease with more than 1100 deaths. Quite how the virus crossed the Atlantic is unknown though it has been suggested that it was probably imported in a live bird. Infection is diagnosed clinically (fever >38.8°C, neurologic symptoms, elevated CSF cell count and protein, possible muscular weakness) and serologically. Vaccines and immunotherapeutic agents are being developed.

Arboviruses and haemorrhagic fevers

Arboviruses are major causes of fever in endemic areas of the world

Arbovirus infections are often subclinical or mild, but occasionally there is a severe haemorrhagic illness. Some of the best known of these infections are listed in Table 27.2. Laboratory diagnosis by isolation of virus, by detection of viral genome or by demonstration of a rise in antibody is possible in special centres.

INFECTIONS CAUSED BY RICKETTSIAE

The rickettsiae are a group of intracellular, arthropod-transmitted Gram-negative aerobic rods (see Ch. 2 and Appendix). Previously the group included, among others, the genera *Rickettsia*, *Bartonella*, *Coxiella*, *Ehrlichia* and *Orientia*. Genomic-based analysis has resulted in a complete reclassification of the group, but for convenience, these genera are all included here. These organisms are 'debilitated' in the sense that all, except *Bartonella*, are obligate intracellular parasites. All are carried in arthropod or animal reservoirs (Fig. 27.2). All are transmitted to humans by arthropods except *Coxiella*, which appears to infect following inhalation from environmental sources; thus person-to-person transmission does not occur.

The rickettsiae are small bacteria and infections tend to be persistent or become latent

Howard T. Ricketts identified 'Rocky Mountain spotted fever' in 1906 and showed that it was transmitted transovarially in ticks. Rickettsiae probably arose as parasites of blood-sucking or other arthropods in which they were maintained by vertical transmission, transfer to the arthropod's vertebrate host being initially 'accidental' and not necessary for rickettsial survival. The infected arthropod does not appear to be adversely affected. *Rickettsia prowazekii* is perhaps a more recent parasite of the human body louse, because the louse dies 1–3 weeks after infection. As with most arthropod-borne infections, transmission from person to person does not occur.

Table 27.1 Arboviruses causing encephalitis

Virus and disease	Geographic distribution	Vector for human infection	Vertebrate reservoir	Severity of infection
Easter equine encephalitis (alphavirus)	USA (Atlantic Gulf states)	*Aedes* spp. mosquitoes	Wild birds, horses (dead-end hosts)	50% case fatality
Western equine encephalitis (alphavirus)	USA (west of Mississippi)	*Culex* spp. mosquitoes	Wild birds, horses (dead-end hosts)	Up to 2% case fatality
West Nile encephalitis (flavivirus)	Africa, Europe, Central Asia, USA	*Culex* spp. mosquitoes	Birds	Up to 5% case fatality
St Louis encephalitis (flavivirus)	USA (Southern, Central and Western States)	*Culex* spp. mosquitoes	Wild birds	10% case fatality
California encephalitis (bunyavirus)	USA (Northern and Central States)	*Aedes* spp. mosquitoes	Small mammals	Fatalities rare
Japanese encephalitis (flavivirus)	Far East, South East Asia	*Culex* spp. mosquitoes	Birds, pigs	Greater than 10% case fatality
Murray valley encephalitis (flavivirus)	Australia	*Culex* spp. mosquitoes	Birds	Up to 70% case fatality
Tick-borne encephalitis (flavivirus)	Eastern Europe	Tick	Mammals, birds	Up to 10% case fatality (variable)
Venezuelan encephalitis (alphavirus)	Southern USA, Central and South America	Mosquito	Rodents	70% case fatality (cases rare)
Powassan (flavivirus)	USA, Canada	Tick	Rodents	Cases rare

The great majority of infections are either subclinical or are associated with non-specific febrile illness (e.g. 70% case fatality in encephalitis due to Venezuelan encephalitis virus, but only 3% develop encephalitis).

Table 27.2 Arboviruses causing fevers and haemorrhagic disease

Viruses	Disease reservoir	Geographic distribution	Vector	Animal
Yellow fever (alphavirus)	Fever, hepatitis	Africa, Central and South America	Mosquito *Aedes* spp.	Nil (monkeys for jungle type)
Dengue (4 serotypes) (flavivirus)	Fever, rash (haemorrhagic shock syndrome)	India, southeast Asia, Pacific, South America, Caribbean	Mosquito	Nil
Kyasanur forest (flavivirus)	Haemorrhagic fever	India	Tick	Monkeys, rodent
Ross river (alphavirus)	Fever, arthralgia, arthritis	Australia, Pacific Islands	Mosquito	Birds
Rift Valley fever (bunyavirus)	Fever, sometimes haemorrhage	Africa	Mosquito	Sheep, cattle, camels
Sandfly fever (bunyavirus)	Fever (mild disease)	Asia, South America, Mediterranean	Sandflies	Gerbils
Congo-Crimean haemorrhagic fever (bunyavirus)	Fever, haemorrhage	Asia, Africa	Tick	Rodents
Colorado tick fever (reovirus)	Fever, myalgia	USA (Rocky Mountains)	Tick	Rodents
La Crosse (bunyavirus)	Fever	USA	Mosquito	Rodents

There are many other less important arboviruses. For example, there are almost 200 in the bunyavirus family, most of which are arthropod-borne, with about 40 occasionally causing human disease.

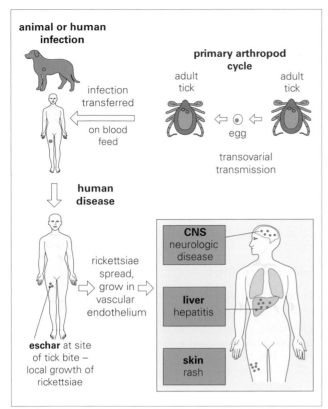

animal or human infection

infection transferred on blood feed

primary arthropod cycle

adult tick

adult tick

egg

transovarial transmission

human disease

rickettsiae spread, grow in vascular endothelium

CNS neurologic disease

liver hepatitis

skin rash

eschar at site of tick bite – local growth of rickettsiae

Figure 27.2 Typical events in rickettsial infection. There is no direct person-to-person spread. Q fever is atypical (see text). Typhus is unusual because the infected arthropod transmits from person to person, eventually dies and there is no eschar. CNS, central nervous system.

Typical clinical symptoms of rickettsial infection are fever, headache and rash

Rickettsiae multiply in vascular endothelium to cause vasculitis in skin, CNS and liver, and hence are multisystem infections (Table 27.3). In spite of immune responses, there is a tendency for rickettsial infections to persist in the body for long periods or become latent.

Except for Q fever (caused by *Coxiella burnetii*), the typical clinical features are fever, headache and rash. A history suggesting contact with rickettsial vectors or reservoir animals may suggest a diagnosis (e.g. camping, working, engaging in military activities in endemic areas).

Laboratory diagnosis is based on serologic tests

Complement fixation tests are specific for different rickettsiae. However, microimmunofluorescence methods are the most common serological approach, and demonstration of a fourfold or greater rise in titre is considered to be a positive result. Infected patients also make antibody to the rickettsiae that cross-react with the O antigen polysaccharide of various strains of *Proteus vulgaris*, as detected by agglutination in the Weil–Felix test. The agglutination pattern with three strains of *Proteus* can be used to identify the rickettsiae. Although the phenomenon is of interest, the test is not of great value, because of false-positive and false-negative results. Earlier diagnosis can often be made by fluorescent antibody staining of skin biopsy material. PCR diagnostic tests are now available. Isolation of rickettsiae is difficult and dangerous, and laboratory infections have occurred.

Table 27.3 The principal rickettsial diseases in humans

Organism	Disease	Arthropod vector	Vertebrate reservoir	Clinical severity	Geographic distribution
Spotted fevers[c]					
R. rickettsii	Rocky Mountain spotted fever	Tick[a]	Dogs, rodents	+	Rocky Mountain states, eastern USA
R. akari	Rickettsial pox	Mite[a]	Mice	–	Asia, Far East, Africa, USA
R. conorii	Mediterranean spotted fever	Tick	Dogs	+	Mediterranean
Typhus					
R. prowazekii	Epidemic typhus	Louse	Human[b]	+ +	Africa, South America
R. typhi	Endemic typhus	Flea	Rodents	–	worldwide
Orientia tsutsugamushi	Scrub typhus	Mite[a]	Rodents	+ +	Far East
Others					
Coxiella burnetii	Q fever	None	Sheep, goats, cattle	+	worldwide
Bartonella quintana	Trench fever	Louse	Human	+	Asia, Africa, Central and South America[d]
Ehrlichia chaffeensis[e]	Fever (ehrlichiosis)	Tick	?		USA, Japan (E. sennetsu)

[a]Vertically transmitted in arthropod.
[b]Non-human vertebrates are possibly also involved.
[c]Other rickettsiae cause similar tick-borne fevers in Africa, India, Australia.
[d]Multiply extracellularly; 1 million soldiers infected in the First World War.
[e]Isolated at Fort Chaffee, Arkansas; parasitizes lymphocytes, monocytes, neutrophils.

All rickettsiae are susceptible to tetracyclines

Prevention is based on reducing exposure to the vector (e.g. ticks). A killed *R. prowazekii* vaccine is available for the military, and a killed *C. burnetii* vaccine is available for those at high risk (e.g. military, veterinarians, etc.) with no demonstrated sensitivity to the antigen.

Rocky Mountain spotted fever

Rocky Mountain spotted fever is transmitted by dog ticks and has a mortality of up to 10%

The rickettsiae causing this disease are carried by the dog tick (*Dermacentor variabilis*) or by wood ticks (*Dermacentor andersoni*) and are transmitted vertically from adult tick to egg. Human infection occurs in the warm months of the year as ticks become active. Children are most commonly infected, but their disease is milder.

The rickettsiae multiply in the skin at the site of the tick bite, then spread to blood and infect vascular endothelium in the lung, spleen, brain and skin. After an incubation period of about 1 week, there is onset of fever, severe headache and myalgia, and often respiratory symptoms. A generalized maculopapular rash appears a few days later, often becoming petechial or purpuric (Fig. 27.3). There is splenomegaly, and neurologic involvement is frequent, with later onset of clotting defects (disseminated intravascular coagulation), shock and death. Fatal cases are usually those with a delayed diagnosis. Peak mortality is seen in 40–60-year-olds.

Mediterranean spotted fever

Mediterranean spotted fever is transmitted by dog ticks

Mediterranean spotted fever is caused by *Rickettsia conorii*, carried by the dog tick *Rhipicephalus sanguineus*. Human infection, which occurs mainly in October, is known in all Mediterranean countries and can occur in urban as well as rural areas. After an incubation period of about 1 week, 50% of cases develop fever, headache and myalgia, and 2–4 days later a rash, especially on the palms and soles. The bite usually goes unnoticed as it is caused by immature ticks and is painless; a local lesion is not usually seen.

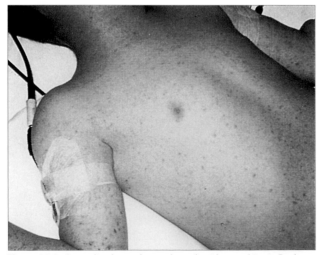

Figure 27.3 Generalized maculopapular rash with petechiae in Rocky Mountain spotted fever. (Courtesy of T.F. Sellers, Jr.)

African tick-bite fever

Four rickettsial species are found in Africa. *R. africae* is found mainly in urban areas and *R. conorii* in semi-rural and rural areas. African tick-bite fever is regularly seen in travellers returning from Africa to the temperate zone.

Rickettsialpox

Rickettsialpox is a mild infection

About 5 days after the bite of a rodent-associated mite (*Allodermanyssus sanguineus*) infected with *R. akari*, a local eschar develops with fever and headache occurring approximately 1 week later. After a few more days, a generalized papulovesicular rash then appears. The disease is, however, mild and usually lasts for about 1 week.

Epidemic typhus

Epidemic typhus is transmitted by the human body louse

Epidemic typhus is transmitted from person to person by *Pediculus humanus*. The rickettsiae (*R. prowazekii*) multiply in the gut epithelium of the louse and are excreted in faeces during the act of biting. The rickettsiae enter the skin when the bite is scratched. The disease cannot maintain itself unless enough people are infested with lice. Epidemic typhus is therefore classically associated with poverty and war, when clothes and bodies are washed less frequently. There were 30 million cases in Eastern Europe and the Soviet Union from 1918 to 1922. The disease is seen in Africa, Central and South America, and sporadically (as a sylvatic form) in the USA. As there is no direct person-to-person spread, outbreaks can be terminated by delousing campaigns.

Untreated epidemic typhus has a mortality as high as 60%

Rickettsiae proliferate at the site of the bite and then spread in the blood to infect vascular endothelium in skin, heart, CNS, muscle and kidney. About 1 week after the louse bite (there is no eschar) the infected person develops fever, headache and flu-like symptoms. The generalized maculopapular rash appears 5–9 days later and sometimes there is severe meningoencephalitis with delirium and coma. In untreated cases, mortality can range from 20% in healthy individuals to as high as 60% in elderly or compromised patients, due to peripheral vascular collapse or secondary bacterial pneumonia.

Convalescence may take months. In some individuals, the rickettsiae are not eliminated from the body on clinical recovery and remain in the lymph nodes. As much as 50 years later, the infection can reactivate to cause Brill–Zinsser disease, and the patient once again acts as a source of infection for any lice that may be present.

Endemic (murine) typhus

Endemic typhus is caused by *Rickettsia typhi* and is transmitted to humans by the rat flea. The disease is similar to epidemic typhus, but is less severe.

Scrub typhus

Scrub typhus is a severe illness caused by *Orientia tsutsuga-mushi* and is transmitted to humans by trombiculid mites (chiggers). It occurs only in the Far East; cases were seen in American soldiers in Vietnam. The rickettsiae are maintained in the mites by transovarial transfer and are transmitted to humans or rodents during feeding. There is fever and an eschar, and a macular rash appears after about 5 days of illness. Pneumonitis, meningitis, disseminated intravascular coagulation and circulatory collapse may ensue. Treatment is with tetracycline or doxycycline and must be given early. Vaccines based on recombinant antigens or on DNA are being developed.

BORRELIA INFECTIONS

Relapsing fever

The epidemic form of relapsing fever is caused by *Borrelia recurrentis*, which is transmitted by human body lice

Borrelia recurrentis is a Gram-negative spirochete consisting of an irregular spiral, 10–30 μm long, and is highly flexible, moving by rotation and twisting.

Epidemics of relapsing fever (Fig. 27.4) are due to transmission of infection by the human body louse. Bacteria multiply in the louse, and when louse bites are rubbed, the lice are crushed and the bacteria are introduced into the bite wound. Lice are essential for person-to-person transmission of louse-borne relapsing fever. As with other louse-borne infections (e.g. typhus), spread of the disease in humans is favoured when people rarely wash and when clothes are not changed (e.g. in wars, natural disasters). The last great epidemic in North Africa and Europe during the Second World War caused 50 000 deaths.

The endemic form of relapsing fever in humans is transmitted by tick bites

Infections with other species of *Borrelia* are endemic in rodents in many parts of the world, including western USA, and are transmitted by soft ticks of the genus *Ornithodoros*. In the tick, the bacteria are transmitted transovarially from generation to generation, which, together with their ability

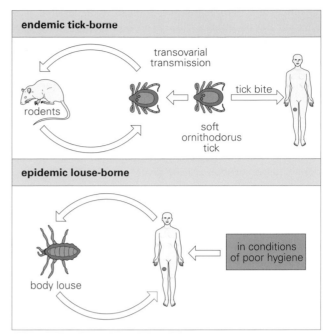

Figure 27.4 Transmission in relapsing fever.

to survive for up to 15 years between feeds, helps maintain the endemic cycle of this form of relapsing fever.

Relapsing fever is characterized by repeated febrile episodes due to antigenic variation in the spirochetes

The bacteria multiply locally and enter the blood. After an incubation period of 3–10 days, there is a sudden onset of illness with chills and fever, lasting for 3–5 days (Fig. 27.5). The afebrile period lasts about a week before there is a second attack of fever, which is followed by another afebrile period. Generally, there are 3–10 such episodes, of diminishing severity. More serious illness can occur if there is extensive growth of bacteria in the spleen, liver and kidneys.

Agglutinating and lytic antibodies are formed against the infecting bacteria, which are cleared from the blood. Under the 'pressure' of this immune response, a new antigenic type emerges and is free to multiply and cause a fresh febrile episode.

Figure 27.5 Course of events in relapsing fever.

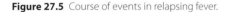

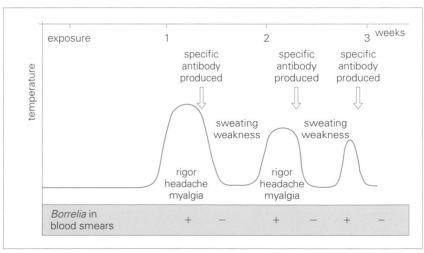

Antigenic variation involves switching of variable proteins on the bacterial surface. The Borrelia have arrays of genes (variable large proteins (Vlp) and variable small proteins (Vsp)) that are altered and activated by gene conversion involving plasmids carrying collections of these genes. The result is that a single cloned bacterium can give rise spontaneously to approximately 30 serotypes and switching occurs at a rate of 1:1000 to 1:10 000 per cell generation. Similar phenomena are seen in trypanosomes. Direct person-to-person transmission does not occur. Mortality with endemic (tickborne) relapsing fever is <5%, but may be up to 40% in epidemic (louse-borne) relapsing fever.

Relapsing fever is diagnosed in the laboratory and treated with tetracycline

The bacteria can be cultivated in the laboratory and can be seen in Giemsa-stained smears of blood taken during the febrile period (Fig. 27.6). Complement fixation antibody tests are available, but are rarely useful because of the problem of antigenic variation.

Tetracycline is used in treatment and to prevent relapses. The best preventative measure is avoidance of arthropod vectors.

Lyme disease

Lyme disease is caused by *Borrelia* spp. and is transmitted by *Ixodes* ticks

Lyme disease (or Lyme borreliosis) occurs in Europe, the USA and most continents of the world, and is named after the town in Connecticut, USA, where the first cases were recognized in 1975. It is caused by *Borrelia burgdorferi* in the USA; in Europe by *B. garinii, B. afzelii predominate*, with *B. burgdorferi* less common. The natural cycle of infection takes place in small mammals in which it is transmitted by hard ticks of the genus *Ixodes* (Fig. 27.7). Human infection follows the bite of an infected tick (most commonly the nymph). In Europe and the USA, infection is more common in summer months when recreational exposure to infected ticks is more likely. Person-to-person transmission does not occur.

Erythema migrans is a characteristic feature of Lyme disease

The bacteria multiply locally, and after an incubation period of about 1 week, fever, headache, myalgia, lymph-

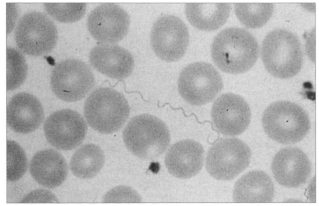

Figure 27.6 Tightly coiled helical spirochetes of *Borrelia recurrentis* in the blood of a patient with relapsing fever. (Courtesy of T.F. Sellers.)

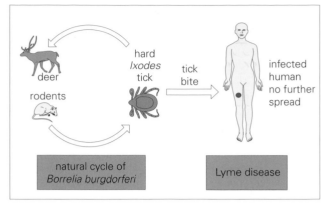

Figure 27.7 Transmission of Lyme disease.

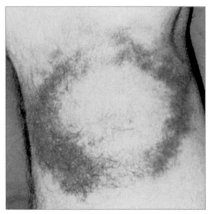

Figure 27.8 Rash of erythema chronicum migrans on the leg in Lyme disease. (Courtesy of E. Sahn.)

adenopathy and a characteristic lesion at the site of the tick bite develop. The skin lesion is called erythema migrans (Fig. 27.8), its name describing its main features. It begins as a macule and enlarges over the next few weeks, remaining red and flat, but with the centre clearing, until it is several centimeters in diameter. In 50% of patients, fresh transient lesions appear on the skin elsewhere in the body. Immunologic findings include circulating immune complexes and sometimes elevated serum IgM levels and cryoglobulins that contain IgM. *Borrelia* is capable of evading the human immune response and mechanisms include antigenic variation and the ability to evade complement-mediated killing.

Lyme disease commonly causes additional disease 1 week to 2 years after the initial illness

In 75% of untreated patients, in spite of antibody and T-cell responses to the *Borrelia*, there are additional later manifestations of disease. These are seen from 1 week to >2 years after the onset of illness. The first of these manifestations to appear are neurologic (meningitis, encephalitis, peripheral neuropathy) and cardiologic (heart block, myocarditis). The second of these manifestations to appear are arthralgia and arthritis, which may persist for months or years. Immune complexes are found in affected joints. These late manifestations are immunologic in origin and are probably due to antigenic cross-reactivity between *Borrelia* and host tissues. The *Borrelia* themselves are rarely detectable at this stage.

Lyme disease is diagnosed serologically and treated with antibiotic

Borrelia can be cultured (in NSK medium) from early-stage cutaneous tissues but is rarely seen at later stages; culture may take several weeks. Thus, Lyme disease is primarily diagnosed on clinical presentation and known exposure. When indicated, serologic tests such as enzyme-linked immunosorbent assay (ELISA) are useful, with Western blot confirmation of all positive and equivocal results. Specific IgM antibodies are detected 3–6 weeks after infection and IgG antibodies at a later stage. PCR diagnosis has been disappointing.

Doxycycline or amoxicillin are effective in treatment of early disease. Late disease, especially with neurologic complications, may require more aggressive therapy, for example, with intravenous ceftriaxone for 30 days.

Prevention of Lyme disease is by avoidance of tick bites.

PROTOZOAL INFECTIONS

Malaria

Malaria is initiated by the bite of an infected female anopheline mosquito

Malaria is restricted to areas where these mosquitoes can breed, i.e. the tropics between 60°N and 40°S (except areas higher than about 2000 m). It is of major importance in Africa, India, the Far East and South America. Drug and insecticide resistance present major challenges to malaria control. About 35% of the world's population is estimated to be infected, with some 10 million new cases annually and perhaps 2 million deaths. Increased air travel means malaria is regularly seen as an imported disease in non-malarious countries, and unless the possibility of malaria is constantly borne in mind, the diagnosis may be delayed or missed altogether, with fatal results. Malaria can also be transmitted by blood transfusion, needlestick accidents or from mother-to-fetus or neonate.

The life cycle of the malaria parasite comprises three stages

Five species of *Plasmodium* cause malaria in humans, of which *P. falciparum* and *P. knowlesi* are the most virulent (Table 27.4). All have similar life cycles, which are the most complex of any human infection, comprising three quite distinct stages and characterized by alternating extracellular and intracellular forms (Figs 27.9, 27.10).

Invasion of red cells requires at least two separate receptor–ligand interactions; the lack of one red cell surface receptor, the Duffy antigen, explains the resistance to *P. vivax* of most West Africans. Other genetic traits that contribute to resistance to malaria include haemoglobin S (sickle cell), β-thalassaemia, and glucose-6-phosphate dehydrogenase deficiency.

Clinical features of malaria include a fluctuating fever and drenching sweats

Symptoms range from fever to fatal cerebral disease or multi-organ failure and are associated exclusively with the asexual blood stage (Fig. 27.9). The clinical picture depends upon the age and immune status of the patient, as well as the species of parasite. The most characteristic feature is fever, which follows rupture of erythrocytic schizonts and is mainly due to the induction of cytokines such as interleukin 1 (IL-1) and tumour necrosis factor (TNF). The synchronous cycle in red cells means that the different species of malaria give characteristic patterns of fever, with either a 48-h (tertian: days 1 and 3) or 72-h (quartan: days 1 and 4) periodicity (Fig. 27.11). However, this classical pattern of fever is seldom seen in clinical practice where a chaotic fever pattern is common. Furthermore, it is possible to be afebrile yet obviously very unwell with malaria. A typical paroxysm starts with a feeling of intense cold with shivering, followed by a hot dry stage and finally a period of drenching sweats. Headache, muscle pains and vomiting are common. The symptoms of malaria closely resemble those of influenza, which is a common misdiagnosis. Jaundice may be present and lead to an

Table 27.4 Human malaria parasites

Species	*Plasmodium falciparum*	*P. vivax*	*P. malariae*	*P. ovale*	*Plasmodium knowlesi*
Major distribution	West, East and Central Africa, Middle East, Far East, South America	India, North and East Africa, South America, Far East	Tropical Africa, India, Far East	Tropical Africa	Asia-Pacific region
Common name	Malignant tertian	Benign tertian	Quartan	Ovale tertian	
Duration of liver stage (incubation period)	6–14 days	12–17 days (with relapses up to 3 years)	13–40 days (with recrudescence up to 20 years)	9–18 days (with rare relapses)	9–12 days
Duration of asexual blood cycle (fever cycle)	48 h	48 h	72 h	50 h	24 h
Major complications	Cerebral malaria; anaemia; hypoglycaemia; jaundice; pulmonary edema; shock		Nephrotic syndrome		Respiratory distress; renal failure

The most important and life-threatening complications occur with *Plasmodium falciparum*, hence its old name 'malignant tertian malaria'.

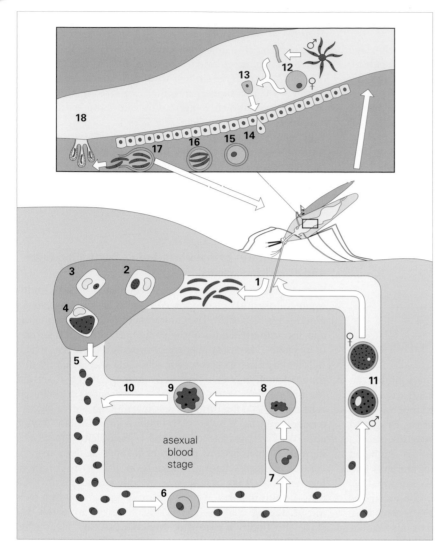

Figure 27.9 The life cycle of malaria in human and mosquito. In the symptomless pre-erythrocytic stage, sporozoites from the saliva of an infected *Anopheles* mosquito are injected into the human bloodstream when the mosquito bites (1). They then enter the parenchymal cells of the liver (2), where they mature in approximately 2 weeks into tissue schizonts (4), finally rupturing to produce 10 000– 40 000 merozoites (5). These circulate in the blood for a few minutes before entering the red blood cells (6) to initiate the asexual blood stage. For *P. vivax* and *P. ovale* only, some parasites, however, remain within the liver to lie dormant as hypnozoites (3), which are the cause of relapses. Once in the red blood cells, the merozoites mature into the ring form (7), trophozoite (8) and schizont (9), which complete the cycle by maturing to release merozoites back into the circulation (10). This cycle may last for months or even years. Some merozoites, however, go on to initiate the sexual stage, maturing within the red blood cells to form male and female gametocytes (11), which can be taken up by the *Anopheles* mosquito on feeding. On entering the gut of the insect, the male gametocyte exflagellates (12) to form male microgametes, which fertilize the female gamete to form the zygote (13). This then invades the gut mucosa (14), where it develops into an oocyst (15). This develops to produce thousands of sporozoites (16), which are released (17) and migrate to the salivary glands of the insect (18), whence the cycle begins again.

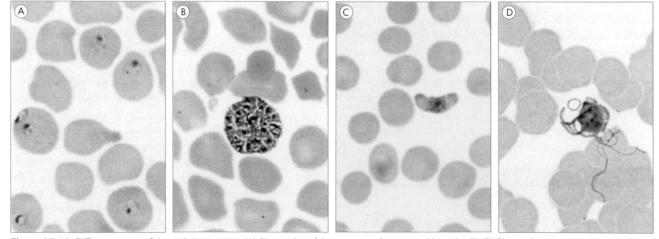

Figure 27.10 Different stages of the malaria parasites. (A) *Plasmodium falciparum* ring forms in red blood cells. (B) *Plasmodium vivax* erythrocytic schizont. (C) *P. falciparum* female gametocyte. (D) *P. vivax* male gametocytes exflagellating to form microgametes 20–25 μm long.

erroneous diagnosis of viral hepatitis. Fever may be the only physical sign in early malaria, but later enlargement of the spleen and liver is common and anaemia almost invariable.

In the absence of reinfection, *P. vivax*, *P. ovale* and *P. malariae* malarias are normally self-limiting though debilitating infections. *P. malariae* may persist in the blood at a low level for decades and recrudesce to cause symptoms from time to time. Relapses (defined as hypnozoite-induced) may occur with *P. vivax* and *P. ovale* months or even 1–2 years after the initial malarial illness.

Figure 27.11 Malaria fever charts showing cyclical fluctuations in temperature. The peaks coincide with the maturation and rupture of the intraerythrocytic schizonts, occurring every 48 h (*Plasmodium falciparum*, *Plasmodium vivax* and *Plasmodium ovale*) or every 72 h (*Plasmodium malariae*), when the cycles are synchronized.

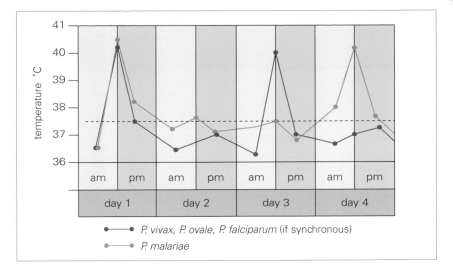

P. vivax, P. ovale, P. falciparum (if synchronous)

P. malariae

P. falciparum malaria is frequently fatal during the first 2 weeks due to a variety of complications (Table 27.4). In hyperendemic areas, complicated falciparum malaria is most common in children aged between 6 months and 5 years, and in pregnant, particularly primigravid, women. However, it can occur at any age in the non-immune (e.g. tourists). The most dangerous complication is cerebral malaria, with convulsions and diminished level of consciousness progressing to coma. Possible causes include binding of parasitized red cells in cerebral capillaries, increased permeability of the blood–brain barrier, and excessive induction of cytokines such as TNF. If successfully treated, there is usually little or no impairment of cerebral function, although neurologic and psychiatric sequelae may occur in 5–10% of childhood cases.

Severe anaemia is also common, due partly to red cell destruction and partly to dyserythropoiesis in the bone marrow. Of the other complications, hypoglycaemia and lactic acidosis are thought to be important contributors to mortality. Acute renal failure due to acute tubular necrosis is an important complication of falciparum malaria and nephrotic syndrome may occur with *P. malariae* (quartan malarial nephropathy).

Malaria has an immunosuppressive effect and interacts with HIV infection

The strong epidemiologic correlation between malaria and endemic Burkitt's lymphoma probably reflects reduced T-cell cytotoxicity against Epstein–Barr virus (EBV)-infected cells. Malaria may also interfere with the efficacy of vaccines against common viral or bacterial infections.

In pregnant females, HIV-1 infection is associated with more peripheral blood malaria, more placental malaria, higher parasite densities, more fever, and increased risk of adverse birth outcomes. In semi-immune non-pregnant adults, HIV-1 infection is associated with higher rates of malaria infection and higher rates of clinical disease. In non-immune, non-pregnant adults, HIV-1 infection is associated with higher rates of severe malaria and death.

Immunity to malaria develops gradually and seems to need repeated boosting

Immunity to malaria develops in stages, and in endemic areas, children who survive early attacks become resistant to severe disease by about 5 years. Parasite levels fall progressively until adulthood when they are low or absent most of the time. However, 1 year spent away from exposure is sufficient for most of this immunity to wane, i.e. repeated boosting is needed to maintain it. The actual mechanisms are still controversial and seem to involve both antibody and cell-mediated immunity (Fig. 27.12).

stage	mechanism
sporozoites	antibody
liver stage	cytotoxic T cells TNF IFN-α IL-1
merozoites	antibody
asexual erythrocyte stage	antibody ROI RNI ECP TNF
gametocytes	antibody ?cytokines
gametes	antibody

Figure 27.12 Immunity to malaria. The principal mechanisms thought to be responsible for immunity at each stage of the cycle. IFN, interferon; IL, interleukin; TNF, tumour necrosis factor; ROI, reactive oxygen intermediates; RNI, reactive nitrogen intermediates; ECP, eosinophil cationic proteins.

Malaria is diagnosed by finding parasitized red cells in thin and thick blood films

Later (schizont) stages may be sequestered in deep tissues, so parasites may be deceptively scarce in, or even absent from, the peripheral blood. A single negative blood film does not exclude malaria. Further samples should be taken 12–24, and 48 h later. Any case of fever, especially with anaemia, splenomegaly or cerebral signs, in a patient who conceivably could have malaria is therefore best treated as malaria, while continuing to look for other diagnoses and seeking expert help. However, the presence of parasites in the blood of an ill patient from an endemic area does not mean malaria is the cause of the illness, so other causes of fever should still be borne in mind while they receive treatment for malaria. For example, they might have lobar pneumonia and coincidental malarial parasitaemia, since low-grade parasitaemia may be asymptomatic in those with partial malarial immunity.

Where available, intravenous artesunate (in combination with other antimalarials to avoid the development of drug resistance) is the drug of choice for severe malaria. Intravenous quinine is used if artesunate cannot be obtained without delay.

Chloroquine is no longer of value for the treatment of falciparum malaria, but remains the drug of choice for the blood stages of *P. vivax*, *P. ovale* and *P. malariae* infections. Primaquine (contraindicated in G6PD deficiency) is used to kill hypnozoites of *P. vivax* or *P. ovale* in the liver and thus prevent relapses of these infections.

In endemic areas, the most promising method of prevention is the use of bed nets impregnated with an insecticide, e.g. permethrin. DDT is again being recommended for indoor residual spraying, where it does not affect the environment or get into food chains. The prospects for a malaria vaccine are discussed in Chapter 34.

Trypanosomiasis

Three species of the protozoan *Trypanosoma* cause human disease

Trypanosoma brucei gambiense and *T. b. rhodesiense* cause African trypanosomiasis or sleeping sickness, and *T. cruzi* causes South American trypanosomiasis or Chagas disease. The diseases differ markedly in:

- the insect vector
- the localization of the parasite
- the effects on the immune system.

African trypanosomiasis

African trypanosomiasis is transmitted by the tsetse fly and restricted to equatorial Africa

The vector of African trypanosomiasis is the tsetse fly *Glossina*, and there is a reservoir of infection in several domestic and wild animals (cattle, pigs, deer). In humans, *T. brucei* remains extracellular, first in the tissues near the insect bite and then in the blood, where it divides rapidly and continuously.

Clinical features of African trypanosomiasis include lymphadenopathy and sleeping sickness

Following an infected bite, a swollen chancre develops at the site (*T. b. rhodesiense* only), with widespread lymph node enlargement, especially in the back of the neck

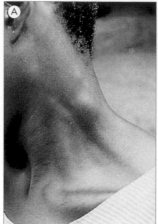
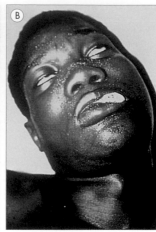

Figure 27.13 African trypanosomiasis. (A) Enlargement of the lymph nodes in the neck (Winterbottom's sign). (Courtesy of P.G. Janssens.) (B) Coma (sleeping sickness) due to generalized encephalitis. (Courtesy of M.E. Krampitz and P. de Raadt.)

(Winterbottom's sign; Fig. 27.13A). The parasite establishes in the blood and multiplies rapidly, with fever, splenomegaly and, often, signs of myocardial involvement. The CNS may become involved (more acutely in the East African *T. b. rhodesiense* than the West African *T. b. gambiense*), with the gradual development of headache, psychologic changes ('silent grief'), voracious appetite and weight loss, and finally coma (sleeping sickness; Fig. 27.13B) and death. Unlike malaria, parasitologically cured trypanosomiasis can leave the patient with severe residual neurologic and mental disability.

T. brucei evades host defences by varying the antigens in its glycoprotein coat

T. brucei survives freely in the blood because of its remarkable degree of antigenic variation, based on switching between some 1000 different genes for the glycoprotein coat. A high concentration of IgM is found in the blood, and later in the cerebrospinal fluid (CSF), and this is manufactured by the plasma cells (Mott cells), which are a feature of the lymphocytic infiltrate seen as perivascular cuffing around blood vessels in the brain (Fig. 27.14).

African trypanosomiasis is diagnosed by demonstrating parasites microscopically in blood, lymph nodes (by puncture) or in late cases in CSF. Detection of antitrypanosomal

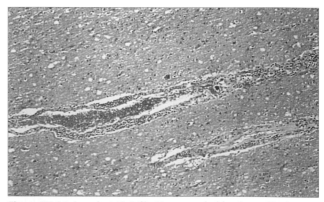

Figure 27.14 Lymphocytic infiltration around a blood vessel in the brain in *Trypanosoma brucei* infection (H&E stain). (Courtesy of R. Muller and J.R. Baker.)

antibody is used to screen populations, with further parasitological examination of those who are seropositive.

East African trypanosomiasis is treated with suramin intravenously for the haemolymphatic stage, followed by melarsoprol intravenously (very toxic) if the CNS is involved. West African trypanosomiasis is treated with pentamidine intramuscularly or eflornithine intravenously for the haemolymphatic stage. CNS involvement is treated with eflornithine intravenously or nifurtimox orally plus eflornithine intravenously (NECT).

Pentamidine prophylaxis is no longer deployed

Control of the tsetse fly vector is difficult, though insecticides are widely used. Bed nets are ineffective, as the flies feed during daylight hours.

Chagas disease

T. cruzi is transmitted by the reduviid ('kissing') bug

T. cruzi is transmitted by reduviid (kissing) bugs, which readily inhabit poor housing, so Chagas disease is characteristically a disease of the rural poor. Almost all species of mammal can act as reservoirs of infection. The parasite invades host cells, notably macrophages and cardiac muscle cells.

Chagas disease has serious long-term effects, which include fatal heart disease

Chancres ('chagomas') may develop at the site of infection, with a transient febrile illness that may rarely lead to death by heart failure. Following invasion of host cells, the disease pursues an extremely slow and chronic course. Some infected individuals remain in the indeterminate phase of the disease and do not develop complications. In cases where the disease does progress, the major complications, which can take years to appear, involve the heart and the intestinal tract. The major cause of death is myocarditis, with progressive weakening and dilation of the ventricles due to destruction of cardiac muscle by the parasite (Fig. 27.15) and probably also to autoimmune mechanisms induced by cross-reacting antigens. Cardiac aneurysm and heart block are particularly serious features. Dilatation of the intestinal tract is due to similar processes in nerve cells, and the organs become incapable of proper peristalsis; megaoesophagus and megacolon are the two commonest manifestations.

Chronic Chagas disease is usually diagnosed serologically

In the acute phase, parasites may be seen in a blood film, but the chronic disease is usually diagnosed serologically or by xenodiagnosis. Clean reduviid bugs are fed on the patient and their rectal contents examined 1–2 months later, or homogenized and injected into mice, in which even a single trypanosome will produce a patent infection. Polymerase chain reaction (PCR) techniques are now in use and may replace or be used in combination with xenodiagnosis.

Chagas disease is very difficult to cure. Children respond better to antitrypanosomal drugs than do adults. Nifurtimox orally or benznidazole orally are the drugs of choice. Side effects are common with both of them. Posaconazole shows promising activity and has been used clinically.

Prevention is achieved by improved housing and living standards, vector control plus active case finding and treatment. However, vector control by insecticides is difficult. *Trypanosoma cruzi* is adept at evading the immune response and thus cannot be eliminated by the human host, a major challenge to vaccine development.

Leishmaniasis

Leishmania parasites are transmitted by sandflies and cause New World and Old World leishmaniasis

Several species of *Leishmania* parasites cause disease in both the New World and the Old World (Table 27.5). In the latter areas especially, dogs can act as an important reservoir of infection. All are transmitted by sandflies.

Leishmania is an intracellular parasite and inhabits macrophages

Leishmania evades the killing mechanisms of macrophages (Fig. 27.16) unless they are strongly activated, e.g. by interferon-gamma (IFNγ). The two principal sites of parasite growth are:

- the liver and spleen (visceral leishmaniasis)
- the skin (cutaneous leishmaniasis).

Untreated visceral leishmaniasis ('kala-azar') is fatal in 80–90% of cases

Visceral leishmaniasis, or kala-azar, usually develops slowly, with fever and weight loss, followed months or years later by hepatomegaly and, especially, splenomegaly. Skin lesions

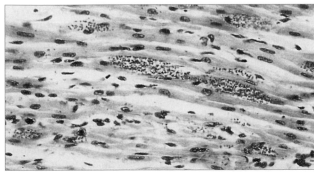

Figure 27.15 Amastigote forms of *Trypanosoma cruzi* in cardiac muscle in Chagas disease (H&E stain). (Courtesy of H. Tubbs.)

Table 27.5 *Leishmania* species – their distribution and clinical syndromes

Species	Distribution	Diseases
L. donovani *L. infantum*	Africa, India, Mediterranean	Visceral leishmaniasis
L. chagasi	South America	
L. major *L. tropica*	Africa, India, Mediterranean	Cutaneous leishmaniasis
L. aethiopica	Africa	
L. mexicana	Mexico and Central America	
L. braziliensis	South America	

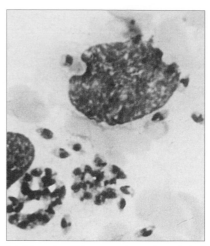

Figure 27.16 *Leishmania* within macrophages in aspirate from a lesion of New World leishmaniasis. (Courtesy of M.J.Wood.)

may appear following treatment; these contain massive numbers of parasites, and the syndrome is known as post-kala-azar dermal leishmaniasis (PKDL). With appropriate treatment, only those who are very ill at diagnosis die.

Cutaneous leishmaniasis is characterized by plaques, nodules or ulcers

Classic cutaneous leishmaniasis progresses insidiously, from a small papule at the site of infection to a large ulcer. This may eventually heal with considerable scarring (Fig. 27.17), leaving the patient relatively immune to reinfection. Old World leishmanial lesions are known as Oriental sores (also 'Baghdad boil' and 'Delhi sore') and New World leishmaniasis as espundia (mucosal leishmaniasis due to *Leishmania (Viannia) braziliensis*) and chiclero ulcer (*Leishmania mexicana* infection of the pinna).

Immunodeficient patients may suffer more severe leishmaniasis

In immunodeficient patients, widespread chronic skin lesions can occur – diffuse cutaneous leishmaniasis – analogous to lepromatous leprosy. Visceral leishmaniasis is a major complication of HIV infection not only in the tropics but also around the Mediterranean, though it is now easier to manage with antileishmanial drugs since the advent of highly active antiretroviral therapy (HAART).

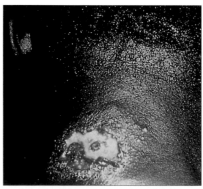

Figure 27.17 Cutaneous lesion on the neck in *Leishmania braziliensis* infection. (Courtesy of P.J. Cooper.)

Leishmaniasis is diagnosed by demonstrating the organism microscopically and is treated with antimonials

Demonstration of the organism by microscopy of splenic aspirate or biopsies of bone marrow or skin lesions (depending upon the clinical picture) is definitive proof of leishmaniasis.

Detection of antileishmanial antibody by the *Leishmania* direct agglutination test is valuable in the diagnosis of visceral leishmaniasis.

A positive delayed hypersensitivity reaction to leishmanial antigens (Montenegro or leishmanin skin test) can be useful in the diagnosis of cutaneous leishmaniasis if parasites are not found.

Where available, the polymerase chain reaction is now the method of choice for the detection and species identification of *Leishmania* in skin biopsies.

Cutaneous leishmaniasis is treated by local injection of the edge of the ulcer with sodium stibogluconate (an antimonial). Intravenous sodium stibogluconate is used to treat multiple or potentially disfiguring lesions. The agent of choice for the treatment of visceral leishmaniasis is intravenous liposomal amphotericin B. Intravenous sodium stibogluconate is an alternative, though there is now significant antimony-resistant visceral leishmaniasis in parts of India.

Impregnated bed nets are effective against the sandfly vector, and the animal reservoir can be eliminated by dog control.

The prospects for vaccination against the cutaneous disease are quite promising.

HELMINTH INFECTIONS

Schistosomiasis

Schistosomiasis is transmitted through a snail vector

All digeneans (flukes) must pass through a mollusc intermediate host in order to complete their larval development. However, schistosomes are the only group in which larvae penetrate directly into the final host after release from the snail.

The life cycle of schistosomes is illustrated in Figure 27.18. Infected snails, which are always aquatic, release fork-tailed larvae into the surrounding water. These penetrate the host's skin, enter the dermis and pass via the blood, through the lungs to the liver, where they mature and form permanent male and female pairs before relocating to their final site:

- the veins surrounding the bladder for *Schistosoma haematobium*
- the mesenteric veins around the colon for *Schistosoma japonicum* and *Schistosoma mansoni*.

The cycle is completed when eggs laid by the female worms move across the walls of the bladder or bowel and leave the body.

Clinical features of schistosomiasis result from allergic responses to the different life cycle stages

The stages of skin penetration, migration and egg production are each associated with pathologic changes, collectively affecting many body systems. Penetration can cause a dermatitis, which becomes more severe on repeated reinfection. The developmental stages are associated with the

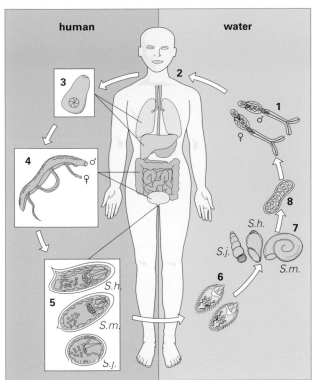

Figure 27.18 Life cycle of schistosomes. Free-swimming cercariae in water (1) penetrate unprotected skin. (2) During penetration, they lose their tails to become schistosomulae. (3) These migrate through the bloodstream via the lungs and liver to the veins of the bladder (*Schistosoma haematobium*) or bowel (*Schistosoma mansoni, Schistosoma japonicum*), where they mature (4), to produce characteristic eggs (5) within 6–12 weeks. The eggs then penetrate the bladder or colon, to be passed in the urine or the faeces (6). Eggs passed into fresh water release miracidia which penetrate snail intermediate hosts (7) where they mature into sporocysts (8). These release cercariae (1) into the water to complete the cycle.

onset of allergic symptoms (fever, eosinophilia, lymphadenopathy, spleno- and hepatomegaly, diarrhea), but the most severe pathology arises following the onset of egg laying. The body becomes hypersensitive to antigens released by the eggs as they pass through tissues to the outside world, or become trapped in other organs after being swept away in the bloodstream.

- In urinary schistosomiasis caused by *S. haematobium*, movement of eggs through the bladder wall causes haemorrhage. With time, the bladder wall becomes inflamed. Infiltrated polyps develop and malignant changes may follow; nephrosis may also occur (see Ch. 20).
- Release of the eggs of *S. japonicum* and *S. mansoni* similarly causes intestinal haemorrhage and inflammation.

A more serious consequence of these infections results from the inflammatory responses to eggs that become trapped in other organs of the body, primarily the liver, but also the lung and CNS. These consequences do not develop in all patients, but if they do, severe disease may ensue (see Ch. 22). Formation of granulomas by delayed hypersensitivity reactions around eggs in the presinusoidal capillaries, interferes with blood flow and, together with extensive portal fibrosis (Symmers' pipestem fibrosis), leads to portal hypertension. As a consequence, there is hepatosplenomegaly, collateral connections form between the hepatic vessels, and fragile oesophageal varices develop. The collateral circulation can lead to eggs being washed into the capillary bed of the lungs.

Intense inflammatory reactions are also provoked when worms killed by anthelmintic treatment are carried back from the mesenteric vessels into the liver.

Schistosomiasis is treated with praziquantel

Treatment of individuals with praziquantel removes the worms, but in advanced cases, the pathology is irreversible. Vaccine research is making progress, but a vaccine may be more useful in minimizing pathology, by reducing the numbers of eggs released, than preventing infection.

Control of infection at a population level is achieved by breaking the transmission cycle, through avoidance of infected water and improvement in sanitation. Mass treatment programmes aim to reduce morbidity but evidence is emerging that they can also reduce transmission.

Filariasis

Filarial nematodes depend upon blood-feeding arthropod vectors for transmission

The filarial nematodes parasitize the deeper tissues of the body (see Ch. 6). The most important species can be divided into those located in the lymphatics (*Brugia, Wuchereria*) and those in subcutaneous tissues (*Onchocerca*). A number of less harmful species also occur. In all species, the female worms release live microfilaria larvae, which are picked up by the vector from the blood (lymphatic species) or skin (*Onchocerca*). Both groups can cause severe inflammatory responses, reflected in a variety of pathologic responses in the skin and lymph nodes, but each is associated with additional and characteristic pathology. (Descriptions of the diseases caused by *Onchocerca* are given in Chs 25 and 26).

Lymphatic filariasis caused by *Brugia* and *Wuchereria* is transmitted by mosquitoes

The mosquitoes introduce the infective larvae into the skin as they feed. These larvae migrate to the lymphatics and develop slowly into long thin adult worms (females 80–100 mm×0.25 mm), found in the lymph nodes and lymphatics of the limbs (usually lower) and groin. Infections become patent after about 1 year, when sheathed microfilariae appear in the blood. Infected individuals may show few clinical signs or have acute manifestations such as fever, rashes, eosinophilia, lymphangitis, lymphadenitis (Fig. 27.19) and orchitis. Later chronic obstructive changes, caused by repeated episodes of lymphangitis, may block lymphatics, leading to hydrocele and to the gross enlargement of breasts, scrotum and limbs, the latter condition being known as elephantiasis (Fig. 27.20). Secondary bacterial infection of the skin, e.g. with streptococci, is a major factor in the development and progression of filarial adenolymphangitis.

A feature of filarial infections in endemic regions is that not everyone exposed develops symptomatic infections. Many, although microfilaraemic, remain asymptomatic, and relatively few show gross pathology (Fig. 27.21). Some individuals develop pulmonary symptoms known as 'tropical pulmonary eosinophilia' (see Ch. 19).

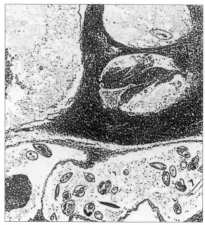

Figure 27.19 Lymph node containing adult *Wuchereria*, showing dilated lymphatics and tissue reaction in the vessel walls. (Courtesy of R. Muller and J.R. Baker.)

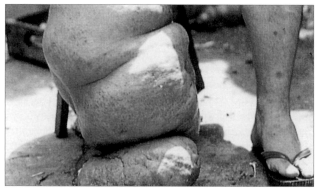

Figure 27.20 Elephantiasis of the leg, caused by *Brugia malayi*. (Courtesy of A.E. Bianco.)

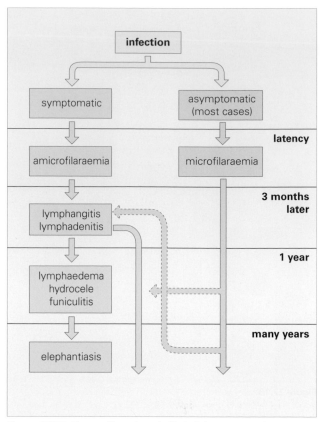

Figure 27.21 Course of lymphocytic filariasis in symptomatic cases. (Redrawn from: Muller R., Baker J.R. *Medical Parasitology*. London: Gower Medical Publishing, 1990.)

Few drugs are really satisfactory for treating filariasis

Diethylcarbamazine (DEC), which primarily kills microfilariae, is no longer used for the treatment of onchocerciasis as it produces a violent allergic response when microfilariae are killed. A single low dose is, however, used in the Mazzotti test for onchocerciasis in patients whose skin snips are negative for microfilariae. Ivermectin is effective against onchocerciasis and has been used to treat lymphatic filariasis as well, in combination with albendazole. Albendazole plus DEC is used in mass drug administration programmes to eliminate lymphatic filariasis. Antibiotics, such as doxycycline, which kill the *Wohlbachia* symbionts, also are effective against the worms in lymphatic filariasis.

It is difficult to prevent transmission of filariasis, although this can be minimized by vector control and prevention of biting.

KEY FACTS

- Many important infections (arboviruses, rickettsiae, *Borrelia*, protozoa, helminths) are transmitted by vectors – insects, ticks or snails.

- Some infections are chronic (Lyme disease, leishmaniasis, schistosomiasis) or can be lethal (malaria, viral encephalitis).

- Often they are restricted to tropical countries because of the distribution of the vector. Climate change may alter this distribution and therefore the pattern of diseases transmitted.

- Strong immune responses are mounted, often leading to immunopathologic complications. Treatment is usually by chemotherapy.

- Vector control is difficult, but can lead to disease eradication.

- With very few exceptions (yellow fever), vaccines are not available for this group of diseases.

Multisystem zoonoses

28

Introduction

Some multisystem infections in humans are animal diseases (i.e. zoonoses)

In these infections, a non-human vertebrate host is the reservoir of infection and humans are involved only incidentally. The human infection follows contact with or ingestion of infective material passed by an infected host, but is not essential for the microbe's life cycle, or for its maintenance in nature. One striking feature of zoonotic infections, and of the arthropod-borne infections described in Chapter 27, is that few are transmitted effectively from human to human.

Sometimes, however, the zoonotic origin of these infections is less clear. For example, tularaemia can be acquired either by direct contact with the reservoir host or from an arthropod vector, and is included in this chapter. Plague is included because it is transmitted from infected rats via the rat flea, although it is also transmissible directly from human to human.

Other zoonoses are dealt with in their relevant chapters (e.g. toxoplasmosis in Chs 23–25, rabies in Ch. 24, salmonellosis in Ch. 22).

ARENAVIRUS INFECTIONS

Arenaviruses are transmitted to humans in rodent excreta

Many zoonoses are caused by enveloped single-stranded RNA viruses with a genome consisting of two RNA segments called arenaviruses. On electron microscopy (Fig. 28.1) these pleomorphic virus particles with a diameter of 50–300 nm can be seen to contain ribosomes that have a sand-like granular appearance, giving rise to the name *arena* (Latin: arena, sand). Arenaviruses are carried by various species of rodent in which they cause a harmless lifelong infection with continuous excretion of virus in urine and faeces of apparently healthy infected animals. Humans may become infected via direct contact with infected rodents, inhalation of infectious excreta, working in agricultural environments or trekking in areas where the rodents exist, and may develop severe and often lethal disease involving extensive haemorrhaging and multiorgan involvement. A selection of arenaviruses and the diseases they cause are included in Table 28.1. Since 2007, nine new arenaviruses have been identified, some as a result of recombination events within one segment. They are divided into the Old and New World groups, of which the Old World viruses, Lassa fever and lymphocytic choriomeningitis virus (LCMV), are associated with the most common human infections involving this family. The distribution of the host is concordant with the distribution of the virus. LCMV is the only arenavirus with a worldwide distribution, the rest being seen in Africa or the New World. Of the New World Tacaribe serocomplex viruses, serious illness is associated with the Junin and Machupo viruses that cause Argentine and Bolivian haemorrhagic fevers, respectively. LCMV can cause acute central nervous system disease. As with most zoonoses, infection is not transmitted, or is transmitted with low efficiency, from human to human. However, healthcare workers have been infected by direct contact with blood or secretions from patients infected with Lassa fever virus, but this can be prevented by using barrier nursing techniques.

Arenavirus infection is diagnosed by viral genome detection, serology or virus isolation

Diagnosis by testing for viral genome or specific antibodies, or by isolating viruses, can be carried out in special centres.

Prevention of infection by reducing exposure to the virus concerned was dramatically illustrated when rodent trapping terminated outbreaks of Bolivian haemorrhagic fever (Box 28.1). Treatment with the antiviral agent ribavirin has been successful if used early in Lassa fever infection. Post-exposure prophylaxis with oral ribavirin has been used. There are no World Health Organization-approved vaccines against arenaviruses. However, a live attenuated Junin virus vaccine was licensed in 2006 for use only in Argentina.

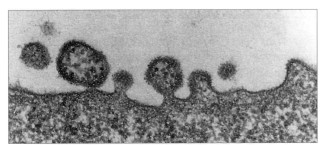

Figure 28.1 Electron micrograph of lymphocytic choriomeningitis virus budding from the surface of an infected cell. The sand-like granules in the virus particles are characteristic of arenaviruses. (Courtesy of K. Mannweiler and F. Lehmann-Grübe.)

Table 28.1 Viral fevers and haemorrhagic diseases acquired from vertebrates or from unknown sources

Virus	Virus group	Disease	Animal of origin	Lethality	Geographic distribution
Lymphocytic choriomeningitis (LCM)	Arenavirus	LCM	Mouse, hamster	−	Worldwide
Lassa fever	Arenavirus	Lassa fever	African bush rat (*Mastomys natalensis*)	+	West Africa
Machupo	Arenavirus	Bolivian haemorrhagic fever	Bush mouse (*Calomys callosus*)	+	NE Bolivia
Junin	Arenavirus	Argentinian haemorrhagic fever	*Calomys* spp., mice	+	Argentina
Hantaan	Bunyavirus	Haemorrhagic fever Fever with renal syndrome (Korean haemorrhagic fever) Severe pulmonary syndrome	Mice, rats	+	Far East, Scandinavia, E. Europe SW USA
Marburg	Filovirus	Marburg disease	Fruit bats	+ +	Africa (lab. infections in Marburg, Germany)
Ebola	Filovirus	Ebola disease	Fruit bats	+ +	Africa (Sudan, Zaire)

Box 28.1 📱 Lessons in Microbiology

Bolivian haemorrhagic fever: a lesson in ecology

In 1962, there was an outbreak of a severe and often lethal infectious disease in the small town of San Joachim, Bolivia. Patients developed fever, myalgia and an enanthem (internal rash), followed by capillary leakage, haemorrhage, shock and a neurologic illness. This disease was termed 'Bolivian haemorrhagic fever' and had a mortality rate of 15%. Extensive investigations failed to incriminate an arthropod vector, but the evidence pointed to a role for mice in the epidemic. Acting on this possibility, hundreds of mouse traps were airlifted to the beleaguered town, and it was soon shown that trapping mice had a dramatic effect on the incidence of the disease. The epidemic was completely halted. Quite separately, a virus was isolated from the tissues of a trapped local bush mouse (*Calomys callosus*). The virus was shown to cause a harmless lifelong infection in this animal, with continued excretion of virus in urine and faeces. The virus (given the name 'Machupo') was an arenavirus, a group that includes lymphocytic choriomeningitis (LCM) virus (infecting mice and hamsters) and Lassa fever virus (infecting an African bush rat). These viruses cause a harmless, persistent infection in the natural rodent host, but an often severe disease in humans exposed to infected animals.

This outbreak of Bolivian haemorrhagic fever provided an important lesson in ecology. Because of the high incidence of malaria in the San Joachim area, extensive DDT spraying had been carried out to control mosquitoes. As a result, geckos (small lizards that eat insects) accumulated DDT in their tissues and the local cats that preyed on geckos began to die with lethal concentrations of DDT in their livers. The shortage of cats, in turn, allowed the bush mice to invade human dwellings. The close vicinity of infected mice to humans and human food led to the epidemic (Fig. 28.2).

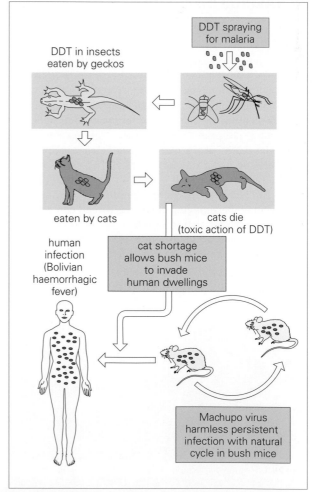

Figure 28.2 Bolivian haemorrhagic fever – a lesson in ecology. DDT, dichlorodiphenyltrichloroethane.

Lassa fever virus is an arenavirus that occurs naturally in bush rats in parts of West Africa

Infection arising from human exposure to infected rats, *Mastomys natalensis*, or their urine results in a febrile disease, which is generally not very severe. Viral entry into host cells is directed by a fusion glycoprotein sited in the viral outer lipid envelope. The cellular receptor for Lassa fever and certain other arenaviruses is α-dystroglycan, a membrane protein found in the mast cells, that anchors the cytoskeleton and the extracellular matrix. There are about 300 000 cases with 5000 deaths/year, and Lassa fever is the commonest febrile illness in hospitals in parts of Sierra Leone. Transfer of virus from hospital patient to healthcare worker via blood or tissue fluids can result in a more severe illness with high mortality. This involves haemorrhage, capillary damage, haemoconcentration and collapse, and was seen when the disease was first recognized in Americans in the village of Lassa in 1969. However, person-to-person transmission via droplet spread is thought to be rare. The usual incubation period is 5–10 days.

Outbreaks have been reported in Central Africa, Liberia, Nigeria and Sierra Leone. An outbreak in Sierra Leone, from January 1996 to April 1997, involved 823 cases with a mortality rate of 19%. The incubation period would allow an infected individual to carry the disease anywhere in the world and, indeed, there have been cases imported into Europe and the USA. Therefore, Lassa fever must be considered in travellers from these endemic areas with fevers of unknown origin.

Lymphocytic choriomeningitis virus occurs worldwide

Lymphocytic choriomeningitis (LCM) has caused sporadic infection in people living in mouse-infested dwellings, and has been reported in children possessing apparently healthy, but infected hamsters. There is generally a non-specific febrile illness, but occasionally an aseptic lymphocytic meningitis occurs, with recovery.

HAEMORRHAGIC FEVER WITH RENAL SYNDROME (HFRS)

The Hantaan and Seoul viruses infect rodents and cause HFRS in Asia

The Hantaan and Seoul viruses are bunyaviruses that causes a harmless persistent infection in various species of mice and rats. They differ from other bunyaviruses as the latter are transmitted by arthropod vectors. After exposure to the urine of infected animals, there is a febrile illness, often with hypotension, haemorrhage and a renal syndrome. Many American soldiers suffered severe infections in Korea, and a milder disease is seen in Eastern Europe and Scandinavia. Related viruses are present in mice and rats in the USA, and outbreaks in the southwestern USA caused 26 deaths with severe pulmonary disease. The latter is called hantavirus cardiopulmonary syndrome and has been reported in the Americas as a result of Sin Nombre virus infection. In Europe, Puumala virus causes a mild form of HFRS known as nephropathia epidemica. Laboratory diagnosis is by molecular and serological methods detecting viral RNA or specific IgM or IgG antibody, respectively.

MARBURG AND EBOLA HAEMORRHAGIC FEVERS

Fruit bats are the reservoir for Marburg and Ebola viruses

Marburg and Ebola haemorrhagic fevers occur in central and east Africa and are caused by filoviruses, long filamentous single-stranded RNA viruses. Patients develop fever, haemorrhage, rash and disseminated intravascular coagulation (see Ch. 17). There is no specific treatment and no vaccine for either virus. The reservoir of origin and natural cycle of maintenance for Marburg virus was not known until Marburg virus RNA was detected in cave-dwelling fruit bats after a small outbreak of Marburg haemorrhagic fever was seen in some miners in Uganda in 2007. A fruit bat reservoir was also found for the Zaire Ebola virus, one of five Ebola virus species.

Infection with Marburg virus was first recognized in 1967 in Marburg, Germany, after exposure of laboratory workers to infected African green monkeys from Uganda. However, these monkeys are not the natural hosts. Mortality was about 20% and, as with Ebola virus infection, it was noted that the virus could be detected in semen for months after clinical recovery; one patient transmitted the infection to his wife by this route.

Outbreaks of a similar disease occurred in 1976 in southern Sudan and in the region of the Ebola River in Zaire (now Democratic Republic of the Congo). Overall, there were 602 cases and 397 deaths. Person-to-person transmission took place in local hospitals via contaminated syringes and needles, burial preparations and, rarely, sexual contact. The virus enters through mucous membranes or abraded skin. Infection does not occur through aerosol transmission. In 1989, monkeys infected with a similar virus were inadvertently imported into the USA from the Philippines. A number of the monkeys died but, although at least four people were infected, none developed disease. In 2004–2005, there was a large outbreak in Angola with a high mortality rate.

A large epidemic was seen in Kikwit, Zaire, in 1995, with 315 cases and 244 deaths. Gabon had three epidemics between 1994 and 1997 and the disease appeared in northern Uganda in 2000. A major outbreak in Congo-Brazzaville in 2003 claimed more than 100 lives, also killing many gorillas and chimpanzees.

Ecological niche modelling models have been used to predict where one might expect to find these filovirus infections. Interestingly, Ebola mapped to the broadleaf tropical rainforest and humid areas in equatorial Central Africa and parts of West Africa (although Angola did not fit this model). Marburg, however, mapped to the opposite, drier, more open areas away from the equator. In these models, bats were thought to be the potential reservoir hosts. Subsequently, tropical rain forest fruit bats were identified as the Ebola virus reservoir.

There is no treatment or post-exposure prophylaxis options for Ebola or Marburg virus infections.

CRIMEAN–CONGO HAEMORRHAGIC FEVER, A TICK-BORNE VIRUS

Crimean–Congo haemorrhagic fever (CCHF), a severe haemorrhagic fever, with shock and disseminated intravascular coagulation, was described clinically during a large outbreak in the Crimea, part of the former Soviet Union, in 1944. The CCHF virus of the Bunyaviridae family, *Nairovirus* genus, was identified in 1967 and has a wide geographic range, including Africa, Asia, Central and Eastern Europe and the Middle East. It is transmitted by the bite of Ixodid ticks (both reservoir and vector), by contact with infected animals or person to person by exposure to infected body fluids including blood. A number of nosocomial outbreaks have been reported around the world. Although mortality rates of up to 80% have been reported, supportive management and the use of ribavirin have been shown to be effective.

Q FEVER

Coxiella burnetii is the rickettsial cause of Q fever

The disease Q fever was first recognized in Australia in 1935, but the cause was unknown for several years – hence Q ('query') fever. The causative rickettsia, *Coxiella burnetii*, differs from other rickettsiae (see Ch. 27) in the following ways:

- It is not transmitted to humans by arthropods.
- It is relatively resistant to desiccation, heat and sunlight, and is therefore stable enough to be acquired from infected material by inhalation.
- Its main site of action is the lung rather than vascular endothelium elsewhere in the body, so that there is usually no rash.

C. burnetii is transmitted to humans by inhalation

C. burnetii can infect many species of wild and domestic animals. In many countries (e.g. USA) infection of livestock is quite common, but there are few human cases (132 reported in 2008 in the USA). Large seasonal Q fever outbreaks occurred in the Netherlands between 2007–2009. Infected dairy goat farms were the source of infection. More than 3500 human infections were notified over that time period. The southern part of the Netherlands was most affected, with >12% of the population found to have *C. burnetii* antibodies. People who come into contact with infected animals, especially their placentas (e.g. veterinarians, farmers, abattoir workers) are at risk from aerosolized organisms. Unpasteurized milk, tissue fluids and dust from infected stock can also transmit the disease.

After inhalation, the microbe multiplies in the terminal airways of the lung, and about 3 weeks later the patient develops fever, severe headache, and often respiratory symptoms and an atypical pneumonia. The rickettsia can also spread to the liver, commonly causing hepatitis. Recovery is usually complete in 2 weeks, but the disease can become chronic. The heart is then sometimes involved (endocarditis), with thrombocytopenia and purpura in some patients, and this condition is fatal if untreated.

Q fever is diagnosed serologically and treated with antibiotics

Polymerase chain reaction (PCR) can be used to determine whether a patient has Q fever; however, the sensitivity of this approach decreases after the first week of illness. *C. burnetii* cannot be detected in blood cultures and cannot be isolated by culture except in specialized laboratories. Thus, serological diagnosis is important. A fourfold or greater rise in complement fixing antibody titre is significant. There are two antigenic forms of the rickettsial lipopolysaccharide (LPS): phase 1 and phase 2. Increased antibody to phase 2 compared to phase 1 is seen in acute Q fever, while the reverse (higher antibody titres to phase 1 than phase 2) is seen in chronic disease. Definitive serological confirmation

of acute Q fever is demonstrated by a fourfold increase in antibody titres measured by indirect immunofluorescence assay (IFA). The Weil–Felix test (see Ch. 27) is not used.

Acute infection is treated with oral tetracyclines; chronic infections may require drug combinations such as rifampin and doxycycline or trimethoprim-sulphamethoxazole. A killed vaccine is available for those at risk. The rickettsiae are destroyed when milk is pasteurized.

ANTHRAX

Anthrax is caused by *Bacillus anthracis* and is primarily a disease of herbivores

Bacillus anthracis is a large Gram-positive rod and is aerobic and non-motile. Most members of the genus *Bacillus* are harmless saprophytes, present in soil, water, air and vegetation. *Bacillus cereus* is a cause of food poisoning, but *B. anthracis* is the principal pathogen and is unique in having an antiphagocytic capsule made of D-glutamic acid. It forms spores, which survive for years in soil.

Anthrax is a disease of herbivores such as sheep, goats, cattle and horses, and bacilli are excreted in faeces, urine and saliva. Humans are relatively resistant, infection occurring following direct contact with infected animals, or by contact with spores present in animal products. The spores can enter the body via the skin and mucous membranes or, less commonly, via the respiratory tract. In resource-rich countries, where animal infection is now uncommon, human infection is rare and has been due to exposure to contaminated imported goods such as hides, skin, wool, goat hair and bristles, bones and bone-meal in fertilizers. Spores have also been used in bioterrorism.

Anthrax is characterized by a black eschar, and the disease can be fatal if untreated

B. anthracis spores germinate in tissues at the site of entry. The bacteria then multiply and produce the anthrax toxin, which consists of a protective antigen, an oedema factor (an adenylate cyclase) and a lethal factor; all are plasmid-coded. Toxic activity requires the protective antigen and at least one of the other two. Host defences are inhibited by the antiphagocytic capsule surrounding the bacillus (see Ch. 14).

The skin is the usual site of entry. As the toxic material accumulates, there is oedema and congestion, and a papule develops within 12–36 h. The papule ulcerates, the centre becoming black and necrotic to form an eschar or 'malignant pustule' (although there is no pus) which is painless and is often surrounded by a ring of vesicles (Fig. 28.3). The bacilli spread to the lymphatics and in about 10% of cases reach the blood to cause septicaemia. Continued multiplication and production of the toxin causes generalized toxic effects, oedema and death.

When the spores are inhaled and enter alveolar macrophages, bacterial growth in the lung leads to pulmonary oedema and mediastinal haemorrhage, with spread to the blood and death. Pulmonary anthrax is now very rare in most resource-rich countries, where it was referred to as 'woolsorter's disease'.

Anthrax is diagnosed by culture and treated with penicillin

Films from skin lesions show Gram-positive bacilli, but diagnosis can be confirmed and the organism distinguished from

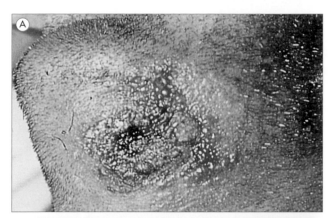

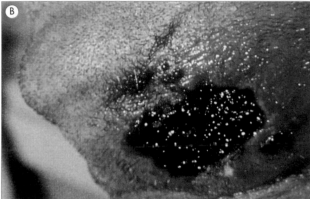

Figure 28.3 Anthrax. (A) Characteristic black eschar surrounded by a ring of vesiculation. (B) Some 8 days later the eschar has enlarged to cover the previously vesicular area, and the surrounding oedema has diminished. (Courtesy of F.J. Nye.)

non-pathogenic bacilli by culture on blood agar or by PCR assay. Antibodies to toxin antigens indicate presence of the bacillus.

Anthrax is successfully treated by ciprofloxacin. Cutaneous anthrax is fatal in 20% of cases when untreated.

Anthrax, as a natural infection, is now mainly confined to resource-poor countries. Vaccines are available. Bioterrorism is an important threat

The disease is largely confined to resource-poor countries (parts of Asia, Africa, Middle East).

Animals can be protected by vaccination with live avirulent bacteria. Infected animals are isolated, killed and buried or cremated without autopsy. A vaccine consisting of purified protective antigen is available for humans at high risk. Human infection is reduced by rigidly controlled disinfection of imported animal products such as hides, hair and wool.

Anthrax is one of the three bacteria categorized by CDC as high-priority bioterrorism threats. Spores sent by mail infected 22 people in the USA in 2001 and this generated renewed interest in antimicrobial post-exposure control (e.g., fluoroquinolone plus doxycycline).

PLAGUE

The plague is caused by *Yersinia pestis*, which infects rodents and is spread from them by fleas to humans

Yersinia pestis is a small Gram-negative rod with a surrounding antiphagocytic capsule that is associated with virulence. The sylvatic reservoirs are rodents such as rats, squirrels, gerbils and field mice, in which the infection is generally mild, the bacteria being spread between animals and to humans by fleas (Fig. 28.4). Infections in urban rats have been the most important sources of plague in humans, and the disease has at times decimated populations and influenced the course of history. In the fourteenth century, about 25% of the population of Europe died in plague epidemics (Box 28.2). Early in the twentieth century, the disease arrived in North America and is at present endemic in wild rodents in western USA. Plague in humans is now extremely rare in Europe and uncommon in the USA.

The rat flea (*Xenopsylla cheopis*) carries infection from rat to rat and from rat to human. *Y. pestis* causes blood to clot in the gut of the flea, multiplies profusely in the clot and eventually blocks the gut lumen, so that the flea regurgitates infected material as it attempts to feed. As infected rats sicken, their fleas leave and may bite humans, thus transmitting 'bubonic' plague. This disease is not generally transmitted from person to person. However, when there is extensive replication of bacteria in the lung, with bronchopneumonia and large numbers of bacteria in the sputum, the infection can spread from person to person by droplets, causing 'pneumonic' plague, with extremely rapid onset.

Rodent infection is endemic in India, SE Asia, central and southern Africa, South America, Mexico and the western states of the USA. Sporadic plague continues to occur in these parts of the world, for instance, in over an 8-week period in 2010, 31 cases of plague were reported in Peru leading to three deaths in a province containing important export harbours. In 2009, a plague outbreak in a farming area of northwestern China resulted in three deaths.

Clinical features of plague include buboes, pneumonia and a high death rate

The infecting bacteria multiply at the site of entry in the skin, and spread via the lymphatics to local and regional lymph nodes. They produce a number of virulence factors, including an antiphagocytic capsular antigen (fraction 1, coded by a plasmid), endotoxin and various other protein toxins. Lymph nodes in the armpit or groin become very tender and enlarge to form 'buboes' with haemorrhagic inflammation 2–6 days after the flea bite. The patient develops fever. In mild forms, the infection is arrested at this stage, but spread to the blood often occurs, with septicaemia, haemorrhagic illness and multisystem involvement (spleen, liver, lungs, CNS).

Common complications are disseminated intravascular coagulation, pneumonia and meningitis. The death rate is about 50% in untreated bubonic plague, and nearly 100% in pneumonic plague. On recovery, there is solid immunity, and bacteria are eliminated from the body.

Plague is diagnosed microscopically and treated with antibiotics

Organisms can be recovered in fluid aspirated from lymph nodes, or from sputum in pneumonic plague and stained with Giemsa, Gram or fluorescent antibody (the staining is bipolar); they can also be cultivated. Streptomycin is the standard treatment; doxycycline or ciprofloxacin are also used.

Plague has been prevented by the following measures:

- classically, by quarantine measures in ports and on ships
- by rodent control, especially of rats at the site of entry of ships and aircraft into plague-free countries

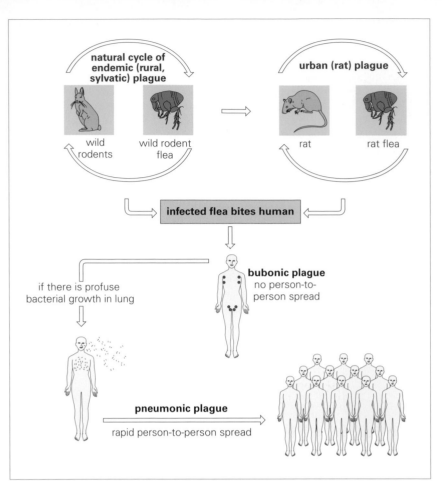

Figure 28.4 The epidemiology of plague.

Box 28.2   Lessons in Microbiology

The Black Death in fourteenth-century England

For thousands of years, *Yersinia pestis* has been endemic in rodents in the Far East, with occasional epidemic spread into Europe and elsewhere. In January 1348, three galleys laden with spices from the East brought the plague to the port of Genoa, Italy. The disease, for reasons that are not clear, became known as 'The Black Death' and soon spread to the rest of Europe, arriving in London in December 1348. To the medieval mind, the speed and violence with which the illness passed from person to person (in the pneumonic form in the winter) was its most terrifying feature. The bubonic form was also important, especially in the warmer summer months, there being at least one family of black rats per household and three fleas to a rat.

The disease was attributed to earthquakes, to the movement of the planets, to a Jewish or Arab plot (350 massacres of Jews took place during the Black Death in Europe), and most commonly to God's punishment for human wickedness. One could become infected without touching a plague victim, and to many it seemed that there was something – a miasma or a poison – in the air. Physicians wore strange masks, and infected houses were labelled and boarded up, together with the inhabitants. But it was impossible to isolate all those who were sick. Rich and poor perished.

The population of England was about 4 million, and over a period of 2.5 years, approximately 35% (more than 1 million) died. The clergy, for unknown reasons, suffered an even greater mortality of nearly 50%. Altogether in Europe, at least 25 million people died. The Black Death was a major human disaster, with lasting effects on economic and social structure.

There were a further five, less severe, outbreaks in England in the fourteenth century. The epidemic in 1665, the year before the Great Fire of London, was graphically described by Daniel Defoe (who was only 5 years old at the time) in his *Journal of a Plague Year in London*. The last pandemic arose in China and reached Hong Kong in 1894, where Yersin and (independently) Kitasato described the causative bacillus.

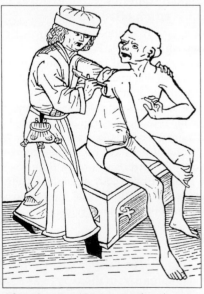

Figure 28.5 Fifteenth-century German woodcut showing incision of a bubo. (Courtesy of the World Health Organization.)

- by strict isolation of patients with plague
- by chemoprophylaxis (doxycycline) during an epidemic or visit to an affected area
- by vaccination of military personnel and of certain workers in endemic areas.

An older vaccine formulation consisting of formalin-killed bacteria has been replaced by efforts to develop a more effective (recombinant) formulation.

YERSINIA ENTEROCOLITICA INFECTION

Yersinia enterocolitica is a cause of diarrheal disease (see Ch. 22) and is mentioned here because it has a reservoir in rodents, rabbits, pigs and other livestock.

TULARAEMIA

Tularaemia is caused by *Francisella tularensis* and is spread by arthropods from infected animals

Tularaemia is caused by the small Gram-negative rod *Francisella tularensis*, first isolated from rodents in Tulare County, California, in 1912 and later shown by Edward Francis to cause human disease. It is present in rodents and in a wide variety of other wild animals in many countries in the northern hemisphere, including the USA (especially Arkansas and Missouri), Russia, Scandinavia and Spain, and can occur in contaminated water. The variety found in North America causes a more severe disease than that found in Europe and Asia. In the infected animal, it causes a plague-like disease and is spread via ticks, mites, lice and biting flies. In *Dermacentor* ticks, the bacteria are transmitted vertically by infected female ticks to her offspring via the ovum. Human infection is sporadic, the normal means of infection being contact with the carcass of an infected animal (e.g. skinning of hares, rabbits, muskrats) or the bite of an arthropod vector. There is no spread from person to person.

Clinical features of tularaemia include painful swollen lymph nodes

F. tularensis parasitizes the reticuloendothelial system and lives intracellularly in macrophages, inhibiting phagosome–lysosome fusion. It spreads at the site of entry, aided by an antiphagocytic capsule, and after 3–5 days forms a skin ulcer. There is a febrile illness, and lymphatic spread results in swollen painful regional lymph nodes. Blood invasion and involvement of lungs, gastrointestinal tract and liver is not uncommon, with the formation of granulomatous nodules around infected reticuloendothelial cells. There may be a rash. Mortality in untreated patients is 5–15%. The conjunctiva or oral mucosa can be infected via contaminated fingers, resulting in ocular or oral manifestations. Infection by inhalation is less common and gives a febrile illness with respiratory symptoms.

Tularaemia is diagnosed clinically and serologically. Streptomycin is the drug of choice, although other antimicrobials have been used (doxycycline and gentamicin)

Infected tissues can be examined by fluorescent antibody staining, but isolation of bacteria is not often attempted, because of the high risk of laboratory infection. Antibody tests are more commonly used in diagnosis.

Streptomycin is an effective treatment. A live attenuated bacterial vaccine is available for people with an occupational risk (e.g. fur trappers) but has issues of toxicity and incomplete protection, prompting efforts to develop a more effective preparation. Handling animals with gloves, particularly when skinning or eviscerating, gives protection, and contact with ticks should be avoided.

PASTEURELLA MULTOCIDA INFECTION

***Pasteurella multocida* is part of the normal flora of cats and dogs and is transmitted to humans by an animal bite or scratch**

Pasteurella multocida is an encapsulated Gram-negative rod and is distributed worldwide. A number of capsular types exist. It is part of the normal oral flora in cats, dogs and other domestic and wild animals, in which it can also cause pneumonia and septicaemia. It is transmitted to humans by animal bites (especially cat bites) or scratches.

***P. multocida* infection causes cellulitis, is diagnosed by microscopy and treated with amoxicillin/clavulanate**

Local multiplication of bacteria leads within a day or two to cellulitis and lymphadenitis; other types of bacteria including anaerobes are often present in the lesion. Infection can become systemic in patients with compromised immune systems. Virulence factors include endotoxin and the capsule.

P. multocida can be cultivated and identified in material from the wound.

Amoxicillin/clavulanate is an effective treatment, and has also been used in prophylaxis after cat or dog bites. Bite wounds should be cleansed and debrided.

LEPTOSPIROSIS

Leptospirosis is caused by the spirochete *Leptospira interrogans*, which infects mammals such as rats

Leptospires are tightly coiled spirochetes 5–15 μm long. They show active rotational movement and have two flagella, originating at each end but located within the cell as in *Borrelia*. Their delicate outline is best seen by dark field microscopy because they are not very well stained by dyes. There are many species, each with several serotypes. The *biflexa* complex is free-living, the *interrogans* complex is pathogenic. The ends of *L. interrogans* are bent into a question-mark shape, hence the specific name. This species infects many domestic and wild mammals in various parts of the world (Table 28.2), dogs and rats being important sources of infection. Infected animals develop a chronic kidney infection with excretion of large numbers of bacteria in urine. The spirochetes are soon killed on drying, heating and exposure to detergents or disinfectants, but they remain viable for several weeks in stagnant alkaline water or wet soil. Humans are infected by ingestion of, or exposure to, contaminated water or food. The bacteria, aided by their motility, enter through breaks in skin or mucosae, so infection can be acquired by swimming, working or playing in contaminated water. Therefore, miners, farmers, sewage workers, and water sports enthusiasts are especially at risk. There are about 50 cases/year in England and Wales, and about 100/year are reported in the USA. Bacteria are excreted in human urine, but person-to-person transmission is rare. Immunity is serotype specific.

Table 28.2 Disease caused by the three main serogroups of the *Leptospira interrogans* complex

Leptospiral serogroups	Animal host	Distribution	Clinical features
Canicola	Dog	Worldwide	Influenza-like illness ('canicola fever', '7-days fever') is the commonest; can progress to aseptic meningitis, liver and kidney damage (Weil's disease)
Icterohaemorrhagiae	Rat	Worldwide	
Hebdomadis	Mice, voles, rats, cattle	Japan, Europe	

There are 19 different serogroups of this organism, other serogroups including Seroja (pigs) and Pomona (swine and cattle in USA and Europe). Among the serogroups, there are 172 different serotypes.

Clinical features of leptospirosis include kidney and liver failure

The bacteria reach the blood and, after an incubation period of 1–2 weeks, cause a febrile, influenza-like illness. In about 90% of cases, this resolves uneventfully, but multiplication can cause:

- hepatitis, jaundice and haemorrhage in the liver
- uraemia and bacteriuria in the kidney
- aseptic meningitis and conjunctival or scleral haemorrhage in the cerebrospinal fluid (CSF) and the aqueous humor (Fig. 28.6).

The main clinical signs result from damage to the endothelia of blood vessels, the clinical picture depending to some extent upon the particular type of leptospire involved. Weil's disease, the severe form with haemorrhagic complications and kidney and liver failure, occurs in only 5–10% of patients with leptospirosis.

Leptospirosis is diagnosed by microscopy and serologic tests and treated with antibiotics

There is often a history of exposure. Bacteria can be isolated from blood, CSF and urine, and a rise in agglutinating serotype-specific antibody can be demonstrated.

Penicillin and doxycycline have been valuable in treatment when given within a day or two of the onset of illness, and doxycycline will prevent disease in those exposed to infection.

Measures for prevention include:

- rodent control
- protective clothing
- prophylactic penicillin after cuts and abrasions in those at risk.

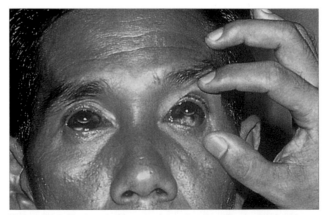

Figure 28.6 Conjunctival haemorrhages in a jaundiced patient with leptospirosis. (Courtesy of D. Lewis.)

RAT-BITE FEVER

Rat-bite fever is caused by bacteria transmitted to humans by a rodent bite

This uncommon but worldwide condition is caused by one of two species: *Spirillum minus*, a Gram-negative spiral-shaped organism (spirillar fever), or *Streptobacillus moniliformis*, a Gram-negative filamentous bacillus (streptobacillary fever). These bacteria are found in the oropharyngeal flora of 50% of healthy wild and laboratory rats and also in other rodents. Transmission to humans is by biting.

Clinical features of rat-bite fever can include endocarditis and pneumonia

After an incubation period of 7–10 days there is an onset of fever, headache and myalgia. Bacteria multiply at the site of the bite, and in the case of *S. moniliformis*, cause an inflamed local lesion. Spread of infection to lymph nodes and the blood leads to lymphadenopathy, rash and arthralgia. Fever may be recurrent if untreated.

Complications include endocarditis and pneumonia, and there is a mortality of up to 10% in untreated patients.

Rat-bite fever is diagnosed by microscopy or culture and is treated with antibiotics

S. moniliformis can be cultured from the wound site, lymph nodes and blood, but *Spirillum minus* cannot be cultivated and must be demonstrated in tissues by dark field microscopy.

Penicillin and streptomycin are effective treatments.

Measures for prevention include:

- rodent control
- prevention of rat bites in laboratory workers.

BRUCELLOSIS

Brucellosis occurs worldwide and is caused by *Brucella* species

Brucellae are small Gram-negative non-motile coccobacilli, adapted to intracellular replication. Four 'species' cause disease in humans: *Brucella abortus*, *B. melitensis*, *B. suis*, *B. canis*, but, on the basis of DNA homology, these are all variants of *B. melitensis*. The first three share common A and M antigens (*B. abortus* primarily A and *B. melitensis* primarily M); *B. canis* is distinct.

Brucellae are primarily animal pathogens, infecting humans after contact with infected animals or their products (Fig. 28.7):

- *B. abortus* infects cows worldwide, but has been eliminated from several resource-rich countries. It causes mild disease in humans.
- *B. melitensis* infects goats and sheep and is common in Malta and other Mediterranean countries, Mexico and South America. It causes more severe disease in humans.

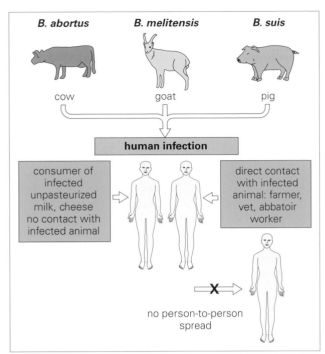

Figure 28.7 Transmission of brucellosis. Human infection follows contact with infected animals or consumption of infected animal products.

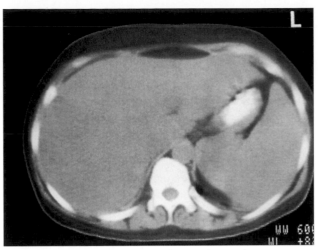

Figure 28.8 Computerized tomographic scan showing hepatosplenomegaly in Brucella melitensis infection. (Courtesy of H. Tubbs.)

- *B. suis* infects pigs in the USA, South America, and SE Asia. It causes severe disease with destructive lesions in humans.
- *B. canis* infects dogs and is an uncommon cause of mild disease in humans.

In cows and goats, brucellae localize in the placenta, causing contagious abortion, and also in mammary glands, from where they are shed for long periods in milk. They are present in uterine discharges, faeces and urine.

Human brucellosis (undulant fever, Malta fever) occurs when the bacteria enter the body via abrasions in the skin, via the alimentary tract or, most commonly, via the respiratory tract. Infection is therefore more common in farmers, veterinarians and abattoir workers. Unpasteurized cows' milk (UK, USA), goats' milk or cheese (Mediterranean countries) are less frequent sources of infection. There is no spread from person to person. Infection is common worldwide, but incidence is low in the resource-rich world.

Clinical features of brucellosis are immune-mediated and include an undulant fever and chronicity

The infecting bacteria pass from the site of entry into local and regional lymph nodes, the thoracic duct and thus the blood (septicaemic phase). Reticuloendothelial cells are infected (liver, spleen, bone marrow, lymphoid tissues) and here the bacteria can survive for prolonged periods. The result is an inflammatory (granulomatous) reaction with epithelioid and giant cells, central necrosis and peripheral fibrosis.

Quite commonly, the infection is subclinical. The symptoms of acute brucellosis begin after an incubation period of 2–6 weeks with a gradual onset of malaise, fever, drenching sweats, aching and weakness. A rising and falling (undulant) fever is seen in a minority of patients. Enlarged lymph nodes and spleen may be detected and hepatitis can occur (Fig. 28.8). The bone marrow lesions may progress to osteomyelitis, and cholecystitis, endocarditis and meningitis are occasionally seen. Abortion occurs in infected cows, sows and goats, but not in humans, who lack the sugar compound erythritol, which stimulates bacterial growth in the placenta.

The patient generally recovers after a few weeks or months, but a chronic stage (more than 1 year's illness) can develop with tiredness, aches and pains, anxiety, depression and occasional fever. Relapses and remissions may occur. Brucellae cannot be isolated at this stage, and chronic brucellosis is often a difficult diagnosis. Agglutinin titres are generally high, but antibodies are less relevant than cell-mediated immunity for this intracellular parasite.

Brucellosis is diagnosed by culture and by serologic tests and treated with antibiotics

Brucellae can be isolated in some cases from blood cultures (or from bone marrow or lymph nodes), and urine culture may be successful. This takes up to 4 weeks. IgM antibodies are present in acute brucellosis, IgG and IgA in chronic brucellosis. A rising titre suggests a current infection.

Brucellosis is typically susceptible to tetracycline and streptomycin; co-trimoxazole is also used. Because of the intracellular location of the bacteria, brucellosis is typically treated with combination therapy (e.g., doxycycline plus streptomycin) for a minimum of 6 weeks.

Brucellae in milk are destroyed by pasteurization. In the USA and UK, brucellosis has gradually declined (about 100 cases/year now reported in the USA) following eradication and control programmes. Protective clothing and goggles may be used by those in close contact with infected animals (farmers, veterinarians, abattoir workers). There is no satisfactory vaccine available for humans. Indeed, veterinarians may develop illness when accidentally infected with the live RB51 animal vaccine.

HELMINTH INFECTIONS

Few helminth infections are true multisystem diseases

It is a somewhat arbitrary decision to include a particular helminth infection in a chapter on multisystem zoonotic infections. Many of the worm parasites that can be acquired from animals have stages that invade a number of the body systems. Others are primarily located in a particular organ, but cause pathologic changes that can be widespread in their effects. Conversely, although stages of certain worms may be widely distributed in the body, their pathologic effects are most commonly associated with a particular organ.

For example:

- The larvae of the pork tapeworm *Taenia solium*, which cause the disease cysticercosis, develop in a variety of tissues, including muscle. However, the most serious pathology is caused by larvae found in the CNS. Accordingly, this infection is discussed in Ch. 24.
- After infection with eggs of the dog nematode *Toxocara canis*, larvae migrate through the body, causing visceral larval migrans or ocular larva migrans. Again, the most serious effects are associated with larvae in the CNS (see Ch. 24) and the eye (see Ch. 25).

However, three helminths can be considered as genuinely multisystem in their effects. These are:

- the tapeworm *Echinococcus granulosus*
- the nematode *Trichinella spiralis*
- the nematode *Strongyloides stercoralis*.

Echinococcus

Echinococcus adults are tiny tapeworms in the small intestine of dogs or foxes, and their larvae cause hydatid cysts in humans. They cause two major types of echinococcosis, both of which result in significant human morbidity.

Echinococcus granulosus (cystic echinococcosis; cystic hydatid disease)

The adults of this species live as tiny (3–5-mm long) tapeworms in the intestine of the dog. Eggs laid by the worm are passed in faeces, surviving for long periods. If swallowed (by sheep or accidentally by humans), the eggs hatch, releasing larvae which then penetrate the small intestinal mucosa to enter a blood vessel. Larvae then lodge in a capillary bed, most commonly in the liver, with the lung next most common, but any organ can potentially be affected. They then grow slowly into large, thick-walled, fluid-filled hydatid cysts, the resulting symptoms and signs being largely due to the mechanical pressure exerted by the cysts (Fig. 28.9).

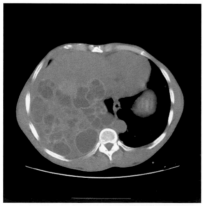

Figure 28.9 Extensive cystic hydatid disease of the liver (courtesy of P. Chiodini).

Cystic hydatid disease is diagnosed by ultrasonography, CT or MRI scans and serologic tests assist diagnosis, but sensitivity and specificity are variable. Finding hooklets and protoscoleces in aspirated cyst fluid provides confirmation, but suspected hydatid cysts in the lung must never be aspirated. Treatment is according to WHO CE ultrasound classification (see bibliography). Depending on cyst type, therapy is with albendazole, plus praziquantel in some cases, with or without PAIR (**P**uncture, **A**spiration, **I**njection, and **R**easpiration) or open surgery. Dead cysts do not require treatment. Special care must be taken during aspiration or surgical removal to prevent leakage of fluid from the cysts. Not only may this trigger anaphylactic responses in sensitized individuals, but the numerous larvae present in the fluid (produced by asexual division) can cause local recurrence or metastatic infection in other sites.

Echinococcus multilocularis (alveolar echinococcosis; alveolar hydatid disease)

Echinococcus multilocularis results in the formation of a multilocular mass lesion consisting of hundreds of small vesicles. The parasite generally occurs as a fox–rodent cycle in China, North Europe, Siberia and parts of North America, and human infections occur via contamination by fox faeces. The macroscopic appearance is similar to that of a hepatic carcinoma. Almost all cases occur in the liver where the parasite leads to obstructive jaundice and weight loss. Treatment is with radical excision plus albendazole. Inoperable cases require life-long albendazole therapy. Liver transplantation is sometimes needed.

Trichinella

Trichinella spiralis is transmitted in undercooked pork and causes the disease trichinosis

T. spiralis is capable of infecting almost any warm-blooded animal. Its natural cycle involves predators (e.g. bears, seals) and their prey, or scavengers and the carrion they feed on, but a domestic cycle has become established in pigs and rats.

Humans are infected by eating undercooked meat (pork or wild animal) containing the encysted infected larval stages. These larvae mature rapidly into adults in the small intestine, their invasion of the mucosa causing an acute enteritis.

The clinical features of trichinosis are mainly immunopathologic in origin

Female worms release live larvae into the mucosa, which invade the blood vessels and become distributed around the body. The larvae attempt to invade the cells of many organs (including the heart and CNS), although they can mature only in striated muscles, where they form the characteristic cysts (Fig. 28.10). There is a wide spectrum of pathologic signs, such as fever, joint and muscle pains, eosinophilia, periorbital oedema, myositis, petechial haemorrhage; encephalitis and cardiac abnormalities may also occur. These signs are mainly caused by hypersensitivity and inflammatory responses.

Trichinosis is diagnosed by microscopy and serologically and treated with anthelmintics and anti-inflammatories

Diagnosis of trichinosis is by muscle biopsy and demonstration of specific antibody by ELISA. Treatment is possible with benzimidazoles in the early stages of infection, but

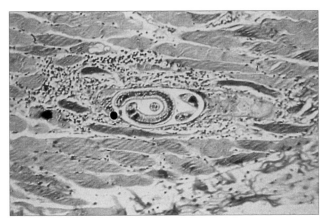

Figure 28.10 Inflammatory reaction around a nurse cell containing a coiled larva of *Trichinella spiralis*. Trichrome stain. (Courtesy of I.G. Kagan.)

symptomatic treatment with anti-inflammatories is helpful during the muscle phase.

Strongyloides

Strongyloides infections are generally passed between humans, but can develop in animal hosts including dogs

Strongyloides infection is acquired by the penetration of infective larvae through the skin. The larvae migrate to the lung, enter the alveoli, pass up the bronchi and trachea, and are then swallowed. Only females develop parthenogenetically in the human host, and they lay strings of eggs into the intestinal mucosa (Fig. 28.11). The eggs hatch within the intestine to release larvae that pass out with the faeces and require warm moist soil to become infective. The geographic distribution of strongyloidiasis is similar to that of hookworm (tropical areas and in rural southern states of the USA).

Infections are most often passed between humans, but the two species can also develop in animal hosts including dogs (*S. stercoralis*) and African primates (*S. fulleborni*). Faecal larval stages may develop directly into the infective stage and penetrate the mucosa or perianal skin to reinfect the host – the process of autoinfection.

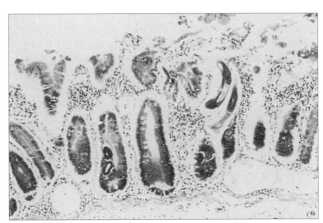

Figure 28.11 *Strongyloides stercoralis*. Adults and larvae in the mucosa of small intestine, showing disruption of the villous surface.

Strongyloides infections are usually asymptomatic, but can cause disseminated disease in patients with immunodeficiency states or malnutrition

Many infected individuals are asymptomatic, though vomiting or diarrhea may occur. However, in immunodeficiency due to corticosteroid therapy, immunosuppression for transplantation, advanced malignancy, HTLV infection and malnutrition, autoinfection can lead to hyperinfection or disseminated strongyloidiasis, the larvae invading almost all organs and causing severe and sometimes fatal pathology. Infected patients may show vomiting, abdominal pain, diarrhea with malabsorption and dehydration, and pneumonitis. Eosinophilia is often absent in *Strongyloides* hyperinfection. Disseminated strongyloidiasis can arise long after initial infection. It has been firmly established that infections can persist for many years (>30), being maintained by low-level autoinfection, then disseminate once the patient's immune defences are reduced. HTLV-1 antibody testing should be advised in this setting, as the two infections are associated.

Strongyloides infection is diagnosed by microscopy and *Strongyloides* culture of faeces to detect larvae. Serology for IgG antibody to *Strongyloides* is helpful in migrants from endemic areas, but less sensitive in travellers. It may be negative in hyperinfestation.

Treatment of *Strongyloides* infection is with ivermectin. Thiabendazole is also effective but much less well tolerated by the patients.

KEY FACTS

- The multisystem infections described in this chapter are zoonoses, being maintained naturally in a reservoir of non-human vertebrates.

- Humans are infected incidentally, generally from rodents (arenaviruses, hantaviruses, plague, tularaemia, leptospirosis) or from domestic animals (brucellosis, leptospirosis, trichinosis).

- There is generally no transmission from person to person (plague is an exception).

- The nature and the extent of human–animal contact are determining factors.

- Some of these infections are highly virulent.

- When the reservoir host is common in crowded human communities (e.g. plague), disease epidemics have been major events in history.

- When humans have less extensive contact with the reservoir host, the infection, even when virulent, has less impact (e.g. Lassa fever, Ebola fever).

- Most of these infections are now less frequent in resource-rich countries (e.g. anthrax, brucellosis, hydatid disease), but remain as frequent causes of disease in other parts of the world and thus may present in migrants from those regions.

- Anthrax is seen as a major bioterrorism threat.

- There are satisfactory antimicrobial agents for most of the non-viral infections, but effective vaccines are generally not available.

Fever of unknown origin

29

Introduction

Fever is an abnormal increase in body temperature and may be continuous or intermittent

The homeostatic mechanisms of the body maintain a constant body temperature with daily fluctuations (circadian temperature rhythm) not exceeding ± 1–1.5°C. Although 37°C (98.6°F) is taken as 'normal', individuals vary in their body temperature; in some it may be as low as 36°C, in others as high as 38°C. Fever is defined as an abnormal increase in body temperature – an oral temperature higher than 37.6°C (100.4°F) or a rectal temperature higher than 38°C (101°F) – and may be continuous or intermittent:

- In continuous fever the body temperature is elevated over the whole 24-h period and swings less than 1°C; this is characteristic of, for example, typhoid and typhus fever.
- In an intermittent fever the temperature is above normal throughout the 24-h period, but swings more than 1°C during that time. A swinging fever is typical of pyogenic infections, abscesses and tuberculosis.

Fever may be produced in response to:

- exogenous pyrogen such as endotoxin in Gram-negative cell walls
- endogenous pyrogen such as interleukin 1 (IL-1) released from phagocytic cells.

It is thought that fever may be a protective response by the host (Fig. 29.1).

DEFINITIONS OF FEVER OF UNKNOWN ORIGIN

Fever is a common complaint of patients presenting to a doctor. The cause is usually immediately apparent or is discovered within a few days, or the temperature settles spontaneously. However, if the patient's fever is > 38.3°C (101°F) on several occasions and continues for more than 3 weeks despite 1 week of intensive evaluation, a provisional diagnosis of 'fever of unknown origin' (FUO) is made based on the classic definition of FUO. However, an increasing number of patients with serious underlying diseases are successfully kept alive by modern medicine necessitating a revision in FUO terminology, especially with regard to particular patient risk groups (Table 29.1).

CAUSES OF FUO

Infection is the most common cause of FUO

For centuries, fever has been recognized as a characteristic sign of infection and, historically, infection has been the most common cause of FUO, especially in children. However, there are important non-infectious causes of fever, most notably:

- malignancies
- collagen-vascular diseases.

These non-infectious causes need to be differentiated from infections during the investigation of a patient with a FUO. Despite intense and prolonged investigations, the cause of fever remains undiagnosed in a significant number of patients. However, in the absence of significant weight loss or indication of severe underlying disease, the outcome, though potentially long term, is generally positive. The reported incidence of different FUO aetiologies has varied over time (Fig. 29.2) due in part to patient demographics and advances in medical diagnostics. One must also consider that patients may have a factitious fever (produced artificially by the patient, e.g. in Munchausen syndrome).

Infective causes of classical FUO

The most common infective causes of classic FUO are shown in Table 29.2. These can be divided into two main groups:

- infections such as tuberculosis and typhoid fever caused by specific pathogens
- infections such as urinary tract infections, biliary tract infections and abscesses, which can be caused by a variety of different pathogens.

Most of these infections are described in detail elsewhere in this book. Bacterial endocarditis is discussed below.

Significant infection may be present in the absence of fever in some groups of patients, notably:

- seriously ill neonates
- the elderly
- patients with uraemia
- patients receiving corticosteroids
- those taking antipyretic drugs continuously.

In these people, other signs and symptoms of infection have to be sought. This chapter deals only with patients whose presenting complaint is fever.

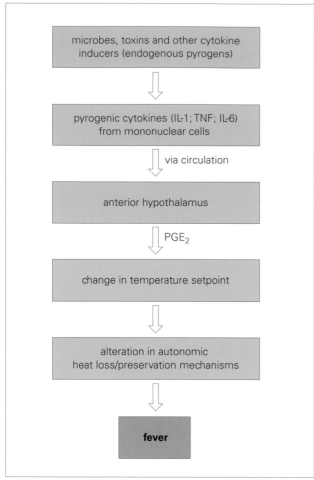

Figure 29.1 Mechanisms of fever. Fever may be induced either by exogenous pyrogens such as microbes or their toxins or by endogenous pyrogens released in the host, and may have a protective effect. IL-, interleukin; PG, prostaglandin; TNF, tumour necrosis factor.

INVESTIGATION OF CLASSIC FUO

Steps in the investigative procedure

Because of the many possible infectious and non-infectious causes of FUO, it is clearly not practical to attempt specific investigations for each at the outset. However, an example of the minimum diagnostic evaluation necessary to categorize a presenting case as FUO is shown in Box 29.1. In addition, the diagnostic pathway can be divided into a series of stages, each stage attempting to focus the investigation on the likely causes (Fig. 29.3).

Stage 1 comprises careful history-taking, physical examination and screening tests

Careful history-taking is essential and should include questions about travel, occupation, hobbies, exposure to animals and known infectious hazards, antibiotic therapy within the previous 2 months, substance misuse and other habits. Some of the infections listed in Table 29.2 are zoonoses (e.g. leptospirosis, spotted fevers), whereas others are vector-borne (e.g. malaria, trypanosomiasis) and/or of limited geographic distribution (e.g. histoplasmosis), hence the importance of a travel history.

In the light of the history and the differential diagnosis, a complete physical examination of the patient with FUO is essential, in particular:

- the skin, eyes, lymph nodes and abdomen should be examined
- the heart should be auscultated.

It is also important to confirm that the patient does have a fever. In some series, as many as 25% of patients whose presenting complaint was an FUO did not have a fever, but had a naturally exaggerated circadian temperature rhythm. The possibility of a factitious fever must also be considered.

Routine investigations such as chest radiography and blood tests should be performed at this stage.

Table 29.1 Definitions of fever of unknown origin (FUO)

Definition	Symptoms	Diagnosis
Classical FUO	Fever (>38.3°C) on several occasions and more than 3 weeks' duration	Uncertain despite appropriate investigations after at least three outpatient visits or 3 days in hospital, including at least 2 days' incubation of microbiologic cultures
Nosocomial (hospital-acquired) FUO	Fever (>38.3°C) on several occasions in a hospitalized patient receiving acute care; infection not present or incubating on admission	Uncertain after 3 days despite appropriate investigations, including at least 2 days' incubation of microbiologic cultures
Neutropenic FUO	Fever (>38.3°C) on several occasions; neutrophil count <500/mm³ in peripheral blood, or expected to fall below that number within 1–2 days	Uncertain after 3 days despite appropriate investigations, including at least 2 days' incubation of microbiologic cultures
HIV-associated FUO	Fever (>38.3°C) on several occasions; fever of more than 4 weeks' duration as an outpatient or more than 3 days' duration in hospital; confirmed positive HIV serology	Uncertain after 3 days despite appropriate investigations, including at least 2 days' incubation of microbiologic cultures

The classic definition of FUO requires that the fever is of 3 or more weeks' duration, but in compromised patients infections frequently progress rapidly because of inadequate host defences. Consequently, the pace of the investigations needs to be rapid if appropriate therapy is to be initiated.

Figure 29.2 Causes of fever of unknown origin over time. Historically, infection has been the single most common cause but a significant number of fevers remained undiagnosed. (Data from Mourand, O., Palda, V., Detsky, A.S. 2003. *Arch. Intern. Med.* 163: 545–555; Bleeker-Rovrs, C.P., Vos, F.J., de Kleijn E.M, Mudde, A.H., Dofferhoff, T.S., Richter, C., Smilde, T.J., Krabbe, P.F., Oyen, W.J., van der Meer, J.W. 2007. *Medicine* 86:26–38.)

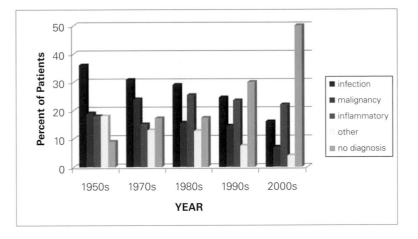

Table 29.2 Representative infective causes of fever of unknown origin (FUO)

Infection	Usual cause
Bacterial	
Tuberculosis	*Mycobacterium tuberculosis*
Enteric fevers	*Salmonella typhi*
Osteomyelitic	*Staphylococcus aureus* (also *Haemophilus influenzae* in young children, *Salmonella* in patients with sickle-cell disease)
Endocarditis	Oral streptococci, *Staph. aureus*, coagulase-negative staphylococci
Brucellosis	*Brucella abortus, B. melitensis* and *B. suis*
Abscesses (esp. intra-abdominal)	Mixed anaerobes and facultative anaerobes from gut flora
Biliary system infections	Gram-negative facultative anaerobes, e.g. *E. coli*
Urinary tract infections	Gram-negative facultative anaerobes, e.g. *E. coli*
Lyme disease	*Borrelia burgdorferi*
Relapsing fever	*Borrelia recurrentis*
Leptospirosis	*Leptospira interrogans* serovar icterohaemorrhagiae
Rat bite fever	*Spirillum minus (Spirillum minor)*
Typhus	*Rickettsia prowazekii*
Spotted fever	*Rickettsia rickettsii, Rickettsia conori*
Psittacosis	*Chlamydophila psittaci*
Q fever	*Coxiella burnetii*
Parasitic	
Malaria	*Plasmodium* species
Trypanosomiasis	*Trypanosoma brucei*
Amoebic abscesses	*Entamoeba histolytica*
Toxoplasmosis	*Toxoplasma gondii*
Fungal	
Candidiasis	*Candida albicans*
Cryptococcosis	*Cryptococcus neoformans*
Histoplasmosis	*Histoplasma capsulatum*
Viral	
AIDS	HIV
Infectious mononucleosis	Epstein–Barr virus, cytomegalovirus
Hepatitis	hepatitis viruses

A wide range of infections can present as FUO. Some, such as brucellosis, are zoonoses, and many are vector-borne. Therefore the patient must have had appropriate exposure to contract these infections. For example, there are about 2000 cases of malaria annually in the UK (ca.1300 in the USA), the overwhelming majority of which are contracted outside the country. A travel history is therefore very important.

Stage 2 involves reviewing the history, repeating the physical examination, specific diagnostic tests and non-invasive investigations

A review of the patient's history, particularly after discussion with colleagues and perhaps carried out by a second physician, is valuable to check for omissions such as exposure to particular risk factors in the recent or more distant past. The physical examination should also be repeated because rashes and other signs of infection can be transient.

Clues to the diagnosis elicited by careful history-taking should direct specific investigations. As the most common

Box 29.1 **Example of Minimum Diagnostic Evaluation Necessary to Categorize a Case as Classical Fever of Unknown Origin**

- Comprehensive history (including travel history, risk for venereal diseases, hobbies, contact with pet animals and birds, etc.)

- Comprehensive physical examination (including temporal arteries, rectal digital examination, etc.)

- Routine blood tests (complete blood count including differential, ESR or CRP, electrolytes, renal and hepatic tests, creatine phosphokinase and lactate dehydrogenase)

- Microscopic urinalysis

- Cultures of blood, urine (and other normally sterile compartments if clinically indicated, e.g. joints, pleura, cerebrospinal fluid)

- Chest radiograph

- Abdominal (including pelvic) ultrasonography

- Antinuclear and antineutrophilic cytoplasmic antibodies, rheumatoid factor

- Tuberculin skin test

- Serological tests directed by local epidemiologic data

- Further evaluation directed by abnormalities detected by above test, e.g.:
  - HIV antibodies depending on detailed history
  - CMV-IgM and EBV serology in case of abnormal differential WBC count
  - Abdominal or chest helical CT scan
  - Echocardiography in case of cardiac murmur

(Adapted from, Knockaeert, D. C., Vanderschuern, S., Blockmans, D. (2003) Fever of unknown origin in adults: 40 years on. From the Department of General Internal Medicine, Gasthuisberg University Hospital, Leuven, Belgium. *J Intern Med* 253:263–275.)

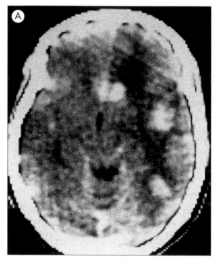
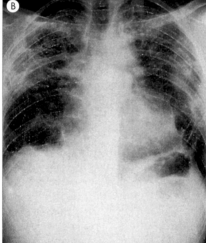

Figure 29.3 Computerized tomography (CT) scans help in the demonstration of abscesses. The patient in (A) has a tuberculoma of the brain, but the CT appearance is not sufficiently characteristic to distinguish this from a pyogenic abscess or a meningioma. (Courtesy of J. Ambrose.) The chest radiograph in (B) shows a patient with sarcoidosis. The differential diagnosis between infective and non-infective causes of granulomas is important, and can be difficult in the early stages of the investigation. (Courtesy of M. Turner-Warwick.)

cause of unexplained fever is infection, collection and careful examination of appropriate specimens are essential. Skin tests may also be appropriate at this stage. The most important specimens include:

- blood for culture
- blood for examination of antibodies. A sample of serum collected when the patient presents should also be stored for comparison with later samples to detect rising antibody titres even if the patient is some weeks into the infection. Serologic tests are helpful, particularly in the diagnosis of cytomegalovirus (CMV) and Epstein–Barr virus (EBV) infection, toxoplasmosis, psittacosis and rickettsial infections. Positive results in syphilis serology should be viewed with caution as other infections can cause biologic false-positives (see Ch. 21)
- direct examination of blood to diagnose malaria, trypanosomiasis and relapsing fever.

Repeated sampling of blood, urine and other body fluids is often required, and the laboratory should be alerted to search for unusual and fastidious organisms (e.g. nutritionally variant streptococci as a cause of endocarditis; see below). If possible, serial cultures should be collected before antimicrobial therapy is commenced.

Technical advances in diagnostic imaging techniques have provided the physician with a wide range of non-invasive investigative methods (e.g. ultrasound, CT scan, MRI, etc.). Some radiologic procedures such as chest radiographs are routine in the work-up of patients with FUO (Fig. 29.4), while others such as gallium or technetium scans may be applied depending on the likely diagnosis (Table 29.3).

Stage 3 comprises invasive tests

Biopsy of liver and bone marrow should always be considered in the investigation of classic cases of FUO, but other tissues such as skin, lymph nodes and kidney may also be sampled. It is undesirable or impossible to repeat biopsies, and therefore it is important to organize the laboratory examination of material carefully to maximize the information obtained.

Figure 29.4 Gallium concentrates in many inflammatory and neoplastic tissues and is a useful non-invasive technique in the investigation of a patient with fever of unknown origin. (A) Retroperitoneal lymphadenopathy of Hodgkin's disease highlighted by a gallium scan. (Courtesy of H Tubbs.) (B) Intra-abdominal abscess shown by a gallium scan. A, abscess; G, gallium in colon. (Courtesy of W.E. Farrar.)

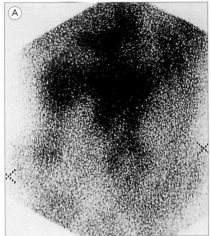
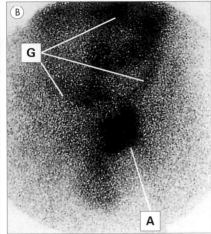

Table 29.3 Representative infective causes of fever of unknown origin (FUO) in specific patient groups

Category of FUO	Infection	Usual cause
Nosocomial	Vascular-line related	Staphylococci
	Other device related	Staphylococci, *Candida*
	Transfusion-related	Cytomegalovirus
	Cholecystitis and pancreatitis	Gram-negative rods
	Pneumonia (related to assisted ventilation)	Gram-negative rods, including *Pseudomonas*
	Postoperative abscesses, e.g. intra-abdominal	Gram-negative rods and anaerobes
	Post-gastric surgery	Systemic candidiasis
Neutropenic	Vascular-line related	Staphylococci
	Oral infection	*Candida*, herpes simplex virus
	Pneumonia	Gram-negative rods, *Candida*, *Aspergillus*, CMV
	Soft tissue, e.g. perianal abscesses	Mixed aerobes and anaerobes
HIV-associated	Respiratory tract	Cytomegalovirus, *Pneumocystis*, *Mycobacterium tuberculosis*, *M. avium-intracellulare*
	Central nervous system	*Toxoplasma*
	Gastrointestinal tract	*Salmonella*, *Campylobacter*, *Shigella*
	Genital tract or disseminated	*Treponema pallidum*, *Neisseria gonorrhoeae*

Patients who contract their FUO in hospital are most likely to be infected with 'hospital pathogens', either from their own normal flora or from the hospital environment. This also applies to neutropenic patients if they are hospitalized, but some are treated as outpatients and may therefore be exposed to a wider range of pathogens. People with AIDS commonly become infected with opportunistic pathogens, though an increasing range of organisms is now implicated. It is important to take a detailed history, as latent infections can become florid as the patient's immune status deteriorates. CMV, cytomegalovirus.

Stage 4 involves therapeutic trials

Trials of corticosteroids (e.g. prednisone, dexamethasone) or prostaglandin inhibitors (e.g. aspirin, indometacin) may be indicated if a non-infectious cause is suspected. There are few indications for empiric antimicrobial or cytotoxic chemotherapy in the management of classic FUO. However, a trial of antituberculosis drugs may be advocated in patients with a history of tuberculosis in the absence of supporting microbiologic evidence. Infections can progress very rapidly in people who are neutropenic or have AIDS, and 'blind' therapy is warranted (see below).

TREATMENT OF FUO

The investigation and management of a patient with FUO requires persistence and an informed and open mind in order to reach the correct diagnosis. As the range of infective causes of FUO is enormous, the correct diagnosis is an essential prelude to the choice of appropriate treatment. As soon as the cause has been identified, specific therapy, if available, should be given.

FUO IN SPECIFIC PATIENT GROUPS

The main difference between FUO in these groups and classic FUO is the time course

As mentioned above, an increasing number of people are surviving with severe underlying disease that predisposes them to infection or are receiving treatment, such as cytotoxic drugs, that compromises their defences against infection. These groups of patients are discussed in more detail in Chapter 30, but are included here because, in addition to classic FUO, other classifications of FUO (see Table 29.1) define:

- nosocomial FUO
- neutropenic FUO
- HIV-associated FUO.

Table 29.4 Causative agents of endocarditis in different groups of patients (in general order of decreasing importance)

Patient group	Major etiologic agents of infective endocarditis
Native valve	Oral streptococci and enterococci *Staph. aureus* Coagulase-negative staphylococci Gram-negative (enteric) rods Fungi (mainly *Candida*)
Intravenous drug misuser	*Staph. aureus* Oral streptococci and enterococci Gram-negative (enteric) rods Fungi (mainly *Candida*) Coagulase-negative staphylococci
Prosthetic valve (early)	Coagulase-negative staphylococci *Staph. aureus* Gram-negative (enteric) rods Oral streptococci and enterococci Fungi (mainly *Candida*)
Prosthetic valve (late)	Oral streptococci and enterococci Coagulase-negative staphylococci *Staph. aureus* Gram-negative (enteric) rods Fungi (mainly *Candida*)

Although almost any organism can cause endocarditis, the majority of cases are caused by a relatively small range of species. The relative importance of these species varies depending upon whether the patient has his/her own heart valves or a prosthetic valve.

Classically, a FUO may exist for weeks or months before a diagnosis is made, whereas for hospital-acquired (nosocomial) FUO and in neutropenic patients the time course is hours to days. The more common infective causes of FUO in these groups are shown in Table 29.4.

Investigation should proceed in the stages listed above, but with the particular emphasis depending upon the patient. In hospital patients the emphasis will depend upon:

- the type of operative procedures performed; fever is a common complaint in patients who have received transplants and may indicate graft-versus-host disease rather than infection
- the presence of foreign bodies, especially intravascular devices
- drug therapy, as drug fevers are a common non-infective cause of FUO
- the underlying disease and stage of chemotherapy in neutropenic patients
- the presence of known risk factors such as intravenous drug misuse, travel and contact with infected individuals in patients with HIV. Although the major opportunist infections in people with AIDS are well described (see Ch. 30), common infections can present atypically and new infections continue to emerge.

INFECTIVE ENDOCARDITIS

Infective endocarditis is an uncommon disease that often presents as an FUO and is fatal if untreated. The infection involves the endothelial lining of the heart, usually including the heart valves. It may occur as an acute, rapidly progressive disease or in a subacute form. The majority of these patients have a pre-existing heart defect, either congenital or acquired (e.g. as a result of rheumatic fever), or a prosthetic heart valve in situ. However, the patient may be unaware of any defect before the infection.

Almost any organism can cause endocarditis, but native valves are usually infected by oral streptococci and staphylococci

Infection of native valves is most commonly caused by species of oral streptococci (viridans group) such as *Streptococcus sanguis*, *Strep. oralis* and *Strep. mitis* and by *Staphylococcus aureus*. Intravenous drug misusers have the added complication of infection due to organisms they inject into themselves. Coagulase-negative staphylococci are common causes of early prosthetic valve endocarditis and are probably acquired at the time of surgery. The species causing late infections – more than 3 months after cardiac surgery – are somewhat more like those causing native valve endocarditis (Fig. 29.5).

Endocarditis is an endogenous infection acquired when organisms entering the bloodstream establish themselves on the heart valves. Therefore, any bacteraemia can potentially result in endocarditis. Most commonly, streptococci from the oral flora enter the bloodstream, for example, during dental procedures or vigorous teeth cleaning or flossing, and adhere to damaged heart valves. It is thought that fibrin-platelet vegetations are present on damaged valves before the organisms implant, and that adherence is probably associated with the ability of the organisms to produce dextran as well as adhesins and fibronectin-binding proteins. Having attached themselves to the heart valve, the organisms multiply and attract further fibrin and platelet deposition. In this position, they are protected from the host defences, and vegetations can grow to several centimetres in size. This is probably quite a slow process and correspondingly the time period between the initial bacteraemia and the onset of symptoms averages around 5 weeks (Fig. 29.6).

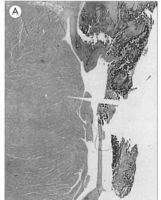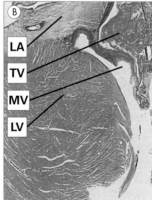

Figure 29.5 Bacteria circulating in the bloodstream adhere to, and establish themselves on, the heart valves. Multiplication of the microbes is associated with destruction of valve tissue and the formation of vegetations, which interfere with, and may severely compromise, the normal function of the valve. These histologic sections show the virtual destruction of the leaflet at the mitral valve by staphylococci. (A) Gram stain. (B) Eosin–Van Gieson stain. LA, left atrium; LV, left ventricle; MV, remnant of mitral valve; TV, thrombotic vegetation. (Courtesy of R.H. Anderson.)

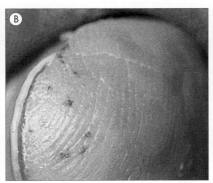
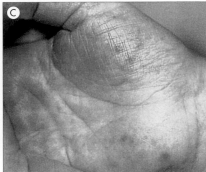

Figure 29.6 Outward signs of endocarditis may be helpful in suggesting the diagnosis. These result from the host's response to infection in the form of immune complex-mediated vasculitis, focal platelet aggregation and vascular permeability. (A and B, different views.) Splinter haemorrhages in the nailbed and petechial lesions in the skin. (C) Osler's nodes. These are tender nodular lesions that tend to affect the palms and fingertips. (Courtesy of H. Tubbs.)

A patient with infective endocarditis almost always has a fever and a heart murmur

The signs and symptoms of infective endocarditis are very varied, but relate essentially to four ongoing processes:

- the infectious process on the valve and local intracardiac complications
- septic embolization to virtually any organ
- bacteraemia, often with metastatic foci of infection
- circulating immune complexes and other factors.

The patient almost always has a fever and a heart murmur and may also complain of non-specific symptoms such as anorexia, weight loss, malaise, chills, nausea, vomiting and night sweats, symptoms that are common to many of the causes of FUO listed in Table 29.2. Peripheral manifestations may also be evident in the form of splinter haemorrhages and Osler's nodes (Fig. 29.6). Microscopic haematuria resulting from immune complex deposition in the kidney is characteristic (see Ch. 17).

Blood culture is the most important test for diagnosing infective endocarditis

Microbiologic and cardiologic investigations are of critical importance. The blood culture is the single most important laboratory test. Ideally, three separate samples of blood should be collected within a 24-h period and before antimicrobial therapy is administered. Isolation of the causative organism is essential so that antibiotic susceptibility tests can be performed and optimum therapy prescribed. Nutritionally variant strains of oral streptococci are known to cause infective endocarditis. These may fail to grow in blood culture media unless pyridoxal is added. Alternatively, they grow as satellite colonies around *Staph. aureus* colonies on blood agar.

The mortality of infective endocarditis is 20–50% despite treatment with antibiotics

In the past, most organisms causing infective endocarditis have been susceptible to a range of antimicrobials. However, antibiotic resistance has become an increasing issue (see Ch. 33). Even with appropriate treatment, complete eradication takes several weeks to achieve, and relapse is not uncommon. This is probably due to factors such as:

- relative inaccessibility of the organisms within the vegetations both to antibiotics and to host defences
- the organism's high population density and relatively slow rate of multiplication.

Before the advent of antibiotics infective endocarditis had a mortality of 100%, and even today, despite treatment with appropriate antibiotics, the mortality remains at 20–50%.

The antibiotic treatment regimen for infective endocarditis depends upon the susceptibility of the infecting organism

For prosthetic valve endocarditis with penicillin-susceptible streptococci, high-dose penicillin is the treatment of choice. Patients with a good history of penicillin allergy can be treated with ceftriaxone or vancomycin. MIC (minimum inhibitory concentration) and MBC (minimum bactericidal concentration) tests (see Ch. 33) should be performed to detect organisms that are less susceptible or tolerant to penicillin (inhibited, but not killed; e.g. MBC = $32 \times$ MIC). Organisms less susceptible to penicillin and enterococci, which are always more resistant to penicillin, are treated with a combination of a beta-lactam antibiotic and an aminoglycoside. Combinations such as this act synergistically against streptococci and enterococci (see Ch. 33). However, vancomycin-resistant enterococci (VRE; usually *E. faecium*) pose a therapeutic challenge and require linezolid or daptomycin.

Staphylococcal endocarditis, particularly in prosthetic valve endocarditis when the organisms may be hospital-acquired and consequently often resistant to many antibiotics, often presents a more difficult therapeutic challenge. The increasing incidence of methicillin-resistant staphylococci requires a combination approach (vancomycin plus rifampin and gentamicin). A number of sources exist for detailed treatment regimens including the American Heart Association and the British Society for Antimicrobial Chemotherapy.

People with heart defects need prophylactic antibiotics during invasive procedures

People with known heart defects should be given prophylactic antibiotics to protect them during dental surgery and any other invasive procedure that is likely to cause a transient bacteraemia.

Most people with an FUO have a treatable disease presenting in an unusual manner

The clinical investigation needs to be individualized, but this chapter outlines the essential stages in the investigation of every patient and draws attention to the important infective causes of FUO.

Although classically a patient with FUO presents with a long history (weeks or months of fever), patients also present with fevers that are not immediately diagnosed by routine laboratory investigations. Definitions of FUO have also been proposed for these groups (nosocomial, neutropenic and HIV-associated). The list of pathogens causing fever in these patients is growing.

The clinician's aim in the investigation of every patient with FUO should be to discover the cause, i.e. to change a FUO to a fever of known origin, and to initiate appropriate treatment.

KEY FACTS

- Fever is the body's response to exogenous and endogenous pyrogens. It is a common symptom and may have a protective effect.

- The term fever of unknown origin (FUO) is used when the cause of fever is not obvious, has classically exceeded 3 weeks' duration, and is not revealed by routine clinical and laboratory investigations.

- Increased numbers of immunocompromised patients have prompted the definition of FUO groups other than classical (i.e. nosocomial, neutropenic and HIV-associated FUO).

- Among the causes of FUO, infection is the most common, but neoplasms and autoimmune diseases are also significant. Cases of FUO often remain undiagnosed.

- The list of infective causes is long; therefore the first stage of investigation (i.e. the patient's history and results of physical examination and screening tests) is a critical pointer to subsequent specific diagnostic tests.

- Therapeutic trials may be indicated if a diagnosis has not been achieved, but may confuse the results of further tests.

- The correct diagnosis is paramount to direct appropriate specific therapy.

- Infective endocarditis is an uncommon, but classic, example of an FUO. It is usually caused by Gram-positive cocci, the species depending upon the patient's underlying predisposition, and is fatal unless treated.

Infections in the compromised host

Introduction

The human body has a complex system of protective mechanisms to prevent infection. This involves both the adaptive (cellular and humoral) immune system and the innate defence system (e.g. skin, mucous membranes). (These have been described in detail in Chapters 9, 10 and 11.) So far, we have concentrated on the common and serious infections occurring in people whose protective mechanisms are largely intact. In these circumstances, the interactions between host and parasite are such that the parasite has to use all its guile to survive and invade the host, and the healthy host is able to combat such an invasion. The focus of this chapter involves the infections that arise when the host defences are compromised, resulting in the host–parasite equation being weighted heavily in favour of the parasite.

THE COMPROMISED HOST

Compromised hosts are people with one or more defects in their body's natural defences against microbial invaders. Consequently they are much more liable to suffer from severe and life-threatening infections. Modern medicine has effective methods for treating many types of cancers, is improving organ transplantation techniques and has developed technology that enables people with otherwise fatal diseases to lead prolonged and productive lives. A consequence of these achievements, however, is an increasing number of compromised people prone to infection. In addition, viral infections including HIV and HTLV result in a compromised immune system referred to as AIDS and adult T-cell leukaemia/lymphoma (ATLL), respectively.

The host can be compromised in many different ways

Compromise can take a variety of forms, falling into two main groups:

- defects, accidental or intentional, in the body's innate defence mechanisms
- deficiencies in the adaptive immune response.

These disorders of the immune system can be further subclassified as 'primary' or 'secondary' (Table 30.1):

- Primary immunodeficiency is inherited or occurs by exposure in utero to environmental factors or by other unknown mechanisms. It is rare, and varies in severity depending upon the type of defect.
- Secondary or acquired immunodeficiency is due to an underlying disease state (Table 30.2) or occurs as a result of treatment for a disease.

Primary defects of innate immunity include congenital defects in phagocytic cells or complement synthesis

Congenital defects in phagocytic cells confer susceptibility to infection, and of these perhaps the best known is chronic granulomatous disease (Fig. 30.1), in which an inherited failure to synthesize cytochrome b$_{245}$ leads to a failure to produce reactive oxygen intermediates during phagocytosis. As a result, the neutrophils cannot kill invading pathogens.

The central role of complement in the innate defence mechanisms is undisputed, and inability to generate classical C3 convertase (see Ch. 10) through congenital defects in the synthesis of the early components, particularly C4 and C2, is associated with a high frequency of extracellular infections.

Secondary defects of innate defences include disruption of the body's mechanical barriers

A variety of factors can disrupt the mechanical non-specific barriers to infection. For example, burns, traumatic injury and major surgery destroy the continuity of the skin and may leave poorly vascularized tissue near the body surface, providing a relatively defenceless site for microbes to colonize and invade. In health, the mucosal barriers of the respiratory and alimentary tract are vital to prevent infection. Damage sustained, for example, through endoscopy, surgery or radiotherapy, provides easy access for infecting organisms. Devices such as intravascular and urinary catheters, or procedures such as lumbar puncture or bone marrow aspiration, allow organisms to bypass the normal defences and enter normally sterile parts of the body. Foreign bodies such as prostheses, e.g. hip joints or heart valves, and cerebrospinal fluid (CSF) shunts alter the local non-specific host responses and provide surfaces that microbes can colonize more readily than the natural equivalents.

The adage 'obstruction leads to infection' is a valuable reminder that the defences of many body systems work partly through the clearance of undesirable materials, e.g. by urine flow, ciliary action in the respiratory tract, and peristalsis in the gut. Interference with these mechanisms as a result of pathologic obstruction, central nervous system dysfunction or surgical intervention tends to result in infection.

Table 30.1 Factors that make a host compromised

Factors affecting innate systems	
Primary	Complement deficiencies, phagocyte cell deficiencies
Secondary	Burns, trauma, major surgery, catheterization, foreign bodies (e.g. shunts, prostheses), obstruction
Factors affecting adaptive systems	
Primary	T-cell defects, B-cell deficiencies, severe combined immunodeficiency
Secondary	Malnutrition, infectious diseases, neoplasia, irradiation, chemotherapy, splenectomy

Table 30.2 Infections that cause immunosuppression

Viral	Bacterial
Measles	*Mycobacterium tuberculosis*
Mumps	*Mycobacterium leprae*
Congenital rubella Epstein–Barr virus Cytomegalovirus HIV-1, HIV-2 HTLV-1	*Brucella* spp.

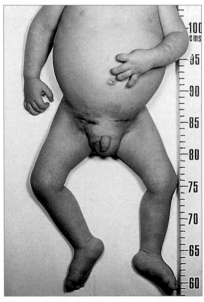

Figure 30.1 Bilateral draining lymph nodes in an 18-month-old boy with chronic granulomatous disease. Abscesses caused by *Staphylococcus aureus* had developed in both groins and had to be surgically drained. (Courtesy of A.R. Hayward.)

Primary adaptive immunodeficiency results from defects in the primary differentiation environment or in cell differentiation

The major congenital abnormalities arising in the adaptive immune system are depicted in Figure 30.2. A defect in the stromal microenvironment in which lymphocytes differentiate may lead to failure to produce B cells (Bruton-type agammaglobulinaemia) or T cells (DiGeorge syndrome).

Differentiation pathways themselves may also be affected. For example, a non-functional recombinase enzyme will prevent the recombination of gene fragments that form the B-cell antibody or the T-cell receptor variable regions for antigen recognition, with a resulting severe combined immunodeficiency (SCID).

The most common form of congenital antibody deficiency – common variable immunodeficiency – is characterized by recurrent pyogenic infections and is probably heterogeneous. Although the number of immature B cells in the marrow tends to be normal, the peripheral B cells are either low in number or in some cases absent. Where present, they are unable to differentiate into plasma cells in some cases or to secrete antibody in others.

Transient hypogammaglobulinaemia of infancy, characterized by recurrent respiratory infections, is associated with a low serum IgG concentration, which often normalizes abruptly by 3–4 years of age (Fig. 30.3).

Immunoglobulin deficiency occurs naturally in human infants as the maternal serum IgG concentration decays. It is a serious problem in very premature babies as, depending on the gestational age, maternal IgG may not have crossed the placental barrier.

Causes of secondary adaptive immunodeficiency include malnutrition, infections, neoplasia, splenectomy and certain medical treatments

Worldwide, malnutrition is common and the most important cause of acquired immunodeficiency. The major form, protein–energy malnutrition (PEM) presents as a wide range of disorders, with kwashiorkor and marasmus at the two poles. It results in:

- drastic effects on the structure of the lymphoid organs (Fig. 30.4)
- gross reductions in the synthesis of complement components
- sluggish chemotactic responses of phagocytes
- lowered concentrations of secretory and mucosal IgA
- reduced affinity of IgG
- in particular, a serious deficit in circulating T-cell numbers (Fig. 30.5), leading to inadequate cell-mediated responses.

Infections themselves are often immunosuppressive (see Table 30.2), and none is more so than HIV infection, which gives rise to AIDS (see Ch. 21). Neoplasia of the lymphoid system frequently induces a state of reduced immunoreactivity, and splenectomy, for whatever reason, results in impaired humoral responses.

Treatment of disease can also cause immunosuppression. For example:

- Cytotoxic agents such as cyclophosphamide and azathioprine cause leukopenia or deranged T- and B-cell function.
- Corticosteroids reduce the number of circulating lymphocytes, monocytes and eosinophils and suppress leukocyte accumulation at sites of inflammation.
- Radiotherapy adversely affects the proliferation of lymphoid cells.

Therefore a patient receiving treatment for neoplastic disease will be immunocompromised as a result of both the disease and the treatment.

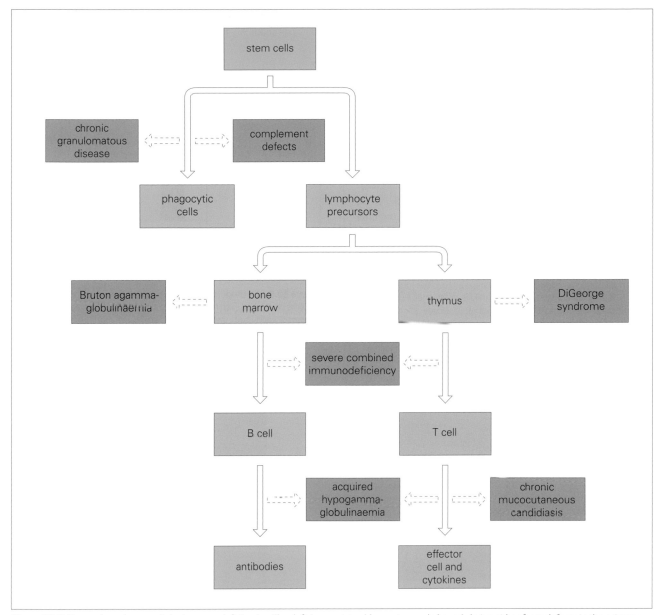

Figure 30.2 The major primary cellular immunodeficiencies. The deficiency states (shown in purple boxes) derive either from defects in the primary differentiation environment (bone marrow or thymus) or during cell differentiation (shown as dashed arrows derived from the differentiation state indicated).

It is important to recognize immunodeficiencies and to understand which procedures are likely to compromise the natural defences of a patient. Due to improvements in medical technology, many immune defects, particularly immunosuppression resulting from radiotherapy or cytotoxic drugs, are transient, and patients who survive the period of immunosuppression have a good chance of a complete recovery.

Microbes that infect the compromised host

Immunocompromised people can become infected with any pathogen able to infect immunocompetent individuals as well as those opportunist pathogens that do not cause disease in a healthy person. They may be lethal when the host defences are lowered. Different types of defect predispose to infection with different pathogens depending upon the critical mechanisms operating in the defence against each

microorganism (Fig. 30.6). Here, we will concentrate mainly on the opportunist infections and refer to other chapters for information about other pathogens.

INFECTIONS OF THE HOST WITH DEFICIENT INNATE IMMUNITY DUE TO PHYSICAL FACTORS

Burn wound infections

Burns damage the body's mechanical barriers, neutrophil function and immune responses

Burn wounds are sterile immediately after the burn is inflicted, but inevitably become colonized within hours with a mixed bacterial flora. Burn injuries cause direct damage to the mechanical barriers of the body and abnormalities

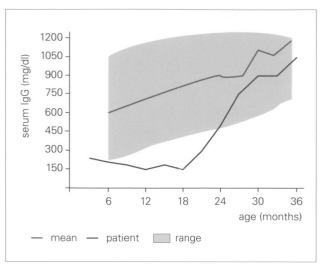

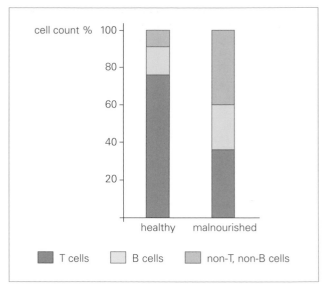

Figure 30.3 Serum immunoglobulin concentrations in a boy with transient hypogammaglobulinaemia compared with the range of normal controls. The patient developed mild paralytic polio when immunized at 4 months of age with live attenuated (Sabin) vaccine.

Figure 30.5 The proportion of T cells is decreased in malnourished patients compared with healthy controls. B-cell counts are usually unaltered, and lymphocytes lacking T- and B-cell markers are increased.

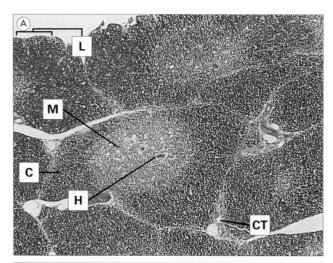

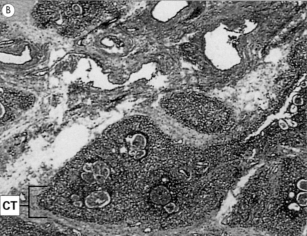

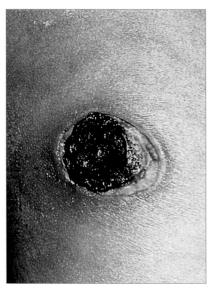

Figure 30.6 Ecthyma gangrenosum in a child with *Pseudomonas* septicaemia associated with immunodeficiency. (Courtesy of H. Tubbs.)

Figure 30.4 Thymic histology in normal children and children with protein–energy malnutrition (PEM). (A) Normal thymus showing a cortex and medullary zones. (B) Acute involution in PEM characterized by lobular atrophy, loss of distinction between cortex and medulla, depletion of lymphocytes and enlarged Hassall's corpuscles. C, cortex; CT, connective tissue; H, Hassall's corpuscle; L, lobule; M, medulla. (Courtesy of R.K. Chandra.)

in neutrophil function and immune responses. In addition, there is a major physiologic derangement with loss of fluids and electrolytes. The burn provides a highly nutritious surface for organisms to colonize, and the incidence of serious infection varies with the size and depth of the burn and the age of the patient. Topical antimicrobial therapy should prevent infection of burns of <30% of the total body area, but larger burns are always colonized. Non-invasive infection is confined to the eschar, which is the non-viable skin debris on the surface of deep burns. It is characterized by rapid separation of the eschar from the underlying tissue and a heavy exudate of purulent material from the burn wound. The systemic symptoms are usually relatively mild. However, organisms can invade from heavily colonized burn eschars into viable tissue beneath and rapidly destroy the tissue, converting partial-thickness burns into full skin-thickness destruction. From here, it is a small step to invasion of the lymphatics and thence to the bloodstream or direct invasion of blood vessels, and to septicaemia. Septicaemia in patients with burns is often polymicrobial.

The major pathogens in burns are aerobic and facultatively anaerobic bacteria and fungi

The most important pathogens in burn wounds are:

- *Pseudomonas aeruginosa* and other Gram-negative rods
- *Staphylococcus aureus*
- *Streptococcus pyogenes*
- other streptococci
- enterococci.

Candida spp. and *Aspergillus* together account for about 5% of infections. Anaerobes are rare in burn wound infections. Herpesvirus infections have been reported and are most likely due to reactivation at a damaged skin site.

P. aeruginosa is a devastating Gram-negative pathogen of burned patients

P. aeruginosa is an opportunist Gram-negative rod that has a long and infamous association with burn infections. It grows well in the moist environment of a burn wound, producing a foul, green-pigmented discharge and necrosis. Invasion is common, and the characteristic skin lesions (ecthyma gangrenosum) that are pathognomonic of *P. aeruginosa* septicaemia may appear on non-burned areas (see Fig. 30.6). Host factors predisposing to infection include:

- abnormalities in the antibacterial activities of neutrophils
- deficiencies in serum opsonins.

Added to these are the virulence factors of the organism, which include the production of elastase, protease and exotoxin. This combination makes *P. aeruginosa* the most devastating Gram-negative pathogen of burned patients. Treatment is difficult because of the organism's innate resistance to many antibacterial agents. A combination of aminoglycoside, usually gentamicin or tobramycin, with one of the beta-lactams such as azlocillin, ceftazidime or imipenem is usually favoured, but several units have reported strains resistant to these agents.

It is virtually impossible to prevent colonization. Prevention of infection depends largely on inhibiting the multiplication of organisms colonizing the burn by applying topical agents such as silver nitrate.

Staph. aureus is the foremost pathogen of burn wounds

The most important predisposing factor to *Staph. aureus* infection in burns patients appears to be an abnormality of the antibacterial function of neutrophils. Infections follow a more insidious course than streptococcal infections (see below), and it may be several days before the full-blown infection is apparent. The organism is capable of destroying granulation tissue, invading and causing septicaemia. *Staph. aureus* infections of skin are discussed in detail in Chapter 26. Treatment with antistaphylococcal agents such as cloxacillin or nafcillin (or a glycopeptide if methicillin-resistant *Staph. aureus* is isolated) should be administered if there is evidence of invasive infection. Every effort should be made to prevent the spread of staphylococci from patient to patient. Although transmissible by both air-borne and contact routes, the contact route is by far the more important.

The high transmissibility of *Strep. pyogenes* makes it the scourge of burns wards

Strep. pyogenes (group A strep) infections of skin and soft tissue are discussed in some detail in Chapter 23. *Strep. pyogenes* was the most common cause of burn wound infection in the pre-antibiotic era and is still to be feared in burns wards. The infection usually occurs within the first few days of injury and is characterized by a rapid deterioration in the state of the burn wound and invasion of neighbouring healthy tissue. The patient may become severely toxic and will die within hours unless treated appropriately. *Strep. pyogenes* rarely infects healthy granulation tissue, but freshly grafted wounds may become infected, resulting in destruction of the graft. Every effort should be made to prevent spread. Penicillin is the drug of choice for treatment, and erythromycin or vancomycin can be used for penicillin-allergic patients.

Beta-haemolytic streptococci of other Lancefield groups (notably groups C and G) and enterococci are also important pathogens of burn wounds.

Traumatic injury and surgical wound infections

Both accidental and intentional trauma destroy the integrity of the body surface and leave it liable to infection. Accidental injury may result in microbes being introduced deep into the wound. The species involved will depend upon the nature of the wound, as discussed in Chapter 26.

Staph. aureus is the most important cause of surgical wound infection

Staph. aureus surgical wound infection (see Ch. 36) may be acquired during surgery or postoperatively and may originate from the patient or from another patient or staff member. The wound is less well defended than normal tissue; it may have a damaged blood supply and there may be foreign bodies such as sutures. Classic studies of wound infections have shown that far fewer staphylococci are needed to initiate infection around a suture than in normal healthy skin. Wound infections can be severe and the organisms can invade the bloodstream, with consequent seeding of other sites such as the heart valves, causing endocarditis (see Ch. 29) or bones, causing osteomyelitis (see Ch. 26), thereby further compromising the patient.

Catheter-associated infection of the urinary tract is common

Urinary catheters disrupt the normal host defences of the urinary tract and allow organisms easy access to the bladder. Such catheter-associated infection of the urinary tract is especially common if catheters are left in place for > 48 h (see Ch. 20). The organisms involved are usually Gram-negative rods from the patient's own faecal or periurethral flora, but cross-infection also occurs (see Ch. 36).

Staphylococci are the most common cause of intravenous and peritoneal dialysis catheter infections

Intravenous and peritoneal dialysis catheters breach the integrity of the skin barrier and allow organisms from the skin flora of the patient or hands of the carer easy access to deeper sites. Staphylococci are the most common cause of infection, but coryneforms, Gram-negative rods and *Candida* are also implicated.

Coagulase-negative staphylococci, particularly *Staph. epidermidis*, account for more than 50% of the infections (Table 30.3). These opportunists are members of the normal skin flora and for many years were considered to be harmless. However, they have a particular propensity for colonizing plastic and can therefore seed sites adjacent to plastic devices and thence cause invasive infections. Their virulence factors are not well understood, but their ability to produce an adhesive slime material and grow as bio films on plastic surfaces is likely to be important. Infections are characteristically more insidious in onset than those caused by the more virulent *Staph. aureus*, and recognition is hampered by the difficulty in distinguishing the infecting strain from the normal flora. Treatment is also difficult because many *Staph. epidermidis* carry multiple antibiotic resistances, and agents such as a glycopeptide (vancomycin or teicoplanin) and rifampicin may be required (see Ch. 33). Whenever possible, the plastic device should be removed.

Infections of plastic devices in situ

The technical developments in plastics and other synthetic materials have enabled many advances in medicine and surgery, but in the process have produced further ways of introducing infectious agents. *Staph. epidermidis* is an important cause of infection of cardiac pacemakers, vascular grafts and CSF shunts.

Staph. epidermidis is the most common cause of prosthetic valve and joint infections

Patients with prosthetic heart valves or prosthetic joints are compromised by:

- the surgery to implant the prosthesis
- the continued presence of a foreign body.

Staph. epidermidis is again the most common pathogen, gaining access either during surgery or from a subsequent bacteraemia originating from, for example, an intravascular line infection. Endocarditis associated with prosthetic heart valves is discussed in Chapter 29.

Table 30.3 Percentage of infections caused by *Staph. epidermidis* in patients with plastic devices *in situ*

Infection of:	Infections caused by *Staph. epidermidis* (%)
Prosthetic heart valve	
Early (<2 months postoperatively)	30–70
Late (>2 months postoperatively)	20–30
Prosthetic hip	10–40
Cerebrospinal fluid shunt	30–65
Vascular grafts	5–20
Peritoneal dialysis related	30
Intravascular catheters	10–50

Data from Gemmell and McCartney.

The most common complication of joint replacement is loosening of the prosthesis, while infection is the second most common complication and is much more likely to lead to permanent failure of the procedure. The difficulties of treatment have been outlined above, but there is understandably great reluctance to remove a prosthetic device, even though it is sometimes the only way to eradicate an infection.

Infections due to compromised clearance mechanisms

Stasis predisposes to infection, and in health the body functions to prevent stasis. In the respiratory tract, damage to the ciliary escalator predisposes the lungs to invasion, particularly in patients with cystic fibrosis, who are infected with *Staph. aureus* and *Haemophilus influenzae* and later with *P. aeruginosa* (see Ch. 19).

Obstruction and interruption of normal urine flow allows Gram-negative organisms from the periurethral flora to ascend the urethra and to establish themselves in the bladder. Septicaemia is an important complication of urinary tract infection superimposed on obstruction.

INFECTIONS ASSOCIATED WITH SECONDARY ADAPTIVE IMMUNODEFICIENCY

The underlying immunodeficiency state determines the nature and severity of any associated infection, and in some cases infection is the presenting clinical feature in a patient with an immunologic deficit. However, septicaemia and related infectious complications of immunodeficiency are most commonly encountered in patients hospitalized for chemotherapy for malignant diseases or organ transplantation. In these patients, infection continues to be a major cause of morbidity and mortality (Table 30.4). Increasingly, these infections are iatrogenic and caused by opportunist pathogens acquired in hospital.

Haematologic malignancy and bone marrow transplant infections

A lack of circulating neutrophils following bone marrow failure predisposes to infection

Susceptibility to infection of patients with leukaemia is primarily due to the lack of circulating neutrophils that inevitably follows bone marrow failure. Septicaemia may be the presenting feature, but is much more common when the patient has been exposed to chemotherapy to induce a remission of the disease (remission-induction chemotherapy). Neutropenia, defined as a count of $<0.5 \times 10^9$ neutrophils/L, may persist for a few days to several weeks. Similarly, prolonged periods of neutropenia occur after bone marrow transplantation.

The length of time over which the patient is neutropenic influences the nature of any associated infection and the frequency with which it occurs. For example, fungal infections are much more common in patients who are neutropenic for more than 21 days. Although Gram-negative rods such as *Escherichia coli* and *P. aeruginosa* from the bowel flora have

Table 30.4 Examples of opportunistic pathogens in immunocompromised hosts

Bacteria
Gram-positive
Staphylococcus aureus
Coagulase-negative staphylococci
Streptococci
Listeria spp.
Nocardia asteroides
Mycobacterium tuberculosis
Mycobacterium avium-intracellulare
Gram-negative
Enterobacteriaceae
Pseudomonas aeruginosa
Legionella spp.
Bacteroides spp.
Fungi
Candida spp.
Aspergillus spp.
Cryptococcus neoformans
Histoplasma capsulatum
Pneumocystis jirovecii[a]
Parasites
Toxoplasma gondii
Strongyloides stercoralis
Viruses
Herpesviruses, e.g. HSV, CMV, VZV, EBV, HHV-6, HHV-7, HHV-8
Hepatitis B
Hepatitis C[b]
Polyomaviruses, e.g. BKV, JCV
Adenoviruses
HIV[b]

[a]Formerly *P. carinii*. BKV, BK virus; JCV, JC virus; CMV, cytomegalovirus; EBV, Epstein–Barr virus; HHV, human herpesvirus; HSV, herpes simplex virus; VZV, varicella-zoster virus.
[b]HIV and HCV have been transmitted via organ transplantation and unscreened blood.

in the past been the most common cause of septicaemia in neutropenic patients, Gram-positive organisms such as staphylococci, streptococci and enterococci are also important. *Staph. epidermidis* septicaemia associated with intravascular catheters (see above) is common. Infections caused by fungi are also increasing, partly because more patients are surviving the early neutropenic period with the aid of modern antibacterial agents and granulocyte transfusions. Viruses such as CMV infections are an important feature of bone marrow transplantation and are associated with graft-versus-host disease as well as immunosuppressive therapy. In addition, adenovirus, EBV and BK virus infections may be seen, especially in allogeneic bone marrow transplant recipients.

Solid organ transplant infections

Most infections occur within 3–4 months of transplantation

Suppression of a patient's cell-mediated immunity is necessary to prevent rejection of a grafted organ, and the cytotoxic regimens used usually suppress humoral immunity to some extent as well. In addition, high doses of corticosteroids to suppress inflammatory responses are required. The combination of these factors results in a severely compromised host, and those that have an effect on infection in recipients of solid organ transplants include:

- the underlying medical condition of the patient
- the patient's previous immune status
- the type of organ transplant
- the immunosuppressive regimen
- the exposure of the patient to pathogens.

The organisms that cause the most common and most severe infections are shown in Table 30.4. Some of the viral infections are latent and reactivate when cell-mediated surveillance is suppressed.

From 3 to 4 months after transplantation, the risk of infection is reduced, but remains for as long as the patient is immunosuppressed.

HIV infection leading to AIDS

The clinical definition of AIDS includes the presence of one or more opportunistic infections

People with AIDS are often infected concomitantly with multiple pathogens, which they fail to eradicate despite prolonged, appropriate and aggressive antimicrobial chemotherapy. Most of the pathogens involved are intracellular microbes that require an intact cell-mediated immune response for effective defence. As the HIV-infected individual progresses to AIDS (see Ch. 21), organisms that are usually controlled by cell-mediated immunity are able to reactivate to cause disseminated infections not seen in the immunologically normal individual. Improved immune surveillance as a result of antiretroviral therapy has reduced the incidence of infections that are the hallmark of AIDS including *Candida*, Kaposi's sarcoma and other opportunist pathogens described in more detail below.

Many of the pathogens that cause infections in the immunocompromised host (Table 30.4) are described elsewhere in this book.

OTHER IMPORTANT OPPORTUNIST PATHOGENS

Fungi

Candida is the most common fungal pathogen in compromised patients

This yeast is an opportunist pathogen in a variety of patients and in various body sites. It is the cause of:

- vaginal and oral thrush (see Ch. 21)
- skin infections (see Ch. 26)
- endocarditis, particularly in intravenous drug users (see Ch. 29).

Candida manifests itself in different ways depending upon the nature of the underlying compromise:

- *Chronic mucocutaneous candidiasis.* This is rare and is a persistent but non-invasive infection of mucous membranes, hair, skin and nails in patients, often children, with a specific T-cell defect rendering them anergic to *Candida* (Fig. 30.7). It may require repeated or long-term treatment with azole antifungal drugs. Diminished sensitivity to these agents may occur after repeated use.

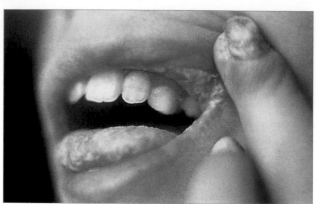

Figure 30.7 Chronic mucocutaneous candidiasis in a child with impaired T-cell response to antigens. (Courtesy of M.J. Wood.)

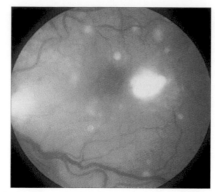

Figure 30.9 *Candida* endophthalmitis. Fundal photograph showing areas of white exudate. (Courtesy of A.M. Geddes.)

- *Oropharyngeal and oesophageal candidiasis.* This is seen in a variety of compromised patients, including HIV-infected individuals (Fig. 30.8), people with ill-fitting dentures, diabetes mellitus or on antibiotics or corticosteroids. Oropharyngeal candidiasis generally responds to treatment with antifungal mouthwashes (nystatin or an azole compound). Those cases which do not respond can be treated with fluconazole. Oesophageal candidiasis requires systemic therapy.
- *Gastrointestinal candidiasis.* This is seen in patients who have undergone major gastric or abdominal surgery and in those with neoplastic disease. The organism can pass through the intestinal wall and spread from a gastrointestinal focus. Antemortem diagnosis is difficult, and as many as 25% of patients do not have any symptoms in the early stages of disease. If there is dissemination from the gut, blood cultures may become positive and *Candida* antigens may be detectable in the serum. A high index of suspicion is required to initiate antifungal therapy early in these patients, but disseminated disease is often fatal.
- *Disseminated candidiasis.* This is probably acquired via the gastrointestinal tract, but also arises from intravascular catheter-related infections. Patients with lymphoma and leukaemia are most at risk. Blood-borne spread to almost any organ can occur. Infections of the eye (endophthalmitis; Fig. 30.9) and the skin (nodular skin lesions; see Ch. 26) are important because they provide diagnostic clues, and without these the non-specific symptoms of fever and septic shock make early

diagnosis difficult. Immunocompromised patients are often given antifungal therapy 'blindly' if they have a fever and fail to respond to broad-spectrum antibacterial agents (Fig. 30.10).

Cryptococcus neoformans infection is most common in people with impaired cell-mediated immunity

C. neoformans is an opportunistic yeast with a worldwide distribution. It can cause infection in the immunocompetent host, but infection is seen more frequently in people with impaired cell-mediated immunity. The onset of disease may be slow and usually results in lung infection or meningo-encephalitis; occasionally other sites such as skin, bone and joints are involved (see Ch. 26).

C. neoformans can be demonstrated in the CSF and is characterized by its large polysaccharide capsule (see Fig. 24.6). Rapid identification can be made by antigen detection in a latex agglutination test using specific antibody-coated latex particles. Treatment involves a combination of amphotericin and flucytosine (see Ch. 33) and can be monitored by detecting a fall in CSF antigen concentration. The prognosis depends largely upon the patient's underlying disease; in the severely immunocompromised, mortality is approximately 50%. In patients with AIDS it is almost impossible to eradicate the organism even with intensive treatment. Fluconazole can be given as post-treatment prophylaxis.

Disseminated *Histoplasma capsulatum* infection may occur years after exposure in immunocompromised patients

This is a highly infectious fungus that causes an acute but benign pulmonary infection in healthy people, but can produce chronic progressive disseminated disease in the compromised host. The organism is endemic only in tropical parts of the world and notably in the so-called 'histoplasmosis belt' of the central USA, particularly in the Ohio and Mississippi river valleys. The natural habitat of the organism is the soil. It is transmitted by the air-borne route and the fungal spores are deposited in the alveoli, from whence the fungus spreads via the lymphatics to the regional lymph nodes. As disseminated disease may occur many years after the initial exposure in immunocompromised patients it may present in patients who have long since left endemic areas. The infection may occur in HIV-infected individuals who have visited such regions.

Cultures of blood, bone marrow, sputum and CSF may yield *Histoplasma*, but biopsy and histologic examination

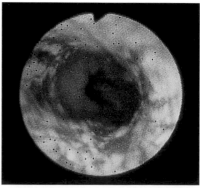

Figure 30.8 *Candida* oesophagitis. Endoscopic view showing extensive areas of whitish exudate. (Courtesy of I. Chesner.)

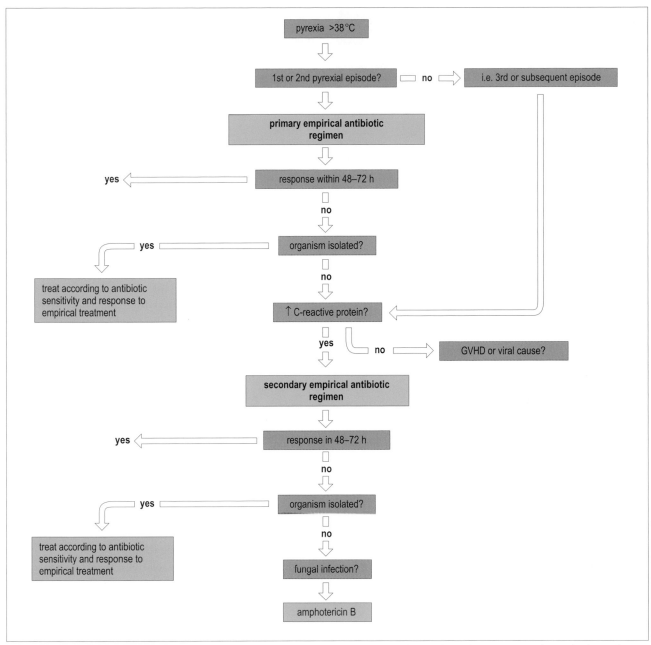

Figure 30.10 Neutropenic patients succumb very rapidly to infections, and decisions to treat have to be made on an empiric basis. This figure shows one example of such a decision-making tree. GVHD, graft-versus-host disease. (Adapted from: Rogers.)

of bone marrow, liver or lymph nodes is often required to make the diagnosis (Fig. 30.11). Approximately 50% of cases of progressive disease in the immunocompromised are successfully treated with amphotericin. Itraconazole can be given for post-treatment prophylaxis.

African histoplasmosis, caused by *Histoplasma duboisii*, is found in Equatorial Africa. Patients may present with localized cutaneous or disseminated disease.

Invasive aspergillosis has a very high mortality rate in the compromised patient

The role of *Aspergillus* spp. in diseases of the lung has been outlined in Chapter 19, but this fungus is now increasingly reported as a cause of invasive disease in compromised patients, usually in profoundly neutropenic patients or those receiving high-dose corticosteroids (Fig. 30.12). Like

Histoplasma, aspergilli are found in soil, but have a worldwide distribution. Infection is spread by the air-borne route, and the lung is the site of invasion in almost every case. Dissemination to other sites, particularly the central nervous system (Fig. 30.13) and heart, occurs in about 25% of compromised individuals with lung infection. Diagnosis involves microscopy, culture, antigen detection and PCR on bronchoalveolar lavage specimens. Lung biopsy may be required to make a tissue diagnosis.

Invasive aspergillosis has a high fatality rate in the compromised patient. Prophylactic antifungal agents such as caspofungin, posaconazole and voriconazole, early diagnosis and institution of treatment using an intravenous lipid formulation of amphotericin B known as liposomal amphotericin B complexes or AmBisome (see Ch. 33), together with a reduction in corticosteroid and cytotoxic

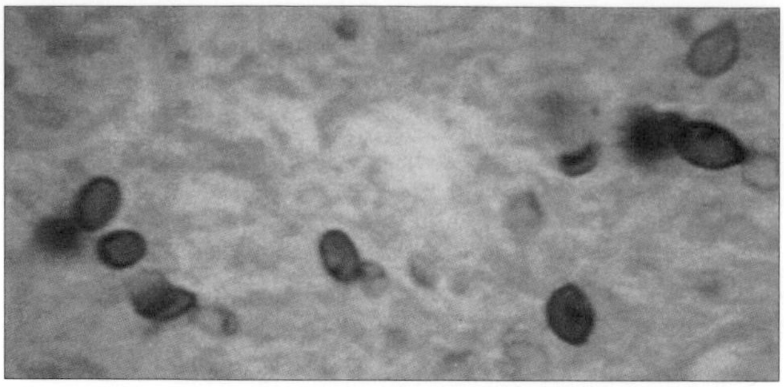

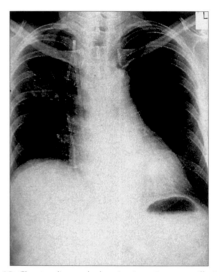

Figure 30.11 Histologic section of the lung showing yeast forms of *Histoplasma capsulatum*. Methenamine silver stain. (Courtesy of T.F. Sellers, Jr.)

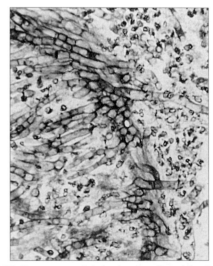

Figure 30.12 Chest radiograph showing invasive aspergillosis in the right lung of a patient with acute myeloblastic leukaemia. (Courtesy of C. Kibbler.)

Figure 30.13 Numerous septate hyphae invading a blood vessel wall in cerebral aspergillosis. (Periodic acid-Schiff stain.) (Courtesy of W.E. Farrar.)

therapy wherever possible, appear to improve the prognosis. Outbreaks of hospital-acquired infection have been reported (see Ch. 36), especially in relation to recent building work.

Pneumocystis jirovecii (formerly *P. carinii*) only causes symptomatic disease in people with deficient cellular immunity

P. jirovecii is an atypical fungus which appears to be widespread; a large proportion of the population has antibodies to the organism, but it only causes symptomatic disease in people whose cellular immune mechanisms are deficient. There is therefore a high incidence of *P. jirovecii* pneumonia in patients receiving immunosuppressive therapy to prevent transplant rejection and in people with HIV. It is very rare to find *Pneumocystis* infection in any other site in the body, but the reason for this is unknown.

Diagnosis is not easy and requires a high index of suspicion. The symptoms are non-specific and can mimic a variety of other infectious and non-infectious respiratory diseases. In addition, unlike the other fungi described above, the organism cannot be isolated in expectorated sputum using conventional culture methods, and invasive techniques such as bronchoalveolar lavage or open lung biopsy are required. In samples obtained by these techniques, the organism can be demonstrated by silver or immunofluorescent stains (Fig. 30.14). DNA amplification by the polymerase chain reaction improves the sensitivity of the diagnostic tests.

Treatment is with high dose co-trimoxazole (trimethoprim-sulfamethoxazole). Pentamidine is an alternative (see Ch. 33). Adjunctive corticosteroid therapy is given in moderate to severe infections in HIV co-infected individuals. Co-trimoxazole is used prophylactically.

Bacteria

Nocardia asteroides is an uncommon opportunist pathogen with a worldwide distribution

The family Actinomycetes, relatives of the mycobacteria, but resembling fungi in that they form branching filaments, contain two pathogenic genera, *Actinomyces* and *Nocardia*. *N. asteroides* infections have been reported in the immunocompromised, especially in renal transplant patients. The lung is usually the primary site, but

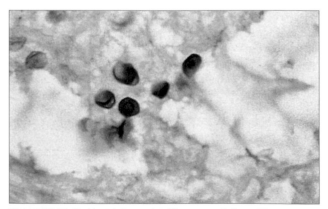

Figure 30.14 Darkly staining cysts of *Pneumocystis jirovecii* in an open lung biopsy from an AIDS patient with pneumonia. (Grocott silver stain.) (Courtesy of M. Turner-Warwick.)

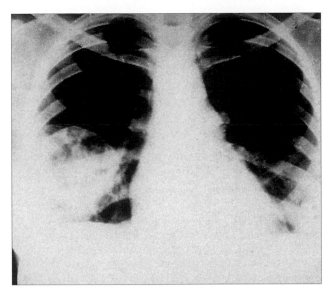

Figure 30.15 Pulmonary nocardiosis. Chest radiograph showing a large rounded lesion in the right lower zone with multiple cavities. (Courtesy of T.F. Sellers, Jr.)

infection can spread to the skin, kidney or central nervous system (Fig. 30.15). As with *Aspergillus*, hospital outbreaks of nocardiosis have been described.

Nocardia can be isolated on routine laboratory media, but is often slow to grow and is consequently easily overgrown by commensal flora. Therefore the laboratory staff should be informed if nocardiosis is suspected clinically, so that appropriate media are inoculated. The organism is a Gram-negative branching rod and weakly acid fast (Fig. 30.16).

Sulphonamides or co-trimoxazole are the drugs of choice, but treatment can be difficult and various other regimens involving tetracycline, aminoglycosides or imipenem have been described.

Mycobacterium avium-intracellulare disease is often a terminal event in AIDS

Although mycobacterial infections are well documented in immunosuppressed patients, the association between AIDS and mycobacteria includes disseminated infection with *Mycobacterium tuberculosis* and *Mycobacterium avium-intracellulare* (*Mycobacterium avium* complex or MAC). These organisms can be isolated from blood cultures from patients with AIDS. *M. tuberculosis* has been described in detail in Chapter 19. *M. avium-intracellulare* belongs to the so-called 'atypical' mycobacteria or mycobacteria other than tuberculosis (MOTT). It resembles *M. tuberculosis* in that it is slow-growing, but it is resistant to the conventional antituberculosis drugs. Multidrug therapy with combinations such as clofazimine or rifamycin derivatives together with macrolides such as azithromycin or clarithromycin, quinolones, isoniazid, ethambutol, cycloserine or pyrazinamide have been recommended.

Protozoa and helminths

Cryptosporidium and *Isospora belli* infections cause severe diarrhea in AIDS

Cryptosporidium (Fig. 30.17) is a protozoan parasite that causes human disease, and is well known to veterinarians as an animal pathogen. It causes significant but self-limiting diarrhea in healthy normal people (see Ch. 22), but severe and chronic diarrhea in people with AIDS. Highly active antiretroviral therapy in individuals with AIDS infected with *Cryptosporidium* has been reported to improve the diarrhea symptoms. Paromomycin reduces oocyst output but does not clear infection. Nitazoxanide is effective in

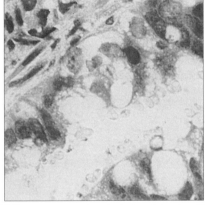

Figure 30.17 Numerous organisms in the brush border of the intestine in cryptosporidiosis. (Courtesy of J. Newman.)

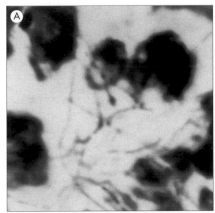

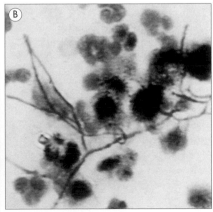

Figure 30.16 *Nocardia asteroides* in sputum. (A) Acid-fast stain. (Courtesy of T.F. Sellers, Jr.) (B) Gram's stain. (Courtesy of H.P. Holley.)

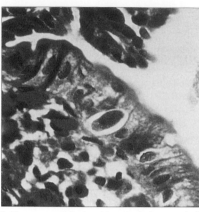

Figure 30.18 Human coccidiosis, with a single *Isospora belli* organism within an epithelial cell and a chronic inflammatory reaction in the lamina propria. (Courtesy of G.N. Griffin.)

HIV-negative patients but is only partially active in those co-infected with HIV. *Isospora belli* (Fig. 30.18) is a parasite very similar to *Cryptosporidium* and also produces severe diarrhea in people with AIDS. Unlike *Cryptosporidium*, however, it is susceptible to co-trimoxazole.

Cyclospora cayetanensis, also related to *Cryptosporidium*, likewise produces prolonged and severe diarrhea in immunosuppressed individuals. Co-trimoxazole treatment is effective. Ciprofloxacin is partially effective.

Infections with microsporidia also cause diarrhea in people with AIDS and other immunosuppressed patients. *Enterocytozoon bieneusi* is the most common cause, although *Encephalitozoon intestinalis* also occurs. Albendazole treatment is effective against *Encephalitozoon intestinalis* but has disappointing activity against *Enterocytozoon bieneusi*. Where feasible, immune reconstitution is the mainstay of treatment.

Immunosuppression may lead to reactivation of dormant *Strongyloides stercoralis*

Strongyloides stercoralis is a parasitic roundworm that remains dormant for years following initial infection, but may be reactivated to produce massive autoinfection in the immunosuppressed patient. Although rare in the UK and most of the USA, it should be borne in mind in patients who have lived in endemic areas such as the tropics and southern USA, even if this was many years before their immunosuppression. Human T-cell lymphotropic virus type 1 (HTLV-1) infection is associated with disseminated strongyloidiasis due to the modified immune response to this enteric helminth. The lungs, liver and brain are the most common organs affected.

Viruses

Certain virus infections are both more common and more severe in compromised patients, and regular surveillance is critical

The virus infections that are more common or more severe in the compromised patient (see Table 30.4) have been described in detail elsewhere in this book. Many of these represent reactivation of latent infections. Pre-transplantation baseline serology is carried out to determine both the donor and recipient status for a number of virus infections, including HIV, hepatitis B and C, CMV, EBV and HSV.

Suppression of specific virus infections using antiviral agents is part of the management of the recipient in conjunction with regular virological surveillance post-transplantation using viral genome or antigen detection methods.

As part of a pre-emptive treatment strategy, blood samples are collected for early detection of viraemia or antigenaemia which precedes disease. For example, transplant donors and recipients are screened for CMV IgG. CMV causes a broad spectrum of clinical disease in this setting, including pneumonitis, oesophagitis, colitis, hepatitis and encephalitis. If there is a transplant mismatch, i.e. the donor is CMV IgG positive and the recipient CMV IgG negative, the infection may be acquired from the donor organ or bone marrow. If possible, transplant centres try to avoid this situation, as the risk of a primary CMV infection in the first month post-transplantation is extremely high, as is the morbidity and mortality. In this case, CMV DNA monitoring is carried out on blood samples on a regular basis post-transplantation to detect early infection and start antiviral therapy as soon as possible. Some centres offer antiviral therapy in the immediate post-transplant period in this clinical setting to delay the onset of infection to a time when the recipient is less immunosuppressed. CMV IgG positive recipients are at risk of reactivation or reinfection and will also be monitored regularly post-transplantation. A primary CMV infection is usually detected around 4 weeks, compared with reactivation at around 6–8 weeks, post-transplantation, respectively.

Antiviral prophylaxis for HSV reactivation that may occur in the immediate post-transplantation period is often given to bone marrow transplant recipients for prolonged periods post-transplantation. Aciclovir is given at a low dose and is effective in preventing HSV and VZV reactivation. Virus surveillance is therefore not carried out, but if a breakthrough infection occurs it is important to collect material from the lesions for virus isolation or genome sequence analysis to determine the antiviral susceptibility. Herpetic lesions can be persistent and involve the lips, oesophagus and other parts of the gastrointestinal tract, and may cause a pneumonitis, hepatitis or encephalitis.

Herpes zoster, a reactivation of VZV infection, may occur within a few months post-transplantation, affecting the skin dermatome supplied by the involved nerve. Sometimes the distribution may be multidermatomal and dissemination can occur to other sites.

HHV-6 and HHV-7 infection, reinfection or reactivation has been reported in transplant recipients, in particular with neurologic conditions including encephalitis. HHV-8 has been associated with the development of Kaposi's sarcoma (KS) in individuals with AIDS as well as classic and endemic KS in HIV-uninfected individuals.

EBV infection can lead to tumour development

EBV infection has been associated with the development of Hodgkin's disease, non-Hodgkin's lymphomas in individuals with HIV infection, post-transplantation lymphoproliferative disease and smooth-muscle tumours in immunosuppressed children. EBV-associated post-transplant lymphoproliferative disorder (PTLD) has a broad spectrum of clinical syndromes ranging from infectious mononucleosis to malignancies containing clonal chromosomal abnormalities with a high mortality rate, especially with the monoclonal tumours. The risk factors recognized for PTLD development in solid organ transplant recipients include post-transplantation primary EBV infection, mismatched donor and recipient CMV status, CMV disease, and intensity and type of immunosuppressive therapy. With respect to EBV infection, EBV-susceptible recipients have a 10–76-fold higher risk of PTLD compared with recipients with previous EBV exposure.

As the two peaks of primary EBV infection are in children and adolescents, the incidence of PTLD is higher in paediatric transplant recipients. In addition, without an effective cytotoxic T-cell response due to post-transplant immunosuppression to prevent graft rejection, the EBV-infected B lymphocytes may proliferate in an uncontrolled fashion. This results in B-cell hyperplasia with CD20-positive lymphocytes that ranges from polyclonal and benign to developing a monoclonal or oligoclonal B cell lymphoma. The prevalence of PTLD in paediatric liver transplant recipients ranges from 4% to 14%, depending on the immunosuppressive regimen. Retrospective studies have shown that up to 50% of paediatric transplant recipients with primary EBV infections are at risk of developing PTLD. The infection may be acquired in the community or, in the transplant setting, from the donor organ or blood products. The natural history of EBV infection and pathophysiology of post-transplant EBV-driven lymphoproliferation is not well understood.

Diagnostic criteria for EBV-associated PTLD have been developed. However, in the absence of randomized, placebo-controlled trials, there is little information on the efficacy of specific treatment protocols. The treatment of PTLD includes reducing immunosuppression to allow a better host response to control the infection, although there is a risk of rejecting the graft, using rituximab, an anti-CD20 monoclonal antibody that targets the B cells with the EBV receptor, and chemotherapy. Treatment of post-transplant lymphomas by adoptive transfer of EBV-specific cytotoxic T lymphocytes has been reported.

Respiratory virus infections

Immunocompromised patients, especially transplant recipients, are at increased risk of pneumonia and death if they develop respiratory tract infections with viruses such as RSV, influenza, parainfluenza and adenoviruses. Preventive measures include influenza immunization, prophylaxis with palivizumab, an RSV-specific monoclonal antibody that is used in specific clinical settings, and early diagnosis of an upper respiratory tract infection using sensitive tests such as viral genome detection. There are some specific antiviral treatments that include oseltamivir for influenza and ribavirin for RSV infections.

Adenovirus infection has a high mortality rate

Primary and reactivated adenovirus infections can result in disseminated disease in immunocompromised hosts, in particular paediatric and adult bone marrow transplant recipients. Hepatitis and pneumonia are most frequently reported. Again, adenovirus surveillance is often carried out in centres by collecting blood samples post-transplantation which are tested for adenovirus DNA in order to detect early viraemia. Where adenovirus viraemia is detected, management options include reducing immunosuppression and treating with an antiviral agent such as ribavirin or cidofovir. However, there are few reports of successful outcomes in patients with disseminated infections.

Hepatitis B and C infection in transplant recipients

Hepatitis B virus infection has an immunopathologic pathogenesis, with jaundice occurring after cytotoxic T cells have lysed the hepatitis B surface-antigen-bearing hepatocytes. The virus is integrated in the hepatocytes after acute hepatitis B. Bone marrow transplant recipients with evidence of previous, not current, hepatitis B infection are likely to suffer a hepatitis B reactivation post-transplantation. They will be asymptomatic as they are immunosuppressed and will not mount a cytotoxic T-cell response until they have engrafted. It is at this stage they will become symptomatic, develop jaundice and the morbidity and mortality can be high. Antiviral prophylaxis with antiviral agents such as lamivudine or tenofovir is given to prevent reactivation, together with HBV DNA monitoring. Antiviral treatment will be given pre- and post-transplant if a transplant recipient has a current HBV infection, i.e. is hepatitis B surface antigen positive.

The most common reason for liver transplantation in the USA and Europe is hepatitis C-related end-stage liver disease. HCV reinfection of the graft post-transplantation is common and within 5 years nearly one-third of these transplant recipients may develop cirrhosis and subsequently suffer liver decompensation and lose their graft.

Hepatitis C virus infection is also associated with veno-occlusive disease in bone marrow transplant recipients. Venous congestion occurs in the liver due to a non-specific vasculitis and results in liver necrosis. Multiorgan failure can be precipitated due to increased capillary permeability throughout the body.

Polyomaviruses can cause haemorrhagic cystitis and progressive multifocal leukoencephalopathy

BK or JC viruses are polyomaviruses acquired via the respiratory tract that lie latent in the kidney, and may be detected in the urine of bone marrow transplant recipients (see Ch. 20). BK viruria is associated with haemorrhagic cystitis.

JC virus can reactivate and disseminate to cause central nervous system infections such as progressive multifocal leucoencephalopathy (PML) in individuals with AIDS. However, since the advent of highly active antiretroviral therapy resulting in higher CD4 counts and suppressed HIV load, PML is seen less often.

KEY FACTS

- A compromised person is one whose normal defences against infection are defective. Immunodeficiencies may involve the innate or adaptive immune systems and may be primary or secondary.

- Compromised patients can be infected with any of the pathogens capable of infecting immunocompetent individuals. In addition, they suffer many infections caused by opportunist pathogens. The type of infection is related to the nature of the compromise.

- Effective antimicrobial therapy is often difficult to achieve in the absence of a functional immune response, even when the pathogen is susceptible to the drug in vitro.

- Important bacterial opportunists include *P. aeruginosa*, especially in neutropenic patients and those with major burns, and *Staph. epidermidis* in patients with plastic devices in situ. In AIDS, the predominant bacterial opportunists are intracellular pathogens benefiting from the lack of cell-mediated immunity.

- AIDS, and neutropenia (particularly following cytotoxic therapy), predispose to fungal infections (e.g. *Candida*, *Aspergillus* and *Cryptococcus*) especially when the patient has received previous antibacterial therapy.

- Viral infections are more common and severe in immunodeficient patients than in immunocompetent patients, particularly reactivation of latent infections (e.g. herpes simplex virus, CMV, JC virus).

Diagnosis of infection and assessment of host defence mechanisms

31

Introduction

Good quality specimens are needed for reliable microbiologic diagnoses

The precise identification of the causative organism in infection has become increasingly important now that therapeutic intervention is possible. The ability to achieve this depends upon a positive interaction between the clinician and the microbiologist; the clinician must be aware of the complexity of the tests and the time required to achieve a result. In turn, the microbiologist must appreciate the nature of the patient's condition and be able to assist the clinician in interpreting the laboratory report. A fundamental step in any diagnosis is the choice of an appropriate specimen, which ultimately depends upon an understanding of the pathogenesis of infections.

Microbiology differs from other clinical laboratory disciplines in the amount of interpretative input required. When a specimen is received, decisions are made regarding the appropriate processing pathway, and when the result is received, it must be interpreted in relation to the specimen and the patient.

AIMS OF THE CLINICAL MICROBIOLOGY LABORATORY

The aims of the microbiology laboratory are:

- to provide accurate information about the presence or absence of microorganisms in a specimen that may be involved in a patient's disease process
- where relevant, to provide information on the antimicrobial susceptibility of the microorganisms isolated.

Identification is achieved by detecting the microorganism or its products or the patient's immune response

Laboratory tests are carried out:

- to detect microorganisms or their products in specimens collected from the patient
- to detect evidence of the patient's immune response (production of antibodies) to infection.

While there are different protocols for different specimens (e.g., urine, faeces, genital tract, blood, etc.), the tests fall into three main categories:

1. *Identification of microorganisms by isolation and culture.* Microorganisms may grow in artificial media or, in the case of viruses, in cell cultures. In some instances, quantification is important (e.g. more than 10^5 bacteria/mL of urine is indicative of infection whereas lower numbers are not; see Ch. 20). Once an organism has been isolated in culture, its susceptibility to antimicrobial agents can be determined.
2. *Identification of a specific microbial gene or product.* Non-cultural techniques that do not depend upon the growth and multiplication of microorganisms to detect microorganisms have the potential to yield more rapid results. These techniques include the detection of structural components of the cell (e.g. cell wall antigens) and

extracellular products (e.g. toxins). Alternatively, molecular approaches are increasingly available such as the detection of specific gene sequences in clinical specimens using DNA probes or the polymerase chain reaction (PCR; see below). They are potentially applicable to all microorganisms, but antimicrobial susceptibilities cannot be determined without culture (although the presence of resistance genes may be detectable by specific probes).

3. *Detection of specific antibodies to a pathogen.* This is especially important when the pathogen cannot be cultivated in laboratory media (e.g. *Treponema pallidum*, many viruses) or when culture would be particularly hazardous to laboratory staff (e.g. culture of *Francisella tularensis*, the cause of tularaemia, or the fungus *Coccidioides immitis*). Detection of IgM and/or IgG antibodies in a single serum collected during the acute phase of illness can be helpful in diagnosis of, for example, rubella by specific IgM, hepatitis A by IgM and hepatitis B by HepB surface antigen, or in rare diseases such as Lassa fever. The classic diagnostic method is by detection of a rise (fourfold or greater) in antibody titre between 'paired' sera, collected in the acute phase of an infection (5–7 days after onset of symptoms) and in convalescence (after 3–4 weeks). Such tests therefore tend to result in a delayed or retrospective diagnosis and are therefore of limited help for clinical management.

SPECIMEN PROCESSING

Specimen handling and interpretation of results is based upon a knowledge of normal flora and contaminants

Specimens intended for cultivation of microorganisms can be divided into two types:

- those from sites that are normally sterile
- those from sites that usually have a commensal flora (Box 31.1; see also Ch. 8).

Box 31.1 Sampling Sites, The Normal Flora and Interpretation of Results

Body sites that are normally sterile

- Blood and bone marrow
- Cerebrospinal fluid
- Serous fluids
- Tissues
- Lower respiratory tract
- Bladder

Body sites that have a normal commensal flora

- Mouth, nose and upper respiratory tract
- Skin
- Gastrointestinal tract
- Female genital tract
- Urethra

Some sites in the body are sterile in health so that growth of any organism is indicative of infection provided that the specimen has been properly collected and transported, and examined in the laboratory without delay. The significance of isolates from sites that have a commensal flora depends upon the identity of the isolate and the quantity, as well as the immune status of the patient.

Box 31.2 Important Steps in Specimen Collection and Delivery to The Laboratory

- Take the appropriate specimen, e.g. blood and cerebrospinal fluid in suspected meningitis.
- Collect the specimen at the appropriate time, during the acute phase of the disease, e.g. malarial films, virus isolation, viral genome detection, IgM detection.
- If possible, collect specimen before patient receives antimicrobials.
- Collect enough material and an adequate number of samples, e.g. enough blood/serum for more than one set of blood cultures.
- Avoid contamination:
  - from normal flora, e.g. midstream urine
  - from non-sterile equipment.
- Use the correct containers and appropriate transport media.
- Label specimens properly.
- Complete request form with enough clinical information and a statement of possible aetiology.
- Inform the laboratory if special tests are required.
- Transport specimens rapidly to the laboratory.

The responsibility of the clinician does not end with collection of the specimen and requesting tests. Good communication with the microbiologist is essential.

A thorough knowledge of the microorganisms normally isolated from specimens from non-sterile sites, and the common contaminants of specimens collected from sterile sites, is important to ensure that specimens are properly handled and the results are correctly interpreted. Some specimens from sites that should be sterile (e.g. bladder urine, sputum from the lower respiratory tract) are usually collected after passage through orifices that have a normal flora, which may contaminate the specimens. This needs to be considered when interpreting the culture results of these specimens.

In an ideal world, each specimen arriving in the laboratory would be considered in turn together with the information provided about the patient on the request form so that the microbiologist could assess the pathogens likely to be present and devise an 'individualized' processing plan. However, in reality, this approach is not practicable because of constraints on time and money. Thus, specimens tend to be processed by type (e.g. urine, blood, faeces) and the microbiologist looks for easily cultivated pathogens known to be associated with each sample type. However, if the laboratory is provided with suitable information, such as a statement of possible aetiology, more fastidious or unusual pathogens can be sought and relevant antibiotic susceptibilities assessed. To obtain a test result that correctly identifies the infection, it is important to collect an appropriate specimen, to use the appropriate transport conditions and to deliver specimens rapidly to the laboratory. These conditions all affect the accuracy of the laboratory report, and therefore its value to the clinician and ultimately to the patient. Key points to remember about specimen collection are summarized in Box 31.2.

Routine culture takes at least 18h to produce a result

Time is a key factor because the conventional methods of microbiologic diagnosis depend upon growth and identification of the pathogen. Results of routine culture cannot be achieved in <18h and may take much longer (e.g. several weeks) for a minority of pathogens such as the mycobacteria, which grow very slowly. Thus, specimen processing can be categorized according to the time required to achieve a result and the method – cultural or non-cultural. An alternative route to the diagnosis of an infection is an immunologic one, relying on the detection of an antibody response to the putative pathogen in the patient's blood. These diagnostic routes are summarized in Figure 31.1, but rapid technologies (e.g. PCR, nucleic-acid probes, microarrays, etc.) have had a major influence on this process.

NON-CULTURAL TECHNIQUES FOR THE LABORATORY DIAGNOSIS OF INFECTION

Non-cultural techniques do not require microorganism multiplication before detection

Although medical microbiology has long been synonymous with the cultivation of microorganisms from patients' specimens, these techniques are labour-intensive and slow to produce results (days rather than hours) because replication of organisms is a necessary, but rate-limiting, step. In addition, some microorganisms cannot be cultured in artificial media, and viable organisms may be difficult to recover from specimens of patients who have received antimicrobial

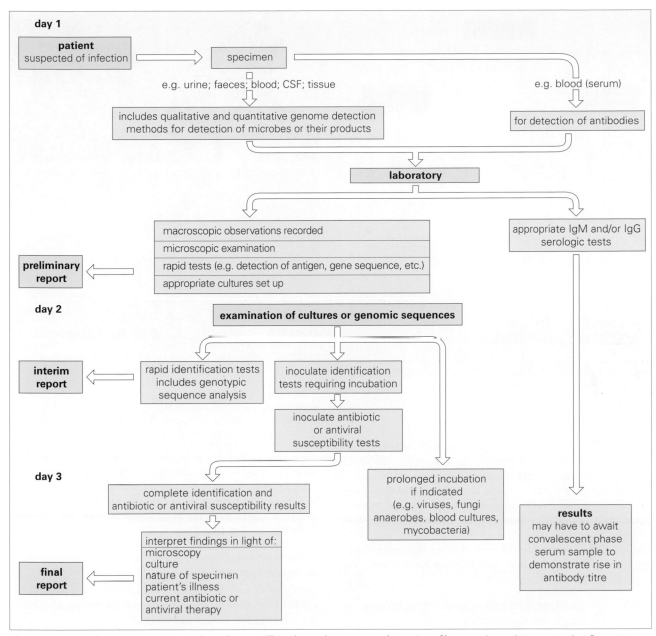

Figure 31.1 Route from patient to microbiologic diagnosis. This scheme shows a general overview of key steps in specimen processing. Some tests can be performed on the specimen immediately and yield 'same day' results. Culture of specimens usually involves a minimum of 18 h incubation before colonies are visible and can be identified. Antibiotic susceptibility tests involve a further incubation period. Alternatively, the diagnosis may be based on the detection of specific antibodies in serum samples: cerebrospinal fluid (CSF), genomic sequences, etc.

therapy. Non-cultural techniques do not require multiplication of the microorganism before its detection. Some techniques, such as microscopy and detection of microbial antigens in specimens, can provide very rapid results (i.e. within 2 h). Other non-cultural methods such as the use of DNA probes and amplification of DNA by the polymerase chain reaction (PCR) may also provide a rapid answer in a matter of hours.

Microscopy

Microscopy is an important first step in the examination of specimens

Microscopy plays a fundamental role in microbiology. Although microorganisms show a wide range in size (see Ch. 1) they are too small to be seen individually by the naked eye, and therefore a microscope is an essential tool in microbiology. The various types of microscopy are summarized in Figure 31.2. The light microscope magnifies objects and therefore improves the resolving power of the naked eye from about 100 000 nm (0.1 mm) to 200 nm; the electron microscope can improve this to 0.1 to 1.0 nm.

Light microscopy

Bright field microscopy is used to examine specimens and cultures as wet or stained preparations

Wet preparations are used to demonstrate:

- blood cells and microbes in fluid specimens such as urine, faeces or cerebrospinal fluid (CSF)
- cysts, eggs and parasites in faeces

421

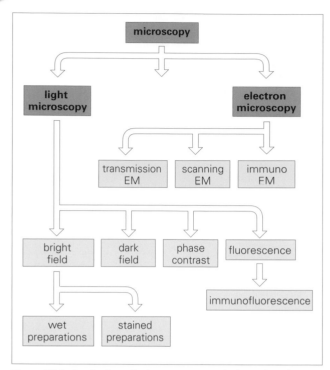

Figure 31.2 Applications of microscopy to microbiology. The scheme shows the different uses of light and electron microscopy (EM) for looking at microbes, although the latter is much less frequently used.

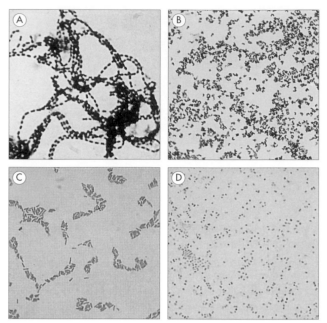

Figure 31.3 The Gram stain is the most important stain for studying bacteria. The combination of the violet dye (crystal violet) and iodine (acting as a mordant) binds to the cell wall. Gram-positive cells retain the stain when challenged with acetone and remain purple. Gram-negative cells lose the purple stain and appear colourless until stained with a pink counterstain (neutral red or safranin). Examination of Gram-stained films also allows the shape of the cells to be noted. Some examples are shown: (A) Gram-positive cocci in chains (*streptococci*); (B) Gram-positive rods (*Listeria*); (C) Gram-negative rods (*E. coli*); (D) Gram-negative cocci (*Neisseria*).

- fungi in skin
- protozoa in blood and tissues.

Living organisms can be examined to detect motility.

Dyes are used to stain cells so that they can be seen more easily. Stains are usually applied to dried material that has been fixed (by heat or alcohol) onto the microscope slide. Samples from specimens themselves, or pure cultures, can be stained. The slide can then be viewed in the light microscope with an oil immersion lens, which improves the resolving power of the microscope.

The most important differential staining technique in bacteriology is the 'Gram' stain

Differential staining procedures exploit the fact that cells with different properties stain differently and thus can be distinguished. Based on their reaction to Gram's stain (Fig. 31.3), bacteria are divided into two broad groups:

- Gram positive (stain purple)
- Gram negative (stain pink).

This difference is related to differences in the structure of the cell walls of the two groups (see Ch. 2).

Acid-fast stains are used to detect mycobacteria

Some organisms, particularly mycobacteria, which have waxy cell walls, do not readily take up the Gram stain. To demonstrate their presence, special staining techniques are used which rely on the ability of such organisms to retain the stain in the presence of 'decolourizing' agents such as acid and alcohol. The Ziehl–Neelsen stain (see Fig. 19.20) is a classic differential staining procedure that uses heat to drive the fuchsin stain into the cells; mycobacteria stained with fuchsin withstand decolourization with acid and alcohol and

are therefore known as 'acid-' and 'alcohol-fast', whereas other bacteria lose the stain after acid and alcohol treatment. Alternatively, many laboratories use the fluorescent dye auramine, which has a strong affinity for the waxy cell wall of mycobacteria, to demonstrate these organisms by fluorescence microscopy (Fig. 31.4).

Other staining techniques can be used to demonstrate particular features of cells

Examples of such features to aid identification include the volutin (polyphosphate) storage granules in *Corynebacterium* spp. and lipid in *Bacillus* spp. (Fig. 31.5).

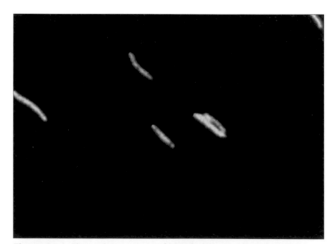

Figure 31.4 Fluorochrome stain of *Mycobacterium tuberculosis* with a mixture of auramine O and rhodamine B. *Mycobacteria* appear fluorescent under ultraviolet light. (Courtesy of D.K. Banerjee.)

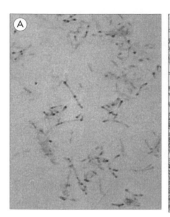
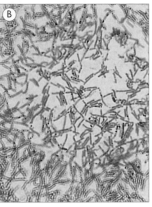

Figure 31.5 Special staining techniques can be used to demonstrate particular features of bacterial cells. (A) Corynebacteria stained to demonstrate polymetaphosphate storage granules (volutin granules), which appear as dark spots in blue-green cells (Albert's stain). (B) Lipid storage granules in *Bacillus cereus* stained with Sudan black (black lipid against red cells).

Dark field (dark ground) microscopy is useful for observing motility and thin cells such as spirochetes

The light microscope may be adapted by modifying the condenser so that the object appears brightly lit against a dark background. Living organisms can be examined by dark field microscopy and thus motility can be observed. The method is also used for visualizing very thin cells such as spirochetes because the light reflected from the surface of the cells makes them appear larger and therefore more easily visible than when examined by bright field microscopy (Fig. 31.6).

Phase contrast microscopy increases the contrast of an image

This technique enhances the very small differences in refractive index and density between living cells and the fluid in which they are suspended and therefore produces an image with a higher degree of contrast than that achieved by bright field microscopy.

Fluorescence microscopy is used for substances that are either naturally fluorescent or have been stained with fluorescent dyes

If light of one wavelength shines on a fluorescent object, it emits light of a different wavelength. Some biological substances are naturally fluorescent; others can be stained

with fluorescent dyes and viewed in a microscope with an ultraviolet light source instead of white light (see Fig. 31.4).

Fluorescence microscopy is widely used in microbiology and immunology and has been developed to detect microbial antigens in specimens and tissues by 'staining' with specific antibodies tagged with fluorescent dyes (immunofluorescence). The method can be made more sensitive or can be adapted to the detection of antibody by labelling a second antibody in an indirect test (Fig. 31.7).

Electron microscopy

The specimen needs to be cut into thin sections for electron microscopy

The electron microscope uses a beam of electrons instead of light, and magnets are used to focus the beam instead of the lenses used in a light microscope. The whole system is operated under a high vacuum. Electron beams penetrate poorly, and a single microbial cell is too thick to be viewed directly. To overcome this, the specimen is fixed and mounted in plastic and cut into thin sections, which are examined individually. Electron-dense stains such as osmium tetroxide, uranyl acetate or glutaraldehyde are applied to the specimen to improve contrast. The electrons pass through the section and produce an image on a fluorescent screen. Images are photographed and enlarged so that the original specimen is magnified many thousandfold (Fig. 31.8).

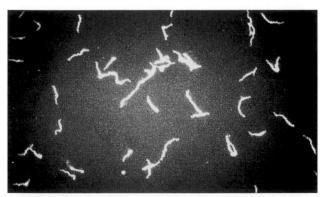

Figure 31.6 Spirochetes visualized by dark ground microscopy. Spirochetes and leptospires are much thinner than most bacterial cells (approximately 0.1 μm in diameter compared with 1 μm for *E. coli*), but they appear larger when viewed by dark ground illumination.

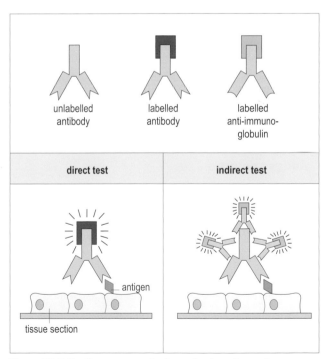

Figure 31.7 The fluorescent antibody test for detection and identification of microbial (or tissue) antigens or antibodies directed against them. In the direct test, antibody labelled with a fluorescent dye is applied to a tissue section bearing the antigen, unbound antibody is washed away, and the bound antibody showing the presence and location of the antigen is visualized by fluorescence microscopy. In the indirect test, antigen is revealed by successive treatments with unlabelled antigen-specific antibody and then fluorescent-labelled anti-immunoglobulin which amplifies the signal (thus if the first antibody is human, the labelled antibody will be an anti-human Ig).

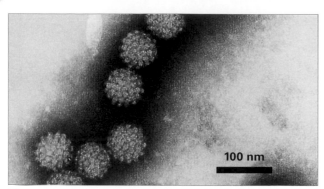

Figure 31.8 Electron micrograph of papillomavirus, the human wart virus. (Courtesy of the Regional Virus Laboratory, Birmingham, UK.)

Although not routinely used in the clinical laboratory, electron microscopy can aid in the identification of virus particles

Direct examination of specimens allows rapid identification of virus particles and detection of viruses that are difficult or impossible to cultivate (e.g. rotaviruses). Fluid for examination is dried onto a copper grid and examined. About one million virus particles per millilitre are needed if they are to be detectable. The sensitivity can be increased by reacting the fluid with antiviral antibody so that clumps of virus particles are visible. This is known as immunoelectron microscopy, a technique analogous to immunofluorescence in light microscopy.

Detection of microbial antigens in specimens

Detection of specific microbial antigens can be a more rapid method for detecting the presence of an organism than attempting to grow and identify the microbe. The methods include:

- those that detect antigens by their interaction with specific antibodies
- those that detect microbial toxins.

They are summarized in Box 31.3. Detection of microbial genes using DNA probes is discussed later in this chapter.

Specific antibody coated onto latex particles will react with the organism or its product, resulting in visible clumping

For example, the common causative agents of bacterial meningitis (*Streptococcus pneumoniae*, *Haemophilus influenzae* and *Neisseria meningitidis* types A and C) can be detected in CSF by mixing the specimen with specific antibody coated onto latex particles. If the antigen (i.e. the organism or its product) is present, the particles will clump together (Fig. 31.9). These tests give results within minutes of receipt of the specimen, but their sensitivity is not significantly greater than that of the Gram stain, and false-positive results may occur because of cross-reacting antigens. However, they can be a useful diagnostic aid when the patient has received antibiotics and organisms may appear morphologically unidentifiable in the CSF and fail to grow in culture.

Box 31.3 📱 Non-cultural Techniques for Detection of Microbial Products

Non-specific techniques for detection of microbial products

Fatty acid end-products of metabolism of anaerobes can be detected in fluid specimens (e.g. pus, blood) by gas liquid chromatography.

Antigen detection

Detection of soluble carbohydrate antigens by agglutination of antibody-coated latex particles or red blood cells (see Fig. 31.9) e.g.:

- *Streptococcus pneumoniae* capsule in CSF and urine
- *Haemophilus influenzae* type b capsule in CSF and urine
- *Neisseria meningitidis* capsule in CSF and urine
- *Cryptococcus neoformans* capsule in CSF and urine
- *Strep. pyogenes* group antigen in throat swabs.

Detection of particular antigens by binding to antibodies labelled with:

- Enzymes (see Fig. 31.11), e.g. ELISA for hepatitis B, rotavirus
- Fluorescent molecules (see Fig. 31.7)

Toxin detection

Detection of exotoxins

- *Clostridium botulinum* toxin by injection of patient's serum into mice (unprotected and protected with specific antiserum)

- *Clostridium difficile* cytotoxin in faeces by addition of suspension to cell culture
- *Clostridium perfringens* and *Staphylococcus aureus* enterotoxins in faeces by agglutination of antitoxin-coated latex particles
- *Escherichia coli* enterotoxin detected by tissue culture or animal model.

Detection of endotoxin

- Endotoxin from cell walls of Gram-negative bacteria detected by *Limulus* lysate assay conventionally tested by clotting of amoebocyte extracts of the horseshoe (*Limulus*) crab but also by colorimetric and turbidimetric assays.

Identification of specific microbial products can be a more rapid method for detecting microorganisms than isolation and culture. The available techniques vary in their specificity. Toxins may be detected either by virtue of their antigenic properties or by demonstrating their action. CSF, cerebrospinal fluid; ELISA, enzyme-linked immunosorbent assay. Alternatively, molecular methods such as PCR (see Fig. 31.12) may be used to assess the potential of microorganisms to produce specific microbial products (e.g. toxins) by detecting the presence of their respective genes.

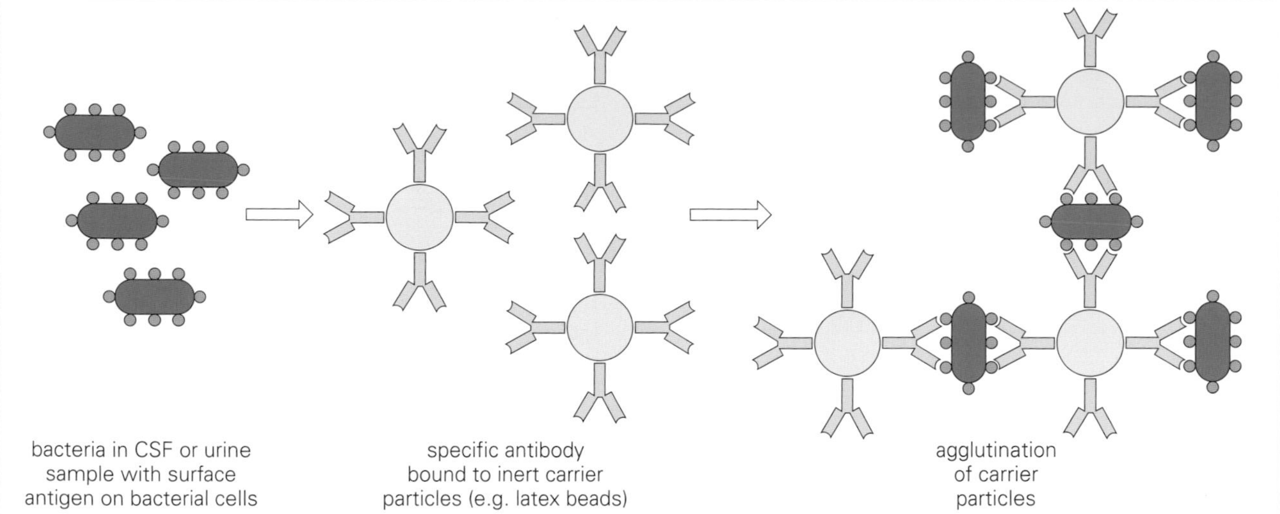

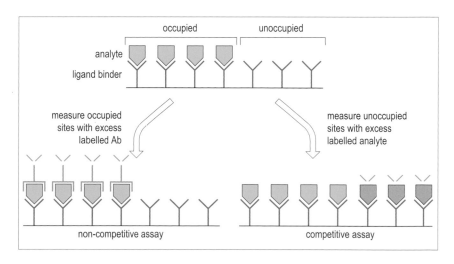

Figure 31.9 When a specimen of cerebrospinal fluid (CSF) containing bacteria (e.g. *Haemophilus influenzae*) is mixed with a suspension of latex particles coated with specific antibody (e.g. *H. influenzae* anticapsular antibodies), the interaction between antigen and antibody causes an immediate agglutination of particles, which is visible to the naked eye.

Immunoassay can be used to measure antigen concentration

Antigens can be measured by their binding to a standard amount of antibody, the fractional occupancy of the available antibody binding sites being a measure of the antigen concentration (Fig. 31.10). Usually, the antibody is adsorbed for convenience to a solid phase and the amount of antigen bound assessed using a second antibody labelled with an enzyme which acts on a substance to produce a colour or luminescence (Fig. 31.11) or a fluorescent probe.

- The test employing an enzyme label is referred to as an enzyme-linked immunosorbent assay (ELISA).
- The use of chemiluminescent or time-resolved fluorescent labels gives assays of very high sensitivity.

Earlier forms of immunoassay used labelling with a radioisotope rather than an enzyme or a fluorescent probe.

With modern techniques, multiple assays can be performed on single samples (see below and Fig. 31.19).

Monoclonal antibodies can distinguish between species and between strains of the same species on the basis of antigenic differences

Hybridomas produced by the fusion of 'immortal' B-cell tumours and individual normal antibody-producing cells provide a copious source of monoclonal antibodies, all with identical specificities for their relevant antigen. These monoclonal antibodies can be used as diagnostic tools. In direct ELISA (see above), enzyme-conjugated monoclonal antibodies are frequently employed to detect antigens in specimens from patients. Rotaviruses, HIV, hepatitis B virus, herpesvirus and respiratory syncytial virus (RSV) can all be detected directly with monoclonal antibodies in ELISAs. *Chlamydia trachomatis* infection can be diagnosed within a few hours by a direct fluorescent antibody test employing a monoclonal antibody labelled with fluorescein (see Fig. 31.7; Ch. 21).

Figure 31.10 The principle of ligand-binding assays. The ligand-binding agent may be in the soluble phase or bound to a solid support as shown, the advantage of the latter being the ease of separation of bound from free analyte. After exposure to analyte, the fractional occupancy of the ligand-binding sites can be determined by competitive or non-competitive assays using labelled reagents (in orange) as shown. In principle, non-competitive assays are more sensitive.

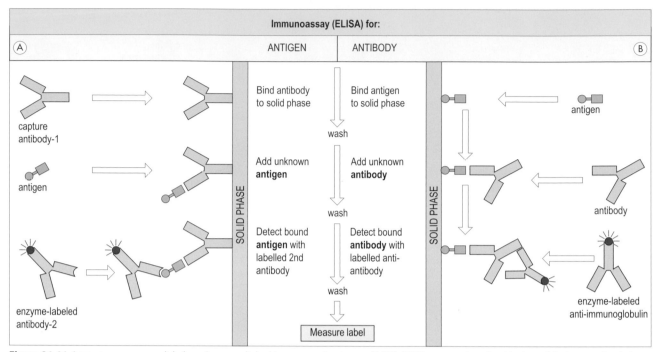

Figure 31.11 Immunoassay on a solid phase (enzyme-linked immunosorbent assay, ELISA). (A) The test antigen is added to solid-phase antibody-1 and the occupancy (see Fig. 31.10) measured by adding an enzyme-labelled second antibody and reading bound enzyme (e.g. peroxidase or alkaline phosphatase) through a colorimetric or luminometric reaction. In some cases, particularly with small antigens, unoccupied sites can be detected by adding a standard amount of labelled antigen. (B) Antibody to be tested is added to solid-phase antigen and is detected by addition of an enzyme-labelled anti-immunoglobulin. (Compare with the indirect test in Figure 31.7, which uses a fluorescent anti-immunoglobulin to detect bound antibody. Similarly, the label in the above assays can be a fluorescent probe rather than an enzyme.)

Detection of microbes by probing for their genes

Organisms carrying genes for virulence factors can be detected by nucleic acid probes for the virulence factors

A gene probe is a nucleic acid molecule that, when in the single-stranded state and labelled, can be used to detect a complementary sequence of DNA by hybridizing to it. Polynucleotide probes may be obtained from naturally occurring DNA by cloning DNA fragments into appropriate plasmid vectors and then isolating the cloned DNA. However, more typically the sequence of the gene of interest is known and oligonucleotide probes can be synthesized or generated by PCR (see below). The single-strand probes are labelled either with a radioactive isotope or with compounds that give fluorescence or colour reactions in suitable conditions (e.g. biotin streptavidin) and hybridized to the extracted microbial nucleic acid which has first been heat-denatured to make single strands and then immobilized onto a nitrocellulose membrane. Such 'blotting' techniques are time consuming and prone to contamination in routine use and have now been largely superseded by PCR methods.

Polymerase chain reaction can be used to amplify a specific DNA sequence to produce millions of copies within a few hours

Polymerase chain reaction (PCR) can theoretically, and often in practice does, detect a single gene-target, i.e. a single organism in the sample being analysed (Fig. 31.12). The method is also rapid; results can be obtained within 1–3 hours, depending on the type of technology used. It is particularly useful

for diagnostic work in virology, where many pathogens are difficult to culture. Earlier methods required the PCR products to be analysed on agarose gels and, for diagnostic certainty, some form of nucleic acid probe technique to unequivocally identify the target. This added a considerable amount of time to the analysis and has more recently been replaced by real-time PCR. This approach uses the same basic reagents and techniques as the original method, but with the addition of fluorescently labelled sequence-specific probes. These hybridize to the amplified product (amplicon) as it accumulates and allows the reaction to be monitored in real time (hence the name). The amount of fluorescence accumulated during the reaction is directly proportional to the amount of amplicon produced. By including a set of pre-quantified DNA standards, co-amplified during the reaction, the copy number of nucleic acid in the original sample can be estimated. Because there is no need for post-PCR analysis, the reaction tubes do not need to be opened, which reduces the potential for contamination and provides results in as little as 1 hour. If the pathogen's nucleic acid is in the form of RNA, it must first be converted into complementary DNA (cDNA), before it can be amplified. This is achieved in an enzymatic step using a reverse transcriptase, prior to the PCR (termed RT-PCR).

The specificity of PCR is determined by careful choice of primers

The primers and probes, which are short DNA sequences (ca. 20 nucleotides) must be exact complementary matches to the region requiring amplification and detection. There are now a number of commercial PCR assays available for pathogen detection including *C. trachomatis*, *N. gonorrhoeae*,

Figure 31.12 The polymerase chain reaction. Short oligonucleotide (ca. 20 bases of DNA) anneal or hybridize to complementary sequences on each DNA strand to be amplified. The strands are separated (denatured) enabling the primers to bind, which are extended by the thermostable polymerase adding complementary nucleotides by repeating the thermal cycling rounds of denaturation, annealing and extension 30–60 times. The original strands to be amplified are shown in the figure as A and B, Subsequent amplified copies are numbered, after early rounds of amplification the desired fragment of DNA to be amplified (amplicon) accumulates and goes on to be copied exponentially.

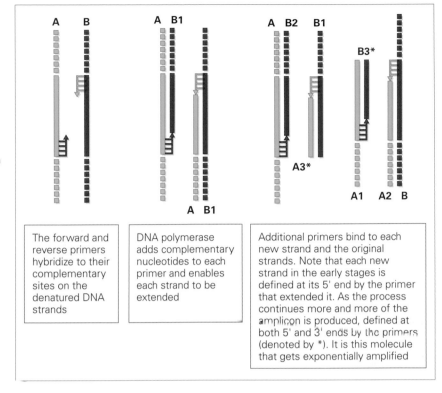

| The forward and reverse primers hybridize to their complementary sites on the denatured DNA strands | DNA polymerase adds complementary nucleotides to each primer and enables each strand to be extended | Additional primers bind to each new strand and the original strands. Note that each new strand in the early stages is defined at its 5' end by the primer that extended it. As the process continues more and more of the amplicon is produced, defined at both 5' and 3' ends by the primers (denoted by *). It is this molecule that gets exponentially amplified |

M. tuberculosis and viruses such as cytomegalovirus, hepatitis C virus, herpes simplex virus and HIV (Fig. 31.13). Both qualitative and quantitative detection can be carried out (e.g. HIV-1 RNA load). However, many laboratories continue to design their own primers and probes, particularly for new or re-emerging pathogens. To do this the sequence of the target region must be known. This can be obtained either from DNA sequence databases, or for novel pathogens, where the sequence is unknown, by de novo sequencing in the laboratory. The pathogen nucleic acid can be fragmented by enzymatic methods and cloned into a suitable vector and sequenced using commercially available primers that flank the cloning site. For long regions, new primers can be designed based on the initial data obtained from the first round of sequencing. Thus, DNA sequence analysis is becoming an increasingly important tool in the diagnosis and characterization of infectious pathogens.

Dideoxy chain terminator sequencing

This method was developed in the 1970s and, although newer methods are being developed, it is still the cornerstone of routine sequencing technology (Fig. 31.14). The reaction is similar to PCR; a DNA polymerase is used to make copies of the nucleic acid to be sequenced. However, in addition to the four standard nucleotide bases, four dideoxynucleotide base analogues are also used. Dideoxynucleotides lack the 3'-OH group on the sugar moiety necessary for extending the DNA molecule, when one of these molecules is incorporated into the growing chain, extension is terminated, hence the name. Each of the four deoxynucleotides is labelled with a different fluorescent dye, each of which emits light at a different wavelength. The fragments are separated according to their lengths by electrophoresis through a

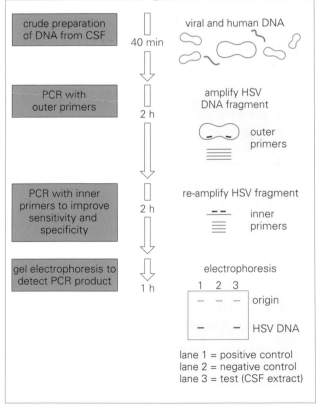

Figure 31.13 Nested polymerase chain reaction (PCR) for the detection of herpes simplex virus (HSV) DNA in cerebrospinal fluid (CSF) from a patient with encephalitis. Nested PCR is a modification of the original PCR technique in which the DNA of interest is amplified first with two primers which recognize sequences some distance apart and then, in a second reaction, with a further pair of primers which recognize sequences within the length of the DNA amplified by the first pair. This technique improves the sensitivity and specificity of PCR.

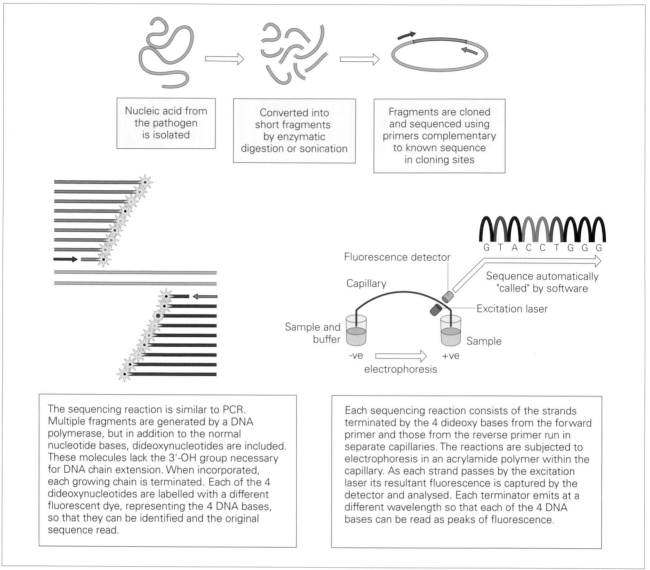

Figure 31.14 Dideoxy capillary sequencing.

polyacrylamide matrix contained within a capillary tube. A laser excites the different fluorescent dyes and the resulting different wavelengths emitted are picked up by a detector and the sequence of the original nucleic acid is read as a series of fluorescent peaks.

CULTIVATION (CULTURE) OF MICROORGANISMS

Bacteria and fungi can be cultured on solid nutrient or liquid media

While cultures can be made in liquid media (broth), it is not possible to tell whether there is more than one species present. Therefore, solid media are more useful in diagnostic microbiology. Bacteria and fungi grow on the surface of solid nutrient media (agar-based) to produce colonies composed of thousands of cells derived from a single cell implanted on the surface. Colonies of different species often have characteristic appearances, which can give a clue to their likely identity (Fig. 31.15).

Different species of bacteria and fungi have different growth requirements

It is possible to grow the majority of species of bacteria and fungi of medical importance in artificial media in the laboratory, but there is no one universal culture medium that will support the growth of them all, and there are still some species that can only be grown in experimental animals (e.g. *Mycobacterium leprae* and *Treponema pallidum*). Some bacteria that cannot be cultivated on artificial media (e.g. chlamydia and rickettsia) can be grown in cell cultures (see below).

Many culture media are designed not only to support the growth of the desired organisms, but also to inhibit the growth of others (i.e. they are 'selective media').

Specimens collected from body sites that have a normal commensal flora will contain a mixture of organisms from which the pathogen has to be recognized. Specimens are 'plated out' on a carefully chosen range of nutrient and selective media to produce single colonies to insure a pure culture. These are subcultured to fresh media for identification and antibiotic susceptibility tests (see below), a procedure which

Figure 31.15 Bacterial colonies. A bacterial cell implanted on a solid nutrient medium will multiply to produce a colony containing millions of cells. Different species produce characteristically different colonies, and this feature can be used as a preliminary clue to the identity of the organism. (A) Golden colonies of *Staphylococcus aureus*. (B) Additional features such as the ability to lyse red blood cells can be demonstrated by culturing bacteria on blood-containing media. Here, β-haemolysis (complete haemolysis) is produced by *Streptococcus pyogenes* on horse blood agar. (C) Culture media can be made selective by including agents that are inhibitory to some species. For example, MacConkey agar contains bile salts so only those organisms tolerant to bile will grow. In addition, it contains lactose and a pH indicator. Species that ferment lactose change the indicator to bright pink. (D) Non-lactose-fermenting species, such as *Salmonella* and *Shigella*, form yellowish colonies.

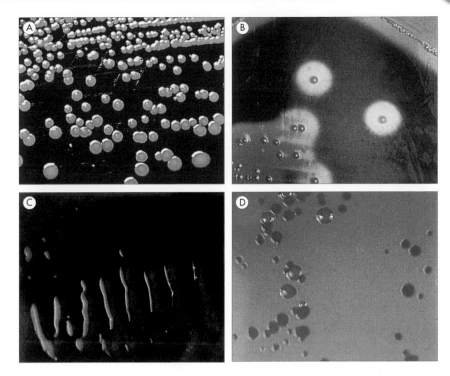

can take 48h or longer by conventional (non-molecular) approaches (see Fig. 31.1).

Parasites such as *Leishmania*, *Trypanosoma* and *Trichomonas* can be cultivated in liquid media to allow small numbers present in the original specimen (e.g. blood or vaginal secretions) to multiply and thus become easier to detect by microscopic examination. Parasites do not form colonies on solid media in the same way as bacteria and fungi.

Viruses, chlamydia and rickettsia must be grown in cell or tissue cultures

This is because these organisms are incapable of a free-living existence. Most cell cultures used in the diagnostic laboratory are continuous cell lines – human or animal cells adapted to growth in vitro that can be stored at −80°C until required. The specimen is introduced into the cell culture medium and the presence of viruses detected by observing the cells for a 'cytopathic effect' (CPE).

Cell culture techniques are specialized and labour-intensive, and some viruses either cause no CPE or cause a CPE that takes >1 week to evolve (e.g. cytomegalovirus, although CMV antigens can be detected after 1–2 days in cells). Therefore, alternative methods such as antigen detection (see above), antibody detection (see below) and PCR-based approaches are important for diagnosis.

IDENTIFICATION OF MICROORGANISMS GROWN IN CULTURE

Bacteria are identified by simple characteristics and biochemical properties

A preliminary identification of many of the bacteria of medical importance has traditionally been made on the basis of the following few simple characteristics of the cells (Fig. 31.16):

- Gram reaction
- cell morphology (e.g. rod or coccus) and arrangement (e.g. pairs or chains)

- ability to grow under aerobic or anaerobic conditions
- growth requirements (simple or fastidious).

Further identification is made on the basis of biochemical properties such as:

- ability to produce enzymes that can be detected by simple tests
- ability to metabolize sugars oxidatively or fermentatively (aerobically or anaerobically)
- ability to use a range of substrates for growth (e.g. glucose, lactose, sucrose).

While these tests can be done individually (e.g. in broth media containing the specifically required reagents), they are more commonly performed using commercial kits or automated systems which have the potential to give a rapid (e.g. 2–4h) indication of pathogen identity based on biochemical profiles.

Some species are identified on the basis of their antigens by reacting cell suspensions with specific antisera.

Antibiotic susceptibility can only be determined after the bacteria have been isolated in a pure culture

A variety of methods are available for antimicrobial susceptibility testing, including broth microdilution and automated instrument approaches. However, the most widely employed method assesses antibiotic susceptibility by applying filter paper disks, which contain different antibiotics, onto a lawn of the test organism which has been seeded onto an agar plate (i.e. disk diffusion). During overnight incubation, the organisms grow and multiply and the antibiotics diffuse out from the disks and inhibit growth around the disk. Therefore, after isolation of bacteria from a specimen, a further incubation period (overnight for disk diffusion testing) is required before antibiotic susceptibility results are available. Methods for antibiotic susceptibility tests are described in more detail in Chapter 33.

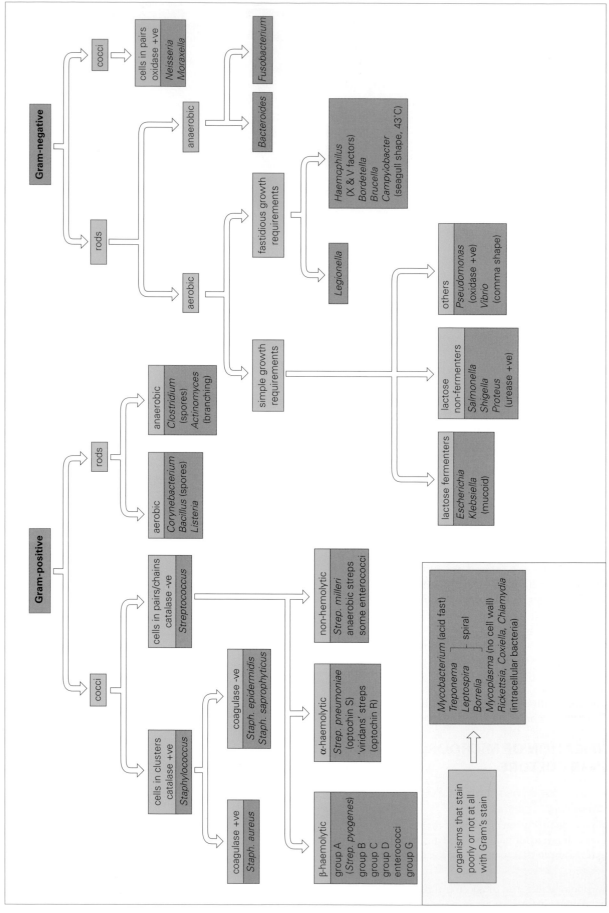

Figure 31.16 Identifying bacteria. The preliminary investigation of the bacteria of medical importance has traditionally been made on the basis of a few key characteristics (see text). Further identification may then be made on the basis of biochemical and serologic tests.

Fungi are identified by their colonial characteristics and cell morphology

Fungi are identified from colonies or pure cultures largely on the basis of colonial characteristics (e.g. colour) and the morphology of the individual cells viewed under the microscope (Fig. 31.17). Biochemical tests (substrate assimilation) can be used for detailed identification of yeasts of medical importance. In general, fungi grow more slowly than bacteria, and final identification may take up to 2 weeks.

Protozoa and helminths are identified by direct examination although newer molecular methods are also available

Many protozoa and parasites can be identified by direct examination of specimens without resorting to culture, and therefore the results can be obtained on the day of receipt of the specimen in the laboratory:

• Protozoa are traditionally identified on the basis of their morphologic characteristics – different stages of the lifecycle may be visible in different specimens from the same patient and at different stages in the disease (Fig. 31.18)

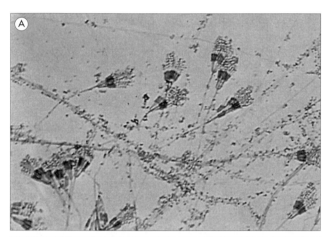

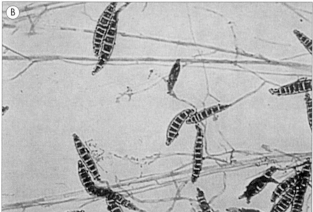

Figure 31.17 Fungi under the microscope. Fungi can be grown on agar culture media in the same way as bacteria, but most species grow much more slowly than bacteria and it may take up to 2 weeks for a colony to form. Colonial characteristics (such as colour) are helpful in the identification of fungi, but confirmation depends upon microscopic examination of the hyphae and sporing structures. (A) Penicillium in a wet preparation showing the conidiophores and free conidia. (B) Macroconidia of *Microsporum canis* stained with lactophenol cotton blue.

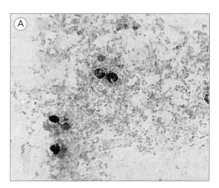

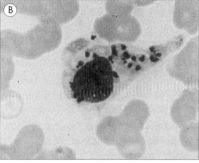

Figure 31.18 Although some parasites can be cultivated in the laboratory, identification is usually based on microscopic appearances in the specimen. (A) Acid-fast stain of *Cryptosporidium* in faeces. Like mycobacteria, this organism is able to retain the pink carbol fuchsin stain when challenged with acid alcohol. (B) *Leishmania donovani* (Donovan bodies) in a stained preparation from a specimen of bone marrow.

• Helminths are commonly identified by the macroscopic appearance of the worm (e.g. *Ascaris* or *Enterobius*) or by microscopic examination of specimens (e.g. faeces or urine) for eggs of, for example, schistosomes (see Ch. 22).

However, molecular approaches to diagnosis are becoming increasingly more common including PCR detection and differentiation of *Entamoeba* species, *Giardia*, and *Cryptosporidium*.

Viruses are usually identified using serologic tests

Viruses may be identifiable by their cytopathic effect in cell culture and their morphology in electron microscopic preparations (Fig. 31.8). A number of viruses may now be identified by nucleic acid-based tests (e.g. probes and PCR; see above), but diagnosis is also often made by detecting viral antigens or by testing for the presence of specific antibodies in the patient's serum (see below).

Mass spectrometry heralds a novel diagnostic era

One of the most promising new approaches to the identification of bacteria and fungi involves the use of mass spectrometry or, more specifically, matrix-assisted laser desorption-ionization time-of-flight mass spectrometry (MALDI-TOF). As MALDI-TOF equipment becomes more widely available, it is being employed increasingly for the identification of microbial pathogens through analysis of their predominant mass spectral protein fingerprints. The field is being heavily researched and the potential value of identifying a variety of smaller molecules is also being explored with the promise of exciting new developments in the future.

ANTIBODY DETECTION METHODS FOR THE DIAGNOSIS OF INFECTION

Serologic tests (the study of antigen–antibody interactions) are used:

- to diagnose infections
- to identify microorganisms (see above)
- to type blood for blood banks and tissues for transplantation.

Diagnoses based on detecting antibodies in patients' sera are retrospective

The major disadvantage of a diagnosis based on the detection of antibodies in a patient's serum is that it is retrospective, as 2–4 weeks must elapse before IgG antibodies produced in response to the infection are detectable. What is more, a positive result indicates only that the patient has come into contact with the infection at some time in the past. However, IgM antibodies are detected earlier in the infection (7–10 days) and are usually indicative of active, as opposed to past, infection. It may also help to show that the patient has 'seroconverted' by demonstrating a fourfold or greater rise in antibody titre between sera collected in the acute and convalescent phases of the disease.

Antibody detection can be invaluable for identifying organisms that grow either slowly or with difficulty

Despite the drawbacks mentioned above, antibody detection is the main method for the laboratory diagnosis of viral infections. The techniques employed often allow several different infections to be screened for simultaneously (e.g. causes of atypical pneumonia, see Ch. 19). Sera should be collected during the acute phase of the disease and stored at −20°C until a convalescent-phase serum is available; the two sera are then tested in parallel. Few diagnoses can be made with any confidence on the results of single serum samples, but sometimes early testing is justified if there is a clinical suspicion of a rare infection that the patient is unlikely to have encountered before (e.g. legionellosis). Previous immunization makes it difficult if not impossible to interpret some serologic tests, because antibodies detected may be the result of immunization or infection (e.g. the Widal test for the serologic diagnosis of enteric fever, see Ch. 22).

Common serologic tests used in the laboratory to diagnose infection

Solid-phase immunoassays can be used to estimate antibody in a given sample

These assays have been described previously (see Fig. 31.11). The amount of antibody binding to the solid-phase antigen is a measure of the antibody content of the original sample, and can be detected by adding a second antibody conjugated with a fluorochrome or an enzyme (e.g. phosphatase or peroxidase) that produces a colour or luminescent reaction with a given substrate.

Modern techniques permit the simultaneous assay of several analytes in the same sample. Examples of two current multiplexing technologies are presented in Figure 31.19.

A variety of tests assess the ability of antibodies to inhibit microbial activity

A number of tests focus on the ability of antibodies in a patient's serum to inhibit some biologic faculty of the microorganism in question. An example is the anti-streptolysin O test, in which the streptolysin O toxin is neutralized by antibody. The extent to which the test serum can be diluted before it fails to prevent the toxin from lysing red cells provides a convenient titre (Fig. 31.20). The ability of a patient's serum containing specific antibody to immobilize motile bacteria – for example, the *Treponema pallidum* inhibition (TPI) test – is another example.

Antibodies can also mask viral molecules such as the influenza haemagglutinins, which are involved in specific adherence to cells, allowing the development of a haemagglutination inhibition test (Fig. 31.21). This assay is a classic technique only in use in reference laboratories.

Antibodies to cytopathic viruses can be detected by the ability of the patient's serum to prevent virus infectivity

In the case of cytopathic viruses, antibodies can be detected by the ability of the patient's serum to prevent the development of a cytopathic effect. These antibodies are called neutralizing antibodies. The important applications of these methods are referred to in the appropriate systems chapters (see Chs 18–30).

Point of care tests

New simpler diagnostic tests are being developed that can be used at the point of care

For example, clinicians increasingly exploit simple dipsticks to directly measure sugar in urine. Much current research aims to design new diagnostic assays that could be performed by non-laboratory staff in a clinic, surgery, or other point-of-care setting. Using lateral flow technology (similar to that used in pregnancy tests), microorganisms might be detected via antibodies to particular antigens. Such tests are already in use for HIV, although they should be confirmed by a second assay and all doubtful or uncertain results referred to the laboratory. Even more miniaturized 'lab on a chip' technology is in development, where reactions take place within a piece of plastic rather than the laboratory.

ASSESSMENT OF HOST DEFENCE SYSTEMS

The opsonic activity and activities of individual components of complement can also be assessed

Although assessment of overall serum complement activity is a relatively uncommon procedure at the present time, it is often of value to assess the opsonic activity of complement in the serum sample by measuring its ability to facilitate the uptake of a microbial particle by a phagocytic cell (Fig. 31.22).

The activities of individual components of the complement system can be evaluated either by:

- their ability to be titrated into a complement-dependent lytic system in which the component to be tested is lacking
- direct immunochemical measurement, often using gel precipitation reactions.

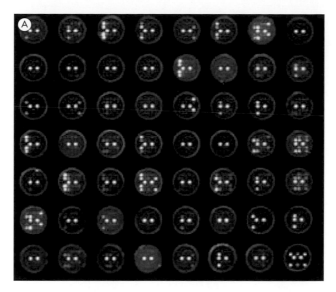

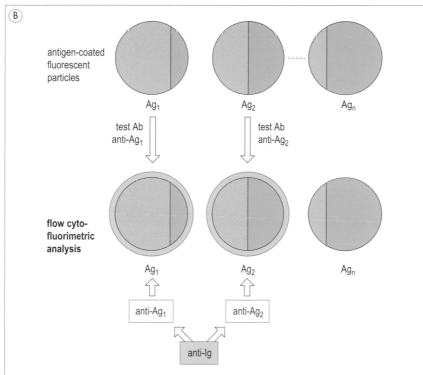

Figure 31.19 Multiplex (i.e. multiple) solid-phase immunoassays on single test samples. (A) A diagnostic antigen microarray permitting the assay for multiple antibodies within each individual serum sample tested on a 5×5 array of antigen dots in each well of a membrane-based microtitre plate using a luminescent enzyme-linked anti-immunoglobulin readout. Twenty of the dots in each well simultaneously evaluate 10 markers in duplicate with 5 dots being used as controls, two of which give strong luminescence signals in two central control spots in all wells, the other 3 in the equatorial row being buffer spots used for the background subtraction value. Varied intensities of other spots correlate with the level of antibodies present in each patient's serum (Courtesy of J. McBride). (B) *Luminex* system in which a variety of particles, each bearing single antigens on their surface, are identified by their individual ratio of two different fluorochromes using flow cytometry (see Fig. 31.25). When antibodies in the test serum bind to a particle, they can be revealed by coating with an anti-immunoglobulin bearing a third fluorochrome. In this way, antibodies to several different antigens within a given test sample, of blood for instance, can be quantitatively assayed.

The nitroblue tetrazolium (NBT) test is used to assess phagocytic activity

The ability of neutrophils to become phagocytic and to concurrently reduce molecular oxygen can be assayed by the nitroblue tetrazolium (NBT) test. When yellow NBT dye is added to blood, it forms complexes with heparin or fibrinogen in the sample. These complexes are then phagocytosed by neutrophils that have been activated by the addition of exogenous endotoxin. The dye complex is taken into the stimulated neutrophils and substitutes for oxygen by acting as a substrate for the reduction process, forming as a result a blue insoluble formazan (Fig. 31.23).

Lymphocytes

The development of T-effector cells to an antigen can often be revealed by intradermal challenge with that antigen. Such

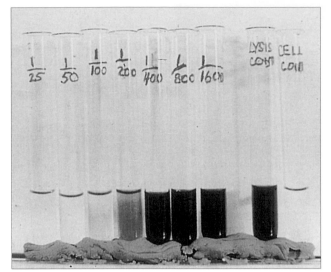

Figure 31.20 Illustration of the anti-streptolysin O (ASO) test which is now performed primarily by automated instrumentation. The O-toxin lyses red cells. Test serum is diluted until the antibodies it contains it no longer inhibit lysis by a standard concentration of toxin. Positive and negative controls are included in the test (right).

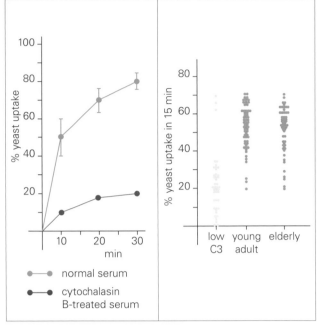

Figure 31.22 Opsonic activity of serum. (A) Time course for the uptake of yeast opsonized with a normal serum by polymorphonuclear neutrophil leukocytes (PMNs) from 12 healthy donors, and uptake of yeast by PMNs from one donor after treatment with cytochalasin B (40 mg/mL), which inhibits phagocytosis. (B) The distribution of opsonic activity for 150 sera from young healthy, elderly and pathologic sera. (Data from Kerr et al., *Clin Exp Immunol* 54:793–800, 1983.)

an intradermal challenge usually gives rise to erythema and induration, peaking at around 48h (Fig. 31.24). This time course has led to the reaction being described as 'delayed-type hypersensitivity', and is the basis of the Mantoux skin test for tuberculosis (see Chapter 19).

Overall responsiveness of the T-cell population can be probed by using materials such as phytohaemagglutinin or concanavalin A, which are polyclonal stimulators in the sense that they activate T-cell populations independently of their precise antigen specificity. However, when peripheral blood cells are incubated with antigen in vitro, the specifically sensitized T cells, which represent only a very small fraction of the total, become activated and divide. Examination of the cultures will reveal blast cells and mitotic divisions, but the response can also be detected by the incorporation

of radiolabelled thymidine, or of a fluorescent dye, such as CFSE, which provides a measure of cell proliferation.

Lymphocytes are counted and classified by detecting their cell surface molecules

Lymphocyte differentiation is accompanied by the expression of related molecules on the cell surface. Detection of these molecules by immunofluorescent techniques allows their enumeration and, in addition, their classification into

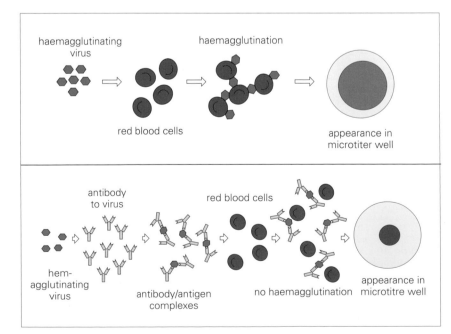

Figure 31.21 Haemagglutination inhibition. Some viruses (e.g. influenza) have haemagglutinin molecules on their outer surface, and when virus particles are mixed with red blood cells, they cause haemagglutination. In the presence of specific antibody, however, haemagglutination is inhibited. This test can therefore be used to detect the presence of antibodies to influenza virus in a patient's serum. Note that the routine test for influenza is PCR but that haemagglutination inhibition is used as a confirmatory test by the reference laboratory.

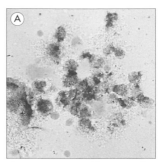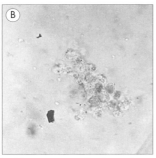

Figure 31.23 Nitroblue tetrazolium (NBT) test. In normal polymorphs and monocytes, reactive oxygen intermediates (ROIs) are activated by phagocytosis, and yellow NBT is converted to purple-blue formazan (A). Patients with chronic granulomatous disease (CGD) cannot form ROIs and so the dye stays yellow (B). (Courtesy of A.R. Hayward.)

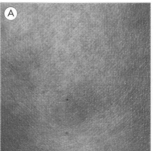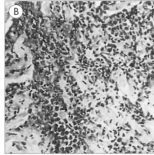

Figure 31.24 Tuberculin-type delayed sensitivity. The dermal response to antigens of leprosy bacillus in a sensitive subject (the Fernandez reaction) is characterized by (A) red induration maximal at 48–72 h and (B) dense infiltration of the injection site with lymphocytes and macrophages. (H&E, ×80.)

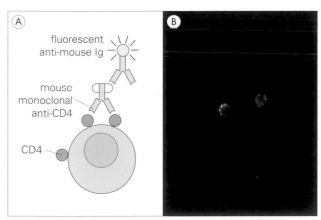

Figure 31.25 Visualization of lymphocyte surface differentiation molecules by immunofluorescence. (A) The double antibody test using mouse monoclonal antibodies to the required surface molecule. Another example of the indirect fluorescent antibody test (Fig. 31.7). (B) Direct demonstration of immunoglobulin receptors on the surface of two B lymphocytes by fluorescent anti-immunoglobulin. Aggregation and capping of the immunoglobulin surface receptors by the anti-immunoglobulin reagent is evident.

different subpopulations (Fig. 31.25). Monoclonal antibodies are widely used to define these differentiation molecules, using flow cytofluorimetry (Fig. 31.26), which is a more rapid and less laborious means of analysing lymphocyte subpopulations than conventional fluorescent microscopy. The fluorescence-activated cell sorter (FACS) separates subpopulations delineated by their cytofluorimetric parameters.

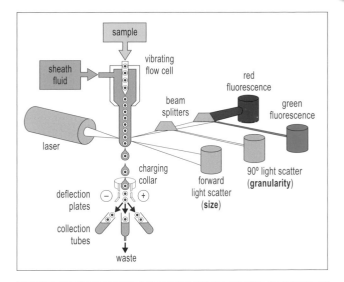

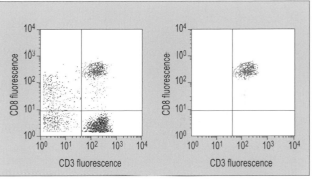

Figure 31.26 Flow cytofluorimetry. Cells in the sample are stained with specific fluorescent reagents to detect surface molecules and then stream one at a time past a laser. Each cell is measured for size (forward light scatter) and granularity (90° light scatter), as well as for red and green fluorescence, to detect two different peripheral blood surface markers, in this instance, CD8 and CD3, respectively (but modern instruments can detect many more different fluorophores). In a cell sorter, the flow chamber vibrates the cell stream, causing it to break into droplets which are then charged according to an arbitrary cut-off 'gate' and can then be steered by deflection plates under computer control to collect different cell populations according to the parameters measured. In the example shown in the left panel, four populations can be seen and after appropriate gating, the CD8 population in the right upper quadrant can be selected; reanalysis gives the plot seen on the lower left panel. (Redrawn from Male D, Brostoff J, Roth DB, Roitt I. *Immunology*, 7th edition, 2006. Mosby Elsevier, with permission.)

Newer FACS machines can measure 10–18 different fluorescent labels simultaneously, allowing both the surface phenotype of the cells and its function to be assessed.

Individual cells secreting antibodies or cytokines can be counted by the ELISPOT technique or by flow cytometry

The lymphocytes are incubated on a membrane impregnated with antigen, for antibody detection or anticytokine monoclonal antibody to detect cytokines (Fig. 31.27). The secreted product is identified by conventional ELISA-type readout.

Recently, two alternative approaches have been developed. One utilizes inhibitors of cytokine export (e.g. metabolic poisons such as brefeldin A that trap cytokines within the endoplasmic reticulum) to block cytokine secretion so that these molecules can be immunostained after cellular

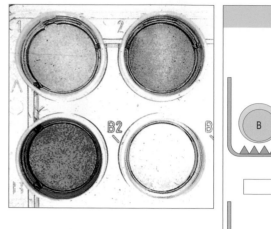

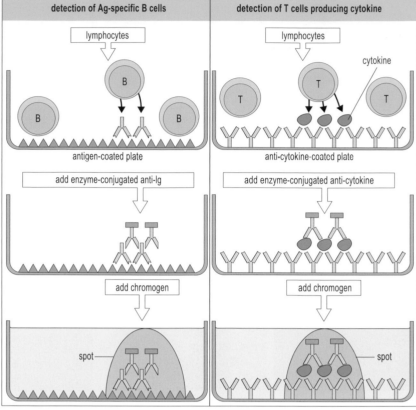

Figure 31.27 The ELISPOT assay for counting lymphocytes secreting antibodies or cytokines. The secreted products (antibodies from B cells and cytokines from T cells) are bound by the solid-phase capture molecules immediately beneath the cell and revealed by a colour reagent as a spot corresponding with the secreting cell. Wells with different numbers of ELISPOTs are shown top left. (Redrawn from Male D, Brostoff J, Roth DB, Roitt I. *Immunology*, 7th edition, 2006. Mosby Elsevier, with permission.)

permeabilization. Cells can then be stained for intracellular cytokines using specific antibodies, followed by flow cytometric analysis, as described earlier. The other approach makes use of bispecific antibodies that can simultaneously bind to a T-cell surface marker (such as CD4) while the other Fab arm is specific for a cytokine. The cytokines are captured as they are secreted from cells but, due to the bispecific nature of the antibody, the cytokine becomes stably attached to the cell making it and can then be detected with a different cytokine-specific antibody conjugated to a fluorochrome, again using a flow cytometer.

The ability of cytotoxic T cells to attack targets is conventionally assayed using a radioisotope

Cytotoxic T cells attack targets such as virally infected cells, and this ability is conventionally assayed by prelabelling the target with a radioisotope such as ^{51}Cr, and then looking for release of the isotope into the supernatant from damaged cells (Fig. 31.28). Cytotoxicity can also be measured by nonradioactive techniques using dyes.

PUTTING IT ALL TOGETHER: DETECTION, DIAGNOSIS, AND EPIDEMIOLOGY

As seen more fully in Chapter 32, understanding the epidemiology of an infection can help to define the correct strategies for control at the population level. However, this understanding, and decisions about control, both depend heavily upon

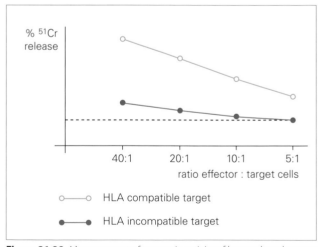

Figure 31.28 Measurement of cytotoxic activity of human lymphocytes against influenza-infected target cells. Only those targets that share human leukocyte antigens (HLA) haplotype with the cytotoxic cell donor are attacked (haplotype restriction) with consequent release of ^{51}Cr. The dotted line indicates background release of isotype from target cells incubated in the absence of effector cells.

the ability to recognize outbreaks of disease, to follow their progress and to identify the causative organism concerned. Detection and diagnosis are therefore key activities here, as they are for treatment of infection at the level of the individual.

Descriptive epidemiology involves asking questions about an outbreak of disease that will help to identify the pathogen and the source of infection. It is important to have a *case definition*, which includes the symptoms of the disease as well as details of the individuals involved and the timing of events. Analysis of these data should make it possible to say where and how the outbreak has arisen, who is at risk and what treatment is necessary to control further infection (see Box 31.4 on Legionnaires' disease for an example). Measures used may involve antibiotic treatment of those immediately affected, or vaccination if a large number are at risk (e.g. meningitis outbreaks in university students). For sexually transmitted disease (see above) an important element of detection is to establish contact patterns, or mixing matrices, so that individuals who may acquire an infection can be treated and further transmission prevented.

This approach to outbreaks of known or new disease follows their chance discovery as a result of clinical observations, exemplified by the discovery of AIDS in 1981 through the increased occurrence of *Pneumocystis carinii* (now known as *Pneumocystis jirovecii*) infection and of Kaposi's sarcoma in homosexual males. A more systematic approach to detection relies on a regular notification system – a surveillance system that routinely records episodes of a number of legally notifiable diseases. Such systems operate nationally through government or federal health organizations, as well as internationally through the World Health Organization for diseases such as cholera, yellow fever and plague. Regular monitoring of this kind makes it easier to identify outbreaks, because it provides the baseline against which 'the occurrence of cases in excess of expectancy' (the definition of an epidemic) can be measured.

Once outbreaks of infectious disease have been detected, the pathogen concerned can be identified by conventional diagnostic procedures, to ensure that the appropriate antibiotic or vaccination is given.

Box 31.4 Lessons in Microbiology

Legionnaires' disease – a case study

Background

War veterans of the Pennsylvania American Legion held their convention at a hotel in Philadelphia on 21–24 July 1976. By early August, an outbreak of severe pneumonia (cause unknown) among participants was reported. Deaths occurred despite antibiotic treatment.

Case definition

- Attendance at the convention or presence at the hotel between 1 July and 18 August
- Onset between those dates of cough, fever, verified pneumonia.

A total of 182 patients met this definition, of whom 149 had attended the convention and nine had been at the hotel for other conventions in the time period. An additional 39 patients had the clinical condition, but had not been in the hotel. They had, however, been within one block of the hotel in the relevant time period.

The epidemic

Cases appeared in late July, peaking between the 25th and 27th. A total of 78% of the cases were male, most were older than 50. The incubation period was between 2 and 10 days. A significant proportion of cases had spent time in the lobby or stood outside the hotel to watch the parade. There was no significant person-to-person spread.

Conclusion

The evidence pointed to an air-borne infectious agent, most likely acquired in the hotel lobby or immediately outside, entering the body via respiration. Initially, although the clinical evidence suggested a bacterial infection (large numbers of neutrophils in the sputum), no organisms could be demonstrated. *Legionella*, a previously unknown bacterium, was isolated and identified shortly afterwards. Erythromycin was found to be effective. The biology of *Legionella* pointed to control through disinfection and high-temperature treatment of water supplies and air-conditioning plant.

KEY FACTS

- Microbiologic confirmation of a clinical diagnosis of infection depends upon the collection of high-quality specimens and their rapid despatch to the laboratory with all the necessary supporting information.
- Laboratory tests detect microorganisms or their products or evidence of a patient's immune response to infection.
- While coming from different perspectives, culture and serologic methods are important, cooperative approaches to the identification of clinically important pathogens.
- Newer molecular techniques (e.g. involving PCR and mass spectroscopy) are increasingly used to detect pathogens rapidly; however, antimicrobial susceptibility can only

be determined and appropriate treatment information provided by isolating organisms in pure culture.

- Growth of bacteria requires at least 18 h (isolation of viruses and of fungi may take much longer); therefore standard culture results cannot be expected in less than 24 h although newer diagnostic tests are more rapid.
- Interpretation of culture results depends upon the source of the specimen. From sites that are normally sterile, any isolated organism is significant. From sites colonized by commensal flora, isolating and identifying the pathogen can be more difficult.
- Good communication between the clinician and the microbiologist is extremely important.

Epidemiology and control of infectious diseases

32

Epidemiology is defined as 'The study of the distribution and determinants of health-related states or events in specified populations and the application of this study to control of health problems' (Last, *Dictionary of Epidemiology*).

In epidemiology, we are concerned with populations rather than individuals. What we want to know of a disease in a population is: *who*, *where* and *when*. Hepatitis A outbreaks are often associated with institutions, restaurants and specific food. It is therefore important to determine who – which individuals ate potato salad, where – in a nursing home, when – 1 February 2010 – developed hepatitis A.

The field of epidemiology is divided into observational and interventional epidemiology. Observational studies are either descriptive, describing the frequency of a disease in the population, or analytical, investigating associations between risk factors and disease. Disease surveillance describing the number of notifiable disease cases such as measles, meningitis, or cholera is an example of observational descriptive epidemiology. Studies showing an association between human papillomavirus infection and cervical cancer are examples of analytical epidemiological studies. Interventional or experimental epidemiological studies are designed to test a hypothesis by allocating an exposure or intervention to one group of people but not the other and measuring the disease outcome. Examples of intervention studies are randomized–controlled trials investigating vaccine efficacy.

Epidemiologists talk about outcomes and exposures. The outcome is usually a disease or event such as death, infection or onset of new symptoms. Sometimes outcomes are laboratory markers, for example C-reactive protein (an acute-phase protein) or HIV viral load. These outcomes are called intermediate outcomes as they do not represent a definite endpoint. Exposures are either risk factors, for example a specific behaviour or harmful substance, or interventions such as drugs, vaccines or health education.

OUTCOME MEASUREMENTS

It is important to clearly define health-related outcomes. A definition should include the methods used to identify a case, the boundaries of a case and the unit of analysis.

Eye disease secondary to *Chlamydia trachomatis* (Chapter 25) is an important public health issue globally. The trachomatous inflammation is graded clinically into whether it involves follicular inflammation of the eyelid, abnormally positioned eyelashes or corneal scarring. When defining a case of trachomatous inflammation, it is important to describe (1) the methods and procedures used to determine a case: clinical examination versus direct immunofluorescence microscopy of conjunctival smear, (2) the boundaries of a case: follicular inflammation only versus all 3 grades, and (3) the unit of analysis: one or two eyes.

Disease prevalence and incidence are the two main types of measure of occurrence used in epidemiology. Prevalence is the number of existing cases in a population at a given point in time. Incidence is the number of new cases occurring in a population during a specified period of time.

Prevalence is influenced by occurrence of new cases (incidence) and the duration of each case. Prevalence of diseases with short durations such as viral gastroenteritis is mainly influenced by incidence. Prevalence of chronic diseases with relatively low mortality is likely to be high even if incidence is low. An example of the interaction between prevalence, incidence and mortality is shown in Box 32.1.

TYPES OF EPIDEMIOLOGICAL STUDIES

Cross-sectional study

Cross-sectional studies measure the frequency of an outcome and/or exposure(s) in a defined population at a particular point in time (Fig. 32.2A). These studies can be either descriptive, measuring the burden of disease, or analytical, comparing the frequency of disease in people exposed and unexposed to a risk factor.

Examples of study questions addressed by cross-sectional studies are:

- What proportion of the population has evidence of a past infection with Lyme disease?
- Is hepatitis B associated with hepatocellular carcinoma?

Cross-sectional studies are relatively cheap and quick to do. They are particularly useful to determine the scale of a

The interaction between prevalence, incidence, mortality and treatment

When HIV is introduced into an HIV-negative population HIV prevalence and incidence grow exponentially (Fig 32.1). As more people become infected the proportion of individuals not infected decreases. With fewer individuals susceptible to infection the likelihood that an infectious HIV-positive individual will be in contact with an HIV-uninfected individual is reduced. This in turn reduces incidence, but prevalence continues to rise. The median time of survival in the natural course of HIV disease is 6–8 years. Thus, after a time-lag, HIV mortality grows, which reduces HIV prevalence. However, if HIV treatment becomes available, survival is prolonged and prevalence grows.

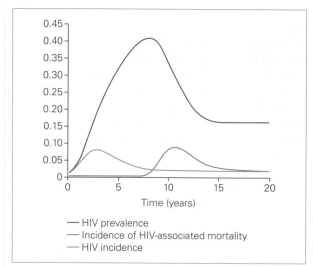

— HIV prevalence
— Incidence of HIV-associated mortality
— HIV incidence

Figure 32.1 HIV prevalence, incidence and mortality in a hypothetical population. (Based on data from: Trends in HIV incidence and prevalence: natural course of the epidemic or results of behavioural change? unaids *in collaboration with Wellcome Trust Centre for the Epidemiology of Infectious Disease,* 1999.)

problem, to generate hypotheses for possibly causal associations and to evaluate diagnostic tests (Box 32.2). Cross-sectional studies measure disease prevalence. It is therefore difficult to differentiate between exposures causing the disease and improving the survival. With outcome and exposure determined at the same time, there remains uncertainty if the exposure preceded the outcome, which is a crucial requirement for causality. Sometimes it is difficult to exclude reverse causality (the outcome caused the exposure).

Case–control study

Case–control studies identify people with the outcome (cases) and a representative group of people without the outcome (controls). Cases and controls are then compared with regards to differences in their past exposure (Fig. 32.2B). These studies are always analytical studies, as they ask the question, 'Does exposure A cause disease B?'

Examples of study questions addressed by case–control studies are:

- Are women with cervical cancer more likely to be infected with human papillomavirus than women without cervical cancer?
- Is injecting drug use associated with hepatitis C?

Case–control studies are usually less expensive and time-consuming than cohort or intervention studies. Rare diseases and diseases with long duration between exposure and outcome are best investigated using a case–control design, as case–control studies start with diseased and non-diseased individuals. However, when the exposure is rare, case–control studies are impractical. Unbiased ascertainment of exposure is often difficult, especially when it relies on the participant to self-report. Neither disease prevalence nor incidence is measured in a case–control study. Exposure is determined when the outcome has occurred and thus reverse causality might be the reason for an association between an exposure and disease.

Cohort study

Cohort studies follow a group of people who do not initially have the outcome of interest and determine whether they develop the disease (descriptive cohort study). Analytic cohort studies classify people at the start of the study as exposed or unexposed to a certain risk factor. Both groups are followed over time and the occurrence of disease is compared between the exposed and unexposed group (Fig. 32.2C).

Examples of study questions addressed by cohort studies are:

- How high is the mortality among patients with methicillin-resistant *Staphylococcus aureus* septicaemia?
- Does infection with human herpesvirus-8 cause Kaposi sarcoma in HIV-infected individuals?

Cohort studies measure disease incidence and ascertain risk factors before the outcome occurred. Thus they provide more robust evidence that an association between disease and exposure is causal. As cohort studies select disease-free exposed and unexposed individuals they are particularly useful to investigate associations between rare exposures and disease, but are inefficient when investigating rare diseases. Minimizing loss to follow-up is sometimes challenging, but important to ensure comparability between exposure groups and generalizability of study results. Cohort studies are often expensive in terms of the costs and manpower needed, as well as time consuming.

Intervention study

In an intervention study, disease-free and exposure-free individuals are actively allocated an exposure (intervention) or no exposure (no intervention). The two groups are then followed over a period of time and the frequency of the outcome is compared between the two groups (Fig. 32.2D). Randomized–controlled studies are a subtype of intervention studies and are considered the 'gold standard' type of study because, when rigorously designed and conducted, they provide very strong evidence of causal associations. The intervention is allocated at random which means that every participant has the same chance of receiving the intervention. This ensures that the group receiving the intervention and the group not receiving the intervention are equally balanced and comparable. The control group often receives a placebo, which is a tablet or injection containing no active compounds. Some intervention studies are double-blinded which means that neither investigator nor participant knows who receives the active intervention and who receives the placebo.

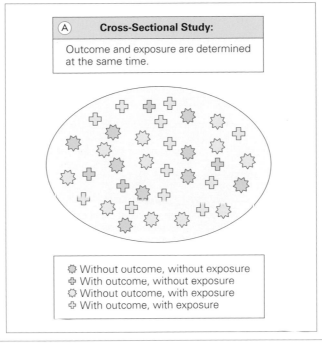

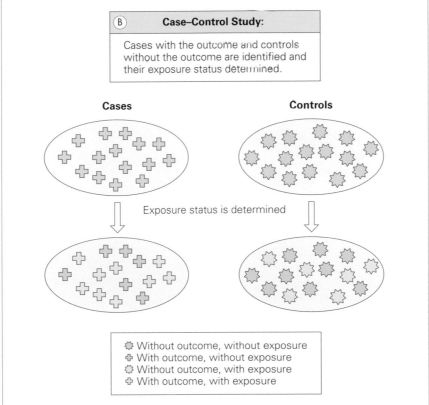

Figure 32.2 (A) Cross-sectional study: Outcome and exposure are determined at the same time. (B) Case–control study: Cases with the outcome and controls without the outcome are identified and their exposure status determined.

(Continued)

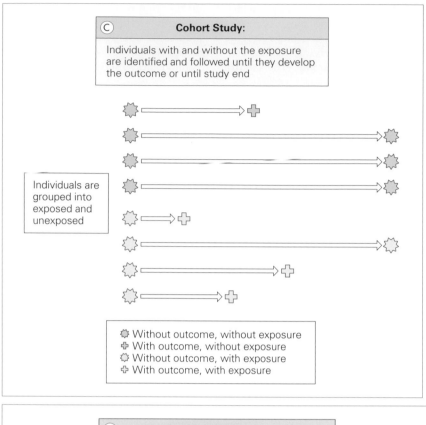

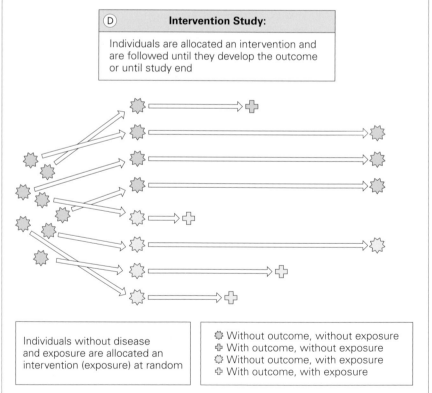

Figure 32.2—Cont'd (C) Cohort study: Individuals with and without the exposure are identified and followed until they develop the outcome or until study end. (D) Intervention study: Individuals are allocated an intervention (exposure) and are followed until they develop the outcome or until study end.

Box 32.2 Lessons in Microbiology

Sensitivity, specificity, positive and negative predictive value

New diagnostic tests are usually evaluated using a cross-sectional study design. The new test is compared against a gold standard test and sensitivity and specificity are determined.

Sensitivity is the proportion of true positives correctly identified by the new test and specificity is the proportion of true negatives correctly identified by the new test. Both sensitivity and specificity are intrinsic to the test and do not vary according to disease prevalence. However, they can be influenced by operators and environmental conditions.

From the patient's and physician's point of view, the more interesting question is, 'What are the chances for me having the disease if I have a positive test result?' This question is answered by the positive predictive value (PPV) which is the proportion of individuals with a positive test result who actually have the disease. The negative predictive value (NPV) is the proportion of individuals with a negative test result who are free of disease. Both PPV and NPV are related to sensitivity and specificity of a test but also to the prevalence of disease in a population.

The Xpert MTB-RIF is a new automated molecular test for diagnosis of *Mycobacterium tuberculosis* (Chapter 19). Diagnosis of tuberculosis (TB) relies on smear microscopy in most resource-limited settings and liquid culture in resource-rich settings. Smear microscopy has a low sensitivity and detects only patients with relatively advanced disease. Liquid culture is the gold standard of TB diagnosis, but takes days to weeks to become positive. A hypothetical evaluation study in 7000 TB suspects in a high TB prevalence setting revealed a sensitivity of the Xpert MTB-RIF of 92% and a specificity of 98% (Table 32.1A). The prevalence of TB among these 7000 TB suspects was 10%. PPV was 93% and NPV 99%.

The evaluation study was repeated in a population survey with 10 000 participants, among whom TB prevalence was 1%, sensitivity and specificity remained the same, but PPV was 53% and NPV 100% (Table 32.1B).

Table 32.1A Results of the Xpert MTB-RIF evaluation among tuberculosis suspects

		Liquid culture (gold standard)		
		Positive	**Negative**	**Total**
Xpert MTB-RIF	Positive	645	50	695
	Negative	55	6250	6305
	Total	700	6300	7000

Sensitivity = 645/700 = 92%
Specificity = 6250/6300 = 98%
Positive predictive value = 645/695 = 93%
Negative predictive value = 6250/6305 = 99%

Table 32.1B Results of the Xpert MTB-RIF evaluation in a population survey

		Liquid culture (gold standard)		
		Positive	**Negative**	**Total**
Xpert MTB-RIF	Positive	92	80	172
	Negative	8	9820	9828
	Total	100	9900	10 000

Sensitivity = 92/100 = 92%
Specificity = 9820/9900 = 98%
Positive predictive value = 92/172 = 53%
Negative predictive value = 9820/9828 = 100%

Examples of study questions addressed by intervention studies are:

- Is a new vaccine effective in preventing pneumococcal disease in children?
- Do steroids improve the outcome in children with meningococcal disease?

Randomised, placebo-controlled, double-blinded studies potentially deal with most problems experienced in observational studies: confounding, recall and observer bias. Confounding occurs when there is unequal distribution of a risk factor between exposed and unexposed individuals and thus the observed association between exposure and disease is due to a third factor. Recall bias is a systematic error which occurs when the way a participant answers a question is affected by either the disease status (in case–control or cross-sectional studies) or the exposure status (cohort studies). Observer bias arises when the accuracy of exposure (in case–control or cross-sectional studies) or outcome (cohort studies) data recorded by the investigator differs systematically between subjects in different outcome or exposure groups. Outcome data are determined prospectively in intervention studies and thus standard case definitions can be applied. Intervention studies may be expensive and time consuming and loss to follow-up can be challenging. Large sample sizes or long follow-up may be needed if disease incidence is low or duration between exposure and disease is long. Allocation of a harmful exposure or withholding of a beneficial intervention is unethical and thus intervention studies cannot be conducted under these circumstances.

TRANSMISSION OF INFECTIOUS DISEASE

An infectious disease is transmitted from one person to another either directly or indirectly. Indirect transmission occurs when the infectious agent is transferred from one person to another via an intermediary (e.g. vector or vehicle). The occurrence of a case depends on the occurrence of at least one previous case (source) and each case can itself lead to another case. Disease events in infectious diseases are dependent. We therefore need to investigate the spread of infectious diseases through a population over time (Fig. 32.3).

Infectiousness (Box 32.3)

The infectiousness of a disease in a population depends on several factors:

- the infectious agent:
  - time between infection of a person and becoming infectious

- duration of infectiousness
- the probability of transmission given a contact between an infectious person and a susceptible person
- the environment:
  - the type of contacts between infectious and susceptible individuals
  - the number of contacts
- the characteristics of the individuals in the population:
  - susceptibility of the population (number of susceptible individuals and degree of susceptibility)
  - infectiousness of the infected person.

Time periods of infections

When a susceptible individual becomes infected, he or she enters the latent period (Fig 32.4, Box 32.4). The latent period is the period between infection and becoming infectious (able to transmit the infection). This period is followed by the infectious period during which the infected individual is able to transmit the infectious agent. This is followed by the non-infectious period due to death or recovery. If the individual survives, he or she might be immune or remain susceptible to reinfection.

The sum of the average latent and infectious periods is called the average generation time of the infection.

Latent and infectious periods are different for different diseases (Table 32.2). For measles the latent period is 6–9 days followed by an infectious period of 6–7 days. In contrast the latent period of hepatitis B is 13–17 days and the infectious period 19–22 days.

Time periods of infectious disease

Not all infected individuals will develop the disease. Disease and infection differ with regards to symptoms and clinical signs. Infected individuals without symptoms and signs have asymptomatic infections. For some infectious agents such as cytomegalovirus the majority of infections will be asymptomatic.

The incubation period starts with the time of infection and ends when the individual develops symptoms (Fig. 32.4).

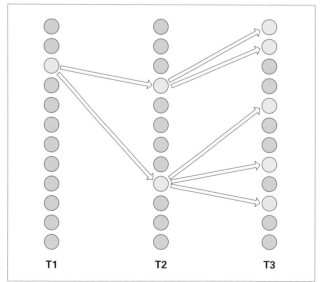

Figure 32.3 Transmission of an infectious disease in a population. One case of disease (source) at T1 transmits the disease to two cases (secondary cases) at T2; those cases transmit the disease to 5 cases at T3. Note that individuals who had the disease at T1 and T2 do not have the disease at T3 due to immunity.

Box 32.3 📱 **Lessons in Microbiology**

Infectiousness – example syphilis

An individual infected with syphilis develops a painless very infectious sore (chancre) at the site of infection on average 3 weeks following infection. The lesion may persists for 3–6 weeks. The individual cannot transmit the infection before the chancre develops. Thus the duration between infection and becoming infectious is important for transmission. The likelihood of transmitting the infection is increased the more frequent the individual has sexual intercourse and the longer the lesion persists (if the frequency of intercourse remains constant). Therefore the duration of infectiousness and the number of contacts influence transmission. The probability of transmission is reduced if the individual uses condoms.

Figure 32.4 Time periods of infections and infectious diseases.

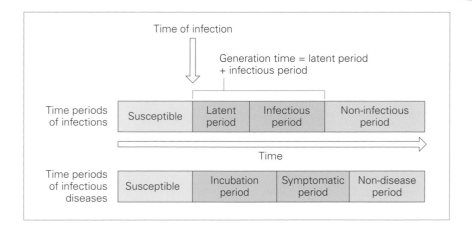

Table 32.2 Latent, infectious and incubation periods for a variety of viral and bacterial infections

Infectious diseases	Latent period (days)	Infectious period (days)	Incubation period (days)
Measles	6–9	6–7	8–13
Mumps	12–18	4–8	12–26
Whooping cough (pertussis)	21–23	7–10	6–10
Rubella	7–14	11–12	14–21
Diphtheria	14–21	2–5	2–5
Varicella	8–12	10–11	13–17
Hepatitis B	13–17	19–22	50–110
Poliomyelitis	1–3	2–3	7–12
Influenza	1–3	2–3	1–3

It is followed by the symptomatic period. The symptomatic period ends with death or recovery.

The incubation period is 8–13 days and 50–110 days for measles and hepatitis B, respectively. Thus an individual infected with measles is infectious before developing symptoms, as persons become infectious after 6–9 days.

Therefore isolation at the time of symptoms will not prevent transmission.

Basic and net reproductive rate

The basic reproductive rate (R_0) is the average number of infected secondary cases produced by each infectious case in a totally susceptible population.

Disease incidence:

- is static if each case leads to one new case ($R_0 = 1$)
- increases if each case leads to more than one infective secondary case ($R_0 > 1$)
- decreases if each case leads to less than one infective secondary case ($R_0 < 1$), which will result in disease control and eradication.

The basic reproductive rate depends on the duration of infectiousness of the case (d), the number of contacts per unit time (c) and the transmission probability (p): $R_0 = c*p*d$. This formula shows that the basic reproductive rate is not specific to an infectious agent only, but also to a specific host population at a particular point in time. R_0 for HIV is different for women, men and commercial sex workers. Table 32.3 shows basic reproductive rates for different diseases. Measles has a very high basic reproductive rate of 15–17, whereas influenza has a basic reproductive rate of 2–3.

A completely susceptible population is unusual. More commonly, a population consists of susceptible and immune individuals. The net reproductive rate (R) is the average number of secondary cases in a population where not

---

Box 32.4 📱 **Lessons in Microbiology**

Terminology: latency

In general, latency is a time delay. The term is frequently used in infectious disease terminology. Strictly speaking, the latent period is the time from infection until the infected individual is able to transmit the disease. However, sometimes the incubation period is called the latent period even though the two periods are differently defined and might differ in duration. A child infected with measles becomes infectious before symptoms occur. Thus the latent period is shorter than the incubation period. In contrast, an individual infected with falciparum malaria will experience symptoms 7–14 days following infection, but will only be infectious after 24 days. Sometimes, disease stages are called latent, such as latent tuberculosis or syphilis. Latent disease in that context describes periods of inactivity of the disease with regards to signs and symptoms.

Table 32.3 Basic reproductive rate for a variety of infectious diseases

Infectious disease	Basic reproductive rate (R_0)
Measles	15–17
Mumps	10–12
Whooping cough (pertussis)	15–17
Rubella	7–8
Diphtheria	5–6
Poliomyelitis	5–6
Influenza	2–3

all individuals are susceptible. The net reproductive rate depends on the basic reproductive rate (R_0) and the proportion of susceptible individuals (x): $R = R_0 * x$. The lower the proportion of susceptible individuals in a population, the lower the probability that an infectious individual will be in contact with a susceptible individual. Thus, if the proportion of susceptibles (x) is small enough, R will be less than 1 and the disease will be eradicated. The proportion of the population immune to an infection is called herd immunity (HI): $HI = 1-x$. The herd immunity threshold is the proportion of the population that need to be immune in order for a disease to die out (R<1): $HIT = R_0 - 1/R_0$. Susceptible individuals

become immune once they are vaccinated with a highly effective vaccine. The basic reproductive rate allows us to estimate the vaccination coverage which needs to be achieved in order to control an infectious disease. The critical vaccination coverage needs to be very high (92–95%) for measles due to the high reproductive rate (15–17). Rubella has a lower reproductive number (7–8) and thus for disease control vaccination coverage needs to be only 85–87%.

VACCINE EFFICACY

Vaccines protect individuals directly by making them less susceptible (more immune) to the disease. They also protect individuals indirectly (even individuals who did not receive the vaccine) through increased herd immunity.

Vaccine efficacy is the most commonly used measure of effect when evaluating vaccines and is often determined in randomized, controlled trials. Vaccine efficacy is the reduction in the incidence of disease in vaccinated individuals compared to unvaccinated individuals:

Vaccine efficacy = (incidence of disease in unvaccinated individuals – incidence of disease in vaccinated individuals)/ incidence of disease in unvaccinated individuals. Thus vaccine efficacy only measures the direct effect of the vaccine. Measurement of the indirect effect of vaccines requires more complex study designs.

KEY FACTS

- Epidemiological studies can be observational or interventional.

- Prevalence is the number of existing cases in a population at a given point in time. Incidence is the number of new cases occurring in a population during a specified period of time.

- Infectiousness depends on the infectious agent itself, the environment, and the characteristics of the individuals in the population, such as whether they are immune or susceptible.

- Infections can also be characterized by the latent period, the infectious period, the incubation period and the symptomatic period: individuals can become infectious before they develop symptoms.

- Vaccine efficacy is the reduction in the incidence of disease in vaccinated individuals compared to unvaccinated individuals. When a significant proportion of the community is protected by vaccination, unvaccinated individuals are also less likely to acquire disease; this is called herd immunity.

Attacking the enemy: antimicrobial agents and chemotherapy

33

Introduction

The interactions between host, microbial pathogen and antimicrobial agent can be considered as a triangle, and any alteration in one side will inevitably affect the other two sides (Fig. 33.1). In this chapter, two sides of the triangle will be examined in greater detail:

- the interactions between antimicrobial agents and microorganisms
- the interactions between antimicrobial agents and the human host.

Laboratory aspects of antimicrobial susceptibility tests and assays will also be outlined. The third side of the triangle, the interactions between microorganisms and the human host, has been considered in detail in the preceding chapters. The concluding part of the present chapter will draw together the three sides of the triangle.

SELECTIVE TOXICITY

The term 'selective toxicity' was proposed by the immunochemist Paul Ehrlich (Box 33.1, Fig. 33.2). Selective toxicity is achieved by exploiting differences in the structure and metabolism of microorganisms and host cells; ideally, the antimicrobial agent should act at a target site present in the infecting organism, but absent from host cells. This is more likely to be achievable in microorganisms that are prokaryotes than in those that are eukaryotes, as the former are structurally more distinct from the host cells. (A comparison of the cellular organization of prokaryotic and eukaryotic cells is given in Ch. 1.) At the other end of the spectrum, viruses are difficult to attack because of their obligate intracellular lifestyle. A successful antiviral agent must be able to enter the host cell, but inhibit and damage only a virus-specific target. The desirable features of ideal antimicrobial agents are summarized in Box 33.2.

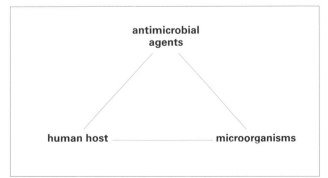

Figure 33.1 The interactions between antimicrobial agents, microorganisms and the human host can be viewed as a triangle. Any effect on one side of the triangle will have effects on the other two sides.

DISCOVERY AND DESIGN OF ANTIMICROBIAL AGENTS

The term 'antibiotic' has traditionally referred to natural metabolic products of fungi, actinomycetes and bacteria that kill or inhibit the growth of microorganisms. Antibiotic production has been particularly associated with soil microorganisms and, in the natural environment, is thought to provide a selective advantage for organisms in their competition for space and nutrients. Although the majority of antibacterial agents in clinical use today are derived from natural products of fermentation, most are then chemically modified (i.e. semi-synthetic) to improve their antibacterial or pharmacologic properties. However, some agents are totally synthetic (e.g. sulphonamides, quinolones). Therefore, the term 'antibacterial' or 'antimicrobial' agent is often used in preference to 'antibiotic'. Agents used against fungi, parasites, and viruses can also be included under antimicrobials, but the terms antifungals, antiprotozoans, anthelmintics, and antivirals are more often used.

The discovery of new antimicrobial agents used to be entirely a matter of chance. Pharmaceutical companies undertook massive screening programmes searching for new soil microorganisms that produced antibiotic activity. In the light of our greater understanding of the mechanisms of action of existing antimicrobials, the processes have become rationalized, searching either for new natural products by target-site-directed screening or synthesizing molecules predicted to interact with a microbial target. Genomic approaches to the identification of novel targets have revolutionized this approach. In addition, knowledge of the crystal structure of the key enzymes involved in viral replication such as protease, reverse transcriptase and helicase leads to the design of new drugs. The steps in a rational design programme are summarized in Box 33.3.

Box 33.1 Lessons in Microbiology

Paul Ehrlich (1854–1915)

Just as Pasteur towers over immunomicrobiology, Ehrlich (Fig. 33.2) is the father figure of immunochemistry. His contributions to the science of medicine at all levels are quite extraordinary. He was the first to propose that foreign antigens were recognized by 'side-chains' on cells (1890), a brilliant insight that took 70 years to confirm. He also discovered the mast cell, invented the acid-fast stain for the tubercle bacillus, and devised a method to manufacture and

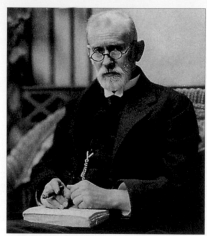

Figure 33.2 Paul Ehrlich (1854–1915).

commercialize a strong diphtheria antitoxin. He pioneered the development of antibiotics with his work on '606' (or 'Salvarsan'), a treatment for syphilis, for which he was denounced by the church for interfering with God's punishment for sin.

While working on the treatment of infections caused by trypanosomes he set forth the concept of 'selective toxicity', as illustrated by the following quote: 'But, gentlemen, it should be made clear that in general this task is much more complicated than that using serum therapy. These chemical agents, in contrast to the antibodies, may be harmful to the body. When such an agent is given to a sick organism, a difference must exist between the toxicity of this agent to the parasite and its toxicity to the host. We must always be aware of the fact that these agents are able to act on other parts of the body as well as on the parasites.'

Like Pasteur, he had a grasp of the continuum from the whole body to the cell and the three-dimensional structure of molecules, and throughout his life, he stressed the importance of molecular interaction as the basis of all biologic function; this is summed up in his famous maxim *corpora non agunt nisi fixata* or 'things do not interact unless they make contact'. A Nobel Prize winner in 1908, his name was systematically eliminated from the records by the Nazi regime on account of his Jewish birth, but he was restored to honour by a reconstruction of his laboratory at the Seventh International Congress of Immunology in Berlin in 1989.

Box 33.2 Desired Properties of a New Antimicrobial Agent

In the design of new antimicrobial agents, both antimicrobial activity and pharmacologic properties of the antibiotic for the host have to be considered.

Antimicrobial properties

- selectivity for microbial rather than mammalian targets
- cidal activity (antibacterial and antifungal agents)
- slow emergence of resistance
- narrow spectrum of activity.[a]

Pharmacologic activities

- non-toxic to the host
- long plasma half-life (once-a-day dosing)
- good tissue distribution including CSF
- low plasma-protein binding
- oral and parenteral dosing forms
- no interference with other drugs.

[a] The desired attribute depends on drug usage. Narrow-spectrum drugs cause less disturbance to normal flora and may contribute less to emergence of antibiotic resistance, whereas broad-spectrum compounds are more useful for empiric therapy and treatment of polymicrobial infections. CSF, cerebrospinal fluid.

Box 33.3 Rational Design of an Antimicrobial Agent

The discovery process of new antimicrobial agents has moved away from the random screening of soil microorganisms towards a rational design programme. From discovery to development and marketing can take up to 15 years and cost US$800 million. This list identifies different steps in this programme (average 10 years).

- Select an appropriate target.
- Identify a chemical lead (i.e. a new molecule with inhibitory activity on the target).
- Modify the lead compound to enhance potency.
- Evaluate in vitro activity.
- Evaluate in vivo activity and toxicity.
- Test in clinical trials and develop.

CLASSIFICATION OF ANTIBACTERIAL AGENTS

There are three ways of classifying antibacterial agents:
1. according to whether they are bactericidal or bacteriostatic
2. by target site
3. by chemical structure.

Some antibacterial agents are bactericidal, others are bacteriostatic

Some antibacterial agents kill bacteria (bactericidal), while others only inhibit their growth (bacteriostatic). Thus, the bactericidal process is irreversible, while bacteriostasis is reversible. Nevertheless, bacteriostatic agents are successful in the treatment of some infections because they prevent the bacterial population from increasing and host defence mechanisms can consequently cope with the static population. However, in immunocompromised patients, bacteriostatic drugs may be less efficacious, and certain infections (e.g., endocarditis) require a bactericidal drug even in an immunocompetent patient.

As a means of classification, the distinction between bactericidal and bacteriostatic agents is blurred because some agents are capable of killing some species, but are only bacteriostatic for others, e.g. chloramphenicol inhibits growth of *Escherichia coli*, but kills *Haemophilus influenzae*.

There are five main target sites for antibacterial action

A convenient way of classifying antibacterials is on the basis of their site of action. This classification does not allow an accurate prediction of which antibacterials will be active against which bacterial species, but it does help in the understanding of the molecular basis of antibacterial action, and conversely in the elucidation of many of the synthetic processes in bacterial cells. The five main target sites for antibacterial action are:

- cell wall synthesis
- protein synthesis
- nucleic acid synthesis
- metabolic pathways
- cell membrane function.

These targets differ to a greater or lesser degree from those in the host (human) cells and so allow inhibition of the bacterial cell without concomitant inhibition of the equivalent mammalian cell targets (selective toxicity).

Each target site encompasses a multitude of synthetic reactions (enzymes and substrates), each of which may be specifically inhibited by an antibacterial agent. A range of chemically diverse molecules may inhibit different reactions at the same target site (e.g. protein synthesis inhibitors).

Antibacterial agents have diverse chemical structures

Classification based on chemical structure alone is not of practical use, because there is such diversity. However, a combination of target site and chemical structure provides a useful working classification to organize antibacterial agents into specific families which will be discussed later in this chapter.

RESISTANCE TO ANTIBACTERIAL AGENTS

Resistance to antibacterial agents is a matter of degree. In the medical setting, we define a resistant organism as one that will not be inhibited or killed by an antibacterial agent at concentrations of the drug achievable in the body after normal dosage. 'Some men are born great, some achieve greatness, and some have greatness thrust upon them' (William Shakespeare, *Twelfth Night*). Likewise, some bacteria are born resistant, others have resistance thrust upon them. In other words, some species are innately resistant to some families of antibiotics because they lack a susceptible target, are impermeable to or enzymatically inactivate the antibacterial agent. The Gram-negative rods with their outer membrane layer exterior to the cell wall peptidoglycan are less permeable to large molecules than Gram-positive cells. However, within species that are innately susceptible, there are also strains that develop or acquire resistance.

The genetics of resistance

In parallel with the rapid development of a wide range of antibacterial agents since the 1940s, bacteria have proved extremely adept at developing resistance to each new agent that comes along. This is illustrated for *Staphylococcus aureus* by the timeline shown in Figure 33.3. The rapidly increasing incidence of resistance associated with slowing down in the discovery of novel antibacterial agents to combat resistant strains is now recognized worldwide as a serious threat to the treatment of life-threatening infections.

Figure 33.3 'Time line' illustrating the chronological emergence of antibiotic resistance in Gram-positive cocci.

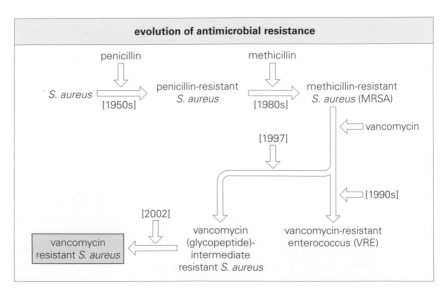

Chromosomal mutation may result in resistance to a class of antimicrobial agents (cross-resistance)

Resistance may arise from:

- a single chromosomal mutation in one bacterial cell resulting in the synthesis of an altered protein: for example, streptomycin resistance via alteration in a ribosomal protein, or the single amino acid change in the enzyme dihydropteroate synthetase resulting in a lowered affinity for sulphonamides. A mutational event could also alter (i.e., increase or decrease) the production of a protein resulting in increased resistance.
- a series of mutations, for example changes in penicillin-binding proteins (PBPs) in penicillin-resistant pneumococci.

In the presence of antibiotic, these spontaneous mutants have a selective advantage to survive and outgrow the susceptible population (Fig. 33.4A). They can also spread to other sites in the same patient or by cross-infection to other patients and therefore become disseminated. Chromosomal mutations are relatively rare events (i.e. usually found once in a population of 10^6–10^8 organisms) and generally provide resistance to a single class of antimicrobials (i.e. 'cross-resistance' to structurally related compounds).

Genes on transmissible plasmids may result in resistance to different classes of antimicrobial agents (multiple resistance)

Not content with surviving the antibacterial onslaught by relying on random chromosomal mutation, bacteria are also able to acquire resistance genes on transmissible plasmids (Fig. 33.4B; see also Ch. 2). Such plasmids often code for resistance determinants to several unrelated families of antibacterial agents. Therefore a cell may acquire 'multiple' resistance to many different drugs (i.e. in different classes) at once, a process much more efficient than chromosomal mutation. This so-called 'infectious resistance' was first described by Japanese workers studying enteric bacteria, but is now recognized to be widespread throughout the bacterial world. Some plasmids are promiscuous, crossing species barriers, and the same resistance gene is therefore found in widely different species. For example, TEM-1, the most common plasmid-mediated beta-lactamase in Gram-negative bacteria, is widespread in *E. coli* and other enterobacteria and also accounts for penicillin resistance in *Neisseria gonorrhoeae* and ampicillin resistance in *H. influenzae*.

Resistance may be acquired from transposons and other mobile elements

Resistance genes may also occur on transposons; the so-called 'jumping genes', which by a replicative process are capable of generating copies which may integrate into the chromosome or into plasmids (see Ch. 2). The chromosome provides a more stable location for the genes, but they will be disseminated only as rapidly as the bacteria divide. Transposon copies moving from the chromosome to plasmids are disseminated more rapidly. Transposition can also occur between plasmids, for example, from a non-transmissible to a transmissible plasmid, again accelerating dissemination (Fig. 33.4C).

'Cassettes' of resistance genes may be organized into genetic elements called *integrons*

As discussed previously, antibiotic-resistance genes may individually reside on plasmids, the chromosome, or on transposons found in both locations. However, in some instances multiple resistance genes may come together in a structure known as an integron. As shown in Figure 33.5A, the integron encodes a site-specific recombination enzyme (int gene; integrase), which allows insertion (and also excision) of antibiotic-resistance gene 'cassettes' (resistance gene plus additional sequences including an 'attachment' region) into the integron attachment site (att). In classic operon fashion, a strong integron promoter controls transcription of the inserted genes. Based on their integration mechanism (integrase, etc.), integrons have been organized into different classes found in both Gram-negative and Gram-positive organisms. Whether acting as independent mobile genetic elements or inserted into transposons, integrons are capable of moving into a variety of DNA molecules, the overall hierarchy of which is depicted in Figure 33.5B. With their ability to capture, organize and rearrange different antibiotic-resistance genes, integrons represent an important mechanism for the spread of multiple antibiotic resistance in clinically important microorganisms.

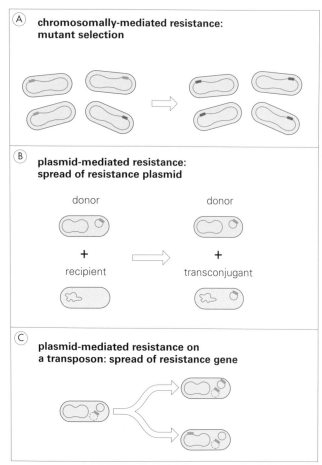

Figure 33.4 A chromosomal mutation (A) can produce a drug-resistant target, which confers resistance on the bacterial cell and allows it to multiply in the presence of antibiotic. Resistance genes carried on plasmids (B) can spread from one cell to another more rapidly than cells themselves divide and spread. Resistance genes on transposable elements (C) move between plasmids and the chromosome and from one plasmid to another, thereby allowing greater stability or greater dissemination of the resistance gene.

Figure 33.5 (A) Basic integron structure and (B) overall interrelationship between integrons and other DNA elements. att, integron attachment site; int, integrase.

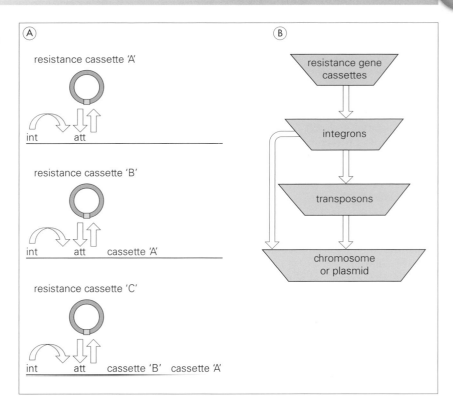

Staphylococcal genes for methicillin resistance are organized into a unique cassette structure

Staphylococcal genes responsible for resistance to the antibiotic methicillin (discussed below) are found in a specialized cassette arrangement termed staphylococcal chromosomal casette *mec* (SCC*mec*). SCC*mec* inserts into a unique target site on the staphylococcal chromosome. The cassette represents a highly recombinogenic region which may not only rearrange internally but also serve as a target for the insertion of other resistance elements (e.g, transposons and plasmids).

Mechanisms of resistance

Resistance mechanisms can be broadly classified into three main types. These are summarized below, in Table 33.1 and described in more detail where relevant for each antibiotic in later parts of this chapter. Where bacterial mechanisms of

Table 33.1 Mechanisms of resistance can be classified into three main types

Antibacterial	Mechanism of resistance		
	Altered target	**Altered uptake**	**Drug inactivation**
Beta-lactams	+	+	+
Glycopeptides	+		
Aminoglycosides	+	+	+
Tetracyclines	+	+	
Chloramphenicol		+	+
Macrolides/ketolides	+	+	+
Lincosamides	+		
Streptogramins	+		
Oxazolidinones	+		
Fusidic acid	+		
Sulphonamides/trimethoprim	+	+	
Quinolones	+	+	
Rifampicin	+		
Cyclic lipopeptide	+		

For antibiotics where more than one mode of resistance exists, drugs vary as to which is more frequently encountered.

antimicrobial resistance have been elucidated, they appear to involve the synthesis of new or altered proteins. As mentioned above, the genes encoding these proteins may be found on plasmids or the chromosome.

The target site may be altered

The target may be altered so that it has a lowered affinity for the antibacterial, but still functions adequately for normal metabolism to proceed. Alternatively, an additional target (e.g. enzyme) may be synthesized.

Access to the target site may be altered (altered uptake or increased exit)

This mechanism involves decreasing the amount of drug that reaches the target by either:

- altering entry, for example by decreasing the permeability of the cell wall
- pumping the drug out of the cell (known as an efflux mechanism).

Enzymes that modify or destroy the antibacterial agent may be produced (drug inactivation)

There are many examples of such enzymes, the most important being:

- beta-lactamases
- aminoglycoside-modifying enzymes
- chloramphenicol acetyl transferases.

These will be described in the relevant parts on these antibiotics.

CLASSES OF ANTIBACTERIAL AGENTS

The following parts of this chapter deal with groups of antibacterial agents based on their target site and chemical structure. In each case, the discussion attempts to summarize the answers to the questions set out in Table 33.2, reviewing the interactions between antibacterial agent and bacteria and between the antibacterial and the host (i.e. two sides of the triangle in Fig. 33.1).

INHIBITORS OF CELL WALL SYNTHESIS

Peptidoglycan, a vital component of the bacterial cell wall (see Ch. 2), is a compound unique to bacteria and therefore provides an optimum target for selective toxicity. Synthesis of peptidoglycan precursors starts in the cytoplasm; wall subunits are then transported across the cytoplasmic membrane and finally inserted into the growing peptidoglycan molecule. Several different stages are therefore potential targets for inhibition (Fig. 33.6). The antibacterials that inhibit cell wall synthesis are varied in chemical structure. The most important of these agents are the beta-lactams, the largest group, and the glycopeptides which are active only against Gram-positive organisms. Bacitracin (primarily used topically) and cycloserine (mainly used as a 'second-line' medication for treatment of tuberculosis, discussed later in this chapter) have many fewer clinical applications.

Beta-lactams

Beta-lactams contain a beta-lactam ring and inhibit cell wall synthesis by binding to penicillin-binding proteins (PBPs)

Beta-lactams comprise a very large family of different groups of bactericidal compounds, all containing the beta-lactam ring. The different groups within the family are distinguished by the structure of the ring attached to the beta-lactam ring – in penicillins this is a five-membered ring, in cephalosporins a six-membered ring – and by the side chains attached to these rings (Fig. 33.7).

PBPs are membrane proteins (e.g. carboxypeptidases, transglycosylases and transpeptidases) capable of binding to penicillin (hence the name PBP) and are responsible for the final stages of cross-linking of the bacterial cell wall structure. Inhibition of one or more of these essential enzymes results in an accumulation of precursor cell wall units, leading to activation of the cell's autolytic system and cell lysis (Fig. 33.8).

Most beta-lactams have to be administered parenterally

Although the majority of beta-lactams have to be administered intramuscularly or intravenously, there are some orally active agents. Most achieve clinically useful concentrations in the cerebrospinal fluid (CSF) when the meninges are inflamed (as in meningitis) and the blood–brain barrier becomes more permeable. In general, they are not effective against intracellular organisms.

A few of the cephalosporins, notably cefotaxime, are metabolized to compounds with less microbiologic activity. All beta-lactams are excreted in the urine, and for some, such as benzylpenicillin, this is very rapid; hence the need for frequent doses. Probenecid can be administered concurrently to slow down excretion and maintain higher blood and tissue concentrations for a longer period of time.

Table 33.2 In order to understand the nature and optimum use of an antibacterial agent, the questions listed here must be answered

What is it?	Chemical structure: natural or synthetic product
What does it do?	Target site, mechanism of action
Where does it go? (and therefore preferred route of administration)	Absorption, distribution, metabolism and excretion of the drug in the body of the host
When is it used?	Spectrum of activity and important clinical uses
What are the limitations to its use?	Toxicity to the human host; lack of toxicity, i.e. resistance of the bacteria
How much does it cost?	Great variation between agents but cost is a serious limitation on availability of some agents in resource-poor countries

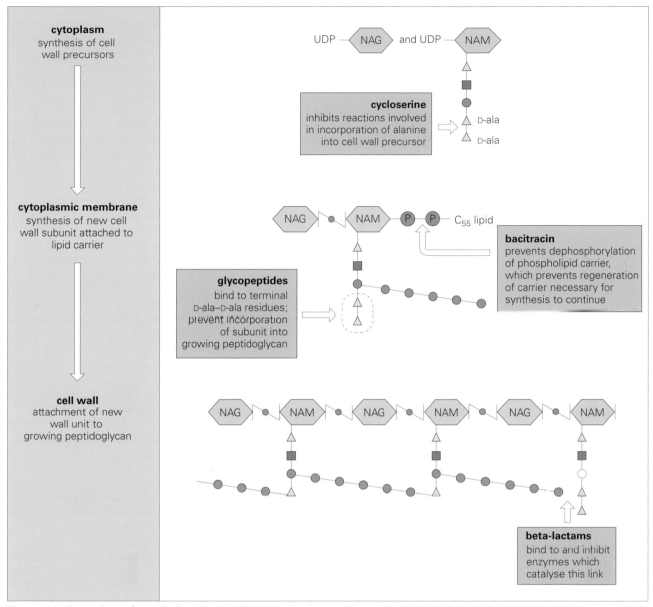

Figure 33.6 The synthesis of peptidoglycan is a complex process that begins in the cytoplasm, proceeds across the cytoplasmic membrane and leads to the attachment of new wall units to the growing peptidoglycan chain. This synthetic pathway can be inhibited at a variety of points by antibacterial agents. The precise mechanism of inhibition caused by glycopeptides such as vancomycin is unknown, but the mechanism of action of beta-lactams has now been fully elucidated (see text). NAG, N-acetyl glucosamine; NAM, N-acetyl muramic acid; UDP, uridine diphosphate.

Different beta-lactams have different clinical uses, but are not active against species that lack a cell wall

A vast array of beta-lactam antibiotics are currently registered for clinical use. Some, such as penicillin, are active mainly against Gram-positive organisms, whereas others (e.g. semi-synthetic penicillins, carboxypenems, monobactams, second-, third- and fourth-generation cephalosporins) have been developed for their activity against Gram-negative rods. Only the more recent beta-lactams are active against innately more resistant organisms such as *Pseudomonas aeruginosa* (Table 33.3).

It is important to remember that beta-lactams are not active against species that lack a cell wall (e.g. *Mycoplasma*) or those with very impenetrable walls such as mycobacteria, or intracellular pathogens such as *Brucella*, *Legionella* and *Chlamydia*.

Resistance to beta-lactams may involve one or more of the three possible mechanisms

Resistance by alteration in target site

Methicillin-resistant staphylococci (e.g. *Staph. aureus*, *Staph. epidermidis* – MRSA, MRSE, respectively) synthesize an additional PBP (PBP2a) which has a much lower affinity for beta-lactams than the normal PBPs and is therefore able to continue cell wall synthesis when the other PBPs are inhibited. Although the *mecA* gene which codes for PBP2a is present on the chromosome in all cells of a resistant population, in many instances it may only be transcribed in a proportion of the cells, resulting in a phenomenon known as 'heterogeneous resistance'. In the laboratory, special cultural conditions are used to enhance expression and demonstrate resistance. Methicillin-resistant staphylococci commonly produce beta-lactamase (see below) and are resistant to all other beta-lactams with the exception

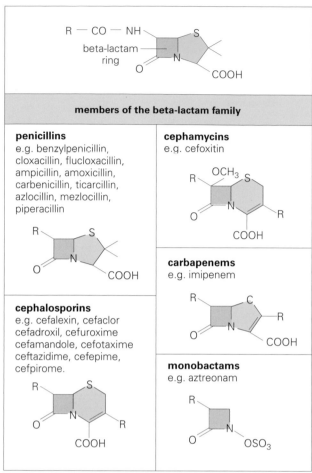

Figure 33.7 The beta-lactam family. The ring structure is common to all beta-lactams and must be intact for antibacterial action. Enzymes (beta-lactamases) that catalyse the hydrolysis of the beta-lactam bond render the agents inactive. The penicillins and cephalosporins are the major classes of beta-lactam antibiotics, but other members of the family, particularly the carbapenems and monobactams, are the focus of new developments.

of ceftaroline, the first cephalosporin approved by the US FDA for activity against MRSA. This cephalosporin binds to PBP2a with an affinity 2000-fold better than other beta-lactams, and is thus effective in treating infections caused by MRSA.

Other organisms such as *Streptococcus pneumoniae*, *Neisseria gonorrhoeae* and *Haemophilus influenzae* may also utilize PBP changes to achieve beta-lactam resistance, which may vary depending on the compound employed.

Resistance by alteration in access to the target site

This mechanism is found in Gram-negative cells where beta-lactams gain access to their target PBPs by diffusion through protein channels (porins) in the outer membrane. Mutations in porin genes result in a decrease in permeability of the outer membrane and hence resistance. Strains resistant by this mechanism may exhibit cross-resistance to unrelated antibiotics that use the same porins.

Resistance by production of beta-lactamases

Beta-lactamases are enzymes that catalyse the hydrolysis of the beta-lactam ring to yield microbiologically inactive products. Genes encoding these enzymes are widespread in the bacterial kingdom and are found on the chromosome and on plasmids.

The beta-lactamases of Gram-positive bacteria are released into the extracellular environment (Fig. 33.8A) and resistance will only be manifest when a large population of cells is present. The beta-lactamases of Gram-negative cells, however, remain within the periplasm (Fig. 33.8B).

To date, hundreds of different beta-lactamase enzymes have been described. All have the same function but with differing amino acid sequences that influence their affinity for different beta-lactam substrates. Some enzymes specifically target penicillins or cephalosporins, while others are especially troublesome in broadly attacking most beta-lactam compounds (i.e. extended-spectrum beta-lactamases, ESBLs). Some beta-lactam antibiotics (e.g. carbapenems) are hydrolysed by very few enzymes (beta-lactamase stable), whereas others (e.g. ampicillin) are much more labile. Beta-lactamase inhibitors such as clavulanic acid (Fig. 33.9) are molecules that contain a beta-lactam ring and act as 'suicide inhibitors', binding to beta-lactamases and preventing them from destroying beta-lactams. They have little bactericidal activity of their own.

Side effects

Toxic effects of beta-lactam drugs include mild rashes and immediate hypersensitivity reactions

Statistics regarding allergy to beta-lactam drugs are complicated by the fact that the problem historically involves self-reporting by patients who are often mistaken in their 'diagnosis'. Nevertheless, serious allergy to beta-lactam drugs in the form of an immediate (type 1) hypersensitivity reaction may occur in ca. 0.5–4% of patients, although anaphylaxis occurs much less frequently (ca. 0.004 to 0.04% of penicillin treatment courses). Mild idiopathic reactions, usually in the form of a rash, are more common (ca. 25% of treatment courses), especially with ampicillin. Patients who are allergic to penicillin are often allergic to cephalosporins (less with third-generation compounds) and vice versa, but aztreonam, a monobactam, shows negligible cross-reactivity.

Neurotoxicity and seizures can occur with all the beta-lactams if improperly dosed for body weight and kidney function, especially in patients with renal impairment. This toxicity is manifest as fits, unconsciousness, myoclonic spasms and hallucinations. Carbenicillin can cause platelet dysfunction and sodium overload (because it is given as a sodium salt), especially in patients with liver failure, renal failure and congestive heart failure.

Glycopeptides

Glycopeptides are large molecules and act at an earlier stage than beta-lactams

Glycopeptides include vancomycin and teicoplanin. Both are very large molecules and therefore have difficulty penetrating into Gram-negative cells. Teicoplanin is a natural complex of five different but closely related molecules.

Glycopeptides are bactericidal and interfere with cell wall synthesis by binding to terminal D-alanine-D-alanine at the end of pentapeptide chains that are part of the growing bacterial cell wall structure (see Fig. 33.6). This binding inhibits the transglycosylation reaction and prevents incorporation of new subunits into the growing cell wall. As glycopeptides act at an earlier stage than beta-lactams, it is not useful to combine glycopeptides and beta-lactams in the treatment of infections.

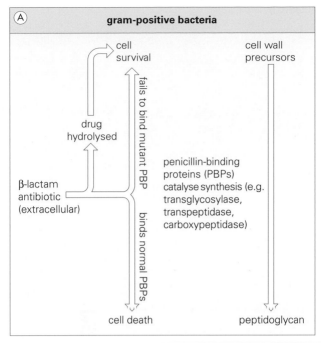

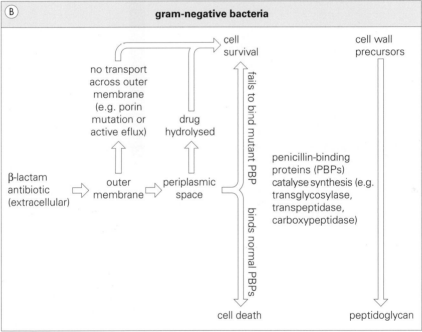

Figure 33.8 Penicillin-binding proteins (PBPs) play a key role in the final stages of peptidoglycan synthesis. They catalyse the cross-linkage of wall subunits, which are then incorporated into the cell wall. Beta-lactams are able to enter the cell (e.g. through pores in the outer membrane of Gram-negatives) and bind to the PBP. This prevents it from catalysing the cross-linkage of subunits, leading to their accumulation in the cell and the release of autolytic enzymes, which causes cell lysis. Within the periplasmic space of Gram-negatives (b1) beta-lactamases can inactivate beta-lactams before they reach their target PBPs, thereby protecting the cell from antibiotic action. Alternatively, mutant PBPs fail to bind beta-lactase, thus allowing peptidoglycan synthesis to occur. In Gram-positive bacteria (b2) beta-lactams may be extracellularly destroyed by beta-lactamases or rendered ineffective, as in Gram-negatives, by mutant PBPs.

Vancomycin and teicoplanin must be given by injection for systemic infections

Vancomycin and teicoplanin are not absorbed from the gastrointestinal tract and do not penetrate the CSF in patients without meningitis. However, bactericidal concentrations are achieved in most patients with meningitis because of the increased permeability of the blood–brain barrier. Excretion is via the kidney.

Both vancomycin and teicoplanin are active only against Gram-positive organisms

Vancomycin and teicoplanin are used mainly for:

- the treatment of infections caused by Gram-positive cocci and Gram-positive rods that are resistant to beta-lactam drugs, particularly multiresistant *Staphylococcus aureus* and *Staphylococcus epidermidis*
- for patients allergic to beta-lactams

Table 33.3 Characteristics of representative beta-lactams

Drug class	Category	General spectrum of activity
Penicillins		
Penicillin G, V[a]	Natural penicillin	Gram-positive bacteria
Cloxacillin[a] Dicloxacillin[a] Nafcillin[a] Oxacillin[a]	Semisynthetic (beta-lactamase resistant) penicillin	Gram-positive bacteria (incl. beta-lactamase producers)
Amoxicillin[a,b] Ampicillin[a,b]	Semisynthetic (amino) penicillin	Gram-positive bacteria Gram-negative bacteria, including spirochetes, *Listeria monocytogenes*, *Proteus mirabilis* and some *Escherichia coli*
Carbenicillin[a] Ticarcillin[b]	Semisynthetic (carboxy) penicillin	Gram-positive bacteria Enhanced coverage of Gram-negatives, including *Pseudomonas* and *Klebsiella*
Mezlocillin Piperacillin[b]	Semisynthetic (ureido) penicillin	
Cephalosporins		
Cefadroxil[a] Cefazolin Cephalexin[a] Cephalothin Cephradine[a]	First generation	Gram-positive bacteria
Cefaclor[a] Cefamandole Cefonicid Cefprozil[a] Cefuroxime[a]	Second generation	
Cefdinir[a] Cefditoren[a] Cefoperazone Cefpodoxime[a] Cefotaxime Ceftazidime Ceftibuten[a] Ceftizoxime Ceftriaxone	Third generation	
Cefepime Cefpirome	Fourth generation	Improved activity against Gram-negative bacteria
Ceftaroline	Anti-MRSA	Improved activity, especially against MRSA
Cephamycin[c]		
Cefmetazole Cefotetan Cefoxitin		Gram-positive bacteria Improved activity against *Bacillus fragilis*
Carbapenems		
Ertapenem Imipenem Meropenem Doripenem		Gram-positive and Gram-negative bacteria
Monobactams		
Aztreonam		Gram-negative bacteria including *Haemophilus influenza* and *Pseudomonas aeruginosa*

Although there are many beta-lactam agents available, the most commonly used ones are listed, together with their main indications.
[a]Oral formulation available.
[b]Can be formulated in combination with beta-lactamase inhibitors (see Fig. 33.9).
[c]Often classified with second generation cephalospoxins.

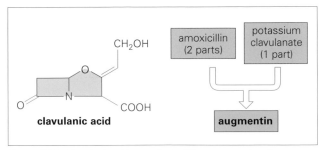

Figure 33.9 Clavulanic acid, a product of *Streptomyces clavuligerus*, inhibits the most common beta-lactamases (e.g. TEM enzymes) and allows amoxicillin to inhibit cells producing these enzymes. Augmentin is the most widely used of these combination drugs. Other combinations include ticarcillin and clavulanic acid, and piperacillin and tazobactam.

- the treatment of *Clostridium difficile* in antibiotic-associated colitis, although concerns that this may promote emergence of glycopeptide-resistant enterococci in the gut flora have led to the increasing use of alternative compounds.

Resistance

Some organisms are intrinsically resistant to glycopeptides

As mentioned previously, Gram-negative bacteria are 'naturally' resistant to the glycopeptides, since these compounds are too large to efficiently move through the outer membrane to the peptidoglycan. Other organisms have an altered glycopeptide target, such as pentapeptides, terminating in D-alanine-D-lactate (e.g. *Erysiplothrix*, *Leuconostoc*, *Lactobacillus* and *Pediococcus*) or D-alanine-D-serine (e.g. *Enterococcus gallinarum*, *Enterococcus casseliflavus*).

Organisms may acquire resistance to glycopeptides

Historically, the most clinically relevant acquired glycopeptide resistance has been observed in *Enterococcus faecium* and *Enterococcus faecalis* (vancomycin-resistant enterococci; VRE), first reported by investigators in the UK in 1986. Since that time, a variety of resistance phenotypes have been described which can be differentiated by transferability (e.g. plasmid association), inducibility and extent of resistance (Table 33.4). The genes associated with the highest levels of glycopeptide resistance are *vanA*, *vanB*, and *vanD* which encode a ligase producing pentapeptides terminating in D-alanine-D-lactate.

VanA is the best understood mechanism of acquired glycopeptide resistance

VanA-type glycopeptide resistance has been the most extensively studied and is characterized by inducible high-level resistance to both vancomycin and teicoplanin. *VanA* is associated with transposable elements related to Tn1546 (ca. 11 kb in size) which may be chromosomal or plasmid (transferable) in nature.

VanB is associated with inducible high-level resistance to vancomycin but not teicoplanin (although teicoplanin resistance can be induced by prior exposure to vancomycin). *VanB* resistance may be chromosomal or plasmid linked and is associated with very large transposable elements such as Tn1549 (34 kb).

VanD is chromosomal in nature and thus non-transferable, resulting in constitutive resistance to high levels of vancomycin but low levels of teicoplanin.

Glycopeptide resistance in the staphylococci occurs by mutation or by acquisition from the enterococci

Within the coagulase-negative staphylococci (CNS), *Staphylococcus epidermidis* and *Staphylococcus haemolyticus* are especially prone to development of glycopeptide resistance by mechanisms which remain incompletely understood. Nevertheless, resistant clinical and laboratory-generated isolates have been shown to differ from their susceptible counterparts in a variety of ways including changes in glycopeptide binding capacity, membrane proteins and cell wall synthesis and composition.

Coagulase-positive staphylococci (i.e. *Staphylococcus aureus*) showing decreased susceptibility to glycopeptides (but not fully resistant) were first described by Japanese investigators in 1996. The reduced susceptibility of these vancomycin-intermediate or glycopeptide-intermediate isolates (VISA or GISA, respectively) may be either homogeneously or heterogeneously expressed. In either case, 'resistance' is not associated with *VanA*, *B*, or *D* but, instead, appears to involve other mechanisms affecting cell wall composition (e.g. leading to increased thickness, etc.).

Unfortunately, high-level glycopeptide resistance has also been observed in *Staph. aureus*. This is due to the *vanA* gene (apparently acquired from VRE) residing on a staphylococcal plasmid.

Side effects

The glycopeptides are potentially ototoxic and nephrotoxic

Vancomycin is usually given by intravenous infusion, administered slowly to avoid 'red-man' syndrome due to histamine release. Particular care must be taken to prevent toxic concentrations accumulating in patients with renal impairment. Oral vancomycin is used for treatment of antibiotic-associated pseudomembranous colitis due to *Clostridium difficile*. Teicoplanin is less toxic than

Table 33.4 Characteristics of glycopeptide resistance in enterococci

Type	Resistance	Expression	Transmissible
VanA	Vancomycin Teicoplanin	} Inducible	+
VanB	Vancomycin	Inducible	+
VanD	Vancomycin (variable) Teicoplanin (variable)	} Constitutive	−

vancomycin and can be given by intravenous bolus and by intramuscular injection.

INHIBITORS OF PROTEIN SYNTHESIS

Although protein synthesis proceeds in an essentially similar manner in prokaryotic and eukaryotic cells, it is possible to exploit the differences (e.g. 70S vs 80S ribosome) to achieve selective toxicity. The process of translation of the messenger RNA (mRNA) chain into its corresponding peptide chain is

complex, and a range of antibacterial agents act as inhibitors, although the full details of their mechanisms of action are not yet known (Fig. 33.10).

Aminoglycosides

The aminoglycosides are a family of related molecules with bactericidal activity

The aminoglycosides contain either streptidine (streptomycin) or 2-deoxystreptamine (e.g. gentamicin; Table 33.5). The original structures have been modified chemically by

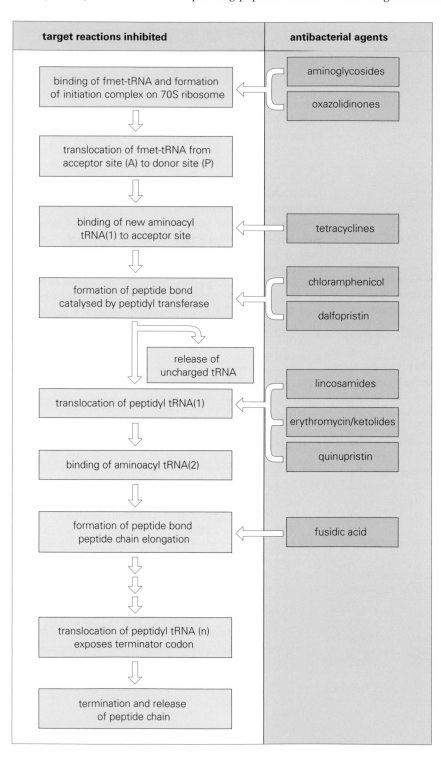

Figure 33.10 The synthetic pathway leading to the production of new protein in bacterial cells is extremely complex and still not fully elucidated. A number of different groups of antibacterial agents act by inhibiting proteins with specific reactions in this synthetic pathway. They can be grouped into those that act on the 30S subunit of the ribosome (e.g. aminoglycosides and tetracyclines) and those that act on the 50S subunit (e.g. chloramphenicol, lincosamides, erythromycin and fusidic acid). fmet-tRNA, formylmethionyl-transfer RNA.

Table 33.5 Aminoglycoside-aminocyclitol antibiotics classified according to their chemical structure

4,6-distributed 2-deoxystreptamines	
Gentamicin[a]	Complex of 3 closely related structures; first aminoglycoside with broad spectrum
Tobramycin[b]	Activity very similar to gentamicin but slightly better against *Pseudomonas aeruginosa*
Amikacin	Semi-synthetic derivative of kanamycin; active against many gentamicin- resistant Gram-negative rods
Netilmicin[b]	Activity spectrum similar to amikacin: possibly lower toxicity
4,5-disubstituted 2-deoxystreptamines	
Neomycin[b]	Too toxic for parenteral use but has topical uses in decontaminating mucosal surfaces
Streptidine-containing	
Streptomycin[b]	Oldest aminoglycoside; now use restricted to treatment of tuberculosis

They are also differentiated by the genus of microorganisms that produces them, and this is reflected in the spelling of the names.
[a]Micins from *Micromonospora* species.
[b]Mycins from *Streptomyces* species.

changing the side chains to produce molecules such as amikacin and netilmicin that are active against organisms that have developed resistance to earlier aminoglycosides.

Aminoglycosides act by binding to specific proteins in the 30S ribosomal subunit, where they interfere with the binding of formylmethionyl-transfer RNA (fmet-tRNA) to the ribosome (Fig. 33.10), thereby preventing the formation of initiation complexes from which protein synthesis proceeds. In addition, aminoglycosides cause misreading of mRNA codons and tend to break apart functional polysomes (protein synthesis by multiple ribosomes tandemly attached to a single mRNA molecule) into non-functional monosomes.

Aminoglycosides must be given intravenously or intramuscularly for systemic treatment

Aminoglycosides are not absorbed from the gut, do not penetrate well into tissues and bone, and do not cross the blood–brain barrier. Thus, they are usually administered as an intravenous infusion. Intrathecal administration of streptomycin is used in the treatment of tuberculous meningitis, and gentamicin may be administered by this route in the treatment of Gram-negative meningitis in neonates. Aminoglycosides are excreted via the kidney.

Gentamicin and the newer aminoglycosides are used to treat serious Gram-negative infections

Gentamicin, tobramycin, amikacin and netilmicin are important for the treatment of serious Gram-negative infections, including those caused by *P. aeruginosa* (Box 33.4). They are not active against streptococci or anaerobes, but are active against staphylococci. Against *P. aeruginosa*, amikacin is most active. Amikacin and netilmicin may be active against strains resistant to gentamicin and tobramycin (see below). Streptomycin is now reserved almost entirely for the treatment of mycobacterial infections. Neomycin is not used for systemic treatment, but can be used orally in gut decontamination regimens in neutropenic patients.

Box 33.4 **Indications for Aminoglycoside Therapy**

Aminoglycosides are valuable additions to the clinician's armamentarium despite their potential toxicity. They are important agents active against Gram-negative facultative bacteria and are often used in combination with beta-lactams to broaden the spectrum to include streptococci and some anaerobes, which are not susceptible to aminoglycosides alone. Resistance to aminoglycosides, particularly among enterobacteria and staphylococci, is mediated by the production of aminoglycoside-modifying enzymes, which react with groups on the aminoglycoside molecule to yield an altered aminoglycoside product. This competes with the unmodified aminoglycoside for uptake into the cell and binding to the ribosome.

Basic rule: use only in severe, life-threatening infections

- Gram-negative septicaemia (including *Pseudomonas*) usually in combination with beta-lactam

[a]Every effort should be made to establish aetiology.

- Septicaemia of unknown aetiology arising from:[a]
  - hospital-acquired infection
  - malignancy
  - immunosuppressive therapy
  - major trauma, major surgery or major burns
  - intravenous catheter
  - urinary catheter
  - extremes of age
- Bacterial endocarditis for synergy with beta-lactam
- *Staphylococcus aureus* septicaemia in combination with beta-lactam
- Pyelonephritis for difficult cases
- Post-surgical abdominal sepsis in combination with anti-anaerobe therapy.

Production of aminoglycoside-modifying enzymes is the principal cause of resistance to aminoglycosides

Although relatively uncommon, resistance to aminoglycoside antibiotics may occur by alteration of the 30S ribosomal target protein (e.g. a single amino acid change in the P12 protein prevents streptomycin binding). Resistance may also arise through alterations in cell wall permeability or in the energy-dependent transport across the cytoplasmic membrane.

Production of aminoglycoside-modifying enzymes is the most important mechanism of acquired resistance (Fig. 33.11). The genes for these enzymes are often plasmid-mediated, located on transposons, and transferable from one bacterial species to another. The enzymes alter the structure of the aminoglycoside molecule, thus inactivating the drug. The type of enzyme determines the spectrum of resistance of the organism containing it.

The aminoglycosides are potentially nephrotoxic and ototoxic

The therapeutic 'window' between the serum concentration of aminoglycoside required for successful treatment and that which is toxic is small. Blood concentrations should be monitored regularly, particularly in patients with renal impairment. Netilmicin is reported to be one of the less toxic aminoglycoside antibiotics.

Tetracyclines

Tetracyclines are bacteriostatic compounds that differ mainly in their pharmacological properties rather than in their antibacterial spectra

Tetracyclines are a family of large cyclic structures that have several sites for possible chemical substitutions (Fig. 33.12).

Tetracyclines inhibit protein synthesis by binding to the small ribosomal subunit in a manner that prevents aminoacyl transfer RNA from entering the acceptor sites on the ribosome (see Fig. 33.10). While this process may occur with both prokaryotic and eukaryotic ribosomes, the selective action of tetracyclines is due to their much greater uptake by prokaryotic cells.

Tetracyclines are usually administered orally. Doxycycline and minocycline are more completely absorbed than tetracycline, oxytetracycline and chlortetracycline and so result in higher serum concentrations and less gastrointestinal upset because there is less inhibition of normal gut flora. Tetracyclines are well distributed and penetrate host cells to inhibit intracellular bacteria. They are excreted primarily in bile and urine.

Tetracyclines are active against a wide variety of bacteria, but their use is restricted due to widespread resistance

Tetracyclines are used in the treatment of infections caused by mycoplasmas, chlamydiae and rickettsiae. Resistance in other genera is common, due partly to the widespread use of these drugs in humans and also to their use as growth

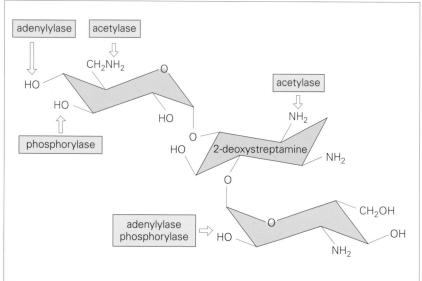

Figure 33.11 Prototype structure of aminoglycoside consisting of aminohexoses linked via glycosidic linkage to a central 2-deoxystreptamine nucleus. Hydroxyl and amino groups are sites at which these compounds can be inactivated by phosphorylation, adenylation or acetylation catalysed by enzymes produced by resistant strains.

aminoglycoside modifying enzyme	reactive group on aminoglycoside	co-factor	modified aminoglycoside product
acetylase	$-NH_2$	acetyl CoA	$-NHAc$
adenylylase (nucleotidyl transferase)	$-OH$	ATP	$-O-AMP$
phosphorylase	$-OH$	ATP	$-O-PO_2-OH$

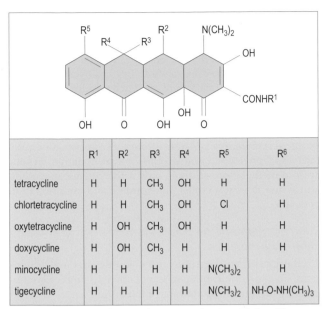

	R¹	R²	R³	R⁴	R⁵	R⁶
tetracycline	H	H	CH₃	OH	H	H
chlortetracycline	H	H	CH₃	OH	Cl	H
oxytetracycline	H	OH	CH₃	OH	H	H
doxycycline	H	OH	CH₃	H	H	H
minocycline	H	H	H	H	N(CH₃)₂	H
tigecycline	H	H	H	H	N(CH₃)₂	NH-O-NH(CH₃)₃

Figure 33.12 Tetracyclines are four-ring molecules with five different sites for substitution, thereby giving rise to a family of molecules with different substituents at different sites. Members of the family differ more in their pharmacologic properties than in their spectrum of activity.

promoters in animal feed. The resistance genes are carried on a transposon, and new cytoplasmic membrane proteins are synthesized in the presence of tetracycline. As a result, tetracycline is positively pumped out of resistant cells (efflux mechanism). Although included with the tetracyclines (Fig. 33.12), tigecycline is a new member of a related class of compounds (glycylcyclines), derived from minocycline, with activity against bacteria resistant to tetracyclines.

Tetracyclines should be avoided in pregnancy and in children under 8 years of age

Tetracyclines suppress normal gut flora, resulting in gastro-intestinal upset and diarrhea and encouraging overgrowth by resistant and undesirable bacteria (e.g. *Staph. aureus*) and fungi (e.g. *Candida*).

Interference with bone development and brown staining of teeth occurs in the fetus and in children. Systemic administration may cause liver damage. The potential for photosensitization is another caveat associated with the use of tetracyclines in all patients.

Chloramphenicol

Chloramphenicol contains a nitrobenzene nucleus and prevents peptide bond synthesis, with a bacteriostatic result

Chloramphenicol is a relatively simple molecule containing a nitrobenzene nucleus, which is responsible for some of the toxic problems associated with the drug (see below). Other derivatives have been produced, but none is in widespread clinical use.

Chloramphenicol has affinity for the large (50S) ribosomal subunit where it blocks the action of peptidyl transferase, thereby preventing peptide bond synthesis (see Fig. 33.10). The drug has some inhibitory activity on human mitochondrial

ribosomes (which are also 70S) which may account for some of the dose-dependent toxicity to bone marrow (see below).

Chloramphenicol is well absorbed when given orally, but can be given intravenously if the patient cannot take drugs by mouth. Topical preparations are also available. It is well distributed in the body and penetrates host cells. Chloramphenicol is metabolized in the liver by conjugation with glucuronic acid to yield a microbiologically inactive form that is excreted by the kidneys.

Resistance and toxicity have limited the use of chloramphenicol

Chloramphenicol has been used in the treatment of bacterial meningitis (particularly *H. influenzae*) since the drug achieves satisfactory concentrations in the CSF. Chloramphenicol is active against a wide variety of bacterial species, both Gram-positive and Gram-negative, aerobes and anaerobes, including intracellular organisms. However, its potential serious toxic effects (see below) and issues of resistance have all but eliminated the systemic use of chloramphenicol in countries where alternative agents are readily available.

The most common mechanism of chloramphenicol resistance involves the inactivation of the drug by a plasmid-mediated enzymatic mechanism which is easily transferred within Gram-negative bacterial populations. Chloramphenicol acetyl transferases produced by resistant bacteria (Fig. 33.13) are intracellular, but are capable of inactivating all chloramphenicol in the immediate environment of the cell. Acetylated chloramphenicol fails to bind to the ribosomal target.

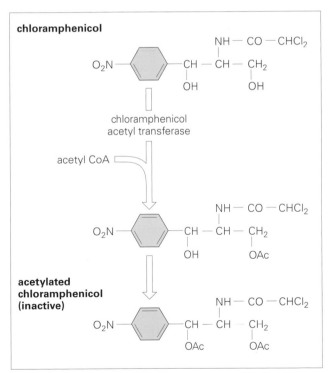

Figure 33.13 Resistance to chloramphenicol is mediated in some organisms by the production of a chloramphenicol acetyl transferase enzyme, which catalyses the addition of acetyl groups to the chloramphenicol molecule. This is a two-stage reaction producing acetylated chloramphenicol, which is inactive.

The most important toxic effects of chloramphenicol are in the bone marrow

Nitrobenzene is a bone marrow suppressant, and the structurally similar chloramphenicol molecule has similar effects. This toxicity takes two forms:

- dose-dependent bone marrow suppression, which occurs if the drug is given for long periods and is reversible when treatment is stopped
- an idiosyncratic reaction causing aplastic anaemia, which is not dose dependent and is irreversible. It can occur after treatment has stopped, but is fortunately very rare, occurring in about 1 in 30 000 patients treated.

Chloramphenicol is also toxic to neonates, particularly premature babies whose liver enzyme systems are incompletely developed. This can result in 'grey baby syndrome'. Thus, chloramphenicol serum concentrations should be monitored in neonates.

Macrolides, lincosamides and streptogramins

These three groups of antibacterial agents share overlapping binding sites on ribosomes, and resistance to macrolides confers resistance to the other two groups. The clinically important drugs are the macrolide erythromycin, the lincosamide clindamycin, and the streptogramin combination quinupristin-dalfopristin.

Macrolides

Erythromycin is a widely used macrolide preventing the release of transfer RNA after peptide bond formation

The macrolides are a family of large cyclic molecules all containing a macrocyclic lactone ring (Fig. 33.14) and are bacteriostatic in activity. Erythromycin is the best known and most widely used, but some of the newer agents, such as azithromycin and clarithromycin, with improved activity and pharmacology may substitute erythromycin for specific indications. Spiramycin is another macrolide used in the prevention of congenital toxoplasmosis.

Erythromycin binds to the 23S ribosomal RNA (rRNA) in the 50S subunit of the ribosome and blocks the translocation step in protein synthesis, thereby preventing the release of transfer RNA after peptide bond formation (see Fig. 33.10).

Erythromycin is usually administered by the oral route, but can also be given intravenously. It is well distributed in the body and penetrates mammalian cells to reach intracellular organisms. The drug is concentrated in the liver and excreted in the bile. A small proportion of the dose is recoverable in the urine.

Erythromycin is an alternative to penicillin for streptococcal infections, but resistant strains of streptococci are common

Erythromycin is active against Gram-positive cocci and is an important alternative treatment of infections caused by streptococci in patients allergic to penicillin. It is active against *Legionella pneumophila* and *Campylobacter jejuni*. It is also active against *mycoplasmas*, *chlamydiae* and *rickettsiae* and is therefore an important drug in the treatment of atypical pneumonia and chlamydial infections of the urinogenital tract.

Resistance is primarily due to either plasmid-encoded *mef* or *erm* genes, for efflux or alteration in the 23S rRNA target by methylation of two adenine nucleotides in the RNA, respectively. The methylase enzyme may be either inducible or constitutively expressed. Erythromycin is a better inducer of resistance than the lincosamides, but strains resistant to erythromycin will also be resistant to lincomycin and clindamycin, so-called 'MLS (macrolide-lincosamide-streptogramin) resistance'. Induction also varies between bacterial species, and resistant strains of Gram-positive cocci such as staphylococci and streptococci are common. In contrast to methylation, efflux is only active against macrolide drugs and does not confer lincosamide and streptogramin resistance.

Newer generation macrolides have fewer side effects than erythromycins

Erythromycin causes nausea and vomiting after oral administration in a significant number of patients. Jaundice is associated with some formulations of the drug.

Ketolides are new semi-synthetic derivatives of erythromycin with improved activity against respiratory pathogens

Modification of the macrolide ring structure (Fig. 33.14) provides ketolides with increased activity against a variety of Gram-positive (and some Gram-negative) bacteria, especially those associated with respiratory infections. Ketolides are administered orally and act in a manner similar to erythromycin. However, their higher affinity for the 50S ribosomal subunit allows them to bind to ribosomes which are resistant to erythromycin. While active against methicillin-susceptible *Staph. aureus* that are either susceptible or inducibly resistant to erythromycin, ketolide activity is poor against erythromycin-resistant MRSA. In addition, telithromycin has had issues related to toxicity.

Lincosamides

Clindamycin inhibits peptide bond formation

Clindamycin is a chlorinated more active derivative of lincomycin and represents the most important drug in this class.

Lincosamides bind to the 50S ribosomal subunit and inhibit protein synthesis in a manner similar to erythromycin (see Fig. 33.10), hence the MLS resistance combination noted above. The selectively toxic action results from a failure to bind to the equivalent mammalian ribosomal subunit.

Clindamycin is usually given orally, but can be administered intramuscularly or intravenously. It penetrates well into bone, but not into CSF, even when the meninges are inflamed. Clindamycin is actively transported into polymorphonuclear leukocytes and macrophages. It is metabolized in the liver to several products with variable antibacterial activity, and clindamycin activity persists in faeces for up to 5 days after a dose.

Clindamycin has a spectrum of activity similar to that of erythromycin

Clindamycin is much more active than erythromycin against anaerobes, both Gram-positive (e.g. *Clostridium* spp.) and Gram-negative (e.g. *Bacteroides*). However, *Cl. difficile* is resistant and may be selected in the gut, causing pseudomembranous

Figure 33.14 (A) The macrolides are antibacterial agents composed of large structures, which may be 14-, 15- or 16-membered rings. Erythromycin is the oldest and most widely used of these, but new agents with improved activity and fewer side effects are being developed. (B) Major differences in ketolide chemical structure compared to erythromycin (i.e. positions of 3-keto and carbamate on the 'backbone' ring structure).

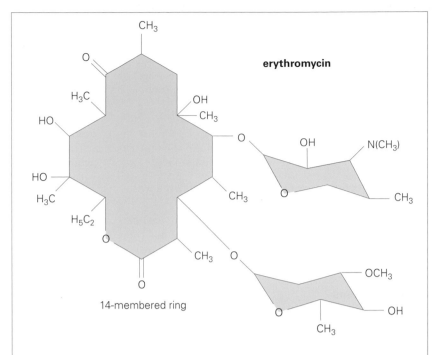

erythromycin

14-membered ring

new macrolide	in vitro activity compared with erthyromycin	human pharmacokinetics
roxithromycin (14-membered ring)	comparable	high peak serum concentrations $T^{1}/_{2}$ = 12 h
azithromycin (15-membered ring)	improved against Gram-negative bacteria	high tissue concentrations, once-daily administration
clarithromycin (14-membered ring)	improved against Gram-positive bacteria and *Legionella* spp.	improved peak serum concentration compared with erythromycin

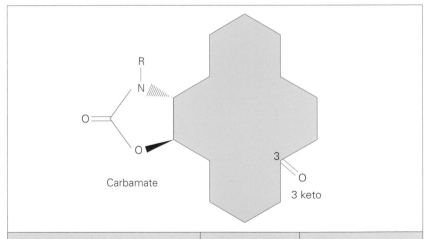

Carbamate

3 keto

new ketolide	in vitro activity compared with erthyromycin	human pharmacokinetics
telithromycin (14-membered ring)	improved activity against respiratory pathogens including *Streptococcus pneumoniae*	high and sustained concentrations in bronchopulmonary tissues and fluids with once daily oral dose

colitis (see below). The activity of clindamycin against *Staph. aureus* and its penetration into bone make it a valuable drug in the treatment of osteomyelitis. Clindamycin is not active against aerobic Gram-negative bacteria because of poor penetration of the outer membrane.

As clindamycin is a less potent inducer of 23S rRNA methylase (see MLS resistance above), erythromycin-resistant strains may appear susceptible to clindamycin in vitro. However, resistance will be manifest in vivo.

Pseudomembranous colitis caused by *Cl. difficile* was first noted following clindamycin treatment

Pseudomembranous colitis caused by *Cl. difficile* follows treatment with many antibiotics. The pathogenesis of this complication is described in Chapter 22, and it should be treated with metronidazole or oral vancomycin.

Streptogramins

The streptogramin formulation currently available is a mixture of streptogramin B and A compounds – quinupristin and dalfopristin, respectively (Fig. 33.15) – that are bacteriostatic individually but synergistically bactericidal in combination. Both compounds bind to 23S RNA in the large (50S) ribosomal subunit (dalfopristin facilitates binding of quinupristin). Dalfopristin inhibits protein synthesis at an earlier stage than quinupristin (see Fig. 33.10), and they together interfere with elongation and extension of peptide chains.

Resistance is relatively uncommon but may develop by altering the quinupristin binding site (MLS resistance described above), enzymatic inactivation, or efflux.

The quinupristin–dalfopristin combination is active against Gram-positive cocci, including multidrug-resistant isolates. Activity is good against *Enterococcus faecium* but not *E. faecalis* (most probably due to an intrinsic efflux mechanism). However, there has been concern that commercial use of streptogramin compounds (e.g. virginiamycin) to prevent disease and promote growth in poultry could contribute to quinupristin–dalfopristin resistance among Gram-positive pathogens in humans.

Quinupristin–dalfopristin is administered intravenously and primarily metabolized in the liver.

Oxazolidinones

Oxazolidinones are a new class of synthetic bacteriostatic antimicrobial agents (Fig. 33.16). Linezolid, the oxazolidinone currently available, is active against a wide range of Gram-positive bacteria, including multiresistant strains. Linezolid inhibits initiation of protein synthesis (see Fig. 33.10) by targeting 23S ribosomal RNA in the 50S subunit in a manner which prevents formation of a functional 70S complex.

Due to the drug's unique mechanism of action, resistance mutations (i.e. altered target) are rare and seen primarily in *Enterococcus faecium*.

Linezolid is administered orally or intravenously and is metabolized in the liver.

Fusidic acid

Fusidic acid is a steroid-like compound that inhibits protein synthesis

Fusidic acid is a bacteriostatic agent that inhibits protein synthesis by forming a stable complex with elongation factor EF-G (the bacterial equivalent of the human EF-2), guanosine diphosphate and the ribosome.

Fusidic acid can be administered orally or intravenously. It is well absorbed and penetrates well into tissues and bone, but not into the CSF. Topical preparations

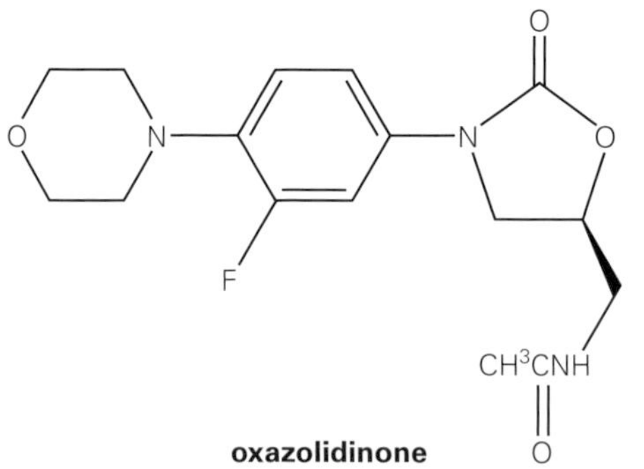

quinupristin
(streptogramin B)

dalfopristin
(streptogramin A)

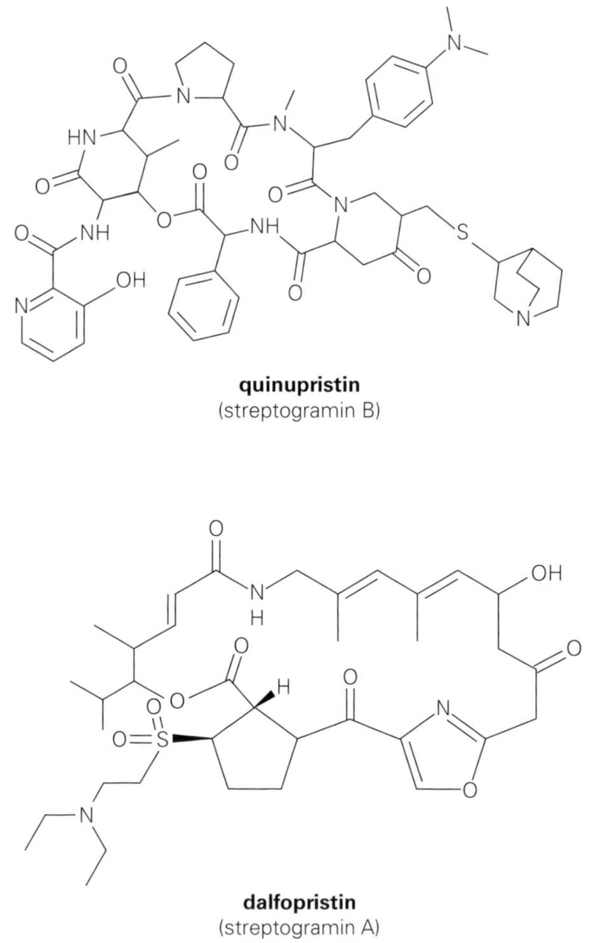

Figure 33.15 Chemical structure of the streptogramins.

oxazolidinone

Figure 33.16 Chemical structure of oxazolidinones.

are also available, but their use should not be encouraged, because of the rapid emergence of resistance (see below). Fusidic acid is metabolized in the liver and excreted in the bile.

Fusidic acid is a treatment for staphylococcal infections, but should be used with other antistaphylococcal drugs to prevent emergence of resistance

Fusidic acid is active against Gram-positive cocci, and its most important use is in the treatment of staphylococcal infections resistant to beta-lactams or in patients who are allergic to alternative staphylococcal agents. Fusidic acid should be given in combination with another antistaphylococcal agent to prevent the emergence of resistant mutants with altered EF-G, which emerge rapidly in staphylococcal populations exposed to the drug.

Fusidic acid has few side effects

Occasionally, fusidic acid causes jaundice and gastrointestinal upset.

INHIBITORS OF NUCLEIC ACID SYNTHESIS

Antibacterial agents that act as inhibitors of nucleic acid synthesis do so in one of three main ways, as listed in Box 33.5.

Box 33.5 **Inhibition of Nucleic Acid Takes Place at Different Stages in its Synthesis and Function, and Different Groups of Antimicrobial Agents are Involved**

Inhibitors of DNA replication

- Quinolones

Inhibitors of RNA polymerase

- Rifampicin

Antimetabolites inhibiting precursor synthesis

- Sulphonamides, trimethoprim.

Quinolones

Quinolones are synthetic agents that interfere with replication of the bacterial chromosome

Quinolones represent a large family of bactericidal synthetic agents which, in a manner similar to the cephalosporins, can be generally grouped in categories or 'generations' based on their spectrum of activity (Table 33.6). Nalidixic acid is the first-generation prototype, but the addition of fluorine at position 6 of the main quinolone ring (i.e. fluoroquinolones) (Fig. 33.17) has improved antibacterial activity, leading to the synthesis of many additional, more commonly used, compounds.

The antibacterial activity of quinolones is due to their ability to inhibit the activity of bacterial DNA gyrase and topoisomerases. During replication of the bacterial chromosome, DNA gyrase produces and removes supercoils in DNA ahead of the replication fork to maintain the proper 'tension' required for efficient DNA duplication. Topoisomerase IV similarly acts to remove supercoils and to separate newly formed DNA 'daughter' strands after replication (Fig. 33.18). These enzymes thus act in concert to insure that the DNA molecule has the proper conformation for efficient replication and packaging within the cell. Quinolones are able to interfere with these essential enzymes in bacteria while not affecting their counterparts in mammalian cells.

Resistance to quinolones is usually chromosomally mediated

Chromosomally mediated resistance is exhibited in two forms:

- mutations, which change the target enzymes in a manner that affects quinolone binding
- changes in cell wall permeability, resulting in decreased uptake, or by efflux. These mechanisms may also lead to cross-resistance to other unrelated agents affected by the same process.

Plasmid-encoded quinolone resistance involves production of a protein (termed qnr) that protects the target DNA from quinolone binding. This protein has been shown to act in concert with a plasmid encoded enzyme capable of reducing the activity of some fluoroquinolones, resulting in increased levels of quinolone resistance.

Table 33.6 Characteristics of representative quinolones

Drug	Category[a]	General spectrum of activity
Nalidixic acid	First generation	Gram-negative bacteria (excluding *Pseudomonas*)
Ciprofloxacin Enoxacin Lomefloxacin Norfloxacin Ofloxacin	Second generation	First-generation coverage but including *Pseudomonas* spp., and some Gram-positives (*Staphylococcus aureus* but not *Streptococcus pneumoniae*)
Levofloxacin Gatifloxacin Moxifloxacin Gemifloxacin	Third generation	Second-generation coverage but improved Gram-positive coverage (penicillin-sensitive and resistant *Strep. pneumoniae*) and some activity against anaerobes
Trovafloxacin	Fourth generation[b]	Third-generation coverage, expanded activity against anaerobes

The most commonly used agents are listed, together with their main indications.
[a]All but first-generation compounds are fluoroquinolones.
[b]Associated with cases of acute liver failure; use reserved for life-threatening situations.

Figure 33.17 The quinolones form a large group of synthetic antibacterial agents.

nalidixic acid

ciprofloxacin

moxifloxacin

trovafloxacin

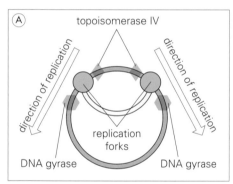

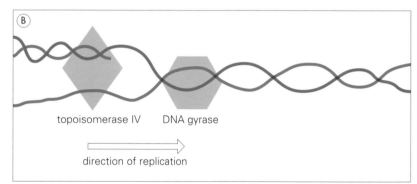

Figure 33.18 (A) An overview and (B) an enlarged view of the role played by bacterial gyrase and topoisomerase enzymes in replication of the bacterial chromosome.

Because of their safety and tolerability, quinolones are commonly used as alternatives to beta-lactam antibiotics for treating a variety of infections

Quinolones are primarily administered orally since they are readily absorbed from the gastrointestinal tract, achieving significant serum concentrations and good distribution throughout the body compartments. Excretion is mostly in the urine; however, drugs such as gatifloxacin and moxifloxacin are excreted to a significant amount in faeces.

Nalidixic acid does not achieve antibacterial systemic concentrations. It is only active against enterobacteria, and, although occasionally employed in treatment of urinary tract infections (see Ch. 20), its use has largely been replaced by the newer fluorinated compounds.

The newer quinolones have improved activity against Gram-negative rods, including *P. aeruginosa*. In addition to the treatment of urinary tract infections, the newer quinolones are useful for systemic Gram-negative infections and in the treatment of chlamydial and rickettsial infections. They are also useful in infections caused by other intracellular organisms, such as *L. pneumophila* and *S. typhi*, and in combination with other agents for 'atypical' mycobacteria. They have activity against staphylococci, but overall have only limited use against streptococci and enterococci (see Table 33.6).

Fluoroquinolones are not recommended for children or pregnant or lactating women because of possible toxic effects on cartilage development

Gastrointestinal disturbances are the most common side effect of quinolones. Neurotoxicity and photosensitivity reactions are less common. However, a notable exception is the potential for liver toxicity associated with trovafloxacin (see Table 33.6) which has prompted severe restrictions on its use. Gemifloxacin is associated with development of a rash which in some cases may be serious enough to require steroid treatment. This is especially a problem of women of child-bearing years or post-menopausal on hormone therapy. Gatifloxacin use has been impacted by issues of glucose homeostasis, sometimes severe enough to produce a coma. All fluoroquinolones have the potential to cause tendon ruptures in active patients who may tend to push their workout regimens. This risk is increased when quinolones and corticosteroids are simultaneously administered.

Rifamycins

Rifampicin is clinically the most important rifamycin and blocks the synthesis of mRNA

Rifampicin is the most important member of the rifamycin family in clinical use. It is a large molecule with a complex structure. Other family members such as rifabutin and rifapentine are also available. All are bactericidal in activity.

Rifampicin binds to DNA-dependent RNA polymerase and blocks the synthesis of mRNA. Selective toxicity is based on the far greater affinity for bacterial polymerases than for the equivalent human enzymes.

Rifampicin is administered orally, is well absorbed and is very well distributed in the body. It crosses the blood–brain barrier and reaches high concentrations in saliva. It also appears to have an affinity for plastics, which can be valuable in the treatment of infections involving prostheses.

Rifampicin is metabolized in the liver and excreted in bile. The compound is red, and urine, sweat and saliva of treated patients turns orange. This is harmless, although disturbing for the patient, but is good evidence of patient compliance.

The newer rifamycins, rifabutin and rifapentine are excreted more slowly than rifampicin, thereby allowing less frequent administration – a feature particularly attractive in the treatment of tuberculosis.

The primary use for rifampicin is in the treatment of mycobacterial infections, but resistance is a concern

While used primarily against mycobacteria, rifampicin may also be used for the prophylaxis of close contacts of meningococcal and *Haemophilus meningitis*. However, highly resistant meningococcal strains may emerge; thus short courses only (maximum 48 h) should be given (see Ch. 24).

While staphylococci rapidly develop resistance to rifampicin, the drug can be efficacious if used in combination with another agent, particularly in the treatment of prosthetic valve endocarditis (see Ch. 29).

Resistance is provided by chromosomal mutations that alter the RNA polymerase target, which then has lowered affinity for rifampicin and escapes inhibition. The prevalence of rifampicin-resistant *M. tuberculosis* is increasing, threatening the future of its use in antituberculosis therapy.

Rashes and jaundice are side effects of rifampicin treatment

Intermittent rifampicin can lead to hypersensitivity reactions.

ANTIMETABOLITES AFFECTING NUCLEIC ACID SYNTHESIS

Several commonly used antimicrobial agents inhibit bacterial metabolic pathways including those which produce precursors for nucleic acid synthesis.

Sulphonamides

Sulphonamides are structural analogues of and act in competition with *para*-aminobenzoic acid

This group of molecules is produced entirely by chemical synthesis (i.e. they are not natural products). In 1935, the parent compound sulphanilamide became the first clinically effective antibacterial agent. The *p*-amino group is essential for activity, but modifications to the sulphonic acid side chain have produced many related agents (Fig. 33.19).

Sulphonamides are bacteriostatic compounds that act in competition with *para*-aminobenzoic acid, PABA, for the active site of dihydropteroate synthetase, an enzyme that catalyses an essential reaction in the synthetic pathway of tetrahydrofolic acid (THFA), which is required for the synthesis of purines and pyrimidines and therefore for nucleic acid synthesis (Fig. 33.20). Selective toxicity depends on the

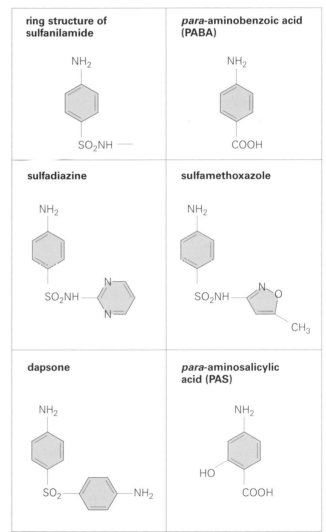

Figure 33.19 The ring structure of the sulphonamides is very similar to the structure of the normal substrate (PABA) of the dihydropteroate synthetase enzyme, which the sulphonamides inhibit. There are many different sulphonamides available and they differ in their pharmacologic properties more than in their spectrum of activity. Relatively few are now in common clinical use. Dapsone is important in the treatment of *Mycobacterium leprae*, and para-aminosalicylic acid is used for the treatment of *M. tuberculosis*.

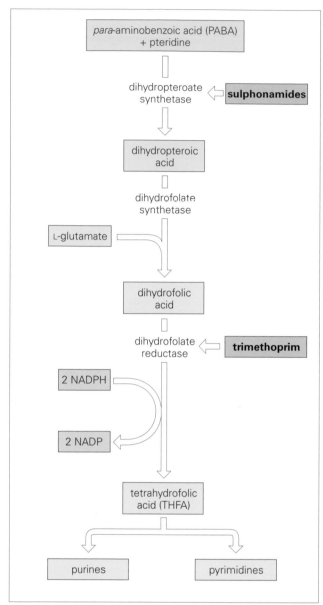

Figure 33.20 Sulphonamides and trimethoprim inhibit in series the steps in the synthesis of tetrahydrofolic acid by interacting with key enzymes in the pathway.

fact that many bacteria synthesize THFA, whereas human cells lack this capacity and depend on an exogenous supply of folic acid. Bacteria that can use preformed folic acid are similarly unaffected by sulphonamides.

Sulphonamides are usually administered orally, often in combination with trimethoprim as co-trimoxazole (see below). Different molecules within the family differ in their solubility and penetrability. Metabolism occurs in the liver, and free and metabolized drug are excreted by the kidneys.

Sulphonamides are useful in the treatment of urinary tract infection, but resistance is widespread

The sulphonamides have a spectrum of activity primarily against Gram-negative organisms (except *Pseudomonas*). They are therefore useful in the treatment of urinary tract infections (see Ch. 20). However, susceptibility cannot be assumed, as resistance is widespread with plasmid-mediated

genes coding for an altered dihydropteroate synthetase. This is essentially unchanged in its affinity for PABA, but has a greatly decreased affinity for the sulphonamide. A resistant cell therefore possesses two distinct enzymes: a sensitive chromosome-encoded enzyme and a resistant plasmid-encoded enzyme.

Rarely, sulphonamides cause Stevens–Johnson syndrome

Sulphonamides are relatively free of toxic side effects, but rashes and bone marrow suppression can occur.

Trimethoprim (and co-trimoxazole)

Trimethoprim is a structural analogue of the aminohydroxypyrimidine moiety of folic acid and prevents the synthesis of THFA

Trimethoprim is one of a group of pyrimidine-like molecules analogous in structure to the aminohydroxypyrimidine moiety of the folic acid molecule (Fig. 33.21). Other agents with a similar structure and mechanism of action include the antimalarial pyrimethamine and the anticancer drug methotrexate.

Trimethoprim, like sulphonamides, prevents THFA synthesis, but at a later stage by inhibiting dihydrofolate reductase (Fig. 33.20). This enzyme is present in mammalian cells as well as bacterial and protozoan cells, and selective toxicity depends upon the far greater affinity of trimethoprim for the bacterial enzyme.

Trimethoprim is often given in combination with sulphamethoxazole as co-trimoxazole. The advantages of this combination over either drug alone are:

- Mutant bacteria resistant to one agent are unlikely to be resistant to the other (i.e. double mutation).
- The two agents act synergistically against some bacteria (i.e. the combined action of the two bacteriostatic agents has a bactericidal effect that is greater than the action of either agent alone).

Trimethoprim can be given orally (either alone or as co-trimoxazole) or by intravenous infusion (alone or accompanied by sulphonamide). Trimethoprim is excreted in urine,

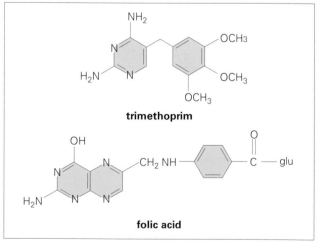

Figure 33.21 Trimethoprim resembles the aminohydroxypyrimidine moiety of folic acid and in this way antagonizes the enzyme dihydrofolate reductase.

and in patients with severe renal failure it is excreted more rapidly than sulphonamide so that the synergistic ratio of the combination may be lost.

Trimethoprim is often given with sulphamethoxazole as co-trimoxazole for urinary tract infections

Trimethoprim alone is active against Gram-negative rods with the exception of *Pseudomonas* spp. and its main use is in the treatment (and long-term prophylaxis) of urinary tract infection (see Ch. 20); however, the development of resistance is a concern.

Co-trimoxazole is active against a wide range of urinary tract pathogens and against *S. typhi*. This combination is also valuable for the treatment of pneumonia caused by the fungus *Pneumocystis jirovecii* (formerly *P. carinii*), although pentamidine, another pyrimidine derivative, is probably the preferred alternative (see Ch. 30). Co-trimoxazole is also useful for the treatment of nocardiosis (see Ch. 30) and chancroid (see Ch. 21).

Resistance to trimethoprim is provided by plasmid-encoded dihydrofolate reductases

Plasmid-encoded dihydrofolate reductases with altered affinity for trimethoprim allow the synthesis of THFA to proceed unhindered by the presence of trimethoprim. The 'replacement enzymes' are approximately 20 000-fold less susceptible to trimethoprim while retaining their affinity for the normal substrate. Bacteria that are resistant to sulphonamide and trimethoprim are also resistant to co-trimoxazole.

People with AIDS seem to be more prone to the side effects of trimethoprim and co-trimoxazole

Trimethoprim alone and in combination with sulphamethoxazole can cause neutropenia. Nausea and vomiting may occur.

OTHER AGENTS THAT AFFECT DNA

Nitroimidazoles

Metronidazole is a nitroimidazole with antiparasitic and antibacterial properties

After entry into the microbial cell, the molecule is activated by reduction, and the reduced intermediate products are responsible for antimicrobial activity, probably through interaction with, and breakage of, the cell's DNA. The reactive intermediates are short-lived and decompose to non-toxic inactive end-products. Metronidazole is active only against anaerobic organisms because only these can produce the low redox potential necessary to reduce the parent drug.

Metronidazole has also been used as a hypoxic cell sensitizer in radiotherapy.

Metronidazole is usually given orally or rectally. It is well absorbed and well distributed in tissues and CSF. The drug is metabolized and most of the parent compound and metabolites are excreted in the urine.

Metronidazole was originally introduced for the treatment of the flagellate parasite *Trichomonas vaginalis*

Metronidazole is also effective against other protozoan parasites such as *Giardia intestinalis* and *Entamoeba histolytica*. It is an important agent for the treatment of infections caused by anaerobic bacteria.

Metronidazole resistance is of increasing concern in *T. vaginalis*, *G. intestinalis*, and several anaerobic and microaerophilic bacteria, and commonly involves either an alteration in uptake or a decrease in cellular reductase activity, thereby slowing the activation of the intracellular drug. *Helicobacter pylori*, a microaerophilic bacterium causing ulcers and gastritis, has been frequently treated with metronidazole. However, resistance can rapidly develop.

Rarely, metronidazole causes central nervous system side effects

The most serious side effects of metronidazole involve the central nervous system and include peripheral neuropathy. However, these are relatively uncommon and usually seen only in patients on large doses or prolonged treatment.

INHIBITORS OF CYTOPLASMIC MEMBRANE FUNCTION

The cytoplasmic membranes that encompass all kinds of living cells perform a variety of vital functions. The structure of these membranes in bacterial cells differs from that in mammalian cells and allows the application of some selectively toxic molecules, but these are few in number compared with those acting at other target sites.

Lipopeptides

Lipopeptides are a new class of membrane-active antibiotics

Daptomycin is a lipopeptide antibiotic with bactericidal activity against a wide variety of Gram-positive bacteria including vancomycin-resistant *E. faecalis* and *E. faecium* and methicillin-resistant *Staph. aureus* and *Staph. epidermidis* (Fig. 33.22). The compound acts in a calcium-dependent matter to insert and depolarize the bacterial cytoplasmic membrane. This action leads to a number of consequences including the inability to synthesize ATP and interference with uptake of nutrients. At present, resistance to daptomycin has been rare.

Polymyxins

Polymyxins act on the membranes of Gram-negative bacteria

In addition to the polymyxins, the polyene antifungal agents (amphotericin B, nystatin) also act by inhibiting membrane function (see below). Polymyxins are bactericidal cyclic polypeptides that disrupt the structure of cell membranes.

The free amino groups of polymyxins act as cationic detergents, disrupting the phospholipid structure of the cell membrane. Polymyxin B is the most common member of the family still in clinical use.

In the past, polymyxins have been used systemically, but due to poor distribution in tissues, neurotoxicity and nephrotoxicity, they have been superseded by less toxic agents.

Polymyxins are primarily used topically but have also been used in the past for gut decontamination, wound irrigation and as a bladder washout

Polymyxins are active against most Gram-negative organisms except *Proteus* spp. They are primarily used topically in ointments. After oral administration, polymyxins are not absorbed

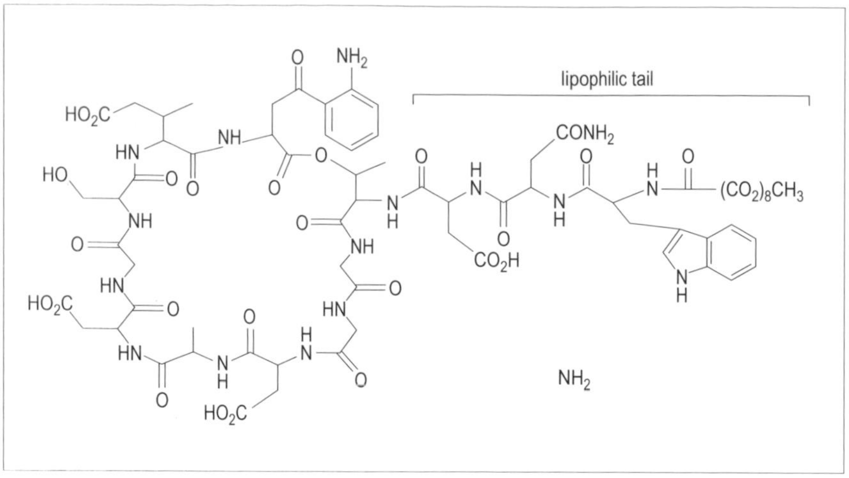

Figure 33.22 Chemical structure of the cyclic lipopeptide, daptomycin, consisting of a 13-member amino acid cyclic lipopeptide with a lipophilic tail which attacks the bacterial cell membrane, causing depolarization and a potassium iron efflux.

from the gut, and polymyxin E (colistin) has been used in some gut decontamination regimens for neutropenic patients, although with caution due to concerns regarding renal toxicity. Concerns regarding the lack of effective antibiotics for treating multidrug resistant Gram-negative bacteria have led to renewed interest in polymixin/colistin combination therapy.

Resistance is due to chromosomally mediated alterations in membrane structure or antibiotic uptake.

URINARY TRACT ANTISEPTICS

Nitrofurantoin and methenamine inhibit urinary pathogens

Nitrofurantoin and methenamine are both synthetic compounds that, when taken orally, are absorbed and excreted in the urine in concentrations high enough to inhibit urinary pathogens. Nitrofurantoin has activity only in acid urine. Methenamine is hydrolysed at acid pH to produce ammonia and formaldehyde; it is the formaldehyde that has the antibacterial activity. Nitrofurantoin is used to treat uncomplicated urinary tract infection, and both agents are used to prevent recurrent urinary tract infections. While resistance rarely develops in susceptible bacterial populations, resistance to nitrofurantoin prior to treatment is a concern.

ANTITUBERCULOSIS AGENTS

M. tuberculosis and other mycobacterial infections need prolonged treatment

The treatment of infections caused by *M. tuberculosis* and other mycobacteria presents an enormous challenge to medicine and the pharmaceutical industry because these organisms:

- have a waxy outer layer that makes them naturally very impermeable and difficult to penetrate with antibiotics
- have an intracellular location, often in cells surrounded by a mass of caseous material, that also makes it difficult for antibiotics to get to them
- grow and multiply extremely slowly, and effective inhibition (and therefore cure) takes weeks or months to achieve. Long-term therapy is therefore a challenge for drug delivery, and orally administrable drugs are consequently highly desirable. It also follows that the emergence of resistance among the mycobacteria and

toxicity in the patient are more likely than with the 'short sharp shock' treatment more often administered for bacterial infections
- are common and increasing in the wake of the AIDS epidemic in resource-poor countries, where the cost of drug treatment can be prohibitive.

The drugs for first-line therapy of tuberculosis are isoniazid, ethambutol, rifampicin, pyrazinamide and streptomycin

Treatment regimens vary between countries but, with susceptible strains, a 9-month course of isoniazid and rifampicin is an approach that has been used with good success. Pending results of susceptibility tests, a three- or four-drug combination is the common initial treatment, and this is continued for resistant isolates. The structure and mechanism of action of rifampicin and streptomycin have been described in preceding parts of this chapter.

Isoniazid

Isoniazid inhibits mycobacteria and is given with pyridoxine to prevent neurologic side effects

Isoniazid is isonicotinic acid hydrazide, a compound that inhibits mycobacteria, but does not affect other species of bacteria or humans to any great extent. Its bactericidal activity results from inhibition of mycolic acid synthesis, which also accounts for its specificity. It is well absorbed after oral administration, and a single daily dose is usually prescribed except in more difficult cases such as meningitis or miliary tuberculosis. The main toxic effects in humans are neurologic complications, which can be prevented by the concurrent administration of pyridoxine, and hepatitis.

Ethambutol

Ethambutol inhibits mycobacteria, but can cause optic neuritis

Ethambutol is a synthetic molecule that inhibits, but does not kill, mycobacteria. It acts by inhibiting the polymerization of arabinoglycan, a critical constituent of the mycobacteria cell wall. It is well absorbed after oral administration and well distributed in the body, including the CSF. Resistance appears fairly rapidly if the drug is used alone. Thus, it is combined with other drugs in antituberculosis therapy. An important toxic side effect is optic neuritis, and visual acuity should be monitored during therapy.

Pyrazinamide

Pyrazinamide is a synthetic analogue of nicotinamide which appears to target mycolic acid synthesis. After oral administration, the drug is readily absorbed from the gastrointestinal tract and well distributed in body tissues and fluids. It is primarily metabolized in the liver and excreted by the kidney. As with ethambutol, resistance during monotherapy requires that the drug be used in combination with other first-line agents. The most important toxic side effect of pyrazinamide is hepatotoxicity.

Mycobacterial resistance

Drug resistance and immunocompromised patients complicate tuberculosis therapy

Despite the use of antibiotics in combination, the incidence of resistance among mycobacteria is a persistent and increasing problem. Infections with mycobacteria other than *M. tuberculosis* are on the increase as opportunist infections in people with AIDS, and these organisms tend to be innately more resistant than *M. tuberculosis*.

Treatment of leprosy

The development of resistance during dapsone monotherapy for leprosy has led to its use in combination with rifampicin

Infection caused by *M. leprae* is characterized by persistence of the organism in the tissues for years and necessitates very prolonged treatment to prevent relapse. For many years dapsone, related to the sulphonamides (see Fig. 33.19), has been used. This drug has the advantages that it is given orally and it is cheap and effective. However, widespread monotherapy has resulted in the emergence of resistance, and a combination of dapsone, rifampicin and clofazimine, a phenazine compound is now commonly used as multidrug therapy.

ANTIBACTERIAL AGENTS IN PRACTICE

It is clear from the preceding sections of this chapter that although there are certain 'rules of thumb' about the resistance of bacteria to an antibiotic, it is often impossible to do more than guess in the absence of laboratory tests. Susceptibility tests performed in the laboratory examine the interaction between antibiotics and bacteria in an isolated and rather artificial fashion. At best, the results are a helpful guide to the likely outcome of therapy; at worst, they are misleading. Patient factors such as age, underlying disease, site and type of infection, renal and liver impairment, and drug pharmacodynamics must be taken into account in the antibiotic management of an infection.

Susceptibility tests

Laboratory tests for antibiotic susceptibility fall into two main categories:

- diffusion tests
- dilution tests.

Diffusion tests involve seeding the organism on an agar plate and applying filter paper disks containing antibiotics

The isolate to be tested is seeded over the entire surface of an agar plate, and filter paper disks containing the antibiotics are applied. After overnight incubation the plate is observed for zones of inhibition around each antibiotic disk (Fig. 33.23). The amount of antibiotic in the disk is related to, among other things, the achievable serum concentration and therefore differs for different antibiotics. In addition, antibiotics differ in their ability to diffuse in agar, so the size of the inhibition zone (and not simply its presence) is an indicator of susceptibility of the isolate. The zone sizes are compared with those for reference organisms (either tested in parallel or established previously and published in reference tables) and the result recorded as 'S' (susceptible), 'I' (intermediate) or 'R' (resistant). An 'I' result indicates that the isolate is less susceptible than the norm, but may respond to higher doses of antibiotic or in sites where the antibiotic is concentrated (e.g. in urine in the bladder for antibiotics excreted by the kidneys).

A dilution test provides a quantitative estimate of susceptibility to an antibiotic

A more quantitative estimate of the susceptibility of an organism to an antibiotic can be achieved by performing a MIC (minimum inhibitory concentration) test (i.e. a test to find the lowest concentration that will inhibit visible growth of the bacterial isolate in vitro). Serial dilutions of the test antibiotic are prepared in broth or agar medium and inoculated with a suspension of the test organism. After overnight incubation, the MIC is recorded as the highest dilution in which there is no macroscopic growth (Fig. 33.24). These tests can be performed in a microtitre plate format and form the basis of some automated susceptibility test systems. An alternative approach is the E test in which a filter paper strip impregnated with a gradient of antibiotic is laid on an agar plate seeded with the test isolate. The concentration on the strip at which growth is inhibited indicates the MIC.

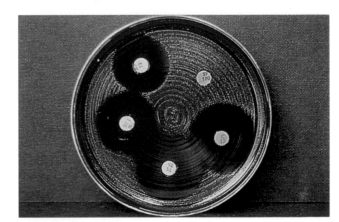

Figure 33.23 The antibiotic susceptibility of an organism can be tested by the application of filter paper impregnated with antibiotic onto a lawn of the organisms seeded on an agar plate. After overnight incubation the organism grows and the antibiotics diffuse to produce a zone of inhibition that indicates the degree of susceptibility: disk susceptibility test indicating sulphonamide resistance. SF100 is the sulphonamide disk. (Courtesy of D.K. Banerjee.)

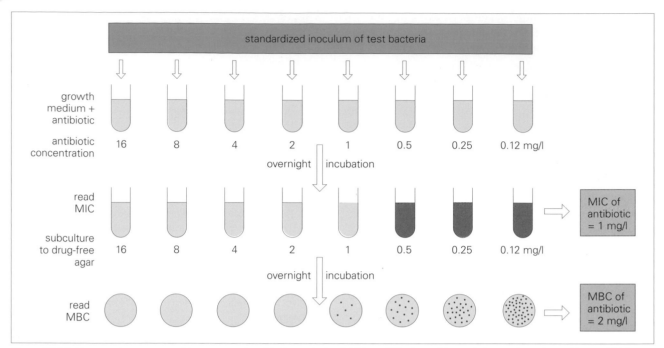

Figure 33.24 More precise measures of the amount of antibiotic required to inhibit and kill a bacterial population can be estimated by establishing the minimum inhibitory concentration (MIC) and minimum bactericidal concentration (MBC) of the antibiotic. Using the standard method as outlined in this illustration, the MIC result is available after 24 h and the MBC result after 48 h. A number of variables such as the inoculum size, the growth medium and the interpretation of the results affect the outcome of MIC tests.

MIC tests are clearly more costly than diffusion tests in terms of time and materials and are not required or used for every isolate from every patient, but they yield useful information for the management of difficult infections or for patients who are failing to respond to apparently appropriate therapy.

An advantage of an MIC test is that it can be extended to determine the MBC (minimum bacterial concentration), which is the lowest concentration of an antibiotic required to kill the organism. In order to discover whether the agent has actually killed the bacteria rather than simply inhibited their growth, the test dilutions are subcultured onto a fresh drug-free medium and incubated for a further 18–24 h (Fig. 33.24). The antibacterial agent is considered to be bactericidal if the MBC is equal to or not greater than fourfold higher than the MIC.

Killing curves provide a dynamic estimate of bacterial susceptibility

One of the disadvantages of MIC and MBC tests is that the result is read at only one point in time. A more dynamic estimate of bacterial susceptibility can be gained by measuring the decrease in viability of the population with time (Fig. 33.25). As with MIC tests, it is not feasible to perform killing curves manually for every test isolate, but they can provide useful information for difficult treatment problems. A number of the automated susceptibility test systems use a measure of bacterial viability (e.g. turbidity, electrical impedance) in the presence of an antibacterial as their indicator system. These machines can produce results more rapidly (e.g. within a few hours) than conventional susceptibility tests. However, automated systems do not work well with fastidious organisms (e.g. *S. pneumoniae*, *N. meningitidis*, etc.) or with resistance that is characteristically difficult to detect (e.g. borderline oxacillin MICs in *Staphylococcus aureus*, ESBLs in Gram-negative isolates, etc.).

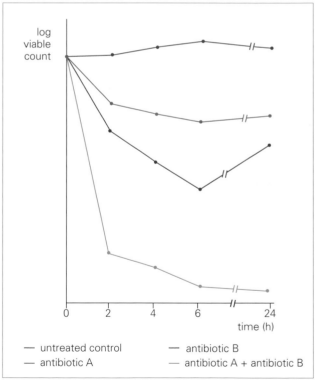

Figure 33.25 A more dynamic picture of the interaction between an antibiotic and a bacterial population can be gained from producing killing curves. In these experiments a culture of 2×10^6 colony forming U/mL was treated with antibiotics A and B alone and in combination. Compared with the untreated control, both A and B inhibit the growth of the bacterial culture, but B is more active than A. However, in combination, the activity of A plus B is synergistic (i.e. it is more active than the sum of the activities of the two antibiotics alone). The combination also prevents the re-growth seen after 6–24 h when the antibiotics are used singly.

Combining antibacterial agents can lead to synergism or antagonism

Hospital patients frequently receive more than one antibacterial agent, and these agents may interact with each other (and also with other drugs such as diuretics).

Antibacterial combinations are described as:

- 'synergistic' if their activity is greater than the sum of the individual activities
- 'antagonistic' if the activity of one drug is compromised in the presence of the other.

Both diffusion and dilution tests allow the action of combinations of antibiotics to be studied. Although synergy can often be demonstrated in vitro (Fig. 33.26), it is difficult to confirm in vivo. Co-trimoxazole is an example of a combination that is frequently used (see above). Another example is the combination of penicillin (or ampicillin) with gentamicin in the treatment of endocarditis caused by *Enterococcus* spp., as this combination has been shown to be clearly superior to the effect of the beta-lactam alone (Box 33.6).

Antagonism can be demonstrated between some pairs of antibiotics in vitro but is rarely evident in vivo.

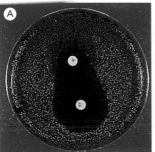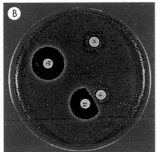

Figure 33.26 (A) Synergy of two antibacterials. Disks containing sulphonamide and trimethoprim have been placed to demonstrate the synergistic activity of these two agents against *E. coli*. Synergy can be recognized by the fact that the zones of inhibition become continuous between the two disks. (B) Antagonism. Nitrofurantoin is capable of antagonizing the activity of nalidixic acid. When the disks are placed far apart, nalidixic acid inhibits the test organism, but when placed close together this inhibition is antagonized by the presence of nitrofurantoin, as demonstrated by the foreshortening of the zone of inhibition.

Box 33.6 **Use of Antibiotic Combinations**

Reasons for using antibiotic combinations. Ideally, single drugs are used, but antibiotic combinations are justifiable under certain circumstances:

- to obtain a synergistic effect, e.g. co-trimoxazole
- to prevent or delay emergence of persistent organisms, e.g. isoniazid, rifampicin and ethambutol for tuberculosis
- to treat polymicrobial infections, e.g. intra-abdominal abscesses where the different microbes have different susceptibilities
- to treat serious infection in the stage before the infectious agent is identified.

ANTIBIOTIC ASSAYS

In the preceding parts of this chapter, the pharmacokinetic properties (absorption, distribution, excretion) of antibacterial agents have been summarized. Some antibacterials have a narrow 'therapeutic index', i.e. the concentration required for successful treatment and the concentration toxic to the patient are not very different. The concentrations of such antibiotics should be monitored both to prevent toxicity and to ensure that therapeutic concentrations are achieved. Other less toxic agents should be monitored in some circumstances in some patients (Box 33.7). Serum concentrations are usually measured, but urine, CSF and other body fluids can be assayed if applicable.

Antibiotic assays may be performed by a variety of methods such as high-performance liquid chromatography and direct assays for biological activity (bioassay). However, the most common approach uses immunologic methods which can be automated. In this method, the antibiotic in the patient specimen is an 'antigen' that competes with a specific level of labelled 'tracking' antibiotic for binding sites on an 'anti-drug' antibody. Thus, increased antibiotic levels in a patient sample result in decreased binding of tracking antibiotic, etc. Such assays are rapid, require only small volumes of serum, and are highly specific. However, they are obviously only applicable to instances where specific anti-drug antibody is available.

ANTIVIRAL THERAPY

The last two decades have seen a range of new antiviral agents licensed for use against a number of virus infections, including HIV, hepatitis B (HBV), hepatitis C (HCV), herpesviruses and influenza A and B (Fig. 33.27). The current

---

Box 33.7 **Importance of Antibiotic Assays**

Assays of antibiotics in clinical practice are particularly important when the antibiotic is potentially toxic, but there is a variety of other situations in which assays are important:

- when an antibiotic has a narrow therapeutic index, e.g. aminoglycosides
- when the normal route of excretion of antibiotic is impaired, e.g. in patients with renal failure for agents excreted via the kidney
- when the absorption of the antibiotic is uncertain, e.g. after oral administration
- to ascertain concentrations in sites of infection into which penetration of antibiotics is irregular or unknown, e.g. in cerebrospinal fluid
- in patients receiving prolonged therapy for serious infections, e.g. endocarditis
- in neonates with serious infections
- in patients who fail to respond to apparently appropriate therapy
- to check on patient compliance.

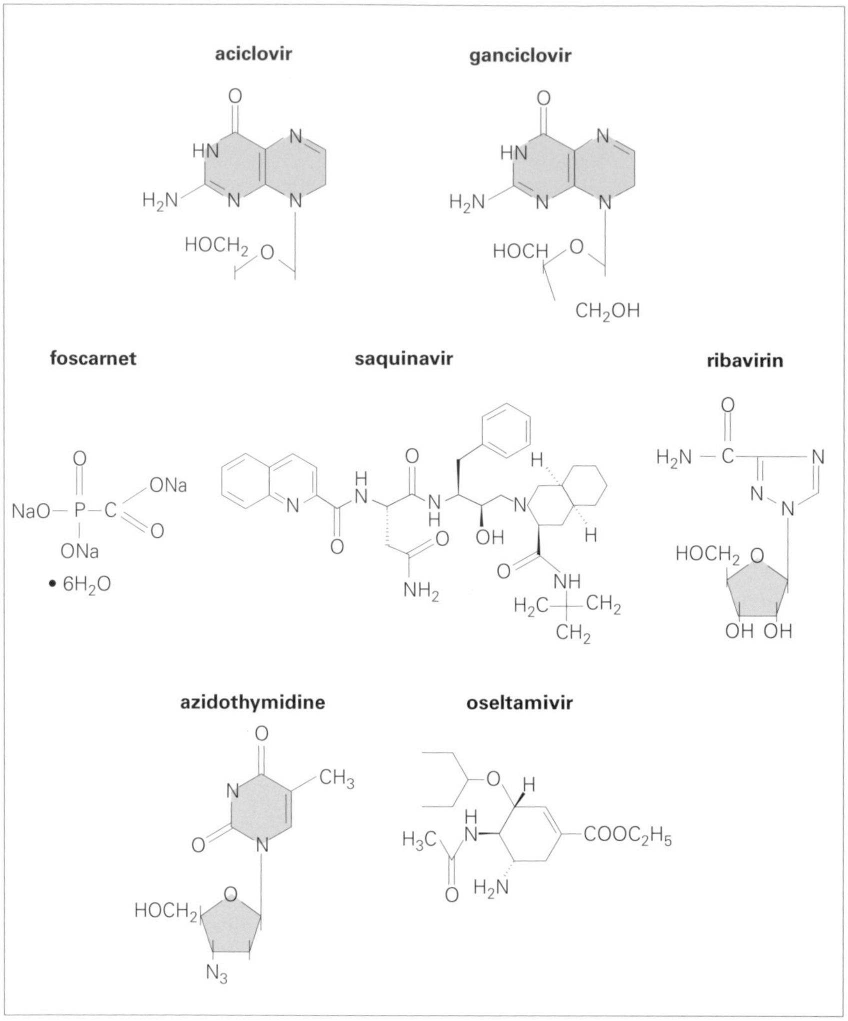

Figure 33.27 Antiviral agents are few in number and narrow in their spectrum of activity, e.g. amantadine is effective against influenza A, but not influenza B, while acyclovir is effective against herpes simplex virus (HSV) and varicella-zoster virus (VZV), but not cytomegalovirus (CMV) or Epstein–Barr virus (EBV).

antivirals for treating individuals with virus infections are all virustatic rather than virucidal, in other words, they do not kill viruses but suppress their replication. Of the increasing array of antiviral agents licensed for treatment, more than half are used in the management of HIV-infected individuals. As of 2011, there were 23 antiretroviral agents, excluding the fixed-dose combination agents, that constitute six different classes of drug (summarized in Table 33.7)

The problem in developing new antivirals has been mostly due to the difficulty of interfering with viral activity in the cell without adversely affecting the host. This is because viruses are dependent on the host cell's protein synthetic machinery. Directions taken in the development of new antivirals include:

- Adsorption inhibitors
- CCR5 and CXCR4 antagonists that target HIV-1 attachment, co-receptor binding and fusion referred to as entry inhibitors
- Blocking viral mRNA with short nucleotide sequences that are complementary to viral sequences. These antisense oligonucleotides bind to newly transcribed viral RNA and block its action
- Using compounds that inactivate virus when used topically.

Reports have highlighted the importance of making an early diagnosis in short-incubation-period viral infections, such as

influenza, in order for antiviral treatment to be successful. Moreover, virus-specific replication steps can be identified (Fig. 33.28), and more of these will doubtless be exploited, such as identifying virus-induced enzymes. In addition, apart from improving the ease of administration of those drugs where the pill burden is high, as in HAART, the lack of therapeutic options for a number of viral infections, including human papillomaviruses and adenovirus infections, is an area for further research and development.

Bearing in mind that antivirals can be used to treat acute and chronic viral infections, and in the latter case may be given for many years or for life, considerations include the length of the treatment course, single versus combination therapy, drug pharmacokinetics and interactions, adverse effects and antiviral resistance. Monitoring viral load as a marker of prognosis and treatment response is important in chronic viral infections such as HIV, HBV and HCV, together with therapeutic drug monitoring and genotypic and phenotypic resistance tests.

Antiviral resistance occurs with varying prevalence in different patient populations: for example, acyclovir-resistant HSV and ganciclovir-resistant CMV are mostly seen in immunocompromised individuals at a low level. Antiretroviral resistance is seen across all the main classes of agents – nucleoside reverse transcriptase inhibitors, non-nucleoside reverse transcriptase inhibitors, and protease

Table 33.7 Antiviral drugs

HIV	
Nucleoside reverse transcriptase inhibitor (NRTI)	Zidovudine (AZT) Didanosine (ddI) Stavudine (d4T) Lamivudine (3TC) Abacavir (ABC) Emtricitabine (FTC) Abacavir/Lamivudine/Zidovudine (Trizivir) Lamivudine/Zidovudine (Combivir)
Nucleotide Reverse Transcriptase Inhibitor (NRTI)	Tenofovir (TDF)
Combinations	
NRTI	Tenofovir/Emtricitabine (Truvada)
NRTI and NNRTI	Tenofovir/Emtricitabine/Efavirenz (Atripla)
Non Nucleoside Reverse Transcriptase Inhibitor (NNRTI)	Nevirapine Efavirenz Delavirdine Etravirine
Protease inhibitors	Indinavir Nelfinavir Ritonavir Saquinavir Amprenavir Lopinavir/Ritonavir (Kaletra) Atazanavir Fosamprenavir Tipranavir Darunavir
Fusion inhibitor	Enfurvitide
Integrase inhibitor	Raltegravir
Chemokine co-receptor inhibitor	Maraviroc
HCV	
	Ribavirin Boceprivir Telaprevir Pegylated interferon alpha 2a Pegylated interferon alpha 2b
Combination	Ribavirin/Pegylated interferon alpha 2b
HBV	
	Lamivudine Adefovir Entecavir Telbivudine Emtricitabine Tenofovir Pegylated interferon alpha 2a
Herpesviruses: HSV, VZV	
	Acyclovir Valaciclovir Famciclovir Penciclovir Idoxuridine Trifluridine Brivudin

(Continued)

Table 33.7 Antiviral drugs—cont'd

CMV including HSV and VZV	
	Ganciclovir
	Valganciclovir
	Foscarnet
	Cidofovir
Influenza A and B viruses	
Neuraminidase inhibtor	Oseltamivir
Neuraminidase inhibtor	Zanamivir
Influenza A viruses	
	Amantadine
	Rimantadine
RSV (also can be used in measles, Lassa fever, adenovirus and HCV infections)	
	Ribavirin

replication stage	drugs available
1 Adsorption	fusion inhibitors, e.g. T-20*
2 Penetration and uncoating	amantadine
3 Viral DNA/RNA synthesis	examples include: aciclovir zidovudine lamivudine nevirapine ribavirin
4 Viral protein synthesis	interferons
5 Assembly	protease inhibitors
6 Release	none available

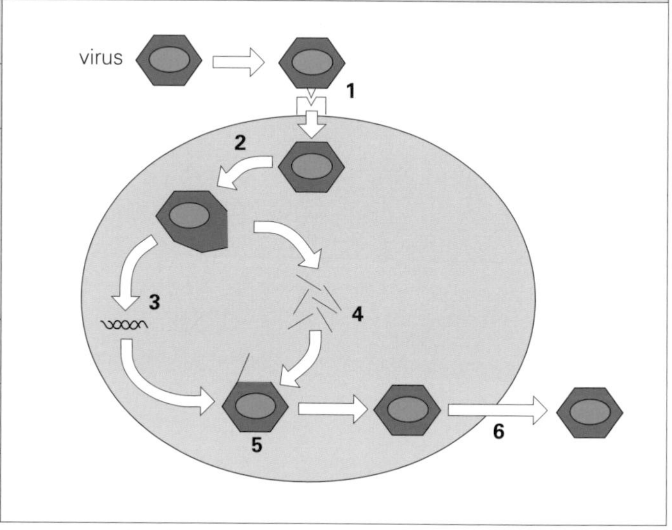

Figure 33.28 The site of action of antiviral agents. Resistance to agents is uncommon, but does occur (e.g. cytomegalovirus strains resistant to ganciclovir, herpes simplex virus strains resistant to acyclovir). Adsorption of virus to cell can be blocked by virus-specific antibody. * T-20 binds to the HIV gp41 site, preventing attachment to the T cell.

inhibitors – with increasing frequency in resource-rich countries. Lamivudine-resistant HBV is well recognized and is usually detected after a couple of years of treatment. Drug resistance involving most of the other agents used to treat HBV carriers also occurs. One issue with antiviral resistance is that the replication fitness of the drug-resistant variants is often less than the wild-type strain. In addition, in the case of a number of viruses, including HBV and HCV, the response varies depending on the viral genotype.

Some viral infections have an immunopathologic basis, such as CMV pneumonitis, in which case an antiviral is given in combination with an immunoglobulin preparation. This may be human normal immunoglobulin or virus-specific immunoglobulin, i.e. CMV hyperimmune globulin. Moreover, an immunomodulator may be given in conjunction with an antiviral such as pegylated interferon and ribavirin to treat hepatitis C virus infection.

Palivizumab is an example of a humanized monoclonal antibody produced to prevent infection. It is directed against the respiratory syncytial virus (RSV) fusion protein and has potent neutralizing and fusion inhibitory activity. It is used in specific clinical settings to prevent severe lower respiratory tract infections caused by RSV requiring hospitalization in children born at 35 weeks' gestation or less who are less than 6 months old at the onset of the RSV season. In addition, it may be used in children less than 2 years of age with specific respiratory and cardiac conditions such as broncho-pulmonary dysplasia.

Finally, in the case of some viral respiratory tract infections, antibiotics are often given to control or act as prophylaxis against a secondary bacterial infection. Influenza infection is an example where staphylococcal and streptococcal pneumonia may occur after the initial virological insult.

It is difficult to group the antiviral drugs in the same way as the antibiotics. One can either look at them as, for example, anti-HIV, anti-HBV and anti-HCV or group them under mechanism of action. The following are classified using the latter heading.

Prodrugs that target the viral DNA polymerase

Acyclovir, valaciclovir, penciclovir, famciclovir, ganciclovir, valganciclovir, cidofovir.

Acyclovir (acycloguanosine)

Acyclovir inhibits HSV and varicella-zoster virus (VZV) DNA polymerase

Acyclovir is used in the treatment of HSV and VZV infections. A number of other agents include valaciclovir, the L-valyl ester of acyclovir, and famciclovir. Acyclovir is inactive until phosphorylated and is an example of a prodrug. Acyclovir (Fig. 33.29) is phosphorylated by the herpesvirus thymidine kinase and the monophosphate is then converted by cellular kinases to the triphosphate, which inhibits the herpesvirus DNA polymerase. As it is taken up and efficiently phosphorylated by HSV-infected cells, the action on cellular DNA polymerase is minimal and toxic side effects such as neutropenia and thrombocytopenia are rare. The drug is also incorporated into viral DNA, resulting in chain termination. As it is excreted by the kidney, the drug can crystallize in the renal tract in individuals with renal failure, causing acute tubular necrosis. Otherwise, acyclovir has an excellent safety profile.

Systemic acyclovir revolutionized the treatment of HSV encephalitis, and HSV and VZV infections in immunocompromised patients. It is effective in treating primary and recurrent genital herpes. In shingles (herpes zoster), recovery is accelerated and post-zoster pain reduced. As with HSV, the varicella-zoster virus remains latent in ganglia and can reactivate.

As the oral bioavailability is only 15–20%, acyclovir is given intravenously in a number of clinical settings initially. Valaciclovir and famciclovir have improved bioavailability profiles in comparison with acyclovir, resulting in less frequent daily dosages.

Ganciclovir (dihydroxypropoxy-methylguanine, DHPG)

Ganciclovir is structurally similar to acyclovir but has an extra hydroxyl group. The range of activity is broader than that of acyclovir, and the drug is active against CMV infections. CMV does not encode a thymidine kinase, but the drug is monophosphorylated by a virus UL97 gene-specified kinase and then further phosphorylated by cellular kinases. However, selective toxicity is not seen, and it is myelosuppressive, its main adverse effect being bone marrow toxicity. Ganciclovir triphosphate inhibits CMV DNA polymerase. It is given intravenously because of limited oral bioavailability. However, an oral agent, valganciclovir, has improved the outpatient management of individuals with CMV infections, as it has equivalent activity to intravenous ganciclovir.

Ganciclovir is given to treat CMV retinitis, encephalitis and gastrointestinal disease seen in immunocompromised individuals. It is also used as pre-emptive therapy in bone marrow transplant as well as solid organ transplant recipients, who are monitored regularly for the presence of CMV in their blood as this leads to CMV dissemination.

Valganciclovir

Valganciclovir is the valine ester of ganciclovir, has similar bioavailability but has the advantage of being given orally.

Cidofovir (HPMPC)

Cidofovir is another chain terminator that targets the viral DNA polymerase. It is phosphorylated intracellularly to the diphosphate form and is then added to the 3' end of the viral DNA chain. It is effective against CMV and has been used to treat adenovirus infections. When given topically or intralesionally, it has activity against genital warts and can be used to treat acyclovir-resistant HSV infections. It has to be given intravenously and is nephrotoxic.

Pyrophosphate analogue that blocks the pyrophosphate binding site on the viral DNA polymerase

Foscarnet (phosphonoformate)

This compound attaches to the pyrophosphate-binding site of the herpesvirus DNA polymerase, preventing nucleotide binding and therefore inhibiting viral replication. It is used in treating CMV infections and is active against HSV and VZV and can be used to treat acyclovir-resistant HSV infections. It is nephrotoxic and is often used as a second-line agent.

Nucleoside and nucleotide reverse transcriptase inhibitors (NRTIs)

The aim of antiretroviral therapy is to lower and keep the plasma HIV-1 RNA load below the limit of assay detection and therefore maintain the CD4 count. There are a number of treatment guidelines, examples of which can be found

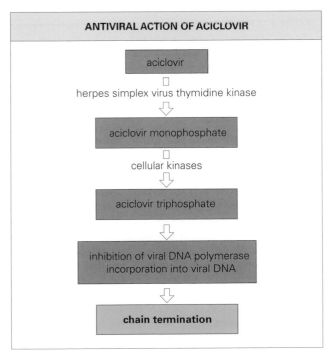

ANTIVIRAL ACTION OF ACICLOVIR

aciclovir
↓ herpes simplex virus thymidine kinase
aciclovir monophosphate
↓ cellular kinases
aciclovir triphosphate
↓
inhibition of viral DNA polymerase incorporation into viral DNA
↓
chain termination

Figure 33.29 The activity of an antiviral agent against different herpes viruses is correlated with the ability of the viruses to induce a thymidine kinase; hence acyclovir is most active against herpes simplex virus and least active against cytomegalovirus.

in the bibliography: zidovudine (azidothymidine, AZT), didanosine (ddI, deoxyinosine), lamivudine (3TC, thiacytidine), stavudine (d4T, didehydrodideoxyuridine), abacavir, emtricitabine, and tenofovir. These drugs have similar modes of action and are mostly used in conjunction with the other main classes of antiretroviral drugs: the non-nucleoside reverse transcriptase inhibitors and protease inhibitors to treat HIV-1-infected individuals.

Zidovudine (azidothymidine, AZT)

Zidovudine is an analogue of the nucleoside thymidine in which the hydroxyl group on the ribose is replaced by an azido group. After conversion to the triphosphate by cellular enzymes (Fig. 33.30) it acts as an inhibitor of, and substrate for, the viral reverse transcriptase. The azido group prevents the formation of phosphodiester linkages. Proviral DNA formation is blocked because AZT triphosphate is incorporated into the DNA, with resulting chain termination.

Zidovudine is given orally. Toxicity is a problem, with bone marrow suppression (macrocytic anaemia, neutropenia, leucopenia) and less commonly nausea, vomiting, headache, myalgia and malaise. This was more often seen in the early days of HIV treatment when the drug was given at a high dose. Other adverse events include lactic acidosis, hyperlipidaemia, lipoatrophy and insulin resistance or diabetes mellitus. Regular blood tests are necessary to detect anaemia and myelosuppression.

Like zidovudine, the other nucleoside analogues are converted to triphosphates and inhibit the HIV reverse transcriptase. Some of these agents have been combined as fixed-dose treatments such as combivir (AZT and 3TC), truvada (emtricitabine and tenofovir), and trizivir (AZT, 3TC and abacavir).

There are a number of adverse effects shared by this class of drugs but the more specific side effects include pancreatitis (ddI), peripheral neuropathy (d4T, ddI), lipodystrophy, i.e. fatty tissue redistribution from subcutaneous areas such as the face and limbs, to the neck and abdominal viscera (d4T), and hypersensitivity (abacavir). Mitochondrial toxicity due to inhibition of the mitochondrial DNA polymerase and lactic acidosis is also reported.

Drug resistance can lead to cross-resistance to other nucleoside analogues.

Tenofovir is a nucleotide reverse transcriptase inhibitor and is phosphorylated to the diphosphate form that acts as chain terminator.

The nucleoside and nucleotide RTIs and most of the protease inhibitors can be used to treat HIV-2-infected individuals. The non-nucleoside RTIs cannot be used and the fusion inhibitor, enfuvirtide, has reduced HIV-2 activity.

Non-nucleoside reverse transcriptase inhibitors (NNRTIs)

Nevirapine, efavirenz (EFV), delavirdine and etravirine

These are used in combination with the nucleoside analogues and may be used as first-line drugs before moving to the protease inhibitor class. This is because they lead to a rapid fall in the plasma HIV-1 RNA load, especially in those individuals with very high HIV loads for whom protease inhibitor treatment is being considered, and have fewer side effects. They act as non-competitive inhibitors of HIV-1 reverse transcriptase by binding to a hydrophobic pocket proximal to the enzyme catalytic site. They are inactive against HIV-2. The NNRTIs are inducers of cytochrome P450 and it is important to consider potential drug interactions. The most common adverse effect with nevirapine is a skin rash. Efavirenz may cause vivid dreams and sleep disturbance initially and should not be used in the first trimester of pregnancy.

A single mutation in the reverse transcriptase leads to resistance to these drugs, effectively removing this class of drug from the treatment regimen. In 2006–07, primary NNRTI resistance rates were about 8% in the USA and 2% in Europe.

Protease inhibitors

Nelfinavir, saquinavir, indinavir, ritonavir, lopinavir plus ritonavir (Kaletra), atazanavir, amprenavir, darunavir, fosmaprenavir, tipranavir

The protease enzyme acts in the post-translational cleavage of the *gag* and *gag-pol* polyproteins into the structural proteins and enzymes critical for viral replication. The result of protease inhibition is the production of immature, defective viral particles. Protease inhibitors (PIs) were introduced to HIV treatment combinations in 1996 and had a great effect on the control of HIV infection. Their use led to the term highly active antiretroviral therapy (HAART). They are peptidomimetic inhibitors of the viral protease and prevent the cleavage of the *gag* and *gag-pol* polyproteins into functional structural proteins and enzymes. They are very potent drugs which lead to a rapid fall in the plasma HIV RNA load, especially in those individuals with very high HIV loads. They are usually given in combination with nucleoside analogues. They are metabolized and excreted rapidly and have to be

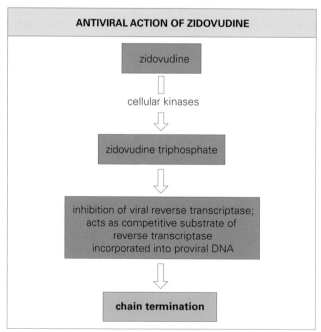

ANTIVIRAL ACTION OF ZIDOVUDINE

zidovudine

⬇

cellular kinases

⬇

zidovudine triphosphate

⬇

inhibition of viral reverse transcriptase; acts as competitive substrate of reverse transcriptase incorporated into proviral DNA

⬇

chain termination

Figure 33.30 HIV reverse transcriptase is 100 times more sensitive than host cell DNA polymerase to zidovudine triphosphate, but toxic effects are not uncommon.

taken several times daily. Side effects include gastrointestinal disturbances, the lipodystrophy syndrome (body fat redistribution), increased triglycerides, and insulin resistance leading to diabetes.

Drug resistance is well recognized and a number of protease mutations result in cross-resistance. Boosting atazanavir and darunavir with low-dose ritonavir leads to greater virological activity due to improved pharmacodynamics. However, higher rates of side effects are seen. Darunavir and ritonavir is useful for treating patients with PI-resistant HIV. Kaletra is a combination of lopinavir and ritonavir and is associated with sustained viral suppression as well as less drug resistance.

Fusion inhibitors

Enfuvirtide, also known as T-20, is a peptide that blocks HIV before it enters the host cell by competitively binding to *gp*41, the transmembrane glycoprotein and blocking the post-fusion structure from forming. It therefore should not cross-react with the other classes of antiretroviral drugs. It is given twice daily as a subcutaneous injection and is approved for salvage therapy in those treatment-experienced individuals with resistance mutations to the other drug classes. Adverse events include pain at the injection site and rare hypersensitivity reactions.

Integrase inhibitors

Raltegravir is an HIV integrase strand transfer inhibitor (INSTI). Integration involves transferring virally encoded DNA into the host chromosome. It is a three-step process including the formation of a preintegration viral DNA complex; 3' processing; and strand transfer. Raltegravir inhibits the strand transfer step. It is thought that it interacts with divalent cations of the catalytic core of the integrase. INSTIs are also active against HIV strains resistant to other classes of antiretroviral agents. Three major resistance mutations have been reported leading to integrase inhibitor resistance. Side effects are mostly gastrointestinal.

Chemokine receptor antagonists

HIV-1 entry into host cells involves the viral envelope protein binding to the CD4 receptor and subsequently to a chemokine co-receptor. Two co-receptors identified are called CCR5 and CXCR4. Tests that identify the viral phenotype have been used to determine the populations of virus in someone with HIV and these are referred to as R5-tropic, X4-tropic or dual/mixed. Diagnostic laboratories use genotypic tests to predict viral co-receptor tropism, R5 or X4, based on the sequence of the viral envelope on the basis of algorithms.

Maraviroc is a CCR5 chemokine co-receptor antagonist and was approved originally for adults who had been given HAART and had R5 HIV-1 infection.

Inosine monophosphate dehydrogenase inhibitor

Ribavirin (tribavirin)

This guanosine analogue is triphosphorylated by cellular enzymes. It has various actions including inhibition of production of guanosine triphosphate pools needed for viral nucleic acid synthesis. Ribavirin can target both RNA and DNA viruses. Once triphosphorylated, it can also interfere with the viral RNA polymerase. It is used clinically as an aerosol for treating severe respiratory syncytial virus (RSV) infection in infants and for arenavirus infections such as Lassa fever (see Ch. 26). Oral ribavirin could be used as post-exposure prophylaxis for Lassa fever in the case of high-risk exposure incidents. It is also active against measles virus and hepatitis C virus infection (see below).

Antivirals targeting influenza viruses

Amantadine, rimantadine, zanamivir, oseltamivir, and peramivir. These drugs have selective activity against influenza viruses and so have been grouped together with this header rather than by their mode of action. Amantadine and rimantadine only have activity against influenza A. The neuraminidase inhibitors, zanamivir, oseltamivir, and peramivir have increased the range of activity by inhibiting both influenza A and B viruses.

Amantadine and rimantadine

These drugs specifically inhibit the replication of influenza A viruses, but have no effect on influenza B and other respiratory viruses. They act by inhibiting the penetration of virus into the cell, or its uncoating. Fusion of the viral envelope with a cell membrane, which normally occurs at a low pH, is prevented. Amantadine acts on the viral matrix protein ion channel, thus stopping hydrogen ion passage, raising the pH in intracellular vacuoles, and therefore blocking infection. The standard dose can cause minor neurologic side effects such as insomnia, dizziness and headache, especially in elderly patients, and this has discouraged its widespread use. Amantadine can be given prophylactically during community outbreaks of influenza A. It can also be used for treatment, and if taken within 48 h of symptoms there is a reduction in disease severity. However, rapid emergence of drug-resistant variants can occur, and due to the inactivity against influenza B and central nervous system side effects, and the development of the neuraminidase inhibitors, this class of drugs is of less importance in the influenza armamentarium.

Neuraminidase inhibitors: zanamivir, oseltamivir, and peramivir

Neuraminidase is one of the two surface glycoproteins studded on the influenza virus surface. It cleaves N-acetylneuraminic acid, also known as sialic acid, residues from the host cell, thus releasing the virus and allowing further spread in the respiratory tract.

The neuraminidase inhibitors (NAIs) are N-acetylneuraminic acid analogues and act as competitive reversible inhibitors of the neuraminidase enzyme active site. Zanamivir is an inhaled agent and can be given intravenously, oseltamivir is an oral drug and peramivir is an intravenous agent, all of which are cleaved by esterases to the active carboxylate form and act on influenza A and B. The importance of having an increased armamentarium of NAIs was demonstrated during 2007–08 and 2008–09 as oseltamivir resistance emerged globally amongst the influenza A H1N1 viruses. In the USA, oseltamivir resistance was seen in around 20% and 90% of influenza A H1N1 viruses tested during both the above seasons, respectively.

These drugs reduce viral shedding, disease severity, duration and symptoms if given early in infection and can be used as prophylaxis. They are effective against the circulating influenza strains including the avian influenza H5N1 virus.

Hepatitis B treatment

The aim of treating individuals with chronic hepatitis B and C virus infections is to reduce the risk of cirrhosis and hepatocellular carcinoma by suppressing HBV DNA and HCV RNA levels, respectively.

Treatment regimens offered to hepatitis B virus carriers include nucleoside and nucleotide analogues such as lamivudine, adefovir entecavir, telbivudine and emtricitabine. After stopping treatment, this response may be reversed and continuing treatment long term may lead to the development of antiviral resistance, although the virus will be less fit than the wild type. Lamivudine, emtricitabine and adefovir monotherapy is not recommended.

Immunomodulation using pegylated interferon alpha, which has a longer half life than interferon preparations that do not include polyethylene glycol, enhances the innate immune response by binding to the type 1 interferon receptor. This leads to up-regulation of multiple interferon-stimulated genes limiting viral replication. In hepatitis B e antigen positive and negative carriers, 48 weeks of pegylated interferon alpha results in HBV DNA loss in 25% and 63% of patients, respectively. However, interferons have a large side effect profile.

Of the nucleoside analogues, lamivudine therapy results in improved liver histology and liver enzyme levels in 56% and 72% of patients, respectively. The genetic barrier to resistance is low as only one mutation is needed to lead to lamivudine resistance, compared with entecavir which has a higher barrier as three mutations are needed.

Emtricitabine cannot be used as single-agent therapy due to high rates of resistance. Telbivudine is effective but has a low genetic barrier to resistance.

Adefovir and tenofovir are acyclic diphosphonates with tenofovir being more effective than adefovir. They are prodrugs as they need to be phosphorylated to become active and are analogues of adenosine monophosphate. They affect the HBV polymerase by competitively inhibiting deoxyadenosine 5'-triphosphate, resulting in chain termination. The major side effect is nephrotoxicity.

Entecavir is a guanosine analogue that is one of the more effective drugs. It inhibits the HBV DNA polymerase by preventing the following functions: priming of the HBV DNA polymerase, reverse transcription of the negative strand from the pregenomic messenger RNA, and synthesis of positive-strand HBV DNA.

These oral antiviral agents have changed the treatment landscape in chronic hepatitis B carriers, and the role of combination therapy needs to be investigated.

Hepatitis C treatment

Pegylated interferon alpha combined with ribavirin is the standard treatment of chronic HCV infection. Antiviral treatment may lead to a sustained virological response (SVR) and long-term clinical benefit shown by the serum HCV RNA being below the limit of assay detection 24 weeks after starting treatment. HCV genotype 1 is the most common genotype globally and 48 weeks of the above combination treatment can lead to SVRs of only up to 50%. However, SVRs are seen in 75–90% of infected individuals with HCV genotype 2 and 3 infections.

Determining the liver histology by carrying out a liver biopsy may not be necessary. This is not the case in genotype 1, 4, 5 and 6 infection, although the development of non-invasive markers of liver fibrosis, serological markers and ultrasound techniques reduce the need for a liver biopsy. Identifying the HCV genotype is critical, as it assists the decision as to whether treatment is indicated and the length of the treatment course.

The HCV nonstructural (NS) NS3/4A serine protease is an enzyme that cleaves the HCV-encoded polyprotein leading to mature viral proteins. NS3/4A protease inhibitors include telaprevir, boceprevir and danoprevir and although they can result in improved SVRs, resistance develops rapidly if given as monotherapy. Boceprevir is a competitive inhibitor of the NS3 protease of HCV genotype 1 but does not have clinically significant activity against other HCV genotypes. Studies in which, for example, telaprevir was given in combination with pegylated interferon and ribavirin, showed good SVR rates. Anaemia is a significant side effect with this class of drugs.

Intereferons – immunomodulatory agents

Interferons (see Ch 9) are natural glycoproteins produced by the innate immune system in response to infections. They have a non-virus-specific antiviral and immunomodulatory actions and trigger a cascade of intracellular reactions that activate IFN-inducible genes. These genes encode proteins thought to inhibit intracellular virus multiplication by inhibiting translation initiation and assisting RNA degradation. IFN-alpha also binds to immune cells resulting in class I MHC antigen expression, activation of effector cells and a cytokine cascade. Production of TH1 cells is stimulated, in contrast to TH2 suppressor cells that are reduced. IFNs are generally given as subcutaneous injections and the side effects are significant and include tiredness, headache, myalgia and psychiatric symptoms.

IFNs have been used to treat individuals with chronic HBV and HCV infections and have an effect on human papillomavirus infections, given by intralesional injection, but are not used routinely.

When given in the past as monotherapy, success was limited due to the poor SVR rates for both HBV and HCV infections.

Other targets

Drugs targeting post-translational processing, virus entry, RNA translation and virus assembly and release are being developed in addition to host cell-targeting compounds. Nucleic acid-based antiviral agents including antisense oligonucleotides and RNA interference-based agents have been synthesized for clinical trials. Other potential therapeutic options include immunotherapy using antibody-based preparations and therapeutic vaccines.

Clinical management of antiviral therapy

Viral load and antiviral resistance tests as well as therapeutic drug monitoring assist in clinical management

Qualitative and/or quantitative nucleic acid tests are critical in the diagnosis, treatment decision, assessment of response to treatment and prognosis for a number of viral infections. This is true for HIV load testing, together with the CD4 count and percentage. With HCV, the main determinant of HCV treatment response and duration is the HCV genotype, having determined the plasma HCV RNA load. However, monitoring the HCV RNA level during therapy is not recommended for patients with genotype 2 or 3 infections, as most become HCV RNA negative early during treatment. For HBV infection, plasma HBV DNA load and antiviral resistance testing are part of the clinical management strategy. Genotypic analysis is also helpful. Another example is CMV DNA monitoring in post-transplant populations to detect early viraemia in order for pre-emptive treatment to be given.

The main causes of treatment failure in HIV infection are either compliance issues or the development of antiviral resistance.

Highly active antiretroviral therapy (HAART) has had an enormous impact on HIV disease progression. However, HAART can fail in up to 50% of individuals on treatment, especially if they have failed on previous treatment regimens. The development of drug-resistant virus will lead to treatment failure as seen by an increase in HIV load and reduction in CD4 count. Specific mutations can be detected in the drug target sites, i.e. reverse transcriptase and protease regions, by nucleic acid sequencing. This is referred to as a genotypic resistance assay. Key mutations known as primary resistance mutations at specific codons have been associated with a reduction in susceptibility to the various clans of antiretroviral drugs. Some mutations are unique to certain drugs, but many confer cross-resistance, resulting in a clan of drugs, such as the NNRTIs, being removed from the treatment regimen. In addition, viral tropism assays are carried out in diagnostic laboratories to identify co-receptor use which is critical when deciding on using chemokine receptor antagonists. HIV-1 entry into lymphocytes and monocytes involves binding of the gp120 envelope glycoprotein to the CD4 receptor, followed by interaction with one of two main co-receptors, CCR5 or CXCR4. This is referred to as viral tropism and whether the virus is X4 or R5 is mainly determined by the amino acid sequence of the V3 region of gp120. Dually tropic strains can use both receptors. In later-stage HIV-1 infection, the CD4 cell count falls and the minority population X4 or R5/X4 strains rises within the viral quasispecies and can finally emerge as a majority population. HIV-1 tropism can be determined using phenotypic and genotypic methods. Genotypic tropism testing can be carried out in laboratories and predictions of co-receptor use are based on the amino acid sequence of the gp120 V3 loop using interpretative algorithms. Antiretroviral drug regimens are based on the results of antiretroviral resistance sequencing assays as well as viral tropism assays.

As HIV drug resistance can be transmitted, and the prevalence of resistant viruses is increasing in individuals with a new HIV diagnosis, baseline genotypic resistance testing is very important in order to tailor HAART appropriately. In addition, this is being used more frequently to optimize the treatment regimen during drug failure episodes. Details of the key mutations can be found on specialist HIV websites together with guidelines for managing HIV infected individuals.

It is important in HIV infection to continue the drugs whilst carrying out resistance tests, as without the 'driver' there is a reversion to the wild-type strain as the minor viral populations that contain the mutations are deselected. Phenotypic analysis may also be helpful.

The effectiveness of HAART is dependent on good drug plasma concentrations. Keeping drug concentrations within a therapeutic range is critical and drug interactions and compliance issues may result in high or low drug levels, leading to toxicity or virological failure, respectively. Therapeutic drug monitoring is carried out in specialist laboratories and is helpful in finding and correcting any such problems.

ANTIFUNGAL AGENTS

Compared with antibacterials, the number of suitable antifungal drugs is very limited. Selective toxicity is much more difficult to achieve in the eukaryotic fungal cells than in the prokaryotic bacteria, and although the available antifungals have greater activity against fungal cells than they do against human cells, the difference is not as marked as it is for most antibacterial agents. Treatment of fungal infections is further hampered by problems of solubility, stability and absorption of the existing drugs, and the search for new agents is a high priority. Drug resistance is also increasing.

Antifungals can be classified on the basis of target site and chemical structure

Like antibacterials, antifungals can be classified on the basis of target site and chemical structure. This immediately reveals a major difference between antibacterial and antifungal agents, with the major antifungals acting on the synthesis or function of the intracellular membranes. The exceptions are flucytosine (5-fluorocytosine) and griseofulvin, which interfere with DNA synthesis, and caspofungin, which inhibits cell wall formation. There are currently no inhibitors of fungal protein synthesis that do not also inhibit the equivalent mammalian pathway.

Azole compounds inhibit cell membrane synthesis

Azole antifungals act by inhibiting lanosterol C14-demethylase, an important enzyme in sterol biosynthesis. Clotrimazole and miconazole are useful as topical preparations. Ketoconazole and fluconazole are used in treatment of a variety of serious fungal infections (Table 33.8), and fluconazole is often used in the treatment of *Candida* infections. Resistance to the azoles is becoming more widespread and threatens to compromise this group of compounds. Newer azole compounds include posaconazole, which is used in aspergillosis unresponsive to amphotericin B, and voriconazole, which is used against invasive candidiasis resistant to fluconazole.

Table 33.8 The major therapeutic applications of antifungal drugs

Infection	Antifungal of choice	Route of administration	Adverse effects
Superficial mycoses			
Ringworm (dermatophytes)	Griseofulvin	Oral	Mild
	Ketoconazole	Oral	Anorexia, nausea, vomiting; dose-dependent depression of serum testosterone leading to gynaecomastia
Candidiasis	Fluconazole	Oral	Inhibits metabolism of ciclosporin when given at high doses
	Nystatin	Topical	Mild
Systemic mycoses			
Histoplasmosis	Ketoconazole	Oral	See above
Blastomycosis	Ketoconazole	Oral	See above
Coccidioidomycosis	Ketoconazole (amphotericin B for CNS involvement) Fluconazole	} Oral	Do not use ketoconazole and amphotericin B together (some evidence of antagonism)
Paracoccidioidomycosis	Ketoconazole	Oral	See above
Aspergillosis	Amphotericin B Fluconazole Caspofungin acetate	} IV (now available in liposomes)	Nephrotoxicity and potassium loss; acute reactions within $1/2$–$1\frac{1}{2}$ h of injection include rigors and hypotension
Candidiasis	Fluconazole Amphotericin B1 Flucytosine	Oral IV Oral	} Flucytosine may cause neutropenia and jaundice; emergence of resistant mutants is common if drug is used alone; combination with amphotericin B can be synergistic
Cryptococcosis	Amphotericin B1 Flucytosine	IV Oral	
Zygomycosis	Amphotericin B	IV	
Pneumocystis pneumonia	Trimethoprim-sulfamethoxazole	IV or orally	Significant toxicity
	Pentamidine isethionate	IV	

Orally active agents are important for the treatment of superficial mycoses, which are often minor but troublesome infections and may require prolonged treatment. Amphotericin is the most important agent for the treatment of severe systemic mycoses, but is toxic. The azoles, particularly fluconazole and ketoconazole and some of the newer agents, provide suitable alternative therapy in some instances.

Echinocandins interfere with cell wall synthesis

The echinocandins caspofungin, micafungin and anidulafungin inhibit the enzyme β-(1,3)-D-glucan synthase which is required for synthesis of an essential part of the fungal cell wall. This important group of compounds offers new therapeutic options against infections such as invasive *Aspergillus* infections, candidaemia and invasive candidiasis and *Pneumocystis*. However, they are not active against *Cryptococcus neoformans*.

Polyenes inhibit cell membrane function

Amphotericin B and nystatin act by binding to sterols in cell membranes, resulting in leakage of cellular contents and cell death. Their preferential binding to ergosterol over cholesterol is the basis for selective toxicity. Amphotericin remains the drug of choice for the treatment of serious systemic fungal infections despite its serious toxic side effects; lipid formulations have lower toxicity and are increasingly preferred. Nystatin is used only in topical formulations.

Flucytosine and griseofulvin inhibit nucleic acid synthesis

Flucytosine (5-fluorocytosine) is deaminated to 5-fluorouracil, which inhibits DNA synthesis. Selective toxicity is based on the preferential uptake by fungal cells compared with host cells. Flucytosine is active only on yeasts (e.g. *Candida* spp. and *Cryptococcus*). Resistance emerges rapidly to flucytosine, which should therefore be used in combination with amphotericin B (whereby it is sometimes possible to reduce the dose of amphotericin B and therefore the toxic side effects).

Griseofulvin appears to inhibit nucleic acid synthesis and to have antimitotic activity, possibly by inhibiting microtubule assembly. It may also have effects on cell wall synthesis by inhibiting chitin synthesis. In the host, griseofulvin binds specifically to newly formed keratin and is active in vivo only against dermatophyte fungi (see Chs 4 and 26).

Other topical antifungal agents include Whitfield's ointment, tolnaftate, ciclopirox, haloprogin and naftifine

A variety of agents such as Whitfield's ointment (a mixture of benzoic and salicylic acids), tolnaftate, ciclopirox, haloprogin and naftifine are available as creams for the topical treatment of superficial mycoses. These are usually available over the counter, and there is little to choose between them.

No single antifungal agent is ideal

The main uses and adverse effects of antifungals are summarized in Table 33.8. Although there are several effective preparations available, some conditions such as ringworm infection of the nails or recurrent vaginal candidiasis are frequently intractable to treatment. The number of antifungal agents for systemic fungal infections is limited, and their adverse effects are considerable.

Fungi develop resistance to antifungal agents

Although much less studied than resistance to antimicrobials used against bacteria, there is evidence that many similar mechanisms operate in resistance to antifungals. These include:

- enzyme modification
- target modification
- reduced permeability
- active efflux pumps
- failure to activate antifungal agents.

Resistance involving some or all of these mechanisms has been described in *Aspergillus*, *Candida* and *Cryptococcus*, particularly in the case of the azole compounds.

There is an urgent need for safer more efficacious antifungal agents

Invasive fungal infections are a significant cause of morbidity and mortality in patients undergoing chemotherapy, immune suppression and transplantation. The incidence of these infections is increasing in parallel with the increasing numbers of such patients and their improved survival due to effective antibacterial therapy. New agents to control these infections (e.g. *Aspergillus*) are needed.

ANTIPARASITIC AGENTS

Parasites pose particular problems

Any consideration of antiparasitic agents must take into account the very large number of different parasites capable of infecting humans, the complexities of their life cycles and the differences between them in their metabolic pathways. Thus, drugs acting against protozoa are usually inactive against helminths and vice versa. Additionally, protozoa and helminths are eukaryotes and therefore metabolically more similar to humans than are bacteria. Although some antibacterials do have antiprotozoal activity (e.g. metronidazole, tetracycline), in general antibacterials are ineffective against parasites. A major challenge has been to identify targets where there are sufficient differences between host and parasite to facilitate safe drug activity. Some of these targets include:

- unique drug uptake: chloroquine, mefloquine, primaquine in malaria
- differences in folic acid metabolism: pyrimethamine in malaria, sulphonamides in toxoplasmosis, trimethoprim in cyclosporiasis
- polyamine uptake: pentamidine in leishmaniasis
- unique trypanothione-dependent reduction mechanisms: fluoromethylornithine against trypanosomes
- unique neurotransmitters: piperazine, ivermectin, pyrantel against nematodes
- cytoskeletal proteins (tubulin): benzimidazoles against nematodes
- intracellular calcium levels: praziquantel against flukes and tapeworms
- oxidative phosphorylation: niclosamide against tapeworms.

Despite differences between host and parasite in these targets, it remains true that a number of the more effective antiparasite drugs carry the risk of significant toxicity.

The wide array of different drugs that have been developed is summarized in Tables 33.9 and 33.10.

Drug resistance is an increasing problem

As with the antibacterials, drug resistance is a significant problem in the treatment of parasitic infections, particularly with malaria. There are four different indications for antimalarial chemotherapy:

- prophylactic: to prevent infection
- therapeutic: to treat infection (applies to all human malarias)
- radical cure: to prevent relapse following the treatment of acute infection (applies to *Plasmodium vivax* and *P. ovale* only)
- killing malarial gametocytes: to prevent transmission.

Falciparum malaria resistant to one or more antimalarial agents is now widespread. Chloroquine-resistant falciparum malaria occurs worldwide and *P. vivax* also shows focal resistance to this agent, notably in the Asia-Pacific region. The usual alternative to chloroquine in the tropics was combined sulphadoxine/pyrimethamine but there is now significant resistance to the antifolate compounds. Mefloquine-resistant falciparum malaria is found in parts of SE Asia and parts of South America. Quinine, the original antimalarial, is still a first-line agent for severe malaria though it requires careful monitoring during treatment to avoid toxicity. Development of antimalarials from natural products has provided new compounds, the most important being derivatives of artemisinin (from the Chinese drug, quinghaosu, produced from the plant *Artemisia annua*). Where available, intravenous artesunate has supplanted quinine as the agent of choice for the treatment of severe falciparum malaria. Drug combinations are now deployed for the treatment of falciparum malaria to reduce the chance of developing drug resistance after monotherapy, as happened with chloroquine, and artemisinin combination therapy (ACT) is already replacing quinine. Drug resistance is less of a problem with other protozoa and, although widespread in animal parasitic nematodes, has yet to become a serious issue with human infections.

Protozoa make use of enzyme and target modification to develop resistance (e.g. against antifolates and sulphonamides), but in addition active efflux pumps have been described in resistance of *P. falciparum* to chloroquine and mefloquine. Resistance to benzimidazole anthelmintics involves target modification, arising from mutations in cuticular tubulins.

CONTROL BY CHEMOTHERAPY VERSUS VACCINATION

While vaccination is discussed in detail in Chapter 34, it is important to note the role both chemotherapy and vaccination play in protecting individuals. An important difference is that chemotherapy is usually given after exposure to infection, whereas vaccination is usually given before exposure. Chemotherapy essentially offers short-term protection, which wanes once the drug is no longer given; vaccination

Table 33.9 Therapeutic applications of the major antiprotozoal drugs

Disease/site	Agent	Route of administration	Safety
Amoebiasis:			
Asymptomatic cyst passers	Diloxanide furoate	Oral	Safe
Invasive	Metronidazole followed by diloxanide furoate	Oral	} Treatment of amoebic dysentery and of extra-intestinal infections, all safe
	Tinidazole followed by diloxanide furoate	Oral	
Cryptosporidiosis	Nitazoxanide the agent of choice Spiramycin (limited activity) Paromomycin (limited activity)	} Oral	} Safe
Cyclosporiasis	Trimethoprim-sulphamethoxazole	Oral	Some toxicity
Giardiasis	Metronidazole Tinidazole Nitazoxanide	} Oral	} Safe
Leishmaniasis			
Cutaneous leishmaniasis	local infiltration with sodium stibogluconate (an antimonial) sodium	} Local injection	Safe
	stibogluconate for multiple, potentially disfiguring lesions	} IV	Some toxicity
Visceral leishmaniasis	liposomal amphotericin B (agent of choice); or sodium stibogluconate	IV	Some toxicity
Malaria			
Blood stages	Chloroquine (*P. vivax*, *ovale* or *malariae* ONLY)	Oral	Generally safe
	Quinine	Oral, IV	Some toxicity, used against drug resistant *P. falciparum*
	Mefloquine	Oral	Used against *P. falciparum*
	Atovaquone/proguanil	Oral	Used against *P. falciparum*
	Artemisinins; artemether/lumefantrine	Oral	Used against *P. falciparum*
	Artesunate	IV	Used to treat severe *P. falciparum* malaria
	Tetracycline	Oral	Used with or after quinine against drug resistant *P. falciparum*
Pre-erythrocytic stages	Primaquine	Oral	Used following chloroquine to kill hypnozoites in the liver and achieve radical cure after chloroquine therapy. Required for *P. vivax* and *P. ovale* ONLY, some toxicity (risk of haemolytic anaemia in G6PD-deficient patients)
Toxoplasmosis	Pyrimethamine plus sulfadiazine	Oral	Some toxicity
Microsporidiosis	Albendazole	Oral	Variable, species-dependent response
Trichomoniasis	Metronidazole	Oral	Safe
	Tinidazole	Oral	Safe
Trypanosomiasis			
East African	Suramin	IV	} Toxic – for haemolymphatic stage.
	Followed by melarsoprol if CNS involved	IV	} Followed by melarsopol IV (very toxic) if CNS involved
	Pentamidine or	IM	Very toxic
	Eflornithine for hemolymphatic stage	IV	Toxic
West African	Eflornithine or melarsoprol if CNS involved	IV	Toxic, passes blood–brain barrier
American (Chagas disease)	Nifurtimox	Oral	Side effects common
	Benznidazole	Oral	Side effects common

Several are potentially toxic and must be given under supervision. Some also have antibacterial activity and have been described in detail earlier in the chapter. Drug resistance is a problem, particularly in the treatment of malaria. G6PD, glucose-6-phosphate dehydrogenase.

Table 33.10 Therapeutic applications of the major anthelmintic drugs

Disease	Agent	Safety
Cestodes (tapeworms)		
Adult stage infection	Niclosamide Praziquantel	Safe Safe, avoid praziquantel in intestinal *Taenia solium* infection unless concomitant cerebral cysticercosis has been excluded
Larval stage cerebral cysticercosis	Albendazole or Praziquantel	} Under corticosteroid cover, some toxicity
Hydatid disease	Albendazole	Some toxicity
Trematodes (flukes)		
Schistosomiasis	Praziquantel	
Intestinal flukes	Praziquantel	
Lung fluke	Praziquantel	} Safe
Liver flukes except *Fasciola hepatica*	Praziquantel	
Fasciola hepatica	Triclabendazole	Safe
Nematodes (roundworms)		
Ascariasis and pinworm infection	Mebendazole Albendazole Pyrantel pamoate Piperazine	} All are safe drugs[b], mebendazole drug of choice Safe[b], mild side-effects, not used in children < 2 years Safe[b], except in epilepsy
Hookworm infection	Mebendazole Albendazole Pyrantel pamoate	} All are safe drugs[b], mebendazole drug of choice Safe[b], mild side-effects, not used for children < 2 years
Strongyloidiasis	Ivermectin Albendazole Thiabendazole	 Less effective Effective but poorly tolerated due to side-effects[b]
Trichinosis	Albendazole Mebendazole	} Both are safe drugs[b]
Trichuriasis	Albendazole Mebendazole	} Both are safe drugs[b]
Cutaneous larva migrans (infection with animal hookworm)	Ivermectin orally Albendazole orally Thiabendazole paste[a]	Mild side effects[b]
Toxocariasis (visceral larva migrans)	Albendazole	Safe[b]
Lymphatic filariasis	Diethylcarbamazine Ivermectin plus albendazole	Allergic side effects as worms killed Mild side effects
Onchocerciasis	Ivermectin	

All are administered orally except thiabendazole paste for cutaneous larva migrans, which is administered topically. Note that many of these drugs are not safe in pregnancy.

[a]Topical administration.

[b]Not used in pregnancy.

can give long-term protection without repeated treatment. Vaccination is therefore more effective than chemotherapy in protecting populations.

There are, of course, exceptions to these: passive antibody can be used to treat acute infection just as a drug can, while drugs like pyrimethamine and chloroquine are used for prophylaxis against malaria, almost as if they were short-term vaccines. However, in most cases there is a clear-cut distinction between the one- or two-shot vaccine, conferring protection for years, and the daily or twice-daily drug dose. Naturally, patients and doctors favour the former, whereas the pharmaceutical industry prefers the latter. Therefore, while drug development is carried out by industry without the need for external encouragement, vaccine development needs an outside stimulus in the form of earmarked funding; a field in which the World Health Organization, in particular, has performed with great distinction.

The concept of selectivity, or specificity, is central to both chemotherapy and vaccination

Although they appear so different (Table 33.11), both chemotherapy and vaccination developed together from the intensive study that followed the demonstration in the late 1800s that diseases could be caused by microbes. Pasteur (Box 33.8, Fig. 33.31) showed that killed or weakened microbes (e.g. anthrax, rabies) could be used to induce immunity that was active against that disease, while Ehrlich's work with histologic dyes led him to the idea that particular chemicals ('drugs') might bind specifically to particular microbial structures and damage them, thus being active against several diseases (see Ch. 33). Both therefore established the concept of selectively or specifically targeting infectious organisms within the body as a means of controlling disease.

The specificity of an antimicrobial drug resides in its ability to damage the microbe and not the host

As noted earlier, antimicrobial drugs should ideally bind to a molecule present only in the microbe to ensure specificity for the microbe and not the host. The extent to which this can be achieved varies from microbe to microbe. Bacteria, with their prokaryotic cell structure, are much more remote from humans than fungi, protozoa or worms (which are all eukaryotic). It is not surprising, therefore, that the most effective antibiotics are generally those used against bacteria. As much of the viral life cycle uses host cell components, antiviral chemotherapy has been much less successful than antibacterial therapy.

Many antimicrobial agents are products of microbes themselves or derivatives of these products. It is presumed that they form part of the self-preservation mechanism by which the microbes prevent overcrowding with their own or other species.

Table 33.11 Comparison of chemotherapy and vaccination

	Chemotherapy		**Vaccination**	
Specificity	Usually high		Very high	
Toxicity	Potentially high		Usually low	
Duration of effect	Usually short		Usually long	
Duration of treatment	May be prolonged		Usually short, but may need boosting	
Effectiveness	Bacteria	High	Viruses	High
	Viruses		Bacteria	
	Fungi	} Moderate	Fungi	} Low/moderate
	Parasites		Parasites	

Box 33.8 Lessons in Microbiology

Louis Pasteur (1822–1895)

The science of microbiology was established in the nineteenth century by the work of many distinguished scientists. However, one such scientist, Louis Pasteur, may legitimately be regarded as a founding father of this discipline (Fig. 33.31). He, along with Robert Koch, a German doctor (see Ch. 12), was able to show that living organisms or 'microbes' were the cause of disease, and provided a firm scientific basis for their study and control.

Pasteur began work at a time when spontaneous generation was still an accepted explanation for the appearance of microorganisms in decaying material. His elegant experiments showed that sterile organic infusions would not putrefy or ferment if there was no subsequent contact with airborne contaminants, proving that spontaneous generation did not occur, and that all microbes must come from pre-existing microbes. This discovery contributed to many fields of science, both basic and applied. Perhaps most important was the contribution Pasteur made to the work of Lister on antiseptics, which revolutionized approaches to surgery.

Pasteur worked in an amazing variety of microbiologic fields, from fermentation in the brewing of beers and production of wines, to identification of silkworm diseases,

bringing to each a penetrating scientific insight and making discoveries that brought him national and international renown. His understanding of the roles of organisms in causing diseases, and his acute scientific perception, enabled him to grasp from a series of 'mishaps' with experiments on chicken cholera that attenuated microbes could induce not disease, but immunity from disease. His ideas generated powerful opposition, but his belief then was strong enough to encourage him in 1881 to take part in a public trial of his vaccine against anthrax in domestic animals. Later, he used his insight into rabies, caused by organisms he could not see or culture, to develop an attenuated vaccine made from the dried spinal cords of infected rabbits. This was proven effective in humans in 1885, when Pasteur inoculated Joseph Meister, a 9-year-old boy who had been badly bitten by a rabid dog. Meister survived, and Pasteur's views on vaccination became universally accepted.

Pasteur ended his life as a national hero in his native France, and with a worldwide reputation for his work. His name is immortalized not only in the process of sterilization ('pasteurization') that he developed, but in the Institut Pasteur in Paris, which remains one of the most important international centres of microbiologic work.

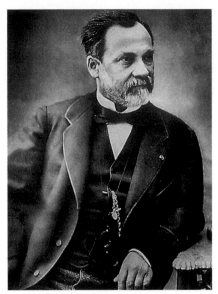

Figure 33.31 Louis Pasteur (1822–1895).

Although it is possible to administer antimicrobial agents in ways that prolong their presence in the body, they are no longer active once concentrations fall below a critical threshold. Continuing antimicrobial activity therefore requires repeated administration as opposed to vaccines which can provide long-term protection with far less re-administration (see Ch. 34).

CONTROL VERSUS ERADICATION

Control and eradication are different objectives, although eradication is always an ideal endpoint

Many infections can be controlled (at least in some parts of the world) by the use of a combination of strategies, including chemotherapy and vaccination (see Ch. 34) (Table 33.11), but are certainly not eradicated, even in those countries where control is most effective. Epidemiologic theory (see Ch. 31) predicts that once transmission rates fall below a threshold value, the infection should die out, and this may certainly be true at a local level. However, reservoirs of infection persist where treatment is non-existent or ineffective, or infection is re-introduced by the movement of peoples, and new epidemics may therefore develop. To date, only one disease – smallpox – has been taken to the point at which the organism has been eliminated. What are the chances that other infectious diseases will follow smallpox into oblivion? Various factors are important in determining the effectiveness of any eradication programme (Table 33.12).

Realism is required when considering the long-term aims of antimicrobial control strategies

Hopes raised by the early success of antibiotics were soon dashed by the emergence of resistance, and far from the microbial load borne by the human race being diminished in recent years, it has if anything increased. Many infections covered in this book, HIV, Legionnaires' disease, Lyme disease, to name but a few, do not feature in older textbooks of microbiology. Infections previously well controlled by antibiotics have become serious problems in hospitals (MRSA, *C. difficile*). Approaches to the control of infectious diseases are therefore a matter of identifying priorities such as:

- Which diseases could, with suitable effort, be eradicated?
- Would the cost of eradication be justified?
- Which diseases need urgent measures to stop them getting worse?
- Which diseases are responsible for the most human suffering and economic loss?

Inevitably, some diseases will not feature strongly on any such list, and it must be accepted that they may always be with us.

USE AND MISUSE OF ANTIMICROBIAL AGENTS

Much has been said in this chapter about the interactions between antimicrobial agents and microbes – the mechanisms of selective toxicity and the defences put up by resistant organisms. The distribution, metabolism and excretion of agents by the host have been considered briefly, together with the important toxic side effects of the agents. The choice

Table 33.12 Strategies for control of infectious diseases

General features	Water purification (water-borne diseases) Sewage disposal (enteric infections) Improved nutrition (host defence) Improved housing (less crowding, dirt, etc.)
Food	Cold storage Pasteurization (milk, etc.) Food inspection (meat, etc.) Adequate cooking
Zoonoses and arthropod-transmitted infections	Control of vectors (mosquitoes, ticks, lice, etc.) Control of reservoir animal (rabies, bovine TB)
Specific disease treatment or prevention	Chemotherapy Vaccines
Miscellaneous measures	Changes in personal habits (reduced promiscuity, use of condoms, improved personal hygiene, etc.) Control of intravenous drug abuse Screening of transfused blood and organs

of antimicrobial for treating specific infections is dealt with in the appropriate systems chapter (Chs 18–30). Dosage regimens have not been included because they vary with the agent, the infection, the age and the underlying condition of the patient, and sometimes from one country to another. Practitioners should consult appropriate local pharmacy guidelines.

Antimicrobial agents should only be used appropriately for prophylaxis or treatment

In conclusion, we should stand back and ask 'Is antimicrobial therapy necessary for this patient, and, if so, which agent is appropriate?' Antimicrobial agents can be used:

- to help prevent infection (prophylaxis)
- to treat infection.

Prophylactic use of antibiotics is appropriate only in a few clearly defined circumstances and is usually of limited duration (e.g. 1–2 days). Specific examples include: (1) patients of normal susceptibility who have been exposed to specific pathogens (e.g. bacterial meningitis or tuberculosis), (2) individuals with increased susceptibility to infection (e.g. neutropenic patients), and (3) perioperative antibiotic 'cover' for patients undergoing surgery.

Antimicrobial use results in the selection of resistant strains

If antibiotic treatment is necessary, several factors must be considered, and these are summarized in Figure 33.32. It is important to recognize that during treatment not only the infecting microbe, but also the patient and all his or her normal microbial flora are being exposed to the effects of the antimicrobial agent. Use of antimicrobials has been clearly shown to select for resistant strains, both in the individual and in the community, and overuse or inappropriate use only increases this risk. History suggests that microbes will never run out of ways of developing resistance, but we may run out of effective antimicrobials.

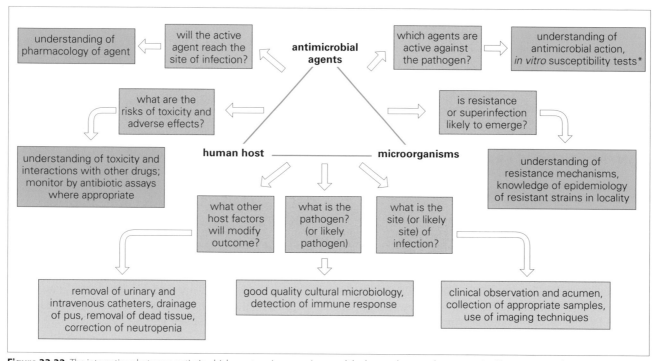

Figure 33.32 The interactions between antimicrobial agents, microorganisms and the human host can be summarized by examining the answers to several questions affecting each side of the triangle of interaction. * Other tests include phenotypic and genotypic antiviral susceptibility tests and viral load tests.

KEY FACTS

- Infection is unique among the diseases which afflict mankind because it involves two distinct biological systems. Antimicrobial agents are designed to inhibit one system (the microbe) while doing minimal damage to the other (the patient). Antimicrobial agents require selective toxicity.

- Antimicrobial agents are often themselves products of microorganisms (natural products) although most are chemically modified to improve their properties. Other agents are entirely synthetic. Antibacterials are the most

numerous; designing antiviral, antifungal and antiparasitic drugs which are selectively toxic provides much greater challenges.

- Antibacterials are classified by their target site and their chemical family; this helps us to understand better their mode of action and the mechanisms of resistance.

- Antibacterials have four possible sites of action in the bacterial cell: cell wall, protein, nucleic acids and cell membrane. The majority act at the cell wall or inhibit protein or nucleic acid synthesis. At each site there are many different molecular targets (enzymes or substrates) which can be specifically inhibited.

- Development of resistance is the major limiting factor of antibacterials. It arises through random mutation of bacterial chromosomal genes but more importantly through acquisition, from other bacteria, of resistance genes on integrons, transposons and plasmids.

- Mutated or acquired genes confer resistance by altering the target site of the antibacterial, altering the uptake of the drug, or producing drug-destroying enzymes.

- The emergence of AIDS has provided an enormous stimulus to research in antivirals (especially anti-HIV drugs). Selective toxicity is again a major challenge. Drug combinations show promise in the treatment of HIV, but there is no specific therapy for the majority of viral diseases. Effective therapy is available for other viral infections, including hepatitis B and C, influenza A and B, HSV and CMV.

- The number of classes of antifungal molecules is very limited. Toxicity (all), difficulty of formulation (polyenes), and emerging resistance (azoles) make effective treatment of fungal infections a serious challenge.

- Although there are many antiparasitic drugs available, a number show toxicity and others are becoming increasingly ineffective because of the development of resistance. This is particularly so in malaria infections, where parasites show resistance to almost all drugs presently available.

- Bacteria can be tested in the laboratory for their susceptibility to antibacterials. The results of well-controlled tests provide a valuable guide to appropriate treatment. In vitro tests with antifungals are less reliable and are rarely performed with antivirals in the clinical laboratory setting.

Protecting the host: vaccination

34

Introduction

Vaccines are one of the most effective public health tools. This chapter will review how vaccines work, and the vaccines in current use. However, although vaccination is very cost-effective as a public health measure, saving many lives (immunization saves an estimated 2.5 million deaths each year from diphtheria, tetanus, pertussis and measles), in 2008 an estimated 1.8 million people died from a vaccine-preventable disease, as a result of poor vaccine uptake. Many others die from infectious diseases such as HIV for which there is as yet no effective vaccine, so new vaccines are also needed (Table 34.1).

Vaccination exploits the ability of the immune system to develop immunological memory, so that it can rapidly mobilize its forces to fight infection when required. Vaccines can be of different types, including live attenuated organisms, killed organisms, or subunit vaccines. Depending on the vaccine type, more than one dose may be needed to achieve or maintain optimal protection. Adjuvants are often required to increase immunity. A lot has been learnt about how to make a good vaccine, but for some vaccines we lack measurable correlates of protection. It is therefore no surprise that the development of new and more effective vaccines is a major area of research. Successful vaccination also requires an understanding of the epidemiology of disease transmission, for example, to estimate what proportion of a given population needs to be vaccinated to produce herd immunity, as discussed in Chapter 31.

VACCINATION – A FOUR HUNDRED YEAR HISTORY

'Never in the history of human progress', wrote the pathologist Geoffrey Edsall, 'has a better and cheaper method of preventing illness been developed than immunization at its best'. The greatest success story in medicine, the elimination of smallpox, began before either immunology or microbiology were recognized as disciplines – indeed before the existence of microbes or the immune system was even suspected. As a result of the pioneering work of Jenner with vaccinia (Box 34.1),

all forms of specific, actively induced immunity are now referred to as 'vaccination'.

The principle of vaccination is simple: to prime the adaptive immune system to the antigens of a particular microbe so that on first contact with the live organism a rapid and effective secondary immune response will be induced by memory T and B cells. Vaccination therefore depends upon the ability of lymphocytes, both B and T cells, to respond to specific antigens and develop into memory T and B cells, and represents a form of actively enhanced adaptive immunity. The passive administration of preformed elements, such as antibody, is considered in Chapter 35.

AIMS OF VACCINATION

The aims of vaccination can vary from preventing symptoms to eradication of disease

The most ambitious aim of vaccination is eradication of the disease. This has been achieved for smallpox, the eradication of polio is being attempted, and there has clearly been a dramatic downward trend in the incidence of most of the diseases against which vaccines are currently in use (Fig. 34.2). However, as long as any focus of infection remains in the community, the main effect of vaccination will be protection of the vaccinated individual against infection.

In certain cases, the aim of vaccination may be more limited: namely, to protect the individual against symptoms or pathology. For example, diphtheria and tetanus vaccines only induce immunity against the toxins produced by the

Table 34.1 Infectious agents that are major killers

Organism	Disease	Estimated annual deaths (millions)
HIV	AIDS	1.8
Mycobacterium tuberculosis	Tuberculosis	1.7
Plasmodium spp.	Malaria	0.8
Total		4.3

We currently lack effective vaccines against these organisms, although bacille Calmette–Guérin (BCG) vaccination can provide protection against disseminated forms of childhood tuberculosis, and pulmonary tuberculosis in some parts of the world. Most of the deaths from HIV are in Africa, and most of the deaths from malaria are in African children. *Sources*: Figures for 2009 from WHO.

Box 34.1 Lessons in Microbiology

Edward Jenner (1749–1823)

The English physician Edward Jenner (Fig. 34.1) is regarded as the founder of modern vaccination, but he was by no means the first to try the technique. The ancient practice of 'variolation' dates back to tenth-century China, and arrived in Europe in the early eighteenth century via Turkey. The technique involved the inoculation of children with dried material from healed scabs of mild smallpox cases, and was a striking foretaste of the principles of modern attenuated viral vaccines. This practice was, however, both inconsistent and dangerous, and Jenner's innovation was to show that a much safer and more reliable protection could be obtained by deliberate inoculation with cowpox (vaccinia) virus. Milkmaids exposed to cowpox were traditionally known to be resistant to smallpox and so retained their smooth complexions. In 1796, Jenner tested his theory by inoculating 8-year-old James Phipps with liquid from a cowpox pustule on the hand of Sarah Nelmes. Subsequent inoculation of the boy with smallpox produced no disease. Although greeted with scepticism at first, Jenner's ideas soon became accepted, and he went on to inoculate thousands of patients in a shed in the garden of his house at Berkeley, Gloucestershire.

He ultimately achieved world fame, though his fellowship of the Royal Society was conferred for a quite different piece of work on the nesting habits of the cuckoo!

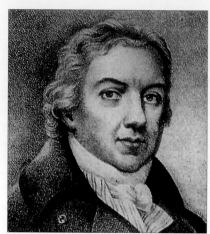

Figure 34.1 Edward Jenner (1749–1823).

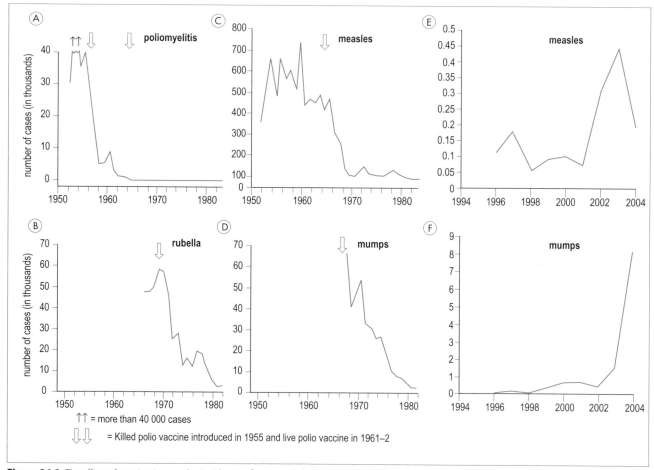

↑↑ = more than 40 000 cases

⇩⇩ = Killed polio vaccine introduced in 1955 and live polio vaccine in 1961–2

Figure 34.2 The effect of vaccination on the incidence of various viral diseases in the USA and the UK. Most infections have shown a dramatic downward trend after the introduction of a vaccine (arrows), but the right-hand panels show the resurgence in disease when vaccine uptake is reduced following vaccine 'scares'. (Data from Mims and White and the Health Protection Agency, UK.)

bacteria, as it is the effect of these toxins rather than the simple presence of the microbe itself that is harmful.

The importance of herd immunity

Successful vaccination programmes rely not only on the development and use of vaccines themselves, but also on an understanding of the epidemiologic aspects of disease transmission. If enough individuals in a population are immunized, this will reduce or stop transmission of the infection. This is called herd immunity. By having your own child immunized, you therefore help protect the whole community – but conversely, when too many parents decide that their child will not be immunized, because they think the risk of their child getting the disease is low, this may contribute to the disease becoming more common (Fig. 34.2)

It is therefore important to know how many individuals in a population must be immunized to produce herd immunity, and also whether immunity should be boosted by re-vaccination.

VACCINES CAN BE OF DIFFERENT TYPES

Vaccines can be based on whole organisms, either live or inactivated, or components of the infectious agent (Table 34.2).

Live vaccines are designed to induce immunity in a similar way to the actual infection. Most live vaccines use attenuated organisms that were attenuated using culture in eggs, animals or in tissue culture (Fig. 34.3); these attenuated organisms replicate to a limited extent in the vaccinated individual but do not cause disease in healthy people. However, the immunosuppression associated with HIV infection can produce problems with live vaccines. For example, infants

Table 34.2 Types of vaccine

Types of vaccine	Examples
Live attenuated	
Viral	Measles, mumps, rubella, vaccinia, varicella, yellow fever, zoster, oral polio, intranasal influenza, rotavirus
Bacterial	BCG, oral typhoid
Inactivated	
Whole virus	Polio, influenza, hepatitis A, rabies
Whole bacteria	Pertussis, cholera, typhoid
Fractions	
Toxoids	Diphtheria, tetanus
Protein subunits	Hepatitis B, influenza, acellular pertussis, human papillomavirus
Polysaccharides	Pneumococcal, meningococcal, *Salmonella typhi* (Vi), *Haemophilus influenzae* type b
Conjugates	*Haemophilus influenzae* type b, pneumococcal, meningococcal

Note that not all types of vaccine are available in all countries. Vaccines are also available for bioterrorism agents such as anthrax and plague, and for vaccinia.

with HIV infection given BCG vaccination can develop disseminated BCGosis. HIV-infected individuals with severe immunosuppression should not be given live vaccines such as measles or varicella, but they can be given inactivated vaccines.

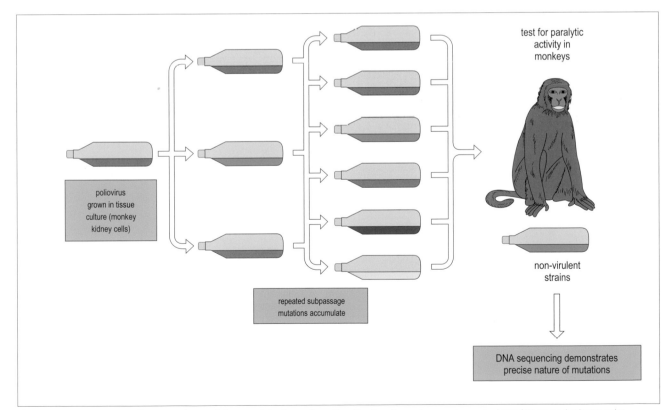

Figure 34.3 Live attenuated vaccines (e.g. polio) were originally produced by allowing viruses to grow in unusual conditions, and selecting the randomly occurring mutants that had lost virulence.

Table 34.3 Fixatives and preservatives used in current vaccines

Fixatives	
Formalin	TdaP, HepA, Hib, influenza, polio
Glutaraldehyde	DtaP, DtaP-HepB-IPV
Preservatives	
EDTA	Rabies, varicella
Phenol	Pneumococcal, inactivated typhoid
2-phenoxyethanol	DtaP, HepA, HepA-HepB, inactivated poliovirus
β-propiolactone	Rabies
Sodium deoxycholate	Influenza
Thiomersal	DtaP, DtaP-Hib, HepB, influenza, meningococcal vaccine

TdaP, combined tetanus, diphtheria and pertussis; DtaP, combined diphtheria, tetanus and pertussis; HepA, hepatitis A; HepB, hepatitis B; Hib, *Hameophilus influenzae* type b; IPV, inactivated polio vaccine.

Inactivated vaccines are safe to use in the immunocompromised, although they may not be as immunogenic, and a good adjuvant may be needed. Inactivation can use heat or fixation, for example, with formalin. Types of fixatives and preservatives in use in vaccines are given in Table 34.3. Another difference between live and attenuated vaccines is that inactivated vaccines are not affected by circulating antibody, but live attenuated vaccines may be.

Individual antigens or toxins can also be used as a vaccine, with adjuvant. Purified proteins are used in the acellular pertussis vaccine and recombinant proteins are used in the vaccines for hepatitis B. A number of protein antigens can also be joined together as a fusion protein and given with adjuvant. Polysaccharides form the basis of the pneumococcal vaccine, but as polysaccharide vaccines are not immunogenic in children under 2 years of age, conjugate vaccines that use a polysaccharide linked to a protein have been developed for pneumococcal and meningococcal disease, and for *Haemophilus influenzae* type b (Hib). For some bacteria, it is the toxin that is pathogenic – so this can be inactivated to make a toxoid, as in the tetanus toxoid vaccine. If individual components of an organism form the basis of a vaccine, an adjuvant will be needed to boost immune responses. Multiple doses of protein or polysaccharide are usually needed, as these vaccines are less immunogenic than vaccines with whole organisms.

One or more vaccine antigens can also be delivered by a viral vector, such as modified vaccinia virus Ankara (MVA) that was safely used in humans at the end of the smallpox eradication campaign.

Some vaccines are designed to boost immunity using only selected antigens or by using a different delivery route. For example, some new TB vaccines in development would boost the immunity induced by BCG by giving key antigens delivered by a viral vector (Fig. 34.4), or a fusion protein with adjuvant.

Recipients of haemopoietic stem cell transplants may need to be revaccinated after the infusion of haemopoietic stem cells, as otherwise antibody titres to vaccine-preventable diseases decline.

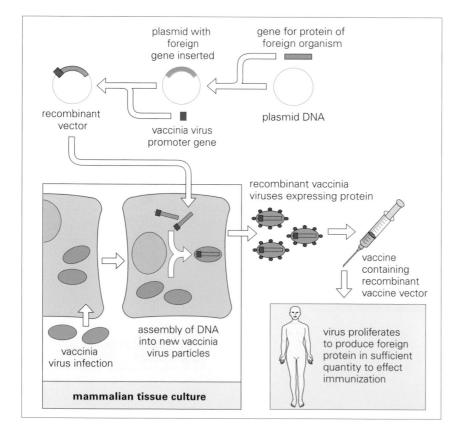

Figure 34.4 It is now possible to insert genes coding for antigens of one or more microorganisms into a large virus such as modified vaccinia virus Ankara (MVA), so that they replicate and are released into the host. A new MVA vaccine is currently being developed for TB that expresses a secretory TB protein.

Adjuvants

Adjuvants increase the immunity induced by a vaccine in a number of ways. Adjuvants can improve the immune response to the vaccine antigens through inducing activation of Toll-like receptors (TLR) on dendritic cells to improve antigen presentation, or by forming an antigen depot which allows antigen to persist and to leak out slowly over time. The earliest adjuvants consisted of water in oil emulsions, and Freund's complete adjuvant which included dead mycobacteria in a water in oil emulsion is very effective, although not suitable for use in humans. Other adjuvants increase antigen presentation, or enhance particular types of immunity, such as antibodies or Th1 immunity. The dramatic effect of adding an adjuvant to a vaccine is shown in Figure 34.5. Aluminium salts are powerful adjuvants and used in many vaccines (Box 34.2). Experimentally, cytokines such as IL-1, IL-2, IFNγ, IL-12 and IL-18, as well as some chemokines, have been tested as adjuvants. Compounds such as liposomes, lipid containing vesicles, have also been used, but so far only monophosphoryl lipid A has been used in a licensed vaccine (HPV, Cervarix).

Vaccine safety

As vaccines are given to healthy individuals, it is important that they are safe. In 1926, live *M. tuberculosis* was inadvertently given to healthy children instead of BCG, leading to the Lubeck disaster, and in 1942, US military personnel were vaccinated with yellow fever virus contaminated with

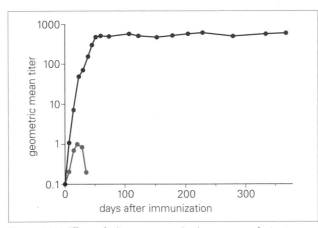

Figure 34.5 Effects of adjuvants on antibody responses of mice to egg albumin. Mice were injected subcutaneously with egg albumin in saline or in Freund's incomplete adjuvant. Antibody titres at intervals over time are shown. The blue symbols represent antigen in saline, and the red symbols antigen in adjuvant. (Redrawn from: Hunter, R. (2002) Vaccine 20:S7–S12.)

Box 34.2 Adjuvants in Currently Used Vaccines

Aluminium salts*	DTaP, Hib, HepA, HepB, HPV, MMR, rabies, rotavirus, rubella, varicella
Monophosphoryl lipid A (MPL)	HPV (Cervarix)

*aluminium hydroxide, aluminium hydroxyphosphate sulphate, aluminium phosphate, aluminium potassium sulphate

Box 34.3 Problems with Vaccine Safety

Both living and non-living vaccines require rigorous quality and safety control. Some of the more common problems are listed below:

Live attenuated vaccines

- Insufficient attenuation
- Reversion to wild type
- Administration to immunodeficient patient
- Persistent infection
- Contamination by other viruses
- Fetal damage

Non-living vaccines

- Contamination by toxins or chemicals
- Allergic reactions
- Autoimmunity

Genetically engineered vaccines

- Possible inclusion of oncogenes

hepatitis B virus (see Ch. 15). Safety testing is now rigorous, requiring extensive quality controls and animal testing, prior to trials or use in humans. Some of the more important issues are summarised in Box 34.3. It is particularly critical that vaccines derived from live organisms are inactivated to ensure they are safe and that vaccines are preserved appropriately to ensure that vaccine immunogenicity is retained. Examples of fixatives and preservatives used in current vaccines are given in Table 34. 3.

Vaccines in current use

Diphtheria, tetanus and pertussis

The diphtheria vaccine consists of the inactivated toxoid. Toxigenic *Corynebacterium diphtheriae* is grown in liquid culture and the filtrate inactivated with formaldehyde to produce the toxoid. This is a highly effective vaccine, giving >90% protection. Three or four doses are required to give good protection, with a booster every 10 years. It is now given in different formulations with other vaccines.

The inactivated toxin from *Clostridium tetani*, inactivated using formaldehyde, is used to vaccinate against tetanus. Tetanus toxoid was first produced in 1924. Again, this is a very effective vaccine, but boosters are required every 10 years. In some developing countries neonatal tetanus is still a problem; if the mother has been immunized against tetanus this will protect the newborn baby but, in 2009, the World Health Organization estimated that only 83% of newborn babies were protected against neonatal tetanus.

The first vaccine developed against pertussis was a whole cell vaccine, which was available from the mid 1940s and introduced in the UK in 1957 (Fig. 34.6). However, although four doses of vaccine induced 70–90% protection against serious whooping cough, concerns over the safety of the vaccine in the UK in the 1970s led to resurgence of disease.

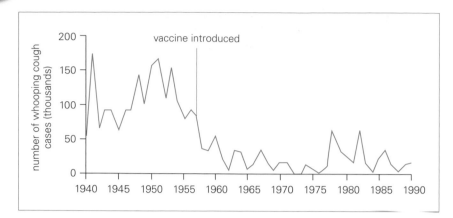

Figure 34.6 The number of cases of whooping cough notified fell steadily after the introduction of mass immunization in the UK in 1958, although epidemics continued to occur at approximately four-year intervals. Following the scare about the possible adverse effects of pertussis vaccine, the number of cases rose, and there was a large epidemic in the winter of 1978–79.

Whether the vaccine did induce brain damage is unclear, but concerns did lead to the development of a safer acellular pertussis vaccine.

Coverage of the combined DTP or diptheria tetanus acellular pertussis (DTaP) vaccines is now good, with an estimated 109 million children under the age of 1 year receiving a third dose of vaccine, equivalent to 82% global coverage.

Measles, mumps and rubella vaccines

Live attenuated measles vaccine was introduced in the USA in 1963, using the Edmonston B vaccine, which has since been replaced by the more attenuated Edmonston–Enders strain, which is grown in tissue culture. Children should be given two doses of vaccine, as the first dose fails to induce protective antibodies in about 15% of those vaccinated. Vaccination is safe and effective, either given on its own or as part of the MMR vaccine with mumps and rubella and mumps, or the MMRV vaccine containing measles, mumps, rubella and varicella. However, maternal antibodies inhibit the induction of immunity, so the first dose is generally given at 12–15 months of age, once maternal-derived antibodies have declined, and the second at 4–6 years of age. In lower-income countries where the risk of contracting measles is higher, the vaccine may be given at about 9 months, in an attempt to protect children whose levels of maternal antibodies are declining.

Vaccine-induced immunity to measles is long-lived and after two doses, probably life-long. Between 2000 and 2008, there was a 78% drop in measles deaths worldwide, as a result of measles vaccination. In this period, approximately 700 million children were vaccinated, with 83% of all children vaccinated before 1 year of age in 2008. Nevertheless, it was estimated that about 450 children were still dying every day as a result of measles – measles is the leading cause of death in young children from a vaccine-preventable disease – and as many as 10 million people still catch measles every year. In the UK there were 1144 cases of measles in 2009 – with some clusters of cases in schools or nurseries.

As shown in Figure 34.2, cases of measles increased in the UK after 2001, following reduced vaccine uptake. This resulted from the suggestion that the MMR (measles, mumps and rubella) vaccine caused autism, as there was an apparent rise in autism in both California and the UK that seemed to coincide with the introduction of the MMR vaccine. However, further studies have failed to show an increased risk of autism after MMR. It had also been suggested that the measles virus

could be detected in the gut following vaccination and that this might lead to inflammatory bowel disease – but, again, this was not confirmed by independent testing. It is no wonder that parents get worried when bombarded with these scare stories – but they forget that measles infection can kill healthy children. In a measles outbreak in Ireland in 2000, nearly 1500 cases were notified and three children died.

Mumps vaccine

The current mumps vaccine is a live attenuated virus (Jereyl Lynn strain), which was licensed in 1967. Over 97% of those vaccinated make antibodies after a single dose of vaccine, and a study in the UK showed that 88% of those receiving two doses were protected. The importance of receiving two doses of MMR is illustrated by a mumps outbreak in Northern Ireland where 55.4% of the confirmed cases had received one dose of vaccine, compared with 0.9% in those who had received two doses. After two doses, protection is thought to last at least 25 years and may be life-long. This vaccine is much more effective than an earlier inactivated vaccine.

Rubella vaccine

The current rubella vaccine is a live attenuated virus, strain 27/3, licensed in 1979. The virus was attenuated by 25–30 cell culture passages in human diploid fibroblasts. Over 90% of those vaccinated have at least 15 years of protection from clinical rubella or viraemia. Although rubella itself is a relatively mild infection, it causes real problems if pregnant woman become infected in the first trimester of pregnancy, when congenital rubella syndrome can cause serious damage to the fetus. Thankfully, there has been a dramatic reduction in confirmed cases of congenital rubella syndrome due to vaccination: cases were reduced by 98% in the Americas between 1998 and 2009.

Although a combined MMRV vaccine with measles, mumps, rubella and varicella is available, the risk of post-vaccination seizures seems slightly higher if this vaccine is given as the first vaccine dose at 12–15 months of age compared to giving the MMR and varicella vaccines separately. The combined vaccine can be given as the second dose at 4–6 years of age.

Polio vaccine

The first polio vaccine was a killed vaccine (inactivated polio vaccine, IPV) developed by Salk; this was first licensed in 1955, and was very effective at reducing the risk of contracting polio. Later, the oral polio vaccine (OPV) was developed by Sabin, and licensed in the 1960s. Giving the vaccine on sugar lumps or directly into the mouth was much easier than giving it by injection and the live vaccine also gives better intestinal immunity. However, the live poliovirus used in OPV vaccine is not genetically stable and can cause vaccine-associated paralytic polio (VAPP) in approximately 1 per million doses administered (Table 34.4). It has long been recognized that OPV is transmissible from vaccinees to their close contacts,

and it is now known that such transmission can persist in the community as circulating vaccine-derived polio viruses (cVDPV). Extensive use of trivalent OPV in routine services and national immunization day campaigns, organized through the Global Poliovirus Eradication Initiative, has succeeded in reducing the number of polio cases worldwide by over 99%, from an estimated 350 000 cases in 1988 to only 1783 reported cases in 2009 (Fig. 34.7). Of the three wild polio serotypes, type 2 transmission was interrupted in 1999, but types 1 and 3 have continued to circulate in Afghanistan, India, Nigeria and Pakistan, and have caused outbreaks in some neighbouring countries.

Low effectiveness of trivalent vaccines in some populations (in particular India), and the elimination of type 2 virus, has led to the development of mono and bivalent vaccines with types 1 and 3 Sabin viruses. These are now widely employed in the Global Poliovirus Eradication Initiative. However to eradicate polio, the world may have to shift to IPV to avoid circulation of vaccine-derived polio viruses. Most wealthy countries have already shifted to IPV vaccines in recent years for this reason. The routine IPV vaccination schedule in the United States consists of four doses given at ages 2 months, 4 months, 6–18 months, and 4–6 years.

Table 34.4 Oral and inactivated polio vaccines compared

	Inactivated (IPV)	**Attenuated (OPV)**
Introduced	Salk 1954	Sabin 1957
Route	Injection plus alum	Oral
Advantages	Can be given with other childhood vaccines	Boosts IgA immunity Herd immunity
Disadvantages	Risk if inadequately killed	Reversion to virulence*

*Although vaccine-associated paralytic polio only occurs in < 1/million vaccinated, vaccine-derived polio viruses can circulate within the community.

Figure 34.7 Progress towards polio eradication. The progress towards the eradication of polio is illustrated by the increase in certified polio-free countries from 1988 (top map) to 2009 (bottom map). (Redrawn from www.who.int/immunization_monitoring/data/SlidesGlobalImmunization.pdf; data from WHO/Polio database, as at August 2010.)

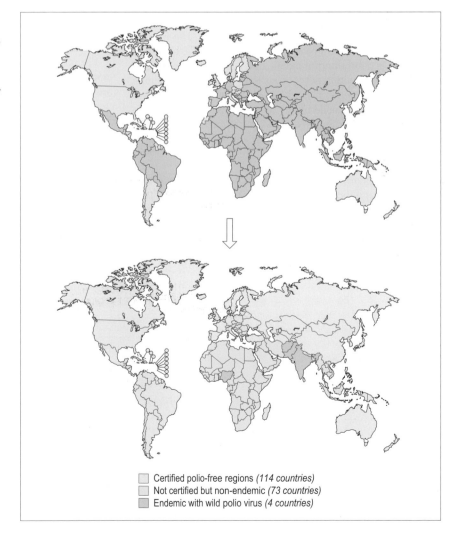

☐ Certified polio-free regions *(114 countries)*
☐ Not certified but non-endemic *(73 countries)*
☐ Endemic with wild polio virus *(4 countries)*

Pneumococcal vaccines

The challenge in making an effective vaccine against pneumococcal disease is that there are 90 serotypes of *Streptococcus pneumoniae* – but luckily a few serotypes cause most infections. The first vaccine was a pneumococcal polysaccharide vaccine with capsular polysaccharide from 14 serotypes. This was replaced in 1983 with a formulation containing 23 capsular polysaccharides from 23 serotypes. However, although this vaccine induced antibodies in >80% of adults, it was not immunogenic in children aged less than 2 years. A conjugate vaccine is now available in which capsular polysaccharides from seven serotypes are conjugated to a non-toxic form of the diphtheria toxin. The conjugate vaccine is highly immunogenic in infants and young children, and new formulations containing more serotypes are being developed. One interesting question is whether the rates of carriage of the different serotypes may be affected by vaccination.

Meningococcal vaccines

As for pneumococcal vaccine, the first vaccine against meningococcal disease consisted of purified capsular polysaccharides for four of the five serotypes, A, C, Y and W-135. Again, similar to the pneumococcal polysaccharide vaccine, the meningococcal polysaccharide vaccine was not immunogenic in young children, as seen for other T-independent antigens. A conjugate vaccine containing capsular polysaccharides from the same four serotypes conjugated to diphtheria toxoid was licensed in the USA in 2005, and shown in trials to induce four times more antibody than the polysaccharide vaccine. The B strain is not covered in either of these vaccines, as the B group polysaccharide is poorly immunogenic and may have some cross-reactivity to the human nervous system. A vaccine containing just the C serotype is currently used in the UK. Vaccination against meningitis is compulsory for pilgrims visiting Mecca in Saudi Arabia for the Umrah and Haj pilgrimages, as there was a *N. meningitis* W-135 outbreak in pilgrims in 2000.

Haemophilus influenzae type b (Hib)

Haemophilus influenzae mainly affects children under 5 years of age. Although there are six capsular serotypes, one, type b composed of a phoshodiester-linked polymer of ribose and ribitol, causes 95% of disease, and so has been the basis of Hib vaccines. The introduction of Hib vaccines has dramatically reduced the incidence of bacterial meningitis from Hib (Fig. 34.8). The first polysaccharide vaccine introduced in the USA in 1985 was not immunogenic in children under 18 months of age, similar to other antigens inducing T cell-independent immune responses. Conjugating the polysaccharide to a T cell-dependent antigen overcomes this problem. Even so, three or four doses are needed to induce good immunity, as this is another example of how a sub-unit vaccine is less immunogenic than a live vaccine. Two conjugate vaccines are currently available, one conjugated to tetanus toxoid and one to meningococcal group B outer membrane protein. Another Hib capsular polysaccharide vaccine conjugated to inactivated tetanus toxoid is now available and can be used as the last booster dose.

Influenza

Flu generated a lot of alarm in 2009, when the first flu pandemic since 1968 was caused by a new influenza A (H1N1) virus. The threat from this new virus, and from avian influenza (H5N1), has highlighted the limited world capacity to produce new flu vaccines quickly in the quantities needed. Another result of the 2009 pandemic was a change to vaccination policies for flu in countries such as the USA. Two types of vaccine are currently available: a trivalent inactivated vaccine that can be given to anyone over the age of 6 months by intramuscular injection, and a live attenuated influenza vaccine, that can be given by intranasal spray to those aged 2–49 years of age who are healthy and not pregnant.

Flu is a tricky customer, as it changes its antigens due to both point mutations and to recombination events, resulting in antigenic drift (Fig. 34.9) and antigenic shift. The recommended composition of current flu vaccines can be found on the WHO website. The 2010–11 trivalent vaccines for the northern hemisphere contained A/California/7/2009 (H1N1)-like, A/Perth/16/2009 (H3N2)-like, and B/Brisbane/60/2008-like antigens. The influenza A (H1N1) vaccine virus was derived from a 2009 pandemic influenza A (H1N1) virus. Different formulations can be used for the southern hemisphere. Flu vaccination policy varies in different countries: for example,

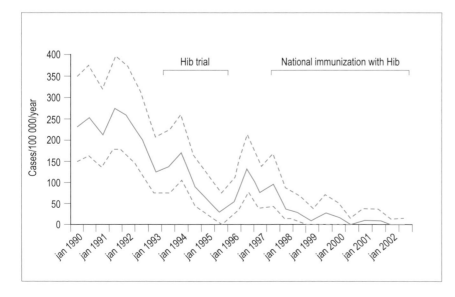

Figure 34.8 Vaccination with a *Haemophilus influenzae* type b (Hib) polysaccharide-tetanus toxoid conjugate vaccine has produced a dramatic decrease in the incidence of Hib meningitis in children >1 year old in The Gambia. Dotted lines represent pointwise 90% likelihood-based confidence limits. (Data from: Adegbola, R. et al. (2005) Lancet 366:144–150.)

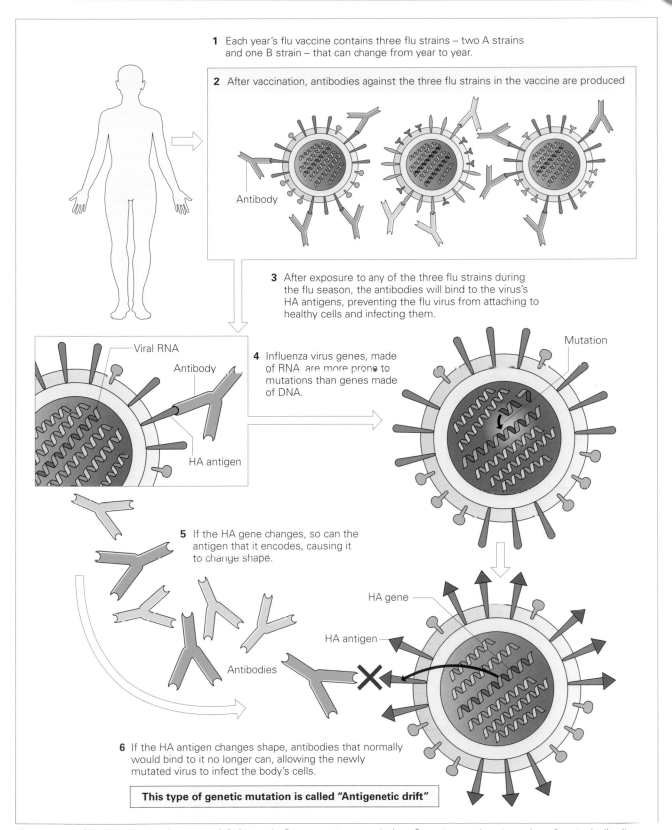

1. Each year's flu vaccine contains three flu strains – two A strains and one B strain – that can change from year to year.

2. After vaccination, antibodies against the three flu strains in the vaccine are produced

Antibody

3. After exposure to any of the three flu strains during the flu season, the antibodies will bind to the virus's HA antigens, preventing the flu virus from attaching to healthy cells and infecting them.

Viral RNA

Antibody

HA antigen

4. Influenza virus genes, made of RNA, are more prone to mutations than genes made of DNA.

Mutation

5. If the HA gene changes, so can the antigen that it encodes, causing it to change shape.

HA gene

HA antigen

Antibodies

6. If the HA antigen changes shape, antibodies that normally would bind to it no longer can, allowing the newly mutated virus to infect the body's cells.

This type of genetic mutation is called "Antigenetic drift"

Figure 34.9 Influenza vaccines and antigenic drift. Seasonal influenza vaccines contain three flu strains, two A strains and one B strain. Antibodies to these strains induced by vaccination will protect against infection, but mutations in the influenza genes can cause antigenic drift leading to infection. (Modified from National Institute of Allergy and Infectious Diseases. Flu (Influenza): Antigenic Drift. Bethesda, MD: U.S. Department of Health and Human Services; 2011.) HA haemagglutinin.

in 2010 in the USA, vaccination was offered to everyone aged over 6 months, whereas in the UK vaccination was restricted to those aged over 65 years or who fell into an at-risk group, such as those with asthma, but for the first time vaccination was offered to previously unvaccinated pregnant women. Children aged 6 months to 6 years (in the USA) or 12 years (in the UK) who are being vaccinated for the first time are now given two doses of vaccine. A new high-dose trivalent inactivated vaccine is also available for use in those over 65 years of age.

BCG and new vaccines for TB

The oldest vaccine still in use is the BCG vaccine, derived following extensive culture of *M. bovis* on potato bile medium by Calmette and Guérin, which resulted in its attenuation. The genetic deletions that this involved have since been mapped, and include the loss of the RD1 region that encodes the ESAT-6 and CFP-10 antigens that are used in the two currently available commercial diagnostic tests for *M. tuberculosis* infection, the QuantiFERON test and the TSPOT-TB ELISPOT assay. A number of different BCG strains are used as vaccines, which have some other minor genetic differences (Table 34.5), although there is no evidence

Table 34.5 Genetic deletions in different strains of BCG vaccine

Strain	Region			
	RD1	**RD2**	**RD8**	**RD14**
M. bovis	+	+	+	+
M. bovis BCG (pre-1931)	−	−	+	+
M. bovis BCG Glaxo	−	−	+	+
M. bovis BCG Danish	−	−	+	+
M. bovis BCG Pasteur	−	−	+	−
M. bovis BCG Connaught	−	−	−	+

A number of genetic regions have been deleted from different BCG strains since the original attenuation. Regions RD1, 2, 8 and 14 contain 9, 11, 4 and 8 open reading frames, respectively. (Data from Behr, M. A. et al. (1999) *Science* 284:1502.)

that these affect the protective efficacy of BCG. BCG was first used as a vaccine in 1921!

BCG is usually given to babies shortly after birth and is given to over 100 million children annually. It provides good (and very cost-effective) prevention of the disseminated forms of childhood tuberculosis, but variable protection against pulmonary TB in adults. For example, it induced good protection (>80%) in trials in adolescents in the UK, but no protection in South India or Malawi. The reasons for this may include exposure to environmental mycobacteria that can induce a masking or a blocking effect on the immunity induced by BCG. When BCG is protective, this is associated with induction of a TH1 immune response – although simply measuring the IFNγ induced in response to mycobacterial antigens does not provide a correlate of protection. When induced, protective immunity lasts for 10–15 years and in one study was shown to last for over 50 years. In settings where BCG is protective, it may protect against infection as well as against disease. There is no evidence that revaccination is helpful. In children over 6 years of age, or in those known or likely to have been infected with *M. tuberculosis*, skin testing with *M. tuberculosis* purified protein derivative (Mantoux skin test) should be performed and BCG vaccination only given to those with a negative test result.

Because of the variable protection that BCG vaccination gives against tuberculosis in adults, the search is on for a new TB vaccine. Candidate vaccines in development include genetically modified BCGs, attenuated *M. tuberculosis*, viral vectors expressing key antigens of *M. tuberculosis*, and fusion proteins in adjuvant. A modified vaccinia virus Ankara expressing Ag85A is now in Phase IIb trials in children and in HIV-infected adults in Africa. This vaccine would be given as a boosting vaccine following BCG vaccination, and has been shown to boost the numbers of Ag85A-specific T cells secreting IFNγ (Fig. 34.10). Other promising vaccine candidates include genetically modified BCGs that express haemolysin or perfringolysin, that are designed to enhance activation of CD8 T cells through escape of antigens into the cytoplasm of the infected macrophage, and a fusion protein of Antigen85A with ESAT-6.

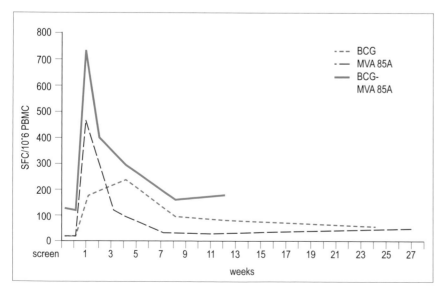

Figure 34.10 The prime boost strategy is being exploited in the design of new vaccines. A new candidate vaccine for TB uses modified vaccinia virus Ankara that expresses Antigen 85A (MVA85A) of *M. tuberculosis* to boost immunity in people previously vaccinated with BCG (BCG). The prime boost group of vaccinees (BCG-MVA85A) show the greatest numbers of spot-forming cells (SFC) making IFNγ in an ELISPOT assay in which peripheral blood mononuclear cells were stimulated with the Antigen 85 protein. (Data from: McShane, H et al. (2004) *Nature Medicine* 10:1240–1244.)

Vaccines against hepatitis

The first vaccine for hepatitis B virus (HBV) consisted of the surface coat antigen of HBV purified from the plasma of virus carriers. This vaccine was protective, but required very careful purification and inactivation to ensure it was safe, and was expensive to produce. A recombinant hepatitis B vaccine was first licensed in the USA in 1986, and was the first vaccine produced using genetic engineering (Fig. 34.11). Recombinant HBV vaccines have an efficacy of 95% with immunity lasting at least 20 years after three doses of vaccine.

Inactivated whole cell vaccines are available for hepatitis A. The virus is grown in human cells, purified, inactivated with formaldehyde and adsorbed onto alum. Again, these vaccines induce excellent immunity. However, as yet there is no vaccine available for hepatitis C.

Human papillomavirus (HPV)

New HPV vaccines have been introduced in the last decade, due to the association between HPV infection and cervical cancer. The first quadrivalent vaccine (Guardisil™), which induces immunity against four types of HPV, was licensed in 2006. This contains the L1 capsid protein of HPV from two oncogenic types of virus HPV16 and HPV18 as well as two non-oncogenic types, HBV6 and HPV11. It is made by recombinant DNA technology, expressed in yeast cells, and forms virus-like particles. This vaccine is being given to females aged 12–13, before they become sexually active, and can induce antibody responses in over 99.5% of vaccinees. The quadrivalent HPV vaccine is now also given to males aged 9–26 years of age in the USA to prevent genital warts as HPV6 and HPV11 cause approximately 90% of genital warts. A bivalent HPV vaccine containing L1 from HPV16 and HPV18 was approved for females aged between 10 and 25 years of age in the USA in 2009. This vaccine is cheaper, but most countries have opted for the quadrivalent vaccine, as it also prevents genital warts.

Rotavirus vaccine

Rotavirus is the cause of most serious gastrointestinal disease in infants. Trials of an earlier vaccine were stopped when it caused intussusception, a rare cause of bowel obstruction. Two new rotavirus vaccines were recommended for use by the WHO in 2009. Such viruses illustrate the difficult decisions to be made when there is a small risk of a vaccine-induced complication, but protection from disease would save many lives. Two new live vaccines are now in use: the RV5 oral vaccine (RotaTeq™) contains five reassortant rotaviruses developed from human and bovine parent strains, while the RV1 vaccine (Rotarix™) contains one live attenuated rotavirus strain. Trials of RV1 vaccine in 11 countries showed that three doses gave 98% protection against severe rotavirus gastroenteritis, while two doses of RV1 vaccine were shown to provide 85% protection against severe rotavirus gastroenteritis in Latin America.

Vaccines that are required for entry into particular countries, or for particular regions

The yellow fever vaccine is required for entry into certain countries. A vaccination certificate may be required for all those entering a particular country, or for individuals coming from a country where yellow fever is endemic. The certificate lasts for 10 years although immunity is probably life-long.

Pilgrims to Saudi Arabia for the Umrah or Haj may be required to show evidence of vaccination, for example, against meningitis (see above).

Travellers spending longer periods in areas of rural Asia, where Japanese Encephalitis (JE, a mosquito-transmitted flavivirus) is common, can be vaccinated with an inactivated JE virus vaccine. A cell-culture derived inactivated vaccine is now replacing an earlier mouse brain-derived inactivated vaccine. The cell-culture-derived vaccine requires two doses and is only given to those over 17 years of age; the mouse brain-derived vaccine requires three doses, and can be given to children and those under 17 years of age.

Vaccines for subgroups at high risk

Rabies vaccination is available for those exposed to rabies, or whose work or travel puts them at increased risk. Two types of vaccine are available: inactivated virus from cell cultures (from human diploid cells or chick embryo cell); intradermal vaccination may be more effective than intramuscular injection. Vaccine has also been prepared in human Vero cells. The cell culture-derived vaccines are considered safer than nerve tissue-based vaccines.

A vaccine has been produced for those working with *Bacillus anthracis*, such as laboratory or animal workers, or some military personnel. To ensure protection, five doses of vaccine are given and a yearly booster is necessary.

Complexity of vaccine schedules

An increasing number of vaccines are being given to infants – at a time when their immune system is not fully mature. However, studies have shown that pre-term babies can still be vaccinated safely at the right chronological age for vaccination. Table 34.6 gives an overview of vaccines being given to infants, children and adolescents in the USA and UK. The detailed schedules can be found on the WHO website (www.who.int).

It is important to ensure that all these vaccines do not interfere with each other, and thus reduce vaccine-induced immunity. It is therefore important to test for non-interference before a new vaccine is introduced.

There may be other factors that affect how well a vaccine works in the real world. Some studies have reported sex differences in vaccine-induced immunity, and seasonal effects, so some vaccines may not induce equivalent immunity in all settings. Vaccination is a very powerful public health tool, but not all infants and children will get their vaccines at the right ages or in the recommended order. Vaccines for developing countries therefore need to be tested in the

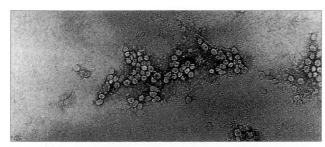

Figure 34.11 Electron micrograph of purified 22-nm hepatitis B surface antigens expressed in yeast cells. (Courtesy of J.R. Pattison.)

Table 34.6 Examples of vaccination schedules in the UK and the USA

Vaccine	UK	USA
Diphtheria, tetanus, acellular pertussis	2, 3, 4 months	2, 4, 6, 15–18 months, 4–6 years
Inactivated polio vaccine	2, 3.4 months	2, 4, 6–18 months, 4–6 years
Haemophilus influenzae type b	2, 3, 4, 12–13 months	2, 4, 6, 12–15 months
Pneumococcal conjugate vaccine	2, 4, 12–15 months	2, 4, 6, 12–15 months
Meningitis C	3, 4, 12–13 months	11–12 years, 16 years
Measles, mumps and rubella	12–13 months	12–15 months, 4–6 years
Hepatitis B	Not used	0, 1–3 months, 6–18 months
Hepatitis A	Not used	12–13 months, 18–19 months
Human papillomavirus*	12–13 years	11–12 years × 3**
Varicella	Not used	12–15 months, 4–6 years
Rotavirus	Not used	2, 4, (6) months***
Influenza	From 6 months (pandemic vaccine only)	From 6 months (seasonal vaccine)

Note that the schedules and vaccines given differ. These indicative schedules are based on recommendations in April 2011; up-to-date- schedules can be found at http://www.nhs.uk/Planners/vaccinations/Pages/Vaccinationchecklist.aspx for the UK, http://www.cdc.gov/vaccines/recs/schedules/child-schedule.htm for the US and http://apps.who.int/immunization_monitoring/en/globalsummary/scheduleselect.cfm for all other countries.
*For human papillomavirus vaccine, the vaccine is routinely given to girls, but can be given to boys to prevent genital warts.
**Three doses given at 0, 1–2 months and 6 months schedule.
***Different formulations of rotavirus vaccine require 2 or 3 doses.

populations most at risk, where other factors as well as infections such as malaria and intestinal helminths may modulate the immunity they induce.

Changes in demography means new vaccine strategies are needed

In many countries, the proportion of older individuals is increasing. With age, immunity can be lost, and in particular, T-cell immunity is weakened. Hospitalizations for infections such as pneumonia and influenza in older people place a burden on health systems. One strategy is to vaccinate older individuals against these diseases – but, due to the reduced efficiency of the immune system in old age, new vaccine strategies may be needed to overcome this immunosenescence, and the World Health Organization has identified the development of effective vaccines for the elderly as a research priority for 2010–2020.

New vaccines in development

Figure 34.12 shows that if effective vaccines were developed against HIV/AIDS, malaria and tuberculosis, many lives could be saved. The development of new vaccines against tuberculosis was covered above – but what about HIV and malaria?

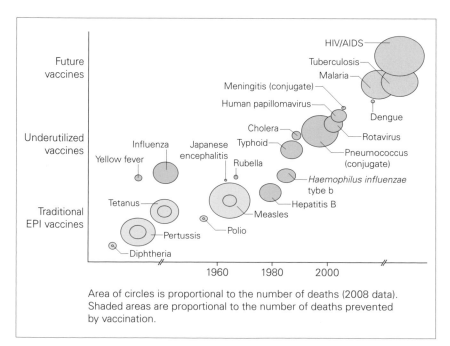

Figure 34.12 Deaths that could be averted by vaccination. Effective vaccines against HIV/AIDS, malaria and tuberculosis could save many lives, and a number of existing vaccines are underused. The area of the circles is proportional to the number of deaths in 2008, and shaded areas are proportional to the number of deaths prevented by vaccination. (Redrawn from World Health Organization. The Initiative for Vaccine Research Strategic Plan 2010-2020. http://whqlibdoc.who.int/hq/2010/WHO_IVB_10.02_eng.pdf)

Area of circles is proportional to the number of deaths (2008 data). Shaded areas are proportional to the number of deaths prevented by vaccination.

HIV vaccines

HIV has proved to be a real challenge in terms of vaccine development. Since 1987, over 30 vaccines have been tested in phase I or phase II trials, but despite all this effort, and two large-scale trials of vaccine based on the envelope gp120 protein, no effective vaccine is yet available. To date, vaccines based on recombinant Env gp120 proteins with adjuvant, HIV-1 DNA plasmids, antigens delivered by a variety of viral vectors, and varying prime-boost regimens have been tested. A trial in Thailand using a priming canary pox vaccine encoding the genes for HIV envelope, core and regulatory proteins and a boosting vaccine with recombinant gp120 showed that modest protection of 31.2% was achieved. However, a trial using a recombinant adenovirus 5 was not only not protective but seemed to increase the risk of infection in those who had antibodies to the adenovirus 5 strain before vaccination. Part of the problem is that the gp120 molecule mutates and circulating HIV viruses are highly variable; the killed virus is not sufficiently immunogenic to use as a vaccine, and the route of infection, mostly through the genital tract, means localized mucosal immunity is needed. This illustrates that despite huge advances in molecular biology and immunology, it can be difficult to design a protective vaccine. Some of the new strategies being investigated include novel antigen design strategies to induce neutralizing antibodies, and strategies to modify the body's response to infection, for example to reduce the viral load in T cells in infected individuals or to stimulate the activity of the antibody-producing B cells.

Malaria

Malaria has been another tricky disease against which to develop an effective vaccine. Most efforts have been directed against antigens expressed during the sporozoite stage in the liver, or the blood stage. There are currently 11 such vaccines in clinical development. The RTS,S vaccine based on the liver-stage circumsporozoite protein has shown 30–50% efficacy in phase II trials – in challenge studies in the USA and in field trials in Africa (Fig. 34.13), and a phase III trial is underway in Africa. In one respect, it should be possible to develop a vaccine against disease, if not against infection, as most individuals living in endemic areas develop a way of remaining well despite sometimes having circulating parasites in their blood. On the other hand, immunity is never complete in these people, and those who move away from endemic areas quickly lose this immunity. It has been suggested that a vaccine may need to induce immunity against malaria antigens that are not normally immunogenic and therefore may be under less immune pressure to change. A transmission-blocking vaccine against the sexual forms of malaria in the mosquito could also help reduce transmission.

Vaccines for neglected tropical diseases

Some infections such as leishmaniasis, leprosy, and helminth infections are described as neglected tropical diseases, neglected while most emphasis is put on HIV, malaria and TB. Schistosomiasis, leishmaniasis and trachoma are examples of neglected tropical diseases where there is no vaccine available. A vaccine against hookworm based on two key antigens is currently being developed. Leprosy also has no vaccine, but luckily the BCG vaccine has been shown to provide partial immunity to leprosy – hopefully any new TB vaccine will do even better.

New delivery systems and technologies for future vaccines

Adenoviruses are being tested as vaccine vectors, as they induce good CD8 T-cell responses. Some adenoviruses are not ideal vaccine vectors as too many individuals already have antibodies to them, which may reduce the efficacy of the vaccine. For example, although only 20% of individuals in the Netherlands have antibodies to type 5 adenovirus, this rises to 80% in sub-Saharan Africa, so some new vaccine trials are using the Ad35 strain instead, as the seroreactivity to Ad35 is lower in Africa. Delivery by MVA (see Fig. 34.10) or adenovirus is being used in the design of new vaccines for TB.

Genetic engineering can be used to make more effective vaccines. Viral recombinant vaccines are being developed as new RSV vaccines – using parainfluenza virus expressing key RSV proteins. Codon optimization can also be used, for example, for poliovirus, where reversion to virulence can be reduced by altering the codon usage.

Virus-like particles can be made that express the key viral proteins, yet are replication deficient. The latest papillomavirus vaccines are virus-like particles made from recombinant HPV coat proteins. This approach is being used for blue tongue virus vaccine for sheep, and is being considered for flu.

DNA vaccines were thought to hold great promise – but so far have not been licensed for use. They are good at priming the immune system and can induce good memory responses and TH1 responses in immunologically naive recipients.

Gentically modified or transgenic plants can be used to produce immunogens, including glycosylated proteins, and even virus-like particles. For example, the recombinant HBV vaccine could be produced in plants rather than in yeast.

New routes of vaccination

The oral polio vaccine was not the first vaccine to be given orally – the BCG vaccine was originally given by mouth. Dissolvable tablets or wafers may be used under the tongue in future. Some new work is even investigating expressing vaccine antigens in edible fruit or vegetables, such as tomatoes or lettuce!

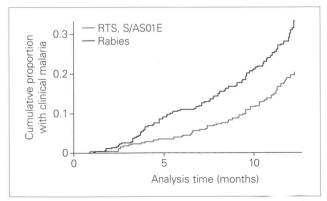

Figure 34.13 A new candidate vaccine for malaria that uses parts of the circumsporozoite protein fused to the hepatitis B surface antigen reduces the prevalence of malaria infection in young African children. Children given three doses of the RTS,S vaccine had a longer delay before they developed clinical malaria infection compared with controls given rabies vaccine. (Data from Olutu, A. et al. (2011) *Lancet Infect Dis* 11: 102–109.)

If protection is needed in the mucosal-associated lymphoid tissues, then to prime cells in this region is very sensible, and nasal sprays can be used, as in one current formulation of the seasonal flu vaccine in the USA. Another approach is to use skin patches – these deliver the vaccine antigens through the transcutaneous route. Vaccines of the future may even use nanoparticles, or be injected using dissolving microneedles, said to be relatively painless. This is clearly an area where molecular science and technological developments can make a real impact.

The Decade of Vaccines

The Bill and Melinda Gates Foundation called in 2010 for this to be the Decade of Vaccines. As a result, the World Health Organization (WHO), UNICEF, the National Institute of Allergy and Infectious Diseases (NIAID) and the Bill & Melinda Gates Foundation are collaborating to produce a Global Vaccine Action Plan. The technology to make many new vaccines is now available, but many challenges remain including how to shorten the gap between vaccine discovery and licensing, how to provide equitable access to vaccines at an affordable price, how to overcome 'vaccine hesitancy' within communities, and how to strengthen health systems so that the vaccines we have, and that work, can be fully utilized.

KEY FACTS

- Vaccination aims to prime the adaptive immune system to the antigens of a particular microbe so that a first infection induces a secondary immune response.

- Vaccines can use live attenuated organisms, killed whole organisms, subcellular fractions or antigens produced artificially by gene cloning or chemical synthesis.

- In general, live vaccines are more effective than other types, but carry the risk of reverting to virulence or inducing disease in immunocompromised patients.

- The details of vaccine choice, route, dose and risks have to be considered for each disease individually.

- Overall, vaccination is a very effective public health tool, but many challenges remain, including the effective implementation of existing vaccines worldwide and the design of new vaccines against those infections for which they are not yet available.

Passive and non-specific immunotherapy

35

An alternative to vaccination is needed for those who are already infected or are immunodeficient

The most dramatic and successful form of immunotherapy is vaccination, as described in the previous chapter. However, there are some situations where a different approach may be necessary. For instance:

- The patient may already be infected and so a more rapid build-up of immune effector mechanisms than occurs naturally may be needed.
- Alternatively, the patient's immune system may be inadequate and unable to respond either to the infection or to a vaccine, through immunodeficiency or some especially resistant property of the parasite.

This chapter deals with such situations.

PASSIVE IMMUNIZATION WITH ANTIBODY

Certain diseases are treated by a passive transfer of immunity, which can be life-saving

Before the introduction of antibiotics, acute infectious diseases were often treated by the injection of preformed antibody on the principle that the patient was already ill and it was too late for 'active' vaccination. Indeed, the demonstration that immunity to tetanus and diphtheria could be transferred to mice with serum from vaccinated rabbits was a key experiment in the discovery of antibody in the 1890s. Subsequently, the production of antiserum for the passive treatment of diphtheria, tetanus and pneumococcal pneumonia, and against the toxic effects of streptococci and staphylococci, became an important industry, and generations of horses that had retired from active duty were kept on as the source of 'immune serum'. The introduction of antitetanus serum in the early months of the First World War reduced the incidence of tetanus dramatically by up to 30-fold (Fig. 35.1).

The advent of penicillin and other antibiotics has, of course, changed the picture considerably, and passive immunotherapy is now used for only a select group of diseases (Table 35.1). The serum may be specific or non-specific and of human or animal origin.

The use of antiserum raised in animals can cause serum sickness

The use of antiserum raised in horses or rabbits has largely been abandoned because of the complications resulting from the immune response to the antibody, which is of course a foreign protein. These include progressively more rapid elimination (and therefore reduced clinical effectiveness) and, more seriously, serum sickness due to immune complex deposition in, for example, the kidney and skin (see Ch. 17), and even anaphylaxis. These complications can be avoided by using human serum taken during convalescence or following vaccination – to prevent infection after exposure (e.g. rabies) or to minimize its severity (e.g. varicella in immunodeficient children).

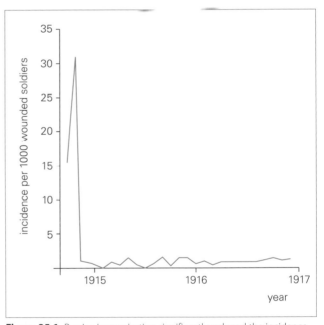

Figure 35.1 Passive immunization significantly reduced the incidence of tetanus in the early months of the First World War. The figure shows the incidence of tetanus per 1000 wounded soldiers in British hospitals during 1914–1916. There was a dramatic fall after the introduction of antitetanus serum in October 1914.

Antibody in pooled normal serum can provide protection against infection

With common infections, it can be assumed that most normal people have antibody to the pathogen in their serum. The clearest proof of this is that patients with hypogammaglobulinaemia can be kept free of recurrent infection by regular injections of IgG from pooled normal serum, and that immunodeficient children can be protected against measles in the same way (Box 35.1). Immunoglobulin is prepared from batches of plasma from 1000–6000 healthy donors after screening for hepatitis B and C and HIV. With improvements

Table 35.1 Specific passive immunotherapy with antibody

Infection	Source of antibody	Indication
Diphtheria	Human, horse	Prophylaxis, treatment
Tetanus	Human, horse	
Varicella-zoster	Human	Prophylaxis in immunodeficiencies
Gas gangrene	Horse	Post-exposure
Botulism		
Snake bite		
Scorpion bite		
Rabies	Human	Post exposure (plus vaccine)
Hepatitis B	Human	Post-exposure
Hepatitis A	Pooled human immunoglobulin	Prophylaxis (travel)
Measles		Post-exposure

Although not so commonly used as 50 years ago, passive injections of specific antibody can still be a life-saving treatment.

Box 35.1 📱 **Indications for Normal Immunoglobulin Therapy**

Sufficient antibody to protect immunocompromised patients against common infections can be obtained from pooled normal human plasma.

- X-linked agammaglobulinaemia/hypogammaglobulinaemia
- Common variable deficiency
- Wiskott–Aldrich syndrome
- Ataxia telangiectasia
- IgG subclass deficiency with impaired antibody response
- Chronic lymphocytic leukaemia
- Post-bone marrow transplantation (for CMV pneumonitis)

CMV, cytomegalovirus.

---

in methods of preparation, intravenous injection is now preferred to intramuscular injection in most cases. Dosages for this type of therapy range from 100 to 400 mg IgG/kg per month.

In healthy individuals the probability of contracting hepatitis A in an endemic area is enormously reduced by a single injection of as little as 5 mL of IgG. The immunity conferred by mothers on their newborn infants by placental transfer of IgG and subsequently by colostral IgA (though the latter is not absorbed, but remains in the intestine) is further evidence for the protective effect of relatively small amounts of antibody.

Theoretically, the most effective therapy is provided by one or more monoclonal antibodies specific for a known target antigen

In practice, a mixture of several monoclonal antibodies mimicking just the relevant clones in a polyclonal serum might be required in situations where individual antigens are

expressed in low quantities on the microbe or where binding to more than one epitope is required for full effectiveness. We have previously described the derivation of mouse monoclonal antibodies, but a serious complication is that they are highly immunogenic in humans and give rise to human anti-mouse antibodies (HAMA) which accelerate clearance of the monoclonal from the blood and possibly cause hypersensitivity reactions; they also prevent the mouse antibody from reaching its target and, in some cases, block its binding to antigen. Logic points to removal of the xenogeneic (foreign) portions of the monoclonal antibody and their replacement by human Ig structures using recombinant DNA technology. One refined approach is to graft the six complementarity determining regions (CDR) of a high-affinity rodent monoclonal onto a completely human Ig framework without loss of specific reactivity (Fig. 35.2). This is not a trivial exercise, however, and the objective of fusing human B cells to make hybridomas is still appealing, taking into account not only the gross reduction in immunogenicity but also the fact that, within a species, antibodies can be made to subtle differences such as major histocompatibility complex (MHC) polymorphic molecules and tumour-associated antigens on other individuals, whereas xenogeneic responses are more directed to immunodominant structures common to most subjects. Notwithstanding the difficulties in finding good fusion partners, large numbers of human monoclonals have been established.

A radically different approach involves the production of transgenic XenoMouse strains in which megabase size unrearranged human Ig H and κ light chain loci have been introduced into mice whose endogenous murine Ig genes have been inactivated. Immunization of these mice yields high-affinity (10^{-10}–10^{-11}M) human antibodies which can then be isolated using hybridoma or recombinant approaches. Potent anti-inflammatory (anti-IL-8) and antitumor

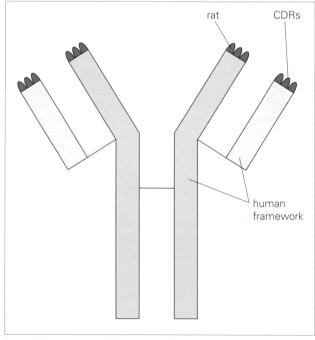

Figure 35.2 Grafting of all six rat complementarity determining regions (CDRs) onto a human Ig framework to create a 'humanized' rat monoclonal antibody.

(anti-epidermal growth factor receptor) therapeutic agents have already been obtained using such mice. There is still a snag in that even human antibodies can provoke anti-idiotype responses; these may have to be circumvented by using engineered antibodies bearing different idiotypes for subsequent injections. Many human monoclonals are being evaluated for clinical use; one can cite IgG anti-RhD for the prevention of rhesus disease of the newborn, and highly potent monoclonals for protection against varicella-zoster, cytomegalovirus, group B streptococci and lipopolysaccharide endotoxins of Gram-negative bacteria.

Not only can the genes for a monoclonal antibody be engineered for expression in bulk in the milk of lactating animals but plants can also be exploited for this purpose, even producing secretory IgA. So-called 'plantibodies' have been expressed in bananas, potatoes and tobacco plants. Just imagine a high-tech farmer with one field growing antitetanus toxoid, another antimeningococcal polysaccharide, and so on – the very stuff of science fiction!

Engineering antibodies

Bacteriophage libraries provide an invaluable technology for engineering new antibody fragments

There are other ways around the problems associated with the production of human monoclonals which exploit the wiles of modern molecular biology. Reference has already been made to the 'humanizing' of rodent antibodies, but an important new strategy based upon bacteriophage expression and *selection* has achieved a prominent position. In essence, mRNA, preferably from primed human B cells, is converted to cDNA, and the antibody genes, or fragments therefrom, are expanded by the polymerase chain reaction (PCR). Single constructs are then made in which the light and heavy chain genes are allowed to combine randomly as *Fab* or single chain *Fv* (scFv) fragments in tandem with the bacteriophage coat protein gene (Fig. 35.3). This *combinatorial library* encodes a huge repertoire of antibody fragments expressed as fusion proteins with a filamentous coat protein on the bacteriophage surface. The extremely high number of phages produced by *Escherichia coli* infection can now be panned on solid-phase antigen to select those bearing the highest-affinity antibodies attached to their surface (Fig. 35.3). Because the genes which encode these highest-affinity antibodies are already present within the selected phage, they can readily be cloned and the antibody fragment expressed in bulk.

It should be recognized that this selection procedure has an enormous advantage over techniques which employ *screening*, because the number of phages which can be examined is several logs higher. Although a 'test-tube' operation, this approach to the generation of specific antibodies does resemble the affinity maturation of the immune response in vivo in the sense that antigen is the determining factor in selecting out the highest-affinity responders. In order to increase the affinities of antibodies produced by these techniques, antigen can be used to select higher-affinity mutants produced by random mutagenesis (or even more effectively by site-directed replacements at mutational hot spots), again mimicking the natural immune response which involves random mutation and antigen selection.

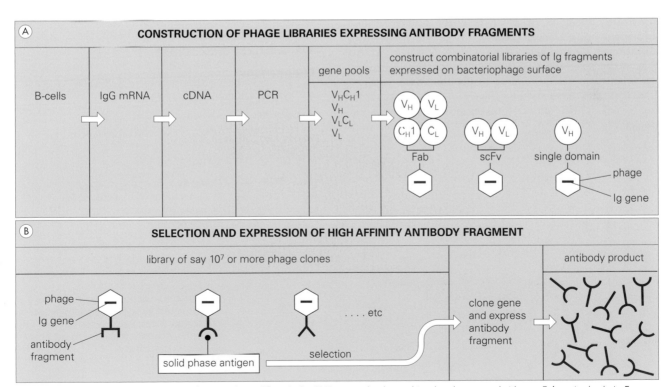

Figure 35.3 Pools of genes encoding Ig domains derived from IgG mRNA are randomly combined and expressed either as *Fab* or single chain *Fv* (scFv) fragments on the surface of the bacteriophage. Libraries expressing single domains of the heavy chain variable region (V$_H$) (human or llama, usually) can also be constructed. Phage clones containing genes encoding high-affinity antibody fragments can be selected from these extremely large libraries using solid-phase antigen. The appropriate Ig genes can then be cloned and expressed in suitable vectors to produce abundant antibody fragments.

Single domain variable region fragments have several advantages

Phage libraries have been created which express just single heavy or light chain variable region domains (V_H or V_L dAbs). When selected from large naive human phage libraries and fine-tuned by random mutation and further selection, dAbs of surprisingly high affinity, sometimes in the low nanomolar range, can be obtained, clearly without the need for prior immunization. Camelids are immunologically curious in that one half of their antibodies are conventionally composed of heavy and light chains but the other half are just heavy chains, albeit with unusual CDRs which can subserve high-affinity interactions with antigen. Thus a parallel technology has developed in which high-affinity V_{HH} (variable domains from heavy chain antibodies) have been selected from immunized llamas.

Both human and llama V_H dAbs have several advantages. They are easy to engineer in bulk cheaply, they can readily be custom-tailored by molecular biological manipulations, they are small and robust in their ability to withstand variations in temperature and acidity, making them relatively insensitive to environmental conditions and the need for refrigeration, and permitting their use for oral therapy and for repeated affinity chromatographic purification of antigens. Another advantage is their low immunogenicity.

Antibody fragments lacking the Fc structures required for secondary activity obviously will not provide protection where complement fixation, phagocytic uptake or extracellular killing is required to eliminate a pathogen. Where they are effective is in blocking cognate enzyme–substrate, hormone or toxin–receptor and microbial addressin–epithelial cell receptor interactions. The latter situation is particularly relevant to mucosal infections where specific adherence to a cognate epithelial receptor is an essential initial step in the infectious process. Initial studies have shown efficacy of dAbs in preventing experimental rotavirus infection and vaginal candidiasis (Fig. 35.4).

NON-SPECIFIC CELLULAR IMMUNOSTIMULATION

Cytokines and other molecular mediators stimulate the immune system

The demonstration by William Coley almost one century ago that crude extracts of bacteria could induce remission and sometimes cure cancers indicated the extent to which the immune system can be non-specifically 'overstimulated', with potentially beneficial results. Until recently, many of the compounds used in this way have been of microbial origin, but current interest is directed mainly at cytokines and other molecular mediators, on the principle that their induction was probably the basis of action of the older crude materials (Box 35.2).

Most of the applications of this type of immunostimulation have been in the tumour field, but some infectious diseases respond to treatment with cytokines (Table 35.2). Foremost among these are the interferons (IFNs), notably

---

Box 35.2 📱 **Non-specific Immunostimulators**

A variety of foreign and endogenous materials have been used in an attempt to raise the general level of immunologic competence.

Microbial

- Coley's toxin (filtered cultures of *Streptococci* and *Serratia marcescens* used against tumours)
- BCG (bacillus Calmette–Guérin)
- Corynebacterium parvum
- Endotoxin (lipopolysaccharide)
- Streptococcal-derived OK432

Endogenous

- Thymus factors and hormones
- Cytokines

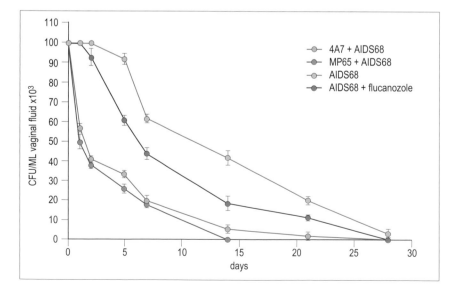

Figure 35.4 Protective activity of an anti-Sap2 (4A7) and an anti-MP65 human variable region single domain antibody (dAb) against rat vaginal infection by a *C. albicans* fluconazole-resistant strain (AIDS 68). Five rats per group were used. Each animal was administered intravaginally 20 μg of each dAb 30 min before intravaginal challenge with 10^7 fungal cells. Fluconazole was used as a single intravaginal dose of 50 μg, 30 min before challenge. Irrelevant dAbs were not protective. Efficacy in protection against infection paralleled the ability of the dAb to inhibit the adherence of *Candida* to cultures of epithelial cells. (Courtesy of F. de Bernadis, and A. Cassone et al.).

Table 35.2 Potentially therapeutic cytokines and their antagonists

IFNα, IFNβ	Hepatitis B (chronic) Hepatitis C Herpes zoster Papillomavirus Rhinovirus (prophylactic only) HIV Warts
IFNγ	Lepromatous leprosy Leishmaniasis Toxoplasmosis (brain) Chronic granulomatous disease
IL-2	Leprosy (local treatment to skin lesions)
IL-10, TGFβ	Septic shock
CSFs	Bacterial infection due to neutropenia in irradiated patients
Anti-TNF	Septic shock
IL-1 receptor antagonist	Septic shock

Cytokines are increasingly used to improve immunity to infection as well as for some cancers and haematologic disorders. CSFs, colony stimulating factors; IFN, interferon; IL, interleukin; TGF, transforming growth factor; TNF, tumour necrosis factor

IFNα, which is effective in a number of virus infections, though less than might have been predicted from the importance of its normal role in inhibiting viral replication. IFNγ has recently been found to benefit many cases of chronic granulomatous disease (CGD), though the mechanism is unclear. The unpleasant side effects of high-dose therapy with interleukins or IFNs restrict their casual use (Table 35.3).

There is an interesting 'grey area' where immunostimulation and nutrition overlap

It has been claimed for many years that transfer factor (TF), a dialysed extract of peripheral leukocytes from normal patients, will restore T-cell responses in unresponsive recipients, and some dramatic cures (e.g. of chronic mucocutaneous candidiasis) have been reported. Whether this restoration is antigen specific or non-specific has been the subject of great controversy, and in the absence of proper molecular characterization, TF is no longer regarded as an orthodox treatment.

Equally unorthodox, but attracting increasing attention, are a variety of plant products (e.g. saponins, ginseng,

Table 35.3 Some common side effects of cytokine therapy

Interferons	Fever
	Malaise
	Fatigue
	Muscle pains
	Toxicity to:
	    Kidney
	    Liver
	    Bone marrow
	    Heart

IL-2	Vascular leak syndrome
	    Hypotension
	    Oedema
	    Ascites
	    Pulmonary oedema
	    Renal failure
	    Hepatic failure
	Mental changes; coma

Treatment with cytokines, especially if prolonged, can lead to serious side effects. IL, interleukin.

Chinese herbal remedies). These substances appear to improve resistance to infection and in some cases also act as adjuvants when combined with vaccines, but the complexity and variability of the extracts makes the active components difficult to track down.

CORRECTION OF HOST IMMUNODEFICIENCY

Antibody defects are the easiest to treat

This subject is discussed in more detail in Chapter 30, and will only be briefly summarized here:

- Antibody defects are the easiest to treat, since immunoglobulin can be transferred and has a reasonably long half-life (about 3 weeks for IgG).
- Treatment of T-cell defects is more difficult, though thymus or bone marrow grafting has been tried in certain cases with some success (Table 35.4).
- Phagocytic defects are the most difficult to correct, and in practice antibiotics remain the mainstay of therapy, though the future may lie in gene replacement.

Gene defects have recently been identified in certain serious immunodeficiency diseases including hyper-IgM syndrome, CGD and Bruton's agammaglobulinaemia.

Table 35.4 Treatment of immunodeficiency: an overview

	B-cell defects	T-cell defects	Phagocytes defects	Complement defects
Correction of defect	Bone marrow graft (SCID)	Thymus graft (DiGeorge)	?Bone marrow graft (CGD)	
Replacement therapy	Pooled normal IgG Specific IgG	Blood transfusion (ADA, PNP deficiency)	Blood transfusion	Not successful
Symptomatic therapy	Antibodies	Antivirals	Antibiotics	Antibiotics Steroids (for immune complex disease)

The treatment of immunodeficiency depends upon knowledge of the element at fault, some being more easily restored than others. ADA, adenosine deaminase; CGD, chronic granulomatous disease; PNP, purine nucleoside phosphorylase; SCID, severe combined immunodeficiency.

PROBIOTICS

Probiotics are dietary supplements containing potentially beneficial bacteria or yeast of which lactic acid bacteria are the most common microbes used. The gut flora can be thrown out of balance by a wide range of circumstances including the use of antibiotics or other drugs, excess alcohol, stress, disease, exposure to toxic substances or even the use of antibacterial soap. In cases like these, the 'friendly' bacteria, which work well with our bodies, may decrease in number, so allowing harmful competitors to thrive to the detriment of our health. Probiotic bacterial cultures are intended to assist the body's naturally occurring flora within the digestive tract to re-establish themselves. They are sometimes recommended by doctors, and more frequently by nutritionists, after a course of antibiotics or as part of the treatment for candidiasis. Many probiotics are present in natural sources such as yoghurt, commonly used microbes being *Lactobacillus acidophilus* and *Bifidobacterium bifidum*.

A range of potentially beneficial medicinal uses for probiotics have been explored and these include managing lactose intolerance, prevention of colon cancer, cholesterol lowering, improving immune function and preventing infections, and reducing inflammation. It is also possible to increase and maintain a healthy gut flora by increasing the amounts of prebiotics in the diet, such as inulin, raw oats and unrefined wheat; a combination of the two should prove to be synergistic since prebiotics are only effective in the large intestine, whereas probiotics exert their influence in the small bowel. It must be said that robust evidence to support these claims is still being acquired.

KEY FACTS

- Transfer of normal pooled IgG is the most widely practised type of passive immunotherapy and is used to treat most forms of antibody deficiency.

- Specific antibodies can be used for certain defined conditions. Such antibodies can be produced as mouse or human monoclonals, as rodent complementarity determining regions (CDRs) grafted onto a human Ig framework.

- Antibodies can be engineered for expression in bulk in conventional vectors in vitro, or in vivo in the milk of lactating animals or in plants.

- Fab, single chain Fv (scFv) or heavy chain variable region domain fragments can be selected by antigen from expression libraries of bacteriophages bearing the antibody fragments as a surface protein.

- These fragments are effective in blocking cognate interactions such as microbial addressin adherence to mucosal epithelial cells as a precursor to invasion. Single domain human and llama variable region antibody fragments are robust and have several advantages.

- Non-specific stimulation of T-cell-mediated immunity is still experimental, but cytokines show some promise, particularly IFN for viral infections.

Hospital infection, sterilization and disinfection

36

Introduction

Infections associated with healthcare settings are an increasingly complex issue

Amassing sick people together under one roof has many advantages, but some disadvantages, notably the easier transmission of infection from one person to another. In the past, the major environment for this interaction has been the hospital, which led to the term nosocomial infection (i.e. any infection acquired while in hospital). Increasing numbers of individuals in skilled nursing and homecare settings have prompted the more recent use of the term healthcare-associated infections (HAI). Nevertheless, hospitals remain the major environment associated with HAI. Hospital infection is generally defined as any infection acquired while in hospital (e.g. occurring 48 h or more after admission and up to 48 h after discharge). Most of these infections become obvious while the patient is in hospital, but some (e.g. postoperative wound infections) may not be recognized until after the patient has been discharged. Earlier discharges, encouraged to reduce costs, contribute to these unrecognized infections, although a shorter preoperative stay reduces the chance of acquiring hospital pathogens (see below).

Healthcare-associated infection may be acquired from:

- an exogenous source (e.g. from another patient – cross-infection – or from the environment)
- an endogenous source (i.e. another site within the patient – self- or auto-infection) (Fig. 36.1).

An infection that is incubating in a patient when he or she is admitted into hospital is not a hospital infection. However, community-acquired infections brought into hospital by the patient may subsequently become hospital infections for other patients and hospital staff.

Many hospital infections are preventable

In 1850, Semmelweiss demonstrated that many hospital infections are preventable when he made the unpopular suggestion that puerperal fever (an infection in women who have just given birth, see Ch. 23) was carried on the hands of physicians who came directly from attending an autopsy to the delivery ward, without washing. A death rate of 8.3% was reduced to 2.3% by introducing the simple measure of handwashing before and after any clinical examination. Recent studies in the USA suggest that about one-third of all infections acquired in hospital can be prevented. Current US estimates place HAI costs associated with hospital infection at approximately 2 million infections leading to nearly 100 000 deaths at a cost of US$4–5 billion annually.

COMMON HOSPITAL INFECTIONS

Urinary tract infections are the most common hospital infections in adults

The infections most commonly acquired in hospitals are:

- surgical wound infection
- respiratory tract infection
- urinary tract infection (UTI)
- bacteraemia.

The relative frequencies of these infections are illustrated in Figure 36.2. Each may be acquired from an exogenous or endogenous source, and even the 'self-source' may be derived from outside by the patient who becomes colonized with pathogens during his or her stay in hospital. Bacteraemia may arise from a variety of sources and may be:

- primary – due to the direct introduction of organisms into the blood from, for example, contaminated intravenous fluids
- secondary to a focus of infection already present in the body (e.g. UTI).

Other infections that may cause outbreaks in the hospital setting include gastroenteritis and hepatitis.

IMPORTANT CAUSES OF HOSPITAL INFECTION

Staphylococci and *Escherichia coli* are the most important Gram-positive and Gram-negative causes of infection, respectively, in hospitals

Almost any microbe can cause a hospital infection, though protozoal infections are rare. The pattern of hospital infection has changed over the years, reflecting advances in medicine and the development of antimicrobial agents. In the pre-antibiotic era, the majority of infections were caused by Gram-positive organisms, particularly *Streptococcus pyogenes* and *Staphylococcus aureus*. With the advent of penicillin and other antibiotics active against staphylococci, Gram-negative organisms such as *Escherichia coli* and *Pseudomonas aeruginosa*

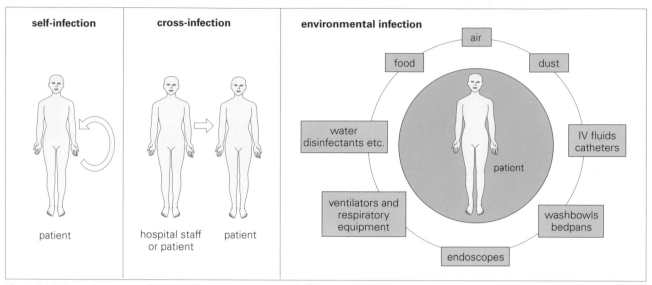

Figure 36.1 Hospital-acquired infection can be endogenous (i.e. self-infection from another site in the body) or exogenous (i.e. from another person or from an environmental source). The sorts of organisms acquired from environmental sources depend upon the nature of the source, e.g. moist areas tend to be colonized with Gram-negative rods (e.g. *E. coli*, *Klebsiella*, *Pseudomonas*) whereas air- and dust-borne organisms are those that can withstand drying (e.g. *streptococci*, *staphylococci*, *mycobacteria* and *Acinetobacter*). I, intravenous.

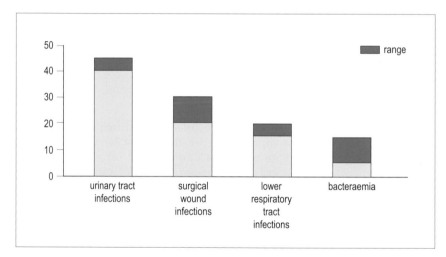

Figure 36.2 The relative frequencies of different kinds of hospital infection vary in different patient groups, but urinary tract infections are the most common hospital-acquired infections.

emerged as important pathogens. More recently, the development of more potent and broad-spectrum antimicrobials and the increase in invasive medical techniques has been accompanied by an increase in the incidence of:

- antibiotic-resistant Gram-positive organisms such as coagulase-negative staphylococci, enterococci (especially those resistant to vancomycin; VRE) and methicillin-resistant *Staph. aureus* (MRSA)
- multidrug-resistant Gram-negative organisms including those producing expanded-spectrum beta-lactamases (ESBLs, see Ch. 33)
- *Candida*.

Many of these organisms are considered as 'opportunists' – microbes that are unable to cause disease in healthy people with intact defence mechanisms, but that can cause infection in compromised patients or when introduced during the course of invasive procedures. Currently, coagulase-negative staphylococci, *Staphylococcus aureus*, and enterococci account overall for most healthcare-associated infections (Box 36.1).

Some infections historically associated with hospitals are now increasingly seen outside of the healthcare setting

Recent reports in numerous countries have documented the emergence of virulent MRSA strains causing infection in individuals outside of the healthcare system. These community-associated MRSA (CA-MRSA) can be transported into the healthcare environment, thus blurring the distinction between community-associated and healthcare-associated infection. This has prompted guidelines for differentiating the increasing number of CA-MRSA infections from those associated with healthcare, summarized in Box 36.2.

Box 36.1 **Order of Pathogen Importance**

The general rank order of pathogen importance is listed for the different infection categories. Although a few species are the most important in all kinds of hospital infection, predominant pathogens vary in different infections. *Staphylococcus aureus* is very important in surgical wound infections and bacteraemia, but much less important in urinary tract infections. The importance of Gram-negative rods has increased since the advent of broad-spectrum antibiotics because these organisms often carry multiple antibiotic resistances.

Urinary tract infections

- *E. coli*
- *Candida*
- Enterococci
- other Gram-negatives (e.g., *P. aeruginosa, K. pneumoniae, Enterobacter* spp.)

Surgical wound infections

- Staphylococci (*Staph. aureus* and coagulase-negative)
- Enterococci
- *E. coli, P. aeruginosa* (other Gram-negatives to a lesser extent)

Lower respiratory tract infections

- *Staph. aureus*
- *P. aeruginosa* (other Gram-negatives to a lesser extent)

Bacteraemia

- Staphylococci (*Staph. aureus* and coagulase-negative)
- Enterococci
- *Candida*
- *K. pneumoniae* (other Gram-negatives to a lesser extent)

Box 36.2 **Criteria for Distinguishing Community-Associated MRSA (CA-MRSA) From Healthcare (Including Hospital)-Associated MRSA (HA-MRSA)**

Individuals with MRSA infections that meet all of the following criteria likely have CA-MRSA infections:

- Diagnosis of MRSA was made in the outpatient setting or by a culture positive for MRSA within 48 h after admission to the hospital
- No medical history of MRSA infection or colonization
- No medical history in the past year of:
  - Hospitalization

- Admission to a nursing home, skilled nursing facility, or hospice
- Dialysis
- Surgery

- No permanent indwelling catheters or medical devices that pass through the skin

---

Viral infections probably account for more hospital infections than previously realized

These affect both patients and healthcare workers and include:

- viruses acquired by the respiratory route, especially influenza, respiratory syncytial virus (RSV), parainfluenza, varicella-zoster virus (VZV); this may also include some of the viral causes of gastroenteritis
- viruses acquired by contact with vesicular lesions such as VZV and herpes simplex virus (HSV)
- viruses acquired by contact with contaminated fomites such as noroviruses and rotavirus
- viruses acquired by contact with blood-contaminated fomites, needlestick injury or splash on mucous membranes, such as hepatitis B virus (HBV), hepatitis C virus (HCV), HIV and human T-cell lymphotropic virus (HTLV). These may also be acquired in countries where blood and blood products are not screened or in the rare instance where the blood donor was in the early incubation period of infection, thereby escaping detection by the screening assay. The latter is referred to

as the window period and may be missed even if a viral genome detection method is used.

The risks of viral infections in hospital are summarized in Table 36.1.

SOURCES AND ROUTES OF SPREAD OF HOSPITAL INFECTION

Sources of hospital infection are people and contaminated objects

As stated above, the source of infection may be:

- *human* from other patients or hospital staff, and occasionally visitors
- *environmental* from contaminated objects ('fomites'), food, water or air (see Fig. 36.1).

The source may become contaminated from an environmental reservoir of organisms, for example, contaminated antiseptic solution distributed for use into sterile containers (Fig. 36.3). Eradication of the source will also require eradication of the reservoir.

Table 36.1 Examples of viruses causing hospital-acquired infection

Virus	Transmissibility	Susceptibility of other patients and staff	Resultant risk of hospital infection
Influenza	+ +	+ / − [a]	+ +
Respiratory syncytial virus	+ +	+ + [a]	+ +
Parainfluenza, adenovirus, rhinovirus	+	+ [a]	+
Varicella-zoster	+ +	− [a]	−
Cytomegalovirus	−	+	− −
Rubella	+ +	+ [b]	+ +
Measles	+ +	− −	− −
Rotavirus	+ +	+	+
Norovirus	+	+	+
Hepatitis A	+	+	+
Hepatitis B	+ + [d]	+ +	+ +
HIV (in countries where not screened)	+ + [e]	+ +	+ +
Hepatitis C	+ [d]	+ +	+ +

Viruses are probably more important causes of hospital infection than generally recognized. The risk of hospital infection is a sum of the transmissibility of the virus and the susceptibility of the patient group. Some viruses, such as varicella-zoster, are of low risk in general, but very important in paediatric units and particularly in immunocompromised children.
[a]High in paediatric age group.
[b]Decreased since immunization programme initiated.
[c]Except for blood transfusion and organ transplantation.
[d]From needlestick injuries and other exposure incidents.
[e]From blood or blood product.

Human sources may be:

- people who are themselves infected
- people who are incubating an infection
- healthy carriers.

The time period for which a human source is infectious varies with the disease (see Ch. 31). For example, some infections can be spread during their incubation period, others in the early stages of clinical disease, while others are characterized by a prolonged carrier state even after clinical cure (e.g. typhoid fever) (Fig. 36.4). Carriers of virulent strains of, e.g. *Staph. aureus* or *Strep. pyogenes*, may act as sources of hospital infection, although they themselves do not develop clinical disease. The carrier state may persist for a long time and go unnoticed unless there is an outbreak or, depending on the significance of the organism, a single case of infection that is traced to the carrier, e.g. a healthcare worker with chronic hepatitis B.

Hospital infections are spread in the air and by contact and common vehicle

The important routes of spread of infection in hospitals are those common to all infections: airborne, contact and common vehicle. Examples of organisms spread by these routes in hospitals are illustrated in Figure 36.3. Although theoretically possible, vector-borne spread is very unusual in the hospital setting, as is sexually transmitted infection. It is important to remember that the same organism may be spread by more than one route. For example, *Strep. pyogenes* can be spread from patient to patient by the airborne route in droplets or dust, but is also transmitted by contact with

infected lesions, for example on a nurse's hand. In addition, a patient or healthcare worker with shingles can transmit VZV to a susceptible person having direct contact with rash blisters.

HOST FACTORS AND HOSPITAL INFECTION

Underlying disease, certain treatments and invasive procedures reduce host defences

Host factors play a fundamental role in the infection equation, particularly in hospitals because of the high proportion of hospital patients with compromised natural defences against infection. The spread of an infectious agent to a new host can result in a spectrum of responses: from colonization, through subclinical infection, to clinically apparent disease, which may be fatal. The degree of host response differs in different people depending upon their degree of compromise. The very young are particularly susceptible because of the immaturity of their immune system. Likewise, the elderly suffer a greater risk of infection because of predisposing underlying disease, impaired blood supply and immobility, which contribute to stasis and therefore to infection in, for example, the lungs. In all age groups, underlying disease and the treatment of that disease (e.g. cytotoxic drugs, steroids) may predispose to infection (Fig. 36.5), while invasive procedures allow organisms easier access to previously protected tissues (Fig. 36.6). The important host factors to be considered in hospital infection are summarized in Table 36.2. Infections in the compromised host are discussed in more detail in Chapter 30.

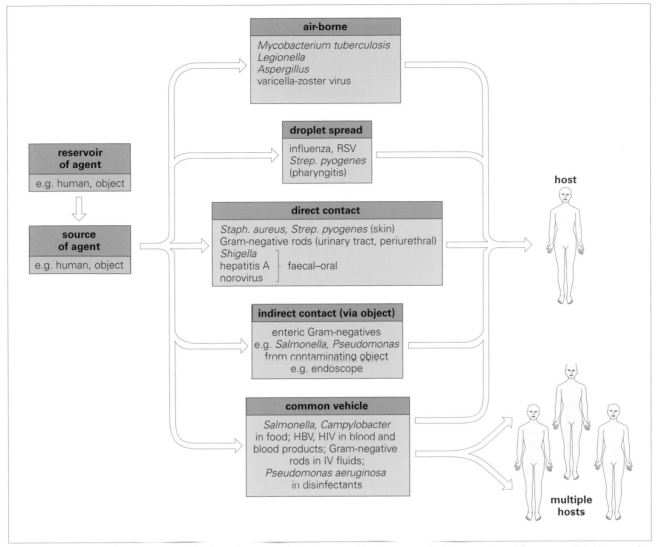

Figure 36.3 Hospital infections are spread by the same routes as infections spread in the community. The reservoir and the source of infection may be human or inanimate and may be one and the same (e.g. a nurse with an infected skin lesion). If the reservoir and source are distinct (e.g. contaminated distilled water supply used to prepare a variety of pharmaceuticals), both must be eliminated if the spread of infection is to be halted, otherwise the reservoir may continue to contaminate new sources. HBV, hepatitis B virus; IV, intravenous; RSV, respiratory syncytial virus.

A variety of factors predispose to wound infection

Wound infection or wound sepsis is characterized by the presence of inflammation, pus and discharge in addition to the isolation of organisms such as *Staph. aureus*. Extensive studies of postoperative wound infection have identified a number of predisposing factors:

- Prolonged preoperative stay increases the opportunity for the patient to become colonized with antibiotic-resistant hospital pathogens.
- The nature and length of the operation also have an effect (Table 36.3 and Fig. 36.7; see also Ch. 26).
- Wet or open wounds are more liable to secondary infection.

From these studies, it has been possible to identify the patients and operations with greatest risk and apply preventive measures such as prophylactic antibiotic regimens and ultra-clean air in orthopaedic operating theatres (see below).

CONSEQUENCES OF HOSPITAL INFECTION

Hospital infections affect both the patient and the community

Hospital infection may result in:

- serious illness or death
- prolonged hospital stay, which costs money and results in a loss of earnings and hardship for the patient and his or her family
- a need for additional antimicrobial therapy, which is costly, exposes the patient to additional risks of toxicity, and increases selective pressure for resistance to emerge among hospital pathogens
- the infected patient becoming a source from which others may become infected, in hospital and in the community.

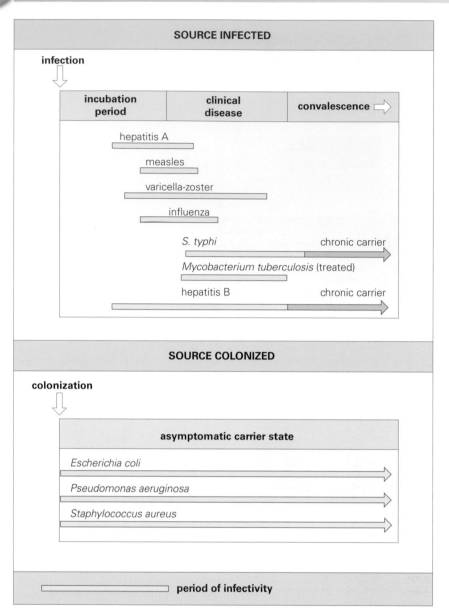

Figure 36.4 Pathogens differ in the time periods for which they can be disseminated from an infected person. For some, it is during the incubation period when infected people may not realize they are ill and infectious. Some people continue to carry organisms such as *Salmonella typhi* and hepatitis B virus long after they have recovered from the clinical disease. Opportunist pathogens are often members of the normal flora and may therefore be carried for long periods without the host experiencing any adverse effects.

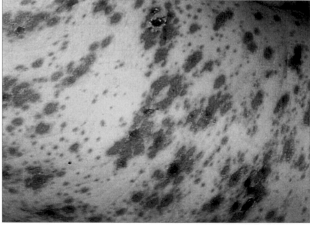

Figure 36.5 Varicella in a patient with chronic myeloid leukaemia resulting in purpuric confluent lesions on the trunk. (Courtesy of G.D.W. McKendrick.)

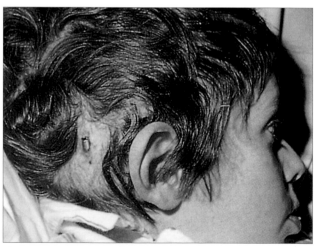

Figure 36.6 Child with infected Spitz–Holter valve used to relieve hydrocephalus. (Courtesy of J.A. Innes.)

Table 36.2 Factors which predispose patients to hospital infection

Age	Patients at extremes of age are particularly susceptible
Specific immunity	Patient may lack protective antibodies to, e.g. measles, chickenpox, whooping cough
Underlying disease	Other (non-infectious) diseases tend to lead to enhanced susceptibility to infection, e.g. hepatic disease, diabetes, cancer, skin disorders, renal failure, neutropenia (either as a result of disease or of treatment)
Other infections	HIV and other immunosuppressing virus infections; patients with influenza prone to secondary bacterial pneumonia; herpes virus lesions may become secondarily infected with staphylococci
Specific medicaments	Cytotoxic drugs (including post-transplant immunosuppression) and steroids both lower host defences; antibiotics disturb normal flora and predispose to invasion by resistant hospital pathogens

Trauma
  Accidental
 	
  Intentional
	Burns, stab or gunshot wounds, road traffic accidents
	Surgery, intravenous and urinary catheters, peritoneal dialysis } Disturb natural/host defence mechanisms

Hospital patients are not all at equal risk of infection. Some factors that predispose to infection can be influenced by, e.g. treating underlying disease, improving specific immunity and avoiding inappropriate use of antibiotics. Other factors such as age are unalterable.

Table 36.3 Risk factors for postoperative infections

Length of preoperative stay	Longer stay – more likely to become colonized with virulent and antibiotic-resistant hospital bacteria and fungi
Presence of intercurrent infection	Operating on an already infected site more likely to cause disseminated infection
Length of operation	Longer – greater risk of tissues becoming seeded with organisms from air, staff, other sites in patient
Nature of operation	Any operation which results in faecal soiling of tissues has higher risk of infection (e.g. postoperative gangrene), 'adventurous' surgery tends to carry greater risks
Presence of foreign bodies	For example, shunts, prostheses, impairs host defences
State of tissues	Poor blood supply encourages growth of anaerobes; inadequate drainage or presence of necrotic tissue predisposes to infection

The risks of infection after surgery have been studied in considerable detail, and surgeons are consequently much more aware of the problems. However, 'high-tech' surgery is often long and difficult and predisposes the patient to postoperative infection.

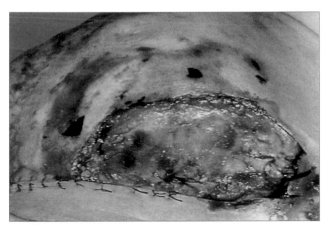

Figure 36.7 Postoperative gangrenous cellulitis. There is a huge area of ulceration filled with gangrenous skin, with sloughing adjacent to the wound and surrounding cellulitis. (Courtesy of M.J. Wood.)

PREVENTION OF HOSPITAL INFECTION

There are three main strategies for preventing hospital infection

For the reasons outlined above, the prevention of hospital infection deserves a very high priority, and the three main strategies are:

- excluding sources of infection from the hospital environment
- interrupting the transmission of infection from source to susceptible host (breaking the chain of infection)
- enhancing the host's ability to resist infection.

Exclusion of sources of infection

Exclusion of inanimate sources of infection is achievable, but it can be difficult to avoid contamination by humans

Exclusion of inanimate sources of infection is both desirable and, to a large extent, achievable. For example, the provision of sterile instruments and dressings, sterile medicaments and intravenous fluids, clean linen and uncontaminated food, and the use of blood and blood products screened for infectious agents. However, many of the sources of infection are human or are objects that become contaminated by humans, in which case exclusion is more difficult. Hospitals must attempt to prevent patient contact with staff who are carriers of pathogens. The problem is the identification of staff who are carriers of pathogens and their relocation to less hazardous positions.

Staff must undergo health screening before employment and should have regular health checks (Box 36.3). For example, in the UK all new healthcare workers (HCWs)

Box 36.3   📱   **Examples of Infectious Diseases where Staff Contact with Patients Should be Avoided**

Recommended work restrictions for staff with infectious diseases. In the event of a member of staff becoming infected, either in the hospital or outside, he or she should be relieved from direct contact with patients. Kitchen staff should also be relieved from duty if they are suffering from diarrhea or hepatitis A, or have infected lesions on their hands.

- Diarrhea
- Hepatitis A
- Herpes simplex on hands (herpetic whitlow)

- *Streptococcus pyogenes* infections
- *Staphylococcus aureus* skin lesions
- Measles
- Mumps
- Whooping cough
- Rubella
- Varicella-zoster infections
- Upper respiratory tract infections (high-risk patients)

---

are offered testing for HIV and hepatitis C. Hepatitis B immunization is offered and HCWs must know their post-immunization status (surface antigen negative or, if positive, e-antigen negative with a viral load of 103 genome equivalents/mL or less) before carrying out exposure-prone procedures (EPPs). It is critical that those carrying out EPPs who either do not know their post-immunization status or have not responded to the hepatitis B vaccine are checked to ensure that they do not have a current HBV infection or have a protective level of hepatitis B surface antibody. This is because HBV could be transmitted to the patients if the HCW carrying out EPPs is a hepatitis B carrier and also because the unprotected HCW is at risk of infection from a hepatitis B carrier patient. New HCWs carrying out EPPs must also be non-infectious for HIV (antibody negative) and hepatitis C (antibody negative or, if positive, negative for hepatitis C RNA).

Hospitals have blood-borne virus exposure policies for the management of healthcare workers and others who may have been exposed to viruses, including HBV, HCV, and HIV, having sustained a needlestick injury or mucous membrane splash from a potentially infected source. Prophylaxis includes active and/or passive immunization against hepatitis B and a short course of antiretroviral therapy for HIV exposure (see later). The risk of transmission is highest, ca. 33%, for HBV in unimmunized recipients, ca. 0.32% for HIV after a single needle stick injury, and HCV is thought to be between 1% and 3%. However, as reporting of exposure incidents and follow-up of the recipient improves, the better our understanding of the outcomes of the incident itself. Fortunately, most HCWs reported have recovered spontaneously or after having had ribavirin and pegylated interferon treatment.

In general, staff should be encouraged to report any incidences of infection (e.g. an infected cut or a bout of diarrhea). Appropriate immunizations should be offered and in some instances made mandatory. Work restrictions for personnel with selected infectious diseases are summarized in Box 36.3. However, healthy carriers of, for example, virulent staphylococci are difficult to identify unless bacteriologic screening is undertaken, which is not feasible on a routine basis. In addition, staff are sources of opportunist organisms such as coagulase-negative staphylococci or enterobacteria, which are part of their normal flora and cannot be excluded.

Breaking the chain of infection

There are two elements to be considered in breaking the chain of infection: the structural and the human. The structure of the hospital and its equipment can play a role in preventing airborne spread of infection and in facilitating aseptic practices by the staff, but this is of no avail if staff do not use the facilities correctly and do not themselves act positively to prevent the spread of infection.

Control of airborne transmission of infection

Ventilation systems and air flow can play an important role in the dissemination of organisms by the airborne route

Wards comprising separate rooms have been shown to afford some protection against airborne spread, and rooms with controlled ventilation are even better. However, neither prevents the carriage of organisms into the room on staff and their clothing, and some studies suggest that this is a more important route of infection than airborne spread. However, *Legionella* infection is acquired by the airborne route, and air-conditioning systems throughout the hospital should be maintained so as to prevent the multiplication of these organisms (see Ch. 19). *Aspergillus* infection in hospitals has been attributed to dissemination of the spores in hospital air, especially when building work is ongoing in the locality.

Ventilation systems in operating theatres must be properly installed and maintained to prevent the ingress of contaminated air and to minimize air currents carrying organisms from the staff in the operating room to the operation site. 'Ultra-clean' air is air passed through high-efficiency filters to remove bacteria and other particles and has been shown to contribute positively to a reduction in the number of postoperative wound infections developing after long orthopaedic operations.

Airborne transmission of infection can be reduced significantly by isolating patients

Patient isolation may be carried out:

- to protect a particularly susceptible patient from exposure to pathogens (i.e. protective isolation)
- to prevent the spread of pathogens from an infected patient to others on the ward (i.e. source isolation).

Isolation also helps to prevent the transmission of infection by other routes by limiting access to the patient and reminding staff of the importance of contact in the spread of infection.

Protective isolation can be provided by a single room on a ward or by enclosing the patient in a plastic isolator. With appropriate positive-pressure ventilation, air should flow from the 'clean' patient area out of the room or isolator. Staff entering the room or in contact with the patient should wear sterile gowns, gloves and masks to prevent organisms they are carrying or have picked up from other patients from coming in contact with the patient.

While source isolation in the past typically involved patient accommodation in an isolation unit in a separate building (e.g, the tuberculosis sanatoria), hospital isolation is typically arranged in a separate ward or in side rooms off the main ward. To prevent airborne transmission of organisms from the patient's room to the ward, air should flow from the ward to the isolation room. In practice, it is difficult to maintain the correct air flows without sophisticated designs, including double doors and air locks.

Facilitation of aseptic behaviour

A general state of cleanliness throughout the hospital is essential, and the design of hospital facilities affects the ease with which the environment can be kept clean and the staff can practise good techniques.

Bacteriologically effective handwashing is one of the most important ways of controlling hospital infection

The hands of staff convey organisms to patients from septic lesions and healthy carrier sites of other patients, from equipment contaminated by these sources and from carrier sites of the staff themselves (Table 36.4 and Fig. 36.8).

Staff should therefore wash their hands:

• before any procedure for which gloves or forceps are necessary

Table 36.4 Contact spread of opportunist pathogens

Patient	Nursing activity	Number of *Klebsiellae* recovered per hand[a]
A	Physiotherapy	10–100
	Taking blood pressure and pulse	100–1000
	Washing patient	10–100
	Taking oral temperature	100–1000
B	Taking radial pulse	100–1000
	Touching shoulder	1000
	Touching groin	100–1000
C	Touching hand	10–100
D	Extubation	100–1000
	Touching tracheostomy	1000

Nursing procedures involving skin contact resulting in contamination of staff hands. These data are derived from experiments performed during an outbreak of *Klebsiella* infection among urology patients.
[a]Control hand washings taken prior to procedure yielded no *Klebsiellae*.
(Data from Casewell and Phillips.)

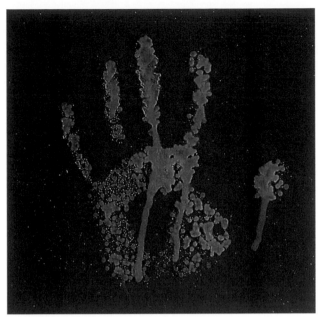

Figure 36.8 Gram-negative rods are not usually part of the resident skin flora except in moist environments, but are readily carried on hands and can be transferred from a source to a susceptible patient. This picture shows an impression of a hand that was inoculated with approximately 1000 *Klebsiella* aerogenes.

• after contact with an infected patient or one who is colonized with multiply-resistant bacteria
• after touching infective material.

While soap and water are adequate in many circumstances, emphasis is shifting to the use of fast-drying alcohol-based gels and solutions which are easier to use and appear to have a more antibacterial result. A mandate from the US Centers for Disease Control, for example, has put this approach into practice in US hospitals. Drying hands after any washing procedure is important. A more prolonged and thorough hand decontamination is required before commencing surgery.

The design of taps, soap dispensers and other washing facilities, including bedpan washers, has reached a high degree of sophistication. However, human behaviour can be influenced by architectural design only to a limited degree, and there is often a disappointingly low compliance with the simple technique of handwashing. Therefore, training and regular reinforcement in appropriate behaviour is essential.

Enhancing the host's ability to resist infection

Host resistance can be enhanced by boosting immunity and reducing risk factors

Although attempts can and should be made to control and prevent hospital infection by removing sources of infection and preventing transmission from sources to susceptible hosts, neither of these strategies is fail-safe. In addition, they do not protect the host from endogenous infection. A way of tipping the balance in favour of the host is to enhance his or her ability to resist infection, both by boosting specific immunity and by reducing personal risk factors. The following aspects should be considered:

• boosting specific immunity by active or passive immunization

- the appropriate use of prophylactic antibiotics
- care of invasive devices that breach the natural defences (e.g. urinary catheters, intravenous lines)
- attention to the risks predisposing to postoperative infection.

Boosting specific immunity

Passive immunization provides short-term protection

Boosting specific immunity by immunization has been discussed in Chapters 34 and 35. The problem for the immunocompromised patient is that they may not be able to mount an antibody response. Passive immunization can afford short-term protection, for example, with chickenpox exposure in susceptible patients who are neutropenic as a result of cytotoxic therapy and whose white cell count should recover after successful treatment. Active immunization with hepatitis B vaccine is recommended for all susceptible patients attending dialysis units. Other immunizations to protect hospital patients are summarized in Table 36.5.

Appropriate use of prophylactic antibiotics

There are well-documented uses for prophylaxis, but antibiotics tend to be misused

This is discussed in Chapter 33. There are several well-documented uses for prophylactic antibiotics in 'dirty' surgery and when the consequences of infection would be disastrous (e.g. in cardiac, neuro- and transplant surgery). However, there is a tendency to misuse antibiotics:

- first, by using them too often or for too long, thereby increasing the selection pressure for the emergence of resistant organisms
- second, by choosing inappropriate agents.

Treatment (as opposed to prophylaxis) of patients and staff who are carriers of pathogens such as *Staph. aureus* or *Strep. pyogenes* has been used successfully to prevent endogenous infection and to control outbreaks of infection with these organisms. Topical preparations of antibiotics such as pseudomonic acid (mupirocin), a fermentation product of

Pseudomonas fluorescens, have been shown to be efficacious. However, resistance (both low and high level) to the drug has occurred.

Gut decontamination regimens and selective bowel contamination aim to reduce the reservoir of potential pathogens in the gut

Gut decontamination regimens to reduce the aerobic Gram-negative flora of neutropenic patients has been practised for some time. With some patients (e.g. liver transplant) in intensive care units (ICU), selective bowel decontamination (SBD) has been employed. The aim is to reduce the reservoir of potential pathogens in the gut by oral administration (or via a nasogastric tube) of a high concentration of a mixture of antibiotics. At the present time, there is still controversy about the efficacy and safety of SBD.

Care of invasive devices

Care of invasive devices is essential to reduce the risk of endogenous infection

It is essential to take care of intravascular devices to reduce the risk of endogenous infection from skin organisms, and of catheters to reduce the risk that the periurethral flora will cause endogenous infection of the bladder in catheterized patients. Guidelines for the care of urinary catheters are discussed in Chapter 20.

The majority of hospital-associated bacteraemias and candidaemias are infusion-related

These infusion-related bacteraemias and candidaemias derive mainly from vascular catheters. Most bacteraemias associated with invasive devices are caused by the patient's own skin flora, although this may be a more resistant flora acquired during the patient's stay in hospital replacing susceptible resident bacteria. Coagulase-negative staphylococci are the most common aetiologic agents, but enterococci, *Candida*, and various Gram-negative rods are also implicated. These infections are largely preventable if appropriate steps are taken. The sources of infection and measures for prevention are shown in Figure 36.9.

Table 36.5 Boosting specific immunity of patients

Patient group	Immunization	
	Active	**Passive**
Elderly (especially those with multisystem disease)	Influenza vaccine	
Pre-splenectomy Pre-renal or bone marrow transplant	} Pneumococcal vaccine	
Haemodialysis patients	Pneumococcal vaccine	
Infants born to HBsAg positive mothers	Hepatitis B vaccine	Hepatitis B immunoglobulin (especially if mother HBeAg positive)
Immunocompromised: exposed to varicella-zoster virus (VZV)	Live attenuated VZV vaccine	Zoster immune globulin as soon as possible after exposure (and within 4 days)
Exposed to measles	measles containing vaccine	Normal human immune globulin within 5 days

Many patients will have been protected against some infections by routine immunization during childhood, but sometimes it is helpful to boost specific immunity by immunization of patients at particular risk of infection.

Figure 36.9 Sources of intravascular device-related infection and opportunities for the prevention of infection.

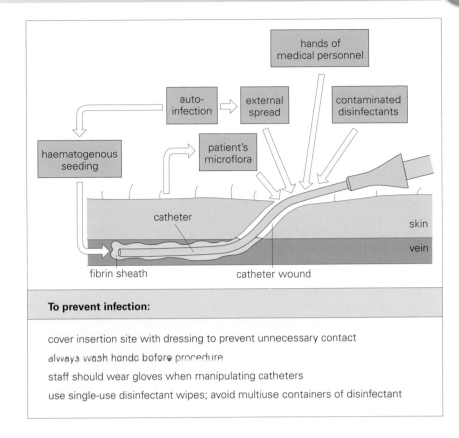

To prevent infection:

cover insertion site with dressing to prevent unnecessary contact

always wash hands before procedure

staff should wear gloves when manipulating catheters

use single-use disinfectant wipes; avoid multiuse containers of disinfectant

Reducing the risks of postoperative infection

Prevention of postoperative infection involves minimizing the risks

Reducing the risks of postoperative infection involves an understanding of the risks and the ways in which they can be circumvented. For example:

- The preoperative length of stay in hospital should be kept to a minimum.
- Intercurrent infections should be treated appropriately before surgery whenever possible (e.g. treatment of UTI before resection of the prostate).
- Operations should be kept to the minimum duration consistent with good operating technique.
- Adequate debridement of dead and necrotic tissue is essential, together with adequate drainage and maintenance or re-establishment of a good blood supply to provide the body's natural defences with optimum working conditions.
- Prevention of pressure sores and stasis by good nursing techniques and active physiotherapy minimizes the risks of developing respiratory tract infection or UTI.

INVESTIGATING HEALTHCARE-ASSOCIATED INFECTION

Many of the epidemiologic principles outlined in Chapter 31 apply to the investigation of healthcare-associated infection. Outbreaks within hospitals are epidemics – they are detected because the incidence of an infection is seen to be above normal levels for that institution. Investigation therefore must determine the extent of the problem, identify the source of infection and the way in which it is spread, identify those at risk, and propose effective methods for control. As with infectious diseases in general, the application of statistical techniques (e.g. calculation of risk ratios) and mathematical modelling has helped to provide an analytical and predictive framework for such infections, but day-to-day investigations still require the application of proven microbiologic approaches.

Hospital infections, like community infections, can involve all the major groups of pathogens, from viruses to arthropods. However, a particular problem with hospital infections, compared with those commonly occurring in the community, is the transmission of antibiotic-resistant bacteria, the emergence of which, and their spread, is favoured by the hospital environment. The recent surge in community-associated MRSA infections is an unfortunate exception to this trend. Epidemiologic investigations of infections place great importance on typing to identify the causative organism. Such molecular epidemiology can make a very important contribution to tracking and controlling infection.

In many hospitals, the responsibility for investigating hospital infection falls on the infection control committee, which includes an infection control officer (who may be a physician or microbiologist) and at least one nurse. The roles of the infection control committee include:

- the surveillance of hospital infection
- the establishment and monitoring of policies and procedures designed to prevent infection (e.g. catheter care policy, antibiotic policy, disinfectant policy, blood-borne virus exposure incidents, including needlesticks and blood splashes)
- the investigation of outbreaks – tracking the source and routes of transmission.

Surveillance

Surveillance allows early recognition of any change in the number or type of hospital infections

National and international surveys continue to highlight the prevalence and importance of hospital infection. By maintaining local surveillance, the infection control team can establish the normal trends in their hospital and proactively recognize any change in the number or type of infections. Sources of surveillance data are:

- Microbiology laboratory reports. These can be used for general surveillance, for example, monitoring haemodialysis patients regularly for hepatitis B surface antigen and HCV antibody, as outbreaks of HBV and HCV infection have been reported in renal units around the world, or for monitoring 'sentinel' or 'alert' organisms such as *Staph. aureus*, *Strep. pyogenes*, *M. tuberculosis*, *Salmonellae* and *Shigellae*.
- Ward rounds. New cases of infection can be identified by direct inspection, and previously identified cases of infection can be followed up. Surveys can also be carried out on the wards (e.g. of wound infections after different practices or procedures).
- Other sources include autopsy reports, staff health records and surveys of patients after discharge from hospital.

Investigation of outbreaks

When an outbreak (or epidemic) occurs or when routine surveillance highlights an increase in the incidence of infection, the infection control team should initiate an investigation. There is no universally applicable routine for finding the cause of an outbreak, but in principle each investigation has an epidemiologic element and a microbiologic element.

There must be a description of an outbreak in epidemiologic terms

This involves obtaining information about a number of relevant factors:

- How many people are infected?
- When were they admitted?
- When did they develop their infection?
- Are they all on the same ward?
- Are they all treated by the same medical or surgical team?
- Have they all been exposed to the same treatments?

The causative organism needs to be isolated and/or detected in all patients in the outbreak

It is the role of the microbiology laboratory to attempt to isolate the causative organism and to show that it occurs in all patients in the outbreak (i.e. they are all infected with organisms that are indistinguishable – see below). The identity of the infecting organism can provide clues as to the possible source:

- Respiratory and intestinal viruses implicate the source of infection as a patient or attending medical staff.
- Hepatitis indicates spread via contaminated blood products or hypodermics.
- An outbreak of wound infection with *Staph. aureus* is likely to be associated with contact spread from staff in theatre or on the ward.

- An outbreak of *Salmonella gastroenteritis* is more likely to originate in the kitchen.
- Infections with *Legionella* or *Pseudomonas* are likely to reflect environmental (especially water) contamination.

In addition, the location of the outbreak, whether in a general ward, a surgical ward, a paediatric unit or intensive care unit (once described as the epicentre of hospital infections) may also provide valuable clues.

Stages in tracking infection

Once the problem has been identified clinically, appropriate specimens should be collected from the patients and, if the indicators are that medical staff are involved, from hospital personnel (see Ch. 31). Likely sources of environmental contamination (surfaces, materials, equipment, water) should also be sampled. This is an important step, as data (using a non-infectious DNA marker as an experimental infectious organism) have shown that after release there is a rapid spread from hands of medical staff to almost all available surfaces (computers, charts, telephones, control knobs, door handles, heater controls, patient monitors). Once samples have been collected, the microbiology laboratory then has the task of identifying and typing the organisms concerned.

While the investigation is proceeding, steps should be taken to contain the outbreak and prevent spread to other patients. Infected patients must be isolated and treated appropriately. Staff who show a similar infection, or who are subsequently found to be carriers, must be suspended from duty until they have been treated. At the end of the investigation, the relevant procedures must be reviewed to try and prevent the reoccurrence of a similar outbreak.

Epidemiologic typing techniques

Bacteria are the commonest causes of nosocomial infections and of the greatest concern because of the prevalence of antibiotic resistance. For example, between January 2006 and October 2007 over 600 hospitals reported more than 28 000 nosocomial infections to the US National Health Safety Network. Of the pathogens involved, 13% were fungi but 87% were bacteria, most commonly coagulase-negative staphylococci, *S. aureus* (e.g., MRSA), *Enterococcus* species (e.g., VRE), *Candida* species, *Escherichia coli*, and *Pseudomonas aeruginosa*. Tracking infection is therefore disproportionately concerned with this group of pathogens, although molecular techniques are also applied to monitoring viral infections.

A variety of phenotypic and genotypic characters are used to 'fingerprint' bacteria for epidemiologic purposes

In epidemiologic studies of the spread of hospital infections, as in the investigation of outbreaks in the community, it is necessary to identify isolates of the infectious organisms to determine whether or not they are distinct (it may not be possible to say that two organisms are the same, only that they are indistinguishable). In the case of bacteria, if the species is a regular member of the normal human flora or is found frequently in the environment, it is necessary to distinguish the 'outbreak' strain from other strains of the same species not involved in the outbreak, but that may also be isolated during the course of the investigation. Essentially, typing is used to look for evidence of a clonal spread of a particular pathogen.

To be valuable in this context, good typing techniques must:

- be discriminatory (i.e. able to show differences between strains of the same species)
- be reproducible (i.e. the same strain gives the same result when tested on different occasions and in different places)
- have a high degree of typability (i.e. capable of assigning a type to all strains).

Antibiotic susceptibility patterns

Antibiotic susceptibility testing is readily performed in the diagnostic laboratory (see Ch. 31) and is useful as a preliminary clue as to whether two isolates are indistinguishable. However, discrimination is poor: many susceptibility patterns are common, and quite different strains may have the same pattern. Conversely, during an outbreak, strains may gain or lose plasmids carrying antibiotic resistance markers. More specialized typing techniques are commonly performed in reference laboratories. This has the advantage that quality assurance can be optimized, but also means that there is an inevitable delay in reporting the results and therefore in learning whether an outbreak of hospital infection is caused by a single strain.

Specialized typing techniques

Serotyping distinguishes between strains, using specific antisera

This classic technique distinguishes between strains by a difference in their antigenic structure, which is recognized by reaction with specific antisera. The 'O' somatic antigens and 'H' flagellar antigens are therefore used to divide salmonellae into types (sometimes referred to as species; see Ch. 22). *Strep. pneumoniae*, *Neisseria meningitidis* and *Klebsiella aerogenes* can be typed on the basis of their capsular (K) antigens, and *Strep. pyogenes* on the basis of their M- and T-cell wall proteins. However, serotyping requires the production and maintenance of appropriate banks of reagents (e.g., antisera), which is both time-consuming and costly. Therefore, this approach, when employed, is usually restricted to reference laboratories.

Bacteriophage (phage) typing has been used to type *Staph. aureus*, *Staph. epidermidis* and *Salmonella typhi*

This technique compares the pattern of lysis obtained when isolates (grown as lawns on agar plates) are exposed to a standard series of phage suspensions (Fig. 36.10). In the past, this method has been important for typing *Staph. aureus*, *Staph. epidermidis* and *Salmonella typhi*, but has also been applied to other species such as *P. aeruginosa*. However, as with serotyping, phage typing requires a reference laboratory for the production, maintenance and testing of the standard phage suspensions and has thus generally fallen out of favour. In the USA, the Centers for Disease Control has forgone the use of bacteriophage typing in favour of molecular techniques such as pulsed field gel electrophoresis (PFGE) (see below).

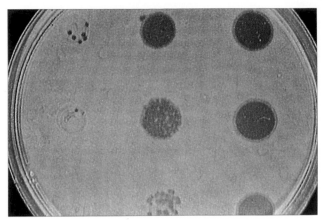

Figure 36.10 Bacteriophage (phage) typing of staphylococci. After seeding the surface of an agar plate with the organism to be typed, suspensions of different phages are dropped onto the surface and the plate incubated. Phages that are able to lyse the strain will produce zones of clearing of the bacterial lawn. The patterns of lysis obtained with the same set of bacteriophages on different isolates of *Staph. aureus* collected, for example, during an outbreak of wound infections, can be compared.

Molecular typing

Molecular typing techniques involve characterizing an organism's DNA

The above methods have been of great use in the epidemiologic analysis of nosocomial pathogens but are all variations on the phenotypic characterization of isolates. Since the chromosome represents the most fundamental 'molecule of identity' in the cell, genotypic approaches are used for characterization, often referred to as 'molecular epidemiology'.

Plasmid profiles are an example of 'first-generation' molecular epidemiology

Comparison of plasmid carriage in different isolates is only useful for species that carry a variety of plasmids and suffers from the drawback that what is actually being characterized is the plasmid and not the organism containing it. Different Gram-negative rods may acquire the same plasmids by conjugation between different species. However, this method has also been used to map the spread of antibiotic resistance plasmids among hospital pathogens (Fig. 36.11).

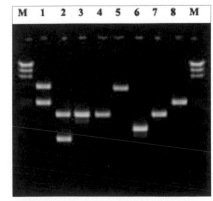

Figure 36.11 Analysis of plasmid carriage in eight bacterial clinical isolates using agarose-gel electrophoresis. Lanes labelled 'M' represent molecular size standards.

Restriction enzymes and probes represent 'second-generation' molecular epidemiology

Restriction-enzyme digestion of total cellular DNA from isolates results in a pattern of different-sized fragments which can be separated and compared by agarose gel electrophoresis-restriction-enzyme analysis (REA). All bacterial cells possess chromosomal DNA and can theoretically be analysed by this process. However, the DNA sequences recognized by most restriction enzymes, such as *Eco*RI, *Hin*dIII, etc. are present in hundreds of copies throughout a typical bacterial chromosome. Thus, the challenge is to compare accurately electrophoretic patterns comprising hundreds of restriction fragments which often co-migrate in clusters of similar size, and may include resident plasmid DNA.

The principle of complementary DNA sequences hybridizing with each other (e.g. Southern hybridization; named after its inventor, Ed Southern) has led to applications where specific DNA appropriately labelled 'probes', complementary to 'target' sequences found at various chromosomal locations, are hybridized against isolate REA patterns. Northern blotting is similar in principle but characterizes RNA sequences. Antibiotic resistance genes, and a variety of repeated sequences (e.g. transposons), have been especially useful targets in this context. The result is a pattern of hybridization with different restriction-fragments, commonly termed restriction-fragment length polymorphism (RFLP) analysis, corresponding to the chromosomal location of the probed sequences, which provides an indication of chromosomal relatedness between different isolates (Fig. 36.12A). For example, copies of the genes for ribosomal RNA (5S, 16S and 23S rRNA) are found at different locations on the chromosome of many medically important bacteria. These highly conserved sequences (i.e. very similar sequences in different species) allow RFLP analysis using a common probe (i.e. ribotyping). However, discrimination between strains of the same species may be less because of the conserved nature of the target sequences. The greatest success with RFLP analysis has primarily involved probes for insertion sequences that provide sufficient coverage (i.e. in number and diversity

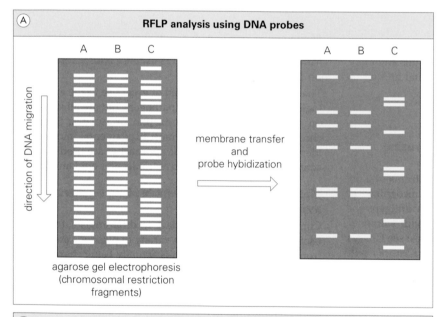

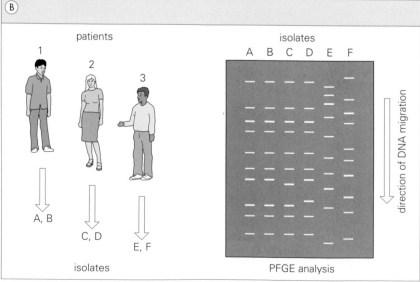

Figure 36.12 (A) Restriction-fragment length polymorphism (RFLP) analysis using DNA probes. An illustration of three nosocomial isolates (A and B epidemiologically related; C unrelated) analysed by restriction-enzyme analysis and subsequently by a specific DNA probe. (B) Pulsed field gel electrophoresis (PFGE) analysis of two bacterial isolates from each of three patients. Isolates in the first two patients are highly related (although slightly different in patient 2). Isolates from patient 3 are epidemiologically unrelated.

Figure 36.12—cont'd (C) In the RAPD/ AP-PCR approach to epidemiologic analysis, PCR products result from the random binding of PCR primers to chromosomal sequences, and the pattern is expected to be similar in epidemiologically related isolates. RAPD, randomly amplified polymorphic DNA; AP-PCR, arbitrarily primed polymerase chain reaction.

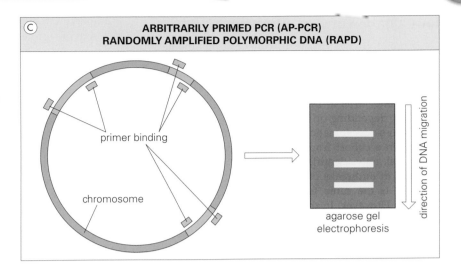

of chromosomal location) to reflect epidemiologically relevant interrelationships. The use of IS6110 probes in the RFLP analysis of *Mycobacterium tuberculosis* isolates is an example of a successful use of this approach. While superior to REA alone, RFLP analysis remains only moderately discriminatory for epidemiologic analysis.

PFGE and PCR are 'third-generation' approaches to molecular epidemiology

Instead of using frequently 'cutting' restriction enzymes, chromosomal DNA may be digested using enzymes with rare recognition sites in bacterial chromosomes (e.g. *Not*I, *Sfi*I, *Spe*I and *Xba*I in most Gram-negatives; *Asc*I, *Rsr*II, *Sgr*AI and *Sma*I in most Gram-positives). The extremely large DNA fragments produced are too large to be separated by conventional agarose gel electrophoresis but may be resolved by electrophoretic current 'pulsed' in different directions for different lengths of time-pulsed field gel electrophoresis (PFGE). PFGE has proved to be a powerful epidemiologic tool. The macro-restriction patterns produced by PFGE provide a sense of 'global' chromosomal monitoring – genetic events that affect distances between rare restriction-site sequences can be inferred from changes in restriction-fragment size (Fig. 36.12B). To date, the major disadvantage to PFGE analysis has been extra time and effort involved in producing unbroken chromosomal molecules necessary for reproducible macro-restriction-fragment patterns. In general, the overall success with which PFGE analysis has been employed has made it the method of choice – the 'gold standard' – for the epidemiologic analysis of most pathogens of clinical concern.

Economy, speed and the relatively low level of technical expertise required by the polymerase chain reaction (PCR) (Ch. 31) have led to a wealth of amplification-based applications for epidemiologic analysis. One of the earliest and most common PCR-based approaches has been randomly amplified polymorphic DNA (RAPD), also called arbitrarily primed PCR (AP-PCR). The method is based on the use of relaxing conditions affecting the stringency (i.e. specificity), with which PCR primers bind to DNA templates. PCR primers are allowed to randomly bind to chromosomal sequences of varying homology, resulting in products which can be comparatively analysed by agarose gel electrophoresis. A group of clinical isolates representing inter-patient transfer of a single strain would thus be expected to exhibit

the same degree of 'randomness', resulting in identical PCR products (Fig. 36.12C). However, several studies have shown that this method is especially prone to artefact and inter- and intra-laboratory variation. Nevertheless, the overall simplicity and utility of PCR continues to drive development and refinement of additional epidemiologic approaches which are beyond our ability to explore here.

'Fourth-generation' molecular epidemiology is based on DNA sequence analysis

Since the chromosome is the most fundamental molecule of identity in the cell, a comparison of actual chromosomal sequences would seem the most fundamental means of assessing potential interrelationships in nosocomial isolates. While a comparison of total chromosomal sequences is not a practical option, analysis of a subset of nucleotide sequences is the basis for what one could consider fourth-generation molecular epidemiology. Thus, recent years have seen a variety of sequence-based approaches to assessing microbial relatedness. These have included:

- microarrays, capable of comparing bacterial isolates for the presence or absence of specific genes (e.g., virulence, antibiotic resistance)
- a comparison of specific chromosomal regions in isolates looking for changes in DNA base (A, T, G, or C) coding, termed single nucleotide polymorphisms (SNPs)
- multi-locus sequence typing (MLST), where differences in the sequences of several (e.g., 6 or 7) essential 'housekeeping' genes serve as the basis for an assessment of isolate relatedness.

However, issues related to the choice of epidemiologically relevant sequences, method of analysis, data output, and interpretation continue to be explored and optimized, a process being greatly facilitated by current developments in microbial whole genome sequencing.

Molecular techniques for epidemiologic fingerprinting have many advantages

Although molecular techniques may require expertise and equipment, they have several advantages. They can be extremely precise, can be performed rapidly, do not involve handling infectious organisms and can be used to type all of the relevant isolates.

Investigation of viral infections

Nosocomial viral infections usually occur via the airborne route, contaminated fomites or blood-to-blood contact as outlined previously with, for example, RSV, noroviruses or hepatitis B, respectively. These are investigated mostly by detecting virus in samples from symptomatic patients and then, depending on the clinical setting, collecting samples from asymptomatic patients when deciding whom to include in a cohort from whom isolates can be obtained. In general, only identification of the microbe as a virus is required in outbreaks of viral gastroenteritis, as the management is the same for all the viral causes of gastroenteritis. However, in this setting it is important from an epidemiologic perspective to identify the cause of the outbreak. Surveillance is critical to monitor any changes in the virus as these alterations to parts of its genome may result in the virus evading detection as the primers used in the diagnostic test may no longer match the complementary sequence of the template. In addition, for those viruses for which we have a vaccine, it is important to know which strains are circulating currently to ensure a good antigenic match with the vaccine strains.

In an outbreak of respiratory infection, identification and typing of the virus is important not only for epidemiological purposes but also for issues of treatment and prophylaxis.

Molecular detection and typing methodologies such as sequencing may be required, usually for epidemiologic purposes rather than direct management of patients. However, in a setting such as postoperative acute hepatitis B infection, an intensive investigation will be carried out covering the possible routes of transmission. This may include investigating blood products, healthcare workers who were involved in exposure-prone procedures, other patients on the operating list, sexual contacts, and other risk activities involving potentially blood-contaminated needles. Once the potential sources have been identified, serologic tests may be carried out to seek evidence of current, recent or past hepatitis B infection. Genome detection methods and sequencing of blood samples from the individual with acute hepatitis B, as well as the potential source or sources, will help to confirm the transmission event or events.

Corrective / Preventive measures

Once tracking is complete, corrective and preventive measures can be introduced

Typing of the aetiologic agent responsible for the outbreak and knowledge of its characteristics and mode of transmission allow preventive measures to be taken. What these include depends to a great extent on the pathogen involved, but all must aim to improve basic hygiene, from more effective handwashing and improved general cleaning to more effectively regulated sterilization of equipment. Hygiene is a crucial factor since agents of nosocomial infection can be spread between patients by hospital staff. With some organisms that are widely distributed in the environment (e.g. *P. aeruginosa*) or occur in water supplies (e.g. *Legionella*), corrective measures may involve radical improvements to facilities.

As noted earlier, awareness of the risks of being exposed to blood-borne virus infections in a hospital setting is important to prevent blood-borne virus exposure incidents. Important protective measures include immunization of HCWs, wearing appropriate personal protective equipment (PPE) for procedures that could result in a break in the skin or exposure of mucous membranes, and appropriate post-exposure steps in the case of an incident.

Nosocomial transmission of SARS (see Ch. 19) has shown how easily airborne infection can be transmitted in a hospital setting. The use of PPE that included an N95 respirator, eye protection, mask, gloves and gown was mandatory to reduce the chance of transmission. Disposable second layers of clothing were also used, for example outer gloves, a gown and hand and foot covering.

STERILIZATION AND DISINFECTION

It is clear that the prevention of hospital infection depends in part upon the availability of clean, and where necessary, sterile equipment, instruments and dressings, isolation facilities and the safe disposal of infected material. Sterilization and disinfection are often talked about by microbiologists in relation to the production of sterile culture media and other laboratory activities, but it must be stressed that the concept of sterility is central to almost all areas of medical practice. An understanding of the rationale of sterilization and disinfection will aid intelligent use of the range of sterile equipment (from needles to prostheses) and techniques (from surgery to handwashing) employed in medical practice.

Definitions

Sterilization is the process of killing or removing all viable organisms

An item that is sterile is free from all viable organisms – in this sense, viable means capable of reproducing. Sterilization is achieved by physical or chemical means, either by the removal of organisms from an object or by killing the organisms in situ, sometimes leaving toxic breakdown products (pyrogens) in the object.

Disinfection is a process of removing or killing most, but not all, viable organisms

Disinfection employs either:

- a chemical 'disinfectant', which kills pathogens but may not kill viruses or spores
- a physical process such as boiling water or low-pressure steam, which reduces the bioburden (i.e. the load of viable organisms).

Antiseptics are used to reduce the number of viable organisms on the skin

Antiseptics are a particular group of disinfectants. Some act differentially, destroying the transient flora but leaving untouched the normal skin flora deep in the skin pores and hair follicles (Fig. 36.13). It is impossible to sterilize the skin, but thorough washing with antiseptic soaps can reduce the numbers of organisms on the surface considerably and therefore reduce contact spread of infection (see above). However, the resident bacteria in the hair follicles and ducts of sweat glands can recolonize the skin surface within hours.

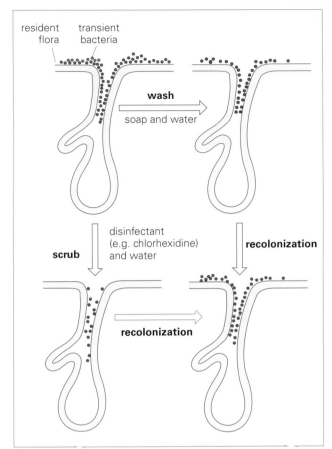

Figure 36.13 Normal skin is colonized with bacteria both on the surface and deep in the pores and ducts of the sweat and sebaceous glands. In addition, bacteria may be carried transiently on the skin surface and may be transmitted from a contaminated source to a susceptible patient. Careful handwashing with soap and water removes the transient flora and some of the superficial resident flora. Scrubbing the hands with disinfectants removes more of the resident flora, but the skin surface is recolonized within hours from the normal flora deep in the skin pores.

Pasteurization can be used to eliminate pathogens in heat-sensitive products

Pasteurization reduces the total numbers of viable microbes in bulk fluids such as milk and fruit juices without destroying flavour and palatability. It does not affect spores, but is effective against intracellular organisms such as *Brucella* and mycobacteria and many viruses.

Since the beginning of recorded history, various other techniques have been used to prevent the multiplication of microorganisms, such as drying and salting of food.

Deciding whether sterilization or disinfection should be used

Sterilization and disinfection processes are costly, and so it is important to choose the appropriate method and the one that causes the least damage to the material involved. A variety of considerations influence the choice of method. The detailed mechanisms of the death process of microorganisms may vary with the sterilizing technique used, but the net effect is similar in that essential cell constituents (nucleic acids or proteins) are inactivated.

It is easier to sterilize a clean object than a physically dirty one

This is because organic matter protects microbes and hinders penetration of heat or chemicals and may inactivate certain chemicals. In other words, a low bioburden is a prerequisite for cost-effective sterilization.

The rate of killing of microorganisms depends upon the concentration of the killing agent and time of exposure

The number of organisms surviving sterilization can be expressed by the equation: N is proportional to $1/CT$, where N is the number of survivors, C is the concentration of agent and T is time of exposure to the agent. If a population of microbes is exposed to a sterilizing technique, and the number of survivors, expressed as a logarithm, is plotted against time, the slope of the graph defines the death rate (Fig. 36.14). These lines may be sigmoid or have shoulders, indicating that individual cells respond slightly differently, some being killed more easily than others. In the case of bacteria, the physiologic state of the organisms influences the

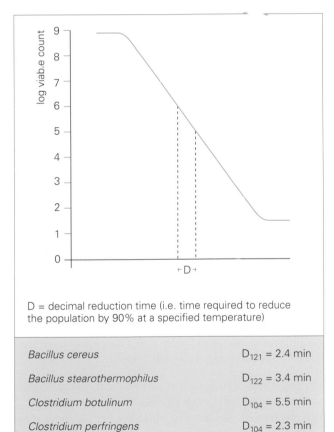

D = decimal reduction time (i.e. time required to reduce the population by 90% at a specified temperature)

Bacillus cereus	$D_{121} = 2.4$ min
Bacillus stearothermophilus	$D_{122} = 3.4$ min
Clostridium botulinum	$D_{104} = 5.5$ min
Clostridium perfringens	$D_{104} = 2.3$ min

Figure 36.14 Theoretically, there is a straight-line relationship between the log viable count of a bacterial population and time when the population is exposed to a lethal temperature. In practice, these lines are usually sigmoid. The D value is the time required to reduce the population by 90% at a specified temperature. *Bacillus stearothermophilus* spores are used as biologic indicators of effective heat sterilization by including filter paper strips carrying a standard number of spores into the autoclave cycle. The strips are then incubated to attempt to recover viable organisms. The usual autoclave cycle of 121°C for 15 min is adequate to kill *B. stearothermophilus* with a margin of safety.

shape of the killing curve; young, replicating cells are usually more vulnerable than stationary or decline-phase organisms or those that are sporing. Graphs like those shown in Figure 36.14 can be used to predict the conditions necessary to achieve sterility. However, these experimental data are usually based on pure cultures in the laboratory (bacterial spores are often used as model systems), whereas in real life, the bioburden is mixed. Therefore, predictions from such data may be inappropriate for mixed populations.

Techniques for sterilization

Sterilization may be achieved by:

- heat
- irradiation (gamma or ultraviolet)
- filtration
- chemicals in liquid or gaseous phase.

Other techniques of doubtful efficiency include freezing and thawing, lysis, desiccation, ultrasonication and the use of electrical discharges, but these are not applied in hospital practice.

Ultraviolet irradiation is inefficient as a sterilant, and its important uses in the hospital setting are in inhibiting growth of bacteria in water in complex apparatus such as auto-analysers and in air in safety hoods in virology laboratories. The potential for damage to the cornea and skin precludes wider use of ultraviolet irradiation. It should be remembered that the agents of Creutzfeldt–Jakob disease (CJD), bovine spongiform encephalopathy (BSE) and scrapie are highly resistant and are not completely inactivated by formalin, ultraviolet irradiation, ionizing radiation or regular autoclaving. Sterilization can be achieved by boiling in 1 N NaOH for 10 min at atmospheric pressure followed by autoclaving at a higher than normal temperature for a longer period than usual (134°C for 18 min), but obviously this technique cannot be applied to living tissues or materials that are damaged at high temperatures.

Heat

Heat, as a way of transferring energy, is the preferred choice for sterilization on the grounds of ease of use, controllability, cost and efficiency.

Dry heat sterilizes by oxidation of the cell components

Incineration and the use of the laboratory Bunsen burner are examples of sterilization by dry heat. Glassware can be sterilized in a hot air oven at 160–180°C for 1 h.

The most effective agent for sterilization is saturated steam (moist heat) under pressure

This can be achieved using an autoclave. Steam under pressure aids penetration of heat into the material to be sterilized (such as dressings), and there is a direct relationship between temperature and steam pressure. Steam under pressure has a temperature in excess of 100°C, which results in increased killing of microbes.

Sterilizing efficiency is improved by evacuating all of the air from the autoclave chamber. The subsequently introduced high-pressure steam rapidly penetrates to all parts of the chamber and its load, and results in predictable rises in temperature in the centre of articles to be sterilized. The

length of an autoclave cycle is determined by the holding time plus a margin of safety, and is derived from the thermal death curves for heat-resistant pathogens such as clostridia. Therefore, the usual cycle of 121°C for 15 min is sufficient to kill the spores of *Cl. botulinum* with an adequate margin of safety. However, the spores of some bacterial species, especially soil organisms, are able to withstand this temperature. The safety margin is reduced in the presence of large numbers of organisms because there is a greater probability of more heat-resistant individuals existing in a large population; hence, the importance of cleaning instruments, whenever possible, before sterilization.

Moist heat in an autoclave is used to sterilize surgical instruments and dressings and heat-resistant pharmaceuticals. A method for the sterilization of heat-sensitive instruments such as endoscopes uses a combination of low-temperature (subatmospheric) steam and formaldehyde.

All of these processes need to be carried out in a suitable pressure vessel and are therefore usually available in the hospital central sterile supply department.

Immersion in boiling water for a few minutes can be used as a rapid emergency measure to disinfect instruments

Immersion in boiling water for a few minutes will kill vegetative bacteria and many, but not all, spores. The addition of 2% sodium carbonate to the water potentiates the sporicidal effect.

Pasteurization uses heat at 62.8–65.6°C for 30 min

This technique was devised by Pasteur to prevent the spoilage of wine by heating it to 50–60°C. It is now used for fluids such as milk to reduce the number of bacteria. This helps to eliminate pathogens present in small numbers and to improve the shelf-life of milk. The fluid is held at a temperature of 62.8–65.6°C for 30 min or may be 'flash' pasteurized at 71.7°C for 15 s. After either process, the fluid should be kept at a temperature below 10°C to minimize subsequent bacterial growth.

Irradiation

Gamma irradiation energy is used to sterilize large batches of small-volume items

The use of gamma irradiation energy for sterilization is an industrial process that works well with products such as needles, syringes, intravenous lines, catheters and gloves. It can also be used for vaccines and to prevent food spoilage. Although the capital cost of the equipment is high, the process is continuous and 100% efficient. Articles are sterilized while sealed in their original packaging, without any heat gain. The process must be conducted in a suitably constructed building, usually at a location distinct from the hospital and usually outside the hospital administration. However, irradiation can cause materials to deteriorate and is thus not suitable for resterilization of equipment. The killing mechanism involves the production of free radicals, which break the bonds in DNA. Irradiation kills spores, but at a higher dose than vegetative cells because of the relative lack of water in spores.

Sterilization using ultraviolet irradiation is discussed above.

Filtration

Filters are used to produce particle- and pyrogen-free fluid

Solutions that are heat-sterilized will contain pyrogens. These heat-stable breakdown products of microbes are capable of inducing fever and are therefore undesirable in products such as intravenous fluids. Filtration or separation of the product from the contamination has a long history in the clarification of water and wine. Modern filters composed of compounds such as nitrocellulose or mixed cellulose ester work by electrostatic attraction and physical pore size to retain organisms or other particles. The resulting fluid should be particle-free. Filtration is used in some parts of the world to purify drinking water.

Filtration techniques are also used to recover very small numbers of organisms from very large volumes of fluid (e.g. *Legionella* from cooling tower water) and can be used as a method for quantifying bacteria in fluids.

Chemical agents

The gases ethylene oxide and formaldehyde kill by damaging proteins and nucleic acids

The need for sterilization by gaseous chemicals has been greatly reduced by the success of gamma irradiation (see above), but two alkylating gases, ethylene oxide and formaldehyde, are still used:

- Ethylene oxide is used in some centres to sterilize single-use medical requisites such as heart valves. However, it is toxic and potentially explosive.
- Formaldehyde is not explosive, but has an extremely unpleasant odour and is an irritant to mucous membranes. It has been used as a disinfectant to decontaminate rooms (such as isolation rooms) and in the laboratory to disinfect exhaust-protective cabinets. A high relative humidity is essential for effective killing.

The liquid glutaraldehyde is used to disinfect heat-sensitive articles

Glutaraldehyde is less toxic than formaldehyde and can be stabilized in solution to remain active for up to several weeks at in-use concentration. It is used for the disinfection of, but does not sterilize, heat-sensitive articles such as endoscopes and for inanimate surfaces.

Many different antimicrobial chemicals are available, but few are sterilant

Some, like the derivatives of pine and turpentine, have been known since ancient times, and chloride of lime and coal tar fluids were in use before the germ theory of disease was established. Most fall into the category of disinfectant or antiseptic, but a few are capable of rendering articles sterile. Factors that affect their efficacy include:

- physical environment (e.g. porous or cracked surfaces)
- presence of moisture
- temperature and pH
- concentration of the agent
- hardness of water
- the bioburden on the object to be disinfected
- the nature and state of the microbes in the bioburden
- the ability of the microbes to inactivate the chemical agent.

It is obvious that the above factors are difficult to control in every circumstance. The main groups of chemical agents are shown in Table 36.6. They act by causing chemical damage to proteins, nucleic acids or cell membrane lipids. The activity of a given disinfectant may result from more than one pathway of damage.

Controlling sterilization and disinfection

In general, it is preferable to control the process rather than the product

This means that it is better to run checks on the technique while it is in operation rather than attempting to recognize process failure by isolating microorganisms from the product. Trying to discover whether one or a few viable organisms remain is analogous to trying to find a needle in a haystack. It is known that damaged bacteria can recover, given time and special nutrient recovery media, but it may not be feasible to hold back a batch of product for such tests. In addition, how many samples of the product should be tested? If too few are examined, the likelihood of missing a failed sample is high; if too many are examined, too much of the batch is used up in quality control to be economically sensible.

Table 36.6 Examples of disinfectants for use in hospitals

Group	Examples	Advantages and disadvantages
Phenolics	Clear-soluble phenolic compounds, white fluids Chloroxylenols	Good general-purpose disinfectants, not readily inactivated by organic matter, active against wide range of organisms including *mycobacteria*, not sporicidal Inactivated by hard water and organic matter, *Pseudomonas* grows readily in chloroxylenol solutions, limited activity against other Gram-negatives
Halogens	Hypochlorites (chloramine)	Cheap, effective, act by release of free chlorine, active against viruses and therefore recommended for disinfection of equipment soiled with blood (because of hepatitis and HIV risk), inactivated by organic material, corrode metals
	Iodine and iodophors	Useful skin disinfectants, sporicidal
Quaternary ammonium compounds	Benzalkonium chloride, cetyltrimethylammonium bromide	Have detergent properties, activity against Gram-negative ← Gram-positive, improved by combination with biguanide, e.g. chlorhexidine, useful as skin disinfectants, inactivated by hard water and organic materials, contamination of stock solutions with Gram-negative rods can be a problem

(Continued)

Table 36.6 Examples of disinfectants for use in hospitals—cont'd

Group	Examples	Advantages and disadvantages
Diguanides	Chlorhexidine	Useful disinfectant for skin and mucous membranes, inactivated by many materials and too expensive for environmental use, alcoholic solutions are less easily contaminated, combinations of chlorhexidine and detergent highly effective for disinfection of hands
Alcohols	Ethyl alcohol, isopropyl alcohol	Good choice for skin disinfection and for clean surfaces, sometimes used in combination with iodine or chlorhexidine (see above), water must be present for bacterial killing (i.e. 70% ethanol best), isopropyl preferred for skin and articles in contact with patient
Aldehydes	Formaldehyde/formalin Glutaraldehyde	Too irritant for use as general disinfectant Kills vegetative organisms, including mycobacteria, slowly but effectively, more active, less toxic than formaldehyde, sporicidal (within 6 h when fresh), slightly irritant, used in alkaline solution which is stable for 1–2 weeks, expensive, limited use, e.g. disinfection of endoscopes
Chlorinated bisphenols	Hexachorophene	Activity against Gram-positive → Gram-negative, used in soap or dusting powder as skin disinfectant (use restricted after potentially toxic blood levels found in infants who had hexachlorophene emulsion spread over whole body) Triclosan, a polychloro phenoxy phenol is used as substitute for hexachlorophene in personal products, antibacterial effect on repeated use

Note that no one group of disinfectant has all the properties desirable for use both on skin and on inanimate surfaces.

The usual process controls are either physical or chemical checks on the technique, for example, tests that show that the autoclave reached the desired temperature for the desired time. They do not show that there are no viable organisms remaining after the process, but this is assumed if the process satisfies the controls. However, the stringency of the controls can be altered intentionally or accidentally to give either an undersensitive or oversensitive test.

Disinfectants can be monitored by microbiologic 'in-use' tests

These tests involve challenging the solution with a bacterial suspension and withdrawing samples, which are then treated to prevent carryover of the disinfectant and cultured. However, these tests are rarely performed in the hospital setting, where the use of disinfectants is guided largely by the manufacturer's recommendations.

 KEY FACTS

- Realization that infection can be associated with a variety of institutional settings has resulted in a preference for the term 'healthcare-associated infection' rather than hospital-acquired infection.

- Nosocomial infection refers to infection acquired in hospital.

- Hospital infections often have serious consequences for the individual, for the hospital community and for the community at large. They may be caused by almost any organism, but a few species cause the vast majority of infections.

- The hospital environment favours the survival of resistant strains and therefore infections are often caused by organisms with limited antibiotic susceptibility.

- MRSA, traditionally viewed as a problem in hospital infection, are increasingly seen in community-acquired infections in the absence of healthcare contact.

- Most common hospital infections are UTIs, respiratory tract infections, surgical wound infections and bacteraemia (septicaemia).

- The most important bacterial causes are Gram-positive cocci (*staphylococci* and *streptococci*) and Gram-negative rods (e.g. *E. coli*, *Pseudomonas*). Multiply-antibiotic-resistant organisms are common. *Candida* is the significant fungal cause, and viruses probably cause more hospital infections than previously recognized.

- Infecting organisms originate from the patient's own flora (endogenous infection) or from other human or inanimate sources (exogenous or cross-infection). Airborne and contact spread are the most important routes of transmission.

- Host factors are of critical importance in determining susceptibility to infection.

- Surveillance should be an ongoing activity to facilitate early recognition of outbreaks of infection. Investigation of outbreaks involves both epidemiologic and microbiologic expertise. Molecular techniques to 'fingerprint' the causative organism are becoming increasingly sophisticated.

- Prevention of hospital infections by excluding sources, interrupting transmission and enhancing the patient's resistance is fundamental to improving patient care and reducing costs.

- Sterilization and disinfection are key processes in the control and prevention of hospital infections as well as being central to many areas of medical practice.

Bibliography

INTRODUCTION

Updates on infectious diseases can be obtained via www.who.int (worldwide); www.cdc.gov; www.niaid.nih.gov (USA); www. hpa.org.uk (UK), www.euro.who.int (Europe).

CHAPTER 1

Topley and Wilson's Microbiology and Microbial Infections. 10th edition. Hoboken: Wiley-Blackwell, 2007.

A multi-volume text which, though published some years ago, still gives detailed accounts of all the organisms covered in Medical Microbiology.

Updates on progress with genome sequencing of infectious organisms are available on the websites of the Wellcome Sanger Institute (www.sanger.ac.uk) and The J. Craig Venter Institute (www.jvci.org).

CHAPTER 2

Beiting DP, Roos DS. A systems biological view of intracellular pathogens. Immunol Rev 2011; 240:117–128.

Gomez JE, Clatworthy A, Hung DT. Probing bacterial pathogenesis with genetics, genomics, and chemical biology: past, present, and future approaches. Crit Rev Biochem Mol Biol 2011; 46:41–66.

La MV, Raoult D, Renesto P. Regulation of whole bacterial pathogen transcription within infected hosts. FEMS Microbiol Rev 2008; 32:440–460.

Pallen MJ, Loman NJ, Penn CW. High-throughput sequencing and clinical microbiology: progress, opportunities and challenges. Curr Opin Microbiol 2010; 13:625–631.

Shames SR, Auweter SD, Finlay BB. Co-evolution and exploitation of host cell signaling pathways by bacterial pathogens. Int J Biochem Cell Biol 2009; 41:380–389.

CHAPTER 3

Zheng Z-M. Viral oncogenes, non coding RNAs and RNS splicing in human tumor viruses. Int J Biol Sci 2010; 6:730–755.

Moore PS, Chang Y. Why do viruses cause cancer? Highlights of the first century of human tumour virology. Nature Reviews 2010; 10:878–889.

CHAPTER 4

Howard DH, ed. Pathogenic fungi in humans and animals. New York: Marcel Dekker, 2003.

A multi-author update on recent work in fungal research.

Merz WG, Hay RJ, ed. Topley and Wilson's Microbiology and Microbial Infections: Medical Mycology. 10th edition. London: Hodder Arnold, 2007.

A detailed account of those fungi which cause disease in humans.

Hibbett DS, et al. A higher level phylogenetic classification of the fungi. Mycol Res 2007; 111:507–547.

CHAPTER 5

Cox FEG, Wakelin D, Gillespie SH, Despommier DD eds. Topley and Wilson's Microbiology and Microbial Infections: Parasitology, 10th edition. London: Hodder Arnold; 2007.

Wiser MF. Protozoa and Human Disease. New York: Garland Science, 2010.

CHAPTER 6

Brindley PJ et al. Helminth genomics: the implications for human health. PLoS Negl Trop Dis 2009; 3:e538.

Cox FEG, Wakelin D, Gillespie SH, Despommier DD, eds. Topley and Wilson's Microbiology and Microbial Infections: Parasitology. 10th edition. London: Edward Arnold, 2007.

A multi-author update including sections on all the important helminth parasites of humans.

Despommier DD et al. Parasitic Diseases, 5th edition. New York: Apple Trees Productions, 2006.

Spielman A et al. Arthropod vectors and human disease: an epidemiological approach. Oxford: Oxford Univ. Press, 2010.

A well-illustrated text on human parasitology.

CHAPTER 7

Clewley JP, Kelly CM, Andrews N et al. Prevalence of disease related prion protein in anonymous tonsil specimens in Britain: cross sectional opportunistic survey. BMJ 2009; 338:1442.

Wadsworth JDF, Asante EA, Collinge J. Review: Contribution of transgenic models to understanding human prion disease. Neuropathol Appl Neurobiol 2010; 36:576–597.

Ironside JW. Variant Creutzfeldt-Jakob disease. Haemophilia 2010 Jul; 16(Suppl 5): 175–180.

CHAPTER 8

Murray PR. Human microbiota. In: Borriello SP, Murray PR, Funke G, eds. Topley and Wilson's Microbiology and Microbial Infections: Bacteriology. 10th edition. London: Hodder Arnold, 2007.

Webster JP. Natural History of Host-Parasite Interactions. In: Advances in Parasitology. vol. 68. London: Elsevier, 2009.

CHAPTER 9

Alt F, Marrack P, eds. Curr Opin Immunol. ISSN: 0952-7915. *Appears bi-monthly. Issue no. 1 of each volume deals with 'Innate Immunity'.*

Male D, Brostoff J, Roth DB, Roitt IM. Immunology. 7th edition London: Mosby Elsevier; 2006.

Kaufmann SHE, Medzhitov R, Gordon S, eds. The Innate Immune Response to Infection. Washington: ASM Press; 2004.

CHAPTER 10

Alt F, Marrack P, eds. Curr Opin Immunol. ISSN: 0952-7915 *Appears bi-monthly. Issue no. 4 of each volume deals with 'Immunity to Infection'.*

Bottazzi B, Doni A, Garlanda C, Mantovani A. An integrated view of humoral innate immunity: pentraxins as a paradigm. Annu Rev Immunol 2010; 28:157–183.

Creagh EM, O'Neill LA. TLRs, NLRs and RIRs: a trinity of pathogen sensors that co-operate in innate immunity. Trends Immunol 2006; 8:352–357.

Delves PJ, Roitt IM, eds. Encyclopedia of Immunology, 2nd edition London: Academic Press, 1998. *Contains articles on IgG, IgA, IgM, IgD and IgE and immunoglobulin function and domains.*

Delves PJ, Martin S, Burton D, Roitt IM. Roitt's Essential Immunology, 12th edition. Oxford: Blackwell Science, 2011 Chapters 1–5.

Flannagan RS, Cosio G, Grinstein S. Antimicrobial mechanisms of phagocytes and bacterial evasion strategies. Nat Rev Microbiol 2009; 7:355–366.

Medzhitov R. Origin and physiological roles of inflammation. Nature 2008; 454:428–435.

Palm NW, Medzhitov R. Pattern recognition receptors and control of adaptive immunity. Immunol Rev 2009; 227:221–233.

Ricklin D, Hajishengalis G, Yang K, Lambris JD. Complement; a key system for immune surveillance and homeostasis. Nat Immunol 2010; 11:785–797.

Schroeder HW Jr. Cavacini L. Structure and function of immunoglobulins. J Allergy Clin Immunol 2010; 125:S41–S52.

CHAPTER 11

Alt F, Marrack P, eds. Curr Opin Immunol. ISSN: 0952-7915 *Appears bi-monthly. Issues 1, 2 and 3 of each volume contain critical reviews.*

Batista FD, Harwood NE. The who, how and where of antigen presentation to B cells. Nat Rev Immunol 2009; 9:15–27.

Delves PJ, Martin S, Burton D, Roitt IM. Roitt's Essential Immunology, 12th edition. Oxford: Blackwell Science, 2011.

Korn T, Bettelli E, Oukka M, Kuchroo VK. IL-17 and Th17 cells. Annu Rev Immunol 2009; 27:485–517.

Littman DR, Rudensky AY. Th17 and regulatory T cells in mediating and restraining inflammation. Cell 2010; 140:845–458.

Male D, Brostoff J, Roth DB, Roitt IM, eds. Immunology, 8th edition. London: Mosby Elsevier, 2011 Chapters 1–6.

Mueller DL. Mechanisms maintaining peripheral tolerance. Nat Immunol 2010; 11:21–27.

Rudensky AY. Molecular analysis of Tregs. Annu Rev Immunol 2011; 29.

Smith-Garvin JE, Kennedy GA, Jordan MS. T cell activation. Annu Rev Immunol 2009;27:591–619.

CHAPTER 12

Jong EC, Stevens DL. Netter's Infectious Diseases. Philadelphia: Elsevier; 2011.

Schlossberg D, ed. Clinical Infectious Disease. New York: Cambridge University Press, 2008.

Williams JV. Deja vu all over again: Koch's postulates and virology in the 21st century. J Infect Dis 2010; 11:1611–1614.

CHAPTER 13

Beiting DP, Roos DS. A systems biological view of intracellular pathogens. Immunol Rev 2011; 240:117–128.

Hunstad DA, Justice SS. Intracellular lifestyles and immune evasion strategies of uropathogenic Escherichia coli. Annu Rev Microbiol 2010; 64:203–221.

Keele BF, Derdeyn CA. Genetic and antigenic features of the transmitted virus. Curr Opin HIV AIDS 2009; 4:352–357.

Lavine JS, Poss M, Grenfell BT. Directly transmitted viral diseases: modeling the dynamics of transmission. Trends Microbiol 2008; 16:165–172.

Peleg AY, Hogan DA, Mylonakis E. Medically important bacterial-fungal interactions. Nat Rev Microbiol 2010; 8:340–349.

Pulzova L, Bhide MR, Andrej K. Pathogen translocation across the blood-brain barrier. FEMS Immunol Med Microbiol 2009; 57:203–213.

Vandemark LM, Jia TW, Zhou XN. Social science implications for control of helminth infections in Southeast Asia. Adv Parasitol 2010; 73:137–170.

Wang LJ, Cao Y, Shi HN. Helminth infections and intestinal inflammation. World J Gastroenterol 2008; 14:5125–5132.

CHAPTER 14

Maizels RM, Pearce EJ, Artis D, Yazdanbakhsh M, Wynn TA. Regulation of pathogenesis and immunity in helminth infections. J Exp Med 2009; 206:2059–2066.

Rouse BT, Sahrawat S. Immunity and immunopathology to viruses: what decides the outcome? Nat Rev Immunol 2010; 10:514–526.

Vivier E, Raulet DH, Moretta A, Caligiuri MA, Zitvogel L, Lanier LL, Yokoyama WM, Ugolini S. Innate or adaptive immunity? The example of natural killer cells. Science 2011; 331:44–49.

Immunological Reviews Special issue: Intracellular Pathogens 2011; 240:5–317.

CHAPTER 15

McColl BW, Allan SM, Rothwell NJ. Systemic infection, inflammation and acute ischemic stroke. Neuroscience 2009; 158:1049–1061.

Teeling JL, Perry VH. Systemic infection and inflammation in acute CNS injury and chronic neurodegeneration: underlying mechanisms. Neuroscience 2009; 158:1062–1073.

Loutet SA, Valvano MA. A decade of Burkholderia cenocepacia virulence determinant research. Infect Immun 2010; 78:4088–4100.

Somerville GA, Proctor RA. At the crossroads of bacterial metabolism and virulence factor synthesis in Staphylococci. Microbiol Mol Biol Rev 2009; 73:233–248.

Simpson RJ. Aging, persistent viral infections, and immunosenescence: can exercise "make space"? Exerc Sport Sci Rev 2011; 39:23–33.

CHAPTER 16

Lambris D, Rickin D, Geisbrecht BV. Complement evasion by human pathogens. Nat Rev Microbiol 2008; 6:132 doi:10.1038/nrmicro1824.

Tritonov V, Khiabanian H, Rabadan R. Geographic dependence, surveillance, and origins of the 2009 Influenza A (H1N1) Virus. N Engl J Med 2009; 361:115–119.

CHAPTER 17

Le Douce V, Herbein G, Rohr O, Schwartz C. Molecular mechanisms of HIV-1 persistence in the monocyte-macrophage lineage. Retrovirology 2010; 7:32.

Moir S, Chun TW, Fauci AS. Pathogenic mechanisms of HIV disease. Annu Rev Pathol 2011;6:223–48.

Wilke GA, Wardenburg JB. Role of a disintegrin and metalloprotease 10 in Staphylococcus aureus alpha-hemolysin-mediated cellular injury. PNAS 2010; 107:13473–13478.

CHAPTER 18

Bermon S. Airway inflammation and upper respiratory tract infection in athletes: is there a link? Exerc Immunol Rev 2007; 13:6–14.

Jackson SJ, Steer AC, Campbell H. Systematic Review: Estimation of global burden of non-suppurative sequelae of upper respiratory tract infection: rheumatic fever and post-streptococcal glomerulonephritis. Trop Med Int Health 2011; 16:2–11.

Kimura H. Pathogenesis of chronic active Epstein-Barr virus infection: Is this an infectious disease, lymphoproliferative disorder, or immunodeficiency? Rev Med Virol 2006; 16:251–261.

Ryan MW. Evaluation and management of the patient with "sinus". Med Clin North Am 2010; 94:881–889.

CHAPTER 19

Alonzo de Velasco E, Verheul AF, Verhoef J, Snipple H. Streptococcus pneumoniae: virulence factors, pathogenesis, and vaccines. Microbiol Rev 1995; 59:591–603.

Couch RB, Kasel JA, Glezen WP, et al. Influenza: Its control in persons and populations. J Infect Dis 1986; 153:431–447.

Department of Health and Welsh Office. The control of legionellae in health care premises. London: HMSO, 1988.

Fauci AS. Seasonal and pandemic influenza preparedness; science and countermeasures. J Infect Dis 2006; 194(Suppl 2):S73–S76.

Fauci AS. Emerging and re-emerging infectious diseases: influenza as a prototype of the host-pathogen balancing act. Cell 2006; 124:665–70.

Govan JRW, Glass S. The microbiology and therapy of cystic fibrosis lung infections. Rev Med Microbiol 1990; 1:19–28.

Hayden FG. Antivirals for influenza: historical perspectives and lessons learned. Antiviral Res 2006; 71:372–378.

Hutchinson DN. Nosocomial legionellosis. Rev Med Microbiol 1990; 1:108–115.

Jacobs E. Mycoplasma pneumoniae virulence factors and the immune response. Rev Med Microbiol 1991; 2:83–90.

Kash JC, Tumpey TM, Proll SC, et al. Genomic analysis of increased host immune and cell death responses induced by 1918 influenza virus. Nature 2006; 443:578–581.

Kawaoka Y, Webster RG. Molecular mechanisms of acquisition of virulence in influenza virus in nature. Microb Pathog 1988; 5:311–318.

Kunst H, Mack D, Kon OM et al. Parasitic Infections of the Lung: a Guide for the Respiratory Physician. Thorax 2010; epub ahead of print.

La Via WV, Marks MI, Stutman HR. Respiratory syncytial virus puzzles. Clinical features, pathophysiology, treatment and prevention. J Pediatr 1992; 121:503–510.

Marrie TJ, Grayston JT, Wang P, Kuo C-C. Pneumonia associated with the TWAR strain of Chlamydia. Ann Intern Med 1987; 106:507–511.

Miller R, Huang L. Pneumocystis jirovecii infection. Thorax 2004; 59:731–733.

Moser MR, Bender TR, Marelolis NS, et al. An outbreak of influenza aboard a commercial airliner. Am J Epidemiol 1979; 110:1–7.

Pedersen SS. Clinical efficacy of ciprofloxacin in lower respiratory tract infections. Scand J Infect Dis 1989; 60(Suppl):89–97.

Sudre P, ten Dam G, Kochi A. Tuberculosis: a global overview of the situation today. Bull WHO 1992; 70:149–159.

Webster RG, Bean WJ, Gorman OT et al. Evolution and ecology of influenza viruses. Microbiol Rev 1992; 56:152–179.

Van den Hoogen BG, de Jong JC, Groen J et al. A newly discovered human pneumovirus isolated from young children with respiratory tract disease. Nat Med 2001; 7:719–724.

CHAPTER 20

Dielubanza EJ, Schaeffer AJ. Urinary tract infections in women. Med Clin North Am 2011; 95:27–41.

Foxman B. The epidemiology of urinary tract infection. Nat Rev Urol 2010; 7:653–660.

Larcombe J. Urinary tract infection in children. Am Fam Physician 2010; 82:1252–1256.

Litza JA, Brill JR. Urinary tract infections. Prim Care 2010; 37:491–507.

CHAPTER 21

Barouch DH. Challenges in the development of an HIV-1 vaccine. Nature 2008; 455:613–619.

Cohen MS, Shaw GM, McMichael AJ, Haynes BF. Acute HIV-1 infection. NEJM 2011; 364:1943–1954.

Greer L, Wendel Jr. GD. Rapid diagnostic methods in sexually transmitted infections. Infect Dis Clin North Am 2008; 22:601–617.

Hay P, Ugwumadu A. Detecting and treating common sexually transmitted diseases. Best Pract Res Clin Obstet Gynaecol 2009; 23:647–660.

Health Protection Agency. Health Protection Report. vol. 4, No. 47. Published on: 26 November HIV in the United Kingdom: 2010 Report.

Johnson VA, Brun-Vezinet F, Clotet B, Gunthard HF, Kuritzkes DR, Pillay D, Schapiro JM, Richman DD. Update of the drug resistance mutations in HIV-1: December 2010. Top HIV Med 2010; 18:156–163.

Moir S, Chun T-W, Fauci AS. Pathogenic mechanisms of HIV Disease. Annu Rev Pathol Mech Dis 2011; 6: 223–448.

Sadeghi-Nejad H, Wasserman M, Weidner W, Richardson D, Goldmeier D. Sexually transmitted diseases and sexual function. J Sex Med 2010; 7:389–413.

Tebit DN, Arts DJ. Tracking a century of global expansion and evolution of HIV to drive understanding and to combat disease. Lancet Infect Dis 2011; 11:45–56.

Thompson MA, Aberg JA, Cahn P, Montaner JS, Rizzardini G, Telenti A, Gatell JM, Gunthard HF, Hammer SM, Hirsch MS, Jacobsen DM, Reiss P, Richman DD, Volberding PA, Yeni P, Schooley RT. Antiretroviral treatment of adult HIV infection: 2010 recommendations of the International AIDS Society-USA panel. JAMA 2010; 304:321–333.

CHAPTER 22

Ghoshal UC, Ranjan P. Post-infectious irritable bowel syndrome: the past, the present and the future. J Gastroenterol Hepatol 2011; 26(Suppl 3):94–101.

Ham M, Kaunitz JD. Gastroduodenal mucosal defense. Curr Opin Gastroenterol 2008; 24:665–673.

O'Brien SJ, Halder SL. GI Epidemiology: infection epidemiology and acute gastrointestinal infections. Aliment Pharmacol Ther 2007; 25:669–674.

Pawlotsky JM. Virology of hepatitis B and C viruses and antiviral targets. J Hepatol 2006; 44(Suppl 1):S10–S13.

Pawlotsky JM, Gish RG. Future therapies for hepatitis C. Antivir Ther 2006; 11:397–408.

Phillips A. Pathogenesis of gastrointestinal infection. Clin Med 2008; 8:299–300.

Radford DA, Gaskell RM, Hart CA. Human norovirus infection and the lessons from animal caliciviruses. Curr Opin Infect Dis 2004; 17:471–478.

Verna EC, Brown RS Jr. Hepatitis C virus and liver transplantation. Clin Liver Dis 2006; 10:919–940.

CHAPTER 23

Dammann O, Leviton A, Gappa M, Dammann DE. Lung and brain damage in preterm newborns, and their association with gestational age, prematurity subgroup, infection/inflammation and long term outcome. BJOG 2005; 112(Suppl 1):4–9.

Edwards AD, Tan S. Perinatal infections, prematurity and brain injury. Curr Opin Pediatr 2006; 18:119–124.

Griffiths PD. Progress towards interrupting intrauterine transmission of CMV? Rev Med Virol 2006; 16:1–4.

Lam NC, Gotsch PB, Langan RC. Caring for pregnant women and newborns with hepatitis B or C. Am Fam Physician 2010; 82:1225–1229.

Larsen JW, Sever JL. Group B Streptococcus and pregnancy: a review. Am J Obstet Gynecol 2008; 198:440–448.

Noyola DE, Jimenez-Capdeville ME, Demmler-Harrison GJ. Central nervous system disorders in infants with congenital cytomegalovirus infection. Neurol Res 2010; 32:278–284.

Tharpe N. Postpregnancy genital and wound infections. J Midwifery Womens Health 2008; 53:236–246.

CHAPTER 24

Aiken AH. Central nervous system infection. Neuroimaging Clin N Am 2010; 20:557–580.

Beer R, Lackner P, Pfausler B, Schmutzhard E. Nosocomial ventriculitis and meningitis in neurocritical care patients. J Neurol 2008; 255:1617–1624.

Chuka KB, Bellini WJ, Rota PA, et al. Nipah virus: a recently emergent deadly paramyxovirus. Science 2000; 288: 1432–1435.

Cook TM, Protheroe RT, Handel JM. Tetanus: a review of the literature. Br J Anaesth 2001; 87:477–487.

Prusiner SB. Human prion diseases. In: Zuckerman AJ, ed. Principles and Practice of Clinical Virology. 4th edition. Chichester: Wiley, 2000.

Roos KL. West Nile encephalitis and myelitis. Curr Opin Neurol 2004;17:343–6.

Tunkel AR. Bacterial Meningitis. Philadelphia: Lippincott Williams & Wilkins; 2001.

Walker MD, Zunt JR. Neuroparasitic infections: nematodes. Semin Neurol 2005; 25:252–261.

Whitley RJ. Herpes simplex encephalitis: adolescents and adults. Antiviral Res 2006; 71:141–148.

Whitley RJ, Gnann JW. Viral encephalitis: familiar infections and emerging pathogens. Lancet 2002; 359:507–514.

Ye S, Yang CD. Central nervous system infections in the systemic vasculitides. Curr Opin Neurol 2008; 21:342–346.

CHAPTER 25

Cox FEG, Wakelin D, Gillespie SH, Despommier DD, eds. Topley and Wilson's Microbiology and Microbial Infections: Parasitology, 10th edition. Hoboken: Wiley-Blackwell, 2007.

Chapters deal with the major parasite groups that have representatives associated with infections of the eye.

Cronau H, Kankanala RR, Mauger T. Diagnosis and management of red eye in primary care. Am Fam Physician 2010; 81:137–144.

Gregory M, Callegan MC, Gilmore MS. Role of bacterial and host factors in infectious endophthalmitis. Chem Immunol Allergy 2007; 92:266–275.

Kalkanci A, Ozdek S. Ocular fungal infections. Curr Eye Res 2011; 36:179–189.

Mueller JB, McStay CM. Ocular infection and inflammation. Emerg Med Clin North Am 2008; 26:57–72.

CHAPTER 26

Curcio D. Resistant pathogen-associated skin and skin-structure infections: antibiotic options. Expert Rev Anti Infect Ther 2010; 8:1019–1036.

Grice EA, Segre JA. The skin microbiome. Nat Rev Microbiol 2011; 9:244–253.

Kish TD, Chang MH, Fung HB. Treatment of skin and soft tissue infections in the elderly: A review. Am J Geriatr Pharmacother 2010; 8:485–513.

Kujath P, Kujath C. Complicated skin, skin structure and soft tissue infections - are we threatened by multi-resistant pathogens? Eur J Med Res 2010; 15:544–453.

Menendez-Arias L. Evidence and controversies on the role of XMRV in prostate cancer and chronic fatigue syndrome. Rev Med Virol 2011; 21:3–17.

Roberts DT, Taylor WD, Boyle J. Guidelines for treatment of onychomycosis. Br J Dermatol 2003; 148:402–410.

Rodgers S, Leslie KS. Skin infections in HIV-infected individuals in the era of HAART. Curr Opin Infect Dis 2011; 24:124–129.

Uldrick TS, Whitby D. Update on KSHV epidemiology, Kaposi Sarcoma pathogenesis, and treatment of Kaposi Sarcoma. Cancer Lett 2011; 305:150–162.

CHAPTER 27

Chiodini PL, Moody AH, Manser DW. Atlas of Medical Helminthology and Protozoology, 4th edition. Edinburgh: Churchill Livingstone, 2001.

Cleri DJ, Ricketti AJ, Porwancher RB et al. Viral hemorrhagic fevers: current status of endemic disease and strategies for control. Infect Dis Clin North Am 2006; 20: 359–393.

Daneshvar C, Davis TM, Cox-Singh J et al. Clinical and laboratory features of human Plasmodium knowlesi infection. Clin Infect Dis 2009 Sep 15; 49(6):852–860.

Goodman JL, Dennis DT, Sonenshine DE, eds. Tick-borne diseases of humans. Virginia: ASM Press, 2005.

Kiauss H, Weber A, Appel M et al., editors. Zoonoses. Infectious diseases transmissible from animals to humans. Virginia: ASM Press, 2003.

Labeaud AD, Bashir F, King CH. Measuring the burden of arboviral diseases: the spectrum of morbidity and mortality from four prevalent infections. Popul Health Metr 2011 Jan 10; 9(1):1.

Murray KO, Mertens E, Despres P. West Nile virus and its emergence in the United States of America. Vet Res 2010 Nov-Dec; 41(6):67.

Ndip LM, Biswas HH, Nfonsam LE et al. Risk Factors for African Tick-Bite Fever in Rural Central Africa. Am J Trop Med Hyg 2011 Apr; 84(4):608–613.

Petersen LR, Marfin AA, Gubler DJ. West Nile virus. JAMA 2003; 290:524–528.

Service MW, editor. Encyclopedia of Arthropod-Transmitted Infections of Man and Domesticated Animals. Wallingford, Oxon: CABI Publishing, 2001.

Thiboutot MM, Kannan S, Kawalekar OU et al. Chikungunya: a potentially emerging epidemic? PLoS Negl Trop Dis 2010 Apr 27; 4(4):e623.

Whitty CJ, Lalloo D, Ustianowski A. Malaria: an update on treatment of adults in non-endemic countries. BMJ 2006; 333:241–245.

WHO. Dengue Guidelines for Diagnosis, Treatment, Prevention and Control. Geneva: WHO, 2009.

Available at http://apps.who.int/tdr/publications/training-guideline-publications/dengue-diagnosis-treatment/pdf/dengue-diagnosis.pdf

Yun O, Priotto G, Tong J et al. NECT is next: implementing the new drug combination therapy for Trypanosoma brucei gambiense sleeping sickness. PLoS Negl Trop Dis 2010 May 25; 4(5):e720.

Updates on arbovirus infections are available at: www.CDC.gov/ncidod/dvbid/arbor.

CHAPTER 28

Chomel BB, Sun B. Zoonoses in the bedroom. Emerg Infect Dis 2011; 17:167–172.

Christou L. The global burden of bacterial and viral zoonotic infections. Clin Microbiol Infect 2011; 17:326–330.

Coker R, Rushton J, Mounier-Jack S, Karimuribo E, Lutumba P, Kambarago D, Pfeiffer DU, Stark K, Rweyemamu M. Towards a conceptual framework to support one-health research for policy on emerging zoonoses. Lancet Infect Dis 2011; 11:326–331.

Feng Y, Xiao L. Zoonotic potential and molecular epidemiology of Giardia species and giardiasis. Clin Microbiol Rev 2011; 24.110–140.

Hartskeerl RA, Collares-Pereira M, Ellis WA. Emergence, control and re-emerging leptospirosis: dynamics of infection in the changing world. Clin Microbiol Infect 2011; 17:494–501.

Prugnolle F, Durand P, Ollomo B, Duval L, Ariey F, Arnathau C, Gonzalez JP, Leroy E, Renaud F. A fresh look at the origin of Plasmodium falciparum, the most malignant malaria agent. PLoS Pathog 2011; 7:e1001283.

Singh BB, Sharma R, Sharma JK, Juyal PD. Parasitic zoonoses in India: an overview. Rev Sci Tech 2010; 29:629–637.

Vrbova L, Stephen C, Kasman N, Boehnke R, Doyle-Waters M, Chablitt-Clark A, Gibson B, FitzGerald M, Patrick DM. Systematic review of surveillance systems for emerging zoonoses. Transbound Emerg Dis 2010;57: 154–61.

WHO Informal Working Group. International classification of ultrasound images in cystic echinococcosis for application in clinical and field epidemiological settings. Acta Trop 2003 Feb; 85(2):253–61.

CHAPTER 29

Antonyrajah B, Mukundan D. Fever without apparent source on clinical examination. Curr Opin Pediatr 2008;20: 96–102.

Bleeker-Rovers CP, van der Meer JW, Oyen WJ. Fever of unknown origin. Semin Nucl Med 2009; 39:81–87.

Chow A, Robinson JL. Fever of unknown origin in children: a systematic review. World J Pediatr 2011;7:5–10.

Dimopoulos G, Falagas ME. Approach to the febrile patient in the ICU. Infect Dis Clin North Am 2009;23:471–84.

Tolan RW Jr. Fever of unknown origin: a diagnostic approach to this vexing problem. Clin Pediatr (Phila) 2010; 49:207–213.

Williams J, Bellamy R. Fever of unknown origin. Clin Med 2008; 8:526–530.

CHAPTER 30

Fishman JA. Overview: fungal infections in the transplant patient. Transpl Infect Dis 2002; 4(Suppl 3):3–11.

Fishman JA. Infection in solid-organ transplant recipients. N Engl J Med 2007; 357:2601–2614.

Fishman JA. Infection in renal transplant recipients. Semin Nephrol 2007; 27:445–461.

Fishman JA. New technologies for infectious screening of organ donors. Transplant Proc 2011; 43:2443–2445.

Groll AH, Walsh TJ. Uncommon opportunistic fungi: new nosocomial threats. Clin Microbiol Infect 2001; 7(Suppl 2):8–24.

Ison MG, Fishman JA. Cytomegalovirus pneumonia in transplant recipients. Clin Chest Med 2005; 26:691–705.

Kotton CN. Vaccination and immunization against travel-related diseases in immunocompromised hosts. Expert Rev Vaccines 2008; 7:663–672.

Linden PK. Approach to the immunocompromised host with infection in the intensive care unit. Infect Dis Clin North Am 2009; 23:535–556.

Spencer SP, Power N. The acute abdomen in the immune compromised host. Cancer Imaging 2008; 8:93–101.

CHAPTER 31

Forbes BA, Sahm DF, Weissfeld A. Bailey & Scott's Diagnostic Microbiology, 12th edition. St Louis: Mosby, 2007.

Garcia LS, ed. Clinical Microbiology Procedures Handbook, 3rd edition. Washington: American Society for Microbiology, 2010.

McPherson RA, Pincus MR, eds. Henry's Clinical Diagnosis and Management by Laboratory Methods, 21st edition. Philadelphia: WB Saunders, 2006.

Larone DL. Medically Important Fungi: a Guide to Identification, 5th edition. Washington: American Society for Microbiology, 2011.

Persing DH, Tenover FC, Versalovic J, et al., eds. Molecular Microbiology: Diagnostic Principles and Practice, 2nd edition. Washington: American Society for Microbiology, 2010.

Rose NR. Manual of Clinical Laboratory Immunology, 6th edition. Washington: American Society for Microbiology, 2002.

Versalofic J, ed. Manual of Clinical Microbiology, 10th edition. Washington: American Society for Microbiology, 2011.

CHAPTER 32

Gordis L. Epidemiology, 4th edition. Philadelphia: Elsevier, 2008.

CHAPTER 33

Brunton L, Chabner BA, Knollmann BC. Goodman & Gilman's The Pharmacological Basis of Therapeutics, 12th edition. New York: McGraw-Hill, 2011.

Dienstag JL, Hepatitis B. virus infection. NEJM 2008; 359:1486–1500.

Ghany MG, Strader DB, Thomas DL, Seeff LB. Diagnosis, management, and treatment of hepatitis C: an update. Hepatology 2009; 49:1335–1374.

Gilbert DN, Moellering RC, Eliopoulos GM, Chambers HF, Saag MS. The Sanford Guide to Antimicrobial Therapy. 41st edition Sperryville, Virginia: Antimicrobial Therapy Inc; 2011.

Saag MS, Chambers HF, Eliopoulos GM, et al. The Sanford Guide to HIV/AIDS Therapy 2011, 19th edition. Sperryville, Virginia: Antimicrobial Therapy Inc, 2011.

Sucher AJ, Chahine EB, Balcer HE. Echinocandins: The Newest Class of Antifungals. Ann Pharmacother 2009; 43:1643–1657.

Thompson MA, Aberg JA, Cahn P, et al. Antiretroviral treatment of adult HIV infection: 2010 recommendations of the International AIDS Society-USA panel. JAMA 2010; 304:321–333.

Versalofic J, ed. Manual of Clinical Microbiology, 10th edition. Washington: American Society for Microbiology, 2011.

CHAPTER 34

Centres for Disease Control and Prevention, Atkinson W, Wolfe S, Hamborsky J eds. Epidemiology and Prevention of Vaccine-Preventable Diseases ("The Pink Book") 12th edition. Washington DC: Public Health Foundation. 2011.

Also available at: http://www.cdc.gov/vaccines/pubs/pinkbook/default.htm.

Crompton PD, Pierce SK, Miller LH. Advances and challenges in malaria vaccine development. J Clin Invest 2010; 120:4168–4178.

McElrath MJ, Haynes BF. Induction of immunity to human immunodeficiency virus type-1 by vaccination. Immunity 2010; 33:542–554.

CHAPTER 35

Casadevall A, Dadachova E, Pirofski LA. Passive antibody therapy for infectious diseases. Nat Rev Microbiol 2004; 2:695–703.

Chan AC, Carter PJ. Therapeutic antibodies for autoimmunity and inflammation. Nat Rev Immunol 2010; 10:301–316.

Chapman CM, Gibson GR, Rowland I. Health benefits of probiotics: are mixtures more effective than single strains? Eur J Nutr 2011.

Coley WB. The therapeutic value of the mixed toxins of erysipelas and Bacillus prodigiosus in the treatment of inoperable malignant tumours. Am J Med Sci 1986; 112:251.

Hudson PJ, Souriau C. Engineered antibodies. Nat Med 2003; 9:129–134.

Nowakowski A, Wang C, Powers DB et al. Potent neutralization of botulinum neurotoxin by recombinant oligoclonal antibody. Proc Natl Acad Sci U S A 2002; 99:11346–11350.

Parker MT, Collier LH, editors. Topley and Wilson's Principles of Bacteriology, Virology and Immunity, 9th edition, vol. 1, London: Edward Arnold, 1997.

Petrovsky N, Aguilar JC. Vaccine adjuvants: current state and future trends. Immunol Cell Biol 2004; 82:488–496.

Reid G, Younes JA, Van der Mei HC et al. Microbiota restoration: natural and supplemented recovery of human microbial communities. Nat Rev Microbiol 2011; 9(1):27–38.

Shanahan F. Probiotics in perspective. Gastroenterology 2010; 139:1808.

CHAPTER 36

Alangaden GJ. Nosocomial fungal infections: epidemiology, infection control, and prevention. Infect Dis Clin North Am 2011; 25:201–225.

Cook E, Marchaim D, Kaye KS. Building a successful infection prevention program: key components, processes, and economics. Infect Dis Clin North Am 2011; 25:1–19.

Mandell GL, Bennett JE, Dolin R, eds. Principles and Practice of Infectious Diseases, 7th edition. New York: Churchill Livingstone, 2010.

Mayhall CG. Hospital Epidemiology and Infection Control, 3rd edition. Baltimore: Lippincott Williams & Wilkins, 2004.

Sydnor ER, Perl TM. Hospital epidemiology and infection control in acute-care settings. Clin Microbiol Rev 2011; 24:141–173.

Wenzel RP, Bearmann GML, Brewer TF, Butzler JP. A Guide to Infection Control in the Hospital, 4th edition. Boston: International Society of Infectious Diseases, 2008.

Zuckerman JM. Prevention of health care-acquired pneumonia and transmission of Mycobacterium tuberculosis in health care settings. Infect Dis Clin North Am 2011; 25:117–133.

USEFUL WEBSITES

ACGM Compendium of Guidance
www.hse.gov.uk/biosafety/gmo/acgm/acgmcomp/
AJIC – American Journal of Infection Control
www.apic.org/ajic/
AMEDEO free medical literature service
www.amedeo.com
American Society for Microbiiology
www.asm.org
AMM home page
www.amm.co.uk
Bioterrorism Preparedness and Response
www.bt.cdc.gov/
BMJ publishing group reviews of clinical evidence for medical practice
http://www.clinicalevidence.org
British Society for Antimicrobial Chemotherapy
www.bsac.org.uk
(Contains latest advice on susceptibility testing)
CDC-Emerging Infectious Diseases Journal Homepage
www.cdc.gov/ncidod/eid/index.htm
Centers for Disease Control and Prevention
www.cdc.gov
Directory of medical and veterinary ecto and endoparasites.
www.soton.ac.uk/~ceb/
Doctor's Guide Personal Edition
www.docguide.com
Electronic Guidelines on effective healthcare

info@eguidelines.co.uk or www.eguidelines.co.uk
EPIC – Evidence Based Practice in Infection Control
www.epic.tvu.ac.uk
Federation of the European Societies for Chemotherapy and Infections
www.fesci.net
Fit for travel
www.fitfortravel.scot.nhs.uk
Food Standards Agency
www.foodstandards.gov.uk
Free medical journals
www.freemedicaljournals.com
The Global Alliance to Eliminate Lymphatic Filariasis
www.filariasis.org
Health Protection Agency England, Wales and Northern Ireland
www.hpa.org.uk/
Hospital Infection Society
www.his.org.uk/
IDSA Home Page
www.idsociety.org/
Infection Control Nurses Association – UK
www.icna.co.uk
Infectious Disease News from WHO
www.who.int/infectious-disease-news
International Travel and Health
www.who.int/ith/
Intestinal Parasites
www.who.int/ctd/intpara
Johns Hopkins Division of Infectious Diseases Antibiotic Guidelines
www.hopkins-abxguide.org
Leprosy Info
www.who.int/lep/
Metaregister of controlled trials
www.controlled-trials.com
Morbidity and Mortality Weekly Report
www.cdc.gov/mmwr/
National Institute for Clinical Excellence summary of guidance issued to the NHS in England and Wales
www.nice.org.uk
National Nosocomial Infections Surveillance System (NNIS)
http://www.cdc.gov/ncidod/dhqp/nnis_pubs.html
National Travel Health Network and Centre, UK, for online information on vaccines required for travellers
http://www.nathnac.org/
Rila Publications Ltd
www.rila.co.uk
Roll Back Malaria
www.rbm.who.int
Royal College of Pathologists website for information on courses, links to other learned societies and discussion sites
www.rcpath.org
Sanford Guides – Antimicrobial Therapy & HIV/AIDS Therapy
www.sanfordguide.com/.
Scottish Intercollegiate Guidelines Network
www.sign.ac.uk
SHEA – Society for Healthcare Epidemiology of America
www.shea-online.org/
The Stop Tuberculosis Initiative website
www.stoptb.org

Surveillance and Response
www.who.int/csr/en/
TDR Home Page: The UNDP-World Bank-WHO Special Programme for Research and Training in Tropical Disease
www.who.int/tdr
Therapeutic Guidelines
www.tg.com.au/home/index.html
UK Clinical Virology Network
www.clinical-virology.org/
UK HPA Malaria Reference Laboratory
www.malaria-reference.co.uk
UK NEQAS Microbiology home page
www.ukneqasmicro.org.uk
Update on current literature and meetings reports, can be focused to infectious diseases
www.medscape.com
WHO Child Health and Development

www.who.int/child-adolescent-health/
WHO Infectious Diseases report
www.who.int/infectious-disease-report/
WHO Influenza virus vaccine compositions
http://www.who.int/csr/disease/influenza/vaccinerecommendations/en/index.html
WHO International Travel and Health
http://www.who.int/ith/en/
WHO Tuberculosis – Prevention and Control
www.who.int/gtb/
WHO Weekly Epidemiological Record
www.who.int/wer/
WHO/OMS Vaccines and Biologicals
www.who.int/immunization/en/
WHO/OMS: World Health Organization
www.who.int

Index

Note: Page numbers followed by *f* indicate figures, *t* indicate tables and *b* indicate boxes.